D1736066

FREEDOM'S PROGRESS?

To be governed is to be watched, inspected, spied upon, directed, law-ridden, regulated, penned up, indoctrinated, preached at, checked, appraised, seized, censured, commanded, by beings who have neither title nor knowledge nor virtue.

To be governed is to have every operation, every transaction, every movement noted, registered, counted, rated, stamped, measured, numbered, assessed, licensed, refused, authorized, indorsed, admonished, prevented, reformed, redressed, corrected.

To be governed is, under pretext of public utility and in the name of the general interest, to be laid under contribution, drilled, fleeced, exploited, monopolized, extorted from, exhausted, hoaxed, robbed; then, upon the slightest resistance, at the first word of complaint, to be repressed, fined, vilified, annoyed, hunted down, pulled about, beaten, disarmed, bound, imprisoned, shot, machine-gunned, judged, condemned, banished, sacrificed, sold, betrayed, and, to crown all, ridiculed, derided, outraged, dishonored.

—Pierre-Joseph Proudhon

FREEDOM'S PROGRESS?

A HISTORY OF
POLITICAL THOUGHT

Gerard Casey

imprint-academic.com

Published in the UK by
Imprint Academic, PO Box 200, Exeter EX5 5YX, UK

Distributed in the USA by
Ingram Book Company,
One Ingram Blvd., La Vergne, TN 37086, USA

ISBN 9781845409425

Set in Times New Roman and Gill Sans Bold

A CIP catalogue record for this book is available from the
British Library and US Library of Congress

Contents

Acknowledgements

I owe a debt of gratitude to many people for helping me along the way in the composition of this book. First and foremost, thanks must go to Dr Thomas E. Woods for getting the whole thing started. While I was captive in his car on the journey from Atlanta to Auburn in March 2013, he made me an offer which I couldn't refuse to draft a series of lectures on the history of political thought for his **LibertyClassroom** website (www.libertyclassroom.com). I was gratified to be invited to contribute to this superb resource for lovers of liberty and I accepted the invitation. The lectures I produced for **LibertyClassroom** provide the foundation for this book. Some parts of the material have remained relatively constant over time but I have made significant additions and alterations to other parts, specifically to the material on Christianity and on Marx. Some material, such as that on Kant, Hegel, Rand, Hayek, Nozick, Rothbard and Rawls, is completely new. All in all, the material in this book is a much revised, expanded and more extensively researched and documented version of the **LibertyClassroom** lectures.

Thanks are also due to my last PhD student, Jason Walsh, for holding up his end of our many conversations and for his eminently practical help in bringing this book into the world; to my son, Gerard Casey, for drawing the diagrams in the Plato chapter; to Andy Curzon and Garrett Barden for heroic and supererogatory feats of proof-reading; to Nikos Sotirakopoulos, author of *The Rise of Lifestyle Activism*, for his comments and criticisms on the Introduction and the chapters on Marx, Twentieth-Century Tribalism and Ayn Rand et al; to Carl Watner for his helpful suggestions in connection with the journal *Liberty* and its writers; to my University College Dublin colleague, Timothy Crowley, for his provision of links to stimulating and controversial material and for his psychic support; and to all the students, undergraduate and postgraduate, in University College Dublin who took my courses on *Anarchy, Law and the State* and *Law, Liberty and the State* and who, by their questions, objections and stout resistance, forced me to be less incoherent than I might otherwise have been.

A very special thanks is due to the indefatigable Dr Walter Grinder for his circular emails with their extraordinarily helpful bibliographical suggestions, from many of which I have profited immensely. Also, in that connection, I thank the Book Depository for all the books (see the bibliography!) delivered to me post free but not, alas, cost free; as I have been intellectually enriched, so have I been financially impoverished. Actually, now that I come to think of it, perhaps the people at the Book Depository should be thanking me!

I steadfastly refuse to allow anyone else to claim credit for any errors, omissions, inaccuracies and distortions; they're mine, all mine. More to the point, no one besides me shoulders the responsibility for the frankly partisan nature of the text which, at some point or other, is sure to annoy or even upset not only those who hold views on the nature and importance of liberty that are diametrically opposed to mine but even some whose views on the topic of liberty largely coincide with mine. But then, I am of one mind with Kingsley Amis who once said, 'If you can't annoy somebody with what you write…there's little point in writing.'

PREFACE

Freedom is the right to live as we wish. Nothing else
—Epictetus

Most people want security in this world, not liberty
—H. L. Mencken

I tell Thee that man is tormented by no greater anxiety
than to find someone quickly to whom he can hand over
that gift of freedom with which the ill-fated creature is born
—Dostoevsky

On the British quiz programme, *Tipping Point*, the following question was once asked of two young contestants: 'Which Duke of Normandy invaded England and became its king?' In a stunning tribute to the efficacy of the English education system,[1] the first contestant said, 'Haven't a clue!'; the second asked, plaintively, 'Was it Harold?' The first contestant was right; right, that is, about not having a clue; the second at least identified a person who was associated in some way with the historical event in question, if not William the Bastard, Duke of Normandy himself. Now it would be unrealistic to expect even those purporting to be educated[2] to have a detailed knowledge of *every* aspect of their country's history—as Will Rogers noted, 'Everybody is ignorant, only on different subjects—but there are certain seminal historical events in the past of any country that it would seem could not possibly be unknown to any educated adult with a pulse and a functioning cerebellum. In English history, what W. C. Sellar and R. J. Yeatman, in their hilarious 1930's spoof, called *1066 and All That*, is just such an event.

It may be some consolation—then again, it may not—to realise that the great British public's knowledge of Britain's geography would appear to be just as bad as its knowledge of its history. A 2016 Ordnance Survey test of people's knowledge of the geography of the United Kingdom showed that 40% of respondents were unable to locate London on an unlabelled map! Edinburgh fared worse, with only 14% of those surveyed getting its location right but, then again, Edinburgh *is* a fairly exotic location. Even so, the humdrum cities of Birmingham and Manchester didn't fare much better than the more outlandish Edinburgh, garnering correct scores of just 15% and 22% respectively. One in ten respondents placed the Scilly Isles in the Irish Sea in the spot normally occupied by the Isle of Man, while one in twenty put them off the coast of Scotland, forcing the Hebrides to scrunch up to make room for them. [Bingham 2016] All of which leads one to conclude that Oscar Wilde may have been right when he quipped, 'In England, at any rate, education produces no effect whatsoever,' before adding, gratefully, 'If it did it would prove a serious danger to the upper classes, and probably lead to acts of violence in Grosvenor Square.'[3]

In the 'more-schooling = more-ignorance stakes,' the British don't have it all their own way. Two out of three seventeen-year old Americans can't place the Civil War within fifty years of when it occurred; one in five cannot say which countries the US fought against in World War II. 'Progressive education reform,' writes Josha Foer, 'made school a lot more pleasant, and a lot more interesting. But it's also brought with it costs for us as individuals and as citizens. Memory is how we transmit virtues and values, and partake of a shared culture.' [Foer 2012, 208] It can't be denied that, all things considered, it is better that schools be pleasant and interesting rather than not, but not if such pleasantness and interestingness comes at the cost of obliterating the school's basic function. I am reminded of the passage in *Pride and Prejudice* in which the pretentious Caroline Bingley attempts to impress Mr Darcy: 'I should like balls infinitely better,' Miss Bingley remarked, 'if they were carried on in a different manner; but there is something insufferably tedious in the usual process of such a meeting. It would surely be much more rational if conversation instead of dancing made the order of the day.' Her brother's reply deflates her pretensions: 'Much more rational, my dear Caroline, I dare say, but it would not be near so much like a ball.'[4]

It might appear at first glance that the kind of ignorance I have just mentioned is indicative of a failure of the education system but Patrick Deneen, Professor of Politics at the University of Notre Dame, disagrees. He writes, 'Our students' ignorance is not a failing of the educational system – it is its crowning achievement. Efforts by several generations of philosophers and reformers and public policy experts whom our students (and most of us) know nothing about have combined to produce a generation of know-nothings. The pervasive ignorance of our students is not a mere accident or unfortunate but correctible outcome, if only we hire better teachers or tweak the reading lists in high school. It is the consequence of a civilizational commitment to civilizational suicide. The end of history for our students signals the End of History for the West.' [Deneen, 2016] Deneen's 'End of History' conclusion might be ever-so-slightly hyperbolic but it can't be denied that such widespread ignorance of basic geography and history is not a cause for celebration. The practical downside of geographical ignorance can be partially remedied by a good map (assuming people know how to read a map) or a reliable GPS device; however, ignorance of basic history is not so easily remediable. History is to a society what memory is to the individual: without memory, an individual cannot sustain a personality[5] or a character or maintain enduring personal relationships; similarly, without a knowledge of its history, a society has no substance and no character, since it does not know what it has been, what it is, or, in a non-geographical sense, where it is going.

THIS BOOK IS SELECTIVE

This book is a history of Western political thought, a conceptual map as it were, tracking the fitful journey of one particular concept—liberty—through time.

As is the case with any map, its usefulness is to be judged as much by what is omitted as by what is included. Not everything can be or should be included on a map, otherwise the map and that which is mapped begin to coincide and the synoptic viewpoint which is the aim of a history becomes unattainable. Moreover, history is essentially a narrative, a story, and any story worth its salt resembles what Hitchcock thought was the essence of drama: life with the dull bits cut out. The thinkers I choose to discuss in this history should not come as a surprise to the reader—it is hard to see how any reasonable history of political thought could ignore, for example, Machiavelli, Hobbes and Locke—though there may be some writers in my account who do not normally appear among the great and the good, thinkers who, if they appear at all, do so only as items in footnotes or are such as to merit the most cursory of mentions, for example, Johannes Althusius. Even in a book as long as this, selections must be made and much that is both interesting and important must be omitted.

In his *The Evolution of Political Thought*, C. Northcote Parkinson remarks, sapiently, that histories of political thought tend to suffer from a number of recurrent fallacies. These are: first, that political thinking is limited to those who write about it; second, that those who write about politics exert an especially powerful influence on political developments; third, that political institutions have progressed steadily and inexorably from the past to the present; and fourth, that such political thinking as there has been has been confined to Europe and America. [see Parkinson 1958, 7-10]

Whatever other shortcomings this work may exhibit, I am reasonably confident that I do not commit the first and second Parkinsonian fallacies of assuming that political thinking is confined solely to those who have written about it and that those writers exert a uniquely significant effect on actual political developments. Walter Grinder is of the belief, a belief I fully share, that it was never the case that 'the movement that we know as liberalism ever grew out of books only.' To the contrary, he writes, 'I believe that liberalism grew primarily out of struggle—the councils against the popes and the people against the Kings and their states and their government.... It was, of course, Conciliarism that led, both directly and indirectly, to popular sovereignty, both inside and outside the Church and to the Reformation itself, which led, in turn, to the Catholic Counter-Reformation and then to the Catholic Enlightenment, a little-understood occurrence...'[6] I, too, most emphatically do not believe that political thinking is confined solely to those who have put their thoughts on paper, nor do I believe that those published thoughts play a uniquely significant role in political developments. To give effect to my disbeliefs and to leaven what might otherwise be an exclusively literary dough, I have included in this history thematic chapters on prehistory, slavery, Christianity, the institutions of the university, the city, feudalism, law and kingship, the English Revolution, twentieth century forms of tribalism, and war.

While the word *progress* appears in the title of this work, thus appearing to constitute the work as a whole as an example of Parkinson's third fallacy, it does so with a question mark attached to it. Furthermore, even to the qualified extent that the word *progress* in the book's title applies to anything, it applies to liberty and not to political institutions as a whole. I am not a political Couéist, believing that, to adapt Coué's famous mantra to my purposes, *tous les jours à tous points de vue les institutions politiques vont de mieux en mieux*—each day in every way political institutions get better and better.[7] The *progress* in the book's title, qualified even as it is by a question mark, is likely to induce apoplexy in those whose thought has been formed by the anti-progressivist relativist orthodoxy dominant in history and anthropology circles since the 1960s, for whom any suggestion that there can be such a thing as progress is ethnocentrically judgemental and culturally benighted. As I use the term *progress*, it has both the relatively neutral descriptive meaning of a journey or a procession, as well as the considerably less neutral and normative meaning of movement towards a better state or condition. In both senses of the term, I will attempt to show that in the last 2,500 years, liberty *has* made progress, even if that progress has been fitful, intermittent, and not always readily apparent.

Apart from a few glancing references, I do not include accounts from Near or Far Eastern traditions in my narrative, thus appearing to commit the fourth Parkinsonian fallacy. However, this omission implies no disrespect on my part for or disparagement of those traditions—I taught an elementary course in Eastern Philosophy for over 30 years—rather, it indicates only my lack of expertise in these areas, coupled with a desire to keep the extent of this book within manageable boundaries. Readers are warmly encouraged to explore the richness of these traditions for themselves.[8]

Even within my self-imposed limits, I have had to be extremely selective. With one or two exceptions, every thinker in this history has been the object of extensive scholarly endeavours, so much so that one could spend one's whole life and career studying the critical literature on a single thinker, and many have done exactly this. I cannot address all the scholarly issues raised nor all the scholars who have written on any given thinker or topic. My account, then, is selective, partial and limited but not, I hope, false. I would urge readers to take what I have to say here as a starting point for their own investigations and not a stopping point. I have tried to keep the treatment as short and as uncomplicated as is consistent with reasonable completeness but more can always be said and other views always invite consideration. 'What we call "history" can be nothing but our weak conceptualization of a few mostly random fragments we have plucked out of the tiniest sliver of the past.' So writes the legal scholar Paul F. Campos. He continues, 'We use such concepts to order the intolerable complexity of things into an apparent pattern, telling ourselves, absurdly enough, that something called "the Middle Ages" was succeeded by "the Renaissance." What an infinite array of precious, irretrievable knowledge is buried beneath those flimsy formulations. And how well the Talmud puts it when it says that with every man's death, a whole universe passes away.' [Campos, 147-148]

THIS BOOK IS BIASED

What makes this history different, or should do if it is in any way successful, is the angle it approaches its topic from. Surely history doesn't have angles?

Well, yes it does. Every judgement is made from a particular standpoint and no standpoint is neutral. To think that one's standpoint is neutral is fundamentally to deceive oneself; it is to adopt a very particular standpoint, the 'no standpoint' standpoint, somewhat like those annoying people who block supermarket aisles with their trolleys, evidently under the impression that they and their shopping devices take up no space. 'Much of what we read in the history books is guesswork (sometimes good, sometimes not so good),' I wrote some years ago, 'reconstructions based on hearsay, and even in the best histories, a narrative framed by a particular human being at a particular time, the whole enlivened by that writer's cultural prejudices, biases and interests.' [Casey 2009a, 249] Everybody approaches history from a particular perspective and the perspective I have chosen is that of liberty. Not only have I chosen a particular perspective, I make no (or at least, very little) effort to conceal my estimations of the thinkers I discuss, so this is not a neutral history either. John Vincent writes, 'History is about evidence, and evidence flagrantly distorts. There is a bias in the creation of evidence, and a bias in the survival of evidence.' He notes that 'our culture has a bias against bias' despite its being difficult to name 'any historical writers who are not well and truly biased. Worse still, their bias is not some shameful blot upon their reputations, but no small part of their reputation itself.'[9] The most potent of all biases is our ill-founded belief that we are more resistant to bias than others.[10] Moreover, as Herodotus remarked a long time ago, 'very few things happen at the right time and the rest do not happen at all. The conscientious historian will correct for these defects.'

To hold that history has angles and perspectives and to believe that historians are subject to bias, however, is *not* equivalent to allowing oneself to be sucked into the black hole of postmodern historiography. The laws of logic hold in the writing of history as much as anywhere else and two contrary historical propositions cannot both be true though both, of course, may be false.[11] Few if any historians hold to the absurd position, the straw-man position attacked by the postmodernists, that what they write is the truth, the whole truth and nothing but the truth. As Richard Evans notes, 'No historians really believe in the *absolute* truth of what they are writing, simply in its probable truth, which they have done their utmost to establish by following the usual rules of evidence.'[12] [Evans 1997, 219] In any event, you, of course, must make up your own mind on all the thinkers and topics discussed in this book but, if I have succeeded at all in what I've set out to do, you should have no difficulty in coming to know what I think about them. [see Tavris & Aronson, passim]

There are two extremes that can be taken in approaching the past. One is to think of the past as being so different from the present as to have nothing in common with what concerns us today. On such an approach, the knowledge we can obtain from our predecessors is of purely antiquarian interest and we can learn nothing from them that we can apply to our own circumstances. On the other hand, we can treat the past as if it simply went on all fours with our own concerns in every salient respect. If we adopt this approach, we flirt with anachronism, the temptation to read things into the past that have no place there. For example, to talk of the state in connection with the writings of Aristotle or Aquinas and to mean by it what the term signifies as it is used in the twenty-first century is to court confusion. It is not always practically possible, however, to avoid such casual anachronism and I apologise if I have fallen victim to this trap from time to time. [see Vincent 9-31, 77-82] If the use of the term 'state', writes Alexander d'Entrèves, 'should lead us to ignore the substantial differences which exist between the political structures of those periods and our own, then to speak of the 'State' in referring to the Greek *polis*, or to the *res romana*, or to the medieval *communitas perfecta*, would have to be condemned out of hand as an abuse of language.' But, he continues, 'this abuse vanishes, or is at least greatly diminished, when the word 'State' is accepted as a brief, almost a shorthand, indication of what is common to these different experiences. This common element is the basic fact of organised force....The notion of the State...always comes back ultimately to the successful carrying out of man's will, to a relation of command and obedience in a social context.' [d'Entrèves 1967, 34]

The history of political philosophy is, of course, only part of a much broader and much more complicated story. I will, from time to time, refer to broader historical themes and topics but the specific focus of this work, together with considerations of space, will limit the number and length of these references. Readers who are interested in the broad historical context within which the history of political philosophy sits should consult the appropriate general histories.[13]

Concepts of Liberty

Since the concept of liberty or freedom (I use the terms interchangeably) is central to my project and since, even by philosophical standards, it is a contested term, it might be as well for me to indicate which conception of liberty I am working with.[14] The concept of liberty can be understood in various senses, as many as two hundred of them if Isaiah Berlin is to be believed! [Berlin, 121] From this very large number, I am going to set my working concept of liberty—thin liberty—against what I take to be its four most significant rival conceptions: metaphysical liberty, liberty as autonomy, republican liberty and substantive (or thick) liberty.[15]

Metaphysical Liberty

Metaphysically, liberty can be understood as encompassing freedom of the will in some sense or other. Throughout the history of philosophy, whether or not human beings are completely determined in their choices by factors such as their environment, their conditioning, their education, their genetics or God's predetermination has been exhaustively discussed. An extensive, if not always illuminating, philosophical literature has been produced on this topic.[16] The discussion is no longer confined to philosophers. Recently, natural scientists are getting in on the act. Nicolas Gisin, the renowned Swiss physicist, asks, 'Are we passive laundry machines through which thoughts happen to pass? Or are we active agents free to influence our thoughts and decisions? The ability even to ask the question seems to require the second interpretation, yet modern science...almost unanimously plumps for the first.' Does science explain free will? No, says Gisin, making the point that it is 'free will that allows us to put trust in science in the first place. Free will doesn't require explanations any more than mathematical axioms require justifications.' [Gisin 2016a] 'Without free-will,' he writes elsewhere, 'there is no way to make sense of anything, no way to decide which arguments to buy and which to reject. Hence, there would be no rational thinking and no science. In particular, there would be no understanding.' [Gisin 2016b, 2] Another physicist, George Ellis, agrees with Gisin: 'We should also recognize that the enterprise of science itself does not make sense if our minds cannot rationally choose between theories on the basis of the available data. A reasoning mind able to make rational choices is a prerequisite for the discipline of physics to exist.' [Ellis 2005, 53]

I argued in a similar fashion in my *Libertarian Anarchy*. There, I presented the following maxim: '*No theory can be seriously maintained such that, if it were to be true, its very maintenance would become impossible, meaningless, contradictory or self-refuting.*' I continued: 'Apart from the formal constraints on theories of the necessity for consistency and coherence, and the material constraints of explanatory adequacy and coverage, there is also a self-referential constraint on theories, namely, that such theories must not render impossible the conditions of their own statement or the conditions of their being maintained. If they do so, they are theoretically self-stultifying. Unless human beings are fundamentally free in their choices and decisions, it is not possible for statements to be meaningfully asserted: that includes the statement of a radical determinism.... The statement of a radical determinism is undermined by its own content's rendering pointless the act of its assertion or by its assertion's rendering meaningless the content of that assertion....Strict determinism falls foul of the maxim since, of necessity, the very attempt to argue for determinism is itself a free act by the arguer which commends itself to the rational judgement of its intended audience. If it is not a free act, we need not regard it; it is only the sighing of the breeze in the vocal chords of the determinist.' [Casey 2012b, 48-49]

In a similar vein, in her *Metaphysics as a Guide to Morals*, Iris Murdoch writes: 'As a philosophical theory, as contrasted with a theological view or an assumption of popular science or an emotional intuition about fate, *determinism fails because it is unstateable.* However far we impinge (for instance for legal or moral purposes) upon the area of free will we cannot philosophically exhibit a situation in which, instead of shifting, it vanishes. *The phenomena of rationality and morality are involved in the very attempt to banish them.*'[17]

So too, without claiming to show that determinism is false, Isaiah Berlin remarks that it seems 'patently inconsistent to assert, on the one hand, that all events are wholly determined to be what they are by other events....and, on the other, that men are free to choose between at least two possible courses of action—free not merely in the sense of being able to do what they choose to do (and because they choose to do it), but in the sense of not being determined to choose what they choose by causes outside their control.' [Berlin, xi] I consider Berlin to be over-modest in his disclaimer, perhaps because the inconsistency to which he points is not a purely logical one involving two contradictory propositions but what has sometimes been termed a pragmatic or existential inconsistency, an inconsistency between a proposition asserted and what is required if that proposition is to be meaningfully asserted.

In any event, whatever the ultimate determination (pun intended) of this question may be, metaphysical freedom is *not* the notion of freedom that I am primarily concerned with in this book.

Liberty as autonomy

Liberty can be understood as *autonomy*,[18] where autonomy is to be thought of not merely as the absence of constraint but rather as the ability to set one's goals in a way that is genuinely in accord with one's status as a rational being. Some such conception of liberty is to be found in various forms in the writings of the German Idealists and in those inspired by them. On one view of autonomy, it is a kind of mastery over oneself commensurate with one's being 'the sole and sufficient source of the actions one performs.' [Dreyfus & Kelly, 138] On this view of things, nothing outside oneself can be allowed to determine one's actions in any way. If this were to happen, we would have heteronomy instead of autonomy. On another, slightly different view of things, freedom as autonomy is not merely the absence of compulsion or constraint that enables a man to do as he likes but is rather the power or ability to do something truly worth doing, where what is truly worth doing is to be determined not by the prejudices of the common mob but by the considered judgement of those who really know. As Tom Palmer characterises it, autonomy, for its defenders is 'true' freedom, 'the freedom to do what is good and not merely "whatever one wants".' [Palmer 2009, 14]

Liberty as autonomy, in either of these senses, is *not* the conception of freedom I am operating with in this book. For me, liberty is entirely compossible with our recognising goods as goods and allowing them to inform our choices—indeed, it is hard to see how our actions could be rational unless this were so. In holding this, I am substantially in agreement with Hegel's account of freedom in *The Philosophy of Right*. However, whether or not the goods that inform one's choices are *truly* good according to the judgement of those who are supposed to know makes no difference to the freedom of choice involved in its selection. In holding this, I am substantially in disagreement with Hegel's account.[19] For my conception of liberty, anything recognised by a human agent as a good (and the recognition of something as a good is, I believe, necessarily a determining factor in our choosing of it)[20] whether true or not (from the perspective of those who know) is freely chosen if chosen without constraint or coercion. In saying this, I do not wish to be understood to deny that there are goods which are truly perfective and fulfilling of the human agent and goods which, ultimately, are not, whether in themselves or in the manner of their pursuit and appropriation. That is an important matter, indeed, a very important matter but it is, for my purposes, another matter.

Republican or neo-roman liberty

Liberty can be understood in a republican or neo-roman sense, as in the writings of Cicero or, more recently, Quentin Skinner.[21] Here, one is thought to be free if one is part of and able to participate in a political structure in which no other person has the political or legal power to determine one's actions. Under this conception of liberty, one would not be free even if in fact one's actions were not constrained as long as the overall institutional context was such that one's action could be constrained if others so chose. 'What, then,' asks Quentin Skinner, 'divides the neo-roman from the liberal understanding of freedom? What the neo-roman writers repudiate,' he writes, 'is the key assumption of classical liberalism to the effect that force or the coercive threat of it consti-tute the only forms of constraint that interfere with individual liberty. The neo-roman writers insist, by contrast, that to live in a condition of dependence is in itself a source and a form of constraint. As soon as you recognise that you are living in such a condition, this will serve in itself to constrain you from exercising a number of your civil rights. That is why they insist…that to live in such a condition is to suffer a diminution not merely of security for your liberty but of liberty itself.' [Skinner 1998, 84] Skinner clarifies what he means thus: 'One might say that the neo-roman and classical liberal accounts of freedom embody rival understandings of autonomy. For the latter, the will is autonomous provided it is not coerced; for the former, the will can only be described as autonomous if it is independent of the danger of being coerced.' [Skinner 1998, 84-85, n. 57] The contemporary political philosopher, Philip Pettit, has also written extensively about the republican or neo-roman concep-tion of liberty, which is not just a matter of non-interference but of not being subject to the arbitrary will of others. A slave with a benign master who allows him to do whatever he wishes but who remains legally a slave is not free under this conception of freedom because his master is still in a position to constrain his action, even if, as a matter of fact, his master never chooses so to do. The threat of coercion may be remote to the point of invisibility but as long as it exists, so the argument goes, the slave is still not free.

I find it difficult to appreciate the particularly austere conception of freedom as expounded by Skinner and Pettit. If the slave owner's benignity is such that he not only is not initiating aggression against the slave now but will never do so in the future, either directly or through the instrumentality of the law, then, whatever the law may say about the relationship between the slave and his erstwhile owner, *he is not a slave*. He can go where he likes, doing what he likes, when he likes without needing permission and without being subject to limitation or recall. But if the mere *possibility* that someone may initiate aggression against me is enough to render me unfree (or, as Skinner puts it, if 'the will can only be described as autonomous if it is independent of the danger of being coerced') then we are all always unfree since anyone at any time may threaten to initiate aggression against us. The mere possibility of coercion is not enough. There has to be an actual initiation of aggression or threat of

aggression for my freedom to be limited. Benjamin Constant famously distinguished between ancient and modern conceptions of liberty. [Constant 1819]
'The first major postrevolutionary liberal in France was Benjamin Constant,'
writes Brian Doherty, 'who celebrated what he called "the liberty of the
moderns" (actual liberty in day-to-day affairs) in contrast to the classical
"liberty of the ancients" that the French revolutionaries relied on overmuch,
which merely meant "equal powerlessness before the state and equal participation in public affairs"' [Doherty, 31-32]

For Constant, modern liberty 'is the right to be subjected only to the laws, and to
be neither arrested, detained, put to death or maltreated in any way by the arbitrary
will of one or more individuals. It is the right of everyone to express their opinion,
choose a profession and practise it, to dispose of property, and even to abuse it; to
come and go without permission, and without having to account for their motives
or undertakings. It is everyone's right to associate with other individuals, either
to discuss their interests, or to profess the religion which they and their associates prefer, or even simply to occupy their days or hours in a way which is most
compatible with their inclinations or whims.'[22] For the ancients, on the other hand,
liberty was primarily a collective or republican matter and was consistent with the
almost complete subjection of the individual to the authority of the community.
According to Constant, the liberty of the ancients consisted in 'deliberating, in the
public square, over war and peace; in forming alliances with foreign governments;
in voting laws, in pronouncing judgements; in examining the accounts, the acts, the
stewardship of the magistrates; in calling them to appear in front of the assembled
people, in accusing, condemning or absolving them.'[23]

What elements of modern liberty do we find among the ancients. Almost
none! 'All private actions,' writes Constant, 'were submitted to a severe
surveillance. No importance was given to individual independence, neither in
relation to opinions, nor to labour, nor, above all, to religion….In the domains
which seem to us the most useful, the authority of the social body interposed
itself and obstructed the will of individuals. Among the Spartans, Therpandrus
could not add a string to his lyre without causing offence to the ephors….
The young Lacedaemonian could not visit his new bride freely. In Rome, the
censors cast a searching eye over family life. The laws regulated customs, and
as customs touch on everything, there was hardly anything that the laws did not
regulate.' [Constant 1819, 311]

The nineteenth-century French historian, Numa Denis Fustel de Coulanges,
concurs with Constant, asserting roundly that in the ancient world, the state was
omnipotent and that the ancients knew nothing of individual liberty. He notes
that the ancient city was as much a church as a state so that citizens belonged
to it body and soul. Every citizen was a soldier, if soldiers were needed. Everyone's possessions were at the disposal of the state, if the state required them.
Modes of dress were fixed and enforced, education was (as we shall see with
Plato) a matter of state control, and no one was permitted to live his life apart
from his fellows. He concludes, "It is a singular error, therefore, among all
human error, to believe that in the ancient cities men enjoyed liberty. They had

not even the idea of it. They did not believe that there could exist any right as against the city and its gods.' [de Coulanges, 223; see 219-223]

What I attempt in this book is, in part, to trace the transition from ancient liberty to modern liberty, from the individual in thrall to his community to the individual capable of exercising the rights noted by Constant. In using the term 'individual' as a focal point for my discussion, I am aware of the danger of lapsing into anachronism. Our modes of thinking are expressed in language, and language is a social entity, shaped by, and shaping, the very possibilities of thought at any given time so that our thinking is always, to some extent, socially and historically contingent. The very idea of the individual is not something that would have been immediately perspicuous to our remote ancestors although, as Thomas Szasz notes, for those of our ancestors closer to us in time, 'Christianity was invaluable for raising man's moral sensibility and laying the foundation for individualism and freedom' which judgement, if true, would give the notion of the individual a respectable historical pedigree. [Szasz, 151] Owen Barfield, one of the Inklings,[24] remarks that 'The consciousness of "myself" and the distinction between "my-self" and all other selves... the observer, and the external world...is such an obvious and early fact of experience to every one of us...that it requires a sort of training of the imagination to be able to conceive of any different kind of consciousness.' Yet it is the case, he remarks, that 'this form of experience, so far from being eternal, is quite a recent achievement of the human spirit. It was absent from the old mythological outlook; absent, in its fullness, from Plato and the Greek philosophers' although, echoing Szasz's judgement, he notes that 'it was beginning to light up in the Middle Ages, as we see in the development of Scholastic words like *individual* and *person*.'[25]

In any event, the republican or neo-roman conception of liberty, while not without interest, is *not* the conception of freedom I am operating with in this book.[26]

Substantive (or thick) liberty

Substantive or thick liberty is liberty understood not just as the absence of external constraints on my actions outside the scope of the zero-aggression principle but as a lack of anything that limits my actual choices, whether that is lack of money, ill health, or a bad choice of parents. Thomas Sowell, characterising this idea of freedom as 'unconstrained freedom' writes, 'the illusory nature of freedom or equality to the poor has been a recurrent theme of the unconstrained vision for centuries....one is not "really" free, in the unconstrained vision, merely because the political process does not legally confine one's action. If the actual means of achieving one's goals are lacking, then there is no freedom in *result*, even if there is freedom in the *process*.' [Sowell 1987, 88] Liberty thus understood in a thick or substantive sense is the capacity to be able to perform certain acts or to make use of certain resources. On this conception of liberty, it is to be parsed out in terms of some other entity—wealth or knowledge or beauty or health or power. But desirable as all these things may be, and granted that freedom may well lead to them or bring them into being or sustain them, for me, they are not what liberty is. Liberty is, well, just liberty and should not be confused with 'ability, capability, knowledge, virtue, health, or wealth.' [Palmer 2009, 28] Hayek is good on this point. He writes, the 'confusion of liberty as power with liberty in its original meaning inevitably leads to the identification of liberty with wealth....Yet, though freedom and wealth are both good things which most of us desire and though we often need both to obtain what we wish, they still remain different. Whether or not I am my own master and can follow my own choice and whether the possibilities from which I must choose are many or few are two entirely different questions. The courtier living in the lap of luxury but at the beck and call of his prince may be much less free than a poor peasant or artisan, less able to live his own life and to choose his own opportunities for usefulness.' [Hayek 1960, 16] The thick conception of liberty, if indeed it is a conception of liberty at all and not a conception of something else entirely, is most definitely *not* the conception of liberty operative in this book.

Thin liberty

The conception of liberty that I am concerned with in this book—thin liberty—is simply this: to the extent that an agent is unconstrained in his actions by force or by the threat of force, he is free or, as Thomas Hobbes puts it, a free man is one who, 'in those things, which by his strength and wit he is able to do, is not hindred to doe what he hath the will to.'[27] [Hobbes, chapter 21, 146] Developing the Hobbesian idea, Isaiah Berlin, in his well-known essay on 'Two Concepts of Liberty,' limits what he calls 'political liberty' to those situations in which the hindrance to action is not the outcome of some natural force but specifically the result of human agency. 'I am normally said to be free to the degree to which no man or body of men interferes with my activity,' he writes. 'If I am prevented by others from doing what I could otherwise do, I am to that degree unfree; and if this area is contracted by other men beyond a certain minimum, I can be described as being coerced....Coercion implies the deliberate interference of other human beings within the area in which I could otherwise act. You lack political liberty or freedom only if you are prevented from attaining a goal by human beings. Mere incapacity to attain a goal is not lack of political freedom.' [Berlin, 122] In a similar vein, Orlando Patterson remarks that 'Personal freedom, at its most elementary gives a person the sense that one, on the one hand, is not being coerced or restrained by another person in doing something desired and, on the other hand, the conviction that one can do as one pleases within the limits of that other person's desire to do the same.' [Patterson 1991, 3]

Friedrich Hayek writes, 'This oldest meaning of "freedom" has sometimes been described as its vulgar meaning; but when we consider all the confusion that philosophers have caused by their attempts to refine or improve it, we may do well to accept this description [viz. 'independence of the arbitrary will of another']. More important, however, than that it is the original meaning is that it is a distinct meaning and that it describes one thing and one thing only, a state which is desirable for reasons different from those which make us desire other things also called "freedom."' Of these erstwhile freedoms, Hayek writes, 'strictly speaking, these various "freedoms" are not different species of the same genus but entirely different conditions, often in conflict with one another, which therefore should be kept clearly distinct.' [Hayek 1960, 12]

If you are held up at gunpoint and threatened with violence unless you hand over your wallet, and if, responding to the threat, you do in fact hand over your wallet, have you acted freely or not? The answer to this question depends on whether one considers freedom from a metaphysical perspective or from a moral/political perspective. From the metaphysical perspective, I believe (with Hobbes[28]) that the action should be considered to be voluntary. You were presented with a choice and, having considered all the options, you made what you believed to be the best choice in the circumstances. True, all things considered, you would have preferred not to part with your wallet to a total stranger and so, to capture this aspect of the situation, your action might be described as being, in Aristotle's classification, nonvoluntary rather than simply voluntary. In the end, however, Aristotle accepts that, properly speaking, nonvoluntary actions are a species of voluntary action; the point of the *non* in *nonvoluntary* is intended to capture the difference between those actions which we choose to perform outside the scope of external coercion or duress and those that are so constrained. A ship's captain who jettisoned his supercargo in a storm to save the ship and its crew would probably be judged to have acted reasonably; a ship's captain who jettisoned his supercargo just to contemplate the pretty pattern the jetsam made on the surface of the sea would normally incur censure. Metaphysically, both have acted freely; morally or politically, however, the action of the first is a response to duress of circumstances; the action of the second is merely capricious.

Returning to our example: if you would not have done what you did do— hand over the wallet—*but for* the threat, then you have acted under duress and so, morally and politically, your action is not free. 'Free agency does not depend on whether a person's choice is driven by a *strong* or a *weak* cause or no *cause* at all. It depends on the agent's capacity to choose from whatever alternatives he faces. He must be a sane adult and not be under duress.' [de Jasay 1991, 19] An individual's *legitimate* freedom ranges over the set of his unconstrained actions limited only by the zero-aggression principle. Every individual may live his own life as he sees fit provided he does not aggress against others, aggression being the initiation or the threat to initiate physical force against the person or property of another. [see Justinian's *Institutes* I.3.1-2]

This thin notion of liberty, obvious as it may appear, yet seems inadequate to some who would characterise it as substantively empty. For these others, such a conception of liberty, perhaps necessary in some measure or other for human flourishing, is certainly not sufficient. The advocate of thin liberty doesn't assume that men are necessarily wise, still less that they are infallible, but he does take their actions to be theirs, for good and, significantly, for ill. The advocate of thin liberty operates with a correspondingly thin conception of justice, confining it to those matters that can be satisfied simply by *not* doing something: not killing, not injuring, not stealing, and not cheating. The advocate of thick liberty typically operates with a thick conception of justice. For him, justice is not merely a matter of refraining from killing and stealing and the like; it also requires us, in a legally enforceable manner, to help the poor and the hungry and the disenfranchised. Even if this vision of justice were otherwise acceptable, at this point the ineliminable knowledge problem kicks in. Which poor? Poor in what way? How many of them? To what extent? For how long? [see Otteson 2014, passim]

Advocates of substantive or thick liberty are willing, in principle, to intervene to override the thin liberty of some in order to bring about the thick liberty of others. But to be willing to intervene in the freedom of other human beings, even for what is conceived to be their own good, is to be committed to a radical kind of inequality, the inequality that subsists between the controller and the controlled, an inequality much more radical and destructive than any mere inequality of access to goods and services. To the extent that we are forced to subordinate our goals, our desires, our wishes and our actions to the commands of others, to that extent is our freedom fatally compromised and with it, our dignity as human beings.

Boundary Problems, Exclusion and Sexist Language

I would like to take a few moments here to consider some issues that crop up with distressing regularity and which, given their ability to confuse and distract, it might be expedient to dispose of summarily. These issues are: the boundary problem (or the *sorites*), claims of exclusion, and the issue of so-called sexist language.

Boundary Problems: Socrates and the Sorites

The first issue I would like to consider is a recurrent methodological stratagem, a failure to appreciate which can lead to our inability to robustly reject a particularly insidious and prevalent form of fallacious argumentation. A problem bequeathed to philosophy by Socrates (through Plato) is the belief, still held by some philosophers to this day, that in order to know what a given concept means and to be justified in using it, one has to be able to produce on demand the necessary and sufficient conditions for its instantiation. This may well be in order for certain disciplines, such as mathematics, where one can often state such conditions—for example, a triangle is a plane figure bounded by three straight lines—but it is most certainly *not* the case in more humdrum and empirically messy areas of life. Who, offhand, can give the definition of a tree? But one's inability to define a tree satisfactorily does not significantly prevent one from identifying an entity as a tree or speaking meaningfully about trees, and having one's identification be accurate for practical purposes most of the time. Of course, there may occasionally be boundary problems so that while there are trees that are unambiguously trees and bushes that are unashamedly bushes, there may be bushes that are suspiciously arboreal, not to mention trees that appear to have a hankering to transgenerate into bushes. But this confused and confusing boundary area between trees and bushes does not prevent us from being clear about most trees and most bushes most of the time. The classical argument form known as the *sorites*—a first cousin of the Socratic obsession with necessary and sufficient conditions—uses the phenomenon of borderline cases between bushes and trees (or any other two pertinent entities) to conclude that, in the end, there's really no difference between bushes and trees at all.

To see the *sorites* in action, try the following experiment on a captive audience. Ask people to raise their hands if they would consider men 6' 6" and over to be tall. My guess is that you will get a 100% positive response. Now ask people to raise their hands if they consider men 4' 4" and under to be short. Once again, a 100% positive response.[29] Move your suggested heights progressively downwards from 6' 6" and upwards from 4' 4" and watch the percentages drop progressively from 100% the more you move away from your starting points. (Even more interesting, perhaps, is to watch how some hands will raise, then lower, then settle at a kind of half-mast!) What this experiment demonstrates is that along any given continuum (let's stick with "short" and "tall"), we can move progressively from a given point that can correctly and unanimously be described as short to a point that can correctly and unanimously be described as tall so that as we move along the line change *does* occur from one to the other; however, it doesn't follow that the change occurs *at a point*. Some people are clearly and unambiguously short, others clearly and unambiguously tall, and others—well, who can tell? But there is no reason to allow the problematic borderline cases to support the claim that there really is no difference between short and tall after all.

The same considerations hold for the application of many contested concepts in ethics and politics. Take the notion of aggression, central to libertarianism. Aggression is defined by the libertarian as the initiation of, or the threat to initiate, physical force against the person or property of another. Walking up to a total stranger and punching him in the face is, under this definition and under normal circumstances, clearly an act of aggression; sitting quietly in one's garden contemplating the beauty of the night sky is clearly not. Threatening to disembowel your next-door neighbour with a blunt knife if he doesn't cut his side of the boundary hedge between your properties may be a joke or an act of aggression, depending on circumstances. Are you and your neighbour close friends who regularly employ extravagant hyperbolic language in your dealings with each other? Have you been engaged in acrimonious disputes for years? Is this the first time you've communicated? But whatever the ultimate judgement on the aggressive or non-aggressive nature of the threatened disembowelling, punching a total stranger in the face is still an act of aggression and contemplating the night sky is not.

Exclusion: Is Philosophy Androcentric and Leukocentric?

The second issue to concern us is that of exclusion. Accusations are regularly levelled against the philosophy 'establishment' that it is exclusively white and exclusively male, so too the authors who receive its attention.[30] Christopher Lasch remarks that some would-be radicals assert that 'knowledge is merely another name for power. The dominant groups—white Eurocentric males, in the usual formulation—impose their ideas, their canon, their self-serving readings of history on everybody else' thus keeping 'women, homosexuals, and "people of color" in their place.' But when the discredited dominant worldview is replaced by some or all of 'black studies, feminist studies, gay studies, Chicano studies, and other "alternative" ideologies' and when it is realised that 'knowledge is equated with ideology, it is no longer necessary to argue with opponents on intellectual grounds or to enter into their point of view. It is enough to dismiss them as Eurocentric, racist, sexist, homophobic—in other words, as politically suspect.' [Lasch, 12-13]

The claim of exclusion is intended to suggest that there are rich veins of non-male and non-white philosophical thought that are either simply unknown or worse, deliberately ignored, or worse still, concealed or destroyed by the white, male philosophy 'establishment'. These accusations range from not unreasonable suggestions that we might look outside the usual male, white suspects to consider the contributions of non-male and non-white thinkers, to hyperbolically unreasonable claims of the 'systemic killing of female philoso-phers' and 'massacres of some of our earliest thinkers such as the Aztec.' [see Salami] I am always willing to be persuaded that some hitherto undiscovered thinker has something of value to contribute to the philosophical conversa-tion (witness my inclusion of the relatively little-known Johannes Althusius in this history) but I do not believe that I am being unreasonable in requiring some direct evidence of this in place of mere generalities inspired by dubious ideological prejudices.

To see this ideological phenomenon operating at a broader cultural and histor-ical level, consider the phenomenon of Afrocentrism. Understood moderately, Afrocentrism amounts to 'an emphasis on the shared African origins of all "black" people', a pride in the cultural contributions of people of African origin and a belief that there is more to be known about Africans and their cultures than has hitherto been appreciated in a world constituted largely by European values. [Howe, 1] In its extreme form, however, Afrocentrism involves belief in 'fundamentally distinct and internally homogeneous "African" ways of knowing and feeling about the world, ways which only members of the group can possibly understand.' This belief is often accompanied by 'a mythical vision of the past, and by a body of racial pseudo-science…' [Howe, 2] The resemblance between this extreme form of Afrocentrism and some extreme forms of nationalism is striking. As someone who was schooled in Ireland in the 1950s and 1960s, I can testify from experience that the history to which I was exposed was a creature of nationalist myth and a vehicle for the assertion of Irish (Celtic) cultural and religious superiority. This bizarre form of indoc-trination was, it appears, more widespread than I had suspected. Stephen Howe remarks that 'Virtually every European state and ethnic group has drawn on and abused the discipline of archaeology in its search for historical roots, often involving straightforwardly racist ideas about the origins and destiny of itself and its neighbours…In the cases I know best, those of Britain and Ireland, very long histories of utterly fantastic racial myth and ideas about the national pasts and origins can be traced, involving all the elements of mysticism, claims of racial primacy and superiority, and promiscuous borrowings from esoteric lore and Masonic tradition which we shall observe operating in the African-American case.' [Howe, 7; see Keating, passim]

So, who deserves to be heard, taken seriously, and accorded a place at the top table of intellectual discourse? Is there systematic exclusion of particular groups of people, based upon their sex, skin colour, ethnic origin, place of birth? I believe the answer to this question is—no. Perhaps an example from another relatively non-contentious field will make my point clear. The invention of the compact disc (CD) made it possible to record and distribute the work of many previously unheard composers. Despite the welcome availability of new musical experiences made possible by the CD, and the re-discovery of many good composers, the received wisdom as to who does and who does not count among music's greats has not been substantially disturbed. Very few of the newly heard composers can make a plausible claim to sit at music's top table—Franz Berwald being a possible exception. The reason is very simple. The top table has a limited seating capacity and very few people *of any kind, ethnicity, sex, age, or nationality* can reasonably claim a seat. Have you ever heard of Robert Ashley, Carlo Arrigoni, Ivor Atkins, Charles-Auguste de Bériot, Hippolyte André-Baptiste Chelard, Isaak Iosifovich Dunayevsky, Armando Gentilucci, Antonín Kammel, Shaiva Mikhaylovich Mshvelidze, Ernest Pingoud, Johan Helmich Roman, Mazimierz Sikorski, Jenö Takács, Moyssey Samuilovich Vatnberg? I found these composers by opening my copy of *The Grove Concise Dictionary of Music* at random and sticking my finger somewhere on the page. These composers were all significant and prolific enough to merit a place in *Grove*, but had you ever heard of any of them before reading their names just now? I hadn't, and I have been an avid music lover for over fifty years. Have you seen their names on any concert programmes? Have you ever heard any of their music? No? What a surprise! Even with the increased availability of recordings of obscure music made possible by the CD and by online streaming services, I wish you good luck trying to find recordings of any of their music. I am not saying it's impossible, just very difficult. You might argue that despite their entries in *Grove*, all these neglected composers are deservedly neglected. A large claim and one hard to justify since we haven't heard their work but, for the sake of argument, suppose it to be so. But what then are we to make of such as Louis Théodore Gouvy (1819-1898), the Franco-German composer, with two hundred compositions to his credit, including nine symphonies, a requiem and many large scale religious and choral works, two operas, dozens of lieder and a half ton of solo piano music, quartets and quintets? Gouvy's music was highly regarded (except perhaps in France) during his lifetime and esteemed by such as Brahms and Berlioz but, despite this, after his death, his music disappeared from the concert hall and the recording studio until the end of the 20th century when a partial recovery began.

The same is true of philosophy. Although it may be correct in some sense to say, as feminist and race critics do, that the works of white male thinkers dominate[31] philosophy, it should also be noted that the works of many, perhaps most, white male thinkers never achieve recognition except, occasionally, for a few lines in the more comprehensive histories of philosophy, even though I suspect that many of these 'excluded' white male thinkers have a plausibly greater claim to philosophical relevance than either the Aztecs or the supposed murder-victims of anti-female philosophical pogroms.

Here's a list of philosophers, whose surnames begin with the letter A, who were born in the twentieth century and who were considered by its compiler to be important enough to make it onto a Wikipedia[32] page: Elisa Aaltola, Nicola Abbagnano, Bijan Abdolkarimi, Taha Abdurrahman, David Abram, Gerd B. Achenbach, Peter Achinstein, Hans Achterhuis, H. B. Acton, Marilyn McCord Adams, Robert Merrihew Adams, Mortimer Adler, Theodor Adorno, Sediq Afghan, Michel Aflaq, Giorgio Agamben, Hans Albert, Rogers Albritton, Virgil Aldrich, Gerda Alexander, Aleksandr Danilovich Aleksandrov, Robert Alexy, Diogenes Allen, William Alston, Louis Althusser, Günther Anders, Alan Ross Anderson, C. Anthony Anderson, G. E. M. Anscombe, Karl-Otto Apel, Kwame Anthony Appiah, Hannah Arendt, David Malet Armstrong, Zaki al-Arsuzi, Raymond Aron, Pandurang Shastri Athavale, Robert Audi, John Langshaw Austin, Alfred Jules Ayer and Joxe Azurmendi. How many of these forty one philosophers (six women and thirty five men) have you ever heard of? Of those you might have heard of, how much of their work have you read or do you know about, even at second hand? If I were to answer these questions, I would say that I have heard of ten of the men and four of the women and I have read the work of five of the men that I have heard of and the work of three of the women. Who, if any, among these forty one philosophers will enter the pantheon of the philosopher gods? Whose work will, in the future, be reckoned important enough to rank beside that of Aristotle, Kant, Hegel or Wittgenstein?

Sexist Language?

The third, and final issue, I'd like to address is the supposed problem of sexist language. It is sometimes claimed that English has no third person singular sex-neutral personal pronoun, that the use of *he* (and its associated forms) is ineluctably sexist and that it has contributed and still contributes to the social oppression of women. Apart from certain neologisms,[33] some of them proffered as early as the mid-nineteenth century and none of them successful, many putatively non-sexist alternatives have been suggested, such as the use of the compound phrase *he or she* (and its associated forms). In a single instance, this is perhaps acceptable, but in a passage with repeated pronouns, it quickly becomes unwieldy, indeed comical.[34] Pluralisation is sometimes possible but even when possible it is not always stylistically elegant. *One* can sometimes be used but it is very formal and, in some contexts, unidiomatic. The simple and radical substitution of *she* for *he* (popular in politically-correct academic circles, as if an injustice long inflicted is now to be remedied at a single stroke) would appear to be as objectionably sexist as *he*, without the saving grace of *he*'s historical justification. *They* (and its associated forms) is increasingly being used in conjunction with a singular antecedent, even in contexts which are exclusively male—so, for example, in relation to men's rugby, you might hear someone say, 'If a player is tackled, they must release the ball immediately.' The lack of agreement in number between the pronoun and its antecedent is as painful to my ears as the scratching of fingernails on a blackboard but my students appear to be oblivious to such discordance. I suspect that this usage will become increasingly common and will eventually be accepted as grammatically in order. After all, we have before us in English the example of the originally plural *you* now used for both singular and plural, albeit with agreement between the pronoun and verb.[35]

As long ago as 1924, Otto Jespersen noted that 'In the personal pronouns for the third person *he* and *she* are distinguished in English as in the other languages of our family; when a common-sex pronoun is wanted, *he* may be used instead of *he or she*, but colloquially the pl. *they* is often used...'[36] The compilers of the Merriam-Webster dictionary, saying 'We're descriptivists. We follow language, language doesn't follow us,' have accepted *they* as singular. The Merriam-Webster Descriptivist policy presents itself as plain, no nonsense, anti-elitist and democratic. Despite its bluff demotic credentials, however, it is not an entirely innocent project, responding in a calm, detached and scientific way to the general linguistic will of the people. As David Foster Wallace notes, 'the very language in which today's socialist, feminist, minority, gay, and environmental movements frame their sides of political debates is informed by the Descriptivist belief that traditional English is conceived and perpetuated by Privileged WASP males and is thus inherently capitalist, sexist, racist, xenophobic, homophobic, elitist: unfair.' [Wallace 2006b, 81] The action of the American Dialect Society (ADS) bears out Wallace's point. Firmly mixing identity politics with linguistics, the ADS salutes the singular *they* for its 'emerging use as a pronoun to refer to a known person, often as a conscious choice by a person rejecting the traditional gender binary of he and she.'

Hidden political agendas aside, it may still appear that Descriptivists have right and reason on their side. It cannot be denied that language changes constantly, sometimes radically. [see Aitchison, passim] The word *obsequious* used to mean *obedient* or *compliant* but it now signifies *sycophantic*; *pretty* originally meant *deceitful* or *sly* and now signifies merely *transient beauty*.[37] One might think that a change in the meaning of random words such as *obsequious* or *pretty* is of no great significance but hold to the view that the core elements of our language must remain constant over time. Alas, not so. Our personal pronouns—core to the language if anything is core—have been far from constant. The original Old English personal pronouns underwent substantial change, being affected, not least by Old Norse, to which language we largely owe the now normal third person plurals, *they*, *them*, *their*. [see Jespersen, 66]

Language does indeed change, sometimes quickly, sometimes slowly, sometimes a little, sometimes a lot. The question that arises for the Descriptivist is—*which* changes are to be accepted by the Dictionary, and *when*, and on the basis of *what principle* or *principles*? [see Wallace 2006b, 83-84] All changes? Some? Immediately? Later? But if not all and not immediately, why not? It is increasingly the case, for example, that the preterite and the past participle are confused in spoken English, with the preterite well on the way to supplanting the past participle almost entirely ['I should have went' and 'they had ran' and 'He's took the wrong option!'] although, bizarrely and bravely, if erroneously, the past participle in a few cases has mounted a countermovement ['I seen' and 'he done'.] And then we have the grammatical cleansing of irregular verbs, the slow, lingering death of the adverb and the increasingly random and bizarre use of prepositions. Should the compilers of a Descriptivist Dictionary not reflect *all* these usages and do so *now*? In not accepting any and every change and in not doing so immediately, the Descriptivist turns out to be a closet Prescriptivist; it's just that she makes her decisions along carefully concealed politically correct Prescriptive grounds. To paraphrase Milton Friedman, 'We're all Prescriptivists now.'[38]

But is it not the case, the Descriptivist will gently urge, that spoken language is primary and that what is to be taken to be grammatically acceptable at any given time depends upon the usage of native speakers? Leaving to one side the not unimportant question of *which* native speakers we are to pay attention to—for not every native speaker speaks in the same way; are we to take some latter-day Eliza Doolittle as our model?[39]—it may be granted that spoken language is (in some sense, at least) primary. But, while people may speak as they damn well please (and they do),[40] and do so in an astonishing variety of ways, the standard written form of the language is the battleground on which the privileged, capitalist, sexist, racist, xenophobic, homophobic, elitist WASP[41] male Prescriptivist is prepared to fight and die. Here, once again, Prescriptivism of some form or other, overt or covert, is unavoidable, so you pays your money and you takes your choice. Despite Descriptivist dogmatism, there is no way on earth I am ever going to accept *enormity* to mean *very large* when we have to hand *immenseness, immensity, largeness, massiveness, vastness,* and *hugeness*, or that I am going to think that to describe a judge as *uninterested* is merely an elegant variation on describing him as *disinterested*, or—and you can see where I'm going here—that I shall consider acceptable in formal writing the use of *they* as a third person singular pronoun.[42]

In the meantime however, a point that many people fail to grasp is that all these solutions to the supposed problem of sexist pronouns, whatever other merits they might have, are essentially solutions in search of a problem because, first, as David Crystal notes, 'There is no necessary correlation between grammatical gender and sex'[43]—indeed, Eric Partridge noted many years ago that '*Gender* refers to words; as a synonym for *sex* it is jocular and archaic'—and second, the claim upon which all the proposed changes are based, namely, that English has no third person sex-neutral personal pronoun, is simply not true![44] Let us take these points in turn.

The linkage of sex and gender in the minds of native English speakers is an instance of linguistic parochialism. Insofar as there is a close relationship between grammar and sex, it is, as Frank Palmer notes, 'largely restricted to languages with which scholars are most familiar, those of the Indo-European and Semitic groups. In other languages, especially in Africa, gender in a strict grammatical sense has nothing to do with sex but is concerned with the distinction between living and non-living creatures and even between big and small.'[45] In a later work, Palmer notes that 'If masculine, feminine and neuter are defined in terms of male, female and sex-less creatures we have no explanation at all for the use of the feminine *la sentinelle* in French to refer to the very male guardsman, while a young lady in German is referred to by the most inappropriate neuter nouns *Fräulein* and *Mädchen*. Clearly, then, the categories of number and gender are formal categories—based upon the form and in particular, the syntax of the language…'[46] [Palmer 1975, 30]

Even in German, a second cousin once-removed of English, the link between sex and gender is tenuous. Mark Twain demonstrates this point humorously in his paper, 'That Awful German Language,' translating the *Tale of the Fishwife and its Sad Fate* thus: 'It is a bleak Day. Hear the Rain, how he pours, and the Hail, how he rattles; and see the Snow, how he drifts along, and of the Mud, how deep he is! Ah the poor Fishwife, it is stuck fast in the Mire; it has dropped its Basket of Fishes; and its Hands have been cut by the Scales as it seized some of the falling Creatures; and one Scale has even got into its Eye, and it cannot get her out. It opens its Mouth to cry for Help; but if any Sound comes out of him, alas he is drowned by the raging of the Storm. And now a Tomcat has got one of the Fishes and she will surely escape with him. No, she bites off a Fin, she holds her in her Mouth,—will she swallow her? No, the Fishwife's brave Mother-dog deserts his Puppies and rescues the Fin,—which he eats, himself, as his Reward….' [Twain, 18]

The second point of which I made mention was that the claim upon which all the proposed changes are based, namely, that English has no third person sex-neutral personal pronoun, is simply not true. The third person sex-neutral personal pronoun in English is *he* (and its associated forms). What is true, however, is that English has no third personal sex-neutral personal pronoun that is *morphologically distinct* from *he*, *him*, and *his*, which is also the third person masculine pronoun. The description of the President in the English-language version of the Irish Constitution [*Bunreacht na hÉireann*] as *he* and references to *his* duties and *his* prerogatives have not prevented the election of two female Presidents by the votes of any citizen, male or female, who has reached *his* thirty-fifth year of age.[47] Neither of the two successful female candidates declined to stand (or serve) on pronominal or adjectival grounds, nor did many female voters decline to cast their ballots because the relevant constitutional article linguistically prevented them from so doing. To move from the constitutional plane to the literary: Elizabeth Bowen, the novelist, in her essay on writing a novel, remarks unselfconsciously of the writer of the novel that 'He is forced towards his plot' and speaks of the 'novelist's perception of his characters.' [Bowen, 1, 3] Similarly, Patricia Highsmith, the crimewriter, notes, without evident discomfort, that 'In the second draft, a writer makes all the changes and improvements he knows how to make.' [Highsmith, 103] Patently, neither of these female authors can, without existential contradiction, be taken by their use of the neutral *he* and *his* to exclude the possibility of female writers.

There is nothing fundamentally mysterious or sinister about this process. Consider this uncontroversial example. The word *bank* can refer either to a financial institution or to the land bordering the side of a river. If I were to say,

'I'm going to deposit my money in the bank this morning,' most people would take me to signify that I am going to my local financial institution to deposit my money there rather than signifying my intention to dig a hole in the land bounding the edge of a river and put my money into it although the recent history of exciting events in banks around the world may make this assumption less obviously likely than it might otherwise be. The word *bank*, used in two distinct significations, is both a homophone (same sound) and a homograph (same spelling) but context disambiguates the relevant signification. Similarly, the word *he* (and its associated forms) is also both a homophone and a homograph signifying, according to context, either human beings indifferently or just male human beings. So too, the word *man* in English signifies, according to context, either human beings in general or adult male human beings. Other languages mark this distinction by using morphologically distinct words; so, Latin, for example, has *homo* for human beings generally and *vir* for a male human beings, while Greek makes the same distinction with ἄνθρωπος (anthropos) and ἀνήρ (aner). In English, the context makes it clear which sense of the homophone/homographs *he* and *man* we are to understand, just as context does for the word *bank*. In addition to all this, the causal link between supposedly sexist words in a language and the social status of women is less than obvious. Peter Farb, noting attempts to introduce completely new third-person pronouns into English, remarks that 'no evidence exists that [such changes] would necessarily improve the status of women.' Turkish has a personal pronoun, *o*, that can mean either 'he' or 'she' yet 'the status of women…in Turkey is certainly lower than that of women in most English-speaking countries….The problem of woman's status in English-speaking communities will not be solved by dismantling the language—but by changing the social structure.' [Farb, 136]

   Given, then, that *he* and *man* have two distinct significations, that there is no necessary causal link between linguistic change and the removal of state-imposed legal impediments to the freedom of women to make whatever non-aggressive choices they wish to make—a removal which I, as a libertarian, fully support—and that none of the proposed solutions to what is essentially a non-problem is without stylistic drawbacks, I shall, when appropriate, use *he* and *man* (and their associated forms) throughout this work. Any reader who has not been persuaded by the foregoing considerations is, of course, free when reading this history to substitute any alternative form of noun or pronoun that takes her, or its, or their fancy.[48]

THE REALITY OF COLLECTIVES

At times in this history, I shall speak of various forms of collective: government, state, nation and the like. It is important to be clear just what the status (no pun intended) of such collectives is. Are groups, corporations, tribes, clans, nations and states just convenient ways of organising the lives of individuals, or do these collectives have a measure of real existence of their own? If so, are they at least as real, or perhaps even more real, than the individuals who constitute them? The dispute about the ontological status of groups or collectives is a reenactment of the classic battle between Platonists and Aristotelians transferred from the empyrean heights of metaphysics to the sublunary arena of human action.[49] Are the Forms, à la Plato, more real than the things of this world, existing apart from them yet giving them the small measure of reality that they have; or are forms in things, *à la* Aristotle, making them to be what they are but having no independent real existence apart from them? This argument is not merely of historical interest; it is a perennial area of philosophical dispute.[50] Today, as Tom Palmer notes, 'An army of illiberal academics have posited an array of "social forces" of domination—including class, gender, race, and other categories—that are more active and real than the mere flesh-and-blood "individuals" that surround us (although it takes the hard work of tenured professors to see those social forces properly and without distortion).' [Palmer 2014b, 113] For such latter-day Platonists, reality is a bloodless ballet of intersecting and interacting abstractions, a phantasmagoria of forms, whereas the concrete chattels of our everyday world are things of little or no real significance.

It is certainly true that we speak of groups or associations and that these groups or associations can constitute the subject or object of sentences with action verbs, for example: 'The State today recognised its obligation to care for the long-term disabled' or 'The Government issued instructions to all local authorities concerning levels of local taxation' or 'The University has adopted a new entrance policy for disadvantaged students.' What is the ontological, moral, or legal status of the subjects of these sentences? In answer to this question, we might adopt a position—call it *collective nominalism*—that denies that these groups or associations have any mode of existence at all, being merely a convenient way of speaking of individuals cooperating with each other; or we could subscribe to *collective realism* and hold that such groups have a transcendent reality above and beyond the members who constitute them or the relationships (informal or contractual) that bind those members together; or, finally, we could accept *collective epiphenomenalism*, which is the position that social groups and associations are entities of a sort, created and sustained by the network of intentions (often embodied in rules, laws and constitutions) of those who compose them, either informal (as with football supporters) or formal (as with members of a corporation).

Of these three positions on the ontological status of collectives, collective epiphenomenalism seems to me to be the most defensible, at once reflecting our lived experience while avoiding the obvious shortcomings of both collective nominalism and collective realism. 'One's ordinary common sense baulks,' Ervin Laszlo remarks, 'at treating what appear to be merely associations between individual human beings as entities in themselves.' [Laszlo 1972b, 98] Some social wholes—teams, corporations, even nations—can, once established, maintain a coherent ethos and mode of existence even as the personnel of whom they are composed changes over time. Such relative stability, which includes a capacity for self-perpetuation, is 'typical of all groups of interacting parts when the parts maintain some basic sets of relationships among themselves.' [Laszlo 1972a, 7; see 44] While there are material elements associated with such social groups—football grounds, company headquarters, bank accounts and the like—the principal sustaining element in the creation and maintenance of social wholes are the beliefs of its personnel and of those who relate to it. 'Attitudes, beliefs, world views—these all play a vital role in determining the environment of social systems. Not that the real and objective factors can be neutralized, but they are overlaid by what people believe about them, and thus their effect is modified (cushioned or sharpened) by the dominant culture.' [Laszlo 1972a, 62]

Larken Rose points out repeatedly that the idea of political authority is a myth created and maintained by the beliefs of those who are prey to the illusion that it really exists and who thereby feel under an obligation to respect it. Remove that belief, and the idea of political authority—and the institutions built upon it—collapse. 'When a mind has always thought of something in one way, that mind will imagine evidence and hallucinate experience supporting the idea.... To most people, "government" feels like an obvious reality, as rational and self-evident as gravity. Few people have ever objectively examined the concept, because they have never had a reason to. Everyone assumes that it is, and talks as if it is, so why would anyone question it?....If enough people recognize and let go of the "authority" myth, there is no need for any election, any political action, or any revolution. If the people did not imagine themselves to have an obligation to obey the politicians, the politicians would literally be ignored into irrelevance.' [Rose 2011, 45; 146] I believe Rose's position should perhaps be described as a form of collective nominalism rather than a form of collective epiphenomenalism but, whichever it is, he is surely correct to maintain that unless the appropriate belief system concerning political authority is widely held by the subject population over which a government exerts control, that government could not survive. In thinking this, Rose echoes the thoughts of Étienne de la Boétie.

Human action, whatever else it may be, is ineluctably particular. One cannot take a dog in general for a walk in general or post a letter in general to no one in particular; it has to be this particular dog, now, in this particular park, and this particular letter to this particular person posted in this particular box. Collectives have a secondary mode of existence, consisting ontologically of a network of relationships subsisting among individual human beings. These relationships are real and so to the same extent are the collectives constituted by them.

A family is a set of human beings related by genetics (usually), social catego-ries, upbringing and a shared social environment. A football team is a set of human beings related by a particular purpose that is determined by the consti-tutive rules of the game and the organisational rules of football's governing associations. We can say that the family did that or that the football team did this but, in the end, only individual human beings act. When we make a collective the subject of a sentence, what we are describing is the action of an individual or individuals *under a certain description*.[51] 'If a crowd, a town, a nation,' writes Auberon Herbert, 'is not in each case a collection of individ-uals—more or less acted upon, it is true, by certain common feelings, more or less possessing certain common interests—what can it be?' [Herbert 1899, 247] He continues:

There, at the bottom of it all—whether it is a crowd shouting for war, a political party rejoicing over an election victory, a body of schoolboys triumphant over the victory of their eleven or their eight, a professional body clamouring for some professional interest, a clerical meeting denouncing some heresy, a socialist congress rejoicing in the onward march of universal coercion, a trades unionist body denouncing nonunionists, or a gathering of capitalists drawing tighter the bonds of their organization— there in every case are the individuals sharing in some common aim, and therefore sharing in the same feelings—the John Smiths and the Thomas Robinsons, exciting both themselves and their fellows by the old love of strife, or the old craving for utopia, and borrowing what is both good and bad—sometimes ugly passions, and sometimes splendid devotions, from one another. [Herbert 1899, 248]

Murray Rothbard posits methodological individualism as the first implication of the concept of human action. 'The first truth to be discovered about human action,' he says, 'is that *it can be undertaken only by individual actors.*' Only individuals have ends and can act to attain them. There are no such things as ends of or actions by 'groups,' 'collectives,' or 'states,' *which do not take place as actions by various specific individuals.*' [Rothbard 2004, 2 Emphasis added] Although football teams or universities or society are not completely non-existent, for Rothbard they certainly do not possess a mode of reality over and above that of the individuals and the relationships among those individuals who constitute them: '[T]o say that "governments" act is merely a metaphor; actually, certain individuals are in a certain relationship with other individuals and act in a way that they and the other individuals recognize as "govern-mental." The metaphor must not be taken to mean that the collective institution itself has any reality *apart from the acts of various individuals.*' [Rothbard 2004, 3, emphasis added] It should be noted that Rothbard does not deny the reality of groups or aggregates completely. What he denies is that they have a mode of reality *apart from* or *superior to* that of individuals.

The British Prime Minister, Margaret Thatcher, is notorious for having once remarked that there was no such a thing as society and she has been roundly sneered at for making that remark ever since. What she in fact said in an interview was, 'Who is society? There is no such thing! There are individual men and women and there are families and *no government can do anything except through people.*'[52] Later in the interview, she went on to say again 'There is no such thing as society. There is a living tapestry of men and women and people and the beauty of that tapestry and the quality of our lives will depend upon how much each of us is prepared to take responsibility for ourselves and each of us prepared to turn round and help by our own efforts those who are unfortunate.' What is usually presented as an example of stone-cold heart-lessness on Thatcher's part is, in fact, a call to take responsibility for oneself and to help one's neighbours and to stop shuffling your problems and their problems off onto somebody else.[53] The mischievous misinterpretation of Mrs Thatcher's comments was instantaneous and egregious, so much so that she took the unprecedented step of issuing a clarification. 'All too often the ills of this country are passed off as those of society,' she said. 'Similarly, when action is required, society is called upon to act. But society as such does not exist except as a concept. Society is made up of people. It is people who have duties and beliefs and resolve. It is people who get things done.'[54] Roger Scruton notes that 'what Thatcher meant on that occasion was quite true, though the opposite of what she said. She meant that there *is* such a thing as society, but that society is not identical with the state. Society is composed of people, freely associating and forming communities of interest that socialists have no right to control and no authority to outlaw.' [Scruton 2014, 8]

Mrs Thatcher might have spared her breath. As the newspaper reporter in *The Man Who Shot Liberty Valence* says when the truth of who really shot Liberty Valence is finally revealed, 'when the legend becomes fact, print the legend.' Mrs Thatcher might have been surprised (and pleased) to discover that her views on society echoed those of the eminent psychiatrist and psychotherapist, Carl Gustav Jung. He believed that 'society is nothing more than an abstract idea like the State. Both are hypostatized, that is, have become autonomous. The State in particular is turned into a quasi-animate personality from whom everything is expected. In reality it is only a camouflage for those individuals who know how to manipulate it. Thus the constitutional State drifts into the situation of a primitive form of society—the communism of a primitive tribe where everybody is subject to the autocratic rule of a chief or an oligarchy.' [Jung 1957, 357]

As might be expected, Murray Rothbard's mentor, Ludwig von Mises, supports the principle of methodological individualism. [Mises 1996, 41-43] He considers the common objections to that principle: human beings are always part of a greater social whole; it is impossible to conceive of man as an isolated individual; language is a social phenomenon; and reason can only emerge 'within the framework of social mutuality.' [Mises 1996, 41] He responds by noting that the evolution of reason, of language, and of cooperation are all real processes but they are the outcome of processes of change *in individuals*. Mises is quite willing to ascribe a measure of reality to groups and even to grant them a determining role in human history. 'Methodological individualism,' he says, 'far from contesting the significance of such collective wholes, considers it as one of its main tasks to describe and to analyze their becoming and their disappearing, their changing structures, and their operation". [Mises 1996, 42]

Are Mises and Rothbard at loggerheads on this matter? No. Just as Rothbard does, Mises asserts that 'all actions are performed by individuals' and that 'a social collective has no existence and reality outside of the individual members' actions.' [Mises 1996, 42] What determines an action to be merely the act of an individual or, on the other hand, to be the act of a group—a state—is the meaning that is ascribed to that action. 'The hangman, not the state, executes a criminal. It is the meaning of those concerned that discerns in the hangman's action an action of the state.' [Mises 1996, 42] To recognise collectives is to exercise an act of understanding, not perception. Collective wholes 'are never visible; their cognition is always the outcome of the understanding of the meaning which acting men attribute to their acts. We can see a crowd.... Whether this crowd is a mere gathering…or an organized body or any other kind of social entity is a question which can only be answered by understanding the meaning which they themselves attach to their presence. And this meaning is always the meaning of individuals.' [Mises 1996, 43][55] 'On a purely factual plane,' writes Alexander d'Entrèves, 'the State does not "exist": it is nowhere to be found, a real person of flesh and blood. Only individuals can be found.' And while it may be that, as with all corporations, 'the State is said to have capacities and liabilities,' this is so only because 'the law, and the law alone… creates and determines them.'[56]

To return for a moment to the discussion of the merits of thin versus thick liberty in a way that links it to this discussion of the individual and the collective, I think it worth pointing out that the interventionist vision of the advocates of thick liberty, appealing as it may at first appear, is guilty of a serious defect. Its paternalism (or, more often nowadays, its maternalism), overt or covert, embodies a serious and ineliminable lack of respect for the autonomy and judgment of those it claims to help. It suffers from the problem of seeing people as being primarily instances of types or kinds or classes rather than the unique individuals they are.[57] James Otteson argues, and it is hard to disagree with his judgement, that 'one of the great triumphs of human civilization [has been] to conceive of human beings not as members of classes but as individual and unique centers of moral agency.' [Otteson 2014, 120] The collectivist vision of the advocates of thick liberty and their ideological allies in the several splintering schools of identitarian politics leads, literally, to a regression to a type of tribalism.

In a Word or Two…

In this history, I will discuss many topics but the overarching theme of the work is the story of the slow, fitful, emergence of the free individual from a background of group-identity and groupthink. In the beginning was the group, and the group, the tribe, the kin, were all in all. Individuality was practically non-existent. The history of human social development is not just the spasmodic transition from status to contract but the fitful emergence of the individual from the group. When we look at the prehistoric and ancient worlds, we must, Larry Siedentop writes, 'imagine ourselves into a world of humans or persons who were not "individuals" as we would understand them now' [Siedentop, 7; Hoffer, passim]

To libertarians, freedom is a constituent condition of individuality and thus, for a libertarian, the most fundamental of social values. But it is not necessarily the only social value that libertarians value. In an earlier work, to anticipate and counter possible misunderstandings, I remarked that 'liberty is the *lowest* of social values, lowest in the sense of being most fundamental, a *sine qua non* of a human action's being susceptible of moral evaluation in any way at all. Human freedom can be used for all sorts of actions directed to all sorts of purposes which are then susceptible to moral evaluation but, unless human action is free from coercion, moral evaluation is intrinsically impossible.'

'Libertarians value freedom as a hard core without which morally significant human action is simply not possible but, while libertarian*ism* as such has
nothing to say beyond asserting and defending individual liberty, this is not at
all the same as thinking that libertarians in living out their lives are concerned
with nothing other than liberty. This would be as absurd as to think that someone
who insisted on the absolute necessity of water for human survival should be
taken to assert that water was the only thing needed for a rich and interesting
diet....Murray Rothbard, whose credentials as a libertarian none can doubt,
remarked that "Only an imbecile could ever hold that freedom is the highest or
indeed the only principle or end of life".'[58] [Casey 2012b, 53-54]

While the desirability and necessity of individual liberty may be obvious
to libertarians, however, it is not quite so obvious to everyone else. As H. L.
Mencken noted, most people want security in this world, not liberty.[59] 'Libertarians,' writes Max Eastman, 'used to tell us that "the love of freedom is the
strongest of political motives," but recent events have taught us the extrav-
agance of this opinion. The "herd-instinct" and the yearning for paternal
authority are often as strong. Indeed the tendency of men to gang up under a
leader and submit to his will is of all political traits the best attested by history.'
[Eastman, 37] As Brian Doherty notes, '…many people loathe and fear liberty,
and not just for others—that tyrannical impulse is easy enough to recognize—
but even for themselves.' [Doherty, 509] Not everyone values freedom, then,
for with freedom comes responsibility, and the necessity to accept that success
or failure are, in part at least, a function of one's own actions and abilities.
'Freedom aggravates at least as much as it alleviates frustration,' remarks Eric
Hoffer. 'Freedom of choice places the whole blame of failure on the shoulders
of the individual. And as freedom encourages a multiplicity of attempts, it
unavoidably multiplies failure and frustration....Unless a man has the talents
to make something of himself, freedom is an irksome burden.' [Hoffer, 35, §26]
In a revealing statement made shortly before the Second World War, a young
Nazi remarked to Ida Wylie, 'We Germans are so happy. We are free from
freedom.'[60] [Wylie, 2]

The libertarian vision, or at least, my libertarian vision, is not of rugged John
the Baptists living alone in the wilderness dining on locusts and wild honey but
rather one of individuals integrated into society by virtue of voluntary association, not just because of their status, personal history, family connections, place
of birth or other adventitious circumstances. 'No man is an island, entire of
itself. Every man is a piece of the continent, a part of the main.' [John Donne]
The completely isolated individual is a creature of fiction; the dichotomy—
either group or individual—is false. Some libertarians are so concerned to
defend the individual against subsumption into the group that they can give the
impression that the ultimate human *desideratum* is a kind of social atomism,
while reluctantly conceding that we must, regrettably, associate with other
human beings from time to time! But few men, if any, can be satisfied with their
own narrow, time-bound and limited lives and most seek some way in which
to transcend their individual limitations. Self-transcendence can come in many
forms—social, sporting, military, religious or other. In his legitimate quest for

self-transcendence, the contemporary isolated individual risks being resubmerged once more in the group, only this time in much larger and more dangerous groups than his predecessors. The nineteenth and twentieth centuries have seen more than their fair share of such cancerous forms of self-transcendence—Militant Nationalism, Fascism, National Socialism and Communism.[61] Liberty's progress throughout history has been real and substantial, but it is still a far from complete and its advances are yet capable of reversal.

A Note on the Text

The road of the history of political thought is a road well travelled. As might be expected, I have made extensive use of the works of original political thinkers and have cited freely from them so that readers may be satisfied that the views I attribute to these thinkers are indeed theirs. I also wanted this book to be a conversation and not a monologue so I have engaged in a dialogue with other historians and with historians of political thought—R. W. and A. J. Carlyle, Francis Oakley, David Boucher & Paul Kelly, J. S. McClelland, David Knowles, Quentin Skinner, John Plamenatz, Henry Sumner Maine, George Sabine, Eric Voegelin, Numa Fustel de Coulanges, Harold Berman, John M. Roberts, Peter H. Wilson and many others—all of which means that there is perhaps more direct citation in this history than would normally be stylistically desirable.

If originality is the art of concealing one's sources, this book should score an A+ for unoriginality. To the best of my knowledge and recollection, everything relevant that I have read or consulted in the writing of this book can be found in the bibliography.

Where it seemed appropriate, I have made occasional use of material that I have published elsewhere but only because I could think of no better way of making the points at issue than the way in which I had originally expressed my thoughts. I have kept these instances of self-citation to a minimum.

Wherever possible, I locate references within the body of the text, allowing them to appear in footnotes only when they would be visually distracting in the text. I have reserved footnotes primarily for parenthetical material and diversionary comments or perhaps, as some disgruntled and cynical readers might think, as a form of 'corroborative detail, intended to give artistic verisimilitude to an otherwise bald and unconvincing narrative.'[62] In my early days as a lecturer, one of my academic superiors sardonically remarked to me that footnotes in French books might safely be ignored, as they were there only for decoration! On the other hand, he counselled that I should completely ignore the main text in German books and read *only* the footnotes! I leave it to readers to decide whether, on the basis of this chauvinistic and tendentious taxonomy, my footnotes follow the French or the German model or if they manage to strike out boldly to achieve a *tertium quid*.

There are few things more daunting than opening a big, fat book at page one and thinking, with a sinking feeling, 'Just another 900 pages to go!' Other things being equal, it makes sense when reading a history to take matters in chronological order but, on the other hand, reading a book shouldn't be a penitential exercise so if, let's say, you are passionately interested in Machiavelli, don't wade through twelve chapters before satisfying your appetite, just go and read the chapter on Machiavelli. Feel free to be selective and unhistorical! If a history of political thought from the perspective of liberty isn't liberty hall, then that fabulous building is nowhere to be found. Here are five suggested short-cuts through the book—Route I, *Historical*: chapters 1, 5, 7, 10, 14, 15, 20, 28-29, 32-35; Route II, *Philosophical*: chapters 2, 3,4, 6, 8-9, 11-13, 17-19, 21-31, 34-35; Route III, *Ancient*: chapters 1-6; Route IV, *Medieval*: chapters 7-13; and Route V, *Modern* 14-34.

I have tried to write this history in a language that resembles idiomatic English and not in one of those strange and incomprehensible dialects common in the Academy, but only you can judge whether I have succeeded. Authors are advised by Sir Arthur Quiller-Couch to 'murder their darlings' and I have tried to comply with Sir Arthur's sage, if sanguinary, advice. I freely confess that the final redaction of this book conceals the graves of quite a few literary corpses, but I should probably have been a little more bloodthirsty. Be that as it may, the book is what it is; *quod scripsi, scripsi*. 'Writing a book is an adventure,' according to Sir Winston Churchill. 'To begin with it is a toy and an amusement. Then it becomes a mistress, then it becomes a master, then it becomes a tyrant. The last phase is that just as you are about to be reconciled to your servitude, you kill the monster and fling him to the public.' The book in your hand turned into a tyrannical monster quite some time ago and so it is with a sense of relief at a burden lifted and, perhaps ironically, a practical appreciation of my newly recovered freedom that I unleash the monster on the unsuspecting public.

Ecce monstrum.

Notes

1 To be fair to the United Kingdom, I suspect that many if not most other state education systems are similarly inefficacious. Over sixty years ago, in his dystopian novel *Fahrenheit 451*, Ray Bradbury remarked presciently that in his dystopia, 'School is shortened, discipline relaxed, philosophies, histories, languages dropped, English and spelling gradually neglected, finally almost completely ignored. Life is immediate, the job counts, pleasure lies all about after work. Why learn anything save pressing buttons, pulling switches, fitting nuts and bolts?' [Bradbury 2008, 73]
2 Most people we think of as educated should perhaps more properly be described as schooled; whether they are also educated is a moot point. Mark Twain is reputed to have remarked that he never let his schooling get in the way of his education but for many people, schooling and education are separated by an hermetically sealed barrier.
3 Oscar Wilde, 'The Importance of Being Earnest'.
4 Jane Austen, *Pride and Prejudice*, chapter 11.
5 Or at best, a shrunken and static personality. See Foer 2012, 69-87.
6 Walter Grinder, private communication to the author. See Oakely 2003 and Lehner, passim.
7 Émile Coué de la Châtaigneraie (1857-1926) was a French psychologist who popularised a method of self-improvement based on auto-suggestion.

8 See Butterworth, Wong, Akhavi and Dalton for brief contemporary introductions to some of these traditions, and see Parens and Macfarland for textual excerpts. See Bernal and McCord for criticisms of the limited range of Patterson's seminal 1991 work, *Freedom*. See Duchesne for a stimulating defence of the uniqueness of Western civilisation, especially his treatment of 'The "Rise" of Western Reason and Freedom' [Duchesne, 231-284] See Parkinson 1958, passim for a treatment of political thought which includes many references to non-Western traditions. In particular, Parkinson notes the Chinese contribution to political thought under a number of headings: the selection of officials by means of competitive examinations, a system that prevented nepotism and favouritism; a method of overseeing officials; and a means of ascertaining the tendencies of public opinion. [Parkinson 1958, 55-57]

9 Vincent, 77, 78; see Frayn, 192.

10 'Our default position tends to be that our opinions are the result of learning, experience and personal reflection. The things we believe are obviously true — and everyone would agree if only they could look at the issue with clear, objective, unimpeded sight. But they don't because they're biased.' [Storr, 112; see Casey 2012c]

11 Postmodernism is just another form of epistemological relativism and, as with all other forms of that dubious doctrine, it is committed to holding to the truth-relativity of all claims *except* the central claims of postmodernism itself—which is, of course, self-referentially incoherent.

12 For a critique of a specific form of history that is constructed explicitly on the basis of political commitment, detached from any reasonable effort to relate to evidence, see Stephen Howe's *Afrocentrism*.

13 J. M. Roberts's *Penguin History of Europe* has a strong claim to be the best single-volume history of its kind. Not only does it have an excellent index and a semi-analytical table of contents, each section in each chapter is clearly set off so that you can read just those parts that you want or need without getting lost in a mass of irrelevant detail. 'The past,' Roberts writes, 'is never a simple influence. Even when its effect seems most obvious and direct, it works on us in many ways, through the circumstances it creates, the material culture it leaves behind, its physical relics and articulated doctrines and ideas, its superstitions and errors, its teaching and propaganda, its example for good or ill, the picture we have of it.' [Roberts 1997, 22]

14 For a treatment of this topic that is by and large consistent with mine, see Hayek 1960, 11-21. For a useful and accessible selection of primary material on liberty, readers are referred to David Boaz's *The Libertarian Reader*. [Boaz 1997] In that volume, Tom Palmer provides a superb review of some of the essential literature on liberty. [Palmer 1997] For a critique of libertarianism, see Haworth's *Anti-Libertarianism* [Haworth 1994] and for the consequent exchange of (re)views see Lester 1997, Haworth 1998, and Lester 2002.

15 It is quite easy to conflate the various different conceptions of liberty. Kent Greenfield does so at book length in his *The Myth of Choice*, sliding frictionlessly from the metaphysical to the social to the cultural to the legal to the economic to the political and back again, with consummate ease.

16 For a very accessible approach to this topic, see Julian Baggini's *Freedom Regained*, in which, in addition to expressing some scepticism about strong metaphysical libertarianism, he also expresses doubts about the validity of the rigid separation of political freedom and freedom of the will. [see Baggini, 103]

17 Iris Murdoch 1994, 203, emphasis in original.

18 See, for example, the discussion of Hegel's conception of freedom, below.

19 *The Philosophy of Right*, §§5-7. See also Rose 2007, 31-56.

20 According to St Thomas Aquinas, man's choices operate *sub ratione boni*, under the aspect of the good. [See *Summa Theologiae*, I-IIae, q. 19, a. 3]

21 Skinner regards the term *republican* as 'liable to mislead' and now prefers to use the term *neo-roman* instead. [see Skinner 1998, 11, n. 31]

22 Constant 1819, 310-311; see Droz, 48-49.

23 Constant 1819, 311. See also Hayek 1960, 13-14.

24 The Inklings—the name has a whimsical J. B. Priestley *Good Companions* ring to it!—was an informal group of individuals that met fairly regularly in Oxford in the 1930s and 1940s to discuss each other's work. In addition to Owen Barfield, the more prominent members of the group were J. R. R. Tolkien, C. S. Lewis and Charles Williams, the author of a number of exceptionally strange metaphysical novels.

25 Barfield, 169; also 133-134. On this important topic, a topic central to the purpose of this book, see Morris 1972, Gurevich 1995 and Black 1988b. See also Parkinson 1958, 171. It is noteworthy that in Smith & Moore's selection of texts on the topic of individualism in their edited volume entitled *Individualism*, only one of the twenty-six excerpts is pre-modern and even that is somewhat dubiously on topic. Of the remaining excerpts, we find one each from the sixteenth and seventeenth centuries, six from the eighteenth, twelve from the nineteenth, and the remaining six from the twentieth century. [see Smith & Moore (eds) 2015, passim]

26 For more on this topic, see the chapters on Kant and Hegel.

27 Skinner remarks that, for Hobbes, 'it makes no sense to speak of being coerced into acting against your will, since the will lying behind your action will always be revealed by your action itself.' [Skinner 1998, 7-8]

28 And with Hayek. See Hayek 1960, 117.

29 I'm assuming the experiment takes place in Europe or North America. If you were to run it in parts of Central Africa, you might well get different results.

30 For a balanced evaluation of the claim that philosophy is androcentric, see Landau. For a robust (and exhaustive) account of the pervasive misandry underlying much gender or radical feminism, see Nathanson & Young, 2001, 2006 & 2015.

31 The word 'dominate' is, of course, tendentious, suggesting the (illegitimate) exercise of power, when all that the evidence justifies is the normatively neutral phrase, 'constitute in large part' or the equivalent. If the tendentious term 'dominate' is justifiable in this context, then it is equally true to say that women 'dominate' the teaching profession and that they increasingly 'dominate' the medical, veterinary and legal professions.

32 'List of Philosophers born in the 20th century', available at https://en.wikipedia.org/wiki/List_of_philosophers_born_in_the_20th_century, accessed 23 April 2016. There are, of course, other lists that one could use but this one will serve to make my point.

33 Such as the inelegant *co* for *she*, *he*, *her* and *him*, and *cos* for *his*, *her*; or *tey* for *he* or *she*, *ter* for *his* or *her* and *tem* for *him* or *her*. [see Beard & Cerf, 1992]

34 'Our beautiful American language,' writes David Mamet, ' is now subject to revision by those screaming loudest, and we have the enormity of s/he, the clunky continuous reiteration of his-or-her, and so on. This revision is presented by the Left as an aid of equality, but its result is an atmosphere not of happy compliance, but of anxiety, circumlocution, and a formalism destructive of the free exchange of ideas.' [Mamet, 108]

35 Otto Jespersen notes that 'the habit of addressing a single person by means of a plural pronoun was decidedly in its origin an outcome of an aristocratic tendency towards class-distinction....In England as elsewhere this plural pronoun (*you*, *ye*) was long confined to respectful address.' Over time, however, 'the pronoun *you* was gradually extended to lower classes and thus lost more and more of its previous character of deference.' [Jespersen 1982, 223]

36 Jespersen 1992, 233; see 226-243.

37 Copley, 110-111; 126-127.

38 And this is not even to give the attention it deserves to the inadvertent invention of a completely new tense form by football (soccer) and snooker commentators, which consists of a combination of the auxiliary ['he has....'] together with the present tense of the verb in place of the more usual past participle ['give' instead of 'given], producing sentences such as, 'He's give it his best shot, Mark!' We might call this the Historic Perfect, combining the dramatic immediacy of the Present Tense with the completed aspect of the Perfect. The same class of bold linguistic pioneers have given (or, if you prefer, 'have give') us what we might call the Perfect Pluperfect, where the 'had' of the normal pluperfect is felt to be insufficiently adequate to its task and in need of support from a neighbouring 'have,' producing such utterances as 'If he hadda passed the ball earlier....' This appears to be an eroded form of 'If he had have passed the ball earlier', journeying through the intermediate form 'If he had of passed the ball earlier' before arriving at its final linguistically innovative destination.

39 'Look at her, a prisoner of the gutter, condemned by every syllable she utters. By right she should be taken out and hung, for the cold-blooded murder of the English tongue.' [*My Fair Lady*, Alan Jay Lerner]

40 'An Englishman's way of speaking absolutely classifies him. The moment he talks he makes some other Englishman despise him.' [*My Fair Lady*, Alan Jay Lerner]

41 Or in my case, WIC: White, Irish, Catholic.

42   A few more of my pet aversions: a *crescendo* is not something that can be reached but is rather the gradual approach towards a state of ever greater volume; *dangling participles* should be dangled from the end of a noose; *envy* and *jealousy* are not synonyms (we are jealous of what belongs to us, envious of what belongs to others—the Lord our God is a jealous God, not an envious God); *fulsome* is not a fancy way of saying *very full* or *generous* but rather signifies language that is unctuous or sycophantic; *imply* and *infer* are not synonyms; *irregardless* is either gibberish or the reverse of what is normally intended by its user; *less* is used with quantity, *few* and *fewer* with number—we can handle a similar distinction between *much* and *many*, why not with *less* and *few*?; *lay* is a transitive verb (preterite *laid*, past participle *laid*), *lie* is an intransitive verb (preterite *lay*, past participle *lain*), and neither is to be confused with *lie* as the deliberate telling of an untruth (preterite *lied*, past participle *lied*); *may* is not a genteel and always-interchangeable synonym of *might*—'He might have scored a goal if he had volleyed the ball' (but, in fact, he didn't score), 'He may have scored a goal (we're not sure but time may tell); and *refute* is a achievement word, meaning a successful rejection—it is not a stylistically forceful way of saying *deny*.

43   'French people,' writes Robert S. Conway, 'do not think of *le ciel* ("the sky") as a man because it is masculine nor of *la douleur* ("pain") as a woman because it is feminine.' He adds, 'It is true that fem. forms in Latin and other Indo-European languages do sometimes denote female sex, and that the neut. forms do nearly always denote something which is not living, but this was not the original meaning of the endings, and they have only been forced into denoting it in a limited number of words and forms.' [Conway, 84, 85]

44   Crystal, 97; Partridge, 129.

45   Palmer 1971, 38; see Jespersen 1992, 226.

46   Otto Jespersen notes that 'masculine pronouns and endings were found with names of a great many things which had nothing to do with male sex (e.g. *horn*, *ende* "end", *ebba* "ebb", *daeg* "day") and similarly feminine pronouns and endings with many words without any relation to female sex (e.g. *sorh* "sorrow", *glof* "glove", *plume* "plum", *pipe*). [Jespersen 1982, 180] Until around AD 1600 and the invention of the neuter *its*, *his* was neuter as well as masculine.

47   See Anon. 1937, Art. 12, §3.1°, §4.1°, §7, §11.3°.

48   In some places, the personal pronominal police-actions have now reached a level of insanity that makes satire almost impossible. Failure to use so-called 'gender-neutral' pronouns, such as *xu, hir, ze, nir, hiser* and so on, by which a given person desires to be addressed, can be (and has been) deemed a form of discrimination and a breach of human rights. [see Wente] Of course, a moment's thought will reveal the absurdity of the policy of demanding, on pain of sanctions, that person X be addressed by his chosen pronoun, Y. Apart from the practical problem of requiring innocent third parties to remember an impossibly large number of possible pronouns, thus defeating one of the purposes for which pronouns came into being in the first place, what is to prevent a pronoun warrior from demanding to be addressed as *gutface, glinky* or *gloopiness the 3rd*? [see Starnes 2016 for an amusingly subversive guerilla attack on this nonsense. See also Murphy 2016] Taken to its extreme, such Humpty-Dumptyish linguistic voluntarism will inevitably lead to the decline of personal pronouns altogether and saddle those of us who wish to avoid persecution with the unenviable task of endlessly repeating name after name after name—*nom d'un nom d'un nom…*.

49   See Shand, 4-6 for a succinct treatment of this topic. For a relentless and devastating attack on the fundamental unreality of authority and government, see Larken Rose's *The Most Dangerous Superstition* (see also his delightfully satirical *How to be a Successful Tyrant*); and for an entertaining and (literally) graphic treatment of the fundamental ghostly nature of government, see Zander Marz's *Beyond the Government-Haunted World*.

50   See Pettit and List, passim.

51   See Shand 1984, 4-6, also, Bunge.

52   *Woman's Own,* 31 October 1987; emphasis added.

53   To some libertarians, Mrs Thatcher's libertarian credentials are suspect. Sean Gabb writes, 'The Thatcher Government made a century of [constitutional] changes in eleven years. These were carried through with an almost gloating disregard for the proprieties, and were generally to enhance the power of the State. We were given pre-publication censorship for the first time in three hundred years, and a real War on Drugs, and *ex-post facto* criminal laws, and punishment without conviction or trial, and reversals of the burden of proof in criminal cases. The ancient right to peremptory challenge of jurors was abolished, together with the ancient right of an inquest jury to find a general verdict. The rights to political speech and association were curbed. The agreed

rule that police officers were civilians employed and given uniforms to do what everyone else had the right to do was swept aside for the creation of an increasingly armed pro-State militia.' [Gabb, 2016]

54 *The Sunday Times*, 10 July 1988.

55 For a detailed, critical discussion of the Austrian conception of methodological individualism, see Nozick 1977, 353-361. See, in response, Block 1980, 398-408.

56 See d'Entrèves 1967, 19; but see also Gierke 1900, and Gierke 1913.

57 The current popularity of identity politics based on factors such as race, religion, sex, gender, sexual orientation, ideology, ethnicity, or any combination of these, is merely the latest in the recurrent tendency to subsume individuals into categories, classes or types to the detriment of their individuality. 'Identity politics,' writes Cressida Heyes, as a mode of organizing 'is intimately connected to the idea that some social groups are oppressed; that is, that one's identity as a woman or as a Native American, for example, makes one peculiarly vulnerable to cultural imperialism (including stereotyping, erasure, or appropriation of one's group identity), violence, exploitation, marginalization, or powerlessness....' [Heyes, 2] See the discussion of false consciousness in chapter 27 below.

58 'It cannot be too heavily emphasized,' I continued, that 'libertarianism is not intended to deny the importance of love, community, discipline, order, learning, or any of the many other values that are essential to human flourishing. Libertarians as much as anyone else can cherish these values but, however much they might cherish them, they reject any and all attempts to produce them by force, coercion or intimidation. They regard such attempts at coercion as both wrong in themselves and as ineffective.' [Casey 2012b, 54]

59 'When Moses led the Israelites from Egypt there were those among them, as there have always been men through history, who preferred security with slavery to the uncertainties of freedom.' [Vawter, 301] 'And all the children of Israel murmured against Moses and against Aaron: and the whole congregation said unto them: Would to God that we had died in the land of Egypt! or would to God we had died in this wilderness! And wherefore irksome burden hath the LORD brought us unto this land, to fall by the sword, that our wives and our children should be a prey? Were it not better for us to return into Egypt? [*Numbers* 14: 2-3]

60 We find the same point made by the Grand Inquisitor in Dostoevsky's *The Karamazov Brothers*. Nothing, says the Grand Inquisitor, 'has been more insupportable for a man and a human society than freedom.' In the end, he says, men 'will lay their freedom at our feet, and say to us, "Make us your slaves, but feed us."' And when the burden of freedom was removed from them, 'men rejoiced that they were again led like sheep, and that the terrible gift that had brought them such suffering was, at last, lifted from their hearts.' [Dostoevsky, Book 5, Chapter 5, 276, 277, 281]

61 See chapter 31 below on 'Twentieth-Century Tribalisms'.

62 W. S. Gilbert, *The Mikado*, Act II.

Chapter 1

THE DAWN OF HISTORY

To-day all our novels and newspapers will be found to be swarming with
numberless allusions to the popular character called a Cave-Man.
He seems to be quite familiar to us, not only as a public character
but as a private character
—G. K. Chesterton

No state, no government exists. What does in fact exist is a man,
or a few men, in power over many men
—Rose Wilder Lane

The emergence of this disposition to be an individual
is the pre-eminent event in modern European history
—Michael Oakeshott

With these words—'It is there, in Ancient Greece, that our story begins'—
Sheldon, the socially-challenged theoretical physicist of *The Big Bang
Theory*, begins his instruction of his academically challenged neighbour Penny,
who wants to impress her boyfriend Leonard, Sheldon's roommate, by learning
'a little something' about physics.[1] Since all she wants to do is to pick up a few
scraps of knowledge so that she can appear informed, she doesn't see the need to
go all the way back to a warm summer evening somewhere in Ancient Greece.
Many people with an interest in political theory are as keen as Penny is to begin
somewhat closer to the present than a warm summer evening in Ancient Greece
but, in an alarming escalation of the Sheldonian strategy, in this chapter, I am
going to begin, not on a warm summer evening in Ancient Greece, but much,
much further back.[2] The first three sections in this chapter—Early Man, Anthropology, and Man & Language—provide the broad speculative background on
which the next six relatively concrete scenes—The Agricultural Revolution,
From Village to City: The Urban Revolution, City State and Territorial State,
Violence and Predation, Kings, Law—are painted.

EARLY MAN

Our story begins with the appearance of Homo sapiens around 200,000 years
ago, about the time when the so-called 'Mitochondrial Eve' lived. As in all such
matters, dates and times are contested but there appears to be a broad, general
consensus on this point.[3] Around 60,000 years ago man began his exodus from
Africa. According to a 2016 article in *Nature*, 'Modern humans arrived in
Europe 45,000 years ago, but little is known about their genetic composition
before the start of farming 8,500 years ago.' The authors of this article argue that
'all individuals between 37,000 and 14,000 years ago descended from a single

founder population which forms part of the ancestry of present-day Europeans' but they go on to note that 'During the major warming period after 14,000 years ago, a genetic component related to present-day Near Easterners became widespread in Europe.' [Qiaomei et al.] Another 2016 article in *Nature* argues that, based on genomic evidence, 'most present-day Europeans derive from at least three highly differentiated populations: west European hunter-gatherers, who contributed ancestry to all Europeans but not to Near Easterners; ancient north Eurasians related to Upper Palaeolithic Siberians who contributed to both Europeans and Near Easterners; and early European farmers, who were mainly of Near Eastern origin but also harboured west European hunter-gatherer related ancestry.'[4] Around 40,000 years ago, we went into the cave-painting business, as well as into the production of sophisticated artefacts such as ropes and sewing needles. [see Storr, 91] Around 30,000 years ago, during the last Ice Age, Palaeolithic (Old Stone Age) culture flourished.

As late as 20,000 years ago, the ocean level was 120 metres *lower* than it is today so that many land masses now separated by water were accessible to each other by foot: Great Britain was linked by a land bridge to the Continent, Ireland to Britain, and Asia to North America. You might have had to take your shoes off and roll up your trouser legs to get to places now separated from each other by bodies of water but the risk of wet feet trumped the need to dig out a canoe and paddle it for miles. 'Global sea level has fluctuated widely in the recent geologic past,' writes Vivien Gornitz of the NASA Goddard Institute for Space Studies and Columbia University. 'It stood *4-6 meters above the present* during the last interglacial period, 125,000 years ago, but was *120 m [meters] lower at the peak of the last ice age*, around 20,000 years ago.'[5]

Presumably working off essentially the same geological evidence, Robin Edwards concurs: 'At the height of the last Ice Age a little more than 20,000 years ago, global sea levels were over 120m lower than present levels.' [Edwards, 2013] 120 metres is almost 400 feet! Without wishing to start any fights on the issue of climate change and its supposedly apocalyptic conse-quences (seemingly always bad,[6] never good), it would seem to me that a couple of inches one way or another in the context of 400 feet doesn't seem all that dramatic.[7] Sea levels today are still 13-20 feet *below* the levels they reached during the last interglacial period so that if any surf-loving members of early *homo sapiens* had built themselves some beachfront huts at that period, their descendants living in the same huts today would need to get on their bikes to get to the water's edge![8] The most recent Ice Age ended about 12,000 years ago and its end signalled the arrival of Mesolithic (Middle Stone Age) culture. The intercontinental land connections disappeared under water when the sea levels rose and the geographical configurations of our continents and our islands took on the shape that they have, in large part, retained to the present. 'The English Channel came and went more than once in prehistoric times, but last appeared again about 8,000 years ago (though only in about 4000 BC did the seas reach their present level.)'[9] Geologically speaking, we are still living in a warm, interglacial period.

Human beings are singularly badly constructed for survival. If the design of man was an engineering student's degree-year project, he might well find himself in academic trouble. Human beings are not, as are most animals, naturally or instinctively well adapted to a particular supportive environmental niche. David Hume comments, 'Of all the animals, with which this globe is peopled, there is none towards whom nature seems, at first sight, to have exercis'd more cruelty than towards man, in the numberless wants and necessities, with which she has loaded him, and in the slender means, which she affords to the relieving these necessities....Not only the food, which is requir'd for his sustenance, flies his search and approach, or at least requires his labour to be produc'd, but he must be possess'd of cloaths and lodging, to defend him against the injuries of the weather; tho' to consider him only in himself, he is provided neither with arms, nor force, nor other natural abilities, which are in any degree answerable to so many necessities.'[10] The fourteenth-century Muslim writer, Ibn Khaldûn, notes that 'When God fashioned the natures of all living beings and divided the various powers among them, many dumb animals were given more perfect powers than God gave to man....To man, instead, He gave the ability to think, and the hand.... The power of one individual human being cannot withstand the power of any one dumb animal, especially the power of the predatory animals....When, however, mutual co-operation exists, man obtains food for his nourishment and weapons for his defence.' [Ibn Khaldûn, 45-46]

In many ways, man is a stranger in a strange land. 'It is remarkable,' Christopher Booker comments, 'how many of the forms of behaviour which distinguish human beings from all other animals consist of creating a consciously-contrived framework for some activity which in the life of every other species is wholly instinctive.' [Booker, 551] The human infant is uniquely dependent upon its parents and is so for an exceptionally long period. Gordon Childe notes that, 'in the case of human infants the condition of dependence lasts exceptionally long. The hardening and solidification of the human skull are retarded longer than in other animals, to allow for the greater expansion of the brain. At the same time, man is born with relatively few inherited instincts.'[11] William McNeill remarks on the helplessness of the human young which, he says, 'must at first have been an extraordinary hazard to survival. But this handicap had compensations, which in the long run redounded in truly extraordinary fashion to the advantage of mankind. For it opened wide the gates to the possibility of cultural as against merely biological evolution.' [McNeill, 20] It would seem, in fact, as if, biologically speaking, human infants are born about twelve months earlier than they should be. 'The human infant,' writes Frank Tallis, ' is extremely vulnerable because of its prematurity. Moreover, its big brain—which grows at an incredibly fast rate in the first two years of life—has a large metabolic requirement. The human infant must have a high quality of care, and this is best delivered by two parents working together for an expended period of time—in effect, two parents in a monogamous relationship, sharing a strong pair-bond...' [Tallis 2005, 81]

William Graham Sumner goes so far as to claim that 'the interests of children and parents are antagonistic....It may well be believed that, if procreation had not been put under the dominion of a great passion, it would have been caused to cease by the burden it entails.' [Sumner, 310] Expressing more or less the same judgement in somewhat franker terms, Philip Stanhope, the fourth Earl of Chesterfield, is reputed to have remarked of sexual congress that 'the pleasure is momentary, the position ridiculous, and the expense damnable.' Lord Chester-field may perhaps have had expenses other than those of child-rearing in the front of his mind when he made this observation but I am sure that even if that were so, an appreciation of the cost of raising the products of sexual congress to maturity when measured against its fleeting pleasure couldn't but have given an additional edge to his remark.

In prehistoric times, pregnancy and the production of children was likely to be a constant condition for most women of child-bearing age, especially given the evolutionary loss of oestrus by human females. 'Man,' writes John M. Roberts, 'is the only animal in which the mechanism of the oestrus (the restriction of the female's sexual attractiveness and receptivity to the limited periods in which she is on heat) has entirely disappeared. It is easy to see the evolutionary connexion between this and the prolongation of infancy...' [Roberts, 10] Roberts believes that this loss of oestrus has had radical social implications. 'The increasing attractiveness and receptivity of females to males make individual choice much more significant in mating. The selection of a partner is less shaped by the rhythm of nature; we are at the start of a very long and obscure road which leads to the idea of sexual love. Together with prolonged infant dependency, the new possibilities of individual selection point ahead also to the stable and enduring family unit of father, mother and offspring, an institution unique to mankind.' [Roberts 1993, 10] The physically debilitating (and oftentimes dangerous) effects of pregnancy and childbirth, and the subsequent demands of childcare extending over a long time, produced a differentiation of social function along sexual lines. The sex-based division of labour meant, Azar Gat remarks, that 'women specialized in child bearing and rearing and in foraging close to the home base, whereas men specialized in long-distance hunting and in the struggle to acquire and defend women and children....' Despite the cooperation of both parents in child-rearing, it is signif-icant that 'the father...was more expendable than the mother' so that when the group came under attack, 'the men formed the group's main line of defence, while the women covered the children to the best of their abilities.' [Gat, 80, 81] C. Northcote Parkinson remarks that 'women and children must be kept out of danger if the family group is to survive. If men are killed in hunting, the survivors may still be enough for breeding purposes. The same is not true of women, upon whose number the natural increase must depend.' [Parkinson 1958, 17]

Not everyone is persuaded by this line of reasoning. Rosalind Miles considers the argument that 'Mother Nature having saddled women with an unequal share of the work of reproduction...[women] had to consent to male domination in order to obtain protection for themselves and for their children' but she counterargues that 'the historical record clearly shows that women in "primitive" societies have a better chance of equality than those in more "advanced" cultures.' She believes that it's a paradox of our age that 'women were freer in earlier times than in our own. Prehistoric women hunted and ran at will, roamed where they would and freely lay down with the partner of their choice. They created pottery and cave painting, they planted and wove, danced and sang.'[12]

As I remarked earlier, prehistory is *pre*history and so we have no written records to rely on to prove or to disprove such claims. But while it isn't necessarily a reliable procedure to take the constitutions of traditional societies that have survived into modernity as a guide to the constitutions of those of the remote past, in the absence of hard data, a consideration of their customs and *mores* would suggest that there is more than an element of wishful thinking and anachronistic retrojection, perhaps—dare I say it?—even of feminist fantasy, in Miles's imaginative account of the 'primitive' woman. 'What egalitarian feminist ideology fails to realize,' writes Camille Paglia, 'is that tribal cultures suppress individuality.[13] The group rules. Our distinct, combative, introspective, conflicted, and highly verbal and creative personalities are a product of Western culture. Feminism itself has been produced by Western culture.' [Paglia 1992]

In hunter/gatherer societies, in respect of the three essential social roles of procreation, provision and protection, men played two roles that were dangerous and arduous (provision [hunting] and protection) and one that was normally neither dangerous nor arduous (procreation), whereas women played one role that was dangerous and arduous (procreation), one that was neither dangerous nor arduous (protection) and one that was arduous but not dangerous (provision [gathering]).

	Men	*Women*
Procreation	Neither dangerous nor arduous	Dangerous and arduous
Provision	Both dangerous and arduous	Not dangerous but arduous
Protection	Both dangerous and arduous	Neither dangerous nor arduous

The burdens and responsibilities of social life were thus roughly equal for both sexes, men having slightly the worst of the bargain, with two dangerous roles to women's one.[14] After the Agricultural Revolution and the relative decline in the importance of hunting, men's role in provision remained arduous but was no longer inherently dangerous so that the number of dangerous and arduous roles of men and women effectively balanced. And so things remained (with minor local variations) until the occurrence of the Reproductive and Technological Revolutions of the second half of the twentieth century, the social and cultural consequences of which we are still working out with fear and trembling.[15]

The depth and extent of the changes wrought by these Revolutions and their social implications cannot be overstated. In the space of forty years, abortion has gone from being either illegal or exceptional to being in effect a relatively routine backup form of contraception. Divorce no longer has any social stigma attached to it and is generally available in 'no-fault' form, that is, on demand by one or other of the parties. The concept of illegitimacy, even the use of that term, is *streng verboten* and in its place we have the brave new world of single-motherhood, stigma-free and state supported. Homosexual conduct has moved from being vilified and illegal to being tolerated to being valorized, with the state offering its support to the new normative environment in its recognition of so-called gay marriage. All these changes, and others, stem from our increasing ability to separate sex and reproduction. Sex without reproduction has been commonplace for almost fifty years; reproduction without sex is already with us and will become increasingly common. The biological constraints that informed human sexual morality from our very beginnings are no longer operative.[16]

I say again; it is impossible to underestimate the importance of these two seismic developments whose social, economic and political consequences rank in significance with the Agricultural and Industrial Revolutions. The Technological Revolution freed men in large measure from the exhausting and debilitating physical toil that made so many of the men of my father's generation physical wrecks by the time they were in their forties; it also drastically expanded the job opportunities open to women while simultaneously placing at a steep discount the economic value of men's superior muscle power. The Reproductive Revolution gave women the power to control their fertility and thereby freed them, in some ways at least, from the biological imperatives that have cabin'd, cribb'd and confined them since sentence was first pronounced on Eve. Chemical contraception, together with the widespread acceptance of effectively unrestricted (in its earlier stages, at least) abortion, constitutes an experiment in radical social re-engineering whose personal, social, sexual, demographic and political implications are difficult to foresee.

The *Times*'s columnist, Caitlin Moran, remarks that 'It's not a coincidence that efforts towards female emancipation only got going under the twin exegeses of industrialisation and contraception—when machines made us the equal of men in the workplace, and The Pill made us the equal of men in expressing our desire.' [Moran, 138] 'The so-called "sexual revolution" of the 1960s,' writes Catherine Hakim, 'was made possible by the contraceptive revolution. For the first time in history, the pill and other modern forms of reliable contraception controlled by women gave women easier access to recreational sex without fear of pregnancy. The uncoupling of sexuality and fertility led to an increase in marital sexual activity in the West. It also made premarital sex more common, and eventually facilitated extra-marital sexuality as well. Possibly for the first time in history, recreational sex became far more important than reproductive sex—for people of all ages, and in all socio-economic groups. Marriage is no longer the precondition for an active sex life.' [Hakim, 8] These revolutions also irrevocably altered the relationship between the sexes— in precisely what ways and whether for good or for ill only time will tell. [see Penman, 549-550]

All that can be said with certainty is that since the 1960s, in the matter of sexual relationships, all is changed, changed utterly: a terrible bemusement is born.

John M. Roberts lists three factors he believes to have contributed to the social emancipation of women, two of which coincide with the factors I have already identified. These factors are: first, the creation of the advanced industrial economy which provided women with significant numbers of new jobs, none of which had existed even a century earlier; second, contraception, which gave rise to a 'revolution in outlook as more women absorbed the idea that they might control the demand of childbearing and rearing which hitherto had throughout history dominated and structured the lives of their sex'; and third, technological changes, such as piped water, gas, imported foods, detergents, gas cookers, vacuum cleaners, washing machines—'Historians who would recognise at once the importance of the introduction of the stirrup or lathe in earlier times, have strangely neglected the cumulative influence of such humble agencies.' [Roberts 1997, 475-476] It may, perhaps, be worth pointing out that all three factors indicated by Roberts—the advanced industrial economy, chemical contraception and the technological inventions which have transformed our lives—were the product of male energy and ingenuity.

'Patriarchy,' Lisa Tuttle tells us, is 'the universal political structure which privileges men at the expense of women.' [Tuttle, 342] You will note that this gender feminist zero-sum definition of patriarchy[17] makes no mention of men's burdens or responsibilities nor of women's corresponding benefits and privileges. A somewhat more conceptually and historically adequate account of patriarchy might see it as rooted in the protective function of the male, specifically fathers, in the cause of which they have to be prepared to sacrifice their health, their safety and their lives. Beard & Cerf's 1994 *Sex & Dating: The Official Politically Correct Guide* will take you on a light-hearted tour through the chilling fields of gender feminism which is, in essence, a mutated form of cultural Marxism. What is disturbing is that the delusional insanity exhibited (humorously) in the entries in this dictionary is still with us (non-humorously) some twenty years later and, although the theorists of gender feminism are largely confined to the rarified hothouse environs of the academic asylum, it has had a generally malign misandric effect outside academia on the law, on the general culture and on the world of work.[18]

The feminist myth of the Patriarchy derives what little evidential support it has (assuming that its adherents require it to have any evidential support at all) from a selective focusing on the supposed benefits accruing to men in traditional social configurations while completely ignoring their associated burdens. [see Harari, 161-178] It takes a curiously creative capacity malformed by preconceptions to see the patriarchy at work in the face of what, to a simple-minded observer, would seem to be a mass of countervailing evidence.[19] For example, in a display of what must seem to third-wave[20] (or later wave) feminists like low and devious cunning, nineteenth-century British parliamentarians, all of them men, attempted to conceal their male dominance by legally prohibiting women from working in coal mines and reserving those delightfully dirty and dangerous jobs for their brother patriarchs. One might have expected the dominant patriarchal group to send members of the dominated group to do their dirty work—literally their dirty work—for them but, to those in the grip of the latest-wave feminist theory, such an expectation is naïve, and the apparently pro-woman actions of the male parliamentarians are merely cloaking devices that serve to conceal their deep-rooted fear and hatred of women. The same patriarchal deceptive strategy employed by those dim and distant British parliamentarians would appear to have been consistently employed in men's historical domination of the military professions in times when, to the eye of the simple-minded, the military life was degrading and physically demanding when not actually dangerous.[21] The patriarchal deception appears to continue today for, even now, the bulk of physically demanding and dangerous jobs are dominated by men, resulting in a wildly disproportionate rate of workplace fatalities between the sexes. Occupational fatalities in the USA in 2013 were 93.1% male, 6.9% female, and this ratio of 13:1 is broadly consistent over time and in different places. [see Anon 2011]

An online cartoon purports to show the patriarchy at work.[22] In attendance at the Monthly Patriarchy Meeting are a top-hatted, robber baron, money-grubbing capitalist; a *doppelgänger* of Ernst Stavro Blofeld (the cat-petting Spectre supervillain from the James Bond films); a Spockoid alien; and someone who looks suspiciously like Milo Yiannopoulos. The Chairman speaks: 'Now let's see…Johnson, excellent work promoting rape culture by getting film and game developers to put lots of hot women in their products. Rapes are at an all time low so we must do something to bring our numbers back up. Pearson, your initiative to get men to spread their legs on public transit has really started to pick up steam. Those microaggressions are a great way to assert our patriarchal power. Wilson, your idea to harass feminists online by disguising arguments with reason and evidence is really paying off. We've fooled a lot of people into thinking there isn't a large organized conspiracy against women.'

The Irish Central Statistics Office report of 2011, 'Women and Men in Ireland,' provides some interesting information about males, females and work that, I suspect, would broadly be replicated in most modern Western societies. Women dominate health and social work, accounting for almost 82% of the workers in that category. Education comes next, still heavily dominated by women, where they account for just over 73% of the workers. The ratio of men to women is closest to 50/50 in accommodation and food services, financial, insurance and real estate, administrative and support services, and the wholesale and retail trade. It starts to edge towards a male preponderance in professional, scientific and technical areas, where men account for 60% of the workers, and continues moving in that direction for information and communication (70%, 30%), industry (72%, 28%), transportation and storage (82%, 18%), agriculture, forestry and fishing (89%, 11%) and construction (92%, 8%)[23] What are we to make of these figures? Well, unless there's some particularly insidious and undetectable form of coercion going on, women by and large choose to work almost exclusively inside buildings, men choose to work both inside and outside of them; men have a preference for technical, industrial and agricultural work, women for social work, health and education.[24]

An obvious but not-often-adverted-to fact is that the infrastructural environment in which radical feminists operate has been designed, constructed and maintained almost entirely by men: the lecture halls in which radical feminist doctrines are espoused; the roads that radical feminists drive on to get to their universities; the iPads, iPhones and the computers on which they write papers about the all-encompassing and all-powerful patriarchy; the airplanes they fly in to attend radical feminist conferences—all are the product of largely male ingenuity and labour. Writing of Suzanne Gordon, the founder of *Women*, one of the first feminist journals in the USA, Camille Paglia notes that while Gordon thinks of the patriarchy as tyrannically oppressive, she 'never pauses to note the benefits, gifts, and privileges she takes for granted in the male-created world around her—the hot showers, flush toilets, automatic washers and dryers,[25] electric lights, telephones, automobiles, the grocery stores overflowing with fresh, safe food, the high-tech network of medicines and life-saving hospital equipment.'[26] In an earlier publication, Paglia had remarked, perhaps provocatively, that 'If civilization had been left in female hands, we would still be living in grass huts.'[27] Using the pregnant words of Francis Urquhart in the original British version of *House of Cards*, I can only say that whereas Paglia might very well think that, I couldn't possibly comment.[28]

Men, it is said, have all the power.[29] If power is defined as *the possession of superior upper body strength*, then men as a whole are indeed in a position to dominate over women as a whole although, as with all such aggregates, any given woman may well be physically stronger than any given man. If, however, one thinks of power not just as raw physical strength but as *an aspect of the complex of sexual psycho-social relationships*, then, given the existence and persistence of the radical imbalance in the demand for sex by men and by women, women, as a whole, are in a position to dominate over men, as a whole and thus might be said to have, if not quite all the power, at least a preponderance of it.[30] As Catherine Hakim notes, 'male demand for sexual entertainments and activity greatly outstrips female sexual interest even in liberal cultures. This gives women an edge, although many are still unaware of it.' [Hakim, 9] Hakim provides conclusive evidence, if evidence of such an obvious fact were needed, of the persistent and significant difference in demand for sex by men and by women. [Hakim, 12-20] This difference in demand, she believes, is 'not due to socialisation, the repression of female sexuality, or women's lesser sexual enjoyment, and may be due to the female sex drive being more plastic, malleable, responsive to social influences, whereas the male sex drive is less compliant.' [Hakim, 19]

If power is defined as *political dominance* then, while most of the politically powerful human beings may be men, it's perhaps worth noting that most men are *not* among the politically powerful! The ruler-ruled relationship is one of domination and subordination and it is of little or no consolation for politically subordinated men to reflect that the orders they have to obey emanate from a male rather than a female. It's also worth noting that, at the time of writing (November 2016), the Prime Minister of the UK and the first Ministers of Scotland and Northern Ireland are women, so too the German

Chancellor, and there are twenty-one other female monarchs, Governors-General, Executive Presidents, Presidents and Prime Ministers.

It would seem that, at least from the ordinary man's perspective, the perspective of those men (almost *all* men) who do *not* have (and never have had) all the power, sexual or political, that the patriarchy isn't all it's cracked up to be. Men must be the only supposed oppressors in history that are *less well-served by the education system* they have permitted to be created than the allegedly oppressed other,[31] are *greater victims of physical violence* than the allegedly oppressed other,[32] are *treated with greater severity by the justice system in respect of divorce and custody and in criminal sentencing* than the allegedly oppressed other,[33] do a *staggeringly greater proportion of society's dirty jobs* than the allegedly oppressed other,[34] *are less well treated by their health systems* than the allegedly oppressed other and live *statistically significantly shorter lives* than the allegedly oppressed other.[35] If patriarchy is all-powerful and all pervasive, as some feminists claim, it would seem to be correspondingly all-stupid and omni-ineffective in its manifest inability to construct and maintain a social order that transparently benefits all and only men, which, given that Patriarchy is supposed to be 'the universal political structure which *privileges men at the expense of women*,'[36] makes no sense.

ANTHROPOLOGY

Gordon Childe believes that anthropological data show the biological changes that have taken place in man in recent years (speaking geologically) to have been either non-existent or negligible. He remarks, 'since the time when skeletons of *Homo sapiens* first appear in the geological record, perhaps 25,000 years ago, man's bodily evolution has come virtually to a standstill, though his cultural progress was just beginning.' [Childe, 33] In saying this, Childe is giving expression to what many take to be the orthodox position, that 'human evolution ground to a halt in the distant past.' [Wade, 5] John M. Roberts agrees with Childe: '[T]he last twelve thousand years, he writes, 'register nothing new in human physiology comparable to the colossal transformations of the early Pleistocene....Man has almost certainly not shown any improvement in innate capacity since the Upper Palaeolithic. His physique has not changed fundamentally in forty thousand years or so and it would be surprising if his mental capacity had done so.' [Roberts 1993, 29] Nevertheless, some contemporary research has indicated that human evolution may be continuing and, if so, is both copious and regional. Wade instances a genetic development among Tibetans, not much older than 3,000 years, that allows them to live at high altitudes. [see Wade, 2, 3] In a recent review article, the evolutionary biologist Stephen Stearns and his co-authors remark, 'Knowing that we are currently evolving and understanding our responses to selection changes our basic concept of the human condition from static to dynamic.'[37]

In many discussions on the 'nature versus nurture' debate, there's a tendency to suggest that human nature is either something wholly or substantially genetically determined and thus unalterable, or else that it's nothing more than a product of our history and cultural environment and thus essentially plastic.

Neither of these extremes would seem to be correct. [see Duchesne, 33] The genetic basis of human beings is effectively identical; however, the epigenetic expression of those genes is the function of the dynamic interaction of those genes and their environment, resulting in relatively specific character types that, in turn, facilitate character traits (such as trust, capacity for hard work, a disposition to self-restraint and delayed gratification in respect of sex, food and money, etc.) that in their turn, give rise to socio-political institutions such as war, religion, trade and law. Genes hold human culture on a leash, but the leash, as E. O. Wilson remarks, is very long.[38] What one takes human nature to be has a significant effect on one's thinking about human action. To show this, here is a sketch of two different approaches to human action premised on very different conceptions of human nature; the first that of Karl Polanyi, the second, that of Hans-Hermann Hoppe.

Karl Polanyi created a sensation in his book, *The Great Transformation*[39] (1944), by asserting that the so-called free market wasn't an eternal aspect of uncoerced human behaviour but was, in fact, a social construct—a great transformation—that was invented and implemented in the wake of Adam Smith's *The Wealth of Nations*.[40] Before this seismic event, markets hardly existed and even when they did, their role in human affairs was insignificant.[41] 'According to Polanyi,' writes Alex Nowrasteh, 'pre-modern humans did not behave according to a profit-maximizing model and were very different from the later evolved *homo economicus*, who supposedly behaves as a rational utility maximizer in all economic circumstances. What were the economic mentalities of pre-modern humans identified by Polanyi? Reciprocity and redistribution—primarily through gifts intended to cement social, familial, and political relationships according to conservative norms of established tradition.'[42] But what serious thinker has ever denied that modern market economies have elements of reciprocity and redistribution deeply embedded in them, the primary agent of which is the family, together with charitable associations, cooperatives and friendly societies.[43] The sex-based division of labour created a need for stable pair bonding that resulted in the distinctively human form of social organisation that would, in due course, result in the institution of the family based on marriage.[44] When I speak of the family in this context, I mustn't be understood to export, anachronistically, a twenty-first century Western conception of the residual nuclear family—father, mother, children— into other times and places. I acknowledge the institutions of the extended family, of patrilineality and matrilineality, and the activities of reciprocity, gift-giving and all the other social complexities well documented by anthropologists such as Bronislav Malinowski, E. E. Evans-Pritchard and others.

None of these institutions and activities, however, undermines the essentially praxeological character of human action. Praxeology studies the *formal* implications of the fact that men use means to attain various chosen ends—it is, as it were, a grammar of human action. Economics is a subdivision of praxeology, to date, its only fully elaborated one and it is important not to allow it to colonise the whole field of praxeology. [see Casey 2010, 23-38] Human action may not always be guided by a desire to bring about profit maximisation, if profit is understood to be limited to material gains, but human action is always and everywhere guided by a desire to bring about a future condition that is thought to be better than the existing one. 'Profit, in the broader sense,' writes Ludwig von Mises, 'is the gain derived from action; it is the increase in satisfaction (decrease in uneasiness) brought about; it is the difference between the higher value attached to the result attained and the lower value attached to the sacrifices made for its attainment; it is, in other words, yield minus costs. To make profit is invariably the aim sought by any action....Profit and loss in this original sense are psychic phenomena and as such not open to measurement....We cannot even think of a state of affairs in which people act without the intention of attaining psychic profit and in which their actions result neither in psychic profit nor in psychic loss....But every individual derives a psychic profit from his action, or else he would not act at all.'[45]

The second part of Hans-Hermann Hoppe's *A Short History of Man* is largely concerned with offering an explanation of why the Industrial Revolution occurred when it did and not earlier. Hoppe's answer is that it wasn't because of an increase in the amount of leisure time nor because of more clearly defined and protected property rights (however necessary such things might ultimately be) but was rather due to the development of human intelligence to a certain critical level. 'A certain threshold of average and exceptional intelligence had to be reached first for this to become possible,' he writes, 'and it took time (until about 1800) to "breed" such a level of intelligence.' [Hoppe 2015, 98] Hoppe realises that this thesis is controversial, containing, as it does, 'a fundamental criticism of the egalitarianism rampant within the social sciences generally but also among many libertarians,' but what is overlooked by such egalitarians, non-libertarian and libertarian alike, he believes, is that 'we, modern man, are a very different breed from our predecessors hundreds or even thousands of years ago.' [Hoppe 2015, 100]

Controversial though it may be, Hoppe's thesis should not be summarily dismissed. I am disinclined, however, to believe that the historical and theoretical evidence available to us shows that human intelligence as a basic capacity is the kind of thing that can be raised in an entire population except within certain narrowly defined limits. Instead, I think it more likely that human progress is the result of the accumulation of technological developments and the refinement of social institutions over time that, as it were, raise a platform upon which the next generation can work. No one, no matter how individually brilliant, could invent the electric light bulb before it became possible to generate and control the flow of electricity. Isaac Newton famously remarked, 'If I have seen further than others, it is by standing on the shoulders of giants.' I suspect that during man's prehistory, to paraphrase Thomas Gray, full many a mute, inglorious Aristotle, Newton and Beethoven were born to blush unseen and waste their sweetnesses on the desert air. Human progress isn't so much a matter of a rising level of intelligence in a group as a whole, I believe, as it is the presence of an appropriate level of technology and social institutions that provide the combustion chamber ready to explode from the spark of individual intelligence. It is interesting to note just how often the same thought occurs to more than one person at roughly the same time when the achievement and diffusion of a certain level of technological, scientific and scholarly thought has prepared the ground. Such simultaneous discoveries or inventions (sometimes called 'multiples') are commonplace in technology, as the history of patent applications will substantiate. Even in the more refined area of purely intellectual achievement we have, as examples, the simultaneous invention or discovery of the calculus by both Isaac Newton and Gottfried Wilhelm Leibniz, the simultaneous formulation of the theory of evolution by both the self-effacing Alfred Russel Wallace and Charles Darwin,[46] and the more or less simultaneous discovery of marginal utility by Léon Walras, Carl Menger and William Stanley Jevons.[47] The resultant theoretical advances and technological developments are subsequently diffused throughout society and so the platform is raised yet again for other individuals to make new discoveries and new advances.

Political theory is, to some extent at least, an outgrowth of our anthropology. Politics, ethics and anthropology go hand in hand. Some see ethics as a thin veneer laid over a brutish and selfish nature, hence, Frans de Waal's term, 'Veneerism' for this view. This veneeristic view of man is that he is something like a layer cake—boring and dull cakebread underneath with a delicious icing on top, the two only adventitiously connected. Others see ethics as an outgrowth of social instincts we share with other animals. De Waal takes T. H. Huxley and Richard Dawkins as exponents of Veneerism, and Mencius and Adam Smith as exponents of the opposing school.

Many political theories work off the assumption that human beings are essentially asocial or even antisocial creatures. Thinkers as diverse as Augustine, Machiavelli, Hobbes and Nietzsche, for example, all agree on this point to a greater or lesser extent and conservatives as a whole tend to take a dim view of man's untutored moral character. Hobbes held that the state of nature was such that 'there is no place for Industry; because the fruit thereof is uncertain; and consequently no Culture of the Earth; no Navigation, nor use of the commodities that may be imported by Sea; no commodious Building; no Instruments of moving, and removing such things as require much force; no Knowledge of the face of the Earth; no account of Time; no Arts; no Letters; no Society; and which is worst of all, continuall feare, and danger of violent death; And the life of man, solitary, poore, nasty, brutish, and short.'[48]

We must distinguish between what it is to be selfish and what it is to be self-serving. Only intentional beings can be selfish because selfishness requires knowledge, whereas both intentional and non-intentional beings can be self-serving. This being so, one cannot literally have a selfish gene. Genes just aren't the kinds of thing that can be selfish. Richard Dawkins waits until the end of *The Selfish Gene* to tell us that we need not be bound by those pesky elements. Our genes may be selfish but we, somehow, are able to transcend them. In our social and political world, we do not have to be Darwinian. But if our genes are the all-powerful things they are portrayed as being by Dawkins, how would we ever be able to transcend them? I am largely on de Waal's side on this topic. Veneerism is a non-starter.

Dawkins's argument exemplifies the fallacy of composition: our genes are selfish so we, being made up of our genes, must be selfish too. Even if it made sense to say that our genes were selfish (and it doesn't), it wouldn't necessarily follow that we as a whole would have to be selfish also. But, in any case, our genes are not and cannot be selfish, not because they are stellar moral exemplars but because they are simply not the kind of thing to which the term *selfish* can sensibly be applied. To attempt to do so is to be guilty of a glaring category mistake, as if one were to talk (non-metaphorically) about a thoughtful cigarette or a meditative foot.[49]

Human beings have never made a transition from being asocial to being social for the simple reason that we have always been social; we have, as de Waal notes, 'been group-living forever.' [de Waal 4] Life outside the human group isn't an option for man, except in the most artificial of situations that are themselves rather post-social than asocial. Indeed, given the length of human gestation and the dangers of human birth, together with the ridiculously long childhood of the human young, we might well be the most necessarily social of all animals. 'Humans started out…as interdependent, bonded and unequal. We come from a long lineage of hierarchical animals for which life in groups is not an option but a survival strategy. Any zoologist would classify our species as *obligatorily gregarious*.'[50] Psychologically, socially, and spiritually, we are designed for life with other human beings. One of the most severe punishments that can be imposed on any individual is exile, exclusion or shunning. 'Our bodies and minds are not designed for life in the absence of others. We become hopelessly depressed without social support: our health deteriorates.'[51] Human society isn't the product of a rational convention but of the exigencies of nature—physical and human. Alone, man can hardly survive, still less flourish; with others, his chances of both are much greater: more and better food, dangers more easily circumvented, the social and psychic support of companionship, and culture.

The Chinese philosopher Mencius believed that we had a natural inclination towards the good. 'All men,' he says, 'have a mind which cannot bear to see the sufferings of others.' He takes the example of a child in danger to illustrate his point. 'When I say that all men have a mind which cannot bear to see the sufferings of others, my meaning may be illustrated thus:—even now-a-days, if men suddenly see a child about to fall into a well, they will without exception experience a feeling of alarm and distress. They will feel so, not as a ground on which they may gain the favour of the child's parents, nor as a ground on which they may seek the praise of their neighbours and friends, nor from a dislike to the reputation of having been unmoved by such a thing. From this case we may perceive that the feeling of commiseration is essential to man, that the feeling of shame and dislike is essential to man…'[52] Similarly, Adam Smith opens his *Theory of Moral Sentiments* by remarking that 'How selfish soever man may be supposed, there are evidently some principles in his nature, which interest him in the fortunes of others, and render their happiness necessary to him, though he derive nothing from it, except the pleasure of seeing it. Of this kind is pity or compassion, the emotion we feel for the misery of others, when we either see it, or are made to conceive it in a very lively manner. That we often derive sorrow from the sorrows of others is a matter of fact too obvious to require any instances to prove it; for this sentiment, like all the other original passions of human nature, is by no means confined to the virtuous or the humane, though they perhaps may feel it with the most exquisite sensibility. The greatest ruffian, the most hardened violator of the laws of society, is not altogether without it.' [Smith 1759, 11] Smith's Scottish compatriot, David Hume, agrees with him. 'So far from thinking that men have no affection for any thing beyond themselves, I am of opinion, that tho' it be rare to meet with one, who loves any single person better than himself; yet 'tis as rare to meet with one, in whom all the kind affections, taken together, do not over-balance all the selfish.'[53] As social animals, our survival and our flourishing depend as much on our having the appropriate emotional responses to others as on having the correct beliefs about the world around us. Pre-linguistic children exhibit expressions of sympathy in the appropriate circumstances. It's as natural for them to do so as it is for them to walk. Human language and human culture emerge from our proto-social connections. Once they emerge, of course, they can recursively modify (although within limits) those proto-social connections. Empathy, remarks de Waal, 'is the original, pre-linguistic form of inter-individual linkage that only secondarily has come under the influence of language and culture.' [de Waal, 24] Emotions, then, do not necessarily conflict with reasoning. Morality has to do with the disciplining and directing of, not the suppressing of, the emotions.

De Waal points out the limitations of our spontaneous inclinations, as indeed does Adam Smith. Spontaneously, we favour insiders over outsiders, kin rather than non-kin. Homicide is universally prohibited but only within the kin group, not outside it. The moral progress of humanity has been the gradual (if fitful) extension of the within-kin *mores* to include non-kin. We might call what happens within the kin group, particular universalism (for example, the prohibition of in-group homicide) and what happens outside it as true universalism (the prohibition of all homicide). Given that morality is, in origin, oriented towards the survival and flourishing of the in-group, it is only incidentally extended towards members of out-groups. 'Government, law, order, peace, and institutions were developed in the in-group,' writes William Graham Sumner. 'The insiders in a we-group are in a relation of peace, order, law, government, and industry to each other. Their relation to all outsiders, or other-groups, is one of war and plunder, except so far as agreements have modified it.' [Sumner, 499, 12] Charity, then, begins at home—it may not end there, but it begins there. Furthermore, charity not only begins at home—it ought to, otherwise, we end up as Mrs Jellyby, a character in Charles Dickens's *Bleak House*, more concerned about the state of some group of people she has never met than with her own ragged and starving children and suicidal husband.

Another factor that enhances group solidarity is the real or merely perceived enmity of another group. 'In our own species,' says de Waal, 'nothing is more obvious than that we band together against outsiders. In the course of human evolution, out-group hostility enhanced in-group solidarity to the point that morality emerged.' [de Waal, 54] I am not sure I agree fully with de Waal on this point. Yes, conflict with another group tends to submerge or crush in-group differences. It is a commonplace for people to remark on how close they felt to their fellow countrymen when they were under attack. Yet I do not think it leads to the *emergence* of morality—morality has to be present already. At most, it can lead to its enhancement or refinement.

Morality, like language, logic and law, is a group phenomenon. Morality, language, logic and law are all embedded in and constitutive of human life long before any of them are reflectively appropriated.[54] If we were really isolatable individuals, morality wouldn't be necessary. It is because we have to live with one another that morality is both possible and necessary. Morality, remarks de Waal, 'places boundaries on behavior, especially when interests coincide.... the moral domain of action is Helping or (not) Hurting others.' [de Waal, 162] The 'non-hurting' element of this assertion is consistent with the libertarian zero-aggression principle, and the 'helping' element is consistent with the remainder of morality. Appearances to the contrary notwithstanding, then, and despite what Hobbes has to say on the matter, human beings have been quite successful in keeping *individual* deviant behaviour under control. For a social group to exist at all implies that the modes of social control, formal or informal, are effective. If not, the group would cease to exist.

Whatever the nature, proximity or rate of human evolution, and whether our biological evolution has slowed to a standstill (Childe and Roberts) or is still taking place (Wade and Stearns), it's reasonably clear that human beings as a whole have resisted the limitations imposed by the biological specialisation characteristic of other animals. Lewis Mumford notes, 'Biologically, man has developed farther than other species because he had remained unspecialized—omnivorous, free-moving, "handy," omni-competent, yet always somewhat unformed and incomplete, never fully adapting himself to any one situation, even though it might continue as long as the last Ice Age. Instead of cramping his activities by producing specialized organs to ensure effective adaptation, man put all his organic capital, so to say, into one feature of animal development that could invent substitutes for such specialized organs—the central nervous system.' [Mumford, 106] The unspecialised human being is none the less firmly constrained by a number of physical and physiological constants. The basic biophysical conditions limiting man have not changed significantly since he first appeared on this earth. He has to eat, drink, seek shelter and companionship, mate, produce and rear children and live in community with others. All these are constants. In addition, he needs protection from wild beasts and from a frequently hostile natural environment. Given these constraints, life is hardly possible without a supportive social group, and the good life is impossible outside society unless, as Aristotle says, one is either an animal or a god—and man is neither. [see Sowell 1987]

Man and Language

If man's recent biological changes have been negligible, the same cannot be said for the cultural, social and political changes[55] that have taken place over

the last 25,000 years, for these have been dramatic.[56] Man's singular advantageous endowment is his mind, with its capacity for abstract thought linked, in
a way not fully understood, with his massively developed brain.[57] This development of the human brain made possible complex social behaviour, some of
it good, some of it not so good. Human beings learn from each other not only
by example but also by means of language, itself a social product, perhaps *the*
most significant social product of all. 'Language,' writes Thomas Sowell, 'is
perhaps the purest example of an evolved social process—a systemic order
without a deliberate overall design....Language is, in effect, a model for social
processes in legal, economic, political, and other systems...' [Sowell 1987, 68,
69] Our possession of language is so commonplace as to appear to be entirely
unremarkable but, as Jeffrey Kluger notes, 'There is no real reason you should
be able to talk....Speech is one of the best and smartest adaptations humans
have, but it's also far and away the most complicated one. Indeed, most ways
you look at it, it's too complicated even to exist.'[58] It is worth noting, in passing,
that the physiological structures that permit human speech come at a cost of
'less efficient breathing, chewing, and swallowing. Modern man can choke
from food lodged in the larynx: monkeys cannot,' so that 'Speech is not merely
the incidental result of a system designed for breathing and eating.'[Crystal,
301]

Language is as close to a cultural universal as one can get. There are no
human societies without language. Although there are conceptual issues associated with the criteria for the identity of a language and empirical problems
associated with counting them, it seems that there are close to 6,000 distinct
languages in the world, over 800 of them in Papua New Guinea alone! David
Crystal, in his monumental *Cambridge Encyclopedia of Language* gives 6,000
as a safe twenty-first century estimate. [Crystal, 295] Of these 6,000 or so
languages, roughly half have already ceased to be the first languages of those
who do speak them, and 2,400 of the remaining 3,000 have fewer than 100,000
speakers. These languages are in imminent danger of disappearing; only 600
languages are outside the linguistic extinction danger zone. [see Aitchison, 247]

Human language is essentially social both in origin and in function. The
philosopher, Ludwig Wittgenstein, showed definitively in his *Philosophical
Investigations* that there could be no such thing as a language that could in
principle be known to only one person. The American novelist and philosopher Walker Percy remarks that our capacity for language 'seems to be, in the
evolutionary scale, a relatively recent, sudden, and explosive development....
it appears to have occurred in Neanderthal man as recently as...75,000 to
35,000 years ago.' [Percy 2000a, 118] Or perhaps it happened a million years
ago, or maybe between 100,000 and 200,000 years ago—R. L. Trask speaks
of a lack of consensus on this issue 'since the new data available to us point
in different directions.'[59] David Crystal is of the opinion that while there is
'general agreement on a time-scale from 100,000 to 20,000 BC for the development of speech....Human language seems to have emerged within a relatively
short space of time, perhaps as recently as 30,000 years ago.' [Crystal, 301]
Whether as long ago as a million years, or as recently as 30,000 years, in evolu-

tionary terms, our capacity for language is a recent acquisition, something that occurred, biologically speaking, only yesterday.[60]

Why is it that human animals speak and non-human animals do not? Is it just that animals do not have the requisite physiological equipment? If so, perhaps we could devise some technological way of surmounting this obstacle. This isn't a new idea. Over two hundred years ago, impressed by the ability of vocally incapacitated human beings to communicate with others by means of signs, Julien de la Mettrie, wondered if 'it be impossible to teach this animal [the ape] a language? I do not think so….Why then should the education of monkeys be impossible? Why might not the monkey, by dint of great pains, at last imitate after the manner of deaf mutes, the motions necessary for pronunciation?' [de la Mettrie, 100-101] De la Mettrie's research strategy was rediscovered by Beatrix T. Gardner, R. Allen Gardner, David Premack and D. M. Rumbaugh in the 1960s. Various sub-strategies were devised. The chimpanzee Washoe was allegedly taught a version of American Sign Language (Ameslan); another chimpanzee, Lana, was taught to enter sequences at a console, and yet another, Sarah, was taught to manipulate items on a visual display. The early reports were astounding; it seemed as if the chimps demonstrated a linguistic ability comparable to that of children. However, as time passed and the initial flurry of excitement subsided, significant differences emerged in the interpretation of the chimpanzees' activities and some researchers began to modify their original strong claims regarding their supposed linguistic abilities.

Taking everything into consideration, it would seem that, unless there are other rational species in the universe as yet unknown to us, language is unique to man. Animals can communicate by means of fixed signals but human language isn't just a signalling system. Fairly obviously, languages have words, and lots of them—animal communication doesn't. The words of human languages can be modified in various ways—they can be singular or plural, vary in tense, mood, and have suffixes and prefixes attached to them—but animal signals are substantially unmodifiable. Similarly, human language is essentially open-ended, permitting us to say things that have never been said before—animal communication is limited to a fixed repertoire. Languages have ways of indicating negation; a monkey's screech might signal 'Look out! Eagle!' but animal signalling doesn't appear to include a way of communicating 'No eagles. Hang loose!' Language allows man to ask and answer questions, to discuss abstractions such as justice and jealousy, to talk about events that are remote in time and space and even about objects or events that are non-existent, hypothetical, fictional, conditional and counterfactual—animal communication has nothing that can compare with this.[61] The capacity for language, then, appears to be unique to man and, despite its mist-shrouded origins, uniquely constitutive of what man is.[62] 'Speech,' writes Peter Farb, 'is not merely some improved form of animal communication; it is a different category altogether that separates human beings, inhabiting the far side of an unbridgeable chasm, from the beasts. [Farb, 16-17] 'The study of animal communication,' Farb notes elsewhere, 'reveals that human communication is not simply a more complex example of a capacity that exists elsewhere in the living world. One animal or another may share a few features with human language, but it is clear that language is based on different principles altogether.'[63]

THE AGRICULTURAL REVOLUTION

The story I tell in what follows is one that has, in different versions, been told before. Rousseau, in the second part of the *Discourse on Inequality*, has an account that in many ways resembles mine, but he draws radically different philosophical conclusions from it. So too, Friedrich Engels tells the story from yet another perspective in his *The Origin of the Family, Private Property, and the State*.[64] For Engels, a study of prehistory demonstrated that matriarchy and primitive communism were the earliest forms of socio-economic formation. This claim, nor surprisingly, is controversial.[65] The opposing, perhaps dominant view, is that 'patriarchy was the original form of social organization. Consequently, the institution of private property and its private inheritance is a natural social phenomenon going back to the very dawn of man's history or pre-history. It is also pointed out that at no stage was matriarchy a universal form of social organization. It existed only among some of the most primitive races, while patriarchy prevailed elsewhere.'[66] As this clash of views demonstrates, almost any statement one might care to make about prehistory is likely to be controversial. This is so for a number of reasons, not least that pre-history is *pre*-history and so, by definition, something for which we have no written records. Even when we do have archaeological and artefactual evidence, the explanations such evidence support are often merely conjectural and subject to contestation and radical revision. As the renowned anthropologist Bruce Trigger remarks, 'The study of early civilizations often reminds me of the proverbial blind men trying to understand an elephant.' [Trigger 2005, 256] In particular, the place of origin of the Indo-Europeans, their culture, their social structures, their military prowess, their patterns of migration and their relationship to indigenous populations are all highly contestable (and contested) issues.[67]

Archaeologists and anthropologists talk about various ages—Old Stone Age (Paleolithic), Middle Stone Age (Mesolithic), New Stone Age (Neolithic), Bronze Age,[68] and so on, but the change from one of these ages to the other did not take place instantaneously nor did it take place everywhere at the same (slow) time. 'It must not be imagined,' remarks Gordon Childe, 'that at a given moment in the world's history a trumpet was blown in heaven, and every hunter from China to Peru thereupon flung aside his weapons and traps and started planting wheat or rice or maize and breeding pigs and sheep and turkeys.'[69] Hunter-gatherer societies—or close facsimiles thereof—are still to be found today. The Hadzas of Northern Tanzania may perhaps give us a glimpse of what life was like for most of mankind for most of its history. Although anthropology professor, Frank Marlowe, who has studied the Hadza for an extensive period of time, very properly warns us that we should be wary of viewing contemporary hunter-gatherers as 'living fossils,' he concedes that even though time may not have stood still for them 'they have maintained their foraging lifestyle in spite of long exposure to surrounding agriculturalist groups' and, he adds, 'it's possible that their lives have changed very little over the ages.'[70]

Childe applied the political idea of 'revolution' to the social and cultural events of prehistory. The first significant revolution was, he thought, the Agricultural Revolution associated with the arrival of the Neolithic. This produced a major transformation of human economies, giving man a measure of control over his food supply. What man did at this time was to 'plant, cultivate, and improve by selection edible grasses, roots and trees' and to domesticate 'certain species of animal in return for the fodder he was able to offer, the protection he could afford, and the forethought he could exercise.'[71] Instead of chasing after their moveable food-source and collecting what non-moveable food items lay about until either or both were exhausted, some group of early human beings had the bright idea of domesticating both animals and plants, so guaranteeing for themselves, natural disasters apart, a reliable supply of food. This revolution in human culture—I do not think it an exaggeration to call it a revolution—provided for those human beings who adopted it a relatively more secure source of food than did hunting and gathering or simple pastoralism and, crucially, for the first time permitted them to settle permanently in one place. The increased productivity resulting from this first Agricultural Revolution made possible a more sophisticated division of labour than that which allocated hunting tasks to men and gathering tasks to women and, for the first time in human history, a significant number of people were released from the time-consuming burden of earning their livings by the sweat of their brows.

Whereas most scholars are prepared to accept the revolutionary nature of the development of agriculture, not all are prepared to see it as a great leap forward. We shall see that Jean-Jacques Rousseau identified agriculture as the cultural snake in the Garden of Eden. A latter-day Rousseauean, Yuval Harari, adopts essentially the same perspective. 'Rather than heralding a new era of easy living,' he writes, 'the Agricultural Revolution left farmers with lives generally more difficult and less satisfying than those of foragers. Hunter-gatherers spent their time in more stimulating and varied ways, and were less in danger of starvation and disease. The Agricultural Revolution certainly enlarged the sum total of food at the disposal of humankind, but the extra food did not translate into a better diet or more leisure. Rather, it translated into population explosions and pampered elites. The average farmer worked harder than the average forager, and got a worse diet in return. The Agricultural Revolution,' he concludes ringingly, 'was history's biggest fraud.'[72] Michael Finkel quotes Jared Diamond as suggesting, in a hyperbolically neo-Rousseauean manner, that the Agricultural Revolution was 'the worst mistake in human history' a mistake from which, again channelling Rousseau at his most romantic, he asserts we have never recovered.[73]

Whether or not the Agricultural Revolution was a fraud, it did indeed make it possible for larger populations to exist[74] while, at the same time, providing by means of the family based on marriage, a check on runaway population expansion. 'The invention of agriculture and animal husbandry,' writes Hoppe, 'allowed for a larger number of people to survive on the same, unchanged quantity of land, and the institution of the family, in privatizing (internalizing) the benefits as well as the costs of the production of offspring, provided a new, hitherto unknown check on the growth of the population.' [Hoppe 2015, 78-79] Hoppe concedes the essence of Harari's point, however, when he admits that neither the agricultural revolution nor the institution of the family yielded a permanent solution to the problem of excess population; for that, we needed another revolution, one that was to be a very long time a-coming. As a result of the Agricultural Revolution, a 'significantly larger number of people could be sustained on the globe than before,' writes Hoppe, 'but mankind did not yet escape from the Malthusian trap—until some 200 years ago with the beginning of the so-called Industrial Revolution.' [Hoppe 2015, 79]

Despite the long history of man on this planet, his overall economic situation would seem to have changed little from his earliest beginnings until about the beginning of the nineteenth century. Gregory Clark believes that 'the average person in the world of 1800 was no better off than the average person of 100,000 BC.'[75] But, with the arrival of the modern Industrial Revolution,[76] all that changed. The average man in the industrial or post-industrial West is now somewhere between ten to twenty times richer than his forebears of just two hundred years ago. It is true that before AD 1800, a small number of elite people had rich and wealthy lifestyles but we are concerned with the average. It might be offered against these claims that the Agricultural Revolution surely changed things for the better. In a sense, that's true. Productivity increased but, as Harari has pointed out, so did the population so that, apart for the wealthy elite, no one was substantially better off. There was a dramatic increase in population but the average standard of living did not increase as it has done dramatically in the last two hundred years. [see Wade 150-197].

It is sometimes suggested that agriculture provided a more reliable and secure source of food than did hunting and gathering and that this was the trade off that Neolithic man was prepared to pay for giving up the somewhat riskier, if more interesting, delights of hunting. But some, such as Yuval Harari, argue that agriculture did not in fact provide a better diet, did not underpin economic security, nor did it provide a means of protection against violence. If this is so, if the negative aspects of agriculture outweighed its positive aspects, how then was it possible for the agricultural revolution ever to take place? The answer, Harari suggests, is that while agriculture was far from beneficial to individuals, it benefitted the human race as a whole inasmuch as it permitted a huge expansion in the numbers of human beings who could exist and reproduce: 'The currency of evolution,' he remarks, 'is neither hunger nor pain, but rather copies of DNA helixes.'

The plausibility or otherwise of this explanation may be judged by Harari's subsequent (and possibly contradictory) judgement: 'Yet why should individuals care about this evolutionary calculus? Why would any sane person lower his or her standard of living just to multiply the number of copies of the Homo sapiens genome? Nobody agreed to this deal: the Agricultural Revolution was a trap.' [Harari, 83] Just so. Harari has precisely pointed out the flaw in his own position.

In a somewhat similar vein, Colin Renfrew asks the searching question: 'If the arrival of the new species, *Homo sapiens*, with its higher level of cognitive capacity, its new kinds of behaviour, its sophisticated use of language, its enhanced self-consciousness, was so significant, why did it take so long for these really impressive innovations, seen in the accompanying Agricultural Revolution, to come about? What accounts for the huge gap from the first appearance of *Homo sapiens* in Europe 40,000 years ago (and earlier in western Asia) to the earliest Agricultural Revolution in western Asia and Europe of 10,000 years ago?'[77] 'Why,' asks Hans-Hermann Hoppe, 'did it take so long until we gave up a hunter-gatherer existence in favor of an existence as agricultural settlers?' [Hoppe 2015, 83] 'That it took 185,000 years for people to take the seemingly obvious step of settling down and putting a permanent roof over their heads,' writes Nicholas Wade, 'strongly suggests that several genetic changes in social behaviour had to evolve first.'[78] A Marxist-type answer to this question would appear to be unavailable—one cannot, without vicious circularity, explain a fundamental change in the modes of production by appealing to a change in the modes of production! No answer to this question is universally accepted but one possible response might be that given by Leopold Kohr who argues that it was the increasing size and complexity of social groups that pushed man towards the adoption of the new technologies, an idea that Rousseau also flirted with in his *Second Discourse*. [see Kohr, passim] Whatever the truth of the matter here—and, I believe, at best we can only conjecture—it is true that not everyone chose to make use of the new technologies, not least because of their preparedness to trade off wealth for leisure. Michael Finkel, for example, remarks that farming has never appealed to the Hadza, who live around Lake Eyasi in the central Rift Valley and on the Serengeti Plateau. They are aware of farming—how could they not be—but 'growing crops requires planning; seeds are sown now for plants that won't be edible for months. Domestic animals must be fed and protected long before they're ready to butcher. To a Hadza, this makes little sense. Why grow food or rear animals when it's being done for you, naturally, in the bush? When they want berries, they walk to a berry shrub. When they desire baobab fruit, they visit a baobab tree. Honey waits for them in wild hives. And they keep their meat in the biggest storehouse in the world—their land. All that's required is a bit of stalking and a well-shot arrow.' [Finkel, 8]

The assumption is often made that people in hunter/gatherer societies lived a precarious existence from hand to mouth and readily embraced the Neolithic revolution. Some argue that this assumption is ungrounded. Marshall Sahlins points out that 'there are two possible routes to affluence. Wants may be "easily satisfied" by producing much or desiring little' so that either option appears reasonable. [Sahlins, 1-2] The consensus of opinion is that the transition from the Paleolithic (old stone age) to the Neolithic (new stone age) was precipitated by the poverty, deprivation and food insecurity of the former age compared to the relative wealth and food security of the latter. Robert Wright, for example, claims that 'the layperson's common-sense notions about life among prehistoric hunter-gatherers is on target: adversity was part of life, shortage loomed over the horizon, and fortune favored the prepared.' [Wright, 73; see 74-7] Marshall Sahlins isn't part of this consensus.[79] According to him, the wants of the hunter are few and his means plentiful. [Sahlins, 13] It isn't that the hunters and gatherers are poor 'because they don't have anything; perhaps better to think of them for that reason as *free*.' [Sahlins, 14] He adds, 'the world's most primitive people have few possessions, *but they are not poor*. Poverty is not a certain small amount of goods, nor is it just a relation between means and ends; above all it is a relation between people. Poverty is a social status. As such it is the invention of civilization.' [Sahlins, 37] On the other hand, it can be argued against such as Sahlins that changing climatic conditions made the life of the hunter/gatherer progressively more difficult. With the retreat of the ice, the forests advanced and reduced the area of land available for animal grazing so that man had little choice but to adapt or die. Instead of its being, as often portrayed, an inexplicable transition of intellectual brilliance to move towards the cultivation of plants (or social stupidity, if one adopt Sahlins's Rousseauean perspective) perhaps it was really more a matter of practical necessity. Davidson & Rees-Mogg make precisely this point. 'The transition to agriculture was not a choice of preference, but an improvisation adopted under duress to make up for shortfalls in the diet.' [Davidson & Rees-Mogg, 66]

Without succumbing to an excessively romantic picture of early man, it seems that the earliest pre-agricultural human societies, though as prone to individual violence as any other human society, were also marked by some degree of matter-of-fact egalitarianism. Renfrew says that 'Most anthropologists agree that many small-scale societies are broadly egalitarian. Their members are more or less equal in status, and they operate without hereditary distinctions of rank or prestige.'[80] On the other hand, although it is true that hunter-gatherer human groups were relatively egalitarian, they 'still displayed significant status differences'. [Gat, 88] Robert Wright roundly rejects as a misconception the idea that hunter/gatherer bands were egalitarian. [Wright, 71] It may be that the view that hunter/gatherers were, on the whole, better off than their agricultural confreres might not be true, that it wasn't, to quote Robert Wright, the case that hunter/gatherers 'work just a few hours a day—hunting, digging roots, harvesting mongongo trees—and then it's Miller time.' [Wright, 66] As Wright goes on to make clear, the estimation of the short time that hunter/gatherers were deemed to spend on food collection did not 'include the time spent processing the food, making spears, and so on. It now appears that these hunter gatherers [the !Kung San][81] at least, work roughly as hard as horticulturalists.' [Wright, 73]

Are these various positions inconsistent? If so, which, if any, is correct? Were our early pre-agricultural societies Edenic oases of equality or were they the scenes of brutal and primitive violence? Was the transition to the Neolithic a matter of choice—good or bad—or a necessity? Who can tell for sure? Nicholas Wade, for example, argues that 'The decision to settle cannot have been in any way simple or a matter of pure volition, or it would have taken place many millennia previously' and he may well have a point in so thinking. [Wade, 82] Robert Wright appears to agree, arguing that it is a misconception to think that '*change is guided by farsighted reason*.'[82] 'No prehistoric hunter-gatherers assembled a committee to decide whether a growing reliance on starchy foods would eventually promote tooth decay. Planted food slowly replaced wild food over many generations….The question isn't why hunter-gatherers "chose" farming, but why they chose the long series of tiny steps leading imperceptibly to it.' [Wright, 67] On the other hand, Hans-Hermann Hoppe, describes the Neolithic Revolution as 'a fundamental cognitive achievement' that resulted in the creation of two enduring social institutions: private property in land, and the family and family household. [Hoppe 2015, 47]

Azar Gat rejects the tendency evident in some scholars to conjoin hunter-gatherers and pre-state agriculturalists into one homogenised mass. In evolutionary terms, this 'lumps together the aboriginal condition of all humans with a quite recent cultural innovation. Agricultural society, even more recently topped by the growth of the state and of civilization, is the tip of the iceberg in human history…' [Gat, 4] The typical hunter-gatherer local group had between 20 and 70 members, averaging around 25. Some of these local groups might come together in a regional group, whose population might extend from 175-1400, with 500 as the average. [see Gat, 13; 44-45; see also Hoppe 2015, 25 ff.] Although small, local groups have been characteristic of human society from the beginning, regional groups would appear to have originated in the Upper Paleolithic, as recently as 35,000 years ago. [see Gat, 52] Hunter-gatherer homelands have typically low population densities but such low densities 'do not necessarily mean lack of competition and territoriality.' [Gat, 18] In fact, most hunter-gatherer groups operate with quite sharply defined notions of territory, and their wandering isn't random or haphazard but takes place within tightly circumscribed boundaries.[83] The Rousseauean idea of a more or less infinitely elastic frontier into which hunter-gatherer groups could wander isn't so. 'Our Paleolithic ancestors has no empty spaces to move to,' writes Gat, and 'resource competition and conflict existed in most hunter-gatherer societies.' [Gat, 62; 64]

In summary, then, for almost the whole of human history—99.5% of it—man has lived by hunting and by gathering. [see Harari, 77] The transition from a hunting and gathering economy to either pastoralism (based on the domestication of animals) or agriculture (based on the domestication of plants) was the first major revolutionary development in human society. [see McIntosh & Twist, 22-33] One of the earliest and most primitive forms of land cultivation involved a light use of available land until it was chemically exhausted, followed by a move on to other virgin land, the process being repeated as necessary. 'A particular woodland clearing could not have been exploited continuously for more than a few years since primitive agriculture demanded that the land be allowed to recover after a while. That meant moving on to another easily-worked patch.' [Roberts 1997, 14] This primitive form of cultivation, sometimes called 'hoe-culture' has been common throughout human history. As many scholars have noted, the transition from hunting and gathering to pastoralism and farming did not take place all at once or everywhere at the same time but it was none the less revolutionary for all that. As Michael Finkel notes, 'Food production marched in lockstep with greater population densities, which allowed farm-based societies to displace or destroy hunter-gatherer groups. Villages were formed, then cities, then nations. And in a relatively brief period, the hunter-gatherer lifestyle was all but extinguished. Today only a handful of scattered peoples—some in the Amazon, a couple in the Arctic, a few in Papua New Guinea, and a tiny number of African groups—maintain a primarily hunter-gatherer existence. Agriculture's sudden rise, however, came with a price. It introduced infectious-disease epidemics, social stratification, intermittent famines, and large-scale war.' [Finkel, 4]

Pastoralism preceded and, later, coexisted with agriculture. The different requirements of the (usually) nomadic tribes and the (relatively) sedentary agricultural communities gave rise to different modes of social and political organisation and relations between the different types of community weren't always amicable. The farmer and the cowman don't have to be friends and, indeed, there would appear to have been tensions between them extending from the disturbances recorded in the earliest books of the Bible (Cain and Abel)[84] up to the conflicts on the American western ranges in the nineteenth century. It mustn't be assumed that plant cultivation is a necessarily sedentary activity and pastoralism necessarily nomadic. Pastoralism can exist in a relatively confined geographical area where animals are moved from one location to another and back again, depending on the availability of food, water and shelter. [see Childe, 71]

Transhumance is the system in which flocks are moved up the mountains in the summer and taken down again in the winter; physical movement, yes, but not geographically significant movement. All that being said, however, it still remains that the cultivation of crops tends towards the settled life and pastoralism tends towards the nomadic. In any event, both pastoralism and agriculture put a premium on the accumulation of surpluses. Surpluses are required simply for the continuation of the primary activity. Some plant material must be retained as seed for next year's harvest, and not all animals in the herd can be slaughtered for food if a supply is to be available for the future.

William McNeill believes that the shift from hunting (and pastoralism, hunting in a domesticated form) to agriculture brought about significant changes in Neolithic cults. 'In proportion as women became the major suppliers of food for the community, their independence and authority probably increased; and various survivals in historic times suggest that matrilineal family systems prevailed in many Neolithic communities. Correspondingly, the spread of agriculture was connected everywhere with the rise of female priestesses and deities to prominence.' [McNeill, 35] Perhaps so, perhaps not—the point is arguable. Matrilineality isn't necessarily the same thing as matriarchy. In any event, even McNeill is prepared to admit that with the introduction of certain technologies to agriculture, in particular the traction plough, the relative contributions of males and females to agricultural production shifted. 'Hunting and tending animals had always been primarily a man's job; and when animals came into the fields, men came with them. Women lost their earlier dominion over the grain fields; and as followers of the plow, men became once again the principal providers of food. Therewith they were able to reinforce or restore masculine primacy in family and society.' [McNeill, 42]

Significant technological developments from around this time included the invention of the plough and the use of animal power to operate it. Animals began to be used as beasts of burden and as forms of transport. Sailing and river navigation came into existence as the commonest means of transport and remained the commonest and cheapest form of transport until the invention of the railway. [see Sowell 2011, 13ff.] One important element of the Neolithic revolution involved the developments of technologies that we now take for granted. Pottery is seemingly a simple process but it is, in fact, one that's both practically and technologically sophisticated. It contributed hugely to every society in which it was discovered. Childe notes that 'the potter's craft, even in its crudest and most generalized form, was already complex.' [Childe, 92] The discovery and use of textiles, especially wool, required yet more technological inventions—the spindle and the loom. And finally, we come to that form of technology that finally moved man out of the Stone Age completely—metallurgy. It is only in an urban environment that this most sophisticated of all primary technologies can properly flourish. 'Metallurgy was important in Europe at a very early date. Copper was the first widely used metal. Objects made of it by hammering were available in the Near East around 7000 BC, but soon after 5000 BC, it was being mined in the Balkans.'[85]

The technological developments of this period were significant; equally significant was the discovery of the social and economic value of trade. Gordon Childe remarks that the Agricultural Revolution marked a change from mere self-sufficiency in food production to 'an economy based also on specialized manufacture and external trade.' [Childe, 143] Matt Ridley argues that the conventional account of the relationship between agriculture, surpluses and trade is only partially correct. 'In the conventional account it was agriculture that made capital possible by generating stored surpluses and stored surpluses could be used in trade. Before framing, nobody could hoard a surplus. There is some truth in this, but to some degree it gets the story the wrong way around. Agriculture was possible because of trade. Trade provided the incentive to specialize in farmed goods and to generate surplus food.' [Ridley, 123]

Trade or commerce seems to be a relatively simple, indeed obvious, idea but it isn't.[86] 'At human sites (but not at Neanderthal sites), archeologists find tools made hundreds of miles away. Trade goods, then, travelled long distances, linking together different language groups and different cultures. To see how other groups do things is to see new, and sometimes better, ways of doing things. This very idea—that there may be better ideas out there—may itself have been the most inspiring of all.' [Schmidtz & Brennan, 33] For trade to occur, one has to have commodities to exchange, a market in which this exchange can take place, an agreed upon system of valuation, an agreed-upon system of weights and measures and the social, linguistic and political preconditions which make all this possible. [see Renfrew, 169-173] As modern man began to reach outside his immediate social group and relate to non-kin, the need for reliable information on the trustworthiness of potential trading partners became urgent.

One can make a living in two ways: one way is to produce goods or to exchange services for goods and vice versa; the other, operating on the principle that only fools and horses work, is to allow others to work and produce and to take the fruits of their labour from them by force. Franz Oppenheimer famously remarked, 'There are two fundamentally opposed means whereby man, requiring sustenance, is impelled to obtain the necessary means for satisfying his desires. These are work and robbery, one's own labor and the forcible appropriation of the labor of others.' Oppenheimer termed one's own labour and the exchange of that labour for another's labour the *economic means* for the satisfaction of needs; the unilateral appropriation of another's labour he termed the *political means*.[87] For some people, theft or robbery is always more attractive than solid toil, and if human nature hasn't changed fundamentally over the last 50,000 years, it is safe to assume that even in pre-agricultural societies, human predation upon human was a reasonably popular option, at least outside one's immediate kinship group. As Thomas Hobbes noted, 'And in all places, where men have lived by small Families, to robbe and spoyle one another, has been a Trade, and so farre from being reputed against the Law of nature, that the greater spoyles they gained, the greater was their honour...' [Hobbes, 118] Nevertheless, given the small scale, transient character and low productivity of such societies, the prospects for long-term large-scale predation was severely limited. With the coming of the Agricultural Revolution and the eventual emergence of cities and states, all that changed forever. 'One could see...why the hunting tribes and primitive peasants never formed a State. Primitive peasants never made enough of an economic accumulation to be worth stealing.' [Nock, 151]

FROM VILLAGE TO CITY: THE URBAN REVOLUTION

As already mentioned, hunting and gathering groups require extensive territories over which to roam. These groups must be small and mobile and not dragged down by extensive possessions. The first evidence we have of permanent human settlement comes from about 15,000 years ago. Around this time we see the first evidence of clearings for agricultural purposes and animal domestication. By the time we come to the early Neolithic, we find evidence of the collection and selection of certain plants and their cultivation, and the use of animals not only for consumption but also as sources of power. All these developments require the abandonment of a nomadic way of life, or at least, its severe limitation. Mumford notes that 'Domestication in all its aspects implies two large changes: permanence and continuity in residence, and the exercise of control and foresight over processes once subject to the caprices of nature.' [Mumford, 12] The village comes into being as a permanent settlement of families and neighbours, together with their animals and their land. Morality, as something over and above basic familial relations, emerges in the social environment of the village, this morality being the settled customs or *mores* of the villagers by which they are enabled to live together in relative amity. Timothy Earle believes that at this time your average political group numbered in the hundreds so that there would have been somewhere in the order of 100,000 such groups scattered over the earth.

Elman Service had provided a classic (if not uncontroversial) typology of social and political orders: bands, tribes, chiefdoms and states.[88] These different orders are distinguished based on size, subsistence type, political centralisation and the existence and level of social stratification. Bands are groups of extended families, usually numbering between 50 and 150 individuals, who live and work together, that work typically being hunting and gathering. Bands have no formal leadership structure and all members of the band know one another. At a higher level of complexity are tribes.

Tribes are groups based on real or nominal kinship structures. Their mode of subsistence is usually sedentary, either agriculture or pastoral. Here too, there is no permanent central political authority. In both bands and tribes, law is essentially custom and is enforced, not by a central authority, but by consensus and convention. Chiefdoms are large groups of people living under a permanent, often hereditary, political leadership. The mode of subsistence produces a surplus, the disposal of which lies in the hands of the leadership and which is often used to support or reward the chief's followers or warriors. [see Service, 15-16] Whereas bands and tribes are essentially egalitarian, chiefdoms instantiate differences in status. States are the largest of the orders, having many thousands of individuals in them, with some form of central government which has the power to levy taxes and to decree and enforce laws. [see Wade, 26-27]

In hunter-gatherer groups, the cost of children was effectively socialised. Up to a certain level of population, children were a group asset; beyond that level, a group burden. The shift from hunting and gathering to agriculture and husbandry brought about not only the emergence of private property in land, but also, as it were, the emergence of private property in children. The costs and benefits of children were de-socialised, privatised, and this required the invention of a social institution to make this privatisation possible—the family based on marriage. The advantage of the institution of the family based on marriage to men was a greater degree of sexual access to women who hitherto would have been monopolised by more powerful men; the advantage to women was, in conditions of relative scarcity, a guarantee of support for themselves and for their children. [see Hoppe 2015, 59-68] The normalisation and valorisation of single-motherhood in contemporary Western society is, in many ways, a return to a pre-Neolithic stage of social development in which the children of single mothers are, from an economic point of view, everyone's and their maintenance costs de-privatised and re-socialised. [see Penman, 565-566]

After the Agricultural Revolution and in part because of it, the second significant transformation to occur in human culture was the Urban Revolution.[89] The social units at the start of the Neolithic period were small and more or less horizontally organised as had been the hunter-gatherer societies that preceded them. Among the contemporary Hadza people, 'camps are loose affiliations of relatives and in-laws and friends. Each camp has a few core members… but most others come and go as they please. The Hadza recognize no official leaders. Camps are traditionally named after a senior male…but this honor does not confer any particular power. Individual autonomy is the hallmark of the Hadza. No Hadza adult has authority over any other. None has more wealth; or, rather, they all have no wealth.' [Finkel, 5] As the Agricultural Revolution took hold, however, cities began to be formed as centres for specialised activities and as the place of residence of the warrior class. The city, as distinct from the village, may well have begun as a sacred spot, a place of gathering, and a meeting place but, however that may be, the Urban Revolution took our simple pastoralists and agriculturalists, and eventually transformed their habitations and villages into cities and their cities into proto-states.

There is a certain irony in the realisation that the first group of human beings who had no option but to settle permanently in one spot was the dead! But there appears to be a connection between these communal burial sites—whether in caves, cairns, barrows or mounds—and the permanent residences of the living. 'In these ancient paleolithic sanctuaries,' writes Mumford, 'as in the first grave mounds and tombs, we have, if anywhere, the first hints of civic life, probably well before any permanent village settlement can even be suspected.' [Mumford, 8] These burial sites are meeting places to which people return again and again, 'a site to which family or clan groups are drawn back, at seasonable intervals, because it concentrates, in addition to any natural advantages it may have, certain "spiritual" or supernatural powers.' [Mumford, 10]

Although certain elements of village life are carried over into the city, these elements are transmuted into higher and more potent forms of social organisation. The transition from village to city isn't merely a matter of greater size or of increasing numbers; it is more a matter of organisation and control producing a highly differentiated community whose purpose extends beyond mere survival.[90] 'This new urban mixture,' writes Mumford, 'resulted in an enormous expansion of human capabilities in every direction. The city effected a mobilization of manpower, a command over long distance transportation, an intensification of communication over long distances in space and time, an outburst of invention along with a large scale development of civil engineering, and, not least, it promoted a tremendous further rise in agricultural productivity.' [Mumford, 30]

The ancient city resulted from a kind of fusion of various elements: agricultural, economic, political, religious and military. 'The early city, as distinct from the village community, is a caste-managed society, organized for the satisfaction of a dominant minority; no longer a community of humble families living by mutual aid.' [Mumford, 38] The tribal leader now becomes a king. The horizontal facilitating social arrangement that is the village now becomes, in the city, a vertical relationship of dominance and control between rulers and ruled. 'The rise of the first city-states, based on large scale agriculture, required a new kind of social structure, one based on large, hierarchically organized populations ruled by military leaders. The states overlaid their own institutions on those of the tribe. They used religion to legitimate the ruler's power and maintain a monopoly of force.' [Wade, 63] At a certain stage, writes Mumford, the 'king becomes a mediator between heaven and earth, incarnating in his own person the whole life and being of the land and its people.'[91] In the standard story, chiefdoms are forms of political organisation midway between village-based polities and fully-fledged states. Earle believes, controversially, that the dynamics of chiefdoms and states are pretty much the same and that 'the origin of states is to be understood in the emergence and development of chiefdoms.'[92]

What marks a city off from a rural environment is that its inhabitants perform specialised functions vis-à-vis the city's hinterland. Such functions could include crafts of various kinds, education, religious rituals and, of course, political and administrative functions. Life in the village wasn't marked by any great specialisation; at most, a rudimentary and sporadic division of labour. Life in the city, by contrast, cannot exist without the permanent division of labour, a division that made possible a distinction between rich and poor. Specialisation resulting from the division of labour, coupled with the fact that although the village is a place one belongs to by birth, the city is, for most people, an adopted place, a place of choice, led to a loosening of small-scale social bonds. 'The very notion of a settled division of labor, of the fixation of many natural activities into a single life occupation, of confinement to a single craft,' Mumford writes, 'probably dates, as Childe indicates, from the founding of cities. Urban man paid for his vast collective expansion of power and environmental control by a contraction of personal life.' [Mumford 102]

It can be hard to draw a sharp line between a large village and a small city, such as the Mesopotamian city of Lagash. All the structural elements of the city are present embryonically in the village: the containers, the houses, the shrines, and the meeting place which is, however, not yet a market place. The *mores* of the social life of the village are the beginnings of ethics and the roots of law and justice and a certain kind of government. The government of the village isn't a specialised function exercised by a professional group but rather a way in which the group consensus, expressed in custom and usage, is given expression. Individuality wasn't encouraged in the village. An individual was an *idiotes*, someone standing outside the group consensus and refusing to take part in public affairs. I already mentioned Camille Paglia as remarking that 'egalitarian feminist ideology fails to realize…that tribal cultures suppress individuality. The group rules. Our distinct, combative, introspective, conflicted, and highly verbal and creative personalities are a product of Western culture. Feminism itself has been produced by Western culture.'[93] The individuality of the villager is more or less completely dissipated in his village community; his personality, such as it is, is largely one with the personality of the group. In the city, by contrast, for the first time, man was partially emancipated from the vise-like grip of the family and the clan. At first, such individuality was possible only for those at or near the top of the social scale but in time, it became the possession of more and more people. 'One by one, the privileges and prerogatives of kingship were transferred to the city, and its citizens. Thousands of years were needed to effect this change; and by the time it was consummated men had forgotten where and how it had begun.'[94]

The creation of cities was to have significant consequences for intra-human violence. Once a city came into being, it had to secure its material supply base. If its population grew, then its supply lines had to be extended and the areas of food production increased. Was this to be done by predation or by some kind of process of symbiosis? 'A power myth, says Mumford, 'knows only one answer. Thus the very success of urban civilization gave sanction to bellicose habits and demands that continually undermined it and nullified its benefits. What began as a self-contained urban droplet would be forcibly blown into an iridescent soap bubble of empire, imposing in its dimension, but fragile in proportion to its size.' [Mumford, 53] The increase in power and production capacity made possible by the invention of the city also made possible for the first time the mass extermination and mass appropriation that is war, as distinct from the border skirmish or occasional cattle raid.

CITY STATE AND TERRITORIAL STATE

We might adopt as a working definition of the state,[95] that given by Bruce Trigger, who describes it as, 'a politically organized society that is regarded by those who live in it as sovereign or politically independent and has leaders who control its social, political, legal, economic, and cultural activities.' [Trigger, 92] The earliest civilisations took the form either of a state based upon a city, or one based upon a territory. It should be noted that some archaeologists and anthropologists see city-states and territorial states not as co-equal and independent forms of political structure but as various stages in a single line of social progression. One possible progression might be—pre-state module; city-state; territorial state; empire. Others, although agreeing that city-states and territorial states are not co-ordinate polities, would reverse some of the stages in the previous example. Instead of city-states moving upwards and onwards towards becoming territorial states, some—Joyce Marcus for one—see city-states emerging rather from the disintegration of territorial states. [see Feinman & Marcus, 98]

A city-state is a relatively small polity consisting of an urban centre located within a hinterland of farmland with possibly outlying minor settlements. (We may note in passing that most Greek city-states were only dubiously states and many had no urban core to speak of.) In city-states, the leading citizens tended to know one another personally. Perhaps as a result, there was a markedly diminished tendency to divinise its rulers. It is hard to believe that the man you have known as an uncouth child is really a god. A territorial state, on the other hand, generally occupied a relatively large area and was governed by a ruler who ruled through a hierarchy of sub-rulers or administrators located in a corresponding hierarchy of urban centres. [see Trigger, 92]

According to Trigger, city-states tended to exist in a kind of geographical network. Their territory was relatively compact, perhaps less than 10 kilometres across, with a modest population of between 5,000 to 20,000 people. Some, of course, had larger territories and larger populations. The urban centres of these city-states attracted artisans and encouraged specialisation. In its Early Dynastic phase, southern Mesopotamia (Sumeria) consisted of a network of quasi-independent city-states.[96] Territorial states (Trigger is thinking primarily of Shang China, Egypt and the Inka) had to develop an effective bureaucracy in order to persist. Egypt may have begun in the form of embryonic Mesopotamian like city-states but even if this were so, those city-states were quickly subsumed under a central government. [see Roberts 1993, 38-51]

The territory governed by territorial states was significantly larger than that controlled by city-states. Territorial states were also less populous than city-states. They were governed by an upper class—a ruling family and other leading families. The rulers of territorial states had access to a much greater surplus that did the rulers of city-states. In territorial states, a relatively large degree of economic control was required in accumulating the surpluses, running the administration, supplying the army, paying for public works projects, and so on. Political control was in large part indirect in territorial states. Whereas in city-states, rulers and ruled were relatively close socially, in territorial states, there was a significant social gap between the rulers and the workers.

Across the various early civilisations, despite their manifold individual differences, certain matters appear to be relatively constant. All had a single supreme ruler; all were based on social and economic inequalities, both in society at large and within the family. Trigger notes that 'ideas of inequality and obedience to authority were inculcated in everyone from earliest childhood.... the concept of obedience was reinforced in schools, social life, and relations with government officials.' [Trigger, 264] In all these societies, a small number of extremely wealthy and powerful people were supported by very large number of producers and taxpayers. The position of the upper class was protected by military force and by law. All this has a depressing air of familiarity!

In many cases, the internal relationships of the state were modelled on that of the family and vice versa. This was explicitly the case in China but also appeared in one form or another in other early states. There was a 'pervasive tendency to model family relations on those that characterized the state. Families were conceptualized as miniature kingdoms in which the father had the same relation to his wife (or wives), children, and other dependents that a monarch had to his subjects.' [Trigger, 271]

With the striking exception of the Meso-American[97] civilisations, all the major ancient civilisations centred themselves around river valleys. Childe points out that such river-valley communities provided the nascent conditions for coercion. Outside the horizons of the river lies desert or wilderness so those who work the land are geographically circumscribed. [see Carneiro, passim.] Although even the strongest of rulers cannot prevent the raindrops from falling on your head, they can restrict your access to irrigation. 'So when the social will comes to be expressed through a chief or a king, he is invested not merely with moral authority, but with coercive force too; he can apply sanctions against the disobedient.' [Childe, 109] Those who controlled access to the water also controlled the land and its products. Individual farmers, write Davidson & Rees-Mogg, 'faced a very high cost for failing to cooperate in maintaining the political structure. Without irrigation, which could be provided only on a large scale, crops would not grow. No crops meant starvation.' [Davidson & Rees-Mogg, 65]

Though sharing certain similarities, Egypt and Mesopotamia differed from one another in certain respects,[98] Egypt being a territorial state and Mesopotamia a city-state, or rather, a collection of city-states.[99] We often have the impression that the use of the fertile land adjoining the Nile was a simple matter of accepting Nature's bounty but this wasn't so.[100] The land on the riverbank would originally have been a tangle of swamps and reeds that needed to be reclaimed before it could be used and this reclamation was no simple undertaking; in fact, this reclamation was, according to Childe, 'a stupendous task: the swamps had to be drained by channels, the violence of flood-waters to be restrained by banks, the thickets to be cleared away, the wild beasts lurking in them to be eliminated. No small group could hope to make headway against such obstacles. It needed a strong force capable of acting together to cope with recurrent crises...' [Childe, 107] Much the same comments could be made about Mesopotamia, the land between the rivers Tigris and Euphrates. There, the land had not just to be cleared but it had to be created more or less *ex nihilo*. Originally consisting of swamps lying just above the level of the Persian Gulf, the Tigris-Euphrates delta needed to be reclaimed, a dry land created out of a watery chaos. The words of *Genesis* appear to be particularly applicable to this process: 'And God said, "Let the water under the sky be gathered to one place, and let dry ground appear."' [*Genesis* 1: 9] Some of the earliest cities in the region[101] were constructed on platforms of reeds laid out on the alluvial mud. Just as in the case of the Nile communities, so too in Sumeria, reclamation required large-scale social cooperation. The drainage, irrigation and protection of this land gave rise to a centrally controlled economic system.[102] Raw materials were needed and so regular systems of trade had to be created to obtain them, requiring merchants, transport workers, specialist craftsmen, and those willing and able to provide security, people to keep records and, most interesting for our purposes, state officials to reconcile conflicting interests. [see Childe, 141-142] Although the Egyptian state seems to have been produced directly from a condition of villagisation without going through intermediate city conditions,[103] in Sumeria, some fifteen to twenty different city-states emerged more or less simultaneously, all politically independent, although sharing a common religion and language as well as being economically interdependent. From time to time, one of these cities would achieve ascendency over the others. The Sumerian economic unit, writes Childe, 'is a city with outlying fields and hamlets which could and did function by itself. In Egypt, on the contrary, the unit is the kingdom as a royal estate;[104] the manors or cities into which it may be subdivided would cease to function if isolated from it, or rather would relapse into more or less self-sufficing peasant communities.' [Childe, 166-67]

VIOLENCE AND PREDATION

A 2014 article in *Nature* argues that while 'the nature of inter-group relations among prehistoric hunter-gatherers remains disputed, with arguments in favour and against the existence of warfare before the development of sedentary societies,' the analysis of skeletons from Nataruk in Kenya dating from the late Pleistocene or early Holocene period (about 14,000 years ago) presents evidence that 'warfare was part of the repertoire of inter-group relations among prehistoric hunter-gatherers.' [Lahr et al.] Evidence supplied by the study of the two best living laboratories of surviving hunter-gatherer societies, Australia and the north west coast of North America, show that 'hunter-gatherers, from the very simple to the more complex, fought among themselves. Deadly conflict, if not endemic, was ever to be expected. The fear of it restricted people to well-circumscribed home territories and necessitated constant precaution and special protective measures....rather than being a late cultural "invention", fighting would seem to be, if not "natural", then certainly not "unnatural" to humans.' [Gat, 35] Hunter-gatherer war consisted mainly of raids on the relatively defenceless. Gat writes, 'the most lethal and common form of warfare was the raid, using surprise and taking place mostly at night....the camp of the attacked party could be surrounded, and its unprepared, often sleeping, dwellers massacred indiscriminately (except for the women who could be abducted).' [Gat, 117] Formal confrontation between equally well-armed groups was not the norm. Disputing the neo-Rousseauean romanticism of Karl Polanyi, Murray Rothbard remarks, 'Curiously, in his idyllic picture of tribal life, Polanyi never seems to mention pervasive inter-tribal warfare. Such warfare is almost necessary, because groups of people are fighting over scarce resources: water holes, hunting, etc. Tribalism, not capitalism, is the "rule of the jungle," for warfare and extermination of the "unfit" is the only way that some of the tribes can keep alive. It is the capitalist market economy, which increases resources by mutual benefit, that is able to bypass the rule of the jungle, and to rise above such animal-like existence to the status of advanced civilizations—and amicable relations among men.' [Rothbard 2004]

What occasioned such of inter-group violence? Property, women, trespass, murder and the desire for revenge.[105] Hunter-gatherer warfare was often about the theft of women (and revenge for the same): 'wife stealing was widespread, and probably the main cause of homicide and "blood feuds" among the Eskimos....Revenge has probably been the most regular and prominent cause of fighting cited in anthropological accounts of pre-state societies. Violence was activated to avenge injuries to honour, property, women, and kin.'[106] It is also the case, as Hans-Hermann Hoppe has pointed out, that the hunter-gatherer lifestyle is essentially parasitic and non-productive and so, given a relatively fixed supply of food, and a tendency of groups to approach super-optimal population density, food acquisition becomes a zero-sum game. As population increased, members of different hunter-gatherer groups would encounter each other with increasing frequency and 'their competition for food was necessarily of an antagonistic nature: either I pick the berries or hunt a given animal or you do it....In this situation, where everything appropriated by one person (or tribe) was immediately consumed and the total supply of goods was strictly limited by natural forces, only deadly antagonism could exist between men.' [Hoppe 2015, 30]

The Agricultural and Urban Revolutions brought many social and political consequences in their train. Apart from the agricultural surpluses that made craft specialisation possible, it also saw the emergence of a special class, for whom the manipulation and control of violence was the key to social domination.

Where aggression brings successful results, incentives abound to increase the size of the aggressing group, for God (or the Devil) is usually on the side of the big battalions. Since not everyone has the time, the disposition or the capacity to exercise violence successfully, the incentive arises for some to specialise in this area. These specialists, which Davidson & Rees-Mogg characterise as the forefathers of government, 'increasingly devoted themselves to plunder and protection from plunder. Along with priests, they became the first wealthy persons in history.'[107]

Just as agriculture involves the shift from hunting animals to domesticating them, so too, the political means, the method of the incipient state, originates in the move from simply robbing and killing other people more or less indiscriminately to, as it were, domesticating them and milking a portion of their produce at regular intervals. We might call this the *domestication of predation* which, as a long-term strategy, is much more productive than outright confiscation and destruction. Just as farmers have domesticated animals over which they exercise control, so too, the specialists in violence have their own domesticated animals, the farmers, over whom *they* exercise control. Violence isn't necessarily pathological but can be used as an instrument of spoliation. 'The powerful were now able to organize a new form of predation: a local monopoly of violence, or government.' [Davidson & Rees-Mogg, 80] For a latter-day (fictional) example of this, think of the film *The Magnificent Seven* in which the valley-dwelling villagers grow the crops that the bandits who live in the hills take from them by force, leaving them just enough to live on so that they may continue to produce and be robbed repeatedly. The bandits, if they can establish themselves permanently in their position, fighting off rival bandits and preventing uprising by the villagers, will form a kind of aristocracy. As Childe notes, writing in 1936, the domestication of predation is quite common, 'it survives in a very simple form in East Africa; it was characteristic of mediaeval Europe and was widespread in antiquity.' [Child, 132] Oppenheimer argues that the state is ultimately dependent and parasitic upon the economic means generated by society so that no state can come into being 'until the economic means has created a definite number of objects for the satisfaction of needs, which objects may be taken away or appropriated by warlike robbery.'[108] Since farmers, unlike hunter/gatherers, were effectively tied to the land, the chance that others would seek to exploit them is high. In the face of aggression, escape by migration wasn't an attractive option, even assuming it were possible. As escape became more difficult, opportunities for organized shakedowns and plunder increased. Farmers were subject to raids at harvest-time. Domestic animals living on the land and the crops grown on it are valuable possessions that could be stolen and hence had to be guarded from predators, and the land itself now became an asset, worthy of being stolen and therefore worthy of protection.[109]

In his comprehensive tome, *The Origins of Political Order*, Francis Fukuyama refers to an article by Mancur Olson that makes more or less the same point that I have been making about the transition from sporadic banditry (the politico-economic equivalent of hunting and gathering) to domestic predation (the politico-economic equivalent of agriculture).[110] Fukuyama rejects Olson's thesis on the grounds that the rulers of traditional agrarian societies, which Olson calls 'stationary bandits', did not tax their subjects to the maximum. But it isn't necessary to commit to the thesis that stationary bandits will always employ their power maximally. 'Stationary bandits' can predate within a range without, as it were, killing the goose that lays the golden egg: above this range, their subjects cannot survive; below this range, the bandits cannot survive. It would be a minor miracle if these two points were always to coincide.

One finds an astonishing degree of agreement among scholars that the state and violence are intimately related.[111] If one were to ask David Hume how the state originated he would say that 'Almost all the governments which exist at present, or of which there remains any record in story, have been founded originally in usurpation or conquest or both, without any pretense of a fair consent or voluntary subjection of the people.' [Hume, 471] Anthony de Jasay writes that, as a matter of fact, the real-life states that people in fact endure have come into existence because their ancestors 'were beaten into obedience by an invader, and sometimes due to Hobson's choice' had to take one king so as to escape the threat of getting another [de Jasay, 36] And Crispin Sartwell remarks that 'Almost any realistic view of the origin of states will attribute their founding or at any rate their development and preservation, to the large-scale application of violence.' [Sartwell, 39] The renowned attorney, Clarence S. Darrow rejects as a tale told by an idiot, full of sound and fury, signifying nothing, the idea that states came into existence to discourage and punish the evil and the lawless and to protect the weak and helpless. On the contrary, he argues, history shows that 'the state was born in aggression, and that in all the various stages through which it has passed its essential characteristics have been preserved.' [Darrow, 3] The actions of the state rest 'on violence and force; is sustained by soldiers, policemen, and courts; and is contrary to the ideal peace and order that make for the happiness and progress of the human race.' Albert J. Nock writes that 'The State[112] originated in conquest and confiscation, as a device for maintaining the stratification of society permanently into two classes—an owning and exploiting class, relatively small, and a propertyless dependent class....No State known to history originated in any other manner, or for any other purpose than to enable the continuous economic exploitation of one class by another,' and James Scott notes that 'much, if not most, of the population of the early states was unfree; they were subjects under duress.' To live in such a state rendered you liable for 'taxes, conscription, and corvée labor' and implied for most a 'condition of servitude.' In substance, then, these early states were 'warmaking machines…producing hemorrhages of subjects fleeing conscription, invasion and plunder.'[113]

The warrior class coeval with these emergent states demanded a portion of the agricultural produce, a portion that steadily rose in tandem with an increase in overall population so that 'where productive capacity was at a premium, the warrior group could take a large fraction of total output. These warriors founded the first states with the proceeds of this rake-off, which reached as high as 25 percent of the grain crop and one-half the increase in herds of domesticated animals. Farming, therefore, dramatically increased the importance of coercion. The surge in resources capable of being plundered led to a large surge in plunder.'[114] Another popular form of aggression was the capture of human beings for use as slaves. Childe remarks that 'war helped to a great discovery—that men as well as animals can be domesticated. Instead of killing a defeated enemy, he might be enslaved; in return for his life, he could be made to work….by early historic times slavery was a foundation of ancient industry and a potent instrument in the accumulation of capital.' [Childe, 134] Earle concurs, writing 'Warfare procured slavery, by which a political economy could be reconstructed, intensified, and tightly controlled.' [Earle, 107]

In pre-state societies, there generally is no segment of the society that's dedicated exclusively to military pursuits. When necessary or when desired, all suitably qualified members of the society can be called upon for military service. As states begin to emerge, one significant characteristic of them is the corresponding emergence of a specific military class whose role it is to attack outsiders, defend against attacks and, significantly, to provide internal policing services, including the intimidation of their fellow citizens. It isn't without interest that our modern police forces began as paramilitary bodies.[115] [see Casey 2102, 80-82] Any group of people may conceivably need protection from aggression by other groups. In many cases, this is provided by the group itself as need be. Where a community possesses a quasi-specialised group of hunters, it is likely that such will provide the core of any defensive unit. There are, however, in human history, many examples of would-be protectors going into the aggression business themselves and turning from watchdog to wolf. 'But the very prosperity and peaceableness of the neolithic village may have caused its protectors to exchange the watchdog's role for the wolf's, demanding "protection money," so to say, in an increasingly one-sided transaction.' [Mumford, 23] What originally were voluntary offerings would eventually become coercively extracted taxes and tributes.

The Agricultural and Urban Revolutions made possible for the first time significant inequalities of wealth, class and power. Renfrew writes, 'after the agricultural revolution…we see the development of communities with leaders and followers where the high ranks often become hereditary. The state societies that sometimes subsequently developed were class societies, in which people were born to a high or low class, and where mobility between classes could be difficult.' [Renfrew, 160] In both Egypt and Sumeria were to be found, above the food-producing class, a class of specialised craftsmen, bureaucrats, courtiers and rulers. At the bottom of the social hierarchy, farmers tended to group in villages and to deal with their social and military superiors as a unit. Nearer to the top of the social hierarchy, however, property took on a more individualistic form with something like a freehold or allodial system of land ownership emerging from time to time.

Much of the wealth produced by these civilisations was appropriated by the small ruling class. 'In all early civilizations,' writes Bruce Trigger, 'a small privileged class appropriated, in ways that were deemed to be socially acceptable, a disproportionate share of the available wealth. Ownership of land was not the key to this process. In earlier civilizations, agricultural produce and manufactured goods were appropriated by the state in the form of taxes in kind, while surplus labour was appropriated by imposing corvées.' [Trigger, 385] The farmers produced most of the wealth but lived just above subsistence level. There were merchants but they lived a relatively precarious existence depending on the goodwill and protection of rulers and officials. But not only the peasants, farmers and merchants were taxed; the heavy hand of the state fell upon all—'All, from the highest to the lowest, were ruthlessly taxed...' [Cottrell, 160] Of course, since government officials, soldiers and other functionaries produced nothing themselves and were paid[116] from taxes extracted from primary producers, the taxes levied on them simply amounted to a difference between their nominal and their real salaries. Then, as now, people were reluctant to give up their hard-earned wealth to others. Trigger again: 'Some ancient Egyptian farmers habitually tried to conceal part of their harvest to avoid having that portion taxed by government officials. Tax collectors for their part, sought to stop such evasion by calculating harvest yields as accurately as possible and forcing farmers who claimed to have produced less to reveal their hiding places.' [Trigger 376] Very little, it seems, has changed.

The wealth appropriated by the governing classes came in the form of taxes (including sales and transaction taxes), rents, fees for licences for various services or legal fees, and tribute. Unlike modern governments, the rulers of ancient civilisations were mercifully inefficient in their ability to monitor and tax the resources of their primary producers. The rulers of these early states also attempted to increase their wealth not just by the exaction of taxes[117] and levies from their own subjects but by the tried and true method of extracting wealth by force from other states. This they did in the form of tribute, the coercive transfer of wealth from the upper class in a weaker state to the upper class in a stronger, resulting in pressure on commoners in those weaker states 'to work harder and pay more taxes.' [Trigger, 394] Again, very little seems to have changed! As one of my old professors used to say, the basic principle of political economy is that the peasant always pays! Commenting on the origins of taxation, Margaret Atwood remarks that 'Taxes fell most heavily on the peasants—those who produced the actual food that kept the superstructure going—and so it remains today.' She notes, as others have done, that, in origin, 'taxation was a sort of protection racket: if the taxes were paid to the religious establishment, you were supposed to get the protection of the gods; if they were paid to a king or emperor, you were supposed to get the protection of his armies.' Musing on the difference between taxation and theft, she comments, 'In theory, taxes are different from someone merely walking into your house and taking your stuff. That's called "robbery," whereas with taxes you're supposed to be getting something in return. What exactly you do get in return provides the chattering points for many a modern election.'[118] In another place at another time, I wrote, similarly, 'the modern state came into being by means of what we would now call a protection racket. While it may be worthwhile to pay someone to protect you from real threats or imminent dangers, there is something delightfully quixotic, almost Gilbertian, when the danger or threat from which your protector is protecting you originates primarily or solely from your would-be protector.'[119] The historian, Charles Tilly too notes that 'Since governments themselves commonly simulate, stimulate, or even fabricate threats of external war, and since the repressive and extractive activities of governments often constitute the largest threats to the livelihoods of their own citizens,[120] many governments operate in essentially the same ways as racketeers.' [Tilly 1985, 171]

When it comes to explaining the origin of leadership in societies, there are two types of explanation. One sees leadership emerging naturally as an adaptive response to increasing social complexity, so that the many in society are willing to cede authority to the one or the few in return for increased wealth or security; the other type of explanation holds that people do not yield their autonomy unless forced to do so and that one way in which this force may be exercised is through economic pressure. Regardless of whichever of these is the more likely, the activities of the leader of the society and his administrative machinery must be financed. This can be done by means of a payment in money or, more commonly in kind, either in goods or in labour, from those who are subject to the leader. Earle notes that 'Effective staple finance must be based on a property system through which staples are mobilized from commoners as "rent" in return for access to subsistence resources. The critical problem is to maximize the gross "surplus" from the subsistence economy that can be deployed to support elite projects ranging from ritual occasions to craft activities to a warrior cadre.' [Earle, 71] Economic power is based on incentives, positive and negative. Whoever controls the production and exchange of goods, especially subsistence goods, exercises significant power over others. The word 'lord' in English is derived from the words for 'bread' and 'giver'; the lord is the one who gives and, significantly, the one who can also *withhold* bread.

It should come as no surprise to anyone to find that military power and the control of that power was a vital aspect of all these early states. Military forces defended borders, imposed tribute on conquered peoples and maintained internal order. Ensuring the collection of taxes and preventing the outbreak of rebellions or crushing them was a vital part of maintaining internal order. One of the tasks of the Egyptian army was, as Trigger notes, 'to assist government officials to collect the grain tax from recalcitrant Egyptian farmers, whom the soldiers would arrest, flog, and imprison until they delivered what bureaucrats had estimated was the government's share of the harvest.' [Trigger, 253] The soldiers making up these early armies were, for the most part, conscripts, officered by members of the upper classes. This pattern of supplying officers from the upper classes persisted in one form or another until relatively recently. In the British Army, until late in the nineteenth century, officers' commissions, and promotion up to the rank of Lieutenant Colonel, were available for purchase so that those with the requisite wealth and social standing were in a position to acquire them more quickly and much earlier than those relying purely on merit.

Military power is overtly coercive and 'A key part of the political process is to be able to assert coercive power.' [Earle, 8] Although it may be an obvious source of power, military might isn't without its own problems. Those who live by the sword risk dying by it and leaders have to reward and control their troops in such a way as to prevent their military subordinates from becoming a threat to them. It was vitally important for the rulers of the state to retain ultimate control of their armies and to ensure that their army commanders wouldn't be in a position to become independent of the state and threaten it.

The leader of the state offered a protection service against aggression by other polities, whether such aggression was real or imagined, provoked or unprovoked. 'Another aspect of intimidation is the fear of attack that herds people together under the leader who offers them protection. Gilman describes the evolution of stratified and centrally organized society as a protection racket. Leaders provide protection from attacks by social predators (including themselves) in return for tributary payoffs.'[121] 'If protection rackets represent organized crime at its smoothest,' writes Tilly, 'then war making and state making—quintessential protection rackets with the advantage of legitimacy— qualify as our largest examples of organized crime.' [Tilly 1985, 169] In their policing functions, the military cohort not only maintains civil order but also, act as an instrument of intimidation. They ensure that commands are followed and tribute paid, 'the person who resists authority is hammered down by the power of the ruling institutions.' [Earle, 105] C. Northcote Parkinson notes the obvious fact—obvious but still worth noting—that war requires leadership. 'In war,' he remarks, 'it is usually better to decide *something*, even mistakenly, than to argue for long as to what is best. So the first effect of war is to transform the character of kingship. The king who leads his people in war becomes something less than a god but gains enormously in actual authority…' [Parkinson 1958, 49-50]

It has been said that, to a man with a hammer, every pointed object looks like a nail. Even if military forces originate as defence options in anticipation of attack, once in existence, the temptation to use them for aggressive purposes is practically irresistible. Speaking of your typical oriental empire, Gordon Childe remarks that 'empires thus established were mere tribute-collecting machines. Normally the imperial government interfered in the internal affairs of subject peoples only in so far as was necessary to ensure obedience and the regular payment of taxes.' [Childe, 234] He also makes the point that such empires did not, for the most part, make any positive contribution to wealth creation. All that happened was that wealth was forcibly redistributed from the relatively poor to the relatively rich, a practice not unknown in our own times.

KINGS

The institution of kingship (or its functional equivalent—emperor, duke, prince) extends across time and space as the most common form of government that we can find, from the Neolithic to the nineteenth-century, from Japan westwards through China, India, the Middle and Near East, Africa and the Americas. Similarly temporally and spatially extended was the system of thought that supported the institution of kingship: the core of this ideological system hinged on the sacred character of the king.[122] Shang China, Southern Mesopo-

tamia, Egypt, Yoruba-Benin, Valley of Mexico (Aztec), Inka and Maya—all
had kings. 'It therefore seems reasonable,' Trigger remarks, 'to conclude that
all early civilizations probably had monarchs, even if kingship was defined
somewhat differently and the actual political power exercised by such rulers
varied considerably from one to another. While some small, non-state societies
may have survived within or on the borders of city-state systems, republican
forms of sovereignty within states, whether they took the form of despotisms,
oligarchies, or democracies, arose from and replaced monarchies.'[123]

The duties of kings varied from polity to polity but all seemed to converge on
the maintenance of internal order, the provision of protection against external
aggression and guaranteeing the link between society and the supernatural.[124]
'The king,' says Trigger, 'standing at the apex of society, constituted the most
important link between human beings and the supernatural forces on which
the welfare of both society and the universe depended. These relations were
mediated by rituals that only kings or their deputies were able to perform.'
[Trigger, 79] Given their intermediary role, kings were often taken to possess
some of the attributes of divinity themselves, in some cases, even to be divine!
The greater the distance between the king and ordinary people, the more likely
this was to be the case. In other cases, the king was thought of as a son of god.
'The rulers of early civilizations invariably claimed divine support, and most of
them were believed to be endowed with divine powers. The most far-reaching
claims were made in Egypt and among the Inka, both large states in which
rulers tended to be remote from their subjects, but even here the human nature
of the individual ruler was acknowledged…The weakest claims were found
among the Mesopotamians, who in early Dynastic times had become the most
urbanized people…and therefore best able to observe their rulers at close range'
[Trigger, 85-86]

In fact, Mesopotamian rulers stood out from rulers of other early civilisations in not normally claiming to be descended in any robust sense from a
god. 'Although some Mesopotamian rulers named deities as their fathers or
mothers, they did not, in doing so, pretend to godliness. When we refer back,
once more, to Egypt, we find that Pharaoh could appear as the son of any god
or goddess but that he counted specifically as the child (in the literal sense) of
certain deities.…In Mesopotamia we do not find equivalents for the unchanging
precisely defined relationships which connected Pharaoh with Amon-Re and
Osiris, with Hathor, and with Isis.' [Frankfort 1948, 299-300]

In considering this vexed matter of the divine status of kings or their relationship to the divine, we have to realise that we moderns start with the presumption
that there is no identity, no relationship of descent, no special appointment of
rulers by the gods or by God, and we wonder how the ancients could ever
have thought otherwise. But for the ancients, no synthesis of the sacred and the
profane was required; for them, the political and the sacred were simply two
dimensions of the same phenomenon. To that synthesis of the social and the
divine you can usually add the world of nature, as the gods were both identified with and distinguished from nature in all its aspect. The sub-title of Henri
Frankfort's *Kingship and the Gods: A Study of Ancient Near Eastern Religion*

as the Integration of Society & Nature reveals the nexus between the natural and the social.

A defining aspect of early states is their claim to exercise not just naked force but legitimate power, and this legitimacy came not least from their rulers' relationship to the gods. 'In many early state societies,' writes Colin Renfrew, 'it was recognised that there was in fact a cosmic order, upon which the welfare and sometimes the continued existence of the earth and of human society depended. It was held also that the ruler—whether pharaoh, emperor or king—had a special role, a divinely ordered status, in seeking to maintain that order and in ensuring that its benefits were felt by the community of which he (or sometimes she) was the divinely sanctified leader. Sometimes the ruler himself assumed the status of a god, as in later Roman times. Alternatively, the mortal status of the ruler was protected by divine sanctions—a view that persisted in a modified form until relatively recent times in Europe with the notion of the 'divine right of kings'. [Renfrew, 186] It doesn't take much reflection to realise just how much it was in the interest of the ruler and his supporting cast that this claim to be divine or to be connected with the divine should be believed by the many.

Ideology, often but not always by means of religion, is used to establish structures of authority. Earle describes an ideology as 'a system of beliefs and ideas presented publicly in ceremonies and other occasions. It is created and manipulated strategically by social segments, more importantly the ruling elite, to establish and maintain positions of social power.' [Earle, 149] For most of human history, religion has been a constituent feature of daily life—in Greece, in Rome and in Medieval Europe. Our present day Western society is perhaps the first to try the experiment of trying to live life with religion pushed to the margins. If ideology works, it's cheaper and more effective than military power. 'To the degree that an ideology, the cultural perspective of a ruling segment, can be imposed as the set of ordering principles for the broader society, it facilitates and legitimizes domination.' [Earle, 9] One can force someone to submit to one's demands by the use or threat of the use of violence. This is effective as long as one can continue to exert that violence—ineffective otherwise. If submission can be had without the use of force, this is more effective and much less expensive.

Such submission can be had if submission is ideologically mandated, for example, if the commoners believe that God should be obeyed and that their leader is a god.

Law

The function of law in early societies wasn't only to maintain order within the social group or between social groups but also to align the social group as a whole with the principles of cosmic order. This link between the order constitutive of society and the cosmic or transcendent order isn't just a feature of archaic societies but something that persisted until historical times. The swearing of an oath is, in essence, the calling down of divine retribution if one should fail to keep one's word.

Crime isn't a modern invention. Our distant ancestors were as prone to start fights with and to steal from one another as we are. Houses had walls to protect against neighbourly depredations; cities had walls too to protect against external marauders. Given the difficulties of communication and the elementary nature of bureaucracy, law enforcement in such societies was largely a matter of self-regulation or local control. 'Significant state intervention at the lowest level of a polity was difficult where collecting information and conveying decisions were cumbersome and expensive' says Trigger. 'In keeping with their approach to administration generally, kings and government officials tolerated and encouraged self-regulation in legal matters at the local and family levels and by craft and other local organizations....The state intervened only when lower-level controls failed to function or the interests of the upper classes were at risk.' [Trigger, 222-223] Justice at the bottom level of society was often enforced through the pressure of public opinion whereas justice at higher levels could be maintained through coercive force.

Law codes began to appear in these civilisations, the best known of these being the Code of Hammurabi, a Mesopotamian King (c. 1700 bc). This code, avowedly, had the purpose of defending the weak against the strong but here the reality was at variance with the Code's stated purpose. All these early civilisations were status-based and how the law was applied depended to a large extent on who and what the offender was and who and what the offended. [see Casey 2012b, 102-110] The nature and the severity of punishments depended on the status of victim and perpetrator, with crimes against those higher up the social scale being punished more severely than crimes against those lower down. Sometimes, however, as among the Aztecs, some offences (such as public drunkenness) were punished more heavily if committed by the upper classes than if committed by the lower. In most of these societies, women were regarded as less legally significant than their male peers in the social order and, of course, slaves were right down at the bottom. All in all, law in these early societies was oriented strongly towards preserving and reinforcing the existing social order. Trigger remarks, 'Far from being a means of securing justice for the weak, the upper levels of the legal system were a powerful instrument of intimidation and control in the hands of the upper classes....the important function of the legal system was to reinforce the power and privileges of the state and upper class.' [Trigger, 238]

Let this suffice, then, for a sketch of the prehistory and early history of man's forms of social and political organisation. Now let us turn to consider the earliest example we have of sophisticated political reflection in the thought of the Greek Sophists and in the institution of the Greek *polis*.

Notes

1 *The Big Bang Theory*, Season 3, Episode 10, 'The Gorilla Experiment'.

2 Readers who, like Penny, are anxious to get down to specifics are recommended to go straight to Chapter 2, 'The Sophists and the *Polis'*.

3 As this chapter is heavily reliant on works produced by specialist scholars, readers can expect to see a greater number of footnotes here than in later chapters.

4 Lazaridis et al. For an accessible account of the genetic composition of the stone age immigrants to Britain and Ireland and their descendants, see Brett, 52-70. What is most striking is the genetic stability of the population over time. Brett writes, 'a recent study [by the] Institute of Molecular Biology, Oxford, has established a common DNA going back to the end of the last Ice Age, shared by 99 per cent of a sample of 6,000, confirming that successive settlement of Celts, Saxons, Vikings and Normans did little to change that make-up.' [Brett, 24]

5 Gornitz 2007, emphasis added.

6 The earth, writes David Mamet, 'has, at many times during recorded history, and before any emission of manmade carbon, been markedly warmer than it is now....This supposed warming is a story known of old as the history of Chicken Little—it means the End of the World. And to the Left, those denying it are classed as heretics...' [Mamet, 40]

7 See Ridley, 328-347. The swift progression of man along the Asian coastline 'has left few archaeological traces, but that is because the then coastline is now 200 feet under water.' [Ridley, 67] The speed of this movement, made possible in large part by the depressed sea level, has been called the 'beachcomber express." Human beings travelled from Africa to Australia, writes Nayan Chanda, in 'just seven hundred generations....Of course, the ancestors did not know they were headed to Australia: they were just following food. But the eastward movement of generations of people along the Indian and South-east Asian coasts brought them to a continent twelve thousand miles from their East African origins.' [Chanda, 9]

8 There is no shortage of material on the topic of climate, climate change and the connection between climate change and the emergence of human civilisations. For a brief introduction to the topic of civilisation and climate, see Fagan 2004; for the general topic of ice ages, see Imbrie and Imbrie, 1986.

9 Roberts 1997, 6. At around this time, North Africa began its transformation from savannah to desert.

10 Hume 1740, 484, 485.

11 Childe, 27; see Storr, 93.

12 Miles, 5. Some much-lauded anthropological works of the twentieth century were perhaps more vehicles of what Christopher Forth terms 'retrospective prophecy' than they were objective academic studies. One thinks, for example, of Margaret Mead's notorious *Coming of Age in Samoa*, the romantic neo-Rousseauean findings of which were robustly challenged in two books by the New Zealand anthropologist, Derek Freeman, a native Samoan speaker. [Freeman 1983 & 1999; see also Appell] So too, Sir Arthur Evans, amateur classicist and excavator of Knossos, produced a future-oriented idealised image of ancient Crete that found its way 'into numerous "alternative" movements in the 20th century, from feminism, ecopolitics, and the peace movement to New Age spiritualism and Afrocentrism.' [Forth, 677] Cathy Gere, writing a cultural history on the relationship between Knossos and prophetic modernism 'remarks on how such 'fantasies about a peaceful human past were intimately bound up with speculations about the future of the West.' [Forth, 677; see Gere 2009, passim] Evans can be forgiven much for having allegedly remarked of an undistinguished fragment of Cretan pottery that it was 'An ill-favoured thing, but Minoan.'

13 Commenting on the sexual division of labour, Matt Ridley remarks, 'Hiwi women in Venezuela travel by foot to dig roots, pound palm starch, pick legumes and collect honey, their men-folk go hunting, fishing or collecting oranges by canoe; while Ache men in Paraguay hunt pigs, deer and armadillos for up to seven hours a day, the women follow them collecting fruit, digging for roots, gathering insects or pounding starch—and sometimes catching armadillos, too; while Hadza women in Tanzania collect tubers, fruit and nuts, men hunt antelope, while Greenland Inuit men hunt seals, woman make stews, tools and clothing from the animals....Even the apparent exceptions

to the rule, where women do hunt, are instructive, because there is still a division of labour. Agta women in the Philippines hunt with dogs; men hunt with bows.' [Ridley, 61-62]

14 I had written the foregoing paragraph before coming across this passage from George Catlin who, writing of his experiences among the Sioux in the 1830s, says, 'It is proverbial in the civilized world that "the poor Indian woman has to do all the hard work." Don't believe this, for it is not exactly so. She does most of the drudgery about the village and wigwam and is seen transporting heavy loads, etc....*His* labours are not seen, and therefore are less thought of, when he mounts his horse with his weapons in hand, and working every nerve and every muscle, dashes amongst the herds in the chase, to provide food for his wife and his little children, and scours the country both night and day, at the constant risk of his life, to protect them from the assault of their enemies.... The education of woman in those countries teaches her that the labours are thus to be divided between herself and her husband; and for the means of subsistence and protection, for which she depends upon his labours, she voluntarily *assumes* the hard work about the encampment, considering their labours about equally divided.' [Catlin, 60-61; emphasis in original; see also Purdy, 90-145]

15 See Nathanson & Young 2001, 2006 & 2015, passim.

16 See O'Hear, 54-88. As I wrote these words on the first day of 2017, an article appeared in *The Guardian* which began, 'Sexual equality—the right for consenting adults to love who they want, the way they want it—is a human right.' Ignoring the logical solecism of using the same term ('right') in the *definiendum* and the *definiens* (so that a right is defined as a right—true but vacuous), the author continues, 'Attempts to re-establish a notion of "normal", "conventional" and "responsible" sexuality comes at a time in which consensus about what an adult life should look like is rapidly dissolving....A shift in cultural morals has opened space for the articulation of a broad spectrum of sexual identities, orientations and gender identifications.' [Witt, 2017] Just so.

17 See Purdy, 93; see also Goldberg 1973, passim. My subsequent comments on patriarchy refer to the fantastic incubus that is the stuff of feminist nightmares.

18 See Nathanson & Young 2006 for an in-depth scholarly treatment of the increasingly pervasive first-world legal and cultural entrenchment of misandry.

19 An example of the gender feminist mind set—not especially important in itself but illustrative—is a 2015 letter of protest from almost 200 members of staff, students and alumni at York University to the University authorities, demanding an explanation of the University's decision to mark International Men's Day, a decision the University subsequently rescinded. The letter contains the following articles of the Feminist Creed: '...the patriarchal structures which underpin society are inimical to both male and female advancement and well-being...the achievements of men are celebrated and disproportionately highlighted as a matter of course. We believe in a critical approach towards equality and diversity, which seeks to understand the structural causes of disadvantage....A day that celebrates men's issues...does not combat inequality, but merely amplifies existing, structurally imposed, inequalities..."gender equality is for everyone" - echoes misogynistic rhetoric that men's issues have been drowned out by the focus on women's rights.... We believe that men's issues cannot be approached in the same way as unfairness and discrimination towards women, because women are structurally unequal to men.' [Adam & Anguita et al.] As it happens, I too believe that the notion of an International Men's Day is fatuous; but then I also believe that the notion of an International Women's Day is equally fatuous.

20 See Rebecca Walker's 1992 paper, 'Becoming the Third Wave,' for the genesis of this category. Feminism may have started as a movement for legal equality in the treatment of men and women—which I, as a libertarian fully support—but it has long transcended that boringly bourgeois ambition. Feminism now, as Herbert Purdy notes, 'has nothing to do with equality, and it is not about fairness. Neither is it egalitarianism, nor is it born of the liberalism of the enlightenment. Feminists are not interested in equality of opportunity, irrespective of race, colour, creed—or sex—principles that are universally accepted as right. Theirs is the communist-utopian definition of equality qua sameness: parity of numbers disconnected from achievement through merit and ability, and divorced from skills and attributes.' [Purdy, vi]

21 Another panel from AntiFemComics: 'Patriarchy: While the men had fun dying, the females were oppressed....inside "comfortable concentration camps" called HOMES.' Of course, from time to time, women have found their way on to the battlefield. Tales of Amazonian warriors are entertaining but mythical, and although there have been isolated individual women (such as Augustina Domonech, Loreta Velasquez and Kit Cavanagh) who have fought in disguise alongside men, the systematic employment of women in military forces is very much the exception. Instances are few:

Dahomey (now Benin) had a female regiment in the nineteenth century and, more recently, the South Vietnamese Army had a brigade of almost 3,000 female soldiers. Currently, Israel appears to be the only country that has mandatory military service for females.

22 From AntiFemComics [Anon, no date B]. The other cartoons at this site are equally offensive (to contemporary feminist sensibilities) and (from my point of view) equally amusing.

23 Incidentally, in Ireland in 2011, men worked an average of 39.4 hours a week on aggregate, compared with 30.6 hours per week on aggregate for women, and married men worked longer hours than married women, with nearly half (44.5%) of married men working for 40 hours or more a week compared with only 14.7% of married women.

24 See the paper by Su, Rounds and Armstrong, passim. The authors of this meta-study conclude that 'Results showed that men prefer working with things and women prefer working with people, producing a large effect size (d=0.93) on the Things-People dimension. Men showed strong Realistic (d=0.84) and Investigative (d=0.26) interests, and women showed strong Artistic (d=-0.35) Social (d=0.84), and Conventional (d=-0.33) Sex differences favoring men were also found for more specific measures of engineering (d=1.11), science (d=0.36) and mathematics (d=0.34) interests….The present study suggest that interests may play a critical role in gendered occupational choices and gender disparity in the STEM fields.' On the related topic of taking correlation to imply causation (a basic logical fallacy) see Haidt, between 46 and 57 minutes.

25 Steven E. Landsburg describes the typical laundry day for a housewife in the 1900s: 'First, she ports water to the stove, and heats it by burning wood or coal. Then she cleans the clothes by hand, rinses them, wrings them out…then hangs them to dry and moves on to the oppressive task of ironing, using heavy flatirons that are heated continuously on the stove. The whole process takes about eight-and-a-half hours and she walks over a mile in the process….By 1945, our heroine probably had a washing machine. Now her laundry chores took just two-and-a-half hours instead of eight-and-a-half and instead of walking a mile, she walked just 665 feet.' [Landsburg, 29-30]

26 Paglia 1992, 88.

27 Paglia 1991, 38; but see Miles 2001 for another perspective. According to Caitlin Moran, 'even the most ardent feminist historian, male *or* female…can't conceal that women have basically done **** all for the last 100,000 years….Our empires, armies, cities, artworks, philosophers, philanthropists, inventors, scientists, astronauts, explorers, politicians and icons could all fit, comfortably, into one of the private karaoke booths in SingStar. We have no Mozart; no Einstein; no Galileo; no Gandhi. No Beatles, no Churchill, no Hawking, no Columbus. It just didn't happen. Nearly everything so far has been the creation of men…' [Moran, 134, 135]

28 See https://www.youtube.com/watch?v=Oz8RjPAD2Jk, accessed 6 June 2016. Camille Paglia's *Sexual Personae* and her collection of essays, *Sex, Art and American Culture*, should be required reading for anyone who wants to think about men, women, sex, power, art and history in a non-stereotypical way. If the 673 pages of *Sexual Personae* are too much to digest, at least its very first chapter, 'Sex and Violence, or Nature and Art' should be read, as well as 'The M.I.T. Lecture' in Paglia's *Sex, Art and American Culture*. [Paglia 1991, 1-39; Paglia 1992, 249-298]

29 But see Farrell, passim.

30 This point is made, humorously in the film, Annie Hall. Alvy (Woody Allen) and Annie (Diane Keaton) are each at their psychiatrist's. On a split screen, Alvy's psychiatrist asks him: 'How often do you sleep together?' Annie's psychiatrist ask her: 'Do you have sex often?' Alvy replies: 'Hardly ever. Maybe three times a week.' Annie replies: 'Constantly! I'd say three times a week.'

31 A German friend of David Mamet told him, 'Boys are different.' 'And indeed they are,' he agrees. 'Very like each other, and very different from girls….Our American school system (public and private) is against them. It is no wonder the boys have developed or been diagnosed (which is to say marginalized) as possessing a whole alphabet full of acronyms, which may be reduced to "I give up, drug them."….A blunter writer might conflate our school's anti-male bias with a societal inclination to cease exploration and production, and let the land revert to fallowness.' [Mamet, 130, 131] Steven Pinker quips that the technical term for people who believe that little boys and little girls are born indistinguishable and are moulded by parental socialisation is 'childless'.

32 …including the socially sanctioned violence of military conscription and military service which was, and still largely is, exclusively applied to disposable men.

33 …not to mention the patent inequality that in rape trials, the (usually male) accused is named and shamed ever before there's any conviction and often even after acquittal [see Hopkins 2016], whereas the alleged (usually female) victim remains anonymous throughout.

34 ...as they have done throughout history.

35 There is a danger in recognising these facts that one may be tempted to be sucked into playing the absurd game of 'I'm a bigger victim than you are' or 'My identity is more special than yours.' The absurdity of identity politics and victimology isn't effectively countered by harping on one's own special identity and boasting about one's superior form of victimhood; that is merely to play the same absurd game as all the other groups or victims. But the point isn't to compete in this zero-sum game; it is to refuse to recognise it as a game worth playing. Claire Fox writes, 'With no hint of irony, there are demands for male-only safe spaces, for formal recognition of International Men's Day on university campuses, and a litany of complaints centring on how hard it is to be a man: shorter life expectancy, higher suicide rates, negative media portrayals, and so on. This aping of feminism's victimhood, by stressing that young men are suffering more than their female counterparts, can only further entrench Generation Snowflake tendencies in our culture. In this worldview, we are all encouraged to wallow in our vulnerability; we are all pathetic.' [Fox 2016, 167]

36 Tuttle, 342, emphasis added. See Lloyd, passim.

37 Stearns, 611. For some detailed book length studies in the intersection between physical and cultural anthropology, see Crawford 2007, Wells 2004 and Marks 2003.

38 Wilson 1978, 167; see also Penman 2015, Carey 2012, Francis 2011, Wade 2014, and Duchesne 2012, 32-38.

39 With typical understatement, Murray Rothbard remarks of Polanyi's *The Great Transformation*: 'I have read few books in my time that have been more vicious or more fallacious.' [Rothbard 2004]

40 Douglass North summarises Polanyi as arguing that 'markets have only dominated resource allocation for a brief span in history centering on the nineteenth-century Western World. Before that time—and increasingly in the twentieth century—other allocative systems have characterized economic organization and these systems are not grounded in economizing behaviour. Accordingly, the theoretical apparatus of economists, both neo-classical and Marxian, is useful to explain only a minute portion of the five millenia of history. It is inappropriate for past societies and increasingly irrelevant for the twentieth century as well.' [North, 703]

41 'For your understanding of the past,' writes Deirdre McCloskey, 'you would be foolish to depend mainly on Polanyi or Weber or even my beloved and liberal Macaulay, or even my worshiped and liberal Adam Smith. But people do. And so the theory of capitalism that educated people to this day carry around in their heads springs from the antibourgeois rhetoric of Polanyi, Marx, St. Benedict, Aristotle. It is economically mistaken. And the point here is that it is historically mistaken as well.' [McCloskey 2011, 143]

42 Nowrasteh 2013. 'Polanyi's thesis or those of his fellow "substantivists" hasn't stood the test of time well. It now seems that the state did not so much sponsor trade, as capture it. The more that comes to light about ancient trade the more bottom-up it looks....Polanyi depicted a reflection of his own planning-obsessed times. The dirigiste mentality that dominated the second half of the twentieth century was always asking who is in charge, looking for who decided on a policy of trade. That is not how the world works. Trade emerged from the interaction of individuals. It evolved. Nobody was in charge.' [Ridley, 164-165]

43 The existence and mode of operation of mutual aid societies or friendly societies is one of the best-kept secrets in social history. These societies originated as early as the sixteenth century and continued to operate well into the twentieth. By 1801, in Britain, there were 7,200 societies with around 700,000 adult male members, in a society of nine million people. By 1872, there were as many as four million members of such friendly societies, four times as many members as there were trade unionists. In 1920, some eighteen million Americans belonged to fraternal societies, approximately 30% of all adults over 20. These societies provided death benefits (often as much as was equivalent to a year's salary at the time) payable to survivors, unemployment assistance, accident insurance, financial aid to those seeking work, and health cover by means of contracts entered into between the societies and physicians. In the late nineteenth century, some of the larger societies built orphanages and old-age homes. [See Beito 1990 & 2000, Green 2000, and Seaman, 97-99]

44 Azar Gat locates the tendency towards human pair bonding in the demands made of parents by slowly maturing offspring. [Gat, 65] Nicholas Wade argues that pair bonding facilitated an extended juvenile dependence. Biologically, children 'could be born at an earlier stage in their development since they would be more protected, and earlier birth enabled the brain to do more of its growing outside the womb.' [Wade, 45] See Sumner, 345f.; 493ff.; see also Locke, §§ 77-83.

45 Ludwig von Mises 1949/1998, 286, 287.

46 Other so-called 'multiples' noted by Matthew Syed include the precursor to the electric battery discovered independently by Ewald Georg von Kelist and Andreas Cuneus in 1745 and 1746, respectively; the more or less simultaneous discovery of sunspots by four independent observers in 1611; yet another quartet proposed the law of conservation of energy in the 1840s. Matthew Syed writes, 'In the 1920s William Ogburn and Dorothy Thomas…found as many as 148 examples of independent innovation. Multiples are the norm; not the exception.' [Syed, 216]

47 Not everyone is completely persuaded that the discoveries of Jevons, Walras and Menger were discoveries of one and the same principle. Phyllis Deane writes, 'On the face of it, the marginal revolution in economics fits rather uneasily into the grand role of a total *Gestalt* shift. For one thing the three agents in the so-called revolution—Jevons, Walras and Menger—did not share the same constellation of beliefs, values, techniques etc. Menger in particular stood apart from the other two. It is debatable whether Menger and his followers were even marginalists in the sense in which this term is generally applied to Jevons, Walras and the neo-classical school generally. For another thing their direct influence on the subsequent development of orthodox economists' views on the scope and methodology of economics was clearly rather limited….Finally and in the third place it took more than twenty years for the methodological innovations associated with the marginal revolution to make sufficient impression on the current orthodoxy to justify the view that a substantive new paradigm was taking over.' [Deane 1978, 97]

48 Hobbes, *Leviathan*, Chapter 13, §9.

49 I salute P. G. Wodehouse, whose books have been my constant and delightful companions for over fifty years. Described by Hilaire Belloc as 'the best writer of English now alive', Wodehouse included among his technical accomplishments the mastery of the transferred epithet: 'I lighted a thoughtful cigarette and, dismissing Archimedes for the nonce, allowed my mind to dwell once more on the ghastly jam into which I had been thrust by young Stiffy's ill-advised behaviour.' [*The Code of the Woosters*]; 'As I sat in the bathtub, soaping a meditative foot and singing…' [*Jeeves and the Feudal Spirit*]

50 de Waal, 4; see Holmes, 225ff.

51 de Waal, 5; see Holmes, 234-235.

52 Mencius, Book II (A), chapter 6: 3-4, 38.

53 Hume 1740, 487; see Sowell 1987, passim. De Waal uses the term 'emotional contagion' to describe the induction in one member of a species of an emotional state present in another. [de Waal, 26] Emotional contagion isn't quite empathy but rather an earlier stage of emotional resonance that may develop into empathy. Empathy requires an additional level of cognition.

54 David Lewis notes that 'Language is only one among many activities governed by conventions that we did not create by agreeing and that we cannot describe.' [Lewis 2002, 3]

55 The climatic changes during this time have been no less dramatic and significant than the cultural, social and political changes, and are probably not unconnected to them. Vivien Gornitz notes that 'The Earth's climate warmed abruptly, starting around 11,500 years ago after the final stages of the last glaciation. The Holocene climatic amelioration following the last ice age coincided with a major transition in human history—from the hunting-gathering lifestyle of our ancestors to the onset of agriculture, permanent settlements, and the beginnings of civilization. Early populations depended on hunting, fishing, and foraging for wild plants. The abundances of these resources were strongly influence by seasonal cycles and multi-decadal climate trends. Even after the development of agriculture, ancient societies were probably more vulnerable to the impacts of sudden climate change than modern societies since they were predominantly agrarian and dependent on weather-sensitive crops.' [Gornitz 2009a, 6] She adds, 'Many authors have pointed out apparent relationships between the rise and fall of ancient civilizations and climate change….However, changes in those societies could have also been instigated by the interaction of a number of other factors, including economic and/or political instability, diseases, human migrations, wars, cultural innovations, and environmental degradation…which may have been only indirectly related to climate, if at all.' However, she concludes, 'Climate change by itself may not have been enough to initiate major population shifts or topple an otherwise stable civilization; however, it could have provided the final straw in environmentally marginal regions or in conjunction with one of the other destabilizing influenced listed above.' [Gornitz 2009a, 7]

56 For ease of exposition, I am assuming that human consciousness hasn't changed radically over time. Nevertheless, the case can be (and has been) made that human consciousness has in

fact evolved historically and that a significant aspect of that evolution has been the emergence of the ability (expressed in and made possible by language) to distinguish self from others and self from world. The positive side of this evolution is the emergence to full reflective awareness of the individual; the negative side is an impoverishment and diminution of the individual's connection to other human beings and to the world if the original unreflective attachment, lost in the evolution of consciousness, isn't re-established at a higher reflective level. Considerations such as these would seem to be at the root of Nietzsche's ambivalent attitude to Socrates who, he believed, had brought the light of reason to bear on the nexus of traditional Athenian ethical thought but, in so doing, had made it impossible for the Athenians (and for us) to rest content with a life lived unreflectively according to tradition. Our specifically human freedom comes, it seems, at the cost of expulsion from the innocence of Eden. As we shall see, Rousseau too had reservations similar to those of Nietzsche. However, critical as Nietzsche and Rousseau might be of our move away from original pre-reflective innocence, neither is willing to endorse a return to it, even if such were possible.

57 See James Le Fanu's *Why Us?* for a stimulating if controversial account of some issues in human origins.

58 Kluger, 210; see Trask and Mayblin.

59 Trask & Mayblin, 159; see 83.

60 Hans-Hermann Hoppe notes that while archaic man could exercise the 'expressive or symptomatic function and the trigger or signal function' of language, he was incapable of exercising the higher 'descriptive and especially the argumentative function.' [Hoppe 2015, 22-23]

61 See Trask & Mayblin, 62-68, and Farb, 214; see also Crystal, 422.

62 For an illuminating discussion of the relationship between language and the apparently insoluble problems of free will, intentionality and *a priori* knowledge, all of which bear on the relationship between mind and world, see Baker 2002, 227ff.

63 Farb, 214; see 206-216, passim.

64 See Engels 1884; see also Marx & Engels 1968, 468-593.

65 The substance of the present chapter was written before Hoppe's *A Short History of Man* (2015) appeared. The first part of Hoppe's book is essential reading for anyone interested in this period of human life, inasmuch as it appears to present a rational counterpoint to Engel's work. It can scarcely be coincidental that this part of Hoppe's book is entitled 'On the Origin of Private Property and the Family.'

66 Wilczynski, 421, 410, and 457-458.

67 A thorough examination of the scholarly arguments would take us too far afield for our present purposes but interested readers could consult Ricardo Duchesne's *The Uniqueness of Western Civilization* for an overview of the issues in the debate. See Duchesne, 341-418. See also Cochran & Harpending, 175-186. For a pictorially and graphically rich introduction to many of the topics treated in this chapter, see McIntosh & Twist's *Civilization*. See also Parkinson 1958, 17-44.

68 A book could be written on the importance of various materials to the character and progress of civilizations. In fact, a book *has* been written on precisely this subject. Stephen Sass, in *The Substance of Civilization* writes 'History is an alloy of all the materials that we have invented or discovered, manipulated, used, and abused, and each has its tale to tell. The stories of some materials, like diamonds and gold and platinum, involve opulence and mystery. The stories of iron and rubber are more mundane, reflecting the fact that they are industrial, indecorous substances. But all these materials have had a profound influence on human history, and to tell the story of each one means spanning many centuries and crossing enormous geographical areas, from South America—source of platinum and rubber, and the great quantities of gold and silver that supported Spain's adventures and misadventures beginning in the sixteenth century—to Great Britain, where the very modern problem of shortages of natural resources triggered a sequence of events leading to the Industrial Revolution, and finally, to the United States, center of material innovation for much of this century, home to the computer and information revolutions ushered in by silicon and optical fibers.' [Sass, 6]

69 Childe, 43. David Brett argues that we ought to think of the various Ages (Stone, Bronze and Iron) 'as interpenetrating and overlapping in time. The use of stone tools did not cease when bronze became available, nor did iron render bronze unusable. We should not assume any great caesura between one stage and the next. Any one group might be living, technically in all three at once. The idea of an "age" is not so much a feature of reality as a device to help us think and classify.' [Brett, 33]

70 Finkel, 4; see Diamond 2012, passim.

71 Childe, 66; but see Harari, 77-97.

72 Harari, 79; but see Ferguson 2008, 18-20.

73 See Finkel, 4 and Diamond 1987, passim.

74 'Agriculture....released the brake on population growth, which had held down hunter-gatherer populations, dependent and parasitic as they were on herds of game.' [Roberts 1997, 11]

75 Clark 2009, 1. I regard the increasingly common politically-correct practice of substituting BCE (before the common era) for BC (before Christ) and CE (common era) for AD (*Anno Domini*—in the year of the Lord) as a sublime exercise in fatuity and condescension. If one's objection to the use of BC and AD is that they instantiate the perspective of Christianity in historical periodisation, that objection is hardly likely to be overcome by the transparently disingenuous ruse of changing the *names* of the periods, thereby pretending that the periodisation has thus somehow become neutral and unobjectionable, while retaining the *focal point*—the conventional date of the birth of Christ—around which the periods pivot. I shall therefore continue to use BC and AD, and I respectfully invite adherents of other religious and cultural traditions with different dating conventions—Roman (+753), Islamic (-622), Jewish (+3760/1), Coptic (-284), Parsee (-632), Japanese (+660)—to convert my dates into a format more acceptable to them by adding or subtracting the number within brackets from the dates I supply.

76 I write 'modern' Industrial Revolution because it is generally not realised that the high Middle Ages saw the first significant post-Neolithic technological revolution. [See Gimpel, passim] Nicholas Wade notes that the modern Industrial Revolution 'was caused not by events of the previous century but by changes in human economic behavior that had been slowly evolving in agrarian societies for the previous 10,000 years.' [Wade, 161]

77 Renfrew, 84; but see also Duchesne 348-353.

78 Wade, 62; see also 127ff.

79 'The tradition among many anthropologists and archaeologists has been to treat the past as a very different place from the present, a place with it own mysterious rituals,' writes Matt Ridley. 'To cram the Stone Age or the tribal South Seas into modern economic terminology is therefore an anachronistic error showing capitalist indoctrination. This view was promulgated especially by the anthropologist Marshall Sahlins, who distinguished pre-industrial economies based on "reciprocity" from modern economies based on markets. Stephen Shennan satirizes the attitude thus: "We engage in exchanges to make some sort of profit; they do so in order to cement social relationships; we trade commodities; they give gifts." Like Shennan,' continues Ridley, 'I think this is patronizing bunk. I think people respond to incentives and always have done. People weight costs and benefits and do what profits them. Sure, they take into account non-economic factors, such as the need to remain on good terms with trading partners and to placate malevolent deities. Sure, they give better deals to families, friends and patrons than they do to strangers. But they do that today as well. Even the most market-embedded modern financial trader is enmeshed in a web of ritual, etiquette, convention and obligation, not excluding social debt for a good lunch or an invitation to a football match. Just as modern economists often exaggerate the cold-hearted rationality of consumers, so anthropologists exaggerate the cuddly irrationality of pre-industrial people.' [Ridley, 133-134]

80 Renfrew, 164; see Hoppe 2015, 25-26.

81 There are methodological problems in assuming that the patterns of behaviour of surviving primitive tribes are a reliable guide to pre-history. As Murray Rothbard remarks in a review of Karl Polanyi's *The Great Transformation*, 'it is absolutely illegitimate to do, as Polanyi does, and infer the history of pre-Western civilization *from* analysis of *existing* primitive tribes. Let us never forget that the existing primitive tribes are precisely the ones that *didn't* progress—that remained in their primitive state. To infer from observing them that this is the way our ancestors behaved is nonsense—and apt to be the reverse of the truth, for our ancestors presumably behaved in ways which quickly advanced them *beyond* the primitive stage thousands of years ago.' [Rothbard 2004]

82 Wright, 67, emphasis in original.

83 See Gat, 18-19. Hans-Hermann Hoppe rejects the assumption that for hunter-gatherers, land ownership was either private or collective [communist]. Instead, he argues that land 'was neither private nor collective property but instead constituted part of the *environment* or more specifically the *general conditions* of action or what has also been called "common property" or in short "the commons."' [Hoppe 2015, 49] The emergence of property in land was coeval with the emergence

of agriculture and animal husbandry.

84 'The early Israelites were the natural children of the desert, and even when they were all becoming farmers they felt an instinctive contempt for the peasantry.' [Vawter, 297]

85 Roberts 1997, 13; see also Roberts 1993, 27-28.

86 Ridley points out, correctly, that barter/exchange isn't just a specialised form of reciprocity. 'Barter,' he writes, 'is a lot more portentous than reciprocity. After all, delousing aside, how many activities in life are there where it pays to do the same thing to each other in turn? "If I sew you a hide tunic today, you can sew me one tomorrow" brings limited rewards and diminishing returns. "If I make the clothes, you catch the food" brings increasing returns. Indeed, it has the beautiful property that *it does not even need to be fair*. For barter to work, two individuals do not need to offer things of equal value. Trade is often unequal, but still benefits both sides.' [Ridley, 57; emphasis in original] In this otherwise acute and accurate observation, Ridley fails to appreciate the point that exchange, being positive sum, *necessarily* depends upon the parties to the exchange having different and unequal estimations of the value of the things exchanged. In an uncoerced exchange, fairness is an issue only if one receives something other than that for which one bargained, not if what one gives and receives are not identical.

87 Oppenheimer, 1975/1919, chapter 2a.

88 See Diamond 2012, 12-19 for a brief and accessible introduction to Elman Service's typology.

89 Childe, 140ff. Mumford gives credit to Childe for his insight and originality but denies that the transition just described was a revolution. 'The rise of the city, so far from wiping out earlier elements in the culture, actually brought them together and increased their efficacy and scope.' [Mumford, 31] It is commonly assumed that the Neolithic revolution occurred when nomadic tribes settled down, grew crops, forming first villages and later cities. However, some, such as Jane Jacobs, have argued that cities had to come first because agriculture is scarcely possible without the goods and services that can be provided only by a city—I do not find this argument even remotely plausible.

90 Not everyone is happy to link the development of civilisations with urbanisation. Elman Service even goes so far as to claim that 'Cities were not…either essential to the development of the archaic civilisations or even closely correlated with that development. [Service, xii]

91 Mumford, 38; see also Siedentop, 19-33.

92 Earle, 14; see Wright, 78-92.

93 Paglia 1992, 32; see Chadwick, 113.

94 Mumford, 110; see Patterson 1991, passim.

95 It is common to associate civilisation with the rise of the state, the state being that form of socio-political control defined by a monopoly (or an attempted monopoly) of control based on physical force. Elman Service made just such an association when he began his research but he eventually came to the conclusion that the 'repressive-force concept of the state…is not useful in defining archaic civilization; it does not describe the origin of civilization, nor is it an identifying criterion of civilization.' [Service, xi-xii; see also 280-281] On the other hand, Thomas Patterson writes, 'Civilization….is an elitist idea, one that is defined by creating hierarchies—of societies, of classes, of cultures, or of races. For the elites that coined the idea, civilizations are always class-stratified, state-based societies, and civilized people always belong to the [*sic*] those classes whose privileged existences are guaranteed by the institutions and practices of the state.' [Patterson 1997, 10]

96 'Throughout the third millennium B.C. Mesopotamia was made up of small political units, the so-called "city-states". Each such state consisted of a city with its surrounding territory, cultivated by the people of the city….From time to time conquerors arose who succeeded in uniting most of the city-states into a single large national state under their rule; but these national states usually lasted for a relatively short time, after which the country would divide into city-states again.' [Jacobsen, 201; see 200-216]

97 For a highly readable recent account of these and several other early civilisations–including Shang China, Yoruba and Inka—see Bruce Trigger's *Understanding Early Civilizations*. For a different (and amusing perspective) on Egypt, see Kealey 2008, 60ff. For a scholarly, yet accessible, introduction to many aspects of Egyptian civilisation, see the beautifully illustrated volume edited by Schultz & Seidel. For more on Mesopotamia see McIntosh & Twist, 46-57 and Service, 203-204; for more on Egypt see McIntosh & Twist, 82-93 and Service, 225-237. For more on early Meso-American and Peruvian civilisations, see Service, 166-202.

98 The differences between the two civilizations went all the way to their very foundations. Thork-

ild Jacobsen writes, 'Were the Egyptian to come back today, he would undoubtedly take heart from the endurance of his pyramids, for he accorded to man and to man's tangible achievements more basic significance that most civilizations have been willing to do. Were the Mesopotamian to return, he could hardly feel deeply disturbed that his works have crumbled, for he always knew, and knew deeply, that as for "mere man—his days are numbered; whatever he may do, he is but wind". To him the centre and meaning of existence always lay beyond man and his achievements, beyond tangible things in intangible powers ruling the universe.' [Jacobsen, 137]

99 We mustn't be misled, Francis Oakley thinks, 'by the obvious commonalities of pattern between the kingships of Egypt and Mesopotamia to overlook the real differences that distinguished one from the other.' [Oakley 2010, 23; see also Roberts, 52-70] For an intensive and extensive account of kingship in the ancient Near East, see Frankfort 1948, passim.

100 For a comprehensive account of the history and culture of the Nile and its peoples, see Ludwig, passim.

101 Abraham's home city, Ur, was located in Sumer, in the southern part of Mesopotamia. There are, says Bruce Vawter, 'countless links with Mesopotamia in the old traditions, which eventually became the first eleven chapters of Genesis.' [Vawter, 116]

102 Speaking of Mesopotamia, Thorkild Jacobsen remarks that 'In the economic sphere appeared *planned large-scale irrigation by means of canals*, a form which forever after was to be characteristic of Mesopotamian agriculture. [Jacobsen, 140-141]

103 'Memphis and Thebes,' writes John M. Roberts, 'were great religious centres and palace complexes; they did not really progress beyond this to true urbanism. The absence of cities earlier was politically important, too. Egypt's kings had not emerged like Sumer's as the "big men" in a city-state community which originally deputed them to act for it. Nor were they simply men who like others were subject to gods who ruled all men, great or small. The tension of palace with temple was missing in Egypt and when Egyptian kingship emerges it is unrivalled. The Pharaohs were to be gods, not servants of gods.' [Roberts, 54]

104 'In Egypt…all property was technically at least crown possession….In keeping with this, the Egyptians were Pharao's property. One Egyptian might own another as his slave, but every Egyptian possessed his freedom at the Pharao's good pleasure. He ruled as an absolute despot, could conscript any of his subjects for public works or other services.' [Vawter, 288]

105 See Gat, 21. Contrary to the Rousseau-inspired portrayal of original innocence, fighting among our hunter-gatherers isn't 'a recent invention, associated with the emergence of sedentary settlement, food storage, property, high population densities, and social stratification.' [Gat, 25; see also 30]

106 Gat, 71; 92; see Whelan, passim and Hoppe 2015, 27-29.

107 Davidson & Rees-Mogg, 79. See also Wade, 130.

108 Oppenheimer, 13; see Davidson & Rees-Mogg, 80.

109 In a comment which is borne out by much that we know of history, F. C. S. Schiller remarks that 'the early nomad tribes were able to congregate in much larger bodies than the hunters, and were much more mobile than the agriculturalists, because they could carry their food-supplies with them. They could thus become a conquering class of rulers.' [Schiller, 269]

110 Fukuyama 2011, 303-304.

111 Some of the material in this paragraph first appeared in Casey 2012b.

112 It *is* possible to distinguish between the state and government. As Brian Doherty writes, Nock 'carefully distinguished the state, to which he was bloodily opposed, from government—the necessary functions for an orderly civilization historically usurped by the state.' [Doherty, 53]

113 Nock, 150; Scott, 7. 'Conscription…was an accepted institution during the earliest period of Egyptian history.' [Cottrell, 90] The *corvée*, likewise, was an established institution.

114 Davidson & Rees-Mogg, 79. The surpluses produced by the Neolithic Revolution may, remarks John M. Roberts, 'have encouraged Man's oldest sport after hunting, warfare. New prizes must have make raids and conquest more tempting. Perhaps, too, a conflict, which was to have centuries of vitality before it, finds its origins here—that between nomads and settlers.' Roberts notes, percipiently, that 'Political power may have its origin in the need to organize protection for crops and stock from human predators.' [Roberts, 27] The history of politics has shown us that these predators need not always be external to a given society but, ironically, are often to be identified with those whose task it is to provide protection.

115 See Casey 2102, 80-82. 'If the original policemen had been started with the present helmets,'

writes Walter Bagehot, 'the result might have been dubious; there might have been a cry of military tyranny, and the inbred insubordination of the English people might have prevailed over the very modern love of perfect peace and order.' [Bagehot, 187]

116 The Pharaoh 'endowed deserving officials and their families with agricultural land to be put to economic use; if they behaved disloyally, however, they were stripped of their possessions and expelled from the ranks of the property-owning classes.' [Gutgesell, 375] 'The state paid officials for their services in kind. They received estates whose produce served to keep them economically prosperous, and they were the beneficiaries of the economic success of their state institutions.' [Pardey, 363]

117 Roberts notes that 'even in the most ancient records there seems to be an unchecked trend towards a greater regularity in government and greater institutionalizing of power. Kings surround themselves with bureaucracies and *tax-collectors find the resources for larger and larger enterprises...*' [Roberts, 75, emphasis added]

118 Atwood, 77-78. Given the colonisation of the academy by thinkers of the left, particularly in continental Europe, it is astonishing to find Professor Peter Sloterdijk, professor of philosophy at the University of Art and Design, Karlsruhe, writing that 'the direct and selfish exploitation of a feudal era has been transformed in the modern age into a juridically constrained and almost disinterested state kleptocracy....' We do not, he writes, 'live in a capitalist system but under a form of semi-socialism that Europeans tactfully refer to as a "social market economy." The grasping hand of government releases its takings mainly for the ostensible public interest, funding Sisyphean tasks in the name of "social justice."' Income tax, especially in its so-called progressive form is, he says, 'the functional equivalent of socialist expropriation. It offers the remarkable advantage of being annually renewable--at least, in the case of those it has not bled dry the previous year....a handful of productive citizens provide more than half of national income-tax revenues.' [Sloterdijk, 5-7]

119 Casey 2012b, 22. For an amusing treatment of the irrational and socially destructive enterprise of taxation, one cannot do better than spend a few pleasant and instructive hours with C. Northcote Parkinson's *The Law and the Profits*. Here are some sample quotations to tempt your appetite: 'Taxation is as old as time and takes its earliest form in the action of the petty chief who builds himself a stockade at the estuary, the river junction, or mountain pass and levies a toll on the passing traveller or merchant.' [Parkinson 1965, 24] The tax on land 'is akin to protection money paid to the gangster, the basic idea of feudalism.' The amount our erstwhile cultivator of the land in question will pay 'is roughly equivalent to the cost of moving to another area beyond the gangster's reach...' [Parkinson 1965, 24-25] The level of taxation 'rises in time of war without falling to the same extent in time of peace.' [Parkinson 1965, 25] Most taxes, Parkinson notes, 'clearly come within the category of burdens imposed by some people upon others. The taxes decreed by ancient monarchies were all of this type and so are the graduated taxes of today at all levels above the average, being voted by those to whom the heaviest rates will not apply.' [Parkinson 1965, 69] By way of contrast, for an egregiously naïve and unwittingly humorous attempt to justify taxation, see Richard Murphy's *The Joy of Tax*. Among other singularities, Murphy purports to show that taxation is not compulsory because people (a) have the right to vote in the elections which generate the governments of the countries in which they reside, or (b) can seek to influence the democratic process by either standing for election themselves or writing books as Murphy has done, or (c) can leave their countries if they really feel they're being compelled to do something they don't want to do. [see Murphy 2016a, 35]

120 Governments may have been repressive and extractive in the benighted past but surely, in our enlightened times, things have changed for the better? Alas! Time passes, and change and decay in all around we see, but amidst all this change, governments and their taxes are islands of stability. David Mamet notes, sardonically, that 'President Obama, in a speech in July 2010, declared that the Government should be ready to support Green Business—that if anyone wanted to create these jobs, the government would be there to help. What was the help? He was offering rebates. But what are rebates but tax cuts? To suggest that giving back (to approved entities) some of the money drained from them in taxes, and to characterize this as "help," is like a mugger pausing in administering his beating and characterizing this pause, to his victim, as assistance.' [Mamet, 113]

121 Earle, 105; see Parkinson 1958, 50.

122 See Oakley 2010, 1, 2; see also Parkinson 1958, 28-44.

123 Trigger, 73; see Parkinson 1958, passim.

124 The personal lives of the Pharaohs were anything but a riot of dissipation; on the contrary,

they could have been models for the ritual-ridden Earls of Groan in Mervyn Peake's *Gormenghast* series. John Wilson notes that 'Diodorus paints a dreadful picture of the king of Egypt as the slave of regulations which controlled his every hour and every act. "The hour of both the day and night were laid out according to a plan, and at the specified hours it was absolutely required of the king that he should do what the laws stipulated and not what he thought best" (i. 70-1). Diodorus goes on to state that these regulations covered not only the king's administrative actions but also his own freedom to take a walk, bathe, or even sleep with his wife. He was allowed no personal initiative in his governmental functions but was required to act only in conformance with the established laws.' [Wilson 1949, 91]

Chapter 2

THE SOPHISTS AND THE *POLIS*: THE BEGINNINGS OF POLITICAL LIBERTY

The edicts of the laws are imposed artificially, but those of nature are compulsory.
And the edicts of the laws are arrived at by consent, not by natural growth,
whereas those of nature are not a matter of consent
—Antiphon

If...[the Sophists] were willing to state the facts
instead of making greater promises than they can possibly fulfill,
they would not be in such bad repute with the lay-public.
As it is, however, the teachers who do not scruple to vaunt their powers
with utter disregard of the truth have created the impression that
those who choose a life of careless indolence are better advised
than those who devote themselves to serious study
—Isocrates

In the six hundred years, from roughly 800 to 200 BC, there occurred developments in fundamental human thought that have provided the intellectual, theological and ideological foundations for every subsequent major civilisation. Karl Jaspers, the Swiss philosopher, called this uniquely intellectually fertile time the Axial Period and Eric Voegelin referred to it as the Great Leap of Being. Significantly, Jaspers also described this period as 'a pause for liberty.' [Jaspers, 51] This was the time of Confucius and Lao Tzu in China, of the transcription of the Vedas in India and the emergence of Buddhism, of Zoroaster in Persia, of the Hebrew prophets in Israel and the Greek philosophers in Greece and Asia Minor. The names from this period resonate with historical significance: Lao Tzu, Confucius, Siddhartha Gautama, Parmenides, Socrates, Plato, Aristotle, Thucydides, Elijah, Isaiah, Zoroaster, Jeremiah, Pythagoras, and Heraclitus. Robert Nisbet notes that 'The whole course of humanity was reshaped by a major revolution in Eurasia in the sixth century B.C. That was when a small number of geniuses and prophets—Confucius, Lao-Tzu (or Lao-Tse or Laozi), Buddha, Zoroaster, Mahavira, Thales, Ezekiel, and Pythagoras—spread out over a vast continent nevertheless simultaneously introduced a revolution in ideas, one in which the individual was for the first time liberated from the role of automaton in a heavily oppressive culture and brought face to face with the entire cosmos, or its ruler at any rate.' [Nisbet 1988, 139]

The intellectual explosions in these various areas and cultures seem to have taken place relatively independently of one another yet the conditions giving rise to them and the social, political, religious and intellectual effects resulting from them exhibit common elements. In India, China, and the Near East, the political condition was one of military struggle between relatively small competing states, with resulting social dislocation and the upsetting of traditional modes of thought. Wandering scholars emerged, willing to teach all and sundry—Confucius in China and the Sophists in Greece—whereas before this time, scholarship and learning had been the privilege of the political elite. And in each of these widely separated areas, we had the beginnings of commerce, made possible by the creation of money and coinage. [see Ober 2015, passim] David Graeber argues that the invention of money and coinage created a 'division of spheres of human activity that endures to this day...' [Graeber, 224] Tempting as it is to wander along the highways of cultural, religious and philosophical speculation, that temptation must be sternly resisted. Our particular concern in this chapter is limited to the implications for political thought of the emergence of the Greek city-state, the *polis*, and the Greek wandering scholars, the Sophists.

The *Polis*

Greek political theory was inevitably conditioned by its time and its circumstances, yet the problems and issues it dealt with have a significance that transcends, at least to some extent, its particularity. 'It is true,' writes Ernest Barker, 'that political theory varies with the variations of the State. Aristotle's theory of the self-sufficient *polis* differs from Dante's theory of the universal Empire, and Dante's theory of the Empire from Hobbes' theory of the national State. Yet, through all its mutations, political theory has a fundamental unity. It is always occupied with the same problem—the problem of the relations of man to the state in which he lives.' [Barker, 17] In making these remarks, Barker flirts with anachronism. It is undeniable that the language of politics we use is heavily reliant on our Greek inheritance and it is also true that there are elements of continuity between ancient Greek civilisation and ours. So used are we in the West to think of Greece and Rome as our intellectual forebears that we allow ourselves to take what we know politically of Greece (limited, by and large, to the Athens of Pericles and Cleisthenes) and the Roman Republic as being in some sense the standard pattern of classical polities. In fact, the truth is rather the reverse. Considered historically, Greece (Periclean Athens) and Rome (early republican Rome) were a-monarchical ripples in a steady stream of monarchy.[1] As Francis Oakley notes, 'the era of the Greek polis and the Roman republic...stands out in bold relief as something of a fleeting episode, a beleaguered island lapped at by the waves of an engulfing monarchical sea.' [Oakley 2010, 3]

Even what we do know of Athens and republican Rome tends to be viewed through the reversed telescope of modern political orthodoxy so that our knowledge, like Barker's, is continually teetering on the brink of anachronism. This is particularly so when it comes to the notion of the individual. All things considered, it does not appear that ancient societies—including Greece and Rome, societies whose essential strangeness is masked by familiarity—entertained a notion of individuality that can in any real way be compared to the modern and contemporary commonplace that individuality has become for us, an individuality characterised by what some have termed 'reflective inwardness' and which is the obvious and ineliminable starting point for most contemporary political theory. 'Few today,' writes Oakley, 'would wish to deny that the average inhabitant of the Greek polis was conceived...less as an individual possessed of a personal history unique to him and standing ultimately alone than as an integral part of the society to which he belonged, deriving therefrom his identity and whatever value he possessed.' [Oakley 2010, 5] It isn't, however, a matter of all or nothing, and here and there in the ancient world we can detect hints of a beginning of a grasp of the importance of the individual. We find these embryonically in the thought of the Sophists, fitfully in certain aspects of the thought of Plato and Aristotle (though for both thinkers, the individual is still almost entirely submerged in the *polis*), and emerging more clearly, if still indistinctly, in the thought of the Cynics, Epicureans and Stoics.[2] We must overcome our cultural myopia and realise just how much of an aberration Greek political life and thought was (and similarly the political life and thought of the Roman Republic) when set in the context of what came before it and after it and, indeed, what coexisted with it. That being so, it isn't entirely accurate to say, as Barker does, that the relation of man to the state is *the* political problem and has always been so. This point will, I hope, become clearer as we proceed.

From about the eighth century BC onwards, the characteristic form of social and political organisation in Greece was the *polis* (plural *poleis*), a term often translated, somewhat misleadingly in English, as 'city-state'. The problem with the use of the term 'city-state' as a translation of *polis* is that many of the *poleis* weren't cities, and none was what we would now recognise as a state! The term 'city-state', however, misleading as it may be, is too well entrenched in the literature to be simply abandoned. The *polis* emerged over a quite short period from what has sometimes been described as Dark-Age chiefdoms. Whereas these chiefdoms would, for the most part, have been based on kinship relations, the emergence of the *polis* 'did not involve the immediate triumph of territorial community identities over those of kinship.' [Ferguson 1963, 192] For Ferguson, the factors that contributed to the emergence of the predominantly territorially based rather than kinship-based *poleis* were a felt need for a cultic centre and a dramatic increase in population not unconnected to the change from a pastoral economy to one based on agriculture.

As I have just mentioned, it's important to understand that the *polis* wasn't a city in the modern sense of that term. It was *not* primarily an urban complex as distinct from a rural wilderness although, by Aristotle's time, most *poleis* had an urban centre;[3] it was, rather, an ethical fellowship, the purpose of which was the attainment of the excellence of the whole political community. This can be an alien notion for us moderns to grasp when we find ourselves more often in conflict with the state and its officials and their aims than in sympathy with them and when we would resent any attempt on the part of the state to interfere in what we believe to be our private affairs—or at least some of us would. In part, this is because today we make a clear distinction not only between the individual and the state but also between society and the state. These sharp distinctions either did not exist for the Greeks or, if they did, did so only in a nascent way. Although it's clearly impossible not to have some idea of an individual, 'the fact remains that in the political thought of Greece the notion of the individual is not prominent...Society must be one with the State, because there was no room for differentiation.' [Barker, 7, 13,] In our contemporary liberal democracies we start with the individual and tend to view the state as having the primary and essentially negative function of providing the basic conditions of peace and justice that will allow us to get on with our private business; the Greeks in their *poleis*, on the other hand, living with other like-minded people, tended to see the function of the state as the furtherance of their common *ethos*.

Despite having had kings at one stage in their political development, the Greek *poleis* were not, except accidentally and incidentally, despotisms in which the mass of the people was subjected to the capricious will of one man, as was the case in the neighbouring Persian Empire. They were, rather, fellowships (*koinonias*). Because the notion of sovereignty is so central to modern and contemporary political thought, it's tempting to look for it in the world of the Greeks. We tend to see the sovereignty of the state as limited because we recognise other forms of sovereignty in individuals and in groups but, as McClelland notes, 'The ancient Greeks did not think about sovereignty in that way because a distinction between public and private in our sense was not available to them. The *polis* based on law was above all other things designed to judge and control the characters of its members in the widest sense.' [McClelland, 12]

The common purposes of the *polis* received attention in many ways, not least in their common public worship of the city's gods. This is another respect in which life in the world of the Greeks differed significantly from ours. For us, religion is largely a private and interior matter and in most Western societies today, apart from ceremonial occasions, religion has little or no intrinsic connection with the state. But for the ancients, as Peter Nicholson notes, 'religion dominated and permeated the life of the *polis*. All social activities had a religious significance. Ritual communal practices, such as banquets and games, produced social cohesion, and also defined one's status as a citizen….the different *poleis* were obliged to respect each other's shrines and religious sanctuaries or the wrath of the gods would be visited upon the offenders. Exclusion from the religious practices of the *polis* was tantamount to the loss of citizenship.'[4] Modern and contemporary Western political thought is the product of a long period of historical, practical, political and theoretical vicissitudes, and one of its distinctive characteristics (so obvious to us that we perhaps don't even realise that it *is* distinctive) is a sharp separation between the political and the religious. Whatever may be the intrinsic merits of this separation, it must be realised that most societies throughout most of history have made no such separation. Even in classical Athens and republican Rome, the religious dimensions of their social order (which can seem to us as decorative irrelevancies) were critically important and constitutive elements of the life of those societies.[5] Francis Oakley employs the term 'cosmic religion' to name what he takes to be the archaic interpenetration of religion and politics, particularly evident in the enduring notion of sacral kingship. He goes so far as to say that 'for the greater part of human history it is an egregious anachronism even to make use of the words "politics" and "religion," the very definitions of which presuppose our modern Western distinction between the religious and the political and inevitably evoke misleading intimations of the modern church-state dialectic.' [Oakley 2010, 19]

There were many *poleis*[6] and they varied considerably in their modes of political organisation. By modern standards, they were small, small in extent and small in population.[7] The multiplicity of *poleis* and their stubborn clinging to independence can seem to us in the twenty first century to be a sign of political immaturity and a failure to learn the lessons of *realpolitik*. It might be, however, as Josiah Ober suggests, that 'Ancient Greek history points to a possible alternative to the dominant narrative of political and economic development, based primarily on the history of early modern Europe...' [Ober 2016, 11]

Not only were there many *poleis* but such *poleis* as there were varied enormously in size. Much of our knowledge about classical Greece comes to us from the literary and philosophical productions of Athens but Athens was in no way typical of the size of the average Greek *polis*. Athens covered an area of around 2,500 square kilometres, just under a 1,000 square miles,[8] and had a population in the region of 250,000. Small as Athens might have been in relation to your average modern state, it was gigantic in area and population when compared to a more average *polis* such as Plataea which covered an area of about 170 square kilometres, around 65 square miles, with a population under 10,000. Plataea would be comparable in size to Liechtenstein, the sixth smallest country in the contemporary world. Plataea in turn dwarfed the tiny *polis* of Koresia which covered an area of only 15 square kilometres, just under 6 square miles, about 75% the size of the City of Westminster. [see Ober, 7]

Every *polis* had its own distinct *ethos* or character and, being as small as they were, *poleis* operated in an atmosphere of intimacy scarcely imaginable to us today. Again, in a way difficult for us to grasp, each *polis* was self-sufficient (*autarkeia*) or largely so and also self-governing (*autonomia*). Although in most of the *poleis* the nobility had lost or had been stripped of their legal and political privileges, they still retained enormous social power connected to their birth and their wealth. In Athens, the partially successful reforms of Solon were more or less effectively completed by Cleisthenes (c. 508/507 BC). In a radical, indeed revolutionary move, Cleisthenes replaced the old religious and exclusionary tribal divisions, which were based upon traditional family or kinship allegiances, with a new set of tribes and demes to which all Athenian free men belonged.[9] Cyril Parkinson comments, 'The essential point in the reforms of Solon and Cleisthenes was the abolition of the clans. Democracy in the Greek sense was incompatible with communal organisation or with the continued influence of the areopogus (sic).'[10] Fustel de Coulanges remarks that 'the suppression of the old tribes, replaced by new ones, to which all men had access, and in which they were equal, was not a fact peculiar to the history of Athens. The same change took place at Cyrene, Sicyon, Elis, and Sparta, and probably in many other Greek cities.'[11] Aristotle, for whom Cleisthenes's reforms were a matter of recent history, commented on the usefulness of his methods in the establishment of democracy: 'Fresh tribes and brotherhoods [phratries] should be established; the private rites of families should be restricted and converted into public ones; in short, every contrivance should be adopted which will mingle the citizens with one another and get rid of old connexions.'[12]

Under the new Athenian constitution, which lasted until the mid fourth century BC, all free Athenian men were equal before the law (*isonomia*). [see de Coulanges,

278-283] Much has been made by many of the supposed birth of democracy in ancient Athens but even if we accept that Parkinson is correct in holding that democracy did not first see the light of day in Athens, what was significant about the reforms of Solon and Cleisthenes was the enshrinement of the individual rather than the family or tribe at the centre of political life. This welcome development wasn't without its dangers as the naked individual, detached from family, community and all other intermediate social groups, is easy prey for a state that will willingly accept his entire loyalty. It isn't surprising that all erstwhile totalitarian states make it their business to destroy the natural pieties of family life. [see Parkinson 1958, 171]

What will seem strange to modern eyes is that Athenian democracy was largely non-elective. The Council (βουλή) with 500 members, the Supreme Court (Ηλιαία) with six thousand members and roughly six hundred of the seven hundred magistracies (to be held only once by any one citizen) were filled by casting lots, the remaining magistracies, including the ten *strategoi* (the generals or diplomats) and the officials responsible for financial matters, were filled by election. The allotment of the non-technical responsibilities was intended to prevent the domination of governance roles by the rich or the well-born which, it was feared (with some justification) would happen under an elective system. As Aristotle remarked, 'the appointment of magistrates by lot is thought to be democratical, and the election of them oligarchical...'[13] Since not every citizen participated in every aspect of government at all times, it would perhaps be something of an exaggeration to describe Athenian democracy as direct. Van Reybrouck suggests that it might be described as a 'non-electoral representative democracy' or, indeed, given the use of lots, as an 'aleatoric representational democracy.'[14]

The basic tension within *poleis*, then, was between the men of birth and property (usually, the few) and those of no social distinction and little wealth (usually the many). The struggle between the few and the many, writes Ernest Barker, 'gave an impulse to the development of political theory in Greece in much the same way as popular revolts against monarchy have in modern times produced, or at any rate stimulated, political theories like that of the Social Contract.' [Barker, 4] The class character of politics was self-evident to the ancients. As they saw it, 'Oligarchy was a conspiracy of the rich to rob the poor and democracy was a conspiracy of the poor to rob the rich.' [McClelland, 8] The natural instinct of the poor, remarks Cyril Parkinson, was 'to tax or fine the rich out of existence. The reaction of the more prosperous was to form societies for mutual protection and political reform.' [Parkinson 1958, 173] Class conflict wasn't the only weakness of the newly emergent Athenian democracy. As tends to happen in all popular forms of government, the number of those on the public payroll rose alarmingly as the class of those in receipt of government largesse overlapped significantly with those who made the decisions on the distribution of that largesse. [see Parkinson 1958, 174]

In Athens, citizens believed themselves to be free to act as they wished in social matters and to have a say in the determination of the direction of the political community. They valued equality in different ways: equality before the law, fundamental equality of regard for all as citizens, and equality in respect of freedom of speech. Not everyone was enthusiastic about this emphasis on freedom and political equality. As we shall see, part of what Plato is doing in the *Republic* is postulating the construction of his ideal city on a model not all that far removed from that provided by Sparta because, for him, Sparta, firmly subordinating the individual to the State and its goals, had the distinct advantage of having little or no truck with all this proto-liberal nonsense about freedom.

It is easy to be misled about the character of Greek political life as a whole and to think of it as being all of a piece with the way things were organised at Athens or Sparta but, as I have already mentioned, there were many *poleis* and each differed from the other, sometimes radically. And as much as these *poleis* differed from one another, they differed again from the Persian Empire and from Egypt and from Carthage and the various barbarian tribes living in the hinterland of the civilised Greek-speaking world. Looking outward, the educated or travelled Athenian couldn't but be aware that customs, habits and laws differed, often widely, from society to society. Looking around him, an educated Athenian could hardly fail to appreciate the dramatic changes that had taken place in his own *polis* in a relatively short space of time. George Sabine remarks that 'The final triumph of democracy was not much older than the political career of Pericles; the constitution itself went back only to the last years of the sixth century; and the beginning of the democracy, counting from the establishment of popular control over the courts by Solon, was less than a century older.' [Sabine, 23] It is also evident from the tragedies and comedies of the Greek playwrights, that the Athenian public must have been well aware of the on-going controversies and the continuing critical debate on all matters of politics.

It is tempting to conclude that the glory days of the Greek *poleis* came to a halt after the Macedonian and Roman conquests but this temptation should be resisted. Josiah Ober argues, I believe correctly, that 'the classical economic and cultural efflorescence continued into the postclassical era as a result of an equilibrium struck between ambitious Hellenistic monarchs and the city-states within their kingdoms....The perpetuation of efflorescence in the Hellenistic era, long past the moment of political fall, made possible the "immortality" of Greek culture.' [Ober 2015, 19]

SOPHISTS

There can be no denying that the Sophists have a bad reputation. To be accused of sophistry isn't to be complimented, and to have your reasoning described as sophistical is to have it damned for being speciously clever but fundamentally wrong. Ordinary language-use mirrors the more sophisticated (pun intended) philosophical depreciation. In common speech, one can be a smart alec, a know-it-all, a wise guy, too clever for one's own good or too clever by half or, in the case of Douglas Adams's self-description, too clever by 40%.[15]

The interpretation of the ideas of the Sophists, perhaps, even more than that of most thinkers, is controversial and disputed, not least because of the paucity of surviving first-hand material. The fragments of the writings of the so-called

Pre-Socratic philosophers have been collected in the Diels-Krantz authoritative edition of *Fragmente der Vorsokratiker* (hereafter, DK). In Kathleen Freeman's *Ancilla to the Pre-Socratic Philosophers*, a translation of Diels-Krantz, the writings of the Sophists occupy a mere thirty seven pages. One can see why Max Salomon says 'the picture of the individual Sophists which we construct on the basis of such of their dicta as are preserved is, in so far as it is determined by the vicissitudes of the tradition, the result of pure chance.'[16] In the case of many of the Sophists, we have to rely largely on the account given of them in Plato's dialogues and although the extent to which Plato was prejudiced in his portrayal of the Sophists is a matter of some controversy, I think it fair to say that his attitude towards them was less than enthusiastic. [see Guthrie, 11-13]

The Sophists did not form a school of philosophy with distinctive doctrines as later would be the case with the Epicureans, the Cynics and the Stoics. Despite this, they shared a common interest in practical rather than theoretical matters, focusing their attention on ethics, politics, and education rather than on physics or cosmology; man, rather than the world around them, was their core concern. If they did have an attitude towards physics and cosmology it was, in the main, sceptical despite which most of them shared a similar approach to that of the physicists. Just as the early Greek physicists had attempted to find an under-lying stable principle beneath the flux of change in the physical world around them, a principle that could explain and support those changes, so too some of the Sophists, keenly aware of the multiple and various social, political and legal realities, sought to find an underlying practical principle that could explain and support the manifold social realities. Still, it's one thing to agree that there must (or might) be some such principle; it's quite another thing to find it.

The Sophists were first and foremost teachers of rhetoric—the art of persuasive public speaking.[17] We might wonder why public speaking should have been regarded as a worthwhile accomplishment. This is because of the changed political circumstances in the Greek *poleis* such that the power of words 'became closely identified with the public sphere, with speaking in the assembly and with the political role of a superior class.' [Siedentop, 35] 'Why did rhetoric catch on so rapidly in Athens?' asks Sam Leith, rhetorically. 'For a start, here was a place that was just getting used to a radical and unprece-dented experiment with democracy. It was only in the early fifth century BC that the popular assembly became the central repository of power in the Athenian state, and the oligarchies and tyrannies that had preceded it, pretty much by definition, weren't fertile ground for the growth of public speaking. Now the principle of persuasive speech was at the heart of government. Those aristocrats who regretted the waning of their influence saw a chance to claw some back, if they could master the skills required to dominate the assembly.' [Leith, 22-23]

With the social disturbances caused by war and the increasing cosmopol-itanism of Athens resulting from its leadership of the Delian League, it had become readily apparent that laws differed from city to city as did customs and habits. This cultural comparison disturbed settled convictions regarding the nature of law. Was there some settled human and social substratum or nature (*phusis*) beneath all the various systems or was it all merely a matter of convention (*nomos*)? Enter the Sophists. What was new and revolutionary wasn't so much *what* they taught, startling as that might be on occasion, but simply *that* they taught at all. Some of the more prominent Sophists were Protagoras, Gorgias, Prodicus, Hippias, Antiphon, Callicles, Diagoras, Critias, Alcidamas and Thrasymachus. With the exception of Antiphon (and Critias, if he is taken to be a Sophist), almost all the Sophists were non-Athenians, attracted to Athens because it had become the intellectual centre of Greece and, let us not be coy about it, because of its wealth. Kerferd notes that we have the names of twenty-six or so Sophists active between 460-380 BC; after this date, the individual Sophists tended to be replaced by the various schools, such as the Academy of Plato and Aristotle's Lyceum.

As itinerant teachers, the Sophists travelled all over the Greek world, visiting all the major cities. Almost all the Sophists visited Athens at one time or another between 460-400 BC because the increasingly dominant cultural position of Athens and the wealth of its citizens made it an attractive base of operations. Given the developing character of democracy in Athens and the possibilities opening to those able to control discussions of policy, the rhetorical skills that the Sophists claimed to teach were extremely valuable. Persuasion isn't necessary where one can command. In a modern army, a general does not have to persuade his troops to obey his commands; he can simply order them about. Similarly, a king who can command does not need to persuade. The shift in Greek society from a royal-through-aristocratic-to-democratic structures meant that those who wished to be the determiners of public policy had to do so by persuading others to support their proposals. 'The prevalence of public speaking that leaves its traces everywhere in Greek literature,' writes Steven Robinson, 'indicates a fundamental shift in political consciousness away from a previous deference to powerful elites (who were accountable to no one) and towards the self-conscious rejection of absolute authority by the masses of Greek citizens.'[18]

The Sophists, then, were responding to market demand. But they were also promoted by individual sponsorship, not least that of the great Pericles. According to G. B. Kerferd, 'it was not merely the general situation at Athens but also the direct encouragement of Pericles that brought so many of the sophists to Athens. Their coming was not simply something from without, but rather a development internal to the history of Athens. They were a part of the movement that was producing the new Athens of Pericles, and it was as such that they were both welcomed and attacked.' [Kerferd, 22]

Part of the contempt of such as Plato for the Sophists [see Plato 282D] appears to have been that the Sophists had the temerity to charge money for their services. Plato's aristocratic disdain for trade and commerce comes through strongly in such contempt. When we consider that other professionals such as doctors, poets and artists received payment for their services while still being highly respected, this objection seems somewhat specious. Perhaps it was the Sophists' claim to teach wisdom and virtue that was problematic? Once again, given that the Greek poets had been doing precisely this since time immemorial, this objection seems specious. What then *was* the objection? It seems that it wasn't that the Sophists expected to be paid for teaching or the content of what they taught or the effect of their teachings upon their students—it was, rather, that they were willing to teach all and sundry, the low and baseborn as well as the noble and the well connected, even though the evidence, as we find it in Plato's *Protagoras*, suggests that the Sophists, though willing in principle to teach anyone who was willing to pay to be taught, were in actual fact selective in their choice of students.

In Athens, all citizens might be equal (in theory) but some citizens were more equal than others. From the beginnings of Athenian democracy in 507 BC, the question was—who gets to speak in the Assembly and the Council; who makes the decisions? The answer was, of course, the citizens. But which citizens? As mentioned already, even though the members of the aristocracy has lost their legal and political privileges, they still retained enormous social power because of their wealth and birth so that when money and birth talked, people listened. The art of the Sophist, by threatening to empower the poor and the poorly born, was a direct challenge to the power and influence of the aristocracy. It isn't coincidental that, although Sophistry did not begin in Athens, the rise of Athenian democracy and the emergence of the Sophists to prominence go hand in hand.

A key incident that shows that there was one law for the aristocracy and another for the common man comes not from history but from literature. At the siege of Troy, when Agamemnon, to test the morale of the Greeks, lets it be known that he is about to lift the siege of Troy and order a return home, he is unpleasantly surprised to find both officers and men only too ready to take to the ships! Odysseus undertakes to stem the rout. He cajoles the other kings and chieftains into returning to duty with mild and persuasive language but he sternly rebukes and physically assaults the rank-and-file, bidding them to listen to better men than themselves, telling them that they cannot all be kings and that one king must be supreme. When Thersites, a soldier, has the temerity to rebuke Agamemnon and to counsel an end to the pointless war, Odysseus strikes him to the ground with his staff and rebukes him with these words: 'Check your glib tongue, Thersites….Drop this chatter about kings, and neither revile them nor keep harping about going home.' [*Iliad*, Book 2, 252-334] Homer is remarkably unkind to Thersites, describing in some detail his repulsive, almost sub-human, physical appearance. Even in later literature, Thersites gets a bad press. He appears in Shakespeare's *Troilus and Cressida* where he is described by Nestor as 'A slave whose gall coins slanders like a mint/ To match us in comparisons with dirt/ To weaken and discredit our exposure/ How rank soever rounded in with danger.'[19] Thersites's protest is, says I. F. Stone, 'the debut of the common man in written history, the first exercise of free speech by a commoner against a king, and it is suppressed by force: Odysseus answers the speech not by argument but with a beating.' [Stone 1989, 32] Frank Furedi notes the tendency of modern readers of the *Iliad* to interpret Thersites's outburst as a challenge to elite authority. As against that, he remarks that Thersites, despite the dislike in which his companions hold him, is 'not a marginal commoner consigned to the bottom of the heap' but a freeman and a warrior, bearing his own arms, and thus belonging to the *aristoi* than *hoi polloi.*' [Furedi, 23-24] Still, he has to concede that 'the silencing of Thersites does not resolve the profound issues to do with leadership, obedience and authority in the *Iliad*....While Odysseus could easily force Thersites into submission, the questions raised by this subversive figure could not be answered.' [Furedi, 19; see 16-30]

The methods of teaching employed by the Sophists included not only the set-piece lecture but also instruction by means of question and answer. If this method sounds familiar to us, it's because it is the method commonly known as Socratic. Did this method predate Socrates? Some, such as Diogenes Laertius, say that Protagoras was the first to use this method. This judgement has generated much heat among those who wish to defend what they see as the originality of Socrates but, without going into tedious detail, we can, I think, agree with Kerferd, who says 'The Socratic method, to the extent that it may have originated with Socrates, none the less originated from within the Sophistic movement, if only because Socrates himself was a part of that movement.' [Kerferd, 34] Socrates a Sophist? Given the hostility of Plato to Sophists as a whole, surely this is a nonsensical suggestion? Whether nonsensical or not, it's clear that to many of his contemporaries Socrates appeared to be indistinguishable from the rest of the Sophists. George Kerferd remarks, 'It is thus clear that Socrates *was* quite widely regarded as part of the sophistic movement.... his intellectual and educational impact on the aspiring young men at Athens was such that *in function* he was correctly so regarded. The fact that he took no payment does not alter his function in any way.' [Kerferd, 57] This view of Socrates is shared by the editors of the Loeb Classical Library volume on the Sophists who write, 'Although chronologically Socrates (469-399) is a central figure of the period considered in this collection, Plato's sustained attempts to set him as an authentic philosopher in the strongest possible contrast to the "sophists" and the historical success of those attempts have made it difficult to recognize what they in fact had in common. To be sure, there are significant differences between the other "sophists" and Socrates....but Socrates' interests and teaching like those of the other members of this loose groups of intellectuals, revolve around the questions of moral and political excellence and the use of language and argument in order to obtain the agreement of listeners or interlocutors. Thus is makes most sense to see Socrates as an idiosyncratically Athenian "sophist."' [Laks & Most, 293]

LAW AND NATURE: *NOMOS* AND *PHUSIS*

The legitimacy of political power was based on law (*nomos*) and this law, as with all early societies, was a mixture of custom, habit, morality, convention and social expectations, almost always unwritten.[20] 'For the Greeks,' writes W. K. C. Guthrie, 'law, however much it might be formulated in writing and enforced by authority, remained dependent on custom or habit.' [Guthrie, 57] In the *polis* law was sovereign and the citizens of the *polis* needed to be educated in that law. Law, for the Greeks, as it has been for most people in history, was something simply given, coeval with and constitutive of their society. It wasn't something to be made or unmade, not least because the intrinsic and normative coercive power of the law lies in its being conceived of as holding from time immemorial, as something permanent and abiding. Our contemporary view of law, in contrast, is that law is a set of flexible regulations, constantly changing to accommodate itself to changing circumstances.[21]

Greek customary law was essentially negative, ruling out such socially disruptive activities as murder, or the stealing of another man's wife, or fraud. Furthermore, 'law was usually strict about religious observance because failing to give the gods their due was always a sign that worse was to follow. But beyond that, men were expected to compete for those things which men called good.' [McClelland, 10] If people live as hermits, law isn't needed, but if people are to live together without conflict, or with minimal conflict, then law is essential. If social and political life is to be possible at all, laws there must be. *Who* should make that law or, more properly, *how* that law should be made and *what* that law should contain—these were highly contentious matters, then as now.

The Sophists systematically raised questions about morality and politics that set the agenda for subsequent philosophical debate. Plato and Aristotle can often be understood as responding polemically to the Sophists' arguments. In his well-known discussion of slavery in his *Politics*, Aristotle refers to some unnamed persons who regard the control by masters over slaves as contrary to nature.[22] These unnamed persons Aristotle later refers to as 'men of judgment', in Greek, *sophoi*, which seems to be a strong indication that this critique originates with the Sophists. Peter Garnsey remarks, 'The intellectual origins of the critique [of slavery] lie ultimately in the activity of the sophists…' [Garnsey, 76] If there is, then, one thing for which the Sophists are well known, it is the distinction they draw between nature (*phusis*)[23] and convention (*nomos*). Is it better to follow the moral and legal rules of one's society or to exist according to nature? Ernest Barker remarks, 'The tendency to oppose Nature to Law not only resulted in views subversive of the State, but also in opinions destructive of many institutions and beliefs. Once oppose Nature to Convention and the whole inherited tradition of the ages goes by the board.' [Barker, 86] Even though the Sophists did not constitute a philosophical school as did, say, the Epicureans or Stoics, there being no canonical set of doctrines to which a Sophist had to subscribe, the distinction between *phusis* and *nomos*, nature and convention/law, was more or less a constant theme of sophistic thought. That there *was* such a distinction is clear enough; just *what* that distinction amounted to is quite another matter.[24]

There are at least two ways in which the *nomos/phusis* distinction can operate, corresponding, roughly, to a division between the thought of the earlier and the later Sophists. 'Before the close of the fifth century,' writes George Sabine, 'the contrast of nature and convention had begun to develop in two main directions. The one conceived nature as a law of justice and right inherent in human beings and in the world….The other conceived nature non-morally, and as manifested in human beings it was self-assertion or egoism, the desire for pleasure or for power.'[25]

In one way, what is natural can be thought of as giving us an account of justice that is independent of and superior to the more specific and limited conceptions of justice that can be found in particular *poleis*. This is how it appears in Sophocles's *Antigone* in the famous passage where Antigone rejects the binding force of her uncle Kreon's laws. Kreon asks Antigone if she knew of his proclamation forbidding what she had done. She answers: 'How could I not? It was public knowledge....[but] Zeus did not announce those laws to me. And Justice living with the gods below sent no such laws for men. I did not think anything which you proclaimed strong enough to let a mortal override the gods and their unwritten and unchanging laws. They are not just for today or yesterday, but exist forever, and no one knows where they first appeared.' [Sophocles, *Antigone*] Commenting on the Sophists, Heinrich Rommen[26] remarks, 'the Sophists had much in common with the revolutionary natural-law ideas of the eighteenth-century Enlightenment....To the Sophists the laws were not venerable because of tradition or by reason of having stood the actual test of life in the city-state: they were artificial constructs and served the interests of the powerful....' [Rommen, 8] In so doing, the Sophists contrasted the laws of the particular city-state with the natural law as they conceived of it. Hippias, for example, talked of unwritten laws that were eternal and unalterable and had a source above that of the municipal laws of the political community. But the contrast between nature and convention can be drawn in another way. In this way of drawing the distinction, nature isn't thought of as having a moral character and so does not stand in judgement over the morality of the *polis*. In effect, this results in denying the status of 'natural' to any social teaching. Notoriously, Alcidamas denied that any man was naturally a slave and Antiphon, even more outrageously, denied that there was any natural distinction between Greeks and barbarians! In one of the longest fragments we have of any of the Sophists, Antiphon states baldly that all law is convention and, as such, *contrary* to nature!

W. K. C. Guthrie presents us with one of the most sophisticated (though, by his own admission, intellectually non-coercive) accounts of the *phusis-nomos* distinction. A *conventionalist* view of the *phusis-nomos* distinction characterises our original primitive human condition as *phusis* and our civilised condition as *nomos*. Such might be the opinion of Protagoras. A *realist* view of the distinction would take *phusis* to be our native self-interest in contrast to our behaviour under public inspection and social control (*nomos*). Such a view might be attributed to Thucydides, and to Thrasymachus and Glaucon in Plato's *Republic*. A third *antinomian* view of the *phusis-nomos* distinction is a more extreme form of the second, seeing *phusis* as our original condition of self-seeking by the strong and independent as opposed to the conventions (*nomoi*) that society attempts to impose on the strong. It wouldn't be inappropriate to attribute such a view to Callicles, in Plato's *Gorgias*.

Whatever the correct view of the *phusis/nomos* distinction, if indeed there is a correct view, or the best view if there isn't a correct view, it cannot be denied that this distinction operated as a kind of intellectual wrench to loosen the bolts of tradition. Heinrich Rommen sees three revolutionary ideas emerging from the thought of the Sophists: first, the laws of the *polis* are artificial and tend to serve class interests; second, all men are free and equal and are citizens of the *civitas maxima* or cosmopolis, which transcends the limitations of the local *polis*; and third, the *polis* comes into being as the result of agreement or convention and not by nature. [Rommen, 9] It is easy to see how opposed such ideas are to the political thought of Plato and Aristotle. Rommen writes, 'Wherever the idea of human rights forced its way through (among the moderate Sophists and in Stoicism), its effect was revolutionary: either it dissolved the city-state or it encouraged dreams of the great society (*civitas maxima*) of mankind...' [Rommen, 29] As already remarked, the Sophists formed no formal school of their own but it isn't too much to say that the force and vitality of aspects of their thought would find renewed expression in various ways in the Hellenistic schools of the Epicureans, Cynics, Sceptics and Stoics.

SOME INDIVIDUAL SOPHISTS

Protagoras (490-420 BC), a native of Abdera in the northeast corner of the Greek world, was among the earliest of the Sophists and is arguably the most famous of them. Only a dozen or so fragments of his work survive but he features in Plato's *Protagoras*, *Euthydemus*, *Cratylus* and *Theaetetus* and is mentioned in Aristotle's *Metaphysics* and *Rhetoric*. He claimed to be able to teach certain skills in political matters. Such skills are necessary in any political community, especially in any democratic political community, and are therefore worth paying to acquire. To the objection that perhaps such skills aren't communicable, otherwise, why would the sons of expert politicians not become experts themselves, Protagoras responds blandly that not everyone has the same capacity to be taught.

Protagoras is often thought of as a relativist, someone to whom the truth of the matter is dependent upon whoever is doing the judging. He is, perhaps most well known for his statement that 'Of all things the measure is man, of things that are that they are, and of things that are not that they are not.'[27] This cryptic statement can be variously interpreted: broadly, as the claim that we have no access to non-human judgements on contested matters; or more narrowly, as the claim that there is no way to distinguish definitively between individual human judgements. It may well be that what, on the face of it, looks like a radically relativist claim simply amounts to the prosaic judgement that the common perceptions of ordinary people must be accorded priority.

What Protagoras appears to have been contesting was, to him and to many others, the metaphysical and unprovable claims about an unknown substance underlying all perceptible things. And just as he rejected this idea of a unitary principle underlying a changeable nature, so too he rejected the idea of a single natural human society distinct from the many forms of state and society he saw around him. To call him a relativist without qualification is, I believe, to overstate the case. He does not appear to be a relativist about matters of fact, such as that certain substances are poisonous to human beings. He is, however, a social/legal relativist, holding that whatever a given city holds to be just simply *is* just for it and its citizens.[28] Odd as it may seem, this social/legal relativism leads him to espouse a fundamentally conservative and communitarian philosophy. 'Protagoras,' writes Peter Nicholson, 'thinks that, in order to live together as a single political entity, the members of the community must agree on a common measure and work constantly to ensure that it is effective.' [Nicholson, 34] If indeed man is the measure of all things, then it is man-in-community who measures things in social and political terms, not some idiosyncratic individual. Those trained in the art of politics will benefit themselves and, in so doing, will also benefit the city, being able to persuade the people to adopt rules and laws (*nomoi*) that are more likely than not to lead to their advantage. Private advantage and public advantage are mutually reinforcing.

Protagoras endorsed no specific political regime, rejecting only tyranny, defined in the usual way as a system of government in which those who govern do so for their own advantage and not for the advantage of the community. He was of the view that all men simply by virtue of family and social life develop a measure of political insight that's capable of development through education. Even so, not everyone's views are equally worthy of respect. Among those who have some measure of political insight, some will have more than others and those should be the ones to give a lead. 'Thus an ideal Protagorean society is not ultimately egalitarian,' writes Kerferd, 'it is to be guided by those with the most wisdom on each and any occasion.' [Kerferd, 144] Despite this elitist bias, Protagoras is still a democrat, unlike Plato who believes, as we shall see, that by and large, your average citizen-in-the-street has little or nothing of value to contribute to the *polis* by way of leadership.

Gorgias was a contemporary of Protagoras. He came from Leontini in Sicily, a colony of Chalcidian Naxos, and so was ethnically an Ionian. He was a brother of Herodicus, the physician. He studied under Empedocles and taught Alcidamas and Antisthenes. Those influenced by him include: Isocrates, Lycophron, Prodicus, Hippocrates, Pericles, Alcibiades, Critias, Proxenus and Meno.

By the standards of other pre-Socratics, we have a substantial amount of extant material from the pen of Gorgias. [DK 82; Freeman, 127-39] He wrote an anti-Parmenidean tract, the substance of which is that nothing exists; that even if something existed, it cannot be known, and if it could be known, it couldn't be communicated. He denied any intention of teaching his pupils excellence (*arête*); rather, his job was to teach people how to speak persuasively. 'At any rate,' writes Guthrie, 'whereas rhetoric was in the curriculum of every Sophist, Gorgias must have put it more prominently in his shop window than any of the others.' [Guthrie, 272] The art of rhetoric he saw as being morally neutral, concerned with means and not ends.

Hippias belonged to the younger generation of Sophists. He came from Elis and so was a Dorian. He served as an Elean ambassador to Athens and claimed to have made a lot of money from his teaching activities. Most of our knowledge about Hippias comes from Plato's dialogues. He appears in the *Protagoras* and in two dialogues called after him that may not be genuinely Platonic. Although Plato shows a measure of genuine respect for Protagoras and, to a lesser extent, Gorgias, and even seems to share some of Prodicus's predilections, he makes relentless fun of Hippias who, in the dialogues, seems to be completely unaware of the ironical flattery that Socrates heaps on him. Xenophon regarded Hippias as a polymath and it was commonly believed that he had a remarkable memory. He taught not only rhetoric but also astronomy, geometry, arithmetic, grammar, rhythm, music, genealogy, mythology and history. It is claimed that he made some significant mathematical discoveries though this has been disputed. Kerferd says that 'his knowledge was not merely superficial' but was 'based on scholarship that was both wide and deep.' [Kerferd, 47]

Hippias seemed to be an early expositor of a theory of natural law. In Xenophon's *Memorabilia*, Hippias and Socrates agree that unwritten laws are divine and god-ordained. [IV iv 19] These laws are observed everywhere without negotiation or promulgation and so cannot be the result of enactment but must have their source elsewhere. This provides for an antithesis between this natural law and the positive law of particular political communities. In typical Sophist fashion, Hippias contrasted law (*nomos*) and nature (*phusis*) and came down on the side of nature (*phusis*) on moral grounds. He held that the divisions among the human race are artificial and a matter of *nomos*. In Plato's *Protagoras* [337D], Hippias intervenes in a dispute. He calls all those present kinsmen by nature, not by law. Law is a despot constraining men to act against nature.

Little was known about Antiphon until the discovery in 1915 of two relatively large fragments from his treatise *On Truth* so that, unlike his fellow Sophists Protagoras and Thrasymachus, we have some relatively substantial material to reflect upon.[29] He draws the standard Sophistic distinction between *phusis* and *nomos*, his particular take on that distinction being that not only are nature and convention different, they are in fact opposed. He seems to have adopted a utilitarian and somewhat cynical approach to *nomos*, arguing that we should follow it only if failing to do so brings more pain than pleasure. 'In Antiphon,' write Andrew Shortridge and Dirk Baltzly, 'we have the first available formulations of a reasoned critique of custom justified at least in part in terms of human nature….he helped give a first, perhaps primitive, shape and form to the antithesis of law and nature: one of the most influential controversies in the history of philosophy.' [Shortridge and Baltzly, 91]

Justice, Antiphon defines, as not violating the legal rules of one's city or, as he adds somewhat cynically, not being known to transgress those rules. These rules are conventional, not natural. We know this because every city has its own rules and they aren't all the same. They cannot, therefore, all be natural since what is natural is common to all. To obey the rules, then, is to go against nature and no one should do so unless he is being observed, for then he is subject to shame and punishment. Those who transgress the laws of nature suffer evil consequences whether observed or not; those who transgress the laws of the city suffer only if their transgressions are witnessed.

Not only do the rules prevent one from acting according to nature and so are the opposite of life enhancing, they do not even protect those who act according to them. 'Now if those who adopted such courses [brought their cases to the courts] received any help from the laws, or those who did not adopt such course, but took the opposite line, suffered any loss from the laws, there would be some use in paying obedience to the laws. But, as a matter of fact, it is

obvious that legal justice is inadequate to help those who adopt such courses....
it permits the injured party to be injured and the offending party to commit his
offence.' Even if the case comes to court matters are no better: '[The injured
party] can only affirm the fact of injury, and endeavour to persuade the court of
the fact.' On the other hand, the offending party can seek to persuade the court
of the truth of his denial. What finally determines the court is the greater ability
of one or other of the parties; and there is no guarantee that the greater ability
will be found on the side of the injured party.' [in Barker, 97-98] In agreement
with Hippias, Antiphon contends that *phusis* recognises no distinction of class
or race.

We rely for our knowledge of Thrasymachus on Plato's presentation of his
ideas in the *Republic*. How accurate this presentation is we cannot know, as we
have no other source of information. Thrasymachus came from Chalcedon, a
Megaran colony and was a teacher of rhetoric who travelled widely. Notoriously, he argues that justice is the advantage of the stronger. In every society,
the rules are made by those with power—the stronger—and are always made
to their own advantage. Since the rules determine what is just in a political
community, justice is to the advantage of the stronger. If one isn't a member
of the stronger group, acting justly is, by definition, to act against one's own
interest. Those who make the rules or, when they cannot make them, evade
them, win; those who follow rules made by others, lose. [see Siedentop, 41-47]
A version of the Thrasymachian idea can be found in the speech of the Athenian
envoys to the citizens of Melos, in Thucydides's *History of the Peloponnesian
War*. The envoys say, bluntly, 'In the case of the gods we believe, and in the
case of humankind it has always been obvious, that as a necessity of nature
wherever anyone has the upper hand they rule. We were not the ones to lay
down this law, nor the first to take advantage of its existence. We found it
already established, expect to leave it to last for ever, and now make use of it,
knowing full well that you and anyone else who enjoyed the same power as we
do would act in just the same way.'[30] This expression of brutal power-realism,
though perhaps shocking to modern sensibilities, was entirely characteristic of
the attitude of all *poleis*, including Sparta. Whatever furthered the interests of
a *polis* was right.[31]

It seems that Thrasymachus makes certain assumptions in the course of his
argument. One is that each individual is isolated and competes with others
for a limited set of goods. The interest of each person is his and his only and
there are no common interests. Politics on this conception is a zero-sum game
in which my gain is your loss and *vice versa*. This position, interestingly, is in
stark contrast to that of his fellow Sophist, Protagoras, who had expounded a
conception of justice that made it to be a communal and reciprocal matter. For
Protagoras, politics is a positive-sum cooperative venture; for Thrasymachus, it
is conflictual and zero-sum. Given Protagoras's social relativism, it's going to
be difficult for him to defend himself against the Thrasymachian arguments. If
justice is only what people collectively think it is and if people think that justice
isn't for the collective good, then what ground does Protagoras stand upon? It
is important to see that Thrasymachus isn't advocating the crude idea that a

physically stronger person has right on his side over the physically weaker. His point is political, not physical, and it is that each ruling group necessarily makes laws for its own advantage. One thing all political systems have in common is that they all embody a struggle for control between those in power and those not in power. Thrasymachus vehemently disputes Socrates's image of the ruler as a kind of doctor, whose actions are motivated by a concern for his patients. He substitutes his own image, of the ruler as a shepherd, whose concern for his sheep is to ensure that they are brought safely to slaughter! [*Republic* 343B]

We know nothing of Callicles except what we read about him in Plato's *Gorgias*. Callicles was a politician and follower of the Sophists rather than a Sophist himself but listening to him, one could fancy oneself listening to a younger, more energetic and less restrained Thrasymachus. For Callicles, conventional morality is simply *nomos* that has supplanted the true morality that's based on *phusis*. This morality of *nomos* is a snare by which the weak trap and tame the strong. But 'nature makes it plain that it is right for the better to have the advantage over the worse; the more able over the less. And both among all animals and in entire states and races of mankind it is plain that this is the case—that right is recognised to be the sovereignty and advantage of the strong over the weaker.' [*Gorgias* 483D] Callicles believes that he is merely saying openly what everyone thinks in secret. Our public defence of morality is simply a mask behind which we conceal our true motivation.

Callicles regards law as the effect of agreement made by the weak to defraud the strong. Conventional law supports a slave morality of equality; inequality is the law of nature. The strong for Callicles aren't just those who are physically stronger but those who have dominant wills or personalities like the *virtù* that Machiavelli discerned in Cesare Borgia. We can draw a line of intellectual succession from Callicles to Machiavelli to Stirner to Nietzsche to Sorel. Callicles is a stout defender of liberty, perhaps too stout, failing to differentiate it from licence. He prizes freedom as the complete absence of external constraint. For him, a freeman is one who can do and can say whatever it is he wants to do and say. Libertarianism endorses freedom too but recognises an intrinsic limit that differentiates liberty from licence. To be free is to be able to do whatever it is one chooses, provided that in so doing one does not entrench upon the like liberty of others. Callicles seems to deny the limiting libertarian condition of zero-aggression.

In addition to the foregoing well-known Sophists, there is a small group of not so well known Sophists that includes Prodicus, Antisthenes, Alcidamas and Lycophron. Prodicus was an Ionian, from Ceos. He was born around 470-460 BC and came to Athens as an ambassador from Ceos. Socrates describes himself as a pupil of Prodicus in the art of drawing fine verbal distinctions (see *Protagoras*, *Meno* and *Charmides*) and in the *Hippias*, he calls him his friend, with what degree of sincerity, one may perhaps question. Prodicus seems to have been concerned, like Confucius, with the rectification of names. 'To Socrates,' writes Guthrie, 'correct language...was the prerequisite for correct living and even efficient government, and it may well be that this truth first dawned on him while listening to the one-drachma discourse of Prodicus.' [Guthrie, 276] Antisthenes was a pupil of Socrates and reputed to be the teacher of Diogenes and founder of the Cynic school. Before associating with Socrates, he had been a pupil of Gorgias. He seems to have been attracted by Socrates's asceticism, an attraction that would give credence to his being credited as the founder of the Cynics, though this claim is doubtful. Alcidamas was a native of Elaea near Pergamo and a pupil of Gorgias. He is well known for his assertion, quoted by Aristotle in his *Rhetoric*, that God made men free and thus no man is by nature a slave. [1373b18] The most interesting of this miscellaneous group is Lycophron a pupil of Gorgias who held a 'night watchman' view of the state that is startlingly modern. He held that the *polis* exists merely to prevent crime and to guarantee each man's right against all others.

Despite their individual differences, one particular way in which the Sophists as a whole differed from thinkers such as Plato and Aristotle was in their understanding of the relative importance of the individual and the *polis*. 'The Sophists,' Rommen remarks, 'started from the freedom of the individual, who had to be liberated from traditional religious and politico-legal bonds.' [Rommen, 14] For Plato and Aristotle, the *polis* was 'the great pedagogue, against which, strictly speaking no natural, subjective right of the citizen could be admitted. They acknowledged no goal of man that transcends the ideal polis. They remained state socialists.' [Rommen, 17]

Notes

1 Cyril Parkinson notes, however, the credulity of many scholars in their subscription to the 'surprising widespread belief that the Athenians were the inventors of democracy. That they were nothing of the kind is tolerably clear. What we owe to the Athenians is not the thing itself or even its name but the earliest detailed account of how a democracy came into being.' [Parkinson 1958, 168]

2 See Oakley 2010, 6-7; and de Coulanges, passim, in particular 352-359.

3 This urban centre was typically surrounded by walls and was big enough to accommodate about half of the population of the *polis*. [see Ober 2015, 7]

4 Nicholson, 26; see also de Coulanges, passim.

5 'In the first place,' remarks Leonard Cottrell, 'his [the Pharaoh's] function was fundamentally religious....To the Ancient Egyptians, their King was not a human being but a god, the son of Amun-Re himself.' [Cottrell, 165, 166] 'On his accession to the throne,' writes Thomas Schneider (quoting Erik Hornung), 'the king became "a human in the role of a god", the successor on earth of the god Horus "upon the throne of (the god) Geb."' [Schneider, 323]

6 'Classical Greece was not a state or a nation; it was an extensive social ecology of many independent city-states with citizen-centered governments.' [Ober 2015, xv] Hansen & Nielsen's magisterial *Inventory of Archaic and Classical Greek Poleis* lists over a thousand *poleis* scattered around Greece, Sicily and the south of Italy, Asia Minor and elsewhere.

7 The population of the Greek *poleis* taken all together did not exceed nine million.

8 At 1,000 square miles, Athens was about one third the size of my home county of Cork which nobody, except the most insanely chauvinist of Corkmen with an inverted inferiority complex (a Corkman with an inferiority complex is one who thinks he is just as good as any other man) would today consider a viable independent political entity.

9 Cleisthenes's reforms, writes Josiah Ober, 'introduced novel features that reconceptualized Athenian citizenship on a federalist model....Under Cleisthenes' reformed constitutional order, 139 villages, towns, and neighborhoods of Attica were designated "demes." An average deme had a free adult male population of 150-250....Each Athenian was thus treated as a citizen at different levels: locally in his deme and at the federal level of the polis....Two intermediate levels of belonging connected the demes

to the federal state. Citizens of each deme were assigned to one of ten newly created artificial "tribes."…
Several geographically contiguous demes…constituted a *third* of a given tribe. Each tribe was made up
of three roughly equal-sized thirds located, respectively, in the coastal zone of Attica, the inland zone,
and the city or its immediate suburbs. Each tribe was, there, regionally diverse in its membership.' [Ober
2015, 162, 164]

10 Parkinson 1958, 172. The Council of the Areopagus was a body that exercised a fluctuating but
generally aristocratically-inclined authority from the archaic period through to the period of Roman
political domination. Ober remarks that the Areopagus 'whose membership was drawn from ex-
magistrates, continued to play a significant role for a long generation after the reforms.' [Ober 2015,
166]

11 de Coulanges, 283; see Ober 2015, 224.

12 Aristotle *Politics*, VI, 4; 1319b22-2.

13 *Politics*, 1294b6-10. 'Democracy,' writes Aristotle in his *Rhetoric*, 'is that constitution in which
offices are assigned by lot. Oligarchy that in which they are assigned by men of property and aristocracy that in which they are assigned by those of upbringing….Monarchy is, as its name suggests, the
constitution in which one man is master of all; of this there are two kinds, that with a certain regularity
being kingship and that without limits being tyranny….the purpose then, of democracy is freedom, that
of oligarchy is wealth, that of aristocracy has to do with education and customs, and that of tyranny is
security.' [Aristotle 1991, 102, 1365b32-1366a6]

14 van Reybrouck, 67. In late medieval times, the Italian city-states of Venice and Florence had robust
sortitional systems which were exported to Parma, Ivrea, Brescia and Bologna (Venice), and Orvie-
to, Siena, Pistoia Perugia and Lucca (Florence). A sortitional system was also used in parts of Spain.
[see van Reybrouck, 73ff.]

15 See Guthrie, 27-54; Kerferd, 24-4.

16 Salomon, 131, cited in Guthrie.

17 The *locus classicus* for anyone interested in investigating the theory of persuasive speech is Aristotle's *Rhetoric*. [Aristotle 1991] Unlike his teacher Plato, for whom rhetoric exemplified everything that
was rotten about the Sophists, Aristotle recognised the practical value of rhetoric as the art of finding
and using the available means of persuasion. 'How,' asks Hugh Lawson-Tancred, 'can a man who, for
a significant phase of his formation, shared his master's opposition to rhetoric have in maturity composed a masterpiece of the formal study of rhetoric?' He did so 'to counterbalance the effectiveness of
rhetoric as a form of tertiary education as established by his rival Isocrates.' [Lawson-Tancred, 7] That
may well be so, but Aristotle's interest in rhetoric was more than merely practical or a matter of disciplinary one-upmanship. He liberated rhetoric 'from its place as a purely instrumental art: the highest
rhetorical accomplishment, for Aristotle, was an expression of *aretē*, or virtue.' [Leith, 30] Like many
of Aristotle's works, the *Rhetoric* can be heavy going but it is worth the effort required to read it. Two
very readable recent works provide an entry route to an understanding of this invaluable art: Sam Leith's
You Talkin' to Me? takes the reader systematically through the structural aspects of rhetoric whereas
Mark Forsyth's *The Elements of Eloquence* presents the techniques of rhetorical figures in an amusingly
self-exemplifying way.

18 Robinson, in O'Grady, 21.

19 *Troilus and Cressida*, Act I, Scene 3.

20 For a formal analysis of the concept of law that should be of particular interest to those concerned
with liberty, see van Dun 2009.

21 'The folkways are the "right" ways to satisfy all interests, because they are traditional, and exist in
fact,' writes William Graham Sumner. 'The "right" way is the way which the ancestors used and which
has been handed down. The tradition is its own warrant.' [Sumner, 28]

22 See Aristotle, 1253b20-23; 1255a3-12.

23 Though the term *phusis* is generally (and correctly) translated as 'nature', when contrasted with
nomos (law or convention) it may on occasion be rendered as 'reality.' [see Guthrie, 55]

24 See Shortridge, passim; Guthrie, 55-134.

25 Sabine, 32. Another set of ways to characterise the distinction between *nomos* and *phusis* comes
from John Walter Beardslee. He gives us four possible contrasts: *phusis* as normal behaviour as distinct
from *nomos* as erratic behaviour; *phusis* as indicating a class of self-moving things in contrast to things
moved by external factors (*nomos*); and *phusis* as reality in contrast to *nomos* as opinion. The fourth
contrast, that between *phusis* as one's natural character as distinct from *nomos* as one's character modified by one's social environment, is also germane to our concerns. [see Beardslee, 70; 76-77]

26 Rommen goes so far as to use the word 'libertarian' to characterise some aspects of Sophist thought, remarking that the Sophists' 'libertarian ideology, directed in the name of the natural law against law and custom, called into question the value of the *nomoi*.' [Rommen, 11]

27 DK 80: 1; Freeman, 125; see Schiller, 105, 159.

28 F. C. S. Schiller presents Protagoras as a proto-Pragmatist, writing that he 'proclaimed the universal right of every man to find his own truth, and was martyred for making man the measure of all things by the Athenian oligarchs....' [Schiller, 105; see also 159, 162]

29 DK 87; Freeman, 144-53; see Barker, 95-98.

30 Thucydides 2013, V, 105 (2), 382. In the Penguin translation this passage reads: 'Our opinion of the gods and our knowledge of men lead us to conclude that it is a general and necessary law of nature to rule wherever one can. This is not a law that we made ourselves, nor were we the first to act upon it when it was made. We found it already in existence, and we shall leave it to exist for ever among those who come after us.. We are merely acting in accordance with it, and we know that you or anybody else with the same power as ours would be acting in precisely the same way.' [Thucydides 1957, 404-405]

31 See Siedentop, 31-32; see also d'Entrèves 1967, 15-20, and Parkinson 1958, 176-177.

Chapter 3

PLATO: FROM KALLIPOLIS TO MAGNESIA

The human race will have no respite from evils until those who are really philosophers
acquire political power or until, through some divine dispensation, those who rule and
have political authority in the cities become real philosophers
—Plato

If I wished to punish a province, I would have it governed by philosophers
—Frederick the Great

Plato's political programme, far from being morally superior to totalitarianism,
is fundamentally identical with it
—Karl Popper

Students coming to philosophy for the first time typically 'do' Plato's most
well known work, the *Republic*, often in their first year of studies; whether
they ever read it again is a moot point, and that's assuming that they have in
fact read it in the first place and not just a summary of it or selected bits of it. In
contrast with the relative notoriety of the *Republic*, Plato's other major works
on political philosophy, the *Statesman* and the *Laws*, are almost completely
unread, unless by Plato specialists or those with a keener than usual interest
in ancient philosophy. In this chapter, I will give an account of all three of
these works, focusing not only on their content but also on the continuities and
discontinuities that run through them.

Plato was born in Athens into a wealthy and influential family around 427
BC and died in 347 BC at the ripe old age of 80. His real name appears to have
been Aristocles, 'Plato' merely a nickname referring, if the accounts are to be
believed, either to the breadth of his shoulders, the expanse of his forehead, or
the extent of his knowledge. His father, Ariston, was wealthy and his mother,
Perictione, was politically very well connected, being a sister of Charmides
and a niece of Critias, two men associated with the short-lived pro-Spartan
oligarchy called the Thirty Tyrants. (404-403 BC) A career in public life was
clearly open to him and, under normal circumstances, he probably would have
taken the road well travelled by his family. A number of events, however,
conspired to push him into a completely different career. The first significant
event that disturbed the even tenor of Plato's life was the outcome of the war
between Athens and Sparta. When the Peloponnesian war ended in defeat for
Athens, Plato was 23 years old. The Athenian defeat was a shock for the young
Plato who, along with many well-to-do citizens, was inclined to blame the
democratic rulers of Athens for it. 'The Peloponnesian war,' writes Trevor
Saunders, 'was one of the two major formative influences on Plato in his youth

and early manhood. He can hardly have failed to sense and share the bitterness and despair felt in Athens at the collapse and defeat of so many high ideals. Yet he was never an admirer of the Athenian democracy ...like many of the Athenians, he felt that Athens' defeat was the defeat of laxity and incompetence by Spartan discipline and good order.' [Saunders 1970, 19] It isn't unreasonable to conclude that this early bitter personal experience gave him distaste for involvement in the day-to-day world of practical politics, a distaste reinforced by his futile visits to Syracuse as a would-be political advisor to the Syracusan political elite, and helped to turn his attention to more theoretical matters.

Plato was influenced philosophically by the Pythagoreans, not least by their emphasis on the metaphysical significance of mathematics and what would now be recognised as a generally rationalist approach to philosophy. He also inherited from the Pythagoreans (and from Orphism) a non-standard conception of the soul as that which the individual person really was and not just a principle of life within the person or a shadowy post-death survival. 'It is reported of Plato,' writes Cicero, 'that he came into Italy to make himself acquainted with the Pythagoreans; and that when there, among others, he made an acquaintance with Archytas and Timæus, and learned from them all the tenets of the Pythagoreans; and that he not only was of the same opinion with Pythagoras concerning the immortality of the soul, but that he also brought reasons in support of it...'[1]

Without doubt, however, the single most important political and ethical influence on Plato wasn't the outcome of the Peloponnesian war and the humiliation of Athens, shocking though that was, but his encounter with Socrates. This encounter was to provide him with his basic philosophical outlook, that virtue is primarily a matter of knowledge, that no one knowingly does wrong and, above all, the conviction that what is really real isn't anything changeable and tangible, such as Minnie the moggie or your temperamental Mac, but something intangible and unchangeable—catness, rather than your psychotic cat, and Macness, rather than the ailing machine on your desk. Plato went on to develop Socrates's ideas in ways that Socrates himself perhaps never envisaged; we have no definite way to tell whether this is so or not because our ideas of what Socrates said and did are largely derived from Plato, the only other accounts we have of Socrates coming from Aristophanes's comedy *The Clouds* (amusing but scarcely historically reliable!) and Xenophon's *Memorabilia*. Whatever the ultimate truth of the matter in terms of particular details, no one denies that Plato was influenced by Socrates and was himself, in turn, through the Academy that he founded, a significant influence on Aristotle and on the whole of subsequent Western philosophy.

Plato left us an unparalleled body of philosophical work in his dialogues covering just about every area of philosophy—epistemology, metaphysics, ethics, philosophy of language and philosophy of science. The pre-eminence of Plato in philosophy is such that the twentieth century philosopher, Alfred North Whitehead, notoriously remarked that 'The safest general characterization of the European philosophical tradition is that it consists of a series of footnotes to Plato,' which, if true, hasn't altogether been an unmixed blessing. [Whitehead,

39] The al division of his dialogues is into early, middle and late, though some commentators insert a transitional category between the early and middle. Whether or which, the overall chronology of the dialogues isn't seriously in dispute. The early dialogues would include the *Crito*, the *Euthyphro* and, perhaps most famously, the *Apology*, an account of Socrates's last moments before he drinks the hemlock. The middle dialogues include the *Phaedo*, the *Theaetetus* and, a dialogue that will be of major interest to us, the *Republic*. Some see this dialogue as coming early in Plato's middle period with some parts of it (Book I) belonging to the early Plato. The late dialogues include the *Timaeus*, the *Sophist* and the *Statesman*, the *Philebus* and the *Laws*. Of these later dialogues, two—the *Statesman* and the *Laws*—are of interest to students of politics.

It is important to remember when reading Plato that his dialogues are works of art, not monographs or treatises or lectures. As it happens, we have Plato's dialogues (all of them, it seems) but not the lectures he gave in the Academy. In contrast, when it comes to Aristotle, Plato's most famous student, we have his lectures or lecture notes but none of his other literary works. This accident of literary history tends to exaggerate the literary and, to some extent, philosophical differences between the philosophies of the two men perhaps more than would be justified if we had access to their entire body of work. None the less, despite the close connection between them, there are, as we shall see, real differences between the thought of the two men. In reading a literary work it is crucial to ask whose voice we are listening to. Just as in reading a novel, we wouldn't necessarily assume that the author is expressing his own views through the mouth of a particular character, so too we musn't assume that any particular character in the dialogues is speaking for Plato, not even Socrates. Some commentators take an extreme view on this topic and appear to believe that the dialogues are a mask for Plato's real views or, at best, a popular and perhaps superficial exposition of them. I would certainly not want to go as far as this. Despite the literary form of Plato's works, they have a clear didactic intent and I am going to take it, in agreement with most critics, that in them Plato is expressing his own views, primarily, though not necessarily exclusively, through the mouth of Socrates. The reason I say 'not necessarily exclusively through the mouth of Socrates' is that, after the early dialogues, Socrates tends to recede somewhat as the principal interlocutor and indeed does not appear at all in some of the dialogues of particular interest to us, such as the *Laws*.

Some readers are more impressed with the purely literary quality of Plato's dialogues than I am or have ever been. I have never found them particularly dramatic or the dialogue within them realistically reflective of actual conversations. Moreover, whatever liveliness we may or may not find in the early dialogues, this seems to evaporate almost completely by the time we come to the later ones. As Saunders puts it, 'In these late productions, philosophical analysis and exposition far outweigh dramatic interest,' which seems to me to be a very polite British way of saying that the later dialogues aren't particularly well written or stylistically engaging—a point even the most devoted Platonist would find hard to deny.[2]

THE *REPUBLIC*

Plato's *Republic* is, through and through, an anti-Sophist tract. Democracy, Plato thinks, is essentially mob rule and the Sophists are the facilitators of democracy. But Plato believes that only those who possess the requisite political expertise can and should rule for political expertise, as with any other form of expertise, isn't a matter of popular opinion. 'Fear of the people as a mob is at the back of Plato's distaste for Sophism,' writes J. S. McClelland. 'He never doubts that mob oratory can be taught. It is a very inferior science, but it is based on a psychology of the common man that is in all respects essentially true. The common man cannot think things out for himself and is therefore incapable of judging whether others have thought anything out properly; he does believe he can understand public affairs and will only listen to those who tell him that he can; he likes things put to him simply, and he likes simple answers to complex questions because he is really bewildered underneath his own self-confidence. *En masse* the common man is a great beast who needs to be stroked, fed, flattered and led by the nose.' [McClelland, 15]

The *Republic* begins with Socrates and his friends in Athens's seaport, the Piraeus, engaged, as usual, in intense conversation. The topic of justice emerges and Thrasymachus presents a version of the thesis that, whatever flattering unctions we may wish to lay to our souls, justice turns out to be whatever is to the advantage of the strong in society. Socrates attempts to confute him using the elenchic technique that is Plato's standard operating procedure in the early dialogues. The *elenchus* is a style of argument that works by getting one's interlocutor to exhibit his ignorance of that which he claims to know by showing that he is unable to give a coherent abstract account of it. Thrasymachus retires from the dialogue at the end of the first book but his arguments are taken over and refined by Glaucon and Adeimantus (Plato's brothers) and, for the first time in his dialogues, Plato's Socrates moves beyond the *elenchus* to put forward a positive account of his own.

The central proposition in Plato's thought about the state or *polis* appears to be that the mass of people do not know what is good for them, therefore, it is only right and proper that their lives be directed by those who *do* know what is in fact good for them, a point made subsequently in different ways by others such as Rousseau and Mill. [see Sowell 1987, 46-47] If this paternalistic idea sounds familiar and you haven't read Plato, perhaps the familiarity is to be accounted for by your hearing something similar elsewhere. In a famous, even notorious passage of his *Democracy in America*, Alexis de Tocqueville writes: 'Above this race of men stands an immense and tutelary power, which takes upon itself alone to secure their gratifications and to watch over their fate. That power is absolute, minute, regular, provident, and mild. It would be like the authority of a parent if, like that authority, its object was to prepare men for manhood; but it seeks, on the contrary, to keep them in perpetual childhood; it is well content that the people should rejoice, provided they think of nothing but rejoicing. For their happiness such a government willingly labors, but it chooses to be the sole agent and the only arbiter of that happiness; it provides for their security, foresees and supplies their necessities, facilitates their pleasures, manages their principal concerns, directs their industry, regulates the descent of property, and subdivides their inheritances; what remains, but to spare them all the care of thinking and all the trouble of living?' [de Tocqueville, 318]

This Platonic theme of ignorance, of false consciousness, of an agent's not knowing what it is he *really* wants, is a commonplace of much modern thought which can be found in, among other 'isms', Marxism, Freudianism, in German Idealism and its latter-day manifestations, and in the more 'advanced' forms of feminism.[3] The British Idealist Thomas Hill Green produced the following persuasive redefinition of 'freedom' in 1881: Freedom, he said, 'rightly under-stood[4]...does not mean merely freedom from restraint of compulsion....[it means]...a positive power or capacity of doing or enjoying something worth doing or enjoying...'[5] Here is a contemporary example. C. D. C. Reeve writes, 'brought up in a capitalist democracy, which arguably does not provide optimal conditions for developing one's needs, wants, and interests, a person may desire profit above everything else. The more he deliberates under the aegis of that desire, the clearer it may become that his desire is perfectly rational. Yet it may not be in his real[6] interest to make profit his goal. But to discover this he would have to begin deliberating already possessed of desires other than those he actually has. His desire for profit is deliberatively rational, then, but not crucially rational. Freedom to have and satisfy this desire is deliberative freedom not *critical freedom*, or the freedom to have and to satisfy only desires sanctioned by the critical theory of rationality.'[7] This, again, is a blatant attempt to justify paternalism. What are a person's *real* interests? *Who* is to determine what these real interests are? For Plato, the answer is clear—the ruler of the *polis*, the philosopher-king.

Why this combination of philosopher and king? To begin to answer this question, let us consider the idea of authority. We can think of authority as occurring in two modes. The first is the authority of the expert. Let us call this authority-E. You believe what your car mechanic tells you because he knows about cars and you do not or, perhaps more accurately, you *believe* that he has this knowledge. So too with your doctor and your dentist. They have authority and you believe what they tell you because you believe they know more than you do about a particular subject matter. Others, however, have an authority that isn't necessarily connected to any actual or reputed knowledge or expertise. It is merely a matter of social or political organisation and the role a person plays in that organisation. Let us call this authority-P. A policeman has this kind of authority. He may be an idiot or a genius—it doesn't much matter which—either way he has authority. It is possible to have neither kind of authority; or authority-E in some specific area without authority-P; or author-ity-P in some respect without authority-E; or, in rare cases, both authority-E and authority-P. What is unique about Plato's account of political authority in the *Republic* is that he conflates both kinds of authority. One has, or should have, authority-P only if one has authority-E. Political authority isn't, then, a matter of having the ability to use force (à la Thrasymachus) or a matter of cajoling the mob into deferring to you by means of your flattery or your promises; in the end, it's a matter of possessing the requisite kind of expertise.

Not all philosophers must be kings (indeed, not all philosophers could be kings) but all kings must be philosophers.

What kind of knowledge or expertise is it that our would-be rulers must possess? They must know how things really are, as distinct from how they merely appear to be. Plato's ideal of objective knowledge was mathematics, a study that, in many of its branches, deals with ideal types that cannot necessarily be instantiated in the real world. My secondary school mathematics teacher once drew what looked to us like a triangle on the blackboard and asked us what it was. Puzzled, and suspecting a trick question, we responded, 'It's a triangle!' 'Really?' he said. 'What's the definition of a triangle?' 'A plane figure bounded by three straight lines,' we answered. 'Right' he said, 'and the definition of line is…?' 'Length without breadth.' 'So,' he asked 'don't the 'lines' I have drawn on the board have breadth? How would you be able to see them if they didn't? And if they have breadth, they can't be lines. And if they're not lines, what I have drawn on the board isn't a triangle. You cannot see a triangle! Not because of some defect of vision; it's just not the kind of thing you can see.' In the *Republic,* Plato attempts to come up with an account of the state that is ideal in the same way that the triangle is ideal. He wants to know what a state has to be in order to be a state and what a good state has to be in order to be a good state, regardless of the messy details of contingent human experience.

Plato gives us two well-known images to illustrate this point: the allegory of the cave, and the image of the divided line.

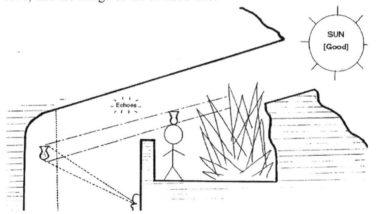

In the cave, the unenlightened prisoners are held in position so that all that they can see are the shadows cast on the back wall of the cave by objects placed behind them lit by the artificial light of a fire. If they were to free themselves, stand up and turn around, they would see the objects whose shadows had formerly been their only source of information. But if they were to leave the cave altogether, they would realise that everything that took place within the cave occurred in a world of shadow and darkness compared with the radiant outside world illuminated by the sun. Plato believes that in our everyday lives we are all, as it were, cave dwellers. In our world of everyday experience, we see shadows, reflections and images of objects and the objects that are the source of those shadows images and reflections. But the everyday changeable objects of our experience are what they are only because they embody certain unchanging elements (Forms) that are themselves stable and abiding. These Forms are the proper objects of real knowledge, as distinct from the products of mere belief or imagination. But even these Forms aren't the ultimate source of knowledge; that source is the Form of the Good which, in Plato's story, is the sun shining outside the cave, the ultimate source of all the light that illuminates all that is real.[8]

Plato gives us a somewhat less metaphorical account of the same issue in his image of the divided line. Draw a horizontal line. Divide it into two parts, one left, one right. Divide each of these parts in turn into two, one left, one right. The original division separates knowledge (on the left) from opinion (on the right) and the other divisions are sub-divisions within knowledge and opinion respectively. A is the realm of imagination and perception. Here, seeing is imagining both in respect of physical objects and in matters of morality. (see *Republic*, 514ff) B is the realm of common-sense beliefs where seeing is believing, without any reasoned grasp of the grounds we might have for those beliefs. C is the scientific realm in which we come to grasp by the use of our intellect the reasons for the beliefs and opinions we have in A and B (if there are any); and D is the highest realm of knowledge in which we grasp by rational intuition the ultimate reason for whatever is in fact physically and morally real. The rulers of Plato's beautiful city (*kallipolis*) will be those who have left the cave, those who have access to the highest level of the divided line, those who know, *really* know, what is true and beautiful and good—good in itself and good for us.

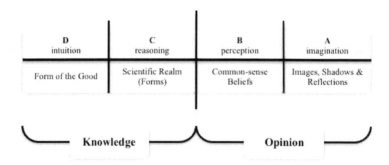

Plato begins his creation of *kallipolis* by noting that human beings need one another: 'The origin of the city…is to be found in the fact that we do not severally suffice for our own needs, but each of us lacks many things….As a result of this…we…gather many into one place of abode as associates and helpers, and to this dwelling together we give the name city or state do we not.' [*Republic* 369b-c] The creator of the city, then, is in a sense our human need for food, housing and clothes. In the course of this discussion, Socrates outlines an embryonic version of the principle of the division of labour and the principle of comparative advantage—it's better for us all if we do not all attempt to do everything for ourselves; and it is more productive if among the things we are good at we work at that which is best: 'Would one man do better at working at many tasks or one at one? ...more things are produced, and better and more easily when one man performs one task according to his nature, at the right moment, and at leisure from other occupations.' [*Republic*, 370b-c] C. D. C. Reeve believes that Plato accepts an 'unique upper-bound doctrine according to which a person's ruling desires set a distinct upper limit to his cognitive development....he also accepts the principle of quasi-specialization, which states that each person in the *kallipolis* must practise exclusively throughout life whichever of producing, guardianship or ruling demands of him the highest level of cognitive development of which he is capable...' [Reeve, 69] Such a city will need many specialists working at their professions. It will also need traders and, to facilitate trade, a market and money, and merchants. [*Republic*, 371b-c] All this seems perfectly reasonable but though such activities are necessary for a city to come into being, they aren't sufficient. Once our basic producers and traders are in place, there will arise a whole host of service providers and with the consequent increase in wealth, an increasing desire on the part of many for more and more wealth so that among the service providers we shall need specialists in the provision of security to protect our property from predation. The desire to possess more than we need thus gives rise to a class of people specialising in security. The existence of this class in turn gives rise to inordinate desire on the part of some to have more and more honour and respect. To hold this in check, we need another level of organisation: 'Unless...either philosophers becomes kings in our states or those whom we now call our kings and rulers take to the pursuits of philosophy seriously and adequately, and there is a conjunction of these two things, political power and philosophical intelligence...there can be no cessation of troubles...' [*Republic*, 473d] Looking then at the requirements of a state, Plato sees that three distinct kinds of service must be provided. The material necessities of life must be produced and distributed; those engaged in the practical activities of production or distribution, the producers, must be protected as they go about their business and that in itself is a specialist task which requires a distinct form of expertise—those who provide this service are called auxiliaries; and, finally, someone must exercise overall control over both producers and auxiliaries and direct the activities of all for the good of all, and these are the guardians of the state.

It is perhaps ironic that this highly intellectualised and paternalistic account of politics is derived from a sound analysis of the practical exigencies that force men into society in the first place. Plato notes correctly that the good life requires a division of labour so that we do not all have to spend all our time trying to do everything for ourselves. Moreover, if we are to make the best of things, we should, to the extent that it is possible, do more or less exclusively that at which we are most competent. So, just as we get our shoes from a shoemaker and not the butcher because the shoemaker is the one who really knows how to make shoes, so too, we should get our government from those who really know what the good for man is, and not some second rate amateur. This bottom-up account of the origination of society is largely agreeable to lovers of liberty for it implies that social life is natural to man and that our natural condition isn't, as Hobbes or Machiavelli would have it, a war of all against all. The problem with Plato's account comes, however, with his conclusion that statesmanship or governance requires a special kind of intellectual knowledge which only some people have and that they are to exercise governance just as the shoemaker is to be allowed to get on with making shoes. Plato wants us to believe, then, that his account of the ruler is no different in essence from his account of every other specialist in society.

It may occur to you that there is one obvious disanalogy between Plato's correct account of the division of labour and comparative advantage and his account of the ruler of the state, which is that our dealings with shoemakers and suchlike are voluntary but our dealings with states are not. We enter into arrangements for the purchase or repair of shoes voluntarily and we can alter those arrangements voluntarily. Not all shoemakers are equally competent or equally reasonable in their charges, nor is there one and only one shoemaker available to all. If the analogy were pursued thoroughly, we would have contingent arrangements with our rulers, subject to change or alteration as necessary. Rulers would vary in their abilities and competences and their charges and there could be more than one ruler at our disposal.

Plato in the *Republic* is notorious for advocating what has come to be called 'the noble lie', this being deemed to be a kind of *realpolitik* procedure to deceive enemies and keep the lower classes in their places. Matters however aren't quite as simple as they first appear. The paradoxical-sounding true-lie, for Plato, is a verbal deception intended to bring about someone's true welfare, whatever that person may believe to be the case about that welfare.

This is a conception of truth-telling which is such that if the end or purpose of the literal untruth is the genuine good of the other, then we aren't only entitled to utter it but it may even be our duty so to do. Perhaps one way to think about the 'noble lie' is to think of it as a kind of constitutive myth that, although literally false, is none the less useful in bringing about the cohesion and solidity of the people in the city. 'The noble lie,' writes d'Entrèves, 'is now termed "ideology", or "myth", or "political formula".' [d'Entrèves 1967, 17] Can we think of anything in use in our own society that might correspond to this idea? Well, what about the idea of a 'nation', the conception that all the people living in a particular area with similar customs and language are, as it were, all part of the same family, all born (*natus*) from the same stock. This is literally not true. Even in clan systems such as that of Scotland, not everyone with the same last name was in fact descended physically from the same ancestor. But if you believe yourself to belong to the same nation as another, the nation being, as it were, a large family, you are likely to be better to disposed to accept quasi-family responsibilities towards that other, more so than you would towards a complete stranger.

In this context, C. D. C. Reeve has a typology that might be useful to bear in mind. He distinguishes between being the victim of a false ideology, having an ideology that's falsely maintained, and being ideology-free. You have a false ideology if you believe that you live in a good society when you don't and believe this because what you are told by your leaders is false; you have an ideology falsely maintained when you believe that you live in a good society and you in fact do, even though you believe this because of falsehoods told you by your leaders; and you are ideology-free when you believe you live in a good society and you in fact do, and your belief is sustained by a world-view that's in fact true. Being the victim of a false ideology is having the wrong beliefs for the wrong reasons; being the victim of an ideology falsely maintained is having the right views for the wrong reasons; whereas being ideology-free is having the right views for the right reasons (the fourth possibility—having the wrong views for the right reasons—seems to be an empty set!)

In the end, the acceptability of all this depends upon a certain conception of people at large, one that sees them as being, in effect, moral and political children. Just as we sometimes tell our children what isn't literally true (think of Santa Claus) and do so for their own good, so too the leaders in the ideal state will be permitted and may even be obliged to do the same to the masses. Even on the most charitable interpretation, this theory of the use of the true-lie by the state is reprehensible. It is clearly a form of paternalism and paternalism, outside the context of the family, can rarely be morally justified. As we shall see, this theme of the rulers knowing better than everyone else what is good for everyone else is a constant in Plato's thought. Even in the very late dialogue, the *Laws*, he puts forward an account of religion that is purely instrumental.

I think it is fair to say that Plato has the aristocrat's disdain for trade and commerce to an exceptionally high degree. One place in which this comes to be seen is in his treatment of his Guardians. They must be preserved pure and uncontaminated and so can have no connection with the mundane business of making a living. They must have no private property save what is indispensable. They will have no privacy, their houses being open to all. They are to receive just the right amount of food as a stipend and they will eat in a common mess. They will not dirty their hands with money: 'But for these only of all the dwellers in the city it is not lawful to handle gold and silver and to touch them nor yet to come under the same roof with them, not to hang them as ornaments on their limbs nor to drink from silver and gold.' [*Republic*, 417a] Reeve notes that such positions are repulsive to contemporary thought but he asks us to be a little understanding. Why would Plato come to such conclusions? He answers, because of his 'profound suspicion of the appetites, and the politically destructive potential of greed and self-interest.' [Reeve, 73] Unfortunately, this completely fails as a defence inasmuch as it simply erects another target for critical attack. Why should we think that greed and self-interest would *necessarily* lead to political destruction? They may—or, then again, they may not. It doesn't seem obviously absurd to argue that self-interest, suitably enlightened, might very well be the factor that forces men to associate with each other, as Plato himself might be taken to have suggested in the passage already quoted: 'The origin of the city…is to be found in the fact that we do not severally suffice for our own needs, but each of us lacks many things….As a result of this…we…gather many into one place of abode as associates and helpers, and to this dwelling together we give the name city or state do we not.' [*Republic*, 369b-c]

Whoever wants to defend Plato's account of the ideal state has a difficult task on his hands. Plato's state presents itself to us as being both repressive and authoritarian. Is this because that's the way it is or simply the way we judge it to be, given our preconceptions? The liberal conception of the state, to the extent that it has a place in modern thought, sees relatively little place for a state's active concern to implement by law and force a particular conception of the good. This isn't perhaps quite consistent with the facts given that the contemporary state is hardly neutral on many matters; rather, it's just that our leaders are unreflectively unaware that what they take to be neutral positions are, in fact, highly particular moral positions that stand in need of justification. Here I find myself in agreement with Reeve, though for substantially different reasons. He writes of the modern liberal neutral state: 'By seeking neutrality above all, the state may undermine certain conceptions of the good which, even though they do not illegitimately limit the freedom of others, cannot easily survive in a neutral state. Because of the extensive labour mobility necessitated by a free-market economy, for instance, those who want stable neighbourhoods, extended families, close ties between the generations, or collective living are likely to find it very difficult to achieve their goals within the state. From their perspective, the supposedly neutral state is biased against their conception of the good.' [Reeve, 77] Reeve and I are at one in thinking that the state cannot, in fact, be neutral. Where he and I part company is that I take this to be an argument for the limitation or even the dissolution of the state. I am not sure that he has any solution except a negotiated truce between different parties within the state with rival conceptions of the good.

Philosophers who take their inspiration from nineteenth century German thinkers tend to distinguish between mere freedom and autonomy. Mere freedom or instrumental freedom, which is the kind of freedom most people have in mind when the term is used, is our ability to choose to act in this way or that free from restraint, coercion or aggression. Never the less, our German-inspired philosophers think the exercise of such instrumental freedom may not in fact result in our choosing what we would have chosen had we a God's-eye view of what was really and truly fulfilling for us, and so its exercise can, they think, result in a diminution of our autonomy. 'Perhaps,' as Reeve puts it, 'the freedom we should be concerned about is the freedom to have and to satisfy desires we would choose to have if we were aware of the relevant facts, were thinking clearly, and were free from distorting influences.' [Reeve, 77-78] This, of course, is just another form of paternalism, hidden under the mantle of a philosophical distinction. Who is to determine what our counterfactual critical freedom requires? Who, if not the Guardians or their latter-day equivalents—the state or the *cognoscenti*? The passage just quoted from Reeve is very revealing. What is missing in mere instrumental freedom is knowledge instead of ignorance, clear thinking instead of confusion, and detachment from the exigencies of the real world instead of the immersive, messy and radically contingent experience that's our lot. In other words, we would all be better off if we were gods instead of men.

It is at this point that Plato draws his famous comparison between the state and the soul. Just as the state has three functions, so too, the human soul has three parts. It has a bottom-level part that concerns itself with our basic appetites and their satisfaction; another, spirited, part that's concerned with the provision of protection; and a third, intellectual, part that knows, thinks and directs the whole. Despite being famous (or notorious) this comparison is hardly used in any substantive way in the *Republic* and so I simply note it and move on. In fact, if anything, this comparison is somewhat limiting, a point made by George Sabine, when he writes, 'the parallelism assumed between mental capacities and social classes is a restricting influence which prevented him [Plato] from doing justice in the *Republic* to the complexity of the political problems under discussion.' [Sabine, 53]

What, then, are the practical implications of Plato's theory? Well, the Guardians, the rulers, aren't allowed to have any private property, land or money. They live life in common in a kind of barracks and eat together in military style. Marriage is abolished for them and in its place we have regulated and eugenic breeding. Plato makes the common pro-eugenic point that we devote more care and attention to the breeding of our animals than we do to the production of the future generation of human beings and, surely, he thinks, this casual approach cannot be justified! This proto-communistic lifestyle applies only to the Guardians (and Auxiliaries); the producers are exempt from these restrictions. There are two additional striking features of Plato's account that need mention. The first is that women are, by and large, treated in just the same way as men, and are expected to contribute to the state in more or less the same way. The other unusual feature of Plato's account is that he has nothing significant to say about slavery, this in a society in which slavery plays a central role. This is all the more striking when we consider that Aristotle feels it incumbent upon him not only to discuss slavery in his *Politics* but indeed to justify it.

It seems that some of Plato's more radical suggestions in the *Republic* may have been 'in the air' in Athens. There is, of course, the remarkable trio of comedies by Aristophanes—*Lysistrata*, *Thesmophoriazusae* and *Ecclesiazusae*—which are concerned with 'the woman question.' In the *Ecclesiazusae*, Aristophanes uses one of the characters, Praxinoa, to present a social programme that involves the communalisation of all property, food, money, and sex, and it isn't difficult to see this as a satirical anticipation or reflection of what we find in Plato's *Republic*. Something of the same kind is mentioned in a literary mode by Euripides, and historically or pseudo-historically by Herodotus about the Agathyrsi who, he writes, 'live in luxury and wear gold on their persons. They have their women in common, so that they may all be brothers and, as members of a single family, be able to live together without jealousy or hatred.' [Herodotus, 275 (IV. 104)]

A suspicion of family and property is deeply rooted in Plato and finds its way into his later works, the *Statesman* and the *Laws*, albeit in slightly different ways. Moreover, his ruling class, with its guardians of the republic and the sinisterly named Nocturnal Council of the Laws, displays a distinctly clerical-cum-military aspect. Private possessions, property and family are attachments that are likely to disturb the peace and tranquillity of the state. To any Athenian reading the *Republic*, the commonality of life required of the guardians, the prohibition of their use of money and, of course, their exclusion from trade or commerce, must have called to mind vividly an image of Sparta in which such restrictions or limitations were a well known feature.

Given that virtue is knowledge and that knowledge is the key to a good human life, education is and has to be pre-eminent. It should come as no surprise to learn that Plato demands that the state provide just such an education as is right and proper and that such education should be compulsory. Just as indiscriminate human breeding is to be reprehended, so too is the indiscriminate and disorderly way in which parents provide for the education of their children. The state requires virtue, virtue is knowledge, and knowledge comes from education so that state must control education. To lovers of liberty everywhere this account will come as no surprise. The modern state has made the provision and control of the educational curriculum a central part of its role. Students are educated in a state curriculum by teachers trained in a state-sponsored training establishment and what students are taught and the way in which they are taught it serves to make unquestionable the existence and nature of the state.

Let us return to our ideal state with its three classes of inhabitants: the Producers, the Auxiliaries and the Guardians. If the Guardians know what is really good in itself and for everyone, what need have we of laws? What need have we, indeed, of consent? If Plato is correct—and that's a big if—then we do indeed have no need of law. Law, which in Greek society meant largely custom and habit, was just another part of the grubby reality of day-to-day social life. If, however, we have a different conception of the good, a conception in which part of what it means to live a good life is to makes choices for oneself and to take responsibilities for those choices, then Plato's vision is less a vision than a nightmare. Indeed, reverting to a point made earlier, the whole ideal orientation of Plato's account, with its deliberate disdain for the murky reality of social and political life as it is in fact lived, is wrong-headed from beginning to end. A suspicion of something like this, albeit a grudging admission, is revealed by the later political works of Plato in which he attempts to provide an account of the second-best type of state, the first, for obvious reasons of practicality, not being available. He never really lets go of the vision of the state he outlines in the *Republic* but he ruefully accepts that such an ideal is scarcely capable of being realised, a conclusion for which lovers of liberty should be eternally grateful.

THE *STATESMAN* AND THE *LAWS*

The political theory of the *Republic* is a paradigm example of a top-down philosophy, starting in the empyrean heights of intellectual definitions and then proceeding downwards with, for the most part, a sublime disregard for the actualities of human social and political life. Indeed, as Sabine remarks, Plato's theory is 'far too much dominated by a single idea and far too simple to do justice to Plato's subject, the political life of the city-state.' [Sabine, 40] This might explain why he felt it necessary to return to the subject in a partial way in the *Statesman* and at great and tedious length in the *Laws*. Truth to tell, the *Statesman*, despite its name, isn't so much a treatise on politics or statesmanship as it is an exercise in Platonic dialectic with the statesman as the object of its dialectical search. We will take from it what we can, concentrating most of our effort on the *Laws*. I might mention once again that it is generally agreed that the literary quality of these later works, in particular that of the *Laws*, is far below that of the *Republic*; in fact, on first reading, it is hard to believe that the two dialogues are by the same author. The *Laws* is a dialogue more in name than in reality, lacking dramatic power, being in fact more a lecture than a literary work. It is very long and very hard to read but, despite this, within the mass of ore that it contains, there are some real nuggets of Platonic genius that are worthy of consideration. Yet another reason for paying some attention to the *Laws* is that Aristotle's work in his *Politics* is a critical continuation from Plato's later work rather than from his earlier. That being so, given the seminal importance of Aristotle's work on politics, it helps to have some understanding of what Plato gets up to in these later dialogues.

The *Statesman* is a late Platonic dialogue whose interlocutors are a young Socrates, the stranger from Elea and a mathematician, Theodorus. Truth to tell, there isn't very much dialogue about it; it's really more of a monologue lacking the conversational liveliness of many of the earlier Platonic texts. This is all the more ironic as a sub-theme of the dialogue is the idea of the dialectic, the art of hunting down one's intellectual quarry, truth, by means of careful analysis and the drawing of significant distinctions. Statesmanship, or kingship, turns out to be a form of knowledge. Those familiar with Plato's thought won't be surprised at this although the form of knowledge relevant to the statesman isn't without its practical dimension. The statesman's knowledge turns out to be the kind of knowledge that a herdsman has, the ability to care for his herd. A salient difference between, say, a shepherd and a statesman is that in the case of the latter, the herder and those who are herded are of the same species whereas very few sheep interview for the job of shepherd. Another important different is that the statesman isn't concerned with the total care of his charges but only with a partial form of this practical art, namely, the ruling of cities.

The metaphor shifts from sheep to their wool so that the statesman is now to be compared to a weaver. Plato gives an account of the different forms of political rule that's uncannily like that which will be given by Aristotle in the *Politics*. We can have rule by the one, by the few or by the many. In each of these cases, the rule can be lawful and voluntary or lawless and violent. Rule by the one, then, is either kingship or tyranny; rule by the few is either aristocracy or oligarchy. Interestingly, Plato refuses to distinguish terminologically between legitimate and illegitimate rule by the many, calling both cases democracy indiscriminately! Since the task of the statesman is based on knowledge rather than on experience artfully developed, it turns out to be irrelevant whether or not those subject to the rule of the statesman give their consent to such rule or not, just as in being treated by a physician, what is important is the physician's knowledge of health restoration and not the patient's views on the matter. What really counts is whether the rule of the statesman really benefits the public at large and if this requires some tactical executions or banishments then so be it.

We might be somewhat shocked by this apparent *realpolitik*, and Socrates *is* shocked—but not so much by the suggestion that strong-arm tactics might be resorted to by the statesman as by the idea that rule without laws might be in order. The Eleatic Stranger makes the point that laws are somewhat over-rated, given that they are of necessity crude and general, whereas the living intelligence of the wise is flexible, adaptable and can always take account of circumstances. One bad thing about laws, the Stranger thinks, is that they might be held to circumscribe the actions of the one possessing the kingly art. All this being so, it is better to have the lawless rule of the one rather than the lawless rule of the few or the many. On the other hand, a law-abiding rule of the many is inferior to the law-abiding rule of the few, which, in turn, is inferior to the law-abiding rule of the one. What the Eleatic stranger really wants is for our statesman to have the power to dispense with laws whenever he judges it wise to do so. Where does the weaver image fit into all this? Well, the task of the weaver is to combine the warp and the woof and to make cloth by keeping the tension right between the various strands. Similarly, the statesman's role is to keep the various elements in the *polis* in a kind of creative tension.

Unlike the *Republic*, the *Statesman* seems unconcerned with detailing the ideal state, being more concerned with delineating the knowledge-based character of the ideal ruler. Nevertheless, those who know what is good for us better than we know ourselves are to be conferred with the power to act, ruthlessly if necessary, but always for our good. We saw that Plato, in the *Republic*, thought of governance as a special task to be allocated to those with the right kind of knowledge. If there are any such, then we have no need of law or rules. We have those who know in charge and they will make the right decisions for all in the right way to the right degree and the right time. 'The fundamental difference between the theory of the *Republic* and that of the *Laws*,' writes Sabine, 'is that the ideal state of the former is a government by specially chosen and specially trained men, quite untrammelled by any general regulations, while the state sketched in the latter is a government in which law is supreme, ruler and subject alike being subject to it.' [Sabine, 68]

Putting laws back into a central position in the state isn't, however, a minor addition, which can be accommodated without much readjustment to the overall theory laid out in the *Republic*; it requires a major re-think of Plato's whole approach. 'If the line of reasoning followed in the *Republic*…was sound,' writes Sabine, 'there was no place in the state for law. Conversely, if a place had to be made for law, then there was nothing for it but to modify profoundly the whole philosophical structure and to admit principles which, to say the least, would greatly complicate it.' [Sabine, 70] Even so, Plato never explicitly abandoned his *Republic* position and some commentators argue for an essential continuity between his earlier and his later work. [see Saunders 1992, passim] Even as late as the *Laws*, Plato argues that law is essentially a blunt instrument that is insufficiently flexible to accommodate the fine details of individual circumstances so that it would still be better overall to have a competent ruler unbound by laws if such could be found. And that, of course, is the rub. By the time he comes to write the *Laws*, Plato seems to have despaired of ever finding such a ruler, assuming that he had ever thought it a realistic possibility. Metaphysically, the divide between the ideal state governed by those who know and the second-best state governed by laws is a mirror image of the divide between true knowledge, which is of the permanent and unchanging Forms, and sense perception, which is an apprehension of the ever-changing everyday world. The law belonging to the inferior side of this division would have been clearer in Plato's day where law was essentially the contingent outcome of custom and habit rather than the legislative product of professional legislators.

By the time Plato came to write the *Statesman*, he has still not abandoned the *Republic*'s theory of the ideal state as the one ruled by those who know what is truly good and who are empowered to bring men to desire that good even against their natural wishes and desires. Even so, though still thinking that the *Republic*'s theory is the best, he is prepared to put forward a second-best, an account that comes to fruition in the *Laws*. Justice, by which Plato means giving and expecting from each man his due, is still the prime virtue but it is to be developed not by the wise rule of those who know but by laws which embody, in a detached and static way, the wisdom that would characterise the ideal ruler, if we could ever find such. As grudging and inconsistent as the *Laws*' account may be, it is none the less a revolutionary change in method for Plato involving, as it does, an acceptance of the reality of the non-ideal, of the changeable and impermanent.

As already mentioned, the *Laws* is a long, very long, and not particularly well written dialogue, even by the relatively low literary standards of the late dialogues. Its first two books review the Spartan and Cretan codes of law, which explains why the Athenian Stranger's interlocutors are a Cretan and a Spartan. Having reviewed the codes of Crete and Sparta, Plato begins his own account by giving us a sort of conjectural history of how men came to live together in society. The story he tells here—a move from a state of nature to society, from simplicity to complexity, from individuals to families to villages to the *polis*—is nothing very remarkable in itself but it does have the distinction of being one of the first of its kind. Power, or more properly, authority, may be located in various more or less natural relationships—parents and children, age and youth, free and enslaved, noble and peasant, strong and weak, the elected and the rest and, not least important, the wise and the ignorant—with the first in each pair being taken to exercise authority and (legitimate) power over the second. The last of these pairs is the source of the authority that Plato would have instantiated in his ideal city which he now thinks is practically unattainable so that his task is now to devise a state which accommodates the various possible authoritative relations in some combination which best realises justice.

In the *Republic*, Plato disbarred his Guardians from the possession of private property and money and from the exercise of trades or engagement in commerce because of the corrupting and distorting effect such things would have on their ability to rule. His basic approach in the *Laws* isn't wholly different except that he has come, reluctantly, to accept the necessity of property and family to any actual society. If we cannot have a communistic system then we will have an equal division of land that cannot be further divided or alienated so that no one may accumulate more than the original allotment. Manual labour is still unbefitting the freemen and women of this city and so we have the usual slaves to do such menial work. The exclusion of citizens from craft and commerce is still in place, such activities being undertaken by a class of resident aliens. In a curious anticipation of measures taken during the 1930s New Deal in the USA, citizens may not have gold or silver, only token money being permitted.

The complicated details of the various levels of governance such as the familiar Guardians (of the law) and the operations of the Nocturnal Council need not concern us save to say that as might be expected, the result of the complicated system is to give relatively more power to the wealthier of the citizens of Magnesia, Plato's imagined new city, within the severe limitations on wealth that obtain in this society. It seems reasonably clear that the Nocturnal Council, untrammelled by the restraints of law, is a kind of second-best substitute for the philosopher-king of the *Republic* and as such, in conflict with the overall thrust of the *Laws*.

The emphasis on education, so much a theme of the *Republic*, is found also in the *Laws*. The poets are still under suspicion, women are to be educated equally with men, and state sponsored and state regulated education is compulsory for all. Religion has an important role to play in the society of the *Laws* but it is a civic and frankly utilitarian religion that supports and validates the state by providing a basis for morality. Such a religion has three central tenets: that the gods exist; that they are concerned with our conduct; and, significantly, that they cannot be, as it were, bought off from exercising judgement on us by prayer and sacrifice. To deny any of these tenets is to be guilty of atheism and atheists are to be subject to severe punishment.

Perhaps the most alarming section of the *Laws* for a lover of liberty is the section on punishment. Plato took from Socrates the doctrine that no one knowingly does wrong; that being so, the actions of wrongdoers must originate in ignorance. The cure for ignorance is education or re-education so wrongdoers in Magnesia won't be punished but rather cured.[9] This sounds all very caring and concerned until one realises that those who refuse to be re-educated or are deemed incapable of being re-educated are to be killed! Plato's account, enlightened as it may sound, can be every bit as savage as more openly retributive theories of punishment. C. S. Lewis clearly expressed the problem with the Platonic 'therapy instead of punishment' approach to wrongdoing when he wrote:

> According to the Humanitarian theory, to punish a man because he deserves it, and as much as he deserves, is mere revenge, and, therefore, barbarous and immoral. It is maintained that the only legitimate motives for punishing are the desire to deter others by example or to mend the criminal. When this theory is combined, as frequently happens, with the belief that all crime is more or less pathological, the idea of mending tails off into that of healing or curing and punishment becomes therapeutic. Thus it appears

at first sight that we have passed from the harsh and self-righteous notion of giving the wicked their deserts to the charitable and enlightened one of tending the psychologically sick. What could be more amiable? One little point that's taken for granted in this theory needs, however, to be made explicit. The things done to the criminal, even if they are called cures, will be just as compulsory as they were in the old days when we called them punishments. If a tendency to steal can be cured by psychotherapy, the thief will no doubt be forced to undergo the treatment. Otherwise, society cannot continue. My contention is that this doctrine, merciful though it appears, really means that each one of us, from the moment he breaks the law, is deprived of the rights of a human being. The reason is this. The Humanitarian theory removes from Punishment the concept of Desert. But the concept of Desert is the only connecting link between punishment and justice. It is only as deserved or undeserved that a sentence can be just or unjust. I do not here contend that the question 'Is it deserved?' is the only one we can reasonably ask about a punishment. We may very properly ask whether it is likely to deter others and to reform the criminal. But neither of these two last questions is a question about justice. There is no sense in talking about a 'just deterrent' or a 'just cure'. We demand of a deterrent not whether it is just but whether it will deter. We demand of a cure not whether it is just but whether it succeeds. Thus when we cease to consider what the criminal deserves and consider only what will cure him or deter others, we have tacitly removed him from the sphere of justice altogether; instead of a person, a subject of rights, we now have a mere object, a patient, a 'case'. [Lewis 1987, 147-48]

It isn't really possible to express this point much more clearly than Lewis has done. In the end, the therapeutic theory of punishment consists in a refusal to recognise our freedom and takes from us, under the guise of an apparently gentler and more humane approach, the very thing that makes us human. We can be free and good, free and evil, but if we aren't free we can be neither good nor evil. In subscribing to the Socratic theory that evil cannot be chosen, Plato conflates a distinction between a subjective and an objective conception of the good. It is true, as Thomas Aquinas points out, that we act *sub ratione boni*, under the aspect of the good. At the moment of choice, what we choose is necessarily for us, at that moment, a good. This subjective conception of the good is conceptually irrefutable. Nevertheless, we know all too well that our choices, however subjectively good they may appear to us to be aren't always good objectively; hence the phenomenon of regret and remorse and, bathetically, the existence in advertising of post-sales reassurance. What is objectively good is that which contributes to our genuine flourishing as creatures with body and mind, the main outlines of which are known to anyone who has lived in the world for more than a few minutes and has reflected on his life.

Even if we are as interpretatively kind to Plato as possible, it is hard not to conclude that his political philosophy, whether early or late, is, to the eyes of modern man, proto-totalitarian. Taking politics to be an exact science and arguing therefore that those with scientific knowledge must rule, his method

is to conceive of a utopia and argue for its implementation. That this implementation will involve force and coercion does not deter him from his aim
for, after all, the rulers in such a utopia will know what is good for all. Not
everyone is prepared to accept a description of the political thought of Plato
as totalitarian. There is, Francis Oakley thinks, 'a great ideological gulf...
between the political views native to the world of the polis and those that...
were to rise to prominence in the early modern era....It is that very fact,
indeed, that helps explain the oddly anachronistic accusation of "totalitarianism" levied periodically against the ideal commonwealth whose lineaments
Plato evokes in the *Republic*, and even more vehemently against that quasi-
theocratic "second-best" commonwealth which he describes in the *Laws*.'
[Oakley 2010, 9] He concedes, however, that 'having endured the apocalyptic
rigors of twentieth century political life, it is understandable that we should
be chilled by the element of thought control that Plato envisaged, with his
provision for a "nocturnal council" of magistrates charged with the task of
punishing, by death if need be, any infringement of the law against impiety.'
[Oakley 2010, 9] Others are less sanguine than Oakley and suspect that the
implementation of Plato's utopian plans would rather lead to a dystopia, a
closed and repressive society: As Trevor Saunders notes, 'once you believe
that you can isolate some sort of 'absolute' moral aim, your great temptation
will be to make a root-and-branch reform of society whatever opposition you
encounter, and refuse to tolerate other views, which, *ex hypothesi*, are wrong.'
[Saunders 1970, 34.]

Francis Spufford, in his brilliant novel, history and fairy tale, *Red Plenty*,
remarks that 'Lenin's state made the same bet that Plato had twenty-five
centuries earlier, when he proposed that enlightened intelligence given absolute
powers would serve the public good better than the grubby politicking of
republics.' [Spufford, 269] He continues, 'the Soviet experiment had run into
exactly the difficulty that Plato's admirers encountered back in the fifth century
BC, when they attempted to mould philosophical monarchies for Syracuse
and Macedonia. The recipe called for rule by heavily-armed virtue—or in the
Leninist case, not exactly virtue, but a sort of intentionally post-ethical counterpart to it, self-righteously brutal....Lenin's core of original Bolsheviks, and the
socialists like Trotsky who joined them, were many of them highly educated
people, literate in multiple European languages, learned in the scholastic traditions of Marxism; and they preserved these attributes even as they murdered
and lied and tortured and terrorised. They were social scientists who thought
principle required them to behave like gangsters. But their successors...were
the most ambitious, the most domineering, the most manipulative, the most
greedy, the most sycophantic...' [Spufford, 271]

Millions of people have lost their lives because of some of the more insane
and nightmarish schemes of social engineering attempted by certain states in the
twentieth century. Despite the death and devastation created by such schemes,
some true believers, it seems, never learn. Steve Ascheim notes that '...for
countless intellectuals and supporters, the redemptive promise, the universalist,
utopian strain of Communism—so obviously lacking in Nazism—rendered

possible a mode of justificatory thinking they would never have dreamed of applying to Nazism. At the end of 1994 (!) a shockingly unrepentant Eric Hobsbawm, one of the century's great historians and a lifelong member of the Communist party, could still argue that the elimination of millions of people in the Soviet experiment was still justifiable in these terms: "Because in a period in which, as you might say, mass murder and mass suffering are absolutely universal, the chance of a new world being born in great suffering would still have been worth backing."' [Ascheim, 10; see West, passim]

In the interview with Michael Ignatieff in the *Times Literary Supplement* (1994) from which the Hobsbawn quote is taken, Ignatieff suggested, it would seem, increduously: 'What that comes down to is saying that had the radiant tomorrow actually been created, the loss of fifteen, twenty million people might have been justified?' to which Hobsbawm replied succinctly and unblushingly, 'Yes.'

Apart from the USSR's disastrous attempts at collectivisation and the death and devastation that it wrought, one may also recall China's ironically titled Great Leap Forward, the romantic 'villagisations' of Tanzania, Mozambique and Ethiopia and the killing fields of Cambodia. James Scott believes that these schemes are 'among the great human tragedies of the twentieth century, in terms of lives lost and lives irretrievably disrupted.' [Scott 1998, 3] Of course, we cannot blame Plato directly for these modern disasters but the kind of thinking that led to them is a lineal descendant of Plato's political thought.

So much for Plato; what of Aristotle?

Notes

1 Cicero 45 BC, 1: XVII; see also Aristotle 1928, 987a-987b and Ferguson 2011, 115-128.

2 Saunders, 1970, 22-23. As I noted earlier, the Greek word *polis* is often translated as 'city-state' or sometimes just 'state'. This is anachronistic since the state as we know it in the twenty-first century, or indeed as we have known it for the last 400 years, simply did not exist in Plato's time or, if it did, the *polis* wasn't that state. Ideally, we should keep the word *polis* untranslated and use it so throughout our account. This is scarcely feasible, however, given the amount of commentary that has accumulated on Plato's work in the last 2,000+ years. No irreparable damage will be done to our discussion provided the anachronism is borne in mind at all times.

3 In the case of the doctrine of false consciousness, the authority of Plato, Hegel, Marx and others gives an unwarranted philosophical weight to what is really nothing more than the fallacy of *ad hominem*.

4 The words 'true', 'real', 'right' are common warning indicators of an upcoming persuasive definition.

5 Green, 370-371; see also Sen 1999, 18.

6 Persuasive redefinition coming up!

7 Reeve, 78, emphasis in original.

8 For what many take to be a dramatic rendition of Plato's allegory, see the film, *The Matrix*. For philosophical reflections on this film, see the collection of papers edited by William Irwin. Many of the contributors to this collection make an explicit connection between the Matrix and Plato's Cave.

9 If this has a contemporary feel, it's because it encapsulates an essential aspect of contemporary social-ism. Dominic Raab notes that socialists tend to view the individuals 'as products of society, conditioned by background and limited by personal circumstances. Anti-social actions are more likely to be excused as a reflection of social conditioning or a deprived background. The state is more likely to be viewed, not as a necessary evil, but rather as a positive force for correcting social inequality.' [Raab, 171]

Chapter 4

ARISTOTLE

A man should live as he likes. This, [democrats] say, is the privilege of a freeman,
since…not to live as a man likes is the mark of a slave….
whence has arisen the claim of men to be ruled by none, if possible,
or, if this is impossible, to rule and be ruled in turn
—Aristotle

Animals are political for whom some single and common work comes into being for all….
Such are the human, the bee, the wasp, the ant, the crane.
Of these, some are under a leader (*hegemon*) and some are without rulers (*anarcha*)—
the crane and the genus of bees are under a leader,
while ants and thousands of others are without rulers
—Aristotle

Go to the ant, thou sluggard; consider her ways, and be wise:
Which *having no guide, overseer, or ruler,*
Provideth her meat in the summer, and gathereth her food in the harvest
—*Proverbs*

One of the delightful quirks of intellectual history is that whereas we have the dialogues of Plato but no record of his Academy lectures, we have Aristotle's lecture notes but none of his polished literary productions. Even though we have a substantial body of work from Aristotle, it still represents only a part of his overall corpus. From his dialogues, some of them on politics, all we have is a few quotations. The effect of this historical literary accident is to distort our perception of the two great philosophers of antiquity: Plato is the imaginative, insightful and entertaining literary artist, whereas Aristotle is the original dry-as-dust dull professor. 'Plato,' writes I. F. Stone, 'is the only philosopher who turned metaphysics into drama….No one reads Aristotle or Aquinas or Kant as literature.' [Stone, 4] Nor is this stylistic contrast all. Although there is some dispute as to whether some minor Platonic dialogues were in fact written by Plato (all his *Letters* are the subject of a lively authentic/inauthentic debate), no one seriously questions the authenticity of any of the major Platonic dialogues. By contrast, Aristotle's extant works are in various states of textual disarray. Some books, such as his *De Anima*, read from start to finish as a more or less coherent whole; others, such as his *Metaphysics*, are admitted by almost all to be a jumble of texts from different times and different original works, cobbled together into a factitious unity. The *Nicomachean Ethics* and *The Politics* are two of Aristotle's works that are significant for his political thought; the *Nicomachean Ethics* is, by general consensus, moderately jumbled whereas the text of the *Politics* is a structural mess. Whether the textually disordered state of the *Politics* is the result of Aristotle's inability to control his material (unlikely) or the result of historical transmission errors (much more likely), it isn't an easy text to give a coherent account of.[1]

ARISTOTLE VERSUS PLATO

Aristotle, a citizen of the *polis* of Stageira, was born there in 384 BC, some thirty five years or so before the area of which it was a part, the Chalcidice Peninsula,[2] was absorbed into the nascent Macedonian empire by Philip, king of Macedon. At the time of Stageira's absorption into Macedonia, Aristotle had already been living for over ten years as a metic (resident alien) in Athens where he was a student in Plato's Academy. Most Greek *poleis* not only restricted the status of citizenship to adult males (no women, no slaves, no children) but confined it to males descended more or less closely from those who were already citizens. 'The Athenians guarded the status of Athenian citizenship jealously,' writes Josiah Ober. 'Indeed, in 451 BCE a new law, passed by the assembly on a proposal sponsored by Pericles, restricted Athenian citizenship to people who could demonstrate that each of their parents had been an Athenian native. Mixed marriages (which had usually been of the form native Athenian male with non-native wife) were no longer recognized as legitimate. The male offspring of a mixed marriage was now legally a bastard. As such, he was ineligible to inherit an equal share in the family property or to be presented by his father before the demesmen as a candidate for inclusion in the ranks of the Athenians.' [Ober 2015, 200]

Given his close association for almost twenty years with Plato and the Academy, the question arises as to whether (and if so, to what extent) Aristotle's own work was influenced by or was produced in reaction to Plato's. Some Aristotelian scholars such as Werner Jaeger have a general interpretative theory that, simply put, sees Aristotle starting his philosophical life as a Platonist, gradually moving away from Platonism to develop his own distinct position.[3] Whether or not this is so, and it's hard to see how it couldn't be true at least to some extent, there are some significant differences between the two philosophers, none perhaps so important as their different philosophical methods. [see Sabine, 88-92]

Plato might be described as a 'unified theory' thinker; for him, all our knowledge is in principle subsumable under some one master principle or science, and mathematics is the paradigm form of knowledge. Aristotle, by contrast, could be described as a 'multiple theory' thinker. His views on methodology are given in a famous passage from the *Nicomachean Ethics* (which, incidentally, employs the *nomos*/*physis* distinction, familiar to us from the writings of the Sophists): 'Our discussion,' he writes, 'will be adequate if it has as much clearness as the subject-matter admits of, for precision is not to be sought for alike in all discussions, any more than in all the products of the crafts. Now fine and just actions, which political science investigates, admit of much variety and fluctuation of opinion, so that they may be thought to exist only by convention (*nomos*), and not by nature (*physis*) ....We must be content, then, in speaking of such subjects and with such premises to indicate the truth roughly and in outline, and in speaking about things which are for the most part true and with premises of the same kind to reach conclusions that are no better. In the same spirit, therefore, should each type of statement be received; for it is the mark of an educated man to look for precision in each class of things just so far as the nature of the subject admits; it is evidently equally foolish to accept probable reasoning from a mathematician and to demand from a rhetorician scientific proofs.'[4]

This contrast in methodology between Plato and Aristotle isn't a mere matter of taste. It fundamentally affects how they approach problems and the solutions they offer. Aristotle clearly recognises the contingent variability of human action, both in individuals and in groups. Given this, we can expect to educe just so much order and no more from individual and group human action. Aristotle thinks it foolish to demand more rigour from a given subject matter than it can provide, and human action, whether in ethics or politics, because of its variety and complexity will allow us to say what is so only for the most part and not necessarily so. Even if this does not match up to some abstract ideal of explanation, it's still worth pursuing. Unless one is somehow persuaded that only that which is mathematically certain is knowledge, the knowledge we can get in these practical areas is still an advance over ignorance. 'Human beings are inherently variable,' writes Carnes Lord, 'and to approach them in the spirit of the physicist or mathematician seeking to discover universal laws is to distort fundamentally the relevant phenomena.' [Lord, 120]

For Aristotle, then, we do not generate our basic theoretical principles by pure reflection and then impose them willy-nilly on each and every area of study regardless of content. Rather, we demand the level of precision that a given subject matter can sustain. In matters of human action, in practical matters, we cannot expect to obtain the kind of rigour that we demand and expect in mathematics. Even in Plato's own political thought, we can see him yielding to a pragmatic necessity to move from the rarefied theoretical purity of the *Republic* to the more breathable air of the second-best option of the *Statesman* and the *Laws* while still hankering after the ideal.

Just as in his *Metaphysics* Aristotle removes Plato's Forms from the transcendental realm and incorporates them in the things of this world, so too he takes Plato's ideal state and embodies it in the context of fourth century BC Greece. The Sophists, who were in some respects (but only in some) deconstructionists before their time, argued that justice was simply a matter of convention, varying from place to place and from time to time. Aristotle was unwilling to accept this view. On the other hand, he was also unwilling to accept the idea that there was or could be only one transcendent ideal political community. Just as the things around us are composed of matter and form—a certain stuff shaped or patterned in a particular way—so too, actual political structures are a combination of material factors (wealth, land, property) organised in a particular way that gives them their characteristic pattern or form or structure. Tony Burns remarks that one of Aristotle's aims in the *Ethics* 'is to provide a refutation of [the] Sophist claim that there is no such thing as natural justice and that all justice is merely conventional. On the other hand, however, Aristotle does not go the opposite extreme and advocate that justice is in its entirety something that is either natural or rational. He does not suggest that the principles of natural justice can provide a rational or ahistorical standard by means of which the positive law or the constitution of any society might be criticized. For in the context of Athenian politics, such a doctrine would have been just as radical as that of his Sophist opponents. It could, for example, have been used (and arguably *was* used by some) to condemn the institution of slavery.' [Burns, 95]

One key difference between Plato and Aristotle, then, has to do with the ideal nature of the state. We saw that for Plato a state governed by laws was a second best compromise, a concession to human limitations. For Plato the choice was disjunctive: rule by man or rule by law. For Aristotle, however, no necessary disjunction exists between rule by man and rule by law. The constitutional ruler rules with the consent and for the good of the ruled and is thus distinguished from the mere tyrant or benevolent despot who, even if he were to rule for the good of the ruled, wouldn't do so with their consent.

On this point, George Sabine remarks that 'The precise moral property which Aristotle means to point out is as elusive as the consent of the governed in modern theories, but no one can doubt its reality.' [Sabine 95] For Plato, wisdom resided in the expert, in the one who really knows. Aristotle, although he doesn't totally reject the idea that the best in society should rule, comes to appreciate what has been called 'the wisdom of crowds', the wisdom that is formed by the living community and embodied in reflectively appropriated custom, custom that isn't simply a matter of just doing whatever has been done before but a living vital activity that sheds the obsolete and adapts itself to the new. 'It is possible to argue, Aristotle says, that in the making of law the collective wisdom of a people is superior to that of even the wisest lawgiver....the reason of the statesman in a good state cannot be detached from the reason embodied in the law and custom of the community he rules.' [Sabine, 96]

As distinct from the modern liberal conception of the state, both Plato and Aristotle agree that it has as one of its functions the moral improvement of its citizens. This is understandable, at least in part, because for both thinkers, the *polis*, the city state, was that form of political organisation that was small enough to allow for the participation of all its citizens while being large enough to provide the conditions necessary not just for life but for the good life. Ethics, politics, custom and law all run together in the *polis*. In respect of a convergence of the political and the personal, the economic and the legal, the historical and the cultural, the contemporary nation-welfare-state is an attempt, an attempt I believe to be both futile and dangerous, to reproduce the *polis* on a gigantic scale. Requiring myth-making of heroic proportions and ignoring the intrinsic physical and demographic constraints of the Greek *polis*, the modern nation-state was a project doomed to failure from the start, all the more so when it added cradle-to-grave welfare to its ever expanding areas of concern. It remains to be seen whether the history of the mid- to late twentieth century has seen its apogee, and the history of the twenty-first century the beginning of its epitaph.[5]

POLITICS

I have pointed out before that the use of the English word 'state' to translate the Greek term *polis* is potentially misleading. This is particularly so in the case of Aristotle. The political entity that Aristotle talks about bears little resemblance to the modern state in either size, mode of governance, or status of citizenship. Only in their both being independent of other states (or *poleis*) can they be said to resemble each other. One of the sayings for which Aristotle is most well known is that 'man is a political animal.' As I. F. Stone notes, 'The English words *political animal* are, it is true, an exact and literal rendering of the Greek term, *zoon politikon*. But in English this conjures up the picture of a ward heeler[6] who spends his life in the seedy chores of a modern political machine.' [Stone, 9] A *polis* was a form of community (*koinonia*) whose constituent members had the right to control their own affairs by debate, discussion and by law making and enforcement.

If the liberal view of the state is that it is an instrument for coordinating and regulating the private associations that make up society, this is certainly not Aristotle's view. 'The very distinction between 'state' and 'society' is foreign to Aristotle's way of thinking,' writes Carnes Lord, 'the city cannot be identified with the state or a form of the state, and the "authoritative" quality Aristotle imputes to it has nothing to do with the juridical "sovereignty" that is essential to the modern conception of the state. Rather, it derives entirely from the circumstance that the city, and only the city, is comprehensively concerned with the comprehensive human good.' [Lord, 134] The *polis* is a kind of community (*koinonia*) among other forms of community and of these, it's the one that aims at the highest and most complete human good.

The household consisting of husband and wife and master and slave is the most elemental social unit and it provides for man's daily needs. The three relationships that obtain in the household are master-slave, husband-wife, and father-children, but Aristotle robustly denies that the master-slave and father-children relationships are a model for political or constitutional rule. The village, consisting of a number of households satisfies a greater range of needs than the family but still not all that is required. The *polis*, however, sets out to meet all human needs and its ultimate goal is the securing of the good life for man. Aristotle writes, 'When several villages are united in a single complete community, large enough to be nearly or quite self-sufficing, the state [*polis*] comes into existence, originating in the bare needs of life, and continuing in existence for the sake of a good life….Hence it is evident that the state [*polis*] is a creation of nature, and that man is by nature a political animal.'[7] He goes on to say that the *polis* is by nature prior both to the family and to the individual since wholes are prior to their parts. This priority is obviously a logical or conceptual priority, not a temporal one. The reason for this priority of the *polis* to all other forms of community is that neither the individual human being nor the household nor even the village is self-sufficing. The *polis*, however, *is* a self-sufficing community whose distinctive function is to make provision not just for human life but also for the good life. The *polis* is a natural entity in the same way as the household or the village is natural; it isn't an artificial or constructed entity. In such a *polis*, we have a union of people in almost all things that matter: in history, language, customs, laws, religion, music, art and culture. This contrasts with the modern liberal conception of the state as a kind of neutral common arena in which the inhabitants are guaranteed some minimal form of justice and law and in which their economic or contractual exchanges can be validated. [see 1280a24-1281a6]

The *polis* is natural inasmuch as the needs that find satisfaction in part in the other and temporally prior forms of community can only be completely satisfied by it. Aristotle has to meet opposition on two fronts to his assertion that the *polis* is a natural form of community whose citizens govern themselves. Against Plato, he denies that rule should be by a class of experts; against the Sophists, he denies that the ruler-ruled distinction is merely conventional. Among free and equal men, there appears to be no natural orientation of ruler and ruled; how then can governing take place? Since organisation of some kind is necessary for the good of the whole and since no one by nature in the *polis* is predestined to rule over another (as distinct say, from the father in the household) the citizens of the *polis* must be alternately ruler and ruled. All must govern and be governed in turn. That a ruler at any given time will, in turn, become one of those who are ruled tends to moderate any tendency towards tyranny and arbitrariness on his part and his rule will be such that it will tend on the whole to be for the good of those ruled rather than for himself.

In constitutional rule, then, citizens are ruled and rule in turn. There are, for Aristotle, situations in which a distinction between ruler and ruled naturally emerges: parents-children, husband-wife, and master-slave. A man governs his children by a royal rule. The rule of the freeman over the slave, remarks Aristotle, is different from rule over one's children or over one's wife, 'although the parts of the souls are present in all of them, they are present in different degrees. For the slave has no deliberative faculty at all; the woman has, but it is without authority, and the child has, but it is immature.' [1260a8-15] Political rule, however, is predicated upon a relationship among equals and so the common mistake of taking the family as the microcosm of the proper order of the state is to be rejected.

ARISTOTLE ON SLAVERY[8]

One of the most interesting things about the *Politics* is that Aristotle feels it necessary to provide a justification for slavery. Apart from the persuasiveness or otherwise of his defence, it is a matter of some interest that Aristotle should feel obliged to offer a defence of such a ubiquitous and widely-accepted institution, an obligation felt by almost no other classical thinker. He could have defended slavery simply on utilitarian grounds but he argues instead, with what persuasiveness one may judge, that whereas some types of slavery are conventional, there are nevertheless some people who are slaves by nature: 'From the hour of their birth, some are marked out for subjection, others for rule.'[9] Aristotle defines the slave as a 'living possession' [1253b1] and the natural slave is one who by nature isn't his own but another man's. That some who are enslaved aren't natural slaves leads some thinkers to condemn slavery as a whole but, according to Aristotle, this condemnation, even though under-standable, is incorrect; the natural slave in fact benefits from subjection to his master! [see Heath, 265-266] Many readers of Aristotle are shocked that slavery could ever have been accepted, still less, defended, by any one as intel-lectually brilliant as Aristotle but, as John McClelland notes, 'If slavery is just another form of rule, then there is no reason in principle why it should not be examined along with the other forms of rule. Of course, slavery…is open to horrible abuses but Aristotle seems to be saying that the existence of a bad master no more vitiates the idea of mastery than a bad father vitiates the idea of fatherhood.' [McClelland, 63]

Malcolm Heath makes a gallant attempt to reconstruct Aristotle's theory of natural slavery—which theory he concedes to be 'full of gaps and apparent inconsistencies'—with a view to showing it to be coherent with Aristotle's overall philosophical position. [Heath, 246] According to Heath, for Aristotle, what makes some human beings to be natural slaves isn't a lack of reason just as such but 'an impairment of the capacity for global deliberation' as a result of which the natural slave 'lacks the capacity to make reasoned judgements about what he should do consistently with his conception of living well in general. And this renders him incapable of living a worthwhile human life.' [Heath, 253] Tellingly, Heath admits that he doesn't believe that any human being fits the reconstructed account of natural slavery. [see Heath, 244, n. 4]

In this matter, Aristotle appears to be trapped by the requirements of his own dialectic. His argument would appear to be something like this. The *polis* is a natural and not a merely conventional form of community. As a form of self-governing community, the *polis* demands the active participation of its citizens in deliberation and judgement and this requires an amount of leisure that isn't commensurate with either manual labour or engagement in business. Somebody has to do this work and, although non-citizen resident aliens (metics) can do some of it, not all that's needed can be done unless we can conscript those who lack the capacity for self-direction to do it, both for our good and for theirs. If slavery was merely conventional then we could have no *poleis*—but that would appear to show that the *polis* isn't, after all, a natural form of community.

One has only to state this argument to see that it has more holes in it than the most panoptical of Swiss cheeses. Even if the *polis* requires the active participa-tion of its citizens, it isn't obvious that such participation is so time-consuming as to leave no time for any other form of work. And even if it were true that to be a citizen one has to be relieved of *all* necessity to work, it doesn't seem fantastic to suggest that the donkeywork in a *polis* could be done by those who *voluntarily* contract for just this purpose with the citizens.[10] 'The Greek philosophers, again, unite in postulating for the citizens of their ideal cities abundant leisure for high things, in admitting slavery as the necessary basis of that leisure, and in excluding from full participation in the State those who have not the leisure they consider necessary; but actual life, in Athens at any rate and in many other cities did not square with their postulates, nor agree with their theories.' [Barker, 33] Although slaves in Athens outnumbered citizens by two to one, they weren't evenly distributed among the citizen population. Many worked for the state in the silver mines of Laurium and for wealthy Athenians. But the mass of citizens had no slaves so that even though 'slavery was necessary to social superiority, it was not necessary for political privilege or intellectual development.' [Barker, 36] To the extent that the political life of Athens depended upon slavery, then, it did so only tangentially.

As we shall see in the next chapter (on slavery), it is impossible to regard Aristotle's defence of slavery, especially natural slavery, as anything other than a form of intellectual scotosis; even to describe his arguments in defence of natural slavery as weak is to be guilty of inverse hyperbole. Even if we grant that slavery was omnipresent and intertwined with every aspect of cultural and commercial life in ancient Athens, we might still have expected something better on this topic from one of the greatest intellects the world has ever seen.

THE HOUSEHOLD AND WEALTH

The household (and the *polis* as a community of such households) requires a material base and for this the art of generating wealth will be necessary. What is the relationship between the art of obtaining wealth (chrematistics) and the art of household management (economics)? Are they the same thing; or is one a part of the other? Aristotle thinks it obvious that they can't be the same since household management uses wealth and does so in a constitutive way. He distinguishes between two kinds of wealth acquisition. On the one hand, we have the acquisition of those things that are necessary for any household. These must be found at hand or produced. Such things, says Aristotle, 'are the elements of true riches; for the amount of property which is needed for a good life is not unlimited...' [1256b31-32] On the other hand, we have that kind of acquisition, more properly called the art of wealth getting, which is related to but not identical with the former kind of acquisition and so is easily confused with it. Whereas the first kind of acquisition is natural, the second kind is artificial. To explain what he means by calling one form of acquisition natural and the other artificial, Aristotle distinguishes between the two uses that can be made of anything: one proper and primary, the other improper and secondary. The proper and primary use of a shoe is for wearing on one's foot. An improper and secondary use of a shoe is for exchange with another. Trade, then, or exchange isn't, according to Aristotle, part of the first, natural kind of acquisition. We can see this, he thinks, if we look at the first community, the family. In the family, everything is held and used in a kind of commonality and trade within the family has no place. Even when the family ramifies and practises a rudimentary form of barter exchange, this is still not the second, artificial, kind of acquisition but just a slightly more complicated version of the natural mode of acquisition. The artificial mode of acquisition Aristotle sees as deriving from long-distance trading which, he thinks, inevitably gives rise to invention of money. 'For the various necessaries of life are not easily carried about, and hence men agreed to employ in their dealing with each other something which was intrinsically useful and easily applicable to the purpose of life, for example, iron, silver, and the like. Of this the value was at first measured simply by size and the weight, but in the process of time they put a stamp upon it, to save the trouble of weighing and to mark the value.' [1257a35-41 Aristotle correctly distinguishes money from wealth—'he who is rich in coin may often be in want of necessary food. But how can that be wealth of which a man may have a great abundance and yet perish with hunger....' [1257b14-15]

Whereas the natural mode of acquisition has intrinsic limits, the artificial mode has none and this, Aristotle thinks, is dangerous, leading men to think that money-making in the service of the satisfaction of insatiable desires is the end of life. 'Hence some persons are led to believe that getting wealth is the object of household management, and the whole idea of their lives is that they ought either to increase their money without limit, or at any rate not to lose it. The origin of this disposition in men is that they are intent upon living only and not upon living well; and, as their desires are unlimited, they also desire that the mean of gratifying them should be without limit. Those who do aim at a good life seek the means of obtaining bodily pleasures; and, since the enjoyment of these appears to depend on property, they are absorbed in getting wealth: and so there arises the second species of wealth-getting. For as their enjoyment is in excess, they seek an art which produces the excess of enjoyment; and, if they are not able to supply their pleasures by the art of getting wealth, they try other arts, using in turn every faculty in a manner contrary to nature.' [1257b37-1258a10]

Aristotle leaves us in no doubt as to what he thinks about all this. The wealth-getting that is part of household management is both necessary and honourable but wealth getting by means of exchange is, he says, justly censured 'for it is unnatural, and a mode by which men gain from one another. The most hated sort...is usury, which makes a gain out of money itself, and not from the natural object of it. For money was intended to be used in exchange, but not to increase at interest. And this term interest [*tokos*—offspring], which means the birth of money from money, is applied to the breeding of money because the offspring resembles the parent. Wherefore of all modes of getting wealth this is the most unnatural.' [1258b1-8] Aristotle is broadly correct in his account of the origin of money but wildly off the mark in his application of a natural/unnatural distinction to its use. His attitude is typical of the approach taken to such matters not only by aristocratic Greeks but by most ruling classes throughout history. He is deeply distrustful of moneymaking and trade. Whereas the agricultural way of life sets some natural limits to men's desire for wealth, the use of goods for exchange rather than for consumption (made possible largely by money) has a tendency to make the acquisition of wealth an end in itself and this, Aristotle thinks, is corrosive of the values of the *polis*.[11] Remarking on the characteristic contempt for labour and distrust of commerce symptomatic of the ancient word, Larry Siedentop remarks, 'Commerce became the enemy of simplicity. It became almost a synonym for decadence. Commerce, along with the taste for luxury it promoted, turned men into quasi-women.' [Siedentop, 38]

BACK TO THE *POLIS*

In the second book of the *Politics*, Aristotle turns his attention to what has already been written about the *polis* by his predecessors. In the *Republic*, Plato wants to have wives and children and property held in common but Aristotle thinks this would be a mistake. Having wives and children be common to all will destroy natural affection. If children are nobody's in particular, then no one will pay proper attention to them. In trying to make all his citizens alike, Plato fails to appreciate that there can be too much unity in a *polis*, if unity is tantamount to uniformity. Uniformity is neither necessary nor desirable.

Moreover, the abolition of property will not only *not* remove the source of dissension, it is likely to produce even more, for 'that which is common to the greatest number has the least care bestowed upon it. Everyone thinks chiefly of his own, hardly at all of the common interest.' [1261b33-34] The basic question that must be answered is whether the citizens in a perfect state should have their posses-sions in common or not. Aristotle notes that 'there is always a difficulty in men living together and having all human relations in common, but especially in their having common property.' [1263a15-16] In the end, what Aristotle recommends is a private property regime but one in which private property is used for the common good: he remarks, 'it is clearly better that property should be private, but the use of it common...' [1263a38]

The *polis* isn't an individual; it is a functional composite of its citizens. What, then, is a citizen? The answer to this question will differ depending upon which form of government one is considering. Aristotle's answer to his own question is, in brief, that a citizen is 'He who has the power to take part in the deliber-ative or judicial administration of any state [*polis*],' the *polis* being a body of such citizens 'sufficing for the purposes of life.' [1275b18-21] On this defini-tion, most citizens (so-called) of modern representative democracies wouldn't be regarded by Aristotle as citizens since they lack the power or right to take part in the deliberations and in judicial administration. Only those who are members of Congress or Parliament (and perhaps not even all of these—do warm-body, voting-fodder backbenchers really count?) would meet the terms of this definition.

Aristotle considers the vexed question of the metaphysical and moral status of a group. How is it possible, he wonders, to attribute actions to a composite entity such as a state or *polis*? He notes that some people will refuse to carry out the terms of contracts of previous tyrannical regimes 'on the grounds that the tyrant, and not the state, contracted them...' [1276a10-11] What is the criterion of identity of the *polis*? What makes a *polis* to be the same *polis* from one moment to the next? Is it having the same inhabitants or occupying the same territory? Aristotle dismisses these material accounts as superficial. His own account is formal. Given that the state is a kind of partnership 'and is a partnership of citizens in a constitution, when the form of the government changes, and becomes different, then it may be supposed that the state [*polis*] is no longer the same.' [1276b1] Anticipating a difficulty already mentioned, namely, whether or not the contracts (and presum-ably decisions, treaties, and the like) arranged by one regime are binding on a successor regime which gives a different form or constitution to the same inhabi-tants occupying the same territory, Aristotle, uncharacteristically, simply refuses to answer: 'It is quite another question,' he says, 'whether a state ought or ought not to fulfil engagements when the form of government changes.' [1276b14-15]

We saw that for Plato, the end of the *polis* is the life of virtue of its citizens. The same is true in general for Aristotle. Nevertheless, he is aware of a problem that only becomes fully articulated in the passage of time. Is a good man necessarily a good citizen? Is a good citizen necessarily a good man? He notes that whereas all citizens of the *polis* must contribute to its end, not all can be expected to do so in the same way or to the same extent. Each citizen, however, is expected to carry out his private business well and to have the virtues associated with so doing. He concludes, 'All must have the virtue of the good citizen—thus, and thus only, can the state be perfect; but they will not have the virtue of a good man, unless we assume that in the good state all the citizens must be good.' [1277a1-4] This modest gap between man as citizen and man as anything else—carpenter, accountant—is something that will become ever more important as time goes by. Only in the perfect state will there be a perfect coincidence of the virtuous man and the virtuous citizen. [see *Politics* III, 18]

As we have seen, a central theme of the *Politics* is that in a constitutional *polis*, rulers and ruled are fundamentally interchangeable.

> The characteristics of democracy are as follows:—the election of officers by all out of all; and that all should rule over each, and each in his turn over all; that the appointment to all offices, or to all but those which require experience and skill, should be made by lot; that no property qualification should be required for offices or only a very low one; that a man should not hold the same office twice, or not often, or in the case of a few except military offices; that the tenure of all offices, or of as many as possible, should be brief; that all men should sit in judgement, or that judges selected out of all should judge, in all matters, or in most and in the greatest and most important—such as the scrutiny of accounts, the constitution, and private contracts; that the assembly should be supreme over all causes, or at any rate over the most important, and the magistrates over none or only over a very few. [*Politics*, 1317b19-30]

'Typical of Athenian democracy,' remarks van Reybrouck, 'was the fact that virtually no distinction existed between politicians and citizens, between the governing and the governed or between holders of power and subjects. The function of "career politician" that we all find so natural today would have seems totally bizarre and absurd to the average Athenian...' [van Reybrouck, 66] The fundamental interchangeability of rulers and ruled, each taking turn and turn about, is the only kind of rule that can be exercised by freemen over freemen. It is true that Aristotle's conception of what constitutes a freeman is severely limited—no women, no children, no slaves, no foreigners—but his formal point is worth considering. The task of the ruler in a constitutional *polis* is to be, for the time being, first among equals. When the time comes, the ruler returns to being one of the ruled. There is, says Aristotle, 'a rule of another kind, which is exercised over freemen and equals by birth—a constitutional rule, which the ruler must learn by obeying, as he would learn the duties of a general of cavalry by being under the orders of a general of cavalry....It has been well

said that "he who has never learned to obey cannot be a good commander".'
The two are not the same, but the good citizen ought to be capable of both; he
should know how to govern like a freeman and how to obey like a freeman.'
[1277b8-15] Given that constitutional rule involves citizens being ruler and
ruled in turn, those incapable of taking part in such activities can't really be
regarded as citizens. So children, for example, can't be full citizens; neither,
however, can those whose work prevents them from taking part in deliberation, such as manual workers. 'It must be admitted that we cannot consider all
those to be citizens who are necessary to the existence of the state….in ancient
times, and among some nations, the artisan class were slaves or foreigners, and
therefore the majority of them are so now. The best form of the state will not
admit them to citizenship.' [1278a3-8] Aristotle admits that matters vary from
polis to *polis*, some having a more relaxed attitude to citizenship than others,
so that in some cases, labourers and mechanics can be citizens but, in the end,
he is unwilling to allow that in the best *poleis*, artisans or mechanics or manual
labourers can be citizens. [1278a15-35]

Is there only one form of government or many; if many, what are the differences between them. He repeats his assertion that man is a creature of the *polis*.
He would live with others even if he did not need another's help although
Aristotle concedes that our need for assistance helps to bind us together. The
chief end of both individuals and the *polis* is well-being. He repeats the point
made on several occasions already that 'when the state is framed upon the
principle of equality and likeness, the citizens think that they ought to hold
office by turns. Formerly…everyone would take his turn of service; and then
again, somebody else would look after his interest, just as he, while in office,
had looked after theirs.'[12] He takes over the classification of forms of government from Plato's *Statesman*. We can have rule by one, by the few and by the
many, and that rule can be for the good of the ruler or for the good of the ruled:

	…for the sake of the ruled	…for the sake of the ruler
Rule by one	(1) Monarchy	(2) Tyranny
Rule by the few	(3) Aristocracy	(4) Oligarchy
Rule by the many	(5) (moderate) democracy	(6) (extreme) democracy

This classification is somewhat mechanical and not particularly insightful. The
distinction between rule by the few and rule by the many does not really show
that what is at issue here is whether political power comes from property and
wealth (aristocracy/oligarchy) or from the claims of the many to some kind of
consideration (moderate or extreme democracy). To displace the problem of
political rule from the number of those exercising power to a system of law
seemingly independent of individuals simply pushes the issue back a step, for
now the question becomes—who makes or moulds the law? Even if it's true
that a good state should be governed according to law, it is perfectly possible to

have bad laws and thus to have a lawfully governed bad state. In his discussion of these various possibilities, Aristotle notes that the form of government can in fact conceal more than it reveals. Nothing prevents a nominally democratic government from ruling in an oligarchic fashion or a nominally oligarchic government from ruling democratically.

Plato tended to run ethics, economics, politics and law together in his conception of the *polis* and we find something of the same tendency in Aristotle. But we also find in Aristotle a countervailing tendency to distinguish these elements, a dawning recognition that to be a good citizen and a good person isn't necessarily the same thing and that politics and ethics may in fact be distinct. We find further the beginnings of, on the one hand, a distinction between political structures and law and, on the other, a distinction between political structures and economics. Nevertheless, the distinction in which all these other distinctions are embraced, the distinction between society and the state, a foundational principle of liberalism in both its classic and libertarian varieties, is hardly one that we could reasonably expect a classical Greek thinker to appreciate. 'The modern distinction between the state and society is one which no Greek thinker made clearly and adequately, and which perhaps could not be made until the state was conceived as a legal structure, but Aristotle at least reached a very good first approximation to it.' [Sabine, 109] Aristotle concedes, however, that ultimately it isn't numbers that matter but whether the poor rule or the rich rule. In fact, more often than not, the rich and the few coincide and the poor and the many do so too. But this is an accidental connection. There is nothing in principle to prevent the many being rich or the few being poor, for 'whether in oligarchies or in democracies, the number of the governing body, whether the greater number, as in a democracy, or the smaller number, as in an oligarchy, is an accident due to the fact that the rich everywhere are few and the poor numerous....the real difference between democracy and oligarchy is poverty and wealth.' [1279b35-1280a1] In the clash between the rich and the poor, we find that while they agree formally on the principle of distributive justice (equals should receive equally), they differ in what they consider relevant to the determination of equality. 'The former [oligarchs] believe that inequality in wealth justifies unequal treatment generally, the latter [democrats] that equality in freedom requires equal treatment in all respects.' [Lord 140] It is important to make it clear that the claim to equal treatment by the many at this period isn't based upon some abstract conception of human rights but derives from the duty that every citizen has to risk his life in defence of the *polis* and thus should have a say in determining its policies and its laws.[13]

Aristotle denies that a *polis* can be constituted simply by agreement or by a nexus of commercial exchanges. Because this denial appears to run completely contrary to the classical liberal or libertarian conception of politics, the passage is worth quoting: 'Let us suppose that one man is a carpenter, another a husbandman, another a shoemaker, and so on, and that their number is ten thousand: nevertheless, if they have nothing in common but exchange, alliance, and the like, that would not constitute a state. Why is this? Surely not because they are at a distance from one another: for even supposing that such a community were to meet in one place, but that each man had a house of his own, which was in a manner his state, and that they made alliance with one another, but only against evil-doers; still an accurate thinker would not deem this to be a state, if their intercourse with one another was of the same character after as before their union.' [1280b20-30] Aristotle's thought experiment imagines his carpenters and shoemakers as constituting, as it were, each his own *micropolis*, with each one relating externally to the others in a set of alliances for defence against evil-doers and the exchange of goods and services. Would such a set of alliances constitute a *polis*? Aristotle thinks not, for apart from their alliance and their trade, the allies have nothing in common. He continues: 'It is clear then that a state is not a mere society, having a common place, established for the prevention of mutual crime and for the sake of exchange. There are conditions without which a state can't exist; but all of them together do not constitute a state, which is a community of families and aggregations of families in well-being for the sake of a perfect and self-sufficing life. Such a community can only be established among those who live in the same place and intermarry. Hence arise in cities family connexions, brotherhoods, common sacrifices, amusements that draw men together. But these are created by friendship (*philia*), for the will to live together is friendship. The end of the state is the good life, and these are the means towards it. And the state is the union of families and villages in a perfect and self-sufficing life...' [1280b30-1281a1] Trade, exchange, and common defence against evildoers are all necessary conditions for the existence of a *polis* but they aren't sufficient. One can't have a *polis* without them but one could have them all and still not have a *polis*, because the *polis* is a community that has ends that go beyond the merely utilitarian, a community founded ultimately on *philia*. *Philia* is often translated as friendship but it means much more than this. *Philia* is used to describe not only friendship but also the relationship of husband and wife, parents and children and, perhaps most significantly, the fellow feeling that people who belong to the same associations have, whether those associations are private groups or, indeed, the *polis* itself.[14]

What Aristotle says here would be a problem for classical liberals or libertarians only if their advocacy of either a minimal state or no state at all were somehow taken to suggest that these conditions were the ultimate fulfilment of the good life. But the classical liberal or libertarian sees the minimal state or no state as a basic condition that permits people to associate in community for the achievement of common goals and purposes of the kind that Aristotle lists. What is distinctive about the classical liberal or libertarian position—and here it may differ from that of Aristotle—is that membership of such communities ultimately has to be voluntary and cannot be coerced.

RULE BY MEN OR RULE BY LAWS?

Should we have rule by the best man or by the best laws? Aristotle is well aware of the limitations of law: its inflexibility, its inability to anticipate all possible circumstances, its Procrustean tendency to ignore significant differences by shoehorning widely differing acts into a small number of ideal types.

Plato in the *Statesman* had characterised the limitations of law in terms very similar to those used by Aristotle and his solution was to make the wise man, he who knows, a kingly ruler. Aristotle comes down, reluctantly, on the side of law, primarily because it is, or at least can be, free from the distorting effects of passion. Since, however, law does not exist in a vacuum and there will always be a requirement for interpretation, Aristotle, showing a nostalgic hankering for the Platonic idea, thinks that a group of the best men rather than a single best man can mitigate the distorting effects of passion and apply the law equitably: 'Laws,' he says, 'when good, should be supreme; and…the magistrate or magistrates should regulate those matters only on which the laws are unable to speak with precision owing to the difficulty of any general principle embracing all particulars.'[15] Aristotle was a realist and he accepted that in the real world, a *polis* with a large and strong middle class was likely to be the best option. It is more than likely that law in such a *polis* would concern itself primarily with the prohibition of acts that were intrinsically destructive of community— homicide, theft, and the like—justice being neither a matter of the will of the majority or of the oligarchs. 'This caution in the business of law-making,' writes McClelland, 'would tend to make law negative, perhaps a list of sensible prohibitions against those things which would make the good life impossible' although, of course, the effect of such negative injunctions is socially positive. [McClelland, 65] Despite recognising that the core political issue in the *polis* is a balancing of the claims of democracy and oligarchy, Aristotle can't resist a nostalgic paean to aristocracy as the ideal form of government. Concluding the discussion of Book III, he writes: 'the true forms of government are three, and …the best must be that which is administered by the best, and in which there is one man, or a whole family, or many persons, excelling all the others together in virtue, and both rulers and ruled are fitted, the one to rule, the others to be ruled, in such a manner as to attain the most eligible life….[the truly good man] will frame a state that is to be ruled by an aristocracy or by a king…' [1288a34-1288b1]

Book IV of the *Politics* seems largely to be either a repetition of matters already discussed or a more detailed inquiry into the mechanics of particular forms of government. Despite occasional flashes of insight, the discussion is long and often tedious—so many kinds of oligarchy, so many kinds of democracy, so many kinds of tyranny, and so on. I am going to take the fast train through this book, stopping only at those stations where something new or interesting is to be seen.

At the end of Book III, we saw that Aristotle thought that in the ideal *polis*, we should be ruled either by a king or by the aristocracy (in the original sense of that term, meaning the best in society). But just like Plato, Aristotle concedes that the ideal isn't always possible (if indeed it ever is) and so he provides us with a pattern for a *polis* populated by average men. [IV 11-12] Leaving aside his disquisition on monarchy/aristocracy, Aristotle has been largely concerned with a duality between rule by the rich and rule by the poor. As Carnes Lord notes, 'The central practical task Aristotle sets himself in the *Politics* is to blunt if not eliminate the political conflict between rich and poor.' [Lord, 144] This is the class struggle or class conflict long before the term to describe it was invented by the nineteenth century French historian Augustin Thierry. It should be appreciated, however, that this struggle isn't just about money or property but more about the strong passions of fear, contempt and anger aroused by a perception of unequal treatment. In this regard, Aristotle is closer to Hobbes than to Marx.

Using the doctrine of the mean that he had developed in the *Nicomachean Ethics*, Aristotle identifies a third element mid-way between rich and poor: the middle class. Those who excel in any sphere are prone to arrogance; those who are very poor find it difficult to follow rational principles. If those who excel rule then we may have a city of masters and slaves; if those who are poor rule, then the city is prey to envy and resentment. Either possibility leaves itself open to tyranny. If follows that in a city with a significant segment of the citizenry which has enough wealth but not too much, it is less likely that factionalism will flourish and much more likely that the *polis* will be stable. This middle element can bridge the gap between rich and poor and avoid the vices characteristic of both these groups because it is disposed to act more reasonably than either the very wealthy or the radically impoverished. Whether there is a strong middle class or not, every *polis* that values stability must recruit the support of the strongest class, whether of the poor or of the rich.

REVOLUTION

In Book V, 1-4, Aristotle turns to consider the cause of revolutions in the *polis*. He locates the principal reason for revolution either in a desire for equality, when men believe that others who are no better than they are have more than themselves, or in a desire for superiority, when men believe that their talents and natural endowments entitle them to more than others who aren't so gifted. 'Inferiors revolt in order that they may be equal, and equals that they may be superior.' [1302a30] This is a very astute sociological observation that will come to the fore again and play a prominent role in the thought of Thomas Hobbes. In democracies, revolutions come from persecution of the rich by demagogues, which forces the rich to combine to resist the democratic depredations, or from military power exercised by a demagogue or by politicians pandering to the mob. In oligarchies, on the other hand, revolution comes from oppression of the common people by the oligarchs or by factions within the oligarchy who have been (in their own estimation) unjustly excluded from power. For the purposes of revolutionary analysis, aristocracies are to be taken as a special form of oligarchy.

If Aristotle anticipates Hobbes in the first four chapters of Book V, he anticipates Machiavelli in the later chapters of that book. How are revolutions to be prevented? Some of Aristotle's advice on this matter is commonsensical and hard to dispute. The spirit of obedience to the law should be sedulously cultivated. Those in power should treat their fellow citizens in a spirit of equality. The ambitious mustn't be wronged in matters of honour, nor the poor in money matters. Other things being equal, short tenure of office has much to recommend it in that it makes it difficult for any one person to do much damage. Officials should keep their hands out of the public till but 'above all every state should be so administered and so regulated by law that its magistrates cannot possibly make money. In oligarchies, special precautions should be used against this evil. For the people do not take any great offence at being kept out of the government—indeed they are rather pleased than otherwise at having leisure for their private business—but what irritates them is to think that their rulers are stealing the public money.' [1308b32-37] In democracies, the rich need to be protected from having their wealth expropriated from them; in oligarchies, the poor need to be taken care of.

So far so good—there's nothing particularly startling in this advice. Now comes the Machiavellian turn! Aristotle notes that since fear keeps people on their toes, 'the ruler who has a care of the constitution should invent terrors and bring distant dangers near, in order that the citizens may be on their guard...'! [1308a26-29] Moreover, since possible disturbances to the state originate with individuals, 'there ought to be a magistracy which will have an eye to those whose life is not in harmony with the government...' [1308b23] Having considered how monarchies in general can be preserved against disturbance, Aristotle turns his attention to tyrannies. The successful tyrant should ensure that no rivals emerge to challenge him, 'the tyrant should lop off those who are too high' [1313a39] He should discourage associations that might provide a focus for resistance against him, clubs, literary societies and the like; sow quarrels among friends; compel people to live their lives in public so that what they do and say may continually be observed; impoverish his subjects (engaging in expensive public works like pyramid-building or temple construction is a good way of using up the people's money); multiply taxes; engage in wars so that the people will be occupied and have constant need of a leader; encourage domestic spying and informing by wives against husbands and slaves against masters 'for slaves and women do not conspire against tyrants' [1313b35]. Above all, the tyrant should simulate virtue, be apparently open, honest, and frank, and in all things appear to act like a king. 'In their stark realism and sure grasp of the preoccupations of day-to-day politics,' writes Carnes Lord, 'these pages have few parallels in the literature of political theory....Particularly striking is Aristotle's willingness to provide advice on the preservation of existing regimes not only to the politicians of imperfect democracies and oligarchies, but even to tyrants.' [Lord, 146]

OLIGARCHY VERSUS DEMOCRACY

In Book VI, Aristotle returns again to *the* constant theme of the *Politics*— the analysis of the merits and demerits of oligarchy and democracy. Much of this has already been covered in the earlier part of his work but some points are noteworthy, especially Aristotle's characterisation of democracy. Liberty, Aristotle thinks, is the root principle of the democratic *polis* and the key to liberty in such a *polis* is for all to rule and be ruled in turn. 'Even among freemen and equals this is a principle which must be maintained, for they cannot all rule together, but must change at the end of a year or some other period of time or in some order of succession. The result is that upon this plan they all govern...it is just that all should share in government.' [1261a32-35; 1261b2] The policies of a democratic *polis* are: the election of all officials by all the people from all the people and not just from some special group; the (by now very familiar) requirement that ruler and ruled take turn and turn about; that appointment to all offices other than those requiring some special skill should be made by lot; that no, or very low, property qualifications be required for office-holding; that no office should be held more than once by any one man; that the tenure of all offices should be brief; and that the assembly should, in the final instance, be supreme over all.

Another important aspect of liberty is that a man should be able to choose to act or not act as he sees fit within the constraints of the law. Aristotle condemns the idea that liberty requires the possibility for a man to be able to do anything at all that he chooses, saying 'men should not think it slavery to live according to the rule of the constitution.' [1310a35] Liberty isn't licence. Libertarians can agree formally with Aristotle in his drawing of a distinction between liberty and licence; however, they are likely to disagree when it comes to indicating precisely where the lines of the distinction must be drawn.

If a democracy of this kind is to be preserved then the rich mustn't be plundered by quasi-legal means. It is important to prevent the growth of what would now be called an underclass, dependent upon a continuous supply of money paid for by confiscatory measures against those with property. Aristotle isn't the first nor will he be the last to note that 'the poor are always receiving and always wanting more and more, for such help is like water poured into a leaky cask.' [1320a30-32]. Such measures as are taken should be such as to enable the poor to achieve some measure of lasting prosperity, 'to purchase a little farm, or, at any rate, make a beginning in trade or husbandry.' [1320a39-1320b1]

Plato's finishing point in the *Laws* is Aristotle's starting point in the *Politics*: Plato's second-best *polis* is Aristotle's ideal. As is generally the case in his relationship to Plato, Aristotle's *polis* is the *polis* of an experiential realist with his feet firmly on the ground where Plato's *polis* floats, Laputa-like, above the grubby world of ordinary experience.

The Sophists, Socrates, Plato and Aristotle all lived in a world in which slavery was a commonplace and largely unproblematic phenomenon. Of all human institutions, slavery is the one most obviously inimical to the progress of liberty. We have considered some aspects of slavery in passing in the earlier chapters of this book; now let us look in more detail at this most omnipresent and long-lasting of human institutions.

Notes

1 Reference to the *Politics* are to the Oxford translation by Benjamin Jowett. For ease of reference to other translations, references shall be by the marginal Bekker number rather than by page number.
2 This peninsula, now generally known as Halkidiki, is located in present-day north-eastern Greece. It comprises three small sub-peninsulas that extend like the tines of Poseidon's trident into the Aegean

Sea. These little peninsulas are the somewhat ominously named Kassandra, the less ominous Sithonia and, perhaps the most well known of them, Mount Athos, where the renowned monastic community of the same name is to be found.

3 One point on which Aristotle clearly diverged from the thought of his mentor was in his approach to rhetoric. As Hugh Lawson-Tancred notes, 'the Platonic tradition, inheriting as it did so much of the perspective of the dissident Athenian aristocrats of the fifth century BC, was profoundly suspicious of the whole activity of rhetoric, and…Plato himself only turned to it with some ambivalence relatively late in his career, though then, admittedly, in one of his most impressive dialogues. After the developments of the mid fourth century, however, the Lyceum could not permit itself the luxury of spurning rhetoric. Isocrates and others had established rhetoric as a legitimate basis for further education and in so doing they were setting a trend that was to last for a millennium. Aristotle was prudent enough to realize that this challenge could not simply be ignored and that is was therefore necessary for him to evolve his own peripatetic doctrine of rhetoric.' [Lawson-Tancred, 14-15]

4 *Nicomachean Ethics* 1094b12-28.

5 See the final two books of the *Politics* in which Aristotle specifies the ideal population of such a *polis*, its optimal geographical extent, its property dispositions and, in agreement with Plato, a system of compulsory education.

6 For those not familiar with the term, a 'ward heeler' is an American expression for someone who works for a political party in a ward, the smallest electoral subdivision of a city, and who adopts, let us say, a relaxed attitude towards corrupt election practices.

7 *Politics* 1252b27-30, 1258a2. Aristotle classifies those animals are political for whom some single and common work comes into being for all; examples of such animals are man, the bee, the wasp, the ant, and the crane. He goes on to say, however, that it's evident that 'man is more of a political animal than bees or any other gregarious animals…Nature, as we often say, makes nothing in vain, and man is the only animal whom she has endowed with the gift of speech. And whereas mere voice is but an indication of pleasure or pain, and is therefore found in other animals…the power of speech is intended to set forth the expedient and inexpedient, and therefore likewise the just and the unjust. And it is a characteristic of man that he alone has any sense of good and evil, of just and unjust, and the like…' [1253a8-16] See Ober 2015, 45-70.

8 The account that follows is a brief and schematic overview of Aristotle on slavery. For a more detailed discussion of Aristotle's conception of slavery within a general consideration of the phenomenon, see the following chapter.

9 *Politics* 1254a23. The *nomos/phusis* distinction at work yet again.

10 For a fuller discussion of this topic, see 'Slavery in Plato and Aristotle' in the following chapter.

11. But see McCloskey 2011, 142.

12 1279a6-10. See also 1261a37-1261b6.

13 An eerily similar set of arguments reappears in the so-called Putney Debates that took place within the ranks of the victorious Parliamentary forces at the end of the English Civil War.

14 See *Nicomachean Ethics* 1155a22-28.

15 1282b1-6. Compare *Nicomachean Ethics* 1137b19.

Chapter 5

SLAVERY

Liberty is not a means to a higher political end. It is itself the highest political end
—Lord Acton

Men fall into two groups: slaves and free men.
Whoever does not have two-thirds of his day for himself, is a slave,
whatever he may be: a statesman, a businessman, an official, or a scholar
—Friedrich Nietzsche

Slavery is, without doubt, one of the oldest and longest lasting of human institutions. 'Slavery,' remarks Thomas Sowell, 'was a virtually universal institution in countries around the world and for thousands of years of recorded history.' [Sowell 2011, 180] It is difficult for us now to realise just how ordinary, how normal, human slavery in one form or another has been for most of human history. [see Sumner, 270-282] It is hard to deny John Vincent's assertion that 'No institution has found wider acceptance over a longer period of time than slavery, unless it be torture. No great religion, no great teacher, opposed either. Christianity did not abhor slavery; even slaves did not wish for slavery to end....Slavery is the norm, from which we have only recently deviated; how then do deviants judge the morality of the norm?' [Vincent, 52-53] The historian of slavery, Orlando Patterson, substantially agrees with Vincent, writing, 'There is nothing notably peculiar about the institution of slavery. It has existed from before the dawn of human history right down to the twentieth century, in the most primitive of human societies and in the most civilized. There is no region on earth that has not at some time harboured the institution. Probably there is no group of people whose ancestors were not at one time slaves or slaveholders.' [Patterson 1982, vii] Among philosophers, Plato, who accepted the institution of slavery without any misgivings, is more representative of the common attitude towards the institution than is Aristotle who, at least, felt a need to provide it with some measure of justification. With the exception of Aristotle and possibly some of the Stoics, few in antiquity, or even long after, ever objected to the institution of slavery or seriously considered its abolition.

Today, the *lex talionis*, which recommends the extraction of 'an eye for an eye, a tooth for a tooth,' is regarded as a crude expression of primitive revenge. What is forgotten, however, is that when the *lex talionis* was introduced into social practice, it marked a moral advance on the previous escalatory social norm of twenty or a hundred eyes for an eye or a mouthful of teeth for a tooth. So too with slavery. Slavery is now universally (and rightfully) regarded with revulsion but when the practice began, it represented a moral advance on the previous custom of killing, torturing and sometimes eating prisoners taken in war. 'The mitigation of the cruelties of war,' writes Maurice Davie, 'received its greatest impetus, however, from the institution of slavery….Slavery put an end to slaughter and alleviated torture and mutilation in order not to impair the efficiency of the captive as a worker.'[1] William Graham Sumner believes that, in its origin, slavery was 'a humanitarian improvement in the laws of war, and an alleviation of the status of women.' [Sumner, 262] Making a similar point in the second century AD, the Roman jurisconsult Florentinus, relying upon some dubious etymology, maintains that slaves (servi) are so-called because 'generals have a custom of selling their prisoners and thereby preserving rather than killing them…'[2] Echoing what by then must have been something of a truism, Augustine offers much the same account, writing, 'those who by the law of war might have been put to death, when preserved by their victors, became servi, slaves, so named from their preservation.' [*City of God*, 19.15]

Not everyone, however, is persuaded on this point. Yvon Garland remarks that to propose that enslavement was a mitigation of the cruelties of war is either to excuse modern slavery or to justify the slavery of ancient times and that such proposals are 'no longer fashionable.' [in Finley 1987, 7] Whether a doctrine is fashionable or not is, of course, supremely irrelevant, a matter at best of chronological snobbery: what matters is whether it is true. To maintain that enslavement was a moral advance on killing, torture and cannibalism is no more to valorise enslavement than to judge that a broken leg is better than pancreatic cancer is enthusiastically to excuse or justify the breaking of legs. William Graham Sumner is careful to note that 'it no more follows from the fact that slavery has done good work in the history of civilization that slavery should forever endure than it follows from the fact that war has done good work in the history of civilization that war is in itself, a good thing.' The abolition of slavery was, he thinks, facilitated primarily by advances in technology that depreciated the value of raw human labour rather than by any refinement of human sensibilities. Lest we congratulate ourselves on our superior moral notions, Sumner suggests that 'as no philosophical dogmas caused slavery to be abolished, so no philosophical dogmas can prevent its reintroduction if economic changes should make it fit and suitable again.' [Sumner, 266] Peter Garnsey makes the apparently paradoxical claim that whereas there have been many societies with slaves, there have been very few slave societies. This claim seems obviously false if not actually self-contradictory until one realises that to Garnsey, for a society to be a slave society rather than just a society with slaves, slaves have to 'play a vital role in production.' [Garnsey, 2] Moses Finley, the pre-eminent scholar of slavery, agrees with Garnsey. Although recognising the ubiquitous presence of slavery in the prehistoric and ancient world, he argues that there have only been five genuine slave societies, among them, Greece and Rome. [see Finley, 77] From my point of view, it isn't a matter of much legal or moral significance whether we choose to discriminate between slave societies and societies-with-slaves on the basis of the economic function of slaves in those societies. I am interested in understanding how and why any society could permit and justify the involuntary ownership of one person by another.

SLAVERY IN GREECE AND ROME[3]

Chattel slavery—the treatment of other human beings as property, on a par with non-human animals and inanimate objects—was only one among many forms of compulsory labour service common in ancient and medieval societies. Other forms of coerced labour included debt bondage (a pledge of labour or services as a repayment for a loan or other debt),[4] clientship (obligations owed by the recipients of patronage to their patrons), peonage (sometimes the same as debt bondage, sometimes a kind of indentured service), helotage (persons tied to land and owned by the state) and serfdom (a kind of modified slavery in which serfs were obliged to supply unpaid labour services). [see Postan, 160-173] Chattel slavery is, however, distinct in kind from some of these other forms of compulsory labour service. The distinction between chattel slave and serf, to take one of the other categories, might seem like a distinction without a difference but serfdom, despite its many degrading and socially incapacitating aspects, still left the serf with some measure of legal personality. 'The serf, even when his status fell so low that he could be bought and sold without land, still had certain individual rights, albeit severely curtailed. The slave, no matter how well off he might be—and there were periods when at least some slaves seem to have enjoyed greater social and economic advantages than did serfs—was in the eyes of the law not a person but a chattel of his owner.' [Blum, 8] Chattel slavery also differed from other forms of coerced labour in other significant ways, one difference being that slaves normally had no settled family life and were isolated from kinship connections, which was not, or not necessarily, the case with other forms of bondage. This lack of a family life derived from the commodity status of the chattel slave, as well as the commodity status of his labour. 'The destruction of family and kinship connections that would otherwise be recognized and protected by the customary and legal apparatuses of the host society is therefore a deliberate and logical part of a slave system.'[5]

One essential element in all forms of slavery was that the slave laboured for another and not for himself. Freemen in Greece and Rome had a rooted antipathy to working for another, even when paid to do so, seeing such work as little different from slavery. 'To work for another was what slaves did, and those who were forced to operate as hired labourers, were likely to feel such conditions of work as slavish, and be attacked as slaves, or virtual slaves, by their enemies.'[6] It seems that the concept of wage-slavery is one that originated well before the nineteenth century! William Graham Sumner notes, somewhat sardonically, that 'the mass of mankind, taught to believe that they ought to have easy and pleasant times here, begin to complain again about "wages slavery," "debt slavery," "rent slavery," "sin slavery," "war slavery," "marriage slavery," etc. What men do not like they call "slavery" and so prove that it ought not to be. It appears to be still in their experience that a free man is oppressed by contracts of wages, debt, rent and marriage, and that the cost of making ready for war and of warding off sin are very heavy.' Sumner concludes, 'slavery, if we mean by it subjection to the conditions of human life, can never be abolished.' [Sumner, 267] Sumner might be surprised to learn that the idea of wage-slavery retains its validity among some thinkers today.

Up to about the second century BC, slavery in Rome was limited and local. By the end of the Republic, however, the number of slaves under Roman control had grown enormously and it continued to increase. 'In 150 B.C. a patrician left to his son only ten. Crassus had more than five hundred. C. Caec. Claudius, in the time of Augustus, had 4116.' [Sumner, 280] Treatment of slaves varied widely. Slaves working in fields could be badly treated, with some Romans, such as the elder Cato, suggesting it was more economical to work a slave to death and replace him rather than to treat him well. Slaves were 'systematically worked as hard as it was possible to make them work, and were sold or exposed to perish when too old to work....it was more advantageous to work them so hard that they had no time or strength to plot revolts.' [Sumner, 280] Household slaves were usually treated better than field slaves but not always so.[7] Jérôme Carcopino, who takes an astonishingly positive view of the treatment and status of Roman slaves, writes in this regard, 'In the great houses where many of the slaves were able specialists and some, like the tutor, the doctor, and the reader, had enjoyed a liberal education, they were treated exactly as freemen.'[8] Yet other slaves, useful because of their intelligence and education, could be treated as if they were, in effect, free and were often manumitted for service. [see Nicholas, 69 ff.] Manumission, however, wasn't necessarily always the triumph of morality over expediency that it might at first appear to be. The slave freed by manumission became his former master's client, bound to his former master by contract while his master was relieved of the necessity of caring for and feeding him. Manumission wasn't a rare event. The number of manumitted slaves could reach astonishing proportions. Frank Cowell estimates that 'in Cicero's lifetime, between 81 B.C. and 49 B.C....half a million slaves were freed and let loose in Rome.' [Cowell 1956, 329] By the device of manumission, as Sumner remarks, the owner made 'a crafty gain.'[9]

Why did chattel slavery arise? The essential conditions seem to have been the military strength of some societies as against others, an elite of property owners with the capacity to use such slaves and the means to acquire them, and the capacity of the receiving society as a whole to absorb and use the labour of such slaves. [see Garnsey, 3 and Davie, passim] In Rome, this last condition was met by the ever-increasing conscription of Roman peasants for military service and in Athens, by Solon's outlawing of debt-bondage and other forms of dependent labour. Moses Finley outlines a similar set of conditions for the emergence of chattel slavery. First, there had to be private ownership of land in such a way that it couldn't be worked efficiently purely by family and kin; second, there had to be a market to permit the exchange and sale of commodities produced by slave labour; and third, the indigenous labour market had to be insufficient. The last of these conditions was met by the post-Solonic elimination of debt-bondage and other forms of involuntary labour in Attica, which necessitated the importation of labour from outside Attic society—and that meant slaves. [see Finley, 154-155] Slavery also seems to have emerged as a corollary of wars of territorial conquest. M. M. Postan remarks that 'it is seldom the object of the conquerors and new occupiers to possess themselves of land and get rid of men cultivating it. Where and when land is relatively abundant acres have little value without labour to work them. Conquering settlers of new lands would as often as not be expected to keep at least some of the conquered population either as independent cultivators or land-working slaves.' [Postan, 12]

Slavery and peasant labour coexisted in both Greece and Rome and in a paradox, often remarked upon, it seemed that some slaves were more secure and economically better off than the mass of the free poor! As a slave, one was fed, clothed and cared for; as a free man, one had to look after oneself. In the early Christian era, Libanius and Theodoret, when comparing the relative benefits of being master and slave, go so far as to give the advantage to the slave! [see Garnsey, 50-51] This ancient argument found expression in the antebellum US South where it was maintained that the millions of free factory workers in the North were objectively in a much worse condition than slaves in Virginia and Mississippi. This claim was made not only by slave owners, which is perhaps scarcely surprising, but it was also made by some former slaves, which is much more surprising! One such former slave, interviewed in 1937, said 'Slavery was better for us than things is now, in some cases.' She went on to say that slaves 'didn't have no responsibility, just work, obey and eat. Now they got to shuffle around and live on just what the white folks mind to give them. Slaves prayed for freedom. Then they got it and didn't know what to do with it. They was turned out with nowhere to go and nothing to live on.' [in Hurmence, 79]

Some slaves cooperated fully and wholeheartedly with their masters, perhaps in the hope of improving their situations and achieving manumission. Others passively acquiesced. Still others engaged in low-level resistance by means of go-slows or sabotage.[10] Yet others actively rebelled by attempting escape or, in extreme cases, by the use of violence against their masters. Despite the romantic images created by film and opera versions of the story of Spartacus, slave rebellions, when they occurred, which was rarely, weren't in fact protests against the institution of slavery, just protests against the slavery of the particular slaves who were revolting.

In the end, what is perhaps most striking about the institution of slavery is the extent to which it was widely accepted as a fact of social life by all and sundry, masters and slaves alike. 'Slavery was a structural element in the institution, economy and consciousness of ancient societies. Within these societies slavery had won broad and deep acceptance...' [Garnsey, 9] There were occasional criticisms of slavery, both of the institution itself (rare) and of its operation (somewhat more frequent) but this criticism was exceptional. As I mentioned earlier, Aristotle's account is a response to some unnamed (probably Sophist) critics of the institution and is 'not only the first but also the last formal, systematic analysis of the subject in antiquity, as far as we know.' [Finley 1980, 120; quoted in Garnsey, 11] By and large, no defence of the institution was offered because it occurred to no one that a defence was needed, which makes Aristotle's account of slavery in the *Politics* all the more striking—not so much *what* he says (interesting if unpersuasive as that is) but *that* he takes the trouble to say it at all.

EXPRESSIONS OF DISQUIET

The first inklings of disquiet with slavery are to be found in the thought of the Sophists. 'Slight hints,' says Fisher, 'of some intellectual unease are to be found from the late fifth century on, as part of the ferment of radical questioning brought to the Greek cities by the Sophists.' [Fisher, 86] Antiphon the Sophist appears to deny any essential distinction between Greek and barbarian when he writes, 'We revere and honour those born of noble fathers, but those who are not born of noble houses we neither revere nor honour. In this we are, in our relations with one another, like barbarians, since we are all by nature born the same in every way, both barbarians and Hellenes. And it is open to all men to observe the laws of nature, which are compulsory.'[11] Nicolas Fisher questions whether Antiphon did, in fact, fundamentally call into question the distinction between Greek and barbarians, high and low birth. That used to be the view, he says but recently discovered material seems to suggest that Antiphon is merely suggesting a kind of co-relativity between Greeks and barbarians to the effect that each social group conceives of others as barbarians in relation to itself.[12] Another familiar and less hermeneutically controversial citation is that of the Sophist Alcidamas, who says that God gave liberty to all and no one is a slave by nature.[13] Some, such as Giuseppe Cambiano, attempt to limit the scope of this citation to a specific historical instance. Peter Garnsey, however, explicitly rejects Cambiano's limited reading of this citation, taking it, as it appears to be, a negative judgement on the idea of natural slavery. W. K. C. Guthrie agrees with Garnsey in taking Alcidamas's assertion to be a universal claim. I find Cambiano's interpretation of Alcidamas completely unconvincing and am persuaded that Guthrie and Garnsey are correct in taking Alcidamas's proposition as the complete rejection of any natural basis for slavery, even though the evidence may not be rationally coercive on either side of the dispute.

We also have some hints of the unease felt about slavery in the plays of Euripides. There, slaves are portrayed as being no different from any free man save in respect of the name of slave; and the enslavement of women and children is exhibited as pitiful in the extreme. Fisher regards the source of such sentiments as deriving from the Sophists, though their precise source can't be identified: He writes, 'it seems likely that sophistic use of the nature/convention distinction in relation to slaves and free men sharpened many Greek's distaste for the enslavement of their fellow Greeks.' [Fisher, 91] Despite this, it does not seem that anyone in Greece proposed the abolition of chattel slavery.

In Roman sources at the highest level we also find suggestions of the fundamental illegality of slavery because of its nonconformity with the natural law. In Justinian's *Digest* it is said that 'Slavery is an institution of the *jus gentium*, whereby someone is against nature made subject to the ownership of another,'[14] 'everyone would be born free by the natural law, and manumission would not be known where slavery was not known....slavery came in by the *jus gentium*,'[15] 'freedom is the condition of natural law and subjection the invention of the law of the world [*jus gentium*]...'[16] In Justinian's *Institutes*, the following appears: 'The law of nations [*jus gentium*] is common to all mankind, for nations have established certain laws, as occasion and the necessities of human life required. Wars arose, and in their train followed captivity and slavery, both which are contrary to the law of nature; for by that law, all men are originally born free.'[17] Despite these statements, none of the eminent jurisconsults seems to be seriously calling legal slavery into question.

In summary, in Roman law, slavery was an institution conceived to be contrary to natural law but sanctioned by the *ius gentium*. Davis notes, 'slavery would not be permitted in an ideal world of perfect justice, but it was simply a fact of life that symbolized the compromises that must be made in the sinful world of reality.'[18] Despite the high-sounding principles just adverted to, then, Roman law permitted chattel slavery. The precise position of the slave in any form of legal classification is always revealing. Varro, in his *Res rusticae* 1:17, written in the late first century BC, distinguished the slave as a man from free men, and as a tool, as something to be used, from other animals and from inert pieces of equipment. Gaius, the second century AD jurisconsult, too, in his *Institutes*[19] displayed a similar ambiguity. Roman law distinguished between laws relating to persons, to things and to actions. Where did slaves fit in this categorisation? Was the slave a person or a thing? Both, it would seem. Within the law of persons, the primary distinction was between the slave and the free; within the law of things, the primary division was between corporeal things and incorporeal things and slaves came under the heading of corporeal things.

SLAVERY IN PLATO AND ARISTOTLE

Plato has little to say about slaves and slavery. One place in which we do find some comment is the *Laws* where, when talking about the kinds of property a married couple should have when starting out their family life together, he remarks that although there is no difficulty in understanding or acquiring most kinds of property, slaves are problematic. [*Laws*, 776B-C, 778A] The reason for this is that some ways of speaking about slaves are right and some are not. This might lead us to think that Plato is going to deal with the difficult question of how one rightly conceives of another human being as property but he talks not about whether there should be such a thing as slavery but only about how slaves should properly be treated. He deprecates any form of master/slave fraternisation and the Athenian interlocutor says that slaves shouldn't be admonished as if they were freemen but speech with them should always be in the form of a command. Aristotle, seemingly with Plato in mind, says this is a mistake and remarks that 'admonition is more properly employed with slaves than with children.'[20]

Aristotle's discussion of slavery takes place in the context of his account of the basic relationships that obtain within the household—master/slave, husband/wife and father/children—and is a response to some unnamed people who hold that the existence of slavery is merely a matter of convention and has no basis in nature, and who object to it on the grounds that it is based on force and so is unjustified. These people also go on the claim that the only difference between kings and slave owners is in the number of subjects they control![21] We do not know for certain who these anti-slavery people were since Aristotle never tells us. Giuseppe Cambiano says that 'All attempts made by historians to identify these opponents have been conjectural. What is certain is that their argument is based on the opposition between nature and *nomos*.' [Cambiano, 22] Given that the distinction between nature (*phusis*) and law or convention (*nomos*) is characteristic of Sophists and that the Sophists provided the immediate dialectical context of the Socrates/Plato/Aristotle philosophical triumvirate, this is, I believe, strong circumstantial evidence that the anti-slavery argument to which Aristotle is responding came either from the Sophists or from their followers. Garnsey seems to be thinking along much the same lines when he says that Aristotle's unnamed persons appear to be 'the heirs of the late fifth- and early sixth century sophists, who were notorious for their criticism of established institutions and beliefs.' [Garnsey, 238]

We do know that Aristotle is aware of Alcidamas's dictum in his *Messeniac Oration* that 'God has left all men free; Nature has made no man a slave' for Aristotle mentions it explicitly in drawing a distinction between two kinds of law: one, local and relative to a particular political community; the other universal. 'For,' Aristotle says, 'there really is…a natural justice and injustice that is binding on all men, even on those who have no association or covenant with one another.'[22] He gives three examples to support his claim that there is such a thing as natural justice: first, Antigone's act of disobedience in burying her brother in defiance of Kreon's edict, as portrayed in Sophocles's *Antigone*; second, Empedocles's injunction that we kill no living creature; and third, the excerpt just mentioned from Alcidamas. This natural justice, binding on all, looks very much like the natural law referred to in the Roman legal texts and is similarly practically ineffectual. In any event, whatever defence it might provide against conventional or merely legal slavery, it isn't in any way effective in undermining what Aristotle calls natural slavery.

In responding to the unnamed critics of slavery, Aristotle does not reject their criticism outright but attempts to sap its force by making a distinction between conventional slavery and natural slavery. Who or what is a natural slave? A man is a slave by nature, says Aristotle, 'who is by nature not his own but another's man…'[23] The heart of the definition is that a natural slave is a human being belonging not to himself but to another, which comes close to, if it doesn't actually coincide with a begging of the question. Note the repetition of the phrase 'by nature': it occurs twice in the passage. The natural slave does not belong to himself *by nature* and he belongs to another *by nature*. That's all very well but how does one identify such human beings? Are there physiological or psychological markers that would allow us to pick out such natural slaves? Aristotle thinks that nature should bring it about that natural slaves are physiologically different in kind from free men. 'Nature would like to distinguish between the bodies of freemen and slaves,' he remarks, 'making the one strong for servile labour, the other upright, and although useless for such services, useful for political life in the arts both of war and peace.'[24]

Nevertheless, as he somewhat ruefully notes, nature doesn't always oblige, so that 'the opposite often happens.'[25] If physiology provides us with no reliable guide to natural slaves, what of psychology? Human beings as human beings are necessarily rational but the natural slave, says Aristotle, somewhat mysteriously, has just enough rationality. This enigmatic claim is parsed out later and turns out to amount to the proposition that natural slaves are those unable to make decisions in respect of themselves and who need direction from others, such direction being for their own good. The natural slave, while rational in some sense, 'has no deliberative faculty at all…'[26] Although human and so presumptively rational, natural slaves function in a way that in essence isn't very different from domestic animals.[27]

Aristotle has to hand a variety of models of authority and subordination: husband and wife, father and children, ruler and ruled, under none of which can the master/slave relationship obviously be subsumed. Aristotle denies that the slave master is a kind of tyrant and the reason for this would appear to be that he envisages the relationship between master and slave to be mutually beneficial, whereas the relation of a tyrant to those he tyrannises is not. The abuse of authority on the part of the slave master 'is injurious to both; for the interests of part and whole, of body and soul, are the same, and the slave is a part of the master, a living but separated part of his bodily frame. Hence, when the relation of master and slave between them is natural they are friends and have a common interest, but where it rests merely on law and force the reverse is true.'[28] This account is not a little odd. The symbiosis between slave master and slave is again asserted, this time because the slave is, as it were, an exteriorised part of his master. Moreover, a relationship of friendship can subsist between a slave master and a natural slave whereas a slave master and a merely legal slave can't be friends. But if the natural slave is sub-rational, how can he be a friend with a rational being except in some seriously attenuated sense. Fido may be man's best friend but do not try to discuss the political implications of climate change with him or the relative merits of socialism and capitalism. On the other hand, even though it mightn't be advisable for all sorts of reasons to be friends with your legal slaves, their being slaves is merely the result of misfortune and they are not, or at least, not necessarily, sub-rational and so could, in principle, be friends with their masters.

Where are these natural slaves to be found? Is it a happy coincidence that all or at least most of the slaves in Athens are natural slaves? We may glean a hint of a possible answer to this question in the *Nicomachean Ethics* where Aristotle refers to people who live by their senses alone 'like some races of distant barbarians…' and so presumably possess just the right amount of rationality—enough to make them human but not enough to make them capable of directing their own affairs.[29] Aristotle defends the method of acquiring slaves by capture in war but only if the war is just. Nevertheless, he seems to think that all wars with barbarians (from which source his natural slaves will come) are in any case just.

There is an air of intellectual desperation about Aristotle's theory of the natural slave. Only too well aware of the arbitrary and possibly unjust nature of slaves taken in war yet unable to conceive of the *polis*'s functioning without the aid of slaves, Aristotle is driven to perpetrate an incoherent account of a kind of slavery that is in accord with nature and so does not violate natural justice. Peter Garnsey concludes that 'Natural slavery as presented by Aristotle is a battered shipwreck of a theory' [Garnsey, 107] and Nicolas Fisher says of Aristotle's account that it is 'flawed by fundamental contradictions and illogicalities, as well as by the standard Greek-centred contempt for foreigners and insensitivity to slaves.' [Fisher, 94]

Even if we give Aristotle every credit for facing up to the theoretical problem of slavery as no one before him had, as we should, it is hard to disagree with Garnsey's and Fisher's negative assessments. I have no wish to be unfair or anachronistic in offering these criticisms of Aristotle's account of slavery. The issues he wrestles with would continue to trouble men of good will and intelligence long after he wrote. In quite another time and in a very different context, Bartolomé de Las Casas, the sixteenth-century Spanish Dominican, concedes that if there were a people who were by nature 'slow-witted, moronic, foolish, or stupid, or even not having for the most part sufficient natural knowledge and ability to rule and govern itself' then such a people would fit Aristotle's description of those who are slaves by nature. Not all barbarians, however, are 'irrational or natural slaves or unfit for government,' so requiring that they be ruled by others. [de Las Casas, 38, 42] In his fascinating and, at times stunningly politically incorrect treatise—Turks and Moors are described by de Las Casas as 'the truly barbaric scum of the nations' and human sacrifice is, at most, a 'probable error,' justifiable on Aristotelian principles [de Las Casas, 47, 224]—de Las Casas none the less stoutly defends the indigenous inhabitants of Latin America against oppression by the invading Spaniards whom he doesn't hesitate to describe as 'torturers'. [de Las Casas, 43]

THE STOICS AND SLAVERY

We have very little first hand material from the Stoics on the topic of slavery. This is particularly the case with the early Stoics and the Stoics of the Middle School (Panaetius and Posidonius). Garnsey remarks, 'there is a penury of collections of snippets culled from the works of substantially later writers, often unsympathetic and tendentious.' [Garnsey, 129] Even though we have somewhat more material from late Stoics, such as Seneca and Epictetus, there is no guarantee that what they have to say mirrors what was said by early members of the school. One might conclude from the paucity of what has survived into the present that although there may have been substantial material available at one time, the exigencies of history have dispersed or destroyed it. The other possibility is that there never was much material, the Stoics having little interest in legal slavery in contrast to their concern with slavery of the soul. [see Garnsey, 131; see also Sumner, 287]

This Stoic attitude isn't peculiar to the phenomenon of slavery but is in fact their regular approach to external circumstances in general. They tended to regard such things as accidents of fortune. Fortune isn't in our control; our response to fortune is. 'To the Stoic,' writes Garnsey, 'legal slavery…is of no significance. It is not in our control, it is one of the externals, like health and illness, wealth and poverty, high and low status. As such, it is to be judged as neither good nor bad, but, rather, indifferent.' [Garnsey, 132]

Did the Stoics reject the theory of natural slavery? It is sometimes assumed that they did but if they did, their rejection isn't obvious. It is certainly true that it's difficult to see how one might hold certain Stoic doctrines, such as the common kinship of all peoples, and not reject the idea of natural slavery, but thinkers aren't always consistent and do not always draw out fully the consequences of their beliefs. In the works of some Stoics, such as Posidonius, we encounter a vision of an apolitical Golden Age in which those less wise voluntarily submitted to the rule of their superiors in wisdom, and those superiors did not exploit their inferiors. 'The first men on this earth…and their immediate descendants,' writes Seneca, 'followed nature unspoiled; they took a single person as their leader and their law, freely submitting to the decision of an individual of superior mind….In that age, then, which people commonly refer to as the Golden Age, government, so Posidonius maintains, was in the hands of the wise.' [Seneca 1969, 162-163] We can find an echo of this view in St Thomas's idea that political society would have existed even if our first parents in Eden had not sinned. But such voluntary subordination, whatever else it might be, isn't slavery.

SLAVERY AMONG THE HEBREWS

In the Old Testament, the term 'slavery' can cover a number of different statuses. There was debt slavery of fellow Jews, which was largely a temporary affair. It could arise by means of self-sale or by the sale of a member of one's family. Debt slaves were supposed to be released after six years although this did not always happen. Philo, early in the first century AD, in his *De Specialibus Legibus*, notes that Jewish slaves were to serve only for six years unless they voluntarily chose to stay in service, for example, to remain with their wife and children. On the other hand, the enslavement of prisoners of war was permanent unless they were redeemed by ransom.[30] Slaves, male and female, might be purchased from the surrounding nations or from sojourners. These were property and might be bequeathed like any other property and, unlike Jewish slaves, could be held forever, not merely for six years. [*Leviticus* 25: 44-6] Enslaving foreigners who had been kidnapped was forbidden, as was allowing the extradition of fugitive slaves.

In his treatise, *Every Good Man is Free,* the first century AD Jewish philosopher Philo distinguished two kinds of freedom: one was the kind that keeps one's body free from the domination of other men (legal slavery); the other kept one's soul free from the domination of vices and passions (moral slavery). In a stoicising vein, Philo argued that legal slaves weren't real slaves, their domination being simply the result of misfortune. Moral slavery, on the other hand, was within our control and those who were moral slaves couldn't blame their condition on misfortune. 'Philo also believed that moral slavery was ordained by God, who has created two natures, one servile, the other blessed. He went on to sanction the subjection of moral slaves to institutional slavery, because they need to be controlled, in their own and in everyone else's interest.' [Garnsey, 172] Commenting on the Essenes, a Jewish sect, Philo observed that they had no slaves and that they denounced slave owners 'not merely for their injustice in outraging the law of equality, but also for their impiety in annulling the statute of Nature' which makes men brothers.[31] Similarly, he noted that the Therapeutae, another Jewish sect, believed that the ownership of men was against nature, nature having made all men free.[32] Does this mean that Philo was committed to the abolition of slavery? Not necessarily. The Essenes and the Therapeutae differed from mainstream communities in almost every respect— in their attitude to money, property and slavery. 'There is no implication that ordinary communities can get by without slaves….Philo is quite clear that they could not.' [Garnsey, 79]

SLAVERY AMONG THE CHRISTIANS

Given what we find in the New Testament and the writings of the Fathers of the Church, it's very difficult to sustain the argument that Christianity made any immediately significant difference to the position of slaves in their societies.[33] It is true that St Paul puts menstealers or enslavers in the same category with 'murderers…whoremongers…them that defile themselves with mankind [and] liars',[34] all of them sinners whose behaviour is contrary to sound doctrine. But this prohibition on enslavement which, if it had been given effect to in law or in private behaviour, would gradually have led to the extinction of slavery for lack of slaves, seems to have been a dead letter from the beginning. In the end, the contribution of early Christianity to the slavery issue amounted to not very much more than an admonition to slave masters to treat their slaves well and advice to slaves to obey their masters willingly. [see Sumner, 289-291] Ernst Troeltsch claimed that 'the Christians changed nothing whatever in the laws affecting slaves,' allowing slavery to endure 'right on into the Middle Ages… yet the Church was fully conscious of the inconsistency between this institution and the inner freedom and equality which was the Christian ideal.' [Troeltsch, 133] Even François Guizot, a resolute defender of the claim that the Christian Church was in large part a creator of European civilisation, has to concede that 'slavery existed for a long period in the heart of Christian society, without it being particularly astonished or irritated. A multitude of causes, and a great development in other ideas and principles of civilization, were necessary for the abolition of this iniquity of all iniquities,' but, although the Church did not abolish slavery, it 'exerted its influence to restrain it.' [Guizot, 117]

The early Church simply accepted the political and social *status quo* and, in so doing, took slavery for granted. 'The ancient world rested civilization on a great exploitation of man by man,' writes John Morris Roberts, 'no other possible way of running things was conceivable….[slavery] was the prevailing social institution almost everywhere well into Christian times…'[35] One could see the Church's acceptance of the *status quo* as a matter of serious scandal or one could, as Orlando Patterson does, regard it as 'a serious anachronism to marvel at the ancient church's lack of interest in the abolition of slavery or the lateness of its interest in promoting manumission.' For Patterson, the question that arises regarding the Church and slavery isn't its failure to denounce it in ancient times but 'why it was that the church, after remaining unbothered (like the rest of the world) by the issue for eighteen hundred years, suddenly in the eighteenth century came to consider slavery not only a problem but the greatest evil.' [Patterson 1991, 321-322] Even when the Roman emperors became Christian, their legislation at best improved the position of slaves—abolition wasn't in question. 'If we ask...whether life was on the whole easier for slaves in Christian times than in pagan, the answer is probably—no,' writes Ramsay MacMullen. 'The new religion introduced no radical innovation, only development along lines laid down earlier....The church itself, corporately, and its priests individually, and its models and heroes as well as at least the richer members of congregations whom church leaders normally address, continued to own, buy, and sell men, women, and children.' [MacMullen, 325]

The distinction between slavery of the body and slavery of the soul received an added impetus with the arrival of Christianity. With the development of Stoicism, Christianity allowed the concept of slavery to be developed in such a way that a distinction came to be drawn between legal slavery—the physically coercive control of one man by another—and moral slavery—the subjugation of one's better self to one's baser self. Using this distinction, it is possible for a slave to be (morally) free, and a free man to be (morally) a slave. Seneca, in his *De Beneficiis*, denies that slavery penetrates to a man's moral interior. 'It is a mistake,' he writes, 'for anyone to believe that the condition of slavery penetrates into the whole being of a man. The better part of him is exempt. Only the body is at the mercy and disposition of a master; but the mind is its own master, and is so free and unshackled that not even the prison of the body, in which it is confined, can restrain it from using its own powers....It is, therefore, the body that Fortune hands over to a master; it is this that he buys, it is this that he sells; that inner part cannot be delivered into bondage.'[36]

As with every other writer and thinker of his period, St Paul accepts the institution of slavery. As is clear from his *First Letter to the Corinthians*, he exhorts his readers to be content to remain in their social condition. 'Everyone should remain in the state in which he was called. Were you a slave when called? Never mind. But if you can gain your freedom, avail yourself of the opportunity.' [1 *Corinthians* 7: 20-21] In *Colossians* and in other epistles, he tells slaves to 'obey in everything those that are your earthly masters...'[37] In *Ephesians*, Paul seems to express complete acceptance of the *status quo* of slavery, admonishing slaves to be obedient to their earthly masters not reluctantly but willingly and from the heart! Masters are counselled to forbear threatening their slaves [*Ephesians* 6: 5-8] but there's no hint at all in this passage (or any other) that there might be anything fundamentally problematic with slavery. Moreover, Paul makes no mention of any restriction on slavery, such as the six-year restriction that we find in the Jewish law. The reason for this acceptance of the *status quo* would appear to be that provided one's relationship to Christ is in order, one's social status is ultimately a matter of no importance. In the context of the fundamental spiritual equality of all human beings, all existing human distinctions—male/female, Jew/Greek, slave/free—are relatively insignificant.

Paul makes this point in *Galatians*, explicitly erasing all social distinctions: 'There is neither Jew nor Greek, there is neither slave nor free, there is neither male nor female; for you are all one in Christ Jesus.'[38] Christ is not only the one who flattens out and erases all human distinctions; he is also the one who through his own voluntary act of abasement (*kenosis*), which ended in a slave's death, shows us that our salvation lies in our becoming slaves of righteousness. 'Christ Jesus…emptied himself, taking the form of a slave…'[39]

Augustine, in his *Commentary on the Psalms*, echoes and indeed amplifies Paul's acceptance of slavery. He remarks that Christ 'did not make freemen out of slaves, but good slaves out of bad slaves' and points out that the rich should be grateful to Christ for 'creating stability in their homes!'[40] Commenting on Psalm 124, he relies on Paul's injunction that slaves should obey their masters to justify his claim that the just should give honour to those who rule over them, even if those rulers are unjust.[41] As should be obvious from these remarks, Augustine, as with most other thinkers of his period, accepted the social fact of slavery which, along with other forms of property, is justified by the positive law of the ruler. What makes my house to be my house and my slave to be my slave is man-made law. 'Take away the laws of emperors, and who will dare say, "that villa is mine, that slave is mine or this house is mine"? People have accepted the laws of kings so that they can possess those very things.'[42] As is the case with Paul, slaves are exhorted to obey their masters and masters to maintain the order of the household. [see *City of God*, 19: 14; 16]

According to Augustine, in the order of creation, no man was intended to be a slave either to any another man or to lust. God did not desire man to dominate over other men but only over irrational creatures. He writes that God 'did not wish the rational being, made in his own image, to have dominion over any but irrational creatures, not man over man, but man over the beasts.' It follows, he thinks, that not only was kingship *not* an original and natural constituent of society but that slavery also isn't natural but rather the result of sin, whether one's own sins or the sins of others. Augustine is sensitive to the claim that the permission of human slavery by a just God is difficult to defend. His solution is to present slavery as a punishment for sin. 'The prime cause of slavery, then, is sin, so that man was put under man in a state of bondage…' [*City of God*, 19.15] This being so, he is content to endorse a version of the 'slavery is for the benefit of the enslaved' theory. [*City of God*, 19.21]

Augustine was aware of, and responded to, the views of some others. In Book III of Cicero's *Republic*, Philus had argued that the state couldn't exist or be properly administered without injustice. It was unjust for some men to be made to serve others, yet no imperial city could exist or function unless this was done. Laelius responded in a quasi-Aristotelian mode that slavery could be beneficial for some.[43] Augustine, commenting on these arguments, takes the side of Laelius, claiming that those who are made to serve are in fact benefitted by this compulsion: 'servitude is in the interest of such men…those subdued will be better off because when not subdued they were worse off.' [*City of God*, 19.21] If we leave aside the question-begging sub-argument in the last part of the quotation, we can see that the counter to the argument that slavery is unjust is simply the re-assertion that those coerced into service are benefitted by that coercion. Augustine isn't the only Church Father to make this point. Ambrose, commenting on the story of Esau's enslavement to Jacob, says 'Isaac was right to deny Esau freedom to make his own choices: else he might drift like a ship in the waves without a helmsman.'[44] Basil of Caesarea initially seems to come down firmly on the side of the rejection of slavery as unnatural—slavery occurs only because of misfortune in war or self-sale in cases of economic distress— but he believes the Jacob-Esau story illustrates the point that some are, by nature, slaves to others because they lack the ability to self-direct. [see *On the Holy Spirit*, 20]

Lactantius, writing in his *Divine Institutes* in the fourth century AD, seems to run counter to the almost universal acceptance of slavery when he states boldly that all men are free by virtue of their Divine creation and when he accuses the Greeks and the Romans of injustice because of their institution of social divisions between man and man.[45] Eventually, however, he falls back upon the distinction between legal slavery and moral slavery, downplaying the significance of the legal form. Garnsey remarks, however, that 'The damage has been done. What stays in the mind is the absence of justice among men.... Despite Lactantius' efforts to repair the damage he has himself inflicted, the logic of his own argument is that spiritual equality is a second-best.' [Garnsey, 80] If Lactantius lets the cat out half of the bag, Gregory of Nyssa let the feline fly free! In one of his homilies, he remarks scathingly that 'God would not therefore reduce the human race to slavery, since he himself, when we had been enslaved to sin, spontaneously recalled us to freedom. But if God does not enslave what is free, who is he that sets his own power above God's?' [*Homilies* IV, 336.16-19] Man is made in the image and likeness of God and all are alike in their bodily frames, their desires, their troubles and their anguish and their joys. He then asks, 'If you are equal in all these ways, therefore, in what respect have you something extra, tell me, that you who are human think yourself the master of a human being....?'[46] This looks very much like an attack on slavery as something so fundamentally opposed to God's design for man that it would seem to merit outright rejection.

On the other hand, Theodoret roundly condemned what he regarded as a class of professional complainers, those who resent taxes and bewail slavery and many other things that, as he says, fit only too well into this life.[47] Who were these fifth century AD troublemakers that merited Theodoret's condemnation? The consensus is that they were Eusthatian (Manichean) heretics. Theodoret wasn't alone in his opposition to the social radicals. The Council of Gangra decreed that 'If anyone, on the pretext of religion, teaches another man's slave to despise his master, and to withdraw from his service, and not to serve his master with good will and all respect, let him be anathema.' This decree was incorporated into the Church's collection of canons and was used for the next 1,400 years![48]

Defenders of New World slavery weren't slow to notice these early Christian sentiments. Thomas Dew, although conceding that slavery is against the spirit of Christianity, noted that there was nothing in either the Old or the New Testament that required slavery to be abrogated. The Hebrews approved of slavery, he says, and there's nothing in the New Testament to disturb the conscience of a slave-holder. Christ himself did not counsel insurrection, even though he lived in the midst of a Roman world. The apostolic writings of Paul and other New Testament writers show clearly, he thinks, that 'slavery in the Roman world was nowhere charged as a fault or a crime upon the holder, and everywhere is the most implicit obedience enjoined.'[49] Orlando Patterson, a preeminent historian of slavery, exposes what he believes to be the anachronism of our modern embarrassment in the face of the existence, toleration and even endorsement of slavery by some of the great figures of the ancient and modern worlds. 'Americans,' he says, 'have never been able to explain how it came to pass that the most articulate defender of their freedoms, Thomas Jefferson, and the greatest hero of their revolution and history, George Washington, both were large-scale, largely unrepentant slave-holders.'[50] But such embarrassment, he believes, results from a failure to grasp the intimate connection between freedom and slavery. 'We assume,' he says, 'that slavery should have nothing to do with freedom; that a man who holds freedom dearly should not hold slaves without discomfort; that a culture which invented democracy or produced a Jefferson should not be based on slavery.' On the contrary, Patterson believes, 'slavery and freedom are intimately connected' and 'it is indeed reasonable that those who most denied freedom, as well as those to whom it was most denied, were the very persons most alive to it. Once we understand the essence and the dynamics of slavery, we immediately realize why there's nothing in the least anomalous about the fact that an Aristotle or a Jefferson owed slaves. Our embarrassment springs from our ignorance of the true nature of slavery and of freedom.' [Patterson 1992, ix]

It is important to note in passing one significant difference between classical and modern slavery which is that slavery in the ancient world was *not* based on racial distinctions or, at least, not directly so. How could it be when those enslaved and those enslaving them were often members of the same race! The operative distinction seems to have been that between insiders and outsiders; in the case of the Greeks, between Greeks and barbarians (non-Greeks); in the case of the Jews, between Jews and non-Jews. Some qualms were felt about the enslave-ment of insiders but very few or no qualms were felt about the enslavement of outsiders. As Thomas Sowell notes, for centuries before the origin of slavery on the North American continent, 'Europeans had enslaved other Europeans, Asians had enslaved other Asians and Africans had enslaved other Africans.' [Sowell 2011, 180] Racism did not give rise to slavery; rather, racism came into being as a convenient tool for defending an institution that would otherwise have had no way to defend itself against libertarian assault. 'Racism became a justification of slavery in a society where it could not be justified otherwise—and centuries of racism did not suddenly vanish with the abolition of the slavery that gave rise to it. But the direction of causation was the direct opposite of what is assumed by those who depict the enslavement of Africans as being the result of racism.' [Sowell 2011, 181] Nor was the importation of slaves to the North American continent the first time that the transport of slaves gave rise to an inter-continental traffic. 'North Africa's Barbary Coast pirates alone captured and enslaved at least a million Europeans from 1500 to 1800, carrying more Europeans into bondage in North Africa than there were Africans brought in bondage to the United States and to the American colonies from which it was formed. Moreover, Europeans were still being bought and sold in the slave markets of the Islamic world, decades after blacks were freed in the United States.'[51]

Slavery is one of the oldest and longest-lasting of human institutions. For most of human history it has been entirely normal and unremarkable that some human beings should have owned and disposed of others. Even slaves, while they might have resented their own enslavement, did not question the normality of slavery! What perhaps needs to be understood is not the existence and widespread acceptance of slavery for almost all of human history but why, as it were in the blink of a moral eye, it should have come to be regarded as the most reprehensible and morally unacceptable of institutions.

Notes

1 Davie, 194. See also 66-67, 75, 89-95, 160-175 and 228-229.

2 *Digest*, I.5.4 in Watson ed., Volume I, 15.

3 For a sophisticated, if somewhat controversial, account of Greek and Roman slavery, see Patterson 1991, 47-263.

4 'Debt slavery,' notes Margaret Atwood, 'is by no means a thing of the distant past. Consider present day India, where a man may be a virtual debt slave all his life—many get into this position through having to provide dowries. Think, too, of the smuggling of illegal immigrants from Asia into North America, where the person smuggled is told he has to work without wages forever in order to pay off the cost of his travel experience.' [Atwood, 57]

5 Shaw, in Finley 1980/1998, 15; see also 143.

6 Fisher, 101; see Garnsey, 135.

7 Some authors, however, are inclined to take a rather more benign, perhaps even rose-tinted, view of Roman slavery. The French historian, Jérôme Carcopino, writes, 'The practical good sense of the Romans, no less than the fundamental humanity instinctive in their peasant hearts, had always kept them from showing cruelty toward the *servi*....slavery in Rome was neither eternal nor, while it lasted, intolerable...' [Carcopino, 69]

8 Carcopino, 71; see 69-74.

9 Sumner, 283; but see Carcopino, 72-73.

10 See Scott 1985 and Scott 2009.

11 DK 87:44, Freeman, 148.

12 Fisher, 89; see Barnes 1987.

13 See Aristotle's *Rhetoric*, 1373b18.

14 *Digest*, I.5.4 in Watson ed., Volume I, 15.

15 *Digest*, I.1.4 in Watson ed., Volume I, 2.

16 *Digest*, I.XII, 64 in Watson ed., Volume I, 388.

17 *Institutes*, I.2.2 in Sanders trans., 89.

18 Davis, in Drescher & Engerman, xv.

19 I. 8-9; 2.1, 12-14, 14a.

20 *Politics* 1260b5-8.

21 *Politics* 1253b20-23.

22 *Rhetoric* 1373b6-9.

23 *Politics*, 1254a15-16.

24 *Politics* 1254b25-31.

25 *Politics* 1254b31.

26 *Politics* 1260a12; 1254b18-19.

27 *Politics* 1254b25-27.

28 *Politics* 1255b9-15. See also 1278b32-8 and *Nicomachean Ethics* 1134b10-13.

29 *Nicomachean Ethics* 1149a8-9; but see Garnsey 114 and 125.

30 See *Exodus* 21: 1-11; *Deuteronomy* 15: 12-18 and *Leviticus* 25: 39-55.

31 Philo, *Every Good Man is Free*, 79.

32 Philo, *On the Contemplative Life*, 70.

33 For a suggestive and provocative treatment of the spiritual and material dimensions of slavery in the Gospels and in St Paul, see Patterson 1991, 293-344.

34 1 *Timothy* 1:9-10.

35 Roberts 1993, 49, 141.

36 Seneca 1964, *De Beneficiis*, 3.20.1-2.

37 *Colossians* 3: 22; see *Ephesians* 6: 5-8, *Titus* 2: 9-13 and 1 *Timothy* 6: 1-2; see also I *Peter* 2: 18.

38 *Galatians* 3: 28. See also 1 *Corinthians* 12:13, *Colossians* 3:11.

39 *Philippians* 2: 5-7; see Romans 6: 18.

40 *Commentary on the Psalms*, 124.7.

41 *Commentary on the Psalms* 124.7.

42 *Tractate on the Gospel of John*, 6: 2.

43 *De Re Publica* 3.35-39, passages preserved in Augustine's *Contra Iulianum*, 4: 12. 61 and *City of God*, 14:23.

44 *De Jacob et Vita Beata*, 2.3. 11.

45 Lactantius, *Divine Institutes*, 5.14.15-15.3.

46 *Homilies* IV, 338.14-16; see Maxwell, 32-33, and Siedentop, 119.

47 *On Divine Providence*, 7 668B, 669B-C; see Maxwell, 36.

48 See Canon 3. C. J. C. *Decreti Gratiani*, II, C.XVII, Q. IV, c. 37. In 1918, the selling of slaves was finally condemned and, in 1965, in Vatican II, all violations of human integrity were condemned, including slavery.

49 See Dew, in Faust, 61-62.

50 Patterson 1982, ix. Louis Menand remarks that 'We think of the Civil War as a war to save the union and to abolish slavery, but before the fighting began most people regarded these as incompatible ideals....Northern business men believed that losing the South would mean economic catastrophe, and many of their employees believed that freeing the slaves would mean lower wages. They feared secession far more than they disliked slavery, and they were unwilling to risk the former by trying to pressure the South into giving up the latter.' [Menand, 4]

51 Sowell 2011, 180. For more on Arab-Islamic black slavery, see Segal, passim and Azumah, passim. For material on Arab-Islamic white slavery see Davis 2003, passim and Milton 2004, passim.

Chapter 6

From *Antipolis* to *Cosmopolis*: Hellenistic and Roman Political Thought

Rehearse death. To say this is to tell a person to rehearse his freedom.
A person who has learned how to die has unlearned how to be a slave.
He is above, or at any rate, beyond the reach of, all political powers
—Seneca

Freedom suppressed and again regained bites with deeper fangs
than freedom never endangered
—Cicero

Many students, when they begin the study of philosophy, have it subtly conveyed to them that nothing much of interest happened in philosophy between the time of Aristotle until the advent of modernity. Plato and Aristotle they must pay attention to, of course, but, having done that, with perhaps a very rapid glance at Hellenistic Philosophy, Neo-Platonism and some random medieval philosophers, they move quickly to restart their philosophical studies in earnest with the seventeenth century French philosopher, René Descartes. This is the softhearted approach! The sterner approach simply ignores the Hellenistic period and the Middle Ages altogether and begins the study of philosophy with Descartes with, at most, a pious bow in the direction of Plato and Aristotle. But the philosophical thought of the Hellenistic period and the Middle Ages can't be ignored. It provided (and provides) a significant contrast with the overly theoretical and abstract political thought of Plato and Aristotle, restoring the practical dimension of philosophy and reconnecting it to challenges and experiences of everyday life.[1] There are those, moreover, such as Harold Berman, who believe that Western civilisation has its proximate source not in Greece or Rome or the Near East but in medieval Europe so that any attempt to grasp the essence of Western civilisation must encompass an appreciation of the history and intellectual life of the Middle Ages, late and early.

In estimating the value of the political thought of Plato and Aristotle it is important to realise that both of them applied their thinking only to the *polis* and not to any other form of political organisation. But even as Aristotle was writing, his erstwhile pupil Alexander the Great was bringing about a new political dispensation in which the *polis* of the Greeks, though it would continue to exist in some form for some time, wouldn't do so exactly as it had done before. Even so, it would be easy to over-dramatise and overestimate the disruptive political significance of the Alexandrian and post-Alexandrian military adventures.

Josiah Ober argues that 'the initial loss of Greek independence turned out to be only partial: Although the power of the Macedonian dynasts was real many postclassical Greek poleis enjoyed considerable independence in the Hellenistic period. Some smaller Greek states were more independent than they had been in the era of hegemonic city-states.' [Ober 2015, 295-296]

Both Plato and Aristotle thought that the good life for man necessarily involved a commitment to and participation in the life of the *polis*—only so was the good life achievable. The man who withdrew from the *polis* to live his life alone was *idiotes*, a term from which we get our word 'idiot'. Not everybody was similarly persuaded. Some thinkers put forward a notion that the good life for man was achievable only by a withdrawal from society. For them, the individual,[2] not the *polis*, was self-sufficient. John Morrall remarks that 'the ancient city was a combination of groups (tribes, families, trades) rather than of individuals, and it seems likely that the reaction in the period between Alexander and Constantine towards more "personalist" philosophies (Stoicism, Epicureanism, Neo-Platonism) was a measure of the frustration of the individual with the collectivist framework of his social life.' [Morrall 1970, 55]

All the Hellenistic schools (with the exception of Stoicism) differ from Plato and Aristotle in rejecting the *polis*. They sought tranquillity, peace, and freedom from yearning. In this, they all echo in one way or another certain themes in Taoism and, in the case of Stoicism, Buddhism. In ancient China, the Taoists distinguished between natural and unnatural desires. If we are to survive we must eat, so the satisfaction of hunger is the fulfilment of a natural desire. But many, perhaps most, of our desires are not in any sense natural and we can spend our lives endlessly and pointlessly in pursuit of their satisfaction. For Taoists, it isn't so much a matter of what one does, even of what one desires; it is more a matter of how one does what one does and how one desires what one desires. In a manner very similar to the Taoists, Epicurus distinguished between desires that are both natural and necessary (food when hungry, drink when thirsty), those that are natural but not necessary (fancy foods and expensive drink), and those that are neither natural nor necessary (the search for honour or esteem). 'Together with the Stoics and Epicureans,' writes Jason Saunders, 'the Skeptics sought a pathway, a way of life, *ars vitae*, the significance of which would mirror the goals of quietude, surcease, *ataraxia* or tranquillity, and the achievement of a euphoric state of mind.' [Saunders 1966, 9] 'Stoicism became a "popular philosophy" in a way that neither Platonism nor Aristotelianism ever did,' writes Dirk Baltzly. 'In part this is because Stoicism, like its rival Epicureanism, addressed the questions that most people are concerned with in very direct and practical ways. It tells you how you should regard death, suffering, great wealth, poverty, power over others and slavery....Historians of philosophy earlier in this century regarded this as a mark against Hellenistic philosophy generally. The notion was that philosophy peaked with Plato and Aristotle and then degenerated into the popular "feel good" philosophy of the Hellenistic period...' [Baltzly, 31-32]

EPICUREANS

Epicurus, the founder of Epicureanism, started a school of philosophy in Athens in 306 BC, some sixteen years after the death of Aristotle. Metaphysically, Epicureanism is materialistic through and through. Adopting the physical theories of Democritus, the Epicureans believed that the world was made up of atoms. Everything—physical, biological, social, historical, political—comes about through the permutations and combinations of matter, without any need for a directing intelligence or orderer. We can see similarities between the Epicureans and Hobbes who was also, or at least attempted to be, a consistent materialist. Hobbes might even be thought of as a latter-day Lucretius.[3] For the Epicureans, the good life is the life of pleasure, pleasure understood not positively as the presence of some good but negatively as the absence of pain or disturbance. 'When we say, then, that pleasure is the end and aim,' writes Epicurus, 'we do not mean the pleasures of the prodigal or the pleasures of sensuality….we mean the absence of pain in the body and of trouble in the soul. It is not an unbroken succession of drinking bouts and of revelry, not sexual-love, not the enjoyment of the fish and other delicacies of a luxurious table, which produce a pleasant life; it is sober reasoning, searching out the grounds of every choice and avoidance and banishing those beliefs through which the greatest tumults take possession of the soul.'[4] Public life, life in the *polis*, involves one in a morass of care and concerns that do not bode well for the equanimity and contentment of the individual.

Diogenes Laertius states that the wise man won't participate in civic life nor will he be a tyrant or a Cynic [Diogenes Laertius, 10.119] and Plutarch noted that the Epicureans urged their followers to avoid public life and expressed disgust for those who participate in it, 'abusing the earliest and wisest lawgivers and urging contempt for the laws.' He commented that when the Epicureans write about politics, they do so 'to discourage us from practicing politics… and about kingship to discourage us from consorting with kings.'[5] For Epicureans, writes Jason Saunders, 'Happiness and pleasure are not to be found in the exercise of the mind nor in man's role as a free citizen and fraternal member of a local assembly.…True happiness is found in withdrawal, and it is perhaps in epicureanism that we find this theme most strongly presented.…Pleasure… is the chief end of man, but pleasure meant the absence of bodily pain and a troubled soul.' [Saunders 1966, 6]

In contrast to Plato and Aristotle, both of whom took man to be by nature a social animal, the Epicureans were radical individualists. Society isn't a natural entity but the result of convention and agreement and is formed, as all else, by man's desire for happiness. Aside from the necessary inclination of human action towards happiness, all other human actions are merely conventional and are to be accepted or rejected inasmuch as they contribute or do not contribute to happiness. In their rejection of any intrinsic human values apart from happiness, the Epicureans made use of the standard relativistic arguments, pointing out the vast variety of what men have accepted or insisted on at various times and in various places.

The Epicurean account of the state anticipates some themes later elaborated by Hobbes. Human nature is rooted in self-interest, the desire, apparently ineliminable, of every individual for his own happiness. To desire the happiness of others is to be every bit as self-interested as to desire one's own happiness or, rather, it is to desire one's own happiness in and through the happiness of others. Self-interestedness and self-centredness are not the same thing. Since all men are motivated by their desire for happiness and since this is likely to clash with the same desires of other men, it is mutually beneficial for all to agree not to inflict harm on others. There's no such thing as injustice in and of itself but the inconvenience of a free-for-all is much greater than any inconvenience resulting from a mutual respect for one another's desires. Morality and justice are, in the end, matters merely of expedience and vary according to time, place and circumstances. Such being the case, the wise man must free himself 'from the prison of general education and politics.'[6] Given that human nature at root is the same for all—all men are moved by self-interest—it isn't surprising that there's a large degree of convergence among different peoples on what self-interest dictates, despite inevitable local variations. The purpose of the state, for the Epicurean, as for Hobbes, is the production and maintenance of security, and whatever form of government works best to produce this is to be preferred. A mild preference for monarchy is characteristic of Epicureans though this may have as much to do with their social class as with the relative efficiency of monarchy in the security business.

CYNICS

If the Epicureans were proto-Hobbesians, then the Cynics might be regarded as the fourth century BC Hellenistic version of your nineteenth century radical anarchists! They originated indirectly from the Socratic tradition and, in turn, gave rise to Stoicism. As with the other Hellenistic philosophies, Cynicism seems to be, at least in part, a product of the individual's feeling of helplessness and homelessness in the face of a hostile universe. Including among their number Diogenes of Sinope (perhaps the most famous of the Cynics), Anthisthenes (the traditional founder of the school), Crates and Menippus, 'they formulated a protest against the city-state and the social classifications upon which it rested, and their escape lay in the renunciation of everything that men commonly called the goods of life, in the levelling of all social distinctions, and in abandoning the amenities and sometimes even the decencies of social conventions.' [Sabine, 136] They rejected property and family, citizenship and reputation or, perhaps, it might be truer to say rather that they ignored such things, for to say that they rejected property and family, citizenship and reputation is to pay such institutions an inverted compliment. Diogenes, notoriously, lived a life according to nature as he saw it, eating and excreting in public and sleeping on the street in his large wine cask. The key ideas of Cynicism are the acceptance of nature as norm and the rejection of culture, self-sufficiency as a key to release from bondage to social control, and a habit of speaking truth to power, most famously exemplified in the notorious (and probably apocryphal) tale of Diogenes's meeting with Alexander the Great in which, when Alexander asked Diogenes if he could do anything for him, Diogenes replied; 'Yes, stand a little out of my sun.'[7]

The Cynics shared with the Epicureans the notion that it was the individual and not the *polis* that should be self-sufficing. They were no social protesters arguing for the righting of wrongs—slave or free, poor or rich, all conditions alike were a matter of indifference to them. It might be something of an exaggeration but then again, perhaps not, to call the Cynics the Hippies of Hellenism. As did the Sophists, the Cynics distinguished sharply between nature and convention. Society gives rise to complex and unnatural desires, for wealth, fame and power, whereas the individual is and can be satisfied by the simple life. They rejected 'The System'—the city, culture, all social conventions and institutions—and practised and preached a return to nature. No longer citizens of the narrow parochial *polis*, Cynics regarded themselves rather as citizens of the world-as-city, the *cosmopolis*. If they were citizens of *cosmopolis*, they were so more in a negative than in a positive fashion, rejecting the limitations and restrictions of the *polis* rather than embracing a positive alternative vision. The positive take on cosmopolitanism belongs to yet another school, Stoicism that in many ways was a product of and reaction to Cynicism.

The Cynics weren't anchorites. They lived *in* society but, as it were, they were not *of* society and their rejection of conventions went all the way down, including the rejection of modesty and manners. What is the point of this simple and non-conventional life? It is to achieve *eudaimonia*, understood not in the Aristotelian sense of that term but as a kind of lived detachment, physical and mental, from the absurdities of conventional life in society. Like the Epicureans, the Cynics believed that we have natural desires, and those are to be satisfied as they occur but not to excess. Unnatural desires are to be rejected completely. Cynic virtues are a kind of independence and indifference towards circumstances. It goes without saying that Cynics reject the notion of property in any full-blooded sense; once again, they teach a detachment from a dependence upon possessions. It is doubtless too far-fetched to suggest, as some have done, that Jesus was himself a Cynic, though there are certain similarities between his indifference to, and detachment from, wealth and that of the Cynics. Of course, there are manifest differences as well, not least of which was the absence of shamelessness in the life of Jesus. Nevertheless, the ever-present emphasis on the moral superiority of poverty that one finds in Christianity, as in the Franciscan tradition, sits surprisingly easily with certain aspects of Cynicism.

SCEPTICS

If Cynicism is an attempt to live a calm and detached life free from the unnatural desires produced by society, Scepticism could perhaps be seen as the desire for intellectual calmness, freedom from the restless and unsatisfiable desire for certainty. Knowledge, certain knowledge at least, is impossible and the desire for it is productive of an intellectual longing that's incapable of being satisfied. The most we can have are beliefs that can be more or less probable and which are a sufficient ground for action. The Sceptics advocated a mental attitude of entertainment, a suspension of judgement (*epoche*), and this, they believed, would lead to *ataraxia*, a form of mental tranquillity or imperturbability.

Sceptics argue that no one position in philosophy is any more believable than another. Does this not lead to a practical paralysis? No. Sceptics simply adapt themselves to the customs and practices of whatever community they happen to be in. Since certainty is unattainable, giving up the fruitless search for it leads to a quiet and simple life. Academic Scepticism was a development of certain elements of Socratic and Platonic philosophy. This may seem surprising at first but it is well known that Socrates is reputed to have said that all that he knew was that he knew nothing! Scepticism became the official philosophical position of Plato's Academy in the mid-third century BC.

Scepticism comes in different forms. The more severe form is characterised by the claim that there is no truth. For well-known self-referential reasons, it is hard to defend this claim. (Is that claim itself true?—then Scepticism is false; is that claim false?—then Scepticism is false. Either way, Scepticism is false.) A less severe form of Scepticism consists in conceding that there may well be truth but that we humans are not in a position to know it. The Sceptics found themselves in opposition to what they regarded as the dogmatism of the Stoics. The Stoics held that our sensory impressions were on occasion so strong that we could be certain of what they told us. The Sceptics, on the other hand, argued that all sensation and all perception is relative and thus couldn't be productive of certainty. Indeed, if the Stoic position amounts to a certain variety of naïve realism, then the Sceptics have a point. Many centuries later, St Thomas Aquinas, not a notorious sceptic, would say that everything that's received is received according to the mode of the receiver. [*Summa Theologiae*, 1a, q. 75, a. 5; 3a, q. 5]

STOICS

Of all the Hellenistic Schools of Philosophy, there can be little doubt that Stoicism was the one with the most influence on its immediate social environment and on subsequent thinkers. Stoicism is a philosophy that originated from early Cynicism with which it continued to share certain characteristics. The founder of Stoicism is commonly taken to be Zeno of Citium who gave birth to this philosophy in Athens in the third century BC. 'The best exponent of anarchist philosophy in ancient Greece,' writes Peter Kropotkin, 'was Zeno (342-267 or 270 BC), from Crete, the founder of Stoic philosophy, who distinctly opposed his conception of a free community without government to the state-utopia of Plato. He repudiated the omnipotence of the state, its intervention and regimentation, and proclaimed the sovereignty of the moral law of the individual—remarking already that, while the necessary instinct of self-preservation leads man to egotism, nature has supplied a corrective to it by providing man with another instinct—that of sociability.' [Kropotkin 1910, 236-237]

There are many famous names to be found attached to this School of philosophy—Cleanthes, Seneca, Epictetus and, of course, the only Roman Emperor ever to have been a practising philosopher, Marcus Aurelius. The Stoics held that truth was, in certain circumstances, attainable, even if, more often than not, we had to be content with belief or opinion. This claim brought them into conflict with the Sceptics. If the default position of Epicureanism, Cynicism and Scepticism was the rejection of the *polis* and with it an attitude of detachment (sometimes rejection) of political life, the default position of Stoicism was the reverse. As Diogenes Laertius says, quoting Chrysippus, 'the wise man will participate in politics unless something prevents him.' [Diogenes Laertius 7: 121]

As was the case with the Cynics, the early Stoics were moved to develop a way of thinking and acting that would buffer them from the disturbing physical and social forces that surrounded them. Stoicism held that knowing how the world worked, in particular, understanding that universal determinism holds sway, helped to produce the right attitude to one's emotional life. Stoicism is often thought to have advocated the extinction of one's emotional life but this isn't so. Jealousy, anger, envy and many other emotions are prone to disturb our equanimity but what the Stoics sought wasn't the extinction of such emotions but a method by which they could be held in proper balance. They *did* propose freedom from passion, where passion is a kind of anguished suffering to which man is subject. Evil in the world is the product of ignorance and it can be avoided or minimised if one brings one's thoughts, actions and desires into conformity with the principle underlying the world, the universal reason or *logos*.

The political implications of Stoicism are that, as all human beings are essentially the same in kind, all are citizens of the universe (*cosmopolis*) and all are called upon to help one another. [see Siedentop, 46] Honours, riches, and pleasure are transient and unimportant aspects of human life and the political world is only a shadow of the universal city. Believing in a universal divine Providence, the Stoics held that human beings had the capacity to develop an awareness of themselves as kindred to one another by virtue of their common rationality. Human rationality, in turn, is a kind of ligament that ties each individual to the universal reason that governs the universe so as to make a great whole in which nothing happens by accident and everything and everybody has it place and its role.[8] Marcus Aurelius writes 'If mind is common to us all, then we have reason also in common—that which makes us rational beings. If so, then common too is the reason that dictates what we should or should not do. If so, then law too is common to us all. If so, then we are citizens. If so, we share in a constitution. If so, the universe is a kind of community.' [*Meditations*, 4: 4]

For Lucius Annaeus Seneca (4 BC-AD 65), one of the most famous of the Stoics, property and coercive government emerge from the loss of our original innocence and yet, somewhat paradoxically, are remedies for it as well. 'Seneca holds of the great institutions of society, property and coercive government, namely, that they are the consequences of and the remedies for vice.' [Carlyle I, 25] In fact, with the addition of slavery to property and coercive government, this view was to become a commonplace among the Christian Fathers. Slavery, private property and coercive government are not aspects of man's original social condition but are the product of some lapse from innocence, some fall from grace. Seneca, as Cicero, holds to what one might term a republican theory of liberty. Whatever about man's natural condition, in the realities of a post-innocent society, liberty is essentially related to being a member of a suitably constituted state. As I already noted, Stoicism had an embryonically enlightened attitude towards slavery. Slaves are not to be despised; their condition results from misfortune rather than from some moral or intellectual defect. Seneca went so far as to write to Lucilius that 'your slave traces his origin back to the same stock as yourself, has the same good sky above him, breathes as you do, lives as you do, dies as you do.' [Seneca 1969, 93] For Seneca, we are all essentially equal. No one is a slave by nature. Slavery is the result of misfortune affecting only the body but not the whole man. He gives us an account of man's original condition that is, in a secular mode, very much like the Christian story of the Fall. In this he differs from Cicero to the extent that Cicero has no developed idea of such a state of innocence and material which we find in his writings that might relate to such a conception is undeveloped. 'Seneca's view is, in all important points, the same as that of the Christian Fathers, that man was once innocent and happy but has grown corrupt.' [Carlyle I, 25] Before the emergence of conventions, men lived in peace and happiness without slavery and without coercive government. This state of innocence is disrupted by the emergence of avarice and uncontrolled desire. The natural voluntary subordination of the not-so-wise to the wise is replaced by tyranny, so that men must have recourse to laws to exercise some control over their rulers.

Cicero

Is the history of philosophy a smooth, unbroken story or are there significant discontinuities? Historians differ on this point. Even among those who support a theory of discontinuity, not everyone locates the breaks in the same place. Carlyle[9] belongs to the discontinuity school but, significantly, he thinks one of the significant breaks occurs between Aristotle and the Roman thinkers of the first century BC and after. [see Carlyle I, 2] 'There is no change in political theory so startling in its completeness as the change from the theory of Aristotle to the later philosophical view represented by Cicero and Seneca.' [Carlyle I, 8] Carlyle sees the continuation of this idea in the Roman Lawyers of the Imperial period. Whereas Aristotle is committed to a theory of the natural inequality of types of men, the Romans believe that since reason is common to all men, all men are, in respect of their humanity, fundamentally equal.[10]

Although Marcus Tullius Cicero was born in the rural backwater of Arpinum in 106 BC, and came from a comparatively modest family that lacked significant wealth or political connections, he made his way in the political maelstrom that was Rome in the century before Christ, and he did it through sheer ability, persistence and force of personality. [see Cowell 1956, 219-269] He became consul in 63 BC and suppressed the Cataline conspiracy, in the process executing several Roman citizens without trial. This unconstitutional action was to dog him for the remainder of his political career. He declined an invitation from Julius Caesar to join what would later come to be known as the first triumvi-rate (Caesar, Pompey and Crassus) only to be proscribed and executed by the second triumvirate (Octavian, Lepidus and Mark Antony), largely at the behest of a vengeful Mark Antony whose political ambitions he had thwarted.[11] His political life and achievements are a matter of public record but, unusually, we know of his interior life through his letters to his friend Atticus. Shortly before he was killed, he was so deeply grieved by the death of his daughter Tullia in childbirth that he withdrew from all public business. 'Cicero was devastated,' writes Anthony Everitt. 'Then, having gained leave of absence from his public duties, he fled the city….Cicero's state of mind during this crisis reveals a new intensity of feeling, too raw and too astonishing to be publicized. He showed little self-pity; his pain was so fierce as almost to be physical.' [Everitt, 243, 244]

The life and writings of Cicero gives the lie to the old canard that nothing of significance in political theory happened between the death of Aristotle and the new philosophy of the sixteenth century. Many think of Cicero as a mere conduit for the ideas of others and although there is a measure of truth in this judgement, it's far from being the whole truth. Cicero's thought isn't original, consisting mainly of compilations and summaries. He regarded himself as an Academic Sceptic and indeed his cast of mind was generally sympathetic to Scepticism. Despite this, in his ethical and political thought he clearly inclined towards Stoicism. His early education in philosophy was wide-ranging but he always claimed an allegiance to the Academic School. His interests were eclectic and he reserved the right to take whatever he saw to be good wherever it might come from. In *De Officiis*, for example, he adopts a more or less consistently Stoic stance. He wasn't, however, attracted to Epicureanism. As a Sceptic, he denied the possibility of absolute knowledge and emphasised the merits of the suspension of judgement but he did not want scepticism to undermine the value of an active political life. 'The philosopher…must be guided by some understanding of the needs of the city and of the practical consequences of this teachings. He must not risk the chaos that might follow a systematic and ruthless public examination of the principles underlying and guiding a particular order, even an order which strikes him as radically defective, without having given some thought to the alternatives. A defective government, a government which falls far short of the best, may be better than no government at all.' [Holton, 157]

Despite his overall commitment to scepticism, Cicero's mode of thought was syncretistic—the wise man could accept any position that seemed probable while remaining open to arguments on the other side. As a philosopher, Cicero was aware of the contested nature of most ethical and political concepts— justice, law, government, authority, freedom—but as a man of affairs, a former consul, he was aware of the need to act and to make decisions and so in practical matters the suspension of judgement had itself to be suspended. The argument for justice in his *Republic,* for example*,* shows little or no trace of the suspended judgement recommended by Scepticism. Whatever the merits of Cicero as an original thinker, he possessed one very important attribute that more than compensated for any deficiencies—everyone read his writings. As a communicator and a transmitter of ideas, he is without parallel. Cicero's use of the dialogue form in his works isn't unrelated to his eclectic philosophical orientation. As with all dialogues, it isn't a simple matter to identify the words of any one interlocutor with that of the author, even when one of the interlocutors is named Cicero! The works of Cicero that principally concern us are *The Republic* (*De Re Publica*), *The Laws* (*De Legibus*) and *On Obligations* (*De Officiis*).[12] The texts of the first two are radically incomplete. Roughly one third of *The Republic* was discovered on a palimpsest in the Vatican Library in 1820. Cicero's model for his *Republic* is the work of the same name by Plato. Despite incidental criticisms, Cicero's work shares a significant number of features in common with Plato's dialogue. But Cicero is influenced not only by Plato but also by Aristotle, Carneades and Polybius. The central topic of Cicero's *Republic* is often taken to be the constitution of the state but this judgement is based on the accident of history that has preserved the portion of the dialogue that deals with that topic. We know that the fourth book concerned itself with education, the fifth and sixth with the character of the ideal statesman. This presentation of topics would seem to suggest that Cicero was well aware that no matter what constitutional provisions one makes, the character of political society is, in the end, determined by the character of those who participate actively in it.

Some parts of the *Republic* are preserved in the writings of Christians of late antiquity: Lactantius, Augustine and Nonius Marcellus. The section of the *Republic* called 'The Dream of Scipio' [vi 9-29] was commented on by Macrobius and thus transmitted to the Middle Ages where it had a great influence. The various bits and pieces of the *Republic* scattered here and there were eventually collected in the sixteenth century but it wasn't until Cardinal Mai, Prefect of the Vatican Library, detected some traces of an earlier text underneath an eighth century copy of St Augustine's commentary on the *Psalms* that the first more or less substantial segment of the work was recovered. Mai uncovered about 25% of the work. Cicero's *Laws* is similarly incomplete. The various extant manuscripts stop after the third book though there were originally at least five books in the dialogue. Rudd notes that, despite their incomplete state, Cicero's *Republic* and *Laws* 'offer considerable rewards to the modern reader, and especially to the student of the history of political thought.' [Rudd, in Cicero 1998, ix] What he thinks is especially noteworthy about these works is their concentration on first principles such as the idea of political legitimacy and justice and the ideas of liberty and equality.

The question underlying both *The Republic* and *The Laws* is, what is the best political order? We know that the Epicureans were inclined to take a dim view of the active political life and, in line with the general trend of post-Aristotelian Hellenistic philosophy, to counsel withdrawal to private life. Cicero tests and rejects the Epicurean arguments. He seems, at this point, to recommend the active life rather than the contemplative life but elsewhere he expresses another point of view. In the passage known as 'The Dream of Scipio,' the contemplative life is presented as being superior to the active life. Despite the assertion sometimes made that Cicero was engaged in a futile and retroactive justification of the dying Roman Republic, he himself thought that what he was doing was trying to articulate principles that underlay the foundation of any state: 'we are framing laws,' he wrote, 'not just for the Roman people, but for all good and stable communities.' [*Laws*, II, 35]

Cicero's mature view on politics can be summed up in five basic theses: *first*, the universe is governed by providence [*Laws* 1, 21]: 'the whole of nature is ruled by the immortal gods, with their force, impetus, plan, power, sway'; *second*, man is an animal but one whose power of reason makes him akin to the gods: 'whereas men derived the other elements in their make-up from their mortal nature…their mind was implanted in them by God. Hence we have what can truly be called a lineage, origin, or stock in common with the gods. [*Laws* 1, 24]; *third*, we have been made to share justice with one another and justice is natural [*Laws* 1, 33]; justice, and its visible expression law, is based on nature not merely on opinion: 'There is one, single justice. It binds together human society and has been established by one, single law. That law is right reason in commanding and forbidding. A man who does not acknowledge this law is unjust, whether it has been written down anywhere or not.…justice is completely non-existent if it is not derived from nature.' [*Laws* 1, 42]; Nature is the criterion by which we can distinguish between good and bad laws: 'We can distinguish a good law from a bad one solely by the criterion of nature.' [*Laws* 1, 44] 'Most foolish of all is the belief that everything decreed by the institutions or laws of a particular country is just.' [*Laws* 1, 42]

Before going on to discuss the fourth and fifth theses, it's worth taking a short detour to note that a case can be made for the claim that Cicero's major contribution to western thought was his transmission to subsequent ages of the Stoic doctrine of natural law. Even though the text of the *Republic* was lost in the twelfth century and only partially recovered in the nineteenth, many of its finest passages had been excerpted and preserved in the works of Augustine and Lactantius. The most famous account of natural law we can find in Cicero, and one that was to have a continuing effect on later thought, is put into the mouth of Laelius: 'law in the proper sense is right reason in harmony with nature. It is spread through the whole human community, unchanging and eternal, calling people to their duty by its commands and deterring them from wrong-doing by its prohibitions. When it addresses a good man, its command and prohibitions are never in vain; but those same commands and prohibitions have no effect on the wicked. This law can't be countermanded, nor can it be in any way amended, nor can it be totally rescinded. We cannot be exempted from this law by any decrees of the Senate of the people; nor do we need anyone else to expound or explain it. There won't be one such law in Rome and another in Athens, one now and another in the future, but all peoples at all times will be embraced by a single and eternal and unchangeable law; and there will be, as it were, one lord and master of us all—the god who is the author, proposer, and interpreter of that law. Whoever refuses to obey it will be turning his back on himself. Because he has denied his nature as a human being he will face the gravest penalties for this alone, even if he succeeds in avoiding all the other things that are regarded as punishments…'[13]

This very Stoic paean to law is put into the mouth of Laelius. Is it Cicero's own view? We might remember that Philus, another interlocutor in the dialogue, expresses *realpolitik* sentiments to the effect that it is neither possible nor desirable always to follow the strict demands of justice. Should we likewise attribute *these* views to Cicero? If one, why not the other?; if not one, why the other? We can find evidence in the *Laws*, however, that this view of law may in fact be Cicero's own. There, in his own person, he remarks: 'according to the opinion of the best authorities law was not thought up by the intelligence of human beings, nor is it some kind of resolution passed by communities, but rather an eternal force which rules the world by the wisdom of its commands and prohibitions. In their judgement, that original and final law is the intelligence of God, who ordains or forbids everything by reason.' [*The Laws* II, 8] Law isn't ultimately derived from the Twelve Tables of the Praetor's edict but from the nature of man. 'We must clarify the nature of justice, and that has to be deduced from the nature of man. Then we must consider the laws by which states ought to be governed.' [*Laws*, 1, 17] This account of law echoes that put into Laelius's mouth in *The Republic* although it is surrounded by the usual sceptical caveat that it may not be wholly correct.

We may remember that Cicero's first three theses were: *first*, the universe is governed by Providence; *second*, man is an animal but one whose power of reason makes him akin to the gods; and *third*, we have been made to share justice with one another and justice is natural. [*Laws* 1, 33] Cicero's *fourth* thesis is that, despite their local differences, human beings are essentially the same: 'there is no essential difference within mankind. Reason in fact—the one thing in which we are superior to the beasts, which enables us to make valid deductions, to argue, refute our opponents, debate, solve problems, draw conclusions—that certainly is common to us all....For the same things are grasped by the senses of all, and those things that act on the senses act on the senses of all alike; and those rudimentary perceptions that are impressed on the mind...are impressed alike on all minds. Speech, which interprets the mind, uses different languages but expresses the same ideas.' [*Laws* 1, 30] This is a vital point, transcending the localism and particularism that has plagued and continues to plague human history. It wouldn't be too far-fetched to take Cicero as deriving his philosophical egalitarianism from the Stoic conception of *oikeiosis*, a process by which every living entity is attached to everything that shares its nature. All men are equal, equal not in character, talents, disposition, appearance, personality, wealth or possessions, but equal in their essential humanity. All men have the same ability to experience the world; all can distinguish between what is right and what is wrong. The fundamental moral identity of all men is expressed very clearly in the following passage: 'Now there is no single thing that is so similar to us, so like anything else as all of us are like one another....Reason in fact...is common to us all.' [*Laws* I, 29-30] The contrast of this idea with that of classical Greek thought, as found in Plato and Aristotle, is stark. For Aristotle, men were not equal and so citizenship had to be restricted. For Cicero, by contrast, all men possess the same reason, are subject to the same universal law and, in those respects, all are equal. From this perspective, a slave can't be seen, as Aristotle has seen him, as a living tool but at worst, as a worker on a lifelong contract on very bad terms!

Cicero's *fifth*, and final thesis is that the development of our human potential demands that we live with one another in community. The most basic reason for the coming together of human beings in community isn't mutual need (though that *is* a factor) but 'a sort of innate desire on the part of human beings to form communities. For our species is not made up of solitary individuals or lonely wanderers.' [*Republic* 1, 39] There are two conceptions of man that are mutually exclusive and universally exhaustive. Whichever of these incompatible conceptions of man one adopts will have a significantly different effect on what one takes to be a plausible political theory. The first conception takes man to be an essentially isolated individual who, out of necessity, associates with others for mutual defence and aid. On this view of things, society and the state are artificial constructs. The other conception takes man to be an essentially social being. On this view of things, society and the state are organic developments of man's natural sociability. The first conception could reasonably be associated with the Epicureans, the second with the Stoics. On this matter, Cicero, the great eclectic, is on the side of the Stoics. Society is natural. The state, the republic, grows naturally from society, in particular, from the family. The republic is founded on justice and law and exists to further human well-being.

	Cicero's 5 theses
1st thesis	The universe is governed by Providence
2nd thesis	Man is an animal but one whose power of reason makes him akin to the gods
3rd thesis	We have been made to share justice with one another and justice is natural
4th thesis	Despite their local differences, human beings are essentially the same
5th thesis	The development of our human potential demands that we live with one another in community

In the *Republic*, Scipio gives a definition of the subject of the discussion. A republic is 'the property of the public. But a public is not every kind of human gathering, congregating in any manner, but a numerous gathering brought together by legal consent and community of interest. The primary reason for human beings coming together is not so much weakness as a sort of innate desire on the part of human beings to form communities.' [*Republic* I, 39] Republics then are not artificial entities but natural outgrowths of human sociability. Human existence is dependent on life in the human community. That being so, 'As magistrates are subject to laws, the people are subject to the magistrates. In fact it is true to say that a magistrate is a speaking law, and law a silent magistrate. Nothing is so closely bound up with the decrees and terms of nature (and by that I wish to be understood as meaning law) as authority. Without that, no house or state or clan can survive—no, nor the human race, nor the whole of nature, nor the very universe itself. For the universe obeys God; land and sea abide by the laws of the universe; and human life is subject to the commands of the supreme law.' [*The Laws*, III, 2-3] The state, then is a corporate body belonging jointly to its citizens. Its purpose is the provision of just government and mutual aid. Political power is the corporate power of the people exercised on their behalf by those chosen to do so. If the magistrate governs the people, the law governs the magistrate. [*Laws* III, 1, 2]

As one might expect, given what Cicero has written about the universal law to which all men are subject, the state and its magistrates are subject to it as well. This universal law transcends particular human choices and particular human institutions. 'These general principles of government—that authority proceeds from the people, should be exercised only by warrant of law, and is justified only on moral grounds—achieved practically universal acceptance within comparatively a short time after Cicero wrote and remained commonplaces of political philosophy for many centuries.' [Sabine, 167] It follows from Cicero's conception of the universal law binding all men that a state can't properly exist unless it gives effect to the mutual obligations and rights that come from this law. 'Unless the state is a community for ethical purposes and unless it is held together by moral ties, it is nothing, as Augustine said later, except "highway robbery on a large scale".' [Sabine, 166]

Cicero has nothing particularly novel to say about the ultimately desirable political regime. He rehearses the usual six types of regime, monarchy, aristocracy and democracy, and their defective counterparts. The best regime for Cicero, is that in which the wise rule. But the best isn't always possible. The mixed regime is a good second-best. The justification of this is by appeal to the settled experience of many generations. 'Cicero's conclusion is fundamentally the same as Plato's,' writes James Holton, 'the perfectly just regime probably lies outside the range of human possibilities. Its demands are too severe. The wise statesman, although seeking to be guided in his practice by such standards, will begin with the understanding that there is little likelihood, given the nature of man and the political community, that they can or will be realized fully in any state.' [Holton 170]

Cicero's conception of the law resonated through the Middle Ages and is reflected in the sophisticated analysis of St Thomas in the thirteenth century. For Cicero, all law is in some sense a reflection of the law of God, the eternal principles of justice. Any law that essentially contradicts these principles isn't just a bad law but is no law at all. The law of the city, the civil law, is an adaptation of these principles to the particular circumstances of a particular people at a particular time. Thus understood, civil law comes down on the rationalistic side of the rationalist/voluntarist debate. It isn't just the will of a person or a community; it's the application to a community of the universal principles of justice.

Cicero tended to conceive of a person's liberty as the having of a share in the state.[14] The Roman lawyers think of the populace as a whole as the ultimate source of authority, even if, as Ulpian states so plainly in the *Digest*, its proximate source is the emperor. 'A decision given by the emperor has the force of a statute. This is because the populace commits to him and unto him its own entire authority and power, doing this by the *lex regia*.'[15] Carlyle notes that 'with the exception of the *Senatus consultum*, every form of law derives its authority ultimately from the *populus*.' [Carlyle I, 67-68] This idea of a popular source for imperial authority—really a somewhat attenuated theory of consent—could provide the starting point for a theory of contract but it wasn't so developed by the Roman jurisconsults. Instead, the contract theory first appears in recognisable form in the eleventh century and then its immediate source is the law of the tribes rather than any Roman source.

THE ROMAN JURISCONSULTS

Carlyle sees the political theory of the Middle Ages as having its origin in three sources: in the writings of the Roman Lawyers, in the thought of the Christian Fathers and, from a libertarian point of view, most significantly, in the tribal law and customs of the post-Western Roman Empire barbarian invaders.[16] We will look at the latter two sources a little later. Let us now look at the thought of the Roman Lawyers.

Although the Roman Jurists do not formally belong to any one philosophical school, their conceptions of justice and law nevertheless align them more with the Stoics than with any other school such as the Epicureans or the Academic Sceptics. In the great collections of Roman law compiled under Justinian in the sixth century AD—the *Digest*, the *Institutes*, the *Code*—we can witness the development of the thought of the Roman jurisconsults. We also have the *Institutes* of the second century AD jurisconsult Gaius (c. AD 130-180), not only the fragments preserved in the *Digest*, as is the case with the others. This gives us a valuable point of comparison. What is of interest to us in these writers is not the detail of law but their conception of what the law is. Their common word for what we call law generally understood was *ius*; when they wanted to refer to a specific enactment of a legislative body, they generally used the term *lex*. In their writing we find them talking about *ius naturale*, *ius gentium* and *ius civile* which we might translate respectively as the law of nature or natural law, the law of nations and the civil law or the law of the city. What constitutes the *ius civile* isn't really a matter of much dispute though its relation to the other two kinds of law is a matter of great interest. The appropriate method of drawing a distinction between the other two kinds of law—the *ius naturale* and the *ius gentium*—is controversial, however, and we find differing accounts of it in the writings of the jurisconsults.

Gaius sees no essential difference between *ius naturale* and *ius gentium* whereas Ulpian, a slightly later second century AD jurist, distinguished between them. Of these two views, Ulpian's was the one to triumph, albeit with some modifications. Gaius's view of the *ius gentium* is that this is a kind of universal law that embodies natural reason. The principles of this law of nations are given to man from the beginning. Gaius's *ius gentium* is 'that body of principles or laws which men have always learned from their reason to recognise as useful and just. The *jus gentium* is primitive, universal, rational, and equitable.'

[Carlyle I, 37] To the extent that he talks of *ius naturale,* which isn't often, it appears to amount to much the same thing as *ius gentium*. In thinking of the *ius gentium* as rational and universal, Gaius is very close to the Ciceronian conception. For both men, law isn't essentially a matter of anyone's will but rather a matter of rational apprehension of a pre-existing order. The division between voluntaristic and rationalistic conceptions of law is a permanent and recurring feature of all jurisprudence, then and now.

At the beginning of the third century AD, a distinction begins to be drawn between *ius naturale* and *ius gentium*. We find this already present to some extent, particularly in the contributions of Ulpian. Although his distinction between the two kinds of law becomes a commonplace of subsequent thought, his manner of drawing the distinction has been a source of confusion. For him, *ius naturale* is whatever nature teaches all animals, including man. Natural law thus covers procreation and the care of offspring, both in animals and in man. The *ius gentium*, by contrast, is peculiar to and is common to all nations, not just Rome. As Ulpian thinks of it, the *ius naturale* is more a matter of instinct than reason. Nevertheless, in other uses of this term, Ulpian characterises *ius naturale* in a manner that makes sense only if it is understood rationally so that it would then have to be peculiar to man and not common to man and animal alike. Ulpian's companion jurisconsults, even though they generally (but not always) draw a distinction between *ius naturale* and *ius gentium*, are no more conspicuously successful in characterising the distinction than he is. By the time we get to the fourth century AD, matters have become a little clearer. By this time, the difference between the two conceptions of law is made to correspond to a distinction between what belongs to man by nature and that which belongs to him by convention. So, for example, man by nature is free and equal but, in the actual conditions of human life, war and slavery have arisen, and around these circumstances, the law of nations has developed.

The distinction between the two kinds of law has particular application to the matter of slavery. For the Roman jurisconsults, slavery is not, as it would have been for Aristotle, something pertaining to the original condition of man but something that arose with the development of complex societies and which is, in some way, a consequence of human failings. As we know only too well, slavery took a long time to disappear and its eventual demise may well be attributed to fundamental changes in the economic circumstances of men. Nevertheless, we find in the Roman Lawyers a rejection of the naturalness of slavery that, together with a similar rejection of slavery's naturalness in the Father of the Church, makes some (small) contribution to slavery's eventual eradication. Even though the jurists (and the Church Fathers) all rejected the naturalness of slavery, they all continued to support it as an institution. That slavery should be the consequence of some declension from the right and the good seems plausible, whether in a secular or religious story. That slavery should also be the cure for the deficiencies giving rise to itself seems to be bizarrely circular!

Finally, those who distinguish sharply between the *ius naturale* and the *ius gentium* generally tend to see private property as an institution of the latter rather than the former. They hold that in man's original condition, all things were held in common. Those who do not make such a sharp distinction between the two kinds of law, such as Gaius and Paulus, tend to see private property as being both primitive and equitable.

Hellenistic philosophy was important in its own right and its re-emphasis on the practical dimension of philosophy was a welcome antidote to the theoretical excesses of academic philosophy. It also provided the philosophical milieu, as the Roman Empire was to provide the political milieu, in which a small and insignificant Jewish sect took root and began to flourish. Greek philosophy, Roman law, and the religious heritage of that fragile Jewish sect would eventually meld to constitute a large part (but not the whole) of what we know as Western civilisation.

Notes

1 Hellenistic philosophy was also the intellectual environment in which an infant Christianity grew to intellectual maturity. [see Taleb, 151-158; 249-262]

2 'While the polis proved robust as a social, political, and cultural form,' notes Josiah Ober, 'Greek elites, and some who expressly rejected elite values (e.g. Diogenes the Cynic) found more freedom to express their individuality. Individuals, rather than collectivities, were now more likely to be regarded by the Greeks as primary agents of historical change.' [Ober 2015, 226]

3 Titus Lucretius Carus, 99-55 BC wrote the Epicurean classic *De Rerum Natura*.

4 Epicurus, *Letter to Menoeceus*, in Saunders 1966, 51-52.

5 Plutarch, *Against Colotes* 1127de(134U); 1127a(8U).

6 The Vatican Collection of Epicurean Sayings, no. 58.

7 Diogenes Laertius, vi. 38; Plutarch, Alexander 14, et al.

8 See Clay xxvi; see Marcus Aurelius, *Meditations*, 10: 6.

9 A three-volume history of medieval political theory was produced by the Carlyle brothers (R. W. & A. J.) between 1903 and 1928. The first two volumes were produced jointly, the third by A. J. Carlyle alone. To avoid having to switch bewilderingly between 'he' and 'they', or 'Carlyle' and 'Carlyles' I attribute material from this history simply to 'Carlyle'. The volume numbers will make it clear whether the attribution is to both brothers or simply to A. J. Carlyle.

10 In his poem, *To Helen*, Edgar Allan Poe remarked on 'the glory that was Greece and the grandeur that was Rome,' but a time-travelling visitor to Rome wouldn't have noticed much grandeur. Instead, he would have found Cicero's Rome to be 'crowded, noisy, dirty, with unusual and forbidding stenches, swarming with vast crowds of people, many of whom would seem almost sub-human types marked by disease, mental deficiency, malformation and mutilation....' [Cowell 1956, 333]

11 For all his faults—and he had many—Cicero deserves the respect of every lover of freedom for his principled opposition to the ambitions of Mark Antony. Frank Cowell writes that, after the death of Caesar, 'Antony...and his fellow thugs cast aside any disguise and appeared as the gangsters they were, determined to run things their own way, to take what they wanted, to have a roaring good time and to murder out of hand anybody who stood in their path....Cicero saw Antony for the unscrupulous adventurer he was and, with tremendous force and courage, denounced him...before the Senate and the people...' [Cowell 1956, 266, 267] When Octavian and Antony formed their coalition, however, Cicero was doomed and his name was on their first proscription list. 'Antony sent a squad to look for his arch-enemy. Octavian, to his eternal shame, made no effort to spare the old man whom he had so recently consulted and flattered....the great orator and spokesman of the liberties of the Roman people was silenced by one stroke of a centurion's sword...the greatest disaster ever to befall the Romans in all their long history mounted to its climax amid bloodshed and degradation. Three hundred Senators and 2,000 *equites*, doomed by Antony's proscription lists, were slaughtered by his thugs. Life in Rome was shattered.' [Cowell 1956, 267-268]

12 Also of interest is his *De Finibus*, concerning which see Tierney 2014, 4-6.

13 *Republic*, III, 33, quoted in Lactantius, *Divinae Institutiones* 6.8. 6-9.

14 For a contemporary treatment of the emergence of non-state law-making in the context of globalization, see Teubner, passim. The central thesis of Teubner's book is that the 'globalization of law creates a multitude of decentred law-making processes in various sectors of civil society, independently of nation-states. Technical standardization, professional rule production, human rights, intra-organizational regulation in multinational enterprises, contracting, arbitration and other institutions of *lex mercatoria* are forms of rule-making by "private governments" which have appeared on a massive global scale. They claim worldwide validity independently of the law of the nation-state and in relative distance to the rules of international public law. They have come into existence not by formal acts of nation-states but by strange paradoxical acts of self-validation.' [Teubner, xiii]

15 *Digest*, 1, 4, 1; see also the *Institutes* 1.ii. 6 and the Institutes of *Gaius* i, 5.

16 Allemanni, Anglo-Saxons, Burgundians, Franks, Ostrogoths, Vandals and Visigoths in the first wave, followed by the Avars and the Lombards.

Chapter 7

CHRISTIANITY

I form'd them free: and free they must remain,
Till they enthrall themselves; I else must change
Thir nature
—Milton

You condemn a person to slavery whose nature is free
and independent, and in doing so you lay down a law
in opposition to God, overturning the natural law established by him
—Gregory of Nyssa

For the first three hundred years of its institutional life, Christianity was a non-establishment, sometimes persecuted, religion.[1] One of the reasons for its persecution was that its adherents were regarded as atheists because they did not worship the gods of the State and so were seen as political subversives.[2] 'During three centuries,' Fustel de Coulanges remarks, 'the new religion lived entirely beyond the action of the state: it knew how to dispense with state protection, and even to struggle against it. These three centuries established an abyss between the domain of government and the domain of religion; and, as the recollection of the period could not be effaced, it followed that this distinction became a plain and incontestable truth, which the efforts of even a part of the clergy could not efface.' [de Coulanges, 394] The Constantinian settlement that instituted Christianity as the official religion of the Roman Empire was undertaken as much with a view to seeing what support Christianity could bring to Rome as with seeing what support the Imperial state could bring to Christianity. Francis Oakley remarks on the startling description that the third/fourth century bishop of Caesarea, Eusebius, gives of the emperor Constantine as 'the image of the One Ruler of All,' comparing Constantine to Moses and likening him to a universal bishop appointed by God.[3] What we have here, says Oakley, 'is a thoroughgoing resacralization of the imperial office in quasi-Christian terms.'[4] 'Through the Edict of Milan, which had legalized the new religion in 313 and made it the emperor's pet,' writes Thomas Cahill, 'Christianity has been received into Rome, not Rome into Christianity! Roman culture was little altered by the exchange, and it is arguable that Christianity lost much of its distinctiveness.' [Cahill, 148] 'The Catholic Church,' writes Lucien Musset, 'won a dominant place for itself by conforming to the framework laid down for it by the civil power…' [Musset, 22] Caesaro-Papism, the arrangement in which the head of state is also the head of the church, immediately became the new norm of Church governance, a norm that continued in the Eastern Roman Empire until its fall in 1453.[5] Siedentop writes, 'The Eastern Empire preserved…relations between the church and state that had been characteristic of the whole empire in the century after Constantine's adopted Christianity. Those relations were marked by a considerable deference of church to the state.' [Siedentop, 136]

In the post-Roman West, the story was somewhat different. The cause, or rather causes, of the fall, collapse or implosion of the Roman Empire in the West are a perennial topic of historical debate. While most reputable historians would doubtless agree that the collapse of the western Roman Empire wasn't an instantaneous event, quite a few non-exclusive causes have been offered by way of explaining it, including: the official acceptance of Christianity, the moral degeneration of Roman society, the rise and rise of a expensive professional army containing many non-Romans whose very existence corrupted the political process, demographic problems, and last, but not least, the rise of taxation to crushing levels.[6] After the collapse of the Western Roman Empire, barbarian kingdoms emerged in the fifth and sixth centuries—Visigothic in Spain, Frankish in Gaul, Lombard in Italy—and their rulers, when they adopted Christianity, retained for a time their originally pagan quasi-sacral functions in a transmuted form, giving us a kind of Caesaro-Papism multiplied and in miniature.[7] 'Germanic kingship from antiquity was such that royal authority was invested with a spiritual function relating to the existence of the tribe or nation,' writes James Greenaway. 'One could even go do far as to say that the kingship that emerged among the pagan Germanic *gentes* was a compact fusion of authority that was simultaneously political and spiritual, but also existential in a surrogate sense. The existence of the individual was dwarfed by the emphasis on collective national or tribal existence, which implied that the meaning of individual existence was sought within the national collective.' [Greenaway, 30] Apart from the somewhat anachronistic use of the term *national*, this statement by Greenaway perfectly describes the interpenetration of religion and politics in the early medieval period. Larry Siedentop writes, 'before the papal revolution spiritual and temporal authority in Europe has been so mixed as to be difficult to separate. Kings had come to understand their role in sacral terms, while emperors had often made and unmade popes,' and Lucien Musset notes that, 'The character of Germanic kinship is twofold, for it is both sacral and military, the relative importance of these aspects varying from people to people....everywhere kingship continued to have a supernatural side...'[8] 'During the late antique and early medieval centuries,' writes Francis Oakley, 'a Christianized version of the archaic pattern of sacral kingship had dominated the political scene in the Latin West no less than the Byzantine East. From the late eleventh century onward, however, in the former region though not in the latter, that was all destined to change; It was not the institution of kingship that was called into question or consigned to a process of marginalization. What was called into question rather, was its age-old sacral dimension.'[9]

The Gregorian Church was heavily influenced by Roman legal and governmental concepts. It conceived of itself as a kind of corporation that required its own form of government. This legal, indeed legalistic, conception of the Church was to reach its highest point in the eleventh century, but elements of such a conception were present in it in embryonic form as early as the sixth century and perhaps even earlier. Tom Palmer regards Gregory VII's issuance of *Dictatus Papae* in 1075, in which the independence of the Church from the state was announced, as 'the first of the most significant moments of the past thousand years.'[10] Over the next 400 years, the Church tried, and to a large extent succeeded, in establishing its independence of the various political orders, whether local, regional or imperial. This commendable effort at achieving independence *from* the secular order was accompanied by a somewhat less commendable attempt to establish dominance *over* the secular order! As the imperial dignity of the German emperors declined from its height in the eleventh and twelfth centuries, so the imperial dignity of the papal monarchy conversely increased until it wielded 'imperial power over a church that knew no national boundaries.' [Oakley 2013, 3] This welcome but double-edged development of ecclesiastical independence came to a shuddering halt with the onset of the Reformation. Leaving to one side the purely religious dimensions of the Reformation and its complicated and convoluted theological debates, one of its most significant and deleterious consequences was the re-emergence of local forms of Caesaro-Papism in the newly emerging autonomous and, more often than not, absolutist states. This regional Caesaro-Papism occurred primarily in the areas under the sway of the Reformed traditions, Lutheran and Calvinist, but was also witnessed even in areas that remained Catholic. To an extent that had not been seen since before the eleventh century, the Church, or rather Churches, now came under pressure to become departments in the various sovereign and independent states, a pressure to which they largely yielded. 'The kings who denied Papal authority and confiscated Church lands,' writes Parkinson, 'added the powers of Pope to the powers of King and used both to stamp out feudalism. But the Papacy was so weakened by this defection that the Catholic Kings gained an almost equal independence as the reward for their loyalty.' [Parkinson 1958, 78] The modern state, in the form in which we have come to know it—the sole sovereign power in a defined territory, exercising a monopoly on (allegedly) legitimate violence, with the power to commandeer the resources, including the persons, of it citizens—had come into existence. But this is to look very far ahead. We will examine these issues in more detail a little later; for the moment, let us concentrate on Christianity in its earliest manifestation.

THE IMPACT OF CHRISTIANITY

With the arrival of Christianity, in some ways, nothing changes; yet in other ways, everything changes. Although ultimately the whole of western history and culture would be radically affected by Christianity, it had no immediately dramatic effect on its social or political environment. John Howard Yoder notes that 'the early church....chose not to challenge the subjugation of woman or the institution of slavery.[11] Thereby it prepared itself gradually to become the religion of the established classes, a development that culminated in the age of Constantine three centuries later.' [Yoder 1994, 166-167] George Sabine goes so far as to write, 'the rise of Christianity did not carry with it a new political philosophy....For purposes of historical accuracy there is no reason why the

Christian era should be taken as beginning a new period in political thought.' [Sabine, 161] Sabine has a point. It isn't unreasonable to ask why it took the long time that it did (almost a millennium, on some estimates) for Christianity to have some palpable effect on its social and political milieu. Siedentop believes it is because the 'implications of moral intuitions generated by Christianity had to be worked out against prejudices and practices sometimes as old as the social division of labour. That, in turn, involved learning how to create and protect a public role for conscience, first of all by forging a conceptual framework that could be deployed to criticize existing social practices.' This wasn't something that could or did happen quickly, involving, as it did, 'fierce controversy, frequent back-tracking and frustration.' [Siedentop, 355] Making a somewhat similar point, albeit more broadly, Oakley maintains that it took centuries for Christians to come to terms with the implications of their faith. [see Oakley 2019, 60]

While conceding as much as possible to Sabine in this matter, in his summary dismissal of the political significance of Christianity he takes a very limited, indeed an oddly blinkered, view of the matter. Even though it is true that Christianity made no *immediately* startling contribution to political theory, and although it is also true that Christianity adopted (and adapted) some ideas, not least the idea of natural law, from its pagan environment, it nevertheless contributed certain distinctive elements of its own that were, in time, to become part of the very fabric of the social and political (as well as religious) life of Christendom. These core elements include, first, the idea that *there are two centres of human allegiance*; second, the development of the gold and silver rules, together *the rule of reciprocity*, as the basis of human conduct; and third (and for my purposes in this history, most importantly) *the value of the individual as a creature made in the image and likeness of God*, whose ultimate goal is to know, love and serve God in this life and be happy with Him in the next. Let us look at these ideas in turn.

Two Centres of Human Allegiance

There are *two centres of human allegiance*, two *loci* of authority, one spiritual (the *sacerdotium*), one temporal (the *imperium*), both of which have a claim on our loyalty and obedience but neither of which can make this claim to the exclusion of the other. Because of the existence of the Church, state idolatry wasn't an option. Without the institutional Church to provide a counterbalance, there was always a danger that the state instead of God would become the source from which all good things come. The state becomes responsible for everything that happens, that which provides security and solves all our problems—'People have faith in the state, obey it' and impute divine attributes to it. [Christoyannopoulos, 125] Greenaway notes, acutely, that Christianity isn't 'a manifesto for the establishment of a Christian politics as attempted in the Middle Ages, but involves a realization that there is no political solution to the problems of human existence....Without the separation of political authority from transcendental authority, there is no limit to what the political is and what it is meant to achieve.' [Greenaway, 81]

Each locus of authority served to limit the achievement of the ambitions of the other. The state, Oakley remarks, 'was gradually stripped of its age-old religious aura' and its claims on the loyalty and obedience of men 'were balanced and curtailed by those advanced persistently by a rival authority'; on the other hand, that rival authority, in turn, had its imperial ambitions thwarted by emperors and kings. [Oakley 2012, 40] In the tension between these rival spiritual and temporal authorities, 'political freedoms in the West were eventually to be forged.' [Oakley 2012, 41] Without this creative (occasionally destructive) tension, Oakley believes that it would have been very unlikely that the early modern period would have inherited a legacy of limited constitutional government from the preceding medieval centuries. I agree with Oakley's judgement but I would go further. The gap between these sometimes cooperating, sometimes competing, centres of authority not only created the space in which limited constitutional government could come to be and to persist but it also provided the social and political space in which individual, not just social, freedom could be conceived and could flourish. 'Two structures of authority were acknowledged,' writes Siedentop, 'and, in the gap between them, an important part of the future of European liberty would be lodged.'[12]

The Rule of Reciprocity

The *rule of reciprocity* comes in two versions, one gold, and one silver. The silver rule is: do *not* do unto others as you would *not* have them do unto you—this is the rule of justice. Cicero wrote, 'The primary function of justice is to ensure that no one harms his neighbour unless he has himself been unjustly attacked. [Cicero 1998, 9 (I, 21)] The silver rule is the essence of all systems of justice—justice being the disposition to give to others what belongs to them. The golden rule is: *do* unto others as you would have them *do* unto you—this is the law of love. The Law and the Prophets are summed up in the so-called Golden Rule: 'whatever you want men to do to you, do also to them...'[13] The Bolognese monk Gratian, in his *Decretum*, otherwise known as the *Concord of Discordant Canons*, assimilates both versions of the rule of reciprocity and describes this assimilation as natural law. 'Natural law is what is contained in the Law and the Gospel by which each is to do to another what he wants done to himself and forbidden to do to another what he does not want done to himself.'[14] In so doing, Gratian 'fused Christian moral intuitions with a concept inherited from Greek philosophy and Roman law. Relations of equality and reciprocity are now understood as antecedent to both positive and customary law.'[15]

Coercive governments necessarily violate the golden rule inasmuch as they do things to others that others aren't allowed to do to them. The golden rule is the essence of all systems of ethics and is based on a principle of enlightened reciprocity. [see Schmidtz 2006, 73-103] When I recognise, as I must do when I put to one side any form of special pleading, the fundamental ontological and ethical equality of all human beings regardless of sex, status, age, and rank, I must also recognise the obligation to treat others as I myself want to be treated. The golden rule emerges spontaneously from the practices of peaceful human social interchange, and its apprehension, fitful and intermittent though it may be, marks the transition in each individual's life from the natural and utilitarian levels (which we never quite leave behind) to the truly moral. The ethical systems of most of the major world religions and cultures converge on this principle.

The Christian emphasis on the golden rule takes us beyond law to love. With its admonition to turn the other cheek, an admonition admittedly not always heeded, Christianity softens the hard edge of law, both Roman and barbarian, thereby defusing disputes and helping to repair the social fabric torn by such disputes. [see Patterson 1991, 298] In *Matthew* 5, we are presented with a whole set of astonishing extensions of what one might take to be the normal moral rules: for example, not only must one not kill but one mustn't even be angry with another; one mustn't only refrain from committing adultery, one mustn't even contemplate it; pluck out your eye and cut off your hand if either should be the cause of offence; not an eye for an eye but rather do not resist evil and turn the other cheek; do not love your neighbour and hate your enemy but love your neighbour *and* your enemy. [*Matthew* 5: 21-44]

The ethical differences that appear between cultures are largely owing to material factors, to limitations that arise from historical circumstances and that prevent some or all in a community from seeing the truly universal nature of the golden rule or prevent its application to all. Whereas libertarianism springs unproblematically from the silver rule, the golden rule could be problematic for it. If it were to be incorporated unalloyed, as a principle of the legal order then some would be required *by law* to do things for others outside the realm of contract and thus their freedom of action or inaction would thus be compromised. Of course, as already mentioned, libertarian principles aren't the only principles one can adopt to guide one's life and there's nothing to stop a libertarian from freely adopting the golden rule—perhaps from religious or humanitarian convictions—but this, of course, is quite compatible with libertarianism since no one else is coercing one so to choose.

The Individual Made in the Image and Likeness of God

The ultimate spiritual destiny of man, as Christianity conceives it, moves him beyond the silver rule of justice and even the golden rule of love, transmuting those necessary but not sufficient elements, elevating them into components of a transcendent love of his Creator in whose image he has been made. The *individual human being*, a creature made in the image and likeness of God [*imago dei*], *is a being of supreme importance*—not the tribe, not the city, not the nation, not even the family. Orlando Patterson speaks of the radical shift of focus from the glory of the tribe or nation to the 'personal history of each individual.' [Patterson 1991, 300] Patterson remarks that even though 'Christianity did not begin as a religion of freedom' it would eventually make freedom 'the doctrinal core of its soteria,' its doctrine of salvation. [Patterson 1991, 295, 294] As God is free, so too, in a limited and derivative but none the less real way, is man, the creature made in his image and likeness. 'Since Christian doctrine was quintessentially a doctrine of freedom,' writes Patterson, 'it would have been extraordinary if the church's all-pervasive influence had not resulted in the perpetuation of the centrality of freedom.' [Patterson 1991, 377] Siedentop concurs, noting that 'If God has created humans as equals, as rational agents with free will, then there ought to be an area within which they are free to choose and [be] responsible for their choices.' [Siedentop, 77]

Augustine invented the literary genre of the confession in his work of that name, although there were anticipations of this genre in Stoicism, especially in Seneca's notion of self-examination (in his *De Ira*), in Marcus Aurelius's *Meditations* and in Cicero's letters to Atticus. And whereas the self of Buddhism is an illusion, the final and most persistent of all illusions, for the Christian, the self is not only *not* an illusion but something all too real! 'The more we discover the truth about ourselves,' writes Michel Foucault, 'the more we have to renounce ourselves; and the more we want to renounce ourselves, the more we need to bring to light the reality of ourselves.' [Foucault, 5] The confessional nature of Christian life requires the constant examination of the thoughts, the words, the acts and the omissions of the self and their realistic evaluation against the demands of Christian morality. A new focus on self was reinforced by the transformation of the sacrament of Penance from a public to a private practice. The Irish monks injected the penitential discipline of the monastery into the secular world 'and thus gave [penance] the form and—in practice—the central importance which it has had since then in the Roman Church.' [Mirgeler, 70]

If the importance of the individual self isn't entirely a Christian invention, it is a principle that attains a pre-eminence in Christian religious thought and culture seldom matched elsewhere.[16] [see Patterson 1991, passim] Larry Siedentop writes, 'Previously in antiquity, it was the patriarchal family that had been the agency of immortality. Now, through the story of Jesus, individual moral agency was raised up as providing a unique window into the nature of things, into the experience of grace rather than necessity, a glimpse of something transcending death. The individual replaces the family as the focus of immortality.' [Siedentop, 58] He adds, 'Christian beliefs...destroyed the ancient family. That is, they destroyed the family as a cult or religious association....This religious character of the ancient family made it, rather than the individual, the fundamental social unit.' [Siedentop, 115-116]

In social and political terms, the realisation of the individualistic implications of Christianity was far from immediate. The case can be (and has been) made that it wasn't until around the twelfth century that the individual began to stand out from his various social groups—family, society, community, guild and city—and a major stimulus to this emergent individualism was the development of commercial activities in which 'Economic changes began to replace the feudal system and traditional communities with a money economy and social mobility.' [Black 1988b, 589] Other no less important factors that contributed to the emergence of individual were the residual insistence on freedom from restraint deriving from Germanic tribal traditions and the germ of a theory of natural rights emerging from the rediscovered and reabsorbed Roman law. This emergence of the individual to political prominence (as against the traditional political centrality of the family, clan or tribe) wasn't without a potential downside as it coincided with the birth of the modern powerful, centralised and jealous state, whose ambition was to emasculate or eliminate all politically significant intermediate social groups that might vie with it for the allegiance of a mass of potentially weak, isolated individuals. [see Siedentop, 92ff.] This ambition was to be realised in the twentieth century in the reversion to tribalism that we witnessed in Fascism, National Socialism and Bolshevism.[17]

SCRIPTURAL INTERPRETATION

Sometimes it is difficult to know what someone means; sometimes it merely appears to be difficult. Consider this masterpiece of hermeneutics from a P. G. Wodehouse short story: Bertie Wooster speaks: "'Jeeves…A rummy communication has arrived. From Mr. Glossop.'" Jeeves replies, "'Indeed, sir?'" Bertie continues: "'I will read it to you. Handed in at Upper Bleaching. Message runs as follows: ""*When you come tomorrow, bring my football boots. Also, if humanly possible, Irish water-spaniel. Urgent. Regards. Tuppy.*"'" What do you make of that, Jeeves?" "As I interpret the document, sir," responds Jeeves, "Mr. Glossop wishes you when you come tomorrow, to bring his football boots. Also, if humanly possible, an Irish water-spaniel. He hints that the matter is urgent and send his regards." "Yes," agrees Bertie, "that's how I read it too…."'"[18] The 'rumminess' of Tuppy's telegram is to be found not in *what* he demands—football boots and an Irish water-spaniel—but in *why* he should demand such mysterious things. The meaning of the telegram is, as Jeeves dryly demonstrates, perfectly clear; what is obscure isn't *what* it says but *why* anyone, even the feeble-minded Tuppy Glossop, would say these things. For Christians, the words of the Bible are normative for belief and practice. It is therefore a matter of some importance to Christian statists to discover, if they can, some Scriptural justification for the state and for coercive government. I know full well how hazardous an enterprise it is to set sail on the controversial and disputed sea of Scriptural interpretation—John Donne remarks, 'Sentences in Scripture, like hairs in horsetails, concur in one root of beauty and strength; but being plucked out one by one, serve only for springes and snares'—but the meaning of Scripture, unlike Tuppy Glossop's telegram, isn't always obvious and some form of hermeneutics is unavoidable.[19]

Over the last twenty years or so, a discipline called Political Theology has witnessed the production of a significant volume of work. In particular, the works of Oliver O'Donovan[20] have created quite a stir in the normally sedate theological community and given rise to extensive commentary—indeed, an entire issue of the journal *Political Theology* is devoted to an appraisal and evaluation of O'Donovan's work.[21] This work contains much of interest to students of philosophy and theology, in particular, a neo-Hobbesian characterisation of political representation as something that was done by governments before ever there was any talk of popular assemblies. What is represented by such political representation isn't a Rousseauean general will or an aggregate of individual preferences but rather a people's identity. Readers might wonder what this identity is, if there is one and only one such identity and, whether one or multiple, how we come to know what this identity is. O'Donovan also attempts to justify a reconceptualised notion of Christendom, one not based on coercion but on harnessing the mighty to the purposes of peace. All well and good, one might think and, depending on one's point of view, perhaps an improvement on the usually dire political situations we find ourselves in, but *who* are the mighty ones and *how* do they get to be mighty? Even if one accepts that Yahweh or Jesus is Lord, it isn't obvious why Joe Bloggs or, even worse, Joe Stalin, should be taken to be invested with his authority.[22]

It is (or should be) well known that St Augustine advanced a sophisticated hermeneutics of scriptural interpretation, particularly in relation to the proper understanding of the first book of *Genesis*. He wrote three works specifically on this topic: *De Genesi Contra Manichaeos* (388-390) (On *Genesis*, against the Manichees); *De Genesi ad Litteram Imperfectus Liber* (393-394) (On the literal interpretation of *Genesis* (incomplete)); and, the most well known, *De Genesi ad Litteram* (AD 410) (On the Literal Interpretation of *Genesis*).[23] As the 'ad litteram' in the title of two of these works might suggest, Augustine believed himself to be advancing a literal interpretation of the first book of the Bible but not a literalistic or hyper-literal interpretation. As Tim Chaffy notes, 'Augustine…differentiated between what he believed was a literal interpretation and what might be called a hyper-literal interpretation, which was practiced by the Manichees. A hyper-literal interpretation takes everything in a strictly literal fashion. For example, a person interpreting this way would believe that Jesus taught He was a physical door when he claimed, "I am the door" (John 10:9).' [Chaffey, 90] Augustine himself advanced the principle that 'We must be on our guard against giving interpretations which are hazardous or opposed to science, and so exposing the word of God *to the ridicule of unbelievers.*' (*De Genesi ad litteram*, I, 19, 21, see n. 39). He rejected the literalistic six days in the *Genesis* account, holding instead to an instantaneous creation of the universe. Moreover, the universe thus created was in an undeveloped state, awaiting the operation of the principles of nature embedded in it.

It must be granted, then, that it isn't possible to give a literal(istic) interpretation of everything in Scripture.[24] Leaving aside questions of whether and to what extent there is a variety of literary genres in the Bible—poetry, novels, and the like[25]—we are still faced with the problem of understanding just what it is that we find on the page. Sometimes the language used is metaphorical, sometimes not. Unless the authors of Scripture have less than common sense, the statement that God is a rock[26] is obviously not to be taken literally; God, whatever else he may be, isn't a lump of granite or sandstone or even marble. The statement that God is good, however, does not seem to be simply metaphorical—could one say that 'God is *not* good' as one could easily say that 'God is *not* a rock'? It would seem not, yet God's goodness, whatever that may be, can't be functional, as is the goodness of an artefact such as a knife, or teleological, as is human goodness.

Straightforward metaphorical language isn't too difficult to deal with but there are times in Scripture when we are faced with a contradiction or at least what

looks like a contradiction. Let us take some examples. We have the commandment to 'honour thy father and thy mother: that thy days may be long upon
the land…' in *Exodus* 20:12. Nevertheless, in Luke's gospel, we have Jesus
addressing the multitude and telling them, 'If any man comes to me without
hating his father, mother, wife, children, brothers, sisters, yes and his own life
too, he cannot be my disciple…none of you can be my disciple unless he gives
up all his possessions.' [*Luke* 14: 26, 33] On the face of it, we have here a
contradiction and such must be either admitted or resolved as in Abelard's *Sic
et Non*. How many Christians take literally these verses from Luke?

And then we are told to sell everything we have and give it to the poor. The
advice to the rich man (or rather the rich *ruler* in *Luke* 18:1—'A certain ruler
[*archon*] asked him, "Good teacher, what must I do to inherit eternal life?"')
proposes that we take all that we have and give it to the poor, whereas in *2
Corinthians* we are counselled merely to give of our excess: 'For I mean not
that other men be eased, and ye burdened. But by an equality, that now at this
time your abundance may be a supply for their want, that their abundance also
may be a supply for your want.' [2 *Corinthians* 8: 13-14] Is God a God of
war or peace? [*Exodus* 15:3—'The Lord is a man of war'; *Romans* 15:33—
'Now the God of peace be with you all'] Is Jesus equal to or less than the
Father? [*John* 10:30—'I and the Father are one'; *John* 14: 28—'my Father
is greater than I'] It seems that wisdom is something to be desired [*Proverbs*
4:7—'Wisdom is the principal thing; therefore get wisdom: and with all thy
getting get understanding'] and also something *not* to be desired [*Ecclesiastes*
1:18—'For in much wisdom is much grief: and he that increases knowledge
increases sorrow']. Should we display our good deeds [*Matthew* 5:16 'Let your
light shine before men, that they may see your good deeds'] or should we
conceal them? [*Matthew* 6:3-4 'But when you give to the needy, do not let your
left hand know what your right hand is doing, so that your giving may be in
secret'].[27]

These few rudimentary comments are certainly not meant to be the final
word on any matter of biblical hermeneutics; the topic is simply too vast and
complicated to be settled here. Still, whatever one's views on particular topics,
it's difficult to deny that *some* interpretation of Scripture is required. Now,
my interest here isn't in the interpretation of Scripture just as such but only
with those passages that have, or have had, a bearing on how Christians have
conceived of the legitimacy of political authority. Following the tradition of *sic
et non* inaugurated by Peter Abelard, I venture to suggest that we can find two
kinds of passage in Scripture relating to the legitimacy of secular authority; one
kind broadly dismissive or sceptical of it, the other kind supportive.[28]

OLD TESTAMENT

I think it fair to say that most relevant Old Testament[29] passages (and many
passages in the New Testament) are sceptical of the value of secular political
rule; for example, the story of *Exodus* is the story of an escape to freedom: 'I
am the Lord your God, who brought you out of the land of Egypt, out of the
house of bondage.' [*Exodus* 20: 2], and the Book of Judges concludes with

these words: "In those days there was no king in Israel; every man did what was right in his own eyes." (*Judges*: 25; see also *Judges* 9: 1-57])[30]

The most obvious place to start is, perhaps, the justly famous passage in the Book of Samuel. The elders of Israel asked Samuel to give them a king, saying to him 'Behold, thou art old, and thy sons walk not in thy ways. Now make us a king to judge us, like all the nations.' Samuel wasn't happy about this demand and consulted God. God told Samuel that this request indicated that the people of Israel had rejected God's reign over them, saying, 'they have not rejected thee, but they have rejected Me, that I should not reign over them… Now therefore hearken unto their voice. However, yet protest solemnly unto them and show them the ways of the king that shall reign over them.' God, then, instructed Samuel to listen to what the people said, first pointing out to them what their request involved. So, Samuel told the people what to expect if they got themselves a king:

And he said, 'This will be the manner of the king who shall reign over you: He will take your sons and appoint them for himself, for his chariots and to be his horsemen; and some shall run before his chariots. And he will appoint him captains over thousands and captains over fifties, and will set them to till his ground and to reap his harvest, and to make his instruments of war and instruments of his chariots. And he will take your daughters to be confectioners and to be cooks and to be bakers. And he will take your fields and your vineyards and your olive yards, even the best of them, and give them to his servants. And he will take a tenth of your seed and of your vineyards, and give to his officers and to his servants. And he will take your menservants, and your maidservants, and your goodliest young men, and your asses, and put them to his work. He will take a tenth of your sheep; and ye shall be his servants. And ye shall cry out on that day because of your king which ye shall have chosen you; and the LORD will not hear you in that day.'[31]

The significance of this passage is worth reflecting upon. First, God clearly sees the demand of the men of Israel for a king to be a rejection of His kingship over Israel. Second, he has Samuel tell the people clearly what to expect from their king when they get him—he will take their sons and daughters, confiscate their property and make them his servants. Nevertheless, if they persist in their desire for a king, God won't interfere with their freedom to choose, even if that choice is foolish. The subsequent history of the kings of Israel, from Saul, through David, Solomon and Rehoboam, followed by the division of the kingdom is very far from edifying and can be seen as the fulfilment of God's warning delivered through Samuel. Samuel's good advice got the reception generally accorded to good advice, which is to say it was completely ignored. The people insisted on having a king so a king they were given.[32]

I am not the first person, and I won't be the last, to be struck by the force of this passage from *Samuel*. Thomas Paine devotes two pages of the introductory chapter to his *Common Sense* to this passage, interpreting it as I have done in the previous paragraph. [see Paine 1995, 13-14] On the other hand, Sir Robert Filmer interprets this passage as rather supporting the legitimacy of royal governance than otherwise! He takes the purpose of this passage 'to teach the people a dutiful obedience to their King, even in those things which themselves did esteem mischievous and inconvenient. For by telling them what a King would do, he instructs them what a subject must suffer. Yet not that it is right for Kings to do injury, but it is right for them to go unpunished by the people if they do it.'[33] Yet again, Francis Oakley reads this passage from *Samuel* as expressing ambivalence.

On the one hand, he says, 'Yahweh is depicted as having recognized the need for kingship, as having accepted the popular desire for it, and in what amounted to a beneficent divine gift, as having anointed Saul to be "ruler over his people Israel".' [Oakley 2010, 50] I believe that the normally sure-footed Oakley has, perhaps in attempting to achieve some kind of scholarly balance, got things badly wrong here. There is nothing in the text to suggest that Yahweh recognized the need for kingship—on the contrary, he says quite explicitly, if I may paraphrase, 'They've already got a king—Me!' He can be said to 'accept' the popular desire for it only in the way in which a father, having tried to prevent his son from buying a powerful motor bike and warning him of the consequences of so doing, could be said to accept his son's decision to go ahead and get the bike. Recall the final words of the passage: 'And ye shall cry out on that day because of your king which ye shall have chosen you; and the LORD will not hear you in that day.' I find it hard to see much recognition and acceptance there, with God regarding the people's demand for a king as derogating from his own kinship.

Oakley does entertain the idea that what we might call, using his interpretation, the 'recognition and acceptance' position comes from a source contemporaneous with the events it describes, while the 'rejectionist' position comes a later period and is the product of sad experience. But even if this were so—and it's by no means certain that it is so—it wouldn't change the tenor of the account as it is rendered and that, as I have already indicated, is in no way two-handed. [see Oakley 2010, 51] In any event, Oakley readily concedes that the ambivalence (as he regards it) in the *Samuel* passage is reflected in many other biblical texts (*Judges*, *Kings* I and II, *Elijah*, *Amos*, *Hosea*, and *Isaiah*) and 'it is almost always reflective of the repeated willingness of the Hebrew kings to accommodate (and even to associate with their own Yahweh worship) the fertility rituals and related practices like sacred prostitution embedded in the cultus of the Canaanite agrarian god Baal.' [Oakley 2010, 51]

The ancient Israelites appear to have had a tribal structure not unlike that which we find among the ancient Irish, Germans and Britons. From time to time, in emergencies such as famine or military defeat, someone would be appointed as a leader to get things back on track, a kind of temporary dictator. [see Clastres, passim] When the task for which they were appointed was done, these leaders returned to the ranks. The reason the Israelites give for wanting a king is that they want to be like other nations. Unfortunately, that isn't what God wanted! He wanted the Israelites to be His people and He to be their God.

Despite their rejection of Him, God grants the Israelites what they require, even choosing the kings for them Himself which, given what has just taken place in Samuel, can hardly be said to be a ringing endorsement of monarchy but rather an indication of God's willingness to tolerate, without necessarily endorsing, the consequences of foolish human choices. In the eleventh century, Cardinal Deusdedit made a very sharp distinction between God's permission or toleration, and God's active approval. On the basis of *Samuel*, he argues that the Jewish kings were *permitted* by God but not *approved* by Him. [See Carlyle III, 99] In evidence for this, he quotes *Hosea* 'They have set up kings, but not by me: they have made princes, and I knew it not.' [*Hosea* 8:4] which clearly indicates the possibility that there can be rulers who have no divine endorsement.

The decisive split between the mundane and the supramundane, between the natural and the divine, comes to us, ultimately, from Hebrew thought. Oakley seems to agree: 'The irruption into the late antique world of the biblical religions was destined eventually to generate seismic activity along that disabling fault and to destabilize the foundations of the edifice of sacral monarchy that Constantine had inherited. But it was to have that effect only centuries later, long after Judaism and Christianity alike had first proved themselves to be in some degree responsive to the allure of the archaic cosmic religiosity and to have been drawn, accordingly and irresistibly, into the strong magnetic field it continued to exert.' [Oakley 2010, 39] One of the most important of the differences between Hebrew thought and that of its neighbours is that, whatever the extent of borrowing or assimilation, Hebrew thought makes a radical distinction between God and creation. God's creation of the universe isn't an aesthetically artistic re-arrangement of pre-existing material, as a potter might impose a shape on a piece of clay, but a constitution of the whole of the non-divine reality from nothingness. For almost all archaic thought, nature, man and the divine intermingled and interpenetrated each other along a continuum. There were, to be sure, boundaries between the various realms but these were semi-permeable, not intrinsically impassible barriers. Because of this interpenetration, nature and man participated by right, as it were, in the divine and so had an intrinsically sacral dimension. 'The biblical idea of creation,' writes Oakley, 'and the notion of God as one, transcendent, and omnipotent, which it both presupposed and entailed, inevitably imposed severe limits on the degree of sacrality that could properly be attached to any truly Israelite king. By destroying the archaic sense that there existed a consubstantiality between God, nature and humankind, it dedivinized or desacralized the two last, engineering in effect what Schiller in a happy phrase called the "disenchantment of the world." As a result, it has a desacralizing or disenchanting effect also on human society and on the political institutions necessary for the maintenance of that society.' [Oakley 2010, 48]

One of the most striking aspects of the Hebrew monarchy is its starkly secular character, this, *despite* the deep religious feelings and experiences of the Hebrew people—or perhaps that should be *because* of the deep religious feelings and experiences of the Hebrew people.

Despite the numerous and increasingly obvious cultural similarities between the Hebrew political experience and that of the other peoples of the ancient Near East, real differences between them did nevertheless exist. And, in the context of world history and of the development in the Latin Middle Ages and early modern centuries of a distinctively Western mode of political thinking, it is to the differences rather than the similarities that real significance attaches. Seek the roots of those differences, moreover, and one will find them embedded in that particular consciousness of the nature of God and of his relationship with the universe and with humankind, which crystallizes slowly, emerging, it may be, in fits and starts but also with growing insistence and clarity, during the long and turbulent odyssey of the Israelites as a self-consciously chosen but frequently faithless people. That consciousness finds a particularly powerful expression in some of the Psalms, in Deutero-Isaiah, and in so many of the prophetic voices transmitted to posterity via the pages of the Jewish Bible/Christian Old Testament. [Oakley 2010, 47; see also 49]

NEW TESTAMENT

When we come to consider the reported acts and sayings of Jesus, we can see immediately that his very life was bookended by acts of political significance, from King Herod's murderous intentions at his birth to the final drama of his politically inspired execution. There is so much material to choose from that I have had, of necessity, to be selective. There are, I believe, five principal passages in the New Testament in which Jesus' words or actions bear on matters political.[34] I think it fair to characterise all these passages as exhibiting, as Jacques Ellul puts it, 'irony, scorn, noncooperation, indifference and sometimes accusation.' [Ellul, 71] Summing up the significance of the New Testament passages that relate to politics, J. L. Houlden says 'What is remarkable…is how little direct interest there is anywhere in ethical questions raised by life in relation to political authority.' [Houlden, 88] Echoing Houlden's point, Cyril Parkinson is robustly dismissive of the attempt to generate political principles from isolated Scriptural texts, remarking that 'Much has been made of particular texts, like that of rendering to Caesar the thing that are Caesar's. But the unreality of conclusions based on such a text is manifest.' [Parkinson 1958, 192-193] He goes on to say that 'Christ was obviously not concerned with politics at all' and that 'Attempts to extract political advice from the new Testament are unscholarly, dishonest or absurd.' [Parkinson 1958, 193] However that may be, the extraction of political advice from the New Testament has been a popular practice—witness the recurrent appeals to *Romans* 13—and so it is necessary, if only for the sake of argument (and without rejecting Houlden's judgement and Parkinson's strictures) to take such attempts at face value and to try to estimate their worth.

The first passage I would like to look at is the one in which the mother of the sons of Zebedee asks Jesus to give her sons a special position at his right and left hand, that is, to place them in the ascendant over the other apostles. The other apostles are understandably annoyed at this request but Jesus overturns the expectations of them all by saying, 'You know that the rulers of the Gentiles lord it over them, and their great men exercise authority over them. It shall not be so among you; but whoever would be great among you must be your servant, and whoever would be first among you must be your slave.' [*Matthew* 20: 25-28] Note especially what is enjoined upon the apostles—they are not to lord it over those in their care nor are they to exercise over them authority-as-coercive-domination—*archein*—that was the norm in the kingdoms of the Gentiles. 'In that kingdom,' remarks Oakley, 'leadership will be a form of *diakonia*, that is to say, it will properly belong to those who serve. In it, certainly, there will be no lordship of the type claimed by the quasi-divinized Hellenistic kings of the day who titled themselves "benefactors".' [Oakley 2010, 57]

A passage indicative of Jesus's attitude to the powerful and the mighty is the account of his temptation in the desert.[35] The incident is recorded thus in Luke: 'And the devil took him up, and showed him all the kingdoms of the world in a moment of time, and said to him, "To you I will give all this authority and their glory; for it has been delivered to me, and I give it to whom I will. If you, then, will worship me, it shall all be yours."'[36] The devil offers Christ all the kingdoms of the world but, since one can't give what one does not have (*nemo dat quod non habet*), it would appear that the kingdoms of the world belong to the devil, a less than edifying estimate of the moral status of the kingdoms of this world! Yoder too notes that 'Jesus did not challenge the claim of Satan to be able to dispose of the rule of all the nations. If one makes this perspective central, all the New Testament texts appear in another light.' [Yoder 1994, 194] Some commentators have argued that the devil is the father of lies and his claim to the possession of the kingdoms of the world is just one more lie so that there's no reason to believe that the kingdoms of the worlds are in fact his to give! But even a liar can on occasion tell the truth and, significantly, Jesus's response to Satan is to reject his offer, not to deny that the offer is his to make. [see Day, 193-194] One could accept such an offer not just for one's own gratification but because one would seek to use this power to do good but, as the characters in Tolkien's *Lord of the Rings* who are offered the one Ring know only too well, it might begin like that but that isn't how it would finish.[37] As Lord Acton wrote in his Letter of 1887 to Archbishop Mandell Creighton, 'Power tends to corrupt and absolute power corrupts absolutely.'

So far, the passages I have considered are indicative of Jesus's generally dismissive attitude to power, authority and status. Now I turn to discuss some New Testament passages that are often quoted in support of the claim that there is scriptural warrant for Christians' obedience to the secular authorities. The first of these is the well-known 'Render unto Caesar' incident. The passage is worth citing in full: 'And they sent to him some of the Pharisees and some of the Herodians, to entrap him in his talk. And they came and said to him, "Teacher, we know that you are true, and care for no man; for you do not regard the position of men, but truly teach the way of God. Is it lawful to pay taxes to Caesar, or not? Should we pay them, or should we not?" But knowing their hypocrisy, he said to them, 'Why put me to the test? Bring me a coin, and let me look at it.' And they brought one. And he said to them, "Whose likeness and inscription is this?" They said to him, "Caesar's." Jesus said to them, "Render to Caesar the things that are Caesar's, and to God the things that are God's." And they were amazed at him.'[38]

There are a number of things to note about the 'Render unto Caesar' passage. First, as the introduction to the passage makes clear, the question wasn't innocent; it was designed to trap Jesus. If he answers 'yes', the zealots will hound him; if he answers 'no', the Roman authorities, who care about the payment of tax more than about anything else, are going to be somewhat less than pleased. [see Atwood, 139-140] 'To Roman magistrates, the peaceful and continuing collection of taxes was more important than the truth or fidelity of religious belief.... tax-gatherers were usually hated.' [Roberts 1997, 70; see Gnuse, 133] The incident as it appears in *Matthew* shows that Jesus is well aware of the non-innocent nature of this question—'Why tempt me, ye hypocrites?' he asks. Second, and more importantly, *Jesus does not answer the question*! But, you might think, this is absurd. Jesus clearly responds to the question that he is asked. Certainly he responds to the question, but not every response to a question is an answer to it. Every question constitutes the centre of a hermeneutic circle within which lie all its possible answers. For example, if one were to ask 'What time is it?' a very large number of possible answers might be given—'4.10 a.m., half past seven, a little after five' and so on. Any of these answers might be true or false, accurate or inaccurate, helpful or otherwise but they are all answers to the question; they all lie within the circumference of the hermeneutic circle. What if one's response to the question were, 'It's half past Spring'? This response does not lie unambiguously within the circle; on the other hand, Spring *is* a measure of time, even if a rather large one, so it doesn't lie unambiguously outside the circle either. One might see this response as straddling, as it were poetically, the circumference of the circle. On the other hand, if one's response to the question were the Zen-like 'Roses are blooming in Picardy' or "Twas brillig and the slithy toves, Did gyre and gimble in the wabe: All mimsy were the borogroves, And the mome raths outgrabe' these responses wouldn't be true, false, accurate, inaccurate, helpful or unhelpful answers to the question; they wouldn't be any kind of answer at all. To say, then, as Jesus does, that we should give to others what belongs to them is unexceptionable—it is, after all, the basic principle of justice. But what Jesus's response *does not* do is to tell his auditors *what* belongs to another. He tells them that they are to give whatever belongs to Caesar to Caesar but he does not say what, if anything, in fact belongs to Caesar. He could just as well have said, 'Give everything to Zaccheus that belongs to Zaccheus' and that formal statement would have been equally true without implying that any particular thing belonged to Zaccheus.

Jesus's non-answer to the question, then, is a classic restatement of the basic principle of justice and nothing more and it is, I believe, as James Redford describes it, 'an ingenious case of rhetorical misdirection.' [Redford, 10] Robert Gnuse writes that Jesus's saying was 'a clever form of articulating passive resistance—give the empire no more than it deserved, and, of course, it really deserved nothing.' [Gnuse, 133] For J. L. Houlden, in a remark that at first appears to be somewhat more sympathetic to the common understanding of this passage, its point isn't that 'the state as well as God has its legitimate claims' but 'The claims of God upon man are absolute…compared with them all other claims are trivial.' [Houlden, 82] Houlden concludes, however, that this passage in fact has 'no explicit implications for a Christian's practical attitude to the state.' [Houlden, 82]

In the end, whatever the merits of these various comments (which show a significant degree of convergence), it is clear that what Jesus's response most definitely is *not* is an answer to the question that he was asked and so is very far from being the straightforward endorsement of state power and authority that it is commonly taken to be.

There is yet another tax passage that isn't quite so well known as the previous one. 'When they came to Capernaum, the collectors of the half-shekel tax went up to Peter and said, "Does not your teacher pay the tax?" He said, "Yes." And when he came home, Jesus spoke to him first, saying, "What do you think, Simon? From whom do kings of the earth take toll or tribute? From their sons or from others?" And when he said, "From others," Jesus said to him, "Then the sons are free."' Clearly, if the sons are free, then the others, those who pay customs and taxes, are not free. But Jesus goes on to say, 'However, not to give offense to them, go to the sea and cast a hook, and take the first fish that comes up, and when you open its mouth you will find a shekel; take that and give it to them for me and for yourself."' [*Matthew* 17: 24-27] Having asserted the freedom of the sons, Jesus's prudential recommendation here is to pay the tax to avoid a scandal that might be detrimental to his mission. I do not think it far-fetched to take Jesus's recommendation here as being limited to its partic-ular circumstances and as having no general political significance.

Francis Oakley acknowledges that Jesus's attitude towards matters political was frankly negative. Unlike the attitude of the Zealots, whose negativity was directed towards Roman (or, more broadly, non-Jewish) authority, Jesus's negative attitude was directed against all government authority. This negative attitude, Oakley thinks, is balanced, albeit to limited extent, by a certain positivity. [see Oakley 2010, 58] The passages Oakley relies upon to support this assertion are the two passages I have just considered—the 'Render unto Caesar' passage, and the passage relating to the payment of the Temple tax. I do not think it necessary to repeat what I have just said about these passages for it to be apparent that if this is the extent of the evidence for Jesus's measured approval of government authority, then the scales on the balance have tipped firmly and decisively on the negative side.

TWO CHAPTERS 13: *REVELATION* AND *ROMANS*

The starkest anti-government passages in the New Testament are to be found in the *Book of Revelation*,[39] from which the people's choice must surely be the famous 'Number of the Beast' chapter 13.

Then I stood on the sand of the sea. And I saw a beast rising up out of the sea, having seven heads and ten horns, and on his horns ten crowns, and on his heads a blasphemous name. Now the beast which I saw was like a leopard, his feet were like *the feet of* a bear, and his mouth like the mouth of a lion. The dragon gave him his power, his throne, and great authority. And I saw one of his heads as if it had been mortally wounded, and his deadly wound was healed. And all the world marvelled and followed the beast. So they worshiped the dragon who gave authority to the beast; and they worshiped the beast, saying, "Who *is* like the beast? Who is able to make war with him?" And he was given a mouth speaking great things and blasphemies, and he was given authority to continue for forty-two months. Then he opened his mouth in blasphemy against God, to blaspheme His name, His tabernacle, and those who dwell in heaven. It was granted to him to make war with the saints and to overcome them. *And authority was given him over every tribe, tongue, and nation.* All who dwell on the earth will worship him, whose names have not been written in the Book of Life of the Lamb slain from the foundation of the world.... Here is wisdom. Let him who has understanding calculate the number of the beast, for it is the number of a man: His number is 666. [*Revelation* 13: 1-8; emphasis added]

If the passage from *Revelation* chapter 13 is full-bloodedly hostile to the reign of the divinised Roman Emperors, then, in apparent stark contrast, stands yet another chapter 13 in the New Testament, this time, chapter 13 of St Paul's *Letter to the Romans*.

John Howard Yoder asserts flatly that '*The New Testament speaks in many ways about the problem of the state; Romans 13 is not the center of this teaching.*'[40] A recent approach to understanding *Romans* 13, in a dialectical engagement with Oliver O'Donovan and John Howard Yoder, is Dorothea Bertschmann's *Bowing before Christ – Nodding to the State?* Bertschmann writes, 'Scholars have made various efforts to tackle this problematic text. Strategies vary, from relativizing the passage either through contextualizing it in a precise historical situation or literary context, to declaring it to be an interpolation; from claiming that most of the weighty and influential *Wirkungsgeschichte* of the text was based on a misreading of it, to seeing the text itself as problematic beyond redemption.' [Bertschmann, 126] Bertschmann herself takes a mainstream position on this passage, holding that it 'deals with political rulers in the narrow sense of the word' and that Paul in this passage 'issues a genuine call for submission with few or no qualifications' although she is aware that others, such as Mark Nanos and Arthur Ogle, read the passage in a radically different way.[41] '[I]n what is probably the oldest part of the New Testament,' Oakley remarks, 'we encounter a stance toward political authority that, while still negative in comparison with archaic and classical views, is a good deal *less* negative.' [Oakley 2010, 61] Well, it is certainly less negative, which isn't saying a whole lot since it would be hard to match the *Revelation* passage for vigour and vitriol; but does it, in fact, give aid and comfort to governmental authority? 'For the first 1,250 years of the Christian era,' writes Wilfrid Parsons, 'the thought of the Catholic Church about the power of the secular state was largely conditioned by two passages in the New Testament. The first of these is found in *Matthew* 22 and is the famous saying of Christ about God and Caesar. The second was the passage in Saint Paul to the *Romans*, 13, 1-7...' [Parsons 1940, 337] It is hard to disagree with this judgement of Parsons except, perhaps, to say that of the two passages, the one in *Romans* is by far the more important. *Romans* 13 is *the* scriptural passage that is used time and time again to justify our obligation to obey government. The narrow Scriptural basis of this doctrine of passive obedience apparently counselled by Paul in *Romans* 13 seems to be buttressed by brief passages in *Titus* 3: 1-2; *1 Timothy* 2: 2 and, perhaps the passage of greatest significance outside *Romans*, *1 Peter* 2: 13-17.[42] The passages from *Romans* and from *Peter*, writes George Smith, 'exerted more influence on Western political thought than any other writings on politics, whether ancient or modern.' [Smith 2013, 73] Of *Romans* 13, Carlyle writes that 'This passage, which is of the greatest importance throughout the whole course of medieval political thought, being indeed constantly quoted from the second century onwards, is indeed pregnant and significant in the highest degree.' [Carlyle I, 90] This text is the root of Augustine's teaching that the state is an instrument devised by God for the chastisement of sinful men. Jacques Ellul remarks that 'the official church since Constantine has consistently based almost its entire "theology of the state" on Romans 13 and parallel texts in Peter's epistles".' [Ellul, 166-167] Let us look at this remarkable text:

> Let every person be subject to the governing authorities. For there is no authority except from God, and those that exist have been instituted by God. Therefore he who resists the authorities resists what God has appointed, and those who resist will incur judgement. For rulers are not a terror to good conduct but to bad. Would you have no fear of him who is in authority? Then do what is good and you will receive his approval, for he is God's servant for your good. But if you do wrong, be afraid, for he does not bear the sword in vain; he is the servant of God to execute his wrath on the wrongdoer. Therefore, one must be subject, not only to avoid God's wrath but also for the sake of conscience. For the same reason you also pay taxes, for the authorities are ministers of God, attending to this very thing. Pay all of them their dues, taxes [tribute] to whom taxes [tribute] are due, revenue to whom revenue is due, respect to whom respect is due, honour to whom honour is due. [*Romans*: 13 1-7]

Whereas some English translations use the word 'governing' in verse 1, the Greek text does not. It reads: 'Let every soul be subject to the superior powers.' Who or what are these superior powers? It is assumed by many commentators that in this passage St Paul was referring to the secular authorities. But why should we make this assumption? Let us place this passage in context. In the previous chapter of *Romans*, St Paul had just written 'Do not be conformed to the world...' (*Romans* 12: 2); why should we think that he would almost immediately contradict himself and counsel conformity to the world? The bulk of chapter 12, and the verses of chapter 13 that occur immediately after the passage just quoted, concern themselves with what is required of the Christian in living a Christian life, of the mutual duties and responsibilities among Christians. There is nothing explicit in these two chapters to support the claim that St Paul has switched his focus in the early verses of chapter 13 to discuss the Christian's relationship to *civil* government. [see Bydeley] In fact, the context seems to support the contrary: St Paul is dealing with spiritual authority within the Body of Christ and the individual members' relationship to that authority. The apostle tells us to submit to the higher powers, then he quotes the law of the higher powers, the love of neighbour of which the particular commandments are only particular exemplifications. What St Paul is talking about here is the Law of God—what does this have to do with the dictates of the secular authorities? We might wonder why St Paul should suddenly switch to a completely different topic, and then back again to what he was speaking of in chapter 12? Why would St Paul encourage the Roman Christians to obey the secular authorities that were persecuting the Church? Of course, if the enemies of the saints in Rome to whom *Romans* is *not* addressed were to come across this letter and read this passage as exhorting Christians to obey the secular authorities and if, deceiving themselves by such a reading, this self-inflicted deception resulted in a lessening of the persecution of Christians, then so much to the good. The technique of deliberate indirection isn't foreign to the writers of the New Testament and, if we accept the words attributed to Jesus Christ himself in Scripture to be His as in the 'Render unto Caesar' passage, not foreign to our Lord Himself either.

In putting forward this contextualisation argument, I am happy to find myself in agreement with John Howard Yoder who writes, 'In the structure of the Epistle, chapters 12 and 13 in their entirety form one literary unit. Therefore, the text 13: 1-7 cannot be understood alone.' [Yoder 1994, 196] Yoder notes that some scholars, such as James Kallas, have taken the passage 13: 1-7 to be an interpolation but he points out, correctly, that such a view is necessitated only if the passage is understood in the way it has come to be understood in later tradition which would make it to be a literary erratic in the context of chapters 12 & 13 of *Romans*. If it isn't so understood, then the problem of accounting for this seeming interpolation simply disappears. Given the overall tenor of his book, Robert Gnuse's treatment of this seminal passage is disappointing. He seems to accept the general understanding of this passage as calling upon Christians to be obedient to the secular authorities, although with some minor reservations. He writes, 'The ultimate irony of his advice in Romans 13 was that Paul was addressing people who had been oppressed by Rome and would ultimately be martyred by Rome.' [Gnuse, 139] My irony gland is particularly well developed but I fail to detect any irony whatsoever in the passage.

All things considered, then, it would seem much less interpretatively arbitrary to take it that St Paul is exhorting those to whom he wrote this letter to be obedient to *their* authorities. I am not alone in thinking this way. Mark Nanos reads *Romans* as a letter from one Jew to other Jews, followers of Christ, who are part of the Roman synagogue communities. According to Nanos, the submission counselled by Paul in *Romans* 13: 1-7 is submission to the leaders of those synagogues, not to Roman government officials. This account isn't obviously implausible given that, when Paul wrote, the followers of Jesus in Rome were, for the most part, Jews who worshipped in synagogues. Coming at this passage from another (but not necessarily contradictory) angle, Arthur Ogle argues that the authorities and rulers referred to by Paul are the service-leaders of the nascent Christian community.[43] To repeat the passage from Matthew that I cited earlier: 'You know that the rulers of the Gentiles lord it over them, and their great men exercise authority over them. It shall not be so among you; but whoever would be great among you must be your servant, and whoever would be first among you must be your slave.' [*Matthew* 20: 25-28] Those who would lead the Christian community are not to lord it over those in their care nor are they to exercise over them authority-as-coercive-domination—*archein*—that was the norm in the kingdoms of the Gentiles. Christian leadership is to be a form of *diakonia*, of service, not domination.

There is yet another passage in the writings of St Paul where he exhorts his readers to 'obey them that have the rule over you.' It is perfectly clear, however, in this passage, that those that have the rule over you are the leaders in the Church, not the secular authorities. 'Obey them that have the rule over you, and submit yourselves: for they watch for your souls, as they that must give account, that they may do it with joy, and not with grief: for that is unprofitable for you.' (*Hebrews* 13:17) There's a similar passage in the Letter to *Titus*: 'Remind them to be subject to rulers and authorities, to obey, to be ready for every good work.' [*Titus* 3: 1] There is no clear indication here that the writer has earthly authorities in mind and, I believe, every likelihood that he does not.

Carlyle takes the standard interpretation of *Romans* 13, commenting that it defines 'in the profoundest way the Christian theory of the nature of political society…' [Carlyle, 90] In taking this approach, the Carlyles are in the majority but, unlike most, they go on to ask why this passage, and the associated passages in *Titus* and *1 Peter*, should endorse political obedience as a religious obligation. The answer, they think, is essentially the one that Augustine gives: the state is necessary to repress the bad and encourage the good. But they go further. They see these passages as evidencing an anti-Roman tendency in some members of early Christian congregations that the writers of these passages are anxious to discourage. More fundamentally, however, they believe that these passages are intended to repress a latent, and sometimes not so latent, general antinomianism in some Christians. It would seem to be the case from what we find in *Thessalonians*, *Corinthians* and *Galatians* that some new Christians understood their freedom from the law to exempt them from observing any moral or ethical standards at all. 'It seems more probable, then,' writes Carlyle, 'that St Paul's vindication of the authority of the civil ruler, with the parallel expression of St Peter's epistle, were intended to counteract some anarchical tendencies in the early Christian societies, were intended to preserve the Christian societies from falling into an error which would have destroyed the unity of human life…' [Carlyle I, 97] These very interesting and acute observations, however, go too far, for rejecting the authority of the state isn't equivalent to rejecting all authority and the account I have just presented could well be taken as recalling Christians to obey the laws of God as embodied in the command to love one's neighbour and not to be conformed to the world, rather than counselling obedience to the secular authorities. Carlyle admits that there is some evidence, some 'germs', as he puts it, in the New Testament that give some credibility to what he terms 'anarchical tendencies' in Scripture, not least among them being the passage from Mark already mentioned in which Christ contrasts the relationships which should obtain between Christians with that which obtains among the Gentiles.

What about the sword verse in the *Romans* 13 passage?—'for he does not bear the sword in vain; he is the servant of God to execute his wrath on the wrongdoer.' Surely this indicates beyond a doubt that the authorities in question here are the secular powers? Are we to understand Paul in this passage to be talking about a literal sword? Once again, context is important. James Redford remarks, 'Paul is not talking about a literal sword, i.e. actual *physical force*, such as used by all the Earthly, mortal governments. Paul is talking about the *Word of God*, which is the sword that Jesus Christ bears, and which figurative sword is none other than simply *the truth*.'[44]

What of verse 7, which speaks of taxes? I understand the verse on taxes/ tribute to parallel in some respects Christ's response to those attempting to trap him [*Mark* 12: 13; 17]. The Romans were relatively relaxed in their approach to those they had conquered, allowing them a measure of self-government and generally being indifferent to the continuation of indigenous religions but, like all governments, they were very touchy about taxes! Paul says: 'Render therefore to all their dues: tribute to whom tribute is due; custom to whom custom; fear to whom fear; honour to whom honour.' [*Romans* 13: 7] Yes, of course. This, once again, is the basic principle of justice: to give to each his due. But the questions are, what, if anything, is due? and to whom? If, as in the case of Christ's response to his would-be entrappers, any snooping official were to read this verse as justifying taxation by the secular authorities and, as a result, were to cease to regard Christians as objects of persecution, all to the good.[45]

If the taxes aren't due to the secular state, are they then owed to the Church authorities in such a way that they can legitimately be coercively extracted? Leaving to one side the very vexed question of tithing, and whether its justifi- cation is strictly derived from and pertinent only to the Old Testament with no implications for Christians, it seems to me to be reasonably clear that Christian pastors are entitled on scriptural grounds to be supported by those to whom they minister[46] (but, even here, not everyone is in agreement). If that is so, then the non-indirect aspect of verse 7 would be applicable to Christian pastors. If pastors are entitled to support, can they extract this support coercively from the Christian community? I think the answer here is—no. Disputes between Christians are not to be taken before the unrighteous [1 *Corinthians* 6:1] There *are* possible sanctions for those who refuse to contribute according to their means—as St Matthew remarks, those who do not listen to the church should be treated as pagans or as tax collectors, an interesting remark, coming from someone who had himself been a tax collector! [*Matthew*: 9: 9]—but those sanctions do not necessarily encompass the enforcement of that support by legal measures. The word usually translated as 'tribute' or 'tax', *phoros,* would seem to connote the idea of a burden or a load and it seems to be usually used in a non-voluntary context. But even granting this point, the phraseology of verse 7 is redolent of the principle of justice, and what one owes another in justice is, strictly speaking, not involuntary, since no one can acquire a positive obligation involuntarily. Even so, our voluntarily acquired obligations can easily be experienced as burdens, and so the use of the term *phoros* isn't inapt.

Let us recall some of the things done by the secular authorities that some interpreters believe *Romans* 1-7 would have us obey: the killing of all the male children in Bethlehem under two (*Matthew* 2: 16); the judicial murder of John the Baptist (*Matthew* 14: 10); the slaughter of the Galileans whose blood Pilate had mingled with their sacrifices (*Luke* 13: 1); the arrest and scourging of the apostles for preaching the gospel (*Acts* 4: 3 and 5:40); the execution of James and arrest of Peter by Herod (*Acts* 12: 2-3); the beating of Paul and Silas with rods and their imprisonment (*Acts* 16: 19-24). In *2 Corinthians*, St Paul speaks of 'far more imprisonments with countless beatings and often near death. Five times I have received at the hands of the Jews the forty lashes less one. Three times I have been beaten with rods; once I was stoned' (23-25), and recounts how he fled from the governor at Damascus (32). Tradition holds that Saints Peter and Paul were judicially executed though Paul, of course, couldn't have known about this when he was writing to the Romans, and there's little reason to doubt that the tradition is correct. And last, and very much by no means least, we have the arraignment of Jesus by the Jewish authorities, and his judicial torture and execution by the Roman Procurator, despite Pilate's not being able to find any case against him. After all this, are we seriously to believe that St Paul in *Romans* is demanding that we obey the secular authorities in any matter in which they care to command us? Surely not! *Arkhones*, the word that is translated as 'rulers' in verse 3 of the passage quoted, which is generally taken to refer to the secular authorities, is everywhere else in the New Testament used to refer to the Jewish religious leaders. In verse 4, are we to suppose that secular rulers are servants (*diakonos*) of the Church? Where in the New Testament is any secular ruler ever described as a servant of the Church? Once again, *diakonos* is a term used to describe Church leaders (see *1 Timothy* 3:8). Are we to suppose that these secular rulers were "God's servant for your good"? St Paul says of the authorities of which he speaks in *Romans* that they 'are not a terror to good conduct but to bad.' So, then, are we to conclude that the conduct for which the apostles and other early Christians were punished was bad? We know from our own experience that the demands of our secular rulers often conflict with the law of the Gospel and have done so throughout the ages.

Are there other possible interpretations of *Romans* 13? Yes, of course. It may well be that the passage means more or less what it has appeared to many to mean but is limited in its application to Paul's immediate circumstances, perhaps because Paul expected the imminent end of the world, a consummation compared to which little else mattered.[47] [see Neufeld, passim.] This is the position taken in the sixteenth century by the Franco-Scottish writer, George Buchanan, who insists that this passage in St Paul has no general application and is addressed to the specific time, place and circumstances of its making. The Church Paul addressed was an infant Church composed, as Buchanan remarks, 'of a promiscuous crowd of plebeians' for whom it would have been extremely foolish to attract the attention of those in government. What advice, he asks, should today be given to Christians living under Turkish rule?; what, indeed, except the advice Paul gives to the Romans 'to omit nothing that could help us to conciliate the good will of all men by honest practices.' [Buchanan 1579, 58] His conclusive argument that Paul's advice was circumstantial and not general is that 'though he [Paul] minutely explains the mutual duties of husbands to their wives, of wives to their husbands, of parents to their children, of children to their parents, of masters to their slaves, and of slaves to the masters, he does not, in describing the duty of a magistrate, address, as in the preceding parts, them expressly by name' Why should he not have done this except that 'there were neither kings nor other magistrates to whom he could write.' If Paul were writing now, Buchanan says, and were there to be a prince 'who thinks that not only human, but also divine laws ought to be subservient to his capricious lusts; who would have not only his decrees, but even his nods, held as laws,' would not Paul 'declare him unworthy of being reckoned a magistrate' and 'put all Christians under an interdict to abstain from all familiarity, all conversation, and all communion with him.' [Buchanan 1579, 59]

Even if we take it that the '*Romans* 13 means what just it says' interpretation in either its limited or global form, it is still possible to ask what 'to be subject' means. To be subject isn't necessarily to endorse or approve. Even if the higher powers are ordained by God, this does not mean that God approves of them any more than he approved of the Israelites' request for a king. Here, then, apart from Buchanan's circumstantial interpretation, are four possible interpretations of *Romans* 13 in order of increasing scope.

First, it requires obedience only to church authorities; second, it requires obedience to any authority to which we have given our consent—but only upon conditions and only for so long as our consent endures; third, it requires unconditional obedience to any ruler, however he may have come to power, but only so long as what he commands is in conformity with his obligation to promote justice or that provide for the regulation of matters that are indifferent but which must be organised in some particular way for the good of the community, or fourth, it requires unconditional obedience to any ruler, however he may have come to power or however he exercises it. The fourth interpretation has been held by some Church leaders from Augustine in the fifth century through to the Reformers in the fifteenth, although, as we shall see, there has been a tendency to move, under pressure, from the fourth interpretation to the third. Neither of these interpretations is acceptable to a libertarian although the third interpretation is clearly less unpalatable than the fourth. The first and perhaps the second interpretations would be acceptable to libertarians generally and even to anarchists, except those who would reject all forms of authority, even authority freely chosen.

As I have already mentioned, there are some other New Testament passages besides *Romans* 13 that are relevant to our topic. Perhaps the most important of these subsidiary passages is that in the First Letter of Peter. The passage reads: 'Be ye subject therefore to every human creature for God's sake: whether it be to the king as excelling; or to governors as sent by him for the punishment of evildoers, and for the praise of the good: For so is the will of God, that by doing well you may put to silence the ignorance of foolish men: As free, and not as making liberty a cloak for malice, but as the servants of God. Honour all men. Love the brotherhood. Fear God. Honour the king.' [1 *Peter* 2: 13-17] This, again, has acquired an interpretation as counselling obedience or subjection to the secular authorities. But it should be noted that Peter himself did not practise what he preached, *if* indeed that is what he preached. He defied the Jewish authorities by preaching about Jesus when they commanded him not to and justified his actions by saying that we ought to obey God rather than men. [*Acts* 5: 29] In any event, Peter counsels subjection to *all* human creatures, not just kings and governors, and the point of this subjection is that it will silence foolish people; there's nothing particularly special in subjecting ourselves to kings and governors. Putting it all together, this amounts to saying that we ought to obey all human ordinances except those that conflict with our God-given liberty and the summary commandment of Jesus to do unto others as we would have them do unto us—which is as much as to require us to obey those ordinances that are required by the golden rule and no others! Once again, what appears to be substantive is in fact politically vacuous. In the end, however, it can't be denied that the fourth, most extensive, interpretation of *Romans* 13, which takes it as requiring unconditional obedience to any ruler however he may have come to power or however he might exercise it, dominated Christian political thinking for sixteen hundred years and that even today that interpretation hasn't yet lost its appeal for many Christians.

One Christian thinker (among many) to whom *Romans* 13 appealed and who made use of it in his political thought was to become the pre-eminent Western theologian and philosopher for more than seven hundred years. His name: Aurelius Augustinus.

Notes

1 The substance of this chapter was largely completed before I had the opportunity to read the work of John Howard Yoder which is, in large part, a not-uncontroversial criticism of Christianity for having compromised its faithfulness to Jesus's message in exchange for a dubious relationship with the state. [see Yoder 2001, passim; see especially Yoder 1994] While our positions are not in complete agreement in all respects—I find Yoder to be insufficiently radical, despite his claim that Jesus is a 'model of radical political action' [Yoder 1994, 2]—I am encouraged to find that our approaches to the seminal scriptural passage, *Romans* 13, are, in many respects substantively coherent, when not in fact identical.
2 See Siedentop, 19-47.

3 See Oakley 2010, 92. John Burrow notes that 'Constantine's conversion became for Eusebius almost like a second Incarnation, and Constantine was clearly God's representative on earth.' [Burrow, 189; see 188-196]

4 Oakley 2010, 95. Even before the official adoption of Christianity, the Roman Emperor Diocletian (who ruled from AD 284-305) had already adopted a sacral role, acting as 'saviour, a Jupiter-like figure holding back chaos.' [Roberts, 225]

5 'Constantine...founded a tradition that Christian emperors enjoyed a special religious authority. It was to last for over 1,000 years.' [Roberts 1997, 78] For an eminently readable account of the (often neglected) history of the Eastern Roman (Byzantine) Empire, see Michael Angold's *Byzantium*. Richard Blake has a series of Byzantine-themed novels that bring this neglected empire and its history to life; see his *Death in Ravenna, Crown of Empire* et al.

6 See Kershaw, 374, and Penman, 570-572, 589, 603.

7 See Canning, 1996, chapter 1, sections 3 & 4 for an extensive discussion of the topic of Christian kingship and the priesthood. See also Tierney 1988, 16-23.

8 Musset, 170; Siedentop, 253.

9 Oakley 2012, 1. 'The idea of ecclesiastical autonomy had deep roots in scriptural authority as well. Yet in fact Frankish emperors, and in the tenth and eleventh centuries German emperors as well as French and English kings—plus Spanish, Norse, Danish, Polish, Bohemian, Hungarian and other rulers—governed bishops even in matters of religious doctrine, just as the Byzantine emperors had done.' [Berman 1983, 92; see also van Creveld, 1999, passim and Siedentop 113-150]

10 Palmer 2009, 287. Among the more significant of the *Dictates* are perhaps number 12, which claims that popes have the power to depose emperors, and number 27, which states that the pope may absolve subjects from their fealty to wicked men. [see Henderson, 366-367]

11 See the discussion of slavery among the Christians in the chapter on slavery.

12 Siedentop, 220. 'If Siedentop's story is persuasive, and our contemporary understanding in the West of liberalism and individualism, society, culture, and nature are fundamentally Christian derived, where does that leave us?' asks Leah Bradshaw. Is it the case that 'the detachment of secular liberalism from its religious foundations in Christianity threatens the future of the West'? [Bradshaw, 489] It is worth noting that over two millenia before Siedentop expressed these sentiments, Polybius had warned of the foolishness of the rejection of religious belief and rites by those in their societies who wanted to be modern and up-to-date. The contemporary West is perhaps the first major world culture to undertake the experiment of systematically dispensing with a religious foundation for its social and political structures.

13 *Matthew* 7: 12; Luke 6: 31.

14 '*Ius naturae est, quod in lege et euangelio continetur, quo quisque iubetur alii facere, quod sibi uult fieri, et prohibetur alii inferre, quod sibi nolit fieri.*' [Gratian, *Distinctio* 1] See Oakley 2012, 83-84.

15 Siedentop, 216; see also 356.

16 However obvious and commonsensical the idea of the individual might appear, it is neither obvious nor commonsensical to all. For Buddhism, in its radically revisionary account of the Hindu concept of *atman*, the self is the last and greatest of illusions. Arthur Schopenhauer is *the* western philosopher who adopts an essentially Buddhistic metaphysics and, channeling him, John Gray declares that 'We think we are separated from other humans and even more from other animals by the fact that we are distinct individuals. But that individuality is an illusion. Like other animals, we are embodiments of universal Will, the struggling suffering energy that animates everything in the world.' The essentially Christian idea that we are free, conscious individuals is, he says, 'an error that conceals from us what we really are.' [Gray 2003, 41]

17 For more on this, see chapter 31 on 'Twentieth-Century Tribalisms.'

18 P. G. Wodehouse, 'The Ordeal of Young Tuppy,' in *Very Good, Jeeves*, chapter XI, (London 1930).

19 'Hermeneutics may be defined as the theory of interpretation. More precisely, biblical hermeneutics inquires into the conditions under which the interpretation of biblical texts may be judged possible, faithful, accurate, responsible, or productive in relation to some special goal.' Thiselton, 279; see also Siedentop, 69.

20 O'Donovan 1996 and O'Donovan 2008.

21 Vol. 9, No. 3. See Chaplin and Wannenwetsch for two contributions to this issue that are pertinent to the concerns of this history.

22 For a popular account of these matters, see Austin; see also Bertschmann.

23 Augustine also dealt with this topic in parts of his *Confessions* and *The City of God*.

24 For a discussion of issues of interpretation in relation to the *Qur'an*, see Abdel Haleem, xxi-xxvi.

25 John Burrow notes that 'the Hebrew scriptures, which Christianity adopted as the Old Testament, are immensely heterogeneous, comprising various genres of ancient literature: creation myth, national epic, wisdom literature, genealogies and king lists, songs and prayers, laws and detailed ritual prescriptions, prophecy and protracted warnings of divine wrath....They also contain something like "political history", especially in the books of Samuel, Kings and Chronicles." [Burrow, 180]

26 'The LORD *is* my rock, and my fortress, and my deliverer; my God, my strength, in whom I will trust; my buckler, and the horn of my salvation, *and* my high tower.' [*Psalm* 18:2]

27 And then there is the vexed question of the composition, authorship and authority of some of the earliest books in the Bible. In *Genesis*, scholars have identified two non-identical accounts of the creation of the world, two non-identical accounts of the Flood, and two non-identical accounts of the history of Joseph. [see Gigot 1901, 103-105] For a sophisticated and relatively modern (1957) account of how to read Scripture, see Vawter's *A Path through Genesis*, in particular, his 'Introduction' to that work.

28 In his remarkable *The Bloudy Tenent of Persecution for Cause of Conscience, Discussed in a Conference between Truth and Peace*, Roger Williams, the founder of Rhode Island, although accepting the thesis that government was necessary and ordained by God, none the less argued strongly on the basis of Scripture for the functional separation of church and state and for the toleration of a variety of Christian denominations, including (unusually for this time) Catholicism.

29 As I am writing this chapter from the perspective of a Christian, I use the terms 'Old Testament' and 'New Testament' in the customary manner. Readers are welcome to substitute 'Jewish Bible' for 'Old Testament' throughout if they so desire.

30 Although for dialectical reasons I am going to discuss particular passages of Scripture and their customary interpretations, I wouldn't wish to be understood to endorse the practice of 'proof-texting,' that method of justifying particular Christian doctrines and practices by reference to Scriptural passages taken out of context. In fact, I shall argue that what is often taken to be the appropriate Christian approach to the justification of political rule rests on, at most, just four such isolated decontextualized passages: *Romans* 13: 1-7, *Titus* 3: 1, 2; 1 *Timothy* 2; 2 and *1 Peter* 2: 13-17. Part of what I shall try to do in this chapter is to attempt to recontextualise these passages, in particular, *Romans* 13, although my effort will necessarily be partial and limited. [see Viola & Barna, 2221-241]

31 1 *Samuel* 8: 11-18. 'The concept of property rights went back to biblical times and was transmitted and transformed by Christian teaching,' writes David Landes. 'The Hebrew hostility to autocracy, even their own, was formed in Egypt and the desert: was there ever a more stiff-necked people....When the priest Korach leads a revolt against Moses in the desert, Moses defends himself against charges of usurpation by saying, "I have not taken one ass from them, nor have I wronged any one of them."' [*Numbers* 16: 15, quoted in Landes, 34]

32 It is perhaps worthwhile to note an earlier unsuccessful attempt to establish Abimelech as king. [see *Judges* 9: 6-15] This abortive attempt provoked Jotham's satirical fable in which the trees set about anointing one of their number as king. All the worthy trees refuse the honour which eventually goes to the worthless bramble. No prizes for guessing whom the bramble represents! Martin Buber (and others) take this passage to be a generic attack on monarchy as such ('the strongest anti-monarchical poem,' say Buber, 'of world literature'!) but, to be fair, it may simply be a warning about placing monarchical power in the wrong hands.

33 *Patriarcha* XXIII, 97. See also XIV and XV.

34 *Mark* 12:13; *Matthew* 20: 20-25; *Matthew* 17: 24; *Matthew* 26: 52 and the accounts of Jesus' trial in the various Gospels.

35 In this connection, it is worth reading the Grand Inquisitor's upbraiding of Christ for his rejection of this temptation in Dostoevsky's *The Karamazov Brothers*, Book 5, Chapter 5.

36 *Luke* 4: 5-7; see *Matthew* 4: 8-9.

37 After a climactic encounter between Frodo, the Ringbearer and Galadriel, the Lady of Lothlórien, when Frodo freely offers Galadriel the one Ring that would enable her to preserve the elven realm of Lothlórien from decay, which offer she refuses, Sam Gamgee urges her to change her mind: 'I think my master was right. I wish you'd take his Ring. You'd put things to rights. You'd stop them digging up the gaffer and turning him adrift. You'd make some folk pay for their dirty work.' Galadriel responds: 'I would,' she said. 'That is how it would begin. But it would not stop with that, alas!' [Tolkien 1954, 357 (Chapter VII)]

38 *Mark* 12: 13-17; *Matthew* 22: 15-22; *Luke* 20: 19-26.

39 In *Revelation* generally, political power is firmly connected with the enemies of God. 'Fallen, fallen is Babylon the great,' and 'Woe, Woe to you, great city, you mighty city of Babylon.'

[*Revelation* 18: 2, 10]

40 Yoder 1994, 194, italics in original.

41 Bertschmann, 127; see 126-170.

42 It is significant, I think, that these passages [*Romans* 13: 1-7; *Titus* 3: 1-2; 1 *Timothy* 2: 2 and *1 Peter* 2: 13-17] assume a prominence in Christian political thought *after* Christianity had become the object of official toleration and support in the fourth century.

43 See Nanos, 302-304, and Ogle, 258.

44 Redford, 16 but see Bertschmann, 127.

45 Margaret Atwood remarks that 'many governments have gone out of their way to give the impression that God and they are firmly in cahoots, so that paying them is the same as paying God. Or almost the same. Or as close as maybe. Just take a look at what governments write on their money, even today. In Canada, it's *Elizabeth D.G. Regina*, short for *Dei Gratia Regina*—Queen by the Grace of God. In Britain, it's a longer inscription that adds initials meaning "Defender of the Faith."' [Atwood, 140]

46 See 1 *Timothy* 5: 18; *Luke* 10:7.

47 It is often argued that since the early Christian community thought the second coming of Jesus was imminent, to have immersed themselves in the things of world, a world that was passing away, would have seemed foolish. On this point, however, see Yoder 1994, 4-8, 104-105, 109-111.

Chapter 8

AUGUSTINE

Charity is no substitute for justice withheld
—St Augustine

The State is the altar of political freedom and, like the religious altar,
it is maintained for the purpose of human sacrifice
—Emma Goldman

In the period immediately after the conversion of the Emperor Constantine (AD 312), one thinker stands head and shoulders above all others. Aurelius Augustinus, later to be known as St Augustine, wasn't only immensely influential in his own time but is a writer who has had a profound effect on theologians, philosophers, political theorists, ethicists, and even upon literary theorists ever since. As a thinker, there is no one to rival him in the early history of the Church in the West. [see Tierney 1988, 7-15] Augustine was born in the Roman province of Africa (present day Tunisia and eastern Algeria) in the city of Thagaste in AD 354. At the time of his birth, Christianity had been accepted and was well on the way to being entrenched as the official religion of the Roman Empire. As a young man, Augustine was attracted to Manichaeism, a dualistic system of thought that posits a radical division between equipotent principles of good and evil. His Manichaean period lasted about ten years after which he became a Neo-Platonist. His Manichaeism and Neo-Platonism left a lasting influence on him. After a spell as a teacher in Carthage and in Rome, Augustine moved to Milan in 384 as a professor of rhetoric where he came under the influence of St Ambrose. He became a Christian and was baptised, together with his son Adeodatus, in AD 387. He returned to Africa to live his life first as a monk, then as a reluctant bishop of Hippo (AD 395/6), a city second in size and importance only to Carthage, where he died in AD 430.

There are writers whose personal lives are radically detached from their literary productions: one such would be St Thomas Aquinas. Augustine is most emphatically *not* one of these. Everything he writes bears the impress of his personality. To discover something of the character of the man, we are fortunate to have his *Confessions*. This intellectual biography, the first example of this literary genre, is essential reading for anyone wishing to come to grips with Augustine's thought. 'For Augustine,' writes Thomas Cahill, 'is the first human being to say "I"—and to mean what we mean today. His *Confessions* are, therefore, the first genuine autobiography in human history. The implications of this are staggering and even today, difficult to encompass....with Augustine human consciousness takes a quantum leap forward—and becomes self-consciousness.' [Cahill, 39. 41] The *Confessions* is both the spiritual autobiography of an individual and a map of the soul's journey to God. In this work, Augustine reveals himself to us as human, all too human, prone to all the temptations of the spirit and the flesh. If to be emotionally transparent is to wear one's heart on one's sleeve, then Augustine could be said to wear a heart on both of his. Consider the following revealing passage: 'The woman with whom I had been living was torn from my side as an obstacle to my marriage and this was a blow which crushed my heart to bleeding because I loved her dearly. She went back to Africa, vowing never to give herself to any other man, and left with me the son whom she had borne me. But I was too unhappy and too weak to imitate this example set me by a woman. I was impatient at the delay of two years which had to pass before the girl whom I had asked to marry became my wife, and because I was more a slave of lust that a true lover of marriage, I took another mistress.' [*Confessions* 6: 15]

It can't be too much emphasised just how unusual, just how ground-breaking a work Augustine's *Confessions* was. It is true that, some fifty years later, St Patrick would write his *Confession* but this is a largely an *apologia pro vita sua*, a defence of his life and mission to convert the pagan Irish, responding to the attacks of his enemies, and Patrick's *Confession* isn't in any way comparable to St Augustine's in its depth of psychological analysis. We do not, as Gurevich points out, 'come across St Patrick indulging in an analysis of his own personality with the same kind of inspiration as St Augustine does.' [Gurevich, 95] 'The inner psychological essence of the human being in the Greek World,' writes Aaron Gurevich, 'was not the object of tenacious questions and investigations. In Ancient Rome the position was slightly different. Certain writers manifested a tendency to engage in self-examination (Cicero, Seneca, Marcus Aurelius), but the genuine break-through to psychological introspection, although it was to remain the only one in that period, was that undertaken by St Augustine.'[1] Gurevich, indeed, goes so far as to argue that that the highpoint of the appearance of the individual occurs at the inception of the Middle Ages, and not towards its end. I can see why he would make this claim and, in fact, given the towering achievement of Augustine I have a certain sympathy with it. However, as I hope to show, the idea of the individual as it was diffused throughout society (and not just the product of the intellectual insight of one man) and incorporated in social and economic institutions was to be the product of almost eight hundred years of cultural and intellectual development.

THE CITY OF GOD

Augustine was a writer with an incredible range of interests and an even more incredible capacity for writing. Writers are sometimes described as volumi-nous; in Augustine's case, this is literally true. In a normal human lifespan, he produced some 117 books—in theology, philosophy, history and rhetoric—yet, despite this vast output, he wrote no single work on what we should now call political philosophy or political theory. To find out what he thought on political matters we have to disentangle and extract the relevant material from his thoughts on ethics, on history, on the nature of man and on theology. Robert

Markus remarks that though there are 'certainly elements of reflection on political theory to be found in his writings...his own explicit remarks in this area constitute no clear body of "political thought".' [Markus 1970, 73]

The *City of God*, perhaps Augustine's most famous work, was occasioned by the Goth's sack of Rome in AD 410 and its political aftermath. [see Oakley 2010, 120ff.] The work that Augustine eventually produced, however, far transcended the limits of its occasion, just as, in the nineteenth century, Newman's *Apologia pro vita sua* was to transcend its occasioning by the remarks of Charles Kingsley.[2] In *The City of God* Augustine produced a work of over a thousand pages about which he himself wryly remarked, 'It may be too much for some, too little for others.' [22: 30] The first 10 books defend the Christian faith against pagan attacks. Christianity, Augustine argues, wasn't responsible for the fall of Rome any more than paganism was responsible for its rise. Popular paganism is in no way satisfactory as a religion although Augustine believes the Neo-Platonism of Porphyry to present a challenge more worthy of his mettle. Having disposed of the claims of the pagans, Augustine turns in the remaining twelve chapters of his book to his proper theme, the tale of two cities, the earthly city and the city of God.

Augustine maintains that mankind is divided into two groups: one belonging to the city of God, the other to the earthly city. He writes, 'although there are many great peoples throughout the world, living under different customs in religion and morality and distinguished by a complex variety of languages, arms and dress, it is still true that there have come into being only two main divisions, as we may call them, in human society: and we are justified in following the lead of our Scriptures and calling them two cities. There is, in fact, one city of men who choose to live by the standard of the flesh, another of those who choose to live by the standard of the spirit.' [14: 1] It is a mistake, one easy to make but one none the less to be avoided, to understand Augustine's distinction to indicate two specific identifiable political entities, church and state. This isn't so. The city of God isn't the Church. The two cities are mixed together in this world: 'those two cities are interwoven and intermixed in this era, and await separation at the last judgement.' [1: 35] At least part of what Augustine is up to in his distinction between the city of God and the earthly city is a denial that any attempt to identify the city of God with any earthly city is likely to lead to idolatry and to an inappropriate attempt at the sacralisation of purely human institutions, mistakes that haven't always been successfully resisted by Christians.

Just as the character of a man's will is determined by the kinds of things he loves, so too, the character of a society is determined by the nature of that common love that is constitutive of that society. Formal membership of the church does not ensure one a place in the ranks of the saints, for some members of the church have in fact turned their wills away from the love of God whereas others, outside the formal structure of the church, have inclined their wills towards God. If we call to mind Augustine's definition of a people which is 'the association of a multitude of rational beings united by a common agreement on the objects of their love,' then it is obvious that those who have turned their wills away from God are not loyal citizens of the City of God. It is, however, important to note that even though the boundaries of the hierarchical Church may not be coterminous with the communion of saints on earth, the Church is still the normal channel of divine grace from God to man. In a sense, then, the Church's mission on earth is irreducibly social in that it is its task to bring as many people as possible into fellowship with the citizens of the City of God.

The citizens of the two cities, then, are ultimately determined by the object of their fundamental and not merely transient love. The city of God is made up of those who love God above all else, 'a love that rejoices in a good that is at once shared by all and unchanging—a love that makes "one heart out of many".' [15: 4] The earthly city is constituted of those who love themselves and thereby love dominion. Augustine writes, 'the two cities were created by two kinds of love: the earthly city was created by self-love reaching the point of contempt for God, the Heavenly City by the love of God carried as far as contempt for self....In the former [the earthly city] the lust for domination lords it over its princes as over the nations it subjugates; in the other, both those put in authority and those subject to them serve one another in love, the rulers by their counsel, the subjects by obedience.' [14: 28] The restlessness that characterises the human heart, if not directed towards its proper object, God, will find some temporary satisfaction in dominion, a dominion that, taken to its conclusion, leads to the creation of kingdoms and empires and an ambition to be their ruler: 'For when can that lust for power in arrogant hearts come to rest until after passing from one office to another, it arrives at sovereignty.' [1: 31]

Man is a social animal and requires society for his development. Augustine sees society as something more than an accidental conglomeration of individuals. Although he recognises the number and the gravity of the disorders that flow from man's social nature, he still asks: 'How could the City have made its first start, how could it have advanced along its course, how could it attain its appointed goal, if the life of the saints were not social?' [19: 5] Justice is the foundational virtue of civil society. It preserves peace, the common good of society, and without peace, no society can subsist, let alone prosper. [19: 13] Although a Roman himself, Augustine is keen to demonstrate that Rome as a state was never actuated by true justice, not even in its early pre-decadent phase. Justice, for Augustine, requires the subordination of the lower to the higher in all things and so the body is to be ruled by the soul, the lower appetites by reason and reason by God. [19: 21] So too in society, virtuous subjects should obey wise rulers, those rulers, in turn, being subject to divine law. In pre-lapsarian society we would have had harmony in society without coercion or the subjection of one man to another but sin has disrupted this original condition and unleashed man's desire to exercise dominion over others. Everywhere, the lower is in rebellion against the higher. The freedom that characterised our original condition has disappeared, to be replaced by coercion and oppression. Perfect justice is practically unrealisable in our workaday world. The city of God is the community of all followers of Christ and there, and there only, is true justice to be found. The earthly city, on the other hand, is guided by self-love. The 'two cities, different and mutually opposed, owe their existence to the fact that some men live by the standard of the flesh, others by the standard of the spirit.' [14: 4]

Augustine believes, then, that human beings are naturally social and that had they not fallen into sin they would have lived together under a benevolent paternal direction. [see Markus 1970, 95] But man did fall, as a result of which his desire for peace is thwarted by his disordered loves. 'The effect of that sin was to subject human nature to all the process of decay which we see and feel, and consequently to death also. And man was distracted and tossed about by violent and conflicting emotions, a very different being from what he was in paradise before his sin...' [14: 12] In this condition, peace can no longer be brought about and maintained by a benevolent paternalism but requires some much stronger means of control. People who are constitutionally inclined to conflict can obtain peace only if someone is authorised to use force to restrain them coercively. 'The great need here, in Augustine's sombre vision of the nasty brutishness of man in his fallen condition,' writes Robert Markus, 'was for bulwarks to secure society against disintegration. In its coercive machinery the state turns human ferocity itself to the limited but valuable task of securing some precarious order, some minimal cohesion.' [Markus 1970, 95] For Augustine, government 'was the consequence of sin and it arose from the lust for power and domination. But in so far as coercive authority restrained further abuse of free will, it was a necessary and legitimate remedy of sin.' [Luscombe 1982, 757]

The relationship between ruler and ruled, then, is analogous to that between slave owner and slave. In both cases, Augustine thinks, those subject to the power of another benefit from that subjection. 'Augustine,' says Weithman, 'does not distinguish clearly between a relationship which is specifically political and other relationships of authority and subjection, especially the relationship between a master and slaves. The qualified assimilation of political subject to slavery is the key to Augustine's views about the purposes of political authority and its origins in human sinfulness.'[3] In our fallen condition we are subject to political domination of some kind or other but it does not follow from this that we can't distinguish better forms of political domination from worse. If human wickedness had been less, 'all kingdoms would have been small and would have rejoiced in concord with their neighbours. There would have been a multitude of kingdoms in the world, as there are multitudes of homes in our cities.' [4: 15] In what must be one of the earliest versions in literature of a 'mirror of princes' passage, Augustine sketches what ideal rulers would be like. Such rulers rule, he says, 'with justice.... they are not inflated with pride, but remember that they are but men....they put their power at the service of God's majesty....they fear God, love him and worship him....more than their earthly kingdom, they love that realm where they do not fear to share the kingship...' [5: 24] Despite these small concessions to political optimism, however, Augustine's political thought is overwhelmingly pessimistic.

Augustine puts forward a theory of passive obedience to the state, whatever the moral character of its leaders. Christians must obey their secular rulers until and unless they require Christians to break God's law. Disobedience is then required but so too is submission to punishment for that disobedience. As McClelland says, 'This is grim doctrine, and not the least of its grimness comes from the lack of any ultimately positive value being attributed to the obligation to obey.' [McClelland, 102] It must be remembered, however, that for Augustine, political events as much as individual human lives are governed by God's providential care: 'we must ascribe to the true God alone the power to grant kingdoms and empires. He it is who gives happiness in the kingdom of heaven only to the good, but grants earthly kingdoms both to the good and to the evil, in accordance with his pleasure, which can never be unjust.' [5: 21] Why he should devolve political authority to such as Nero is, in the end, a mystery whose explanation is hidden from us.

Augustine's political thought is radical, running contrary to the consensus of the classical traditions to which he was heir. [see Markus 1970, 72-104] Paul Weithman comments: 'His arguments that political authority is exercised because of human sinfulness, that it is fundamentally akin to slavery, that it exists to restrain and humble those subject to it, and that citizens do not develop the virtues by dedicating themselves to political life, together constitute a sustained assault on the tradition of political thinking which locates "the good for man" in the common good of an earthly rather than a heavenly city.' [Weithman, 243] Augustine's thinking about politics is a counterweight to those optimistic theories that emphasise rationality and enlightenment and cooperation. To the perennial plaint 'Why can't we all just get along?' Augustine has an answer—it is because of our damaged human nature, damaged by sin and sinfulness.

From Augustine's perspective, the state isn't an institution for inculcating the virtues—that was the Greek view; nor is the state an example of the instantiation of some kind of universal law—that was the Roman view or at least the view of some Romans. It is true that in his earlier writings, Augustine was somewhat more open to conceiving of human law as a reflection of the divine law and thus as a means to man's perfection. In his later thought, however, this conception disappears. [see Markus 1970, 89-90] The purpose of law isn't to make men virtuous but to underpin public order, and the state is the provider of this law. Even when he argues for its practical necessity, Augustine's opinion of the state isn't high. For him, the state is, as McClelland says, 'tawdry in virtue of its function. It can never be much more than a thief-taker, a bent policemen in pursuit of robbers and murderers who do not differ in kind from the pursuer.' [McClelland, 102] As sinful beings we may need the state, but that does not make the state anything other than an institution staffed and operated by sinners. Augustine is convinced that the state's origins are to be found in violence.

Augustine on Man

Augustine's view of man is, in many ways, the key to his political and social thought. For Augustine, man is a creature only somewhat less mysterious than God. Even though we live with ourselves day by day, we are never wholly transparent to ourselves. Augustine's man is decidedly not the detached, bloodless, Cartesian ego; he is an embodied creature with all the opacity to himself that corporeality implies. 'For Augustine, the mind can never be transparent to itself; we are never wholly in control of our thoughts; our bodies are essential to who we are and how we think; and we know that we exist not because "I think, therefore I am" but, rather, "I doubt, therefore I know I exist".' [Elshtain, 121] Augustine has Stoic doctrine firmly in his critical sights when he argues that human beings aren't just rational beings but emotional beings as well. If the Stoic state of *apatheia* (which Augustine, coining a new word, calls 'impassibility') were achievable it would, Augustine thinks, be the worst possible outcome. 'If *apatheia* is the name of the state in which the mind cannot be touched by any emotion whatsoever, who would not judge this insensitivity to be the worst of all moral defects?' [14: 9] On the other hand, if this impassibility were to be understood as a lack of the disturbing emotions that defy reason it would be a good thing but that, Augustine thinks, isn't something achievable in this life.

Human beings are social and relational beings. For Augustine, human beings made in the image of the Trinitarian God, a God who is Himself essentially relational, are themselves relational and are not detached and isolated egos. We are always in society. The question isn't *whether* we shall be social but *how*. Even criminals are social by nature. A thief may be a sole trader, unwilling to trust others to work with him in his enterprises or doubting their competence to do so. But even such a solitary predator requires that his incidental criminal colleagues act according to some kind of order and, if he has a family, he will expect the members of that family to respect his authority.

Society is just one form of friendship, friendship being a kind of union in which a plurality strives for a shared good. Charity begins at home but it does not end there. The natural ties of familial affection are directed outwards towards others, thus binding together an ever-increasing number of individuals. Language aids in this binding but there's always the possibility of being misunderstood. Where languages differ, this difficulty escalates. Life in society is a complex resulting not only from our love for ourselves and others but also—and here we are getting close to the root of Augustine's political thought—our lust for domination.

Man is moved to act by the object of his love. Our love may be a merely fleeting desire, as for an ice cream on a sunny day, or it may be a deeper habitual orientation towards some good, such as for knowledge, or it may be an all-encompassing fundamental orientation, as towards good or evil, God or not-God. Some things we desire are desired merely as a means to something else, other things are desired in themselves; the former are merely used; the latter are enjoyed. Music, for example, though it can be used for various purposes, is essentially useless. So too is a baby. Only something that is lovable in and for itself and not as a means to something else can bring happiness to man. At the start of his *Confessions*, Augustine, addressing God directly, says 'you made us for yourself and our hearts find no peace until they rest in you.' [*Confessions* 1.1] No created thing, however good it may be, is capable of bringing cessation to our restless longings. Augustine, notoriously no despiser of the good things of creation, remarks of physical beauty that it is 'a good created by God, but it is a temporal, carnal good, very low in the scale of goods; and if it is loved in preference to God, the eternal, internal and sempiternal Good, that love is as wrong as the miser's love of gold…though the fault is in man, not in the gold. This is true of everything created; though it is good, it can be loved in the right way or in the wrong way…' [15: 22] Nevertheless, because of sin, original and personal, our loves are disordered so that we crave the merely instrumental and useful as if they were final goods, not only the usual suspects of wealth and sensual pleasure but also the more deadly and less obvious culprits such as glory, reputation and, especially, domination over others. Because of his disordered inner life, man is in conflict with himself and so, not surprisingly, in conflict with others. And that brings us back to Augustine's two cities.

Augustine on History

The course of human history might be described as being, for Augustine, merely the filling in of the temporal gap between two singular states of affairs. One of these singularities is, of course, man's original bliss in Eden: the other is his projected bliss in heaven (or damnation in hell.) The significance of the historical process is to be located in its terminal points, not in any intrinsic features of the events of history themselves. The purpose of history is to give post-lapsarian man the opportunity to become either a citizen of the City of God or a citizen of the City of Man. It is important to realise that for Augustine, human history, in and of itself, has little significance. Whatever meaning or purpose it may have, it has primarily by reference to its ultimate beginning and its ultimate end. Even the Roman Empire lacks any ultimate significance, 'being only an incident, albeit an important one, in the Providential march of universal history,' history being essentially 'a record of the encounters of individuals with God.' [Morrall 1970, 61]

How does Augustine arrive at this view of history? Well, certainly not by some inductive process based on evidence acquired by means of an empirical investigation of the facts of history. Augustine has the truth about history already in his grasp before he begins his study of it. His task is to make sense of the endless succession of historical events in the light of Christian Revelation. Augustine, then, does not take the world at its own valuation; neither does he seek to understand it in terms of its own categories of self-understanding. Rather, being in possession of certain key interpretative principles, he is able to discern the true meaning of history, a meaning that is very different from the meaning it is commonly thought to possess. Christopher Dawson makes this point concisely: 'Augustine did not consider the problem of secular progress, but then secular history, in Augustine's view, was essentially unprogressive. It was the spectacle of humanity perpetually engaged in chasing its own tail. The true history of the human race is to be found in the process of enlightenment and salvation by which human nature is liberated and restored to spiritual freedom.' [Dawson 2009, 209]

Does this mean that the social and political activities of man are devoid of intrinsic significance? Broadly speaking, Augustine has to answer this question in the affirmative. The original blueprint for man contained no specification for the domination of one man over another. The creation and maintenance of political regimes, which depends on the fact of human domination and submission, can be traced back to man's fall. Augustine has a very unflattering opinion of the foundations of political authority. In the last analysis, political authority rests on coercion. But even though political regimes are a consequence of man's fallen nature, they can nevertheless be instruments of God's Providence. One of the useful functions of the political state, perhaps the only one for Augustine, is the likelihood that it will create the peaceful conditions in which the Christian can pursue his true vocation. Any ruler is better than none, even such a one as Nero! [see Markus 1970, 93]

AUGUSTINE ON SLAVERY

Augustine, in his *Commentary on the Psalms*, echoes and indeed amplifies Paul's acceptance of slavery. He remarks that Christ 'did not make freemen out of slaves, but good slaves out of bad slaves' and points out that the rich should be grateful to Christ for 'creating stability in their homes!'[4] He relies on Paul's injunction that slaves should obey their masters to justify his claim that the just should give honour to those who rule over them, even if those rulers are unjust. As should be obvious from this, Augustine, as with most other thinkers of his period, accepted the social fact of slavery which, along with other forms of property, is justified by the positive law of the ruler. There is no slavery by nature; the dominion of one man over another isn't natural. Before man fell into sin, private property wouldn't have been necessary. After sin, men have an unnatural desire for material things which can be abated only if what should have been held in common for all is divided into separate portions. Only in this way can conflict be avoided or, at least, minimised. What makes my house to be my house and my slave to be my slave is man-made law. 'Take away the laws of emperors, and who will dare say "that villa is mine, that slave is mine or this house is mine"? People have accepted the laws of kings so that they can possess those very things.'[5] As is the case with Paul, slaves are exhorted to obey their masters and masters to maintain the order of the household. [see 19: 14, 16]

In the order of creation, no man was intended to be a slave either to any another man or to lust. God did not desire man to dominate over other men but only over irrational creatures. Augustine writes that God 'did not wish the rational being, made in his own image, to have dominion over any but irrational creatures, not man over man, but man over the beasts.' It follows, he thinks, that kingship wasn't an original item of society, but an institution that had developed over time.

Slavery, then, isn't natural but the result of sin, whether one's own sin or the sin of others. Augustine is sensitive to the claim that the arbitrary imposition of slavery on men by a just God is difficult to defend. His solution is to present slavery as a punishment for sin. 'The prime cause of slavery, then, is sin, so that man was put under man in a state of bondage...' [19.15] This being so, he is content to endorse the slavery-is-for-the-benefit-of-the-enslaved theory. [19.21]

ARE RULERS ON A PAR WITH ROBBERS AND PIRATES?

There is a short but shocking chapter in the *City of God* that is worth quoting in full.

> Remove justice, and what are kingdoms but gangs of criminals on a large scale? What are criminal gangs but petty kingdoms? A gang is a group of men under the command of a leader, bound by a compact of association, in which the plunder is divided according to an agreed convention.
>
> If this villainy wins so many recruits from the ranks of the demoralized that it acquires territory, establishes a base, captures cities and subdues people, it then openly arrogates to itself the title of kingdom, which is conferred on it in the eyes of the world, not by the renouncing of aggression [*cupiditas*] but by the attainment of impunity.
>
> For it was a witty and a truthful rejoinder that was given by a captured pirate to Alexander the Great. The king asked the fellow, "What is your idea, in infesting the sea?" And the pirate[6] answered, with uninhibited insolence, "The same as yours, in infesting the earth! But because I do it with a tiny craft, I'm called a pirate: because you have a mighty navy, you're called an emperor". [4.4]

It has been observed that this passage is somewhat ambiguous. It may be taken to suggest that the difference between State operations and criminal undertakings is merely a matter of degree; on the other hand, it may be taken to suggest that the State can be redeemed by subjecting it to justice so that, despite the manifest similarities between robber bands and kingdoms, kingdoms *do* possess the essential difference of being just. [see d'Entrèves 1967, 23] But this latter interpretation can't possibly be correct, for Augustine has been at great pains to argue that no human political order, not even that of Rome, has ever possessed or manifested true justice. Augustine's conception of the state was radical inasmuch as he saw it as having no moral force whatsoever! Although for Cicero, it was essential that the law of the state embody justice and Augustine, echoing Cicero, maintained in one place that there could be no true republic without justice [4:4], he also thought that no state could in fact be just in a Christian sense! [19.24) But if the possession of justice is the only thing that could differentiate a kingdom from a robber band and if, as seems to be Augustine's point, no kingdom can possess such justice, there can be no discernible moral difference between robbers and kings!

Robber Bands [*latrocinia*]	Kingdoms [*regna*]
Groups of men	Groups of men
Under a leader	Under a leader
A compact of association	A compact of association
Spoils divided according to rule	Spoils divided according to rule

Justice does not give us the essential difference between the two groups. What then does? The answer is surprisingly *realpolitik*: it's a matter of size and degree of permanency! A kingdom is simply a robber band on a larger scale than most with a more permanent base of operations![7] That's what makes the difference between a robber band and a kingdom, just as it does between the pirate and Alexander. Though much of Augustine's thought was enormously influential on later thinkers, it is perhaps not surprising that his radical ideas on the state and justice had little or no effect in his own time and in the centuries immediately following.

That this passage isn't just a substantial slip of the pen on Augustine's part but a considered and sober judgement is made clear when, some chapters later, he turns his attention to the career of Ninus, King of Assyria. Having described Ninus's craving for empire, Augustine concludes the chapter by saying, 'to attack one's neighbours, to pass on to crush and subdue more remote peoples without provocation and solely from the thirst for dominion—what is one to call this but brigandage on the grand scale?' [4.6] The point is made yet again when Augustine remarks that a brigand who was offered the control of a city or a whole nation could afford to emerge from the shadows of brigandage but without abating one little bit of the greed and malignity that made him so successful a brigand. The man who would now be king is no different from the man who once used to be a brigand except in size and boldness. [19.12]

Augustine was much influenced by the writings of Cicero, in particular, the *Laws* and *Republic*, in which Cicero proposed a definition of the commonwealth as an association of people bound by an acknowledgement of right and a community of interests. Augustine goes beyond this account to add to it the idea that for something to be a commonwealth there must be a common agreement among its members not only in respect of rights and interest but also as to the object of their love. A people is 'an assemblage of reasonable beings bound together by a common agreement as to the objects of their love...'[8] Augustine, however, is still sceptical of the claims of any state, even Rome, to be the embodiment of justice. In a passage in his *Republic*, Cicero, comparing the original Roman foundation with its current embodiment, laments the fatal decline in virtue that has taken place over the centuries.

This, and similar pieces of nostalgia for the good old days, is the occasion for a magnificent display of irony by Augustine who remarks, 'Sallust says "equity and virtue prevailed among the Romans not more by force of laws than of nature." I presume it is to this inborn equity and goodness of disposition we are to ascribe the rape of the Sabine women. What, indeed, could be more equitable and virtuous, than to carry off by force, as each man was fit, and without their parents' consent, girls who were strangers and guests, and who had been decoyed and entrapped by the pretence of a spectacle!' [3: 14]

Given this, one might expect Augustine to reject kings and kingdoms and all their works and pomps. If one had such an expectation one would be sorely disappointed! Despite his clear-eyed recognition of the dubious moral status of kingdoms, Augustine argues that the essential task of the state, whether ruled by a good prince or a bad prince, is still the same—to maintain peace and justice inasmuch as such is possible in this vale of tears. The moral character of the prince makes absolutely no difference to the legitimacy of his rule and the duty, as Augustine sees it, of the Christian to render obedience to any and every law and command such a prince might make, unless such laws or commands require a Christian to violate his religious duties. And even in this case, although refusing to obey the law, the Christian must willingly accept the punishment he merits by his disobedience and may not rebel against the ruler's authority.

The legitimacy of a ruler's authority is not, Augustine thinks, compromised in the slightest by the roughnesses, uncertainties, and practical injustices that the administration of any state inevitably entails. Judges may convict the innocent or fail to convict the guilty—that is unfortunate but inevitable. He writes, 'those who pronounce judgement cannot see into the consciences of those on whom they pronounce it. And so they are often compelled to seek the truth by torturing innocent witnesses in a case that is no concern of theirs. And what about torture employed on a man in his own case? The question is whether he is guilty. He is tortured, and, even if innocent, he suffers, for a doubtful crime, a punishment about which there is not a shadow of doubt and not because he is discovered to have committed it, but because it is not certain that he did not commit it. This means that the ignorance of the judge is often a calamity for the innocent.' [19.6]

Even with all its manifest imperfections, Augustine thinks the state is essential because without it, sinful men couldn't be suitably restrained. The state is both a consequence of sin and, paradoxically, a means for its restraint. So too, other forms of human domination resulting from sin—property and slavery—are means by which order can be maintained, a relative and imperfect order to be sure but an order none the less. Because men value their possessions, sanctions that threaten their continued ownership or use of those possessions have traction. 'The sanction by means of which the state attempts to insure conformity to the conduct prescribed by the laws,' writes Herbert Deane, 'consists in the ability to deprive the offender of one or more of these possessions—his property, his liberty, his citizenship, or, in the last resort, his life.' [Deane 1963, 139]

Augustine believes that the state, imperfect, limited, and unjust as it may be, is none the less an instrument of Providence. However unjust or wicked a ruler of a state may be, the authority he has comes from God and, as such, the Christian owes him obedience. No disobedience to the ruler's commands is envisaged, much less resistance or rebellion. It should come as no surprise to find Augustine relying on the thirteenth chapter of *Romans* to support this point of view. Origen had held that associations of men to resist unjust laws were worthy of approval but Augustine couldn't agree with this sentiment. 'One of the primary reasons why Augustine insists so strongly on the divine origin of political authority and on the subjects' duty of absolute obedience to it,' writes Herbert Deane, 'is that, like Hobbes, he is so keenly aware of the need for a strong power to restrain the boundless appetites and ceaseless conflicts of men....Only at the end of time will this need for human authority and for absolute obedience to it come to an end.' [Deane 1963, 144]

Despite his insistence on the citizen's obligation to obey his rulers and render obedience to the state, Augustine is never tempted to sacralise secular authority in any way. For him, however essential such authority may be, it is, as Francis Oakley incisively remarks, 'nothing more than a secular instrumentality adapted to the evanescent conditions of the *saeculum* or present age, an essentially limited and necessarily coercive force that lacks both the authority and the ability to reach beyond the imposition of a merely earthly peace and a merely external order to mould the interior dispositions of men.' [Oakley 2010, 130]

It cannot be denied that Augustine's *realpolitik* is, at one level, an expression of his pessimistic anthropology. But at a deeper level, Augustine's passivity and quietism comes not just from his pessimistic anthropology but even more so from his deep conviction that this life is, in the scheme of things, momentary and fleeting.[9] In comparison to our ultimate destiny, the question of who does or who does not rule and the manner in which they exercise that rule is a matter of little significance. He remarks, 'As for this mortal life, which ends after a few days' course, what does it matter under whose rule a man lives, being so soon to die, provided that the rulers do not force him to impious and wicked acts?' [5.17]

A standing liberal reproach to Augustine is that he was prepared to use coercion for religious reasons. He did not always think this was permissible but eventually he reluctantly concluded that it was right, or at least expedient, to use force against the Donatists, a rigorist sect of Christians. In this context, using force meant appealing to the civil authorities for assistance. It would seem that Augustine's decision was a casuistic one, made in light of the concrete circumstances of the Donatist resistance, which appeared to threaten the civil order as well as to disturb the religious peace of the North African church. Augustine concluded that coercion, in some matters, is for the good of the coerced! The Donatists, on the other hand, were unwilling to grant any authority to the state in religious matters. Petilian asks Augustine what Christians have to do with kings who have never shown anything but envy to them. Augustine replies that kings, as kings, can serve God in that capacity.[10] To the charge that Christianity undermined the civic order, Augustine asks those who make such a charge to consider how well Christians fulfil their obligations as soldiers, judges, taxpayers and even tax collectors![11]

By acquiescing in coercion in religious matters, Augustine is firmly in the tradition of previous secular states. 'The idea that there was something especially problematical about religious coercion,' writes McClelland, 'had yet to be invented.' [McClelland, 105] To do Augustine justice, it must be conceded that the struggle with the Donatists wasn't just a courteous exchange of opinions. Physical violence and destruction of property, with consequent disruption of public order, was commonplace and, of course, from a libertarian perspective, one has the right to defend oneself against aggression, using proportionate force so to do. Whether this goes all the way to exculpate Augustine is another matter. [see Morrall 1970, 68-69] McClelland comments: 'We sometimes forget that the modern view of the state's monopolistic right to use violence is only possible if we also take a specifically liberal view of the distinction between society and the state. Most political theory is not liberal, and most political theory denies that the liberal distinction between the state and society is a valid one.' [McClelland, 106] The tenor of this remark seems to suggest that if we accept in principle that the state has a right to use coercion in a given area, we can't deny its right, in principle, to use it in other areas. The libertarian response to this contention, of course, would be to deny that anyone, including the state, has a right to coerce in any area. Defending Augustine against criticism on this matter, Henry Paolucci presents the following argument. What Augustine did, he thinks, was more or less on a par with what Lincoln did in forcing the Southern states to remain in the Union or what the US government did in forcing integration upon schools. Clearly, Paolucci thinks Lincoln's actions to be justified and so, by analogy, Augustine's endorsement of force against the Donatists to be likewise justified. I would run the argument the other way around. Lincoln's use of force cost 500,000 lives; the US government's integration programme disrupted people's free choice and despite the best of intentions, arguably set back race relations in the USA by several generations. So too, Augustine's endorsement of the use of force against the Donatists was a bad mistake, both practically and in principle. Some, such as McClelland, may defend Augustine on this matter by saying that it is anachronistic to expect him to have liberal views that historically could only exist in modern times. There is something to this defence but, in the end, Augustine's vacillation on this matter shows that he wasn't unaware of the tension between his religious beliefs and his political beliefs. [see Markus 1988, 113-115]

The peace of this world, imperfect as it may be, is necessary for man's continued existence, and so must be maintained. If men were perfect and their internal lives properly ordered no laws would be necessary. But men, Augustine believes, are very far from being perfect. Man is a fallen creature, riven by conflicting desires and incapable of restraint, filled with various lusts, among them the lust to dominate others. That being so, political and legal structures must be put in place to restrain us and limit the damage we might do to others; it keeps us, as Irenaeus pleasingly phrased it in his *Against Heresies*, from eating each other like fish.[12] This order imposed by political and legal structures come from outside a man and are experienced by him as repression; it isn't primarily concerned with the inner nature of human beings but with regulating and controlling their outer conduct. Political and legal order is also not something merely proposed for our acceptance; it is inherently coercive. As such, it ultimately relies on force and fear to ensure that its demands are complied with. Finally, political and legal order isn't only external and coercive, it is also unnatural, an order that wouldn't have been required had man not sinned. The state, private property and the institution of slavery are all forms of domination of man by man and the consequences of sin.

Many people have remarked on the similarities between the political thought of Augustine and Machiavelli; Alexander d'Entrèves for example, remarks that the *City of God* 'affords a clear illustration of political realism[13] long before Machiavelli.' [d'Entrèves 1967, 22] Both thinkers are utterly realistic and unsentimental in their estimation of practical politics. Both know only too well the horrors and cruelties that make up the bulk of political history. These horrors and cruelties weren't unknown to classical thinkers but, as James Schall notes, 'The difference between the classical authors and Machiavelli with his influence in modernity is not that Machiavelli knew more about the dark side of human nature than Thucydides, Plato, Aristotle, Augustine, or Aquinas did. Machiavelli is only shocking because, unlike the classical authors, by spelling out in graphic, often historical detail, what a "good" prince did to stay in power Machiavelli approved of those means. It is this latter approval that we do not find in the classical authors' descriptions of tyrants and other forms of disordered rule.' (Schall 1996, §III) Augustine, as fully aware as Machiavelli of the evils of politics, did not lower his moral standards by declaring evil not to be evil.

The game of finding anticipations of later writers in Augustine is endlessly fascinating. Could Augustine really have been a precursor of Machiavelli as Meinecke once suggested? Indeed, in thinking the state necessary for the preservation of peace and order, was he a precursor of Hobbes? In respect of his idea that Providence brings all things to work for God's purposes independently of the particular interests and desires of individuals, did he anticipate Hegel's idea of the cunning of reason? It is true that Augustine, in contrast to his classical forebears, exhibits a stimulating realism in acknowledging that political power consists essentially in coercion. In the *City of God*, he gives an account of human history from its beginnings to the time of Christ and, in a passage the eerily presages both Hobbes and Machiavelli, he notes that 'the society of mortal men spreads everywhere over the earth; and amid all the varieties of geographical situation it still was linked together by a kind of fellowship based on a common nature, although each group pursued its own advantages and sought the gratification of its own desires. In such pursuits not everyone, perhaps no one, achieves complete satisfaction, because men have conflicting aims. Hence human society is generally divided against itself, and one part of it oppresses another, when it finds itself the stronger. For the conquered part submits to the conqueror, naturally choosing peace and survival at any price— so much so that it has always provoked astonishment when men have preferred death to slavery.' [18: 2]

The conflict, the division and the consequent oppression of mankind anticipate Hobbes's war of all against all. The willing if reluctant submission following oppression anticipates Machiavelli. Augustine's notion of Providence, which ensures that whatever men do, God's will always triumphs, also anticipates Machiavelli's concept of *Fortuna*, though without the capricious implications of that concept. This idea is also echoed later by Hegel in a secular mode in his idea of what he calls 'the cunning of reason [*List der Vernunft*]. Our own petty desires and passions are framed and channelled in ways we can't anticipate into the satisfaction of an overall scheme, whether of a quasi-divinised Reason or a more orthodox Christian Providence.[14] Augustine also pre-echoes Machiavelli in acknowledging what would come to be called 'reasons of state.' Paolucci writes: 'at the very top of the social order, in positions of the highest trust, men are often required to commit acts of the very kind that civilizing society, with its laws and education, attempts to repress in the conduct of the mass of its members....political regimes...are able to maintain a semblance of peace and order in the world only by using coercive force, veiled or naked, to restrain coercive force.'[15]

Augustine, then, has a distinctly unflattering conception of secular authority. It exists, he thinks, to restrain the wicked, and to do this even if those doing the restraining are themselves wicked. Christians are bound to cooperate with and tolerate the secular authorities, even those that are vile. 'Christ's servants, whether rich or poor, freemen or slaves, men or women, are bidden, if need be, to endure the wickedness of an utterly corrupt state...' [2: 19] That being so, he is more or less indifferent to the form of government—every government makes use of coercion and it matters little whether it is democratic, oligarchic or monarchical.

The Roman Empire in the west would collapse less than fifty years after Augustine's death (AD 430). Its demise created both a challenge and an opportunity for the Church of which he was a reluctant bishop and would alter irrevocably the political landscape of what was to become Europe.

Notes

1 Gurevich, 91; see also 250.

2 The single most important source for this chapter will be Augustine's treatise on *The City of God* (*De Civitate Dei*) but reference will also be made from time to time to other of his works, including his letters and sermons. *The City of God* is readily available in a translation by Henry Bettenson. There is also a very useful collection of other material relevant to Augustine's political ideas in a volume edited by E. M. Atkins and R. J. Dodaro.

3 Weithman, 238; see also Markus 1970, 93.

4 Augustine, *Commentary on the Psalms*, 124.7.

5 *Tractate on the Gospel of John* 6: 25.

6 The Mediterranean has been a hotbed of piracy for most of its history, apart, perhaps, from the first two centuries of the Roman Empire. [see Ormerod, passim]

7 Readers may be surprised to learn that even pirates obey rules, operating under articles of association! See Leeson, 2007.

8 *Populus est coetus multitudinis rationalis rerum quas diligit concordi communione sociatus.* [19: 24; compare 19: 21]

9 John Morrall argues that Augustine approaches the role of the state from the standpoint of the individual. 'For him [Augustine] society, even Roman society, is above all a collection of *temporarily*....like-minded individuals....The character of the State is determined by the character of its citizens.' [Morrall 1970, 61]

10 Augustine, *Reply to Petilian* II, 92.

11 *Ad Marcellinum*, 138, c. 15.

12 v. 24.2; see Markus 1970, 84.

13 Political realism is the view that 'Political relations are relations of force. Any statement about them is a statement of fact—of the fact that some rule and others obey—not an assessment of means and of ends, nor a statement of value.' [d'Entrèves 1967, 16]

14 Shakespeare captures this common element in Providence, *Fortuna*, *List der Vernunft* when he writes, 'There's a divinity that shapes our ends, rough-hew them how we will.' [*Hamlet*, Act

V, Scene 2] Thomas Sowell writes of what he calls 'evolutionism' that 'People have articulated intentions but history is not a record of those intentions being realized so much as it is a record of entirely different things happening as a net result of innumerable strivings toward mutually incompatible goals. Hegel and Marx called this "the irony of history" and Adam Smith called it "an invisible hand" determining the social result of an individual's action—"a result which was no part of his intention." Darwin's biological generalization of the same principle made the point even more vivid, since his evolutionary theory applied to animals whose intentions (or "instincts") hardly included the evolution of their species, and even to inanimate life such as trees and grasses with no apparent intentions at all, but which develop elaborate ecological patterns nevertheless.' [Sowell 1996, 103]

15 Paolucci, vi. For an in-depth discussion of the problem of 'dirty hands' in politics, see Parrish, passim.

Chapter 9

AFTER ROME

Kreon: 'I'll have no dealings with law-breakers,
Critics of the government:
Whoever is chosen to govern should be obeyed—
Must be obeyed, in all things, great and small,
Just and unjust!'
Antigone: 'Your edict, King, was strong,
But all your strength is weakness itself against
The immortal unrecorded laws of God.
They are not merely now: they were, and shall be,
Operative for ever, beyond man utterly'
—Sophocles

The date customarily given as marking the fall of the Roman Empire is AD 476 but, just as Rome wasn't built in a day, so too, it did not collapse in a day.[1] The deposition of the Emperor Romulus in that year was only the final act in a long series of events that were corrosive of the empire, reaching back well over a hundred years before this date.[2] The barbarians usually get the blame for Rome's demise but, as Terence Kealey notes, 'the empire did not collapse in the face of unstoppable barbarian hordes. The numbers of barbarians were always small....The empire fell because many of its citizens had emigrated to the freer, more pleasant barbarian lands...and, crucially, the invading barbarians found themselves welcomed as armies of liberation by vast numbers of oppressed people.' [Kealey 1996, 27] The late Roman Empire was, according to Lucien Musset, a 'totalitarian state, which was almost constantly in a state of siege, using savage means in its attempt to ensure the survival of a limited ruling class made up of learned senators and uncouth military officers.' It was, he says, 'A régime of appalling social inequality, a political organization which for the previous two centuries had been based on constraint and suspicion, biased courts and laws of an absurd and ever-increasing savagery...'[3] Orlando Patterson too does not believe in the fall of Rome. 'Rome,' he says, 'did not fall. It withered on the vine.' John Morrall notes that 'The barbarian invasion of the Empire was in fact not a cataclysmic Blitzkrieg in its early stages, but a slow process of infiltration across the frontiers, more often than not connived at by the imperial authorities themselves.'[4]

This withering, or rapid decay, of the Western Roman Empire in the fifth century did not all at once precipitate a political or social crisis. People did not wake up one morning to find a sign posted in the Forum saying: 'Roman Empire now under new management. Apply to Barbarian Enterprises, Incorporated.' Some things had changed, however, and had changed fundamentally and forever. The highly centralised, highly bureaucratised, heavily taxed, legally unified political and military entity that had been the Roman Empire in the West was about to disappear. What was to replace it was not yet obvious. It would be wrong, however, to think that Roman culture simply disappeared, to be replaced suddenly by a melange of barbarian *mores*. 'It is impossible, writes Musset, 'to talk of an integral Germanic culture without Roman survivals or influence, just as no Roman culture survived intact without any infiltration of Germanic elements. All the medieval western civilizations are, in different proportions, the heirs both of Rome and of the Germans.' [Musset, 116] Albert Mirgeler goes so far as to say, 'The Germanic peoples…became the creators of a new historical unity in Europe….If the Germans had not accepted Christi-anity and had not been receptive to the learning of the ancient world, what we know as Western Christianity or Western Civilization would simply not have existed.' [Mirgeler, 44] Their acceptance of Christianity and the heritage of the ancient world 'demonstrated their power to create a new civilization.'[5]

Between the fifth and the ninth centuries, the political landscape of the area once controlled by the Western Roman Empire[6] changed forever under the influence of the Germanic tribes now settling there. Whereas the Vandals, Visigoths, Franks and Lombards maintained some measure of central power in the areas they controlled,[7] it nevertheless remained that, as George Sabine remarks, 'The barbarian conquest itself, with its attendant social and economic changes, had made government on a large scale impossible. Both politically and intellectually western Europe was beginning to revolve around a center of its own, instead of being merely the hinterland of a world whose center was the Mediterranean basin.' [Sabine, 198] In cultural terms, the collapse of the Western Roman Empire is often portrayed as if it entailed the end of civilisation and its replacement with chaos, mayhem and disorder. On the contrary, however, compared with the statist, pillaging, slave-based and tax-burdened nightmare that was fifth-century Rome, 'the world of the so-called barbarians was free and enlightened,' with superior economic and personal freedoms. [Kealey 1996, 29] Although Ricardo Duchesne does not support the culturally relativist claim that the barbarians had attained the same level of civilisation as the Romans, he questions 'the still popular perception that the barbarian invasions into Rome were a "regression" because they brought about the collapse of this civilization.' He believes that the barbarian invasions were 'indispensable to the preservation and rejuvenation of the Western aristocratic-libertarian spirit.'[8] So too, François Guizot remarks that 'the sentiment of personal independence, a love of liberty displaying itself at all risks, without any other motive but that of satisfying itself' was introduced by the barbarians and 'deposited in the cradle of modern civilization, wherein it has played so conspicuous a part… that it is impossible to help reckoning it as one of its fundamental elements.' [Guizot, 49]

Even after the disappearance of the Western Roman Empire, between the fifth and seventh centuries, the centre of gravity of the Christian and barbarian world lay principally on the shores of the Mediterranean, just as the Roman Empire had done. After the rise of Islam, however, the centre of gravity of the

Christian barbarian world moved inexorably northwards. Henri Pirenne argues that the rise of Islam effectively separated the Christian East from the Christian West and because the Mediterranean was now a largely Islamic preserve, this turned Western Europe into a land-centred culture. Pirenne's account isn't uncontroversial. John Morrall remarks that 'One of Pirenne's most formidable critics, Robert Latouche, has in fact argued...that the Carolingians, far from retreating to a land-locked economy, promoted economic recovery by their monetary reform and their control of economic development in countryside and town.' Despite this, Morrall concedes that even if the effect of Islam on the West wasn't quite as dramatic as Pirenne would have it, 'yet the Islamic presence was to be a constant feature of the medieval landscape.'[9]

The Moslems controlled Corsica, Sardinia and Sicily and, in the western Mediterranean, the Balearic Islands. By the end of the eighth century, the whole coastline of the Christian West was exposed to constant attack and harassment, an attack it was in no position effectively to repel.[10] Adding to the Moslem pressure from the south, the Slavs and Magyars exerted constant pressure in the east. The Norsemen plundered the northern and western coasts of the Carolingian Empire and anywhere else that could be reached by water, sometimes even competing with the Moslems for a share of Mediterranean booty. Squeezed from the north and the south and unable to defend its borders from the Moslems, Norsemen, Slavs and Magyars, 'The Empire of Charlemagne,' writes Henri Pirenne, 'was essentially an inland one. No longer was there any communication with the exterior; it was a closed State, a State without foreign markets, living in a condition of almost complete isolation.'[11] Making a point very similar to Pirenne's on the isolated and land-locked character of medieval Western Europe, R. W. Southern says, 'the enclosure of western Europe at a critical moment in the development of social and political institutions, the practical exclusion from the Baltic, and very limited access to the Mediterranean, meant that the land was the unique source of political power, and almost the only source of wealth.' [Southern, 73] Guizot, too, notes the fragile character of the post-Roman West, 'pressed on the south by the Mahometans, on the north by the German and the Sclavonic tribes, it was scarcely possible that the reaction of this double invasion should do other than hold the interior of Europe in continual disorder.' [Guizot, 61] The principal social force holding this fragile and threatened society together was the institution of the Christian Church.[12]

One can't study history without making the acquaintance of periods[13]—the Renaissance, the Enlightenment and, of course, that perennial favourite and people's choice, the Dark Ages or, as Montaigne referred to it, the 'black hole of barbarism.'[14] It was a commonplace of Renaissance and Enlightenment thought that the thousand or so years that occurred between the fall of the Western Roman Empire and the Renaissance was a 'an unfortunate interlude, a regression in humanity.'[15] Much historical writing still shows a tendency to 'minimize the moral distance between the modern world and the ancient world, while at the same time maximizing the moral and intellectual distance between modern Europe and the middle ages.' [Siedentop, 350] The historical period labels—Enlightenment, Renaissance, Dark Ages—are so much second nature to us that it may come as a shock to realise that someone, somewhere devised them and that the people who lived during these periods didn't know they were living in the Dark Ages or the Renaissance or the Enlightenment; they thought they were living in the present. Just like us, they tended to regard the manners and *mores* of the previous generations as old-fashioned and to see themselves as modern and up-to-date.[16]

However useful and perhaps indispensable periodisation might be as a tool of historical analysis, it isn't an entirely innocent process. Names often embody negative or positive judgements. Clearly, if an age or period is labelled 'Dark' that isn't a good thing, whereas what historical period could possibly object to being called 'Enlightened'? The theoretician of history, John Vincent, tells us that Herbert Butterfield, the great twentieth–century English historian, 'protested against the ideology, the false judgments, and the unseen and unrecognized distortions implicit in the conventional periodization of history. He opposed "a popular view that is still not quite eradicated—the view that the Middle Ages represented a period of darkness when man was kept tongue-tied by authority—a period against which the Renaissance was the reaction and the Reformation the great Rebellion".' [Vincent, 87-88] In reality, while the period pejoratively referred to as the Dark Ages might have been an unhappy one for the apparatchiks of the Roman State, its soldiers, officials and tax collectors, for the its taxpayers it 'represented nothing but liberation.'[17] It seems that the conception of the 'Dark Ages' was originated by Petrarch in the fourteenth century, at the very beginning of what has now come to be called *the* Renaissance. Theodore Mommsen writes that Petrarch 'never vacillated in his firm conviction that the era following the decline of the Roman Empire was a period of "darkness."….It is logical that the "Father of Humanism" is also the father of the concept or attitude which regards the Middle Ages as the "Dark Ages."'[18] Kenan Malik writes, 'Few historians today would countenance the term "Dark Ages"….the idea of the "Dark Ages" is a self-serving phrase that later thinkers employed to elevate the intellectual standing of their own era by suggesting that, between the glories of Greece and Florence, there had been nothing but cultural darkness. While the first half of the Middle Ages may have lacked intellectual spark…the culture of Europe after the turn of the millennium, a culture that produced Aquinas and Ockham, Giotto and Dante, was unquestionably sophisticated, restless and curious.' [Malik, 163, 164]

To call a period of around one thousand years 'The Middle Ages' is to suggest that it was not much more than a rather long interlude between more important times flanking it on either side, an interlude so unimportant it doesn't even deserve a proper name of its own. Against this cavalier attitude, Robert-Henri Bautier argues that it is 'imprecise to subsume such a long, diverse, and decisive period under the single label of the "Middle Ages"…' Offering us a more fine-grained analysis of this one-thousand-plus years of history, Bautier suggests that if the economic and social evolution of Europe during this period is taken seriously, then we might begin with what he terms an 'early Middle Ages', stretching from the collapse of Rome to the end of the tenth century, a period characterised by a 'slowing down of all economic activity in the barbarian west, and by its retrenchment in the face of the brilliance of the Byzantine and Moslem east,' a period punctuated by two minor renaissances, one in the seventh, the other in the ninth century. This early period was followed by what he calls the 'classical Middle Ages', a period extending from the middle of the tenth to the middle of the fourteenth century. This period was characterised by a general improvement in the quality of life, the cultivation of waste and forest, industrialisation, urban development, trade and communications. This in turn was followed by the 'late Middle Ages', a period extending from the early fourteenth century to the middle of the sixteenth, beginning with 'a severe demographic and financial crisis,' followed by a rapid surge in population growth and 'a development of European techniques and manufacturing processes.' [Bautier, 7, 8]

John Morrall comments that even as early as the middle of the seventeenth century, 'we find "the Middle Ages" cast for what was to be its accustomed role of unwelcome delayer of both cultural "Renaissance" and religious "Reformation".' [Morrall 1970, 17] Norman Davies believes that when it comes to arriving at a balanced evaluation of the cultural, religious and political achievements of the Middle Ages, the English (and, by implication, much of the wider WASPish English-speaking world) have problems peculiar to themselves, deriving in no small part from the exigencies of historical revisionism. 'For centuries after the Reformation,' he writes, 'they [the English] were taught to look askance at an era when England was a minor kingdom in Catholic Europe and when the sun of national greatness had not yet arisen.' [Davies 1999, 327] He singles out John Lingard (1771-1851) as one of the few English historians who, perhaps because he was a Catholic priest and so did not share 'the prevailing Protestant antipathy to the medieval Church,' was able to escape 'the nationalist bias of his contemporaries.' 'It says much for the limited horizons of English historiography,' continues Davies, 'that Lingard never found his way into the company of recognized "greats".'[19] Although the term 'The Middle Ages' is an improvement on 'The Dark Ages', it is still a derogatory label given that this period was not just a relapse into quasi-barbarism between two ages of enlightenment but itself a time of significant change and development during which the foundations of our modern and contemporary world were laid, in law, in philosophy, in the creation of social institutions, in commerce and in technology. Larry Siedentop is of the opinion that during the early Middle Ages 'the moral foundations of modern Europe were being laid, foundations which would later support the individual as the organizing social role, the state as a distinctive form of government, and an exchange or market economy.' [Siedentop, 165]

That there were developments in law, philosophy, and economics[20] during this period many people might be prepared to grant—but developments in technology? Surely not! But yes. 'The Middle Ages,' writes Jean Gimpel, 'was one of the great inventive eras of mankind. It should be known as the first industrial revolution in Europe. The scientists and engineers of that time were searching for alternative sources of energy to hydraulic power, wind power, and tidal energy. Between the tenth and the thirteenth centuries, western Europe experienced a technological boom....capitalist companies were formed and their shares bought and sold....They introduced extensive division of labor to increase efficiency....the growth of capitalism brought about modern methods of accountancy and banking, which in turn led to further expansion.'[21] [Gimpel, viii, ix] Among the seemingly humdrum but in fact significant technological inventions of the period, Terence Kealey lists 'the saddle, the stirrup, the horseshoe, the horse collar, the tandem harness, the water mill, the fore-and-aft sail, soap and, perhaps most importantly, the crank.' [Kealey 1996, 32] To these innovations we might add the invention and use of the heavy plough and, perhaps most significantly, the three-field crop rotation system which was both more productive and more efficient than previous systems of land-use and which also provided a protein-rich diet for the many so that, as Lynn White remarks, 'In the full sense of the vernacular, the Middle Ages from the tenth century onward were full of beans.'[22] The thinkers of the Middle Ages not only produced innovation and invention in commerce and technology but they also made advances in theoretical physics, developing mathematical models to analyse the problems of motion, thereby producing concepts that would later be used in early modern mechanics. It is significant, the historian Joel Kaye believes, that these fourteenth-century innovations in physics were linked to the commercial revolution and the intellectual sophistication demanded by the new market-friendly mentality.[23]

THE EARLY CHURCH AND POLITICS

For the first 300 years of its life, the Church had been a quasi-clandestine organisation, ignored when not actively persecuted by the secular powers. The conversion of the Emperor Constantine in the early fourth century changed everything for both Christianity and for politics—whether for good or for ill is another matter.[24] In the early days of the new rapprochement, the tendency among Christian leaders was to reject completely the idea that secular rulers could in any justified way have any authority in Church matters. But the invocation of the power of the secular ruler to settle intra-church disputes (as, for example, in the case of the Donatist controversy in North Africa) inevitably ceded to the secular powers a measure of authority over the Church. Over time, however, after the Constantinian settlement, a certain amount of mutual inter-penetration developed: the Church became part of the Empire,[25] but the Empire also became part of the Church. Pope Gelasius, in the late fifth century, was one of the first to try to outline an account of the proper relationship between the Church and society's secular rulers. The spiritual and temporal powers were thought of as being given to two different bodies, each supreme and independent in its own sphere. But however independent they might be of each other when considered theoretically, practically, the two powers were interdependent. 'The king is subject to the bishop in spiritual matters, the bishop to the king in temporal matters.' [Carlyle I, 192] The working out of the details of this apparently unambiguous relationship between the spiritual and the temporal powers was to be a constant theme for the next thousand years and more of Western history.

Christianity affected medieval political thought in a number of ways. Despite numerous practical accommodations and compromises, the spiritual life of religion was conceived of in a way that made it, in principle, independent of the secular power. Though often practically intertwined with secular politics, the story of Christianity in the West is, in part, a tale of entanglement, disentanglement, and re-entanglement with politics and its sometimes realised, sometimes not realised, independence. This duality of centres of authority, of allegiance, is central to any understanding of Western thought. Neither the spiritual power nor the secular power could command the total allegiance of any person and the space created by the tension between the two authorities was the breeding ground for liberty.

On the Christian conception, man is a being made in the image and likeness of God. Each individual person reflects and participates in the divine to the extent that any limited creature can do so. Christianity gives to the world a 'conception of individuality or personality which was unknown to the ancient world....The solidarity of the primitive and ancient group was giving way before the development of a new apprehension of individuality.' [Carlyle III, 7; 8] Because it recognised the fundamental worth of every single person, Christianity made possible the emancipation of the individual from the grasp of the tribe and the clan, an emancipation, I hasten to add, that was, unfortunately, neither immediate nor rapid. [see Black 1988b, passim] The social, cultural and political history of the West has been in no small part a working out, a slow and deliberate working out, of the implications of Christian anthropology. [see Siedentop, passim] For most of human history, the individual has been little more than part of a group, whether family, village, clan, tribe or nation. Larry Siedentop remarks that whereas today we see other human beings as 'individuals with rights, rather than family members, each with an assigned status,' for our ancestors 'the family—past, present and future—was the basic unity of social reality.' [Siedentop, 13, 12] Of course, the independence of the individual may be exaggerated to the point where society dissolves into a collection of contingently related human atoms. That is one possible consequence of individualism but it isn't in any way a necessary consequence. Conservatism in its many forms, whether Burkean or Rousseauean or Libertarian, is, at least in part, an attempt to balance the books on this issue and to ensure that individuals are seen as the socially embedded creatures that they are. Conservatism can be presented in such a way that it is tantamount to a return to tribalism, perhaps a sophisticated tribalism, but a tribalism none the less, where the individual is re-subsumed into the group. In any form of conservatism that's consistent with liberty, cultural conservatism rather than political conservatism, all forms of mature human relationships must be voluntary and the methodological priority of the individual must remain front and centre. [see Shaw]

Christianity teaches not only the intrinsic worth of the individual but also the fundamental moral equality of all individuals. This doctrine of the fundamental equality of all human beings is to be found right throughout the New Testament.[26] In the end, all distinctions of sex, status, ethnic roots and the like, though real and important on various levels and in various respects, are ultimately insignificant when compared to the fact that all people have the same value as children of God. One might expect that armed with this conception of human nature, the Christian impact on the social and political world in which it found itself would have been revolutionary. If that is one's expectation, it is going to be disappointed. Instead of turning the social order upside down, Christianity instead seems to have endorsed a passive acceptance of the *status quo*, even where part of the *status quo* was slavery. Here is one point on which the Christian view appears to be, in essence, little different from that of Cicero or Seneca. In fact, Seneca expresses the essential odiousness of slavery much more forcefully than any passage in the letters of St Paul or the Pastoral Epistles.

When it comes to the Christian conception of the nature of government, the most important scriptural text, as already discussed, is *Romans* 13. Carlyle is surely correct when he says that 'This passage, which is of the greatest importance throughout the whole course of mediaeval political thought, being indeed constantly quoted from the second century onwards, is indeed pregnant and significant in the highest degree.' He is less correct when he continues, 'It defines in the profoundest way the Christian theory of the nature of political society, while it furnishes us with the most interesting evidence with regard to the condition of the Christian societies of the apostolic period.' [Carlyle I, 90] As a matter of historical fact, it can't be denied that the influence of *Romans* 13 on all subsequent Christian thought on politics was overwhelming; nevertheless, we need not be overwhelmed with the multiplicity of uses of this passage, for this strategy resembles the process of consulting one copy of a newspaper to check the veracity of a story one has read in another copy of the same issue. In the end, it all comes back to *Romans* 13. What matters is the passage itself and what it says which, as we have seen in an earlier chapter, may well not be what it appears to say or what interpreters have taken it to say. As with the majority of commentators, Carlyle is in no doubt that this Pauline passage demands that Christians obey and respect their secular rulers. 'St Paul's general meaning is,' he says, 'plain and distinct,' a distinctness that has not, Carlyle thinks, prevented later thinkers (he would seem to have the Anabaptists in mind) from perverting it. [Carlyle I, 90; 97] The plain meaning of the passage, he thinks, amounts to this: government is divinely instituted and, because of this, resistance to government is rebellion against God himself because God has instituted government to repress evil and to promote the good.

From the perspective of such as Carlyle, Christian political theory would seem to be a towering edifice constructed on the narrowest of scriptural foundations. The slim Scriptural basis of this doctrine of passive obedience in *Romans* 13 is apparently buttressed by brief passages in *Titus* 3: 1, 2; *1 Timothy* 2; 2 and, with perhaps the passage of greatest significance outside Romans being *Peter* 2: 13-17. It may well be that these passages are directed, at least in part, to repressing a certain tendency towards antinomianism in the infant Christian community. 'It requires only a slight study of the apostolic writing,' notes Carlyle, 'to perceive that if the early Christian teachers had hard work to overcome the traditional legalism of the Jew, they were confronted with an almost equally dangerous tendency to anarchism, especially no doubt among their Gentile converts. This tendency shows itself first in a disposition to slight the ordinary duties of life, to refuse submission to the discipline of the common life.'[27] He remarks, significantly, that 'the early Church was troubled with anarchical tendencies, very similar to those of some of the Anabaptist movements of the sixteenth century...' [Carlyle I, 96] I find little to disagree with in this last claim by Carlyle but its significance, for me, is that it seems to make the requirement to obey the authorities or powers in *Romans* to be an internal Christian matter of church discipline rather than a command to obey the secular authorities. In fact, Carlyle admits that there may be some, just some, indirect justification in Scripture for a less than respectful attitude by Christians to the political authorities. He has in mind Christ's words to his disciples that those entrusted with the rule of Christians were not to be like the Gentile leaders who lord it over others. Christian leaders were called to service, not domination. These words might, Carlyle thinks, induce in the rash and impulsive, contempt for political authorities, as might St Paul's own injunction to his fellow Christians not to go to law. One might wonder why those who take *these* words literally are to be denigrated as rash and impulsive as compared with those who take literally the apparent meaning of *Romans* 13. In the end, whatever the true or the better or the best interpretation of *Romans* 13 may be, the early Church's approach to the political order tended more to the Stoics' relatively positive conception of the state and its purposes than to the Epicurean attitude of indifference or hostility.

NATURAL LAW

On the issue of the natural law, the Fathers of the Church all take their cue from St Paul's Letter to the *Romans* in which the natural law is presented as a law written on men's hearts. The relevant passage runs: 'For as many as have sinned without law shall also perish without law: and as many as have sinned under law shall be judged by law; for not the hearers of the law are just before God, but the doers of the law shall be justified: for when Gentiles which have no law do by nature the things of the law, these, having no law, are a law unto themselves; in that they show the work of the law written in their hearts, their conscience bearing witness therewith.' [*Romans*, 2: 12-14] Does this idea in Paul come from his Jewish heritage or from his Hellenic environment? Who can say?

Whichever, it dovetails neatly into the Ciceronian idea of the natural law. St Hilary goes so far as to give an idea of the content of this law. It includes forbidding a man to injure his fellows, to take from them what is theirs, and to engage in fraud. All these are actions that a libertarian would recognise as falling under the zero-aggression principle.

As mentioned earlier, in the twelfth-century, Gratian's account of natural law is presented in terms of the so-called Golden Rule so that natural law is what is contained in the Law and the Gospels by which each is to do to another what he wants done to himself and forbidden to do to another what he does not want done to himself. In adopting this perspective on natural law, Gratian weaves Christian moral intuitions with the original Stoic concept. The effect of his account is to make relations of equality and reciprocity to be antecedent to both positive and customary law. Gratian's canonist successors developed the concept of natural law in a direction that took it further away from its Stoic roots and moved it in the direction of a early version of natural rights.[28] For these later canonists, natural law is not, as it was for the Stoics, just an objective moral order, nor is it, as it would appear to have been for Gratian, a set of moral precepts on which reason and scripture converge. Rather, it becomes a certain universally present human capacity (or, for Rufinus of Bologna, a force), an aspect of human reason and freedom, the effect of which is to recognise moral precepts. [see Tierney 2014, 23-25] If all men are morally equal by nature, then it would seem to follow that each man has a right to make certain moral and legal claims that are logically prior to particular customs or particular municipal laws.

SLAVERY, COERCIVE GOVERNMENT AND PROPERTY

The issue of slavery has been discussed in detail in an earlier chapter but it might be profitable to reconsider the issue again (briefly) in the context of Christian thought. I have in mind the tendency among early Christian writers to link slavery, coercive government and property together as institutions that both result from sin and, somewhat paradoxically, are also meant to be sin's cure! The writer known as Ambrosiaster, commenting on *Colossians*, makes the following points regarding slavery and human nature: first, men are created free and equal by God; second, slavery is a matter of (mis)fortune—it extends only to man's body; third, slavery is the result of sin; and fourth, masters mustn't treat their slaves with cruelty but with consideration. In respect of the first point, Ambrosiaster is completely at one with the Church Fathers. St Augustine, it will be remembered, noted that God, creating all men equal, had not made man to lord it over other men. [*City of God*, 19: 15] This fundamental human equality persists even in the condition of slavery inasmuch as a man's self or soul can't be enslaved. Given their adherence to Ambrosiaster's first and second points—the basic freedom and equality of all men and slavery's being a matter of misfortune—one might have expected the Fathers to reject slavery forthwith. This did not happen and the reason for this is that slavery, though not an aspect of man's original condition, is the consequence of sin and sinfulness. As the result of sin, man who was once innocent and harmless is now prone to evil. As such, he stands in need of constant restraint. Slavery isn't only the consequence of sin; it is also, in part, a remedy for sin. Those who are vicious are in truth better off in subjection to another; as they can't rule themselves, others may with propriety rule them.

Of course, the third point—slavery being the result of sin—even if it were true, would prove too much or too little. If, as the second point notes, the slavery of this or that man is, in the main, a matter of misfortune, no particular slave is in that condition as the result of his own misbehaviour. Even if it were true that slavery as an institution is rendered possible and necessary for those who are vicious, this wouldn't explain why those who are *not* vicious are being punished for what they haven't done. On the other hand, if all men as such are vicious as the result of sin, then all men, not just the few, should be enslaved. Taken together with the second point, the third point can't explain why some men are slaves and others are not. This being so, it renders somewhat mysterious the endorsement that the Church Fathers give to the institution of slavery when they posit it as a lawful institution and 'constantly urge upon the slave the duty of obedience and submission....The Church, then, so far from repudiating the institution of slavery, accepted the fact, and framed its own canonical regulations in accordance with it.' [Carlyle I, 120, 121]

Ambrosiaster's fourth point, that masters should refrain from cruelty and treat their slaves with compassion does little to undo the damage done by this astonishing and baffling example of conformity by the Church to the norms of the surrounding secular world. At the end of his short but perceptive discussion of the attitude of twelfth-century jurists towards liberty and slavery, Brian Tierney concludes that they 'did not treat slavery as a grievous moral issue; they saw it rather as basically a problem of conflict of laws....But they always started out from the assumption that humans were naturally free, that servitude was something that had supervened on human liberty, something that somehow had to be explained.' [Tierney 2014, 37] On a practical level, the change from the late classical Roman world to the early medieval world saw slavery decline as a significant economic institution. This decline was in large part an effect of economics rather than of ethics. Slave owners could no longer afford to maintain large numbers of slaves whereas serfs, with their allotments, were self-subsistent while still being required to provide services to their social superiors.

Slavery, then, isn't man's natural condition but the result of sin. But slavery isn't the only institution that is justified by man's sinfulness. A similar justification is offered for the existence of coercive government with much the same degree of plausibility or implausibility as that offered for slavery. As Carlyle notes, 'That natural equality which is, in the judgment of the Fathers, contrary to slavery, is also contrary to the subjection of man to man in government.' [Carlyle I, 125] The Fathers are in general agreement that man is naturally social. In this state of nature, men are all free and equal. Although there might well be the exercise of authority of knowledge or skill in such a condition, this authority will not be coercive, but will arise from the uncoerced recognition that some are wiser than others and their counsel should be followed. Coercive government, then, like slavery, isn't natural. But, as with slavery, in the actual conditions of human life, it is something useful and even proper. Saints Ambrose, Augustine, Gregory the Great and Isidore all make the point that coercive government is both a consequence of sin and the remedy for sin. Those who are too foolish to obey the wise spontaneously must be compelled for their own good to do so.

Slavery and coercive government are, then, unnatural to man but justified by the concrete circumstances of man's life in a post-Edenic condition. They aren't, however, the only institutions that are unnatural but useful and thus justified. The Fathers of the Church, for example, St Ambrose, in general hold that private property isn't in itself something naturally justifiable. Nature gives all things to all men and nothing in particular to any one man. Nevertheless, in the actual conditions of life, private property, like slavery and coercive government, is useful and proper. Carlyle notes: 'the Church accepted the institution of property as being in accordance with the actual conditions of life, just as it accepted the institution of slavery or coercive government...' [Carlyle I, 136] This is one area in which the Fathers of the Church diverge sharply from the writings of the Roman jurists. The jurists tended to regard private property, in some form or other, as being justifiable by natural law. The views of the Fathers 'represent a tradition which differs materially from that of the jurists, a tradition probably derived from the same sources as the view of Seneca...they would, with Seneca, have classed the institution of property as one of those which belong to the conventions of organised society, and not to the primitive conditions of the human race.' [Carlyle I, 142]

AUTHORITY AND JUSTICE

The Patristic position on the authority of a ruler may be set out in the following way. On the one hand, there are those who take rulership as very much a factual matter. Whatever rulers we have and whatever their conduct may be, they are appointed by God and therefore must be obeyed and reverenced. On the other hand, there are those, such as Clement, who hold that a ruler can be deemed to be appointed by God only if that ruler rules according to law with the aim of securing justice. This is a quasi-normative notion—an unjust ruler, on this view of things, would be a ruler *de facto* but not *de jure*. 'If indeed there is a difference between good and bad princes,' says Clement, 'it is this; that the good love freedom, the bad, slavery.'[29] St Ambrose even goes a little further; not only must a ruler rule according to law and for the end of justice, he must also love liberty! Augustine seems to waver between the descriptive and the normative view of the state. Is a state *any* organisation of rational beings for the promotion of the objects of their love? If so, is that sufficient? If it isn't to be merely a glorified band of robbers, mustn't a state also promote justice? Isn't this the tenor of the famous passage in the *City of God* where Augustine appears to say that the distinction between a gang of robbers and a state rests entirely on the latter's pursuit of justice? [see *City of God*, 4, 4]

We find Cassiodorus [Flavius Marcus Aurelius Cassiodorus Senator] interpreting *Romans* 13 in more or less the usual way but insisting that it isn't simply to any ruler that we owe obedience but only to the ruler whose commands are just. Wilfrid Parsons writes: 'Cassiodorus (479-572) is particularly concerned that the Pauline precept of civil obedience must have, as its correlative, justice in the ruler. ....Throughout his earlier life, acting as a sort of Prime Minister to Theodoric, in dozens of letters to minor officials and subject peoples, Cassiodorus unceasingly rings the changes on the absolute necessity of justice in government if government is to justify its origin in God.' [Parsons, 338-339] Cassiodorus manages to combine this quasi-normative conception of the genuine ruler with the standard late Roman idea that the ruler is both the source of law and above the law, answerable in the end only to God. Carlyle sums up in the following way: 'We have seen that, with the exception of St. Augustine, they [the Fathers] seem to show the persistence of the conception that the end of the State is the attainment of justice, and that the quality of justice is essential to the legitimacy of any organisation of society. We think it important to observe this, for in some measure it seems to counteract that tendency of some of the Christian Fathers towards the theory of the absolute Divine authority of the monarch, and the consequent obligation of unlimited obedience.' [Carlyle I, 174]

Persuaded of the divine origin of secular authority, some of the Fathers concluded that 'all authority, under all circumstances, was from God, and that even an unjust and oppressive command of the ruler must be obeyed. On the other hand, they were for the most part equally clear that the foundation and end of civil society was the attainment of justice, and some of them more or less distinctly apprehended, as a consequence of this principle, that an unjust authority was no authority at all.' [Carlyle I, 174] The person most associated with the notion that the authority of the ruler is somehow sacred is St Gregory the Great. This view is the culmination of one tendency that can be found in the writings of the Fathers but it is, as we have seen, certainly not the only one. Ambrosiaster expressed an extreme version of the view that the ruler's authority comes from God inasmuch as God's sanction of a ruler is never lost regardless of that ruler's conduct. Augustine seems to hold a similar view, on some occasions at least. Nero receives his power through Divine Providence and, under the provisions of *Romans* 13, must be obeyed and even reverenced.[30]

If one wanted to be somewhat cynical about this one could say that the Christian's duty to obey his secular ruler, given that that ruler's authority derives from God, appears most prominently whenever the secular power is being used to support some faction in an intra-Church dispute. This was the case, for example, in the case of the Donatists in North Africa. The Donatists, needless to say, protested that internal Church affairs were no concern of the Emperor; those opposed to them, not surprisingly, disagreed. (To jump forward a thousand years or so, we find a similar dynamic during the time of the Reformation—when the secular authorities were on one's side, then obedience, absolute and unconditional, was required; when the secular authority was opposed to one's position, then a somewhat less robust theory of obedience was developed. More on this below.)

Carlyle remarks, 'Churchmen would resist the Emperor when he happened to be opposed to their view; but when he agreed with them, they were only too apt to fall into the habit of regarding his action against their enemies as that of a truly sacred authority.' [Carlyle I, 158]

In the various pro-ruler Christian pronouncements, we can detect a failure to distinguish between what God merely permits and what God actively endorses.

If one believes that God is omnipotent then, naturally, everything that occurs happens with Divine concurrence, that is, it happens with Divine permission. It is quite another thing, however, to draw the conclusion that whatever happens with Divine permission is therefore proper, just, and right and is in accord with God's positive will. All sorts of ghastly horrors take place every day and do so under the guiding hand of Providence but it does not follow from this that such activities are morally proper or Divinely approved. The possibility that there might be kings of whom God does not approve is suggested by Scriptural passages such as: 'They have set up kings, but not by me: they have made princes, and I knew it not...' [*Hosea* 8: 4] Citing *Hosea*, Sedulius Scotus can write, 'What are impious kings but the greatest robbers of the earth, fierce as lions, ravening like wolves; but they are great to-day and perish to-morrow, and of them God has said "They reign, but not by Me; they arose as princes, but I knew it not."'[31] The passage from *Hosea* is explained or explained away by St Isidore who says that what God is doing here is setting an evil ruler over an evil people. St Gregory agrees with this view of things: 'a good ruler is God's reward to a good people, an evil ruler God's punishment on an evil people.' [Carlyle I, 152] One might wonder, on the Gregorian and Isidorean accounts, if it is possible to have a good people with an evil ruler. If not, why not? And if so, how would these Fathers account for that situation?

Summing up his discussion, Carlyle says: 'In Gregory the Great, then, we find this theory of the sacred character of government so developed as to make the ruler in all his actions the representative of God, not merely the representative of God as embodying the sacred ends for which the government of society exists. The conception is, as far as we have seen, peculiar to some Christian writers. We haven't observed anything that is really parallel to the conception in the legal writers, and even in Seneca and Pliny, we have only indications of an attitude of mind that might be capable of development in this direction. The theory is a somewhat irregular and illogical development of the Christian conception of the divine character of the civil order.' [Carlyle I, 157] For Gregorians, the ultimate source of a ruler's authority is God; for the Jurists, the ultimate source of that authority is the people. Which party adopts which position depends to a large extent on the *realpolitik* of the day. During the High Middle Ages, we find that the party in support of the Emperor is the one that tends to adopt the Gregorian position, whereas the ecclesiastical party tends to adopt the juristical position.

The political theory of the Church Fathers, insofar as they have one at all, is the political theory of the surrounding secular world, modified in various respects. The questions arising from the relation of a universal religion to the universal empire were unprecedented, as was the matter of whether and to what extent the character of secular government had divine sanction but, apart from these, everything else is relatively unremarkable. When we come to the ninth century, however, we enter a different world of political thought. Just as there's a break between the ancient world and the world of the Roman Lawyers, centred on their differing conceptions of man, so too, as we come to the end of the first millennium, we leave the classical world firmly behind and move towards a world that is recognisably modern, if only in a rudimentary way. 'There is,' writes Carlyle, 'a great gulf between the Teutonic societies of the Middle Ages and the ancient empire, but there are many relations, many traditions which have been carried over from the one to the other.' [Carlyle I, 197] The contribution of these new thinkers to political theory arises from their attempt reflectively to appropriate and to express the principles embodied in the legal and political practices of their quasi-tribal societies. On one signifi-cant point, however, namely that of slavery, the approach of the ninth century thinkers does not differ appreciably from that of the earlier period save that it is, if anything, slighter harsher. One writer, Smaragdus of Saint-Mihiel (around 760-840), differs somewhat from the common view in urging rulers to prohibit the making of any new slaves in their territories and urging slave owners to manumit their slaves, but even he stops short of recommending the abolition of the institution.

It cannot be denied that in many respects, the cultural life of the post-Roman barbarian world, the early Middle Ages, was poorer that it had been under the tutelage of Rome, even if economic and personal freedoms were significantly greater. Even so, this period was to witness two minor renaissances, one in the seventh, the other in the ninth century. I mentioned earlier that Greek philosophy, Roman law, and the religious heritage of a fragile Jewish sect would eventually meld to constitute a large part (but not the whole) of what we know as Western civilisation. The final piece that needed to be added to the contributions of Greece, Rome and Jerusalem to make possible the emergence of European civilisation, a piece that is usually overlooked, was the aristocratic-libertarian spirit of the German tribes. To quote François Guizot once again, 'the sentiment of personal independence, a love of liberty displaying itself at all risks, without any other motive but that of satisfying itself' was introduced by the barbar-ians and 'deposited in the cradle of modern civilization, wherein it has played so conspicuous a part...that it is impossible to help reckoning it as one of its fundamental elements.' [Guizot, 49]

Notes

1 For a comprehensive history of the early Middle Ages, it would be hard to better Chris Wickham's *Framing the Early Middle Ages*. [Wickham, 2005] Especially relevant for the purposes of this history are Wickham's chapters 3 ('The form of the state'), 6 ('Political breakdown and state-building in the North') and 10 ('Cities'). Norman Davies's *The Isles: A History* is also worthy of study. If it is more limited in scope than Wickham's magisterial volume, it is for that very reason somewhat more sharply focused.

2 For a wonderfully detailed yet succinct account of the extraordinarily complex history of the various barbarian groups, their constitutions, their peregrinations and their interactions with the Roman Empire and Roman culture, see Musset, passim.

3 Musset, 22, 167.

4 Patterson 1991, 347; Morrall 1970, 35. On the question of whether the barbarians invaded or merely migrated, see Musset, 158-160. Adopting a long-range perspective on the topic of whether political and demographic stability or political and demographic flux should be taken as the norm, he writes,

'According to the traditional view, the period of the "great invasions" is a time of turmoil sandwiched between two eras of stability and normality: that of the Roman Empire and our own. It would be wise to adopt the opposite attitude and consider the Roman period the exception, a temporary lull in a whirlwind of invasions....This turmoil, which lasted for seven or eight centuries, carried along with it many extremely varied peoples. The interactions between them are so complex that it is rarely possible to say who was responsible for initiating each movement.' [Musset, 3, 4]

5 Mirgeler, 46; see also Lopez and Macfarlane.

6 It shouldn't be forgotten that the Roman Empire waxed and waned in the East for another 1000 years, until Constantinople fell to the Turks in 1453.

7 See Wickham 2005, 56-150. In the early Middle Ages, Chris Wickham distinguishes strong states, weak states and pre-states. His strong states are 'the Roman Empire and its Byzantine and Arab successors', his weak states, the 'Romano-Germanic kingdoms such as Frankish Gaul, Lombard Italy, and Visigothic Spain', and his pre-states, England, Wales, Ireland and Denmark.' [Wickham 2005, 56] In chapter 6 of the same work, he deals in great detail with areas such as Ireland and Denmark which were never under Roman rule. Some of the areas which had been under Roman rule, such as Britain, lost their specifically Roman character very quickly after the departure of the Roman legions.

8 Duchesne, 463; 465.

9 Morrall 1970, 46-47; see Goldberg 2015, passim, and Greif, passim.

10 The land advance of Islam into western Europe was checked in AD 732 at Tours (450 miles north of the Pyrenees!) by Charles Martel, Mayor of the Palace of the Frankish King. If it hadn't been checked, then, according to Edward Gibbon, we'd all be reading the Koran and I wouldn't be writing this book.

11 Pirenne, 19; see Morrall 1970, 50-51, 83; and see Landes, 29-30.

12 See Guizot, passim; see also Morris 1972, 21.

13 'Every student of history,' remarks John Morrall, 'has to come to grips, sooner or later, with the problem of periodization.' [Morrall 1970, 11]

14 In judging the 'Dark Ages' to be the 'black hole of barbarism', Montesquieu spoke for the thinkers of the Enlightenment in general. [see Shklar, 50] For a contemporary take on the 'Dark Ages, see Wright, 139-154.

15 Siedentop, 9. 'In general,' writes James Greenaway, 'medieval political thought has not been adequately treated. For example, a cursory glance at most political philosophy textbooks or course programs demonstrates that the fifteen hundred years from antiquity to Machiavelli, Hobbes, or Locke, with an occasional nod toward Augustine and Aquinas, is simple "leap-frogged" or ignored—as though nothing of significance happened.' [Greenaway, 17]

16 'To the question posed by Huizinga in 1920—"What actually was the cultural transformation we call the Renaissance? What did it consist of, what was its effect?"—no clear answer has been found.' [Eisenstein, 125]

17 Kealey 1996, 29; see also Kealey 2008, 111-122 and Parkinson 1958, 181-184.

18 Mommsen, 241, 242; see Day, 34-38; see also Hannam, 7-8.

19 Davies 1999, 331; see also 338-339.

20 See Bautier, passim.

21 Carlo Cipolla, too, notes the technological innovations of this period, as well as remarking on the effects of international trade and urbanisation. See Cipolla, passim.

22 White, 76 and passim; see Morrall 1979, 132-134.

23 See Kaye, chapters 6 & 7. See also Hannam, passim. For an account of the scientific advances of the later Middle Ages see Haskins, 303-340.

24 Albert Mirgeler writes, 'we must be careful not to commit ourselves to the current impression that the Constantinian turning-point "perverted" Christianity....To demand for that age an unpolitical, still more a purely spiritual Christianity, would mean asking for a Christianity aloof from the destiny of its time and which consequently would itself have been left behind by that destiny. The only solution at the time was the Constantinian. Abelard in his day maliciously observed that the success of Christianity before it received the massive support of the Emperors had been very slight.' [Mirgeler, 28, 29]

25 'A momentous accentuation of the position of the clergy in the hierarchical structure of the Church was brought about by the fact that Constantine made their various grades correspond to the grades of the State hierarchy. Thus the patriarchs came to correspond to the four *praefecti*, the metropolitans to provincial governors, while the bishops began to also to [*sic*] take up important secular positions as a result of the decline of local administration....As a result of the Constantinian turning-point, the clergy, hitherto unquestionably first and foremost the representatives of the Christian people in face of the

persecuting State, were torn away from this anchorage and established in principle above them, holding an authority similar to and in association with that of the State hierarchy: a situation which inevitably diminished their sacred character.' [Mirgeler, 37-38, 38]

26 See *Galatians* 3: 28; *1 Corinthians* 12: 13.

27 Carlyle I, 94; see *1 Thessalonians* 4: 10, 11 & 5: 14.

28 This claim isn't uncontroversial but has been articulated and consistently maintained in several persuasive publications by Brian Tierney. [see Tierney, 2001; see also Siedentop, 245ff.] The complexities of canonistic jurisprudence are elucidated in an elegant and exemplary manner in Tierney 2014.

29 '*Quod boni libertatem amant, servitutem improbi.*' *Letter to Theodosius*, no. 40, §2, in *Migne*.

30 See *City of God*, 5: 21; see Parsons 1941, 332.

31 Migne, *Patrologia Latina*, vol. 103.

Chapter 10

GOWN AND TOWN

Stadtluft macht frei nach Jahr und Tag
—German Saying

There has been no lacuna in the Western idealization of freedom,
certainly not in the medieval world where,
contrary to the common view, commitment to the ideal,
including the notion of negative personal freedom,
was as great as it had been in the ancient past and as it is today
—Orlando Patterson

As was mentioned earlier, historical periodisation is never an innocent enterprise. To speak of *the* Renaissance, for example, is to suggest that there was just one such event, the one that took place between the fourteenth and seventeenth centuries. But this is to conceal with a capital letter the fact that before that large-scale cultural event, there had been many earlier re-births. One of the most significant such renaissances took place in the eleventh and twelfth centuries and it affected almost every area of intellectual life: literature, law, philosophy, theology, mathematics, technology and science.[1] 'The old humanist claim that the recovery and reappropriation of classical learning had had to await the triumphs of the Italian Renaissance in the fifteenth and sixteenth centuries contrived to linger on in pedagogical practice and the public historical imaginary (*sic*) well into the latter years of the twentieth century,' writes Francis Oakley, but, as he points out, Charles Haskins demonstrated almost ninety years ago, the 'twelfth century…was a period of intellectual and cultural renewal.'[2]

It would be true to say that the cultural emphasis of the eleventh and twelfth centuries was primarily literary and was associated with the work of St Bernard, John of Salisbury and William of Malmesbury; philosophy and theology had to wait to attain their high water mark until the early thirteenth and mid-fourteenth centuries. On the other hand, the study of law assumed a position of prominence as early as the eleventh century, a prominence that it rarely lost from that time onward. Whatever the rise to prominence and distinction of this or that discipline, perhaps the most striking aspect of this period was the attainment across most of Europe of a significant level of cultural unity. 'For three hundred years, from 1050 to 1350,' writes David Knowles, 'and above all in the century between 1070-1170, the whole of educated Western Europe formed a single undifferentiated cultural unit.'[3] The names that come down to us from this period would have adorned any age: Lanfranc, Anselm, Peter Abelard, John of Salisbury, Thomas Aquinas, Duns Scotus and William of Ockham. Associated with these intellectual luminaries were various institutions: monasteries, cathedral schools and finally, the university, perhaps *the* most significant and lasting institutional contribution of the age apart from the Church itself.[4]

A single undifferentiated cultural unity medieval Europe may have been, but underlying that cultural unity was an astonishingly varied and diverse set of ethnic, linguistic and quasi-political groups, including (among others), Ålanders, Albanians, Alsatians, Andalusians, Aragonese, Asturians and Cantabrians, Austrians, Basques, Bavarians, Belarusians, Balearic Islanders, Bretons, Bulgarians, Burgenlanders, Carinthians, Castilians, Catalans, Channel Islanders, Cornish, Corsicans, Croats, Czechs, Danes, Dutch, Estonians, Faeroese, Finns, Franconians, French, Frisians, Frulians and Triestines, Galicians, Greeks, Highland and Island Scots, Hutsuls, Boikos and Lemkos, Icelanders, Irish, Karelians, Lapps, Latvians, Ligurians, Lithuanians, Lombards, Lower Austrians and Viennese, Lowland Scots, Luxembourgers, Macedonians, Magyars, Maltese, Manx, Mecklenburgers, Montenegrins, Navarrese, Normans, Norwegians, Piedmontese, Poles, Portuguese, Prussians, Rhinelanders, Romanians, Russians, Ruthenians, Salzburgers, Sammarinesi, Sardinians, Saxons, Serbs, Sicilians, Slovaks, Slovenes, Styrians, Swabians, Swedes, Swiss, Tyrolese, Ukrainians, Upper Austrians, Valdaostans and Waldensians, Valencians, Veneti, Veps, Vorarlbergers, Walloons, Welsh and Wends. [see Fernández-Armesto, passim]

I shall come to discuss the University presently but it should be noted, in passing, that monastic life was to contribute some significant ideas to social and political thought.[5] James Greenaway goes so far as to claim that 'More than any other institution, the driver of major civilizational renovation in early medieval Europe was the monastery,' adding, '…it was the monasteries that led the movement once again toward ecclesial independence and renewal.' [Greenaway, 20, 33] It was also in the monasteries that the rudiments of modern democracy first appeared.[6] Monasteries were, in effect, voluntary associations of equals and in them the principle obtained, sometimes more honoured in the breach than in the observance, that what concerned all should be decided by all. This principle[7] 'was applied over and over by canonists, Catholic theologians, and medieval thinkers' so that 'consent and natural rights theories "had deep roots" in the Middle Ages.' [Watner 2005, 67] Abbots and priors were elected by their brethren and were simply first among equals for the time being. Cyril Parkinson notes that 'The Rule of St. Benedict and its later variants provided the models for a written constitution. The procedure in Chapter provided a model for the orderly conduct of business. The system of Visitation gave precedent for any regular system of inspection. And, finally, the sending of delegates to the annual Conferences or Chapters of the Order…was a thirteenth century experiment in representative democracy.'[8] The monasteries, in particular the Benedictine monasteries, also played a major role in undermining the ubiquitous classical contempt for manual labour. Moreover, the voluntary association of monastic equals was consistent with their freely willed subjection to a freely chosen authority, an authority 'founded on and constrained by the consent of the community.' [Siedentop, 139] Freedom and authority could coexist and, in this coexistence, the notion of autonomy, of self-rule, was born; liberty could be exercised in 'obedience to rules that an individual's conscience imposed on itself...' [Siedentop, 98]

The shift in presumption from the classical natural inequality of people to the medieval/Christian moral equality of all brought about changes in the legal principles structuring corporations. It had been the case in Roman law that corporations, to be corporations, had to be recognised by the appropriate public authority. Canon lawyers rejected this principle and recognised as corporations any voluntarily constituted group directed towards the achievement of a common goal. Such corporations could set out and enforce rules for their constituents without requiring the approval of a public authority. The presumption of moral equality, together with the view that the property of the corporation was the property of all its constituents, made it to be the case that in making certain decisions, corporations had to seek the consent of all their constituent members. [see Siedentop, 234-235]

It has been argued, with some degree of plausibility, that European civilisation as we know it today was born during this period. Harold Berman believes that 'not only modern legal institutions and modern legal values but also the modern state, the modern church, modern philosophy, the modern university, modern literature, and much else that is modern—have their origin in the period 1050-1150 *and not before*.'[9] Hastings Rashdall remarks that 'the beginning of the eleventh century represents, as nearly as it is possible to fix it, the turning-point in the intellectual history of Europe.' [Rashdall 1936a, 33] To move from the early Middle Ages to the later Middle Ages is to go from a world that's foreign to us in many ways to a world that is recognisably ours, even if it is our world at an earlier stage of development. To look at the early Middle Ages is to stare at a photograph of your distant cousin; to look at the later Middle Ages is like glancing through your photo album and admiring your younger self. Harold Berman argues that '...there was a radical discontinuity between the Europe of the period before the years 1050-1150 and the Europe of the period after the years 1050-1150,' and James Greenaway notes that 'The roughly one-hundred-year period from 1050 to 1150 marks an axis-time for Western society: before which the practical fusion of institutional authorities was the norm and the assertion of existential authority was still dull; and after which the resetting of relations between the church and the now multiple royal heads led to a separation of way, which the exercise of existential authority had become one of the dominant characteristics of Western society.'[10]

The struggle between the *sacerdotium* and the *regnum*, sometimes overt, sometimes covert, but always confused because of the existential fusion of the two, wouldn't be reflectively thematised until after—and to a large extent because of—what took place during this axial period. In the gap created by the competing *sacerdotium* and the *regnum*, a space emerged for the development of the individual. So it was that during this period, the individual, submerged for much of the early Middle Ages, finally emerged into the light of day and became present to consciousness. Colin Morris writes, 'The discovery of the individual was one of the most important cultural developments in the years between 1050 and 1200. It was not confined to any one group of thinkers.

Its central features may be found in many different circles: a concern with self-discovery; an interest in the relations between people, and in the role of the individual within society...' [Morris 1972, 158]

Here as elsewhere, it is important to avoid anachronism. I am not arguing that there's just one idea of the individual and that this idea appeared fully grown in the year AD 1139 on the fourth of August at 3.46 p.m. No. The idea of the individual is neither diachronically nor synchronically simple. Aaron Gurevich, the author of *The Origins of European Individualism*, regards Colin Morris's *The Discovery of the Individual 1050-1200* as a 'milestone in the study of the individual in the Middle Ages,' yet his evaluation of Morris's work isn't entirely uncritical. [Gurevich, 6] While he believes that Morris is correct to think that the discovery of individuality 'did not involve a sudden cataclysm' in 1500 and that he is also correct to insist that the twelfth century Renaissance witnessed 'the emergence of an individual with new psychological leanings' and 'a more profound vision of the nature of humanity,' nevertheless, he believes Morris's approach suffers from two defects. First, it is limited to the experience of the great and the good and ignores the lived experience of the humbler members of society, and, second, it is insufficiently appreciative of the subsisting relations between the emergent individuals and their groups. I shouldn't wish to deny that there may well be some grounds for Gurevich's criticisms; still, while appreciating the complexity of this issue and conceding that it is antecedently unlikely that any one writer has got everything right in every respect, it is none the less the case, I believe, that while nature may not make jumps (*natura non facit saltum*), culture sometimes does; and one of those jumps in the direction of a clearer and more robust conception of the individual was made in the period under discussion.[11]

In this chapter I should like to provide a brief treatment of four mediaeval institutions—two relatively concrete (the University and the City), and two somewhat more abstract (Feudalism, and Law and Kingship)—that provide some of the necessary social and legal background to the discovery of the individual, together with a brief overview of the thought of John of Salisbury, a writer who, although in many ways a man of his times and often regarded as the creator of the first medieval treatise on politics, none the less is really a bridge figure between the old and the new.

THE UNIVERSITY

Universities came into being in a haphazard and, dare I say it, anarchic manner.[12] They weren't created from the top-down according to a pre-conceived plan, but grew upwards and outwards, fuelled by a genuinely popular desire for learning, both practical and theoretical.[13] As complicated and disputed as their origins may be, it is without doubt that within a short period of time, emerging institutions of higher education were recognised as universities if law, medicine or theology was taught in them. '[The university] was to prove one of the great European inventions; almost all universities in the world can trace their origins to the models provided by Bologna, Paris and Oxford, the first examples; by 1400 there were fifty-three more.' [Roberts 1997, 216] Among the earliest universities, Salerno was identified with medicine,[14] Bologna with law, and Paris, an outgrowth of the cathedral school of Notre Dame, with theology.[15] At first, the school at Paris was not essentially different or superior to schools in Chartres and Rheims and Laon, but its geographical location and, more significantly, its having the academic superstar Peter Abelard teaching there, gave Paris a position of prominence that it never subsequently relinquished.[16] Whereas Salerno and Bologna were largely what we would today call professional schools, the student at Paris could obtain a general education before embarking on his specific professional studies: 'the number of both students and masters multiplied at Paris, and the majority of the students entered the arts school, which provided the only general education then available, and which was also an indispensable preparation for theology, law and medicine. Paris, in fact, rapidly became a city of students, the first of its kind in Europe; they filled the island around the cathedral, spilling over upon the left bank of the river, the later *quartier latin*.'[17] The creation of universities elsewhere in Europe quickly followed—Cambridge, Coimbra, Montpellier, Naples, Oxford, Padua, Salamanca and Vicenza.[18]

From their very beginning, universities were international institutions, drawing their students from far and wide. The international reach of universities was due in no small part to their having the same language of instruction—Latin. During the Renaissance, the Latin of the medieval universities came in for some radical criticism but, in fact, as Rashdall notes that 'the Latin language, originally rigid, inflexible, poor in vocabulary and almost incapable of expressing a philosophical idea, became in the hands of medieval thinkers flexible, subtle, and elastic' and was a living language until 'killed by the Ciceronian pedantry of the sixteenth or seventeenth century.'[19]

Universities were only one form, if a very important form, of the corporative institutions that emerged during this period; the idea of the corporation, especially of the corporation as a representative body, was to have a resounding effect on subsequent political history. The very term *universitas* means a corporation, an entity made up of one or more persons with the capacity to act in legal matters as if it were a single person. It is difficult to realise just how innovative and indeed singular this idea was in its time, an idea that is now commonplace. 'Occasional claims to the contrary,' remarks Francis Oakley, 'it has to be insisted that neither the great civilizations of eastern and southern Asia or of Mesoamerica, nor our own archaic predecessors in the ancient Near East and the classical world, not the cultures of medieval Byzantium or Islam gave birth to anything truly comparable. Like the university…the species of representative assembly that proved to be the direct forerunner of our modern parliamentary institutions was ultimately a product of the legal and institutional creativity characteristic of western European life in the twelfth and thirteenth centuries.'[20]

The earlier part of the eleventh century renaissance had at its disposal only fragments of the writings of Aristotle, mediated largely through the work of Boethius. When the complete canon of Aristotle eventually became available, as it did over the period of about one hundred years, its effect on Western thought was unprecedented. The renaissance was fuelled by access to this Aristotelian corpus and, in part, by medieval Europe's renewed contacts with Syria, Constantinople, Sicily and Spain, the contact with Sicily and Spain being particularly important.[21] The earliest part of the Aristotelian corpus to be re-discovered was his logic—the *Prior* and *Posterior Analytics*, the *Topics*, and his *On Sophistical Refutations*—and this, when assimilated, became the foundation of what came to be called the scholastic method.[22] This method was a tool for the discovery, articulation and defence of doctrine in theology, law, canon law and philosophy. [see Oakley 2012, 42-65]

The reception of the works of Aristotle, on the face of it merely a recondite academic matter, was in fact a critical moment in the development of Western culture.[23] 'The reception of Aristotle presented a challenge to the West, not so much an intellectual challenge as a spiritual challenge.' [Greenaway, 13] Had the works of Aristotle been rejected as incompatible with Christianity (a policy some advocated at the time), then it is unlikely that the intellectual explosion that was the most significant element in the High Middle Ages would ever have taken place, and the social, religious and political development of Europe would have been substantially different.[24] 'The introduction of Aristotle's work from Islam into the civilization orbit of the West was the occasion for another pattern of thought to challenge the Christian basis of civil theology,' writes James Greenaway. 'The philosopher's writings and the commentaries that accompanied them contained many propositions that were incompatible with those of Christian dogma. In the intellectual climate of the times, a rival narrative presented a stimulating alternative to Christian symbols, while at the same time it was suppressed as heretical. These contrary responses were evidenced in the University of Paris's teaching the *Commentaries* of Averroës and in the 219 propositions of heresy condemned by Bishop Tempier (1277), respectively. A third response to the Aristotelian corpus was represented by Albert Magnus and Thomas Aquinas in which the recognition that this rival narrative was useful and was not going to go away necessitated a serious attempt at assimilation.' [Greenaway, 148]

An apocryphal story is told by Hegel in his *Philosophy of History* of the burning of the library of Alexandria on the orders of the Caliph Omar, who is alleged to have said that if the books it contained agreed with the Qur'an, they weren't needed, and if they were opposed to the Qur'an, they should be destroyed.[25] This would appear to be a garbled version of Ibn Khaldûn's report of what Caliph Omar is reputed to have written to his victorious general in Persia, Sa'd bin Abi Waqqas, who had requested Omar's permission to distribute his booty of books and scientific papers: 'Throw them in the water,' Omar said. 'If what they contain is right guidance, God has given us better guidance. If it is error, God has protected us against it.'[26] In either its genuine or apocryphal version, the story serves to illustrate the tension between a literalist, fundamentalist approach to religion and a considered, rational and critical approach, a tension whose resolution can have immense practical consequences. It is widely believed that the anti-scientific, anti-critical turn in Islamic thinking is to be credited to the renowned Islamic theologian al-Ghazali (Abu Hamid

Al Ghazāli c. 1055-1111) but whereas it's true that the anti-scientific, anti-critical turn in Islamic thought undoubtedly occurred in the eleventh century, after a fertile, if ultimately derivative,[27] period of Islamic science and philosophy, it isn't entirely clear that al-Ghazāli was its agent.[28] Other possible culprits have been identified, such as Abu Ali al-Hasan ibn al-Hasan ibn Ali ibn Ishaq al-Tusi (1018–1092), also known as Nizam al-Mulk, who set up the Nizamiyah education system that prioritised religious studies as against independent rational enquiry. [see Reilly, 43]

In the matter of the relation between the spiritual and temporal realms, Ernest Fortin points to an important difference between Islam and Judaism, on the one hand, and Christianity, on the other.[29] 'The most distinctive feature of Islam and Judaism is that they both present themselves first and foremost as divinely revealed Laws or as all-inclusive social orders, regulating every segment of men's private and public lives and precluding from the outset any sphere of activity in which reason could operate independently of the divine Law. Christianity, on the other hand, first comes to sight as a faith or as a sacred doctrine, demanding adherence to a set of fundamental beliefs but otherwise leaving its followers at liberty to organize their social and political lives in accordance with norms and principles that are not specifically religious.' [Fortin, 251] This theological-legal difference has socio-political consequences. Whereas in Jewish and Islamic societies,[30] there could be only one centre of authority, in Christian society, there came to be two—*sacerdotium* and the *regnum*—and one of the most significant and recurrent features of Western history is the tension between these two centres of authority. Each centre was relatively independent of the other but none the less had to coexist with the other in the same social space. 'The upshot was that one was usually able to study political phenomena in the light of reason alone without directly challenging the established religious authority or running the risk of an open confrontation with it.' [Fortin, 251] Francis Oakley puts forward a controversial argument for the different ways in which the scholastic method was received in Christian and in Islamic circles, with consequent effects upon the development of critical thinking and cultural and political change among the adherents of each of these faiths. Whereas for Christians, the centre of their faith is the person of Jesus Christ, with the Bible taking second place—a close second place but a second place none the less—for Muslims, the Qur'an plays the role that Christ plays in Christianity. If that is so—and the point is arguable[31]—then 'Muslim hesitancies about subjecting Quranic teaching to philosophical analysis—just as the continuing absence from the Islamic world of anything really comparable to modern Western biblical criticism—is entirely understandable.'[32]

Whether Oakley's argument obtains or not, it is clear that in contemporary orthodox Islam there appears to be no operative distinction between its transcendent aspirations and its political expression, nor does there appear to be any possible space for the existence of the autonomous individual.[33] All three elements—the religious, the political and the individual—are fused in a seemingly inextricable and undifferentiated mass. In contrast, the differentiation of the *sacerdotium* and the *regnum* in the West has been a long and complicated process, a process still unfinished, but however incomplete and ragged the differentiation, it created the existential space for the emergence of the individual.[34] Islam too had its opportunity to move in a similar direction, as exemplified by the Mu'tazilites 'who were the adherents of suppressed schools of Shari'a that prioritized reason over the claims of Qu'ranic revelation.' [Greenaway, 282] Greenaway notes that it was from the Mu'tazilites that 'the great flowering of Islamic civilization came which included philosophy, science and mathematics, engineering, medicine, and so forth,' their method being expressed in a saying of Averroës that 'whenever there is a contradiction between the result of a proof (or of rational speculation) and the apparent meaning of a revealed text, the latter must be subject to interpretation.'[35] The most fundamental contrast between Islam and the West, writes Greenaway, 'rests on the phenomenon of differentiation. In contrast to the open-ended process in the West, authority in Shari'a remains both undifferentiated and encrusted in teleological symbolism. Authority is exercised in spiritual, political, and existential spheres, but each of the spheres is effectively fused with the others by the finality of Allah's sovereignty. In Western terms, this means that there is no sphere of temporal-political authority that runs separately from spiritual authority; nor a zone of individual autonomy in Ockham's sense. Any assertion of authority in Islam outside the orthodox codification of Islamic law is an assertion of apostasy and therefore illegitimate...' [Greenaway, 283]

The scholastic method is essentially one in which those thinkers who are accepted as authorities in a given field—philosophy, law and theology— have their pronouncements investigated, rationally organised, disputed and distinguished. It demonstrates a radically changed attitude towards what the medieval scholar regarded as authorities. Up to this period, theology had been primarily a matter of unsystematic scriptural reflection. With the acquisition of Aristotle's logic, reason could be applied to *all* sources of authority, Scripture included, to elucidate, arrange, organise and evaluate it. In the case of Scripture, this period marks the beginning of systematic theology. As in Peter Abelard's notorious *Sic et Non*, it became readily apparent that Scripture (and indeed all the other authorities in Law and Philosophy) contained within it a number of apparent contradictions. Faced with this, a commentator could simply throw up his hands and abandon any prospect of coherence, or he could argue that the contradictions were more apparent than real and seek a method of resolving the tensions. Resolution by rational distinction was the choice that was made, and it was applied not only to Scripture but also to Philosophy (Aristotle), to Law (*Institutes* and *Digest*) and, by Gratian, to Canon Law.

The scholastic method is simple and essentially dialectical and open-ended. A question is posed, let us say, whether God exists. Those authorities that seem to support the claim that God does not exist are quoted (*sic*); those authorities that seem to support the claim that God does exist are quoted (*sed contra*); then the master resolves the question on one side or the other (*respondeo*) and meets the objections from the side rejected, normally by making relevant distinctions. There is a very old (and very mild) joke that St Thomas never met a distinction he didn't like, but much the same could be said of any of the scholastic thinkers. This proclivity for drawing distinctions, sometimes distinctions without a difference, eventually led to accusations, sometimes justified, that the later medieval thinkers were engaged in arid logic-chopping rather than genuine enquiry.[36]

The scholastic method originated in law, specifically in the context of the re-discovery and re-assimilation of Roman law. At the same time, the Catholic Church in the West was beginning to conceive of itself in a juridical manner and, as part of the struggle of emancipation from political control, began to systematise its own customs and legal rulings in its own legal code, canon law. It is, I think, significant, that almost all the popes of the twelfth and thirteenth centuries had been trained as lawyers.[37] It might be true to claim that philosophy and theology mark the highest intellectual achievement of medieval culture but it can not be denied that in practice law was in most universities far and away the most prominent faculty. 'One of the most important results of the universities was the creation, or at least the enormously increased power and importance, of the lawyer-class. Great as are the evils which society still owes to lawyers, the lawyer-class has always been a civilizing agency....Lawyers have moderated or regulated despotism even when they have proved its most willing tools...' [Rashdall 1936c, 457]

Canon law, based on the teachings of the Father, the canons of particular councils and the decrees of various popes, was systematised by Gratian, a Bolognese monk, in or around 1140. Gratian collected, collated and distinguished around 4,000 ecclesiastical legal texts that came to be called *Concordantia discordantium canonum* (*The Concordance of Discordant Canons*) or the *Decretum*. [see Tierney 1988, 150-157] It isn't coincidental that the University of Bologna was to become the preeminent university for legal studies. Gratian's 'method of reconciling, or harmonizing, diverse opinions became a model for the golden age of scholasticism in the schools of the thirteenth century.'[38] Very shortly afterwards, this very same method was applied to Scripture and to theological opinions and judgements by Peter Lombard in his *Sentences*. Both Gratian and Peter were preceded in their development of their dialectical method by the renowned early medieval writer and teacher, Peter Abelard,[39] whose *Sic et Non* was one of the earliest instances of the systematic application of reason to an authoritative source. Peter Lombard's *Sentences* were the application to theology of Abelard's dialectical method and Gratian's *Concordance* (or *Decretum*) was similarly dialectically constructed.

Stadtluft macht frei—The Free Air of the City

Were there cities in the post-Roman barbarian west? If by cities one means fortress-like centres of administration, then the answer is, yes, to an extent; if, however, one means by cities, social entities possessed of their own laws and institutions and devoted primarily to commercial activity, then the answer must be, no.[40] Peter Wilson notes that 'Towns contracted in the Romanized areas during late antiquity as the dwindling population could no longer defend settlements that remained tempting targets for raiders.' [Wilson 2016, 504] Such towns as existed were largely fortress-based defensive enclosures, the seat of the local bishop and a local habitation for the peripatetic local lords. 'The towns had already in the Dark Ages become primarily fortified centres to meet the unsettled conditions of the ages before and after Charlemagne; the connexion is reflected linguistically in such words as the German *burg*, which means both "castle" and "town".' [Morrall 1970, 139] Henri Pirenne writes, 'the Empire itself was without a capital. The counts, to whom the supervision of [the towns] was entrusted, did not settle down in any fixed spot. They were constantly travelling about their districts in order to preside over judicial assemblies, to levy taxes, and to raise troops. The centers of their administrations were not their places of residence but their persons. It was therefore of little importance whether they had or did not have their domicile in a town.' [Pirenne, 44]

Roman towns had largely been places of administration rather than commerce. By the start of the ninth century, most of the old Roman towns had declined in importance while no new towns had really developed in northern Europe. Around the same time, however, trade and commerce revitalised the old Roman towns of the south and created new towns in the north. The social and political significance of this urban revolution can't be overstated. 'By the thirteenth century,' writes Denys Hay, 'the development of towns had reached a point where the whole temper of western European society had been radically affected.' [Hay, 107] The extent of trade and commerce in the period between the ninth and eleventh centuries, however, mustn't be overstated. Although its extent was greater than is commonly appreciated, it was much less than it would become in the high Middle Ages. Summing up, Henri Pirenne says that the populations of such cities weren't city populations but rather fortress populations. 'Neither commerce nor industry was possible or even conceivable in such an environment. It produced nothing of itself, lived by revenues from the surrounding countryside, and had no other economic role than that of a simple consumer.' [Pirenne, 53] Not only were the inhabitants of such cities consumers and not producers but they had no special legal status either that distinguished them in any way from the denizens of the surrounding country-side.

By the early tenth century, the menace of the Norsemen was effectively terminated, in part by the cession of Normandy to them, although the Norse pressure continued on Britain, Ireland, Sicily and southern Italy for some time. The expansion of the Slavs and Hungarians was checked in the East, leaving only the Moslem pressure on the Eastern Empire, the Mediterranean, and, from Spain and the Mediterranean, on southern France. In time, the Moors were checked in Spain and the Mediterranean islands were recaptured by the forces of the Italian cities. 'From the middle of the ninth century to the middle of the tenth,' writes Bautier, 'there was a total collapse of the European economy as a result of the Saracen, Viking and Hungarian attacks. Little by little, a new world emerged from the general chaos, and from the systematic destruction of all that had made western and central Europe a going concern economically. It was, however, a very different world from its forerunner, which still had links with ancient Rome. The process of recovery lasted for two centuries, from the middle of the tenth century to the middle of the twelfth, before the remarkable flowering of the classical Middle Ages could come about.' [Bautier, 57] François Guizot remarks, 'At the beginning of the tenth century…two great results had been obtained.…The movement of the invasion on the north and south has been arrested.…in the south.…The Arabs were quartered in Spain.… but the grand progress of Islamism had evidently ceased.' [Guizot, 68-69] Europe, no longer land-locked, had access to the Mediterranean, the North Sea and the Baltic. By the time the eleventh century rolled around, the West witnessed its first real commercial flourishing. This came from two principal places: Venice, and the lands of the Flemish coast. Venice, founded on some little islands in the northern Adriatic in the sixth century by refugees from the attacks of the barbarian tribes, was from its beginning an outpost of the Byzantine Empire.[41] 'While Western Europe was detaching herself from the east,' writes Pirenne, 'she continued to be part of it. And this circumstance is of capital importance. The consequence was that Venice did not cease to gravitate in the orbit of Constantinople. Across the waters, she was subject to the attraction of that great city and herself grew great under its influence.' [Pirenne, 60] Living on these little offshore islands with little or no natural resources (not even drinking water), the inhabitants of Venice were, from the start, reliant on trade. Constantinople wasn't only an administrative centre of the Eastern Roman Empire but also an industrial and commercial centre without equal. Venice's connection with Constantinople made her rich and powerful.[42] Her trade connections went well beyond Constantinople, reaching out even to their religious opponents. 'No scruple had any weight with the Venetians,' remarks Pirenne. 'Their religion was a religion of businessmen. It mattered little to them that the Moslems were the enemies of Christ, if business with them was profitable. After the ninth century, they began more and more to frequent Aleppo, Cairo, Damascus, Kairwan, and Palermo. Treaties of commerce assured their merchants a privileged status in the markets of Islam.'[43] With wealth came power and that power was used to clear the Adriatic of everything inimical to trade. Settlements were founded wherever Venetian power was felt. In a similar, but smaller way, the proto-Byzantine cities of Bari, Tarentum and Naples also engaged in trade with Constantinople and with the Moslems.

As might be expected, the revitalisation of trade took root first in the cities of the south, especially the Italian maritime cities; Venice, of course, as just discussed, but also Genoa and Pisa, and elsewhere on the Mediterranean, Marseilles and Barcelona. The effects of the commerce thus began in the maritime ports extended inland into the other cities of northern Italy, Provence and the Rhone valley. By the end of the eleventh century, traders were operating in Hamburg, Cologne and Mainz, Paris and Rouen, Cambrai and Ghent, Liege, Dinant and Verdun and Bruges. Even the outer limits of Europe were involved with trading posts in England (London), Scotland and even as far afield as Ireland. The example of Venice was enviously copied by other northern Italian cities; first by Pavia, then by the bitter rivals, Genoa and Pisa[44] which, unlike their Venetian counterpart, were reluctant to trade with Moslems. The Genoans and Pisans, the object of Moslem attack in the tenth century (Pisa was plundered by the Arabs as late as 1001 and 1011) returned the favour with interest in the eleventh! They began by taking Sardinia (1022), Corsica (1091) and then went on to attack the Moslem bases in Africa and Spain, sacking Madhiya (in present day Tunis) in 1088. [see Bautier, 96] 'It wasn't overly difficult for the major Italian seaports to gain mastery of the Mediterranean against the declining Muslim and Byzantine fleets,' notes Robert Lopez, 'and to use their sea power as a bargaining instrument to get what they wanted from territorial lords who needed maritime support.'[45] Finally, the conquest of Sicily by the Normans (1058-1090) took away from the Saracens, the last base of operation in the Mediterranean which, since the ninth century, had enabled them to keep the west in a state of blockage. [see Pirenne, 64-65]

In the northern part of Europe, the Norsemen, who had begun their careers as raiders, began to settle down, in the northern half of England, the maritime regions of Ireland and, most notably, in the land that took their name, Normandy. Once settled, their piratical tendencies turned towards trade. Their eastern cousins established connections through Russia with Constantinople and this was the conduit for trade between the North Sea and Baltic coasts and the capital of the Eastern Empire. The increasingly pacific tendencies of the Norsemen and their repulsion by the new, energised German cities finally made the Baltic and the North Sea a highway for commerce. [see Cipolla, passim]

The effect of all this on the previously land-locked West was revolutionary. The old Roman cities were revitalised and new cities founded far and wide, cities not just as sporadic administrative centres and fortresses but cities as commercial and industrial centres. Cities also developed away from the Mediterranean rim. 'In northern and western Europe,' writes George Holmes, 'urban life in the Middle Ages was in general a secondary phenomenon and cities were overawed by kings.' [see Morris 1972, 37-38] By the early fourteenth century, however, 'a galaxy of city states had emerged...' [Holmes 1975, 67] Peter Wilson notes, 'Whereas there were only 200 German towns in 1025, there were over 600 by 1150, and 15,000 by 1250...' [Wilson 2016, 506]

One of the most spectacular northern European developments was the emergence of the Hanseatic League. The more important cities in the north of Germany were governed by patrician families, much as in Italy, and their wealth was derived from trade in the Baltic and the North Sea.[46] These cities formed an association, the Hanseatic League, originally between the families but later between the cities, to promote their common interests. At its height, the League consisted of about 100 towns and cities—including Arnhem, Bremen, Danzig, Elbing, Hamburg, Kiel, Riga, Rostock and, perhaps most famously, Lübeck—and was able to exercise huge influence in that entire region, sometimes overbearing even national governments, such as that of Denmark.[47] It is perhaps easier to say what the League was not rather than what it was. It met no recognisable set of criteria for unity, yet its very looseness of organisation was its strength. In the League, we had 'a seemingly vague, amorphous sort of group, barely able to organize a meeting every few years to make decisions, and yet able to make war efficiently on Flanders, France, England, Denmark, Norway, Sweden and Holland at various times, to raise money for ships like a nation, sign treaties at the end and even manage kings, imposing them and deposing them.' [Pye, 231] It flourished between the mid-thirteenth century until its decline at the beginning of the seventeenth century and wasn't formally terminated until the nineteenth century, when only Hamburg, Bremen and Lübeck were left as members.[48]

The new cities and the newly revitalized cities were largely, though not exclusively, the creation of the merchants.[49] 'The rise of the merchant class was a function of the growth of towns; merchants were inseparably linked with the most dynamic element in medieval European civilization, the towns and cities which increasingly fostered within their walls so much of the future history of Europe.' [Roberts 1997, 161] Merchants needed a place to live in between their journeys to and from the great fairs; they needed store houses in which to keep their goods; they needed places in which their goods could be manufactured and from which their business could be transacted. City populations increased and extended beyond the historical limits of the old towns. Walls were built to defend the inhabitants and the cities became burgs, fortified places. Because they did not produce their own food, this had to be sourced from outside the city and paid for. Finally, and most importantly, cities needed to be freed from the rule and exactions of the local big man, so, as Morris Bishop remarks, 'They bought the privilege of self-government, substituting a money economy for one based on land...'[50] 'The crucial step in civic emancipation,' notes Peter Wilson, 'was the acquisition of the count's rights over a town when these had passed into the hands of the local bishop....Towns..."communalized" these jurisdictions by assuming responsibility for protecting themselves and handling internal justice and other public functions.' [Wilson 2016, 513]

The new cities were no longer just places for local administration but 'manufacturing and trading cities, associating all citizens, noble and plebeian, for defence, offence, and the pursuit of wealth.' [Bishop, 220] As the economic importance of the newly emerging towns and cities grew, so too did their political aspirations. 'Relief from the jurisdiction and taxation of feudal hierarchical superiors was the immediate prerequisite and, to achieve this, the townsmen formed themselves into associations bound by oath.' [Morrall 1970, 140] Having purchased or won their liberty from political control by the local landed magnate, the cities organised their own forms of governance in which they were unwilling to suffer interference from lord, bishop or king. 'The other liberty which most towns eventually acquired,' writes M. M. Postan, 'was fiscal autonomy, or freedom from interference and control by the royal or feudal agents. This exemption took, as a rule, the form of the "*firma burghi*" which gave the townsfolk the right to discharge their financial obligations to the King collectively, by a fixed annual sum which they levied themselves. The right to tax themselves was, in its turn, a step towards fuller and more general self-government.' [Postan, 240] Long before modern states came to be, the new cities became self-governing entities, 'freed from quasi-religious ideas of lordship and paterfamilias' and acknowledging 'an underlying equality in their inhabitants and the freedom this implied.' [Siedentop, 267] The cities of Greece and Rome had been formed from the association of families or tribes but, as John Morrall notes, 'the medieval town was basically a coming together of individuals bound primarily by an economic nexus.' [Morrall 1970, 140] François Guizot notes the almost revolutionary character of the new cities. Were we to enter such a place, a fortified place, 'defended by armed burghers,' we would see that these burghers 'tax themselves, elect their magistrates, judge and punish, and assemble for the purpose of deliberating on their affairs….In a word, they govern themselves; they are sovereigns.' [Guizot, 135] 'The twelfth century,' writes Peter Wilson, 'saw a change from economic privileges associated with market rights (*Markrecht*) to more general civic rights (*ius civitas*, or *Stadrecht*), making the town and its inhabitants a legal corporation….An important element was the power to raise the taxes and labour needed to sustain self-rule and carry out tasks ranging from street cleaning to building new city walls.' [Wilson 2016, 514]

David Landes uses the term 'commune' to describe the newly-emerging semi-autonomous cities. The essence of the commune, he says, 'lay, first in its economic function: these units were "governments of the merchants, by the merchants, and for the merchants", and second, in its exceptional civil power: its ability to confer social status and political rights on its residents—rights crucial to the conduct of business and to freedom from outside interference.' [Landes, 36]

Why would the powers that be grant liberty to the nascent cities? For one of the most basic of all human motives—for gain. There was profit to be made in city real estate and the burghers were willing to pay for their liberties.[51] Moreover, 'The rivals for the German crown after 1250 granted immunities and privileges to lords and towns to win their support…' [Wilson 2016, 493] In some cases, the local magnate simply lost control. 'Some towns owed their freedoms to the privileges granted to attract their first inhabitants as settlers, such as Freiburg in the Breisgau. In other cases, lords lost control, because their jurisdiction was over the land where the town was built, not the houses within it. Although the inhabitants initially paid ground rent, the value of their buildings soon outstripped that of the land. It became impossible for the lord to recover the ground, because he could not compensate the inhabitants for their 'improvements" to it. This helped establish the rule that residence in a town for a year and a day made a person free, greatly encouraging further immigration.'[52]

The attitude of the nobility and the church towards those involved in trade in the towns was more or less uniformly negative and hostile. The landed magnates appreciated the goods and services that the cities made available and the privileges that the burghers were prepared to pay for; on the other hand, independent-minded burghers threatened the magnates' power and prestige. The merchants were men of no family, landless and thus devoid of respectability, 'workers in the mechanical arts [horror!] who in other nations would be rejected like the plague' but were possessed of money that the nobility often lacked and needed. [Lopez, 69-70] The willingness of the merchant class to supply the nobility with money did nothing to lessen the nobles' disdain for the vulgarity of commerce, an attitude that persisted well into the twentieth century and has still not completely disappeared.[53]

The Church regarded trade as more or less inherently sinful, founded on cupidity and a crude and unchristian desire for wealth. The capital essential to the merchants' operation was, from the Church's point of view, the result of greed. The necessary borrowing and lending involved merchants in the sin of usury, and the active life of the merchant was a standing reproach to the contemplative life favoured by the Church. Despite the disdain of the nobility and the contempt of the clergy, many new cities were created by lay or ecclesiastical lords and, to attract citizens to them, advantages of various kinds were offered, including, very often, exemption from taxes that bore heavily on the rural peasantry. Into a traditional society consisting of nobility, clergy and peasantry, the rise of the cities inserted a middle class that was none of these three. M. M. Postan notes that 'the householders in medieval towns, or burgesses as they came to be known, were deemed to be personally free and held their land by "burgage tenure", a fully-free title which approached very closely the concept of full untrammelled ownership represented by the Roman *proprietas*.' [Postan, 240] The freedom characteristic of this middle class was gradually extended, through a kind of social osmosis, to the rural class. In the old social system, only the clergy and nobility had a hand in government. In the new system, a place had to be found for the burghers. So, says Pirenne, 'a new type of peasant appeared, quite different from the old. The latter had serfdom as a characteristic; the former enjoyed freedom. Like a virus, the freedom of the cities spread outside their walls to infect and disturb the rural tranquillity.' This new freedom, writes Pirenne, 'was not long in making headway even in the old demesnes, whose archaic constitution could not be maintained in the midst of a reorganized social order. Either by voluntary emancipation, or by prescription or usurpation, the seigneurs permitted it to be gradually substituted for the serfdom which had so long been the normal condition of their tenants.' [Pirenne, 156-57]

The Greek and Roman economies had money but little or no credit; the post-Roman western societies had neither money nor credit; the Europe of the revived cities had little money but extensive and sophisticated systems of credit. 'Unstinting credit,' writes Robert Lopez, ' was the great lubricant of the Commercial Revolution.' [Lopez, 72] Unless a city existed purely as an administrative capital subsisting on the forced contribution of its subjects, a city could survive and prosper only if it engaged in reciprocal trade with those that supplied its basic necessities. The rise of commerce had an effect on the development of law. Not only in the creation and operation of the *lex mercatoria* but in forcing a law made for an agricultural society to become more flexible and applicable to the new economic realities created by commerce and trade. The new city of the twelfth century 'was a commercial and industrial community living in the shelter of a fortified enclosure and enjoying a law, an administration and a jurisprudence of exception which made of it a collective privileged personality' [Pirenne, 151]

What was the effect of the rise of the cities on the status of the individual? 'That status was one of freedom,' writes Pirenne. 'It is a necessary and universal attribute of the middle class. Each city established a "franchise" in this respect.

Every vestige of rural serfdom disappeared within its walls. Whatever might be the differences and even the contrasts which wealth set up between men, all were equal as far as civil status was concerned.' [Pirenne, 138] *Stadtluft macht frei*—the air of the city makes one free, says the German proverb.

The city wasn't just an accidental collocation of like-minded people: it was, in effect, a kind of corporation. If nothing else, the walls defending the city had to be paid for and their construction arranged. This required money and organisation. 'The principal burgesses in assembly jointly undertook these charges together with a further programme—the emancipation of all inhabitants of the town from the control of the lord, the responsibility of the town as a whole for the taxes and dues laid on its members, the administration of law within the walls by magistrates chosen by the burgesses and no longer by the bailiff or steward appointed by the lord.' [Hay, 111] Being a citizen of a city carried with it not only privileges but responsibilities, not least, that of contributing to the upkeep of the city's defences. 'Everyone was obliged to participate, according to his means, in the expenses incurred in the interests of all. Whoever refused to support the charges which they involved was barred from the city.' [Pirenne, 144] It is hard to see how a libertarian could object in principle to such an arrangement. The city was a free association which one could join or not as one saw fit. If one did, one was obliged to pay one's dues. The significance of this from the point of view of liberty can't be overstated. The city was a compact between equals, resulting in political emancipation from any superior. 'The towns, fortified, administering their own law, were self-conscious islands of "liberties", that is, of specific exemptions from the normal operation of manor and fief. No more momentous event has occurred in European history than this. For the "liberty" of the town gradually became a status applicable to all its inhabitants.' [Hay, 111-12] Larry Siedentop notes that in the new cities, the 'conception of society as founded on "natural inequality" gradually gave way to a conception of society as found on "moral equality", as an association of individuals rather than an association of families.' [Siedentop, 129] The old social system dependent on land ownership and the control by landowners of those who worked the land, inevitably led to serfdom. The rise of the new cities and their commercial life wasn't simply an addition to the old system but the germ of a new one. Pirenne notes that, 'with the origin of the middle class, there took its place in the sun a class of men whose existence was in flagrant contradiction to this traditional order of things. The land upon which they settled they not only did not cultivate but did not even own. They demonstrated and made increasingly clear the possibility of living and growing rich by the sole act of selling, or producing exchange values.' [Pirenne, 158]

As was perhaps inevitable, distinctions between the haves and the have-nots reappeared within the cities and with it, conflict. The first privileges had been obtained by a small number of people acting in concert, bound together by common interests in trade, moneylending (banking in embryo) and, to some extent, landholding. They were unwilling to share their powers with those they regarded as not being of the same order as themselves. These lower orders tended to ape their betters by banding together in cooperative associations known as guilds. The relationships between the various sectors within the city varied from city to city. It would therefore be a mistake to think that cities were always and everywhere idyllic oases of peace and tranquility. There were tensions between various groups within the cities, between city and city, between the city and the local magnates and between the cities and their surrounding countrysides. George Holmes notes that many towns 'controlled substantial areas of the country outside the city walls. They did not extend the benefits of political enfranchisement to these subject areas. The republicanism of the city state existed only within the city. The role of the population of the *contado*, that is the subject countryside, was to obey and pay the taxes imposed upon them...'[54]

The distinction between 'patricians' and plebeians' wasn't the only way in which cities mirrored certain aspects of Roman history. One matter that tended to recur with distressing frequency was the emergence of a quasi-monarchical system of government within the cities. Although the republican constitutional forms were observed just as in Rome in its transformation from a Republic to an Empire, in the period before and after 1300, 'town after town...succumbed to rule by a dynastic lord and saw its *signoria* in the hands of one man.' [Hay, 117] And as has been known to every would-be ruler since the beginning of time, the 'emergency' was used as an instrument for the consolidation of political rule and many emergencies, real or imagined, were encountered. The larger and more powerful cities, whether republican or monarchical, were unable to resist the temptation to forcefully incorporate their smaller local rivals and so, for example, Florence assimilated Arezzo, Volterra, Lucca and Siena and, somewhat later, Cortona, Pisa and Livorno. This was the political and social context in which Machiavelli wrote *The Prince*.

FEUDALISM

A key element, if not *the* key element, in social organisation during much of the medieval period is often described as feudalism.[55] 'Feudalism' is a word calculated to cause fistfights to break out among respectable and normally peace-loving historians. Oakley notes the 'skepticism of those medievalists who...have launched a frontal assault on the continued deployment of the very notion of feudalism itself' as artificially uniting an infinitely varied set of historical facts. While he isn't unsympathetic to aspects of this scepticism, he notes (I believe rightly) that it is ultimately fuelled by what he calls 'a species of historiographic nominalism.'[56] As I have already mentioned, many historical period terms are radically contested but among such contested terms, 'feudalism' surely has a place of honour. Nevertheless, just as with period labels such as 'Middle Ages', 'Renaissance' and so on, it is scarcely possible to do without the term so, mindful of the limitations of all forms of labelling, I am going to go ahead and use it.

One point I would like to make right at the start is that feudalism cannot be comprehended if it isn't clearly understood that at this time political power in Europe was radically decentralised.[57] The largest and most powerful political organisation, the Roman Empire, had disintegrated and there was nothing in the West to take its place, notwithstanding the attempts of Charlemagne and his successors to do so. 'During the tenth century,' writes Larry Siedentop, 'centralized power in the Carolingian empire withered away. The fragmenting of the empire and the localizing of power led to incessant struggles between rival lords and their unruly retainers.' [Siedentop, 178] The economic circumstances of the time made each village effectively self-sufficient and this continued to be the case until the re-emergence of cities towards the end of this period. As Terence Kealey notes, 'The decline of the Roman Empire bequeathed to Europe a social and economic structure that presaged feudalism.' [Kealey, 37] Land was the source of wealth and the source of power. Whatever needed to be done needed to be done locally, whether this was the production and supply of food or the production and supply of security. If a man had not the wherewithal to provide for his own security then he obtained that security from someone able to provide it by becoming that man's dependent. 'The small man obligated himself to render services to the great man in return for protection, and he surrendered the ownership of his land and became a tenant upon the condition of paying a rent in services or goods.' [Sabine, 214-215] And M. M. Postan notes that before the barbarian conquest was completed, 'informal relations of dependence and subordination could arise between leaders and followers; in the course of the Dark Ages more formal contracts placed large numbers of freemen under the authority of great men.' [Postan, 91] 'A society arose,' writes Francis Oakley, 'in which *divided dominium* had come to be the norm and to be enshrined at the very heart of the law, one in which a multiplicity of rights could exist in any one piece of land, each protected by the appropriate legal remedy. But…feudal relationships were concerned with more than land or the payments arising from the use of land. Of its very nature, and apart from issues pertaining to divided ownership, feudalism had from the start involved a personal element of protection offered in return for services pledged.' [Oakley 2012, 200]

Feudalism, then, was a mode of personal, social, political, economic and military organisation that emerged in the West just before the end of the first millennium. Though it is no longer fashionable to say so, it appears that the source of some of the key feudal ideas can be found in the *mores* of the barbarian tribes. [see Canning, passim] First, there was the loyalty that the war chief's companions ('*comes*' or 'counts') owed to their chief. Then there was the practice of a person's putting himself under the protection of a more powerful man; in return for this protection, the protected one owed his protector goods or services. And then there was the inverse situation in which a lord rewarded by the gift of land the one who, in return, owed him service although it should be noted that vassalage had nothing intrinsically to do with landholding. [see Oakley 2010, 190] Land-gift, when it did occur, was the basis of the land tenure system characteristic of the later Middle Ages. Moreover, as M. M. Postan remarks, 'the German invaders brought with them into erstwhile Roman provinces customs and institutions which were by no means incompatible with dependent cultivation.' [Postan, 91]

What to the modern mind is perhaps most mysterious about feudalism is its combination of the personal and the contractual or, to use other terminology, status relationships and legal agreement. In the modern world, status relationships are largely confined to immediate family connections.[58] Father, mother, son and daughter—these are relationships that aren't chosen by us but are simply given to us. Apart from this limited set of status relationships, the modern mind finds it hard to conceive of anything else that might count as a status relationship. But we have a ready example to hand or, at least, we had until relatively recently. For much of modern history, marriage has been thought of as a status relationship (like family relationships) although it was one that was chosen rather than simply given and hence entered into by means of contract. Although created by contract, its status, once created, was covenantal[59] rather than contractual. This is the conception of marriage that was commonplace among Christians generally until quite recently but one which is now in swift retreat before a view of marriage that tends to regard it as merely a conditional agreement between any two adult human beings that lasts only at the pleasure of the contracting parties. In earlier times, marriage wasn't the only status or covenantal relationship that could be created through contract. The basic idea in feudalism was likewise a status relationship created through agreement, at once personal and contractual. Carlyle remarks, 'nothing could seem further apart than the conception of personal loyalty and the conception of bargain or contract as the foundation of human relations. And yet there's no escape from the conclusion that in the last resort feudal relations were contractual relations, that the vassal was bound indeed to discharge certain obligations, but only on the condition that the lord also discharged his obligations to the vassal.' [Carlyle III, 21]

Francis Oakley detects the roots of feudalism to lie in the centuries before the emergence of the Carolingian empire:

> During these centuries, with the disruption or decline of the tribal bond among the invading peoples and the decay among their Roman (or Romanized) subjects of loyalty to anything as abstract as the state, there was a growth in the practice by which lesser men, some of them warriors, attached themselves by bonds of personal loyalty to the most powerful men in their local communities. This practice, with precedents in both the Roman and German past, was the source of the first and most basic component of the feudal complex, that of the personal dependence of the warrior or vassal upon his lord. In the Merovingian Gaul of the sixth and seventh centuries, the vassals in question—strong-arm men who fought on their lord's behalf in return for protection, maintenance, and a share of the spoils—were by no means aristocratic figures. In the eighth and ninth centuries, however, vassalage appears to have risen steadily in status, and that process was accelerated as it came to be linked with the holding of a benefice (*beneficium*) or fief (*feodum*) as it came eventually to be called. [Oakley 2010, 190]

Owners of great estates could make use of their estates (perhaps could make use of them *only*) by granting part of them to others in return for the provision of services or goods. The relationship of lord and vassal was a mutual relationship, albeit a socially vertical rather than an horizontal relationship. Whatever else it might have been, it wasn't the relationship that obtains between the sovereign state and its citizens in modern times. It was both a property relationship and a personal relationship that was in part status-based and in part contractual. In feudal relationships, writes Sabine, 'there was an aspect of mutuality, of voluntary performance, and of implied contract which has almost wholly vanished from modern political relationships. It was as if a citizen might refuse to pay taxes beyond a certain amount, decline military service beyond a stipulated period, or perhaps refuse both until his liberties were recognized.'[60] Oakley notes that vassals were obliged to give aid to their lords, such aid being primarily military service when required (but for a limited period only) and, secondarily, financial contributions in certain circumstances when a vassal's lord might incur heavier than usual expenses. If a lord wanted to solicit further aids beyond those customarily due, however, these were regarded as 'gracious' aids, that is, aids that, strictly speaking a vassal was not obliged to grant. These gracious aids 'had to be asked for' and 'were to be granted only at the goodwill of the vassals...' [Oakley 2010, 195] In the thirteenth and fourteenth centuries, the consent required from the potential donors of such gracious aids was to become the engine of the rise of representative assemblies to prominence all over Europe. [see Oakley 2010, 199]

It can be difficult to avoid anachronism when evaluating this period and its complex set of social, political and personal relationships. Even the normally perspicacious George Sabine stumbles on occasion. He believes that in feudalism there was a tendency to obscure the distinction between private rights and public duties but such a judgement is anachronistic. [see Sabine, 217] To those who lived at that period, there was no confusion. The distinction Sabine draws belongs to another and a later age and is based on conceptions very different from those available to or comprehensible to medievals.

Medieval courts were made up of a lord and his vassals and their purpose was primarily to resolve disputes arising from their various relationships. This was true as much of the royal courts as of any other and even here the relationship among the members of the court, including the king, were quasi-contractual. This was sufficient to prevent the king achieving, even if he aspired to it, a total control of the reins of power. Sabine remarks with disapprobation that this system lent itself to a kind of legalised rebellion and he regards this as an intolerable inconvenience but, from the perspective of a libertarian, the possibility of what Sabine terms 'legal rebellion' is a positive, not a negative, aspect of feudalism. Once again, Sabine's judgement here is anachronistic.

Carlyle, too, does not always avoid the anachronism trap. He believes that the anarchical tendencies of feudalism tended to undermine the idea of a national society or state. Even leaving aside the objection that talk of a nation state in the context of the twelfth and fourteenth centuries is wildly anachronistic, Carlyle, in adopting this negative view of feudalism, is prey to the preconception that the national state is a consummation devoutly to be wished so that what tends to retard it is necessarily problematic. Nevertheless, there's no obvious reason, certainly not in the twenty-first century, to think of the nation state as having some intrinsic moral pre-eminence and so feudalism's anarchical tendencies (viewed as such by Sabine and Carlyle) may rather be a solution to a problem rather than a problem in search of a solution.

There were two great and all-pervading status systems in operation during this period. First, the distinction between free and unfree (serfs, villeins, sokemen) and second, the distinction between noble and commoner. As status relationships, these conditions were largely hereditary. The status of freedom, however, could be alienated. If this were done, then it affected not only the one doing the alienating but all his descendants as well. Why would anyone voluntarily change his status from free to unfree? Answer: for advantage. Often, the new serf lost his free status but gained some advantage, such as more land. His only real disadvantage in many cases was that he was now tied to this land. That was to the advantage of his master in a situation in which land was plentiful but labourers were few; on the other hand, the new serf advanced economically. M. M. Postan remarks that although 'free status was appreciated and serfdom resented for a variety of reasons….freedom was not always estimated more highly than, or even as highly as, material possessions.' If all this seems strange, a reflection on some contemporary employment practices may diminish its oddity. R. W. Southern puts it well: 'When the employee of a great industrial concern today accepts a substantial sum on condition that he will not move elsewhere, he is doing in a grand way what thousands of men, large and small, were doing in the eleventh century.' [Southern, 99]

Subordination of various kinds was a fact of medieval life. What men feared and resented in serfdom wasn't subordination but subjection to the arbitrary will of another. In fact, in terms of legal subordination, nobles were probably more subject to restricting and restraining conditions than others but these conditions weren't arbitrary. As Southern writes, 'to the medieval mind the conception of mere freedom was colourless, almost meaningless, and it was consequently difficult to imagine a freeman without imagining him a member of some privileged group….Freedom could only be defined by reference to the law, by which those who were free were governed.' [Southern, 105] Freedom wasn't so much a status like that of being a serf, but 'a quality which was attached to the status of all who were not serfs,' not so much free as un-unfree! [Southern, 106] Moreover, even though serfdom and villeinage were prominent features of medieval society, these unfree statuses were only some among many of the 'patterns in the palimpsest of rural society…other patterns, including the purely economic one, entered into the overall design, and could at times over-shadow the imprint of serfdom and freedom.'[61] 'It was,' writes Ullmann, 'these conceptions of the inferior status of the individual and the superior status of ruling authority which explains not only the prevailing medieval view of the inequality of men…but also the development of the conception of *majoritas* and its corollary of *obedientia*.' [Ullmann 1967, 13] It will come as no surprise to readers to learn that, according to Ullmann, 'the layman as such had none of the rights with which even the most insignificant member of a modern society is credited. He had, for example, no right of resistance to superior authority.' [Ullmann 1967, 16]

The personal/contractual relation between a vassal and his lord wasn't necessarily transitive. My lord's lord was not my lord, nor was my vassal's vassal my vassal. 'It was not until the twelfth century,' writes Oakley, 'with the deployment of the historical fiction that all political power had been delegated in hierarchical fashion from king to superior lord and thence to lower lord, that the type of legal systematization presupposed by the notion of the feudal pyramid became possible.' [Oakley 2010, 193] In special circumstances, as in the case of the Crusader Kingdom of Jerusalem, transitivity in lordship and vassalage could be determined by contract but this was a special case. James of Ardizone, writing in the thirteenth century, remarks the sub-vassals aren't obliged to follow their lord against the prince and may well refuse to follow him against another superior. By the thirteenth century, however, the king was understood to have some measure of jurisdiction over all persons in his kingdom; the first steps on the road to the modern state had been taken. When everything has been said, it's hard to deny Walter Ullmann's claim that 'Feudalism was indubitably the most important bridge between the rarefied doctrine of the individual as an inferior and the gradually emerging new thesis of the individual as a full member of the State, as a citizen.'[62]

LAW AND KINGSHIP

In the ninth century, kings came to be kings by a process that to us may appear confused, perhaps even incoherent, but which seemed perfectly in order to the people of that time. The process combined elements of divine sanction, election and hereditary succession, elements that might well appear to be incompatible and even contradictory. The election element in this process is of great interest to those with an interest in the progress of liberty. In this process of election, there was a mutual exchange of promises between king and people or, at least, between king and the great men in the land. This made the kingly appointment both contractual and conditional. Because of the mutuality of the relationship between ruler and people, should the ruler fail in his obligation—and his primary obligation was to rule under the law—then the bargain or compact was broken and the people released from their obligations to obey. 'Men do not undertake so great an obedience except for reasonable causes,' writes Carlyle, 'and it is not reasonable to think that they are bound to obey one who refuses to recognise the principles and conditions in virtue of which they promised obedience.' [Carlyle III, 168] This is a very different conception of kingship from that which we derive from Hollywood films which, inasmuch as it has any historical accuracy at all, is modelled on a version of kingship that's very much later than that of the period with which we are dealing. Indeed, the mutuality of obligations between king and people may be seen as the origin of the idea of the social contract. The social contract is often thought of as a modern artefact, coming to us from Hobbes or Locke or Rousseau. This isn't so. The fact of the matter is that the social contract 'is a mediaeval conception,' one that arose 'primarily out of conceptions and circumstances which were characteristic of mediaeval society.'[63]

A major difference between the medieval conception of kingship and that of the earlier Roman and later European variety was that the transmission of authority from the people to their rulers was deemed in the Roman and later European cases to be once and for all, whereas for the medievals it was continuous and, in principle, revocable. Roman law had indeed portrayed the populace as the ultimate source of imperial authority, but only as a remote and not a proximate source. The transfer of authority from the people to the emperor (the so-called *lex regia*) was once-for-all and unconditional. In contrast, the Germanic idea was that the people were the proximate source of authority and that this transfer was neither once-for-all nor unconditional. As Francis Oakley notes, however, 'It is very difficult...to determine with any degree of confidence what exactly the ancient Roman principle of the derivation of all power from the consent of the people can originally have meant and whether what the medieval civilians made of it was altogether a medieval novelty or in some degree true to its ancient historical roots.' [Oakley 2012, 86]

The choice of king was a matter that custom dictated. Normally, a king would be chosen from within the kinship of an existing ruler. The one chosen might be, but need not necessarily be, his eldest son. The choice of king from within the kinship group was regarded as a form of election, an instance of inheritance and, at the same time, the result of divine approval. 'The striking fact about many medieval kings is that they not only inherited and were elected but ruled also "by the grace of God," the three titles being not alternative but expressing three facts about the same state of affairs.' [Sabine, 210] It is worth remarking that two of the oldest and most important cases of medieval rulership, the emperor and the pope, were (and continue to be in the case of the Pope) matters of explicit election. 'There is no doubt that in the Middle Ages the authority of the ruler was conceived of as normally depending upon the election, or at least the recognition, of the community. The conception of a strictly hereditary right to monarchy is not a mediaeval conception.' [Carlyle III, 150] Not only was popular support required in the form of election or recognition, the king was also obliged to act with the counsel and consent of the great men of the kingdom.[64]

In a letter to the Pope of 1320, signed by most of the nobility of Scotland,[65] and generally known as *The Declaration of Arbroath*, the Scottish Earls and Barons requested the Pope (Pope John XXII) to 'admonish and exhort' the King of the English [Edward II] to 'leave us Scots in peace'. The letter's signatories acknowledge Robert [the Bruce] as their king according to their laws and customs, having given him their consent and assent, for it was he, they say, who relieved them from countless evils[66] and restored their freedom. Even so, they go on to assert, 'Yet if he should give up what he has begun, seeking to make us or our kingdom subject to the King of England or the English, we should exert ourselves at once to drive him out as our enemy and a subverter of his own right and ours, and make some other man who was well able to defend us our King; for, as long as a hundred of us remain alive, never will we on any conditions be subjected to the lordship of the English. It is in truth not for glory, nor riches, nor honours that we are fighting, but for freedom alone, which no honest man gives up but with life itself.' [Various, 1320] The appeal to the Pope must be adjudged a success inasmuch as some four years later, the Pope recognised Robert as the king of an independent Scotland. David Brett claims that the *Declaration* is not a feudal document inasmuch as it makes the nobles's support for the king 'provisional and renders the monarch subordinate, in the last resort to a secular, collective and abstract concept.' [Brett, 226] I believe that Brett here overstates his case, for feudal relationships were *both* status-based *and* also contractual or, better still, status relationships established *via* contract. I can see nothing in the *Declaration* that would subvert what I regard as its essentially feudal character.

The nature and character of original Germanic kingship is much disputed.[67] Among nineteenth-century German scholars, the idea was expressed that German kings were popularly elected and that this kind of elective kingship persisted in the kingdoms that emerged in the wake of the dissolution of the Western Roman Empire. This type of elective kingship was limited and, in the end, could be called to account by a popular assembly. This idea has been called into question by more recent scholarship, largely for the not inconsiderable reason that there appears to be little direct evidence for it. In the twentieth century, a more restricted theory of the elective nature of Germanic kingship has found support, involving not a wide popular election but the support of the king by his nobles. Archbishop Hincmar of Rheims held that 'the sustained support of a sizeable faction of the aristocracy in a particular region was what in fact made a king, both in the sense of installing him and of supplying him with the means to rule.' [Nelson 1988, 217] Still, this was by no means a proto-democratic form of election so that 'Whatever the force of the "elective" process so often associated with the older Germanic kings…and surviving for centuries in the form of the "people's recognition" embedded in the coronation rituals of so many medieval kingdoms, it certainly did not involve anything even roughly approximating to legitimation by consent.' [Oakley 2012, 144]

Throughout history, kings have had not only the obvious functions of political and military leadership but also the sacral role of being, in effect, chief priest for the whole people, their representative to the numinous world.[68] This is so whether we are speaking of the Chinese Emperor, whose right to rule depended on the mandate of heaven, or, in the case of Rome, the Pontifex Maximus, (now a Papal title), whose function, divided in the republic from those who held the various magistracies, was reintegrated with the holder of the imperium under Augustus, or the many and varied minor rulers in other times and places, such as the kings of pre-Christian Ireland. The Chinese Emperor's duty was to 'bridge the gulf between heaven and earth and, by scrupulously performing a cyclic round of rituals and sacrifices geared to significant calendric moments, to secure the maintenance of order, cosmic no less than mundane, natural no less than societal.' [Oakley 2010, 19] The ascription of divinity to the Roman emperors is typically viewed as an uncharacteristically un-Roman aberration, a matter of the down-to-earth Romans being, as it were, contaminated by alien oriental influences. However, given the 'always and everywhere' nature of sacral kingship, the ascription of divinity to the emperors could rather be viewed as a return to a kind of historical normality from the temporary aberration that was the Republic![69]

Any significant natural or social disorder or, in the worst case, disaster, was taken to be an indication that the relationship between earth and heaven was out of joint and, perhaps, a sign that the mandate of heaven had been taken away from its current holder. In the fourth century AD, the historian Ammianus Marcellinus noted that, for the Burgundians 'a king is called by the general name Hendinos, and, according to an ancient custom, lays down his power and is deposed, if under him the fortune of war has wavered, or the earth has denied sufficient crops; just as the Egyptians commonly blame their rulers for such occurrences.' [Marcellinus, 28.5.14] And as Francis Oakley notes, even as late as 1527, the Swedish King was complaining that if the weather was bad, the peasants blamed him 'as if he were a god and not a man.'[70] Denys Hay makes the point that the barbarian kings were as much religious leaders as they were political leaders. [see Hay, 60] However that may be, the early barbarian Christian kings were never regarded as priests in a sacramental sense although they did exercise certain ecclesial or quasi-ecclesial powers, such as issuing ecclesiastical legislation, nominating bishops and so on.[71]

Even if the Germanic kings were elected by the *Thing* and operated within various limits, it doesn't follow, then, that they weren't regarded as sacral figures. 'The *Thing* was itself...a sacred, cultic assembly through which flowed to the monarchy the sacred power of the whole community. It is not to be viewed anachronistically as some sort of "secular" or even "democratic" body.' [Oakley 2010, 149]

Oakley is critical of Walter Ullmann's sharp distinction between the bottom-up naturalistic element of king selection by means of the deliberations of the folk assembly, and the top-down super-naturalistic element of selection 'by the grace of God'. He comments, 'the Germanic peoples of the pre-Christian era knew no sharp distinction between the natural and supernatural and intuited the world of nature itself as pulsating to the rhythm of the divine.' [Oakley 2010, 182]

The theory of the divine right of kings, which came to prominence in the seventeenth century, might seem to have sprung out of thin air. It was, however, in some ways a final, if distorted, expression of a notion, prevalent and popular in the medieval period, that kings had a sacred function.[72] If it isn't seen against its medieval background, the theory of the divine right of kings takes on the appearance of a social and political erratic. Francis Oakley remarks, 'the sacral dimension of kingship, rather than being totally obliterated during the Sturm und Drang of the Investiture Contest, enjoyed for centuries something of an enduring half-life Fluctuating it may have been, but it remained powerful enough to be able to draw the medieval papacy itself into its magnetic field and, later on in the sixteenth and seventeenth centuries, to generate a species of decaying autumnal energy in the theory of the divine right of kings' [Oakley 2012, 39]

But if a king's sacral role, in whatever form it was manifest, provided a note of continuity between medieval and modern notions of kingship, the medieval notion of kingship also differed in significant ways from its early modern incarnation. To state this difference simply, if somewhat crudely: early modern kings aspired, and to some extent realised their aspirations, to become absolute rulers;[73] medieval kings may have had similar aspirations but if they had, given the prevailing laws, customs and the social and economic structures of their realms, they had little hope of realising them.

Even though the barbarian invaders were willing to adopt and adapt elements of Roman culture, not least Roman law, the essential cultural elements of their societies were largely indigenous. The working out of these indigenous cultural elements was to have a major effect on the development of European society. As Sabine puts it, 'allowance must be made for the appearance in the early Middle Ages of ideas about law and government which had not existed in antiquity and which yet, by their gradual incorporation into common modes of thought, had an important influence upon the political philosophy of western Europe.' [Sabine, 199] In their fundamental approach to law, the Germanic peoples weren't essentially different from other groups, such as the Celts, whose mode of life was based on the tribe and whose economic existence was semi-nomadic.[74] Still, it can't be denied that the societies of the Goths, the Franks, the Langobards and the Celts were status-based, just as much as Roman society had been, and that by the fourth century AD 'the Germans had formed veritable, albeit tribal, principalities and evolved complex political systems marked by hierarchical gradations of power and possession. In these gradations, the lowest position was occupied by slaves, the topmost by a tribal aristocracy.'[75]

Perhaps the most significant aspect of archaic law was that it was under-stood as being a constitutive element of the whole social group, not something additional or superfluous but the very thing that made that group to be what it was and gave it its identity. It should be noted that while the embeddedness of the law in customs and *mores* and its separation from political authority gave a measure of freedom to individuals from hierarchical authority, individuals as individuals had little or no status. In early Irish society, as Nora Chadwick notes, 'the individual counted for little in law. It was the kinship group which was ultimately responsible for the actions of its individual members.'[76] To be a member of that social group was to be bound by that law; to reject that law in a serious and permanent fashion was to put oneself outside the group and to become, in fact, an outlaw. This law was originally not written down but was embodied in the day-to-day customs and procedures by which the group operated. To begin with, tribal law was the law of the group, not of the land on which the group live. But gradually, as the tribes settled down, this began to change so that, for example, around the mid 600s, there was a common law for both Romans and Visigoths in Spain.

In these early barbarian kingdoms, law codes were enacted relatively early. The earliest knowledge we have of such barbarian systems of laws is in their reduction to writing in the sixth century and following. In 506, Alaric II produced the Lex Romana Visigothorum whose influence persisted in parts of France for around 700 years. The Burgundian King Gunobad produced the Lex Romana Burgundionum in 517. These codes weren't the production of new law by a ruler or a legislative body but simply the reduction to writing of the existing customary law of the tribe with an admixture of Roman law. Hay notes, 'there is no *legislation* in the Middle Ages proper, the place of law-making in modern society being taken by the interpretation of custom. That is to say, law-making was not regarded as being the function of a sovereign individual or of a sovereign body.' [Hay, 59]

Archaic law wasn't the command of anyone, whether a king or community. It was the communal acknowledgement of that which was already binding on everyone. It was primarily custom and not something made and, to the extent that it was an outcome of a legislative act, it was a record of that which was already binding. 'The notion of law as we have it—of a rule imposed by human authority, capable of being altered by that authority when it likes, and in fact, so altered habitually—could not be conveyed to early nations, who regarded law half as an invincible prescription, and half as a Divine revelation.'[77] It isn't until around the thirteenth century that we have the first glimmerings of laws being made in certain conditions by a suitable authority. Carlyle writes, 'at least as early as the thirteenth century there began to reappear the conception of laws as being made, not that the idea of custom as law disappears, but that there gradually grew up alongside of this the conception that laws could be made under certain conditions and by suitable authority,' and Roberts notes that '…in the eleventh century the Roman Law of Justinian was to begin to be accepted as the basis for good jurisprudence in western Europe too. It was powerfully biased towards seeing law as something made by rulers rather than (as in Germanic tradition) handed down in custom. This would appeal to many later princes, though not always to their subjects.'[78] Even at this late stage, however, these laws were still not the arbitrary dictat of a prince but were made only after suitable deliberation and consultation with the great men and advisors of the prince and they had to be received by the whole people.[79]

Common to all archaic legal thought was one central idea and that was that the law wasn't something that any one person or any group of people made from the beginning. 'It was imagined to be as permanent and as unchangeable as anything in nature,' writes Sabine, '…rather like a circumambient atmosphere which extended from the sky to the earth and penetrated every nook and cranny of human relationship.' [Sabine, 202] Such law wasn't a mere incident of social life; it was constitutive of it. Such a conception of law runs its head straight against our contemporary conception of law as something made by a body specially constituted to make it, a law that is minute, particular, detailed, complex and largely unknowable if not in fact incomprehensible. What is especially true about our contemporary law is that it is protean, ever changing and largely unknowable, even by legal professionals. Archaic law changed too, of course, but it changed slowly and in step with the lived experience of the people whose law it was. If situations arose that weren't simply repeats of previously adjudicated cases, then principles already embodied in legal norms were extended to cover them. If something came up that had very little or perhaps no parallel with anything on record, then the case was decided from the beginning on principles consistent with the existing law. In archaic law, then, custom is king and tradition is normative and prescriptive. Whatever has been done for any considerable period of time is presumptively lawful.

On the other hand, throughout the whole medieval period, for almost a thousand years, the universal reach of the Church and its concern with certain issues—marriage, family, and inheritance—provided a countervailing unifying tendency that operated against the plurality of systems of law. Despite this, however, much law remained particular and local so that it was still true at the time of the French Revolution that almost all private law in France was a function of the locality in which the parties lived. All over the Empire, 'Justice involved finding law appropriate to circumstances. From its foundation, the Empire used an eclectic combination of written and unwritten laws. The latter, often labelled as "customs", were not necessarily inferior to written systems, which themselves should not be interpreted as direct precursors to later practice. Medieval lawyers distinguished between *lex* as law deriving from contracts between rulers and subjects over (usually) specific matters, and *ius* as law in general expressed variously in statutes, court verdicts, and broader concepts of fairness and justice.' [Wilson 2016, 604]

That the law belongs to the people as a whole does not imply any particular conclusions about government. Sabine writes, 'There was, and indeed is, nothing incongruous in the idea that a locality, a borough, or even a whole people, might make decisions, present their grievances, be called to account for their negligence, and give their approval to policies for which they had to provide money or soldiers. It is a modern convention that all this is done by elected representatives, but everyone knows that the convention often is not true.' [Sabine, 206] The key idea here is that the people, or specific groups of people, has a corporate identity the 'mind' of which can be expressed by its leaders. In traditional or customary societies, this may very well be true without there being any formal mode of determining this 'mind', and even today it should be possible to have something like this in voluntary bodies that have a constitutional mode of determining their group thinking. But it isn't at all so obvious today that a modern democratic constituency is any such thing.

The ninth century inherited the Roman and Patristic teaching on the divine source of secular authority and the corresponding obligation on Christians to offer no resistance to their rulers and to obey them in all things save a direct command to violate God's laws. This inherited tradition comes into sharp conflict with the indigenous beliefs and practices of the Germanic tribes, one significant aspect of which is that the authority of rulers is limited and the obligation of obedience to that authority conditional. The clash between these two theoretical tectonic plates is the source of much of the apparently confused political discussions and political practice of this period and the following centuries. The traditions of the Germanic tribes were innocent of any subscription to the theory of unlimited and absolute obedience to one's rulers. The German tradition 'knew nothing of an unlimited authority in the ruler, but a great deal of the relation of the king to his great or wise men, and even to the nation as a whole; for the most part the churchmen outside of Italy, and even to a large extent in Italy, were men of the Teutonic race or tradition.'[80]

For ninth century thinkers, a king without justice was no king but a tyrant. The law is the law of the community and the king, as part of the community, is as bound by that law as anyone else. The law isn't a matter of the king's will. 'So far as laws have been made, they proceed from the whole nation. They have,' says Carlyle, 'been made with the general consent of the faithful subjects of the king....the king does not make laws by his own authority, but requires the consent and advice of his wise men and, in some more or less vague sense, of the whole nation." [Carlyle I, 234; 238] The law of the ninth century was made up of the following elements: traditional tribal law; the remnants of Roman law; and the new laws or amendments of the old laws made with the consent of the people. A new element, canon law or the law of the Church, makes its appearance, at first fitfully, and then with ever greater force. 'The political theory of the ninth century, then, very clearly recognises that there is an authority in the Church which extends over all persons, even the most exalted in society....There is, then, a body of law in the Church which all men must obey and to which all other laws must conform themselves.' [Carlyle I, 275; 277]

Kings, then, were empowered to maintain justice under law, a law that was neither a matter of their devising nor simply an expression of their will. The role of the king in law making in such societies was limited to ascertaining and declaring the pre-existent law, not in making it by the exercise of his own naked will. As a member of the people of which he was king, the king was as much subject to the law as any other. [see Duchesne, 481-488] Sabine notes, 'the king was felt to be obliged not only to rule justly rather than tyrannously, but also to administer the law of the kingdom as it actually was and as it could be ascertained to be by consulting immemorial practice. The king could not lawfully set aside rights which custom guaranteed to his subjects or which his predecessors had declared to be the law of the land.' [Sabine, 207] Kings and those who ruled had mutual obligations to maintain justice and law. Should the king fail to maintain justice then he could be deposed, even slain, if he acted tyrannously, or his subjects could be released from their obligations to him. Manegold of Lautenbach, one of the earliest masters of theology, argued in his 1085 tract *Ad Gebehardum liber* in favour of the possibility of deposition of kings since a king who lapsed into tyranny is no different in principle from a swineherd who fails to look after his pigs. If the swineherd can be dismissed for failing to observe the conditions of his contract, so too can a king![81]

The pre-eminence of the law applied even to the highest in the land. The king was under God and under the law and, as Bracton wrote, 'There is no king where will rules and not the law.' Carlyle concludes, 'the feudal system was in its essence a system of contractual relations...the contract was binding upon both parties, on the lord as much as the vassal....feudalism represents the antithesis to the conception of an autocratic or absolute government.' [Carlyle III, 74] If kings acted capriciously or against the dictates of customary law, then they could be, and were, resisted, this despite whatever St Paul or Gregory the

Great was deemed to have said about the necessity for passive obedience. Of course, the king was granted a great deal of discretion to act in circumstances that of necessity did not permit consultation and this dimension of kingship, not unreasonable in and of itself, was to provide a platform for the gradual extension of kingly powers over the succeeding centuries. Francis Oakley notes that even the staunchest supporters of monarchical rule failed to realise the extent to which, in the emerging feudal system, 'the bonds that united his *fideles* with the king, always in some measure reciprocal, had with the extension of vassalage matured into a relationship that was legally contractual and capable of imposing real limitations on the exercise of royal power.' [Oakley 2012, 139] In a similar fashion, in the first part of his trilogy, Oakley wrote, 'To the older Germanic belief that the king was responsible for the welfare of his people and in some sense accountable if he failed in that responsibility, and to the quasi-reciprocal nature of the bond between the king and his *fideles* so often reaffirmed by oath during the Carolingian era, feudalism eventually added the more specifically legal conviction that the king as feudal lord was himself bound by the laws and customs of this kingdom.' [Oakley 2010, 198]

Koos Malan describes what he calls 'medieval constitutionalism' as comprising 'popular sovereignty' and ' sovereignty of the law'. Such political authority as existed was legitimated by 'a bona fide contractual relationship between the political leadership and the people' and law, 'either as natural law or custom…was a *permanent* and *unchangeable*, or at least slow-moving premise' which was 'not actively created, but merely found and afterwards articulated or promulgated.' [Malan, 22] Political authority rested on three principles: 1. All authority is derived from God; 2. Law, representing the principle of justice, is supreme in political society; 3. The proximate source of political authority is the community, for the law is the law of the community and legitimate authority requires either election or at the very least recognition by the community. One might wonder if there was some tendency in the period under discussion to deny the first of these principles, that all authority is derived from God. In a celebrated, if somewhat anomalous, passage from a letter written at the height of his struggle with the Emperor Henry IV, Pope Gregory VII described secular rulers in the starkest and least flattering of terms. 'Who does not know,' he writes, 'that kings and leaders are sprung from those who—ignorant of God—by pride, plunder, perfidy, murders—in a word by almost every crime, the devil, who is the prince of this world, urging them on as it were-have striven with blind cupidity and intolerable presumption to dominate over their equals; namely, over men? To whom, indeed, can we better compare them, when they seek to make the priests of God bend to their footprints, than to him who is head over all the sons of pride and who, tempting the Highest Pontiff Himself, the Head of priests, the Son of the Most High, and promising to Him all the kingdoms of the world, said: "All these I will give unto Thee if Thou wilt fall down and worship me?"'[82] This startling passage was written by Gregory in defence of his actions against Henry IV. In yet other of his writings, however, Gregory expresses himself more in line with the standard approach to the legitimacy of secular power. Carlyle writes, 'we must not isolate the phrases of the two letters to Hermann of Metz, but must consider them along with the sentiments he expresses at other times….we find that the purpose of [the letters] was to refute the arguments of those who maintained that it was not lawful or proper for the Pope or any one else to excommunicate the king or emperor.' [Carlyle III, 96]

On the other hand, other prominent ecclesiastics were somewhat sceptical about the divine ground of secular authority. Cardinal Deusdedit makes a distinction between God's permission and God's active will— *Eo quidem permittente, non tamen volente*; to permit is not to will—and does so in the context of the famous passage in *1 Samuel* where the Israelites demanded a king. Deusdedit points out that given *Hosea* 8:4 'They set up kings without my consent; they choose princes without my approval,' it simply can't be the case that any king, simply by virtue of being a king, has to be deemed to have God's active support. God's providence rules over all so that everything that occurs happens with Divine concurrence, but it does not follow from this that all that happens is in accord with God's active will and approval, otherwise, murder and theft would have to be regarded as divinely approved! Carlyle tries to explain away Deusdedit's comments by reading them as simply distinguishing between the remote and immediate sources of authority but that isn't what Deusdedit in fact says and the force of his distinction can't be so easily deflected. [83]

Cardinal Deusdedit's distinction between God's permission and God's active will is important. There is an understandable tendency to believe that if all authority comes from God that God must therefore actively approve of that authority. To deny that all authority comes from God would be to question the scope of Providence; but to deny that all such authority is divinely approved appears to be in accord with the words of Scripture in *Hosea*. If secular authority is always and everywhere divinely justified, how could it ever be justly resisted? Some—Augustine (apparently), Atto of Vercelli, and, as we shall see, the magisterial Reformers—seem to think it can't but then what are we to make of the actions and words of Gregory VII? Moreover, it's difficult to deny that *Hosea* 8:4 appears to ground a distinction between God's permission and God's active will. Furthermore, other thinkers believe that the function of kingship is inextricably linked to the promotion and defence of justice so that a king who does not promote justice is, in fact, no king; resistance to such a one would then not fall under any supposed scriptural injunction to obey one's rulers. A real king governs according to law and obeys it himself; a tyrant, in contrast, oppresses the people and voids the law. 'The principle that unless the king is just and rules according to law he is no true king is the first principle of the mediaeval theory of government, and was firmly held even before the great political agitations of the eleventh and twelfth centuries compelled men to think out the real nature of their political convictions.' [Carlyle III, 128]

We can find the differing strands endemic to medieval thought reflected in the writings of Henry de Bracton. Bracton is keen to assert that the king is without equal in the realm because, were it otherwise, he couldn't rule. But if the king is subject to no other man, he is all the more subject to God and to the law, since law is what makes him to be king. Bracton sums up what it is that the king must swear to at his coronation: peace for the Church and for all Christian people, the repression of wrongdoing, and equity and mercy. The king is under no man but under God; he is also under the law. I have already mentioned that Bracton states that 'there is no king where will rules and not the law.' It is worthwhile citing more from the passage in which we find this statement: 'The king has no equal within his realm; subjects cannot be the equals of the ruler, because he would thereby lose his rule, since equal can have no authority over equals; nor *a fortiori* a superior, because he would then be subject to those subjected to him. The king must not be under man but under God and under the law, because law makes the king. Let him therefore bestow upon the law what the law bestows upon him, namely, rule and power; for there is no *rex* where will rules rather than *lex*….There ought to be no one in his kingdom who surpasses him in the doing of justice, but he ought to be the last, or almost so, to receive it, when he is plaintiff.' In another quite remarkable passage, Bracton even goes so far as to assert that though the king has no human superior, his counts[84] constitute, in a way, his master. 'The king has a superior, namely, God. Also the law by which he is made king. Also his curia, namely, the earls and barons, because if he is without bridle, that is without law, they ought to put the bridle on him.'[85] This passage may well be a later interpolation but, even if it isn't by Bracton himself, it illustrates the point that its author thought that the king was under the law.[86]

There was, perhaps, an ineliminable tension between the role of the king, considered as the one assigned the care and guidance of those over whom he was set in authority, and what might be done in the event that a king failed to exercise his functions in an appropriate manner. The king's status as the Lord's anointed, writes Ullmann, 'in practice removed him from the control of the very men for whose guidance and care he was established in the first place; the king as the Lord's anointed could not be withstood or resisted or subjected to any control by those over whom divinity has set him.' [Ullmann 1967, 26]

There can be no doubt that the medieval conception of kingship contained commingled elements capable of development in a number of directions. On the one hand, the king was *primus inter pares*, first among equals, but subject to the law like any other and, in some sense, answerable to his companions. He was also deemed to be elected in some way or other and party to a contract or a quasi-contract. 'There could be no succession to kingship, even in the context of usurped rule, without some recognition of the king's fitness to rule or an election by parts of the community or the making of promises to uphold law and custom.'[87] This element comes from the tribal background and the archaic law tradition. On the other hand, the king was the chief magistrate, accountable to no one and answerable only to his conscience. This element reflects some aspects of the archaic law tradition but, perhaps even more so, the understanding of *imperium* coming out of Roman law and legal institutions. When we come to the high Middle Ages, to the twelfth and thirteenth centuries, the role of the king begins to change, not least because kings can now aspire to model their polities on the legal and administrative pattern provided by the Church. The restricted and bound form of early medieval kingship 'gives way to a new form of kingship, a form involving centralization of authority and the growth of bureaucracy.' [Siedentop, 260]

In summary, then, the legacy of the Germanic tribes to political thought was threefold: first, law was supreme over everyone, including the king; second, the office of king required either election or community recognition in some form; and third, the legitimacy of kingship was conditional upon the king's performance of his obligations under the law.

JOHN OF SALISBURY

John of Salisbury had a stellar diplomatic and administrative career. He was secretary to Theobald, Archbishop of Canterbury and, in that capacity, provided legal advice and acted as the archbishop's envoy. His work brought him into contact with many of the most important men all over Europe, including the first and only English pope, Nicholas Breakspear (Adrian IV). Secretary to yet another archbishop of Canterbury, Thomas Becket, he found himself caught between Becket's zeal (of which he did not entirely approve) and Henry II's attempt to bend the Archbishop to his will.

John is the proverbial man of one book, one very large book, and that book is the *Policraticus* (1159). It is the first and only effort in the medieval period to give an overarching comprehensive and systematic account of political philosophy, all the more significant in that it was produced before the widespread recovery of Aristotle's works in the West. Nevertheless, despite having no direct access to Aristotle's practical writings, he managed to grasp the essence of Aristotle's practical philosophy from those Aristotelian works that were available, notably the *Organon*, Aristotle's six books on logic. At first glance, the *Policraticus* can indeed appear to be a confused *mélange* of disparate and contradictory ideas. Undoubtedly the earliest medieval work of political theory, it is in many ways a throwback to more ancient norms and does not really reflect the socio-political realities of its times. It tries to weld together the received traditions coming from Cicero and Seneca, the Roman lawyers and the fathers of the Church. John blends, or attempts to blend, all these seemingly disparate authorities into a coherent whole, in a manner that was characteristic of the dialectical method developed in the study of theology and law and philosophy. 'This was the first application to politics of the method…which had already been applied—much more rigorously—to Roman law by Irnerius and his successors, to theology by Abelard (under whom John of Salisbury had studied), and to canon law by Gratian…' [Berman 1983, 280] Nederman warns us that in reading the *Policraticus* we should strive to avoid anachronism. John was writing in and for the twelfth century, not the twenty-first. In summary, then, the *Policraticus* isn't just a book on political theory but is much more wide-ranging in its subject matter and although running to around a quarter of a million words it was, by medieval standards, an immediate and runaway best seller.[88]

The organic metaphor that is prominent in Plato's political thought is introduced into Western thought by John, although with his own elaborate, indeed fantastically bizarre, additions.[89] On the basis of this metaphor, political rule is natural to man, not something that is forced upon human societies; on the other hand, it isn't a mere matter of voluntary contract either. Political rule, then, is neither coercive nor contractual. Here is how John expresses his version of the organic metaphor: 'The position of the head in the republic is occupied, however, by a prince subject only to God and to those who act in His place on earth, inasmuch as in the human body the head is stimulated and ruled by the soul. The place of the heart is occupied by the senate, from which proceeds the beginning of good and bad works. The duties of the ears, eyes and mouth are claimed by the judges and governors of provinces. The hands coincide with officials and soldiers. Those who always assist the prince are comparable to the flanks. Treasurers and record keepers...resembles the shape of the stomach and intestines; these, if they accumulate with great avidity and tenaciously preserve their accumulation, engender innumerable and incurable diseases so that their infection threatens to ruin the whole body. Furthermore, the feet coincide with peasants perpetually bound to the soil, for whom it is all the more necessary that the head take precautions, in that they more often meet with accidents while they walk on the earth in bodily subservience; and those who erect, sustain and move forward the mass of the whole body are justly owed shelter and support.' [*Policraticus* 5.2 (67)] Many chapters of the *Policraticus* are devoted to the detailed working out of this metaphor. Alexander d'Entrèves remarks that 'the organic metaphor is intended to stress the point that the State cannot be reduced merely to "force-relations" between individuals. The State is a living, articulate force apparently different from that of the individual who compose it.' [d'Entrèves 1967, 18]

Another of John's key political ideas is based on the opposition between moderation and lack of moderation. The good ruler is characterised by moderation; the tyrant by lack of it. The good ruler allows his subjects enough freedom to fall into sin and error unless such should endanger the Christian faith or the temporal security of the realm. In a refreshingly liberal moment (and anticipating Lysander Spooner), John recommends that a distinction should be made between vices and crimes. Crimes can't be endured but vices may be tolerated. [*Policraticus* 6.26]

In contrast to the good ruler, the tyrant, is one who tries to stifle the liberty of others and, as tyrant, he unfortunately has the power so to do.'There is wholly or mainly this difference between the tyrant and the prince: that the latter is obedient to law, and rules his people by a will that places itself at their service, and administers rewards and burdens within the republic under the guidance of law...princes are concerned with the burdens of the entire community.' [*Policraticus* 4.1 (28)] Tyrants may be public, private or ecclesiastical but only public tyranny is now of political interest. In its day, however, John's characterisation of ecclesiastical tyranny had particular resonance.

The non-tyrannical ruler, the prince, is entitled to obedience and may not be resisted, even if his conduct is less than edifying. [*Policraticus* 6.24] The justification for this position is, of course, the ubiquitous passage from *Romans* 13; since all power is ordained of God, whoever resists this power, resists God. Or so it seems. [see *Policraticus* 5.6] Nevertheless, should the prince command one to break the commandments, then one's allegiance is to God rather than man. [*Policraticus* 6.25]

Another area in which John dialectically synthesises apparently divergent elements is royal succession. A king can be made by descent, by election or by the reception of a divine mandate. These would appear to be three different and mutually exclusive methods. John sees no problem with accommodating all three. 'Heredity creates a presumptive claim to the throne, which must be confirmed by election, but the priesthood—that is, the papacy—has a decisive voice when it is in the overriding interest of the church to exercise it. The theory on which this is based is that royal title is derived from God either through heredity or through election or through such other means as God in a given instance chooses to apply.' [Berman 1983, 285]

Apart from the modernity of his method, what John is most famous, even notorious, for is his apparent defence of tyrannicide. At first, John seems to present an account of rulers that is in accord with the commonly held view that, whatever their character, rulers hold their power from God and therefore must be obeyed. On the other hand, those rulers who command us to do what is contrary to faith must be disobeyed. John can't deny that tyrants are yet ministers of God inasmuch as they punish evil and restrain the wicked. Even so, if they can't be restrained, it is honourable to kill them. [*Policraticus* 8.18] The very title of Book 8, chapter 20 of the *Policraticus* is 'That by the authority of the divine book it is lawful and glorious to kill public tyrants, so long as the murderer is not obligated to the tyrant by fealty nor otherwise lets justice or honour slip.' A tyrant is a ruler whose assumption of power is unjustifiably acquired. This would appear to be based on a distinction between lawful kings whose power is justifiably acquired and tyrants whose power is not. How are we to tell the difference? John writes, 'it is not only permitted, but it is also equitable and just to slay tyrants. For he who receives the sword deserves to perish by the sword. But 'receives' is to be understood to pertain to he who has rashly usurped that which is not his, not to he who receives what he uses from the power of God. He who receives power from God serves the laws and is the slave of justice and right. He who usurps power suppresses justice and places the laws beneath his will. Therefore, justice is deservedly armed against those who disarm the laws, and the public power treats harshly those who endeavour to put aside the public hand.' [*Policraticus*, 3.15 (25)] The tyrant in one who 'oppresses the people by violent domination, just as the prince is one who rules by the laws.' And whereas the prince is to be 'loved, venerated, and respected' as an image of God, 'the tyrant, as the image of depravity, is for the most part even to be killed.' [*Policraticus* 8.17]

Francis Oakley deems what he terms 'John's blunt advocacy of tyrannicide' to have received an excessive amount of comment but, given the uncompromising nature of John's words, it's not difficult to see why they should have fascinated and continue to fascinate readers of the *Policraticus*. [see Oakley 2012, 99] Some, however, go much further and call into question completely John's apparent justification of tyrannicide. Jan van Laarhoven, in his exhaustive analysis of John's writings, argues that the point of John's multiple *exempla*—Roman Emperors, biblical kings and commanders, English barons, and so on—is to demonstrate that tyrants come to a sticky end and that tyrannicide, in fact, often goes unpunished rather than to provide a positive argument for its justification. Van Laarhoven concludes: 'Anyone who has read the long treatise of Book VIII must be disappointed if he had expected an elucidation of a real theory of tyrannicide. Once a little clause of iii.15 is read as a kind of imperative, these 67 pages do not only cause a thorough disappointment, but they pose real troubles for maintaining such a "theory".' He continues: 'There is nothing in these texts on the right of resistance, nothing on other forms of government, nothing on any sovereignty of the people, nothing on practical questions like "Who could be the murderer?" or "Who should be the judge to exonerate him?" [van Laarhoven, 327] John of Salisbury *is* concerned with the phenomenon of tyranny in human history, concerned to show its prevalence, its inhumanity, its embodiment of pride and injustice. Is there, then, a theory of tyrannicide in the *Policraticus*? According to van Laarhoven, the answer to this question is—no. 'The *Policraticus*...is not a handbook for murderers, but a guide book for people in the *polis*, especially for those who *ex officio* have to dominate themselves—rather than others.' [van Laarhoven, 329]

So, the Dark Ages wasn't quite as dark as it is often portrayed as being, and the Middle Ages wasn't just a regrettably long period when the lights went out over Europe. Kenan Malik is, I believe correct, when he writes, 'the idea of the "Dark Ages" is a self-serving phrase that later thinkers employed to elevate the intellectual standing of their own era by suggesting that, between the glories of Greece and Florence, there had been nothing but cultural darkness.' And while it is true, as he notes, that 'the first half of the Middle Ages may have lacked intellectual spark,' he is also correct when he says that 'the culture of Europe after the turn of the millennium, a culture that produced Aquinas and Ockham, Giotto and Dante, was unquestionably sophisticated, restless and curious.' [Malik, 163, 164] To one of these sophisticated thinkers we now turn.

Notes

1 See Roberts 1997, 156-157 and Bautier, 209-226.
2 Oakley 2012, 44; see Haskins, 303-340; see also Luscombe & Evans 1988, passim. No one who appreciates fine writing and keen historical insight should fail to consult Francis Oakley's splendid three-volume series on the emergence of Western political thought in the Latin Middle Ages (Oakley 2010, 2012 & 2015). I am gratified to find that on many salient points, especially the indispensability of grasping the significance of the Middle Ages if one is to understand modern and contemporary political thought, our judgements essentially converge.
3 Knowles, 80; see also Tierney 198.
4 In this chapter, which is more historical than philosophical, I am heavily reliant on writers such as M. M. Postan, R. W. Southern, David Knowles, Henri Pirenne, Morris Bishop, Robert Lopez, Francis Oakley and Brian Tierney.
5 See Parkinson 1958, 92-101.
6 Anyone interested in the dynamic effect of the Cistercians on European culture should consult Berman 2010/2000 and Jamroziak.

7 *Quod omnes similiter tangit, ab omnibus comprobetur*—Codex 5, 59, 5 §§2-3. David van Rey-brouck notes the religious context in which elections originally arose, commenting that, in the eighteenth century, 'To give the people a voice...a formal procedure was invented, the election, a procedure until then mainly used to choose a new pope. Voting was familiar as a means of achiev-ing unanimity among a group of like-minded people, such as cardinals, but in politics it would now have to promote consensus between people seen as virtuous within their own circles.' [van Reybrouck, 46]

8 Parkinson 1958, 96; see Morrall 1970, 114-116. To my set of concrete social institutions of City, University and Monastery, Parkinson adds Chivalry, of which he remarks that it 'implies an idea of equality as between adult and trained members of a particular order or society' and a kind of sportsmanship which 'makes it possible to reconcile conflict...with courtesy, and even friendship between opponents...' [Parkinson 1958, 95; see Morrall 1970, 108]

9 Berman 1983, 4, emphasis in original.

10 Berman 1983, 4; Greenaway, 42.

11 See Gurevich, 5. Alan Macfarlane argues strongly against a Whig interpretation of the devel-opment of individualism, making a case especially for English exceptionalism in this regard. The significant elements of individualism were, he believes, to be found well-developed in England as early as the thirteenth century and stem from, among other things, a blending of persisting German-ic elements with the Judaeo-Christian tradition.

12 See Knowles, passim; see Holmes 1975, 134-142; and see especially all three volumes of Rash-dall. That the University of Bologna was organised for and by students is reasonably well-known, but A. B. Cobban believes that 'The notion of student power is a crucial one for an understanding of university development in the pre-Reformation era' and that 'Organized student protest is vir-tually coeval with the emergence of universities in southern Europe where it became endemic for about two hundred years.' [Cobban, 165]

13 'The universities did not start out as crucibles for an intellectual revolution,' writes David Duncan. 'Originally referred to as *universitas magistrum* or *universitas scholarium*—"university of masters" or "university of students"—at first they were little more than gatherings of students in certain cities, attracted by masters whose fame allow them to charge fees.' [Duncan, 215]

14 Not all scholars are prepared to grant university status to Salerno. Cobban writes that while Salerno 'has sometimes been reckoned among Europe's earliest universities, 'it did not measure up to the normally accepted view of university status.' [Cobban, 37] While it did possess an Arts school, it provided no higher-level instruction in anything other than medicine.

15 See Cobban, 48-95. John Morrall notes that 'It is hard to see how the universities could have come into being in any other *milieu* than that of the towns.' [Morrall 1970, 148]

16 See Rashdall 1936a, 25-73, especially 49-59.

17 Knowles, 164; see Rashdall 1936a, passim.

18 For a comprehensive treatment of the Italian, German-speaking, Polish, Swedish, Hungarian, Danish, Scottish and French universities (Paris excepted), see Rashdall 1936b. The English univer-sities are treated in Rashdall 1936c, 1-324.

19 Rashdall 1936c, 343-344; see also Haskins, 127-152.

20 Oakley 2012, 149; see also Haskins, 368-397.

21 'Texts which became available from Islamic sources were often at first regarded with suspicion. It persisted until well into the thirteenth century, but gradually a search for reconciliation between the classical and Christian accounts of the world got under way. So it came about that the classical heritage was recaptured and rechristened in Europe.' [Roberts 1997, 217]

22 After the reception of Aristotle's logic came the translation and reception of his work on the soul (*De Anima*), his *Metaphysics* and his *Nicomachean Ethics*. Finally, in the middle of the thir-teenth century, the reception of Aristotle's work was completed with the production of Latin trans-lations of his *Politics*, *Economics* and *Rhetoric*.

23 See below the discussion on the challenge presented to the Christian West by the doctrines of the Spiritual Franciscans. See also Mirgeler, 121-129.

24 'Aristotle's writings set a framework for the discussion of biology, physics, mathematics, logic, literature an criticism, aesthetics, psychology, ethics and politics in Europe for 2,000 years....His is a vast achievement.' [Roberts 1997, 38]

25 See Hegel 1956, 355-359. The relevant passage can be located in other editions in Part IV, §1, chapter II.

26 See Reilly, 13, 44. 'Where are the sciences of the Persians that 'Umar ordered to be wiped out at the time of the conquest?', asks Ibn Khaldûn. [Khaldûn, 39]

27 When it came to technology,' writes David Landes, 'Islam knew areas of change and advance: one thinks of the adoption of paper; or the introduction and diffusion of new crops such as coffee and sugar; or the Ottoman Turkish readiness to learn the use (but not the making) of cannon and clocks.' Landes adds, significantly, 'But most of this came from outside and continued to depend on outside support. Native springs of invention seem to have dried up.' He quotes Lynn White to the effect that, '"For nearly five hundred years the world's greatest scientists wrote in Arabic, yet a flourishing science contributed nothing to the slow advance of technology in Islam."' [Landes, 55, citing White 1964, 227]

28 See Griffel, passim; see also Duncan 1998, 175-191. Whether or not al-Ghazali played the role commonly ascribed to him, it is none the less true that the consequence of the triumph of the Ash'arite school of theology (founded by Abu al-Hasan al-Ash'ari, 873/4-935/6) over its Mu'tazi-lite rival (the Mu'tazilite school was founded by Wasil ibn 'Ata, 700-748) resulted in what Robert Reilly describes as 'The Closing of the Muslim Mind.' 'There are,' writes Reilly, 'two fundamental ways to close the mind. One is to deny reason's capability of knowing anything. The other is to dismiss reality as unknowable. Reason cannot know, or there is nothing to be known. Either approach suffices in making reality irrelevant. In Sunni Islam, elements of both were employed in the Ash'arite school. As a consequence, a fissure opened between man's reason and reality—and, most importantly, between man's reason and God. The fatal disconnect between the Creator and the mind of his creature is the source of Sunni Islam's most profound woes.' [Reilly, 4] David Landes notes that, for over three hundred years, 'Islamic science and technology far surpassed those of Europe' but then, he remarks, 'something went wrong. Islamic science, denounced as heresy by religious zealots, bent under theological pressures for spiritual conformity.' [Landes, 54; see also 413-414]

29 See the rich and suggestive discussion of the political implications of Islam in Greenaway, 278-293. For a topical (and controversial) discussion of similar issues, see Hirsi Ali, passim. The renowned historian of the Middle East, Bernard Lewis, remarks that whereas 'throughout Christian history, and in virtually all Christian societies, it has been accepted that there are two authorities, dealing with two different matters—God and Caesar, church and state, religious and secular affairs,' in contrast, there is 'in Islamic history, and more specifically in the early formative events which are the common possession of Muslims everywhere and which shape their corporate awareness, an interpenetration of creed and power, of correct belief and worldly dominance that has no parallel in Christianity and that has had no parallel in Judaism since the earliest books of the Old Testament.' [Lewis 2012, 232, 232-233]

30 'Islam does not, as Christianity does, separate the religious from the secular. The two constitute an integrated whole.' [Landes, 54]

31 If the *Qur'an* were to the play the role that Christ plays in (orthodox) Christianity it would have to be a divine person which, given the fundamental Islamic aversion to *shirk* (anything that might be construed as compromising the unicity of Allah) is hard to credit.

32 Oakley 2012, 59. 'In 1169,' writes Émile Derenghem, 'the Almohad caliph Abu Ya'qûb Yusûf summoned Averroes to Marrakesh. Rather disturbed at first, the latter at last understood that the caliph was about to adopt the bold ideas of the philosophers. It was at the ruler's own wish that he undertook his great commentary on Aristotle....Unfortunately the third Almohad, Abu Yûsuf Ya'qûb....sent Averroes into temporary exile and had his books burnt, just as the Almoravids had burnt those of al-Ghazâli. The liberal free-thinking philosopher and the Sûfis or mystics were likewise condemned. Now these two schools were the living forces in the Muslim civilization of the time. They balanced one another and made progress possible. Their elimination or their eclipse brought about that of authentic living culture.' [Derenghem, 85-86]

33 'The Arabic word for "individual"—*al-fard*—does not have the commonly understood implication of a purposeful being, imbued with the power of rational choice,' writes Ali Allawi. 'Rather, the term carries the connotation of singularity, aloofness or solitariness....*Al-fard* is usually applied as one of the attributes of supreme being, in the sense of an inimitable uniqueness....Therefore to claim the right and the possibility of autonomous action without reference to the source of these in God is an affront and is discourteous to the terms of the relationship between the human being and God. The entire edifice of individual rights derived from the natural state of the individual or

through a secular ethical or political theory is alien to the structure of Islamic reasoning.' [Allawi, 11]

34 See Robert Reilly, passim. Albert Mirgeler comments, 'The stage of development which Christianity had reached already in the thirteenth century involved an inner contradiction. On the one hand, it had succeeded in splitting up the political and cultural unity which had taken shape and on the whole been maintained under the rule of a sacral kingship. Moreover, the process had gone so far that not only was public life divided off into the two spheres of Church and State, but there was also a rift at the very heart of personal and social life: the Christian was bound simultaneously by two loyalties....And yet, on the other hand, Western civilization was maintained as an historical unity and indeed as a Christian historical unity.' [Mirgeler, 130]

35 Greenaway, 282. For an account of the contemporary relevance of this dispute, see Malise Ruthven, 40.

36 Albert Mirgeler remarks that Scholasticism 'at its best first embodied that pioneer achievement which has since been the prerogative of science in the fabric of Western life and society. This achievement rests on the fact that, through the separation of the spiritual and the secular, the first distinction in principle came to prevail against a spiritual and political unity which, although now obsolete from the intellectual standpoint, continued for centuries to dominate European life in practice and found in modern times a very anachronistic resurrection in the secularized form of the totalitarian state.' [Mirgeler, 99]

37 For a brief, yet comprehensive treatment of the scholarship of law, Roman and Canon, in the Middle Ages, see Ullmann, 1975. Ullmann links the emergence of an autonomous science of politics with the development of law, writing that fourteenth century sources reveal, 'the emergence of "politics" as an autonomous science that took its place next to professional jurisprudence....one of the main ideas common to both was that of justice: jurisprudence worked backwards from the law to find the contents of justice, whereas politics operated with the a-legal idea of justice and therefore looked forward to the future law.' [Ullmann 1975, 283-284]

38 Hittinger, in Rommen, xxi.

39 Abelard (1079-1144), apart from being one half of a famous (or notorious) dramatically doomed love affair with Héloïse, was an 'intoxicating lecturer and a proponent of the new-fangled logic of Aristotle' who is credited by some 'with single-handedly attracting the original crowds of students that made possible the university in Paris.' [Duncan 1998, 215]

40 See Guizot, 132-151; see also Wickham, 591-692.

41 Venice was, according to Robert-Henri Bautier, 'the first city in the Middle Ages to live by trade alone.' [Bautier, 65] Not only was Venice an 'outpost of the Byzantine economy', so too were the southern Italian towns of Salerno, Naples, Amalfi and Bari. [Bautier, 67] The southern area of Italy, known in classical times as Magna Graecia had, as this name suggests, been for much of its history associated culturally and economically more with Greece than with the contiguous areas of the Italian peninsula.

42 Venice, writes Robert-Henri Bautier, 'entirely dominated the Adriatic; it ruined Ravenna and Pola, attempted to do the same to Zara, and allowed Ancona only a limited economic life.' In 1187, the Eastern Roman Emperor granted the Venetians 'unlimited freedom to trade in the empire, with total exemption from taxes. As a result, the Byzantine empire came under the economic control of the Venetians before the time of the first Crusade.' [Bautier, 104]

43 Pirenne, 61. 'The Venetians worked their way into the markets of Egypt and the Levant (they never showed the qualms expressed by less successful rivals about trafficking with the infidel) and, above all, those of the eastern empire.' [Roberts 1997, 206]

44 The activities of Pisa were directed largely towards the central Mediterranean, its attention being concentrated 'on the corn lands of the Maremma, Sardinia, Sicily and southern Italy, the iron of Elba and the Lucca district, and wool and leather from the north African ports (Bougie, Bône, Collo, Djidjelli).' [Bautier, 105]

45 Lopez, 69; see Bautier, 98.

46 To take advantage of the rapidly expanding trade in the Baltic, 'new towns were found all along the Baltic shore, notably Rostock (1200), Wismar (1228), Stralsund (1234), Stettin (Szczecin) and Elbing (Elblag: 1237), Danzig (Gdańsk: 1238), Greifswald (1238), and Königsberg (Kaliningrad: 1255). The region between the Elbe and the Oder (Mecklenburg, Pomerania, Prussia and even Poland) was systematically colonized, and towns were found in Baltic and Slav territory to develop

the agriculture and commerce of this vast area: Berlin (1230), Thorn (Toruń: 1233), Frankfurt-on-the-Oder (1253), Breslau (Wrocław) and Cracow (1257).' [Bautier, 122]

47 For a lively account of the central yet generally under-appreciated cultural and economic importance of the North Sea to the development of European civilisation see Pye, 221-241.

48 For more on the Hanseatic League, see Brand (ed.), 93-168. For a standard historical account, see Schildhauer.

49 Chris Wickham makes the point, however, that 'the leadership of medieval Italian cities was not ever exclusively commercial, whether mercantile or artisanal....Most of Italy's major landowners lived in cities...and they always had a central role to play in city politics.' [Wickham 2015, 8; see Morrall 1970, 143]

50 Bishop, 209; see Postan, 240.

51 It is important to understand the particular nature of liberty as it came to be understood in the process of the urbanisation of Europe. Communal self-government wasn't necessarily present from the beginning but 'emerged from the eleventh century, beginning in Italian towns...becoming general by 1200. This complex process frequently pitted lords and commons against each other, and many of the concessions were only won through violent protest....The new freedoms were never equal or universal *Liberty*, but instead local and particular *liberties* that bound the community and its inhabitants within the wider web of rights constituting the Empire's legal order.' [Wilson 2016, 508; see 12]

52 Wilson 2016, 515-516. David Landes argues that rulers were willing to grant privileges to towns and townsmen for two reasons. 'First, new land, new crops, trade, and markets brought revenue, and revenue brought power. (Also pleasure.) Second, paradoxically, rulers wanted to enhance their power within their own kingdom: free farmers (note that I do not say "peasants") and townsmen (*bourgeois*) were the natural enemies of the landed aristocracy and would support the crown and other great lords in their struggles with local seigneurs.' [Landes, 37]

53 Today, critics of capitalism are very happy to express these criticisms from the positions of comfort that capitalism makes possible.

54 Holmes 1975, 77; see also 74-83.

55 See Guizot, 52-69; Duchesne, 466-470; Morrall 1970, 98-134 and Roberts 1997, 149-151.

56 Oakley 2010, 189, 190; see 177-199.

57 'Most people today,' remarks John M. Roberts, 'are used to the idea of the state. It is generally agreed that the world's surface is divided between impersonal organizations working through officials marked out in special ways, and that such organizations provide the final public authority for any given area. Often, states are thought in some way to represent people or nations. But whether they do or not, states are the building blocks from which most of us would construct a political account of the modern world. *None of this would have been intelligible to a European in 1000...*' [Roberts, 402, emphasis added]

58 See Guizot, 77-79 for a brief but illuminating discussion of the differences between the patriarchal family, the clan, and the feudal family.

59 A covenant, writes Jonathan Sacks, 'is a bond, not of interest or advantage, but of belonging. Covenants are made when two or more people come together to create a "We". They differ from contracts in that they tend to be open-ended and enduring. They involve a commitment of the person to another, or to several others. They involve a substantive notion of loyalty—of staying together even in difficult times. They may call, at times, for self-sacrifice.' [Sacks, 151]

60 Sabine, 217; see also Kealey, 33-46.

61 Postan, 136; see also Siedentop, 165-177.

62 Ullmann 1967, 104; see Oakley 2010, 180-181.

63 Carlyle III, 12; see Oakley 2010, 183.

64 For a succinct historically based treatment of the barbarian kingdoms, see King 1988, passim.

65 Duncan, Earl of Fife, Thomas Randolph, Earl of Moray, Lord of Man and of Annandale, Patrick Dunbar, Earl of March, Malise, Earl of Strathearn, Malcolm, Earl of Lennox, William, Earl of Ross, Magnus, Earl of Caithness and Orkney, and William, Earl of Sutherland; Walter, Steward of Scotland, William Soules, Butler of Scotland, James, Lord of Douglas, Roger Mowbray, David, Lord of Brechin, David Graham, Ingram Umfraville, John Menteith, guardian of the earldom of Menteith, Alexander Fraser, Gilbert Hay, Constable of Scotland, Robert Keith, Marischal of Scotland, Henry Sinclair, John Graham, David Lindsay, William Oliphant, Patrick Graham, John Fenton, William Abernethy, David Wemyss, William Mushet, Fergus of Ardrossan, Eustace Max-

well, William Ramsay, William Mowat, Alan Murray, Donald Campbell, John Cameron, Reginald Cheyne, Alexander Seton, Andrew Leslie and Alexander Straiton, and the other barons and free-holders and the whole community of the realm of Scotland.

66 The evils are itemised: 'massacre, violence, pillage, arson, imprisoning prelates, burning down monasteries, robbing and killing monks and nuns and yet other outrages without number which he [the King of the English] committed against our people, sparing neither age nor sex, religion nor rank' and are such that 'no-one could describe nor fully imagine unless he had seen them with his own eyes.' [Various, 1320]

67 Almost the whole of Francis Oakley's *The Mortgage of the Past* is devoted to the theme of the persistence of kingship as the 'dominant form of government in Europe' [Oakley 2013, 1; but see especially 36-37, 133-134, 144-145 and 161-168] Walter Ullman makes the point, a point that to me seems irrefutable, that 'for the greater part of the Middle Ages government and its underlying principles were considered first and foremost as integral parts of applied Christian doctrines...' [Ullmann 1975, 12]

68 See the section on 'Kingship' in Chapter 1.

69 See Oakley 2010, 32-39; 145, 146.

70 Oakley 2010, 147; also, 26-29.

71 For an extensive discussion of the notion of theocratic monarchy, see Canning, chapter 2, section 2. For a discussion of the relationship between kingship and priesthood see Canning, chapter 1, sections 3 & 4.

72 The persistence of the idea that kings had a sacral function does not contradict Malan's claim that the notion of the 'divine right of kings enjoyed no substantial support during the Middle Ages' but that 'it forcefully entered the stage with the Reformation, in particular as a result of Luther's doctrine.' [Malan, 56]

73 We can take the year 1,500 as a pivotal point around which the idea of kingship changed radically. 'The relationship of lord and vassal which, with the vague claims of pope and emperor in the background, so long seemed to exhaust political thought, gave way to an idea of princely power over all the inhabitants of a domain which, in extreme assertions (such as that of Henry VIII of England that a prince knew no external superior save God) was really quite new.' [Roberts, 402]

74 See Berman 1983, passim, Scott 2009 and Chadwick 1970.

75 Postan, 84; see Kelly 1988, passim.

76 Chadwick, 113; see also Casey 2010a.

77 Bagehot, 178. 'The Parliament of today is a ruling body; the mediaeval Parliament was, if I may say so, an *expressive* body,' writes Walter Bagehot. 'Legislation as a positive power was very secondary in those old parliaments. I believe no statute at all, as far as we know, was passed in the reign of Richard I, and all the ante-Tudor acts together would look meagre enough to a modern Parliamentary agent who had to live by them. But the negative action of parliament upon the law was essential to its whole idea, and ran through every part of its use. That the king could not change what was then the almost sacred *datum* of the common law, without seeing whether his nation liked it or not, was an essential part of the "tentative" system.' [Bagehot, 181 182]

78 Carlyle III, 45; Roberts 1997, 93.

79 At this period, law was largely the product of custom, with some royal codes and decrees attached. A sophisticated understanding of the law wasn't really available at this time and the analytic tools necessary to understand just what conception of law was operative at this period only became available in the high Middle Ages. With the emergence of the Dominicans and Franciscans in the high Middle Ages, two distinct intellectual approaches were taken to understanding the nature of law. Broadly speaking, the Dominicans tended to understand law in terms of reason (*lex-ratio*), whereas the Franciscans tended to see it as in terms of will (*lex-voluntas*). This dispute isn't of mere historical interest. Hittinger, in his introduction to Rommen's *The Natural Law*, says that 'Rommen was convinced that the Fascist idea of the state as an organic expression of a collective racial or ethnic will was the legacy not just of Rousseau but of medieval Franciscan mysticism and supernaturalism.' [Hittinger, in Rommen, xxix]

80 The German kings 'have not unlimited or arbitrary powers,' writes Tacitus. When it comes to making decisions, 'About minor matters the chiefs deliberate, about the more important the whole tribe. Yet even when the final decision rests with the people, the affair is always thoroughly discussed by the chiefs....then the king or the chief, according to age, birth, distinction in war, or eloquence, is heard, more because he has influence to persuade than because he has power to com-

mand. If his sentiments displease them, they reject them with murmurs; if they are satisfied, they brandish their spears.' [Tacitus, *Germania*, §§7, 11; 2009, 666, 668-669]

81 See Oakley 2012, 35, 162-163; but see Ullmann 1967, 23. According to David Luscombe, Manegold argued that 'the king is hired or contracted by the people to do a job. The elective principle was an aspect of the making of a king and oaths were taken at royal coronations. If the king chooses to act the tyrant, he can no longer claim fidelity because he has broken faith and the compact. Hence the people should be free of his lordship.' [Luscombe 1982, 769]

82 Letter from Pope Gregory VII to Hermann, Bishop of Metz, 15 March 1081. Original text in *Monumenta Gregoriana*, ed. Jaffe, 453; for a translation of most of this letter, see Tierney 1988, 66-73.

83 See Cardinal Deusdedit, '*Libellus contra invasores et symoniacos*' in ed. Mai, Nova Bibliotheca Patrum, VII, III, 77-114; ed. Sackur, Mon. Germ. Hist. Libelli de lite, II, 300-365.

84 From the Latin *comes*, meaning fellow traveller, comrade or companion.

85 Bracton, Vol. 2, 110.

86 Much later, Calvin employs the same image of the bridle in a related political context.

87 Luscombe 1988, 163. 'The element of election,' writes Peter Wilson, 'was mixed with other forms and the monarchs should not be considered a kind of life president. Those involved never enjoyed an entirely free choice. The number of candidates was always limited to a select group considered *Caesarable*.' He continues, '…it is important to remember that until the late Middle Ages contemporaries did not regard "elective" and "hereditary" monarchies as sharply defined constitutional alternatives.' [Wilson 2016, 296, 301]

88 References to and citations from this text are to and from the abridged (1991) Nederman edition in the CAMBRIDGE TEXTS IN THE HISTORY OF POLITICAL THOUGHT series. Anyone interested in a complete English version of the whole text should consult the Dickinson and Pike translations. See Oakley 2012, 91-99, for a succinct account and evaluation of John's political thought; see also Greenaway, 86-94.

89 For more on the importance of the organic metaphor in John's thought, see Struve, passim.

Chapter 11

THOMAS AQUINAS

By nature all men are equal in liberty but not in other endowments
—Thomas Aquinas

The distinction between freedom and liberty is not accurately known;
naturalists have never been able to find a living specimen of either
—Ambrose Bierce

Thomas Aquinas (1225-1274) was born into a family of minor but socially well-connected Italian nobility of Norman origin. As a very young man, he joined the newly formed and very far from respectable Dominican Order in opposition to his family's wishes, spending the remainder of his life as a mendicant friar working as a university professor, much of the time at the University of Paris. In the space of just thirty years or so, he wrote[1] some eight million words—two massive theological summaries, collected volumes of disputed questions on various topics, and a raft of commentaries on Scripture and on the works of Aristotle. With the exception of an early incident of kidnapping (he was the kidnappee!) and a bit of academic blackleg strikebreaking, Thomas's life was largely socially uneventful. Intellectually, however, he was one of those who led the successful fight to have the newly translated (into Latin) works of Aristotle accepted by the academic and ecclesiastical establishments, a critical moment in the intellectual life of Europe. He lived and worked during one of the most intellectually revolutionary periods in European history. In the fifty years between 1220 and 1270, the period that corresponds with Thomas's life, the Christian West rediscovered almost the entire body of Aristotle's writings. George Sabine writes, 'the extraordinary intellectual rebirth that began in the latter years of the twelfth century…[was]…one of the most brilliant in the history of Europe.' He sees this rebirth as being due 'chiefly to the new universities, especially Paris and Oxford, and to the two great Mendicant Orders in the church, the Dominicans and the Franciscans.'[2]

If the universities and the new mendicant orders were the institutions driving the intellectual ferment, the material on which these institutions fed were the works of Aristotle enveloped in a cocoon of Arabic and Jewish commentary. As one might expect, the arrival of this intellectual material wasn't greeted by everyone with the same degree of enthusiasm. One attitude towards it might be summarised simply but not unfairly as holding that if it contributed something not in the teachings of the Church then it was either false or heretical; if, on the other hand, it was consonant with Church teaching then it was redundant. The Church authorities wavered and the writings of Aristotle were, for a time, prohibited. But nothing could stop the Aristotelian tsunami and before long, the status of Aristotle's writings had moved from prohibition to tolerance, then to acceptance and finally to promotion.

But the works of Aristotle were not the only explosive set of intellectual materials that came into the hands of a world scarcely prepared for it. The *Institutes* and *Digest* of the Emperor Justinian, that great sixth century codification of Roman law, was another source of intellectual stimulation.[3] Here we had a mass of legal material on which human reason might exercise itself. A method was required to deal with this sophisticated philosophical, legal and religious material and one was found—the scholastic method. This was, as I have already mentioned, an essentially dialectical and open-ended procedure, consisting of the assembling of authoritative texts on either side of a given question and the rational resolution of the question in the light of those authorities. To use this method effectively required the development of powers of discrimination and an ability to make distinctions, often subtle distinctions, a practice that could, and did on occasion, collapse into an arid form of logic chopping.

LAW

Thomas wrote little explicitly on politics. Only the first book and the first four chapters of the second book of the *De Regimine Principum* are authentically Thomas's, as are books I, II and III (chapters 1-6) of his commentary on Aristotle's *Politics*. Thomas's treatment of political themes is very much parenthetical to his theological concerns and what he has to say is, with the exception of *De Regimine Principum* and his commentary on Aristotle's *Politics*, largely contained in discussions of other topics. For example, his account of political authority is largely to be found in his treatment of what things were like for men before the Fall. Still other political themes are treated in passing in his discussion on the particular vices and virtues. 'As opposed to his interspersed and fragmented political writings,' writes James Greenaway, 'he [Thomas] presents a coherent legal theory' and this theory of law provides the thread that ties his disparate remarks on politics together into a coherent whole.[4]

For Thomas, political authority can only exist and properly be exercised in accordance with law. That being so, his understanding of what law is cannot but be central to his theory of the political community. Law, for Thomas, is something much more than a system for regulating the affairs of men; it is part of the system of divine government. *Eternal Law* is God's design for the whole of creation. It is 'the ideal of divine wisdom considered as directing all actions and movements' and all other forms of law ultimately derive from it.[5] *Divine Law* is, in effect, what is given to us by revelation in Scripture. *Natural Law* is 'the participation of the eternal law in a rational creature,' a reflection of Eternal Law as we see it manifested in creatures. [1a2ae, q. 91, a. 2] It gives to each kind of thing ends in accordance with its nature. For man, those ends are the preservation of his own life, life in society, the generation and education of children and the search for truth. *Human* (or *Positive*) *Law* is law as it applies specifically to men in their concrete and practical circumstances. It is an ordinance of reason for the common good made and promulgated by those who have charge of the community. [1a2ae q. 90, a. 4] In what follows, we shall be concerned primarily with natural law and positive law and the close relationship between them.

What is this natural law that plays such a foundational role in Thomas's thought on politics? Natural law is participation by man in the eternal law according to reason. But practical reason deals with contingent matters so that, although there is a certain necessity in its general conclusions, the further one moves from generality, the more the conclusions are open to exceptions. Moreover, in practical matters, when it comes to the conclusions of practical reason, not only is it the case that we do not have the same standard of truth or rightness for everyone, it is also the case that the conclusions aren't known by everyone either.

The natural law is by and large incapable of change but it can be modified in two ways. The first way in which the natural law can change is by addition. Examples here would be the institution of slavery (*servitus*) and the institution of private property (*distinctio possessionum*), both issues of concern to libertarians.[6] The natural law can also change by subtraction. Nothing can be taken away from the first principles of the natural law or from its secondary principles inasmuch as these are immediate conclusions from first principles, but in some particular cases or a limited set of examples it can change. [see 1a2ae q. 94, a. 5] It is also possible that the natural law may be practically or prudentially unobservable in certain specific circumstances. Thomas gives us the standard example of the repayment of a debt. Given that it is right to act according to reason, it is right, because reasonable, to repay one's debts. And so it is, in general, but not in every set of particular circumstances, as, for example, if the money were to be used to make war on one's own country. Thomas writes, 'the law of nature, as far as general first principles are concerned, is the same for all as a norm of right conduct and is equally well known to all. But as to more particular cases that are conclusions from such general principles, it remains the same for all only in the majority of cases, both as a norm and as to the extent to which it is known. Thus in particular instances it can admit of exceptions: both with regard to rightness, because of certain impediments, (just as in nature the generation and change of bodies is subject to accidents caused by some impediment), and with regard to its knowability. This can happen because reason is, in some persons, depraved by passion or by some evil habit of nature...'[7]

If it is to have moral force, human or positive law must be derived from natural law. This may happen in two ways. The first way is as a conclusion from general principles. So, from the principle 'Harm no one' we get the more specific 'Don't murder, rape, commit fraud or steal'. Laws thus derived are understood to concern themselves with actions that are *malum in se*—wrong in and of themselves and never justifiable. The second way in which positive law may be derived from natural law is by means of a determination to particular instances so that, from the general principle, 'Transgressors should be punished,' *some* form of punishment is specified but no particular form of punishment more so than any other. Positive laws such as these seem to relate to what is called *mala prohibita*—things that can be one way or the other but not all of which can obtain at the same time, such as which side of the road one is to drive on. [see 1a2ae q. 95, a. 2, c.]

Positive law can be divided into two kinds: the law of nations (*ius gentium*) and the law of the city or municipal law (*ius civile*). All the conclusions that can be derived directly from the natural law belong to the *ius gentium*. These include the norms that govern commerce and other activities necessary for social intercourse. These are derivable from the natural law because man is naturally a social animal. The norms that are derived from natural law as particular applications make up the law of the city, or municipal law, which every city will determine according to its particular requirements. Law should be sufficiently general to cover the various component parts of the city and do so over time as one generation succeeds another. [1a2ae q. 96, a. 1] 'Natural law,' writes d'Entrèves, 'is the pattern of all positive legislation: what is stressed is the duty of the State rather than the right of the individual. Natural law is the basis of political allegiance, the ground upon which social and political relations can be secured and comprehended.' [d'Entrèves 1959, xiv]

Brian Tierney notes that, for Thomas, the positive law 'does not prohibit all evils but only the graver ones that harmed others such as murder or theft.' [Tierney 2014, 73] The reason for such toleration is that the attempt to suppress all evils might be counter-productive, making the bad even worse. [see 1a2ae, q. 96, a. 2] But even though Thomas notes the *practically* ill advised nature of attempting to regulate all vices by law, it does not seem to some interpreters of his works that he rejects it in *principle*. John Finnis believes this interpretation of Thomas's position to be mistaken. Divine law is one thing, human law, another. Human law coercively restricts external acts in civil society by which people relate to one another. This form of external communication is a matter of justice and the other virtues are involved, if they are involved, only incidentally.[8] The object of human law is a specific form of common good which can be called the public good. This public common good is 'distinct from the private good of individuals and the private common good of families and households.' [Finnis, 226] The objects of the public good are interpersonal, person-to-person, other-related external human acts which are to be regulated so as to produce justice and peace. 'The position,' Finnis remarks, perhaps surprisingly, 'is not readily distinguishable from the "grand simple principle" (itself open to interpretation and diverse applications) of John Stuart Mill's *On Liberty*.' [Finnis, 228] In his *De Regimine Principum*, Thomas says that a task of the prince is 'to restrain his subjects from immorality and lead them to virtuous action.'[9] Doesn't this statement support the claim that the objective of political rule goes well beyond merely external and other-related conduct to the promotion of virtue in the fullest and most complete sense of that term? No. The prince's task isn't that 'of leading the people to the fullness of virtue by coercively restraining them from every immorality.' It is, rather, 'leading people to those virtuous actions which are required if the public weal is not to be neglected, and of upholding peace against unjust violations.' [Finnis, 231]

For Thomas, law needs to be adapted to the capacities of those to whom it is to apply. We do not apply the same laws to children that we apply to adults, nor should we make the same demands of those lacking in virtue that we make of the virtuous. 'Now human law is enacted on behalf of the mass of men,' writes Thomas, 'the majority of whom are far from perfect in virtue. For this reason human law does not prohibit every vice from which virtuous men abstain; but only the graver vices from which the majority can abstain; and particularly those vices which are damaging of others, and which, if they were not prohibited, would make it impossible for human society to endure: as murder, theft, and suchlike, which are prohibited by human law.' [1a2ae q. 96, a. 2]

Laws can be **just** by virtue of their *object*, as directed to the common welfare; or by virtue of their *author*, when enacted within the powers of whosoever enacts it; or by virtue of their *form*, when the burdens they impose are distributed in such a way as to promote the common welfare. As all men are part of a community, so everything that a man is or possesses has a relationship to that community. The preservation of the whole may demand the sacrifice of a part and, provided that due proportion is observed, laws of this kind oblige in conscience. Laws can be **unjust** for two reasons. First, they may be detrimental to human welfare, either with respect to their *objects* (when a ruler enacts laws burdensome to his subjects which are designed for his own benefit and not for common prosperity) or with respect to their *author* (if a legislator should exceed his powers) or with respect to *form* (if the burdens, even though connected to the common welfare, are unequally distributed.) Such laws do not generally bind in conscience except when not to observe them would cause scandal or disorder. If this be so, then a man is obliged to give up his right. Secondly, laws may be unjust if contrary to divine goodness—'We must obey God rather than man'[10] The legislator does not have a blank cheque. Laws that would require persons to do things that should never be done should be disobeyed. [see 2a2ae q. 57, a. 2, ad. 2] Generally, laws that are made from greed or vanity and not for the common good, or laws made outside the authority granted to the lawmakers; or laws that apportion burdens unfairly—these aren't so much laws as acts of violence. These can be disobeyed unless disobedience would cause disproportionate disorder. Human law is law properly speaking only if it proceeds from right reason; if not, it's an unjust law and is characterised by violence. Despite saying this clearly (and correctly), Thomas goes on to add that even unjust laws 'to the extent that they retain the appearance of law through their relationship to the authority of the lawgiver, derive in this respect from the eternal law.' The justification for this odd claim is, yes, you've guessed it: *Romans* 13! [1a2ae q. 93. a. 3 ad. 2]

Does Thomas's adoption of the Aristotelian conception of the naturalness of the political community undermine the status of the individual and, if so, how is this reconcilable with the Christian emphasis on the importance of the individual? The answer seems to be as follows. The unity of the state isn't an organic unity, merely a unity of order. In this unity, the individual is neither lost nor absorbed. 'The integration of the individual in the whole,' writes d'Entrèves, 'must be conceived as an enlargement and an enrichment of his personality, not as a degradation to the mere function of a part without a value of its own.' [d'Entrèves 1939, xix] The individual is not completely absorbed by the State. The role of the state isn't to make men perfectly virtuous; it confines its attention only to the outward sphere of human action, not to the inner thoughts and desires of man. Human law is not competent to judge of interior acts, such as acts of the will or intention, which receive no external embodiment. 'For human law does not punish the man who meditates murder but does not commit it, though divine law does punish him...' [1a2ae q. 100, a. 9]

Law directs human action with the power of compulsion. Man is subject to law in two ways: the first way is that in which something that is ruled is subject to the rule, so if anyone is subject to a power, he is subject to the laws coming from that power; the second way is as one who is constrained by the one who constrains him. The virtuous and the just are not subject to law in this sense because constraint is violence against the will, and the wills of the virtuous are at one with the law; the wicked, however, whose wills are opposed to the law, are constrained. [1a2ae q. 96, a. 5]

Human law can be changed, if necessary, and indeed sometimes it must be changed. Thomas, however, prefers not to have too much change in law. Law can be changed either by a development in custom or by some kind of direct legislative action. The latter is something to be resorted to only when the requirements of the common good demand it. It is not to be expected that lawmakers will get their laws perfectly right in the beginning so that laws are bound to be to some extent imperfect and deficient. With increasing knowledge and experience, these can be perfected. Furthermore, if circumstances change then the law should change too but such changes should be made only for the public welfare. Custom being of such importance in matters of law, laws shouldn't be changed lightly, for changes in the law decreases its coercive power. Only if the change is necessary and significantly for the better should the law be changed. 'Thus law should never be changed unless the benefits which result to the public interest are such as to compensate for the harm done. This may be the case if the new statutes contain great and manifest advantages; or if there is urgent necessity due to the fact that the old law contains evident injustice, or it observance is excessively harmful.' [1a2ae q. 97, aa. 1-2] The law is made for the generality of cases and for the common welfare so 'if it should happen that the observance of such a law would be damaging to the general well-being, it should not be observed.' Unless it's a case of emergency, the decision of whether or not to dispense from the law in the common interest isn't one to be made by just anybody. This is a decision for rulers. Nevertheless, if the danger to the common well being is imminent and there is no time to refer the matter to the authorities, then 'necessity itself 6]carries its own dispensation: for necessity knows no law.' [1a2ae q. 96, a.]

AUGUSTINE AND ARISTOTLE—FROM LAW TO POLITICS
St Augustine notoriously thought that the line between what emperors, kings and princes do and what bandits do is very thin. If man had not sinned, political domination of man over man wouldn't have been necessary and couldn't be justified. St Paul too is generally believed to hold that the state, although less

than salubrious in many respects, is necessary to keep sinful men in some kind of order. 'A carnal world is going to be vicious,' writes McClelland, 'so God in his mercy gives men the state to batten down some of the social consequences of man's original sin. The state's law may bear a relationship to God's law in some purely formal sense because everything is related to God but in practice the law and its enforcement can be as ungodly as it pleases and still be law.' [McClelland, 111]

For most of the early medieval period, the Augustinian view of politics had held centre stage. With the recovery of the works of Aristotle, in particular, his *Politics*, all that was to change. In the early thirteenth century, Augustinian pessimism 'was being challenged on all sides….The study of Roman law, which had spread from Bologna, had disclosed new perspectives to government and administration.' [d'Entrèves 1939, x] Believing that, as a result of original sin, human nature had been radically altered for the worse and thus required the need for an institution to repress the consequences of such sinfulness, Augustine's view appears to be completely opposed to the more naturalistic views of Aristotle. How is Thomas going to reconcile this apparent tension?

Thomas agrees with Augustine that human nature has been damaged—our intellect is darkened and our will is weakened—but we are still essentially what God created us to be in the beginning. Thomas quietly and unobtrusively leaves behind a certain element of Patristic thinking and regards political authority as something we would have needed even if Adam and Eve had not sinned, as something integral to the human condition and therefore natural. Although Thomas agrees with Augustine in accepting the fundamental carnality of the world, he is more optimistic than Augustine about its prospects. For Augustine, politics is one of the consequences of the Fall; for Thomas, even life in paradise would have been political.[11] In this, Thomas appears to echo the thoughts of some Stoics. Posidonius had a vision of a Golden Age in which those less wise voluntarily submitted to the rule of their superiors in wisdom, and those superiors did not exploit their inferiors. Seneca wrote, 'The first men on this earth…and their immediate descendants, followed nature unspoiled; they took a single person as their leader and their law, freely submitting to the decision of an individual of superior mind….In that age, the, which people commonly refer to as the Golden Age, government, so Posidonius maintains, was in the hands of the wise.' [Seneca 1969, 162-63] Thomas, then, rejected the Augustinian and traditional medieval view of a discontinuity between pre- and post lapsarian man in respect of his political nature. For Augustine, politics is a remedy for man's sinful nature, a result of the Fall; for Thomas, political society is natural to both post and pre lapsarian man, with this difference, that before the Fall, political rule would have been directive but not coercive. Even in a state of original innocence, there would have been differences between individuals in terms of age, sex and intellectual capacity. 'The concept of political society,' writes John Morrall, 'is thus detached from its previous connection in Christian thought with original sin, its consequences and remedies, and hence from any inherent connection with the economy of redemption and the Church…' [Morrall 1971, 72] Politics, for Thomas, is associated rather with the economy of creation rather than the economy of redemption. Given all this, political society has its own legitimate (if limited) sphere of activity.

Aristotle's thought was capable of bearing an interpretation that fundamentally challenged the Christian culture of the period, especially as refracted through the lens of Islamic scholarship, and the temptation of a Christian society to reject it root and branch was almost overwhelming. Aquinas was one of those who resisted this temptation and he attempted to show how a reconciliation between Aristotle and Christianity was possible. Sabine remarks, 'there is no better evidence of the intellectual virility of medieval Christianity than the rapidity with which Aristotle was not merely received but made the corner stone of Roman Catholic philosophy.' [Sabine, 247] Aquinas's political philosophy 'is best understood as a modification of Aristotle's political philosophy in the light of Christian revelation or more precisely as an attempt to integrate Aristotle with an earlier tradition of Western political thought represented by the Church Fathers and their medieval followers and compounded for the most part of elements taken from the Bible, Platonic-Stoic philosophy, and Roman law.' [Fortin, 248]

Unlike Aristotle, Thomas does not grant any kind of absolute autonomy to the state but he sees it rather as occupying a subordinate and quasi-independent position in relation to man's ultimate ends. As such, the law of the state is presumptively binding on everyone, even doubtful law. Disobedience can be justified only when a law is clearly bad and disobedience to it does not threaten civil stability and peace. Thomas distinguishes between the ultimate end of human life and its proximate end. The ultimate end, perfect happiness, is achievable only in the next life; man's life in the here and now is but a path he must tread on that journey. It has its own proximate ends but they are ultimately subordinate to the overall purpose of life. Politics, then, is not an hermetically sealed set of human activities having nothing to do with religion. Its proximate end is the common good, that being the good of the whole community, not just that of the individual or indeed even of the family. In Thomas's view, grace, the order of the supernatural, does not overwhelm nature, nor is it a substitute for it; rather, grace supervenes upon and perfects nature. Human values and human truths, although not ultimate, are none the less not false but they are, at best, partial and limited.

Thomas agreed with Aristotle that man is a naturally social being or a being with a need for a political community. For Aristotle, he writes, 'man is naturally a political or social animal.'[12] It is significant that Thomas insists not only that man is a political animal but also, going beyond Aristotle, a *social* animal, thereby showing that he saw man's need for society extending beyond the narrow confines of the political community. Man is naturally inclined to be sociable and that natural sociability is essential to perfect his rational nature. The infant human being is bewilderingly helpless and is so for a very long time. The family is the first natural human society that provides the basic necessities for human survival and the minimum degree of sociability in which the young human being learns to relate to others, not least through the medium of language. Although necessary, the family has a limited capacity to provide what man needs; for this, we have the political community, the perfect society, in which man can aspire to a full and complete human life. This political community is a complex and differentiated entity in which individuals and families play their parts. It is possible for these parts to put their own ends before that of the political community as a whole, a tendency that, if unchecked, would lead to its destruction. That being so, it's necessary to have some authority whose job it is to look after the good of the entire community and to moderate the centrifugal tendencies of individuals and inferior forms of organisation.

Public goods do not prevail over private goods in all circumstances. There are, in fact, private goods which 'prevail over public or other common goods; the state's rulers cannot rightly intervene in private relationships and trans-actions to secure purposes other than justice and peace; individual good, the common good of the family, and the common good of the state are irreducibly diverse; and private persons need not regard their lives as lived for the sake of the state or its purposes.'[13] The primary purpose of the political community and its authority is to maintain the conditions that will allow all its parts to function smoothly or, if not smoothly, at least with minimal roughness. As is the case with Aristotle, Thomas sees this as a condition of human flourishing but only as a necessary condition. The political community has higher goals than merely maintaining order and preventing the destruction of the common good—it also aims at the good life for all its citizens.

THE POLITICAL COMMUNITY

Who or what should be the political authority in the political community? Thomas answers: the best man or the best men, if such can be found. Monarchy, if it be good, is the best form of government; if bad, the worst. A *regnum* or kingdom is to be preferred provided that it isn't corrupted [1a2ae q. 105, a. 1, ad. 2] but Thomas seems to accept that in this world, where the possibility of corruption is ever present, a mixed constitution is probably the best we can hope to achieve, a regime with a mixed constitution being one combining monar-chical, aristocratic/oligarchic and democratic elements in which everyone has the right (in principle) to be appointed as a ruler and to play a part in the appoint-ment of a ruler. In this mixed polity, the political community will have stable and abiding laws that are tailored to its ends and which are administered and, when necessary, altered by those charged with the care of the community. So far, this line of thinking follows Aristotle. But Aquinas lived 1500 years after Aristotle and although Aristotle was *the* philosopher to him, there were other traditions that he had inherited, not only and not least his Christianity but also elements of the Roman and Hellenistic culture, such as Stoicism. The Jewish influence comes through strongly in the conception of law as a command of a lawgiver, and from Christianity Thomas gets his understanding of the end of man as extending beyond the confines of this world so that the ends and purposes of the political community, however self-contained they might appear to be, could only be so relatively and not absolutely. In Aristotle's thought, the individual was in danger of being completely subsumed in the societies to which he belonged, the family, the village, and the *polis*. Thomas, in contrast, sees the natural communities as unities of order rather than organic or quasi-organic unities so that each individual is a centre of freedom and action, a centre not completely absorbed by his belonging to any organisation or community.

Government is the institution that exercises the legal, judicial and executive functions necessary to produce and maintain justice and peace. For Thomas, governments aren't above the law but are in fact regulated and limited by law. If law is to be effective, it must have coercive force. That force may not be exercised by any private person but only by the community as a whole or its political representative. [1a2ae q. 90, a. 3 ad. 2] 'Law, strictly understood, has as its first and principal object the ordering of the common good. But to order affairs to the common good is the task either of the whole community or of some one person who represents it. Thus the promulgation of law is the business either of the whole community or of that political person whose duty is the care of the common good.' [1a2ae q. 90, a. 3]

Wherein lies the authority of the human legislator to make laws and the corresponding obligation of the people to obey them? The answer seems to be that certain aspects of the common good cannot be achieved or maintained without some authoritative ordering. Finnis comments, 'social life and common action…cannot be achieved in a group whose members have many ideas about priorities.'[14] In certain circumstances, a decision, even if not absolutely the optimal decision, must be made, otherwise the common good cannot be achieved. The preservation of peace and justice requires cooperation. 'A private person has no authority to compel right living. He may only advise; but if his advice is not accepted, he has no power of compulsion. But law, to be effective, in promoting right living must have such compelling force….But the power of compulsion belongs either to the community as a whole, or to its official representative whose duty it is to inflict penalties…He alone, therefore, has the right to make laws.' [1a2ae, q. 90, ad. 2]

Where does coercion come into all this? The ruler of society has the authority to enforce human law given that human law is a specific application of natural law. One might wonder why we need *coercive* governance. 'Why,' asks Finnis, 'can there be no law, in the focal sense, within families or neighbourhood groups of families?' [Finnis, 249] Thomas's answer seems eerily like the one that John Locke will give some four hundred years later. Individuals and families can't be sufficiently impartial for legal judgement and law enforcement. 'None of us can rightly be simultaneously prosecutor, judge, and witness.' [2a2ae q. 60, a. 6 c. and ad. 1] John Finnis remarks that 'the institution which gives the community its completeness—law and government—needs justification in the face of the natural equality and freedom of persons, and the need to show just why and when their authority overrides the responsibility of parents and the self-possession of free persons above the age of puberty.'[15] 'The rulership of one man over another must not take away the free moral agency of the subject,' writes Sabine. 'No man is bound to obedience in all respects and even the soul of a slave is free.' [Sabine, 256]

So, again, why is coercion needed? The answer to this question appears to be that although individuals and families are able to provide some basic goods for themselves, either directly or through production and exchange, there are other goods that individuals and families are simply not in a position to produce or to produce well. Law and government serve to protect and enhance these basic goods in a way that families and individuals cannot. 'What is it that solitary individuals, families, and groups of families inevitably cannot do well?' asks Finnis. 'In what way are they inevitably "incomplete"? In their inability (1) to secure themselves *well* against violence (including invasion), theft, and fraud, and (2) to maintain a fair and stable system of distributing, exploiting, and exchanging the natural resources which, Aquinas thinks, are in reason and fairness "naturally" (not merely "initially") things common to all.'[16] This line of thinking is broadly compatible with libertarianism, at least in respect of the provision of protection against violence. The public goods of peace and justice must somehow be provided—all are agreed on this point—but libertarian anarchists would argue that these could be supplied without erecting a monopoly government to provide them. They would further argue that the distribution, exploitation and exchange of natural resources are not only possible but also freer and more effective in the absence of a coercive state.[17]

Thomas held the view that no one should be coerced to embrace the Christian faith and he endorsed a limited acceptance of non-Christian cults [2a2ae q. 10, a. 8 & 11]. Nevertheless, heresy was not to be tolerated. In words that have an ominous ring to modern ears, he said 'From the point of view of the heretics themselves there is their sin, by which they have deserved not only to be separated from the Church, but to be eliminated from the world by death.' [2a2ae q. 11, a. 3] The most charitable construction that can be put on this is that heretics are to be considered as a kind of menace to public order as are forgers and so their temporal punishment is a radical kind of quarantine. Similar considerations had prompted Augustine to change his mind on the use of force vis-à-vis the Donatists.

What if men had no evil dispositions and no inclination towards injustice? Would we then have no need of governance? As already mentioned, the common interpretation of Thomas here is that, in contrast to Augustine, he believes that even in a state of innocence we would still need governance. The political rule of man over man would have existed in the pre-lapsarian condition of innocence, because man is a social animal and lives in society, and there can be no society without someone who exercises authority for the sake of the common good [1a q. 96, a. 4] But Thomas does *not* say that the governance of the innocent would be legally coercive since law is for the unjust, not for the just.

Who holds the supreme legislative power in a political community? Thomas answers: either the whole people or those responsible for and representing the whole people.[18] The latter alternative raises the question of representation. How is representation made possible? Finnis argues that this isn't really the issue: 'To extend this idea of representation into an idea that authority must, or should, have been transmitted by some procedure of transference (however implicit or tacit) from the people to their representative(s) is to miss the point of the construction, and to convert it into a fiction or a sometimes inappropriate requirement for just government.' [Finnis, 264] I don't think the issue can be swept under the carpet as breezily as this and Finnis does concede that the question of representation occupied the minds of Thomas's later followers such as Cardinal Cajetan.

The need for a justification of supreme legislative power is made, tongue firmly in cheek, in the film, *Monty Python and the Holy Grail*. King Arthur is searching for knights for his Round Table and comes riding up (without a horse!) to some peasants working in the fields. The following conversation takes place:

> *Arthur*: How do you do, good lady. I am Arthur, King of the Britons. Whose castle is that?
> *Woman*: King of the who?
> *Arthur*: The Britons.
> *Woman*: Who are the Britons?
> *Arthur*: Well, we all are. We're all Britons and I am your king.
> *Woman*: I didn't know we had a king. I thought we were an autonomous collective.

An increasingly frustrating dialogue takes place, in the course of which Arthur again says:

> *Arthur*: I am your king!
> *Woman*: Well, I didn't vote for you.
> *Arthur*: You don't vote for kings.
> *Woman*: Well, 'ow did you become king then?
> *Arthur*: The Lady of the Lake…[*angels start to sing*]…her arm clad in the purest shimmering samite, held aloft Excalibur from the bosom of the water, signifying by Divine Providence that I, Arthur, was to carry Excalibur…[*singing stops*]…That is why I am your king!

At this point, Dennis, the proletarian proto-shop steward, takes up the running:

> *Dennis*: Listen—strange women lying in ponds distributing swords is no basis for a system of government. Supreme executive power derives from a mandate from the masses, not from some farcical aquatic ceremony.
> *Arthur*: Be quiet!
> *Dennis*: Well you can't expect to wield supreme executive power just 'cause some watery tart threw a sword at you!
> *Arthur*: Shut up!
> *Dennis*: I mean, if I went around sayin' I was an emperor just because some moistened bint had lobbed a scimitar at me they'd put me away!

It is hard to disagree with Dennis the prole: strange women lying in ponds distributing swords (or, as he gets increasingly politically incorrect, watery tarts throwing swords, or moistened bints lobbing scimitars) doesn't appear be a sound basis for a system of government. How, then, according to Aquinas, should government be organised? Whatever the ultimate details, any defensible form of government must be based on the principles that government exists for the sake of the common good, not for the good of the rulers; that no one has a natural right to govern; and that people's obligation to obey the government is in effect an obligation to obey themselves and their fellow citizens. The best government is to be had when we have one virtuous person who commands all and has others under him who also govern virtuously and when all participate by electing those who rule. This combines the best of monarchy, aristocracy and democracy. 'This is the best form of constitution which results from a judicious admixture of the *kingdom*, in that there is one person at the head of it; of *aristocracy* in that many participate in the government according to virtue; and of *democracy* or popular rule, in that rulers may be elected from the people and the whole population has the right of electing its rulers.' [1a2ae q. 105, a. 1] Thomas sees this system exemplified in the Old Testament when Moses and his successors ruled the people, aided by seventy-two elders elected by the people.

In his *Commentary on the Sentences of Peter Lombard*,[19] St Thomas asks whether Christians are bound to obey secular powers, especially tyrants. Thomas initially suggests that the answer to this question 'Are Christians bound to obey secular powers?' must be in the negative; 'It seems that they [Christians] are *not* bound to obey secular powers, especially tyrants.' He cites the passage from *Matthew* 17: 25[20] where, in the matter of whether there is an obligation to pay toll or tribute, Jesus remarks that the 'sons are free.' Thomas comments on this passage, remarking 'If then in any kingdom the sons of its king are free, then the sons of the king to whom all kingdoms are subject ought to be free in any kingdom.' He cites *Romans* 8:16 to demonstrate from Scripture that Christians are indeed sons of God and so 'are free everywhere, and are not held to obey secular powers.'[21] Moreover, slavery (in this case, understood as the obligation to obey another) is the result of sin but 'by Baptism people are cleansed from sin. Therefore they are liberated from slavery' and so cannot be obliged to obey secular powers.

In response to these arguments, Thomas says that 1 *Peter* 2: 18 requires the subjection of servants to masters, and that *Romans* 13: 2 tells us that the resistance of power is equivalent to the resistance of God's ordinance, which clearly is not legitimate.[22] Thomas also remarks that 'authority which is instituted for the utility of the subjects does not take away their liberty,' moreover, those who are baptised 'need not be immediately liberated from a servile state, even though that is a penalty of sin.'

In general, Thomas believes that Christians are bound to obey authorities inasmuch as they are from God; but they are *not* bound to obey putative authorities that are *not* from God. There are two ways in which authority may not be from God. First, in 'the *mode* in which authority is acquired, and, second, as to the *use* which is made of authority.' In regard to the *mode* of acquisition of authority, there are two possible defects—first, the unworthiness of the ruler, and second, the acquisition of authority by illegitimate means, such as violence or simony. Personal unworthiness, according to Thomas, does not in itself constitute an obstacle against the acquisition of lawful authority. On the other hand, authority obtained in any illegitimate way is no lawful authority at all. 'He who seizes power by violence does not become a true holder of power. Hence, when it is possible to do so, anybody may repel this domination, unless, of course, the usurper should later on have become a true ruler by the consent of the subjects or by a recognition being extended to him by a higher authority.'

An *abuse* of power might occur in either of two ways. First, 'should the authority command an act of sin contrary to virtue, we not only are not obliged to obey but we are also obliged not to obey, according to the example of the holy martyrs who preferred death to obeying those ungodly tyrants.' Second, an abuse of power can also occur if the authority were to act *ultra vires*, 'for instance, when a master exacts duties which the servant isn't bound to pay, or the like. In this case the subject is not obliged to obey, but neither is he obliged not to obey.'

The question, then, of political obligation to obey authority turns on the answer to the question; what constitutes a legitimate authority? The passage just cited on the legitimation of usurpation—'unless, of course, the usurper should later on have become a true ruler by the consent of the subjects or by a recognition being extended to him by a higher authority'—suggests that one source of legitimacy is the consent of the subjects or the sanction of a yet higher authority which, one supposes, must itself be based upon the consent of subjects if it is not to be the kind of authority acquired by illegitimate means. But *volenti non fit injuria*—to the willing, there can be no injury. If we freely consent to erect an authority, then we have bound ourselves to obedience to it as long as it remains within its proper limits and serves the purpose for which it was erected (acts for the good of the ruled and not the ruler) and as long as our consent remains in effect.

Contract?

As we've just seen in the previous section, one can find some traces of covenant or contract or consent in Thomas's thought on political matters. Even where rulers exercise regal power, the laws that have been put into force constitute a kind of implied contract between the people and their ruler.[23] Nevertheless, it seems we shouldn't get too excited about those passages in Thomas in which he seems to hint at a notion of pact, contract or covenant. John Finnis remarks that 'this is far removed from the theory that some original or standing or foundational "social contract" is or could be a fundamental ground or justification for legislative or other political authority, or for the (defeasible) obligation to respect such authority and obey its laws.' [Finnis, 266] Thomas, however, does make some concessions to popular sovereignty. In the *Summa Theologiae*, he allows that the law-making capacity of society belongs either to the multitude or to the person who has care of the multitude. [1a2ae, q. 90, 3.] Likewise, custom reveals the law-making capacity of the people [see 1a2ae, q. 97, a. 3] According to d'Entrèves, however, Thomas does not endorse the notion that the people have an original or natural right and that they are the ultimate source of authority. All power is from God. Even though this is so formally, it does not prevent there being a material source of authority in man in setting up particular forms of government. Thomas remarks that 'the multitude's consent, manifested by custom, has more weight in observing something than the authority of the prince, who only has the power to make law in so far as he bears the person of the multitude.'[24]

Where we have a free community that has the power to establish its own laws, the consent of the whole community is more valuable than the authority of the ruler, for the power of the ruler comes from the fact that he represents the community. Where we have a community without such power, an established custom makes law if it is in fact tolerated by those whose duty it is to legislate. [1a2ae q. 97, a. 3, ad. 3] Reason can manifest itself in words or in action. Where law is changed by repeated actions it is changed by custom and custom, as manifesting reason, has the power of law. It may in fact interpret law or even annul it. [1a2ae q. 97, a. 3] J. S. McClelland makes the point that 'Much human law, and nearly all of feudal law, arises out of custom. Most of what we call 'legislation' has happened through the expedient of making permanent lists of already well-established customs.' But 'The great law-givers of history are really misnamed if we think of them as law-inventors. Rather, they are law declarers…' [McClelland, 113]

SACERDOTIUM AND REGNUM

Where does Thomas stand in the vexed question of the relationship between the *sacerdotium* and the *imperium* or *regnum*? The *sacerdotium* and the *regnum* aren't two mutually opposed and conflicting orders but two interrelated spheres of human life in one society. He believes that the temporal power is subject to the spiritual power in the same way that the body is subject to the soul. 'Therefore,' he writes, 'there is no usurpation of power if a spiritual Prelate should interest himself in temporal affairs with respect to those things in which the temporal power is subject to him or in matters which have been left to him by the secular power.' [2a2ae q. 60 a. 6, ad. 3] Taken by itself, this passage is ambiguous. The power of the spiritual appears to be limited in two ways; it seems that no aspect of the temporal is subject to the spiritual power, and it seems that the spiritual power has jurisdiction only where such has been permitted by the temporal power. Thomas seems to recognise distinct spheres of authority. 'Just as it falls to temporal princes to enact legal precepts which are particular determinations of the natural law, in all those matters which concern the common welfare in mundane matters; so also it is the province of ecclesiastical prelates to regulate by precept those matters which affect the common interest of the faithful to their spiritual well-being.' [2a2ae q. 147, a. 3]

TYRANNY

When it comes to the question of whether we owe obedience to tyrants, Thomas appears to endorse tyrannicide. 'It is legitimate,' he writes, 'for anyone, who can do so, to re-take what has been taken away from him unjustly. Now many secular princes unjustly usurped the dominion of Christian lands. Since, therefore, in such cases rebellion is legitimate, Christians have no obligation to obey these princes.' Moreover, 'If it is a legitimate and even a praiseworthy deed to kill a person, then no obligation of obedience exists toward that person. Now in the *Book on Duties* Cicero justifies Julius Caesar's assassins. Although Caesar was a close friend of his, yet by usurping the empire he proved himself to be a tyrant. Therefore toward such powers there is no obligation of obedience.'[25] 'An authority acquired by violence,' concludes St Thomas, 'is not a true authority, and there is no obligation of obedience.'[26] Where no recourse can be had to a superior to pronounce sentence upon a usurper, 'he that kills the tyrant for the liberation of the country, is praised and rewarded.'[27]

Some commentators on Thomas assert that he moved from an early and incautious acceptance of tyrannicide to a mature rejection of it. John Finnis isn't persuaded by this assertion, I think correctly, arguing that a textual analysis shows 'no significant shift of that kind and no particular concern that tyrannicide be done on public authority.' [Finnis, 288] Tyranny is government in any form in which the end of government is the good of the ruler rather than the good of the whole community. [2a2ae q. 42, a. 2, ad. 3] The laws of a tyrannical regime are, in fact, not laws at all and 'One is entitled to treat its laws, judgements, and directives as having, in conscience, the same status as a bandit's demand' and there is no requirement to obey these laws except where not to do so would cause disproportionate harm to others. [Finnis, 289] One may use lethal force in one's resistance to the acts of a tyrant. [2a2ae q. 69, a. 4, c.]

For Thomas, it makes a difference whether a tyrant is someone legitimately entitled to rule but who does so in a tyrannical manner (*tyrannus exercitio*), or is someone who, with no right to rule, has illegitimately seized power (*tyrannus sine titulo*).[28] Towards the former, a *tyrannus exercitio*, acquiescence and passive disobedience is recommended, with positive resistance to be taken, if at all, by those with some modicum of public authority on their side. On the other hand, early in his career, it seemed that Thomas supported tyrannicide in certain specific circumstances, namely, where the tyrant had achieved his position by violence and so was *tyrannus sine titulo*. Laws of a tyrant aren't laws properly speaking unless they happen to provide for the well being of the citizen. [1a2ae q. 92, a. 1 ad. 4] Nevertheless, in *De Regimine Principum*, he appeared to retract his earlier endorsement of limited tyrannicide, saying that it went against Scripture, quoting I *Peter*, 2: 19! The multitude could remove a tyrant but no individual person. 'If to provide itself with a king belongs to the right of a given multitude, it is not unjust that the king be deposed or have his power restricted by that same multitude if, becoming a tyrant, he abuses the royal power.'[29] Can one resist a tyrant? Yes, in certain circumstances, because tyrannical rule is unjust and resistance to it isn't sedition. Despite these circumstances, where resistance is accompanied by such disorder that the people would suffer more harm from the resistance than from the continued rule by the tyrant, resistance isn't justified. [2a2ae q. 42, a. 2] Our obligation to obey rulers is limited to the extent to which justice requires it. If rulers have no just title to rule, we aren't obliged to obey, unless not doing so would cause scandal or some other disproportionate danger.[30]

Thomas's comments on the status of the tyrant's laws are exactly what the libertarian anarchist thinks of the state's laws as a whole, outside and apart from the state's enforcement of whatever would fall under the zero-aggression principle. A libertarian anarchist can accept a principle of proportionality in resistance but can see no justification for leaving resistance exclusively up to some public authority. In discussing the matter of tyrannicide, John Finnis instances the assassination plot against Hitler, arguing that Stauffenberg and his co-conspirators constituted a kind of public authority in undertaking their plot. This example seems so completely far-fetched as to constitute a *reductio ad absurdum* of Finnis's claim. Either a public authority is determined by some set of objective criteria, which wasn't the case with Stauffenberg and his fellow-conspirators, or else one runs the risk of circularly describing resistance to tyrants of which one approves as *ipso facto* emanating from a public authority.

Thomas makes a distinction between two types of rule: regal (or royal) and political.[31] Government is political when the laws of the political community limit the ruler. In regal rule, by contrast, the ruler has plenary power. Is a regal government necessarily a tyranny? No. Regal government, though plenary, is limited inasmuch as even though the rulers aren't subject to the coercive force of the law, they are subject to its directive force that exercises a guiding authority upon them. What is the relationship of a ruler to the law? Well, conceptually, a ruler is above the law in the sense that the constraining force of the law comes from the power of the ruler and no one can constrain himself. He is also above the law in the sense that if necessary he may change it or dispense from it. Nevertheless, the ruler is voluntarily subject to the directive force of the law. 'A ruler is not free from the directive power of the law; but should voluntarily and without constraint fulfil it.' [1a2ae q. 96, a. 5, ad. 3] Finnis writes, 'holders of even "plenary power" who demand the obedience of the subject, while themselves defaulting from their own duties under that very law, go beyond the limits of their authority, their rightful power.'[32] Thomas's student, Giles of Rome,[33] carried the distinction between political and regal rule into his own teaching. An example of political rule would be that which subsists between husband and wife, limited as it is by covenants or agreements; an example of regal rule would be that which a father exercises over children which, while directed towards the welfare of the children, isn't constituted by any agreement or contract. Apart from political or regal rule, there is also a kind of rule which is despotic, a *regimen despoticum vel dominativum*, which the head of a household exercises over his servants and which, unlike his rule over his children, isn't intended for their benefit but for his. [see Oakley 2012, 123]

The writings of two of Thomas's contemporaries, the slightly older Henry of Ghent (c. 1217-1293) and the slightly younger Godfrey of Fontaines (1250-1306/9), show the topicality of the issue of whether or not disobedience to the statutes of a ruler can be legitimate. Henry of Ghent considers the question of whether a subject is bound to obey a statute when it isn't clear that it actually promotes the common good. He is prepared to grant a presumption of legitimacy to the edicts of a ruler: 'It is for the ruler, however, and for superiors in

Freedom's Progress?

general, to ordain such things [things ordained towards the peace and well-being of the community]' so that 'every subject is bound to obey statutes issued by superiors on matters necessary for this end or for something without which the end itself can be achieved...even if it is not evident to any of them that this statute is necessary for the end or for something ordered toward it.' [Henry of Ghent, 311, 312] This presumption of legitimacy is rebuttable. Should it happen that 'there is no presumption of a ruler's diligence but rather the reverse, then for as long as he is nevertheless still tolerated he can issue statutes and should be obeyed. It is preferable, though, to act to depose him, however long the line of ancestors through whom he has inherited his kingdom. When a ruler has been deposed, he cannot issue statutes, nor is there a duty (*debitum*) to obey him, because it shouldn't be presumed that his statutes contain virtuous deeds. Nevertheless, if his statutes are not evidently opposed to virtue, then for as long as the superior is tolerated they should be completely obeyed.' [Henry of Ghent, 313] These words can hardly be considered a ringing endorsement of a right of disobedience. The presumption of obedience may be rebuttable but the circumstances that would ground such a rebuttal in practice are difficult to envisage. Indeed, Henry believes that the promotion or maintenance of the common good may require the sacrifice of a subject's goods, some or all of them, and even the subject's life itself! [see McGrade, 309]

Godfrey of Fontaines takes the matter a little further than Henry of Ghent is prepared to go. The rulers of a political community ought to be the best and most prudent of individuals. There is no guarantee, however, that the institution of a monarch on the principle of heredity can produce such an individual because 'the best does not necessarily give birth to the best in the course of natural generation...' [Godfrey of Fontaines, 317] If kings were elected then we might be justified in presuming that they are the best and most prudent of individuals[34] but 'since kings are not generally instituted by election in this way, it should not be presumed from the fact that they are kings that they are the better and more prudent individuals.' [Godfrey of Fontaines, 318] In arguing in this fashion, Godfrey neatly subverts the presumption of the legitimacy of the ruler's issuance of statutes. If the acts of a ruler are to be legitimate and not the acts of a tyrant, then 'he does not have the right to rule except by virtue of the whole community either electing him or instituting or accepting and agreeing on him, and his government ought not to exist except for the sake of the common good and the common benefit.' [Godfrey of Fontaines, 318] Whereas Henry is willing to accept the idea of tacit consent, Godfrey is not. He writes that the ruler 'should not impose anything on the community that weighs heavily on it or harms it, *unless* this proceeds from the consent of his subjects. Inasmuch as they are free, they ought to obey willingly, not by compulsion, knowing the reason for which a burden is imposed upon them and knowing that it is the sort of reason which merits approval.' [Godfrey of Fontaines, 318] How is this consent to be procured or demonstrated? Not merely tacitly! Godfrey argues that consent can be deemed to be given if the burdens proceed from already established and accepted statute law or if the proposed measures have the approval of the ruler's counsellors, where those counsellors are independent of the ruler and have a record of prudent judgement. It is never enough for a ruler simply to declare that the burden he proposes to impose on his subjects is necessary for the common good, for all rulers alike, the good and the tyrannical, make such claims. Godfrey permits disobedience in the following heavily qualified way: 'if what is instituted, or what is announced to the ruler's subjects, is something momentous and burdensome, and if there is no apparent benefit for which so great a burden ought reasonably to be imposed, and if compared with others the ruler is not markedly superior in prudence, faithfulness, and love for the common good, and if those whose counsel is primarily used are not the sort of people who are markedly more trustworthy than others, then, because such an imposition is not reasonable, subjects are not by right (*de iure*) bound to obey.' [Godfrey of Fontaines, 319]

Self-defence and Homicide

Finnis believes that according to Thomas there is an exceptionless moral norm to the effect that I may never choose to kill or harm any human being, innocent or guilty.[35] The obvious objection to this is to ask what I am to do if I am attacked either by someone who is vicious or insane? It turns out that I can use whatever means are reasonably necessary to repel such an attack even where I can foresee that the employment of such means will result in the death of the attacker, but I mustn't intend to kill, only to repel the attack. This account isn't obviously coherent. I must be taken to intend (even if I do not absolutely desire to bring about) whatever can reasonably be foreseen as the result of my action so that if the death of the attacker is reasonably foreseeable as the result of the means I take to repel the attack, then I intend, though I do not necessarily desire, his death.

This distinction between intention and desire can be illustrated, I believe, using Aristotle's distinction between voluntary acts and nonvoluntary acts. The ship's captain who throws his cargo overboard in a storm to save the ship and crew acts, properly speaking, voluntarily rather than involuntarily. No one is coercing him to do what he does and he can choose not to do it if he wishes. His action may be described as nonvoluntary (even though properly voluntary) to indicate the fact that other things being equal, this particular action isn't something he would normally choose to do. His act isn't capricious, prompted by a desire to see what kind of pretty pattern the jettisoned goods will make on the water but is intended to save the ship and its crew. Similarly, a mountain climber who cuts the rope between him and another climber who has lost his foothold and is dangling from him, where it is reasonably certain that unless this is done, all those depending for their support on the rope will fall to their deaths, can be said to intend whatever can reasonably be seen to be the result of that action, namely the death of the stricken climber. He doesn't necessarily *desire* the death of the climber below him and, were things otherwise, wouldn't cut the rope. But, things being as they are, he intends what can reasonably be foreseen. Of course, the usual principle of proportionality applies so that such drastic means can't be employed for the repulsion of a trivial assault or the alleviation of an insignificant threat. This is a matter of judgement and, when such judgment is exercised, considerations must be had of the circumstances of the object of the attack.

Finnis is puzzled by Thomas's apparent disregard of the exceptionless nature of the moral norm never to intend the death of another in the case of its being performed by someone having public authority in war or justice (capital punishment).[36] And he is right to be so puzzled. If the norm is exceptionless then it is exceptionless. So, either Thomas is being inconsistent or the norm is not in fact exceptionless. Why one rule for public authorities and another for private persons? Even if a prudential case could be made for delegating drastic action to public authorities whenever possible, there will be times when this isn't possible, as when one comes under attack and there is no opportunity to refer the matter to some public body. And indeed, in the end, Thomas himself rejects the claim that 'imposing and carrying out capital punishment involves no intent to kill.' [Finnis, 280; 2a2ae q. 64, a. 7] In a footnote, Finnis remarks that 'if executioners have this intention, so too must the judges on whose orders they act…' [Finnis, 280, n. 31] How can this be justified? Thomas's answer is that vicious criminals, having deviated from reason, have acquired the status of a subhuman animal and so may legitimately be intentionally killed. Not only is this killing just but there are consequential reasons for carrying it out: it deters others and removes a danger from society. This 'sub-human' defence of judicial homicide, however, is an act of hermeneutical desperation. Human beings do not cease to be human when they act viciously; in fact, only human beings can act viciously! Thomas's justification is nonsensical, as Finnis himself admits, acknowledging that Aquinas elsewhere explicitly denies this supposed fact![37] None of the conceptual juggling by Thomas or Finnis is necessary if we deny that intentional killing (in the attenuated sense just discussed) is an exceptionless norm. What *is* an exceptionless norm is intentional murder or manslaughter, namely, wrongful killing.

SLAVERY, PROPERTY, USURY AND TRADE

Aquinas has no general treatment of *servitus*, the state or condition of being a *servus*. The term *servitus* can, and sometime does, signify; slavery; at other times, it signifies something less than slavery, some kind of service such as, for example, serfdom. [see Tierney 2014, 75ff.] That the term carries no necessary moral opprobrium is clear from that fact that in marriage and in the religious life one is *quasi-servitus*, a sort of a slave, inasmuch as one has given up certain freedoms to do as one wills. While willingly granting that man, made in the image and likeness of God, is intelligent and free, Thomas, like almost all his contemporaries, simply accepts slavery as a fact of life, a fact that exists only as a consequence of sin and human wrongdoing. [see 1a2ae, q. 1] In the master-slave relationship, the rule of the master over the slave is for the master's convenience. What can be bought and sold is the service of the *servus*, and *servi* retain the right to eat and sleep, marry and have a religious life. Moreover, *servi* can't be killed or deliberately harmed or aggressed against sexually. The condition of servitude exists only in positive law; by nature, all men are equal in liberty.

Aquinas has no specific theory of property acquisition though he nods in the direction of the Roman law concept of *'occupatio'* (occupation or possession). This occupation, which takes from the commonality, is so that the owner can use that which he acquires to share with others.[38] Aquinas allows that the institution of private property is an efficient way to handle resources. His reasons for this are largely pragmatic—commonality in ownership tends towards neglect, work is avoided, projects are confused and ill directed and we will have permanent and unresolvable disagreements and discord. Despite these advantages of private ownership over public ownership, however, the ultimate disposition of goods is still oriented towards the community as a whole.

If we grant that natural resources do not belong to any particular person by nature ('if a particular piece of land be considered absolutely, it contains no reason why it should belong to one man more than to another, but if it be considered in respect of its adaptability to cultivation…it has a certain commensuration to be the property of one and not of another man' [2a2ae q. 57, a. 3]); and if we grant that methods of appropriation are not obviously natural and so depend in some way on moral and legal norms that are for the good of all ('Community of goods is ascribed to the natural law, not that the natural law dictates that all things should be possessed in common and that nothing should be possessed as one's own: but because the division of possessions is not according to the natural law, but rather arose from human agreement which belongs to the positive law…Hence the ownership of possessions is not contrary to the natural law, but an addition thereto devised by human reasons.' [2a2ae q. 66, a. 2, ad. 1]), then we might well wonder why, given all this, anyone should accede to a private property regime?[39]

Man may make use of natural things for his benefit but how does he acquire and dispose of such things? Is private ownership possible? Yes. For three reasons. First, everyone is more immediately concerned with obtaining what he needs than with the common welfare. If everything were common, everyone would be tempted to leave the work to everybody else. Second, matters are arranged in a more orderly fashion if each attends to his own business, 'there would be complete confusion if every one tried to do everything.' Third, private property leads to peace, at least where each is content with what he has. When things are held in common, there are frequent disputes. Despite this, men should hold what they have so that all may benefit: 'men should not hold material things as their own but to the common benefit: each readily sharing them with others in their necessity.' [2a2ae q. 66, a. 2]

Natural law doesn't decree that all things must be held in common; rather, within natural law, no property distinctions are made. This requires human agreement and so belongs to the sphere of positive law. 'Thus private property is not opposed to natural law, but is an addition to it, devised by human reason.' [2a2ae q. 66, a. 2 ad. 1] On the other hand, material goods exist for the satisfaction of human needs. So, whatever dispositions are made regarding private property in positive law can't be such as to obstruct man's ability to satisfy his material necessities. Thomas goes on to say that 'whatever a man has in superabundance is owed, of natural right (*ex naturali iure*) to the poor for their sustenance.' [2a2ae q. 66, a. 7] Still, as many people are in need and a person can't help everyone, it is left to that person's initiative to determine whom he will assist. None the less, where a person is in desperate straits, in imminent danger of privation, he may take what he needs from another person's superfluous possessions and such taking is not, properly speaking robbery.

Why, given the public orientation of all goods, would Aquinas endorse a private property regime? The answer to this seems to be that whatever one holds privately, one holds as it were in trust. That which one needs for one's own survival and that of one's dependents, for the maintenance of one's business and paying one's debts are one's own; whatever is left over after these responsibilities have been met or prepared for is superfluous. Aquinas's position is twofold: (1) *everything* one has is 'held as common [or in common]' in the sense that it's morally available, as a matter of right and justice, to *anyone* who needs it to survive; (2) one's *superflua* are all 'held in common', in the sense that one has a duty *of justice* to dispose of them for the benefit of the poor. [Finnis, 191]

For those who are in extreme necessity, everything is common and they are entitled to appropriate whatever will relieve that necessity, that entitlement overriding titles otherwise legitimate: 'All things are common property in case of extreme necessity. Hence one who is in such dire straits may take another's goods in order to succour himself, if he can find no one who is willing to give him something.' [2a2ae q. 37, a. 7, ad. 3] Apart from situations of dire necessity, resources needed for one's own maintenance and the maintenance of one's family are entitled to be kept by their owner, but the owner's superfluous possessions should be made available to those who, though not in dire straits, can't meet their obligations. The judgement as to what is and what is not *superflua* is to be made prudentially and not according to some mechanical rule. Resources one needs for investment and for the future provision of one's business aren't superfluous, nor are savings for future consumption by oneself or one's dependants. [see Tierney 2014, 89-91]

What does Aquinas think of taxes? He tends to regard them as a kind of stipendiary reward for governing. More than that, as rulers have an obligation to make provision for a distribution of goods for consumption, laws can be made regarding the superfluous possessions of some so that taxes can be imposed legitimately for redistributive purposes. What of the purported rebuttal that Aquinas is economically naïve, that economics isn't a zero-sum game in which if some are too rich, others must be too poor because the being-too-rich of the one is the cause in some way of the being-too-poor of the others? Finnis responds to this question by effectively accepting the zero-sum thesis: 'if some have a superabundance—more than they need for their business, their legitimate savings, and their other responsibilities—then others must, in the real world, be going short of what they are entitled to. For if we set aside the possible world in which everyone everywhere has enough to meet all their needs, *superflua* truly belong to others; anyone who keeps them is depriving, and indeed stealing from, those to whom they should, by one means of another, have been made available.' [Finnis, 195-196]

Given the paucity of Thomas's remarks on economic matters, it would perhaps be unwise to put too much emphasis on them. Raymond de Roover remarks that 'there is very little on economics in the vast works of Thomas Aquinas except some casual remarks buried here and there among extraneous material and two or three more extensive fragments in his *Summa theologica* and his *Commentaries on the Nicomachean Ethics of Aristotle.*' [De Roover 1967, 7] Even though St Thomas's writings aren't free from ambiguity, a reasonably unforced reading of them will show that all things considered, he did not endorse the labour theory of value, despite some lingering inclination to do so. There are two key passages in the works of St Thomas that point in the direction of an embryonic utility theory: In the *Summa Theologiae*, Thomas notes that 'The price of things saleable does not depend on their degree of nature, since at times a horse fetches a higher price than a slave; but it depends on their usefulness to man.' [2a2ae, q. 77, a. 2, ad. 3] And in his *Commentary on Aristotle's Nicomachean Ethics* he notes that 'In economics, things are not valued according to their natural dignity, otherwise a mouse (which is a living creature) would be prized more highly than a pearl (which is an inanimate object); but in fact the price is set with reference to human wants.'[40]

Thomas condemns usury, the demand for any form of interest on the loan of money. The reason for this is that usury involves selling what does not exist and that's contrary to justice. In the case of certain things, we can't sensibly distinguish between their use and the thing itself. So wine is for drinking and when used by being drunk, nothing remains. So to try selling someone wine and the use of wine would be to try to sell the same thing twice: 'for the same reason he commits an injustice who requires two things in return for the loan of wine or wheat, namely the return of an equal quantity of the thing itself and the price of its use.' This is usury. Nevertheless, where a distinction can be drawn between the use of a thing and the thing in itself, we have a different situation. So, we can distinguish between a house and the use of a house. The house is not consumed by its use by any person over a certain period of time. 'for this reason it is permissible for a man to accept a price for the use of a house, and in addition to sell the freehold of the house itself...' The charging of interest on money, however, doesn't seem to be covered by the example of the house. Once again, Thomas goes back to Aristotle for inspiration. 'The proper and principal use of money lies in its consumption or expenditure in the business of exchange. For this reason, therefore, it is wrong to accept a price, or money, for the use of a sum of money that is lent. And just as a man is bound to make restitution of other things which he has unjustly acquired, so also must he restore the money he has obtained from usury.' [2a2ae q. 78, a. 1] Thomas makes a distinction between (a) situations where we can distinguish between the use of a thing and the thing itself and situations where we can't. Money is assimilated to the situation where we can't make this distinction and so usury is condemned.

This is just a mistake, a mistake made practically evident by the rapidly changing economic circumstance of the Middle Ages. As trade and commerce developed, the spirit of the laws against usury were consistently and increasing evaded even though the letter of the law remained. Despite his condemnation of usury, even Thomas concedes its usefulness, thereby effectively vitiating his condemnation. He allows that, even though sinful, usury may go unpunished! 'Human law permits usury, not as though considering it to be just, but to avoid interference with the useful activities of many persons.' [2a2ae q. 78, a, 1 ad, 3] In his evaluation of trading and commerce, Thomas follows the Aristotelian line, writing that 'trading, considered in itself, always implies a certain baseness, in that it has not of itself any honest of necessary object'! Despite this, he goes on to give a grudging acceptance of profit-making, saying that profit doesn't necessarily imply anything vicious or contrary to virtue provided such profits are used for legitimate purposes such as the upkeep of a household or the assistance of the poor. Trade for the public welfare to provide the necessaries of life for the community is permissible. Trading is lawful when a person 'seeks profit, not for its own sake, but as a reward for his labour.' [see Kealey, 38, 39]

The forty nine years of Thomas's life in the middle of the thirteenth century mark in many ways the high point of the intellectual achievements of the Middle Ages. After Thomas, only Duns Scotus and William of Ockham will approach his level of genius. But immediately on the heels of Thomas's death was born a man whose kaleidoscopic mind was to produce a new point of departure in political thought, a point of departure that would eventually contribute in part, even if inadvertently, to the fragmentation of Christendom.

Notes

1 It might be more accurate to say that he dictated eight million words, rather than wrote them. Such autographs as there are of Thomas's are written in a kind of shorthand, the appropriately named *littera inintelligibilis*, but these autographs are all of Thomas's early works. Mary Carruthers suggests that 'There is good evidence in the remembrance of his peers that, certainly later in life, Thomas was not accustomed to writing his thoughts down himself, even in *inintelligibilis*.' She notes that 'no autographs are found of the later major works' and entertains the proposition that the reason for their nonexistence 'is due not to loss but to there having been none in the first place to save.' [Carruthers, 5]

2 Sabine, 244; see also Tierney 1988, 165-171. For a brief, popular introduction to St Thomas see Chesterton's *Saint Thomas Aquinas*. For an equally brief but more scholarly introduction to St Thomas, see Pieper's *Guide to Thomas Aquinas*.

3 For a brief but scholarly overview of Justinian's efforts at legal codification (and, indeed, other important aspects of Justinian's reign), see Ure's *Justinian and his Age*, 139-167.

4 Greenaway, 70; see Tierney 2014, 69-91.

5 *Summa Theologiae*, 1a2ae q. 93, a. 1; a. 3. Citations otherwise unidentified are to this work. *The Summa Theologiae* is divided into parts, those parts into questions, and those questions into articles. References to 1a are to the first part of the *Summa*, IaIIae (or 1a2ae) are to the first part of the second part; IIaIIae (or 2a2ae) to the second part of the second part, and IIIa (or 3a) to the third part. References to questions are given by q. followed by a number; articles by a. followed by a number. So, the citation given at the start of this note is to the first part of the second part of the *Summa*, question 93, articles 1 and 3 respectively. Conventions vary somewhat on references within articles but one system is as follows: pr = prologue; arg. = objections; s.c. = on the contrary (*sed contra*); co. = I respond that (*respondeo*), and ad.x = reply to objection x.

6 See 1a2ae q. 94, a. 5, ad. 3; see Tierney 2014, passim.

7 1a q. 94, a. 4; see 2a2ae q. 57, a. 2, ad. 1.

8 See 1a2ae q. 98 a. 1, c; q. 100, a. 2. C.

9 *De Regimine Principum* II, 4.

10 *Acts* 5: 29; 1a2ae q. 96, a. 4.

11 According to David Luscombe, Aquinas 'distinguished two types of lordship. Lordship in the sense of rule in the interest of the ruler was, as the Stoics and the Fathers and the medieval lawyers had maintained, absent from the state of nature or innocence. But lordship in the sense of the direction of free men for the sake of their common good is, as Aristotle showed, natural, for man is by nature a political animal and the common good of a society requires an organising and directing authority. Moreover, men are by nature unequal in respect of knowledge and the capacity for justice, and it would be unsuitable for the superior members of society not to be able to use their superiority for the benefit of others. Thus subjection is natural, and although slavery is not found in the state of nature, it is not against nature, for it is an addition made to nature by human reason for the benefit of man following the introduction of sin.' [Luscombe 1982, 761]

12 *Homo est naturaliter animal politicum et sociale.* [Ia2ae, q. 72, a. 4]

13 Finnis, 252. See 2a2ae q. 59, a. 3, ad. 2; q. 64 a. 5, c. and ad. 1.

14 Finnis, 270; see 1, q. 96, a. 4, c.

15 Finnis, 242; see 2a2ae q, 88, a, 8, ad. 2.

16 Finnis, 247; see 1a2ae q. 105, a. 4, ad. 5. In his *De Regimine Principum* I 2, Thomas talks about the fruits of good governance being not only peace and justice but also economic abundance. Finnis remarks that the law can permit economic injuries, such as usury, for the sake of economic benefits! [fn. 146, 247]

17 For a particular example of non-government produced order, see Sowell, 202-213, who gives a succinct and persuasive account of the inefficacy, if not counter-productivity, of anti-trust legislation.

18 1a2ae q. 97, a. 3, ad. 3; q. 90, a. 3, c.

19 I *Sent.* D. 44, q. 2, a. 2. The remaining citations from Thomas in this section are from this source.

20 See the discussion of this passage in the chapter on Christianity, above.

21 In his commentary, Thomas also suggests another possible interpretation of Christ's words as reported by St Matthew, namely that Christ is speaking solely about himself and his disciples, 'who were not of servile condition, nor did they have temporal property by which they would be obliged to pay tax to their lords. Therefore it does not follow that every Christian shares in this liberty, but only those who follow the apostolic life, owning nothing in this world, and unaffected by servile state.'

22 Note the citation of the usual authorities here: *Romans* 13 and 1 *Peter* 2. See the discussion of these texts in the chapter on Christianity.

23 See *De Regimine Principum* I, 6.

24 1a q. 97, a. 3. See, below, Hobbes on the sovereign's personation.

25 I *Sent.* D. 44, q. 2, a. 2. The reference to Cicero is to *De Officiis* I, 8, 26.

26 I *Sent.* D. 44, q. 2, a. 2, ad. 4.

27 I *Sent.* D. 44, q. 2, a. 2, ad. 5.

28 See below the discussions of tyranny by Johannes Althusius and Edward Sexby.

29 *De Regno*, Lib I, cap. 6; see Oakley 2012, 114f.

30 2a2ae, q. 104, a. 6, ad. 3. Thomas's student, Giles of Rome, seemed to vacillate between holding in one work that one is obliged to obey even tyrannical rulers and, in another work, to envisage the possibility of a ruler's deposition. [see Oakley 2012, 125, 195-206]

31 This distinction will be adopted and adapted later by the fifteenth century English lawyer and Chief Justice, Sir John Fortescue, in his *De Laudibus Legum Angliae*, written for the instruction of the young Prince Edward, then in exile. The work was published posthumously circa 1543. Eric Voegelin portrays Fortescue as advancing further along the secularising line already sketched out by John of Salisbury and Marsilius of Padua. Whereas John and Marsilius had left the means by which the political substance of a polity was formed somewhat mysterious, Fortescue penetrated more deeply into this obscure problem, as well as fitting his theory to the newly emerging English national realm. [Voegelin III, 157; see 155-162]

32 Finnis, 260. See 1a2ae q. 96, a. 5.

33 Giles, also known as Aegidius Romanus, is perhaps most well-known for his robust claim that the pope isn't just the supreme authority in the Church but also the only legitimate source of all earthly authority. It is possible that he significantly influenced the content of Boniface VIII's bull, *Unam Sanctam*. [See Lambertini, 11-15, Greenaway, 213-218, and Giles of Rome 1986, 2001 and 2004, passim] On the other side of the argument concerning the reach of papal power we find John of Paris, who argues in his *Tractatus de Potestate Regis et Papali* that the political community does not lie within the reach of papal power. The pope may excommunicate but the deposition of a ruler is a matter for others.

34 Godfrey's faith in the efficacy of elective procedures to produce the best and most prudent of individuals is, in the light of our greater experience, touching. Eight hundred years later, we are perhaps somewhat less sanguine about the merits of elections. [see van Reybrouck, passim]

35 2a2ae q. 64 a. 3, ad. 3; q. 65, a. 2, c.; 1a2ae q. 100 a. 3, c. and q. 100, a. 8, ad. 3.

36 See 2a2ae q. 64, a. 6, ad. 3; q. 67, a. 7. c.

37 2a2ae q. 25, a. 6, c., and ad. 1 and ad. 2.

38 See 2a2ae, q. 66, a. 2, obj. 2 and ad. 2.

39 See Tierney 2014. 'The moral or juridical relationships to such an entity that we call property rights are relationships to other people. They are matters of interpersonal justice. Arguments for founding rights on alleged "metaphysical" relationships between persons and the things with which they have "mixed their labour", or to which craftsmen have "extended their personality", are foreign to Aquinas.' [Finnis, 189]

40 *In Decem Libros Ethicorum*, Liber V, lect. 9, 981. Editio Tertia, Marietti, 1964.

Chapter 12

MARSILIUS OF PADUA—INTIMATIONS OF MODERNITY

The gift of liberty is like that of a horse, handsome, strong, and high-spirited.
In some it arouses a wish to ride; in many others,
on the contrary, it increases the desire to walk
—Massimo d'Azeglio

Every citizen would happily obey and accept a law passed as a result of
an audience or consent on the part of all the multitude...
in that with a law of this kind, each can be seen to have laid it upon himself,
and therefore has no cause to protest against it, but rather to accept it with equanimity
—Marsilius of Padua

From the time of the Gregorian Revolution, which began in the eleventh century, a deep tension, latent since the fifth century, had developed between the claims to temporal ascendancy of the Emperor and other secular rulers and the rival claims of the Papacy to *plenitudo potestatis*, to a fullness of power, secular as well as religious. 'The most public battle of the struggle, writes John Roberts, 'was fought just after the election of Pope Gregory VII in 1073.'[1] [Roberts 1997, 143] Gregory VII had 'pronounced the legal supremacy of the pope over all Christians and the legal supremacy of the clergy, under the pope, over all secular authorities.' [Berman 1983, 94] 'Gregory's thought was primarily directed at the freedom, and the renewal, of the church; but the severity of his polemics led to yet another form of the perennial medieval problem: that of claiming the privilege to act in a sphere that does not lend itself to such privileges. Gregory sought to establish the independence and liberty of the church from the supererogatory assertions of the emperor, but his revolutionary temperament in principle carried the Gelasian[2] ideal beyond itself.' [Greenaway, 42] Before 1073, the Church's autonomy was compromised by its existential entanglement with secular politics. Gregory's quest for independence for the Church, legitimate as far as it went, was framed in the context of overturning the superiority of the *regnum* to the *sacerdotium* and attempting to substitute for it not a functional balance or complementarity but the superiority of the *sacerdotium* to the *regnum*. This attempt, though understandable in its historical context, was, according to Albert Mirgeler, a 'sociological self-misunderstanding' which 'made the Church the first example of an attempt to establish a total sovereignty, since she had to try to incorporate all spheres and all the phenomena of life into the whole scheme of her norms and—of greater importance historically—legal sanctions.' [Mirgeler, 105] A struggle between the two authorities ensued over the next 250 years that would eventually result in the so-called Babylonian Captivity of the Papacy (1309-1377), followed by the Great Western Schism, two events that did irreparable damage to papal prestige and authority. The Great Western Schism, which began in 1378, lasted for almost forty years until it was ended in 1417 by the Council of Constance (1414-1418). For those forty years, a lifetime for many people, the question of who was Pope was a matter of fierce religious, political and diplomatic controversy, a controversy that did little to enhance the authority of the papacy. The confusion created by the Schism opened the way for the development of a conciliar theory of Church government, 'the essentially constitutionalist conviction that side by side with the institution of papal monarchy (and in intimate connection with it) it was necessary to give the Church's communal and corporate dimension more prominent and more regular institutional expression.' [Oakley 2003, vii] The 1415 decree of the Council, *Haec Sancta*, which asserted the power of general councils over all, including popes, was declared to be invalid, as was the pope elected by the Council, Martin V. Apart from its practical effect on its immediate contemporaries and succeeding generations, the struggle between the *imperium* and the *sacerdotium* stimulated two important political thinkers—the Italian, Marsilius (of Padua), and the Englishman, William (of Ockham).

The Papacy made its greatest bid for political supremacy[3] with the publication of Boniface VIII's *Unam Sanctam* in 1302, the beginning of a century which, ironically, was also the beginning of the end for papal pretensions to temporal power.[4] The long-running simmering tension between Emperor and Pope came to a head in the early fourteenth century when the exiled Avignon Pope John XXII tried to intervene in a contested imperial election in 1323. The row rumbled on for over twenty years before finally coming to an end in 1347 with victory going to the side of the Emperor, the Imperial Electors utterly repudiating the papal claim that the election of an Emperor required papal confirmation. The two hundred year struggle forced all the parties to it to think long and hard about fundamental political concepts. Under the Roman conception of *imperium*, the objects of legal jurisdiction were social categories or classes, not individuals. In their attempt to assimilate the Roman idea of *imperium* and apply it to papal claims of *plenitudo potestatis* (fullness of power), the canonists made individuals, rather than classes, the subject of jurisdiction and, in so doing, they 'purged Roman law of hierarchical assumptions surviving from the social structure of the ancient world.' [Siedentop, 219] Between one subject and another, regarded just as subjects, there could be no moral or legal difference. By undermining the political force of status relationships, the Church reformers had sown the seeds of a notion of sovereignty that could be applied not only within the Church but also in secular polities. Between the ruler and his subjects too there could be a direct relationship not mediated by intervening structures. 'The papal claim of sovereignty prepared the way for the emergence of the state as a distinct form of government.'

[Siedentop, 219] Jean Bodin's conception of sovereignty—often presented as if it sprang unheralded and unanticipated from Bodin's brain alone—was to be the logical development of these papal claims.[5] Even though the Papal project ultimately ended in failure, its example stimulated the increasingly ambitious but politically enfeebled secular rulers who learned the lesson that 'sovereignty offered them a means of centralizing not only authority but also power in their kingdoms' and 'a basis for undermining "feudal" jurisdictions.' [Siedentop, 229]

'Whatever the success of the Gregorians in reducing the degree of direct royal and imperial control over episcopal appointments (and they could not eliminate it),' writes Francis Oakley 'they did little to undercut the whole system of noble proprietary control over churches.' [Oakley 2003, 23] Oakley identifies two characteristic weakness of the medieval Church: 'the politicization of the Church's self-understanding' and 'the transformation of the very idea of ecclesiastical office itself.' [Oakley 2003, 22] An appreciation of the complex interaction of these two disabilities is, Oakley thinks, essential to 'make sense of the path that led from the great papal successes of the eleventh, twelfth, and early thirteenth centuries to the more questionable achievements of the Avignonese papacy and, thence, to the onset of the Great Schism, to the subsequent demand of church reformers for "reform in head and members", and to the conviction in particular of the reformers whom we know as "conciliarists" that the achievement and enduring effectiveness of such reform would be guaranteed only if significant changes were made in the very constitution of the universal Church.'[6]

Marsilius[7] was born in the northern Italian city of Padua sometime between 1275 and 1280, shortly after the death of Thomas Aquinas. He studied medicine before becoming Rector of the University of Paris and it is not to be wondered at that his writings are replete with medical analogies. He wrote his most famous work *Defensor Pacis* [*Defender of the Peace*] in 1324.[8] Although he is known almost exclusively for this work, he wrote others that also deserve attention. The most significant of these is his *Defensor Minor*, which is at once a recapitulation of some of the principal themes of *Defensor Pacis* and also contains some clarification and extensions of its doctrines. *Defensor Pacis* was originally released into the public realm without any author's name attached to it and it was several years before Marsilius was revealed to be its author, at which time he found it expedient to flee from Paris to the safety of the court of Louis of Bavaria at Nuremberg.[9] Apart from some forays abroad with the Holy Roman Emperor, he spent the rest of his life as an adviser in the imperial court and died around the year 1343.

Such is the fertility of Marsilius's ideas that he risks being all things to all men. His writings have been deemed to foreshadow participatory democracy, Marxism, liberalism and republicanism. [Nederman 2009, 150] Alan Gewirth remarks that 'The modern theory of sovereignty, in its extreme Hobbesian and Rousseauean form, derives from Marsilius…' [Gewirth, lix] 'Marsilio's theory,' writes George Sabine, 'is one of the most remarkable creations of medieval political thought and showed for the first time the subversive consequences to which a completely naturalistic interpretation of Aristotle might logically lead.' [Sabine, 289] And Alexander d'Entrèves notes, somewhat ironically, that 'The author of the *Defensor Pacis* has been hailed in turn as the announcer of most, if not of all, the doctrines which were to become the creative forces of the modern era, a precursor of the Reformation, a theorist of popular sovereignty and constitutional systems, a herald of the modern sovereign state: a rather curious, and even incompatible, assortment of doctrines.' [d'Entrèves 1939, 44] Eric Voegelin notes, tartly, that 'The inclination to read modern ideas into a medieval treatise at all costs was due rather…to the willingness of historians of the progressivist age to enhance the greatness of an earlier thinker by letting him brilliantly "anticipate" later ideas because "later" ideas are supposedly more advanced and enlightened so that their "anticipation" is a particular merit.' [Voegelin III, 85] In any event, Voegelin regards the *Defensor Pacis* rather as the end of an almost century-old battle of ideas rather than the instauration of a new intellectual regime.

What kind of work was it that could give rise to such a range of diverse judgements?

EMPEROR VERSUS POPE

Marsilius's *Defensor Pacis* is just one rivulet in a torrent of writing that rushed out on the rival claims of the *sacerdotium* and the *regnum*.[10] Marsilius's ambition in his *Defensor Pacis* was to undermine as completely as possible any pretensions of the *sacerdotium* (the ecclesiastical hierarchy—particularly the Pope) justifiably to exercise control over the actions of the *regnum* (the secular leaders—in particular, the Holy Roman Emperor).[11] The first part of *Defensor Pacis* lays out the conditions for the stability and unity of secular communities as a preface to its second part in which Marsilius comprehensively repudiates papal authority in secular affairs. In the quarrel between Pope and Emperor as to who was the supreme authority, Marsilius wasn't so much a supporter of the Emperor as an enemy of the Pope. His account of secular politics was taken from and was primarily applicable to the Italian city-states; he had no particular attachment to the Empire except insofar as its activities affected the welfare of the Italian city-states and he gives no clear indication of how the political theory developed in *Defensor Pacis* is to apply to the Empire or even to less extensive political units, such as the kingdom of France.[12] As was the case with the other city-states of northern Italy, Padua, Marsilius's birthplace, had a system of communal self-government that operated by means of a system of councils under an elected official from outside the city who administered the system of justice. [see Morrall 1971, 105] Despite being nominally self-governing, Padua and the other northern Italian cities found themselves caught in the middle of the quarrel between the Pope and the Emperor.

If Marsilius's ambition had been realised, it might appear to have had the consequence of making the Church simply a department of State. To think like this, however, is to run the risk of anachronism. It is important to be clear that the contest between the *sacerdotium* and the *regnum* wasn't a struggle between Church and State, as we now understand those terms. Secular rulers of

Marsilius's time could hardly have imagined how they could manage without the Church, and the Church likewise would have found it hard to imagine how she could do without what we would now call 'the state'. But 'to speak of the "state" in this context can be misleading,' writes McClelland. 'We speak of feudal "societies" rather than "states" because the idea of the state has come to be closely associated with the idea of sovereignty, and it is by no means clear that the medieval rulers were sovereign in anything like the ancient or modern senses.' [McClelland, 131] Moreover, in the fourteenth century, the idea of something like a national church was frankly inconceivable, just as inconceivable as a church deprived of any independent form or organisation of its own. Nevertheless, the inconceivable can become conceivable and in the seventeenth century post-Reformation religious settlement, Churches, Catholic and Protestant, did become, in effect, departments of state. 'Like many Protestants after him,' writes George Sabine, 'Marsilio was really in a position where he ought to have remitted all religious questions to private judgment and regarded the church as a purely voluntary organization, but it is hardly surprising that he did not draw in the fourteenth century a conclusion which Protestants refused to draw in the sixteenth.' [Sabine, 300]

Marsilius's theory was a kind of embryonic Erastianism, the theory that the state is superior to the church in ecclesiastical matters. This theory was later to come to the fore in England in the writings of Richard Hooker (*On the Laws of Ecclesiasticall Politie*) and, most notoriously, in the *Leviathan* of Thomas Hobbes. Among Marsilian scholars, Alexander d'Entrèves seems the most disposed to characterise him as a proto-Erastian, going so far as to argue that 'Marsilius's theory leads, in fact…to a complete absorption of the church into the state. It is here that we must look for the real "modernism" of Marsilius's position. If we are to see in it an anticipation of later systems and doctrines, it is certainly not the modern notion of religious liberty that we can find in it. It is much rather a notion which implies the most radical denial of any such liberty, and expresses that complete subjection of the church to the state, which was to be the outcome of the Reformation in some countries of Europe.' [d'Entrèves 1939, 82]

George McClelland believes that the idea of statehood was lost when the Classical world came to an end and that it had to be re-invented again by Marsilius and others. [McClelland, 136] I do not find this claim plausible, primarily because I believe that the idea of statehood in the relevant sense wasn't known to the classical world at all so that, when the state did eventually come into existence, it wasn't a matter of rediscovery but a matter of invention *ab initio*. Whether or which, McClelland *is* correct in his belief that in Marsilius's day the state as we now know it did not exist and that it is important not to read *Defensor Pacis* as if it did. He remarks, 'it is easy to read *The Defender of Peace* from a modern secular angle and to imagine that in Marsilius's own day truly sovereign states in the modern sense actually existed. Marsilius's own direct transposition of key political terms from the ancient to the medieval world compounds the likelihood of an anachronistically modern reading of the work.' [McClelland, 137]

MARSILIUS'S AUTHORITIES

Marsilius takes as given the truthfulness of Christian revelation; he also takes as given, the core aspects of Aristotle's political thought. If Aristotle and Christian Revelation appear to conflict then one of them must be being misunderstood. If one takes Aristotle as one's starting point in politics, as Marsilius does, then in a case of apparent conflict, it must be that Christian Revelation is being misunderstood. The structure of *Defensor Pacis* mirrors this priority among authorities: Aristotle in Part I, Christian Revelation in Part II. It must be clearly understood, however, that although Marsilius is anti-clerical, he isn't anti-religious.[13] Whatever may be the ultimate truth of religion and its future consequences in another world, its effects in this world are matters for secular regulation. In his *Defensor Pacis* we witness, for the first time in Christian Europe, a dramatic and radical secularisation of politics.

Inasmuch as Marsilius had any immediate intellectual mentor, that mentor was Aristotle, especially, those parts of the *Politics* in which Aristotle discussed the causes of revolution and civil unrest.[14] Of course, Aristotle couldn't have foreseen among the sources of civil dissension a transnational spiritual authority outside the *polis* claiming an ultimate authority over secular rulers but his general account of the causes of revolution and dissension, suitably modified, was applicable to the circumstances of fourteenth-century Europe. When Aristotle's writings descended upon an astonished Europe in the thirteenth century, two extreme reactions to it were possible; on the one hand, to reject it totally as unnecessary, if not dangerous, for the Christian community; on the other hand, to see it as a source of truth parallel to that of Christian Revelation. The ground of Marsilius's theory was an attempt to recover and apply the Aristotelian conception of the *polis* as a self-sufficient political entity to the social and political circumstances of his time, although the temporal and psychic distance of his work from that of Aristotle and the inevitable formation of his ideas by the very different religious and political realities of his time make his ideas anything but a simple re-presentation of Aristotelian ideas. The Aristotelian conception of the *polis* is that it is the self-sufficient community and this is Marsilius's point of departure in his reflection on politics. For Marsilius, the political community exists so that men may lead a life of sufficiency. The elements of the state aren't just isolated individuals but functionally different parts making their contribution to the whole. If one or other of the parts gets out of order, then the whole suffers, as it were, a kind of social cancer. The condition in which all the parts of the political community work together is peace, the primary function of the ruling part of the community being to prevent any disturbance of the peace or to restore peace whenever it has been disturbed.

Even though Aristotle is the pre-eminent authority upon which Marsilius relies, he isn't the only one. Marsilius appeals to Cicero's *De Officiis* to bolster his claim that men exist to serve one another. Following Cicero, he believes that justice not only implies the obvious duty to refrain from injuring others, a claim that libertarians will have no difficulty accepting, but also a positive obligation to protect others from harm, a claim that, if understood legally, no libertarian could accept.[15] Human sociability implies a responsibility to eliminate antisocial beliefs and practices anywhere and everywhere. Marsilius held, as Machiavelli was to hold years later, that the Papacy's claim to exercise supreme secular authority was the root cause of civil and political dissension in Italy. Among the many causes of strife, he writes, there is 'one singular and well-hidden cause, under which the Roman Empire has laboured for a long time and labours still.' [I. i. 3] Papal aggression is a major threat to human happiness and so Marsilius believes, on Ciceronian grounds, that all have a Christian duty to resist papal infringements on secular authority.

A LIFE OF SUFFICIENCY

What, for Marsilius, is a life of sufficiency? For the most part, it is a life in which men have access to the material necessities of human life, 'a plain *bourgeois* desire for sufficient material tranquillity to permit the smooth interchange of economic and social benefits.' [Morrall 1971, 107] Marsilius does not mean by sufficiency what Aristotle means by the good life or Aquinas by the virtuous life. It isn't the political community's job to make the good or virtuous life possible except indirectly by taking care of the conditions that make possible the acquisition of basic material necessities upon which the good or virtuous life may supervene. The rulers of the political community provide peace and order so that men can provide for themselves the good things they can derive from nature. Marsilius exhibits a refreshingly concrete attitude to the aim of politics, 'a down-to-earth concentration on political life dictated by the material human conditions of economics, biology and psychology.' [Morrall 1971, 107] He does not reject any of the higher aims of life; he just doesn't see the cultivation of them as the direct task of the political community and in this he stands in opposition to both St Thomas and Aristotle.

Marsilius accepts as his fundamental principle of human action that all men desire a sufficient life and avoid what is not conducive to this: 'all men not deficient or otherwise impeded naturally desire a sufficient life, and by the same token shun and avoid those things that are harmful to them' [I, iv. 2] and he endorses Cicero's assertion in *De Officiis*, that the most basic purpose of all living creatures is self-preservation: 'all species of living creatures are endowed by nature with the capacity to protect their lives and their persons, to avoid things likely to harm them, and to seek out and procure all life's necessities such as food, hidden lairs, and the like.' [*De Officiis* I, 11] He takes the position that human beings are naturally sociable and cooperate to their mutual advantage in the formation and operation of an organised community: 'For men gathered into a civil community in order to pursue their benefit and the sufficient life and to avoid their contraries. And therefore any convenience or inconvenience that can affect all ought to be known and heard by all, so that they can pursue their benefit and avoid its contrary.' [I, xii, 7]

The original motivation for human association is the mutual advantage that promotes individual self-interest. Something more than mere survival can be achieved in a community when we get differentiation of function and a division of labour. Marsilius adopts an account of human beings that sees them possessed of capacities that fit them for a given specialisation but, unlike many other theorists, he does not believe that this specialisation debars artisans or manual labourers from participating in some way in the political community. 'Marsilio insists that the intercommunication of functions required for the public welfare necessitates a politics of inclusion, and he thus construes citizenship in a remarkably extensive fashion. Citizenship is consequently conferred on a strictly functional basis, judged according to the usefulness of various human activities for the meeting of material human ends.' [Nederman 2009, 154-155]

At this point, a libertarian might well ask: if the advantage of the individual is the end of human association, why is government necessary at all? Marsilius's answer to this question appears to be that in the furtherance of their own interests, individuals are impelled to congregate but, as a result of this very congregation, they are very likely to come into conflict with one another. [see Morrall 1971, 109] Without laws and an executive power to enforce those laws, peace can't be preserved. In an eerily anticipatory echo of Hobbes, Marsilius claims that the basic task of government is to be a defender of the peace—hence the title of his work. Because man is born 'naked and undefended against the excesses of the air which surrounds him, and of the other elements...therefore he stood in need of arts of different kinds and types in order to resist the said damage. And since these arts couldn't be practised except by a large number of men, nor retained except by their mutual communication, men need to gather together to secure the advantage to be had from them and to avoid disadvantage. But because disputes and scuffles break out among men who are gathered together in this way, and these, were they not regulated by a norm of justice, would cause fighting, the separation of men and ultimately the destruction of the city, it was necessary to institute within this community a standard of justice and a guardian and executor of it.' [I, iv. 4] The production and maintenance of peace is the basic reason for which government exists and the condition without which no one can obtain a sufficient life. [I. i. 1] 'Peace for Marsiglio,' writes Cary Nederman, 'is not an end in itself, but a requirement for the realization of stable intercourse within the community towards the end of a materially sufficient life. Whatever threatens the peace is necessarily inconsistent with the natural and proper goal of human society' [Nederman 2009, 157]

The tranquillity of the city can be disturbed from without or from within. External considerations are things such as bad weather or natural disasters that can affect the political community's ability to provide a sufficiency; internal considerations, however, are the human passions that issue in actions that affect others for good or for ill. Employing once more a medical metaphor, he conceives of some human actions as proceeding from an excess that, if not restrained, can lead to conflict and the consequent destruction of the political community. The cure for such excess is the restoration of some kind of balance. 'There are other actions and passions,' he says, 'which come from us or occur within us as a result of our cognitive and appetitive powers. Some of these are called 'immanent', i.e. because they do not cross over into a subject different from the agent nor are they performed by means of an external organ or limb moved in respect of place. Such are the thoughts and desires and inclinations of men. Whereas others are and are called 'transitive', because in one or other of the said ways they are in contrast with those just mentioned.' [I, v, 4] Transitive actions may cause inconvenience or injury to others. In order to moderate excesses arising from some of these transitive actions 'there was of necessity instituted within the city a particular part or office through which the excesses of such acts might be corrected and reduced to equality or due proportion.'[16]

As he was a student of medicine, it is understandable that Marsilius uses the analogy of health and sickness in his evaluation of political regimes. Just as a body can be healthy or diseased, so too can a city. A body will be unhealthy if its constituent parts compete with each other instead of cooperating; so too with the city. The health of a body is the co-operation of all its organs: the health of the city is tranquillity. [see I. ii. 3] In line with Aristotle's distinction between good polities and bad polities,[17] Marsilius thinks of temperate or healthy government as government for the good of all, intemperate or unhealthy government as that which is good only for some of the parts. In order to illustrate what tranquillity and its opposition is, he imagines 'that the city is like a kind of animate or animal nature. For the animal which is in a good condition in respect of its nature is composed of certain proportionate parts arranged in respect of each other, all communicating their action between themselves and towards the whole; likewise too the city which is in a good condition and established in accordance with reason is made up of certain such parts. A city and its parts would therefore seem to be in the same relation to tranquillity as an animal and its parts is to health...'[18] The less picturesque definition of tranquillity is that it is the 'good condition of a city or realm in which each of its parts is enabled perfectly to perform the operations appropriate to it according to reason and the way it has been established.' [I, ii, 3]

Law

Marsilius's sharp division between the spiritual and the secular is applied to law. Though on the surface it appears multifaceted, in the end, Marsilius's division of law reduces to a simple bifurcation; we have divine law and we have human law. [*Defensor Minor*, 1. ii] Both forms of law are presented as the outcomes of commands: the one the result of a divine command, the other the result of a human command. Both forms of law have content but only human law is coercible in this world. In this, as in other matters, Marsilius's thought differs fundamentally from that of Aquinas. [see Voegelin III, 97] For Aquinas, all law was understood to be essentially the same kind of thing albeit requiring to be understood analogously, cascading downwards, as it were, from eternal law through divine law to natural law and human law. For Marsilius, on the other hand, divine law and human law are essentially different. Moreover, for Aquinas, law was an ordinance of reason consonant with the natures of those subject to it and not simply an expression of a legislator's will, whereas for Marsilius, law is essentially a command, an expression of the will of the legislator, the disobeying of which will attract a penal sanction.

Alexander d'Entrèves identifies the dependence of the whole body politic on the will of the legislator as *the* novelty of Marsilius's system. [see d'Entrèves 1939, 59] I am not so sure it is quite the novelty d'Entrèves thinks it is. Cicero, one of Marsilius's sources, had remarked that as the magistrate is under the law, so too the people are under the magistrate. 'As magistrates are subject to laws, the people are subject to the magistrates. In fact it is true to say that a magistrate is a speaking law, and law a silent magistrate.' [*De Legibus*, III, 2] All that is missing to square Cicero with Marsilius is to have the people be the source of law; and that is precisely the direction in which Marsilius goes.

God is obviously the legislator in the case of divine law. Who is the legislator of human law? Ideally, the whole body of the people but where that is not possible (and it isn't often going to be possible) then it is the weightier part of the community (*valentior pars*). Eric Voegelin holds that Marsilius's theory of the legislator is 'the first consistent construction of the intramundane political unit, deriving governmental authority not from an extraneous source but from a specially constructed "whole" of the community behind its single parts.' He continues, 'it is a genuinely medieval idea, using the material of the medieval stratified society for the conception of the "whole," without regard to the possibilities of a populist construction that were present in the politico-religious town movements.' [Voegelin III, 91]

Determining which part of the community is the weightier part is more a qualitative than a quantitative matter. In any political community, there will be those, usually those few, who are best placed and best circumstanced to declare the law. In Marsilius's city-state, those would be the oligarchs of the city. Who was to play this role in the various kingdoms and principalities of the Holy Roman Empire? It isn't so easy for Marsilius to answer this question. The legislator is 'the primary and proper efficient cause of the law…the people or the universal body of the citizens or else its prevailing part, when, by means of an election or will expressed in speech in a general assembly of the citizens, it commands or determines, subject to temporal penalty or punishment, that something should be done or omitted in respect of human civil acts.' [I, xii, 3] The body of the people or its prevailing part give effect to their will in a general assembly operating according to a set of rules. Human law making, then, requires something akin to an executive body whose authority derives ultimately from all the people. Law supported by such authority may be made not only in a formal assembly but can also be expressed through generally accepted custom.

Wisdom is the cumulative possession of a community, not the inspiration of some particularly enlightened person. Marsilius thinks of knowledge as something that is gradually accumulated so that, at the start of an inquiry, we have at best a partial and limited grasp on the truth. Understanding requires a community and is a function of a common history. There will be those in the community who are above average in their grasp and understanding of political matters but they are not and cannot be the only judges of what is good or bad. If the prince were to act as legislator, he would lack the communal wisdom of the whole body of citizens and would be susceptible to partiality in respect of himself and his family and his own interests.

In *Defensor Pacis* Marsilius positioned the people as a whole as the legislator[19] but appears to be somewhat ambiguous as to the actual extent of the people in this context. Should the people be understood narrowly or broadly, inclusively or exclusively? Are artisans and workmen to be included in this body or not? John B. Morrall thinks that the *valentior pars* comprises 'the vast majority of the community—the normal undeformed citizens. In their persons, the claims of both quality and quantity are reconciled.' [Morrall 1971, 113] In the *Defensor Minor*, Marsilius appears to clarify this point. He writes, 'the power and authority to correct rulers who are negligent or irresponsible in performing their duties by restraining them through punishment of their persons or property belongs solely to the human legislator....if such correction pertains to some particular part or office of the civic body, then under no circumstances does it pertain to the priests, but instead to the men of prudence or learned teachers, indeed preferably to the workmen or craftsmen or the rest of the labourers.' [*Defensor Minor*, 2, vii] Nederman takes this passage as indicating that the task of correction should be given for preference to workmen and artisans rather than the men of prudence or learned teachers. The passage is somewhat ambiguous, however, and I think it more likely that Marsilius is counselling that the task of correction be given not to priests but to men of prudence and learned teachers *in preference to* the workmen or craftsmen. This would correspond to what he says explicitly in *Defensor Pacis*: 'it is the province of any citizen to discover the [content of the] law...even if this kind of inquiry can more appropriately be undertaken and more adequately completed through the observations of those who have the possibility of leisure—elders and those experienced in action, who are called "the prudent"—than through the cogitations of mechanical workers who must concentrate on their labours in order to acquire the necessities of life.' [I, xii, 2]

The multiple authorities and legal structures prevalent in the Middle Ages could and did give rise to situations in which rival claims conflicted and were capable of being arbitrated in different ways. Often, of course, agreement was possible, or one or other side would concede, but sometimes agreement wasn't possible and neither side would give way. When the two competing sides were the *regnum* and the *sacerdotium*, specifically the Empire and the Papacy, trouble was bound to ensue. Both laid claim to men's allegiance; both could claim divine support; both had means at their disposal to cause trouble for the other; but, in the end, each had need of the other.

For Marsilius, good government is government by law, not force. Good law should be clear and knowable and it should really be law, not just force masquerading as law. What makes law to be law? One thing on which all the medievals were agreed, though their working out of that agreement was a contentious matter, was that the law wasn't something that could, still less ought to, be made. 'To think otherwise, that human beings really could make law, was to take a position with potentially very radical implications.'[20] Until relatively recently, the task of the judge in common law systems in cases not readily subsumable under existing legal rules was to 'find' the law, the assumption being that the law governing this particular case was there to be found, just that the occasion for finding it hadn't arisen until now. It cannot be too much emphasised that the idea that it is the task of a specific body to *make* law—

as distinct for codifying, clarifying or synthesising aboriginal law—is a very new and a very revolutionary idea. Despite its novelty and its revolutionary character, the idea of law as the product of a legislature is now the dominant conception of what law is in Western societies. McClelland remarks that 'it is not clear when men in the West began to believe that they could truly make new law. The distinction between "law-declarer" and "law-maker" was still alive and well at the end of the eighteenth century...' [McClelland, 140]

VOX POPULI

Marsilius's ideas have often been taken to presage a theory of consent of the governed and it's easy to see why one might think this. All those whose interests are determined in any way by a community must be granted full membership of that community. In Roman law, there was a maxim that *quod omnes similiter tangit, ab omnibus comprobetur*—what touches or concerns all similarly should be approved by all. So, Marsilius gives the following argument: Either the legislator is all, one or a few. If one, the distorting effects of passion and self-interest might induce him to pass a bad law; similarly with the few. 'It belongs, therefore, to the universal body of the citizens or its prevailing part, where the reasoning is different and contrasting. For because all the citizens must be measured by law in due proportion, and no one willingly harms or wants what is unjust for himself, therefore all or most of them want a law that is adapted to the common advantage of the citizens' [I, xii, 8] This passage gives two reasons why the legislator should be the citizen body as a whole. The first is that by having all give their approval, it irons out the idiosyncrasies that might well result if the laws were made by only one or a few. Secondly, since the law that is made by me will apply to me, and that's the case for all citizens, then it is most likely to be made for the advantage of all.

But it might be objected that there's as good a chance of the voice of the people being *vox diaboli* as being *vox dei*. What then? A political community can only come into being if the majority of its citizens are willing to support it and engage with it in such a way that it is truly productive of a sufficiency. That being so, 'citizens in the plural are neither wicked nor undiscerning, at least in respect of most individuals and most of the items: all or most are of sound mind and reason and of an upright desire for the polity and what is necessary for its survival, such as laws and other statutes or customs, as shown before. For although not every citizen, nor the greater multitude, may discover the laws, every citizen is none the less capable of a judgement on those which have been discovered and put to him by another, and of perceiving if something should be added or removed or changed.' [I, xiii, 3] Secondly, even if we have among us those who are wise, it doesn't follow that 'the wise know how to discern what needs to be established better than the entire multitude, which includes them along with the rest of the less learned.' [I, xiii, 4]

As members of a community, individuals must agree to the terms constituting it—the laws by which it is to be regulated and the executive principles by which it is to be governed. Once consent is given, individuals are bound to obey the law and the decisions made by the rulers of the community in conformity with those laws. This account is of particular interest to libertarians inasmuch as it makes the legitimacy of the community a voluntary matter. A regime is well-tempered, Marsilius thinks, to the degree that it is exercised 'over willing subjects and in accordance with a law passed for the common advantage of these subjects' and laws 'must receive their necessary approval from the same primary authority [the universal body of the people or its prevailing part] and no other.'[21] Participation in the political life of the community therefore is, for Marsilius, real and not nominal and even if citizens-in-the-street are not expected to devote themselves full-time to political matters, it is appropriate and expedient for them to delegate this task to 'prudent and experienced men.' [I, xiii. 8]

The legitimacy of any government, then, depends upon the voluntary assent of those over whom government is to be exercised. Once one has assented to a law, one can't afterwards object to its enforcement. 'But every citizen would happily obey and accept a law passed as a result of an audience or consent on the part of all the multitude...in that with a law of this kind, each can be seen to have laid it upon himself, and therefore has no cause to protest against it, but rather to accept it with equanimity.' [I, xii, 6] This idea of legal obligation resulting from the imposition of a law on oneself will echo through the succeeding centuries, resonating in such thinkers as diverse as Rousseau and Kant and Hegel.

Marsilius's account of the popular basis of sovereignty can be made to sound radical and forward-looking but its effect is to strengthen, not weaken, the authority of the secular rulers of the political community. To describe the people as the source of political sovereignty isn't at all the same thing as to say that the people should exercise political sovereignty. Marsilius was no democrat, as that term is understood in the contemporary world, and there was enough of Augustine in him to think that sinful men required a firm hand, otherwise the peace would be disturbed.

The prospects for freedom in Marsilius's world are anything but propitious. Whereas before Marsilius, the *sacerdotium* and the *regnum* worked together to restrain and repress the selfish disruptive tendencies of men, with the removal of the coercive power of the spiritual authority the whole task of repressing and restraining men now falls on the shoulders of the secular rulers and there's nothing to prevent them requiring a stricter and more rigidly enforced obedience to secular law than obtained in the competing and conflicting multiple authorities of the medieval world. Whereas in the pre-Marsilian world, there existed the possibility of playing one coercive authority off against another, in the Marsilian world, that possibility no longer exists.[22] There can be no doubt that Marsilius desires the freedom of every citizen. He writes, 'any and every citizen should be free and not suffer the despotism...of another. But this would not be the case if some one or few of the citizens passed law upon the universal body of the citizens on their own authority, for in legislating in this way they would be despots over the others,' [I, xii, 6] But in the *Defensor Minor*, Marsilius, disappointingly from a libertarian perspective, remarks that 'divine law commands obedience to human rulers and laws which are not contrary to divine law…'[23] In the end, Marsilius appears to have no fully developed theory of freedom. Just as the promotion of the virtuous life, although not rejected by Marsilius, is deferred by him, so too is the ultimate value of freedom.

Would the Marsilian theory lead to an incipient totalitarianism of the majority? Cannot the whole community assent to laws that are morally objectionable? No. The assent of the community to the laws that govern it is a necessary but not a sufficient condition of the validity of those laws. The laws of a community may or may not conform with justice but Marsilius thinks that the greater the level of consent to laws, the more likely it is that the laws approved of do in fact conform with justice. The standard of justice we are to employ in our reflections isn't an abstract conception but one that bears directly on each and everyone's self-interest. Given that communities are formed for the preservation of the individual and the advancement of his interests, this is hardly surprising. 'Those matters, therefore, that can touch upon the advantage and disadvantage of everyone ought to be known and heard by everyone, so that they can obtain advantage and repel its opposite.' [I, xii, 7] The common good of the community, then, isn't something over and above the good of the individuals making up the community; it is, rather, the sum total of advantage over disadvantage of the individuals in the community. In short, if an individual wants to know what the communal benefit is of any proposed law or regulation, he need only consult his own benefit and 'anyone can check whether a proposed law tends more to the advantage of a particular man or men than to that of other or of the community…' [I, xii, 5] Without the test of popular assent, it is likely that the law will lean towards the benefit of the few rather than the many. But where there is none to object to a proposal on the grounds that it is detrimental to his interest, then that law is more than likely to be reasonable. Marsilius does not manifest any strong preference for any particular form of governance, whether monarchy, aristocracy or democracy. He is much more concerned that a government be temperate or healthy than that it have a particular constitution, and no government can be healthy or temperate without the consent of the governed.[24]

However it comes into being, what is most important for the executive isn't only that it give expression to the law as determined by the legislator, it is also that it be supreme. Only if it is supreme or sovereign can it in fact give expression to the law. In considering this aspect of Marsilius's thought, it's difficult not to see this idea of the supremacy of the executive as being, at least in part, a response to the existential conditions of governance in the fourteenth century. Not only was there a division between the authority of the secular and the spiritual, both expressed legally in courts and in claims of jurisdiction, there were also multiple and overlapping forms of each of these two basic types in operation in any given area.[25]

Sovereignty is unitary and the secular authority is sovereign. As such, it and it alone has the coercive power that accompanies sovereignty. The *sacerdotium* then can have no coercive power unless the secular authority delegates such power to it and, of course, whatever is delegated can be un-delegated. Insofar as it claims to have a distinct jurisdiction, canon law is in error unless that jurisdiction is confined to purely spiritual matters with sanctions applicable in the hereafter. If it is to have coercive powers in the here and now it can have them only as delegated to it by the secular power. 'No other writer in the Middle Ages went so far as Marsilio in thus setting apart the spiritual and religious from the legal.' [Sabine, 299]

Anticipating the work of Jean Bodin, Marsilius's theory of sovereignty with its unitary and exclusive character is primarily designed to undermine the claim of the *sacerdotium* to exercise any jurisdiction in the here and now but its consequences would have been startling to the medieval man in the street. Not only is canon law as a separate system of jurisdiction more or less completely invalidated, all the temporal claims that the Church might make, including that of owning property, are seriously undermined. [see Lee] The Church can't lay claim to financial support from the Christian community as a matter of right unless that right be granted and supported by the secular authority. Even the filling of ecclesiastical offices is done only within boundaries set by the secular authority.

We can have peace, then, only if we have a unitary central authority (a prince) with coercive power to enforce the law, and there can be only one law for that authority to enforce. 'This...Marsilian theme is the forerunner of the doctrine of politics centered in considerations of power and stability which have been so characteristic of modern political thought.' [Gewirth, xxxviii] Does this imply that once we have a prince he may do whatever it is he wishes? Marsilius thinks not. And the answer lies in his conception of law. The function of the prince is to execute the law but the law isn't made by him but by the legislator, which is the whole people or the *valentior pars* of the people. Morrall writes that, 'authority is not wholly transferred; the *legislator humanus* retains ultimate sovereignty and can check, even depose, the *pars principans* [the prince] when necessary.' [Morrall 1971, 114] And whereas the transient acts of individuals may clash and lead to conflict, the people as a whole desire a peaceful state in which they may pursue their own ends. So, the will of an individual may be coerced by the prince but only if the prince in so acting is giving expression to the law that has been willed by all. If one were to detect the spectre of Rousseau at this point, one wouldn't be far wrong!

Law has to be given effect through an executive body of some kind or other. Whether this executive body is elected or hereditary isn't the primary consideration for Marsilius; what *is* important is that the executive should act in accordance with the law. That being said, Marsilius clearly has a preference for an elected executive. We need law to regulate excess, and we need someone to do the regulating. There can be only one such regulator or at least, only one supreme regulator in a political community. How does one prevent the prince or the regulator from becoming a tyrant? By means of the law. The prince isn't the legislator and the laws limit the prince's power so that he may act legitimately only in accordance with the law. Gewirth writes: 'The upshot, then, is that the people's will is unchallenged as the possessor of supreme authority. Doctrines of popular control were by no means foreign to medieval political thought. The Roman law tradition of the derivation of the emperor's power from the people, the Germanic tradition of the basis of law in immemorial custom, as well as the development of medieval institutions themselves, all pointed in this direction. Yet in no medieval work had this tendency been given so complete, explicit, and extensive a statement as in the popular sovereignty of Marsilius.' [Gewirth, xlv]

ONLY ONE PRINCE....

Marsilius presents us with six types of regime on the usual Aristotelian model: monarchy, aristocracy and polity (moderate democracy) on the good side, and tyranny, oligarchy and democracy on the bad. Of interest to us is his description of the good regimes as being 'tempered' whereas the bad ones are described as being 'distempered'. When it comes to what Marsilius calls a *regnum*, this term being sometimes translated somewhat anachronistically as 'state' (a better term might be 'realm'), there are four possible ways in which it can be taken: as a 'plurality of cities or provinces contained under one regime'; or a 'temperate regime' which one can have even in a single city; or a temperate regime over a plurality of cities or provinces; or, finally, whatever it is that all temperate regimes have in common, whether over one city or province or many. [I, ii, 2]

Marsilius's political theory is meant to be a 'one-size-fits-all' account inasmuch as it isn't tied to any particular people, nation, area, language or culture, nor does it endorse or recommend any particular form of political constitution. Although he is relatively indifferent to constitutional forms, Marsilius is far from indifferent to the manner in which the authority of a temperate realm is exercised. Any such realm must have a single supreme ruler; otherwise, all will be confusion and chaos. If there are diverse authorities in a given realm, then there must still be a supreme one to which all the others are ultimately subordinate. There can be only one prince in any political community, only one ultimate law-enforcer. In a single city or a single realm, he writes, 'there should be only one single principate; or if there are several, in number or species— as seems expedient in great cities, and most of all in a realm [containing a plurality of cities or provinces under one regime]—then there should be among them one in number that is supreme over all, to which and through which the rest are reduced and regulated, and any errors that arise in them corrected.' [I, xvii, 1] The unity Marsilius is talking about here may be either personal or institutional. What would happen if we did not have such unity? He writes, 'if there were more than one principate in a city or realm, and they were not reduced or ordered towards any one supreme, then the judgement, command and execution of what is advantageous and just would fail, and the result— because of injuries remaining unavenged between men—would be fighting, disintegration and ultimately the destruction of the city or realm.' [I, xvii, 3]

At the end of his book, Marsilius offers us this summary: 'The first citizen... of a civil regime...one man or several...will understand...that they alone have the authority to command the subject multitude, collectively, or individually, and to constrain any individual, if it is expedient to do so, according to the laws that have been laid down.' He goes on to say that 'they can do nothing more than this, particularly anything involving difficulty, without the consent of the subject multitude or the legislator and that the multitude or legislator should not be provoked by injustice, because the force and authority of the principate consists in the express will of this same multitude.' On their part, the subject multitude 'is obliged to obey only the commands of the princely part as being coercive for and in the status of this present world' and 'it will learn to keep as close a watch as possible that the princely or any other part of the community does not presume to be its own arbiter, by judging or taking any other action in the city against or outside the laws.' [III, iii]

Alan Gewirth isolates three theses in Marsilius's work. 1. The state, the political community, exists so that men may live well; 2. Political authority exists to resolve conflicts and so must have coercive power; and 3. The source of legitimate political power is the people. Gewirth notes that even though no one of these theses is particularly novel, the combination of all three in one work is. The first thesis is characteristic of ideal accounts of politics; the second, of positivistic or realistic accounts usually opposed to the idealistic; and the third implies an account of the state or political authority that can be set in opposition to both the first two but, in Marsilius's though, is meant to mediate the first and the second dialectically. [Gewirth, xxx-xxxi] Given this dialectical tension, it is no wonder that similarities between Marsilius and such diverse thinkers as Hobbes, Machiavelli and Rousseau have been drawn. [see Voegelin III, 101f.]

Marsilius starts with the idea that political obligation is based on the moral ends or virtues that a political community can help its citizens achieve. This idealistic conception is quickly moderated to the less lofty idea that political obligation is based on the ability of the executive office of the political community to prevent conflict and settle disputes. It is important to note that Marsilius never rejects the idealistic conception; he just does not pursue it further in *Defensor Pacis*. Although this may seem to be an anticipation of a characteristically Hobbesian theme, it is, in fact, a commonplace of medieval thought. So, for example, Aquinas, in his *De Regime Principum*, says that 'Where there are many men together and each one looks out for what suits himself, the multitude would be broken up onto diverse parts unless there were someone to watch out for that which concerns the good of the multitude.'[26] This theme coheres with the typical Augustinian idea that the sinfulness of men is what makes government necessary.

The approach a political philosopher takes towards this sociological fact (if it is a fact) determines to a large extent the outcome of his philosophy. If he takes it to be something relatively insignificant, something to be dealt with expeditiously before moving on to higher things, we will get a generally more optimistic political philosophy. If, as here, it is a recurring drumbeat that sounds all the way through, then the political philosophy is likely to be much less optimistic. This is what we find in Machiavelli and in Hobbes. Once again, Marsilius does not deny that the content of the law is determined relative to some standard of reason or justice, but the essential characteristic of law is a command backed by coercive force. This is an idea that will echo in Hobbes and others.

George Holmes says of Marsilius's achievements that it was 'an elegant theory and it is surprising that it did not become more popular. But it was too bold in its direct confrontation with the scholastics' ingenious adaptation of Aristotle to monarchical, theocratic end. In fact, Renaissance social ideology was going to advance by another route, by abandoning scholasticism entirely, rather than by adapting it to the city-state environment.' [Holmes 1975, 147] John Morrall reaches much the same conclusion: 'Though even Marsiglio did not realize it, the Christian Commonwealth, in the form in which the Middle Ages had created it, was ceasing to exist and in its place a new political *leitmotiv* was coming into control—the modern State.' [Morrall 1971, 118]

Shortly after Marsilius died, the Black Death pandemic descended upon Europe, having its maximum devastating effect on human mortality from 1346 to 1353. The devastation wrought by the plague consisted not only in the staggering death toll that it produced but also in its long-term social and religious consequences. Crops failed, workers rioted, bankruptcies proliferated, public works were abandoned. In defiance of the most basic human instincts, parents abandoned children and children parents, husbands wives and wives husbands. With some few heroic exceptions such as the nuns of the Hôtel Dieu in Paris, even the clergy and religious reneged on their duties towards their flocks so that to the agony of death, many of the dying died unshriven. The fear inspired by the plague gave rise to a resurgence of religious fanaticism and the usual targeting of suspect social groups.[27] Europe would never be the same again. To those who survived this apocalyptic period, T. S. Eliot's words might have resonated with their experience: 'This is the way the world ends/ Not with a bang but a whimper.'[28]

Notes

1 'Hildebrand...emerges from the records as far from attractive person, but a pope of great personal and moral courage....All his life he fought for the independence and dominance of the papacy within western Christendom.' [Roberts 1997, 143]

2 Pope Gelasius had outlined in a letter of AD 494 to the emperor Anastasius the doctrine that this world is ruled by sacred authority and royal power, the sacred authority supreme in religious affairs, the royal power supreme in secular affairs. '*Famuli vestrae pietatis,*' available at http://www.web.pdx.edu/~ott/Gelasius/, accessed 10 July 2016. See Mirgeler, 96.

3 'Historically, the papal claim to full imperial power was asserted only for a relatively brief period in the thirteenth century—from Gregory IX to Boniface VIII (1227-1303).' [Mirgeler, 106]

4 Greenaway writes, 'the recasting of the papal office as that of an imperial overlord, whose dominium claims a legalistic jurisdiction over church, empire, world, and existence itself...is a remolding that confounds the genuinely Christian foundation of medieval civil theology and the differentiation of authority into distinct but overlapping spheres set in motion from the beginning.' [Greenaway, 215] The papal revolution begun under Gregory VII, a revolution intended primarily towards the achievement of the independence of the church from the power of the temporal authorities, had overreached itself and compromised the differentiation of the various forms of authority.

5 Johannes Althusius's ideas (see below) would reintroduce intervening structures between the ultimate sovereign and the ultimate subject, but each intervening structure would itself have its own direct sovereign-subject structure, although a sovereign conceived in terms of service rather than domination.

6 Oakley 2003, 25; see Roberts 1997, 191-194.

7 Our subject's name was Marsiglio or Marsilio, Latinised as Marsilius or Marsillius.

8 In this chapter, citations within square brackets without attribution are from the *Defensor Pacis*.

9 Marsilius wasn't to have things all his own way. Augustine of Ancona (1270/3-1328) published his *Summa de ecclesiastica potestate* (*Summa on Ecclesiastical Power*), a work directly antithetical to *Defensor Pacis*, some few years after the publication of *Defensor Pacis*. Augustine's treatise is 'the most extensive medieval articulation of the papalist, curialist, or hierocratic conception of spiritual and temporal power earlier advanced by such authors as Giles of Rome and James of Viterbo and developed (with qualifications regarding secular affairs) by Juan de Torquemada, Cardinal Cajetan and Albert Pighi.' [McGrade, 418]

10 It is, perhaps, advisable at this point to state that although the political thought of the late Middle Ages (from around 1300 to 1550) such as we find in Marsilius, Machiavelli and others will produce ideas and theories of politics ever more familiar to us, it is none the less the case that 'kingship, whether tending toward absolutism or limited in nature, remained as heretofore the dominant political form and certainly the one to which the political thinkers of the day devoted by far the greater part of their attention.' [Oakley 2015, 4]

11 See Morrall 1971, 28. For a short but sympathetic treatment of Marsilius's ideas, together with those of his younger contemporary Bartolus of Saxoferrato, in the context of popular associations, customary law and, in particular, their relevance to the conciliar movement, see Part III of Ullmann 1966, 215-305. Ullmann writes, 'What, with the help of Aristotle, Marsiglio ideologically achieved for the political sovereignty of the people his contemporary Bartolus with the help of the Roman law achieved for the legal sovereignty of the people. Bartolus was the exact antipode of Marsiglio: entirely independent of each other they arrived at the same result by entirely different routes.' [Ullmann 1966, 282] The application of Marsilian-Bartolist thought to conciliarism could be summed up in the idea that 'the sum-total of power is located in the *populus christianus* which finds its representative organ in the general council.... The hallmark of the conciliar theme is the denial that the source of power is transmitted downwards through the mediating agency of the priesthood.' [Ullmann 1966, 288]

12 See d'Entrèves 1939, 53; see also Tierney 1988, 172-192.

13 George Sabine, however, is inclined to take the Marsilian moment as having anti-religious consequences: 'Such a separation of reason and faith is the direct ancestor of religious skepticism, and in its consequences amounts to a secularism which is both anti-Christian and anti-religious....The church is a part of the secular state in every respect in which it affects temporal matters.' [Sabine, 294]

14 See d'Entrèves 1939, 87.

15 See Cicero, *De Officiis*, I. 20.

16 I, v, 7; see Aristotle's *Politics* 1291a2-4.

17 Eric Voegelin believes that the antecedents of Marsilius's analogy are to be found in John of Salisbury rather than in Aristotle. [see Voegelin III, 88]

18 I, ii, 3; compare Aristotle *Politics* 1253a18ff.

19 James Greenaway is critical of what he sees as Marsilius's separation of church and state, which leads, he believes, to a 'radical isolation of the political from its own civil theology.' [Greenaway, 169] As a result, existential authority is compromised and the individual disappears into the collective. His treatise is, according to Greenaway, 'a top-heavy edifice that barely notices the underlying human substance of individuals in community.' [Greenaway, 170] If this criticism were valid, Marsilius's work would have the effect of running counter to the general (if fitful) tendency of the age to distinguish and prioritise the individual as against the collective. I am not persuaded of the validity of Greenaway's criticism. Marsilius's treatise, whatever its defects and limitations as a work of political philosophy, does not seem to me to be significantly different in its central focus on governing structures from its predecessors and successors and, if anything, pays rather more attention than less to the importance of concrete individuals. Greenaway concedes that 'The role of the legislator *looks like* it highlights the dignity of persons by recognizing their quality and quantity, but in the end Marsilius is too strongly influence by the Averroist [collectivist] pattern of thought....The existential author of individual persons is flattened into irrelevance by the massiveness of the collective, and the dignity of human participation in transcendental reality is imagined into oblivion. Man is reduced to a function of collective in a way that anticipates later speculation and ideology' [Greenaway, 174, 177-178, emphasis added] I would argue, *contra* Greenaway, that in the case of the legislator, appearances aren't deceptive and that what you see in Marsilius is what you get.

20 McClelland 133. Compare Berman 1983. See also Morrall 1971, 16.

21 I, ix, 5; I, xii, 3. See also I, xii, 7.

22 See Berman 1983, passim.

23 *Defensor Minor*, 8, iii.

24 Some years later, Nicholas of Cusa will argue that 'since by nature all men are free and equal in respect of authority, valid rule and legal coercion can only arise from the voluntary consent of men' and Francisco Suárez will reject the view that political authority is possessed by divine right, holding that 'the decision to create a political jurisdiction must be made by the community.' [Luscombe 1982, 766, 759]

25 See Berman 1983, passim.

26 *De Regimine Principum*, I, i.

27 These results of the plague were not unprecedented. Thucydides, writing of the plague that befell the Athenians during the Peloponnesian War, observed that 'The most terrible things of all was the despair into which people fell when they realized that they had caught the plague; for they would immediately adopt an attitude of utter hopelessness, and, by giving in in this way, would lose their powers of re-sistance. Terrible, too, was the sight of people dying like sheep through having caught the disease as a result of nursing others.' [II, 51, Thucydides 1954, 154] The catastrophe was, he says, 'so overwhelming that men, not knowing what would happen next to them, became indifferent to every rule of religion or of law.' [II, 52, Thucydides 1954, 155] The restraints normally imposed by morality and by law became totally ineffective. 'In other respects also Athens owed to the plague the beginnings of a state of unprecedented lawlessness. Seeing how quick and abrupt were the changes of fortune which came to the rich who suddenly died and to those who had previously been penniless but now inherited their wealth, people now began openly to venture on acts of self-indulgence which before then they used to keep dark. ...No fear of god or law of man had a restraining influence.' [II, 53, Thucydides 1954, 155]

28 See Tuchman, passim.

Chapter 13

NICCOLÒ MACHIAVELLI

Of mankind we may say in general that they are fickle, hypocritical,
and greedy of gain
—Machiavelli

The Swiss are well armed and enjoy great freedom
—Machiavelli

It is difficult to understate the significance of the political changes that took
place in Europe towards the end of the fifteenth century and the beginning of
the sixteenth. One of the most significant of these changes was the increasing
dominance of royal power at the expense of all other forms of social and
political organisation. We can date to this period the rise of the state as we
have come to know and love it (well, perhaps 'love' is a little hyperbolic).
Almost everything that we can see in the modern state is already here in
embryo—centralisation, incipient nationalism, a systematic repression or even
destruction of intermediate social institutions and a desire to domesticate and
control the Church, a policy that reached its apogee in the post-Reformation
settlement in both Catholic and Protestant states. Some things in the modern
state—such as its incipient desire to exert total control over all aspects of social
and political life, including the economy and the family— had to wait for the
development of a sophisticated bureaucracy that did not come into full flower
until the end of the eighteenth century. There is more than a little irony in the
rise of a form of political absolutism that piggy-backed upon a severe restriction of the absolutist claims of the papacy but which was itself merely a secular
reflection of that very absolutism that had been claimed for the papacy itself.

The patchwork quilt that was the late medieval political world was in part
a result of the physical limitations of travel and the difficulties of communication characteristic of this period.[1] It wasn't only political power and control
that was local; everything was local, including commerce, law, and culture.
The economic changes which had been gathering force since the twelfth
century began to take significant effect during this period and saw the development of international trade and banking,[2] together with the emergence of a
new merchant middle class that was neither noble nor peasant, neither clerical
nor royal. Kings with absolutist ambitions and merchants with commercial
ambitions made common cause with each other to restrict and limit the power
of the feudal nobility, each for their own reasons. Kings needed money for their
armies and for the disarming and political neutralisation of an independent
and potentially competitive class of nobles; the merchants desired a greater

and more extensive legal certainty and freedom from what they perceived as restrictive and arbitrary limitations to their activities deriving from local law and administration.

Spain appears as it were from nowhere at this time, resulting from the union of the kingdoms of Aragon and Castile and the consequent extension of their control over most of the Iberian peninsula. So used are we to looking at maps of Europe and seeing Spain occupying the bulk of Iberia that it takes an effort of imagination to realise how recent a reality this is. Absolutism in England dates from the conclusion of the War of the Roses and the accession, the very dubious accession it should be said, of the Tudors under Henry VII. From this time on, the great families of England—the Stanleys (key to Henry's successful effort to acquire the throne at the Battle of Bosworth Field), the Nevilles, the Percys[3] and suchlike—change from quasi-independent rulers of their own regions to become mere courtiers whose position and power depends ultimately upon royal favour.

By far the earliest instance of the development of royal absolutism and central-isation is to be found in France as early as the first third of the fifteenth century. The French king acquired control of the nation's non-feudal and increasingly professional military force together with the authority to impose taxation to pay for it. By the beginning of the sixteenth century, the great quasi-independent regions of Brittany, Burgundy and, later, Lorraine had become mere provinces of a united France. The political, social and cultural particularism of the emergent nation states in the context of an increasingly chaotic and ineffectual Empire provided new material for political thought and reflection. These new absolute or soon-to-be absolute monarchs needed a dignity and style that would elevate them above their increasingly subservient and powerless courtiers. It is no accident that a new style of address, 'Your Majesty', was adopted at this time, first by the Emperor Charles V and then by King Francis I of France and King Henry VIII of England. The reality corresponding to this *majestas* was embodied in clothes, music, buildings, art and elaborate etiquette.

This is the time and these are the circumstances into which Machiavelli was born in 1469. If it is a truism that every man is a creature of his time, this is no less true and perhaps even more true of Machiavelli than of any other thinker. Born into an Italy riven by semi-permanent strife between the major city-states of Florence, Venice, Naples, Milan and, notoriously, the Papal States (stretching right across the belly of the Italian peninsula)—all these city-states being the object of strategic plans of occupation and control by the newly centralised Spain, France and the not-yet centralised German Empire—how could his view of politics and political philosophy not be affected by his upbringing, his social environment and his political experience? Machiavel-li's early public career culminated in his appointment as a kind of minister without portfolio of the Florentine republic, commissioned to go on diplomatic missions to various other states, including the Papal States, France and the Holy Roman Empire. The Medici family came to power when the Florentine republic collapsed in 1512 as the result of complicated manoeuvres by Spain against France, whereupon Machiavelli was accused of conspiring against the

Medici interests, not only losing his position but even undergoing torture and imprisonment. The two works treated in this chapter were written shortly after this devastating personal experience when Machiavelli was in internal exile and they bear the marks of this shattering experience in every line.[4]

Keenly aware and envious of the newly-minted politically united realms of France and Spain, inchoately desirous of a similarly outcome for Italy as a whole (see his passionate appeal to Lorenzo di Medici in the final chapter of *The Prince*), Machiavelli, like Marsilius of Padua before him, was resentful of what he took to be the chief obstacle to that unity, the Papal States. Too strong to be shifted from its central and obstructive position yet not strong enough to be the basis of unification, the Papal States are blamed by Machiavelli for most of Italy's woes. To test the truth of this assertion, Machiavelli asks us to conduct a thought experiment: 'And any one, to be promptly convinced by experiment of the truth of all this, should have the power to transport the court of Rome to reside, with all the power it has in Italy, in the midst of the Swiss, who of all peoples nowadays live most according to their ancient customs so far as religion and their military system are concerned; and he would see in a very little while that the evil habits of that court would create more confusion in that country than anything else that could ever happen there.'[5] Other than resenting the machinations of the Pope as one among many Italian rulers, Machiavelli was singularly blind to the significance of religion and its possible political effects in general.

Was Machiavelli a Christian?

Was Machiavelli a Christian? In *The Prince* we find little or no explicit mention of Christianity except when piety is picked out as a virtue worthy of simulation. Religion is considered of value only insofar as its practice is conducive to good behavior by the public at large but it isn't allowed to be a restraint on the actions of the prince. [see Plamenatz, 32-36] As Napoleon is alleged to have said, 'Religion is excellent stuff for keeping common people quiet' and 'Religion is what keeps the poor from murdering the rich.' We find nothing on the idea of natural law, a commonplace of medieval thought, no references to the Fathers of the Church or to the saints or to Scripture and, above all, no effort to place politics within a larger religious or theological context. Furthermore, Machiavelli directly attacked Christianity for, as he saw it, promoting servility and weakness; in this respect, he anticipates Nietzsche as in other respects he anticipates Hobbes.

All in all, Machiavelli is perhaps best understood as one of the earliest of the new humanists of that movement that would come to be called the Renaissance. Some would hold that the Renaissance humanists as a whole weren't so much anti-Christian as simply a-Christian. For example, McClelland says, 'Machiavelli is probably a Christian about everything important *except* politics' but I don't see how this can be. Being a Christian doesn't really allow one to pick and choose as one likes, and to leave the whole political arena out of the Christian equation is to excise a big lump of human activity and experience from Christian oversight. [McClelland, 157]

WAS MACHIAVELLI AN ARISTOTELIAN?

Machiavelli never refers to Aristotle, which is significant when one reflects that, as George Sabine notes, 'Until the sixteenth century it was scarcely possible to write a treatise on politics which…did not owe a debt to [Aristotle's] *Politics*.' [Sabine, 245] Machiavelli also rejected the classical (and Aristotelian) idea of the *polis* as a natural entity with a common set of ends binding all its members together. For him, the state was an arena of competing interests that had to be resolved in such a way that the existence of the state itself wasn't subverted. The task of the prince was to blend these competing interests together dynamically as Machiavelli thought the competing interests of the Senate and the Roman people had been blended together in the early Roman Republic. Machiavelli thinks that the success of Rome, in its republican phase, was predicated on the incorporation of liberty in large measure into its public proceedings. Unusually, however, he does not believe that this liberty arose from some fundamental identity of purpose among the various groups in Roman society. On the contrary, he believes that it was the fundamental underlying tensions between the Senate and the people, between the patricians and the plebeians, that created the space for liberty by preventing the dominance and hence the tyrannical rule of either group. 'I maintain,' he writes, 'that those who blame the quarrels of the Senate and the people of Rome condemn that which was the very origin of liberty, and that they were probably more impressed by the cries and noise which these disturbances occasioned in the public places, than by the good effect which they produced; and that they do not consider that in every republic there are two parties, that of the nobles and that of the people; and all the laws that are favourable to liberty result from the opposition of these parties to each other, as may easily be seen from the events that occurred in Rome.'[6] This idea is somewhat similar to Plato's image in *The Statesman* of the king as a kind of weaver whose role is to blend the disparate elements in the state into a dynamically stable whole. In recognizing the creative power of competition in the public arena and its contribution to liberty, Machiavelli distinguished himself from the bulk of his predecessors and contemporaries and anticipates a theme that will scarcely receive recognition again until the development of economics as an independent science some three hundred years into the future.

His recognition of the creativity of competition isn't the only instance in which Machiavelli gives evidence of his political prescience. He also recognised very clearly that once a people has lost its liberty by coming under princely government, it is no simple matter to recover it. 'Many examples in ancient history prove how difficult it is for a people that have been accustomed to live under the government of a prince to preserve its liberty, if by some accident it has recovered it, as was the case with Rome after the expulsion of the Tarquins. And this difficulty is a reasonable one; for such a people may well be compared to some wild animal, which (although by nature ferocious and savage) has been as it were subdued by having been always kept imprisoned and in servitude, and being let out into the open fields, not knowing how to provide food and shelter for itself, becomes an easy prey to the first one who attempts to chain it up again. The same thing happens to a people that hasn't been accustomed to self-government; for, ignorant of all public affairs, of all means of defence or offence, neither knowing the princes or being known by them, it soon relapses under a yoke, oftentimes much heavier than the one which it had but just shaken off. This difficulty occurs even when the body of the people isn't wholly corrupt; but when corruption has taken possession of the whole people, then it cannot preserve its free condition even for the shortest possible time, as we shall see further on; and therefore our argument has reference to a people where corruption hasn't yet become general, and where the good still prevails over the bad.'[7] This would seem to be more or less what happened when the Soviet Union collapsed both in Russia and, to a more limited extent, in the former satellite countries of the Soviet Empire. Civic culture, including the ability to exercise liberty, isn't something that can be conjured from nowhere. It is a delicate plant that, once crushed, requires tender loving care if it is to revive and flourish. It isn't sufficient, as some think, simply to install formal democratic procedures and institutions in such countries and expect them to work in the absence of the historical, cultural, and social supports that are a necessary condition of their ability to function elsewhere.

Despite the republican sympathies he displays in the *Discourses*, Machiavelli is unambiguous in contending that if radical change is needed in any political structure, it can be effected only by one single individual: He writes, 'it never or rarely happens that a republic or monarchy is well constituted, or its old institutions entirely reformed, unless it is done by only one individual; it is even necessary that he whose mind has conceived such a constitution should be alone in carrying it into effect. A sagacious legislator of a republic, therefore, whose object is to promote the public good, and not his private interests, and who prefers his country to his own successors, should concentrate all authority in himself; and a wise mind will never censure any one for having employed any extraordinary means for the purpose of establishing a kingdom or constituting a republic.'[8]

Machiavelli redefined the very idea of virtue (*virtù*) so that instead of its being synonymous with prudence and wisdom as would have been the traditional understanding of the term, it is now taken to be descriptive of a collection of practical skills such as courage and energy and willpower, not to mention shrewdness and cunning. Along with the radically redefined *virtù*, the idea of *Fortuna* plays a significant role in Machiavelli's thought. [see Gatti, 16-19] *Fortuna* is not simply a dramatic personification of Christian Providence (of which we find no mention in Machiavelli) but a return of the pagan and capricious goddess who may, or may not, reward the man of *virtù*. Understood non-metaphorically, *Fortuna* appears to be a way of describing the world of change, contingency and accident which spreads itself out in front of Machiavelli's eyes, which isn't a world that is recognisably Christian or the object of a beneficent Providence. He compares *Fortuna* to a 'swollen river, which in its fury overflows the plains, tears up the trees and buildings, and sweeps the earth from one place and deposits it in another. Every one flies before the flood, and yields to its fury, unable to resist it; and notwithstanding this state of things, men do not when the river is in its ordinary condition provide against its overflow by dikes and malls, so that when it rises it may flow either in the channel thus provided for it, or that at any rate its violence may not be entirely unchecked, nor its effects prove so injurious. It is the same with Fortuna, who displays her power where there is no organized valour to resist her, and where she knows that there are no dikes or walls to control her.'[9] Machiavelli's attitude to *Fortuna* is a kind of qualified fatalism. Although he is inclined to agree with those who think there's no point in attempting to resist the decrees of fate, in the end, he thinks that even though the major movement of events lies outside our control, we can still, to a small extent, determine their direction albeit within severe limits.

Was Machiavelli Machiavellian?

Machiavelli has the dubious distinction of contributing his name as an adjective to our vocabularies to describe a person or policy that's devious, underhanded, deceitful, ruthless and cunning, these traits being concealed under a mask of respectability and morality. Whether such a term is justified by the man himself, his life and his writings is a matter of continuing controversy. Was Machiavelli Machiavellian? Was he a proto-Italian patriot? Was he a peace-lover whose writings, misinterpreted as the counsel of the devil, were really meant to be an exposé of the duplicity of princes? There appear to be as many Machiavellis as there are Machiavellian scholars. [see McClelland, 151] The devilish and devious advisor to ruthless rulers of the sixteenth century was gradually transformed over time into a proto-political scientist who merely described the objective conditions relating to the political realties of his time until, in the nineteenth century, based on his impassioned plea in *The Prince* to Lorenzo Medici to rescue Italy from the 'barbarous dominion of the foreigner,' he became transformed into a hero of the incipient Italian nationalism, rather like the enchanted frog which, when kissed by the Princess turns into, what else, a Prince.[10]

Just what are we to make of his major writings—*The Prince*, and *The Discourses on Livy*? Do we take them at face value? If so, do they offer different and perhaps conflicting ideas? Just as German scholars in the nineteenth century discerned an apparently irreconcilable tension in the two major works of Adam Smith, *The Theory of Moral Sentiments* and *The Wealth of Nations*, and christened this tension the *AdamSmith-problem*, so too, we might conjecture, in trying to understand Machiavelli we come face to face with the *Machiavelli-problem*. *The Prince* seems to be an exercise in *realpolitik*, a 'mirror of princes' tract that, unlike the majority of such works, bypasses ethical considerations completely and confines itself to giving advice to rulers on how to acquire and retain power.[11] '*The Prince*,' writes Hilary Gatti, 'has become a famous text in the modern world above all for Machiavelli's claim that politics and ethics cannot easily be conjugated together.' Not everyone accepts this interpretation. Gatti, for example, believes *The Prince* to be 'far more than a handbook of advice,' being 'more in the nature of a close analysis of the logic of a power structure which, as Machiavelli so clearly saw, was going to dominate the European scene for many years—even centuries—to come.' [Gatti, 23] *The Discourses*, in contrast, seems to be a work in republican theory, counselling not just leaders but citizens also on how to hold on to their freedoms. The easy solution of arguing that Machiavelli simply changed his mind from one work to the next isn't available to us as the evidence clearly shows both works to have been composed during the same period, the writing of *The Prince* being a temporary interruption to his work on *The Discourses*.

One consideration that gives a further twist to the question of Machiavelli interpretation is that, as with Plato's dialogues, his two major works aren't straightforward treatises, constructed and expressed in a detached scholarly manner. They exhibit some characteristics of works of literature and, as with all such works, the question of what in them is to be attributed to the author becomes a matter of some controversy. As Joseph Femia notes, 'Like other Florentines of his social standing, Machiavelli was steeped in the rules of Roman rhetoric; vivid imagery and an insincere (sometimes ironic) invocation of values or prejudices dear to the listeners' or readers' hearts were familiar and accepted techniques. No one expected every statement to be a literal expression of the author's beliefs.' [Femia, 166] The problem with the use of irony, as all too many authors have found to their cost, is that there's a danger that some readers will fail to appreciate the author's ironic intent and get things precisely the wrong way around. Once upon a time, in a seminar discussing Jonathan Swift's *A Modest Proposal for Preventing the Children of Poor People in Ireland From Being a Burden to Their Parents or Country, and for Making Them Beneficial to the Publick*, one of the students was asked to comment on Swift's suggestion that eating babies might simultaneously solve the overpopulation problem in Ireland while providing a nutritious source of food to those who remained. He replied, 'Well, that might have been all right in Mr Swift's day but I don't think we could do that now.'

In the end, as seems likely, what appear to be significant differences between the two works may well turn out to be more apparent than real. On this topic, McClelland is clear and unambiguous. Are the two works reconcilable? The answer,' he says, 'is a resounding 'yes!' Not only that, but the *Discourses* themselves provide us with a complete political theory into which Machiavelli's treatment of princely government in *The Prince* can easily be fitted. Far from there being a contradiction between *The Prince* and the *Discourses*, it might be said that *The Prince* is simply one part of the *Discourses* writ large.' [McClelland, 154; see Gatti, 14ff.] John Plamenatz agrees with McClelland: 'The arguments of *The Prince* are perfectly consistent with the arguments of the much longer *Discourses*, in which Machiavelli expresses his strong preference for popular government....there is scarcely a maxim in *The Prince* whose equivalent is not to be found in the *Discourses*.' [Plamenatz, 13] A cynical understanding of *The Prince* might see it as part of a job application by Machiavelli, a selection but not a distortion of material from the *Discourses*. [see Sabine, 338] 'Machiavelli hoped it [*The Prince*] would attract the attention of the Medici and induce them to employ him in affairs of State.' He was disappointed: 'his book did not dispose the Medici to employ him.'[12] Both works are largely aligned on all significant matters with the possible exception of

Machiavelli's approval of republican forms of government that appears only in the *Discourses*.

REASONS OF STATE

Both of Machiavelli's major works are primarily concerned with the ability of a state to maintain its independence and with that the safety of its citizens. To bring that about, a wedge must be driven through the traditional interpenetration of ethics and politics. Reasons of state—*raisons d'état*—dictate that whatever needs to be done to maintain the independence of a state and the safety of its citizens may be done, regardless of ethical concerns. This radical division between the demands of ethics and the requirements of politics is, I believe, what is most characteristic of Machiavelli.[13] That this interpretation of Machiavelli was common can be evidenced by the publication of Giovanni Botero's *Della Ragion di Stato* in 1589 which criticises precisely this element of Machiavelli's thought.

Machiavelli is commonly taken to be the inventor of the doctrine of *raison d'état* but this isn't quite accurate. This idea already existed before Machiavelli. We can see it expressed as early as Plato's *The Statesman* where the young Socrates is shocked by it. In its earlier manifestation, it was seen as something to be used *in extremis* only and ultimately only for the good of the community as a whole. '[T]he Machiavellian influence on the 'ragion di stato' tradition was fundamental,' writes Noel Malcolm, 'But late Renaissance humanists searching for models and authorities in the ancient world, found a near-equivalent to Machiavelli's teachings in the writings of Tacitus…' [Malcolm, 95] In Machiavelli, however, such regrettable departures from normal morality are commonplace and unremarkable. Machiavelli appears to be a political utilitarian; actions and decisions are to be judged not by detached moral standards but by results.[14] The arena of private human relations is suitable for subjection to the normal rules of morality; politics, however, is a dirty business, and here the only relevant consideration is the appropriate and successful exercise of power. The idea of 'reasons of state, then, extends from Tacitus through Machiavelli and right up to the present. No one who has had the opportunity to reflect on historical and contemporary political practice can be unfamiliar with the concept of *raison d'état* and with its importance in domestic and international relations. Are we really shocked by Machiavelli's prescriptions? Are not such political expediencies commonplace? Haven't princes, democracies, tyrants, and oligarchies always acted like this—or are we just shocked by Machiavelli's plain and direct statement of his prescription?

Many would find this doctrine of *raison d'état* to be abhorrent but not everyone. Joseph Femia remarks, 'no one, apart from pacifists, would now deny that deviations from strict moral standards are sometimes necessary to achieve a higher political good.' [Femia, 182] Femia's remark does not appear to be obviously true. Libertarians are not, or at least not necessarily, pacifists and they would deny precisely this, holding that the fundamental moral/political principle, the zero-aggression principle, applies to *all* actors, whether individual or agents of groups, including states or governments.

When one examines the rhetoric of defenders of the doctrine of *raison d'état*, one point that comes across with monotonous regularity is the allegedly unique nature of the state that allows it to operate in ways not available to ordinary people. [see d'Entrèves 1967, 44-49] 'Reasons of State' is a full and complete justification for actions that we would ordinarily condemn as immoral, or criminal or both. The state is different from you and from me. What you and I can't do the state may do with impunity. 'For centuries the State has committed mass murder and called it "war"….for centuries the State has enslaved people into its armed battalions and called it "conscription" in the 'national service.' For centuries the State has robbed people at bayonet point and called it "taxation."' [Rothbard 2006, 56-57] But unless one is a collective realist[15] and also holds to the view that different standards of morality apply to collectives than to individuals, 'Reasons of State' cannot be accepted as a defence for actions that are instances of aggression.[16] And that is precisely the point. Applying the principle of methodological individualism, we can see that there is, properly speaking, no such thing as a state, *if* by that we mean an entity ontologically distinct from and superior to ordinary people. The state is simply a name for a particular group of people acting at a particular time in particular ways. And the moral law, if it applies to any, applies to all, whether they act as agents or principals, on their own behalf or on behalf of others, and whether they benefit personally from their actions or not. As Rothbard points out, 'The distinctive feature of libertarians is that they coolly and uncompromisingly apply the general moral law to people acting in their roles as members of the State apparatus.' [Rothbard 2006, 56]

MIRROR OF PRINCES

Although *The Prince* can be seen as a contribution to the traditional 'Mirror of Princes' literature, Machiavelli is well aware that what he is doing is significantly different from giving the usual run-of-the-mill advice to rulers. In extenuation of his daring novelty, Machiavelli defends himself by noting that he wants to provide something that is really useful to its recipient (a sideways swipe at the presumed uselessness of much of this literature) and so he isn't going to indulge in the favourite philosophical pastime of imaginary and ideal schemes of governance (take that, Plato!) but rather pursue, as he says, the real truth of the matter. Machiavelli isn't interested in how things ought to be but in how things are. This sharp distinction between the factual and the normative, predating Hume's famous distinction to much the same effect by some three hundred years, is entirely characteristic of Machiavelli's whole approach.

In *The Prince*, Machiavelli produces the kinds of statements that have contributed to his reputation for cynical *realpolitik*, remarking, 'a man who, in all respects, will carry out only his professions of good, will be apt to be ruined amongst so many who are evil. A prince therefore who desires to maintain himself must learn to be not always good, but to be so or not as necessity may require.'[17] This advice, of course, runs counter to the usual advice contained in the Mirror of Princes literature that counsels the prince to become a paragon of all the virtues. But Machiavelli is well aware of what he is doing. Other things being equal, it would be wonderful for a prince to possess all the virtues but, as he is a man with all the imperfections that that implies, this is simply not possible. That being so, it's important for the prince to avoid acquiring a reputation for vices that might imperil his rule. It should be noted it isn't important for him *not* to have those vices, merely to avoid their imputation! Any vices which might be necessary for the preservation of the state (presumably Machiavelli has in mind such things as a reputation for cruelty) need not be avoided at all for, as he remarks, 'all things considered, it will be found that some things that seem like virtue will lead you to ruin if you follow them; whilst others, that apparently are vices, will, if followed, result in your safety and well-being.'[18]

In a variation on the saying 'you must be cruel to be kind,' Machiavelli, taking the activities of Cesare Borgia as his example, remarks serenely that if a prince has to be cruel to keep his state in order, even though such cruelty is to be regretted, it is better that we have such cruelty than that we allow rampant disorder its head. 'Cesar Borgia was reputed cruel, yet by his cruelty he reunited the Romagna to his states, and restored that province to order, peace, and loyalty; and if we carefully examine his course, we shall find it to have been really much more merciful than the course of the people of Florence who, to escape the reputation of cruelty, allowed Pistoja to be destroyed. A prince, therefore, should not mind the ill repute of cruelty, when he can thereby keep his subjects united and loyal; for a few displays of severity will really be more merciful than to allow, by an excess of clemency, disorders to occur, which are apt to result in rapine and murder; for these injure a whole community, whilst the executions ordered by the prince fall only upon a few individuals.'[19]

MACHIAVELLI'S VIEW OF MAN

Machiavelli's political thought is grounded ultimately upon his own particular conception of man. Men generally are despicable animals: changeable, greedy, liars, and cowards. They will lick the hand that feeds them so long and only so long as it feeds them and pledge all that they have to support their benefactor provided, as Machiavelli cynically remarks, 'the necessity for it is far off.' When the time comes for them to redeem their pledges, they will rather revolt than gratefully come to the aid of their benefactor.[20] This view of man also finds expression in the *Discourses* though in a somewhat more nuanced way; whereas the claim that men are naturally bad is made categorically in *The Prince*, in the *Discourses* we are advised rather to *assume* that all men are naturally bad[22] and, in an even more nuanced way, that men are rarely either entirely good or entirely bad.[22] Similar sentiments were to be expressed many years later by Arthur Schopenhauer, who wrote that 'the great majority of men are in the highest degree egoistic, unjust, inconsiderate, deceitful, sometime even malicious, and equipped moreover with very mediocre intelligence.' Because of these manifold moral defects, Schopenhauer believes, echoing Hobbes, that if men are to be controlled and ruled 'there exists the need for a completely unaccountable power, concentrated in one man and standing above even justice and the law, before which everything bows and which is regarded as a being of a higher order, a sovereign by the grace of God.' [Schopenhauer

1970, 152-153] When I was learning to drive, I was taught the concept of 'defensive driving'. In essence, this amounts to driving on the assumption that every other road user is an idiot! Expect people to shoot out from their driveways without looking, drivers to swing out from side roads in front of you without warning, children to run out from behind parked cars, and so on. In making the assumption in *The Prince* that men are naturally bad, Machiavelli could be seen, on one version, to advocate a kind of 'defensive rule' for princes. The ruler should, if he wishes to stay in power, operate on the assumption that everyone is opposed to him, or is betraying him, or will betray him. To paraphrase Horace's well-known tag, we might say that as a political thinker, Machiavelli '*odit profanum vulgus*'—he despised the common mob. However Machiavelli's anthropology is to be understood in detail, there can be no doubt that it is a dark, proto-Hobbesian view of man and his nature. There can also be no doubt that Machiavelli's personal experiences coloured his anthropology, something that we shall see was also the case with Hobbes.

Answering the question of whether it is better to be loved rather than feared or feared rather than loved, Machiavelli opts for fear over love. The reason for this is, once again, rooted in his conception of man. The bonds of love will be broken whenever it suits men to break them whereas fear, Machiavelli thinks, never fails to motivate men as they have a lively apprehension of punishment. To be feared isn't necessarily to be hated and Machiavelli advises the prince to avoid incurring the hatred of his people, which he can do very easily by keeping his hands off their property and their women. The appropriation of another's property is habit-forming and the habit is best not started. Besides, Machiavelli remarks with some cynicism, men are more likely to forgive and forget the execution of their fathers than the loss of their patrimonies![23]

Deceit and the breaking of promises are part and parcel of the prince's daily work. Just as Machiavelli believes that the mass of men are untrustworthy and will break their promises when it suits them, so too, a prince must be prepared to do likewise. Machiavelli acknowledges that such conduct would be bad if men were good but, as he says to the Prince, returning to his central theme, 'as men are naturally bad, and will not observe their faith towards you, you must, in the same way, not observe yours to them; and no prince ever yet lacked legitimate reasons with which to colour his want of good faith.'[24]

Hypocrisy, too, is another string to the prince's bow. If a prince were to possess all the virtues, that might (not necessarily would) be admirable. Much more important than possessing such virtues is *appearing* to possess them. The prince should seem all 'charity, integrity, and humanity, all uprightness, and all piety. And more than all else is it necessary for a prince to seem to possess the last quality; for mankind in general judge more by what they see and hear than by what they feel, every one being capable of the former, and but few of the latter. Everybody sees what you seem to be, but few really feel what you are; and these few dare not oppose the opinion of the many, who are protected by the majesty of the state; for the actions of all men, and especially those of princes, are judged by the result, where there is no other judge to whom to appeal.'[25]

Here is Machiavelli's advice to a prince who has just taken over a neighbouring state. Assuming the previous ruler is dead (and if not, why not?), exterminate the remaining members of the ousted dynasty for 'A prince cannot live securely in a state so long as those live whom he has deprived of it.'[26] If the prince's path to power was smoothed by elements in the conquered state that now expect to be rewarded, ignore them. What are they going to do? There will be those in the prince's new state who will be, if not actively disruptive, at best sullenly acquiescent. What should the prince do with these? If some killing has to be done to get people into line, the prince should do it and get it over with. Better still, he should delegate the task to a subordinate who can later be blamed for being overzealous or disobeying orders if too much blood is shed, that way, resentment and anger can be deflected from the prince to his underlings. If the prince must kill, then he should kill quickly; if, on the other hand, he has rewards to allot, he should allot them slowly. The new prince should raise taxes as little as possible and leave the old laws in place—good advice for all rulers at all times and in all places—that way, resentment is minimized and the chance of legitimising his rule is significantly increased.

We have seen that, like Marsilius of Padua before him, Machiavelli was resentful of the Papal States and papal power which he took to be the chief obstacle to Italian unity. What then would his attitude have been to the Reformation and the fracturing of Christendom with its consequent weakening of the power of the Papacy? It is hard not to believe that he would have welcomed it. Moreover, apart from his resentment of the political pretensions of the papacy, Machiavelli certainly had no love for religion for he saw it as promoting weakness and servility so even on those grounds alone we might expect that he would have welcomed its institutional weakening. We shall, however, never know the answer to this question for Machiavelli died in 1527 (the very year that the Medicis were expelled from Florence) just ten years after Luther posted his theses to the door of the Castle Church at Wittenberg but long before the battle lines of the Reformation were definitively drawn. Even a man of Machiavelli's intellectual acuity could hardly have been expected to anticipate the religious (and political) firestorm that was about to convulse Europe for over a hundred years after his death.

Notes

1 See Berman 1983, passim.

2 See Bautier, 146-154.

3 These great family names in time became popular first names, so popular that they eventually overbalanced and fell into naffness. 'Stanley' still gets some use but 'Neville' and 'Percy' (especially Percy) are names you give to your children if you want them to be beaten up at school.

4 For a succinct historically based account of Machiavelli's career and thought, see Rubinstein, 41-58.

5 *Discourses*, Book I, Chapter XII.

6 *Discourses*, Book I, chapter IV.

7 *Discourses*, Book I, chapter XVI. 'A corrupt people that becomes free can with greatest difficulty maintain its liberty.' [*Discourses*, Book I, chapter XVII]

8 *Discourses*, Book I, chapter IX.

9 *The Prince*, chapter XXV.

10 *The Prince*, chapter XXVI.

11 For an engaging latter-day Machiavellian textbook, see de Mesquita & Smith's *The Dictator's Handbook*. See also de Mesquita et al., passim.

12 Plamenatz, 13; see Gatti, 24.

13 For a graphic introduction to the ideas contained in de Mesquita and Smith's *The Dictator's Handbook*, see C. G. P. Grey 2016 & 2016a.

14 See *The Prince*, chapters XVIII & XVIII.

15 As discussed in the Preface, *collective realism* is the position that groups have a transcendent reality above and beyond the members who constitute them or the relationships (informal or contractual) that bind those members together. The contrasting positions are: *collective nominalism*, the position that denies that groups or associations have any mode of existence at all, being merely a convenient way of speaking of individuals cooperating with each other; and *collective epiphenomenalism*, which is the position that social groups and associations are entities of a sort, created and sustained by the network of intentions (often embodied in rules, laws and constitutions) of those who compose them, either informal (as with football supporters) or formal (as with members of a corporation).

16 The fundamental principle of libertarianism is the non- or zero-aggression principle [ZAP]: *no one may initiate or threaten to initiate the use of physical violence [aggression] against the person or property of another.* It should be noted that what is ruled out by the ZAP is the *initiation* of violence (such as murder, rape, theft, assault); libertarianism does *not* rule out the use of violence in *defence* of one's person or property *against* aggression. The practical difficulties of telling the difference in borderline cases between aggression, which libertarianism prohibits, and the forceful resistance of aggression, which libertarianism permits, doesn't tell against the clear conceptual difference between the two. As part of one's fundamental freedom, one has the right to defend one's most basic property, oneself, and any other property that one has rightfully acquired. Of course, one may waive that right if one chooses so that pacifism and libertarianism are compatible, although libertarianism does not require pacifism.

17 *The Prince*, chapter XV.

18 *The Prince*, chapter XV.

19 *The Prince*, chapter XVII.

20 *The Prince*, chapter XVII.

21 *Discourses*, Book I, chapter III.

22 *Discourses*, Book I, chapter XXVII.

23 *The Prince*, chapter XVII.

24 *The Prince*, chapter XVIII.

25 *The Prince*, chapter XVIII.

26 *Discourses*, Book III, chapter IV.

Chapter 14

THE REFORMATION

The right of a nation to kill a tyrant in case of necessity can no more be doubted
than to hang a robber, or kill a flea
—John Adams

It is better that all of the peasants should be killed
rather than that the sovereigns and magistrates should be destroyed,
because the peasants take up the sword without God's authorisation
—Martin Luther

U p to the time of the Reformation there couldn't have been such a thing as a Protestant political theory or a Catholic political theory. What was common to all Christians was an historically mediated understanding or range of understandings of the relationship that should exist between the spiritual and the secular authorities and the manner and mode of authority that each was justified in exercising. Some points were seemingly beyond dispute. 'No Christian, from the time when St. Paul wrote the thirteenth chapter of *Romans*,' writes George Sabine, 'had ever doubted…that authority has a religious origin and sanction.' [Sabine, 392] Even if we take into account the notorious passage from Pope Gregory's second letter to Bishop Hermann of Metz, in which he describes kings and princes as the seed of those who have committed every crime under the sun, it's hard to disagree with the historical accuracy of Sabine's assessment. When we come to the sixteenth century, how the religious origin and authority of secular authority is to be understood and how it is to be practically implemented is going to be a matter requiring some re-evaluation in the light of changed religious and political circumstances. We are so used to thinking of the separation of Church and State as being somehow natural and normal that it takes a huge effort of imagination to return to a time when this distinction did not exist, at least not in the way it does today. Harro Höpfl remarks, 'Such was the interpenetration of the secular and spiritual in the sixteenth century that no reformation of religion could take place without a transformation of the public order of the commonwealths of Christian Europe…' [Höpfl, vii]

As I mentioned before, historical periodisation isn't an entirely innocent process. Seemingly neutral and descriptive period names often embody negative or positive normative judgements—Dark Ages, bad; Renaissance, good. For convenience, I am adopting the standard historical terminology used to describe the momentous religious events of the sixteenth century without necessarily subscribing to any historical or theological presuppositions, positive or negative, embodied in such terminology. [see Davies 1999,

386] In his monumental work, *Reformations*, Carlos Eire writes, 'the name for this transitional moment in history has changed over the years. In the English-speaking world, as in several other European cultures, this era came to be known as the Reformation. Implicit in this designation is the judgement that something corrupt has been reformed or improved. More than that, the singular capitalized name given to this historical period implied that this event was the ultimate, definitive step in the right direction: it was not a reformation but *the* Reformation....In England and all of its colonies, as in all other Protestant cultures, the only true Reformation—with a capital *R*—was that brought about by Protestants. All narratives shaped by this Protestant consciousness shared an unquestioned assumption and a common plot line: some time after the fourth century, the true Christian Church founded by Christ and his apostles fell into gross corruption for a thousand years, a defilement so deep and thorough that the only way to restore the genuine Christian faith on this earth was to reject the church led by the pope in Rome and to replace it with one that had nothing to do with "Romishness' or "popery"....even though Protestants were not always of one mind and actually created a number of distinct competing Reformations and churches, each of which claimed to be the genuine article, they nonetheless took to speaking of the Reformation in the singular rather than the plural, and to assigning it capital letters.' Eire continues,

> Up until the late nineteenth century, then, the term *Reformation* remained strictly Protestant. Catholics used the word *reform* and *reformation* more broadly, without a capital *R*, when referring to the many reforming movements throughout the history of their church, including those of the sixteenth and seventeenth centuries, which tended to be called Tridentine reforms, in reference to the Council of Trent (1545-1563) and all of the many changes and improvements it had set in motion. In contrast, on the Protestant side, whatever Catholics reshuffled within their religion as a response to Protestantism tended not to be considered a reform per se, but rather a reactionary turn. This perspective led Leopold von Ranke...to refer to the inner renewal of Catholicism in the sixteenth and seventeenth centuries as a Counter-reformation (*Gegenreformation*)....for nearly a century, up until the 1970s, historians tended to think of two distinct and opposing Reformations, with the Protestant one being the Reformation and the Catholic one being the Counter-Reformation.[1]

As should be evident from what I have written earlier, the relationship of Christianity to secular authority isn't a simple matter. It became significantly less simple when Christendom splintered and the relationship became not one between a more or less unitary Christianity and a more or less unitary empire, but a series of relationships between different Christian Churches and distinct and independent states. In those circumstances, one's form of Christianity and one's political allegiances were inextricably bound together. 'The upholding of rulers became a primary article of religious faith, while the defense of a religious creed was felt to be, and often in fact was, an attack upon a ruler of a different belief.' [Sabine, 357] Common to almost all the disputants was a belief that everyone could agree on religious matters if only one's opponents would cease being wilfully blind or just plain evil. From the religious side, there was general agreement that the secular authorities had an obligation to maintain religious orthodoxy; from the side of the rulers, there was a belief, all the more powerful for being assumed and not defended, that law and order could hardly be maintained unless all of a ruler's subjects subscribed to the same religion. 'Nearly forty years after Luther's posting of his thesis in Wittenberg, the imperial Diet of Augsburg in 1555 acknowledged that Germany was irreparably divided into Catholic and Protestant states....Nearly ten years after Luther's death, Europe thus institutionalized religious pluralism.' [Roberts 1997, 260]

The late fifteenth and early sixteenth centuries was a time of state centralisation, particularly in France. In contrast to France, the pace and success of centralisation was very different in Germany and Italy. Those who had been feudal lords in these areas were transformed into local magnates with quasi-independent government powers of their own, powers that they were reluctant to cede to a central monarchy. Moreover, the rise of the cities constituted a challenge not only to the monarchical rule of the emperor but even to that of the local magnates. 'Like the Italian city-states,' writes Ellen Meiksins Wood, 'German cities often governed their surrounding villages, exacting taxes from the peasantry by means of a collective urban lordship...' [Wood 2012, 60] Not only did individual cities manifest a relative independence of local political control, in some cases cities banded together for commercial purposes which led to their exercising quasi-political functions as well. Chief among these associations of cities was the already mentioned Hanseatic League which, at the height of its power, had the capacity to engage in blockades, embargoes and even military action. Still, despite these areas of resistance to centralisation, the general tendency of the age was more and more towards the creation of independent territorial kingdoms—each king an emperor in his own kingdom (*rex imperator est in regno suo*)—encapsulating in practice the notion of sovereignty, even if the idea wasn't yet theoretically developed

So, out of the political and religious melange of the Middle Ages, the rise of the modern monarchies was already well in progress before the religious turmoil of the sixteenth century. The Reformation did not create a new political order *de novo*; it simply accelerated a process that was already in being. Sabine remarks, 'the Reformation joined with economic forces already in existence to make royal government, invested with absolute power at home and with a free hand abroad, the typical form of European state.' [Sabine, 357] The fragmentation of the Empire into a complex of multiple sovereign states horizontally related to one another was well underway. 'The decline of Christian unity,' writes Frank Furedi, 'coincided with a powerful momentum for national territorial centralisation...' [Furedi, 156] Given the close connection between religious and political realities, it is perhaps not surprising that the unified (at least in the West) Church should be ripe for fragmentation as well. 'The Jesuits,' writes Edward Norman, 'realized that the old tensions of pope and emperor no longer represented the realities of sixteenth-century Europe. Organic concepts of empire and universal claims of allegiance had passed: Europe was a continent of independent nation-states. The Reformation occurred after this enormous shift in the balance of things had taken place—it was itself a symptom of the new world order.' [Norman 2007, 95] Norman perhaps goes too far in describing Europe as a continent of nation states—nation states were quite some way in the future—but his basic point is indeed correct: political change came first, and religious change followed. It is perhaps an open question whether, as the result of the political and religious changes resulting from the Reformation, Christianity gained in spiritual power, but there can be no doubt, however, that as a result of the Reformation, the embryonic centralising states, both Protestant and Catholic, gained enhanced political power and control. [see Mirgeler, 97] John Neville Figgis perhaps overstates his case somewhat when he remarks that 'had there been no Luther there could never have been a Louis XIV' but his notorious remark, if not entirely accurate, is so only in limiting the causal factor of political absolutism to Luther and the effect to Louis XIV. [Figgis, 71]

WYCLIFFE

The Reformation did not suddenly spring into being, fully armed, like Athena from the head of Zeus. It was presaged in various ways in the centuries that immediately preceded it. One of the more significant of those presagements was the movement inspired by the writings of John Wycliffe (1320-1384).[2] The ecclesiastical life of England was thrown into turmoil in the fourteenth century by the phenomenon known as Lollardism.[3] The Lollards (the term 'Lollard' is derogatory and means something like 'mumbler') were followers of John Wycliffe.[4] Wycliffe was an English Schoolman who attacked the prevailing Catholic orthodoxy on core doctrines such as the nature of the Eucharist, asserted that Scripture and only Scripture was authoritative (an anticipation of the Lutheran doctrine of *Sola Scriptura*) and also attacked the very concept of property. It is not difficult to see that these ideas had political implications, particularly the attack on property.

In some ways, Wycliffe's ideas on property and what he thought the Church's relationship to it should be were a fourteenth century re-enactment of the dispute that had arisen in the thirteenth century upon the emergence of the mendicant Franciscan order.[5] James Greenaway remarks on the connection between the thought of Wycliffe and the earlier Franciscans, noting 'Much of Wycliffe's thought was preformed by others. In the case of his thought on dominium or ownership, the preformation came though the Franciscan problem of poverty.' [Greenaway, 126, n. 16] The original Franciscan charism was tied resolutely to their core belief that the possession of any form of property, whether individual or communal, was inconsistent with their ideals as a religious order. It is perhaps not implausible to see the Franciscan charism as emanating from reflection on the following Scriptural passage: 'And behold, one came up to him, saying, "Teacher, what good deed must I do to have eternal life?" and he said to him, "Why do you ask me about what is good? One there is who is good. If you would enter life, keep the commandments." He said to him, "Which?" And Jesus said, "You shall not commit adultery, You shall not steal, You shall not bear false witness, Honour your father and mother, and You shall love your neighbour as yourself." The young man said to him, "All these I have observed; what do I still lack?" Jesus said to him, "If you would be perfect, go, sell what you possess and give to the poor, and you will have treasure in heaven; and come, follow me." When the young man heard this he went away sorrowful; for he had great possessions.' [*Matthew* 19: 16-22] After the young man had left, Jesus stunned his apostles by saying, '...it is easier for a camel to go through the eye of a needle than for a rich man to enter the kingdom of God.' [*Matthew*, 19: 24] When they then asked, 'Who then can be saved?' [*Matthew* 19: 25] Jesus replied that 'with God, all things are possible.' [*Matthew* 19: 26] In *Mark* [*Mark* 10: 17-22] the corresponding passage is recounted in essentially the same way. Moreover, in both *Matthew* and *Mark*, the questioner is described simply either as a 'young man' (*neaniskos*) or just as 'one' (*eis*). However, the corresponding passage in Luke reads: 'And a *ruler* (*archon*) asked him...' which, with the suggestion that the riches may be ill-gotten, gives quite a different cast to Jesus's admonition.[6] The Franciscans eventually split into two groups, the Spirituals, who held firmly to what they regarded as Francis's authentic teaching and continued to reject all property, and the Conventuals, who took a more pragmatic approach to this matter. The issues at stake were so important and had such damaging potential that the pope intervened. In countering the danger from the Spiritual Franciscans (as he saw it), Pope John XXII,[7] the second Avignon pope, went so far as to declare that private ownership was *not* the consequence of original sin but a condition that would have obtained even in Eden. [see Lahey 2013, 7] In making this claim, he was rejecting a position that had been widely held among theologians to the effect that private property (and coercive government and slavery) were all consequences of sin.[8]

It is important to appreciate the significance of the challenge presented to Christendom by the position taken by the Spiritual Franciscans. It was, says Albert Mirgeler, 'no mere harmless and petty monkish squabble without interest today' but a crisis that turned on the question of whether 'Christianity had to be predominantly personal or institutional.'[9] Had the views of the Spiritual Franciscans prevailed, what would have been the outcome? According to Mirgeler, the result would have been that 'from this time onwards nothing "worldly" would have arisen to confront the "spiritual", and nothing "spiritual" would have been able any longer to find its expression in the field of secular culture. Dante and Giotto, on whose shoulders...Humanism and the Renaissance rest, would then have been impossible or at least have been without any historical importance....Albert the Great and Aquinas likewise would scarcely have succeeded in making Aristotelianism prevail against Plato and Augustine: in other words, the justification in principle of secular activity as "edifying" for the Christian and for Christianity would not have been assured. The development of new, autonomous science—especially the basic natural and historical sciences—was indeed held up, but not completely blocked by the Church, and in the course of time the opposition was worn down; but the victory of the Spirituals would have meant, as in Islam, turning attempts at scientific progress into heresy and thus bringing about their complete failure.' [Mirgeler, 126]

Wycliffe argued that true ownership of anything could only come about through its creation: X truly owns Y if and only if X has created Y. It is easy to see that this claim makes God to be the true and only owner of the universe, human ownership being merely a temporary right to that which one possesses *de facto*. Moreover, human ownership, as limited as that is, is granted only to those who are properly related to God, that is, to those who are in a state of grace. 'I intend,' says Wycliffe, 'to show....that no one while in mortal sin has a simple right to any of God's gifts...'[10] It isn't hard to see the practically disruptive consequences of such a quasi-Donatist[11] doctrine.[12] Whether or not any given person is in a state of grace isn't something evident to the senses. Moreover, since a person could be in a state of grace at one time and not in a state of grace at a later time and later again be once more in a state of grace, he could change, invisibly, from being an owner to being a non-owner to being an owner again.[13] It is easy to see why Wycliffe's arguments on this point were unsettling to the authorities, secular and religious. Wycliffe rejects the position taken a century earlier by John XXII and argues that the natural *dominium* that obtained in Eden was characterised by a lack of any distinction between 'mine' and 'thine'.[14]

The similarities between the original Franciscan teaching and Wycliffe's position are obvious but Wycliffe's position is, in fact, much more radical than that of the Franciscans. Whereas the Franciscans were happy to claim that their constitution required and permitted them to return, as a religious order, to what they believed to be the ownership-free condition of the early Church, Wycliffe claimed that one effect of Christian redemption was that it required everyone, not just the members of a religious order, to return to the pre-lapsarian ideal. The secular and religious authorities in England recognised the revolutionary potential of Wycliffe's teachings and the Lollard movement was extinguished by force and had ceased to be effective by the beginning of the fifteenth century. It played no direct causal role in the English religious transformation of the sixteenth century but it did have an indirect effect on it through the influence that Wycliffe's writings had on such as Jan Hus and others of the continental reformers whose ideas were (re)imported into England. 'The Hussite Movement which surprised and frightened traditional Europe in the first half of the fifteenth century,' writes George Holmes, 'loomed menacingly in the East driving rulers and priests into plans of counter-revolution or conciliation...' It was 'a religious reorganization initiated for reasons of state, but drawing inspiration from both popular feeling and learned theology.'[15]

The claim could be made that Lollardism was among the first expressions of what would later come to be known as the Radical Reformation. Norman Davies notes, 'Once unleashed, Protestantism came in many forms. Luther in Saxony from 1521, Zwingli in Zurich from 1522, the Anabaptists of Münster from 1535, and Calvin in Geneva from 1540, all propagated their views across Europe in an unstoppable flood. For practical purposes, the main divisions lay between the so-called "Magisterial Protestants", like Luther and Calvin, who sought to replace the state-backed monopoly of the Catholic Church with similar monopolies of their own, and the so-called "Radical Protestants", such as the anabaptists and anti-trinitarians, who professed every sort of extreme idea from pacifism to democratic congregationalism and, most dangerously, religious tolerance.'[16]

LUTHER

Without the invention of printing, it is difficult to see how the Protestant Reformation could ever have taken place.[17] 'The advent of printing was an important precondition for the Protestant Reformation taken as a whole,' writes Elizabeth Eisenstein, 'for without it one could not implement a "priesthood of all believers."' [Eisenstein, 171] Seldom has a single technological invention had such a major cultural impact, enabling 'an obscure theologian in Wittenberg' to 'shake Saint Peter's throne' and turning what would otherwise have been a storm in a teacup into the precipitating event in an international revolt that was to shatter Christendom. 'Sixteenth-century heresy and schism shattered Christendom so completely that even after religious warfare had ended, ecumenical movements led by men of good will could not put all the pieces together again.' [Eisenstein, 171, 172]

The core of Luther's theological revolution[18] was the doctrine of salvation by faith alone—*sola fide*. The theological implications of this doctrine aren't the concern of a history of political thought but its social and political implications are. Of these, the religiously grounded obligation of subjects to obey their secular authorities could hardly have been more emphatic. It hardly needs to be said that Luther takes as the ultimate scriptural justification of this doctrine, the opening verses of chapter 13 of Paul's *Epistle to the Romans*. As we have seen already, in this notorious passage, Paul appears to require Christians to give their allegiance to the *de facto* secular authorities and Augustine, at a later date, would go on to use this passage to justify requiring the submission by Christians even to pagan rulers. Luther places himself firmly in the Pauline and Augustinian traditions. If one wanted to find a central example of a resolute and robust defender of the religious obligation to obey secular authority one would have to go very far before one would find someone to trump Luther. As Ellen Meiksins Wood puts it, 'there hardly exists in the Western canon a more uncompromising case for strict obedience to secular authority; and this…belongs to the essence of Lutheran doctrine.' [Wood 2012, 59]

Given that he began his religious life as an Augustinian, it is hardly surprising that Luther takes what is effectively the Augustinian position that the power of the sword is given to secular authorities to control and limit evil. 'If all the world were true Christians, that is, if everyone truly believed, there would be neither need nor use for princes, kings, lords, the Sword or law.'[19] Alas, the world isn't made up of true Christians so that if there were no law and government 'people would devour each other and no one would be able to support his wife and children, feed himself and serve God. The world would become a desert.'[20] We shall see that a similar bleak view of the consequences of an unrestrained human nature will emerge a century later in the writings of Thomas Hobbes. So then, Luther, as everyone else in the Christian world, takes the words of St Paul in *Romans* 13 to mandate Christians to be obedient to their secular rulers. This may be relatively unproblematic where what one's rulers are obliging one to do is in conformity with one's conscience; where it is not, however, there are going to be problems. The Reformers dealt with these problems in different and distinctive ways. Luther's tract, *On Secular Authority,* was an early attempt by him to specify the rights and duties of secular rulers. It doesn't represent his last word on the subject for his beliefs in this area were to shift as the political and religious consequences of the Reformation became more apparent.

Nevertheless, at this early stage, his judgement on the merits of secular rulers is often very negative, indeed sometimes surprisingly hostile. 'God Almighty,' he says, 'has driven our princes mad: they really think they can command their subjects whatever they like and do with them as they please. And their subjects are just as deluded, and believe (wrongly) that they must obey them in all things.'[21] According to Luther in this document, all that the secular rulers of the present do is to 'poll and fleece, heap one tax on another, let loose a bear here, a wolf there. There is no good faith or honesty to be found amongst them; thieves and villains behave better than they do...' This isn't an isolated or rash judgement. A little later in the same work, he comments, 'As a rule, princes are the greatest fools or the worst criminals on earth, and the worst is always to be expected, and little good hoped for, from them, especially in what regards God and the salvation of souls.'[22] Thus, the opinion of the early Luther. Later, as we shall see, his evaluation of secular rulers would become considerably more positive.

For Luther, human beings are irreducibly sinful yet, while still sinful, they can be justified by divine grace. In respect of their ultimate destiny, all men stand on the same horizontal footing but, in a neo-Augustinian moment, Luther argues that the sinfulness of man demands the vertical relationship of ruler and ruled, the existence and operation of secular authorities to whom, as instituted by God, all Christians owe obedience and respect. At the same time as he gives his support to the right of secular governments to demand and receive obedience from the people, Luther attacks the Church's right to exercise any jurisdiction in the external forum—for example, to punish sins or to excommunicate. For him, the Church has no legitimate temporal jurisdiction. Luther's view of the Church in *On Secular Authority* is that it is a free and voluntary association of believers. Such a view of the Church isn't without its political consequences, not least of which is that it is inconsistent with the idea that the membership of the Church is necessarily co-extensive with any given polity.

There are, then, for Luther, two governments in the world: one, spiritual, which addresses itself to the constitution of true and faithful Christians and another, secular, 'which holds the unchristian and wicked in check and forces them to keep the peace outwardly and be still, like it or not.'[23] Would it not suffice to preach the Gospel to such wicked and evil men and by such means bring them to order? Well, yes, but in the meantime, he notes that there are 'always many more of the wicked than there are of the just. And so to try to rule a whole country or the world by means of the Gospel is like herding together wolves, lions, eagles and sheep in the same pen, letting them mix freely, and saying to them: feed, and be just and peaceable; the stable isn't locked, there's plenty of pasture, and you have no dogs or cudgels to be afraid of.'[24]

But if one's rulers are Christian, as they should be, how can they be justified in using coercive power over other Christians, seeing that Christ has told us to turn the other cheek?[25] The distinction Luther draws to solve this problem is between what one does for oneself and what one does for others. 'As far as you and your possessions are concerned,' he writes, 'you keep to the Gospel and act according to Christ's word,' but the coercive actions of secular authority are for the good of others and are, Luther thinks, positively enjoined by *Romans* 13. You are, it would seem, obliged to turn your own cheek but not, if you are a magistrate, your neighbour's.[26]

Luther has already hinted that rulers cannot command us in everything and in certain matters we are not bound to obey them. How are the parameters of obedience to be determined? Rulers who act *ultra vires* are, in that respect at least, no longer rulers and need not be obeyed: *Romans* 13 applies only to rulers and if they act *ultra vires* and are as a result not rulers, it doesn't apply to them. As already mentioned, for Luther, belief cannot be and ought not to be commanded and so if any ruler were to exert his power in this respect, he would have exceeded his authority and become a tyrant. Not only is it the case that obedience in such matters isn't required, Luther thinks that failure to resist would be tantamount to a denial of God![27] What is the position of a Christian who is instructed to obey an order that, in his judgement, is in conflict with the requirements of Scripture? According to Luther, he may disobey the order but then he has to be prepared to accept the consequences of such disobedience. Even more to the point, the issuance of such orders does not constitute any grounds for resistance or rebellion. Doesn't this contradict what Luther had previously stated in his tract? Not quite. The illegitimacy of resistance applies only to the individual Christian acting in a private capacity. Subsidiary rulers may be justified in resisting the commands of their superiors so that princes might not only have a right but even a duty to resist the emperor or, more generally, inferior magistrates, their superiors.

Luther's character drew him towards freedom. Coercive force is to be applied, if at all, only to bringing about outward conformity to right action but what a person believes 'is a matter for each individual's conscience.'[28] Coercion must not be used in matters of belief because 'Faith is free, and no one can be compelled to believe...no one can or ought to be forced to believe anything against his will.'[29]

But Luther couldn't shake off the age-old conviction that heresy must be suppressed, a task which, if not done or not capable of being done by the Church, must be undertaken by the civil power. [see Plamenatz, 54] In undertaking such suppression, kings were 'bishops by necessity'. The upshot of all this, of course, was that secular governments became agents of reform and eventually the arbiters of what reform would take place. As John Plamenatz remarks, 'To us it seems odd that Luther should not have seen that whoever appoints to the ministry and provides for it will in fact decide what it shall teach. How can the Church depend on the secular power in matters of discipline and organization, and yet retain its spiritual independence?' [Plamenatz, 55] This reliance on secular authorities led to the emergence of national churches, something that no one had foreseen and that was hardly immediately comprehensible to anyone on either side of the theological and political disputes, all of whom clung to the core belief that there could only be one true Church until eventually reduced to a position of hostile mutual toleration by war, destruction and death. Whatever Luther's intentions may have been, the result of his efforts and that of the other reformers was the emergence of national churches dominated by their secular rulers.[30]

The Church thus fragmented could offer little or no resistance to the emerging sovereignty of the secular princes. This was true as much in Catholic countries as in Protestant. 'The disruption of the universal church, the suppression of its monastic institutions and ecclesiastical corporations, and the abrogation of the Canon law,' writes George Sabine, 'removed the strong check upon secular power that had existed in the Middle Ages.' [Sabine, 362] Commenting upon this passage from Sabine, Frank Furedi remarks that 'Arguably, the immediate impact of the Reformation was to strengthen absolutist forms of power' and he goes on to note that P. W. Gray 'blames the Reformation and Luther in particular for subordinating the Church to the state.' [Furedi, 163]

It is worth noting the prevalence of a popular but mistaken belief that the Protestant Reformers, in contrast to the repressive Catholic Church, were the apostles of liberty. Even Richard King, in his otherwise excellent *On Offence* writes, 'The clamour for religious liberty that grew out of the Spanish Inquisition and the countless [*sic!*] horrors perpetrated in its name led eventually to the Protestant Reformation which, though it spawned its own atrocities, contained the seeds of a revolution "aiming for liberty in the kingdom of the mind".' [King, 33-34]

The Reformation was many things but by no stretch of the imagination was it the result of a clamour for religious liberty or, indeed, for liberty more broadly construed.[31] John Plamenatz remarks, 'The Catholics, the Lutherans, the Anglicans, the Calvinists, all had this in common: they believed that there could be only one true Church….Luther and Calvin…did not believe that men could receive the Word and be saved outside the Church, or that there could be several Churches, each interpreting the word differently from the other, and yet all equally acceptable to God. Luther and Calvin, no less than the Catholics and Anglicans, believed in uniformity of faith and worship.' [Plamenatz, 62] 'The sixteenth century,' writes Perez Zagorin, 'which witnessed the Reformation and the beginning and spread of Protantism, was probably the most intolerant period in Christian history….When Martin Luther, John Calvin, and other outstanding religious reformers undertook their successful revolt against the Catholic Church and established their own Protestant churches, the latter showed themselves to be no less intolerant of heretics and dissenting Christians than was the Catholic Church.' [Zagorin, 2] And, in respect of the broader social and cultural issues, Hilary Gatti notes that, 'Just as Protestant dogmatism and oppression were often in the period studied here as merciless and unrelenting as those of the post-Tridentine Catholic Church, so the rich texture of Catholic culture produced voices raised in the name of liberty as eloquent and forward-looking as those of Protestant derivation.' [Gatti, 176]

THE RADICAL REFORMERS

It is no secret that Luther and the other major reformers such as Calvin and Zwingli (sometimes referred to as the Magistral or Magisterial Reformers) found themselves in opposition to Catholicism and to Catholic princes, but what is perhaps not quite as well known is that they had to fight battles on not one but on two fronts. The movement of revolt begun by Luther spawned a plethora of splinter groups on his other flank, united only in their belief that he and the other Magisterial Reformers did not take matters as far as they ought to have gone. Höpfl notes, 'The "Radical Reformation" is a term commonly used to refer to those who either sought the take-over of secular authority by the self-selecting members…of churches composed exclusively of "the Elect", or more usually withdrew from contact with secular authority as far as possible…' [Höpfl, viii]

Some took the logic of Luther's theological arguments to imply the illegitimacy of secular authority, an implication that would seem to have some measure of justification if we look to Luther's *On Secular Authority*. 'Luther's attack on the Church could be more readily mobilized against the ecclesiastical hierarchy, princes of the Church and the imposition of tithes, which were indeed a major grievance,' writes Ellen Meiksins Wood. 'But during the peasant revolt the challenge to authority went beyond ecclesiastical jurisdiction to include secular authorities, the ever-increasing burden of taxation and gross inequalities of property and power.' [Wood 2012, 71] Luther emphatically denied that the rejection of secular authority was a consequence of his teaching and he urged the princes on to the most brutal repression of any hint of resistance, rebellion or revolution. The very title of one of his works shows Luther's attitude very clearly—*Against the Robbing and Murdering Hordes of Peasants*. If Luther had little respect for rulers, he had even less respect for the great unwashed. 'Disobedience,' he said, 'is a greater sin than murder, unchastity, theft, and dishonesty, and all that these may include.'[32] Some, such as Ellen Meiksins Wood, believe that the peasants' recruitment of Lutheran support for their political activities wasn't justified on Lutheran principles; others are inclined to take Luther to have been selective in his doctrine of resistance. Whether or which, the actual position of Christian passive obedience eventually promulgated by Luther found favour, not surprisingly, with the German princes, the more so as it freed them and their lands from papal control and the requirement to fund the papacy.

By removing all legal and jurisdictional functions from the Church, Lutherans effectively facilitated the transference of those functions to the state, thus enlarging and extending state power. With the church's legal authority diminished, there was no place outside the secular political structure that could pass judgement on a tyrant. Lutheranism accepted that whatever powers existed were instituted by God and were deserving of all the obedience and respect that they understood *Romans* 13 to mandate. Not only good and just rulers ruled by divine right, tyrants did so too, and no ruler, good or bad could be resisted without violating the explicit commands of Scripture. Although it is true that early Lutheranism, especially after the Peasants' Revolt, endorsed a doctrine of absolute non-resistance, this changed as the political environment changed. Skinner remarks, 'If we turn...to the period after 1530...we find Luther, Melanchthon, Osiander and many of their most prominent followers suddenly changing their minds, and arguing instead that any ruler who becomes a tyrant may be lawfully and forcibly opposed.' [Skinner 1978, 74]

Whether or not Lutheranism over time modified its original stance on the matter of resistance to secular rule, its original conservatism on this matter provoked a more radical reaction that took root especially in parts of Germany and in Switzerland. One of the earliest flashpoints between the magisterial reformers and the radicals took place in Luther's hometown of Wittenberg in 1521-1522. Andreas Karlstadt, who was Luther's replacement in Wittenberg for a short period at this time during Luther's absence, put forward doctrines that were much more radical than those endorsed by Luther himself. On Luther's hasty return to Wittenberg, Karlstadt fled, but not before he had strongly influenced Nicholas Storch and Thomas Müntzer of Zwickau. A parallel separatist anti-Lutheran movement also developed at Zwingli's Zurich under the influence of Conrad Grebel, Felix Manz and Balthasar Hubmaier.[33] The Zwickau radicals and the Zurich radicals were in correspondence with and influenced each other.

Thomas Müntzer had no time for the Lutheran doctrine of the separation of powers—spiritual and secular—and wanted the secular authorities to take an active role in promoting and defending the true faith. False clergy, Müntzer says (and by false clergy he has Luther in mind) have 'made fools of you, so that everyone now swears to the saints that the princes are heathen people insofar as their office is concerned.' [Müntzer, 1524a, 26-27] Müntzer cites the usual passage from *Romans* but he does so *not* to make the usual point about the necessity for Christians to be passively obedient to their rulers; on the contrary, Müntzer interprets this passage as requiring rulers to actively promote a Christian society and, in the event of their failing to do so, he believes that Scripture legitimates rebellion against them! [1524a, 28, n. 18] On the other hand, the Anabaptists Conrad Grebel and Felix Manz also attacked the political attitude of the magisterial reformers but, in contrast to the revolutionary Müntzer, they not only did not want the godly to take control of political power for the advancement of the true faith but, on the contrary, they wanted true believers to ignore secular authority completely! Michael Sattler, in his *Schleitheim Confession*, makes the point that the coercive application of law and order has no role to play in the lives of true Christians. He writes, 'The sword is ordained of God outside the perfection of Christ....In the perfection of Christ, however, only the ban is used for a warning...without putting the flesh to death.' May Christians resort to the law courts to decide their disputes? Sattler thinks not. 'Christ did not wish to decide or pass judgment between brother and brother in the case of the inheritance, but refused to do so. Therefore we should do likewise.' Can a Christian be a magistrate? Again, Sattler thinks not. 'The government magistracy is according to the flesh, but the Christians' is according to the Spirit...'[34] We now had a three-way standoff in respect to the appropriate relation between the spiritual government and the secular government: the Zwickau prophets, so-called, oppose the magisterial reformers and the Anabaptists; the magisterial reformers oppose the Zwickau prophets and the Anabaptists; and the Anabaptists oppose the Zwickau prophets and the magisterial reformers!

Zwickau Prophets	Spiritual government and secular government fused
Magisterial Reformers	Spiritual government and secular government distinguished but cooperating
Anabaptists	Spiritual government disdains secular government

Although the challenge of Müntzer was eliminated effectively with his execution in 1525, and the Anabaptist challenge never amounted to much in terms of the numbers of its adherents, the intellectual challenge of the Anabaptists forced the Magisterial Reformers into forging a closer alliance between the spiritual and secular governments to give the lie to those, not least the Catholic opposition, who wished to tar them with the anti-authority Anabaptist brush.

CALVIN

If justification by faith alone is the Lutheran touchstone, then Divine Sovereignty is the Calvinist equivalent. The spiritual and temporal authorities exercise their jurisdiction under the sovereignty of God. If Luther's vision of the state is a modified version of Augustinianism—the state's function is to prevent or limit evil—the Calvinist vision has a more positive role for the state to play, to wit, the imposition of a godly discipline on the populace as a whole. Civil governors are representatives of God and so must be obeyed. John Plamenatz notes that 'Calvin preached the doctrine of obedience to established civil authority almost as fervently as Luther.' [Plamenatz, 59] Calvin even goes so far as to suggest that such secular rulers are called gods! 'When those who bear the office of magistrate are called gods, let no one suppose that there is little weight in that appellation. It is thereby intimated that they have a commission from God, that they are invested with divine authority and, in fact, represent that person of God, as whose substitutes they in a manner are.' [*Institutes* IV.xx.4]

As was the case with most Christian theologians, Calvin makes use of *Romans* 13 to support his claim that Christians are obliged to obey their political leaders. In the *Institutes*, Calvin is at pains to demonstrate that his variety of Christianity constitutes no threat to royal authority in contrast to, as he thinks, Catholicism. Similarly, he opposes the radicals, such as the Anabaptists, who object to any form of political authority. Just as Luther had prohibited any resistance, disobedience or revolution by individuals, so too does Calvin. Nevertheless, he does allow inferior or lesser magistrates to act as a check on the power of the monarch. This limited power of resistance was later to prove significant. Calvin, then, accepts that Christians have an absolute obligation to submit to temporal authority. Such submission is, for him, consistent with Christian liberty. His position was perhaps even more extreme than Luther's. 'Just as Luther inclined to the providentialist view that Romans 13 refers to whomever we find equipped with power, and that Christians have no business curiously inspecting the titles of those they find in authority, so did Calvin.' [Höpfl, xxi] Together with this standard view on the necessity for submission to secular authorities, Calvin drew a distinction between the realms of secular and spiritual government.[35] Generally, Calvinism supported a position in which state and church were separate but in which the state enforced the church's teaching on faith and morals. As Sabine points out, the consequence of such a policy was 'an intolerable rule of the saints: a meticulous regulation of the most private concerns founded upon universal espionage, with only a shadowy distinction between the maintenance of public order, the control of private morals, and the preservation of pure doctrine and worship.' [Sabine, 363] Later, Calvin was to modify drastically his earlier view that the secular and the spiritual realms were and ought to be separate. In his later views, the authority of secular magistrates extends not only to the ordering and control of relations between man and man but to relations between man and God.

For Calvin, the spiritual kingdom of Christ and the civil government are far removed from each other.[36] Although this is so, the purpose of civil government isn't something that should be shunned by Christians. On the contrary, such a government has among its purposes the fostering and protection of 'the external worship of God' and the defence of 'pure doctrine and the good condition of the Church.'[37] Having separated the spiritual and civil realms, it might seem that Calvin is once again mingling them. He is aware of this criticism and responds, 'Nor ought it to worry anyone that I am now allotting to the human polity that care for the right order of religion, which I seem earlier to have placed outside human determination. I approve a political order that makes it its business to prevent true religion…from being besmirched and violated with impunity by public and manifest sacrilege. But in doing so, I no more allow men to make laws about religion and the worship of God according to their fancy than I did before.'[38] Calvin appears to be making a distinction between the externals of religion, which can come under the care of the civil power, and the internals of religion, which cannot. If that is so, then one might wonder how and where this distinction is to be drawn, who is to draw it, and how one can prevent the incursion of civil powers into areas that should be none of their concern.[39]

Calvin does not regard the civil magistracy as some kind of necessary evil. He notes that 'it is not at all by the perversity of men that kings and other superiors obtain their power over all things on earth; on the contrary it comes about by the providence and sacred ordinance of God, whose pleasure it is to have mankind governed in this manner.'[40] On the contrary, he holds that we should hold it in the highest honour, just as he believes is the case in Scripture.[41] Calvin surely has in mind his Anabaptist adversaries when he rebukes those who reject civil authority as something contrary to the Christian religion and charges them with insulting God by so doing. 'It is impossible to despise God's ministers without dishonouring God himself.'[42] Against the Anabaptist claim that violence must be eschewed by all Christians, Calvin robustly defends the right and duty of the civil powers to punish criminals and even, when necessary, to wage war.[43]

The same problem presented itself to Calvin as it did to Luther and others: what is one to do if one's rulers mandate that which is against conscience or against one's conception of what one's Christian commitment requires? Calvin anticipates this objection. He gives a vivid description of such delinquent princes: 'Some of them live lives of indolence and pleasure, not in the least concerned about all those duties to which they ought to attend. Others, intent only on their own profit, prostitute every right, privilege, judgement and charter by putting them up for sale. Others again drain the poor people of their money, only to squander it in wild prodigality Yet others pillage homes, violate wives and maidens, slaughter the innocent; in short, they engage in what can only be called criminality.' [Höpfl, 76]

Calvin was to adopt a hermeneutical position that the powers to which submission was required were plural rather than singular and that one could distinguish between superior and inferior magistrates, as Luther did, with this difference, that Calvin thought of them on classical models deriving from the Spartan ephors[44] and the Roman tribunes, as ephoral or tribunal magistrates. The Spartan Ephors, 'as representatives of the people, had formidable powers.... every year they declared war on the *helots*...and could execute them without trial; they had disciplinary power over all citizens; they virtually conducted Spartan foreign policy; they presided in the *Gerousia* and the Assembly; they oversaw the training and discipline of the young; the *Krypteia* (Secret Police) was under their orders; and they had interesting powers in relation to the Kings, with whom they exchanged a monthly oath, guaranteeing to support them if they should be true to their oaths.' [Kershaw, 143-144] The Calvinist conception of these inferior magistrates, although functionally similar to the Lutheran, tends to see them as being in some sense a product of or representative of popular support. It is tempting to equate the Calvinist popular magistrates with the Lutheran inferior magistrates but although they may function in more or less the same way as the legitimate locus of resistance, their origin is significantly different: they are appointed, not ordained. They come from the bottom up, not down from the top. In this context, what Calvin in fact says is, 'It may be that there are in our days popular[45] magistrates established to restrain the licentiousness of kings, corresponding to those "Ephors"...which were set against the authority of the kings of the Spartans, or the Tribunes...of the People, set over against the Roman consuls, or the "Demarchs", set up against the Council of the Athenians.'[46]

Calvin hints that the role played by the ephors, tribunes and demarchs might be played in his time by the three estates in individual kingdoms. The inferior magistrates could, if their superiors became tyrannical, legitimately lead resistance to them. Resistance wasn't something permitted to private individuals but only to inferior or popular magistrates acting in their official capacities. Whether or not superior magistrates are evincing tyranny is to be determined by whether they are exercising their authority in the proper way and in the proper areas. Magistrates neglecting their duties or exceeding their authority or commanding men to act against God's will, *to that extent* cease to be magistrates becoming rather 'robbers, usurpers and invaders' and so obedience to their dictates isn't required by Scripture.[47] 'Calvin's doctrine of active resistance by lesser magistrates to the sovereign or supreme magistrate,' writes Plamenatz, 'justified their using their local privileges in defence of their faith. They needed a right of resistance they could use wherever they were socially predominant, but which could not be used to stir up against them the lower classes who were strongly Catholic in almost every part of France....only those who already had authority have the right to resist authority. The mere citizen or subject has no such right.'[48]

So, then, is resistance by individuals justified when one's rulers are such as these? No, says Calvin! Rulers derive their authority from God alone and to God alone are they answerable. We must submit to all our rulers, good and bad alike. Moreover, not only are we required to submit to our rulers but we are also obliged to honour and reverence them, however bad they might be, for 'even the worst of them, and those entirely underserving of any honour, provided they have public authority, are invested with that splendid and sacred authority which God's Word bestows on the ministers of his justice and judgement.... they are to be held in the same honour and reverence as would be accorded an excellent king.'[49] Private individuals have neither a right nor a duty to interfere in public matters, however much provocation they are offered. If some kind of correction is required, this is the task of a magistrate, one who is the 'eyes and ears' of the ruler.[50]

Not only did Calvin and Luther think alike on the matter of passive obedience; they shared an outright contempt for popular democracy and the thinking of the radical wing of Protestantism. On this point, Calvin was in complete agreement with Luther. To resist the magistrate is, in effect, to resist God, since the magistrate is God's vicar. It is the office of magistrate that requires respect, not the individual magistrate, and so that office commands obedience irrespective of the moral quality of its holder. Is the ephoral or tribunal right of resistance not in conflict with this requirement of obedience? Calvin thinks not, because this right is itself God-derived and not an expression of a power emanating from the people as a whole. In effect, this amounts to claiming that sovereignty is held jointly by more than one person and that each holder has a duty to prevent aggression by the others. Not everyone is persuaded that this line of argument is central to Calvinism, nor is everyone persuaded that Calvin and Calvinists necessarily agree on the matter. Sabine writes that 'This theory of the inferior magistrate got an importance among certain Calvinists out of all proportion to the place given it by Calvin.'[51]

By contrast with Calvin's initial rejection of any form of active resistance to one's prince, Lutherans were confronted with this problem when they found themselves protesting against the removal by the Emperor Charles V of the concessions previously granted to them. In this context, the standard interpretation of *Romans* 13 isn't rejected outright but it is modified significantly in a number of respects. First, the powers to which Paul refers are taken to be plural rather than singular so that not only the Emperor but all the local German princes are wielders of the sword in respect of their own jurisdictions. Second, a quasi-contractual idea is introduced which posits that the Emperor has not only authority but also duties and responsibilities towards other rulers and the public at large which, if not observed, may release those others from their duty of obedience. Luther himself was initially resistant to any modification of the duty of obedience deriving from *Romans* but by 1530 he and the other Lutheran theologians ceased to resist. They argued, ingeniously, if perhaps disingenuously, that although they had heretofore counselled absolute non-resistance, that was before they realised that the law itself allowed for the right of armed resistance! Apparently, there was a positive Imperial law to the effect that in cases of notorious injustice, the government might be resisted by force. Thus, paradoxically, the very obedience that was mandated by Scripture could actively require one to resist one's rulers!

PRIVATE RESISTANCE

Even if the principle of legitimate resistance were to be granted, another problem had to be solved. Could such resistance be channelled only constitutionally through public representatives or inferior magistrates or public powers (as with the Lutheran conception of inferior magistrates or the Calvinist conceptions of ephors and tribunes) or could such resistance be offered by any private individual? Although they initially rejected any right of private resistance, the Lutherans (if not Luther himself) appear to have moved slowly but inexorably in the direction of endorsing it. If the Catholic powers were to attempt to aggress against the Lutherans, they would *ipso facto* cease to be lawful magistrates and so resistance to them would not, despite appearances to the contrary, be a violation of Scriptural norms. The Emperor had the powers he had for the defence of the realm. Should he use those powers to attack parts of the realm he may be resisted, just as we may resist anyone who offers us unwarranted violence. Among prominent Lutherans, Melanchthon's attitude was equivocal, inclining to the constitutional (inferior magistrate) position, but appearing to endorse also the private position in its approval of the exercise of the duty of self-preservation by the repulsion of force by force. On the other hand, Bucer and Osiander appear to stick rigidly to the position that legitimate resistance can only be offered by inferior magistrates.

Did the Lutheran ideas on this matter affect the Calvinist position? It would seem that the 'inferior magistrate' interpretation was reflected by the Calvinists but not without some backing and filling, with their sometimes appearing to endorse it, sometimes not. [see Skinner 1978, 216] Eventually, what we see emerging here is a convergence by both Lutherans and Calvinists on a specific interpretation of *Romans* 13. Initially taken to require unconditional obedience to the prince, it appears that this passage, when properly understood, justifies obedience *not to one prince or power but to many* and, moreover, does so *not unconditionally but contingently* upon that power's being exercised for its proper purpose. By the mid-1540s, some Lutherans had made the more radical move to embrace, if only tentatively, the private-law theory of resistance. In the Magdeburg *Confession* of 1550, the argument is proposed that magistrates acting *ultra vires* cease to be 'powers' falling under Paul's injunction. Since they are no longer powers, resistance to them by anyone isn't a violation of Scriptural norms. In Calvinist circles, some of the mid-century Calvinist literary productions also cautiously accepted the principle of private resistance.

Calvin, in the final version of the *Institutes*, seems to grant the private-law argument some validity when he recounts Daniel's denial that 'he was guilty of any offence against the king when he disobeyed an ungodly law the latter had made: for the king had transgressed the bounds set to him and had not only wronged men, but had raised his horns against God, thereby abrogating his own power.'[52] Höpfl sees clearly that the implication of this passage is that 'any ruler who sets himself against God, *ipso facto* ceases to be a ruler.'[53] He denies, however, with what justification one can only imagine, that Calvin does *not* intend this implication even though it was drawn by some of his successors. That Höpfl may be incorrect in his denial that Calvin intends to claim that rulers setting themselves against God cease to be rulers can be gleaned from other works of Calvin, some earlier, some later, than the final version of the *Institutes* where he appears to make much the same point. Skinner notes that 'if we turn from the *Institutes* to the *Commentaries on the Bible* which he [Calvin] began to issue in the closing years of his life, we find him beginning to develop his allusions to the private law argument into a theory of lawful opposition to tyrants. The earliest decisive instance occurs in his *Commentary on the Acts of the Apostles*, first published between 1552 and 1554.' [Skinner 1978, 220] This publication predates the final revision of the *Institutes*. In his *Readings on the Prophet Daniel* and in his *Sermons on the Last Eight Chapters of the Book of Daniel*, which postdate the final version of the *Institutes* by two and six years respectively, Calvin discusses once again the case of Daniel's defiance of Darius's command. Rulers who claim that God is not to be served or honoured are not to be counted as princes. Not only may they be resisted but they should be laid low! Despite this, it is true to say that Calvin's endorsement of the private-law theory is never quite unequivocal.

Whatever may have been Calvin's final thoughts on this matter and however much there remain unresolved ambiguities in his works, there can be no doubt that in some of those influenced by him (and here Höpfl is clearly correct) there is much less ambiguity in their endorsement of private resistance. As we have seen, both Luther and Calvin initially held to a doctrine of passive obedience, both holding that resisting one's rulers was always wrong. Lutheranism and Calvinism as they later developed adopted a less rigorous position. Later Calvinism developed and defended a theory of resistance as an instrument of religious reform. This happened in Scotland where John Knox, an orthodox Calvinist in every other respect, departed from Calvin on this point. Something similar also happened among the French Calvinist, the Huguenots. The common ground for the French and the Scottish Calvinists was that they found themselves subjects to rulers who were Catholic. The effect of the creation of these islands of Protestantism in a Catholic sea or, less commonly, islands of Catholicism in a sea of Protestantism, was to force a reconsideration of the absolute prohibition of active resistance to one's rulers. As Francis Oakley notes, when 'confronted by the hostile apparatus of the persecuting confessional state, those minorities were forced to confront a truly fundamental question. They were forced, in effect, to think the unthinkable and to decide if they might not, after all, disobey a legitimate ruler who sought to deny them the practice of their faith.' [Oakley 2015, 6]

The attitude of Calvinists in Britain was significantly less reticent about private resistance than the non-French Continental Calvinists. In Scotland, says Skinner, 'we find a completely unequivocal statement of the private-law argument being deployed as the main justification for the lawfulness of forcible resistance.' [Skinner 1978, 221] Chief among these more forceful exponents of the private-law argument are John Ponet and Christopher Goodman. 'During the 1550s,' writes Frank Furedi, 'Calvinist theologians John Ponet and John Knox [Furedi doesn't mention Goodman] developed a theory of popular resistance. Ponet argued that since authority was a unique gift from God to the community, those rulers who abused it should be disobeyed and dispossessed of their power.' [Furedi, 154]

Both Ponet and Goodman agree on what should be by now the familiar contention that rulers exist in order to exercise specific duties. Should they fail to do so and instead act in a tyrannical fashion, those rulers lose their special status and become just private citizens. John Ponet is less inclined to make this point explicit than is Goodman but he does say that 'the lawes of many Christiane regions doo permitte, that private men maie kil malefactours, yea though they were magistrates…as when a governour shall sodainly with his sworde renne upon an innocent, or goo about to shote him through with a gonne, or if he should be found in bedde with a mannes daughter; much more if [he] goo about to betraie and make awaie his country to forainers, etc.' [Ponet, 146] Still, he thinks that the killing of errant magistrates by private individuals isn't conducive to good order.

Ponet is critical of the Anabaptists for thinking that men can live together without sin without the need of a civil power; papists, on the other hand, make the mistake of thinking that the civil power is to be obeyed in everything. Both are in error. [see Ponet, 147] Skinner notes that Ponet goes so far as to deny completely that princes are always ordained by God but, not surprisingly, that he is unable to offer any authority for this claim other than citing—in a somewhat embarrassed manner—some Catholic contributions made by Gerson and others to the conciliarist debates! [see Skinner 1978, 227] A distinction is drawn between those rulers whose actions are lawful and those whose actions are not. The former are ordained by God; the latter are not. But that gives rise to another question, namely, if tyrannous rulers aren't ordained by God, how do they come to hold office? This can come about, it seems, only if the people make a mistake in the selection process; and, once again, Ponet has recourse to a Catholic example—if a Pope isn't one who carries out his appointed duties or is one who oversteps his authority, then the cardinals made a mistake in appointing him![54]

Christopher Goodman dispenses entirely with any lingering reluctance to endorse private resistance. He takes his starting point, as usual, from *Romans* 13 but remarks that our rulers aren't merely ordained but ordained for a purpose, namely, the administration of justice. Rulers who become tyrannical or are guilty of murder cease to be public persons. He writes, 'if the Magistrates would whollye despice and betraye the iustice and Lawes of God, you which are subiectes with them shall be condemned except you mayntayne and defend the same Lawes against them, and all others to the uttermost of your powers... for this hath God required of you....Which commandement as it is not geven onely to the Rulers and governours (thoghe I confesse it chieflie apperteyneth to their office to see it executed)...but also is common to all the people, who are likewise bownde to the observation of the same...' [Goodman, 151-52]

Perhaps as a development of the idea that rulers are appointed for particular purposes and not just for their own aggrandisement, the notion of a covenant enters into Calvinist thinking. The writings of Christopher Goodman and John Knox argue that godly citizens—not just magistrates—make a covenant with God, which covenant gives rise to obligations. One of these obligations is the obligation to resist and to remove tyrants. This notion of a covenant enables these Calvinist thinkers 'to reverse the most fundamental assumption of orthodox reformation political thought: they assure the people not that they will be damned if they resist the powers that be, but rather that they will be damned if they fail to do so, since this will be tantamount to breaking what Knox call the "league and covenant" which they have sworn with God himself.' [Skinner 1978, 238]

If it is Scriptural teaching that all rulers, whatever their character and howsoever they execute their offices, are *de facto* appointed of God, then on the standard interpretation of *Romans* 13 they are due obedience and may not be resisted. How can this position be combined with any legitimate theory of resistance? It can't! Or at least it can't, unless the standard interpretation of the Pauline prescription in *Romans* is suitably and radically re-interpreted along teleological lines. The emergence of a doctrine of a right to resistance in Calvinism, especially individual resistance, was due not so much to Calvin's own teaching—he was a resolute supporter of the doctrine of passive obedience—but to the pressure that French and Scottish Calvinists found themselves under to adapt to their particular political situations, opposed, as they were, to governments which they couldn't hope to convert to their cause. Sabine comments, 'It was practically a foregone conclusion, therefore, that a Calvinist church, existing in a state whose rulers refuse to admit the truth of its doctrine and to enforce its discipline, would drop the duty to obey and assert the right to resist.' [Sabine, 368] On the other hand, John Plamenatz remarks, 'Knox went further, much further, than Calvin had done; he was a more violent and reckless controversialist. It wasn't, however, mere recklessness that carried him on, for the Calvinists were stronger in Scotland than in France, and could afford to be bolder. Knox's doctrine of resistance is entirely in keeping with Calvin's conception of the proper relations between Church and State.' [Plamenatz, 60]

VINDICIAE, CONTRA TYRANNOS

The St Bartholomew's Day massacre in 1572 had an invigorating effect on Huguenot political thought. As the prospect of execution is said to sharpen the mind wonderfully, so the imminent prospect of persecution tended to sharpen the minds of the Huguenots. 'It is a striking fact,' says John Allen, 'that a good many of the pamphlets published in the year that followed August, 1572, alleged "necessity" as a sufficient justification under the circumstances for armed rebellion. Self-preservation, it was argued, is a natural right.' [Allen 1928, 307] Of course, as Allen points out, one could preserve oneself by submission or by voluntary exile just as much as by armed rebellion. It is only if it is considered that there's no obligation to submit or to go into voluntary exile that self-preservation could be said to justify armed rebellion.

One of the most significant publications of this period was the anonymous *Vindiciae, contra tyrannos* published in France in 1579 by one Stephanus Junius Brutus, this name being, of course, a *nom de guerre*. The real author of this piece has sometimes been identified as Philippe du Plessis-Mornay, sometimes Hubert Languet, but there's no definitive scholarly consensus on this point. J. W. Allen believes neither of these men to have been the author of this work of which an English translation was published as early as 1648.[55] Taking for granted the belief that rulers must uphold pure Christian doctrine, its author asks: first, are a ruler's subjects are obliged to obey him if he commands something against the law of God?—second, is it lawful to resist a ruler who seeks to set at naught God's law or who attacks the church?—third, is it lawful to offer resistance to a ruler who oppresses or attempts to destroy the state and, if so, who may offer such resistance and in what way? The answer to the first question is no, his subjects are not obliged to obey him, to the second question the answer is yes, it is lawful to offer resistance to such a ruler; and the answer to the third question is, as they say, complicated. This question and its answer is the one most of interest to us.

Because of the contract subsisting between people and ruler, the people are bound to obey only upon condition that the ruler provides a lawful and just government. The *Vindiciae* envisages *two* contracts; one between God and the people as a whole, including the ruler; and another between the ruler and his subjects. The ruler is bound to perform his duties unconditionally; if he fails to do so, the contract between him and his subjects is null and void. A surprisingly utilitarian justification is initially presented to justify the withdrawal of obedience to the ruler. It amounts to the claim that men are willing to bear the cost of a ruler only if they obtain a net benefit by so doing. 'In the first place every one agrees that men, by nature loving liberty and hating servitude, born rather to command than obey, have not willingly admitted to be governed by another, and renounced, as it were, the privilege of nature by submitting themselves to the commands of others but for some special and great profit that they expected from it.'[56] Should that turn out not to be the case, then obedience is no longer required. This, however, isn't the principal justification for the right to resist.

The right to resist is primarily justified because, in the end, the ruler is subject to law, both the law of nature and the municipal law. A ruler who becomes a tyrant loses his claim to rule legitimately. Now comes the critical point. The argument thus far may seem to lead in a direction of justifying individual resistance to the ruler in the appropriate circumstances. But, surprisingly, this is *not* what our pseudonymous author is claiming. It isn't individual citizens but the people as a whole, a corporate whole, who can offer legitimate resistance to their ruler. Their corporate activity is mediated through those who, other than their ultimate ruler, are their natural leaders, such as inferior magistrates, nobles, or local officials. The duty of individuals to render passive obedience to their rulers is asserted just as strongly by the author of the *Vindiciae* as by Luther and Calvin. As Sabine notes, the right of resistance was 'in no sense a claim of popular rights inhering in every individual, nor did the Huguenot party from which it emanated stand for popular rights. It stood rather for the rights (or ancient privileges) of towns and provinces and classes against the levelling effect of royal power. The spirit of the *Vindiciae* was not democratic but aristocratic. Its rights were the rights of corporate bodies and not of individuals...'[57] The corporatism exhibited in the *Vindiciae* envisaged the state as being composed not of isolated individuals but of constituent parts or classes or corporations. Such a conception is capable of being understood and expressed in a federal form, and that, as we shall see, was precisely what was done sometime later by Johannes Althusius.

THE *FRANCO-GALLIA* AND THE *RÉVEILLE MATIN*

François Hotman's *Franco-Gallia* is an attempt to show by means of historical analysis that the King of France was and had always been subordinate to the Estates-General.[58] Whatever its merits as a piece of political theory, as history the *Franco-Gallia* is 'a mass of inaccuracies, confusions and misunderstandings.' [Allen 1928, 309] Whether confused or inaccurate or not, however, it does not seem to have had any significant effect on contemporary Huguenot political thought. Another anonymous piece, the *Réveille Matin*, allegedly composed by someone with the charmingly improbable name of Eusèbe Philadelphe Cosmopolite, is remarkable perhaps more for its paucity of religious references than for its general, if somewhat incoherent, expression of ideas current in the Huguenot community.

It is easy to think of the polemical political writings of this period as being all of a piece but, though there are recurrent themes and indeed striking similarities among these writings, there are also significant differences. Allen remarks that 'Both Hotman's *Franco-Gallia* and the anonymous *Réveille Matin* differ essentially from the tracts of the *Mémoires de l'Estat* and from the *Vindiciae*, in that the views expressed or implied in them are strictly political or juristic and are not radically concerned with any religious conceptions.' [Allen 1928, 308-309] Hotman, making use of the controversial belief that German Völker had chosen their kings,[59] proposed that the people's transference of the right to rule to a king did not in any way involve a permanent transfer of sovereignty. On the contrary, he thought, the people and their representatives have the right to oversee the actions of the king, as well as the right to depose him if necessary. As Calvinists, the Huguenots found themselves dogmatically leg-ironed to Calvin's commitment to complete passive obedience to the powers that be, anything less revolutionary than which it is hard to conceive; however, in their particular political circumstances, this policy was radically inoperable. The French Protestants had three options: submit, go into exile (which many were later to do) or resist. If, despite Calvin's teaching, resistance to political authority were to be a legitimate option for Christians, then it would have to be justifiable. Typically, such justifications propounded either a theory of the original sovereignty of the people, or a thesis that royal governance wasn't absolute but conditional, or both.

THEODORE BEZA

In Geneva, Calvin's successor Theodore Beza (1519-1605) developed a theory of popular sovereignty. He arrived at this conclusion by arguing that since people necessarily preceded their rulers, political power had to have originated with them. Between 1554, when Beza wrote 'On the Authority of the Magistrates to Punish Heretics,'[60] and 1574, when he wrote 'The Rights of Rulers and Duty of Subjects,' the political landscape had changed significantly. Outside France, the Scottish rejection of Queen Mary, begun in 1559, culminated in her abdication in 1567; and at home in France a civil war had broken out in 1562. After the St Bartholomew's Day massacre of 1572 the position of French Calvinists was so perilous that they were finally moved to advocate resistance as religiously justified.

   According to Beza, magistrates are given to men so that the laws necessary to human flourishing might be maintained. 'The Magistrate,' he writes, 'is he who by the public consent of the citizens is declared custodian of that peace and tranquillity. This peace depends on the observation of laws which established the safety of all the citizens.' [Zuck, 143] But what is a citizen to do if his prince or supreme magistrate, either through cruelty or through ignorance, 'combats the reign of Christ'? Beza recommends having recourse to one's local inferior magistrate: 'When then several Princes abuse their office, whoever still feels it necessary to refuse to use the Christian Magistrates offered by God against external violence whether of the unfaithful or of heretics, I charge, deprives the Church of God of a most useful, and...necessary defense...' [Zuck, 144] Beza teaches that 'it shall be lawful and permitted to the subordinate magistrates to take precautions for themselves and for those over whom they exercise guardianship, and to offer resistance to the tyrant of the people.' [Zuck, 170] This referral of the right to resist to inferior magistrates or ephors was one respect in which the Huguenots generally adhered to Calvinist doctrine. For political purposes, the 'people' were taken to be their representatives—ephors, magistrates, estates-general—rather than the common mob, still less individual members of that mob. Resistance, including, in case of extremity, tyrannicide, wasn't something permitted to the common mob or to its members but only to duly constituted assemblies. Murray Rothbard writes in his *Economic Thought before Adam Smith*, 'sovereignty rests in the institutions of duly constituted assemblies or magistrates, only these institutions embodying the sovereign power of the people can properly resist the tyranny of the king.' [Rothbard 1995a, 170] But if those magistrates should refuse to perform their duties then, Beza says, 'let each private citizen bestir himself with all his power to defend the lawful constitution of his country, to whom after God he owes his entire existence.' [Zuck, 169] Zuck writes that 'Beza thus had removed Calvin's doctrinal restraint against resistance at a time when pressure was mounting for military action among Calvinists, and consequently, despite his doctrinal conservatism, he exerted notably radical influence upon the religion and politics of his age.' [Zuck, 142]

GEORGE BUCHANAN

When we examined the Lutheran and Calvinist contributions to political theory, we saw that their thinking was dominated by the traditional understanding of *Romans* 13. I think it is true to say that Calvinists residing in jurisdictions whose secular leaders were unsympathetic to their religious convictions tended, understandably, more towards radicalism than those whose countries, cities or cantons were governed by co-religionists. This was certainly true of the French Huguenots although their radicalism was measured. In Scotland, another country where Calvinists found themselves religiously at odds with their rulers, however, matters were taken somewhat further.

George Buchanan (1506-1582) considered the Calvinist doctrine of the restriction of resistance and tyrannicide to the ephors—and rejected it! Buchanan was perhaps the first to develop and articulate a theory of individual natural rights and to justify tyrannicide not by assemblies or inferior magistrates but by individuals. Buchanan's *The Right of the Kingdom in Scotland* was begun by him in 1567 but only published some twelve years later in 1579. As with many political philosophers before and after him, Buchanan has his account of pre-political man. Taking his inspiration from Stoic sources, he portrays man as a pre-rational animal, outside society, outside religion, solitary and wandering. Such a man isn't only pre-political, he is also pre-social. This type of approach to political anthropology is similar to that of Buchanan's Catholic contemporary, Juan de Mariana and to the account later given by Rousseau in his *Second Discourse*. It is strikingly different from the Aristotelian and Thomist accounts and also from the view of most Huguenots, that man might possibly have been pre-political but not pre-social. Like Hotman in his *Franco-Gallia* and the author of the anonymous *Réveille Matin* and, later, Johannes Althusius, but unlike most Huguenot writing, Buchanan significantly maintains a steadfast reticence on the topic of religious covenants, addressing himself only to the political covenant. Even more significant is that, in Buchanan's thought, the intermediate authorisers, characteristic of much Calvinistic theorising—ephors, lesser magistrates—simply disappear. Buchanan insists that "the whole body of the people' must be pictured as 'coming together' to elect 'someone to deliberate and concern themselves with the affairs of each member of the community" [Skinner 1978, 342]

I discussed Buchanan's contribution to the interpretation of *Romans* 13 in an earlier chapter but it is worth reminding ourselves here of what he had to say.

Buchanan insists that this passage in St Paul has no general application and is addressed to the specific time, place and circumstances of its making. The Church Paul addressed was an infant Church composed, as Buchanan remarks, 'of a promiscuous crowd of plebeians' for whom it would have been extremely foolish to attract the attention of those in government. What advice, he asks, should today be given to Christians living under Turkish rule, what except the advice Paul gives to the Romans 'to omit nothing that could help us to conciliate the good will of all men by honest practices.' [Buchanan 1579, 58] His conclusive argument that Paul's advice was circumstantial and not general is that 'though he [Paul] minutely explains the mutual duties of husbands to their wives, of wives to their husbands, of parents to their children, of children to their parents, of masters to their slaves, and of slaves to the masters, he does not, in describing the duty of a magistrate, address them expressly by name.' Why should he not have done this except that 'there were neither kings nor other magistrates to whom he could write.'? If Paul were writing now, Buchanan says, and were there to be a prince 'who thinks that not only human, but also divine laws ought to be subservient to his capricious lusts; who would have not only his decrees, but even his nods, held as laws' would Paul not 'declare him unworthy of being reckoned a magistrate and 'put all Christians under an interdict to abstain from all familiarity, all conversation, and all communion with him.' [Buchanan 1579, 59] Kings, then, no less than common men, may be called to answer for their actions, for God 'commands the wicked to be exterminated, and excepts neither rank, nor sex, nor condition, nor even person; since to him kings are not more acceptable than beggars,' and Buchanan gives a long and detailed account of kings, princes and rulers who have been justly punished. [Buchanan 1579, 59ff.]

Kings exist only to serve a specific function. Since all men are equal and no one naturally has authority over another, a king can come into being only if given authority by those over whom he is to rule. This authority cannot be unlimited; otherwise, kingship would fail of its function. The king, then, is bound by laws, and his authority is conditional upon the proper performance of his function. The people as a whole are, and remain, superior to the king; he is their agent or delegate. Buchanan argues that there's a mutual compact between king and citizens such that whoever first withdraws from it or acts contrary to it forfeits whatever rights belong to him under that compact. A king who destroys orderly government is a tyrant and as such is a public enemy. In a war against an enemy, it isn't only the people as a whole who have a right to destroy him but *such a right belongs also to individuals.*[61] The coronation promise of the Scottish kings shows, Buchanan thinks, that a covenantal relationship exists between the Scottish people and their king. The obedience of the people isn't absolute but conditional upon the king's performing his side of the bargain. Buchanan is of the opinion, as later will be Johannes Althusius, that when the people *do* select a ruler, they do *not* transfer their sovereignty to him but merely delegate their authority to a person who isn't sovereign but simply a minister and hence bound by the laws of the commonwealth.

Buchanan's theory has radical, perhaps even anarchic, implications. Skinner notes that 'As Suarez was shortly to point out in *The Law and God the Lawgiver*, an appallingly anarchic view of political obligation seems to be implied if one concedes that "the power of a whole community of individuals assembled together must be derived from men as individuals" for this suggests that the reason for setting up a commonwealth must be to protect individual rights rather than the common good, thus leaving open the alarming possibility that the whole body of the people, and even individual citizens, may be said to have the authority to resist and kill a legitimate ruler in defence of their rights.' [Skinner 1978, 343] For Suarez, this conclusion was a *reductio ad absurdum*. Not so for Buchanan. For him, 'one of the reasons for insisting on a stoic rather than an Aristotelian account of man's pre-political condition may well have been the fact that it helped him to legitimate a highly individualist and even anarchic view of the right of political resistance.' [Skinner 1978, 343]

After the 1570s, Protestant political theory crosses a watershed. Up to this point, political resistance was to be justified solely on religious grounds; after this date, however, this exclusively religious justification is abandoned. 'The result,' according to Quentin Skinner, 'is a fully political theory of revolution, founded on a recognizably modern, secularized thesis about the natural rights and original sovereignty of the people.' [Skinner 1978, 338] Some elements of pre-1570s thinking remain (there is still a lingering tendency to make the locus of legitimate resistance some intermediate body or other—ephors, Estates-general or lesser magistrates—rather than individuals) but this tendency too will diminish in time.

A Catholic Aside: Juan de Mariana and Étienne de la Boétie

The first book of Juan de Mariana's tome on *The King and the Education of the King* is the source of his controversial reputation as an apologist for tyrannicide. Given this reputation, it's not a little ironic that this work was dedicated to Philip III. In his philosophical anthropology, Mariana echoes certain aspects of Buchanan's thought and anticipates aspects of the thought of Johannes Althusius. Mariana believed early men to be solitary wanderers without any settled abode. Self-preservation and procreation are their primary interests and such lives as they live, they live apart from laws and from any source of authority. They live as animals, being, in fact, very little more than animals. What drives men out of this original brutish condition is its inconvenience, exacerbated by the depredations of other men and wild animals. But if the advantages of civilisation are absent in this natural condition, so too are its disadvantages. In man's original condition, there is no lying, cheating, stealing, ambition or avarice—and, significantly, there is no private property. Still, man's needs outstrip the bounties of nature and his position vis-à-vis other animals is precarious, lacking, as he does, the natural advantages of many of these animals. These disadvantages act as a stimulus to human cooperation under the leadership of those best able to promote men's welfare. Men are driven into society by fear, desire and need, forced to co-operate for self-protection. According to John Allen, Mariana was 'more dispassionate than the author of the *Vindiciae*, more subtle than Buchanan and had more imagination than either....Perhaps the most original thing in his book is the dim vision of man emerging from the semi-brute of the State of Nature into a consciousness of himself and of right and so into full humanity.' [Allen 1928, 365]

Despite the similarities between the thought of Mariana, and that of Buchanan and the anonymous author of the *Vindiciae*, Mariana's account of the political order is in no way theocratic. 'It is perhaps significant,' writes Allen, 'that for him the inner light by which we know right from wrong was *vox naturae* rather than *vox Dei*....political authority needs no further justification when it corresponds to general needs and is directed by the will of the community. In thinking thus he resembled Buchanan, but was far from the thought of the *Vindiciae* and yet further from that of the [Catholic] League.' [Allen 1928, 366] Monarchy is the earliest and most obvious form of political rule but its manifest imperfections quickly give rise to the necessity for law. Such laws are, in the beginning, simple but become more complex as society develops. Since the people are the ones to give themselves a king to serve their purposes, they are also entitled to remove him, since what they give they can take away. The prince or king isn't the owner of his realm, not *dominus*, but rather a guide, a *rector*. 'His status can never be higher than that of an elected official who is paid a salary by the citizens in order to look after their interests.' [Skinner 1978, 347]

Like his Protestant contemporaries, Mariana is of the view that the popular will is expressed in representative bodies such as the Estates of the Realm. The Estates are the formulators of the fundamental law within which the monarch and all others must operate. Moreover, the Estates controlled matters of taxation, succession to the throne and the religious establishment. The monarch, then, according to Mariana, is very far from being *legibus solutus* (not bound by the laws). The people as a whole are sovereign. The rights of the ruler have their roots in a grant of authority by the people but such rights do not include taxation and legislation. The people as a whole are above the monarch. Rothbard writes, 'In contrast to other scholastics, who placed the 'ownership" of power in the king, he [Mariana] stressed that the people have a right to reclaim their political power whenever the king should abuse it.' [Rothbard 1995a, 117]

Mariana is notorious for his justification of tyrannicide, a tyrant for Mariana being any ruler who violates the laws of religion or, and this is significant for libertarians, who imposes taxes without the consent of the people. One of the powers reserved by the people when they appoint a king is the power to regulate taxes. Because the monarch is given the authority he has for a purpose, the promotion of the welfare of the people, a monarch whose actions run directly contrary to this purpose may be reprimanded. First comes a warning from the assembly, which, if not heeded, justifies sterner action. 'When, however, the people through its assembly has spoken,' writes Dunning, 'then, and not till then, may the private individual justly slay the tyrant. If, however, as is likely to be the case, the assembly is not permitted to meet or to act, the private citizen is justified in killing the tyrant at discretion.' [Dunning 1905, 71] Mariana is aware of the practical dangers of such a doctrine but, on the other hand, he thinks that if monarchs are aware that tyranny on their part will warrant assassination, this will give them furiously to think! The removal of a tyrant normally requires the assent of an assembly but where this assent isn't forthcoming, then anyone may act to remove the tyrant. There is, then, an ultimate right of tyrannicide that can be exercised by anyone.[62]

We have seen that Luther and Calvin were inclined to confine the right to resist to those already invested with some form of inferior authority although later Lutherans and Calvinists tended to be less circumspect. In contrast, as John Plamenatz points out, 'the Jesuits, who had not to suit their doctrine to the conditions of any particular country, always insisted on the popular origins of temporal power, and never confined the right of resistance to inferior magistrates.' [Plamenatz, 61] Around this time, the idea of contract as the basis of political order came into prominence, deriving from reflections on Scripture and, perhaps most significantly, from Roman law. Since all men by nature are equal, if one is to have authority over another, this must be the result of agreement. Significantly, during this period, in both Catholic and in Protestant circles, there's a secularisation of the source of political authority. 'The construction put by Luther and Calvin on the teachings of Scripture in this respect is dropped, and submission to any particular ruler as the representative of God's will ceases to be the presumptive duty of a Christian.' [Dunning 1905, 78]

The *Mémoires de l'Estat de France sous Charles IX* is a miscellany of various writings published in 1576. Lovers of liberty will be especially interested to note that Étienne de la Boétie's *Discours de la servitude Volontaire ou le Contr'un*, though perhaps written earlier than 1550 when Boétie was still a teenager, appeared in print for the first time in this collection of writings.[63] Although Boétie wasn't a Huguenot, his *Discours* gave a measure of support to the idea expressed in some Huguenot tracts that forcible resistance to tyranny could be justified by appeal to natural law and natural rights. Boétie was perhaps the first thinker[64] to explore systematically what may well be one of the most fundamental mysteries of politics—how is it that the few, or the one, succeed in dominating the many? For Boétie, human beings are naturally free and equal: 'we are all naturally free, inasmuch as we are all comrades. Accordingly it should not enter the mind of anyone that nature has placed some of us in slavery, since she has actually created us all in one likeness....Since freedom is our natural state, we are not only in possession of it but have the urge to defend it. [de la Boétie, 51-52] Being thus free and equal, if one man dominates another, that domination stands in need of explanation and justification. Perhaps that man is stronger than his victim. That may well be so one on one, but it can scarcely explain how, as in the case of political rule, one man or a small group of men succeeds in dominating thousands or millions. 'For the present,' he writes, 'I should [desire] to understand how it happens that so many men, so many villages, so many cities, so many nations, sometimes suffer under a single tyrant who has no other power than the power they give him; who is able to harm them only to the extent to which they have the willingness to bear with him; who could do them absolutely no injury unless they preferred to put up with him rather than contradict him. Surely a striking situation!' [de la Boétie, 42] In words that are eerily reminiscent of *1 Samuel* 8: 11-18, too reminiscent perhaps to be entirely coincidental,[65] Boétie details the depredations typically inflicted on subjects by their ruler: 'You sow your crops in order that he may ravage them, you install and furnish your homes to give him goods to pillage; you rear your daughters that he may gratify his lust; you bring up your children in order that he may confer upon them the greatest privilege he knows—to be led into his battles, to be delivered to butchery, to be made the servants of his greed and the instruments of his vengeance; you yield your bodies unto hard labor in order that he may indulge in his delights and wallow in his filthy pleasures; you weaken yourselves in order to make him the stronger and the mightier to hold you in check. From all these indignities, such as the very beasts of the field would not endure, you can deliver yourselves if you try, not by taking action, but merely by willing to be free. Resolve to serve no more, and you are at once freed.' [de la Boétie, 48]

The mystery of political domination becomes even more enigmatic when the people are dominated not by some alien conqueror but by one of their own, one who owes his power precisely to the obedience of those whom he dominates. 'All this havoc, this misfortune, this ruin,' writes Boétie, 'descends upon you not from alien foes, but from the one enemy whom you yourselves render as powerful as he is, for whom you go bravely to war, for whose greatness you do not refuse to offer your own bodies unto death.' [de la Boétie, 48] This enemy is only one man or, at most, a few, staggeringly outnumbered by the subject population. 'He who thus domineers over you has only two eyes, only two hands, only one body, no more than is possessed by the least man among the infinite numbers dwelling in your cities; he has indeed nothing more than the power that you confer upon him to destroy you. Where has he acquired enough eyes to spy upon you, if you do not provide them yourselves? How can he have so many arms to beat you with, if he does not borrow them from you? The feet that trample down your cities, where does he get them if they are not your own? How does he have any power over you except through you? How would he dare assail you if he had no cooperation from you? What could he do to you if you yourselves did not connive with the thief who plunders you, if you were not accomplices of the murderer who kills you, if you were not traitors to yourselves?[66]

Boétie believes, correctly, that it is *not* by primarily by force that the many overbear the few. 'Whoever thinks that halberds, sentries, the placing of the watch, serve to protect and shield tyrants is, in my judgment, completely mistaken. These are used, it seems to me, more for ceremony and a show of force than for any reliance placed in them....It is not the troops on horseback, it is not the companies afoot, it is not arms that defend the tyrant.' [de la Boétie, 71] The real political structure isn't a direct relationship between the one and the many, but rather a human cascade, with the ruler being supported by a small number of supporters or collaborators (sometimes rivals), they, in turn controlling a rather larger number of supporters or clients, and so on downwards. Boétie remarks that 'there are only four or five who maintain the dictator, four or five who keep the country in bondage to him. Five or six have always had access to his ear, and have either gone to him of their own accord, or else have been summoned by him, to be accomplices in his cruelties, companions in his pleasures, panders to his lusts, and sharers in his plunders. These six manage their chief so successfully that he comes to be held accountable not only for his own misdeeds but even for theirs. The six have six hundred who profit under them, and with the six hundred they do what they have accomplished with their tyrant. The six hundred maintain under them six thousand, whom they promote in rank, upon whom they confer the government of provinces or the direction of finances, in order that they may serve as instruments of avarice and cruelty, executing orders at the proper time and working such havoc all around that they could not last except under the shadow of the six hundred, nor be exempt from law and punishment except through their influence.' [de la Boétie, 71-72]

If it is not by superior force that rulers keep their subjects in submission; what is the source of the ruler's power? In an anticipation of a theme that would later emerge in the writings of David Hume, Boétie believes rather that political rule is grounded in the voluntary subjugation of the many, based upon a habit of obedience deriving from prescription, custom and habit, the whole psycho-social edifice propped up by an array of ideological supports. '[T]he essential reason why men take orders willingly,' Boétie writes, 'is that they are born serfs and are reared as such. From this cause there follows another result, namely that people easily become cowardly and submissive under tyrants.' [de la Boétie, 62] Astonishing as it may seem, the mass of men actually consent to their own servitude, and Murray Rothbard notes that 'this consent is engineered, largely by propaganda beamed at the populace by the rulers and their intellectual apologists. The devices—of bread and circuses, of ideological mystification—that rulers today use to gull the masses and gain their consent, remain the same as in La Boétie's days. The only difference is the enormous increase in the use of specialized intellectuals in the service of the rulers. But in this case, the primary task of opponents of modern tyranny is an educational one: to awaken the public to this process, to demystify and desanctify the State apparatus.' [Rothbard 1975, 35] If customary obedience is the ground of political rule, then disobedience is the means by which political rule can be undermined; 'if tyranny really rests on mass consent, then the obvious means for its overthrow is simply by mass withdrawal of that consent.[67] The weight of tyranny would quickly and suddenly collapse under such a non-violent revolution.' [Rothbard 1975, 16-17] Once again, and not surprisingly, Boétie anticipates a theme that will find anglophone expression in the writings of David Hume.

RETURNING TO THE HUGUENOTS

The other most significant works contained in the *Mémoires de l'Estat* were *Du Droit des Magistrats sur les sujets* and the *Dialogue d'Archon et de Politie*. John Allen believes the *Mémoires de l'Estat* to be a much more significant work in Huguenot political theory than the more well known, indeed notorious, *Vindiciae* which appeared three years later. He writes, 'The writings included in the *Mémoires* of 1576 almost completely anticipate the *Vindiciae* of 1579. To isolate the latter is a mistake and gives a wrong impression. It should be considered along with the writings that it at once expanded and reduced to order. Its superior importance is hardly at all due to any originality, but primarily to the fact that it states the case of the earlier writers more completely and systematically than was done by any one of them.' [Allen 1928, 314]

The author of the *Du Droit* (perhaps Theodore de Beza) and the author of the *Dialogue d'Archon*, and indeed the author of the *Vindiciae*, all accept the traditional tenet that obedience to political authority is required, even when, as is the case with the author of the *Dialogue d'Archon*, attempts are made to explain, or explain away, Scriptural texts that can be used to condemn rebellion in whatever circumstances. Still, only God's sovereignty is and can be absolute. All earthly sovereignty is limited and conditional and all rulers are subject to Divine and to natural law. Any particular political constitution is created and sustained by the will of the people, so much so that even in hereditary monarchies, the king may be deemed to be elected. But the king is not only an agent of the people, holding his authority from them, he also, in some way, has his authority from God. In the end, it's hard to disagree with Koos Malan when he comments that Huguenot political theory was 'an eclectic concoction of mostly unconvincing claims to popular sovereignty, on the basis of the antique constitution of the Middle Ages.' [Malan, 61]

The *Mémoires de l'Estat* might be said to encompass not so much a purely political as a politico-theological conception of authority in which a number of not very clearly distinguished notions of covenant, compact and contract between people, ruler and God intermingle. As far as determining who the 'people' were in their deliberations, these various authors were committed not to some radically democratic conception, tending, rather, to think of the people as being represented by existing institutions, whether nobles, Estates, or local magistrates. The right to resist one's ruler was vested not in the people as a whole but in some or other of these representatives. This idea is neither Catholic, nor Protestant, nor modern; it is medieval. If these representatives fail to act to resist tyranny then the people *en masse* have no recourse. 'So expressly is it the duty of the magistrates to resist a tyrant, says the *Vindiciae*, that they have no possible excuse for not doing so. But if the magistrates, nevertheless, fail in their duty, the community has no remedy against them. It may not rise and depose its magistrates.' [Allen 1928, 325] This position is, as we have seen, rejected both by the more radical views of the Protestant Buchanan and the Catholic de Mariana who allowed for individual resistance in cases of necessity.

John Allen writes that the authors of the *Mémoires de l'Estat* believed that there could be no merely human obligation. 'Hence, though the people could set up a government and endow it with force, they could not give it real authority. They could not create an obligation to obey it, for all obligation is to God.' So, even though a ruler receives his office and power from the people, 'the obligation to obey the command of the Prince…is derived not from the people but from God.' [Allen 1928, 318] In time, however, the theological element of these reflections diminished or disappeared and the contractual dimension increased in clarity and in importance. 'The use of such terms as pactum and foedus seemed to imply that political sovereignty was established by a deliberate act of will and with a consciousness of the ends to be realized through it. This, whether he exactly meant it or not, is, practically, what the author of the *Vindiciae* contributed to the theory by his use of the word pactum. And this, it would seem, is the essence of what is loosely called the "contract theory".' [Allen 1928, 329]

A significant strand of thought in the *Vindiciae*, perhaps not very clearly expressed but none the less there, was a defence of the rights of natural communities. This was later to be developed in some detail by the neglected German Calvinist writer, Johannes Althusius. But before Althusius we come to the work of one of the most prolix and disorganised but yet most influential writers on political matters, one who introduced to political thought and practice a notion that subsequent writers and practitioners of politics would take for granted and upon which the idea of the modern state crucially depends—the notion of sovereignty.

Notes

1 Eire, ix, x. In his magisterial account of traditional religion in England in the fifteenth and sixteenth centuries, Eamon Duffy, Professor of the History of Christianity at Cambridge, writes 'the Reformation as actually experienced by ordinary people was not an uncomplicated imaginative liberation, the restoration of true Christianity after a period of degeneration and corruption, but, for good or ill, a great cultural hiatus, which had dug a ditch, deep and dividing, between the English people and their past.' [Duffy, xiv]

2 See Voegelin III, 168-175; 184-192, and Greenaway, 125-133. See Conti passim.

3 Duffy judges that 'the impact of Lollardy on fifteenth- and early sixteenth-century religious awareness has been grossly exaggerated.' [Duffy, xxi]

4 Wycliffe's name also appears as Wyclif, Wycliff, Wiclef, Wicliffe, Wickliffe. I shall use the form Wycliffe but I shall keep the alternative spellings of his name when they are used by others. [see Davies 1999, 386]

5 'Wyclif's elaborate treatment of lordship, divine and civil, is largely inspired by the treatise *On the Poverty of the Savior* by Richard FitzRalph, Bishop of Armagh, a contribution to the controversies over Franciscan poverty in which Marsilius of Padua and William of Ockham had also taken part.' [McGrade et al., 587]

6 For a magisterial treatment of this and related issues, see Brown 2012 and Brown 2015.

7 'In Pope John XXII (1316-34) [the Spiritual Franciscans] had an enemy who was determined to stamp them out. His most important statement was the Bull *Cum Inter Nonnullos* of 1323 which authoritatively destroyed the whole basis of the strict interpretation of the Franciscan Rule by declaring that it was heretical to deny Christ the right of property.' [Holmes 1975, 157; see 157-167]

8 See Mäkinen, 141-190; see also Tierney 2014, 95-121 and Coleman 1988, 631-643.

9 Mirgeler, 122, 123. Some readers may be familiar with some (fictionalised) elements of this dispute from their reading of Umberto Eco's novel, *The Name of the Rose*.

10 Wyclif, 591. In true Scholastic style, Wycliffe presents nine dialectically elaborated arguments to support his claim. See Wyclif, 592-628.

11 The Donatists (4th century North African Christian sect) held that the effectiveness of sacraments depended on the moral character of the minister of the sacrament.

12 Arthur McGrade et al. believe that the implications of Wycliffe's thesis are unclear but conclude that 'it seems most likely that Wyclif thought sinners should be deprived of civil lordship' given that he argues that 'the civil judge should award civil lordship to Peter against Paul if he knows that Peter is in grace and Paul in mortal sin...' [McGrade et al, 590]

13 'The work of Wycliffe is marked by a spiritual sensitivity to the problems of the time, on the one hand, and, on the other hand, an intellectualism that elevates the spiritual authority of the individual in a "state of grace" over the papal magisterium, simultaneously rendering the authority carried by the sacred tradition redundant.' [Greenaway, 126]

14 Alessandro Conti writes, 'Wyclif defines dominion as the right to exercise authority and, indirectly, to hold property. According to him, there are three kinds of possession: natural, civil, and evangelical. Natural possession is the simple possession of goods without any legal title. Civil possession is the possession of goods on the basis of some civil law. Evangelical possession requires, beyond civil possession, a state of grace in the legal owner. Thus God alone can confer evangelical possession....On the other hand, a man in a state of grace is lord of the visible universe, but on the condition that he shares his lordship with all the other men who are in a state of grace, as all men in a state of grace have the same rights. This ultimately means that all the goods of God should be in common, just as they were before the Fall. Private property was introduced as a result of sin.' [Conti, 38]

15 Holmes 1975, 195; see 195-213.

16 Davies 1999, 386; see Zagorin, 83.

17 'Luther and Zwingli's generation was the first to fully benefit from the invention of the printing press....By the time Luther and Zwingli's generation began their university studies, the printing revolution was already well under way....By 1517, when Luther and Zwingli were poised to challenge the status quo, a network was already well set in place for the rapid production and distribution of their writings.' [Eire, 9, 10-11]

18 Not only a theological revolution but, as it was to turn out, a *political* revolution. Koos Malan writes, 'From a political perspective, the Protestant Reformation should rather be characterised as a revolution. The medieval universalism of the ecclesiastic-imperial unity—in Luther's time already an eroded concept—was abrogated with the Protestant revolution....Through the Lutheran revolution the church became a mere association within the state. It no longer existed as an independent entity alongside the state.' [Malan, 51]

19 *On Secular Authority*, in Höpfl, 9; 13.

20 *On Secular Authority*, in Höpfl, 10.

21 *On Secular Authority*, in Höpfl, 27.

22 *On Secular Authority*, in Höpfl, 30; see 32.

23 *On Secular Authority*, in Höpfl, 11.

24 *On Secular Authority*, in Höpfl, 11.

25 *On Secular Authority*, in Höpfl, 18.

26 *On Secular Authority*, in Höpfl, 19-20.

27 *On Secular Authority*, in Höpfl, 29.

28 *On Secular Authority*, in Höpfl, 25.

29 *On Secular Authority*, in Höpfl, 26.

30 It should be noted that the direction of causality can run from political to religious change as much as from religious change to political change so that secular state concerns were, in some circumstances at least, in whole or in part productive of religious change. 'The English Reformation,' writes Zagorin, 'did not originate as a widespread popular movement of discontent with Catholicism. It began as the work of the state and monarchy, which initiated, imposed, and enforced it.' He notes that while the English government 'executed about 189 Catholics as traitors,' in fact 'most of them were in reality religious victims who died for their faith.' [Zagorin, 188, 189]

31 Thomas Sowell notes that, as a matter of fact, the Reformation did indeed conduce to freedom, but 'not by intention but systemically from the new diversity of power sources. The Protestant Reformation was as intolerant and bloody as any Catholic Inquisition. Freedom "was the consequence rather than the design of the Reformation."' [Sowell 1996, 350]

32 Luther, *On Good Works*, *Werke*, VI, 250.

33 Hubmaier, notably, in a tract of 1524, rejected the burning of heretics as the appropriate response to heresy, going so far as to suggest that the instinct to punish heretics in this way emanated from the suggestion of the devil! [see Zagorin, 83-84]

34 Sattler, *Schleitheim Confession*, 74 in Suck.

35 See *On Civil Government*, in Höpfl, 47.

36 See *On Civil Government*, in Höpfl, 48.

37 *On Civil Government*, in Höpfl, 49.

38 *On Civil Government*, in Höpfl, 50-51.

39 Whereas the Calvinist theological doctrines of election and foreordination would seem to lead inexorably to a passive resignation to the status quo, in fact the opposite happened! The practical consequence of these doctrines was militancy in the enforcement of orthodoxy in faith and worship and the rigid enforcement of orthodoxy in matters of morals. In a curious and ironical way, the outcome of Calvinism was to give effect, in a Protestant context, to a Hildebrandean conception of the superiority of the spiritual over the secular.

40 *On Civil Government*, in Höpfl, 52; 74.

41 In this chapter in the *Institutes*, *Romans* 13 is cited by Calvin eight times, at §§4, 7, 10, 13, 17, 19, 20 & 22; see also *On Civil Government*, in Höpfl 52, 55, 61, 65, 70, 72 and 74.

42 *On Civil Government*, in Höpfl, 55.

43 See *On Civil Government*, in Höpfl, 62-64; 72-73.

44 Sparta was governed by a pair of kings, a senate, called the gerousia, consisting of twenty eight members, and five ephors, who exercised administrative, financial and judicial powers. The kings were hereditary; the gerousia and ephors were elected. Each element in the Spartan government had different responsibilities—the kings for military affairs and security, the gerousia for law, the ephors for administrative and financial oversight. It is worth noting that the remit of the ephors extended over kings and gerousia.

45 The Latin text has the word 'popular' whereas the French text omits it.

46 *On Civil Government*, in Höpfl, 82-3; see Skinner 1978, 230-34, 324.

47 Höpfl, xxiii; *On Civil Government*, in Höpfl, 83.

48 Plamenatz, 59.For an historically-based treatment of this subject, see Kingdon, passim.

49 *On Civil Government*, in Höpfl, 77; 80.

50 See *On Civil Government*, in Höpfl, 75.

51 Sabine, 367; but see Plamenatz, 59.

52 *On Civil Government*, in Höpfl, 83-84.

53 *On Civil Government*, in Höpfl, 84, n. 110; see Skinner 1978, 219-220.

54 Carl Watner writes, 'the idea of consent played a prominent part in Ponet's thinking. His view of natural law led to a restriction on the power of kings and governors, who derived their authority from the people....The institution of government and its magisterial offices are in the nature of a trust, which ultimately rests upon the consent of the governed.' [Watner 1986, 113-114]

55 See Allen 1928, 319, n. 2.

56 *Vindiciae*, question 32, section 'Why Kings are Created.'

57 Sabine, 383; see Wood 2012, passim.

58 For an accessible collection of relevant texts in this area, see Franklin 1969.

59 This belief, which Oakley calls the 'myth of primordial Germanic "populism" was used not only by Hotman but 'it was in the Leveller literature…that it first rose to real prominence.' [Oakley 2012, 143]

60 Despite his support for a form of popular sovereignty, Beza wholeheartedly upheld the magistrate's right and duty to extirpate heresy and to punish heretics in order to protect the church and preserve civil society from disturbances. [see Zagorin, 122ff.]

61 See Zuck, 160-163; and Buchanan 1579, 73-75.

62 If Mariana's doctrine on tyrannicide is startling, in Book III of *The King* we can find doctrines that are distinctly Machiavellian! A good moral character is essential for judges and churchmen according to Mariana, but not for soldiers or minor administrators. Mariana cannot countenance lying by anyone, including the monarch, but, none the less, dissimulation is not only permitted on occasion but may even be required.

63 Some believe the *Discours* to have been written somewhat later, in 1552 or 1553.

64 If Boétie wasn't the first to raise this problem, then he was the first to raise it clearly, consistently and thematically.

65 The likelihood of a connection between this passage and the famous passage in *Samuel* is supported by Boétie's remark that the Israelites were the only people who, without compulsion or need, sought the appointment of a tyrant. Let us imagine, he says, 'some newborn individuals, neither acquainted with slavery nor desirous of liberty, ignorant indeed of the very words. If they were permitted to choose between being slaves and free men, to which would they give their vote? There can be no doubt that they would much prefer to be guided by reason itself than to be ordered about by the whims of a single man. The only possible exception might be the Israelites who, without any compulsion or need, appointed a tyrant.' [54]

66 de la Boétie, 48. Rothbard notes that 'Boétie's insight that any State, no matter how ruthless and

despotic, rests in the long run on the consent of the majority of the public, has not yet been absorbed into the consciousness of intellectuals opposed to State despotism....only the freemarket economist Ludwig von Mises has sufficiently stressed the fact that all governments must rest on majority consent. [Rothbard, 34-35]

67 'La Boétie was also the first theorist to move from the emphasis on the importance of consent, to the strategic importance of toppling tyranny by leading the public to withdraw that consent. Hence, La Boétie was the first theorist of the strategy of mass, non-violent civil disobedience of State edicts and exactions. How practical such a tactic might be is difficult to say, especially since it has rarely been used.' [Rothbard 1975, 37-38]

Chapter 15

JEAN BODIN—APOSTLE OF SOVEREIGNTY

The most usual way to prevent seditions is to take away the subjects' arms
—Jean Bodin

I believe there are more instances of the abridgment of the freedom of
the people by gradual and silent encroachments of those in power
than by violent and sudden usurpations
—James Madison

After a brief and abortive stab at a life in religion, Jean Bodin (1529/30-1596) began his adult life as a student of law. Despite spending some years teaching at the University of Toulouse, he was unable to find a permanent academic niche for himself as a university professor so, in the 1570s, he changed career and became a government official at the French Court. He published his *Six livres de la République* in 1576, a book that Murray Rothbard described as 'perhaps the most massive work on political philosophy ever written' and 'certainly the most influential book on political philosophy in the sixteenth century.' [Rothbard 1995a, 204] That same year, Bodin's life as a courtier came to an abrupt end when he opposed some tax measures of Henry III. The remainder of his life was devoted mainly to scholarship, apart from some years in the late 1580s and early 1590s when he was once again thrust into the spotlight of royal politics.

Bodin is a bridge figure between the Middle Ages and the Early Modern period. Many elements of medieval thought are present in his work, not least, the idea of quasi-constitutional laws outside the scope of the will of any given legislator, the so-called *leges imperii*, and a belief in both divine and natural law, which laws operate as a constraint on all men, including kings and princes. Bodin was also sufficiently formed by his early scholastic training to make Aristotle's *Politics* the model for his *République*, with recognisably Aristotelian themes, such as the nature of the state, its forms, its purpose and its roots in the family, structuring Bodin's major work.[1]

But Aristotle isn't Bodin's only model. He was well acquainted with Machiavelli's works and, although he couldn't share Machiavelli's disregard for moral principles in politics, his historical predilections inclined him to give the practical purposes of the state a central place in his analysis. The state is the means to the good life for its citizens but not directly. It merely provides the conditions in and by which the state's subjects can live good and pious lives. And whereas Machiavelli had no use for religion except as a propaganda tool for the inculcation of obedience in the state's subjects, Bodin was a genuine believer in Divine law. Just what Bodin's religious views were was (and is) a matter of controversy. He was suspected of being a Calvinist, even a Judaiser. That controversy was aided and abetted by his intellectually and religiously ecumenical *Colloquium of the Seven about Secrets of the Sublime*, a work not published in his lifetime, in which the interlocutors are Catholic, Protestant, Jew, Muslim and Sceptic. The current scholarly view appears to be that Bodin was and remained a Catholic, although a critical one.[2]

Bodin and Machiavelli were both practising civil servants with a practical knowledge of government, and both made extensive use of the historical method, although in different ways. [see Plamenatz, 89-90] Among Bodin's possible influences, not only Machiavelli but also the fourteenth century Islamic philosopher Ibn Khaldûn[3] stood apart from their predecessors and contemporaries in regarding the state from an almost purely secular perspective. 'Bodin's theory of the origins of government,' writes Elman Service, 'was essentially like that of Ibn Khaldûn, that the state rises out of conflict. Also, like Ibn Khaldûn and Machiavelli, Bodin differed from the ecclesiastical dogmas of God-given stasis by recognizing that stability is practically unattainable and that good government must be able to cope with change.' [Service, 23]

It is a commonplace among commentators to note that Thomas Hobbes's political theory in the *Leviathan* was in part an existential response to the confused and fraught religious and political realities of his time resulting from the constitutional (and later armed) struggle between Parliament and King. What isn't so often noted is that some seventy-five years before Hobbes produced his *Leviathan*, Jean Bodin's *République* was a product of very similar existential conditions in sixteenth century religiously conflicted France. Marian Tooley notes, 'Civil war inspired [Bodin] with a horror of rebellion and the anarchy that comes in its train, and convinced him that the *politiques* were right, and that the only remedy was the recognition of the absolute authority of the state "to which, after immortal God, we owe all things".' [Tooley, xii] The *Politiques* were a party in sixteenth century France who, in the context of the religious and political disturbances of that time, took the view that the primary function of the state was the establishment and maintenance of order and not the establishment of the true religion. The most notable member of the *Politiques* was Michel de l'Hôpital, sometime Chancellor of France. Bodin may have shared with the *Politiques* their view that state authority had to be absolute and sovereign but, beyond that, there's little or no evidence that he shared any other of their views. [see Turchetti, 26] Koos Malan remarks, 'With the *Politiques*, religion became a private and individual, or personal matter. Religion lost its public appeal as a political category, because it had to yield to the new value of preference—the unity and stability of the state, which became the foremost interest and highest virtue.' [Malan, 71]

Although Bodin and Hobbes started from much the same political conditions and arrived at much the same conclusions, 'the differences between the two men in method and in general philosophic feeling are as marked as the similarity of some of their conclusions.'[4] Bodin adopted a scholarly approach, a mixture of scholasticism and history, taking Aristotle and Machiavelli as his intellectual mentors and lacing his work with citations, illustrations and digressions; Hobbes, by contrast, a devotee of the new scientific method, applied the method of geometry to political philosophy (as Spinoza was later to apply it to ethics) and one can search the *Leviathan* in vain for historical references or illustrations.

It is generally agreed that Bodin's work is notable for its prolixity and occasional lack of clarity. George Sabine, for example, remarks that Bodin's books are 'unorganized and ill-arranged, repetitious and disconnected, though in parts he was capable of being clear and cogent,' and John Plamenatz remarks that 'it was more than [Bodin] could do to put his ideas into good order,' adding that his writing style is 'tortuous, obscure, repetitious and disorderly.'[5] If Sabine's and Plamenatz's judgements are correct and Bodin's writing was as they describe it, why does he have an honoured place in the history of political thought? First of all, though it can't be denied that Bodin's thought is far from being perfectly consistent, we might charitably judge that such inconsistency as there is results primarily from Bodin's being an intellectual trailblazer, creating the very paths that others would follow. If this is so, it's hardly surprising that on some occasions his intellectual trains of thought should crisscross in a less than perspicuous manner. But whether confused, disorganised and repetitious or not, Bodin is famous for one thing above all and that is his conception of sovereignty, an idea that political theorists and indeed the general educated public now take for granted but which wasn't always either clearly understood or appreciated. The introduction of a single concept to political philosophy might seem to be a very slender basis upon which to build an entire scholarly reputation but, as Julian Franklin notes, 'Bodin's account of sovereignty was a major event in the development of European political thought.' [Franklin 1992, xii] His sharp and clear account of sovereignty was a distillation of elements which had been, as it were, 'in the air' during much of the sixteenth century and for some time before that but which had not, before Bodin put pen to paper, ever been so clearly expressed. The medieval period had been dominated by interminable and unresolvable discussions on the proper relationship between the *sacerdotium*, the spiritual powers, and the *regnum*, the temporal powers. The concept of the state with which we are now all too familiar and which depends crucially on the idea of sovereignty was, at best, embryonic in the thought of Bodin's predecessors; certainly, it was nowhere fully articulated. 'With the possible exception of the author of the *Defensor Pacis*,' Tooley writes, 'no one in the Middle Ages asked, "What is a state and how is it constructed?", but only "Who are the rulers and what are their powers?"' [Tooley, xiv] Bodin changed all this, not only for himself and his contemporaries but for all subsequent political thinkers.

The state that we have come to know if not necessarily to love was a new type of political entity that began to exist embryonically in the fifteenth century and reached maturity two centuries later. The Treaty of Westphalia (1648), which marked the end of the Thirty Years' War, can be taken as the end point of Christendom and the starting point of Europe, now conceived of as a conglomeration of sovereign autonomous states. The state that emerged at this time was 'an impersonal, abstract and permanent constitutional entity that exercised control over a consolidated territory.' [Malan, 6] Older terms that had been used to describe the variety of political orders that existed prior to 1648—*civitas*, commonwealth, and the like—gradually fell into disuse and by the time Hobbes came to write, the term 'state', and the political reality it described—impersonal, autonomous and sovereign—were both firmly established. [see Malan, 7]

SOVEREIGNTY

Sovereignty, Bodin defines as 'the absolute and perpetual power of a commonwealth, which the Latins call *maiestas*; the Greeks *akra exousia*, *kurion arche*, and *kurion politeuma*; and the Italian *segnioria*, a word they use for private persons as well as for those who have full control of the state, while the Hebrews call it *tomech shévet*—that is, the highest power of command.'[6] The use of the word 'absolute' in the account just given may give the not unreasonable impression that Bodin was a supporter of political absolutism as this came to be understood in the political debates of the seventeenth century. This is not so. Bodin's 'absolute' is a somewhat more nuanced notion than that which it is sometimes taken to be. The sovereign who is absolute is *ab-solutus*, that is, set free or made separate or unbound, unbound by positive or municipal law but not unbound by divine or natural law. In addition to this, Bodin envisaged the sovereign as operating in the contexts of traditional restraints of various kinds. 'Bodin ...stood for centralized state authority against feudalist pluralism and decentralization of political authority,' writes Heinrich Rommen, 'but he never doubted that all such authority is subject to and limited by natural and divine law. Therefore the modern concept of absolute sovereignty could appear on the scene only after positivism...had freed sovereignty from the limitations which Christian tradition and the ideas of natural and divine law had placed upon it.' [Rommen, 128] As well as being absolute and perpetual, sovereignty, for Bodin, was indivisible, and necessarily so. By such indivisibility he meant not just that every system of law must embody some principle of ultimate determination but that if political incoherence was to be avoided, the ultimate powers of government must all reside in one entity, whether that entity was to be one human individual or one group. Such a claim wasn't obviously descriptively true even of the quasi-absolutist regimes of his own time, let alone of all the rapidly emerging European monarchies. Still, it might be argued, his thesis is prescriptive rather than descriptive so that its failure to match up the political realities of his day is no great fault.

This account of sovereignty wasn't always held by Bodin in precisely this way but had developed over time. During his time as an erstwhile professor of law at the University of Toulouse, Bodin had encountered the idea, known as *merum imperium*, that certain officers of state exercised the power of their offices by, as it were, the right of the office itself, and not merely as a power delegated to them by the king. In the context of emergent absolutism, some thinkers attacked this notion but Bodin did not entirely concur with this attack, holding that such officers held some undelegated powers but not any powers that could place them in competition with the king. Franklin writes, 'Bodin divided the *merum imperium* into a (minor) part that could be held by magistrates, and a (major) part held only by the prince.' [Franklin 1992, xiv] This distinction, of course, immediately gives rise to the question of which prerogatives belong to which part and it was by attempting to answer this question that Bodin eventually found his way to the doctrine with which he has come to be so closely associated. For methodological reasons that need not detain us here, Bodin engaged in the mid 1550s in an historical and comparative study of different polities with a view to determining a set of the essential elements of sovereignty. By the time he came to write the *Six livres de la République*, these elements included the authority to appoint magistrates and assign them their duties; to make and unmake laws; to initiate and terminate wars; to be the court of last appeal; to make determinations of life and death in situations not envisaged by the law as it stands; the right to receive homage, to tax, and to determine coinage.[7] Bodin's list of elements is a distillation of the writings of various jurists but, significantly, he comments that 'No matter how much power they [rulers] have, if they are bound to the laws, jurisdiction, and command of someone else, they are not sovereign.' [Bodin 1992, 49, §482]

As I mentioned already, Bodin held that sovereignty, to be sovereignty, had to be indivisible. It is true that sovereignty, as Bodin defines it, can only be unitary but it does not follow from this, he thinks, that its unity needs to be embodied in just one person or just one corporate body. For him, there is no logical impediment in having a unitary sovereignty embodied in any arrangement, the parts of which are divisible from each other. It isn't immediately clear how a unitary sovereignty might be embodied in divisible parts and Julian Franklin remarks, bluntly, that 'Bodin's idea that sovereignty is indivisible was thus based on serious confusions.'[8] Again, sovereignty may be absolute in being the locus of all legitimate power but unless one holds to the indivisibility thesis this does not produce an absolute monarch or an absolute assembly. Correlative to the idea of sovereignty is that of subjection. The sovereign is sovereign over subjects and subjects are subjects to a sovereign. No sovereign, no subjects; no subjects, no sovereign. Of course, there are many other relationships that may obtain between individuals—religious, social, fraternal—but none of these involve of necessity the notion of sovereignty. Given the religious (and political) fragmentation that had arisen in the sixteenth century together with the existing local groupings, different patterns of customs and local laws, even different languages, one can see why Bodin is choosing to prioritise one particular relation among all these to constitute *the* political tie that binds.

What is this sovereignty then? It is *supreme power over subjects unrestrained by positive or municipal law*. It is *perpetual* rather than limited in time. It is *primary* rather than delegated. It *cannot be alienated* and *cannot be circumscribed* by prescription. In every state there is a sovereign. This sovereign may not be an individual person; it may instead be an assembly. Whether a sovereign is ontologically singular or plural, sovereignty is always unitary. If no sovereignty to be found, then, Bodin thinks, there is no state. In a sovereign state, all authority other than that of the sovereign is either illegitimate or is delegated. Even if a state to be a state has necessarily to be sovereign and thus possess a unitary centre of legitimate authority, it does not necessarily follow that it must operate directly from this centre. There is no principled objection to decentralisation; in fact, Bodin even favours such a policy. In this, Bodin, a man of his time, recognised the continuing existence of various forms of corporations and had no practical desire to see them prorogued or eliminated. The consequence of his theory of sovereignty was that all such corporations, insofar as they possessed authority, did so ultimately as holding it in a delegated form from the sovereign.

The sovereign is the supreme lawgiver and the law is simply his command. His law-giving requires no consent from anyone—inferior, equal or superior. If customary law continues to function, it does so only with the consent (implied or express) of the sovereign. Thomas Aquinas had held that prescription could alter statute; Bodin denies this and instead asserts that statute can alter custom. Law (*lex*) proceeds from the sovereign; divine law (equity or *ius*) proceeds from God. In an ideal state, there should be no clash between these two types of law. If there is, however, no subject can take it upon himself to remedy that legal dissonance. Bodin's understanding of divine law was taken exclusively from the Old Testament and, despite his acquaintance with Calvin's works and its recurrent themes and topics, it is significant that he never mentions the notorious chapter 13 from St Paul's *Letter to the Romans*. Bodin was sufficiently a creature of his time to believe that the sovereign was responsible to God and encompassed about by the natural law but neither of these constraints affected in any substantive way his sovereignty. Of the three types of law—Divine, Natural and Municipal—only the last is the product of the prince's will.

Bodin's sovereign, unlike Hobbes's ruler, is obliged to keep the covenants he makes with his subjects. (Hobbes's ruler, as we shall see, makes no covenant at all with his subjects but is himself the product of a covenant they make with one another.) In what way is the sovereign obliged by covenants? Not by positive law, for there is no way a sovereign can be obliged to obey his own command. There remains only divine and natural law so that the keeping of covenants is therefore a matter of natural law. Nevertheless, as we have seen, unless the sovereign voluntarily submits to the sanctions of divine and natural law, the subject has no way of enforcing them. Though the sovereign isn't in any way obliged to seek advice or consent, Bodin thinks it expedient for him to do so in normal circumstances. An advice-giving council is desirable, as are the Estates that constitute quasi-representative bodies. If the sovereign's laws are to run, since he can't do everything himself, there must be magistrates to give them effect.

In Bodin's account of sovereignty there is, it would appear, little to prevent the autocratic exercise of power by the sovereign. He has no superior or equal, he is the sole source of municipal law and that law is simply his command. If he is subject to divine law, its sanctions lie beyond the borders of this vale of tears. If the sovereign's law is a matter of his will and if his will isn't in conformity with divine law, how is such a tension to be reconciled? If he is subject to the natural law, who is to enforce its dictates against him? True, by natural law, even a sovereign is obliged to keep to his agreements but should he fail to do so, who will enforce his obligations upon him?

THE STATE AND GOVERNMENT

Bodin agrees with Calvin that the state is a consequence of sin. He differs from Calvin, however, in understanding that sin to be one of injustice against other men rather than an affront to God. The state, he believes, originated in violence and is expressive of man's lust to dominate his fellow men. He writes, 'force, violence, ambition, avarice, and the passion for vengeance, armed men against one another. The result of the ensuing conflicts was to give victory to some, and to reduce the rest to slavery....the man who had been chosen captain and leader by the victors, under whose command success had been won, retained authority over his followers, who became his loyal and faithful adherents, and imposed it on others, who became his slaves. Thus was lost the full and entire liberty of each man to live according to his own free will, without subjection to anyone.'[9]

On the other hand, Bodin sometimes suggests that the state emerged from a desire for mutual association, partly to repel and defeat acts of violence, partly to promote social ends. He writes, 'The origin of all corporate associations and guilds is rooted in the family....with the increase in numbers, it became no longer possible for them all to inhabit and find sustenance in a single place, and they were compelled to spread abroad. Gradually the villages grew into towns, each with its separate interests and distinct locality. As these communities were originally without laws, without magistrates, and without sovereign rulers, quarrels easily arose over such things as ownership of some spring or well.' In response to these occasions for quarrelling, men associated 'for the defence of their homes and families, others to attack those in possession, and to despoil, and destroy them. The activities which were held in the greatest esteem among primitive men, says Plutarch, were the massacre, slaughter and ruin of their fellows, and the reduction of them to slavery.' This same sentiment will be repeated later by Hobbes. Bodin continues: 'This licence and impunity in preying upon one another compelled men, who knew neither rulers nor magistrates, to join together as friends for mutual defence one against another, and institute communities and brotherhoods...' [Bodin 1955, III, vii] The disorder resulting from lawlessness and lack of a common magistrate forced men into associations for mutual defence. In the end, however the state arose, whether by violence or by some form of constrained agreement, is a matter of little consequence for Bodin. What does matter is whether the state 'maintains order and acts for the good of its subjects.' [Plamenatz, 98]

The story Bodin tells resembles that which will be told by Hobbes, except that Bodin recognises, as Hobbes does not, that human associations are held together not only by the necessity to resist common dangers but also by mutual affection. Marian Tooley puts this well when she writes, 'Bodin could not go quite so far as Hobbes and define the commonwealth as a number of individuals united solely by their individual subjection to a common power, for he thought of men as naturally sociable, and any association of men as based on mutual amity even more than on justice. But sharing Hobbes's acute fear of anarchy, he was possessed by the same conviction that the recognition of an absolute sovereign power was the only bulwark against it. Where there is no such power, there can be no political society.' [Tooley, xxvi.]

The family is a natural social entity that is the basis of all other communities, including the state. The boundary of the family is a limit beyond which the state cannot go. Bodin would have liked to restore to the family the old Roman idea of the *pater familias* with all the draconian powers such a personage had. If the family is one rock around which the waters of the state must flow, so too is property. In fact, Bodin links family and property closely together so that the proprietor of property isn't the individual as such but the family. Property thus becomes a family attribute. Though the state is composed of families, none the less, state and family are separate entities and have different attributes. If property is an attribute of the family, sovereignty is an attribute of the state. Political authority, sovereignty, isn't a form of property relation. The prince or king does not own the public sphere and he isn't in a position to alienate any of it. More to the point, he does not own the property of families. The sanctity of property derives from both natural law and divine law (via the Old Testament). Indeed, so great a role does the notion of the family play in Bodin's thought that there's little or no room left for any substantive notion of individual liberty for the mass of human beings. Liberty, for Bodin, is freedom from the authority, from the *imperium*, of any person (except God) and since all the members of a family except its *pater familias* are subject to the authority of the *pater familias*, only the *pater familias* is, properly speaking, free under natural law. [see Dunning 1905, 87]

The state, then, if formed from an association of households, isn't just any association such as a village or a city, or any other form of corporation; such an association of households only becomes a state when the constituent parts are unified by an authority that is sovereign. The state is supposed to provide the conditions in which its subjects may live good and virtuous lives. But a state whose sovereign defies divine and natural law—for Bodin this is a tyranny— can hardly produce these conditions. Echoing Augustine, Bodin distinguished between a state and a band of robbers on the grounds that one was based on justice whereas the other rested merely on violence. Despite making this distinction, Bodin nevertheless recognises tyranny as a form of commonwealth! As Tooley, not unreasonably remarks, 'it is difficult to see why he should have recognized it as a commonwealth while rejecting a robber band, or how it is to be reconciled with the definition of the state as a rightly ordered government.' [Tooley, xxxv]

It is easy to see what Bodin takes sovereignty to be and why he thinks it to be *politically* important; it is also easy to see what Bodin takes the family to be and why he thinks it to be *socially* important; but it isn't easy to reconcile his conception of the role of the family with the sovereign power of the state. Bodin believes that families arise to satisfy natural needs; the state, he thinks, comes into existence primarily through conquest. Are there natural needs that a state fulfils? If Bodin knows what these might be, he isn't telling us. Significantly, he has no use for the usual recourse to the idea of a spiritual sanction for supreme political authority but he is strangely reluctant to supply us with a secular sanction. What the state is for, what its ends and purposes are and why citizens are obliged to obey their sovereign—these aren't questions to which Bodin gives conspicuously clear answers. What the state *is*, however, is a lawful government of several households, its lawfulness, presumably, distinguishing it from unlawful robber bands and the like. He accepted, not with any great degree of willingness, that the state couldn't make its citizens' happiness or goodness its practicable end, but he was also unwilling to restrict the state's purpose to the provision of and maintenance of peace and security.

It is apparent that Bodin's conception of the family as a bulwark against the state sits uneasily with his conception of sovereignty. But there are other flies in the ointment. The *princeps* is circumscribed by divine and natural law, even if such law is practically unenforceable. More practically problematic was a possible conflict between Bodin's conception of the sovereign and the actual constitutional law of the realm. Bodin thought, in fact, that there were certain things that even the king couldn't do and that these were given by law. Nevertheless, if the law in total is of the king's making, then there can *be* no such laws. Bodin attempted to get around this problem by conceiving of the existence of certain laws that were in fact constitutive of the very notion of sovereignty itself so that their violation would be self-destructive. These he called *leges imperii*. Dunning remarks, 'In not explaining fully the conception involved in the term *leges imperii*, Bodin is again guilty of a serious lapse. His anxiety to have something in a state more fixed and permanent than the human will lead him to limit the power *legibus soluta*, by *leges* as well as by *jus*. But who is the law-maker in the case of these *leges imperii?*' [Dunning 1896, 96] The maker of the *leges imperii* can't be either God or nature, for that would make these laws to be either divine or natural which isn't how Bodin thinks of them. Do these laws emanate from the people as perhaps the ultimate source of perpetual sovereignty? Possibly, but Bodin has a marked aversion to any idea of popular authority. Clearly, what Bodin is reaching for in his conception of *leges imperii* is some kind of constitutional law that would provide the framework within which ordinary law-making would take place but his analytical categories provide no secure basis for such.

Bodin's idea of *leges imperii* is patently unsatisfactory. Either the sovereign is the sole source of law with no equal or superior to say him nay; or he is himself subject to certain laws not of his making, in which case he is not, nor can he be, superior to such laws. To be consistent, it seems that Bodin should move in one of two directions: either admit no superior of any kind to the sovereign (and this is the direction Hobbes will take) or else give up the idea of identifying the sovereign with a prince (whether a single person or an assembly).

To compound Bodin's woes, there is the ever-present problem of the family-property nexus that stands opposed to the state in one respect while being a constituent part of it in others. The sovereign–subject relationship isn't one of property owner to property. A sovereign does not own his subjects' property and if he wishes to make use of it, he needs his subjects' consent. But if this is so then, in relation to any laws that a sovereign might make about, let us say, taxation, the sovereign's ability to make such laws is limited by his subjects' property rights—but that's a significant limitation on the sovereign's lawmaking powers. [see Dunning 1896, 95] It would seem that all the king's horses and all the king's men can't yoke the illimitable legislative power of the sovereign together with the apparently indefeasible character of the family-property nexus. If one had to judge which of these two notions—illimitable sovereign power or the family-property nexus—was more fundamental to Bodin, one would have to choose family-property.

Perhaps Bodin's most significant analytical contribution after his account of sovereignty is his sharp distinction between state and government. Instead of Aristotle's six types of *polis*—monarchy, tyranny, aristocracy, oligarchy, moderate democracy and democracy—Bodin holds that there are only three possible forms of the state. If the sovereign is one, the state is a monarchy; if a few, an aristocracy; if all or most, a democracy. [Bodin 1955, II, i] Still, even though the form of a *state* is determined simply by the number of people in whom sovereignty resides, the form of a *government* is given by the way in which the administration of the will of the sovereign is executed. So, one can have a democratic state with an aristocratic government (as in the early Roman republic), or a monarchic state with either an aristocratic or a democratic government; or, as was the case in Athens during the time of Pericles, a democratic state and a democratic government. There can be, then, three and only three kinds of state—monarchic, aristocratic and democratic—and three and only three kinds of government—monarchic, aristocratic and democratic. That gives us nine theoretical combinations of state and government:

State	Government	Historical Examples
Monarchy	Monarchy	Russia under Ivan IV
Monarchy	Aristocracy	Eighteenth Century England
Monarchy	Democracy	United Kingdom
Aristocracy	Monarchy	Imperial Rome
Aristocracy	Aristocracy	?
Aristocracy	Democracy	?
Democracy	Monarchy	?
Democracy	Aristocracy	Republican Rome
Democracy	Democracy	Pericles' Athens

These are all the theoretical possibilities. I leave it to the reader to discover what actual examples there may have been of each of the nine combinations. I have made some speculative suggestions but feel free to add or subtract from my tentative candidates or alter them as seems fit.

FREEDOM AND PROPERTY

The exact distinction between natural law and natural right is one over which philosophers happily squabble. It would be too much to say that Bodin had a clear conception of natural rights as such came to be understood later but it's revealing that, despite the problems they cause for him theoretically, he recognises liberty and property as divinely sanctioned aspects of man in his life in society that can't arbitrarily be taken from him. It might be somewhat anachronistic to describe Bodin's conception of liberty and property as rights but functionally that's what they are for him. Nevertheless, his treatment of the two is dissimilar—he gives a reasonably robust defence of property but a particularly weak defence of liberty.

Liberty, Bodin characterises, as the freedom to live as one chooses subject only to the rule of reason [Bodin 1955, I, iii] So far so good. Nevertheless, that freedom is severely limited by a subject's obligation to obey his ruler, an obligation that isn't in any way contingent upon a subject's consent. This is in stark contrast to the Huguenot-inspired *Vindiciae contra Tyrannos*. In Bodin's account, a subject who wishes to preserve his freedom has no alternative but to rely upon his sovereign's adherence to divine and natural law. Should his sovereign refuse to be bound by such law, the subject has no remedy in the here and now.

Whatever about his admiration for certain classical institutions (such as the Roman family), Bodin wasn't attracted by all aspects of classical life. Strikingly, he robustly rejected slavery as either useful or as justifiable. He considered the more plausible arguments in favour of slavery—its longevity as a social institution, its virtual omnipresence, and the enslavement of prisoners as a morally better option than their death or servitude in place of capital punishment—but he rejects them all. I reproduce excerpts from the relevant section of his work as a model of Bodinian rebuttal:

> I agree that servitude is natural where the strong, brutal, rich, and ignorant obey the wise, prudent, and humble, poor though they may be. But no one would deny that to subject wise men to fools, the well-informed to the ignorant, saints to sinners is against nature…One sees in fact how often quiet and peaceable men are the prey of evildoers. When princes attempt to settle their differences by war, it is always claimed that the victor had right on his side, and the vanquished were in the wrong. If the vanquished did indeed make war without just cause, as do brigands, ought one not rather to make an example of them and put them to death, than to show them mercy? As for the argument that slavery could not have been so enduring if it had been contrary to nature, I would answer that the principle holds good for natural agents whose property it is to obey of necessity the unchanging laws of God. But man, being given the choice between good and evil, inclines for the most part to that which is forbidden, and chooses the evil, defying the laws of God and of nature. …there is no sort of impiety or wickedness which in this way had not come to be accounted virtuous and good….it is sufficiently obvious that there can be no more cruel and detestable practice

than human sacrifice. Yet there is hardly a people which has not practised it, and each and all have done so for centuries under the cover of piety. ... such things show how little the laws of nature can be deduced from the practices of men, however inveterate, and one cannot on these grounds accept slavery as natural. Again, what charity is there in sparing captives in order to derive some profit or advantage from them as if they were cattle? For where is the man who would spare the lives of the vanquished if he saw more profit in killing than in sparing them? [Bodin 1955, I, v.]

Bodin was appalled by the plight of slaves and, in addition to his theoretical rebuttals of the pro-slavery arguments, he gives a moving account of their sufferings, remarking that 'the cruelties one reads about are unbelievable, and yet only the thousandth part has been told.' Moreover, despite the tolerance if not active acceptance of slavery by Christians, Muslims and Jews alike, he stoutly maintains that 'by the law of God it is forbidden to make any man a slave except with his own entire good will and consent.' [Bodin 1955, I, v]

If, apart from his rejection of slavery, Bodin's treatment of liberty is disappointing for libertarians, his account of property is somewhat more red-blooded, if indirect. What he is most concerned to defend against invasion is the family as a social unit in its own right and the basic unit of the state. If the family is to be preserved, then its property—and we may remember that Bodin saw property as an aspect of the family as a unit rather than the individual—must be preserved also. Anna Becker remarks that 'Oeconomics [household management] is the key to understanding Bodin's political thought; the family stood at the centre of his vision of politics, while his thought of the family is central to both his universal claims pertaining to his notion of the political and his more particular interest in sovereignty and the origins of absolutism.' [Becker 2014, 136] The family is constituted as a unity by the authority of husband over wife, father over children, master over servant, and slave-owner over slaves. [Bodin 1955, I, iii]

Despite recognising the importance of property in the family, Bodin was more interested in the political aspects of the family than in its economic aspects. It is in the family that children are inculcated with the habits of obedience to authority, a habit that is then transferred to the ruler of the state. The articulation of political relationships on the model of the family is a frequently recurring theme of many political thinkers and Bodin, in a sense, belongs to this company. He writes, 'the well-ordered family is the true image of the *République*, and the domestic power resembles the sovereign power: equally, the right government of the household is the true model of the government of the *République*.' [Bodin 1955, I, ii] Nevertheless, the modelling does not go all the way through. As Becker remarks, 'Bodin's monarch was not conceived as a father ruling over his citizens as his children but as a *pater familias* ruling over households, whose property he was not allowed to touch....Bodin's sovereign power...did not have its origins in the power of the father to [*sic*] children, but in conjugal power." [Becker 2014, 154]

Taxation

Bodin writes that the state may raise revenue in any one of seven different ways: from the royal domain, by conquest, by the reception of gifts, by subsidies from allies, by directly engaging in commerce, by excise duties on exports and imports, and by taxes. [Bodin 1955, VI, ii] Regarding taxes, Bodin writes, 'One should never have recourse to it [taxation] until all other measures have failed, and only then because urgent necessity compels one to make some provision for the commonwealth. In such a case, seeing that the security and defence of each private citizen depends on the preservation of the common good, each individual must be prepared to assist in the matter.' [Bodin 1955, VI, ii] Such extraordinary means of raising revenue for the defence of the realm in time of war must not be continued in peacetime. Bodin held to the medieval idea that a king should live of his own, that is, that the king should pay for his administration from his own resources, and that taxation should be an extraordinary source of revenue. Libertarian hopes will be raised when it is seen that Bodin denies that a ruler can tax as he wills but requires the consent of those who are to be taxed. Once again, this limitation is less watertight than it might at first appear. Such consent as is required here isn't the explicit consent of the individual subject but the corporate consent of the Estates. As Oakley notes, 'representative assemblies of one sort of another…made their appearance all over western Europe [and] national monarchs and territorial princes became accustomed to making use of these Romano-canonical procedures. They did so because they needed to secure for their increasingly vigorous and ambitious governmental activities, and for the mounting "extraordinary" taxation needed to finance them, the requisite consent not only of the noblemen and bishops who could attend their assemblies as individuals but also of the increasingly powerful corporate (or quasi-corporate) bodies and groupings which could not.' [Oakley 2012, 155] Although Bodin asserted the rights of property and demanded that taxation occur only with consent, his notion of consent was perilously close to being an empty formality. [see Rothbard 1995a, 205] Public revenues, once obtained, are to be used for the upkeep of the king's household and the payment of the army. Any remaining funds are to be used for the general benefit in the construction of fortifications, the building of roads and bridges and public buildings and the foundations of colleges.

A Right to Resist?

Bodin's subjects have no right of resistance against their rulers. The ruler, like the father in the family, is neither chosen, nor elected, nor is he appointed, and his authority isn't dependent on choice, election, appointment or consent. 'All right to command is therefore essentially independent of the consent of the commanded,' writes Tooley. 'The artificial society of the commonwealth should be modeled on the natural society of the family, and no father is appointed by his children to rule over them.'[10]

What was Bodin's approach to tyrannicide? May a tyrant be killed? Bodin's answer depends on distinguishing between a tyrant and a despot. A prince who, as the result of a just war, takes the persons of his enemies as slaves and their goods as his possessions acts legitimately and is a despot but not a tyrant. Nevertheless, a prince who so acted by means of an unjust war or who in some other way seizes the property or persons of a free people is a tyrant. Tyrannicide may be justified, if the tyrant is a usurper, but absolute sovereigns may not be legally or physically resisted. [see Turchetti, 20-22]

We saw in earlier chapters that medieval kings were thought to derive their kingship, at least in part, from a kind of contract with their subjects, this being manifested through election or approval. Bodin rejects this idea completely and in so doing moves most definitely from the medieval to the modern period. Bodin's king makes the law and he does so by his command. Subjects do not make their king and they cannot unmake him. They do not make his laws and they cannot unmake them. Subjects are bound by divine and natural law to obey their rulers, even if those rulers are cruel.

Bodin's thought on sovereignty as legislative power and the idea of law as the command of the lawgiver would re-emerge in the work of Thomas Hobbes (who cites him in his *The Elements of Law*). Hobbes, who follows Bodin in his major conclusions, is conceptually more chaste than Bodin and has no place in his system for any laws outside the reach of the sovereign, nor does he recognise a subject's right to property in such a way that it would necessarily restrict the actions of the sovereign. [see Dunning 1896, 103] Bodin also influenced Filmer, Locke, Harrington and, in respect of his environmental determinism, Montesquieu. Bodin's idea of a natural law circumscribing and limiting even the sovereign (not to mention the limitations imposed by the priority of the family-property nexus) was to re-echo in the work of Locke and Grotius. As we shall see, Johannes Althusius accepted Bodin's theory of sovereignty while locating it in the community as a whole rather than in the prince.

Notes

1 See Becker 2014, passim and Dunning 1905, 89.

2 See Turchetti, 17-20, 29-31.

3 Arnold Toynbee said of Ibn Khaldûn that the loneliness of his star was as striking as its brilliance. Of Khaldûn's *Muqaddimah*, he wrote, with perhaps some degree of exaggeration, that it was 'undoubtedly the greatest work of its kind that has ever yet been created by any mind in any time or place. [*A Study of History*, 2nd ed., London, 1935, III, 322, cited in Khaldûn, xxxv] It is ironic, then, that Khaldûn, the most brilliant Muslim thinker of his time, was a follower of the anti-intellectual Ash'arite school!

4 Dunning 1896, 84; see also 87.

5 Sabine, 402; Plamenatz, 92; see also 97 and 115.

6 Bodin 1992, 1, §345. References to Bodin *Six Livres* are to the translation by Marian Tooley (1955), by book number and chapter number, and Julian Franklin's (1992) translation, by page number and marginal number.

7 Bodin 1992, 47-48, §§479-480.

8 Franklin 1992, xx; see xvii-xxi.

9 Bodin 1955, 1, vi. 'While human society thus arose through the operation of the social instinct, the state, on the other hand, took its origin in force....The view of Aristotle and others, following Herodotus, that the first monarchs were voluntarily chosen by the peoples for their supereminent virtues, is, Bodin holds, wrong.' [Dunning 1905, 89; see Gammie, passim]

10 Tooley, xxiv; see also Becker 2014, passim.

Chapter 16

THE ROAD NOT TAKEN:
JOHANNES ALTHUSIUS

I consider that no polity from the beginning of the world has been more wisely
and perfectly constructed than the polity of the Jews
—Johannes Althusius

When the tyrant has disposed of foreign enemies by conquest or treaty
and there is nothing to fear from them, then he is always stirring up some war or other
in order that the people may require a leader
—Plato

According to Carl Joachim Friedrich, one-time Eaton Professor of the
Science of Government at Harvard University and Professor of Political
Science at the University of Heidelberg, a certain man was 'The most profound
political philosopher between Bodin and Hobbes.' Who was Friedrich talking
about? Johannes Althusius (1563-1638). Who? One might well ask! Some
thinkers are deservedly little known, some are undeservedly well known (I've
got a little list!), and some are undeservedly little known. Johannes Althusius
belongs to the latter class.

Althusius was born in the middle of the sixteenth century, by which time the
part of Germany in which he lived, Diedenhausen in Westphalia, was already
a stronghold of Calvinism. He studied law, logic and philosophy in various
places, including Basel and Cologne, before returning to his home area to
teach law. At around the age of forty, he became a municipal trustee of the city
of Emden in the very north of Germany, close to the Dutch border, and rose
through the city's ranks to become a syndic, a senior administrator, which post
he held for over thirty years until his death in 1638. It can be seen from this
brief biographical resumé that Althusius (like Bodin and Machiavelli) managed
to combine both theoretical and practical experience of politics, and his reflections were no mere idle speculations but were given a sharp practical point by
the Dutch (Calvinist) revolt against (Catholic) Spain which took place during
his early and middle years.

Althusius's ideas were to a certain extent in competition with those of
Jean Bodin. Daniel Elazar notes, and I believe he is correct in this, that the
Althusian view lost out to the Bodinian view of 'reified centralized states
where all powers were lodged in a divinely ordained king at the top of the
power pyramid or in a sovereign center.' [Elazar, xxxviii] Althusius by and
large adopts Bodin's concept of sovereignty, his definition of sovereignty being
the 'universal power of ruling...which recognizes no ally, nor any superior
or equal to itself [*Politica*, 69-70] but crucially, however, he locates it differ-

ently. For Bodin, sovereignty is located in the prince, ruler, or chief officer of the state; for Althusius, sovereignty is to be located in the people taken corporately, not in a ruler, rector, or administrator. This sovereignty of the people is not only *not* alienated to any ruler; it is, in fact, inalienable. Power, yes, is given to the ruler to administer the affairs of the commonwealth; sovereignty, however, remains, and cannot but remain, with the people as a whole.[1] Not only does Althusius accept Bodin's idea of sovereignty (though locating it differently), his entire proto-federalist scheme is consistent with Bodin's view of the state as 'the ultimate form of association, (*caetus*), holding together by a supreme power a mass of lesser associations and individuals.' [Dunning 1905, 90] Even the terminology used by Bodin to describe these lesser forms of association—family, college (*collegium*), corporation (*corpus*) and commune (*universitas*)—is to some extent echoed by Althusius in his own account.

With the triumph of the modern state based on a Bodinian conception of sovereignty, Althusius's ideas were swept to one side and forgotten until the end of the nineteenth century when Otto Gierke drew attention to them once again. As George Sabine notes, Althusius's theory 'had little application in France and England, where the political thinking of the sixteenth and seventeenth centuries mainly took place. This fact was perhaps one of the reasons why Althusius's work fell into oblivion.' [Sabine, 419] In the 1930s, Althusius's reputation was given a boost by the work of Carl Joachim Friedrich who republished the major part of Althusius's principal work, *Politica Methodice Digesta, Atque Exemplis Sacris et Profanis Illustrata*. Over the years, a small but growing band of scholars has dedicated itself to re-establishing Althusius as a thinker whose ideas are worthy of rehabilitation. 'Only at the end of the first century of the Reformation,' writes Daniel Elazar, 'did a political philosopher emerge out of the Reformed tradition to build a systematic political philosophy out of the Reformed experience by synthesizing the political experience of the Holy Roman Empire with the political ideas of the covenant theology of Reformed Protestantism.' [Elazar, xxxv] Had the Althusian and not the Bodinian conception of the locus of sovereignty prevailed, the course of political history might well have been very different.

It should be noted that not everyone is as persuaded of Althusius's eminence as a political thinker as are Friedrich and Gierke. Stephen Grabill notes that 'Eric Voegelin stands alone among twentieth-century political philosophers and intellectual historians with his unilaterally negative assessment of Althusius...'[2] Voegelin writes, 'Althusius' work...is still overrated as a consequence of Otto Gierke's monograph. The *Politica* is by far the most solid work of the Calvinist monarchomachic group; ... it is the work of an experienced practical lawyer who could digest his rich knowledge, with the aid of his 'method,' into a well-ordered book; but it is definitely not the work of a great political thinker." [Voegelin 1998, 56]

As unusual and even startling as Althusius's theory might appear to be, it is, in fact, in many ways simply a theoretical tidying-up of the *de facto* political arrangements that subsisted in the Holy Roman Empire (*Sacrum Imperium Romanum*), a multi-ethnic complex of cities, duchies, principalities, kingdoms, counties and the like, that originated in AD 800 and lasted for more than a thousand years until its eventual dissolution in 1806. 'The Empire was never a unitary state with a homogeneous population, but instead a patchwork of lands and peoples under an uneven and changing imperial jurisdiction.'[3] [Wilson 2016, 179] The key failing of the Empire from the perspective of orthodox political historians was its decentralised and flexible character, a decentralised and flexible character that, from Althusius's perspective, was precisely its strength and virtue. Peter Wilson, in his magisterial study of the Holy Roman Empire writes, '...the Empire has often been judged as ineffectual, because it favoured arbitration rather than swift and unambiguous verdicts. There has also been a tendency to see protest as an intrusion threatening political stability, rather than as a form of negotiation and a check on arbitrary power....legal and judicial arrangements were primarily intended to find and sustain workable compromises, ideally through reconciliation rather than exemplary punishment.' [Wilson 2016, 603] Whereas modern politics, as Wilson notes, 'are largely about determining who controls such states and what policies they should pursue' what we had in the Empire was a kind of 'auto-politics and self-regulation, both of which are closer to the Empire's *regimen* of a broadly inclusive system relying more on consensus than command.' [Wilson 2016, 295]

Although Althusius is a transitional figure between late medieval and early modern times, he is remarkably inclusive in his choice of sources. As one might expect, Aristotle, Bodin, Cicero, Augustine and Seneca feature in his writings but, as a Calvinist, Althusius was also acquainted with the *Vindiciae contra Tyrannos* and the writings of George Buchanan and the French antimonarchists. Althusius also had an extensive interest in and an ecumenical appreciation of some Catholic writers, notably the late Spanish scholastics—Vásquez, Covarrubias and Mariana.

Althusius—Federalist?

It is often held that Althusius's work is one of the first federalist theories of political order based on the concept of subsidiarity. [see Gierke 1957, 70ff.] Daniel Elazar believes that Althusius found a model for his federal design in the Old Testament. 'Biblical thought is federal (from the Latin *foedus*, covenant) from first to last....' [Elazar, xxxvi] Ancient federalism was tribal or corporatist (or status-based), whereas modern forms of federalism tend to emphasise the individual to the detriment of the group. The Althusius model of federalism is an attempt to combine the strengths and to eliminate the weaknesses of the ancient and the modern federalist conceptions. A postmodern federalism must recognize both individuals and their rights and also groups. It must be based on covenant; sovereignty must remain with the people as a whole; there must be some minimal recognition of norms binding citizens and providing a basis for trust and communication; the public and private realms must be distinguished yet connected. Dunning sees Althusius as having a conception of the 'people' that is in fact incompatible with any conception of the state except one that is confederative. [see Dunning 1905, 62]

So, *was* Althusius a federalist? M. R. R. Ossewaarde thinks not. 'Althusius is neither a scholastic subsidiarity thinker, nor "the first federalist", nor is he one of the founding fathers of the liberal constitutional state.' [Ossewaarde, 107] According to Ossewaarde, Althusius structures his political theory on what Ossewaarde calls 'sphere sovereignty', which is independent both of the Bodinian notion of sovereignty and the scholastic notion of subsidiarity. The rights and duties of any given sphere are peculiar to that sphere so that Althusius's state 'has no responsibility for the provision of subsidiary assistance to lower authorities…in order to make citizens flourish or guard the common good. The only responsibility of the state is to administer justice by maintaining law and order in the universal symbiotic association of all spheres in a fight against parasitism.' [Ossewaarde, 123]

In the end, whether federalist or not, whether great and profound or merely workmanlike, what cannot be denied is that Althusius's thought stands out from among the mass of political writing of this period, particularly in its opposition to the increasingly dominant Bodinian conception of sovereignty in respect of its ultimate location. Elazar remarks, 'to read Althusius is to discover how important his ideas are for our times. Eclipsed for three centuries by the major thrust of the modern epoch toward the homogeneous nation-state built around the individual citizen, standing politically naked before the state machinery, Althusian ideas seem much more in place in the postmodern epoch…' [Elazar, xlv]

CONSOCIATION

Althusius's starting point is this: 'Politics is the art of associating[4] [*consociandi*] men for the purpose of establishing, cultivating, and conserving social life among them. Whence it is called "symbiotics".' [*Politica*, 17] For Althusius, symbiotic association isn't just a happenstance fact of living in proximity to other people: 'It indicates a quality of group life characterized by piety and justice without which, Althusius believes, neither individual persons nor society can endure.' [Carney, xv] 'The subject matter of politics is therefore association (*consociatio*), in which the symbiotes [those who live together] pledge themselves each to the other, *by explicit or tacit agreement*, to mutual communication of whatever is useful and necessary for the harmonious exercise of social life.'[5] The idea of agreement is central to Althusius's understanding of all forms of consociation, that consent or agreement being the very thing that brings the consociation into being. Despite the many, the very many, references to Scripture in Althusius's work and his conventional identification of natural law with the second table of the Decalogue, his political theory depends in no essential way upon any religious assumptions. Althusius's political theory, remarks George Sabine, 'depended logically upon the single idea of contract and owed substantially nothing to religious authority.' [Sabine, 417]

Althusius recognises the truism that the individual man is radically insufficient even for his own self-preservation, let alone his flourishing, and that this insufficiency is what moves him towards consociating with others. 'Necessity therefore induces consociation; and the want of things necessary for life, which are acquired and communicated by the help and aid of one's consociates conserves it. For this reason it is evident that the commonwealth, or civil society, exists by nature, and that man is by nature a civil animal who strives eagerly for consociation.' [*Politica*, 25] This voluntary coming together of men, this consociation, is, for Althusius, the subject matter of politics.

As already mentioned, for Althusius, in consociating, the symbiotes 'pledge themselves to each other, by explicit or tacit agreement, to mutual communication of whatever is useful and necessary for the harmonious exercise of social life,' communication being a sharing in common of whatever is communicated. [*Politica*, 17] This communication has three aspects: a communication of *things*, which relates to the production of useful and necessary goods for the common advantage of the symbiotes both individually and collectively; a communication of *services*, which relates to contributions the symbiotes make to their social life by means of their work and occupations; and a communication of *rights*, which is the means by which the symbiotes are ruled by just laws in the life together. [see *Politica*, 19] The third aspect of communication—the communication of rights—is the one that is of most interest to political philosophers. Althusius, typically, divides this communication of rights (which he also calls the law of consociation) into two parts, one common, and one proper. The common part of this law of consociation concerns itself with the highest level of political organisation that supervenes upon every other constituent part— what we would normally think of as the state—while the proper part relates to the laws by which particular forms of consociation are to be governed.

Althusius sees human society as constituted by an ascending order of consociations, with the *family* at the lowest and most particular level, and the *realm or the commonwealth*, at the highest and most universal. Between the family and the commonwealth are the *collegium*, the *city* and the *province*. The *common* part of the law of consociation, then, belongs to the realm or commonwealth, which is the overarching form of consociation, and the *proper* part to the family, the *collegium*, the city and the province. Each of these forms of consociation has the same structure which Althusius explains using the Aristotelian doctrine of the four causes—efficient, formal, material and final. The *efficient* cause of a consociation, what brings it into being, is the consent and agreement of the communicants; the *formal* cause, what the consociation is when it is brought into being, is the institution, cultivation, maintenance and conservation of the fellowship of the communicants by the making of decisions on what is useful and necessary for this life in common; the *material* cause of a consociation is, according to Althusius, the 'aggregate of precepts for communicating the things, services and rights' needed for the common advantages of social life; and the *final* cause, what all of this is for and that towards which it is directed, is 'the enjoyment of a comfortably, useful, and happy life, and of the common welfare,' and the production of a society in which one can 'worship God quietly and without error.' [*Politica*, 24]

Each consociation is constituted by an agreement which has both an horizontal and a vertical dimension. These dimensions result from an agreement or contract that sets out the rules according to which that consociation is to be organised, which rules include the (vertical) administrative machinery for the effective implementation of these rules. The horizontal dimension makes the consociation to be the kind of consociation it is; the vertical dimension 'creates and limits an authority for administering its common affairs.' [Sabine, 418] These five types of consociation are vertically related to each other, the family at the bottom, the realm or commonwealth at the top. Each consociation higher in the scale than the one or ones below it regulates such affairs as are essential to its purposes, leaving all other affairs within the remit of the consociations lower in the scale.

Although Althusius makes contract or covenant to be the efficient cause of all his consociations, this contract or covenant can be either explicit or implicit. As implicit, this seems to amount to pretty much the innate social tendency in man that many writers have remarked upon. 'Althusius' grand design,' remarks Elazar, 'is developed out of a series of building blocks or self-governing cells from the smallest, most intimate connections to the universal commonwealth, each of which is internally organized and linked to the others by some form of consensual relationship.' [Elazar, xxxviii] The basis of each consociation is a covenant, which requires initial and continuing consent from its constituent members. Some forms of consociation, such as the family, are less explicitly voluntary than others such as the *collegium*, but all depend to some extent on needs that the consociations are intended to satisfy. 'This integral relationship between necessity and volition that first finds expression in private consociations carries over into public consociations, and becomes one of the distinctive characteristics of the entire consociational theory of Althusius.' [Carney, xvii] All forms of consociation, from the family to the commonwealth, are grounded upon symbiosis and covenant so that there's no essential difference in kind between them.

Some things should be noted about this multi-causal account. First, and most importantly, every form of consociation is voluntary, requiring either explicit or tacit consent. Second, as sometimes happens, the formal and final causes tend to coalesce, that is to say, what a consociation *is* and what it is *for* are scarcely distinguishable. Third, Althusius's material cause is strangely immaterial. One might have expected him to describe this material cause as being made up of the things, services and rights needed for the common advantage; instead, he describes it as the aggregate of *precepts* relating to these things. Althusius believes that each form of consociation requires *imperium*. Once constituted as the kind of consociation it is, each consociation requires an administration that can give effective leadership and direction so that it may achieve its purposes.

Before discussing what is of most concern to us, namely, the universal form of consociation, the realm or commonwealth, I am going to give a brief account of the less universal forms of consociation, the family and the *collegium*, which are simple and private forms of consociation, and the city and the province which, together with the commonwealth, are mixed and public.

THE FAMILY

Of the two simple and private forms of consociation, the family and the *collegium*, the family is natural and the *collegium* is civil. The family, for Althusius, is the primary form of consociation without which no other form of consociation can come to be or to endure; all other forms of consociation derive from the family. The family is 'rightly called the most intense society, friendship, relationship, and union, the seedbed of every other symbiotic consociation.' [*Politica*, 28]

By family, Althusius means more than the modern nuclear unit of father, mother and offspring—his family includes not only the married parties but also blood relatives and in-laws. None the less, he distinguishes within the general family form of consociation between the conjugal type (husband, wife and children) and the kinship type (relatives and in-laws). The family is brought into being by means of a covenant among individuals in which 'married persons, blood relatives, and in-laws, in response to a natural affection and necessity, agree to a definite communication among themselves.' [*Politica*, 28] Its purpose or end is the communication of each to the other of aid and assistance, station in life, economic condition, solicitude, food, clothing, cohabitation, sexual congress and procreation, education of children, and so on. Within the larger family, the kin, we can add solicitude for one's relatives and the provision of support for those in need in cases of necessity. The husband is the director and governor of the common affairs of the conjugal unit; within the larger kinship group, the paterfamilias assumes leadership. As always with Althusius (and as we shall see very clearly when we come to discuss the commonwealth), leadership is a service which one renders for the good of others and not a status to be had for one's own gratification or aggrandisement.

THE *COLLEGIUM*

The second form of the simple and private form of consociation is the *collegium*, by which Althusius means such voluntary groupings as guilds, corporations, societies, federations, sodalities, conventions or synods. [see *Politica*, 34] There are *collegia* of 'bakers, tailors, builders, merchants, coiners of money... philosophers, theologians, government officials....craftsmen and merchants' and others. Some *collegia* stand alone; others are themselves constituent parts of yet larger collegia. [*Politica*, 38] Such consociations are constituted by the voluntary agreement of individuals to unite for purposes related to their duties or their crafts. In his account of the functioning of the *collegium*, we are given the first hint of Althusius's approach to the broader issue of governance. Each *collegium* will choose one of its members as president to administer the property and functions proper to the *collegium*. As president, he is superior to each of the individuals in the *collegium* but not to the *collegium* itself. His role is one of service to the group; that is the purpose for which he is elected. In its relation-ships to others, the *collegium* forms a unity such that what is owed to it is owed not to the individuals who constitute it but to the *collegium* as a whole. In turn, what it owes isn't owed by the individuals constituting the *collegium* but by the *collegium* as a whole. Althusius gives a detailed account of the inner workings of the *collegium* that need not concern us here. It is enough to take from his account that in matters that pertain jointly and wholly to the *collegium* as a whole, the decision of the majority binds all; however, in matters that bear upon each member individually, a majority won't suffice—here, unanimity is required.

THE CITY (COMMUNITY)

The first form of the mixed and public forms of consociation is the community or city. A city isn't constituted directly from a mass of isolated individuals. Such a mass is more properly called a crowd, a throng, a multitude or a gathering. Rather, the city is a public consociation of private consociations constituted by fixed laws and a commonality of residence: 'The public consociation exists when many private consociations are linked together for the purpose of establishing an inclusive political order....The members of a community [city] are private and diverse consociations of families and collegia, not the individual members of private consociations.' [*Politica*, 39, 40]

As with all other forms of consociation, the city has a president or rector who 'directs the business of the community, and governs on behalf of its welfare and advantage, exercising authority over the individuals but not over the citizens collectively.' [*Politica*, 40] The function of the rectors of *collegia* and the rectors of cities is identical. They exercise their authority for the attainment of the ends of their consociations but, although superior to their constituents taken individually, are none the less inferior to their constituents taken collectively. The rector of the city, who can of course be one or many, is such only by virtue of the consent of the civic community. The unity of the city is a unity of function, not of matter, and so continues in existence as long as that function continues to operate. There must of course be *some* rector and *some* constituent consociations composed of *some* particular individuals or other but not any *particular* person as rector nor any *particular* consociations nor any *particular* individuals.

Althusius envisages a city of any reasonable magnitude as having not only a rector but also counsellors and senators whose function it is to advise and assist the rector and who, in so doing, constitute a senatorial *collegium*. We shall see when we come to look at the universal consociation, the realm or commonwealth, that those who there make up the commonwealth equivalent of the senatorial *collegium* also assist and advise its rector but, significantly, also have functions of supervision and, ultimately, control over the rector.

Just as with the family and the *collegium*, the community or city lives its life in common and its component parts communicate with each other with respect to things, services and constitutive laws. [see *Politica*, 46] These things, services and laws are, necessarily, more extensive and more complex than those obtaining in the constituent consociations but their function is identical. Among the services that Althusius has in mind are the commonplace activities of carpenters, builders, shoemakers, tailors and the like, all specialising in their work but all contributing to the common advantage of the city. The political functions of a city relate to justice, the essence of which Althusius sees outlined in the second table of the Decalogue, about which more later when we come to discuss the commonwealth.

THE PROVINCE, THE COMMONWEALTH OR REALM AND SOVEREIGNTY

Althusius's treatment of the province as an independent level of consociation is perfunctory, a fact that becomes less surprising when one realises that the province made no separate appearance in the first edition of the *Politica* but was treated rather as an administrative and constitutive element of the commonwealth. There is little to distinguish the province from the commonwealth in terms of its function except its having a superior consociation to which it is subordinate (which is as much as to say that it isn't sovereign) and in its having existed in its own right before commonwealths. 'For families, cities, and provinces existed by nature prior to realms, and gave birth to them.' [*Politica*, 66]

The realm or commonwealth is the form of universal consociation, a 'people united in one body by the agreement of many symbiotic consociations and particular bodies, and brought together under one right.' [*Politica*, 66] The immediate consociations that make up the commonwealth are cities, provinces and regions which are to the commonwealth 'as prow, stern, and keel are members of a ship and roof, walls, and floor are essential parts of a house...' [*Politica*, 67] Once again, the foundation of this consociation isn't a mere collection of units but a consensus which Althusius describes as a 'tacit or expressed promise to communicate things, mutual services, aid, counsel and the same common laws to the extent that the utility and necessity of universal social life in a realm shall require.' [*Politica*, 67] He spoils somewhat the bracing effect of the notion of consensus here when he adds that the reluctant 'are compelled to comply with this communication.' The commonality of laws in the commonwealth as a whole does not prevent there being different special laws in the provinces.[6]

It might be useful to remind ourselves of Althusius's thought on sovereignty before looking in more detail at his account of the realm. I mentioned earlier that while Althusius agrees with Bodin as to what sovereignty is, in respect of the locus of sovereignty he differs sharply from Bodin. Althusius defines sovereignty as the 'universal power of ruling...which recognizes no ally, nor any superior or equal to itself [*Politica*, 69-70] The difference between Bodin and Althusius, to state it baldly, is that for Althusius, sovereignty belongs to the people in their universal consociation and not, as it does for Bodin, to the chief officer of that consociation. Sovereignty does not belong to any single member of the realm, immediate or distant, but jointly to all.[7]

Althusius is aware of Bodin's account of sovereignty and knows well what is at issue. He acknowledges that both he and Bodin would accept that human sovereignty has a superior in divine and natural law. Is civil law superior to sovereignty? 'Bodin says no....there is a supreme power above civil law and not limited by it' but, Althusius asserts, 'This is a judgment I would not hold. To liberate power from civil law is to release it to a certain degree from the bonds of natural and divine law. For there is no civil law, nor can there be any, in which something of natural and divine immutable equity has not been mixed. If it departs entirely from the judgment of natural and divine law, it is not to be called law.' [*Politica*, 72] To the extent that civil law partakes of a higher law, to that extent it is superior to the sovereign; where civil law departs from this higher law, then the sovereign isn't necessarily bound by it. Does this concession grant Bodin all that he needs? No, because Althusius does not locate supreme power in a king or optimates but 'only to the body of a universal consociation....From this body, after God, every legitimate power flows to those we call kings or optimates. Therefore, the king, prince, and

optimates recognize this consociated body as their superior...' [*Politica*, 72]
It wouldn't be going too far to say that, for Althusius, the ruler is an agent of
the commonwealth which is and which remains his principal. As an agent, the
ruler is limited in his actions by the terms set by his principal and must render
an account of his administration to his principal. Just as an economic agent may
not wilfully diminish his principal's capital, so too, the ruler may not alienate
the provinces or cities or towns of the realm. Just as an agent serves at the
pleasure of his principal, so too, does the supreme monarch serve the commonwealth and may even be deposed if circumstances warrant such deposition.
[see *Politica*, 73]

Another way of thinking about the Althusian conception of the relationship
between the rector and the constituents of the commonwealth is to see it in
terms of the trustee-beneficiary relationship. A trustee is vested with the legal
ownership of the property of its equitable or beneficial owners but he must
exercise his legal ownership for their benefit and not for his own. Althusius
makes the point very clearly that political power is given not for the advantage
of the persons who exercise it but for the advantage of those who have been
entrusted to their care. Universal administrators and their deputies, delegates
and ministers 'have the use and exercise of power for the benefit of others, not
the ownership of it.' [*Politica*, 74] Althusius can be forgiven for not being fully
aware of the problem that besets all agent-principal relationships, a problem
that we haven't yet learnt satisfactorily to resolve, which is to ensure that agents
as agents act in the interests of their principals and not for their own betterment.

It mustn't be forgotten that Althusius is a Calvinist and so it is perhaps not
surprising, even if it is disappointing, to find that his commonwealth has rights
not only over the body but also over the soul. Somewhat naïvely, he believes
that the true and right religion can be ascertained by reflection on the Word of
God and the commonwealth has the right and power to restore this faith if it
should be corrupted and, somewhat more alarmingly, the right of 'expelling
from the territory those alien to uncorrupted religion' and, even more alarmingly
'of compelling the citizens and inhabitants of the realm, by public ordinances
and even by external force, to worship God' [*Politica*, 76] Religious toleration
is, then, not an aspect of the Althusian commonwealth. Atheists or doubters
cannot be tolerated. There is only one God and only one right way to worship
him so that 'many faiths, and many diverse churches, introduce idolatry and
impiety.' [*Politica*, 78]

The core of public law is to be found in the second table of the Decalogue. It
prohibits homicide and the infliction of bodily injury, offences against chastity,
property, and reputation. More local laws may differ from place to place and
from time to time according to the 'varying circumstances of place, time and
person' within the commonwealth. [*Politica*, 81] The material necessities of life
in a commonwealth require that there be regulations that facilitate commerce,
sound money, a common medium of communication and the equitable allocation of duties and responsibilities, all of this supported by ordinary taxation
or, in cases of emergency, extraordinary taxation. Because the commonwealth,
like all consociations, is based on consent, none of these conditions is neces-

sarily problematic for a libertarian—provided, of course, that the consent is real and continuing.

The commonwealth is entitled to use force to defend itself against violence and rapine and theft and to preserve liberty (all this being defensible on libertarian grounds), but the commonwealth is also entitled to use force to defend the true religion and to produce a right of passage for its citizens through foreign territory if it adjudges that permission to do so has been unreasonably withheld (these latter justifications of force *not* being defensible on libertarian grounds). [see *Politica*, 88-89] The commonwealth requires councils to determine general policy issues such as the commonwealth's fundamental laws and the imposition of taxes, because what concerns all should be deliberated on by all. Furthermore, there is wisdom in crowds. And still further, the executive officers of the commonwealth are held in check by a fear of such councils in which complaints can freely be heard and the administrators are required to give an accounting of their administration.

As is the case with all forms of consociation, the consociation that is the realm is formed by agreement, in this case, an agreement on the basic laws. [see *Politica*, 93] These laws, however, must be administered and, to this end, certain administrators or rectors are chosen and entrusted with this task. The relationship between those electing their rectors and the rectors thus chosen is twofold: the electors taken as a whole are superior to their rectors and are indeed their masters ('for the commonwealth or realm does not exist for the king, but the king and every other magistrate exists for the realm and polity.' [*Politica*, 93]); on the other hand, the individuals constituting the electors are subjects of the rectors. [see also *Politica*, 97] By way of analogy, one might say that the electors as a whole are the beneficial owners of the rights of the commonwealth whereas its rectors are its trustees or legal owners. A king or rector, then, can be said to be simultaneously above and below his subjects, but not in the same respect. He is below his subjects when they are taken collectively or corporately; he is above his subjects taken they are taken individually. 'Therefore, these persons—Caesar, king, and prince—are over (*praeesse*) in one relationship and are under (*subesse*) in another, but not over and under in the same relationship; they are, nevertheless, over and under at the same time and with reference to the same interpretation.' [*Politica*, 113]

If rectors, rulers or kings exceed their authority they lose their status as rectors and revert to being private persons so that they aren't owed obedience in those matters in which they are acting *ultra vires*. They can exceed their powers in at least three ways—first, by commanding that to be done which is prohibited by God or by commanding that to be omitted which is required by God; second, by commanding that to be done which is contrary to charity or by commanding that to be omitted which is required by charity; and third, by seeking their personal profit instead of the good of the realm. Sovereignty, which is the supreme power of doing that which relates to the spiritual and material welfare of the members of the consociation, inheres in the people taken as a whole in its corporative existence. Magistrates and kings are functionaries who are subject to the people as a whole. The king or chief magistrate is in essence merely an executive of the sovereign power of the people. The relationship between king and people is asymmetrical: the king's obligation to the people is absolute whereas the obligation of the people to the king is conditional. Should the king fail in his duty and descend into tyranny, the people may resist and even depose him. Althusius follows the Calvinist (and, indeed, standard medieval) position on resistance to rulers in holding that such resistance belongs to the people in their corporate capacity and is to be exercised through their representatives, the ephors. Private individuals are limited to passive resistance to such commands as are unlawful and to self-defence against the invasion of natural rights.

Althusius conceives of two kinds of rector—ephors and the supreme magistrate. Ephors are the representatives of the commonwealth who are entrusted with the task of appointing the supreme magistrate and in assisting him once appointed. They are chosen by the consent of the whole people. The ephors also exercise a supervisory role, ensuring that the supreme magistrate acts within his powers and does nothing that is ruinous or detrimental to the realm. In case of need, they can remove a tyrannical supreme magistrate. They also act as *de facto* administrators of the commonwealth in the event of an interregnum brought about by the magistrate's captivity, death, insanity, prodigality, or any other impediment that should incapacitate him. [see *Politica*, 103; 107]

Althusius's ruminations on these matters aren't purely theoretical but are, to a certain extent, a theoretical codification of the existing structure of the Holy Roman Empire. This becomes clear when he says that 'In the German polity such general ephors are the electors, or the seven men of the imperium, of which three are ecclesiastical and four secular. The ecclesiastical are the archbishop of Mainz…the archbishop of Cologne, and the archbishop of Treves. The secular ephors are the king of Bohemia, the prince of the Rhenish Palatinate, the duke of Saxony, and the duke of Brandenburg.' [*Politica*, 117] Ideally, a commonwealth or realm will have ephors but where it does not, then the functions of the ephors are undertaken by 'the consent of the entire people, proposed or obtained by tribes, by curial or centurial divisions, or individually…' [*Politica*, 118]

A covenant or contract subsists between the supreme magistrate and his subjects, which covenant imposes obligations on both parties. The obligations fall first upon the supreme magistrate and then upon his subjects for 'the people can exist without a magistrate, but a magistrate cannot exist without a people… the people creates the magistrate rather than the contrary.' [*Politica*, 122] Failure on the part of either party to observe the terms of the covenant releases the other party from its obligations. The supreme magistrate exercises only those powers that have been explicitly conceded to him and cannot exercise absolute power. Althusius believes that absolute power could serve only the pleasure of the supreme magistrate and, if exercised by any magistrate, would destroy justice. Were that to happen then, echoing the words of St Augustine, the realm would become a band of robbers. [see *Politica*, 124-125] In fact, the supreme right in any commonwealth can't be communicated to anyone, not even the supreme magistrate, and remains with the body of the universal consociation. In taking the approach Althusius does to the supreme magistrate,

George Sabine believes that he 'continued and elaborated the anti-royalist theory of the French Calvinists.' [Sabine, 416] An interesting development, resulting from Althusius's theory of the composition of the state not from individuals but from larger bodies is that, in the event of a breach of contract, such bodies may withdraw from the state. This amounts to a justification of secession.

The *Politica* contains an interesting but not particularly novel account of law. What *is* novel, however, is a chapter on tyranny, a chapter that did not appear in the first, 1603, edition of the work. A ruler does not become a tyrant simply because he isn't perfect in the performance of his office. People vary in their abilities and men, even rulers, are sometimes weak and irresolute. Even behaviour tending towards tyranny does not make a ruler a tyrant. Echoing the similar position taken by St Thomas, Althusius observes that 'the wicked life of a magistrate does not invalidate his royal authority, just as a marriage is not dissolved by every misdeed committed by one mate against another.... not every misdeed of a magistrate deprives him of his sceptre, but only that in which he, having accepted and then neglected the just rule of administration, acts contrary to the fundamentals and essence of human consociation, and destroys civil and social life...' [*Politica*, 192]

If a ruler does become a tyrant, either by overthrowing or by destroying the fundamental laws of the commonwealth or by carrying out his functions in a manner contrary to piety and justice, what remedy, if any, is to be had? Resistance, says Althusius, and, if necessary, deposition. By whom? Well, not by any ordinary citizen but by the optimates or ephors or, in cases where there are no ephors, by public defenders constituted as the circumstances require. [*Politica*, 195] In adopting this position, Althusius takes the more or less standard Calvinist line. He writes, 'the position we have thus far taken about the ephors applies only to public persons. It plainly does not apply to private persons when the magistrate is a tyrant by practice [*tyrannus exercitio*] because they do not have the use and right of the sword (*usus et jus gladii*), nor may they employ this right...This is to be understood, however, in such a manner that these private persons are not forced to be servants of tyranny, or to do anything that is contrary to God. Under these circumstances, they should flee to another place so that they avoid obedience not by resisting, but by fleeing. Nevertheless, when manifest force is applied by the magistrate to private persons, then, in case of the need to defend their lives, resistance is permitted to them. For in this case private persons are armed against the magistrate who lays violent hands upon them by the natural law (*jus naturale*) and the arrangements constituting kings.' [*Politica*, 196] It should be evident from this that Althusius allows little scope for individual resistance to misbehaving rulers except in respect of personal self-defence.

As mentioned, one of the functions of the ephors is to supervise the supreme magistrate. Althusius's justification of resistance to tyranny even by the ephors is far removed from the freewheeling account given by Buchanan and it is hedged around with restrictive conditions. In resisting tyranny, the ephors must act as a body and not as individuals. The resistance must be, as far as possible, defensive rather than offensive, and even such defensive action must endure only so long as the tyranny endures and only in respect of the ruler's actions that are tyrannical. For Althusius, a ruler has to behave exceptionally badly before tyrannicide is justified. 'In one instance only can he [the tyrant] justly be killed, namely, when his tyranny has been publicly acknowledged and is incurable: when he madly scorns all laws, brings about the ruin and destruction of the realm, overthrows civil society among men so far as he is able, and rages violently; and when there are no other remedies available.' [*Politica*, 199] One might be forgiven for thinking that if things have to come to such a pass before a tyrant can be killed, it may be a case of too little too late.

Althusius's ideas on sovereignty were to a certain extent in competition with those of Jean Bodin and in that intellectual struggle, Althusius was the loser. Both thinkers thought of sovereignty in more or less the same terms save that where Bodin located it in the chief officer of the state, Althusius located it in the people taken corporately. Had the Althusian and not the Bodinian conception of the locus of sovereignty prevailed, the course of political history might well have been very different. If Althusius was the right man in the wrong place and the wrong time, our next writer most definitely picked the right time and the right place in which to operate. Whether he was the right man is quite another question.

Notes

1 Jacques Almain, rector of the University of Paris in the early sixteenth century, had argued that 'no community can wholly alienate its authority to a ruler any more than an individual can renounce his right to self-preservation...' [Luscombe 1982, 764]

2 Grabhill, n. 54 in Althusius 2006.

3 'The empire was neither a single command chain nor a neat pyramid with the emperor at the pinnacle. Instead, the Empire was an idealized overarching framework encompassing multiple elements that were both internally hierarchical and that interrelated in complex patterns characterized by inequality.' [Wilson 2016, 181-182] 'The imperial constitution,' writes Roberts, 'was supposed to provide the framework for the affairs of about 400 different states, statelets, and notables north of the Alps. There were princes who were the feudal vassals of the emperor but in no other way subordinate to him; dozens of independent imperial cities exercising imperial powers within their territories; the lands of the imperial family, themselves usually scattered and disunited; fifty princes of the Church who ruled in their lands like lay sovereigns; hundreds of minor noblemen—the imperial knights—subject to the emperor as feudal dependants; the Bohemian and Silesian lands which actually belonged to the crown of Hungary (itself outside the empire) and so on and on.' [Roberts 1997, 201]

4 The word which Carney translates as 'association' is *consociandi* for which I am going from here on to use the neologistic transliteration 'consociation' in referencing both Althusius's text and Carney's "Introduction", as the term 'association' for Althusius has the ring of the involuntary whereas what Althusius wants to emphasise is the voluntary coming together of men on various levels.

5 *Politica*, 17; emphasis added.

6 Althusius sees danger in either an excess or deficit of population in any given commonwealth. Too many people and there is a danger of corruption, as happened with Rome; too few, and the commonwealth's safety is compromised.

7 Roger Williams was to make a similar claim in his 1644 *The Bloudy Tenent of Persecution, for Cause of Conscience, Discussed, in a Conference betweene Truth and Peace*, remarking that the sovereign, origin, and foundation of civil power lies in the people. John M. Barry describes this claim as 'original and revolutionary', which in many ways it was but, as we can see, Althusius anticipated him by at least thirty years. See Barry 2012, 335; see also Zagorin, 196-208.

Chapter 17

HUGO GROTIUS

Men did not at first unite themselves in civil society by any special command
from God, but of their own free will, out of a sense of the inability
of separate families to repel violence
—Hugo Grotius

It is lawful for any Man to engage himself as a Slave to whom he pleases; as appears
both by the *Hebrew* and *Roman* Laws. Why should it not therefore be as lawful for
a People that are at their own Disposal, to deliver up themselves to any one or more
Persons, and transfer the right of governing them upon him or them, without reserving
any Share of that Right to themselves?
—Hugo Grotius

To go from Johannes Althusius to Hugo Grotius (1583-1645) is in many ways to step backwards in time and in thought to find oneself, politically speaking, in the company of such as Luther and Calvin. If Althusius can be pedantic and repetitious, Grotius is ponderously prolix. Both writers are prone to stuff their works with supporting citations from classical and contemporary authorities but in any fairly judged contest, Grotius would surely be the winner by a country mile. The work for which Grotius is best known, *The Rights of War and Peace*, comes in at a mentally and physically hernia-inducing 1,900 pages! So much for matters of style; what of the substance? Here, matters are somewhat but not universally better. In fact, Grotius is confused and confusing on the topic of law, the key concept in his most significant work, and on the subject of sovereignty, his views are regressive. Brian Tierney attempts to make the best case for Grotius that he can, remarking that 'The diversity of ideas that one can find in Grotius's writings should not finally be considered a weakness' but this charitable estimate of Grotius's work come perilously close to arguing that incoherence is a virtue. [Tierney 2014, 247] It isn't often that I find myself in sympathy with Jean-Jacques Rousseau but with his judgement on Grotius expressed in his *Émile*, minus its harshness and more than a little suspicion of jealousy, I can find myself in tune. 'Grotius,' he writes, 'the master of all the savants in this subject [*le droit politique*], is only a child; and, what is worse, a dishonest child. When I hear Grotius praised to the skies and Hobbes covered with execration I see how far sensible men read or understand these two authors.' [Rousseau 1969, 836]

If Grotius is a poor writer and a confused thinker, why then does he occupy the position he does in the history of thought? The answer to this question might be that he is famous because he was the inventor or discoverer of the idea of international law. But he wasn't! Much of the work which Grotius gets the credit for originating was done by the Spanish jurists before he ever wrote. With the utmost charity in his heart, William Dunning writes, 'Without detracting from the just fame of Grotius, it is necessary for the careful student to point out the currents that were manifesting themselves in various philosophical channels before he wrote and that set straight toward the system which he presented.' [Dunning 1905, 153] But the work of the Spanish jurists was Catholic and scholastic and on these two counts unacceptable to a northern European culture that was increasingly Protestant and humanistic. On the other hand, there were Protestant writers, such as Oldendorp, Hemming and Winkler who developed theories of law that dovetailed smoothly with the work of their Catholic Spanish contemporaries but which failed to have the effect that Grotius's was to have perhaps because their work was more Protestant than humanistic. Taking everything into account, I think it can fairly be said that Grotius's major claim to fame was that, if he wasn't the first, he was the most influential thinker to re-apply the venerable notion of natural law to the newly emerging field of inter-state relations. [see Tierney 2014, 215-247] Whatever the just solution to this conundrum, Grotius was the right man, at the right time, in the right place, with the right approach.

Even with his limitations as an author, there can be no doubting that Grotius was a man of immense ability. He was a child prodigy, learned from the earliest age in mathematics, literature, jurisprudence and philosophy. At the age of thirty-three he became in effect the principal civil servant for Holland and West Friesland. He took sides in the violently polemical religious, political and economic disputes raging throughout this region and found himself on the losing side, as a result of which he was sentenced to life imprisonment. He escaped to France and it was here that he produced the work that was to bring him universal renown, *The Rights of War and Peace*.[1] In time, he became surplus to requirements in France and emigrated to Sweden only to be returned eventually as the Swedish ambassador to France. Oh, the ironies of Fate!

INTERNATIONAL RELATIONS AND WAR

The Rights of War and Peace is very much wider in its scope than its title might immediately suggest. It is, in fact, a treatise on the law of nature and the law of nations. In the classic debate between *phusis* and *nomos*, between nature and convention, Grotius, for the most part, takes the side of nature. Man is naturally both rational and social. Grotius is willing to accept the cynical position that men associate with each other, driven by a natural desire for self-preservation, but this is only part of the story and not the most interesting part. The natural desire for self-preservation isn't the only natural desire we have. We also desire by nature to live life in association with others and, in so doing, we recognise the good of justice. Justice, then, isn't merely conventional but a necessary constitutive part of social life, such a social life being intrinsic to the good for man.

The time at which Grotius wrote *The Rights of War and Peace* was the time at which it was becoming evident that the religious and political divisions of European Christendom were here to stay and, perhaps more significantly, that the ever more highly centralised post-medieval sovereign states were also here to stay. The practical question then arose: how were these sovereign and independent states to relate to one another lawfully when they acknowledged no common superior? The most spectacular way in which one state can relate to another is through the violence of war, a condition of which Grotius had first-hand experience. Grotius is, of course, best known for his analysis of this particular aspect of inter-state relations, namely the question of whether and in what circumstances violent inter-state action—war—may be justified.

Well, then, can there be just wars? Grotius answers, yes. He accepts that not every use of force or violence by a party is necessarily unjustified. It is so only if it involves an infringement of the rights or the possessions of another. (This is close to the libertarian zero-aggression principle.) Defensive wars to protect persons and property against aggression are clearly just. Offensive wars may be just if they are waged to prosecute injuries or to inflict punishment which is deserved, such being the case when contracts or promises are violated. Defensive and offensive wars are both bilateral affairs, involving a putative injured party and an alleged aggressor. Nevertheless, Grotius allows for third-party interventions where the intervening agent isn't directly the object of any injury. Once again, relying on classical precedents, Grotius here believes that rulers have a duty to enforce the law of nature; if that is being violated by the rulers of another state, intervention is justified. Whether such intervention is expedient or not is, of course, another question. [see Kaldor 1998, passim] This is a particular instance of the limitations of sovereignty as Grotius sees it. Sovereignty does not absolve rulers from adhering to the law of nature as it absolves them from submission to positive law.

On this issue of third party intervention, Grotius finds himself in opposition to those, such as Francisco Vitoria, who hold that force or violence is justifiable only if exercised by those who have been aggressed against (or their agents) or by those who have jurisdiction over those who are aggressed. He writes, 'We must also know, that Kings, and those who are invested with a Power equal to that of Kings, have a Right to exact punishments, not only for Injuries committed against themselves, or their Subjects, but likewise, for those which do not peculiarly concern them, but which are, in any Persons whatso-ever, grievous Violations of the Law of Nature or Nations. For the Liberty of consulting the Benefit of human Society, by Punishments, which at first, as we have said, was in every particular Person, does not, since Civil Societies, and Courts of justice, have been instituted, reside in those who are possessed of the supreme Power....Nay, it is so much more honourable, to revenge other Peoples Injuries rather than their own...'[2]

But war is only one aspect of inter-state relations, even if it is the most spectacular and destructive of them. Grotius's interest extended beyond the issue of war and peace to trying to find a basis for universal legal rules in a reconsideration and reconceptualisation of the venerable notions of *ius naturale* and *ius gentium.* Grotius's most important contribution, then, wasn't so much to an intra-state analysis in matters such as, for example, sovereignty but to an analysis of the relationships *between* the now sovereign states, each free from the legal control of another. With the collapse of a common Chris-tendom, however nebulous Christendom may have been at that stage of history, and with the increasing irrelevance of the Holy Roman Empire, the question of the relationship to one another of the new autonomous states became urgent. Without a common superior, it would appear that their mutual relations would have to be conducted outside the sphere of law, subject only to considerations of expedience and power. 'The rise of the absolute monarchies and the more or less frank acceptance of a Machiavellian conception of the relations between them made force the arbiter in the dealings of states with states,' writes Sabine. 'To this must be added the effects of the religious wars which followed the Reformation, bringing to international relations the intrinsic bitterness of religious hatred and affording the color of good conscience to the most barefaced schemes of dynastic aggrandizement.' [Sabine, 421] If there were to be a source of norms that could govern inter-state relations, then it would have to be found where all could accept it, despite their particular differences of language, culture and religion. That being so, it is scarcely surprising that Grotius turned to the venerable idea of the natural law, this time shorn of any essential connection to religious revelation, a naturalised natural law, as it were.

Of course, the idea of natural law isn't immediately acceptable to everyone so Grotius chooses to confront the sceptical challenge as expressed by Carneades, the critic of Stoicism. For the Sceptics, human action is governed by self-interest, and law is merely a conventional social apparatus whose primary justification is a matter of prudence rather than one of justice. Grotius's response to this criticism is to point out that human society results not just from prudential considerations but from an inherent sociableness, although utility plays a supplementary role. 'Human nature itself is the mother of natural law, as it drives us to seek a common society even if there is no shortage of resources,' he writes, 'But utility is annexed to the natural law: the author of nature willed that as individuals we should be weak and in need of many things if we are to lead a good life, in order that we should be all the more impelled into living in society…' [Grotius 1625b, 1749]

In the *Prolegomena* to *The Rights of War and Peace*, Grotius distinguishes between two possible impulses to social cooperation—a natural inclination towards sociability and an association based on agreement in the service of self-interest. Sometimes he seems to favour one account and sometimes the other. Do human beings come together in society because they have determined that it is in their interests so to do, or do they congregate because they have a natural desire to live with others of their kind? In the end, Grotius seems to believe that human beings live in society simply because that is how they are constructed, whether such cohabitation is in their interests or not. As it turns out, cohabitation *is* productive of utilitarian advantages to all, but that's a happy accident. The appearance of confusion here may, once again, be the result of a failure clearly to draw a distinction that Grotius flirts with, a distinction between society, on the one hand, and the state, on the other. Using this distinction, society would be the outcome of a natural human propensity towards sociability, whereas the state would be the outcome of an explicit contract or agreement. 'Men did not at first unite themselves in Civil Society by any special Command from GOD, but of their own free Will, out of a Sense of the Inability of separate Families to repel Violence...' [I, iv, 7—358] As a rationalist, Grotius has confidence in the power of human reason to hit upon the principles of conduct that will be conducive to the needs of human social existence.

CONTRACT

Whatever the ultimate justification of their theories of natural law, the thinkers of this early modern period, Grotius included, tended to take for granted that the bindingness of an obligation upon an agent derived from that agent's free assumption of that obligation. The moral force of an obligation derives from an inward normative necessity, not merely from an outward threat of sanction. The relevance of this to the matter of political obligation was that it undermined the idea that such obligation could be legitimately imposed without the consent of those on whom it was to be imposed. This idea, the idea of a contract or a compact, was to play a prominent role in political thought from this time forward. It is true, as we have seen, that the germ of such an idea was already present in the thought of the high Middle Ages; however, it comes into renewed prominence during this period, a prominence which, despite much criticism, it has never since quite lost. The dominant anglophone political treatise of the last third of the twentieth century, John Rawls's *A Theory of Justice*, is merely the latest, if not the least bizarre, in a long line of contract theories.

If there is to be a contract that gives rise to political obligation then, of necessity, there must be a prior condition in which such a contract does not exist. This pre-contractual condition is characterised by different thinkers in different ways (see, for example, the very different ways in which Hobbes and Locke treat it) but the term of art by which this pre-contractual condition has generally come to be known is 'the state of nature'. Most thinkers take what they have to explain to be the transition from individuals in a pre-contractual state of nature to the post-contractual social or political order. Grotius, however, realised that not only can individuals be conceived to be in a state of nature vis-à-vis one another but the states resulting from the contract among individuals could themselves be conceived to be in a state of nature in respect of each other and so be in a position to contract with one another.

There are different ways to conceive of these contractual relations. The members of a set of people can contract with each other in a series of independent mutual horizontal relationships. On the other hand, a set of people can agree jointly to organise a group and set it up with a constitution so that they together form a kind of corporation of which each individual contractor is a member. It goes without saying that different political thinkers conceived of the contract (or contracts) in different ways. As we shall see, Hobbes recognised only the horizontal contract that brought the ruler into being, the ruler not being party to the contract and his sovereignty not conditional upon performance. Locke's account of contract is ambiguous. Althusius was of a mind to conceive two contracts; one horizontal, by which a people agreed among themselves to bind themselves together; and a second, vertical, by which this now bound-together corporate body contracted with its rector or rulers. A theory of contract just as such is indifferent in respect of the political character of the resultant state. Whereas Hobbes and Spinoza had it give rise to a form of unlimited absolutism, Locke and Althusius had it give rise to a form of limited power. Grotius emphasised the moral limits that circumscribed rulers without, however, full-bloodedly justifying revolution or resistance.

There are, broadly, two ways in which one can think about the relationship between man and society. One can start with society and take as one's problem the task of finding space within that society for the individual. This is the general trend of classical thought. The modern approach is to start with the individual and then the problem becomes one of justifying or explaining society. 'The individual is both logically and ethically prior,' writes Sabine. 'To the philosophy of the seventeenth century relations always appeared thinner than substances; man was the substance, society the relation. It was this assumed priority of the individual which became the most marked and the most persistent quality of the theory of natural law, and the clearest differentia of the modern from the medieval theory.' [Sabine, 433]

Ius Naturale and Ius Gentium

For Grotius, those acts are right (*ius*) or just which aren't fundamentally destructive of man's life in society, destructive of the essential order which every society requires. Theft, for example, destroys trust and so cannot be just. One can see the libertarian zero-aggression principle assimilating itself to Grotius's notion of justice in this respect. Still more libertarian vistas appear when we come to Grotius's second notion of right (*ius*) which is the right to do and to have, to act and to possess. This looks like an anticipation of the modern, subjective, notion of right that belongs to man as man rather than man as defined by status or property relations. This is perhaps to go further than Grotius was prepared to go though an unambiguously subjective account of right would appear in the work of Thomas Hobbes. And, of course, right (*ius*) has the standard meaning of law.

As law, right (*ius*) is divided by Grotius in the following way which indicates clearly his understanding of the often vexed relationship between the *ius naturale* (natural law) and the *ius gentium* (law of nations). The first division is between the *ius naturale* (natural law) which is an emanation of reason, and volitional law which, as the name suggests, is a creature of the will. Volitional law is of two kinds, human or divine depending on whether the will in question is human or divine. Divine law is given to us through revelation. Human law has three kinds: the first is non-civil law which might be described as the commands issuing from those forms of authority that are natural, such as those of the father in the family; the second is the standard civil or municipal law regulating human affairs within a particular jurisdiction; and the third is the *ius gentium* which derives from the will of all or from the will of many people.

Before we get to a more detailed treatment of the various forms of law, let us broadly consider the relation between the *ius naturale* and the *ius gentium*. The *ius naturale* is grounded on reason while the *ius gentium* is based on will. Their subject matter may well coincide, at least in part, but whereas the *ius gentium* is changeable, the *ius naturale* is not. Moreover, the *ius gentium* belongs on the volitional side of the great divide, attaches to only one part of the basic division within volitional law and is still only one of the three parts of *that* division. Grotius offers an example, not perhaps perfectly perspicuous, to illustrate the difference between the two types of law. By the law of nature, he thinks, one person can't be made responsible for the debts or obligations of another. Nevertheless, by the law of nations, citizens are responsible for the debts and obligations of their rulers.

Although Grotius held that no man is a slave by nature, he conceded that slavery can be voluntarily entered into or inflicted for wrongdoing, and slavery that arises in this way is in accord with natural law. The enslavement of war captives is, however, a matter of the *ius gentium* and isn't an arrangement of which Grotius is particularly enamoured. What Grotius is groping towards here would seem to be a distinction between legal rights and moral rights so that the enslavement of war captives would be legally in order but, at the same time, morally reprehensible. Grotius, however, has but one word at his disposal, *ius*, which word, like charity, has to cover a legal and moral multitude so that there's a constant tendency in his thinking towards the conflation of the legal and the moral orders.

While there's little in Grotius's treatment of *ius naturale* that can't be found elsewhere, his account had the advantage of being tailored to its practical application to the problems of his time. As we have seen, law, for Grotius, was either natural or positive, based on reason or on will. Natural law he defined as 'the Rule and Dictate of right Reason, shewing the Moral Deformity or Moral Necessity there is in any Act, according to its Suitableness or Unsuitableness to a reasonable Nature and consequently that such an Act is either forbid or commanded by GOD, the author of Nature.' [I, i,10,1] The presence of God in this definition is, technically, otiose, because even if there were no God, the law of nature would still be what it is and would still be binding on all. Grotius makes this point clearly in the *Prolegomena*: 'What I have just said would be relevant even if we were to suppose...that there is no God, or that human affairs are of no concern to him...' [Grotius 1625b, 1748] The law of nature is as freestanding and as independent of human variability as are the laws of mathematics. Acts judged according to this standard are right or wrong considered in themselves and not because they violate the command of any legislator, either divine or human. This natural law or natural right is incapable of change, so that not even God can change it any more than he can (*pace* Descartes) make a triangle to have four sides. Grotius writes, 'the Law of Nature is so unalterable that God himself cannot change it. For tho' the Power of God be infinite, yet we may say, that there are some Things to which this infinite Power does not extend, because they cannot be expressed by Propositions that contain any Sense, but manifestly imply a Contradiction. For Instance then, as God himself cannot effect, that twice two should not be four; so neither can he, that what is intrinsically Evil should not be Evil.' [I, i, 10, 5—155]

As we have seen, Grotius divided law into two basic types: natural/rational, on the one hand, and human/volitional, on the other. *Ius gentium* belongs to the human/volitional side of the divide. It derives its authority 'from the Will of all, or at least of many, Nations.' [I, i, 14, 1—163] As the occasion for the emergence of civil law is the aggregated welfare of many individuals, so too, the occasion for the emergence of the *ius gentium* is the aggregated welfare of many nations. Grotius draws a hard and fast distinction between natural law and the law of nations. One is a matter of reason—whatever is rationally consistent with human nature; the other is a matter of will—whatever is in common use among the nations. But as his account of these two different kinds of laws develops, the distinction tends to erode and they begin to converge. William Dunning remarks, 'the rationality of a precept is in last analysis a matter merely of the private judgment of the philosopher; and similarly, in the case of the practice of nations, since uniformity and universality are not deemed discoverable, the usages which constitute the *ius gentium* must be those of the nations which in the judgment of the philosopher are worthy of respect and imitation....The net result of all this elasticity and vagueness in the ultimate standards of both natural and international law is to obliterate all distinction between them and to justify the tendency, which grew continually more manifest after Grotius, to blend the two systems into one, resting upon no deeper an ultimate foundation than the opinions of publicists, among whom Grotius himself always held a first place.' [Dunning 1905, 175-176] This potential confusion between natural law and the law of nations is extremely problematic for Grotius in one of the main uses to which it is to be put, namely, whether a war is to be justified or not. Violations of natural law are a reputable cause for war whereas violations of the law of nations are not necessarily so. That one nation eats its boiled eggs from the little end and another from the big end is scarcely a justification for armed conflict.[3]

Social order, then, is an intrinsic good and the maintenance of that order is the ground of law: 'This care for society,' Grotius writes, 'in accordance with human intellect...is the source of *ius*, properly so-called...' [Grotius 1625b, 1747] The content of that law contains few surprises. It demands that we refrain from taking what belongs to another, restoring whatever we may have that belongs to another, that we keep our promises and make good any losses for which we are responsible. [Grotius 1625b, 1747-1748] The key thing to note about these aspects of the natural law, apart from their complete lack of novelty and surprise, is that they do not result from a compact or agreement. These laws are binding on all men irrespective of whether or not any particular man has explicitly covenanted with another with respect to them. These laws are pre-contractual, universal and unchangeable. All other systems of law—local law, municipal law, and so on—operate within the boundaries set by the natural law.

For libertarians, it is of great interest to note that Grotius clearly rejects certain aspects of the doctrine of 'reasons of state', arguing that the standards of justice that apply to individuals apply equally to states and their rulers. 'If no community can preserve itself without law,' he comments, 'so the community which all human beings, or a multiplicity of nations, construct among themselves certainly requires laws. Cicero recognized this when he said the evil actions should not be committed even for the sake of our country.' [Grotius 1625b, 1751]

RATIONALISM AND CERTAINTY

The seventeenth century was an age whose intellectual life was dominated by the idea of certainty and the centrality of mathematics as the model of rational thought. Political theory and ethics might seem to be only dubiously capable of being arranged on a mathematical model—Aristotle had explicitly denied that the method of mathematics could be applied to the practical sciences—but our seventeenth-century thinkers were impressed by the power of mathematics and the new physics that was coming into being based on it. If axiomatic propositions in law and politics could be discovered then, using reason, theorems could be deduced from them that would share the indubitability of the axioms. Grotius, writes Sabine, 'intended to do for the law just what, as he understood the matter, was being done with success in mathematics or what Galileo was doing for physics.' [Sabine, 425] 'My prime concern,' writes Grotius, 'has been to base my examination of what belongs to the law of nature on ideas which are so certain that nobody can deny them without doing violence to their fundamental being. The principles of natural law are clear and self-evident, to a much higher degree than the things that we perceive with our outward senses...' [Grotius 1625b, 1756] Grotius was somewhat less certain that ethics could attain the rigour of mathematics, a claim that drew upon him the criticism of Samuel Pufendorf. Whatever minor differences may have obtained among our thinkers of this period (apart from Grotius and Pufendorf, one can call to mind Hobbes, Descartes, Leibniz, Galileo and Newton) they all were in thrall to the new mathematical method. 'It would be impossible.' Sabine notes, 'to exaggerate the importance that these conceptions had in the early modern development of social studies. Everywhere the system of natural law was believed to offer the valid scientific line of approach to social disciplines and the scientific guide to social practice....the logical ideals of analysis, simplicity, and self-evident clarity appeared to be equally applicable to all subject-matters. They were...the perfect solvents for authority and mere customary belief." [Sabine, 426, 427]

The characteristics of mathematics most appealing to the Greeks and their modern followers were its certainty and its explanatory power. First, catch a small bunch of axioms.[4] Then, using the heat of reason, cook up a vast structure of theorems, theorems that partake of the same worthiness to be believed that belongs to the original axioms. This mouth-watering prospect made an enormous appeal to Plato and to the members of the Academy whose metaphysics is a philosophical analogue to mathematics. Aristotle's position, of course, differed radically from that of Plato. 'Whereas Plato had maintained that mathematics was the true and deep reality of which the physical world was but a pale reflection, Aristotle claimed mathematics to be but a superficial representation of a piece of physical reality. Such is the contrast between idealism and realism in the ancient world.' [Barrow, 177] With the breakdown of the medieval synthesis and the rise of modern science, the mathematical model re-emerged as the very type of explanation, of power, of clarity. It isn't accidental that two of the three prototypical philosophical Rationalists—Descartes and Leibniz—were first-class mathematicians, inventing or discovering, respectively, co-ordinate geometry and the calculus, and that the third prototypical Rationalist, Spinoza, set out his *Ethics* in a geometrical mode which wasn't just a stylistically charming authorial idiosyncrasy but an acknowledgement of the dominating intellectual position of the mathematical model.

Grotius, then, was a rationalist in an age of rationalism. The attempt to ground law on a rational basis of axiomatic principles from which logical deductions could be made did not, of course, imply a lofty independence of experience and the knowledge to be derived from it. As George Sabine notes, within the boundaries set by rational principles, rationalists 'accepted as a matter of course great bodies of empirical fact that had to be learned by observation.' [Sabine, 427] Although there was a tendency among rationalists of all stripes to regard perceptual experience as a confused form of intellectual knowledge (as the empiricists philosophers of a later age had a converse tendency to regard intellectual knowledge as a refined and effete form of perception) only Leibniz among the great names of the age was inclined to discount empirical knowledge more or less entirely.

Within the category of natural law, Grotius distinguishes, as many of his predecessors had done, between what we might deem to be a basic natural law and a more developed form of natural law which is still not to be confused with positive or civil law. *Basic* natural law designates those matters that flow 'simply and purely from Nature,' while *developed* natural law 'takes Place in Consequence of an established Property, and before all civil Law...' [II, viii, 1—634-635] Basic natural law would obtain in man's pre-political condition while the more developed natural law would obtain in political society but before the development of particular positive laws.

In Grotius's state of nature, where the basic natural law holds sway, every man is the executor of his rights. 'Indeed all Men,' he says, 'have naturally a right to secure themselves from Injuries by Resistance....But civil Society being instituted for the Preservation of Peace, there immediately arises a superior Right in the State over us and ours, so far as is necessary for that End. Therefore the State has a Power to prohibit the unlimited Use of that Right towards every other Person, for maintaining publick Peace and good Order.... for if that promiscuous Right of Resistance should be allowed there would be no longer a State, but a Multitude without Union...' [I, iv, 2—338-339] Although according to Grotius, resistance against other aggressive individuals is to be severely limited in civil society, resistance against one's rulers is completely ruled out, for, as we have seen, he holds to the notion that upon the institution of civil society, individuals irretrievably willed their rights to whoever holds supreme authority. Despite the clear contractual aspects to Grotius's thought, he recognises no form of conditionality that could lead to the revocation of consent and so has a distinctively different perspective on that topic from the anti-monarchic Huguenot thinkers.

Although subject to various usages and interpretations, the idea of *ius gentium* in its original Roman context was applied to private rather than to public law and to that private law inasmuch as it governed non-Roman societies. It took on a further refinement when it came to designate those aspects of the private law of non-Romans that tended to converge on common principles. With the erosion of the distinction between the Roman *ius civile* and the *ius gentium*, the *ius gentium* tended to approach the natural law. 'When under the Empire practically all these peoples became Roman citizens,' writes William Dunning, 'and the dual system of law became unified, *ius gentium* survived as the designation of an ideal hardly distinguishable from *ius naturale*.' [Dunning 1905, 171-172] With the dissolution of the western Roman Empire, the conditions that had given rise to the notion of the *ius gentium* in the first place re-emerged in the newly fragmented political condition of Europe. But now, private relations were extensively covered by the Church's canon law and the Romanised indigenous civil law of the barbarian tribes so that the *ius gentium* tended to be applied not to the relationships between individuals but to the relationship between more or less independent political communities. This inter-national aspect of the *ius gentium* became the common property of the Scholastics generally and eventually found its way to Grotius.

SOVEREIGNTY

Grotius's notion of sovereignty, although superficially allied to the emerging modern notion of that concept, is yet again conditioned by classical norms. The sovereign power is subject to no superior positive legal control (so much is in accord with the modern notion) but it *is* subject to the law of nature and the law of nations (so much is in accord with classical and medieval notions). Civil or municipal law has as its root the idea of obligation arising from consent and that obligation is derived from the natural law; civil or municipal law is thus radically conditioned by natural law.

In respect of his conceptions of sovereignty and the state, Sabine takes Grotius to regress from the clarity achieved by Althusius. Sovereignty is a power free from the legal control of another, a condition of being *sui juris* as it were, and the state is its common subject. Where Althusius took sovereignty to reside in the people as a whole, Grotius, like Bodin, accepted the Roman idea of a *lex regia* by which the people could and did alienate irrevocably their sovereign power to another. Here, Grotius shows his predilection for classical thought. Once transferred from the people to their ruler, power remains with the ruler and isn't capable of being re-assumed by the people whether by revolution or by less drastic means. The primary purpose of government, for Grotius, is the maintenance of peace and this takes priority over one's right to defend oneself against a ruler's abuse of authority. Except in very specific circumstances Grotius says, 'I do not see how it can be lawful for any private Man, either to dethrone or kill an Usurper.' [I iv, 19—381]

Sabine is right. Grotius's discussion of sovereignty is a distinct regression on that proposed by Althusius. He defines sovereignty as the moral power of governing a state. [I, iii, 6—257]. Power is supreme when its acts 'are not subject to another's Power, so that they cannot be made void by any other human Will.' [I, iii, 7—259] Such sovereign power, for Grotius, is a matter of right that attaches to its holder as any other right may attach. It may be completely owned or be had merely as a usufruct or be had for a limited term but, however owned, there's no difference in power. Strangely, Grotius allows that sovereignty may be divided between, say, King and people. 'Though the sovereign Power be but one, and of itself undivided, consisting of those Parts above mentioned, with the Addition of Supremacy, that is…accountable to none, yet it sometimes happens, that it is divided….Thus though there was but one *Roman Empire*, yet it often happened, that one ruled in the *Eastern* Part, and another in the *Western*….so also it may happen, that the People in chusing a King, may reserve certain Acts of Sovereignty to themselves, and confer others on the King absolutely and without Restriction.' [I, iii, 17—305-306] It is hard to escape the suspicion that Grotius's account of sovereignty is a little less than fully coherent. 'That Grotius's conception of sovereignty falls short, in respect to logical precision and coherence of that of Bodin and Althusius, is self-evident,' writes Dunning. 'A power that is supreme, yet bound by pledges; that is at once a unity and divisible; that is complete yet limited to usufruct and terminable at a fixed time; and that inheres equally in protector and protected, in lord and in vassal,—is a confusing kind of concept.' [Dunning 1905, 183]

What *is* clear in Grotius's account is his resolute opposition to any popular account of sovereignty, such as we find in Althusius. He writes, 'here we must first reject their Opinion, who will have the Supreme Power to be always, and without Exception, in the People; so that they may restrain or punish their Kings, as often as they abuse their Power.' [I, iii, 8—260-261] The issue here is whether a people *can* irretrievably transfer their rights to another, that is, whether such rights are completely alienable. Grotius argues that since voluntary slavery is possible for an individual, there can be no principled objection to the idea that a people as a whole, in a manner analogous to slavery, may transfer to another their right to rule themselves. 'It is lawful,' he says, 'for any Man to engage himself as a Slave to whom he pleases; as appears both by the *Hebrew* and *Roman* Laws. Why should it not therefore be as lawful for a People that are at their own Disposal, to deliver up themselves to any one or more Persons, and transfer the right of governing them upon him or them, without reserving any Share of that Right to themselves?' [I, iii, 8—261] Even if the notion of voluntary slavery for an individual is coherent, it doesn't immediately follow that it would be coherent for an entire society. Even if (as seems unlikely) all the individual extant members of that society were to consent to enslavement, how could that bind their future children who weren't party to the contract? It is, I think, not insignificant that these passages reveal a conception of political rule that make it to be analogous to the slavery of an entire people to its ruler, thus conflating the concepts of *imperium* and *dominium*.

Though political society may be entered into by means of a contract, Grotius denies that such a contract entails that there is any necessary reciprocal dependence of King and people such that, if a King were to abuse his power the people would be released from their obligation. Not only does Grotius reject the idea that sovereignty remains in the people, he also rejects a common theme of the antimonarchists that government is for the good of the governed. A ruler may rule in such a way that he brings about the good of those he governs but he isn't in any way obliged so to do. It follows from this that Grotius will have no truck with any supposed right of resistance to one's rulers, save that one is not obliged to obey a command that conflicts with Divine law, although one is obliged to endure the punishment for such disobedience. As we have seen, a distinction is often drawn between legitimate rulers who exceed or abuse their powers and those who usurp power illegitimately. Even those who had scruples about resisting badly behaving legitimate rulers generally accepted a right of resistance against usurpers. But here, again, Grotius is unwilling to endorse resistance. He concedes that there may be some very limited conditions under which such resistance could be justified but he holds that prudentially 'I do not see how it can be lawful for any private man, either to dethrone or kill an Usurper.' [I. iv, 19—381] Dunning concludes, 'By his doctrine of sovereignty Grotius wins no special place in the development of political theory. He ranges himself with Bodin, Suarez, Barclay and the other advocates of monarchy, and hardly strengthens the case that they had already presented. From the scientific point of view his influence on this phase of theory was distinctly reactionary; for his treatment of sovereign power as a private right, subject to the rules of private law, introduced an element of confusion into the conception that has been perpetuated under the influence of his great name, to the present day.' [Dunning 1905, 189]

With the writings of Bodin, Althusius and Grotius, we have moved gradually but inexorably from the end of the Middle Ages to the beginnings of modernity. Whatever lingering remnants of medieval thought may attach to these writers, when we come to the writings of Thomas Hobbes, we find ourselves in a very different intellectual world.

Notes

1 References to Grotius without further ascription will be to *The Rights of War and Peace* and will be given by book, chapter, section and paragraph—so that I, i, 10, 1 signifies book one, chapter 1, section 10 and paragraph 1—and also by page number to the Tuck edition.
2 II, xx, 40, 1—102.
3 See *Gulliver's Travels*, Part 1, chapter 4.
4 Our word axiom comes from the Greek ἀξίωμα, meaning 'that which is thought worthy or fit, that which commends itself as self-evident.' *Oxford English Dictionary.*

Chapter 18

LEVIATHAN—THAT MORTAL GOD: THOMAS HOBBES

A FREE-MAN, is he, that in those things,
which by his strength and wit he is able to do,
is not hindred to doe what he hath a will to
—Thomas Hobbes

War is peace. Freedom is slavery. Ignorance is strength
—George Orwell

W hoever else might possibly be omitted from a history of political thought, Thomas Hobbes (1588-1679) isn't such a one. His ideas—for the most part, clear and consistent but always controversial—have been enormously influential in political thinking and are especially challenging to any libertarian who would wish to see the state minimised or eliminated. That said, there are elements of his thought that any liberal would welcome. He may well be, as George Sabine thinks, 'the greatest writer on political philosophy that the English-speaking peoples have produced,' although I would tend rather to see it as a two-man contest between Hobbes and Locke. [Sabine, 457] In any event, he produced the 'first full-scale politico-theoretical treatise written in the English language,' one which 'explained the fundamental nature of the modern territorial state in a rational way.' [Malan, 78]

Hobbes was born near the little town of Malmesbury in the English West Country in the year of the Spanish Armada. His family circumstances were modest but, despite this, he managed to attend the University of Oxford and graduated from there in 1608. He immediately accepted an appointment to work for the wealthy and politically important Cavendish family with which he was to be closely associated for most of his career. He was an outstanding classical scholar and all his early works were in this area of thought. His employment with the Cavendish family frequently took him to Continental Europe and he became personally acquainted with, among others, Mersenne, Gassendi and Galileo. The writing for which he is best known today dates from his maturity. He was fifty-two years old when the *Elements of Law* was written, fifty-four when *De Cive* was published in Paris, and sixty-three when *Leviathan* appeared. He had an appointment as a mathematics tutor to the Prince of Wales in the exiled English Court in Paris but the publication of *Leviathan* brought about his exclusion from the Court and he returned to England in 1652. Despite this exclusion, when Charles II was restored to the throne, Hobbes was well treated by the returning royalist regime and he died peacefully in 1679.

His three principal works: *The Elements of Law, De Cive* and *Leviathan*, all concern themselves with more or less the same theme, except that *Leviathan* has a whole lot more to say on the topic of religion than the other two.[1] In fact, over one half of *Leviathan* is about religion, which half some take to be the most important part of the book. Richard Tuck, for example, remarks that 'It is reasonable to say that it is Parts III and IV of *Leviathan* which constitute the prime purpose of the work.' [Tuck, xxxix] Whatever justification there may be for this judgement, I think it fair to say that this isn't a view that would command general agreement. In any event, the first two parts of *Leviathan*—'Of Man', and 'Of Common-wealth'—are the ones that attract the attention of political philosophers and it is these parts that will be the focus of attention in this chapter.

Perhaps more than any other political philosopher, Hobbes's political philosophy is meant to be a consistent and integral part of his overall thought. He was, remarks John Plamenatz, 'a philosopher before he became a political theorist, and he applied philosophical methods acquired independently of the study of politics to the solution of political problems.' [Plamenatz, 117] Hobbes's overall thought was fundamentally materialist. In many ways, he could be seen as a seventeenth century reincarnation of Lucretius. For Hobbes, all that ultimately exists is matter in motion. No matter how complicated the world of our experience may seem on first inspection, Hobbes believes it can nevertheless be fully explained in terms of some basic material and the movement of that material. The animate world, he believed, including man's body and his mind, ultimately consisted of forms of matter in motion, although more complicated forms than the merely physical, and even the extremely complex social and political world too was explicable in materialistic terms. 'Hobbes's aim' remarks Elman Service, 'was to describe human behavior in terms of a kind of social physics.' [Service, 24]

Aristotle had postulated that when it came to explanations, there were four basic questions that one could ask and attempt to answer. These were—what is something made of? (material cause); what kind of thing is it? (formal cause); what is its purpose or function? (final cause); and how did it come to be? (efficient cause). As modern science emerged from the medieval world, it did so largely because it rejected as methodologically inappropriate the search for final causes in relation to inanimate objects. Objects did not fall to earth because they desired a resting place on the earth's surface but because of the force of gravity. Teleological explanations—explanations in terms of ends or purposes—however, remained central to the explanation of human action. As a card-carrying materialist, Hobbes treated all of nature—human nature as well as non-human nature—as a vast system of mechanical causes from which purpose was to be excluded. Just as the world of physics is the complex result of a system of mechanical interactions, so too is the world of human beings, individually and collectively. George Sabine remarks that Hobbes 'exhibited human nature as governed by a single fundamental law and in his politics he exhibited the working of this law in the specific case of social groups. The method was fundamentally deductive.' [Sabine, 459] As was the case with many other seventeenth century thinkers, Hobbes was hugely impressed by the power of mathematics and logical deduction. This was the age of the great Rationalists: Descartes, Leibniz and Spinoza, two of whom, as already mentioned, were mathematicians of note. What impressed all these thinkers, Hobbes also, was the power of what we would now call the axiomatic method. In employing this method, a thinker starts with a small number of axioms, as few as possible, and then, using only pure reasoning, deduces from these axioms, a rich and complicated set of theorems (deductions), all interconnected and all derived, in a strict logical chain, from the basic axioms. The *locus classicus* for such a method is, of course, Euclid's *Elements*.[2]

Things can go wrong in attempting to use the axiomatic method in two ways. First, one can make a mistake in reasoning, so that a purported theorem (conclusion) does not in fact follow from what comes before; or, more significantly, one's axioms may not be quite as axiomatic as one think. Putting it more positively, if one gets one's axioms right and doesn't make any mistakes in reasoning, everything will be well; if not, one is going to have problems. Now, whatever might be the position of the axiomatic method in mathematics or logic, its employment as the method of investigation in science generally isn't obviously appropriate. Whatever one's ultimate philosophy of mathematics, there would be general agreement that the material of mathematics and logic is by and large the interrelationship of concepts in terms of consistency and implication. Science, however, is supposed to connect to the world of our experience and, unless one is a card-carrying ultra-rationalist, can never be just a pure play of ideas. This isn't to deny that any given empirical science may have at its theoretical heart a core of conceptually interrelated elements as, for example, does Austrian economics; it is simply to reject the ultra-rationalist idea that the axiomatic method is *the* scientific method par excellence.

HOBBES ON MAN AND THE STATE OF NATURE

Let us take a look, then, at Hobbes's account of man. On the natural level, men are spontaneously self-seeking, acquisitive and aggressive. Such natural and spontaneous self-seeking, acquisitiveness and aggressiveness, though perhaps immediately satisfying, are often counter-productive in the long run. What each man needs isn't just immediate gratification but a longer-term assurance of security and this requires a form of utilitarian calculation that may require the regulation of his natural impulses. It is this latter, utilitarian, motive which moves man into society.[3] The transition from the natural to the utilitarian is mediated by what Hobbes calls the law of nature. This is a general rule discoverable by reason whose function it is to extend and safeguard the self-preservation that Hobbes believes to be at the root of human psychology. Although in a state of nature I may do as I please and others may do so too, and while in such a state there's no right or wrong, in this state my continued existence will ever be precarious. It is to my longer-term benefit, therefore, to give up this natural untrammelled right to do as I please provided—and this is the key point—that others do so too. But how can I be sure that others will keep their side of the bargain and exercise restraint? If I do so and they do not, then I am severely disadvantaged. It is a little like the classic Western standoff—there we stand with our guns trained on each other and the first one to lower his gun stands a good chance of being shot! It is to the benefit of all if we all exercise restraint but who is going to make the first move?

There is a paradox, perhaps an ineliminable bootstrapping paradox, at the heart of Hobbes's thought that many commentators have pointed out and it is this: 'If,' says Sabine, 'men were as savage and anti-social as they are at first represented, they would never be able to set up a government. If they were reasonable enough to set up a government, they would never have been without it.' [Sabine, 465] John Plamenatz frames the problem thus: 'Hobbes tells us that covenants without a power strong enough to enforce them are void, and that in the state of nature there is no such power. And yet a covenant is need to create that power; for in the state of nature men are equal, and can therefore set up a power strong enough to coerce them only by agreement. It would appear, then, at first sight, that the covenant is both necessary and impossible.' [Plamenatz, 134] Hobbes attempts to escape from this conundrum by distinguishing between two types of covenant: one in which the parties to the covenant do not simultaneously perform what they promise, and another in which they do simultaneously perform what they promise. The original covenant is meant to be of the second kind and so to escape the bootstrapping paradox. But, as Plamenatz notes, it does nothing of the sort. What happens in any covenant is the making of a promise, but promises are necessarily futural. In promising to obey I do not yet obey—my obedience lies somewhere in the future. It is not the making of promises by the covenanters that gives a sovereign power but their keeping of those promises. 'If his power alone can make them keep their promise,' writes Plamenatz, 'and yet he has no power unless they keep them, their condition does not change; they remain in the state of nature and have no sovereign over them.' He adds, 'Hobbes has confused himself and his readers by taking it for granted that a simultaneous renunciation of natural rights in favour of a particular person or assembly is equivalent to a grant of power to him or them, even when the persons who renounce the rights have no good reason to trust one another until there is a common power over them.' [Plamenatz, 135] Hobbes's theory is an example of what we might call the Humpty-Dumpty problem. If Humpty-Dumpty falls off the wall, all the King's horses and all the King's men, won't be able to put Humpty together again. If one start, as Hobbes does, with certain assumptions about men as isolated units of aggression and self-seeking energy, ever in pursuit of their own satisfactions to the disregard of others, then it is hardly surprising if one is going to find it difficult to explain how human beings can ever cooperate.[4]

What is the character of man's pre-social condition, the state of nature? Hobbes believes that in such a condition, men are by and large equal in strength, at least to the extent that any one man could, in the appropriate circumstances, kill another. 'Nature,' Hobbes remarks, 'hath made men so equall, in the faculties of body and mind; as that though there bee found one man sometimes manifestly strong in body, or of quicker mind than another; yet when all is reckoned together, the difference between man, and man, is not so considerable, as that one man can thereupon claim to himselfe any benefit, to which another may not pretend, as well as he. For as to the strength of body, the weakest has strength enough to kill the strongest, either by secret machination, or by confederacy with others, that are in the same danger with himselfe.'[5] What each man wants more than anything else is to preserve himself, not only in the present but into the future as well. In a state of nature, fear of sudden and violent death is omnipresent. In Hobbes's view, men in the state of nature would like to have what other men have but fear that others are thinking just the same thought so that men come to fear and distrust each other: 'if any two men desire the same thing, which neverthelesse they cannot both enjoy, they become enemies…'[6] But it isn't only fear that motivates men. Men also seek to be esteemed by others as they esteem themselves and resent any sign of contempt. In such circumstances, no man can afford to let his guard down for a moment lest others take advantage of his lack of vigilance; man's every waking moment is consumed by fear and distrust.

There are, then, three causes of inter-human strife or, as Hobbes terms it, war: competition, fear (diffidence) and glory. Men compete with one another for gain 'to make themselves Masters of other mens persons, wives, children, and cattell'.[7] Men fear other men as threats to their own property and safety and defend themselves against such predation; and they want to be esteemed and valued by others as they value themselves and resent the failure of others so to do. Hobbes writes, 'during the time men live without a common Power to keep them all in awe, they are in that condition which is called Warre; and such a warre, as is of every man, against every man. For Warre, consisteth not in Battell only, or the act of fighting; but in a tract of time, wherein the Will to contend by Battell is sufficiently known: and therefore the notion of Time, is to be considered in the nature of Warre…the nature of War, consisteth not in actually fighting; but in the known disposition thereto.'[8] In a state of war, there is no place for the civic virtues, for agriculture, sea voyages, construction, engineering, or scholarship, and the life of man in this condition is, in Hobbes's famous, memorable and oft-quoted phrase, 'solitary, poore, nasty, brutish, and short.'[9]

It is hard not to see some aspects of Hobbes's thought as being, at least in part, a reflective product of his own particular experiences in the war-torn years of the English Civil War, or the War of the Three Kingdoms as it is now sometimes called.[10] This fraught time saw the destruction or demoralisation of many traditional social institutions leaving only the contending parties of Parliament and King at the top, and the suffering individuals at the bottom, with a ruined social landscape in between. Small wonder then that Hobbes's saw nothing of substance between the monster Leviathan and the individual. 'There is no middle ground between humanity as a sand-heap of separate organisms,' writes George Sabine, 'and the state as an outside power holding them precariously together by the sanctions with which it supplements individual motives. All the rich variety of associations disappears, or is admitted suspiciously and grudgingly as carrying a threat to the power of the state. It is a theory natural to an age which saw the wreck of so many of the traditional associations and institutions of economic and religious life and which saw above all the emergence of powerful states in which the making of law became the typical activity.' [Sabine, 475] Given this absence of intermediate social structures with their own modes of authority (and there can be no such quasi-independent authorities in Hobbes's world where all authority belongs to Leviathan) Hobbes presents us with a clear choice between either the acceptance of Leviathan or a state of ultimate disorder and lawlessness. Take it or leave it—and who, given this stark choice, would be so foolish as to leave it?

In giving this account of man's original condition, Hobbes intends no moral judgement. He sees himself as simply describing how things are or have been. 'The last nominalist,' remarks d'Entrèves, 'Hobbes can equally well be described as the first legal positivist.' [d'Entrèves 1967, 107] If you aren't inclined to believe Hobbes, he asks you to look at seventeenth century America where, apart from the social life of families, there's no government and the 'savage people' live in a 'brutish manner'. Such a state of war is also, Hobbes thinks, the natural condition of international relations where one nation or state relates to another in this natural way. The thought of Hobbes in the *Leviathan* is usually portrayed as starting with the state of nature and working towards civil and political society but it is also possible that what Hobbes characterises as the state of nature is arrived at imaginatively by starting with civil and political society and removing from it the law-making and law-enforcement that Hobbes thinks is the essential function of government until one arrives at chaos.

In this state of nature, there is no right and wrong, no justice or injustice because such concepts have purchase only in civil society. For Hobbes, justice and injustice are a function of law and law, in turn, is a function of what Hobbes calls 'a common Power'. In a state of nature, there can be no such thing as property but mere possession. In this state, men can do whatever is necessary to preserve their lives; so much so that each man has a right to everything, not a right based on law, to be sure, for there is no law, but a right understood in that no one may, except by naked force, prevent them from taking and using whatever they desire. Given the awful situation in which men find themselves in the state of nature, it's hardly surprising that they desire to escape from it. But how is this to be done? On the one hand, men fear death, injury or despoliation; they desire peace and tranquillity and would like to obtain it. On the other hand, they are moved by pride to an aggressive self-assertion.

So, we have a multitude of self-seeking aggressive individuals, each seeking his own long-term preservation but each unwilling to yield his natural right to do as he wishes unless all others do likewise. How is this impasse to be overcome? We could try to reach an agreement with each other but this, Hobbes thinks, is foolish beyond permission. How can we be sure that the others will keep their words? 'Covenants without the sword, are,' he remarks, 'but words, and of no strength to secure a man at all.'[11] What is needed is an institution that can enforce any such agreement that we may make among ourselves. If we are prepared to contract each with the other to give up our natural right to self-help and, at the same time, cede to this institution, Leviathan, the power to enforce our contracts, then we may overcome the impasse created by our conflicting natural impulses. Once again, the paradox at the root of Hobbes's thought rears its head. If men in a state of nature are sufficiently enlightened to subscribe to a contract, then the state of nature can't possibly be a condition in which all are at war with all. And if that is so, what need have we of a contract? That being so, perhaps Hobbes's talk of contract cannot be taken literally. 'Strictly speaking,' remarks Sabine, 'he is saying merely that in order to cooperate men must do what they dislike to do, on pain of consequences which they dislike still more. In no other sense is there logically any obligation whatever in Hobbes's system.' [Sabine, 469] If one is inclined to think that Hobbes isn't, in any real sense, a contractarian, one has to take account of the second half of chapter fourteen of the *Leviathan* which deals extensively and in a sophisticated manner with the notion of contract. It is a little difficult to see why Hobbes should spend so much time on this concept if it weren't to be used in his work. Of course, he may be mistaken in thinking that he does so use the concept of contract; or it may be that the critics of contract in Hobbes are saying rather that he doesn't need such a concept. Whether or which, however, it is plainly there.

McClelland makes the point that it is somewhat ironic that Hobbes's *Leviathan*, usually considered to be a masterpiece of social contract theory, is used by Hobbes to undermine the very thing that social contract was invented to establish, namely, the justification for disobeying our lawfully constituted political superior! [McClelland, 193] I think it fair to say that the import of most social contract theories is to emphasise the equality of *all* the contracting parties and the liberty that they exercise in the making of the contract. This liberty and equality isn't abandoned when they enter civil society. But this is precisely where Hobbes differs from your run-of-the-mill contractualist. What most other political theorists see as an original blessing—namely our original pre-civil equality and liberty—Hobbes sees as a curse, something that men are only too willing to give up to enter civil society.

Who would want to live in such a state? Not too many people, Hobbes thinks. Nobody really wants to be in a state of permanent conflict and there are human passions that move men to leave this state. These passions are a fear of death and the desire and hope to obtain whatever is conducive to living well. Such being what the passions aim at, reason suggests a way out of our natural condition. In using our reason, we discover the fundamental law of nature which is that each should be willing to give up his natural right to everything if all others are simultaneously willing to do so. This can only come about if there is some authority with the power to enforce contracts.

OUT OF THE STATE OF NATURE

The solution is this: men agree not to make law themselves directly but to choose a sovereign by agreement with each other and then let the sovereign make and enforce the law. So far, this could be just another variation on the social contract theme but Hobbes's account has a fateful and unique twist. The sovereign, once chosen, isn't limited by anything or anybody. Social contract theory is normally thought to be a bargain between rulers and ruled from which the ruled may resile upon the non-performance by the ruler of certain conditions. But on Hobbes's account, the contract is between men in a state of nature *and there is no contract at all with the sovereign.* The sovereign is a third-party beneficiary of the contract, not one of the contracting parties, and he makes no agreement with any of the parties. In coming to their agreement, the contracting parties move themselves from the state of nature to civil society but the sovereign who isn't a party to the agreement remains in that state vis-à-vis the contracting parties.

Hobbes defines the Right of Nature as follows: 'The Right of Nature, which Writers commonly call *Jus Naturale*, is the Liberty each man hath, to use his own power, as he will himselfe, for the preservation of his own Nature; that is to say, of his own Life; and consequently, of doing any thing, which in his own Judgement, and Reason, hee shall conceive to be the aptest means thereunto.'[12] By a 'liberty', Hobbes intends the absence of external impediments. Rights, for Hobbes, are liberties, to do or to abstain from doing; in contrast, a law is something that binds or determines. As distinct from a right (or liberty) of nature, a Law of Nature is 'a Precept, or general Rule, found out by Reason, by which a man is forbidden to do, that, which is destructive of his life, or taketh away the means of preserving the same; and to omit, that, by which he thinketh it may be best preserved.'[13] Summing all this up it comes to this: one is free to do whatever it is that in one's judgement is required to preserve one's own life. One is obliged, however, not to destroy one's own life or to refuse to do whatever is necessary to preserve it. Given his characterisation of the state of nature as a state of lawlessness, Hobbes believes that every man has a right to everything else, including the bodies of others!

John Plamenatz judges that Hobbes's account of natural right is 'wonderfully confused.' 'We are told,' Plamenatz says, 'that in a state of nature man has a right to all things....we can see that the word *right* cannot, in this sense mean *power*, because the right to all things is not a power over all things. In the perilous state of nature, where man is said to have a right to all things, he very clearly is not able to get whatever he wants, or even whatever he deems necessary to his security. And yet, if natural right is called a liberty, and liberty is defined as absence of eternal impediments, it follows that natural right is a power.' [Plamenatz, 139]

If peace can't be had, then any man can wage war as he sees fit. Reason, however, suggests to us a way to eliminate war. The law of nature, the rule of reason, can be expressed in two precepts or laws, the first of which is to seek peace and defend oneself by any means. The second law of nature follows hard on its heels, and it is this: '*That a man be willing, when others are so too, as farre-forth, as for Peace, and defence of himselfe he shall think it necessary, to lay down this right to all things; and be contented with so much liberty against other men, as he would allow other men against himselfe.*'[14] The key phrase in this law is 'when others are so too' which implies a fundamental reciprocity. Indeed, Hobbes specifically links this law to the Gospel precept that reads: 'Whatsoever you require that others should do to you, that do ye to them.'[15] In giving up his right under the second law, a man does not empower another to do something he couldn't otherwise do for, as already said, in the state of nature, anyone can already do anything to anyone. All he does is to undertake not to exercise his own right. Nevertheless, not all rights can be alienated. Given that all voluntary acts aim at the good of the agent, no right can be alienated which fundamentally makes it impossible to realise that good—'a man cannot lay down the right of resisting them, that assault him by force, to take away his life; because he cannot be understood to ayme thereby, at any Good to himselfe.'[16] To attempt to alienate such a right is, according to Hobbes, incoherent. For it at once aims at a man's good while bringing about the frustration of that good.

In chapter fifteen of *Leviathan*, Hobbes lays out quite a number of additional laws of nature, bringing the grand total to nineteen in all. Of these, the third is perhaps the most important. This third law is that men ought to perform their covenants and from this requirement, justice proceeds. Without a covenant there is no transfer of right from one man to another, all men having a right to everything, and so no action can be deemed unjust. If covenants are made in a state of nature, each man may fear a lack of performance on the part of the other contractor and such a fear renders the contract invalid. 'Therefore before the names of Just, and Unjust can have place, there must be some coërcive Power, to compell men equally to the performance of their Covenants…where there is no Common-wealth, there nothing is Unjust.'[17]

PERSONATION AND THE SOVEREIGN

The sixteenth chapter of *Leviathan* contains, I believe, the key to Hobbes's account of the Leviathanatic sovereign. It bears the distinctly unenticing title, 'Of Persons, Authors, and things personated.' This chapter really concerns what has come to be called representation or what Hobbes calls 'personation'. He defines 'person' as 'he, *whose words or actions are considered, either as his own or as representing the words or actions of an other man, or of any other thing to whom they are attributed, whether Truly or by Fiction.*'[18] If the words or actions are a person's own, then he is a natural person; if they are those of another, then he is an artificial person.[19] In relation to artificial persons, Hobbes goes on to make the point that some of these have their words or actions owned, as it were, by that other whom they represent, whom Hobbes calls the 'author'. In such a case, that artificial person is called by Hobbes, the 'actor'. This distinction corresponds, in large part, to the familiar modern distinction between principal (author) and agent (actor). When an agent or actor acts or speaks on the authority of the author, then his actions or words bind the author. The manner in which Hobbes makes use of the notion of agency might be problematic for libertarians, in principle, but there's nothing intrinsically objectionable in the notion. Moreover, Hobbes is a methodological individualist and that can't fail to warm a libertarian's heart. In *De Cive*, chapters 5 and 6, he argues that, strictly speaking, a group cannot be said to act. Only individuals act. What makes an action a collective action is that some one individual acts under a certain description, as an agent of the many. Hobbes's individualism, one commentator remarks, makes his philosophy 'the most revolutionary theory of the age.' [Sabine, 467] But representation isn't only a relation between two rational beings. It is possible, Hobbes thinks, for inanimate objects to be represented by a kind of fiction where such objects clearly can't play the role of author. Hobbes instances churches and bridges and the like. So too, animate but irrational beings such as children, 'Fooles and Mad-men' can be represented (or personated) where they aren't in a position to delegate authority. Even the gods, whether false or true, can be personated or represented.'[20]

Now we come to the key point. 'A Multitude of men, are made *One* Person, when they are by one man, or one Person, Represented; so that it be done with the consent of every one of that Multitude in particular. For it is the *Unity* of the Representer, not the *Unity* of the Represented, that maketh the Persons *One*. And it is the Representer that beareth the Person, and but one Person: And *Unity*, cannot otherwise be understood in Multitude.'[21] Now, this passage makes a number of interesting points. If a multitude of people is to be considered as anything more than a mob, it must have a *locus* of concerted action. Someone must act and speak in its name and be authorised so to do. As Hobbes remarks, it is the unity of the representer, whether that representer be a single individual or a single group, that makes into a unity the multitude that is represented. Hobbes initially states very clearly that the commissioning of a person to act or speak for a multitude requires the consent of all—we might call this the *unanimity* principle. Despite this, two paragraphs later, he says: 'And if the Representative consist of many men, the voyce of the greater number, must be considered as the voyce of them all.'[22] This we may call the *majority* principle. What justification does Hobbes offer for the sudden and dramatic transformation of the unanimity principle into the majority principle? None that I can see. He remarks that where the negatives outweigh the affirmatives in an assembly, the negatives are the voice of those represented. But this is either nonsense or else question begging. The negatives *would* be the voice of those represented if the negatives were unanimous but if they are not then, on Hobbes's own unanimity condition, they can't be the voice of the whole. Some smaller points are made towards the end of the chapter but none that explain the substitution for the unanimity principle by the majority principle. Hobbes elsewhere gives an attempted justification for this substitution but he does not do so here.[23]

The reader might well wonder at this point where all this is leading. The answer is—to Leviathan, to the Common-wealth and to the sovereign. The state of nature is a state of war of all against all and reason tells us that the way out of this miserable condition is to bring about a state of peace.[24] We could try to agree among ourselves to restrain the natural passions that lie at the root of our warring condition but, Hobbes thinks, without the existence of some power capable of keeping us to our promises, such agreements will necessarily fail. As already mentioned, Hobbes is notorious for maintaining that 'Covenants without the Sword, are but Words, and of no strength to secure a man at all.'[25] He concedes that *if* it were possible that men could mutually agree to make and enforce agreements, then government would be unnecessary but he thinks this impossible.

Hobbes points to human history to illustrate his argument about the prevalence of human predation. He notes, 'in all places, where men have lived by small Families, to robbe and spoyle one another, has been a Trade, and so farre from being reputed against the Law of Nature, that the greater spoyles they gained, the greater was their honour....And as small Familyes did then; so now do Cities and Kingdomes which are but greater Families (for their own security) enlarge their Dominions, upon all pretences of danger, and fear of Invasion...'[26]

It could be argued against Hobbes that just as other animals are naturally social, so too perhaps is man. Nevertheless, Hobbes believes that man is different from other animals in significant respects. Men strive for honour and dignity, which striving gives rise to envy and hatred. In human life, there's a tension between what is good for me and what is good for the whole community; the two may run together in certain instances but they can and often do diverge. Not having reason, non-human animals do not criticise their leaders and think that they could do better, whereas such criticism is prevalent among men. In the end, the only way to bring about the escape from our natural warring condition, is for men to "conferre all their power and strength upon one Man, or upon one Assembly of men, that may reduce all their Wills, by plurality of voices, unto one Will: which is as much as to say, to appoint one Man, or Assembly of men, to beare their Person; and every one to owne, and acknowledge himselfe to be Author of whatsoever he that so beareth their Person, shall Act, or cause to be Acted, in those things which concerne the Common Peace and Safetie; and therein to submit their Wills, every one to his Will, and their Judgements, to his Judgment. This is more than Consent, or Concord; it is a reall Unitie of them all, in one and the same Person, made by Covenant of every man with every man…'[27] The unity thus produced Hobbes calls the Common-wealth or the great Leviathan, that '*Mortall God*, to which wee owe under the *Immortal God*, our peace and defence.'[28] Whoever it may be that's chosen to 'bear the person' in the commonwealth is the sovereign and all others are his subjects.

So a commonwealth is formed when *all* agree that whosoever (whether a single person or a corporation) shall be conferred with sovereignty by a majority, all shall be bound, those who voted for the proposal and those that did not. This is a return in a qualified way to the unanimity principle enunciated by Hobbes in chapter sixteen of *Leviathan*. Men must unanimously agree in their initial agreement to the binding nature of subsequent majority decisions. Unanimity is necessary initially as a majority vote to accept the binding nature of majority votes would be viciously circular. This isn't Hobbes's last word on this subject.

What are the characteristics of the power that the sovereign exercises—what are the incidents of sovereignty? Hobbes gives an extensive list of such incidents, all of which hinge critically upon the notion of personation or representation outlined in chapter sixteen of *Leviathan*. These may seem strange and perhaps even arbitrary on first glance but Hobbes sees them as simply being deductions from the very concept of sovereignty and thus incapable of being rejected without rejecting the very idea (and thus the reality) of sovereignty itself, with a consequent relapse into the hideous state of nature. These incidents of sovereignty include the inability of those who have covenanted to repudiate it; the inability of the sovereign to breach a covenant since he hasn't been party to it; the inability of the sovereign to wrong any of his subjects since his will is their will and no one can wrong himself; the inability of any of his subjects lawfully to punish the sovereign for what he may do, for whatever he may do is done by the authority of his subjects. The sovereign is the only judge of whatever is needed for the peace and defence of all. He alone may lay out the rules for the possession of property; he alone has the power to judge and adjudicate; he alone has the right to make and unmake war with other commonwealths. No one may choose or impose upon him any counsellor, minister or officer. These he appoints and dismisses himself at his pleasure.

Whoever is sovereign concentrates all power in himself. He may, of course, delegate some of that power for administrative reasons but that delegation can be revoked at will and is always exercised only under licence from him. This account makes short work of the by-now traditional discussion of different forms of government. For Hobbes, this discussion is pointless. Whoever in a society is the ultimate decision maker is sovereign and that's all there is to that. In Rommen's view, 'The absolute power of God in Occam's doctrine became at the hands of Thomas Hobbes the absolute sovereignty of the king.' [Rommen, 54-55] Where we have Leviathan, we have no distinction between morals and law, and law is simply the command of the sovereign. Hobbes is the archetypal legal positivist. Law and morals are merely an expression of the will of Leviathan and as Leviathan is one, so too there can be no fissure in the expression of Leviathan's will. Hobbes rejects any robust conception of natural law or any idea that custom, tradition and habit have any normative force except insofar as the sovereign condescends to enforce it, either explicitly or tacitly. Just as there is no real distinction in Hobbes's thought between morals and law, so too, there is also no real distinction between society and state. Without Leviathan, there is no state; without Leviathan there is no society. Here, Hobbes's individualism produces a result that would be acceptable, I suspect, to very few libertarians. A recurrent libertarian theme is precisely the distinction between society and state, with society being held to emerge from the bottom upwards by means of forms of mutual cooperation and order whereas the state is held to be the top-down imposition of control.

In the question of whether there can be such a thing as a legitimate rebellion, a venerable topic that will be considered in turn by Locke writing some years after Hobbes, Hobbes's thinking once again bears a striking resemblance to certain traditional Chinese ideas. In Chinese political thinking, the Emperor's authority depends upon his having the sanction of the somewhat mystical sounding mandate of heaven. If this is withdrawn, then his rule ceases to be legitimate. The evidence of its withdrawal, however, is somewhat less than mystical and consists largely in the occurrence of widespread social and political disorder. So too, given that Hobbes believes that the function of the state and of government is to provide the security which is the very reason for its being, should it be unable to provide that security then, *de facto*, it has already ceased to govern. So, resistance to the authority of Leviathan can't be prospectively legitimate but, if such resistance is in fact successful, then it thereby becomes, retroactively, legitimate.

There are many other incidents of sovereignty of no great interest but there remains one that is. We saw that Hobbes, in chapter eighteen, had returned, in a qualified way, to the necessity for original unanimity if all are to be subsequently bound by a majority. Nevertheless, when he comes to discuss the third incident of sovereignty he remarks: 'the major part hath by consenting voices declared a Soveraigne; he that dissented must now consent with the rest; that is, be contented to avow all the actions he shall do, or else justly be destroyed by the rest.'[29] We saw that, in chapter sixteen, Hobbes had shifted from the necessity for unanimity to the less stringent requirement merely for majority rule; earlier in chapter eighteen he seemed to have returned to a modified requirement of unanimity—unanimity in respect of a decision to accept a majority decision. Now, however, he seems simply to be reasserting the appropriateness of simple majority decision-making. The reason seems to be that Hobbes thinks that merely turning up and taking part in the discussion of whether or not to set up the common-wealth is, *ipso facto*, a tacit agreement to be bound by the majority decision even if one were in fact a dissenter to the ultimate decision! Moreover, dissenters from the covenant and the new sovereign are in a state of nature in respect of each other and since, in the state of nature, one has a right to every-thing, there's nothing to stop the new sovereign from exercising this right on his part to compel them to recognise his sovereignty. That they might rather not do so is irrelevant. Whereas in the original state of nature, each man was about as strong as any other, in the new dispensation, the individual dissenters are now opposed by an immensely stronger opponent in the new sovereign.

Men then come together in a commonwealth and in so doing form it as a kind of legal person, a sovereign. The will of this sovereign is, as the focus of the union of all, the will of all. The legislation of this sovereign is self-legislation. 'Since the only legitimate obligation is ultimately self-obligation,' writes Laurence Berns, 'the freedom of man in the state of nature must survive, in some form, in his subjection to the government...'[30] Richard Tuck writes: 'In a sense, in *Leviathan* Hobbes was working towards a theory rather like some later discussions of democracy and voting (for example, the theory in Rousseau—who was aware of some similarities between himself and Hobbes), in which he was trying to answer the puzzle about how someone can be said to be our "representative", or how (in a direct democracy) we can be said to have "consented" to the decision of our assembly, when we were outvoted and our apparent wishes were ignored. His answer, like Rousseau's and like that of most modern theorists was that we have a prior and unanimous commitment to be bound by the result of the electoral process, and that it is this unanimity which renders legitimate the representative or the law in question.'[31]

It might be objected that even if Hobbes were correct in thinking that a given civil order had originated in the way he says it does, what of the justifica-tion of sovereignty acquired through conquest? Surely *this* can't be justified? Hobbes denies this. Such sovereignty results from the defeat of one sovereign by another. The defeated sovereign being defeated no longer represents the union of the contracting parties and they return to the state of nature. As such, they may choose to try to remain in this condition (but why would they?) or simply accept the *de facto* sovereignty of the conqueror.

Another objection: are those making this contract not making it in a state of fear, and does that not invalidate the contract? No, says Hobbes. All contracts are made through fear so that if fear were an invalidating condition, no contract of any sort could ever be made. It was precisely fear that, in the original condition, drove men to form their contract that set up their sovereign. Hobbes is anxious to make clear that whether or not such a covenant is entered into willingly or through fear or by coercion is immaterial. It is important to note that the sovereign, whoever he is, is *not* a party to this contract! The contract isn't between men and the sovereign; it is between men only and issues in the assignment of right to the sovereign. Since he hasn't covenanted, his relationship to all others is and remains the original condition of the state of nature. And in any case, it isn't true to say that the adherents of the defeated sovereign have no choice. They can flee if they choose to do so—that's their choice, just as it is a choice of men in the state of nature to remain there rather than to contract out of it.

At this point, Hobbes could have made use of a distinction made by a philosopher he despises, Aristotle. Aristotle distinguished between actions that are involuntary and actions that are nonvoluntary. If a doctor taps my kneecap with a blunt instrument, my lower leg jerks upwards. This is an involuntary action—strictly speaking, it isn't an action at all but merely a happening. If, on the other hand, I am the captain of a ship with cargo stored on deck and I choose to jettison that cargo in a storm for the sake of the ship's safety, I haven't acted involuntarily; I have acted voluntarily but my action wasn't whimsical. The reason for my jettisoning of the cargo was a greater good that I chose. I would rather not have had to make the decision I did, and that's why Aristotle calls such actions nonvoluntary. Returning to Hobbes, the acquiescence of the subjects of the defeated sovereign in the authority of the conquering sovereign is more properly to be understood as a kind of nonvoluntary action rather than an involuntary action. No coercion of the will is required, nor, indeed, on Hobbes's view of things, is it possible. Hobbes happily accepts the notion that one can tacitly assent to a contract by silence, by acquiescence or by forbearance.[32]

When it comes to grasping the nature of sovereignty, Hobbes is remarkably clear and prescient. Ultimate authority is ultimate authority by whomever and by however many people it may be exercised. What matters is that it is ultimate, not the number of people involved. In respect of their sovereignty, democracies are just as sovereign as one-man tyrannies. Modern democratic theory, with its (flawed) concept of representation, is a way in which sovereignty is legitimised while the exercise of that sovereignty in those democracies is Hobbesian through and through. [see McClelland, 202] The key to the justification and popular acceptance of democracy is the idea of representation: those who are ruled are thought to be ruled by those who represent them and thus, it is claimed, in being so ruled they are, in effect, virtually ruling themselves. Hobbes has this to say: 'For he that doth anything by authority from another, doth therein no injury to him by whose authority he acteth: But by this Institution of a Common-wealth every particular man is Author of all the Soveraigne doth; and consequently he that complaineth of injury from his Soveraigne complaineth of that whereof he himself is Author, and therefore ought not to accuse any man but himselfe; no, nor himselfe of injury, because to do injury to ones selfe is impossible.'[33] If rulers and ruled are virtually one and the same, then the problem of justifying one person's or group of person's arbitrarily commanding another disappears. Whatever difficulties there might be about the legitimacy of another person commanding you, there can be no disputing the legitimacy of your commanding yourself. Whether the notion of commanding yourself (as distinct from the notion of self-command) makes any sense is another matter. The justification of political governance by the state, then, rests upon democracy, and the justification of democracy in turn rests upon representation. If the bough of representation were to break, down would come the cradle of democracy, baby and all. Somewhat less metaphorically, if representation can't be satisfactorily accounted for, then representative democracy, the sole viable contender for the justification of political governance by the state, finds itself in no more tenable a position than any of its discredited competitors.

What does it mean for one person to represent another? Under normal circumstances, those who represent us do so at our bidding and cease to do so at our bidding. They act on our instructions within the boundaries of a certain remit and we are responsible for what they do as our agents. The central characteristic of representation by agency is that the agent is responsible to his principal and is bound to act in the principal's interest. Is this the situation with my so-called political representatives? Political representatives are not normally legally answerable to those whom they allegedly represent. In fact, in modern democratic states, the majority of a representative's putative principals are in fact unknown to him. Can a political representative be the agent of a multitude? This also seems unlikely. What if there are multiple principals and they have interests that diverge from each other? A political representative must then of necessity cease to represent one or more of his principals. The best that can be done in these circumstances is for the politician to serve the many and betray the few. In this very normal political scenario, it isn't that it is *difficult* to represent a constituency—it is rather that it is *impossible*. There is no interest common to the constituency as a whole, or, if there is, it's so rare as to be practically non-existent. That being the case, there's nothing that can be represented. Michael Oakeshott remarks that 'the political representative has drawn up his own mandate and then, but a familiar trick of ventriloquism, has put it into the mouth of his electors: as an instructed delegate he is not an individual, and as a "leader" he relieves his followers of the need to make choices for themselves.'[34]

What then are the powers of the sovereign? Well, pretty much everything! As the sovereign is the unitary locus of the covenant of all, then his will is the will of all and his acts the acts of all. As he is in the original condition of nature vis-à-vis all others, he can do no wrong, commit no injustice. Furthermore, as his will is the expression of the will of all, if anyone were to accuse the sovereign of injuring him, that would be tantamount to accusing himself of injuring himself! It follows, then, that the sovereign has the right to do pretty much whatever it is he deems necessary whether others deem it to be so or not. The sovereign is the only ultimate judge of what is or isn't conducive to the peace and so he may censor and regulate opinion as he sees fit, and that includes religious opinion. Whereas Machiavelli had an instrumental view of religion, Hobbes firmly subordinates religion to the power of the sovereign. As his will is law, it makes no sense to speak of the sovereign being subject to the law, for that would subject him to his own will.

Despite all this, Hobbes thinks that some rights of the covenanters are in fact inalienable. Given that self-preservation is the motive force for entering into the compact in the first place, Hobbes believes that there can be no political obligation to do or undertake anything that would take away a man's life. Even to desert while serving in the army (provided one had not volunteered) is, for Hobbes, not unjust but, of course, the sovereign will see to it that the penalties for desertion are more fearful than any fear engendered by serving. Hobbes even thinks that a justly condemned criminal has no obligation to go quietly to execution!

When talking about the traditional typology of kinds of government—monarchy, aristocracy or democracy and their 'bad' versions—tyranny, oligarchy and anarchy—Hobbes remarks that the negative characterisation of the 'bad' versions is merely a way of the speaker's indicating his dislike; in fact, the difference between monarchy and tyranny, let us say, is meaningless, from a political point of view. It is possible to have some divergence on the part of the sovereign between public and private interests; that being so, Hobbes thinks this will be more limited under monarchy than under either aristocracy or democracy since the number of people enriching themselves at the public expense is more limited. [see Hoppe, 2001]

Whatever form of government one ends up with, one must start with a functional democracy, given that the origin of sovereignty lies in a contract between equal individuals. Laurence Berns again: 'Since all men in the state of nature are equal in rights, and all legitimate obligation is ultimately self-obligation, the first part of the social contract, in order to be binding, must be an agreement of each man with every other man to accept as sovereign that person or persons designated by a majority of all of them.' [Berns, 411]

We saw that Machiavelli thought the tension between the Roman Senate and the Roman people was the source of a dynamic energy that kept the Republic going through the centuries. Hobbes disagrees. This tension, he thinks, provided the gap through which the civic disturbances that started with the Gracchi, and continued under Marius and Sulla, Pompey and Caesar, and Octavian and Anthony finally brought about the end of the Republic and the start of the Principate. Setting his face squarely against many traditional themes and doctrines in political philosophy, Hobbes rejects the idea that sovereigns can be subject to the law, that men can have some pre- or apolitical property which gives them rights that a sovereign must observe, that a mixed constitution in which ultimate authority is divided is best and, as should be obvious by now, he totally and completely rejects the idea that resistance to the sovereign can be lawful, still less, that tyrannicide is or could ever be justified. It is a mark of Hobbes's greatness as a political thinker that, as d'Entrèves remarks, his '"invidious truths" have turned into today's generally accepted truisms: and they will remain such, at any rate until a new political situation, which may already be in process of development, has taken the place of the one we still live in. [d'Entrèves 1967, 109]

Notes

1 References without ascription are by chapter and by page number to the 1996 Cambridge edition of *Leviathan*, edited by Richard Tuck.

2 See the section on *Rationalism and Certainty* in the chapter on Grotius.

3 Confucian moral philosophy distinguishes four nested and co-existing levels of moral development, the first two of which are the natural and the utilitarian. Hobbes's account mirrors this analysis closely.

4 How, asks Anthony O'Hear, 'do we imagine that people outside any society could bind themselves or, more to the point, others, by a contract? If they could make a contract, they would already be social beings, and have no need of the primitive contract. But if they were completely outside any society they would have no reason to keep any pseudo-contract they might devise—except force.' [O'Hear, 64]

5 Hobbes, chapter 13, 86.

6 Hobbes, chapter 13, 86-87.

7 Hobbes, chapter 13, 88.

8 Hobbes, chapter 13, 88-89.

9 Hobbes, chapter 13, 89.

10 It should perhaps come as no surprise to find that Hobbes had translated Thucydides *History of the Peloponnesian War*, his own position appearing to mirror to some extent what would seem to be Thucydides's sympathy for *realpolitik*. [see the Mytilenian Debate and the Melian Dialogue in Thucydides 1954, 212-223, 400-408] David Polansky notes the present-day tendency to group Thucydides, Machiavelli, and Hobbes into a kind of 'unholy trinity' but he argues that 'Hobbes never refers to Thucydides as a "realist" (an anachronistic term in his day). Whatever the character of Hobbes's thought, and the uses to which he put Thucydides's work in it, it is far from clear that he endorses Thucydides on the basis of some shared realism—at least not explicitly' and he goes on to claim that, in fact, 'Nietzsche is…the earliest thinker to make the now-common association of Thucydides with Machiavelli.' [Polansky 425, 426-427, 427]

11 Hobbes, chapter 17, 117.

12 Hobbes, chapter 14, 91.

13 Hobbes, chapter 14, 91.

14 Hobbes, chapter 14, 92; emphasis in original.

15 Hobbes, chapter 14, 92.

16 Hobbes, chapter 14, 93.

17 Hobbes, chapter 15, 100-101.

18 Hobbes, chapter 16, 111.

19 As we shall see, the similarities between Hobbes's Leviathan and Rousseau's General Will are striking. It is not surprising that Rousseau is an admirer of Hobbes. 'When I hear Grotius praised to the skies and Hobbes covered with execration I see how far sensible men read or understand these two authors.' [Rousseau 1969, 836]

20 For a contemporary argument that natural objects should have legal standing, see Stone 1972, passim.

21 Hobbes, chapter 16, 114.

22 Hobbes, chapter 16, 114.

23 See Hobbes, chapter 18, 123.

24 The state of nature is not, d'Entrèves thinks, an imaginary state but 'an ever-present menace. It lurks beneath the glossy surface of civilized life.' [d'Entrèves 1967, 107] For a fictional treatment of the superficiality of civilisation, see C. P. Snow's *A Coat of Varnish*.

25 Hobbes, chapter 17, 117.

26 Hobbes, chapter 17, 118.

27 Hobbes, chapter 17, 120.

28 Hobbes, chapter 17, 120.

29 Hobbes, chapter 18, 123.

30 Berns, 405; see Hobbes, chapter 21.

31 Tuck, xxxvi; but see van Reybrouck, passim.

32 See Hobbes, chapter 14, 94.

33 Hobbes, chapter 18, 124.

34 Oakeshott 1991a, 380; see Casey 2012b, 117-128. In his remarkable pro-democratic but anti-electoral tract, David van Reybrouck writes, 'Electoral fundamentalism is an unshakeable belief in the

idea that democracy is inconceivable without elections and elections are a necessary and fundamental precondition when speaking of democracy. Electoral fundamentalists refuse to regard elections as a means of taking part in democracy, seeing them instead as an end in themselves, as a holy doctrine with an intrinsic, inalienable value.' [van Reybrouck, 39]

Chapter 19

THE ENGLISH REVOLUTION

When Adam delved and Eve span,
who was then the gentleman?
—John Ball

I beseech you, in the bowels of Christ,
think it possible that you may be mistaken
—Oliver Cromwell

The glories of our blood and state
Are shadows, not substantial things
There is no armour against Fate
Death lays his icy hand on kings
—James Shirley

The Reformation, with its attendant social, religious and political changes, was the first occasion on which political, religious and social matters became a topic of widespread popular concern. The new technology of printing—the Internet of its age!—made the production and dissemination of pamphlets and controversial literature possible, and the importance of the changes that were taking place or were contemplated provided the energy necessary for authorship. Up to this time, religious and political controversy was, for the most part, a sedate academic matter, written in Latin, the universal medium of scholarly written communication, and thus confined to a tiny section of the population. From now on, anyone who could read had access to copious amounts of material in his native language. [see Eisenstein, passim]

Vast as was the literature relating to the religious changes that swept over Europe in the sixteenth century, it paled into insignificance when compared to the massive output of popular writings relating to the religious and political issues that gripped the English mind in the seventeenth century. An incomplete listing of pamphlets produced in the twenty years between 1640 and 1660, despite restrictive and repressive licensing laws, runs to almost twenty thousand titles! 'This pamphlet-debate,' writes Sabine, 'was the first great experiment in popular political education using the printing press as the organ of government by discussion.' David Wootton writes, 'The Civil War, however, saw the appearance of a quite new type of political theorizing. With the breakdown of central authority, men such as Lilburne, Walwyn and Winstanley, none of whom had much formal education, sought to address a new political audience of craftsmen, apprentices and common soldiers. Writing at speed, often when in prison, and printing on hastily organized clandestine presses, the pamphlets and broadsheets they produced were crudely printed and coarsely illustrated....There is, however, no European parallel to the Putney debates, no

French Lilburne or Spanish Walwyn, and the English Civil War can properly be described as having called forth a revolution in political thought.'[1]

The central bones of contention were religious and political. From the religious perspective, the question was: was the Church in England going to become a modified version of Catholicism, complete with bishops, or was it going to become an English type of Presbyterian Calvinism? What was to be done with those people who wanted neither a quasi-Roman episcopal nor a Presbyterian Church? From the political perspective, the question was: who would eventually triumph in the struggle between the increasingly absolutist Stuart monarchy under the second Stuart king, Charles I, and an increasingly assertive Parliament? The two perspectives weren't hermetically sealed and the interaction of religious and political factors created an explosive situation that was eventually to result in open war.

LEVELLERS

In the late 1640s, a semi-organised group emerged whose adherents were known, pejoratively, as the Levellers because of their presumed intent to flatten all social and religious hierarchies. John Lilburne, William Walwyn and Richard Overton, the most prominent members of this group, all disclaimed (with varying degrees of ingenuousness) any levelling intent.[2] The Levellers gave voice to the political and religious concerns of those on the fringes of the newly emerging middle class. More radical but even less organised than the Levellers (and thus more ephemeral) were the Diggers (sometimes called True Levellers) whose controversial literature appears in the main to have been the production of just one man, Gerrard Winstanley. If the Levellers were lower middle-class men with at least some stake in the community, the Diggers were those with little or no property at all and who thus tended to be socially and economically marginalised. Sabine writes, 'as the Levellers were an early instance of a radical middle-class democracy with political aims, the Diggers are more easily classified as the beginning of utopian communism.' [Sabine, 479] The active involvement of Levellers and Diggers in real-life politics was brief and, in the event, largely ineffectual. Their importance, however, lies not so much in their practical achievements or lack of practical achievements but in the ideas which they were among the first to articulate and which they bequeathed to later generations. It is hard to disagree with Robert Ashton when he remarks, 'it could be argued that the enormous amount of ink which has been spilt on the subject of the Levellers and the Diggers in recent years reflects more nearly current interests in the origins of radical politics, and the political ideas appropriate to them, than the contemporary significance of such movements, important though they undoubtedly were.' [Ashton, viii]

In 1647, after the struggle between Parliament and King had resulted in victory for the Parliamentary forces, Parliament, fearful of the Army it had itself created, ordered its disbandment. The soldiers, who had not been paid and who weren't satisfied that the changes they had fought for would be implemented, revolted and Parliament capitulated. An Army Council representing both officers and rank-and-file was set up. Norman Davies remarks that this

Army Council was 'an extraordinary outfit. It was highly political and given to intense debates; it was highly democratic in respect to its own internal procedures, and yet it was highly despotic in its stance to other institutions and to the nation at large.' [Davies 1999, 499] In October and November of 1647, in an extraordinary and unprecedented turn of events, the Army Council met to discuss proposals contained in a Leveller document entitled 'The Agreement of the People'. The lower ranks and some few officers called, among other things, for the franchise to be widely extended, for equality before the law and for the elimination of religious coercion. Most of the higher officers, including Oliver Cromwell and his son-in-law Henry Ireton, were unwilling to adopt what they saw as sweeping changes to the English Constitution, not least because of its presumed effect on the rights of property holders. The year 1647 was the high-water mark of Leveller influence. Later that year, the escape of the King from his army guards and the resumption of hostilities forced the army to re-unite around their leaders and the Leveller influence was effectively dissipated in the exigencies of meeting the renewed Royalist challenge. Despite this disruption, in the latter part of 1648, the Army, having purged Parliament and seized political power, negotiated a modified form of the 'Agreement of the People' with the Levellers.

Despite the name given to them by their political opponents, the Levellers did not in fact propose the sweeping away of all differences of rank or title, nor did they propose the abolition or radical redistribution of property. One can find constant denials in their literature to this effect and there can be no doubt that these denials were, to varying degrees, sincere. We find them professing that 'we never had it in our thoughts to level men's estates, it being the utmost of our aim that the commonwealth be reduced to such a pass that every man may with as much security as may be enjoy his propriety.' [Sharp, 161] Some of the Levellers, Lilburne, for example, may have been more in earnest with this protestation than others, such as Walwyn. John Gurney believes that we are entitled to some scepticism on this matter, as were many of the Levellers's contemporaries. 'The Levellers' views on private property,' he writes, 'were never wholly consistent: Lilburne was probably the most outspoken in his opposition to the "conceit of levelling of propriety and Magistracie". Overton acknowledged the advantages of opening up impropriated common land and turning it over to the poor (a move that would have infringed the property rights of landowners), whereas Walwyn never convincingly repudiated the accusation that he had—in theory at least—some sympathy for the idea of community of property.' [Gurney, 62]

The truth is more likely to be that the views of many of the radicals, Levellers and Diggers alike, had been rapidly acquired, and being neither fully assimilated nor articulated were capable of development in various directions in the light of circumstances. Henry Brailsford, for example, remarks of the Digger, Gerard Winstanley, that 'his thought was in flux and underwent a rapid development. His voluminous writing was all done, much of it rapidly, in four years; he had little sense for form or order in his compositions and often seemed to be thinking aloud.' [Brailsford, 662]

Whatever differences they may have had on other issues, the Levellers one and all objected to legally created and legally maintained monopolies: the effective monopoly of political power by the nobility and gentry, the economic monopolies enjoyed by the merchants, and the professional monopolies enjoyed by lawyers.[3] Sabine notes, 'the Levellers appear to have grasped with remarkable clearness the point of view of radical democratic liberalism, individualist rather than socialist in its philosophy and political rather than economic in its aims.' [Sabine, 482] The equality they sought, or the equality they said they sought, was not any radical egalitarianism implying wholesale redistribution of property but an equality of all men before the law and in political representation. In the course of the Putney Debates, Henry Ireton was sceptical of the purportedly limited nature of the Leveller claims and urged against them that those claims taken to their logical conclusions *did* in fact undermine the existing, and possibly all, property regimes. The Levellers rejected Ireton's argument, appealing to the law of nature 'to demonstrate that the right to property is guaranteed by the law of nature, and not, as Ireton maintained, merely by positive government laws.'[4]

On what basis did the Levellers make their claims? As one might expect, there are appeals to Scripture in their writings but equally appeals to what is reasonable and natural, reason and nature showing forth self-evidently the basic rights of all men simply as men. For the Leveller writers, reason and revelation coincide, man's rationality being a creaturely reflection of the Divine mind.[5] Consider the following passage from John Lilburne (which I quote in full as the shortest complete passage of its kind) which starts and finishes as a Scriptural reflection but which moves seamlessly from Scriptural quotation to rational considerations and back again, and from the use of Scriptural epithets, such as 'wicked', 'devilish' and 'sinful', to the use of rational epithets, such as 'unnatural' and unjust'. I have italicised the words that appeal to reason and nature.

> God, the absolute sovereign lord and king of all things in heaven and earth, the original fountain and cause of all causes; who is circumscribed, governed, and limited by no rules, but doth all things merely and only by His sovereign will and unlimited good pleasure; who made the world and all things therein for His own glory; and who by His own will and pleasure, gave him, His mere creature, the sovereignty (under Himself) over all the rest of His creatures and endued him with a rational soul, or understanding, and thereby created him after His own image. The first of which was Adam, a male, or man, made out of the dust or clay; out of whose side was taken a rib, which by the sovereign and absolute mighty creating power of God was made a female or woman called Eve; which two are the earthly, original fountain, as begetters and bringers-forth of all and every particular and individual man and woman that ever breathed in the world since; who are, and were *by nature* all *equal* alike in power, dignity, authority, and majesty—none of them having (*by nature*) any authority, dominion or magisterial power, one over or above another. Neither have

they nor can they exercise any but merely by institution or donation, that
is to say by *mutual agreement* or *consent*—given, derived, or assumed by
mutual consent and *agreement*—for the good benefit and comfort each of
other, and not for the mischief, hurt, or damage of any: it being *unnatural*,
irrational, sinful, wicked and *unjust* for any man or men whatsoever to part
with so much of their power as shall enable any of their parliament-men,
commissioners, trustees, deputies, viceroys, ministers, officers or servants
to destroy and undo them therewith. And *unnatural*, *irrational*, sinful,
wicked, *unjust*, devilish, and tyrannical it is, for any man whatsoever—
spiritual or temporal, clergyman or layman—to appropriate and assume
unto himself a power, authority and jurisdiction to rule, govern or reign
over any sort of men in the world without their free consent; and whosoever
doth it—whether clergyman or any other whatsoever—do thereby as much
as in them lies endeavour to appropriate and assume unto themselves the
office and sovereignty of God (who alone doth, and is to rule by His will
and pleasure), and to be like their creator, which was the sin of the devils,
who, not being content with their first station but would be like God; for
which sin they were thrown down into hell, reserved in everlasting chains,
under darkness, unto the judgement of the great day.[6]

The *religious* argument of this passage is this: God, by virtue of his creation of
us, is only natural sovereign. Anyone attempting to exercise dominion over
another without that other's consent is usurping God's position. The *rationalist*
argument of this passage is this: all men are equal by nature, therefore no one
can rightfully exercise authority over another except with the consent of that
other. The word 'nature' or variants thereof occurs four times in this passage,
with two occurrences of 'unjust', 'agreement', and 'consent', and one each of
'equal' and 'rational'.

Lilburne practised what he preached. On the occasion of his first trial before
the Star Chamber, when he was in his early twenties, Lilburne refused to defer
to the court (by bowing) on the grounds that he was the equal of the bishops
and the judges! 'For this shocking snub to the authority of the Chamber,' writes
James Otteson, Lilburne 'was fined, publicly whipped and pilloried, and finally
imprisoned, receiving over time increasingly harsh punishment because he
refused to stop denouncing the presumed authority of the bishops.' [Otteson
2003, 121]

The Levellers' justification for their demands appears to have veered
somewhat erratically between an appeal to traditional or customary liberties,
on the one hand, and, on the other, a much more radical conception of natural
rights apart from any customary or traditional instantiation.[7] In the Putney
debates, Ireton's response to the Leveller demands was to ask them repeatedly which of these two was the source of their proposals. Sabine remarks,
'The distinction between customary and natural right was a bone of contention
between Ireton and the representatives of the regiments.' [Sabine, 484]

Let us look at some examples of the Leveller literature to see for ourselves
just what they proposed. In 'A Remonstrance' written by Overton in 1646 with

the help of Walwyn, we have an fervid calling to account of the House of Commons. What have you done?, the authors ask their elected representatives. We elected you to set us free, 'to deliver us from all kind of bondage and to preserve the commonwealth in peace and happiness.' [Sharp, 33] Remember, 'We are your principals and you our agents....For if you or any other shall assume or exercise any power that is not derived from our trust and choice thereunto, that power is no less than usurpation and an oppression from which we expect to be freed...' [Sharp, 34] That trust which we have given to you, we can revoke if we so choose. [Sharp, 33] If a king is to be a lawful magistrate, then he must demonstrate the lawfulness of his authority 'which must be from the voluntary trust of the people; and then the case is the same with them as between the people and you—they (as you) being possessed of no more power than what is *in* the people justly to entrust.' [Sharp, 44-45] Since the time of the Norman invasion, this country has been held in bondage 'by the policies and force of the officers of trust in the commonwealth, amongst whom we always esteemed kings the chiefest.' [Sharp, 34] The appeal to a supposedly immemorial law pre-dating the Norman invasion, a law that was supposed to undercut the absolutist pretensions of the Stuarts, is a common theme to be found in the Leveller literature. Alas, the claim on which this appeal was based, despite receiving the self-interested *imprimatur* of Sir Edward Coke and being admittedly rhetorically effective, had no basis in history. [see Davies 1999, 328-329]

What, asks Overton impatiently, is all this nonsense you Parliamentarians are telling us about needing the consent of the Lords and King to make laws? 'Ye only are chosen by us the people; and therefore in you only is the power of binding the whole nation by making, altering, or abolishing of laws.' [Sharp, 35] As things stand, the laws of the nation are unworthy of a free people. Magna Carta is 'but a beggarly thing containing many marks of intolerable bondage; and the laws that have been made since by parliaments have in very many particulars made our government much more oppressive and intolerable.' [Sharp, 46-47] Imprisonment for debt is deplorable, as is the practice of the New Model Army of impressment into military service. In words which, suitably updated, could have been written in the turbulent anti-war demonstrations of the 1960s, Overton writes, 'We entreat you to consider what difference there is between binding a man to an oar as a galley-slave in Turkey or Argiere, and pressing of men to serve in your war. To surprise a man on the sudden, force him from his calling where he lived comfortably from a good trade, from his dear parents, wife or children, against inclination and disposition to fight for a cause he understands not and in company of such as he has no comfort to be withal, for pay that will scarce give him sustenance—and if he live, to return to a lost trade, or beggary, or not much better: if any tyranny or cruelty exceed this, it must be worse than that of a Turkish galley slave.' [Sharp, 47-48]

Another Leveller tract, Walwyn's 'Toleration Justified and Persecution Condemned' (1646) contains a plea for religious tolerance which, in the religious context of the period, is little short of astonishing. The tract is essentially a complaint that the Presbyterians, now that they are in the ascendant, are

behaving every bit as intolerantly as the episcopal leaders of the church did
when *they* were in the ascendant. This point was also made by John Milton in
his *Areopagitica*. 'In the *Areopagitica*,' writes Hilary Gatti, 'Milton identifies
the new presbyters as the new enemies of tolerance in England. In this respect,
bishop and presbyters are "the same to us both name and thing"…'[8]

Walwyn argues that 'every man ought to be free in the worship and service
of God—compulsion being the way to increase, not the number of converts,
but of hypocrites.' [Sharp, 15] Against the argument put forward by the
Presbyterian Synod that such toleration as is desired by the Independents is
nowhere else to be found, Walwyn's response is that the practice of states is
to be judged by God's law and the rule of reason, not the other way around.
In passages that anticipate the later writing of J. S. Mill by two hundred years,
Walwyn argues that 'it cannot be just to set bounds or limitations to toleration any further than the safety of the people requires. The more horrid and
blasphemous the opinion is, the easier suppressed by reason and argument.'
The likeliest way to find out the truth 'will be by giving liberty to every man
to speak his mind and produce his reasons and argument, and not by hearing
one sect only.' [Sharp, 20]

The most remarkable piece of Leveller writing of all has to be Overton's
'Arrow Against all Tyrants.' (1646) The majority of Leveller documents
concern themselves with asserting the fundamental equality of all men and
arguing for universal suffrage, equality before the law, limited terms for
members of Parliament, and so on. Overton's 'Arrow against all Tyrants'
is very different.[9] It has without doubt the most philosophically interesting
opening section of any of the many pieces of Leveller literature. The force of
the arguments and assertions here depend in large part on a certain conception of nature. In the first two paragraphs alone, the word 'nature' or one of
its derivatives is used fourteen times! God, of course, enters into Overton's
account but only indirectly as the author and guarantor of man's nature. [see
Sharp, 55] Well, one might think, we have had natural law theories aplenty
already. What is so unusual about Overton's?

The answer lies in Overton's linkage of nature with property, in particular,
with the notion of a property in one's self, a notion that was to achieve prominence in Locke's *Second Treatise on Government* some forty three years later
and which many believe to have originated with Locke but which did not.[10]
In fact, the concept of self-ownership had been clearly articulated over three
hundred years before Overton wrote. The medieval master of the University
of Paris, Henry of Ghent, in a 1289 discussion of whether a man condemned
to death could lawfully flee, argued that whereas others might have the right
to use the criminal's body in certain ways, only the criminal himself had a
property right in his own body. Henry used the word '*proprietas*' to describe
this right, not the more common (and ambiguous) '*dominium*'. The criminal's
efforts of self-preservation (provided he did not thereby injure another) were
equitable (*fas*), permitted by the law of nature and therefore licit (*licitum*) and
right (*ius*) and, Henry argues, even necessary (*necessitas*). [see Tierney 2001,
83-89]

'To every individual in nature is given an individual property by nature not to be invaded or usurped by any,' writes Overton. 'For every one, as he is himself, so he has a self-propriety, else could he not be himself; and of this no second may presume to deprive any of without manifest violation and affront to the very principles of nature and of the rules of equity and justice between man and man. Mine and thine cannot be except this be. No man has power over my rights and liberties, and I over no man's [Sharp, 55] What Overton is saying seems to come to something like this. Simply by being, every man has a property in himself. If he had not, he couldn't be himself. The principles of nature and equity and justice prohibit interference with this self-ownership by any third party. This property in oneself is at the root of all further distinctions between what belongs to you and what belongs to another. By nature, all men have this property in themselves so that all alike are equal and all alike are free. This is self-evident. Overton writes, 'For by natural birth all men are equally and alike born to like propriety, liberty and freedom; and as we are delivered of God by the hand of nature into this world, every one with a natural innate freedom and propriety—as it were writ in the table of every man's heart, never to be obliterated—even so are we to live, everyone equally and alike to enjoy his birthright and privilege; even all whereof God by nature has made him free.' [Sharp, 55] All our human powers have their origin in our self-property and our actions cannot contradict our enjoyment of our liberty. No man can give to another more than he himself has; and no man, Overton thinks, 'naturally would be befooled of his liberty by his neighbour's craft or enslaved by his neighbour's might.' [Sharp, 55] In respect of himself, each man is his own lord and master and any rights that another may come to have over him can come only from that man's consent: 'every man by nature,' writes Overton, 'being a king, priest and prophet in his own natural circuit and compass, whereof no second may partake but by deputation, commission, and free consent from him whose natural right and freedom it is.' [Sharp, 55]

The political implication of all this is as follows. Our rulers, leaders, governors have rightful powers over us only to the extent that we have given it to them. Such power as they have, they have only for our benefit, acting as our agents ['commissioners and lawful deputies'] while we remain principals, and they have it only so long as they act for our benefit ['for our better being, discipline, government, propriety and safety']. Just as no man willingly injures himself ['no man may abuse, beat, torment, or afflict himself'], so no man can willingly communicate a rightful power to another to injure him. Sabine comments, 'The interesting and distinctive feature of the Leveller philosophy is the new form which it gave to the ancient conceptions of natural right and consent. They interpreted the law of nature as endowing human individuals with innate and inalienable rights which legal and political institutions exist only to protect, and they construed consent as an individual act which every man is entitled to perform for himself.' [Sabine, 484] Overton reminds Parliamentarians, the Presbyterian leadership and the Army that the arguments they offered in support of their resistance to Charles can be raised, if need be, against themselves! They rejected the tyranny, oppression and cruelty of Charles as detrimental to the safety and good of the people; so too, their rule can similarly be rejected if it replicates the defects of royal rule, for, comments Overton, 'tyranny, oppression and cruelty whatsoever, and in whomsoever, is in itself unnatural, illegal yea absolutely anti-magisterial; for it is even destructive to all human civil society, and therefore resistible.' [Sharp, 56-57]

With the king in custody, the civil war victors were faced with a 'Now what?' situation. Multi-lateral discussions took place between Charles and Parliament and the Army and the City of London. Within the victorious Army, there were very distinct and opposed points of view as to what should be done next. In 1647, the General Council of the Army met to discuss[11] proposals put to them by the (largely) Leveller element in the Army, which proposals effectively amounted to the following:

- Members of Parliament should be allocated in a manner proportionate to population
- Parliament should sit for a limited (2-year) term and no longer
- Matters of religion and public worship should not and do not come within the remit of Parliament and so were not to constitute the substance of any coercive law
- Impressment to the army is contrary to freedom and cannot be allowed
- Laws are to be made for the good of all and must be applicable to all.[12]

In the light of our subsequent political experience in the last four centuries, these proposals do not seem wildly unreasonable but in the political context of the day they occasioned much heart-searching. The senior army commanders, Ireton and Cromwell included, were essentially socially conservative and inclined to make only those changes that were absolutely necessary to resolve their immediate problems. Needless to say, the representatives of the regiments were in favour of much more sweeping changes.

Both sides in the debate saw Parliament as being representative of the people, but whereas the senior army commanders held to the traditional view that such representation was of estates or of corporations or of property holders or, as Ireton put it, 'those with an interest or share in the disposing or determining of the affairs of the kingdom,' the Leveller interest portrayed the relationship or representation as subsisting between Parliament and the individual person. [Sharp, 103] George Sabine notes that 'These two features of their political philosophy—the delegated power of parliament and the right of every man to consent to law through his representatives—were the grounds upon which they urged the main parts of their radical program.' [Sabine, 487]

Putting it at its simplest, the key issue on representation came to this. The Levellers argued that all men were subject to law and so should be in a position to determine who their lawmakers were. This position was movingly expressed by Colonel Thomas Rainsborough[13] in a passage that has become justly famous: 'I think,' he said, 'that the poorest he that is in England has a life to live as the greatest he; and therefore truly, sir, I think it's clear that every man that is to live under a government ought first by his own consent to put himself under that government; and I do think that the poorest man in England is not at all bound in a strict sense to that government that he has not had a choice to put himself under. And I am confident that when I have heard the reasons against it, something will be said to answer those reasons—inasmuch that I should doubt whether he was an Englishman or not that should doubt of these things.' [Sharp, 103]

The opposing position was articulated clearly by Henry Ireton. He was willing to concede that all those born in England should be protected from ejection from the kingdom, should have 'air and place and ground and the freedom of the highways and other things to live among us.' [Sharp, 104] But, since Parliament disposes of funds raised by taxes from those with a permanent interest in the kingdom, that is to say, from men holding a certain minimum of property, only such as are affected by such taxation should be in a position to determine the lawmakers; no representation without taxation, as it were! Against the Leveller position, Ireton argued forcefully that their demands on representation, if put into effect, could very well result in a situation where no property would be secure since those who wouldn't bear the burden of taxation would be able to lay that burden on others. If all men have a right to a voice in elections simply by nature, then 'by that same right of nature…by which you can say a man has an equal right with another to the choosing of him that shall govern him, by the same right of nature he has the same right in any goods he sees: meat, drink, clothes, to take and use them for his suste-nance; he has a freedom to the land, the ground, to exercise it, till it. He has the freedom to anything that anyone does account himself to have any property in.'[14] One is reminded of Bastiat's aphorism 'Government is that great fiction, through which everybody endeavours to live at the expense of everybody else.' [Bastiat, 99] Anyone who lives in a modern democracy cannot but be aware that one part of the population pays for what another part of the population consumes and that he who robs Peter to pay Paul may always count on Paul's enthusiastic support.

Neither side of this debate is wildly unreasonable.[15] On the one hand, the Leveller position is that those who are permanently to be affected by law should have a say in choosing their lawmakers; on the other hand, Ireton's position is that those who pay the bills should have the final say over what bills are to be incurred. What seems to have occurred to neither party was that the problem lies somewhat deeper than either supposes and that the whole notion of representation is suspect. If Parliament were to have the power to make laws binding on the whole Commonwealth but not to exact taxes or otherwise affect the disposition of property, then the basis of Ireton's objection to universal suffrage would disappear. On the other hand, if Parliament had no power of law-making at all, then the Leveller objection to property-holder-only suffrage would disappear.

The Levellers were suspicious that the outcome of the Revolution would be that the very same powers exercised heretofore by the king would from now on be exercised by Parliament. As it turns out, in the long run their suspicion was justified with this salient difference, that when the king exercised the executive functions of state, Parliament could, with some degree of success, oppose his tax measures; but when the executive functions came to be exercised by a sub-committee of Parliament itself (and that, after all, is just what the Cabinet is) the possibility of Parliament's opposing the will of the executive disappeared like mist on a warm summer's morning. If that were to happen, as it did, all that the Revolution would have effected would have been a change of master and, as Lysander Spooner remarked, 'A man is none the less a slave because he is allowed to choose a new master once in a term of years.'[16] What the Levellers' 'Agreement' was groping towards was the idea of a set of constitutional provisions limiting the power of *any* legislature or *any* executive, something like the 1653 Instrument of Government or the Bill of Rights of 1689, if somewhat more radical.

A 1649 pamphlet, 'An Agreement of the Free People of England' proposed a more extensive list of proposals. Of particular interest is the listing of what Parliament can, and cannot, do. What it *can* do is to preserve peace, international commerce, give effect to the safeguards of life, limb and property requested by Parliament of the King in the 1628 Petition of Right, raise money, provided the burdens would fall equally upon all, and do whatever is conducive to these ends or the enlargement of freedom, redress of grievances and economic prosperity. Among the things that Parliament *cannot* do is to constrain men in matters of conscience regarding religion; impress men into the army or navy; extend special legal privileges to some and not others; give judgement except under law; require self-incrimination in criminal cases; restrain free trade either directly or by means of excises or customs; permit people to avoid paying their debts or imprison people for debt; continue or extend capital punishment to crimes not destructive of society; impose tithes; and appoint clergy. [Sharp, 172-175.] By 1649, however, the Levellers' moment had come and gone. The Army had seized control of the government, various mutinies had been repressed,[17] political dissension stifled,[18] and the indecision stemming from vacillation concerning the fate of the monarchy had been drastically resolved by the execution of the king.

DIGGERS

The Levellers weren't the only radical social movement to flourish at this time. Associated in the popular mind with the Levellers are the group that has come to be known as the Diggers, their name coming from an attempt by a group of more radical reformers to appropriate and use some uncultivated common land with a view to feeding the poor. On 1st April 1649, a small group of radicals, some twenty or thirty men, including Gerrard Winstanley, came together on St George's Hill in Walton-on-Thames and began to cultivate the waste land there by digging, hence their name. After clashes with local landowners, the group moved in August to Cobham Heath, just over a mile from Walton, and continued their activities there. Similar disturbances ensued and by the spring of 1650, the colony was unable to continue. Walton and Cobham were the two most prominent Digger enterprises, though there were also some attempts at other places in other counties, such as Northamptonshire, Kent, Hertfordshire, Middlesex and Bedfordshire. The efforts of the Diggers were ephemeral, the numbers actively involved tiny, and the result a resounding practical failure. As a practical experiment, the whole thing lasted just over a year after which it collapsed under the weight of legal threats and popular resistance. The theoretical outcome was the production of some pamphlets by the writer most closely associated with the Diggers, Gerrard Winstanley.

We have seen that the Levellers were accused of implicitly or explicitly proposing the reduction of all social distinctions to one level, and of envisaging a radical restriction of property rights. We have also seen the leading Levellers vehemently deny that such was their programme although Overton perhaps gave some ground for that suspicion when he proposed that those commons which had been enclosed should be made available once again for the free use and benefit of the poor. [see Gurney, 37] A re-appropriation by the poor of much of the land of England was precisely the programme of the Diggers. To draw a rough but not inaccurate contrast between the two movements, we might say that whereas the Levellers were concerned with political reform first and foremost and with economic reform only in a subsidiary way, the Diggers were concerned with political reform by economic means. If the Levellers were few and the time of their influence brief, the Diggers were even fewer and their time of influence even briefer. The Levellers appealed to the law of nature to support their claims; so too did the Diggers. But whereas the Levellers saw natural law as supporting individual rights, including the right to property, the Diggers saw it as supporting the right of all to the basic means of subsistence which, in the context of the seventeenth century, meant access to land, with the rights of the individual limited to a share in the common produce. From the Digger perspective, land was given to all for the good of all and no one might appropriate to himself alone what belongs to all.

The Digger movement wasn't without historical antecedents. In England, there had been the short-lived Peasants' Revolt of 1381, of course, but much more immediately relevant was the German Peasant Revolt of the sixteenth century. All these disturbances had their theoretical root in the Christian belief that private property was a result of original sin and that common ownership of all natural resources was the original and better disposition of things. In the context of this belief, the standard justification of private property was that it was the practically best way to arrange matters given man's fallen nature. The Diggers believed that private property wasn't so much the product of sin but its cause: private property isn't the result of original sin; original sin is rather the result of private property! Sabine captures this thought well when he writes that for the Diggers, 'The root of all evil is covetousness and greed, which first produced private property while the latter causes all supremacy of one man over another, all manner of bloodshed, and the enslaving of the masses of men, who have been reduced to poverty by the wage-system and are forced to support by their labor the very power that enslaves them. Consequently most social ills and most of human vice can be removed by destroying private property, especially in land.' [Sabine, 492]

A hundred years after the English Civil War, in a different country and in a different language, private property will once again be identified as the root of all social evil. Jean-Jacques Rousseau wrote, 'The first man who, having enclosed a piece of ground, to whom it occurred to say *this is mine*, and found people sufficiently simple to believe him, was the true founder of civil society. From how many crimes, wars, murders, how many miseries and horrors Mankind would have been spared by him who, pulling up the stakes or filling in the ditch, had cried out to his kind: Beware of listening to this impostor; You are lost if you forget that the fruits are everyone's and the Earth no one's.'[19] If the Digger influence ran into the sand, Rousseau's influence (as we shall see) would irradiate all subsequent political thought. Still, Winstanley's position on the land question did have its later followers in English-speaking countries.. The interest taken in Winstanley by late-nineteenth-century British radicals reflected the immense importance of the land question in late-Victorian Britain. Henry George writes, 'Poverty deepens as wealth increases, and wages are forced down while productive power grows, because land, which is the source of all wealth and the field of all labour, is monopolised. To extirpate poverty, to make wages what justice demands they should be, the full earnings of the labourer, we must therefore substitute for the individual ownership of land a common ownership. Nothing else will go to the cause of the evil...'[20]

In the quasi-mythical Digger account of history, the people of England have been held in subjection ever since William the Conqueror and his henchmen arrived in 1066, grabbed all the land of England, and divided it up among themselves. The law is simply a device backed by physical sanctions for preserving the *status quo* and the whole apparatus of persisting robbery is defended by the ideological apparatus of the Church, whose apologists for this flagrant wrongdoing are rewarded by a share of the booty in the form of tithes. Were the Diggers issuing a call to outright revolution? No. In fact, the Diggers tended towards pacifism rather than militancy. What they wanted, in practical terms, was the right to cultivate the extensive acreage of unenclosed common land while leaving the existing enclosed property as it was.

The Levellers had John Lilburne, Richard Overton and William Walwyn to make their case; the Diggers effectively had one man, the semi-mystic Gerrard Winstanley. Winstanley's public activities took place over a very short period, between 1648 and 1652, and the practical side of those activities took place primarily in the year 1649. Winstanley has been claimed by many subsequent thinkers as presaging their particular concerns, not least by Marxists and socialists. George Woodcock, the author of *Anarchism*, sees him as antici- pating Kropotkin's notion of 'Mutual Aid' and thus beginning the anarchist tradition of direct action. George Orwell, too, sees Winstanley as a predecessor of anarchism rather than of socialism. [Woodcock, 43f.]

The tract, 'A Declaration of the Poor Oppressed People of England' (June 1649) written by Winstanley and 44 others,[21] was an appeal addressed to those that are called, Lords of the Manor and is, in the main, a declaration of intent on the part of the Diggers to take and make use of the land, specifically the commons, which, they believe, was given to all for the use of all. Winstanley and his co-authors wrote, 'the main thing we aim at, and for which we declare our resolutions to go forth and act, is this: to lay bold upon, and as we stand in need to cut and fell and make the best advantage we can of the woods and trees that grow upon the commons, to be a stock for ourselves, and our poor brethren, through the land of England, to plant the commons withal; and to provide us bread to eat, till the fruit of our labours in the earth bring forth increase. And we shall meddle with none of your properties (but what is called commonage) till the spirit in you make you cut up your lands and goods, which were got and still is kept in your hands by murder and theft.' [Winstanley 1973, 103] The authors of the Declaration disclaimed any intention to interfere with settled property even though it had been acquired by violence and dishonesty. They wrote, 'For though you and your ancestors got your property by murder and theft, and you keep it by the same power from us that have an equal right to the land with you by the righteous law of creation, yet we shall have no occasion of quarrelling (as you do) about that disturbing devil, called particular property. For the earth, with all her fruits of corn, cattle and such like, was made to be a common storehouse of livelihood to all mankind, friend and foe, without exception.' [Winstanley 1973, 100]

The Diggers took grave exception to money and trade. They wrote, 'we must make use of gold or silver as we do of other metals, but not to buy and sell withal; for buying and selling is the great cheat that robs and steals the earth one from another. It is that which makes some lords, others beggars, some rulers, others to be ruled; and makes great murderers and thieves to be imprisoners and hangers of little ones, or of sincere-hearted men.' [Winstanley 1973, 101]

In another appeal, this one entitled 'A Watchword to the City of London, and the Army' (August 1649) Winstanley defended the Digger's adventure on St George's Hill by reminding the City of London and the Army that they, with others, had given their money and their service to rid England of the royal tyranny; he wrote, 'all sorts…have paid taxes, free-quarter, excise, or adventured their lives to cast out that kingly office' and so 'those from whom money and blood was received ought to obtain freedom in the land to themselves and posterity, by the law of contract between Parliament and people.' [Winstanley 1973, 136] Winstanley vigorously denied that the Digger's activities on St George's Hill were in any way an infringement of the rights of others. [see Winstanley 1973, 137]

Apart from his tractarian literature, Winstanley produced one substantial book, the *Law of Freedom*, his single most sustained piece of writing, which came out in 1651-1652 towards the end of his active involvement in politics. The basic idea of this work is that poverty is the ground of all that restricts and limits human freedom. To be free isn't just to be unfettered but to be able to use the earth and its produce. Politically, Winstanley saw two possible modes of social organisation. One, based around the idea of the preservation of all, is at the root of the commonwealth in which all, strong and weak alike, are protected. The other, based around the idea of self-preservation, is at the root of royal government and is productive of covetousness and of tyranny. In this latter mode, land is held by some to the exclusion of others and bought and sold as any other commodity. There can be no true equality or liberty unless all land is held in common. In a striking anticipation of certain communist tenets, Winstanley would have it that all should have access according to their needs from a common store. In a slightly more chilling anticipation, Winstanley would have it that all should be compelled to work productively up to a certain age. Personal property wouldn't be affected by the communalisation of land. Winstanley's thought, says Sabine, rested upon 'a clear insight into the inevitable dependence of political liberty and equality upon the control of economic causes....Nowhere is there a clearer perception of the incompatibility of economic exploitation with democratic ideals.' [Sabine, 494-495]

True freedom, for Winstanley, isn't a freedom to buy and sell, to be uncoerced in religious matters or the like; it lies, rather, in the free enjoyment of the earth. 'A man,' he wrote, 'had better to have no body than to have no food for it; therefore this restraining of the earth from brethren by brethren is oppression and bondage; but the free enjoyment thereof is true freedom.' [Winstanley 1973, 295-296] He anticipated some obvious objections to the Digger platform—it will lead to idleness if all belongs to all; there will have to be a community of persons as well as of property, 'a community of all men and women for copulation,' and there will be no law for lack of government. [see Winstanley 1973, 302] Winstanley responded that here will be no idleness, for all will be made to work![22] Whereas the storehouses are to be communally furnished, houses and their contents will belong to individual families, and personal relations, conjugal and familial, will remain private. And as for government: 'Government is the wise and free ordering of the earth and the manners of mankind by observation of particular laws or rules, so that all the inhabitants may live peaceably in plenty and freedom in the land where they are born and bred.' [Winstanley 1973, 305] The genuine root of government is a concern for the preservation of all, 'to seek the good of others as himself' but the concern for self-preservation is the root of tyranny. [Winstanley 1973, 315] Magistrates are to be chosen yearly, for long service in office tends towards corruption: 'the heart of man is so subject to be overspread with the clouds of covetousness, pride and vain-glory: for though at the first entrance into places of rule they be of public spirits, seeking the freedom of others as their own; yet continuing long in such a place where honours and greatness is coming in, they become selfish, seeking themselves and not common freedom.' [Winstanley 1973, 319]

Winstanley envisaged a variety of public offices: representatives, peacemakers, overseers, soldiers, taskmasters, and judges. The heart of his scheme, however, lies not in these arrangements but in his pre-romantic vision of a society producing and distributing what they require simply on the basis of need. After a minimal formal education, all children are to be set to occupations connected to the basic activities of husbandry, mining, pastoralism and woodcraft and all trades derivative from those primary activities such as shoemaking, tailoring, carpentry and the like, at which activities and trades they will work until the age of forty. After that, work is optional and only those retired from work shall be eligible to serve as officers. All that is produced is to be placed in storehouses or other depositories from which people are free to take what they need without recourse to buying and selling. If all this sounds suspiciously familiar, it should, for it is a staple of two forms of organisation—communist countries and some religious orders. [see Winstanley 1973, 367-368]

There can be no doubt that there was a strong mystical religious streak in Winstanley, a common enough feature of public life in seventeenth century England. His earliest writings are, to me at least, largely incomprehensible, my opinion being shared by many commentators, though some recent scholarship has claimed to discern elements of Winstanley's later work in these relatively juvenile productions (relatively juvenile because Winstanley was nearly forty years old when he first wrote!). Winstanley's *The New Law of Righteousness* exhibits some of the mystical opacity of his earlier writings but it also contains a clear expression of his fundamental view that no man was made to be lord over another and that all men had been given equal rights to access the earth and its resources.

Apart from being a mystic, Winstanley was also a millenarian. His early publications, *The Mysterie of God* and *Breaking of the Day of God* are described by Gurney as being 'overtly millenarian works, and strikingly anti-clerical and anti-formalist,' and Winstanley's millenarianism was evident in almost all his writings. [Gurney, 27] We can have heaven on earth—the problem of scarcity is ultimately not a problem at all for there is enough and to spare for everyone—all that we have to do is to divide things up equitably—distribution is the only problem we have—production is scarcely problematic once the temptation to idleness is overcome. Winstanley's vision is of a world in which everything is 'restored to perfection and freed from conflict, poverty and oppression.' [Gurney, 29] Winstanley may, perhaps, be forgiven for his economic naïvety. The same forgiveness, however, can hardly be extended to us. We have had extensive experience of just how well communism actually works. The basic problem, apart from the massive and insuperable problem of lack of incentives, is that in such a system, there is simply no way to discover what needs to be produced, how much of it, where, and when. 'From each according to his ability, to each according to his needs': such was Winstanley's ideal; such was the Communistic Commonwealth he evidently imagined would naturally evolve if only the equal claims of all to the use of the Earth were once recognised and respected.' [Berens, 216] Winstanley was a communist, one of the very first and, like all communists, he has a tenuous grasp on economics and, in particular, he lacks any adequate grasp of how people with their real needs and desires have to function in the real world as opposed to how they might do so in a reconstituted Garden of Eden.

Some have discerned a change between Winstanley's earlier writings and *The Law of Freedom*, believing that the latter work 'has often seemed troubling, and less an advance on his earlier positions than a retreat from the optimistic belief in human perfectibility that permeated *The New Law of Righteousness*.' [Gurney, 92] Compared to the anarchic enthusiasm of the writings between 1648 and 1650, the concrete proposals detailed in *The Law of Freedom* can seem authoritarian and domineering. [but see Gurney, 94] Whatever the truth of this matter, Winstanley's essential and unchanging argument was this. The earth belongs to all; it is a common treasury. But covetousness brought it about that some appropriated for themselves what belonged to all. This led to the creation of a power, the state, capable of protecting these ill-gotten gains. Covetous appropriation by a few of what belongs to the many is, according to Winstanley, the source of all wars and bloodshed, theft and slavery. If we desire these evils to be eliminated, then the source of those evils, private property, must be abolished. We have seen that for many Christian thinkers, private property was understood to be a result of original sin, a pragmatic solution to the problems that arise in our post-Edenic existence. For Winstanley, however, covetousness and the private appropriation of property either are the causes of man's first sin or just *are* that first sin.

Winstanley too understood that 'state power is related to the property system' so that, in his view, political freedom cannot be had without substantial economic equality and that this, in turn, requires the abolition of private property. [Hill, 9] Hill goes so far as to claim that 'The Levellers sought to establish political democracy, a state in which the poorest would be as free as the richest. They based this on a system of inalienable natural rights,[23] one of which was a right to property. This at once gave rise to contradictions; in order to safeguard the property rights of small men against the rich and powerful, some Levellers would have withheld the vote from those who were economically dependent, such as servants and paupers. Winstanley, like the Leveller's shrewdest critic, Commissary-General Ireton, saw that a natural right to accumulate property was incompatible with liberty. For Ireton this was a decisive argument against extending the vote to those who weren't landowners or freemen or corporations: for Winstanley it was an argument for complementing political freedom by economic freedom.' [Hill, 49]

In his earlier writings, Winstanley seemed to envisage a reformed society existing without any, or with little, government. In his later writings, he had moved to support at least a minimal state responsible for the preservation of law and order. [see Hill, 41-42] The Diggers and the Levellers agreed on many things. Although there were internal differences between the leading Levellers, with some, such as Overton, more inclined to radicalism, it's true to say that the Levellers by and large sought political reform without any specific intent to disturb the existing property regime. Ireton, in the Putney debates, argued against them that their demands, logically pursued, were incompatible with the rights of property and here, he and Winstanley would appear to agree. The difference between them being, of course, that Ireton took this as a reason to reject the Leveller's political demands whereas Winstanley took it as a reason to link political reform with economic reform.

KILLING NOE MURDER

Once Oliver Cromwell took power, the fluid post-conflict political situation hardened and it seemed for a time as if a new royal dynasty was going to be established. The prospect of this produced one spectacular piece of writing from this period that doesn't fit neatly into either the Leveller or the Digger camp but harkens back to an earlier tradition of the justification of tyrannicide. This is Edward Sexby's (aka William Allen's) 'Killing Noe Murder (1657). This tract has to be one of the most extraordinary productions of the revolutionary period, both in content and in sustained literary sardonic style. It is a general defence of tyrannicide addressed to the specific desired object of that exercise, Cromwell! Nothing in life, Sexby thinks, will become Cromwell better than his leaving of it. 'To your Highness justly belongs the honour of dying for the people,' he says, 'and it cannot choose but be unspeakable consolation to you in the last moments of your life to consider with how much benefit to the world you are like to leave it.' [Sexby, 360]

Sexby believes three questions need to be considered; first, is Cromwell a tyrant?; second, if he is, is it lawful to kill him?; and third, if lawful, would his killing be beneficial or harmful to the commonwealth? [Sexby, 364] Let us take a look at Sexby's treatment of the first two of these questions.[24] Sexby makes the common distinction between two types of tyrant: those who although entitled to govern, do so tyrannically (*tyrannus exercitio*); and those who aren't entitled to govern at all (*tyrannus sine titulo*). To further his accusation of tyranny against Cromwell, Sexby supplies us with a list of characteristics of the tyrant which he has gleaned from a variety of sources, including Plato, Aristotle, Tacitus and Machiavelli. Many tyrants begin their career as military defenders of the people against oppression, which oppression, that battle won, they then themselves resume. They use fraud more than force. They eliminate all possible competitors and all persons of excellence. They limit or prohibit public assemblies. They are always well guarded. They impose burdensome taxes and duties and excise on the people. They use war as a way to divert people from the ills they suffer and as a spurious means of justifying the taxes and levies. They use others to do their dirty work. They pretend to love God and even to be divinely inspired. [Sexby, 368-370] On all these counts, Sexby thinks, Cromwell fits the bill. The answer to the first question, then, is yes— Cromwell is a tyrant.

So, he now asks Cromwell for the source of his authority. Who, he asks, 'made thee a prince and a judge over us?' [Sexby, 366] If God, please show us evidence of this. If the people, how was this done? 'If to change the government without the people's consent; if to dissolve their representatives by force and disannul their acts; if to give the name of the people's representatives to confederates of his own, that he may establish iniquity by a law; if to take away men's lives out of all course of law, by certain murderers of his own appointment, whom he names a High Court of Justice; if to decimate men's estates, and by his own power to impose upon the people what taxes he pleases; and to maintain all by force of arms: if I say, all this does make a tyrant, his own impudence cannot deny, but he is as complete a one as ever has been since there have been societies of men.' [Sexby, 366-367] Cromwell, then, is a tyrant and a tyrant without title.

As a tyrant without title, may Cromwell be lawfully killed? Sexby adheres to the traditional view that a ruler who has degenerated into a tyrant (*tyrannus exercitio*) may be brought to justice by the people's representatives but not by a private individual acting without authority. On the other hand, tyrants without title are simply criminals who deserve 'no benefit from human society' and 'no protection from the law.' [see Sexby, 371] Men enter society to live and to live well and to do so they submit to the law of reason and justice. Without law, Sexby remarks in a Hobbesian manner, men's appetites 'would quickly make society as unsafe, or more, than solitude itself, and we should associate only to be nearer our misery and our ruin.' [Sexby, 371] But a tyrant without title is under no law. He is not only *not* a magistrate, he isn't even a member of society properly conceived. 'A tyrant,' he says, 'being no part of the common-wealth, nor submitting to the laws of it, but making himself above all law, there is no reason why he should have the protection that is due to a member of a commonwealth, nor any defence from laws, that does acknowledge none.' [Sexby, 372] As the tyrant without title, then, isn't under any law, individuals may defend themselves against him by appropriate means including deadly force if necessary. In a passage that recalls the famous interview between Alexander and the Pirate, and which will warm the hearts of libertarians, Sexby writes, 'for what can be more absurd in nature, and contrary to all common sense, than to call him thief and kill him that comes alone with a few to rob me, and to call him Lord Protector and obey him that robs me with regiments and troops….But if it be the number of adherents only, not the cause, that makes the difference between a robber and a Protector, I wish that number were defined, that we might know where the thief ends and the prince begins, and be able to distinguish between a robbery and a tax.' [Sexby, 374]

JAMES HARRINGTON

The English Revolution was a practical success in search of a theory. The establishment of a Commonwealth left Englishmen with a *de facto* repub-lican regime in need of a theoretical justification. The Commonwealth, like Topsy, had just 'growed' without anyone in particular setting out to make it. What was needed was an explanation of how it had come about without, as it were, anyone (or at least very few) in fact desiring it. 'There is a real sense,' writes J. G. A. Pocock, 'in which republican theories were a consequence, not a cause or even a precondition, of the execution of the King and the temporary abolition of the monarchy.' [Pocock, xi) Of those who attempted to provide a theoretical grounding for the Commonwealth during its ten or so years of existence, the most significant thinker was James Harrington.[25] Harrington does not have the same name recognition as, say, Hobbes, his contempo-rary, but according to Sabine, he was 'a political philosopher of first-rate originality, not the equal of Hobbes in the bold sweep of his reasoning but much his superior in the grasp of political realities.' [Sabine, 497] Harrington draws on the classical authors, in particular Plato, for many of his ideas. He was also an avowed admirer of Machiavelli and followed Machiavelli's historical and comparative method, and his thought is permeated by a neo-Machiavellian realism.[26] 'He wanted to know how the English parliamentary monarchy, the government of king, lords and commons, had come to collapse, and he wanted to know what should replace it.' (Pocock, xv)[27]

Harrington's immediate practical influence was negligible but theoretically he contributed two enduring ideas to the republican debate. The first was that the structure of a government is ineluctably determined by the 'balance of dominion in the foundation,' that is, by whom and by how many the material resources in a given state were controlled. The second idea is that a lasting solution to England's political problems has to be located in a government of laws rather than a government of men. [see Scott 2004, 295] What is, perhaps, most interesting about Harrington, is that his account of the change from monarchy to republic is not couched in terms of pure ideas, as if the material, economic and social realities could be moulded into just any shape by the victor in a battle of ideas. Rather, he offered an explanation of the struggle between King and Parliament 'as a revolution, produced by the erosion of one political structure and the substitution of another through processes of long-term social change.' (Pocock, xix)

The key to understanding Harrington's thought is to grasp that he saw government as being essentially determined by a society's underlying social and economic forces.[28] Some inkling of this is present in the thought of the Levellers and especially in the thought of the Digger, Gerrard Winstanley; Harrington, however, is the first to make this thesis explicit, a good two hundred years before Karl Marx. The religious and political issues that drove the Revolution were obvious enough. Lying a little deeper, however, was the fundamental change in social and economic conditions that had slowly and quietly taken place in the sixteenth and early seventeenth centuries. Harrington was perhaps the first person to note clearly this shift in economic power. The way in which property is distributed in a society (and by property Harrington meant ownership of land) has a profound effect on the kind of government that is possible. Those who control the land, control the government.

The Tudor dynasty had emerged from the internecine Wars of the Roses that had resulted in the destruction of the English nobility as a class that could effectively oppose the monarch. The king was no longer *primus inter pares*, that noble who among other nobles just happened to occupy the throne. After 1485, no one in England was in a position militarily to challenge the king. The estates of the great nobles were fragmented and the land allocated to a host of smaller landowners. Much the same thing happened under Henry VIII, this time with the landed estates of the Church. 'The result in both cases was to distribute wealth among a numerous class of landowners from whom the demand for popular rights was certain sooner or later to arise.' [Sabine, 498] Harrington wrote in his *A System of Politics*, 'All government is interest, and the predominant interest gives the matter or foundation of government. If one man has the whole, or two parts in three of the whole land or territory, the interest of one man is the predominant interest, and causes absolute monarchy. If a few men have the whole, or two parts in three, of the whole land or territory, the interest of the few or of the nobility is the predominant interest; and, were there any such thing in nature, would cause a pure aristocracy....If the many or the people have the whole, or two parts in three, of the whole land or territory, the interest of the many or of the people is the predominant interest, and causes democracy.'[29] If the government does not reflect the underlying economic realities then one gets a tyranny, an oligarchy or anarchy.

The Levellers' demand for a government based on laws was, remarks John Gurney, 'famously taken up by James Harrington, whose 1656 work *The Commonwealth of Oceana* provided a detailed model of a system of government based on precisely this principle.' [Gurney, 96] According to Harrington, what distinguishes a commonwealth from all other forms of government is that it is a government of laws and not men. Although Harrington agreed with Hobbes that all government is a matter of control, he did not agree with him in thinking it a matter of irrelevance what kind of control a government exercised. The essential distinction between tyrannical and legitimate government remains inasmuch as that in a tyranny, rule is exercised for the sake of the ruler whereas in a legitimate government it is exercised for the sake of the ruled. 'All forms of government,' writes Sabine, 'including the commonwealth, require the coincidence of power with authority. No amount of wisdom can keep a government going smoothly unless the political power and economic power fall together, but it is equally true that government does not flow spontaneously from a given economic arrangement.' [Sabine, 502]

Harrington agreed with Hobbes that there can be no power without the sword but he adds to this the obvious but often ignored fact that swords must be paid for. As Hobbes said of the law that 'without this sword it is but paper, so he might have thought of this sword that without an hand it is but cold iron. The hand which is either an army in the field, or ready for the field upon occasion. But an army is a beast that hath a great belly and must be fed; wherefore this will come unto what pastures you have, and what pastures you have will come unto the balance of the property, without which the public sword is but a name or a mere spitfrog.' [Harrington 1992, 13]

If a commonwealth is to be established and preserved, then, it is essential to prevent the accumulation of large estates and equally essential to bring about the division of such large estates as already existed. What is the minimum number of landowners one would need in order to provide the economic basis for a commonwealth? Harrington estimated that number to be about 5,000 which, curiously, is more or less the same figure that Plato had given for the ideal number of citizens in his model city in his *Laws*.

Harrington proposed rotation in office, election by ballot, a written constitution,[30] religious freedom and a separation of powers. The separation of powers he proposed wasn't that which was later to be proposed by Montesquieu[31] but a division between the power to propose legislation, the power to adopt it and the power to execute it. [Harrington 1992, 34] Harrington's practical proposal envisaged a complex system of indirect representation in which units would elect representatives to the next highest level, which level would then elect its representatives to the next higher level and so on, giving us, from bottom to top, parishes, hundreds, tribes and senate. On the point at issue between the

Levellers and Ireton, Harrington came down on Ireton's side (and also, ironically, Winstanley's), believing it not to be possible to separate political rights from the rights of property.

SIR ROBERT FILMER

If the name of Sir Robert Filmer is known to students of political philosophy at all today, it will probably be only as the source of provocation that led to John Locke's *First Treatise of Government.*[32] The common estimation of Filmer is that he was something of a village idiot, putting forward a fantastically untenable theory of political obligation that Locke was able to dispatch with consummate panache. There are a number of problems with this estimate. First, if Filmer's views were so self-evidently idiotic, one can only wonder why Locke (and others) devoted so much time and attention to combating them. Second, on closer analysis, when one takes a look at what Filmer in fact wrote, there are elements of his account that his critics appear not to have met at all, in particular his arguments against the notion of contract as the foundation of political obligation.[33] Carl Watner writes, I believe correctly, that Filmer's political tracts 'have an importance far surpassing the mere fact that Locke wrote in rebuttal to his *Patriarcha.* Filmer questioned the principle essential to all accounts of political obligation other than his own, the principle of consent. Perhaps, it could be argued that Locke realized Filmer's uncanny and unerring ways of pushing consent arguments to their radical anarchist conclusions required their own answer.' [Watner 1986, 122]

The basis of Filmer's positive account of political obligation depended upon his assimilation of political authority to paternal authority, taken together with a literalist and authoritarian reading of the Bible.[34] Human society, he argued, originated with Adam to whom was given the whole world, all the land and everything on it. All creatures, human as well as non-human, were subject to his primal and patriarchal authority. His successors to this day inherit this authority and have no need of the consent of those over whom they rule, any more than a father needs the consent of his children to his authority. It should be obvious why Filmer entitled his major work, *Patriarcha.* The premises upon which Filmer's account were based were part of the common sense of his period and so his argument had much more intuitive force then that it has now.

Filmer's defence of patriarchalism as the ground of monarchy has proved an easy target for philosophers from Locke onwards. His argument is manifestly weak, the assimilation of political authority to paternal authority providing a very insecure foundation for the edifice it is required to support. Even if we were to grant its starting presuppositions, it also suffers from the irremediable defect of not being able to identify *who* the legitimate successors to Adam are supposed to be. With a reasonably clear conscience, we can dismiss Filmer's positive argument; the critical side of Filmer's position, his attack on the doctrine of contract or consent, is a different animal altogether. [see Ashton, 3-15]

Filmer was greatly influenced by the writings of Jean Bodin, not least Bodin's unitary conception of sovereignty. Royal power was intrinsically incapable of being participated in by any of the ruler's subjects. [*Patriarcha* XX, 93] Moreover, Filmer maintained against the monarchomachs and some Catholic theorists such as Suarez and Bellarmine that no resistance of any kind to the king's rule could be in any way justified. As part of his effort to defend his positive account of the origin and nature of political obligation against attack, Filmer found it necessary to deflate those rival theories of the origin and justification of political obligation, in particular, those theories that located it in consent of the governed, for such theories made political authority both derivative and conditional. Before going into some detail in respect of Filmer's account, it might be useful to lay out the overall very simple structure of his argument. In effect, it comes to this. Any theory of political authority or political obligation that relies on the notion of contract or consent, invariably leads to anarchy, by which Filmer signifies chaos and disorder. Since anarchy is eminently undesirable, so too is the theory of consent which leads to it.

Filmer begins by attacking the idea that men are by nature free and equal. 'Within the last hundred years,' he writes, 'many of the Schoolmen and other Divines have published and maintained an opinion that 'Mankind is naturally endowed and born with freedom from all subjection, and at liberty to choose what form of government it please, and that the power which any one man hath over others was at the first by human right bestowed according to the discretion of the multitude.' [*Patriarcha*, I, 53] It is bad enough that such an horrendous idea should be entertained by Papists, but it's even worse when some eminent divines in the Reformed Churches come to the same conclusion! Whatever may be the convergence of Catholic and Protestant thought on this matter, Filmer believes it to be in contradiction to the history and doctrine of the Scriptures, and to be inconsistent with 'the constant practice of all ancient monarchies, and the very principles of the law of nature.' [*Patriarcha*, I, 53] From this doctrine of the natural freedom and equality of all, there follows inexorably the right of a people to resist their ruler. As might be expected, Filmer refers to the passages in *Romans* 13 and to *1 Peter* 2 to support his rejection of the doctrine of original freedom and equality but he also appeals to *Samuel* 8 in a surprising fashion. [*Patriarcha*, XXIII, 100-101] Most interpreters take the *Samuel* passage to demonstrate a less than enthusiastic Divine acquiescence in the Israelites's request for a king; Filmer, by contrast, takes the purpose of this passage as being 'to teach the people a dutiful obedience to their King, even in those things which themselves did esteem mischievous and inconvenient. For by telling them what a King would do, he instructs them what a subject must suffer. Yet not that it is right for Kings to do injury, but it is right for them to go unpunished by the people if they do it.' [*Patriarcha* XXIII, 97]

When it comes to the topic of consent or contract, Filmer points out that there is no record of any government ever beginning in this way (a point later made by Hume). Furthermore, even if, despite the manifold practical difficulties amounting almost to an impossibility, all people were to agree at some particular moment, why should the consent of new additions to the population not be required at another particular time, a point that was to be echoed by Thomas Jefferson in a letter to James Madison some one hundred and fifty years later when he wrote, 'it may be proved that no society can make a perpetual constitution, or even a perpetual law. The earth belongs always to the living generation. They may manage it then, and what proceeds from it, as they please, during their usufruct. They are masters too of their own persons, and consequently may govern them as they please. But persons and property make the sum of the objects of government. *The constitution and the laws of their predecessors are extinguished then in their natural course with those who gave them being...*'[35] To assist in the comprehension of his argument, Jefferson came up with a remarkable thought-experiment. He imagined the earth populated by generations of men, all of the same age, that die together, just at the moment that the next generation attains maturity. He writes, 'let us suppose a whole generation of men to be born on the same day, to attain mature age on the same day, and to die on the same day, leaving a succeeding generation in the moment of attaining their mature age all together' One discrete generation would then follow another, with no overlap. He invited Madison to reflect upon and respond to his arguments. Madison's response to Jefferson relies on that old perennial, tacit consent. 'I find no relief from these consequences,' writes Madison, 'but in the received doctrine that a tacit consent may be given to established Constitutions and laws, and that this assent may be inferred, where no positive dissent appears....May it not be questioned whether it be possible to exclude wholly the idea of tacit consent, without subverting the foundation of civil Society?'[36] Without such tacit consent, political society might well be subverted, but we have no reason to think that civil society would likewise fail, unless we make the classic mistake of conflating the civil and the political orders.

Filmer, of course, rejects the whole notion of tacit consent or consent by proxy and also the idea that the consent of one's progenitors can bind their descendants. [see Watner 1986, 119-122] As John Plamenatz notes, with some degree of justification, 'Filmer, when he argues that political authority does not rest on consent, is often forceful and ingenious...' [Plamenatz, 181] In words that anticipate the arguments of Lysander Spooner, Filmer remarks: 'if it were lawful for particular parts of the world by consent to choose their Kings, nevertheless their elections would bind none to subjection but only such as consented; for the major part never binds, but where men at first either agree to be so bound, or where a higher power so commands...'[37] Were it to be argued that the votes of parents can go proxy for their children then 'farewell the doctrine of the natural freedom of mankind; where subjection of children to parents is natural, there can be no natural freedom.'[38]

The core of Filmer's argument is that, if the natural freedom and equality of all were to be granted, then it would never have been possible for any government to get started or if, *mirabile dictu*, to be started, to be maintained. Natural freedom and equality leads straight to anarchy.[39] George H. Smith writes, 'Filmer challenged consent theorists to show how any sovereign government can be justified if we begin with the supposition that people are naturally free and equal. He repeatedly asserted that the doctrine of natural liberty and equality, which was commonly called upon to limit the powers of government, actually destroys the foundation of government itself and will land us in anarchy instead. Those who begin their political reasoning with a state of nature—a society without political authority or dominion in which every person enjoys equal rights—are logically doomed to remain in that anarchistic condition.' [Smith 2013, 99] If such universal unanimity isn't required in order to set up a king, and a part of the whole may legitimately do so, why shouldn't a part of the part have a similar power; indeed, why should it not be possible for everyman to be his own king? Anarchy again. Filmer writes:

> Since nature hath not distinguished the habitable world into kingdoms, nor determined what part of a people shall belong to one kingdom, and what to another, it follows that the original freedom of mankind being supposed, every man is at liberty to be of what kingdom he please, and so every petty company hath a right to make a kingdom by itself; and not only every city, but every village, and every family, nay, and every particular man, a liberty to choose himself to be his own King if he please; and he were a madman that being by nature free, would choose any man but himself to be his own governor. Thus to avoid the having but of one King of the whole world, we shall run into a liberty of having as many Kings as there be men in the world, which upon the matter, is to have no King at all, but leave all men to their natural liberty, which is the mischief the pleaders for natural liberty do pretend they would most avoid.[40]

George H. Smith is prepared to put Filmer on a list of 'the most influential political philosophers of the modern era' on foot of his penetrating criticism of the theory of consent, rescuing him from the outer darkness into which he is cast by most political theorists. [Smith 2013, 101] John Plamenatz's estimation of Filmer is somewhat more muted than Smith's—Filmer, he says, was 'a shrewd critic of doctrines he disliked' but 'he was not a deep thinker.' [Plamenatz, 186] In one form or another, Filmer's anti-contractarian arguments, will be rehearsed by those, such as David Hume and Edmund Burke, who reject contract or consent theories as the ultimate source of legitimate political authority. But before turning to consider Hume and Burke, let us first examine the writings of Filmer's supposed vanquisher, one who is often taken to be, as it were, the 'official' theorist of the new political order.

Notes

1 Wootton, 17; 18. David Brett argues that looked at 'with a Nelsonian eye from the top of his pillar in O'Connell Street, the Civil War was not an English affair at all, but most emphatically pan-British, fought in, around and across the inland [i.e. the Irish] sea.' [Brett, 265] It is hard to disagree with Norman Davies when he remarks that the label '"The English Civil War" must be one of the worst misnomers in the whole historical repertoire. Not much used at the time, the label ill suits the complex chain of conflicts which were fought out between Scotland, Ireland, and England after 1639.' [Davies 1999, 490] He believes that to describe the stirring events of this period as the "English Revolution" is to subscribe to a Marxist slogan which, he says, 'completely misses the point.' [Davies 1999, 490] My use of the term 'The English Revolution' for the title of this chapter is not intended to signify that I have inadvertently joined the Marxist camp but rather to emphasise that what took place in the three kingdoms of England, Ireland and Scotland in the fifty years be-

tween 1639 and 1689 wasn't just another dynastic or quasi-dynastic struggle followed by business as usual but a radical change in political practice and political thought.

2 For a superb collection of Leveller documents, see Otteson 2003. See especially Roger Williams's remarkable *Bloudy Tenent of Persecution for Cause of Conscience, Discussed in a Conference between Truth and Peace* (1644) in which he argues for the functional separation of church and state. Williams was an apprentice and a protégé of Sir Edward Coke; he was also a gifted linguist and the (reluctant) founder of Rhode Island. [see Barry 2012, 315-356]

3 See 'An Agreement of the People' and the Putney debates, passim. It would appear that the Levellers were also opposed to a monopoly of religion by a State Church. '[The Levellers] moved quite close to a voluntaryist conception of the church, and a Leveller petition of March 1647 went so far as to urge "that tithes and all other enforced maintainences may be for ever abolished, and nothing in place thereof imposed, but that ministers may be paid only by those who voluntarily choose them, and contract with them for their labours".' [Watner 1986, 116]

4 Watner 1986, 117. For a succinct account of the broader historical aspects of the intra-New Model Army disputes, see Ashton 290-353.

5 For an historically-based treatment of this subject, see Wootton 1991, passim.

6 Lilburne 1646, 'The Freeman's Freedom Vindicated,' 31-32.

7 See Sabine 483 and Oakley 2012, 143. The eminent historian, John Burrow, commenting on David Hume's *History of England*, remarks that one way in which Hume managed to offend the piety of his contemporaries was by his refusal 'to accept the Whig notion of an enduring "ancient constitution" subverted by the Stuarts. To him, English constitutional precedents, by the early seventeenth century, were chaotically contradictory, reflecting the shifting balance between Crown and nobility over the preceding centuries....The early Stuarts could find precedents for most if not all of what they did, and the Tudors had ruled much more absolutely while avoiding theoretical claims. Essentially it was the parliamentary leaders in the 1640s who became the innovators...' [Burrow, 333]

8 Gatti, 147; see also 140-148.

9 See Smith and Moore, 97-101 for an accessible version of this piece.

10 George Smith remarks, 'Richard Overton and John Lilburne were prominent Levellers who defended self-proprietorship, private property, and government by consent before John Locke was a teenager.' [Smith 2013, 6; see also Smith and Moore, 97-101]

11 These discussions are commonly known as the Putney debates. For an exhaustive account of these debates, see Woodhouse. For excerpts, see Sharp, 102-130 and Wootton, 285-317.

12 These proposals make their appearance in 'An Agreement of the People' 1647 which seems to have been written primarily by Walwyn with contributions from Lilburne and Overton.

13 Rainsborough, who was a thorn in the side of the senior commanders of the New Model Army, died in controversial circumstances in 1648 at the age of thirty eight.

14 Wootton, 291. It is worth noting that well over 200 years after Ireton made these remarks, John Stuart Mill would echo them in a modern mode, arguing strongly that those who receive or stand to receive more benefits from the state than they contribute to it shouldn't be in a position to determine the allocation of state funds. Mill writes, 'It is also important, that the assembly which votes the taxes, either general or local, should be elected exclusively by those who pay something towards the taxes imposed. Those who pay no taxes, disposing by their votes of other people's money, have every motive to be lavish and not to economise. As far as money matters are concerned, any power of voting possessed by them is a violation of the fundamental principle of free government; a severance of the power of control, from the interest in its beneficial exercise. It amounts to allowing them to put their hands into other people's pockets, for any purpose which they think fit to call a public one...That representation should be coextensive with taxation, not stopping short of it, but also not going beyond it, is in accordance with the theory of British institutions.' [Mill, *Considerations on Representative Government*, Chapter VIII, 331-332] He continues, 'I regard it as required by first principles, that the receipt of parish relief should be a peremptory disqualification for the franchise. He who cannot by his labour suffice for his own support, has no claim to the privilege of helping himself to the money of others. By becoming dependent on the remaining members of the community for actual subsistence, he abdicates his claim to equal rights with them in other respects. Those to whom he is indebted for this continuance of his very existence, may justly claim the exclusive management of those common concerns, to which he now brings nothing, or less than he takes away.' [332]

15 It has been suggested that the differences between the views expressed by Rainsborough and by Ireton are significantly less unbridgeable than might at first appear, a matter more of degree than of kind. 'What was at issue at Putney, in Macpherson's view,' writes Robert Ashton, 'was a clash between two restrictive view of the franchise, one of which was simply more restrictive than the other.' [Ashton, 310]

16 Spooner 1870, sect. VI, 24.

17 What has come to be called the Corkbush Field Mutiny took place on 15 November 1647 and was followed two years later by the Bishopsgate mutiny. [see Ashton 312-314]

18 In what I would regard as a tendentious account, Norman Davies writes that Cromwell 'had watched the solidarity of the New Model Army fragment, as radical agitators such as John Lilburne…harangued the troops in their camp at Putney' and so was 'forced to take drastic action… in due course the "Levellers" were repressed.' [Davies 1999, 496]

19 Rousseau, 1754a, 161 (Part II, (1).

20 George 1879, 234 (VI, II, 2). Henry George (1837-1897) was an American economist and social reformer and the author of *Progress and Poverty* (1931 [1879]). The land question loomed large not only in Victorian Britain but also in Victorian Ireland where one reformer, Michael Davitt, proposed a Georgist solution that had the distinction of being roundly rejected by every shade of nationalist! [see Donnelly, 93]

21 Or rather, I suspect, written by Winstanley and signed by the others!

22 Winstanley 1973, 303. The totalitarian impulse is never far below the surface of the communist utopia.

23 For a challenging presentation of the thesis that the idea of natural rights significantly pre-date the onset of modernity, see Tierney 2001.

24 There is no little irony in Sexby's attack on Cromwell, echoing, as it does, Milton's justification of the execution of Charles I in his *The Tenure of Kings and Magistrates*. (see Milton 1649)

25 See Bowle, 392, 395.

26 For a brief historical treatment of Harrington and his work, see Worden, 450-455.

27 It is tempting to devote some space to the only other major attempt to provide a theoretical grounding for the Commonwealth, *The Excellencie of a Free-State*, written by the Machiavellian-admiring journalist, erstwhile Leveller, political hack, satirist, Cromwellian mouthpiece and multiple turncoat who went under the real but unlikely name of Marchamont Nedham, but that is a temptation I must, reluctantly, resist. [see Nedham, passim]

28 Hume seems to have Harrington in mind when he refers to a noted author who has made 'property the foundation of all government.' [Hume 1741b, 33] Hume believes this claim to be overstated but, if expressed more moderately, to be essentially sound. He adds, however, that 'A Government may endure for several ages, though the balance of power, and the balance of property do not coincide.' [Hume 1741b, 35]

29 §§10-12, §14; Harrington 1992, 271-272.

30 The belief that a written constitution can, by itself, bring into being and sustain in being the political order it delineates betrays a touching and naïve faith in the creative power of the written word. 'Can a document restrain a government official?' asks Sheldon Richman. He replies to his own question: 'Obviously not. James Madison understood this when he called the Bill of Rights a "parchment barrier."' [Richman 2016, 130]

31 Andrew Kahn believes Montesquieu to be 'one of the great political thinkers of the modern world.' [Kahn, vii] I can understand why Kahn would make this judgement but, none the less, I cannot agree with it. It is true that Montesquieu's *The Spirit of the Laws* had a significant effect not only on the thinking of the founders of what was to become the United States of America but also on Catherine the Great's legislative reforms in Russia; despite this, Montesquieu's political thought, while influential, was largely unoriginal and so merits no particular attention in this book. For a succinct introduction to Montesquieu's thought, see Shklar.

32 In his introduction to his edition of Filmer's works, Peter Laslett write that Filmer 'was a man of genuine culture, a seventeenth-century literary and intellectual critic. He was personally acquainted with poets, lawyers, theologians, politicians, playwrights and historians and he bought the books of his contemporaries and wrote judicious, critical and often humorous notices of them for his own amusement and for the satisfaction of a small circle of friends. The political events of his last years forced him into more serious controversy and into publication…' [Laslett 1949, 10]

33 Filmer's 'critique of the assumptions his contemporaries were making about political obliga-

tion went to the bottom of the most difficult problem in the whole field of inquiry. It will be seen that neither Locke nor Sidney nor any of a host of others who attacked *Patriarcha* ever attempted to meet the force of these criticisms and that none of them even realized what he meant by his naturalism.' [Laslett 1949, 21] Laslett notes that John W. Allen contends in his *The Social and Political Ideas of some English Thinkers of the Augustan Age* (1928) that, as a political thinker, Filmer '"was far more profound and far more original than was Locke."' [Laslett 1949, 21]

34 John Plamenatz comments: 'Of Filmer's views about what makes government legitimate we need not take long notice. They are simple, and they are less ingenious and persuasive than his criticism of the doctrines he disliked.' [Plamenatz, 182; see 175-186]

35 Letter dated 6 September 1789, in Boyd.

36 Letter of 4 February 1790, in Hutchinson.

37 *The Anarchy of a Limited or Mixed Monarchy*, 286. See above in the chapter on Hobbes, Hobbes's vacillation between the unanimity condition and the majoritarian condition.

38 *The Anarchy of a Limited of Mixed Monarchy*, 287. Filmer, Peter Laslett writes, 'questioned the principle which was essential to all accounts of obligation other than his own, the principle of consent. This to Filmer was an obvious contradiction of the social reality around him. It was simply not true that authority was being exercised by consent. How could it be pretended that the son consented to being commanded by his father? What conceivable sophistry could justify the obedience of the apprentice in going to church at his master's bidding, or the submission of the schoolboy to a beating, on the ground that they had given their assent? If authority could be exercised without consent, if in fact it was perpetually being so exercised, then there must be some other source of obligation.' [Laslett 1949, 31]

39 'In the English-speaking part of the world, the "limited" government versus anarchy controversy has evolved in at least three stages. The first stage was the critique by such people as Sir Robert Filmer...and others that government by consent led straight to anarchy....The second stage of the controversy witnessed both the moral and practical triumph of the libertarian ideal...that each person is unique and possesses proprietorial rights over him- or herself....Finally, after nearly a century and a half of discourse, there arose a group of radical thinkers who were brave enough actually to brandish the *reductio ad absurdum* of anarchy. This constituted the third phase of the limited- versus no-government controversy. People like William Godwin were prepared to accept the logical implications of their beginning premises, namely, that no outside coercive authority had any jurisdiction over the nonconsenting individual and that each person should be left totally free of coercive molestation.' [Watner 1986, 111, 112]

40 *The Anarchy of a Limited or Mixed Monarchy*, 286; see Smith, 100. There is an irony here that appears to have escaped Filmer's notice, namely, that Catholic propagandists had made a very similar objection to the Protestant rejection of the authority of the papacy to the effect that, in their efforts to avoid having one Pope, they brought about (say the propagandists) a situation in which every man is his own Pope!

Chapter 20

JOHN LOCKE

The greatest art of the politician is to render vice serviceable to the cause of virtue
—Lord Bolingbroke

The most dangerous man to any government is the man who is able to think
things out for himself, without regard to the prevailing superstitions and taboos.
Almost inevitably he comes to the conclusion that the government he lives
under is dishonest, insane and intolerable, and so, if he is romantic,
he tries to change it.
And even if he is not romantic personally he is very apt
to spread discontent among those who are
—H. L. Mencken

There must be something in the water or the air of the English West Country to have produced not one but two giants of seventeenth century English political thought: Thomas Hobbes (1588-1679) and John Locke (1632-1704). Whereas Hobbes was born and reared in rural Wiltshire, Locke was a city boy, a Bristol city boy (or almost so). He received his university education at Oxford where he, like Hobbes, was less impressed with its curriculum. He had interests in science and medicine and eventually took a medical degree. His medical competence was to change the course of his life. In 1666, he had the good fortune to come to the attention of the Whig (liberal) politician, Anthony Ashley Cooper, the future Lord Shaftesbury, who was in need of medical services. Cooper was impressed by the young physician and made him part of his retinue. Locke spent most of his active life in Shaftesbury's employment until Shaftesbury's death in 1683. Shaftesbury is often credited with being the founder of the Whig (Liberal) party and there can be little doubt that he influenced Locke's thinking in this regard, some even crediting him with prompting Locke to write his treatises on government. Locke found it prudent to spend some time in the Netherlands in the 1680s, returning to England after the so-called Glorious Revolution of 1688 and the accession to the throne of William & Mary. While in the Netherlands, he worked on the writings for which he is now best known—*The Essay on Human Understanding* and the *Two Treatises on Government*. The last years of his life were spent in relative seclusion in Essex. There can be little doubt that among the ranks of non-anarchist political philosophers, Locke is pre-eminently concerned with freedom, whether that freedom is religious (as in his *A Letter Concerning Toleration*—Catholics excepted of course!), economic (in his *Some Considerations on the Consequences of the Lowering of Interest and Raising the Value of Money*) or political (as in his *Two Treatises on Government*). Locke's *First Treatise,* which is a purported refutation of the ultra-monarchist views of Sir Robert Filmer, generally receives little or no attention, the common view being that Filmer's position is so obviously absurd that one can only wonder that Locke thought it worth the trouble to refute it. On the contrary, however, it could be argued, as it is by Eric Mack (2009) and George Smith (2013), that Filmer makes a reasonable case *against* the claim for the natural equality of all men which, if true, undermines the idea that the consent of the governed is in any way necessary to legitimate government. Since government is necessary, Filmer believes, it follows that it must be false that all men are naturally equal, or, to put it in what, from Filmer's perspective, is a form of *reductio ad absurdum*—if all men are naturally free and equal, then government is illegitimate since government of necessity involves the subordination of some men to others. Of course, if one is a philosophical anarchist, one can happily accept this conclusion, taking it to be not only *not* self-evidently absurd but rather patently obvious. Additionally, Filmer presents a utilitarian argument to the effect that men will more likely flourish under unlimited monarchical power than under popular governance[1] while also arguing for the doctrine of legal voluntarism, the view that law is, in essence, the command of the lawmaker. I agree with Eric Mack that the Filmer-Locke debate is deserving of greater attention than it normally gets and I have made some small effort in that direction in the previous chapter. In this chapter, however, I am going to confine myself to commenting on Locke's *Second Treatise*.[2]

LOCKE ON MAN IN THE STATE OF NATURE

As with all philosophers, Locke has his own specific theory of man and, as we shall see, this theory of man is one thing that, in the end, distinguishes his political philosophy from that of Hobbes, whatever else, apart from their local heritage, they might have in common. To put it simply and a little crudely: Hobbes's conception of man is that he is more or less a wild beast in constant need of restraint so that society and state are required for the creation and maintenance of any order, whereas Locke's conception of man is that he is naturally social and that only certain 'inconveniences' of his naturally social state move him to create and accept a political order.

In the state of nature, Locke believes that all men are free and equal. This state of nature is not, however, without any law at all, as it is for Hobbes, for Locke believes that where there is no law, there can be no freedom. Even in this state of nature there is a law of nature and that law is given to us by reason. Reason teaches us that 'no one ought to harm another in his life, health, liberty or possessions' or, to put it in the language of rights, every man has the right not to be harmed by another in his life, health, liberty and possessions. [§6] If this sounds remarkably like the libertarian principle of non- or zero-aggression, that is surely no accident. The purpose of the law of nature is to bring about 'the peace and preservation of all mankind.' [§7] The justification for the law of nature is that we are all God's creatures and his property and, as such, no man is innately superior or inferior to any other. Given what Locke will say later to the effect that we all of us have a property in ourselves, this 'we are God's property' justification for the law of nature is somewhat surprising but there's no reason to doubt that Locke is perfectly sincere in saying what he does.[3]

Since there are no spontaneously operating law-enforcers in the state of nature, the execution of the law of nature is left to each and every man. This law permits the restraint of those who are prepared to invade another's rights and, where they have done so, the exaction of reparation. Locke is careful to state that the exaction of reparation must be proportionate to the transgression.

How is the physical force used in restraint and reparation to be justified? In violating the law of nature, Locke believes that a transgressor has shown that he does not respect the freedom and equality of others and in so doing has made himself a danger to all. That being so, each man has not only the right to defend himself against aggression directed at himself but may also restrain and punish any person who aggresses against any other. [§§8-10] In the state of nature, then, men have the right to defend themselves against those who violate their rights. Locke writes: '*in the state of nature every one has the executive power* of the law of nature…' [§13; italics in original] This second-level right is essential for, without it, the first level rights of life, liberty, health and possessions couldn't be vindicated. 'And that all men may be restrained from invading others rights,' says Locke, 'and from doing hurt to one another, and the law of nature be observed, which willeth the peace and *preservation of all mankind*, the *execution* of the law of nature is, in that state, put into every man's hands, whereby every one has a right to punish the transgressors of that law to such a degree, as may hinder its violation: for the *law of nature* would, as all other laws that concern men in this world, be in vain, if there were no body that in the state of nature had a *power to execute* that law, and thereby preserve the innocent and restrain offenders.' [§7; italics in original]

Eric Mack identifies four arguments, the intersection of which 'constitutes a powerful case for a natural right to freedom which, given Locke's under-standing of freedom, is also a natural right of self-proprietorship.' [Mack 2009, 46] These four arguments are, respectively: 1. The *Perfect Freedom Argument*—for Locke, the state of nature is one in which men are free 'to order their actions and dispose of their possessions, and person, as they think fit, within the bounds of the law of nature…' [Mack 2009, 25]; 2. The *Reciprocity Argument*—'the logical cost of affirming one's own right not to be subject to force or deceit is one's acknowledgement of other's equal rights.' [Mack 2009, 38]; 3. The *False Presumption Argument*—the phenomenon of subordination falsely presumes that one individual exists to serve the purposes of another; and 4. The *Like Reason Argument*—as a man is bound to preserve himself, by like reason, he is bound, within reason, to preserve others. By the law of nature, every man is bound to preserve himself 'and not quit his station willingly' and, as far as possible, also to preserve all other men.[4] [§6]

Locke's state of nature is, then, a pre-political condition but it isn't lawless because men in this condition can and do relate to each other by means of the law of nature. If the question is asked if there has ever been such a condition, Locke will reply that these conditions exist at present between all those who rule independent governments as well as those who find themselves living in the ever-popular desert island scenarios beloved of political thinkers or in the wild woods of America. 'The promises and bargains for truck, etc. between the two men in the desert island,' he writes, 'or between a Swiss and an Indian, in the woods of America, are binding to them, though they are perfectly in a state of nature, in reference to one another: for truth and the keeping of faith belongs to men, as men, and not as members of society.' [§14]

What of the Hobbesian claim that men in a state of nature are at war with each other? Does Locke deny this? Yes, he does. We have war when one man attempts to get another into his absolute power, to enslave the other. War isn't a temporary or fleeting expression of hostility but 'a sedate settled design upon another man's life.' [§16] The state of nature in contrast, is 'Men living together according to reason, without a common superior on earth, with authority to judge between them...' [§19] The state of nature is opposed not so much to a state of war but rather to civil society in which men do in fact have an authoritative superior who can judge between them. A state of war or peace can in fact be found on occasion in both the state of nature and in civil society. Whether or not we have someone who is authorised to act as judge, if force without authority is used then we have a state of war. 'Want of a common judge with authority, puts all men in a state of nature: force without right, upon a man's person, makes a state of war, both where there is, and is not, a common judge.' [§19] The possibility of war is, for Locke, *the* great incentive for men to enter civil society because there, while war is still possible, its incidence is likely to be substantially decreased. 'To avoid this state of war...is one great reason of men's putting themselves into society, and quitting the state of nature: for where there is an authority, a power on earth, from which relief can be had by appeal, there the continuance of the state of war is excluded, and the controversy is decided by that power.' [§21]

Despite their differences, Hobbes and Locke do agree in some matters. While they differ in their characterisations of the state of nature, both agree that it is something better departed from, either out of strict necessity—Hobbes—or for the remedying of inconveniences—Locke. The state of nature is a state of war for Hobbes while for Locke it is the most likely condition in which war can occur. Both thinkers see our ineliminable desire for self-preservation as the impetus which takes us from the state of nature to another and better condition, that condition being either Leviathan or civil government, which can provide the only sure remedy for man's wolfish nature or the inconveniencies of the state of nature. As already pointed out, Hobbes and Locke differ sharply in their anthropology. For Hobbes, *homo homini lupus*—man is a wolf to man, whereas for Locke, while war is a possibility in the state of nature, it isn't equivalent to it. This difference has profound significance for their political theories. For Hobbes, only an absolute sovereign can remedy the defects of the state of nature as he characterises it; for Locke, something considerably less than Leviathan is either needed or to be desired. One clue, perhaps even the key, to the difference between Hobbes and Locke is Locke's treatment of the concept of property.

PROPERTY

Locke's account of property and its relationship to government is one of the most interesting yet also one of the most controversial aspects of his thought. Property, which isn't so much a thing but more a right to dispose of things without interference from others, is understood very widely by Locke to include not only the obvious material goods which man desires and needs but also the relatively intangible yet very real goods of life and liberty. We might say, crudely, that property comes in two basic varieties—first, the property that one has or can have in oneself; and second, the property one has or can have in things other than oneself, things that derive ultimately from natural resources. I am going to begin by considering the possible positions that might be adopted towards the controversial question of property in natural resources and then return to the even more controversial matter of self-ownership.

Natural resources are either (A) originally owned or (B) they are originally unowned.[5] If natural resources are originally owned (A) then they are either originally owned by all (A1) or by some (A2). A2 has no serious proponents and so will not be considered further. If they are owned by all (A1) then this ownership is either common (A1i); or several and equal (A1ii); or several and unequal (A1iii). If natural resources are originally unowned (B) then they can come to be owned by all (B1) or merely by some (B2). If they can come to be owned by all this comes about either by all doing X (where X is a procedure requiring some intentional action) $+\Delta 1$, where $\Delta 1$ is some *intrinsic* limiting condition (B1i) or by all doing X (where X is some procedure requiring some intentional action) $+ \Delta 2$, where $\Delta 2$ is some *extrinsic* limiting condition. (B1ii)

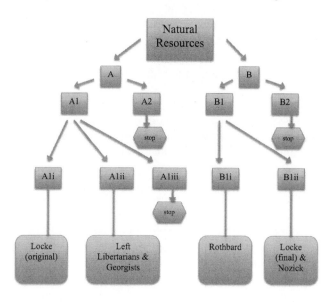

Is it possible to link any political theorists to any of these positions? Original common ownership (A1i) appears to be Locke's opening position, though it may not be his final one. Original several and equal ownership (A1ii) appears to be the position of the so-called left libertarians—Peter Vallentyne, Michael Otsuka and Hillel Steiner—and possibly the position of Henry George. I can't think of anyone who defends the position of original several and unequal ownership (A1iii) or any of the variations of A2, original ownership merely by some.

Position B1i appears to be the Rothbardian position. There is no original ownership; ownership is in principle available to all by employing the requisite procedure (in Rothbard's case, what he calls homesteading, a variation on the Lockean labour-mixing criterion), and the intrinsic condition (which could, in principle, be null) is the deployment of a restriction in initial acquisition emanating from the homesteading procedure, hence, intrinsic. Position B1ii appears to be Locke's final position (and perhaps also that of Nozick). Nothing is in fact owned by anyone originally. Natural resources are acquired by X using the requisite procedure, in this case, the mixing of labour or, understood more expansively, by improvement; and the extrinsic limiting condition is the proviso that enough and as good be left for others. The proviso is extrinsic because it is more than a simple implication from the acquisition procedure. Position B2—no original ownership, ownership available in principle only to some (plus various conditions)— does not appear to have any adherents.

Just as Locke believes that all men are God's creatures, and as such free and equal, so too he thinks that God has given the earth to all men in common. 'Though the earth, and all inferior creatures, be common to all men, yet every man has a property in his own person: this no body has any right to but himself.' [§27] This appears to commit Locke to the position in my taxonomy that I have called A1i. What does this mean? Does it mean that everybody owns every-thing? Probably not, as this would be tantamount to no one's owning anything! Does it mean that all men have a natural right to some particular part of the earth—I'll take Kansas; you can have Alaska? (This is A1ii) Again, this seems unlikely. If not this, just what does it mean?

The claim by any person to the exclusive use of a portion of the earth has to be justified by a procedure in accordance with which *this* particular bit of the earth is withdrawn from the common stock and put to someone's private use. But there is an obvious problem here. In his *First Treatise on Government*, Locke had countered Filmer's claim that God gave the earth to Adam by insisting rather that God gave the earth to all mankind in common. But if the earth belongs to all men in common, no individual may use or appropriate any portion of natural material without everyone's first consenting to such use or appropriation and, of course, such universal consent is practically unattainable. Moreover, even if the consent were obtained at any one time and place, how should it bind future generations who manifestly were not present to give their consent and to whom the earth belongs every bit as much as those who were in existence at the time the claim to particular use was made?

Locke's thesis of God's gift of the world to us all appears to retreat from the expansive claim that everybody owns everything to the more restricted claim that in the beginning no one in particular owns anything in particular. This is B1ii. To remind you of what this says: If something comes to be owned by all (B1), this comes about by all doing X (where X is some intentional action) + $\Delta2$, where $\Delta2$ is some extrinsic limiting condition. (B1ii). Here, the X which is done is the 'mixing of labour; and the Δ, the extrinsic limiting condition, is the notorious Lockean second proviso.

Let us turn our attention to Locke's claim that 'every man has a property in his own person: this no body has any right to but himself.' [§27] You not only control your body as a matter of fact but you and only you have a right to do so. Because of this right, you have a property in yourself, that is, a right to dispose of yourself without interference by others, subject only to God's pre-eminent ownership of all creation. And here we come upon one of the most famous images in all political literature. Not only does a man have an exclusive property in himself but 'The labour of his body and the work of his hands, we may say, are his property. Whatsoever then he removes out of the state that nature hath provided, and left it in, he hath mixed his labour with, and joined to it something that is his own, and thereby makes it his property. It being by him removed from the common state nature hath placed it in, it hath by this labour something annexed to it, that excludes the common right of other men: for this labour being the unquestionable property of the labourer, no man but he can have a right to what that is once joined to…' [§27]

The basic idea here is that I have an exclusive right to the disposition of my body and my body's powers and so also to that part of the external environment that has been significantly modified ('improved' in the terminology of the period) by my action upon it. This image of mixing one's labour with natural objects has been the target of much criticism, not only from those opposed to the very notion of private property, but even from those who are broadly sympathetic to the results of Locke's approach. Locke's theory 'runs into difficulties when one attempts to explain what is meant by "mixing labor with land," write the Tannehills. 'Just how much labor is required, and of what sort? If a man digs a large hole in his land and then fills it up again, can he be said to have mixed his labor with the land? Or is it necessary to effect a somewhat permanent change in the land? If so, how permanent? Would planting some tulip bulbs in a clearing do it? Perhaps long-living redwood trees would be more acceptable? Or is it necessary to effect some improvement in the economic value of the land? If so, how much and how soon? Would planting a small garden in the middle of a 500-acre plot be sufficient, or must the whole acreage be tilled….Would a man lose title to his land if he had to wait ten months for a railroad line to be built before he could improve the land? What if he had to wait ten years? And what of the naturalist who wanted to keep his land exactly as it was in its wild state in order to study its ecology.'[6] In response to this kind of objection, Mack maintains that Locke's notion of mixing of labour is to be understood broadly to encompass the 'purposeful transformation of raw material' by people employing their 'energies, time, natural capacities, acquired skills, and insights about opportunities for transformations.' [Mack 2009, 59] If we take Mack's broadening of Locke's 'mixing of labour' image to extend to purposeful transformation, then it becomes a kind of conceptual *synecdoche*, where the part ('mixing of labour') is taken to encompass the whole ('purposeful transformation').

In citing the passage where Locke talks about 'mixing one's labour with things removed from nature,' I deliberately omitted the final phrase, which adds, 'at least where there is enough, and as good, left in common for others.' [§27] This is Locke's notorious proviso which is intended to limit man's right to acquire external goods.[7] A man may acquire whatever he has mixed his labour with provided he leaves enough and as good for others. The proviso does not, on the face of it, seem unreasonable. Without some such limitation on the right of individuals to acquire external property, it's difficult to see how we could give effect to other individuals' rights to self-preservation.

In any event, it is easy to see why Locke believes that some such proviso is required. For example, it might be objected that whatever about taking an apple from a tree for my own immediate consumption, the fencing off of a parcel of land and claiming of it as my private property permanently deprives others of the opportunity to use that land and does so without their consent. Isn't this problematic for Locke? The short answer is, no, not necessarily, and the reason for this is that Locke views things historically and in our early history my appropriation of land for my own use will *always* leave enough and as good for others. [see §33] In this original situation, land is plentiful—it is labour that is scarce. Can a man then make a claim to as much land as he likes? Locke thinks not. 'As much land as a man tills, plants, improves, cultivates, and can use the product of, so much is his property.' [§32] Note the restrictions here, of which there are two. First, it isn't simply a matter of gazing out upon the horizon and saying 'I hereby claim for my own private use all that I can see!' The amount of land I can claim as mine is limited by my ability to cultivate it and put it to use or, in the vocabulary of the seventeenth century, by my ability to 'improve' it. It isn't just a matter of leaving enough and as good for others; even if there were no others, I would still not be able to establish property rights over any natural resources that I did not in some sense improve. Second, I have to be able to use the product of the natural resources I appropriate. The first restriction is eminently sensible, ruling out what Murray Rothbard called the 'Columbus Complex', the idea that one can land on the shore of a continent, plant one's country's flag and claim the entire continent for one's political masters. The second restriction is a version of Locke's non-spoilage proviso.

The basic idea in Locke's account of property is that my labour is mine and if I, as it were, put it into something material, the resulting transformed material is mine. Robert Nozick offered the well-known counterexample to the 'mixing of labour' account. Suppose, he says, that I own a can of tomato juice and that I pour it into the sea. Does it now follow that the resulting very dilute tomato juice is mine, that I now own the whole ocean? This counter example is ruled out by Locke's first restriction in two ways: one, the mixing of the tomato juice with the ocean isn't an 'improvement' (by which Locke means tilling, planting or cultivating—see §32) and, furthermore, it would fall foul of the Columbus Complex. More pertinently, perhaps, Locke consistently holds that land in our original state is relatively worthless while our labour is valuable so that it can't be considered strange that 'the property of labour should be able to over-balance the community of land: for it is labour indeed that puts the difference of value on every thing…' [§40; see §§40-44]

Although the difficulties created by the Lockean metaphor of mixing one's labour with external resources as a criterion of their ownership have often been pointed out, there none the less remains something intuitively attractive about it. If I pick up a piece of driftwood and carve it into a statue of the Infant Samuel at prayer, it's difficult to see how the statue could be considered anyone's but mine. The core of the Lockean labour-mixing metaphor is that one must *do* something to acquire natural resources—one acquires nothing by sitting around and looking pretty—and that something must have the effect of altering them or controlling them or demarcating them in some significant way so as to exclude others from using them. Exclusion is, I believe, the key element in the notion of initial acquisition. It isn't enough merely to be first; one has to be first *in acquiring* and acquiring means appropriating resources in such a way as to exclude their use by others.[8] How this exclusion is to be manifested depends on the nature of the resources appropriated. Something of this notion of exclusion as a key to property title remains in the common law doctrine of adverse possession. If someone without legal title to a piece of land treats it in such a way as effectively to assert ownership of it—say, for example, by building on it or fencing it off from surrounding land—and if the holder of the title takes no action to assert his rights to the land, then the adverse possessor will, after a certain time, be able to assert a title superior to that of the original holder. The failure of the original titleholder to exclude the adverse possessor is taken to be tantamount to a virtual abandonment of his claim to title.

There is another problem with the Lockean account of property acquisition, or at least with certain version of that account. The account (or certain versions of it) seems to imply that ownership or possession is a direct two-place relationship between a human agent and a thing. But consider the following scenario. Suppose that, living alone on a desert island, you were to clear some ground, plant some carrots and give them the tender loving care that they need until they are ready to be picked and eaten. Would you then own the carrots? I would say that if you were to live in such radical social isolation, you would neither own nor not own the carrots: the question of ownership simply wouldn't arise. But now, suppose another person were to appear and attempt to appropriate the carrots, what then? In that case, you would be in a position to make a counter-claim that, all things considered, would seem to be better grounded than that of the challenger. In so doing, you would be attempting to actualise a kind of latent or virtual ownership that pre-existed any actual claim or recognition of that claim by others.

It would seem that, in the course of human history, after the first Agricultural Revolution, when people began to cultivate crops and domesticate animals, work was required to bring land under cultivation or to make it suitable for pasture. This work represented an expenditure of labour that couldn't easily be recovered if the one who expended it could legitimately be forced to give it up by others. At this stage, however, we still have *de facto* possession rather than ownership or, if ownership, then only virtual or latent ownership. That virtuality became actualised when other land users settled around the original user and, requiring undisturbed possession of their own tracts, were able to demand this only if there was mutual recognition not just of the fact of possession but of the right so to possess, in a word, a recognition of property. These reciprocal claims, of course, require that the boundaries between adjacent properties be reasonably clearly demarcated, a requirement celebrated in the proverb that 'Good fences make good neighbours'. Carol Rose makes a strong case that a possessor of a given portion of land has an obligation to provide a persistent and unambiguous demarcation of that portion's boundaries. [see Rose 1985, passim] 'As people began to lay claims to territory and to mark by signs what they regarded as their territory, neighbors started, in some cases at least, to accommodate themselves to these claims. To do this, though, it had to be true that neighbors could discern and were prepared to respect the boundaries of territorial claims.' [Schmidtz & Brennan, 109]

Acquisition of external resources, including land, is a kind of *virtual* ownership that becomes *actual* ownership by means of reciprocal recognition. My settled use and reuse of my possessions requires you to refrain from interfering with them but your use and reuse of your possessions also requires me to refrain from interfering with them. Mutual recognition of one another's exclusive control amounts to the transformation of factual possession into normative ownership. Cicero wrote that private property has been endowed 'not by nature, but by longstanding occupancy in the case of those who settled long ago on empty land; or by victory in the case of those who gained it in that way; or by law or bargain or contract or lot....since what was by nature common property has passed into the ownership of individuals, each should retain what has accrued to him, and if anyone seeks any of it for himself, he will transgress the law of the community.' [Cicero, I 21] The requirement of reciprocal recognition cannot sensibly be made a universal spatio-temporal requirement but must be limited to one's immediate neighbours in space and time. Recognition of your property claims by those geographically remote isn't required; still less does the validity of your property claims require the recognition of those yet to be born.[9]

The libertarian theorists, Linda and Morris Tannehill, who, as we have seen, are sceptical of the Lockean labour-mixing metaphor as a criterion of resource acquisition, reject the arguments of those who call into question the legitimacy of the 'first come' principle: 'If the first comers were ambitious, quick and intelligent enough to acquire the property before anyone else, why should they be prevented from reaping the rewards of these virtues in order to hold the land open for someone else?' Primary acquisition does not exclude others for all time for it isn't enough to have the luck and skill to acquire property, one must also have the luck and skill to hold onto it. 'And if a large chunk of land is acquired by a man who is too stupid or lazy to make a productive use of it, other men, operating within the framework of the free market, will eventually be able to bid it away from him and put it to work producing wealth.[10] Anthony de Jasay is in sympathy with David Hume who regarded initial exclusion as a simple matter of fact. For Hume, he writes, 'initial exclusion is a matter of fact;

it happens by "first occupation." At that point, society is formed by the "first assignment" to the "present possessor." The morality of these steps is not at issue.' [de Jasay 2010, 147]

The relative valuelessness of unimproved land where there is effectively no scarcity of such is, I repeat, a key point in Locke's account. It must be remembered that Locke was, among other things, an economist and so it isn't surprising that he should be sensitive to the relationship between value and scarcity. But even if we were to accept that Locke's account of the relative valuelessness of land is accurate in man's original sparsely-populated condition, surely the time will come, indeed it *has* come, where land is a scarce commodity so that the appropriation or retention of a parcel of land by one person inevitably disadvantages another, a non-consenting other and so it seems that Locke's proviso (that enough and as good be left for others) cannot be met. How is Locke to meet this looming objection?

Locke's response to this objection is to sketch a conjectural history. Starting, as already noted, with the creation of property in a condition of non-scarcity, once land has become relatively scarce (not least through the invention of money) 'the several communities settled the bounds of their distinct territories, and by laws within themselves regulated the properties of the private men of their society, and so, by compact and agreement, settled the property which labour and industry began...' [§45] This quasi-historical account is important, disputing, as it does, the image common to redistributivists that human beings have, as it were, descended from the heavens *en masse* onto the surface of the earth, without antecedents, without history, and without any particular attachments.

Locke was an economist as well as a philosopher and political theorist. For him, money comes into existence *before* the formation of political society, resulting from what Adam Smith might have termed our natural tendency to truck and barter. It requires no state or central authority to validate it. Recent historical examples show this invention of money to be commonplace so, for example, in the prisoner of war camps of World War II, unopened packets of cigarettes were used as a medium of exchange. Historically, of course, many substances have performed this function: wampum, shells, animal hides, gold, silver and the like. Locke fixes on gold, silver and diamonds as the lasting media of exchange that men can use without spoilage. [§47]

The introduction of money into society has as drastic effect on man's condition as did the introduction of the serpent into the Garden of Eden. The natural limitations of man's condition were altered inexorably. Above all, land became scarce and the accumulation of wealth (and hence disparities of wealth) became possible. Locke writes, 'as different degrees of industry were apt to give men possession in different proportions, so this invention of money gave them the opportunity to continue and reject them...' [§48] In acceding to the use of money, 'men have agreed to a disproportionate and unequal possession of the earth, they having, by a tacit and voluntary consent, found out a way how a man may fairly possess more land than he himself can use the produce of, by receiving in exchange for the overplus gold and silver, which may be hoarded up without injury to any one; these metals not spoiling or decaying in the hands of the possessor.' [§50]

For many people, Locke will have gone much too far and much too fast in this argument. It is one thing to justify the acquisition of property in a state of abundance; it is another to justify large inequalities of property holdings in a condition of scarcity. How is Locke to justify this? Well, his (second) proviso was that enough and as good be left for others and Locke's argument is that, through the appropriation of land, productivity increases spectacularly so that not only is enough and as good left for others, but more than enough and as good is left for others. A common presupposition of redistributionists is to simply assume a fixed stock of stuff that must be continually re-allocated to an ever-changing population. Locke, the economist, is well aware that productivity is the key to wealth. Locke looks at the America of his time and notes that its native inhabitants, while spectacularly rich in land are also spectacularly poor in their possession of the comforts of life and that their richest men are poorer than an English day labourer. [§41] He remarks, 'he who appropriates land to himself by his labour, does not lessen, but increases the common stock of mankind: for the provision serving to the supports of human life, produced by one acre of inclosed and cultivated land are…ten times more than those which are yielded by an acre of land of an equal richness lying waste in common. And therefore he that encloses land, and has a greater plenty of conveniences of life from ten acres, than he could have from an hundred left to nature, may truly be said to give ninety acres to mankind: for his labour now supplies him with provision of our ten acres, which were but the produce of an hundred lying in common.' [§37]

AN ASIDE ON BODY-PART CANNIBALISM

One aspect of theories of property that is of particular interest to libertarians is the relationship between self-ownership and the ownership of external resources. Libertarians tend to take the position that self-ownership is relatively unproblematic and that what needs to be explained is how self-ownership is, as it were, to be projected onto the world to permit the private ownership of external resources. Left libertarians (such as Michael Otsuka, Peter Vallentyne and Hillel Steiner) in their various ways defend self-ownership while at the same time being prepared to countenance significant restrictions on the ownership of external resources.

The claim that if I own anything at all, I own myself and my body is one of those that divides people; to some, it seems nonsensical; to others, more or less self-evident. The analytical Marxist, Gerald Cohen, also affirms the antecedent plausibility of self-ownership, noting that 'leftists who disparage Nozick's essentially unargued affirmation of each person's rights over himself lose confidence in their unqualified denial of the thesis of self-ownership when they are asked to consider who has the right to decide what should happen, for example, to their own eyes.'[11] In his influential book *Self-ownership,*

Freedom, and Equality Cohen writes: 'The thesis of self-ownership has... plenty of appeal....Its antecedent (that is, pre-philosophical appeal) rivals that of whatever principles of equality it is thought to contradict.' [Cohen 1995, 70]

Responding to his own musings regarding the shakiness of the opposition to self-ownership when those who oppose it are confronted with the possibility of having one of their eyes (or kidneys) re-allocated, he continues: 'They [those opposed to the notion of self-ownership] do not immediately agree that, were eye transplants easy to achieve, it would then be acceptable for the state to conscript potential eye donors into a lottery whose losers must yield an eye to beneficiaries who would otherwise be not one-eyed but blind. The fact that they do not deserve their good eyes, that they do not need two good eyes more than blind people need one, and so forth—the fact, in a word, that they are merely lucky to have two good eyes—does not convince them that their claim on their own eyes is not stronger than that of some unlucky blind person. *But if the standard leftist objections to inequality of resources, private property, and ultimate condition are taken quite literally, then the fact that it is sheer luck that these (relatively) good eyes are mine should deprive me of special privilege in them.*'[12] Cohen, it would seem, intends this last remark as an ironic warning against taking what he calls 'standard leftist objections' literally.

But what is irony to one may be the literal truth to another. Such is the case with the contemporary political philosopher Cécile Fabre. Fabre is the author of a paper, innocuously entitled, 'Justice, Fairness and World Ownership,' another paper, rather more ominously entitled, 'Justice and the Compulsory Taking of Live Body Parts,' and a book with the really alarming title, *Whose Body is it Anyway? Justice and the Integrity of the Person.*[13] In contrast to libertarians generally and also to such as Cohen, Fabre denies that the claim of self-ownership is unproblematic and she evacuates the irony from Cohen's warning, arguing that 'if one thinks that the needy have a right to the material resources they need in order to lead decent lives, one must be committed...to conferring on the sick a right that the healthy give them some of the body parts they need to lead such a life.'! [Fabre 2003, 128] Fabre is correct in thinking that the principles that allow for the restriction of, or interference with, the ownership of external resources must, if one is to be consistent, be extendable to issues connected with self-ownership. In the end, however, I believe that what her argument really shows is that in a three-way fight between libertarianism *simpliciter*, left libertarianism and Fabrean liberalism, left libertarianism is incoherent, leaving the choice between her theory of body-part cannibalism, which compromises both self-ownership and the ownership of external resources, and libertarianism *simpliciter*, which defends both self-ownership *and* the ownership of external resources.

Fabre believes that most contemporary theories of justice hold that those who are badly-off have a right to some of the resources of the well off in order to live a decent life.[14] It is also held, Fabre believes, that people should have a considerable degree of self-ownership or autonomy. She sees the right to a decent life and the right to autonomy as being in competition with one another and *the* problem of political philosophy to be able to reconcile the competing rights.[15]

Echoing John Rawls, she presents us with two ordered principles of substantive justice that embody these competing rights. According to Fabre, we have a Principle of Sufficiency—this holds that people have a right to the resources they need in order to lead a decent life, and a Principle of Autonomy—this holds that once the Principle of Sufficiency is satisfied for everyone then everyone should be permitted to follow their ideas of the good and enjoy the fruits of their labour. Note that these principles are ordered in a Rawlsian fashion: the Principle of Sufficiency must be satisfied before the Principle of Autonomy. Some fairly obvious questions about Fabre's Principle of Sufficiency readily come to mind. Where does this principle come from? What is its justification? Is it meant to be self-evident? As the term 'right' is used in this principle, does it signify a claim right? If so, against whom is such a claim to be made—me, you, the state? If the state, why the state? What if there is no state, as has been the case of most of human existence? And if it isn't a claim right, what kind of right is it?

Fabre, then, argues that everyone has an interest in living a decent life and, in order to do so, must have access to an adequate amount of resources—food, clothing, shelter, health care, and so on—as well as a minimal degree of autonomy. She notes that the provision of sufficiency for some may require the curtailment of autonomy for others but, she believes, once everyone has a sufficiency, then everyone should be allowed to maximize his autonomy as a matter of right.

Once again, some obvious questions present themselves. How, one might wonder, is the application of the Principle of Sufficiency supposed to work? How does one determine what is or what isn't a level of decency? Who makes the decisions? Whom does it range over? It is difficult to avoid the suspicion that the notion of basic decency may be so vague as to make it practically impossible to allow for any autonomy at all. As might be expected, these principles of justice have a dramatic effect on property rights. Fabre claims that neither collective ownership nor unrestricted private ownership can satisfy these principles simultaneously. Collective ownership alone violates the Principle of Autonomy, whereas unrestricted private ownership alone violates the Principle of Sufficiency. She argues for a combination of both kinds of ownership rights as a way of satisfying her principles.

Under Fabre's Principle of Sufficiency, all would get equal shares in natural resources. In the event that Peter Pan has insufficient resources, he has a right against Captain Hook that Hook cultivate his share of resources in certain ways or else allow Peter to do so. The Principle of Sufficiency requires that 'neither of us singly has the right to decide by whom, whether and how the world will be used, and to enjoy the whole of the income derived from it. We both have those rights *only* if our life isn't decent under the status quo and if the other's life is better than ours, or more than decent or already decent (and would not get less than decent after the decisions are made.)' Let us imagine a situation in which some people need housing and others have more than one property. In such circumstances, if, for example, redistributive taxation weren't able to do the job, 'justice requires that those houses be requisitioned.'[16]

On the face of it, it looks as if the composite set of private and collective property rights might impinge negatively on autonomy. But individuals may use the world as they wish only if they do so in such a way that the luckless are provided for. Suppose someone were to object that requiring the lucky to work for the unlucky is an infringement of his autonomy. 'If the lucky have to work *most*, let alone *all*, of their time for the unlucky, my Dworkinian opponent would argue, they cannot implement those identity-conferring choices of theirs which do not revolve around work, and they thus do not have a decent life.' [Fabre 2002, 267] This is a pretty potent objection, one might think. Fabre, however, denies that being forced to do work one does not want to do is a form of slavery, provided one's life is still decent. She eventually admits that even where one's life is decent, her composite theory of property rights does, in fact, infringe on the autonomy of the lucky but not, she says, to an unacceptable degree. At which point a libertarian might rudely respond— sez who? 'The criticism that it does [infringe on the autonomy of the lucky] appears to have force only if one focuses on the situation of the lucky and overlooks the fact that if they do not work for the unlucky, the latter are not autonomous either, since they lack the material resources necessary for them to enjoy the opportunities society offers them. Such focus unacceptably fails to live up to what motivates justice in the first instance. Clearly the lucky will suffer a loss of autonomy, but that is an unavoidable condition of securing minimum autonomy for all.' [Fabre 2002, 269] So that's all right then! I am sure that the so-called lucky (perhaps not so lucky after all) will happily accept this argument.

In a bid to make her proposal seem less unappealing and unintuitive, Fabre appeals to what she considers to be our willingness in general to accept the legitimacy of taxation, even when it is onerous, writing, 'conceptions of ownership which disallow restricting the lucky's control rights over the world but allow that they should be taxed can also be detrimental to the autonomy of the lucky if they are designed in such a way as to secure justice. For justice may very well require that the income owners derive from their property be taxed to such an extent that they would have to work, and do nothing but work, in order to meet the needs of the unlucky, which would render their life [*sic*] less than decent.' [Fabre 2002, 269] This is a striking and, to me, damning admission.[17]

This admission, damning or otherwise, isn't the only problem Fabre's account runs into. She breezily dismisses the objection that her proposal may be simply unworkable. Having to check the allocation of ownership rights constantly does not, she believes, 'fall foul of justice and fairness' even if having to constantly modify allocations 'is likely to be very costly and difficult.' 'Perhaps, she concedes, 'those considerations provide good reasons not to implement my proposal.' Nevertheless, considerations of unworkability cannot disqualify her proposal as that form of ownership which 'best satisfies both justice and fairness.'[18] One might be forgiven for thinking a theory's lustre to be somewhat tarnished when the theory in question is a theory of justice that, perhaps naïvely, one might consider is supposed to apply to the rough and ready sublunary world in which we find ourselves.

The standard libertarian view (both left and right) is that our body is beyond the reach of legitimate demands from others, whereas our personal possessions and our money may [left libertarianism] or may not be [libertarianism *simpliciter*]. On the liberal view, by contrast, we are *not* always free to use our bodies in ways we ourselves desire even if in so doing we do not necessarily harm others and may in fact benefit them in some way, as in the case of prostitution or the sale of body organs. The position that holds that people's bodies mustn't be interfered with Fabre calls 'body exceptionalism'. She argues that if we are susceptible to legitimate claims on our material resources from those who would appear to need them, we are also susceptible to legitimate claims on the use of our bodies and our body parts from those who need them. If need be, our personal services may be demanded and our body parts confiscated. Taxation, which liberals and left-libertarians accept in principle, may in fact negatively affect our life plans more extensively than, say, the forcible extraction of one of our kidney so that if taxation is in a principled way unexceptionable, so too must be body-part cannibalism. In a 1963 essay, Ayn Rand, anticipating Gerald Cohen, asked what she thought was a patently absurd question to which the answer was a blindingly obvious (pun intended) no—'Would you,' she asked, 'advocate cutting out a living man's eye and giving it to a blind man, so as to "equalize" them?' [Rand 1963a, 99] If only she had lived another 30 years, she would have realised the error of her ways.

I would run Fabre's argument precisely in the opposite direction to which she runs it. We *do* object to others interfering in our bodies without licence, the level of objection rising with the severity of intrusion. Kidney extraction or forcible eye transplantation ranks pretty high in the objectionability scale. That being so, by parity of argument, we are entitled to object to others interfering with our rightfully acquired possessions also. If the reason for the rejection of kidney extraction or eye transplantation were based on interference with life plans, and taxation is more devastating from that point of view, then taxation, bizarrely would be *more*, not less, objectionable than forced kidney extraction or eye transplantation.

It has been said that there is no position so absurd that some philosopher hasn't held it.[19] Fabre's account is a case in point. Her account, although consistent, is a *reductio ad absurdum* of the standard liberal position. She is right to see a connection between the body and material resources and she is also right to accuse the liberal position of inconsistency. Libertarians, however, would turn her argument around. If conceding the legitimacy of taxation and suchlike leads to our having to concede the right of others to use our bodies without our consent, this shows us that in protecting the autonomy of our bodies, we are also committed to the protection of our ownership of material resources. Fabre's position has, at least, the merit of consistency even if it is the consistency of the ever so slightly mad. If self-ownership implies some reasonably robust account of the ownership of external goods, then, if no such robust account of the ownership of external goods is tenable, self-ownership likewise becomes untenable. The libertarian position is also consistent. The left-libertarian position, however, is incoherent, permitting the non-voluntary redistribution of external resources but denying the permissibility of any such redistribution of body parts.

Summary of Positions

Position re:	Natural Resources	Bodies
I: Left-Libertarian/ Liberal	Non-voluntary redistribution possible	Non-voluntary redistrib-iton NOT possible
II: Fabre	Non-voluntary redistribution possible	Non-voluntary redistribution possible
III: Libertarian	Non-voluntary redistrib-iton NOT possible	Non-voluntary redistrib-iton NOT possible

GOVERNMENT AND CONSENT

Returning to Locke: Money and the increased productivity resulting from the changed property dispositions deriving from money solve one set of problems only to give rise to others. The problem solved is the economic one; the problem it gives rise to is the political one. With the decrease in the abundance of unappropriated land, it will no longer be possible for labour to give title to property. 'Men, by their labor, invention, and arts, make *increase* possible,' writes Robert Goldwin, 'and thereby solve the economic problems that beset them in the original natural condition. But at the same time they also make the continuance of that state impossible. The original common, however dangerous and inconvenient, is tolerable when its conditions are a plenty of raw provisions, few men, lots of room, and a general equality of weakness. But the consequences of *increase* are to make unowned provisions scarcer, men more numerous, and open space harder to come by; and in this new situation there is generated a new inequality of power among men, based on the new inequality of possessions. Under these new conditions, labor can no longer give title to property or be the first measure of value, and spoiling ceases to limit acquisition....Men are "quickly driven into society" (§127) for the protection of their property.' [Goldwin, 494-495]

So far, Locke believes he has established that every man possesses a natural right to life, liberty and estate and that each man's property rights in external things derives ultimately from his property right in himself and his labour. The invention of money and its effect on the distribution of property changes all this, disturbing the fragile social equilibrium and making it necessary to establish a means by which the rights of property, broadly construed, can be more effectively defended. The state of nature, adequate as it might be at a certain stage of human development, suffers, to use Locke's own term, from certain obvious inconveniences. In that state, there is no known or settled law and no known indifferent judge to adjudicate between rival claimants. Since men are partial to their own causes, the lack of settled laws and neutral judges is likely to lead to escalating conflicts for even though all men have the right to execute the law of nature, not all men have the requisite power to do so. [see §§124-126] These drawbacks ('inconveniencies') of the state of nature are sufficient to push men to form a civil society in which they can be remedied. 'And in this we have the original *right and rise of both the legislative and executive power*, as well as of the government and societies themselves.'[20] These inconveniencies are what drive men to take refuge under the established laws of government.

It is hard to disagree with the essence of Locke's analysis of the shortcomings of the state of nature. If indeed there were no settled law, then, given that some men are corrupt, vicious and degenerate our lives would be uncertain and the tensions and ambiguities attending our conduct unendurable. [see §128] Even if there were laws but no independent judges of that law, we wouldn't be much better off. And if we had law and independent judges but no way to enforce that law apart from our own feeble power, then we would live in a pitiable state. All very well. But how does Locke get from here to the establishment of a government? Well, a government for Locke is simply an agency devised by those who desire to escape the inconveniences of nature, that agency being charged with securing everyone's property 'by providing against those three defects…that made the state of nature so unsafe and uneasy' [§131] But, and this is vitally important, the power of government can never go further than is required to remedy those inconveniences. In making this point, Locke shows an awareness of what has come to be called the 'agent-principal' problem, the perennial problem of ensuring that agents as agents act in the interests of their principals and not in their own interests.

There is, then, nothing obviously crazy about people's consenting to the creation of such an agency and surrendering to it certain of their rights. The particular form such an agency might take isn't determined simply by the decision to create it; that requires a further decision. Locke thinks that the initial decision to create an agency requires the consent of all but that the form of the agency can be determined by a majority.[21] In a compact with others, each man transfers to the commonwealth his natural rights to look to his self-preservation and to punish offenders. The right to attend to his self-preservation isn't transferred completely or finally to the commonwealth but only to the extent that such a transfer is consistent with his self-preservation and the preservation of the rest of society. The right to punish offenders, however, is completely and wholly transferred. [§§129-130] The commonwealth thus established by compact is established to defend man's life, liberty and estate or, more succinctly, for the preservation of society, and its powers are therefore limited. The government of the commonwealth is to operate by established and promulgated laws, these laws to be made for the good of the people. Taxes may not be raised on men's property without their consent, which consent is to be given by men themselves or their representatives. [§142]

Here is one clear point where Hobbes and Locke disagree. Hobbes believes that the setting up of a single authority subject to no limitation and from which there can be no secession is the only way to establish peace. Locke, on the other hand, is unable to see how such an arbitrary power could resolve the problems emerging from the state of nature. As Goldwin notes, 'To be subject to the arbitrary power of an uncontrolled ruler without the right or strength to defend oneself against him is a condition far worse than the state of nature; it cannot be supposed to be that to which men consented freely, for "no rational creature can be supposed to change his condition with an intention to be worse"' (§131).' [Goldwin, 497] As Locke himself puts it elsewhere, 'as if when men quitting the state of nature entered into society, they agreed that all of them but one, should be under the restraint of laws but that he should still retain all the liberty of the state of nature, increased with power, and made licentious by impunity. This is to think, that men are so foolish, that they take care to avoid what mischiefs may be done them by *pole-cats*, or *foxes*; but are content, nay, think it safety, to be devoured by *lions*.' [§93]

How does a man make himself subject to a government? Given Locke's presuppositions, the answer can only be by consent. [see Riley, 350-353] If that consent is express, there is no fundamental problem to be addressed although Locke inexplicably argues that such an express consent, once given, binds a man to remain perpetually in subjection to that government [§121]. To say that it isn't obvious why such express consent must be irrevocable is to be guilty of understatement and Locke offers us no justification for this doctrine, certainly not in that part of the text where this claim is made. This brings us to Locke's famous (or notorious) notion of tacit consent. Those who live under a government that, broadly speaking, does what the Lockean agency is supposed to do—protect everyone's property—can be deemed to have given their tacit consent to it since 'someone who was really so opposed to it that he or she would prefer living in the state of nature…could always take up the life of a survivalist.' [Feser 2007, 140] How far does such a tacit consent bind? Every man, Locke says, 'that hath any possessions, or enjoyment, of any part of the dominions of any government, doth thereby give his tacit consent, and is as far forth obliged to obedience to the laws of that government, during such enjoyment, as any one under it; whether this his possession be of land, to him and his heirs forever, or a lodging only for a week; or whether it be barely travelling freely on the highway; and in effect, it reaches as far as the very being of any one within the territories of that government.' [§119]

This tacit consent argument isn't entirely implausible for we can and do enter into contracts by a course of conduct. The argument has often been made against the necessity for explicit consent in all cases of contract that there are well-recognised circumstances in which we can make binding agreements without engaging in any formalities. I freely grant that some contracts can be formed by a course of conduct, one of the most familiar of which is, perhaps, ordering a meal in a restaurant. If William orders a meal in a restaurant and consumes it, then he has incurred an obligation to pay for it; the lack of an explicit verbal agreement does not relieve him of his monetary obligations. One might imagine a visitor from a radically alien culture innocently failing to realise this cultural and legal norm and thinking that he was witnessing a gratuitous distribution of food, with ensuing comical complications, comical at least to onlookers if not to the mystified alien and the out-of-pocket restaurateur. But, of course, we are under no obligation to go to any restaurant at all, still less to go to this particular one rather than another. And if one were to insist that it and only it had the right to feed us and we the corresponding obligation to pay for that food whether we wanted to or not, we might find the argument less persuasive. This is, more or less, the response that David Hume will give to the tacit consent argument, arguing that where there's no real possibility of choice or secession, the most one can claim is that here we have acquiescence rather than consent.

Some, such as Hume, have attempted to defuse Locke's residency argument by arguing that for consent to be genuine it must be voluntary and that, in many cases, the demand that people either stay and obey or leave presents people with alternatives neither of which they can really be said to choose. Hume instances the position of the unskilled peasant presented with such a choice and deems it to be equivalent to that of a man kidnapped and taken aboard a boat without his consent who is given the option of either consenting to the authority of the ship's master or jumping overboard. The choice isn't simply to stay and obey or leave; one may also stay and not obey, a possibility that might have unpleasant consequences but is none the less an option. Attempts by the state to enforce obedience in matters not covered by the principle of zero-aggression will then be coercive and those who remain will have a choice of whether to actively resist such aggression or to acquiesce in it in the face of *force majeure*, without such acquiescence being tantamount to any form of legitimation of the authority of the state to require such obedience.

As if antecedently to rebut Hume's argument that all states that ever have existed have come into being through violence so that the issue of consent is moot, Locke argues that while the evidence of history shows this to be, in the main, true, none the less, consent is still the only sufficient condition for the authority of government: 'such have been the disorders ambition has filled the world with, that in the noise of war, which makes so great a part of the history of mankind, *this consent* is little taken notice of: and therefore many have mistaken the force of arms for the consent of the people, and reckon conquest as one of the originals of government. But *conquest* is as far from setting up any government, as demolishing an house is from building a new one in the place Indeed, it often makes way for a new frame of a common-wealth, by destroying the former, but, without the consent of the people, can never erect a new one.' [§175; Italics in original]

Whatever may be the case in the relatively trivial and transient contractual situations engendered by the purchase of food in a restaurant and such like, in most jurisdictions one cannot form contracts in respect of significant assets, such as automobiles or houses, that saddle one with significant obligations in the same casual existential manner. Randy Barnett notes that even for something as relatively trivial as the lease of a television, most legal systems require a complete account of the obligations one is taking on in return for the benefits received. That being the case, he remarks on the irony of resting our duty to obey the law of the state on such a slender reed as that of 'tacit consent' so that merely by living in a certain town or not leaving our country of birth 'we have "consented" to obey nearly any command that is enacted by the reigning legal system. And the consent of a majority is supposed to bind not only themselves, but dissenters and future generations as well.' [see Barnett 2004, 24] And while it is true that entering a marriage or making a will were activities that once were informally transacted, they have since come to be attended with a significant degree of formality so that one cannot now get married (except perhaps in Las Vegas) or make a will without being explicitly aware of just what it is that one is doing. If such formality with its attendant explicit reflection and consent characterises such important matters, how much more then is explicit reflection and explicit consent required when accepting a constitution, given that it purports to be the fundamental law by which one is to be bound?

The argument is sometimes made (as by Locke) that those who receive benefits from a state, such as the provision of housing or healthcare, the use of roads, and police services, tacitly accept the legitimate authority of that state by their acceptance of such benefits. In response to this argument, it could be argued that such benefits, to the extent that they *are* benefits, could be regarded as positive externalities, much as your neighbour's dazzling flower display is a welcome addition to the visual delights of your neighbourhood. And just as you would be surprised to receive a bill from your neighbour for the pleasure his flower display gives you and rightly resistant to paying it, so too the benefits provided by the state being, as it were, happy accidents, you can neither be legitimately charged for them nor required to submit to the authority of the state in return for them. After all, just as one may acquiesce passively in the negative elements of state action without thereby being taken to legitimate it, so too, one can similarly acquiesce in the positive elements of state action without legitimating the consequences. Simmons remarks that most citizens 'not unreasonably take the public goods they receive to be fully "bought and paid for" (indeed, overpaid for) from governments with tax payments. Mandatory purchase of overpriced public goods with compulsory tax payments does not leave much to account for the alleged additional aspects of political obligation.' [Simmons, 255]

In any event, even libertarians might agree that if a government along Lockean lines were to confine itself to the defence and vindication of our property rights (including, of course, our right to life and person), this is surely something we could live with. Maybe so, maybe not. Consider the following argument. We saw that Locke argues (in what Eric Mack calls the *Like Reason* argument) that just as a man is bound to preserve himself, so too, he is bound to preserve the rest of mankind when such preservation doesn't conflict with his duty of self-preservation. [§6] That being so, what if our Lockean government were to decide, by means of a majority decision, that our particular individual rights to external goods ought to be constrained, say, by taxation or partial confiscation, to ensure the preservation of all. Even if we were to disagree with the reasons for such a decision, as long as we were in the minority we couldn't legitimately object to the government's implementation of such a decision.

Let us return to the inconveniences of the state of nature. These were, let us remind ourselves, no settled law, no independent judges, no means of enforcement. A libertarian can concede that these are, indeed, problems for those of us who wish to live and associate with others. But libertarians aren't necessarily opposed to law, certainly not natural–rights libertarians who willingly concede that the zero-aggression principle is a non-negotiable element of all societies together with whatever other positive arrangements are freely entered into by individuals. [see Casey 2012, chapter 5] Nor are libertarians necessarily committed to the exercise of self-help as the first port of call whenever there's a serious dispute that must be resolved. Just as the principle of the division of labour applies to the production and distribution of material goods, so too, it makes sense to avail of arbitration and dispute resolution services to resolve our more intractable and serious problems rather than undertake to resolve them directly ourselves. Such services, to be effective, must of course be impartial and unbiased. The need for impartiality is satisfied if there is, in any given case, someone who is willing and competent to judge. It does not require that there be some one particular person who, or some one particular agency which, is willing and competent to serve in every case. In Rome, any Roman citizen was deemed competent to act as a judge in disputes between his fellow citizens. Libertarians would readily concede that judgement must be given effect. What is the point in having your dispute resolved and judgement and costs awarded to you if you can't enforce the judgement? But the enforcement of legal judgements also does not require that there be a single person or agency who is competent to do the enforcing, *a* government, one particular agent of governance, to the exclusion of all others. For Locke, the only way to remedy such inconveniences is for individuals to transfer the second-level rights they possess to defend their first order rights to an agency which undertakes to remedy these inconveniencies. This, in brief, is Locke's justification for the commonwealth. Eric Mack is particularly critical of Locke's creation of a super-agent, political society, noting that it gives rise to insuperable problems, no one of which can arise if Locke simply invokes 'the rights of individuals, *as individuals* (to the nonviolation of their rights *and* to the structure of governance that they have individually authorized.' [Mack 2009, 104]

As to which form of government—government by the one, the many or by all—is preferable, Locke has no fixed opinion. He rejects an absolute monarchy but is happy to accept an hereditary monarchy, an elective monarchy, even a democracy. His preferred term for the state is 'common-wealth' which signifies no particular form of government as such but rather any independent political community. [§§132-33] The legislative power is superior to the executive power [§§150; 152] though Locke is comfortable with the exercise of emergency powers by the executive when necessary and indeed even the executive's exercise of a kind of equitable discretion to temper the application of laws when such might be considered too severe. [§§159-60] While the legislative power is supreme, it is only a power taken on trust, a fiduciary power, which leaves unaltered in the people a power, also described as supreme, to remove or alter the legislative power! [§149] We then appear to have two supreme powers, the legislative power and the people. It is obvious that both can't be supreme at the same time and in the same respect, unless Locke is willing to entertain a contradiction. The charitable interpretation is to take the legislative power to be the active supreme power, with the people's power being passive or residual. [see Goldwin, 501]

Again, these themes in Locke aren't unproblematic. What constitutes the limits to the equitable or discretionary exercise of power by the executive? What is to stop the executive usurping the authority of the legislative power? What justifies the executive in such actions is that it acts for the public good in circumstances where the laws do not reach or do reach but aren't fit for purpose. But the plea of 'the public good' is elastic and can, like charity, be made to cover a multitude. In the end, Locke has little more to say than that the people, if they judge that the executive power, the prince, is acting to destroy rather than to defend their lives, liberty and estate, may regard him as a rebel, that is, to be someone who has brought back war or aggression, and as such may resist him. It is important to be clear that Locke isn't providing a charter for revolution but only justifying, *in extremis*, an ultimate resistance to a government which has fundamentally forsaken its constitutive purpose and is actively waging war on its citizens.

Eric Mack provides a useful summary of Locke's fundamental principles in respect of politics. These are (1) that every person possesses a set of natural rights to life, liberty and estate; (2) that a person's property rights derive from his rights over himself and his labour; (3) that the legitimate function of government is the protection of the rights mentioned in 1; (4) that the authority of a government is derived from the consent of those whom it governs; (5) that the failure of a government to protect these rights permits it to be resisted and replaced; and (6) that political authority is narrowly circumscribed and requires religious toleration. There can't be much doubt that this is a succinct and accurate account of Locke's fundamental principles.

What, if anything, is the value of Locke's contribution to contemporary discussions of rights? Communitarians and others criticise rights for promoting individualism at the expense of social solidarity but the pursuit of an individual's welfare based upon their rights (understood in the limited classical liberal sense and not in the expansive and endlessly inventive latter-day sense of the term) isn't only compatible with the pursuit of the welfare of communities, it is foundational to such a pursuit. Rights are 'precisely what enable individuals to discover or create diverse voluntary associations…in which people with all their different proclivities can cooperate to mutual advantage.' [Mack 2009, 139] What is the relevance of Lockean thought in our modern multicultural world? Mack is emphatic in claiming that 'Resolute depoliticalization of decision making rather than a futile search for more enlightened modes of political decision-making is the fundamental Lockean formula for how wider and increasingly diverse ranges of people can peacefully coexist.' [Mack 2009, 141] One can but agree.

Notes

1 See Hoppe, 2001.

2 '§' followed by a number refer to the relevant sections of the *Second Treatise*.

3 Eric Mack provides a fascinating discussion on the tensions in Locke's account between his tendency to accept a form of voluntarism (which Mack terms 'Divine Voluntarism') and the position that some moral norms apply to us simply because of the kind of creatures we are, such that even God couldn't make just any set of moral norms apply to us (which Mack calls the 'Inborn Constitution Program'). [Mack 2009, 28ff] He holds that the Divine Voluntarism elements in Locke's later work are, as it were, conceptual 'erratics' left over from an earlier stage of his intellectual career: 'Locke has no good reason to appeal to his divine voluntarism within his theory of the law of nature' [Mack 2009, 34] and he holds that 'the best construal of his arguments for natural rights will present those arguments as developments of an inborn constitution program that does not need to be supplemented by divine voluntarism.' [Mack 2009, 35] According to Mack, Locke's Divine Voluntarism is not the only example of a conceptual erratic. Another such is the 'Divine Workmanship' argument (we are all the product of God's creative activity; He is the maker of all) which Locke uses to support his argument that we have no right to commit suicide and, perhaps of greater significance politically, that as the product of God's creative activity and therefore, in some fundamental sense, his property, we cannot assign to others what we do not ourselves possess. As God's property we do not have the right to destroy, damage or enslave ourselves and so we cannot convey that right to another, even to a sovereign. As Mack points out, this argument proves too much: 'if we are really God's property and all our seeming rights are really God's rights, then we cannot transfer *any* of the rights which *seem* to be ours in a state of nature. [Mack 2009, 42] As he rejects Locke's voluntarism, so too Mack rejects the workmanship argument.

4 There are broad and narrow ways to interpret this fourth argument. Mack suggests that it mandates that one 'avoids pursuing one's own ends in ways that prevent others from devoting themselves to the pursuit of their respective ends.' [Mack 2009, 45] We shall see a little later that there may be more expansive ways to take the *Like Reason* argument.

5 See O'Keeffe 1992, 1; 5; 9.

6 Tannehill and Tannehill, 57-58.

7 Strictly speaking, it is his *second* proviso but it is the more important of the two that Locke offers and is generally what is meant when people mention 'the Lockean proviso' without qualification.

8 See Kant's account of property, below.

9 The immediately preceding material first appeared in my *Libertarian Anarchy*.

10 Tannehill & Tannehill, 58.

11 Cohen 1995, 70; see O'Keeffe 1992, 2.

12 Cohen 1995, 70, emphasis added.

13 Fabre 2002; 2003; 2006.

14 Even if it were true that *most* contemporary theories of justice held this (just how many theories of justice *are* there?) why should this factual majority be of any significance? Moral issues are not normally resolved by the counting of heads.

15 For a cool and intellectually devastating treatment of what he terms 'rights contagion', see Dominic Raab's *The Assault on Liberty*, 123-168.

16 Fabre 2002, 261. In the film *Shenandoah*, a son asks his father (played by Jimmy Stewart) what 'requisition' means and Stewart replies laconically—did Jimmy Stewart ever respond any other way?—'Steal!' From time to time, tax demands have been resisted by their would-be victims. Perhaps the best known examples of such resistance are Shay's Rebellion of 1786/87 (to which the move to construct and enact the US Constitution was in large measure a reaction) and the Whiskey Rebellion of 1791 (and its mid-nineteenth century successor) [see Adams 1999, 65ff, 117ff, and Slaughter, passim] One of the more colourful instances of such resistance has to be that of Muireadhach Albanach Ó Dálaigh. In early thirteenth century Ireland, Ó Dálaigh, who was the chief poet of Domhnall Ó Domhnaill, considered the demands of Ó Domhnaill's tax-collector to be insolent and he killed the tax-collector with an axe. Ó Domhnaill took exception to the killing of his emissary and Ó Dálaigh expressed his surprise at this, writing: 'Trifling is our difference with [Ó Domhnaill]/A churl [*bachlach*] was affronting me/And I killed that clown [*mogh*]/ O God! Is this a cause for enmity?' [see O'Connor, 252-253] But active resistance to the collection of taxes goes back even further than medieval Ireland. Cyril Parkinson notes that in the middle of the eighth

century BC, an official of Tiglath Pileser III, the king of Assyria, experienced some difficulties collecting taxes in the cities of Tyre and Sidon. One tax collector was killed in Tyre, while another was rescued from a similar fate only with difficulty. [Parkinson 1965, 26] But now, we are reassured by Richard Murphy, the age for tax-resistance is past. 'The notion that tax is compulsorily imposed is anachronistic and should be a remnant of another age, when one class imposed their will on others who were not represented in the decision-making process. Now that we are, or at least can be (although some shamefully absent themselves from it), a part of that decision-making process, tax is not imposed but is consensual.' [Murphy 2016a, 42] So that's all right then. Thank you, Mr Murphy. In the face of such comfortable complacency, I am hesitant to suggest that the notion of representation in representative democracy might be less than completely coherent, that, *pace* Murphy's reassurances, government appears still to involve the imposition by one class of its will on another and that perhaps it might be that we do *not* in fact consent to government's imposition of taxes on us but at best acquiesce in the exercise of *force majeure*. [see Casey 2010b, passim]

17 Is it really necessary to point out how the argument runs neatly in the opposite direction if one were to start from the unacceptability of taxation?

18 Fabre 2002, 271. In contrast to this breezy dismissal of practicability by Fabre, James Otteson believes that any political philosophy, if it is to be taken seriously, must take questions of practicability into account. [see Otteson 2014, passim]

19 *Sed nescio quo modo nihil tam absurde dici potest quod non dicatur ab aliquo philosophorum*—Marcus Tullius Cicero.

20 §127; italics in original.

21 Compare Hobbes's treatment of the unanimity/majority issue.

Chapter 21

JEAN-JACQUES ROUSSEAU

Whoever refuses to obey the General Will shall be constrained to do
so by the entire body: which means nothing other than that
he shall be forced to be free
—Jean-Jacques Rousseau

Not only is democracy mystical nonsense, it is also immoral.
If one man has no right to impose his wishes on another,
then ten million men have no right to impose their
wishes on the one, since the initiation of force is wrong
(and the assent of even the most overwhelming majority
can never make it morally permissible).
Opinions—even majority opinions—neither create truth
nor alter facts. A lynch mob is democracy in action.
So much for mob rule.
—Morris Tannehill

Many thinkers command our admiration and respect even if we do not always find ourselves in agreement with them. Some few, however, do not. Of all the thinkers we have encountered and shall encounter who have written on political philosophy, there can be little doubt that Jean-Jacques Rousseau (1712-1778) can stake a claim to be one of the least likeable. If one had to choose someone to go for a companionable drink with, Rousseau—described by Tibor Fischer as 'a man who made a career out of spite and who could bore a balloon to Mars'—wouldn't be one's first choice. [Fischer, 126] If he had ever been found suffering from a gunshot wound, the question 'Who shot J-JR?' would have elicited a long list of possible suspects. Rousseau is a figure whom many people love to hate. And there's good reason for this. He was self-centred, vain, self-pitying, narcissistic, and he yoked all these unattractive traits to an irrepressible lust for self-publicity. An Angry Young Man before his time, he made the common mistake of confusing rudeness and boorishness with honesty and integrity, betraying a bumptiousness that probably resulted from knowing that he could never hope to move by right in the highest social circles to which he aspired. Iring Fetscher writes of him, 'A Protestant among Catholics, a proud citizen of the tiny republic of Geneva among cosmopolitan fellow travellers of monarchical imperialism, a critic of modernity at its most fashionable eighteenth-century shrine, Rousseau was spiritually estranged from the intellectual circles in Paris to which he had previously been drawn...' [Fetscher, 573]

Rousseau had the Mrs Jellyby-like liberal vice of loving (or claiming to love) all mankind while simultaneously showing a particular propensity for hating particular individuals. He might have been the model for Chesterton's verses:

Oh, how I love Humanity,
  With love so pure and pringlish,
And how I hate the horrid French,
  Who never will be English.

The villas and the chapels where
  I learned with little labour
The way to love my fellow-man
  And hate my next-door neighbour.
[Chesterton, xv]

He was a notorious ingrate, falling out with those who made the fatal error of being kind and helpful to him, including Voltaire, Diderot,[1] Tronchin and that most personally lovable of all philosophers, David Hume. [see Edmonds & Eidinow, passim] J. S. McClelland remarks that 'Hume tried to be decent to Rousseau in his English exile, but the meeting between reasoned moderation and paranoid romanticism ended in disaster.' [McClelland, 403]

His personal life was irregular, to say the least, an irregularity revealed with much pseudo-moralising in his *Confessions,* about which production David Hume remarked astutely, 'I believe, that he intends seriously to draw his own picture in its true colours: but I believe at the same time that nobody knows himself less.'[2] While we might, in the ethically relaxed twenty-first century, be inclined to overlook much in Rousseau's life that scandalised his contemporaries, his callous abandonment of the five children he had with Thérèse Levasseur still has the capacity to shock. Perhaps even more shocking is the patently specious justification Rousseau offered for the abandonment of his children. He claimed that they would be better provided for in every way in the orphanage, a claim that is patently implausible when Rousseau must have been well aware that more than two thirds of the babies deposited in the *Hôpital des Enfants-trouvés* died within the first year.[3] Some might argue that Rousseau's moral failings are irrelevant to a consideration of his ideas[4]—in another context, Arthur Schopenhauer remarked that 'It is therefore just as little necessary for the saint to be a philosopher as for the philosopher to be a saint' [Schopenhauer 1966, 383]—but Paul Johnson is, I believe, entirely correct in believing it entirely appropriate to focus on Rousseau's abandonment of his children 'not only because it is the most striking single example of his inhumanity but because it is organically part of the process which produced his theory of politics and the role of the state.' [Johnson 22] For Rousseau, education was the key to social and moral improvement and therefore education is and should be a concern of the State. In Rousseau's vision, the State becomes father to all and all citizens become children in the State orphanage.

It is not only in respect of his having written a *Confessions* that Rousseau resembles Augustine. The thinking of both men is, to an extraordinary degree, an exteriorisation of their character and personal circumstances. In addition, both men were consumed by the discrepancy between what they aspired to be and what they were. 'All that Rousseau wrote on philosophy and politics,' notes Sabine, 'grew in some devious way from his complex and unhappy personality.' [Sabine, 575] John Plamenatz remarks of Rousseau that he was 'one of the most self-absorbed and emotional of writers, and his political and social theories are deeply affected by his personal difficulties, by his eccentricities and hatreds. What Rousseau wanted was a world fit for himself to live in, a heaven fit for himself to go to, and a God worthy of his love. Nobody who spoke so often of man in the abstract gives so strong an impression that he is speaking always of himself.' [Plamenatz, 364] But if Rousseau resembled Augustine in his confessional mode, what he wrote could scarcely have been more different: the professions of faith of the Savoyard Vicar and that of the Bishop of Hippo are worlds apart. Whereas the medieval period had been an attempt to come to grips with our world by means of reason and revelation, and the early modern period had kept reason while ditching revelation, Rousseau's romanticism went one better than the early moderns and ditched both revelation and reason, seeking and finding its home in sentiment and feeling. [see Sabine 578]

Given the highly peculiar circumstances of his life as recounted in his (admittedly unreliable) *Confessions*[5] and the widely acknowledged problems of interpreting certain aspects of his thought, it is tempting to dismiss Rousseau out of hand as a thinker unworthy of serious consideration. To do so, however, would be a major error. Whatever his personal failings, his profound influence on subsequent thought cannot be denied. Perhaps more than any modern thinker, Rousseau has determined the agenda for all modern and contemporary discussions of political philosophy. 'Rousseau,' writes Victor Gourevitch, 'has permanently altered how we perceive ourselves, one another and the world about us, and in particular how we conceive of politics and what we expect of it.' [Gourevitch1997a, ix] Paul Johnson also testifies to the influence of Rousseau, writing that he was 'the first of the modern intellectuals, their archetype and in many ways the most influential of them all….In both the long and the short term his influence was enormous' [Johnson 2] Among Rousseau's admirers and followers we can find an impressive and diverse range of thinkers and political activists—Robespierre, Kant, Hegel, Schiller, Shelley, Mill, Marx, Levi-Strauss, Foucault and Derrida. He has contributed to, or has been believed to have contributed to, not one but two revolutions, the American and the French, and to have affected not one but several schools of thought, among them Kantianism, German Idealism (directly and also via Kant), the Romantic movement and its progeny, including Nietzsche, twentieth century totalitarianism and, perhaps most surprisingly, modern conservatism and communitarianism.

Rousseau achieved overnight fame as a result of the publication of his *First Discourse*, an outcome that Paul Johnson finds frankly astonishing. 'The essay is feeble and today almost unreadable,' he remarks, adding, 'it seems inexplicable that so paltry a work could have produced such an explosion of celebrity…' [Johnson, 7] Paltry and feeble as it may have been, it also appears to have been plagiarised. Robert Whelan notes that 'the most striking characteristic of Rousseau's prize essay, which appears not to have been noticed by the judges, was its complete lack of originality! There is not a single strand in his account of the noble savage which he had not copied from Montaigne's essay *On the Cannibals*, published 170 years before.' [Whelan, 12] Rousseau's later philosophical works—the *Second Discourse* and the *Social Contract*—were in fact little read during Rousseau's lifetime. Cyril Parkinson remarks, ironically, that the evidence for listing Rousseau's *Social Contract* among the causes of the French Revolution 'is weakened somewhat by the lack of evidence that it was widely read. M. Daniel Mornet analysed the library catalogues of five hundred contemporaries of Louis XV and discovered that whereas 165 of them include *Nouvelle Heloise*, only one contained the *Contrat Social*.' [Parkinson 1958, 203-204] Rousseau's expanding fame after the production of the *First Discourse* was due largely to his novel *La Nouvelle Héloïse* and to a lesser extent to his treatise on education, the didactic novel *Émile*. *Émile* is the source-text for the progressive movement in education, influencing such as Pestalozzi and Montessori and others. *Héloïse*, like the *First Discourse*, is scarcely readable today but in its day, it had an appeal to the prurient cleverly concealed under a mask of morality; the Archbishop of Paris accused it of insinuating the poison of lust while seeming to proscribe it, an accusation which did nothing to depress its sales!

THE *DISCOURSES*

Rousseau's *First Discourse* (*The Discourse on the Sciences and Arts*) was written as an entry in a competition organised by the Dijon Academy on the topic—Has the Restoration of the Sciences and the Arts Contributed to the Purification of Morals? There can be little doubt that the Academy expected contributors to answer *yes* to this question and then go on to describe *how* the Arts and Sciences had made this contribution. Rousseau, however, took the startling and counter-intuitive (but strategically clever) step of answering the question in the negative. Science and culture have not only *not* improved man's moral life, they have, on the contrary, caused it to deteriorate! His *First Discourse* is an attack on reason, on science and, by implication, on the whole Enlightenment project. For reason, science and philosophy, Rousseau substitutes sentiment, even instinct, and recommends an attitude of natural and unspoiled reverence for nature. Those who are simple and thoughtless are to be valued more than the sophisticated and the educated. All Rousseau's moral valuations, writes Sabine, turned upon 'the affections of family life, the joy and beauty of motherhood, the satisfactions of the homely arts like tilling the soil, the universal feeling of religious reverence, above all, the sense of a common lot and the sharing of a common life....By contrast science is the fruit of idle curiosity; philosophy is mere intellectual frippery; the amenities of polite life are tinsel.' [Sabine, 577] This *First Discourse* (together with the *Second Discourse*) is the source of the commonly held idea that Rousseau expounds a theory of the nobility of the savage and recommends a return to man's native simplicity. This idea is not quite accurate. For one thing, whatever the short-comings of cultured society, Rousseau never thought that a return to primitive simplicity, even if desirable, was in fact possible.

All Rousseau's central ideas are in essence a transmutation and projection of his own particular life and circumstances into the life and circumstances of all, so that his hero isn't so much the noble savage as Rousseau writ large, an 'irritated and bewildered bourgeois, at odds with a society that despised and looked down on him, conscious of his own purity of heart and the greatness of his own deserts, and profoundly shocked at the badness of the philosophers to whom nothing was sacred.' [Sabine, 577] The romantic in Rousseau opposed feeling to intellect, tradition to enlightenment, and faith to science. Sabine writes, 'The enormous importance of Rousseau lies in the fact that, broadly speaking, he carried philosophy with him against its own tradition....the distrust of intelligence was written large over the philosophy of the nineteenth century.' [Sabine, 578] It might be more true to say that Rousseau's attitude towards reason was one of profound ambivalence rather than outright rejection. As he saw it, reason was rather like the broom enchanted by the sorcerer's apprentice that, once unleashed, couldn't be restrained or controlled. So too, reason was to be encouraged and welcomed when it attacked and destroyed obvious excrescences such as the Church but not when, like the animated broom, it went on a rampage and threatened to destroy all that was valuable in human life. 'Rousseau first made vocal a newly awakened fear,' Sabine writes, 'the fear that rational criticism, having demolished the more inconvenient pieties like the dogmas and disciplines of the church, might not be made to stop before the pieties which it still seemed judicious to retain.' [Sabine, 577] A century later, we can detect a similar ambivalence towards science and its methods in the attitude of Friedrich Nietzsche.

What Rousseau was driving at was the idea that what society needed to improve its morals wasn't heavier doses of science, technology or philosophy but a re-education of the passions. 'Moral/political excellence....can only be achieved by everyone's recognizing the shared concern for the common interest or good as the organizing principle of their cares and pursuits...' [Gourevitch 1997a, xiv] In our civilised society, there appears to be an ineradicable tension between the good of individuals and the common good. It seems that the good of any individual can only be achieved at the expense of the good of all. If this is so, why, Rousseau asks, is it so? Is there something the matter with human beings so that this tension is irremovable? Or does the problem lie elsewhere?

In the *Second Discourse* (*Discourse on the Origin and Foundations of Inequality Among Men*), Rousseau attempts to answer this question. He distinguishes between what he calls *physical* inequality—all aspects of our physical and psychological being—and what he calls *moral* inequality, by which he means the difference between being ruled and being a ruler. He is concerned primarily with moral inequality. Rousseau adopts Hobbes's term 'state of nature' to describe man's pre-political condition but his account of the state of nature is very different from that given by Hobbes. In fact, he thinks Hobbes got matters precisely the wrong way around by not being sufficiently radical in his account of natural man and imagining him to have desires that can arise only in society. According to Rousseau, Hobbes should have said that 'the state of Nature is the state in which the care for our own preservation is least prejudicial to the self-preservation of others; it follows that this state was the most conducive to Peace and the best suited to Mankind. He said precisely the contrary because he improperly included in Savage man's care for his preservation the need to satisfy a multitude of passions that are the product of society and have made Laws necessary.'[6] Rousseau accepts that man in the state of nature is gifted with a desire for self-preservation (self-love) but he sees this as being balanced by an equally native propensity to feel pity for others. Pity, he writes, is 'a disposition suited to beings as weak and as subject to so many ills as we are; a virtue all the more universal and useful to man as it precedes the exercise of all reflection in him...' If man had needed the assistance of moral philosophy to survive he would have perished forthwith; the state of nature, then, is not a war of all against all—otherwise how would Hobbes explain the survival of man prior to his entry into civil society? 'While Socrates and minds of his stamp may be able to acquire virtue through reason, mankind would long ago have ceased to be if its preservation had depended solely on the reasons of those who make it up.'[7]

It is widely believed that Rousseau's central contention is that man in a state of nature is naturally good. Well, yes, in a way, but this isn't quite the whole story. In the state of nature man isn't good in the way that someone is good who can choose evil but does not; but, rather, good in the way that an entity which hasn't yet eaten of the tree of good and evil can be said to be good. This is a kind of natural goodness rather than a moral goodness, more ignorance than innocence. Pre-social man is pre-moral and, largely, pre-rational as well. Just as an animal, however ferocious it may be, isn't a fit subject for moral evaluation, so too is man in the state of nature. In the state of nature, writes Gourevitch, 'men's natural goodness is perfectly compatible with fierceness, even with ferociousness, cruelty, and a considerable level of violence.... Natural goodness is, then, emphatically not beneficence, the inclination or the steady will to do another's good. Nor is it virtue...let alone the justice that consists in doing unto others as you would have them do unto you. Nothing in Rousseau's account of men in the pre-political state of nature justifies calling them "noble savages."'[8]

Rousseau does not believe, *contra* Samuel Pufendorf and many others, that men are naturally social beings; nor, on the other hand, does he believe, *contra* Hobbes, that men are naturally antagonistic. For Rousseau, man in the state of nature is neither social nor anti-social, neither moral nor immoral; he is, rather, asocial and amoral. Men in this condition are not and cannot be either just or unjust. He writes, 'let us not conclude with Hobbes that because he has no idea of goodness man is naturally wicked...' On his own principles, according to Rousseau, Hobbes should have held that the state of nature 'was most conducive to Peace and the best suited to Mankind,' instead, Hobbes 'says precisely the contrary because he improperly included in Savage man's care for his preservation the need to satisfy a multitude of pasions that are the product of Society and have made Laws necessary.'[9]

Part of Rousseau's criticism of Hobbes is that his state of nature simply did not go deep enough. [see Riley, 365] To get to a state of nature one has to strip off *everything* that society contributes to man, *including* language, reason, and sociability. Natural man is neither moral nor immoral—he is, rather, pre-moral. He is an animal without thought, operating purely on instinct. Rousseau's men in the state of nature have removed from them not only the accoutrements of developed Western civilisation but almost everything that makes them human—morality, language, and rationality. Rousseau's original man, without thought, without language, is scarcely recognisable as human at all, resembling rather a chimpanzee that has been strategically shaved and dressed in a suit. This anthropology is often taken to be unique to Rousseau but it has antecedents, generally, among the Stoics, and, more immediately, in the accounts of early man one can find expressed by George Buchanan and Juan de Mariana. It is important to note that while Rousseau has the concept of a state of nature, just as Hobbes and Locke do, his state of nature is *not* exited by means of a social contract. 'What is remarkable about Rousseau's account of the origins of human society,' writes McClelland, 'is that, although he is a social contract thinker, he does not use the idea of social contract itself to explain the origins of human societies.' [McClelland, 257] In fact, he is remarkably coy about explaining why and how the transition from natural man to social man took place!

In the state of nature, man has two guiding principles; self-preservation, and pity or sympathy. These two principles provide a kind of balance, each preventing the other from being exercised to excess. Neither of these principles is calculating or the product of reason; they are pre-rational. In their natural state, men have the potential to be free, a possibility given to no other animal. This potential is actualised only when man's circumstances change radically. It is only in society that men become 'self-seeking and egoistic, desiring things not because of their intrinsic worth but because they want to excite the admiration of others.' [Boucher, 270] What snake is it, then, that introduces sin into this (relatively) Edenic state?

Agriculture![10]

Agriculture, with property as its inexorable accompaniment, and not the love of money, is, for Rousseau, the root of all evil. In his *Essay on the Origin of Languages*, Rousseau tells us that originally, hunting and herding sufficed for man's needs with relatively little effort. Agriculture, however arose later and 'it introduces property, government, laws, and gradually wretchedness and crimes, inseparable for our species from the knowledge of good and evil.'[11] Man, once self-sufficient, is self-sufficient no longer. This dependence upon others leads to the division of labour which, in turn, leads to inequality, for the once insignificant physical differences between man and man now assume a moral character and become inequalities not of strong versus weak or clever versus stupid but between rich and poor, ruler and ruled, master and slave. Men, he writes in the *Second Discourse*, 'so long as they applied themselves only to tasks a single individual could perform, and to arts that did not require the collaboration of several hands, they lived free, healthy, good, and happy as far as they could by their Nature be, and continued to enjoy the gentleness of independent dealings with one another; but the moment one man needed the help of another; as soon as it was found to be useful for one to have provisions for two, equality disappeared, property appeared, work became necessary, and the vast forests changed into smiling Fields that had to be watered with the sweat of men, and where slavery and misery were soon seen to sprout and grow together with the harvests.'[12]

In asserting that man is naturally good (or, at least, not bad) and that society is responsible for his deformation, Rousseau is taken to often reject the Christian notion of original sin. [see Boucher, 269] But Rousseau's account of natural man is, in many respects, simply a secular version of the Christian story. Rousseau's state of nature is a secularised version of the Garden of Eden—Rousseau's pre-social man isn't so much naturally good as naturally outside the scope of good and evil altogether. In the Christian story, it isn't until Adam and Eve eat of the fruit of the tree of good and evil that they move from their state of original innocence to a state of moral awareness. The Christian's original sin is Rousseau's advent of civilisation with its property and its government; Adam and Eve and their descendants are expelled from Eden never to return while Rousseau's man in society now finds himself prey to vanity, self-seeking and conflict. It isn't until man discovers agriculture that society becomes possible and with it, moral awareness and moral freedom and, with them, the necessity for government and the domination of one man by another. In the Christian story, after the Fall, man must earn his bread by the sweat of his brow and the children of Adam become tillers of the soil and pastoralists; in Rousseau's fable, civilised man is similarly prey to many evils simply unknown to man in the state of nature.

In this no-longer-innocent condition, conflict now arises and since those with property have more to lose than those without property, they propose a compact to set up a supreme power that would rule all men in accordance with law and protect the possessions of each. 'The rich,' writes Rousseau, 'must soon have sensed how disadvantageous to them was a perpetual war of which they alone bore the full cost and in which everyone risked his life while only some also risked goods.'[13] Rousseau regards the proposal to agree to this compact to be one of the all time great swindles by which the rich man's adversaries were turned willy nilly into his defenders. Persuaded that a supreme power would be to their advantage, 'All ran toward their chains in the belief that they were securing their freedom; for while they had enough reason to sense the advantages of a political establishment, they had not enough experience to foresee its dangers...'[14] It is important to realise that this compact does not constitute man as a member of *society*—he is that already—what it does is to constitute men as members of a *political* order. Rousseau's description of man once he has entered society is uncannily similar to Hobbes's description of man in the state of nature. 'In society humans become self-seeking and egoistic, desiring things not because of their intrinsic worth but because they want to excite the admiration of others,' writes Boucher. 'In comparing ourselves with others the self is never satisfied, because in valuing ourselves above others we vainly demand that others value us above themselves. At this point the capacity for both freedom and self-perfection is undermined.' [Boucher, 270]

For Rousseau, property isn't something that belongs to man in the state of nature—possession, yes, property, no. The opening to the second part of the *Second Discourse* is notorious for the following passage: 'The first man who, having enclosed a piece of ground, to whom it occurred to say *this is mine*, and found people sufficiently simple to believe him, was the true founder of civil society. How many crimes, wars, murders, how many miseries and horrors Mankind would have been spared by him who, pulling up the stakes or filling in the ditch, had cried out to his kind: Beware of listening to this impostor; You are lost if you forget that the fruits are everyone's and the Earth no one's.'[15] This passage echoes ideas that came before Rousseau, from the Franciscans, from Wycliffe, from Winstanley, ideas that will be re-echoed later by Henry George and others. Does this put Rousseau in the communist camp? Not necessarily. However regrettable it may have been that man ever invented property and human society, the reality is that that is what we have and we just have to get on with it. What Rousseau is really trying to get across in this passage and in others like it, is that property isn't a right that man holds *against* society but one that he holds only *within* society.

Property is the source of almost all human ills, certainly the ills of inequality and the vain desire for reputation. Rousseau's account of the origin of property is surprisingly close to that of Locke. A claim to property derives from the labour that I expend in making use of the earth's resources. With the advent of agriculture and the longer time span required for the use of natural resources, possession necessarily becomes longer and longer, so much so that it leads eventually to a claim of right, that is, to property. This in turn gives rise to conflicts and a war of all against all from which man desiring to escape agrees to the imposition of the legitimate use of power by one man or a group of men over others. 'What Rousseau wanted to emphasize was that the passions that incline us to violence, aggression, and war are not pre-societal, but actually acquired in society itself.' [Boucher, 271] Violence is *not* an aspect of the condition of man in the state of nature. In particular, war isn't in any way an aspect of the life of natural man. 'For Rousseau, war is the result of a corruption of human nature. It is a condition that prevails among states and not among individuals, and its consequences are far more destructive. Instead of alleviating violence, states accentuate it.' [Boucher, 271]

Readers have often assumed that Rousseau is proposing a return to our condition of original innocence and passages such as the following from the *Second Discourse* give some grounds for thinking this to be so. 'Savage man and civilized man differ so much in their inmost heart and inclinations that what constitutes the supreme happiness of the one would reduce the other to despair. The first breathes nothing but repose and freedom, he wants only to live and to remain idle, and even the Stoic's ataraxia does not approximate his profound indifference to everything else. By contrast, the Citizen, forever active, sweats, scurries, constantly agonizes in search of ever more strenuous occupation: he works to the death, even rushes toward it in order to be in a position to live, or renounces life in order to acquire immortality.'[16] But there is no going back. The liberty that men enjoyed in the state of nature, is, like

my darling Clementine, lost and gone forever. Such liberty as we may find will
be a simulacrum of the original, not its re-installation. 'The clue to Rousseau's
solution to the problem of liberty within a political community,' writes McClelland, 'lies in his assertion that the natural liberty of the State of Nature has gone
for ever; we now live in a social condition from which there is no turning back.
The only way lies forward, so that all this hankering after a so-called 'natural'
liberty has to stop.' [McClelland, 260]

THE SOCIAL CONTRACT AND THE GENERAL WILL

Rousseau's conjectural history of man in the *Second Discourse* was his explanation of how human beings had got themselves into a situation where the
freedom of man-in-nature (or something close to it) could be reconciled with
the obedience required of man-in-society. His *Social Contract*[17] is an attempt
to explain how liberty and order (obedience to the authority of the state) could
be reconciled. By the end of the *Second Discourse*, Rousseau has arrived at
what for Hobbes is his starting point; the insecurity of man versus man which
leads, as it does in Hobbes, to the establishment of the state. But this preserves
order only at the cost of institutionalising inequality, protecting the rich from
the justified revenge of the poor. The poor are faced with an unenviable choice:
either some measure of security with endemic injustice or a Hobbesian war of
all against all.

  Some nineteenth century German scholars saw a fundamental discrepancy
between the Adam Smith of the *Theory of Moral Sentiments* and the Adam Smith
of *The Wealth of Nations*. This discrepancy they christened *Das Adamsmith-
problem*. Some people think there's a *Jean-JacquesRousseau-problem*: we
seem to have one Rousseau, Rousseau the individualist, in the *Discourses*,
particularly the *Second Discourse on Inequality*, and yet another Rousseau,
Rousseau the socialist, in the *Social Contract*. It is hard to reach a scholarly
consensus on whether there is a problem here or not but, if there is, the reason
for it may be that Rousseau's writing is simply inconsistent! Many people have
a suspicion that if you want to become a famous philosopher, the last thing one
should do is to strive for clarity. Ayn Rand sardonically remarks that 'if you
want to propagate an outrageously evil idea…your conclusion must be brazenly
clear, but your proof unintelligible. Your proof must be so tangled a mess that
it will paralyze a reader's critical faculty.'[18] Confusion and contradiction feed
the scholarly industry where professors can argue happily for years as to what
it was that you *really* meant. 'Confusion has always surrounded Rousseau's
political ideas,' writes Paul Johnson, 'because he was in many respects an
inconsistent and contradictory writer—one reason why the Rousseau industry
has grown so gigantic: academics thrive on resolving "problems". In some
passages of his works he appears a conservative, strongly opposed to revolution ….But his writings also abound with radical bitterness.' [Johnson, 23]
Georges Sorel would seem to be of a mind with Johnson. Commenting on
Sorel's *Réflections sur la Violence*, John Bowle says that Sorel maintained that
Rousseau was unintelligible but that this lack of intelligibility did not matter!
'The idea of the General Will and the Marxist theory of value—notable and

perennial torments for students of political thought—both prove, says Sorel, "how important obscurity can be in giving force to a doctrine". Of course, it is quite beside the point to try to understand either.' [Bowle, 406] Heidegger, notoriously if naïvely, remarked in his *Beiträge zur Philosophie*[19] that 'to make oneself understood is suicidal to philosophy.' Sabine remarks of Rousseau, somewhat more charitably, 'The difference between the earlier works and the *Social Contract* is merely that in the former he was writing himself free from an uncongenial social philosophy and in the latter he was expressing as clearly as he could, a counter-philosophy of his own.' [Sabine, 580] The uncongenial social philosophy Sabine has in mind is individualism as we find it in Locke and Hobbes. The thinker who was to release Rousseau from subjection to any lingering disposition he might have had to be individualist was, surprise, surprise, Plato! Sabine may see this return of Rousseau to Plato as a release from bondage; I would see it, rather, as the re-subjection of modern political thought to the collectivism of the Greeks.

For the mature Rousseau, then, the collectivity comes first, the individual a distant second. The naked individual is nothing. Anything an individual has of value—his desire for happiness, his language—all these come from his society. Sabine expresses Rousseau's point clearly: 'Within a society there may be individuality, freedom, self-interest, respect for covenants; outside it there is nothing moral. From it individuals get their mental and moral faculties and by it they become human; the fundamental moral category is not man but citizen.' [Sabine, 581] Here, we can see clearly once again, the egregious conflation of the social with the political that is characteristic of classical thought. We can grant that man is a social animal. It is obvious that language and moral upbringing happen in society. But none of this necessarily implies anything in particular about politics, least of all the legitimacy or priority of the state.

The *Social Contract* opens with a piece of magnificent rhetoric. 'Man everywhere is born free, and everywhere he is in chains. One believes himself the others' master, and yet is more a slave than they.'[20] This resounding claim might, and often does, give the impression that what Rousseau is advocating is a return to the state of nature and the condition of original freedom. But that isn't so. As we have seen, for Rousseau, human beings are not really human unless they are members of society. The state of nature isn't, in fact, a golden age, an Eden, from which we have unaccountably departed and to which we need to return. Looking forward briefly to where Rousseau is leading us, we shall see that he thinks there's no way back to the state of original innocence in which every man is naturally free. The only way is forward and that brings us to his account of the social contract and the General Will.

Rousseau's notion of the General Will may have been clear to Rousseau but I suspect he was just one member—perhaps the only member—of a very small General Will appreciation society. Rousseau's idea of the social contract with the notion of the General Will at its core is, not to put too fine a point on it, simply baffling. If I wanted to be rude I might call it incoherent. It seems to mean something like this. By means of the General Will, which isn't the will of the individual citizen nor even the will of a majority of citizens but somehow a will that transcends the merely empirical, the laws which we are obliged to obey are willed by each and every citizen (not factually but as it were counter-factually) so that obedience to these laws is obedience to our own will and not to the will of another. Thus freedom is preserved together with order.[21] It is doubtful whether any existing state manages to be a complete and pure expression of the General Will. That being so, a paradoxical consequence of his view is to make Rousseau in some sense a philosophical anarchist inasmuch as no existing state exercises legitimate authority over its citizens! In actuality, each man's self-interest is determined by his particular history and circumstances. The General Will, then, isn't simply the will of a majority as is said to obtain in modern democracies—it transcends such mundane realities—though there are passages in Rousseau that seem to support such an interpretation. It is, rather, what all *would* will for all *if* they were to abstract from their individual biases and concerns. In an eerie anticipation of John Rawls's Veil of Ignorance, Rousseau suggests that if we 'posit a moment of equality, then each man, when consulting his own interest, will be consulting exactly the same self-interest as everybody else because he will no longer have unequal self-interest to tell him which way to vote.' [McClelland, 262]

Political society isn't natural, neither is political rule in any way natural. If political rule is to be justified, it can only be justified by some convention requiring the consent or agreement of those who will be subject to such rule. The social contract is, properly conceived, not so much an historic event located at some particular point in the past, as it is the naming of an analytically necessary continuing act by which we constitute and recognise ourselves as members of a political community. By virtue of the social contract, we exchange our natural freedom for civic freedom.

It is difficult to understand why Rousseau makes any use of the notion of a contract, given his perspective on the state of nature. Equally difficult to understand is how his contract is supposed to be a *contract*. Individuals have no rights unless and until they are members of society, so society cannot be constructed by any kind of contract between pre-social individuals. Sabine remarks, 'the imaginary act by which a society is produced is not even remotely like a contract, because the rights and liberties of individuals have no existence at all except as they are already members of the group. Rousseau's whole argument depended upon the fact that a community of citizens is unique and coeval with its members; they neither make it nor have rights against it. It is an "association" not an "aggregation." A moral and collective personality. The word contract was about as misleading as any that Rousseau could have chosen.' [Sabine, 587] These problems to one side, we may ask what the social contract is for? It is to provide a solution to the problem of finding 'a form of association that will defend and protect the person and goods of each associate with the full common force, and by means of which each, uniting with all, nevertheless *obey only himself and remain as free as before.*'[22]

Rousseau's idea of the General Will is, in part, an attempt to capture the idea that a community has a personality of its own that isn't the personality of any of its members, and a good that isn't the good of any of its members; nor are

the community personality and good simply the aggregated sum of the personalities and goods of the individuals that go to make it up. If the community is
in any significant way a unity, it must have a unitary mode of direction. 'If the
State or the City is only a moral person whose life consists in the union of its
members,' writes Rousseau, 'and if the most important of its cares is the care
for its self-preservation, then it has to have some universal and coercive force
to move and arrange each part in the manner most conformable to the whole.
Just as nature gives each man absolute power over his members, the social
pact gives the body politic absolute power over all of its members, and it is
this same power which, directed by the General Will, bears, as I have said, the
name of sovereignty.'[23] Law made by the General Will must be general in scope
and apply to all equally. Although individuals can't but be concerned with their
own circumstances and interests, none the less they can support laws made to
secure the interests of all. This situation is more likely to come about if the
economic and social situation of every citizen is more or less the same.

Rousseau's notion of the General Will was later to find a home away from
home in Kant (and from him to Rawls), in Hegel and, perhaps most surprisingly, even in Burke. Hegel took it to be the spirit of the German nation
whereas Burke tended to see it as being embodied in the culture and traditions
of England. Sabine comments that 'In Burke, the corporate life of England
became a conscious reality. The General Will was released from temporary
bondage to Jacobinism and made a factor in conservative nationalism.' [Sabine,
595] Burke's version of the General Will is also couched in terms of a contract.
For Burke, as we shall see, society is indeed the product of a contract but a very
special kind of contract.

Clearly, then, there can be tensions between the individual will of a citizen or
of particular groups of citizens and the General Will of the whole society. Apart
from rejecting its identity with the will of the majority, Rousseau was conspicuously vague about the method for ascertaining the General Will. Exactly how
is the General Will to be made manifest? How is one to know what it is? Is
it enough that the individual wills of citizens are refined by considerations
of universality so that they converge on, if they do not exactly equate to, the
General Will? Tempting as this sort of explanation is, Rousseau is disinclined
to think that self-interest, however refined, will result in the production of a
General Will because of a lack of the requisite virtues in citizens.

To overcome this problem, Rousseau introduces the puzzling figure of the
Legislator whose task it is to bring about the conformity of diverse wills.[24] This,
while momentarily helpful, is ultimately to explain the obscure by the even
more obscure for if the notion of the General Will is problematic, the notion of
the Legislator is scarcely less so. Rousseau says of the Legislator that he is 'in
every respect an extraordinary man in the State'[25] He has to persuade people
to obey the laws but not by argument, for arguments would be too abstruse.
'The wise who would speak to the vulgar in their own rather than in the vulgar
language will not be understood by them. Yet there are a thousand kinds of
ideas which it is impossible to translate into the language of the people' since
'each individual, appreciating no other scheme of government than that which

bears directly on his particular interest, has difficulty perceiving the advantages he is supposed to derive from the constant privations required by good laws.'[26] Not being amenable to reason, the people must be persuaded by some other means. 'Thus, since the Lawgiver can use neither force nor reasoning, he must of necessity have recourse to an authority of a different order, which might be able to rally without violence and to persuade without convincing.'[27] It is hard to read passages such as this now without being forcibly reminded of the flourishing of National Socialism, Fascism and Bolshevism in the first part of the twentieth century. Robert Nisbet remarks that Rousseau's depiction of his Legislator 'is about nothing else but the absolute and relentless power necessary to remake human nature in order to achieve equality.' [Nisbet 1988, 119]

A common method by which the requisite rallying without violence and persuading without convincing is to be produced is for the Legislator to claim that his laws emanate from God or the gods. While states and tribes in the past have had law-givers who have claimed to receive the laws whole and entire from God, it would be difficult in our more cynical times for any contemporary would-be Legislator to persuade the general public that his laws are God's law. The Legislator will provide the impetus to the creation of a collective identity that will overcome the residual defects in virtue that would otherwise inhibit the achievement of the General Will. The Legislator persuades the citizens to move towards what is really good for them but, worryingly, he does so by non-rational methods. In the end, one might not perhaps be taken to be unduly sceptical if one regarded the Legislator as having the appearance of a *deus ex machina*, appearing from outside the intrinsic dynamics of the drama, to solve the insoluble problems that the characters have got themselves into.

FREEDOM

Rousseau's account of the social contract would seem to make the claims of any particular individual subordinate to the General Will, yet Rousseau could never seem to rid himself completely of the idea that individuals have some rights that even the General Will must respect. Within the confines of a single chapter he writes that 'the social pact gives the body politic absolute power over all of its members' whereas 'each man alienates by the social pact only that portion of his power, his goods, his freedom which it is important for the community to be able to use, but it should also be agreed to that the Sovereign is alone judge of that importance.' A little later on the same page he adds, the Sovereign 'cannot burden the subjects with any shackles that are useless to the community' so that (two pages later) while the Sovereign power is absolute, sacred and inviolable, it 'does not, and cannot exceed the limits of the general conventions, and that everyone may fully dispose of such of his goods and freedom as are left him by these conventions...'[28] Putting these passages together makes it seem as if Rousseau wants to have his cake, indeed several of his cakes, and eat them too.

However odd the conflict, real or apparent, between the operation of the General Will and individual rights may be, it pales into insignificance besides the conceptual juggling Rousseau indulges in with the concept of freedom. One of the most notorious passages in the *Social Contract* says that 'for the social compact not to be an empty formula, it tacitly includes the following engagement which alone can give force to the rest, that whoever refuses to obey the General Will shall be constrained to do so by the entire body: which means nothing other than that he shall be forced to be free...'[29]

What might look like coercion to the untutored eye isn't really coercion at all, it seems, because when an individual sets himself against the General Will he is being merely capricious. It wouldn't be too far wrong to regard this passage from the *Social Contract* as the canonical text that supports the recurrent claims of subsequent social engineering movements to be able to distinguish between what an individual merely *thinks* he wants and what he *really* wants, between a vulgar idea of freedom as the ability to do what you want to do without let or hindrance and a sophisticated idea of freedom as the ability to do what it is that you *really* desire, even if you need to be helped by others so to realise and to do. The judge of the counterfactual claim of what it is that you really desire is, of course, an *ersatz* parent who knows what is good for you even when you do not. Rousseau's passage, then, is an early expression of the doctrine of false consciousness.[30] Rousseau's heirs include Marxists who hold that their opponents are necessarily tools of a capitalist ideology and devout feminists believers in the sexist mind-control exerted by the all-pervasive Patriarchy. Sabine remarks 'Straining language to show that restricting liberty is really increasing it, and that coercion is not really coercion, merely makes the vague language of politics still vaguer. But this was not the worst of it. What was almost inevitably implied was that a man whose moral convictions are against those commonly held in his community is merely capricious and ought to be suppressed....Forcing a man to be free is a euphemism for making him blindly obedient to the mass or the strongest party.' [Sabine, 591]

What, then, is freedom for Rousseau? On the one hand, man, he says, is born free but is everywhere in chains; on the other hand, citizens must be forced to be free.[31] Both of Rousseau's claims are notorious. The first seems to lead us in a libertarian direction; the second, in the direction of totalitarianism. Rousseau sees human freedom metaphysically as emancipation from the dictates of instinct. Morality is possible only because man is metaphysically free, and only as he is metaphysically free can man act and choose. In fact, Rousseau has at least four conceptions of freedom: *natural* freedom, *civil* freedom, *moral* freedom and *republican* freedom. He distinguishes between natural freedom and civil freedom thus: 'What man loses by the social contract is his *natural* freedom and an unlimited right to everything that tempts him and he can reach; what he gains is *civil* freedom and property in everything he possesses. In order not to be mistaken about these compensations, one has to distinguish clearly between *natural* freedom which has no other bounds than the individual's forces, and *civil* freedom which is limited by the General Will, and between possession which is merely the effect of force or the right of the first occupant, and property which can only be founded on a positive title.'[32] Rousseau's idea of natural freedom is similar to Hobbes's conception of the right of nature. Rousseau differs from Hobbes in thinking that this natural freedom won't necessarily result in conflict and disorder. Nevertheless, in his conjectural history, he accepts that, as a matter of fact if not of natural necessity, with the introduction of agriculture, natural freedom results in the well-known inconveniences of conflict and violence. It is in these circumstances that the notorious swindle perpetrated by the idea of property is made possible, in which the mass of men exchanges its freedom for security.

In civil society and only in civil society can man achieve a further kind of freedom, *moral* freedom, which consists of the ability to give a law to himself and to obey it. Rousseau writes, 'one might add to the credit of the civil state *moral* freedom, which alone makes man truly the master of himself; for the impulsion of mere appetite is slavery, and obedience to the law one has prescribed to oneself is freedom.'[33] This notion of moral freedom harks back to what Rousseau had described two chapters earlier as the fundamental problem of political philosophy, which was '"To find a form of association that will defend and protect the person and goods of each associate with the full common force, and by means of which each, uniting with all, nevertheless obey only himself and remain as free as before." This is the fundamental problem to which the social contract provides the solution.'[34]

In the face of all this elaborate theorising, there remains a stubborn practical problem. Suppose that I, or a group of citizens, find ourselves rejecting what purports to be a decision of the General Will. If we are required to obey this, is our freedom not compromised? Rousseau responds: 'each individual may, as a man, have a particular will contrary to or different from the General Will he has as a Citizen. His particular interest may speak to him quite differently from the common interest; his absolute and naturally independent existence may lead him to look upon what he owes to the common causes as a gratuitous contribution, the loss of which will harm others less than its payment burdens him and, by considering the moral person that constitutes the State as a being of reason because it is not a man, he would enjoy the rights of a citizen without being willing to fulfil the duties of a subject; an injustice, the progress of which would cause the ruin of the body politic.'[35] The trend of Rousseau's response to this objection is to say, in effect, that the citizens' prior commitment to the General Will overrides the caprice of their particular inclinations so that in being required to obey the law, they are in fact being required to obey themselves, their better selves, as it were. Is it necessary to point out the intellectual contortions embodied in Rousseau's response? 'It is patently clear,' writes Koos Malan, 'that Rousseau was confronted with a huge dilemma: how could he be an ardent advocate of freedom and then, in the same breath, deliberately subjugate that freedom, as expressed in individual and minority views, to the majority will that appears in the guise of the general will? Rousseau avoided this dilemma by arguing that the minority have squandered and abused their freedom and that the majority merely assist the minority by offering the minority the genuine freedom represented by the majority will, which the minority will then be forced to observe. In this way the minority can also enjoy genuine freedom.' [Malan, 138]

We have already seen Rousseau distinguish three types of freedom: natural, civil and moral. He has yet another type of freedom to add to this list, *republican* freedom, which is a matter of not being subject to the will of another person as if one were a slave. Part of the justification of the 'being forced to be free' aspect of the doctrine of the General Will is that it produces this republican form of freedom. The law of the sovereign makes one free in the republican sense of the term by emancipating everyone from the arbitrary rule of another. Rousseau's admiration for the Greek *poleis* and the Roman Republic is one reason why he valorises a republican conception of freedom and also a reason why his political thought has no direct application to the political realities of his (or our) time. While there is very little direct correspondence between the France of the eighteenth century and fourth century BC Athens, Rousseau's thought is a modern expression of classical ideas, particularly those of Plato. The object of his concern is the city-state, the *polis*, an idealised Geneva, not the modern states by which he was surrounded. "It is clear,' writes Malan, 'that Rousseau should certainly not in any way be regarded as a philosopher of the territorial state. In fact...he reveals himself to be an *opponent* of the territorial state, in which citizenship is deficient and people live as individuals, rather than as citizens. Rousseau is a leading exponent of a close, almost intimate republicanism modelled on the Greek city states of ancient times, or... Rousseau's own romanticised version of his city of birth, Geneva.' [Malan, 133] This adds another layer of complication to the already complicated task of applying Rousseau's ideas to contemporary political realities. [see Sabine, 587] There can be no doubt that Rousseau was an admirer of the ancient Greek *poleis*, even (or perhaps especially, Sparta!) but while he admired greatly 'the general or common good, superior to modern fragmented politics and its political morality of self-interest, at the same time he shared with modern individualist thought the conviction that all political life was conventional and could be made obligatory only though individual consent.' [Riley, 364]

SOVEREIGN, GOVERNMENT AND RELIGION

Rousseau distinguishes between the sovereign, who is the locus of the General Will, and the government, which is simply an agent of the sovereign that is given the task of overseeing the day-to-day administration of the state. The well-known agent-principal problem rears its head. How can the principal, the sovereign, ensure that its agent, the government, doesn't go into business for itself at the expense of the sovereign? The larger the state, the more likely it is that this problem will become severe. For this reason and for others, Rousseau believes (with Aristotle) that there are natural limits to the size of the state. Once again, his model is that of the *polis* and his own native Geneva.

One aspect of Rousseau's thought that runs contrary to the contemporary consensus that representative democracy is a Good Thing but which is likely to find a receptive hearing among libertarians is his rejection of the idea of representative government.[36] Hobbes thought that the people as a whole could transfer their legislative will to a person or body that would then rule over them. Rousseau rejects this idea completely, arguing that if the people were to engage in such a transfer it would be tantamount to enslaving themselves and abdicating their moral agency. Even if citizens vote for representatives in periodic elections, those representatives will of necessity discuss and debate and decide upon issues in respect of which the citizens haven't themselves indicated their individual wills. If representative democracy is unacceptable, what of direct democracy? Given Rousseau's admiration for the Greek *polis*, this is theoretically acceptable but impracticable to any large state such as France or England. Rousseau rejects the sham of political representation since, he thought, the sovereignty of the people cannot in fact be represented. Government isn't an entity with delegated powers to do as it wishes but merely an executive committee at the disposal of the General Will. [see van Reybrouck, passim]

Rousseau takes a dim view of Christianity's impact on political life. 'Jesus came to establish a Spiritual Kingdom on earth, he writes, 'which, by separating the theological from the political system, led to the State's ceasing to be one, and caused the intestine divisions which have never ceased to convulse Christian peoples.'[37] For Rousseau, this division is something to be reprobated; for a libertarian, of course, it's something to be celebrated. In a letter he wrote to Voltaire in 1756, Rousseau goes so far as to say that 'there can exist Religions that attack the foundations of society, and one has to begin by exterminating these Religions in order to insure the peace of the State.'[38] Despite this—or perhaps because of it—Rousseau proposed the erection of a civic religion that would provide a kind of spiritual support for the state. The core elements of this civic religion are a God and a retributive theory of final judgement. In Rousseau's state, anyone dissenting from the tenets of this religion would be severely punished. On this point, we are reminded once again of Rousseau's classical affinities. Plato, it will be remembered, had proposed a civic religion along very much the same lines.

ROUSSEAU: PROTO-TOTALITARIAN?

Rousseau has often been accused of being an incipient totalitarian. Individuals alienate all their resources to the political community and the sovereign imposes the laws. Since, however, the sovereign *is* the people, the laws are imposed by the people upon themselves and so, according to Rousseau, tyranny is avoided. 'The defining features of Rousseau's political teaching,' writes Gourevitch, 'is freedom under self-imposed law: by being a party to the social contract, each one of us is a member of the sovereign; the sovereign's will is the General Will; the General Will declares itself through laws; to obey the law is, therefore, only to obey oneself; and "obedience to the law one has prescribed to oneself is freedom"' [Gourevitch 1997b, xx]

Was Rousseau a proto-totalitarian? Was he a radical liberal democrat? Was he a precursor of modern conservatism/communitarianism? There is certainly matter in his writings to support each of these interpretations. It might be, however, that all such interpretations of his work are misguidedly anachronistic. Rousseau was an admirer of the Greeks and the Romans and it might be more faithful to his writings to see him as endorsing a modern version of a kind of republicanism 'firmly rooted in the republican traditions of virtue, patriotism, and citizenship.' [Boucher, 266] In the end, however, Rousseau's vision of the state is, I believe, both authoritarian and totalitarian. The state orders all human activity. In this, Rousseau anticipates the totalitarian regimes of the twentieth century and foreshadows Mussolini's dictum, 'Everything within the State, nothing outside the State, nothing against the State.' In his idea that everything depends on politics, that the state ought to be father to all the citizens, that virtue is the result of good government, Rousseau is a, if not *the*, source of the damaging regime of social engineering that has dominated liberal Western thought, in particular since the middle of the twentieth century.

Notes

1 Diderot: 'I never want to see that man again. He makes me believe in devils and hell.'

2 This remark is to be found in a letter from David Hume to the Countess de Boufflers, 19ᵗʰ January 1766, in Hume 1820, 125.

3 Even the enthusiastically pro-Rousseau Susan Neiman, remarks that 'There is no good way to square Rousseau's tenderness towards abstract children with the callousness with which he decided the fates of his own very real ones' especially given that 'It was he [Rousseau], after all, who insisted that fathers' responsibility for their children consists of a great deal more than conceiving and providing for them.' [[Neiman, 69-70]

4 In making these remarks about Rousseau's personal life and character, I am aware that I run the risk of committing a version of what has been called the Genetic (or Intentional) Fallacy. [see Wimsatt and Beardsley, 21] In the end, Rousseau's works mean whatever they mean irrespective of his personal history and circumstances and stand or fall on their own merits (or lack of them). Nevertheless, for some writers—not all—their lives and writings are intertwined in a way that may be mutually illuminating. As is the case with many informal fallacies—*argumentum ad hominem*, *argumentum ab auctoritate*—the Genetic Fallacy is not always fallacious.

5 To be fair to Rousseau, it should be noted that autobiographies, when they're not outright fabrications, tend to follow the Hitchcockian maxim that drama is life with the dull bits cut out by foregrounding the artistic and imaginative and backgrounding the mundane and the quotidian. R. F. Foster remarks of Anthony Trollope's autobiography that 'it is a highly disingenuous text and nothing in it should be taken as read.' John Stuart Mill's autobiography, he says, 'contrives never to mention his mother' and 'Evelyn Waugh's…misrepresents most of the background of his youth…' [Foster 2002, 128]

6 Rousseau 1754 [1997a2], I, 35, 151. References to the *Discourses* are given by part and paragraph number for the convenience of those who may not have access to the Cambridge edition edited by Victor Gourevitch—Rousseau 1997a. The page numbers given are to the Gourevitch edition.

7 Rousseau 1754 [1997a2], I, 38, 154.

8 Gourevitch 1997a, xxi. For a wryly amusing cinematic fantasy on Rousseauean themes, see Michel Gondry's 2001 film, *Human Nature*.

9 Rousseau 1754 [1997a2], I, 35, 151.

10 As was mentioned in the chapter *The Dawn of History*, not everyone accepts that the Agricultural Revolution was an unmixed blessing. For a Neo-Rousseauean presentation on this topic, see Harari, 87-178.

11 Rousseau 1781 [1997b3], 9 (18), 272.

12 Rousseau 1754a [1997a], II, 19, 167.

13 Rousseau 1754a [1997a], II, 30, 172.

14 Rousseau 1754a [1997a], II, 32, 173.

15 Rousseau 1754a [1997a], II, 1, 161.

16 Rousseau 1754a [1997a], II, 57, 186-187.

17 References to the *Social Contract* are by book, chapter and paragraph, so that I, i, 1 indicates

Book I, chapter one, paragraph 1. The page references are to the Cambridge edition edited by Victor Gourevitch—Rousseau 1762 [1997b2].

18 'An Untitled Letter' in Rand 1984, 157. Rand's sardonic remark was directed at John Rawls's *A Theory of Justice* but it fits Rousseau like a glove.

19 Section 259, *Gesamtausgabe*, Vol. 65 (1989), 435.

20 Rousseau 1762 [1997b2], I i (1), 41.

21 See van Dun 2009, 52-53.

22 Rousseau 1762 [1997b2], I, vi, 4, 49-50; emphasis added.

23 Rousseau 1762 [1997b2], II, iv, 1, 61.

24 Rousseau's Legislator bears a striking resemblance to Adam Smith's Impartial Spectator in *The Theory of Moral Sentiments*.

25 Rousseau 1762 [1997b], II, vii, 4, 69.

26 Rousseau 1762 [1997b], II ,vii, 9, 70-71.

27 Rousseau 1762 [1997b], II ,vii, 9, 71.

28 Rousseau 1762 [1997b], II iv, 4, 61; II, iv, 9, 63.

29 Rousseau 1762 [1997b], I, vii, (8), 53.

30 For a discussion of this concept, see the chapter *Back to the Future* below.

31 Rousseau 1762 [1997b], I, i 1, 41; I, vii 8, 53.

32 Rousseau 1762 [1997b2], I, viii, 2, 53-54; emphasis added.

33 Rousseau 1762 [1997b2], I, viii, 3, 54.

34 Rousseau 1762 [1997b2], I, 6, 4, 49-50.

35 Rousseau 1762 [1997b2], I, vii, 7, 52-53.

36 'Representative government,' writes Bernard Manin, 'is a perplexing phenomenon, even though its routine presence in our everyday world makes us think we know it well. Conceived in explicit opposition to democracy, today it is seen as one of its forms....We are thus left with the paradox that, without having in any obvious way evolved, the relationship between representatives and those they represent is today perceived as democratic, whereas it was originally seen as undemocratic.' [Manin, 236]

37 Rousseau 1762 [1997b2], IV, viii, 8, 144.

38 Rousseau 1756 [1997a3], §34, 245.

Chapter 22

POLITICS NATURALISED: DAVID HUME

Why should a man be in love with his fetters, though of gold?
—Francis Bacon

It is often better to be in chains than to be free
—Franz Kafka

Scotland in the eighteenth century had a total population of just over a million people, more or less the same number of people who now live in Dallas or San Diego. Yet, this tiny population produced an astonishing outburst of philosophical, economic and historical writing that has radically affected how we think about the world. The two most well-known names from the period of the Scottish Enlightenment are those of Adam Smith and David Hume, but there were many other significant thinkers: Francis Hutcheson, Adam Ferguson, Henry Home, James Steuart, Thomas Reid and John Millar. [see McArthur, passim] The name of Adam Smith can be unknown to few who take even the slightest interest in economics. His 1776 book, *An Inquiry into the Wealth of Nations*, is perhaps his greatest claim to fame but his other major work, *A Theory of Moral Sentiments* (1759) some would judge to be a more significant contribution to human thought than his more well known treatise on economics. [see Casey, 2012] His equally well-known compatriot, David Hume, was born in Edinburgh in 1711 where he attended the University at the age of twelve. After an extensive course of study and some foreign residence, he produced his *A Treatise on Human Understanding* when he was only twenty-six years old. This book, now considered to be one of the most significant works in Western philosophy, made almost no impression upon its publication and what little impression it did make was largely negative. After the disappointment of the reception of the *Treatise*, Hume turned his attention to the production of a series of essays on moral and political topics which were quite well received, and he finally found fame and fortune with the publication of his *History of England*. 'David Hume,' writes John Burrow, 'is now famous as a philosopher; as a historian he is scarcely known. In the eighteenth and nineteenth centuries it was the reverse. Then he was primarily the author of a monumental, authoritative, though much contested six-volume *History of England* (1754-1762).' [Burrow, 332] Repeated efforts by him to be appointed to a university chair all ended in failure and he had to be content with a position as a librarian. Later in life, he spent some time in Paris as secretary to Lord Hertford where he met, among others, Rousseau, who managed to find reason to quarrel with him. He eventually returned to Scotland to take up a position as Under Secretary of State and settled in Edinburgh until his death in 1776.

It may not be immediately obvious why Hume should merit a place in a history of political philosophy given that his writings in this area are neither extensive nor what he is best known for in philosophical circles. Why then are his reflections on political philosophy significant? What makes his political thinking significant is that he issues a fundamental challenge to the assumption made by many modern political theorists that political authority can be legitimate only if it rests on the consent of those over whom it is exercised. Some theorists believe that such consent has to be explicit and when it isn't, which is most of the time for most people, then political authority is illegitimate; others argue that implicit or tacit consent is sufficient to ground political authority and that such consent can be evidenced from people's acquiescence in the activities of the state. Both parties in the explicit/implicit debate assume the necessity of consent for the legitimation of political authority. It is precisely this common assumption that Hume rejects. The consent of the governed, he thinks, isn't in any way a necessary condition of the legitimacy of government. Let us see how his story unfolds.

REASON AND HUMAN NATURE

The concept of reason has been a constituent part of theoretical and practical thought for most of Western history. In the eighteenth century, the nature, scope and limitations of reason became a contentious topic for philosophers, notoriously, for Immanuel Kant, whose first critical work was called *A Critique of Pure Reason*, but also for Kant's predecessor and gadfly inspiration, David Hume. Reason was the watchword and the principal tool of the Enlightenment. If water is the universal solvent, then Reason, for Enlightenment thinkers, was the solvent of superstition, dogma, tradition, custom and habit.[1] Within the broader Enlightenment circle, a reaction set in, in which, without rejecting Reason, its more ambitious claims to universal reach were contested. In the eighteenth century, Hume and Burke, each in his own way, insisted on confining reason within its proper limits in practical matters, as Kant was to do in metaphysics. Hume's principal philosophical works, *A Treatise of Human Nature*, *An Inquiry concerning Human Understanding* and his *An Inquiry concerning the Principles of Morals* are, by common consent, recognised as being a stern attack on the claims of reason to provide a solid basis for intellectual inquiry and morality. The implications of Hume's attack on religion and morality as traditionally defended need not directly concern us, but his criticism was also directed at any and all efforts to construct political theory on a rational basis, in particular, efforts to employ theories of natural rights and contract or consent for that purpose.

One could simply accept Hume's criticism and leave it at that. On the other hand, one could argue that his conception of reason is artificially narrow and that an expanded conception of reason, one that would see reason as embodied not in abstract formulae but in custom and tradition, could rescue man's practical life from the accusation of irrationality. 'Instead of regarding [custom and tradition] as the antithesis of reason,' writes Sabine, 'the new philosophy preferred to see in them the gradual unfolding of a reason implicit in the consciousness of the race or nation. Hence they are no burden which the enlightened individual must shuffle off but a precious heritage to be guarded and into which it the high privilege of the individual to be inducted.' [Sabine, 606]

In the *Treatise*, Hume begins his political reflections with some anthropological comments, noting that man has a seemingly endless stream of desires that he is singularly ill-equipped by nature to satisfy. As he exists by nature, man is provided 'neither with arms, nor force, nor other natural abilities, which are in any degree answerable to so many necessities.' [Hume 1740, 485] The solution to man's perplexity lies in society even though, as James Moore remarks, 'Hume found no natural instinct or passion which would motivate mankind to be naturally sociable.' [Moore, 302] Man's social existence has the effect of amplifying his already extensive natural desires but, on the other hand, it amplifies his ability to satisfy these desires still more, leaving him 'in every respect more satisfied and happy than 'tis possible for him, in his savage and solitary condition, ever to become.' [Hume 1740, 485] In a solitary condition, man's labour is relatively insignificant; having to do all for himself in many things, he is unable to attain perfection in anything and, depending on himself alone, his ability to survive failure is slight. Society remedies all three of these idiosyncratic deficiencies. In cooperating with others, the effect of man's labour is disproportionately increased; in the division of labour made possible by his life with others, his ability to attain perfection increases; and with others to help him, no longer is individual failure tantamount to disaster.

Society, then, is advantageous to man but this isn't a conclusion that can be reached by pure reason alone. Hume thinks that if men had been originally solitary and had had to depend upon a rational calculation of advantage to bring society into being, society would never have been created. If man were reliant upon the slender reed of reason to achieve his ends he would be in trouble but, luckily, what reason can't supply is remedied by a natural necessity. 'This necessity,' writes Hume, 'is no other than that natural appetite betwixt the sexes, which unites them together, and preserves their union, till a new tye takes place in their concern for their common offspring.' [Hume 1740, 486] With the production of children, the conjugal union becomes a family in which the natural authority of the parents, deriving from their physical strength and superior knowledge, is tempered by the natural affection they bear towards their offspring. While Hume is aware that the bonds of family life, if unbalanced, can be inimical to the interests of society at large, and also aware that there are in man centrifugal forces counteracting the centripetal forces that hold the family society together, he none the less believes the asocial account of the human condition given by thinkers such as Hobbes to be distorted.

According to Hume, we have three kinds of good—our subjective mental life, our bodily powers and our external possessions. Our subjective mental life is directly available to ourselves alone and so no one can be tempted to relieve us of it for their own use; our bodily powers can be taken from us through injury or death but that, in itself, brings no particular advantage directly to any would-be assailant; our external possessions, however, *are* detachable from us and their possession *is* valuable to those who would deprive us of them. This wouldn't matter much if we lived in a magical world in which such goods were instantaneously replaceable without cost but that, unfortunately, isn't the case. The facts are, then, that external goods are scarce and because of that scarcity, our possession of them is unstable. We can't appeal to our basic nature to provide for the stability of these external goods because our natural and untutored concerns are directed first to ourselves, second to our relations and friends and finally, and most feebly of all, to strangers. Tom and Dick each desire what only one of them can have and there's no antecedent reason why Tom rather than Dick should have it. This is where, despite Hume's well-known general depreciation of the pretensions of reason, reason rides to the rescue. 'The remedy, then, is not deriv'd from nature, but from artifice, or more properly speaking, nature provides a remedy in the judgment and under-standing, for what is irregular and incommodious in the affections.' [Hume 1740, 489]

If the possession of external goods is naturally unstable then it can be rendered stable only by a convention in which the stability of the possession of external goods is recognised by all in society, conventions being simply the rules that in fact regulate conduct. Significantly, such *conventional rules are not necessarily the result of a contract or an agreement.* One of Hume's examples of a convention is that of two men rowing a boat. Because they share a commonality of purpose, they coordinate their rowing without any need for someone to order them about or without any need for an explicit agreement. It could be argued that the emergence of a convention in respect of external goods is, on Hume's own assumptions, unlikely given our natural self-centred propensities but this, he thinks, is not so. Such a convention is *not* contrary to the passions, it is contrary merely to their 'heedless and impetuous movement' and in abiding by it, we gain more than we lose. [Hume 1740, 489] Hume goes on to say, 'There is no passion, therefore, capable of controlling the interested affection, but the very affection itself, by an alteration of its direction. Now this alteration must necessarily take place upon the least reflection; since 'tis evident, that the passion is much better satisfy'd by its restraint, than by its liberty, and that in preserving society, we make much greater advances in the acquiring possessions, than in the solitary and forlorn condition, which must follow upon violence and an universal licence.'[2]

Ever since the time of Plato, philosophers have drawn a sharp distinction in man between his reason and his passions and have often portrayed the passions as wild and capricious impulses that need to be tamed or controlled by reason. Hume is one philosopher who takes the passions to be simply what they are, a constituent part of man and the moving force at the root of all human action. Most of our passions are social or, at least, not anti-social, but one passion, namely self-interest, *is* essentially anti-social. If it is to be held in check, this can be done only by the influence of another passion, for one passion may be confronted and altered only by another, not by reason. The role of reason is to inform the actor dispassionately where his long-term interests lie.

THE CONVENTIONS OF PROPERTY AND JUSTICE

We are naturally inclined to seek out whatever promotes our self-interest, but this natural inclination is limited in its views and disposed to seek immediate gratification to the detriment of our longer-term interests. At this point, reason enters in to indicate that the idea of property with its correlative three laws of justice is, in fact, conducive to the enlargement of our interests, together with those of others. 'Justice,' writes McClelland, 'is certainly a human invention, and is to that extent unnatural, but justice is also natural in the sense that human reason everywhere has seen the need for justice if human living is ever to advance beyond a very primitive state. ...The discovery of justice may be halting and accidental, but once justice, however primitive, is established, human reason has no difficulty in seeing its advantages.' [McClelland, 410]

How does the convention of property arise? Not by design and not by planning but by a dawning realisation on the part of everyone that the reciprocal recognition of stable rights of ownership is to everyone's benefit. Hume writes, 'Nor is the rule concerning the stability of possession the less deriv'd from human conventions, that it arises gradually, and acquires force by a slow progression, and by our repeated experience of the inconveniences of transgressing it.' [Hume 1740, 490] The emergence of the property convention, then, resembles the way in which languages or money come into being. Languages and money emerge spontaneously as Humean-like conventions[3] from common practices tending towards the promotion of everyone's interests.[4]

Human action can be regarded from different perspectives. Those actions can be said to be primary that make up the bulk of human conduct—eating pizza, talking to friends, shopping for shoes, and so on. Actions that bear on primary actions—encouraging them, discouraging them, punishing them, can be said to be secondary. The difference between primary and secondary actions is similar to what we find in sports where the players are engaged in primary action and the referee or other officials are engaged in secondary action. Of course, secondary actions can themselves become the object of further social controls. Primary actions embody norms in practice—one can play or watch a game without a completely explicit grasp of its rules—whereas secondary actions require explicit reflection on the norms. Logic is the explicit articulation of the practices embodied in reasoning; grammar is the explicit articulation of the linguistic practices embodied in speaking and writing; ethics is the explicit articulation of the socially cohesive practices already embodied in lived interpersonal relations. When we learn logic as a discipline, it enables us to appropriate reflectively what it is we do when we reason and allows us to become better at what we already do; what it does not do is to allow us to learn to do something we have never done before. We learn grammar only after we already speak our language, not before. And ethics is a meaningless enterprise if we haven't already grasped its essence in practice before we begin to think about it. Nobody learns to be ethical by taking Aristotle's 30-drachma course. The sense of the dictum that 'ignorance of the law is no defence' is to be found in the fact that no one who lives in a community can be functionally unaware of how the basic rules for peaceful coexistence function in that community, any more than a native speaker of a language can be functionally unaware of the rules of the language. To know the law in this sense it isn't necessary to be able to state it, defend it or justify it, any more than knowing (implicitly) the rules of English syntax, require a native speaker to be able to state explicitly what those rules are. I can know that 'Boy the deck burning on stood the' is gibberish in English without being able to say precisely why this is so. The claim that one knows something only if one can give the reason for it is false. I can know that some act is just or unjust without being able to give an account of justice or injustice, just as I can know that wine is red without being able to give an account either of redness or wine. Philosophically sophisticated readers will realise that in saying this, I am denying the fundamental presupposition of Socrates's claim, in Plato's early dialogues, that knowledge to be knowledge requires the ability to give a justified account of what it is that one claims to know.

Justice and property (as distinct from mere possession) emerge together, for property is the moral (and subsequently legal) right to make exclusive use of certain goods. Property and justice are covalent notions. ''Tis very preposterous, therefore,' says Hume, 'to imagine, that we have any idea of property, without fully comprehending the nature of justice, and shewing its origin in the artifice and contrivance of men. The origin of justice explains that of property. The same artifice gives rise to both.'[5]

Craig Smith remarks that 'For the Scots, and particularly for Hume and Smith, notions of property and justice are coeval. Their origins are intimately related and indeed explain each other. For Hume the notion of justice can only exist where the conditions for it exist, and as these conditions are the same as those which produce conventions of property, then the origins of the two concepts are mutually explanatory.' [Smith 2006, 48]

Once the correlative notions of property and justice have emerged and are instantiated in society, the most significant impediment to the fruitful cooperation of people has been removed. If man were universally benevolent instead of his benevolence's radiating outwards from himself to his immediate environment and diminishing in intensity as it expands, and if there were no economic scarcity, then the nexus of property and justice would have little or no purchase on the human condition. '[I]f every man had a tender regard for another,' says Hume, 'or if nature supplied abundantly all our wants and desires,' then 'the jealousy of interest, which justice supposes, could no longer have place; nor would there be any occasion for those distinctions and limits of property and possession, which at present are in use among mankind.' [Hume 1740, 494] But man is *not* universally benevolent and scarcity *is* a permanent aspect of the human condition so that the conventions of property and justice are here to stay. The idea of justice, then, isn't derived by any process of *a priori* abstract analysis but is, rather, derived from the natural facts of the limited generosity of man and economic scarcity, nature, as already mentioned, providing 'a remedy in the judgment and understanding, for what is irregular and incommodious in the affections.' [Hume 1740, 489]

The fundamental dynamic underlying the emergence of the convention of property is reciprocity. Andy has an interest in respecting the property of Barbara, Charlie, and Deborah, provided that Barbara, Charlie, and Deborah respect his property. The recognition of a mutual interest is enough to ground the convention. No promises are needed, promise-keeping itself being just another convention. The convergence on mutual interest that grounds the convention of property is liable to fray at the edges under the natural tendency that all men have to prefer their own interests rather than the interests of all. That being so, the artificial virtue of justice arises, again by convention, to strengthen the property convention. There are three rules of justice: stability in possession (the most important rule); consensual property transfer; and the requirement that promises be kept (*pacta sunt servanda*). We observe the rules of justice not because they necessarily maximise our short-term interests (they may do so but, then again, they may not) but because their observance serves our long-term interests.

Friedrich Hayek is one whose thinking in many respects seems to follow that of Hume. 'For Hayek,' writes Paul Kelly, 'regimes of property are part of the spontaneous order of market societies. They grow up as a result of the myriad micro-decisions of individual agents, and therefore represent a convergence of individual wisdom and reason that cannot be fully comprehended by any single mind. Hayek follows Hume both in his conventionalism and in his rejection of rationalism, which Hayek claims re-emerges with the desire for justice as redistribution.' [Kelly 2009a, 242] Spontaneous order is an idea that was publicised by Bernard Mandeville but, while Mandeville may well have been the proximate source of this idea for thinkers such as Hume, it wasn't original with him. Peter Wilson notes that '…well before anglophone writes like Bernard Mandeville or Adam Smith, Germans expressed positive interpretations of self-interest. Leonhard Fronsperger, a military clerk and noted writer, argued in 1564 that divergent individual needs actually created harmony by encouraging mutual interdependence.' [Wilson 2016, 502] Mandeville's idea is accepted, in various forms, by the Scottish philosophers of the eighteenth century and extends downwards through time—from Mandeville and Hutcheson and Smith and Hume and Ferguson to Burke, Darwin (who got the idea from James Hutton), Herbert Spencer, Huxley, and from there on to Menger, Böhm-Bawerk, Wieser and von Mises, to Hayek, Michael Polanyi, Popper, and Oakeshott.

For Hume, then, obligations can arise from conventions without the interposition of promise-keeping, agreement or contract. But this is a direct attack on the fundamental assumption of all forms of contractarianism. The contract theorist holds that obligations can only arise on foot of the promises embodied in contractual agreements. Contract theorists argue that government is justified because men consent to it (or contract for it) either explicitly or implicitly. [see Riley, 355-357] Others, such as Lysander Spooner, argue that there is no contract and, taking as a given that without such a contract there can be no obligation, as there is no contract so there is no obligation. Both parties to the dispute fixate on the necessity for contract for the existence of political obligation. Hume rejects the assumption common to both parties, arguing that obligation can arise without any contract. 'Political legitimacy cannot be based on a contract or promise because the "practice" of promise-keeping itself depends upon a widely accepted convergence of interests that undermines the basic premiss of social-contract-arguments, namely that the natural condition is one of conflict. Whatever convergence of interest is necessary to legitimate a promise is sufficient to legitimize government.' [Kelly 2009a, 234] Hume believes the property/justice-establishing convention to be so obviously benefi-cial for all that he holds that man couldn't for long have lived in a pre-social condition; in fact, he claims that man's 'very first state and situation may justly be esteem'd social.' [Hume 1740, 493] The pre-social state of nature, beloved of philosophers, is a fiction on a par with the idea of the Golden Age.

Hume thinks that he has shown that an enlarged conception of self-interest lies at the root of our notion of justice but that in itself it does not explain why we attach the moral attributes of praise to the observation of justice and blame to its derogation. Hume's explanation is to appeal to sympathy to show why, when particular instances of injustice can in no way personally affect us, we still are displeased. As he writes, '*Thus self-interest is the original motive to the* establishment *of justice: but a* sympathy *with public interest is the source of the* moral approbation *which attends that virtue.*'[6] It should be noted that both Hume and Smith make much of the notion of sympathy in their moral theories. For Hume, sympathy is a more or less natural response to the appreciation of the situation of others, a response that's communicated to us more or less mechanically. For Smith, on the other hand, any sympathy we may have with another, beyond the obvious wince we give when, say, we see someone suffer a blow, requires an effort of imagination. Sympathy, then, for Hume is passive; for Smith, active. For Hume, the sentiments we have are just the sentiments we have; for Smith, there's always a question of whether the sentiments we have are appropriate—and this question is made possible by Smith's idea of the Impartial Spectator. Hume is, in the end, a consequentialist; Smith is not. Happiness for Smith isn't something that can be defined in some brute physical way apart from moral components—happiness is intrinsically connected with having the right moral dispositions. In Smith, the notion of sympathy becomes the motive force of a sophisticated moral theory. [see Casey 2012, passim]

How are we to determine what property goes to whom? Hume remarks that 'first possession always engages the attention most; and did we neglect it, there wou'd be no colour of reason for assigning property to any succeeding posses-sion.' [Hume 1740, 505] We possess not only what is, in fact, within our grasp but whatever it is that is within our power to use, move or destroy. This is, like many other things, a matter of more or less and shades off at the extrem-ities. First possession, then, gives title or, where first possession is obscure, those who are in *de facto* possession if they have been so over a long period of time acquire title by prescription. In an indirect reference to Locke, Hume considers the claim that the 'mixing of labour' is the criterion of ownership but remarks that at best such a criterion covers a limited number of cases. There are many instances in which we make use of things in a manner that involves no mixing of labour at all or, if so, only in a metaphorical or attenuated and figurative sense as, for example, when we graze cattle on a field. Here, possession amounts to a kind of occupation. So, then, the stability of society is founded on stability in the possession of property. To this, Hume adds two more rules: the transference of property by consent and the performance of promises. The observance of these three laws is necessary for the security of human society.

Social life is governed by conventions; those conventions provide the stability that most men desire. Whatever the ultimate origin of a given political authority (and Hume cheerfully grants that most have originated in dubious circumstances), those that persist have obtained the sanction of prescription and prescription brings an end to questions of justification. The order men require, therefore, isn't based upon reason but upon a kind of sentiment, and can be explained historically or psychologically or even anthropologically but not purely rationally. Hume does not discount self-interest as a primary motivation for human conduct but he is much more disposed to see our actions as conforming to what is, for individuals, a social given which, like the language they speak, isn't of their own making but which, again like the language they speak, is accepted as a brute social fact.

Hume recognises that the possession of property isn't without its inconveniences. Possession, followed in due course by occupation, prescription, accession and succession, depends to a large extent on chance and so 'must frequently prove contradictory both to men's wants and desires; and persons and possession must often be very ill adjusted.' [Hume 1739-40, 514] The remedy for this inconvenience, however, isn't the forcible redistribution of property according to the desires of particular individuals, for that would be productive of still further inconveniences that would far outweigh the inconvenience it is intended to remedy, leading inexorably to the destruction of society. The stability provided by possession and its attendant operations outweighs the initial inconvenience, serving 'many good purposes in adjusting property to persons.' [Hume 1739-40, 514] Property is an artificial convention that can arise only when society reaches a certain level of material sophistication. The urgency to satisfy the immediate and pressing requirements of subsistence in a hunter/gatherer society prevents the emergence of anything but the most rudimentary conception of property. Commenting on the Hadza, a contemporary hunter-gather society living in Northern Tanzania, Michael Finkel remarks, 'Traditional Hadza...live almost entirely free of possessions. The things they own—a cooking pot, a water container, an ax—can be wrapped in a blanket and carried over a shoulder. Hadza women gather berries and baobab fruit and dig edible tubers. Men collect honey and hunt. Nighttime baboon stalking is a group affair, conducted only a handful of times each year; typically, hunting is a solo pursuit. They will eat almost anything they can kill, from birds to wildebeest to zebras to buffalo. They dine on warthog and bush pig and hyrax. They love baboon...'[Finkel, 5]

David Hume and Adam Smith are in essential agreement on the artificial and contingent nature of property. Smith believes that the notion of property properly begins to appear at the stage of husbandry when herds of animals need to be controlled and protected. The notion of property comes into central focus with the invention of agriculture and fixed places of habitation. 'The concerted development of private property,' writes Smith, 'is to be found in early urban areas where people living close together found it necessary to define their separate possessions. The notion of private property arose gradually from a sense of the utility of the mutual recognition of claims of right to property.' [Smith 2006, 52] Though private property may originate in the extended self-interest of individuals, the Mandevillian effect is to provide peace and social stability for all, despite its not being the design of any. Private property is, as it were, a product of cultural evolution, not an institution designed by anyone in particular but a convention arising from the realised perception of its usefulness to all. In the context of the emergence of property, and with it the coeval notion of justice, law emerges also. Like language and morality, law too evolves coevally with the level of sophisticated social order.

Suppose that, living alone on a desert island, one were to clear some ground, plant some carrots seeds and give the emerging carrots the tender loving care that they need until they were ready to be picked and eaten. In this case, wouldn't one own the carrots? I would rather say that if one were to live in such radical social isolation, one would neither own nor not own the carrots: the question of ownership simply wouldn't arise. But now, suppose another person were to appear and attempt to claim the carrots for himself, what then? In that case, one would be in a position to make a counter-claim that, all things considered, would seem to be better grounded than that of the challenger. In so doing, one would be attempting to actualise a kind of latent or virtual ownership that pre-existed any actual claim or recognition of that claim by others.[7]

It would seem that following the Agricultural Revolution, when people began to cultivate crops and domesticate animals, a significant amount of work was required to bring land under cultivation or to make it suitable for pasture. This work represented an expenditure of labour that couldn't easily be recovered if the one who expended it could legitimately be forced to give it up by others. 'Hunters and gatherers may have "territory"; pastoralists have grazing and watering-places; agriculturalists have land,' writes John Keegan. 'Once man invests expectations of a regular return on his seasonal efforts in a particular place—lambing, herding, planting, reaping—he rapidly develops the sense of rights and ownership. Towards those who trespass on the places where he invests his time and effort he must equally rapidly develop the hostility of the user and occupier for the usurper and interloper. Fixed expectations make for fixed responses.' [Keegan, 122] At this stage, however, we still have possession rather than property or, if property, then, as in my desert island illustration, virtual or latent property. That virtuality becomes actualised when other land users settle around the original user and, requiring undisturbed possession of their own tracts, are able to demand such only if there's mutual recognition not just of the fact of possession but of the right so to possess, in a word, a recognition of property. Acquisition and subsequent possession is a kind of virtual ownership, a virtual ownership that is transformed into actual ownership by means of the convention of reciprocal recognition. My settled use and reuse of my possessions requires you to refrain from interfering with them but your use and reuse of your possessions also requires me to refrain from interfering with them. Mutual recognition of one another's exclusive control amounts to the transformation of factual possession into normative ownership. Long ago, Cicero wrote that private property has been endowed 'not by nature, but by longstanding occupancy in the case of those who settled long ago on empty land; or by victory in the case of those who gained it in way; or by law or bargain or contract or lot....since what was by nature common property has passed into the ownership of individuals, each should retain what has accrued to him, and if anyone seeks any of it for himself, he will transgress the law of the community.' [Cicero 54-51 BC, I, 21]

This process of mutual recognition of normative claims, of course, requires that the boundaries between adjacent properties be reasonably clearly demarcated, a requirement celebrated in the proverb that 'Good fences make good neighbours.' Carol Rose argues that a possessor of a given portion of land has an obligation to provide a persistent and unambiguous demarcation of that portion's boundaries. [Rose 1985, passim] 'As people began to lay claims to territory,' write Schmidtz & Brennan, 'and to mark by signs what they regarded as their territory, neighbors started, in some cases at least, to accommodate themselves to these claims. To do this, though, it had to be true that neighbors could discern and could afford to respect the boundaries of territorial claims.' [Schmidtz & Brennan, 109] In order for it to be valid, the requirement of reciprocal recognition cannot sensibly be a universal requirement in some absolute spatial or temporal sense but must be limited to one's proximate neighbours in space and time. The recognition of those who are geographically or historically remote is neither possible nor required.

GOVERNMENT AS THE GUARDIAN OF JUSTICE

What has all this to do with government or with the state? Well, property is necessary for society and property depends on certain rules of justice. Men, some men at least, can't seem to abide by these rules. The trouble with such men is that they prefer the present to the future, the immediate advantage to the long-term advantage. 'Men are not able radically to cure, either in themselves or others, that narrowness of soul, which makes them prefer the present to the remote.' [Hume 1740, 537] That being so, although the long-term interests of all would be served by a strict observance of the laws of justice, any one person may seek his own advantage by their transgression. The solution to this problem is, Hume thinks, to make the observance of justice by everyone the immediate concern of some particular party. It is given, then, to some one or some group to execute the laws of justice and also to settle disputes: these are the basic functions of government. The same limited vision in respect of justice that requires the creation of government also prevents the emergence of any spontaneous form of large-scale cooperation so that, in addition to its basic functions of the execution and the arbitration of justice, government must have the ability to perform public works that benefit all. 'Thus bridges are built; harbours open'd; ramparts rais'd; canals form'd; fleets equip'd; and armies disciplin'd, every where, by the care of government, which, tho' composed of men subject to all human infirmities, becomes, by one of the finest and most subtle inventions imaginable, a composition, which is, in some measure, exempted from all these infirmities.'[8] Government, then, for Hume (as for Locke), is a remedy for the inconveniencies of selfishness and the promoter of public goods that otherwise wouldn't be provided.

It would be carping to criticise Hume for not realising that the deficiencies of human nature, which he sees so clearly operating at the primary social level, are likely to be replicated and indeed amplified at the level of government. If individual men can be selfish and disordered in their private dealings, they can be equally or perhaps even more selfish and disordered when entrusted with the provision of public order and justice and public goods. Who will guard the guardians? Despite the praise he gives to government, Hume is surprisingly realistic about its contingent nature, remarking, 'it is not necessary in all circumstances, nor is it impossible for men to preserve society for some time, without having recourse to such an invention [government]….The state of society without government is one of the most natural states of men, and must subsist with the conjunction of many families, and long after the first generation.' [Hume 1740, 539, 541] If government is a remedy for the inconveniences attached to property, it follows that in a society with little or no property, there is little incentive to discover the advantages of government. So natural is a society without government that 'Nothing but an increase of riches and possessions cou'd oblige men to quit it…' [Hume 1740, 541]

For Hume, we need government because it is useful. In small-scale societies, violations of justice are relatively easily remediable because men live face to face with each other. Radical non-cooperation will be sanctioned. 'An interest in reputation and the need for reciprocity is enough to give the normative force of promises,' writes Paul Kelly, 'even without the existence of an external lawgiver threatening physical punishment.' [Kelly 2009a, 237] As society grows larger, however, these informal sanctions lose force and efficacy as we may have little or no contact with others in that society. In that case, government is needed to bridge the gap. According to Kelly, government is needed not only to provide external legal sanctions when the force of informal sanctions diminishes; government also has an educative function, that of extending our imaginative and sympathetic identification with many others.

Government, then, isn't established by any form of explicit agreement or contract but emerges slowly and gradually together with a society's increase in size and in wealth.[9] All large civilised societies require government. Contract, as a form of promising, is an horizonatal mode of relationship between individuals in a natural society none of whom claims to have the authority to command the other; the obligation to obey the civil magistrate is a vertical relationship in a civil society between one commissioned to enforce the laws of justice and those who are bound by those laws. 'To obey the civil magistrate is requisite to preserve order and concord in society,' says Hume. 'To perform promises is requisite to beget mutual trust and confidence in the common offices of life. The ends, as well as the means, are perfectly distinct; nor is one subordinate to the other.' [Hume 1740, 544]

Hume believes that, as a matter of fact, no government requires or finds it necessary to canvass the explicit or even the tacit consent of the governed, yet every government believes that those whom it governs are obliged to obey it. Hume *is* willing to grant that at the very beginning of a government among men there may have been a contract by which men bound themselves to obey but he points out that once government has been established for some considerable time we simply suppose ourselves 'born to submission' and that those who are our governors have, by prescription, a right to command and we, a correlative obligation to obey. [see Hume 1740, 554-555] 'Time and custom give authority to all forms of government, and all successions of princes; and that power, which at first was founded only on injustice and violence, becomes in time legal and obligatory.' [Hume 1740, 566]

When it comes to providing a justification for government, one could hold either that such justification comes from a divine sanction or from the people by means of their agreement to be governed. If people want to insist that government is divinely sanctioned, Hume isn't going to object, provided that such sanction is taken not to be a particular miraculous disposition of Providence but simply part of God's general plan for human subsistence which requires the protection of government. Anyone who rules, in whatever way and in however humble a manner, can be said to act by divine commission. Hume remarks, 'nor has the greatest and most lawful prince any more reason, upon that account, to plead a peculiar sacredness or inviolable authority, than an inferior magistrate, or even an usurper, or even a robber and a pyrate....A constable, therefore, no less than a king acts by a divine commission, and possess an indefeasible right.' [Hume 1748a, 467] Having thus deflated by inflation the notion of any theory of divine right, Hume turns his attention to what he believes to be the most significant theory of the justification of government, the original contract.

CONTRACT?

Although taken to be a resolute critic of any notion of an original contract, Hume in fact *does* allow that only by some such contract, properly understood, could government have received its start! He makes the point, as Hobbes had done before him, that men are more or less equal in their physical powers and their mental capacities so that no natural inferiority could make them subordinate themselves to another man. That being so, if government were ever to arise, there had to have been an original agreement, express or implied, to this government on the part of the governed. 'If this, then, be meant by the *original contract*, it cannot be denied,' says Hume, 'that all government is, at first, founded on a contract, and that the most ancient rude combinations of mankind were formed chiefly by that principle.' [Hume 1748a, 468] Such consent, however, was fitful and opportunistic, relating more than likely to the effective leadership that is necessary in social emergencies such as war. 'No compact or agreement, it is evidenced, was expressly formed by general submission; an idea far beyond the comprehension of savages. Each exertion of authority in the chieftain must have been particular and called forth by the exigencies of the case.' [Hume 1748a, 468-469]

Hume, then, grants that there may in fact have been an historical compact that was the origin of political society but, for him, whether or not this was so is of no great significance. Even had our ancestors agreed among themselves to associate in a particular way, that is no reason why such an agreement should be binding upon us. Hume claims that no extant government indeed asks its citizens to agree to be governed. In a moment that is reminiscent of Hobbes, Hume believes that contracts and compacts bear on the relationships between individuals, not between individuals and their governments. As a matter of fact, Hume thinks, governments subsist on the basis of a more or less inchoate feeling of loyalty or allegiance rather than any idea of an agreement, whether explicit or tacit. Why should one be loyal to a government or why should one keep one's agreements? Both questions are equally pertinent. Hume's answer is that, without some sentiment of political allegiance, however faint, and a general disposition to honour agreements (the sphere of justice), society wouldn't be possible. Political structures provide order, and contracts protect property, and without both order and the protection of property civilised society couldn't function.

While Hume concedes, then, that there has to have been an element of contract or agreement (or, as he says later, acquiescence) at the dim and distant birth of government in the remote past, he nevertheless holds that the situation obtaining at present in our sophisticated modern states cannot be construed on those terms. There are, he says, philosophers (Locke perhaps?) who hold that 'not only that government in its earliest infancy arose from consent or rather the voluntary acquiescence of the people but also, that, even at present, when it has attained full maturity, it rests on no other foundation. They affirm, that all men are still born equal, and owe allegiance to no prince or government, unless bound by obligation and sanction of a promise. And as no man, without some equivalent, would forego the advantages of his native liberty, and subject himself to the will of another; this promise is always understood to be conditional, and imposes on him no obligation, unless he meet with justice and protection from his sovereign.' [Hume 1748a, 469]

So, it comes to this. Hume's objection to an original contract isn't an objection to some antique pre-historical event but to the claim that the existent political order needs to be founded upon a current or continuing contract without which it cannot be considered to be justified. The original contract of interest to philosophers can't be the pre-historic agreement which started governments in business, for such a contract, even if it were less limited and more substantial that it possibly could have been, cannot be held to have any purchase on men now living. Hume asks those philosophers who espouse contract as the basis of political obligation to see if they can discover any historical instance where a current contractual agreement between sovereign and subject is to be found. On the contrary, he believes, everywhere we find princes who claim their right to sovereignty either from conquest or from succession; we find subjects who acknowledge this right of sovereignty and believe themselves born with an obligation to obey their princes. How, in fact, did our present governments come to exist, if not by contract? Hume's answer to this question is refreshingly matter of fact. 'Almost all the governments, which exist at present,' he writes, 'or of which there remains any record in story, have been founded originally, either on usurpation or conquest, or both, without any pretence of a fair consent, or voluntary subjection of the people.' [Hume 1748a, 471] Where in all this force and violence is our mutual agreement or voluntary association or contract to be found? Many people are scandalised by the historically dubious origin of governments. But should they be? Suppose, on the contrary, that our government had been founded upon some kind of election. How much better would things be now? Here, too, Hume finds the process less than appealing, for the result of an election is merely that we end up with a few men who decide for everyone and will brook no opposition, and how much better is that than the rule of an hereditary monarch?

Is Hume a democrat? No. He writes, 'In reality, there is not a more terrible event, than a total dissolution of government, which gives liberty to the multitude, and makes the determination or choice of a new establishment depend upon a number, which nearly approaches to that of the body of the people...' [Hume 1748a, 472] If men were so constituted as naturally to be able to refrain from interfering in other men's properties than government wouldn't have been necessary. If men were so constituted that they knew their own interests, then government could be founded upon consent. But men are not so constituted and, so far from their being consulted about the constitution of a government when there is none, it is rather that 'during the fury of revolutions, conquests, and public convulsions, military force or political craft usually decides the controversy.' [Hume 1748a, 474] But, it might be objected, did we not have the Glorious Revolution[10] of 1688 in which the tyrant James II was replaced by William & Mary? Think again, says Hume. A tiny number determined that change in the royal succession, some seven hundred people out of a total population of some ten million. What say did the other nine million, nine hundred and ninety nine thousand, three hundred have in this process? None. They acquiesced in the change but they did not choose to bring it about.[11]

Contractarians often argue that even if there is no actual explicit consent to government, still, a tacit consent can be deduced from the citizens' continuing to reside in the area under the government's rule. But, Hume points out, such a tacit or implied consent could only be plausible if the citizens thought they had a real choice in the matter. But where a man thinks 'as all mankind do who are born under established governments—that by his birth he owes allegiance to a certain prince or certain form of government; it would be absurd to infer a consent of choice, which he expressly, in this case, renounces and disclaims.' Your average citizen has effectively little or no choice over continued residence in his home place any more than a man 'by remaining in a vessel, freely consents to the dominion of the master; though he was carried on board while asleep, and must leap into the ocean, and perish, the moment he leaves her.' [Hume 1748a, 475] If it were ever the case (as it manifestly is not) that one generation of men passed away to be succeeded instantaneously and completely by another of mature years, then, perhaps a case might be made for voluntary consent. But the generations are inextricably intermingled so that there can be no stability in government unless those born into a given political order conform themselves to the established constitution, whatever that may be. In the end, in response to the question—why are we bound to obey the government?—Hume reaffirms the point he made in the *Treatise* that without such obedience, society couldn't continue to subsist. Men acquiesce in government not because of any contract but because they believe that it provides them with security and protection.

Hume opens his 1741 essay, 'On the First Principles of Government,' with a statement whose truth is hard to dispute: 'Nothing appears more surprizing to those, who consider human affairs with a philosophical eye, than the easiness with which the many are governed by the few; and the implicit submission, with which men resign their own sentiments and passions to those of their rulers.' [Hume 1741b, 32] Clearly, the many are stronger than the few so that the few can ultimately depend not on superior force but on what Hume calls 'opinion'. 'It is therefore on opinion that government is founded; and this maxim extends to the most despotic and most military governments, as well as to the most free and most popular.' [Hume 1741b, 32] Hume distinguishes several varieties of opinion but the most pertinent is that the generality of the people must believe that government as a whole is advantageous to them and that this is true of the particular government in power. Those who govern are men like those they govern and are subject to the same limitations of perspective. Our governors 'do not immediately become of a superior nature to the rest of mankind, upon account of their superior power and authority'; in fact, given the constancy of human nature, our governors 'will neglect even this immediate interest [the preservation of order and the execution of justice], and be transported by their passions into all the excesses of cruelty and ambition.'[12]

In an essay published posthumously a year after his death, 'Of the Origin of Government,' Hume returned to consider the question he had first discussed in his *Treatise* some thirty-six years earlier. What, if anything, of his views had he changed? As it turns out, very little. Society can't subsist without peace and order, and peace and order requires the establishment and maintenance of justice. Every man prefers himself and his own interests to those of others so that if disorder is to be averted, someone must be assigned the task of ensuring that man's narrow and selfish interests do not disturb the peace and order required for the survival of society. Magistrates, then, are instituted to 'punish transgressors, to correct fraud and violence, and to oblige men, however reluctant, to consult their own real and permanent interests.' [Hume 1777, 38]

In this essay, however, Hume adds something he had not considered before. It might be objected that our duty of obedience to our rulers is a weak reed that can't survive the turbulence of our passions. Why should a bad neighbour not be an equally bad citizen? Men love dominion over others so that those who are chosen to fulfil the role of magistrate do so despite all the 'dangers, and fatigues, and cares of government' [Hume 1777, 39] Hume argues that those first chosen for these roles must, of necessity, have had some outstanding personal merit, whether of courage or wisdom and those who succeed them, even if they haven't the same level of merit as their predecessors, will be obeyed by virtue of habit—'men, once accustomed to obedience, never think of departing from that path, in which they and their ancestors have constantly trod, and to which they are confined by so many urgent and visible motives.' [Hume 1777, 39]

When our governors become tyrants, then they may be resisted; we owe them no passive obedience. The doctrine of passive obedience amounts to the claim that it is never lawful for a people to resist the authority of the ruler or his agents. As we have seen, this doctrine is often taken to be implied by the Christian scriptures, in particular, by *Romans* 13. Hume goes so far as to call the doctrine of passive obedience 'an absurdity' although he does hold that resistance to our governors is limited to the case of extremity and in normal circumstances, Hume says, 'nothing could be more pernicious and criminal.' [Hume 1740, 553] In the wake of the Jacobite rebellion of 1745, Hume is somewhat more guarded in his criticism of passive obedience but the general trend of his thought hasn't changed. Quoting the Latin tag *Salus populi suprema Lex* (the safety of the people is the supreme law), Hume argues that since government arises by convention to secure the public utility, if obedience to a government should threaten public ruin and thus the destruction of public utility, then that obedience cannot be required. Nevertheless, as in the *Treatise*, while willing to concede this right to rebellion, Hume is anxious to maintain that such rebellion should be undertaken only in the most extreme of circumstances. Far from its being the case as some have maintained, that the prospect of rebellion, including tyrannicide if needed, would keep incipient tyrants in check, Hume believes that any such rebellious disposition would in fact increase the likelihood of tyranny and make it, if anything, even more severe. 'Thus the tyrannicide or assassination, approved of by ancient maxims, instead of keeping tyrants and usurpers in awe, made them ten times more fierce and unrelenting; and is now justly, upon that account, abolished by the laws of nations, and universally condemned as a base and treacherous method of bringing to justice these disturbers of society.' [Hume 1748b, 490] On the other hand, Hume chastises those who maintain an exceptionless doctrine of passive obedience for provoking those who hold a doctrine of the legitimacy of resistance into maintaining such a doctrine. 'Hume rejects the Tory doctrine of passive obedience just as decidedly as the Whig doctrine that the obligation to obey rests on consent,' writes John Plamenatz. There is a duty to respect the law but 'law can always be rightly put aside when it endangers [the interest common to all men]. But the danger he says, must be extraordinary.' [Plamenatz, 316] Plamenatz also remarks that whereas Hume and Burke are both conservatives by inclination, in his attitude towards the state, Hume, in contrast to Burke, 'is quite without reverence or admiration; he sees nothing divine or majestic about the State; it is merely a contrivance in the public interest.' [Plamenatz, 316; see also 331]

CONCLUSION

What, in summary, does Hume's account amount to? *First*, if man's natural mode of existence were asocial, he would be radically unable to satisfy his desires; moreover, his very existence would be imperilled. Life in society with other humans beings is what is required for human flourishing and, indeed, for human existence. Society is advantageous for man because cooperation with others both disproportionately enhances man's powers and provides insurance against individual failure. Human beings do not need to be persuaded by rational argument to conjoin with others for their mutual benefit; the natural attraction between the sexes spontaneously gives rise to the basic social unit, the family, and that inevitably leads on to larger forms of social organisation.

Second, external goods are scarce and because of that scarcity, our possession of them is unstable. We can't all have everything yet there is no obvious reason why Tom but not Dick or Harriet should have that particular donkey. Our natural instincts won't guarantee stable possession of external goods because our untutored concerns are directed first to ourselves, second to our relations and friends and finally, and most feebly of all, to strangers. This is the point at which reason supplements nature in permitting the emergence of a convention by which stability of possession, in a word, property, with its correlative three laws of justice is, in fact, conducive to the enlargement of our interests and those of others. The conventions of property and justice are so obviously beneficial for all that Hume believes man couldn't for long have lived in a pre-social condition if he ever did so at all. How are we to determine what property goes to whom? Why does Tom get the donkey rather than Dick or Harriet? *De facto* possession is the answer, a *de facto* possession that transforms into *de jure* ownership by prescription over time based on reciprocal recognition.

Third, what has all this to do with government or with the state? Property is necessary for society and property requires the observance of rules of justice. Although the long-term interest of all would be served by a strict observance of the laws of justice, some one person may seek his own advantage by their transgression. The solution to this problem is, Hume thinks, to make the observance of justice by everyone the immediate concern of some particular party. It is given, then, to some one or to some group to execute the laws of justice and also to settle disputes: these are the basic functions of government. Just as property with its associated rules of justice emerges by convention, so too does government. Once a society develops a robust notion of property, one that requires social stability, together with the possibility of its orderly alienation and a notion of contract, then government is needed to overcome the short-sightedness of individuals.

Hume is willing to grant that at the beginnings of a government among men there may have been a contract by which men bound themselves to obey but he points out that once government has been established for some considerable time we simply suppose ourselves 'born to submission' and that those who are our governors have, by prescription, a right to command and we, a correlative obligation to obey. [see Hume 1740, 554-555] 'Time and custom give authority to all forms of government, and all successions of princes; and that power, which at first was founded only on injustice and violence, becomes in time legal and obligatory.' [Hume 1740, 566] Men acquiesce in government not because of any contract they have made among themselves or with it but because they believe that it provides them with security and protection. If Hume is correct then the question of the justification of the legitimacy of government simply does not arise and no contract or consent or agreement is necessary. Just as we do not need to agree with the rules of English syntax in order for the language to exist and function, so too we do not need to agree that we shall be governed by those who, by prescription, exercise authority over us.

There is much that a libertarian would find agreeable in Hume's account. The spontaneous generation of order dear to the hearts of libertarians everywhere is very close to Hume's notion of a convention. It is even possible—at a stretch—to enlist Hume as a supporter of a form of anarchism. Nicholas Onuf writes, 'For Hume, anarchy is a political society, rich in conventions, full of cooperative endeavors, well able to provide a suitable environment for peace, prosperity, and individual accomplishment.' [Onuf, 188] Onuf also notes that 'Hume's conventionalism eliminates political society as such and thus the need for a theory of such. In the place of political society is the aggregate of conventions enabling politics, economy and whatever else is social.' [Onuf, 186] But not everybody would agree with Onuf. Paul Kelly remarks that Hume's cast of mind 'is as hostile to the utopianism of the left as it is to the libertarian fantasies of many on the right who wish to dispense with government except as an enforcer of natural rights.' [Kelly 2009a, 242]

Libertarians can, I think, agree substantially with Hume's account of the necessity of society for human survival and human flourishing. It is only with the last step in Hume's argument that libertarians are likely to demur. Society and government aren't the same thing. Society operates on the basis of love or money. People do things for others either because they love them and disinterestedly desire their welfare (as, for example, parents do for their children for the most part or lovers for each other in the first flush of romantic attachment) or they provide services and goods to others in exchange for money. Governments, by contrast, rely for their effects on force and coercion. If society is necessary for human flourishing, it does not follow that a coercive government, still less *this* particular coercive government, is necessary for society. No society can tolerate the arbitrary initiation of violence against person or property so laws instantiating the zero-aggression principle must be a constituent element of any functioning society. Such laws must be enforceable and enforced. It does not follow, however, that there can only be one enforcer of such laws nor, indeed, that the enforcer in place at any given time is incontestably entitled to its position.

There is a fundamental difficulty with proposing coercive government as the only possible provider of justice and security. Suppose that such a coercive government is instituted to be the protector of property and justice and that part of its role is also to protect us from foreign and domestic threats of violence. But this government now has a monopoly of force. Who or what will protect us against *it*? Who or what, in John Locke's pregnant phrase, will prevent us being devoured by lions? If the answer to this question is that this government can be trusted to be self-restraining, then, given that any such government is composed ultimately of individuals, the same must be true of individuals in society prior to government and so the alleged necessity for a single coercive government to be the provider of justice and security is less than compelling. Nevertheless, if the 'no justice and security without coercive government' problem were in fact genuine, then we couldn't rely on voluntary restraint by coercive governments to prevent them abusing their power and so, logically, we would require a super-government to restrain *them*. But—and you can see where this argument is going—even if we arrived at a One World Government, we would still have a problem of who or what is going to restrain *it*? What we have, then, is a dilemma. Either justice and security can be provided only by a coercive government (A) or it can be provided by voluntary cooperation (B). If B, then a coercive government isn't necessary. If A, this provides us with another public good that can either be provided by voluntary constraint (A1) or that requires restraint by a superior body–that is, another coercive government (A2). A1 short circuits to B and A2, of necessity, leads to A3, etc. and so, either generates an infinite series, which is impossible, or to A which is either self-restraining (and we return to B) or which must frankly be admitted to be unrestrainable.[13] Hume's account, then, appears to be a factually accurate account of people's acquiescence in the political *status quo* but, just as reason has a role in helping to overcome our self-centred and self-defeating limitations vis-à-vis property and justice, so too reason can call into question the advantages of a coercive government, however prescriptively well established it may be. In fact, Hume's conventionalism can be extended to explain the production and operation of a legal system without coercive government so that law and legal institutions, like language, morals and money, spontaneously emerge and operate in society.

Immanuel Kant once wrote that David Hume interrupted his dogmatic slumber. [Kant 1783, 9] There are unkind people who suggest that he promptly went back to sleep again. Let us ignore these cynics and grant that Kant's theoretical philosophy is without doubt an attempt to accommodate Hume's sceptical empiricism. But what of Kant's practical philosophy? Is that in any way a reaction to or an attempt to come to terms with Hume's reflections? It is reasonably well known that Kant's ethics are a prime example of a deontological theory but most people, including quite a few philosophers, would be at a loss to declare what, if anything, Kant had to say about political philosophy. Just what did he say?

Notes

1 In this context, see the remarkably suggestive comments of Albert Mirgeler in the 'The Justification of the Modern World' section of his *Mutations of Western Christianity*, 141-145.

2 Hume 1740, 492; see Moore, 302-304.

3 For a sophisticated account of the phenomenon of convention, inspired by Hume's account of the origin of justice and property, see David Lewis's *Convention: A Philosophical Study*.

4 The phenomenon of spontaneous order on the human, social level is just one aspect of the spontaneous order that, according to Steven Strogatz, 'pervades nature at every scale from the nucleus to the cosmos.' 'At the heart of the universe,' he writes, 'is a steady, insistent beat: the sound of cycles in sync....Every night along the tidal rivers of Malaysia, thousands of fireflies congregate in the man-

groves and flash in unison, *without any leader* or cue from the environment. Trillions of electrons march in lockstep in a superconductor, enabling electricity to flow through it with zero resistance.... Even our bodies are symphonies of rhythm, kept alive by the relentless, coordinated firing of thousands of pacemaker cells in our hearts. In every case, these feats of synchrony occur spontaneously, almost as if nature has an eerie yearning for order.' [Strogatz, 1, emphasis added; see also Capra, passim, and Bertalanffy] For a superb account of how social order has been (and is) created and sustained without central direction, see Stringham 2015, passim.

5 Hume 1740, 491. Plamenatz remarks that 'Hume's account of justice is not entirely original; almost every part of it can be found, somewhere or other, in writings earlier than his own. What is new about it is less the ideas that go to make it up than the clear, systematic and economical exposition of them.' [Plamenatz, 299]

6 Hume 1740, 499-500, emphasis as in original.

7 This paragraph and the subsequent paragraphs in this section first saw the light of day in my *Libertarian Anarchy*. [Casey 2012b, 69-71]

8 Hume 1740, 539. Public Choice theory took another two hundred years to appear!

9 'Hume thinks it probable that government first arose out of quarrels,' writes Plamenatz, 'not among men in the same society, but among men of different societies, and therefore originated to provide military discipline.' But while Hume is willing to speculate on the origins of government 'he does not use these origins to justify authority or to set limits to it. How did government arise? and What makes it legitimate? are, for him, distinct questions.' [Plamenatz, 313]

10 The most significant English political event of 1688 may have been a revolution of sorts and its long-term results may have been good for liberty but, whether revolution or not and whether ultimately good for liberty or not, it was far from glorious. A palace cabal consisting of Thomas Osborne, Earl of Danby; Charles Talbot, Earl of Shrewsbury; William Cavendish, the Earl of Devonshire, Edward Russell; Richard, Baron Lumley; Henry Sidney; and the Bishop of London, Henry Compton, the so-called 'Immortal Seven, issued an invitation to William of Orange, James II's son-in-law, on foot of which he landed in Brixham to begin his conquest of England. 'This was a bloodless conquest,' writes Norman Davies, 'but a conquest all the same; and it was to cause the spilling of much blood. No English Parliament had summoned William to England; it was William who summoned the Parliament before he had any legal pretence for doing so.' [Davies 1999, 517] By no stretch of the imagination could this invitation be described as coming from 'the English People'. Norman Davies rather describes the invitation as 'one of those technicalities which seek to lend respectability to an act of force already decided on. The Stadholder could have had no illusions that he was embarking on a blatant usurpation, which no form of words could conceal.' [Davies 1999, 516]

11 John Burrow remarks that 'The declaration which gave the throne to William and Mary was illogical and contrary to fact....By a benign fiction that no revolution had taken place, the work of the revolution, once done, continued to be ballasted by precedent.' [Burrow, 376]

12 Hume 1739-40, 552. Now this is more like Public Choice Theory!

13 See Casey 2012, passim; see also Kennedy 2001, whose account I am following here.

Chapter 23

KANT: FREEDOM, PROPERTY
AND THE STATE

Out of the crooked timber of humanity, no straight thing was ever made
—Immanuel Kant

Men love liberty because it protects them from control and humiliation from others,
and thus affords them the possibility of dignity.
They loathe liberty because it throws them back on their own abilities and resources,
and thus confronts them with the possibility of insignificance
— Thomas Szasz

To anyone who has ever had to study his *Critique of Pure Reason*,[1] the name of Immanuel Kant is almost guaranteed to inspire a kind of intellectual terror! By common estimation, the *Critique of Pure Reason* is a work of staggering intellectual difficulty while also (unfortunately!) being a work of immense philosophical importance, so much so that any student of philosophy who aspires to competence cannot conscientiously ignore it. Indeed, such is its importance that it tends to occlude the remainder of Kant's works, including even the *Critique of Practical Reason* (1788) and the *Critique of Judgment* (1790). Not all its first readers found the *Critique of Pure Reason* immediately intelligible, so Kant wrote a simplified (well, relatively simplified) introduction to it to which he gave the snappy title *A Prolegomena to Any Future Metaphysics Which Shall Lay Claim to Being a Science* (1783). Students of Kant are never quite sure whether this simplified account really helps or whether all it does is to render the obscure more obscure. Whatever the case may be with his metaphysics, when it came to his discussion of practical matters, specifically to morality, Kant had learned his lesson and he provided an overview of his position in the *Groundwork of the Metaphysics of Morals* (1785) *before* publishing both the *Critique of Practical Reason* and *The Metaphysics of Morals* (1797). Curiously, although the *Groundwork* was meant to be an introduction to *The Metaphysics of Morals*, as Roger Sullivan points out, 'most people interested in Kant's moral theory have tended to neglect *The Metaphysics of Morals* and have devoted themselves instead to analyzing the volume meant to be its introduction.' [Sullivan, vii]

Not only is *The Metaphysics of Morals* something of an orphan child among Kant's works but, even on those rare occasions when it does receive attention, its first part, called the 'Doctrine of Right' [*Rechtslehre*], is usually ignored. This is regrettable for it is in the *Rechtslehre* that Kant gives us his most sustained treatment of political philosophy.[2] The neglect of the 'Doctrine of Right' can be explained in part by what would appear to have been the extremely confused nature of the text as originally published. Katrin Flikschuh writes, 'the main reason behind the almost complete neglect, until recently, of the *Rechtslehre* is the distorted state of the argument in the published text itself.' [Flikschuh, 114] This confusion or distortion some have taken to be the product of Kant's senility[3] but it may, more charitably, be due primarily to editorial errors that occurred during its original printing. In 1986, Bernd Ludwig produced a reordered version of the text that has commanded general assent and which forms the basis for Mary Gregor's 1996 translation. [see Flikschuh, 8-9] All that being said, the text, even when revised and reordered, remains difficult and the argumentation is sometimes less than immediately perspicuous. [see Ladd, xxxiii]

In his 1891 'Translator's Introduction' to Kant's Philosophy of Law, William Hastie waxes lyrical in praise of Kant's political philosophy, writing 'In Kant the student will find the fundamental principles of all the best Political and Social Science of the Nineteenth Century, the soundest exposition of Constitutional government, and the first clear adumbration of the great doctrines of Federation and Universal Right which are now stirring in the hearts of the peoples and taking visible and practical form in society. No political writer has ever expounded more emphatically than Kant, the necessity of social order, the harmony of true politics and morals, the sanctity of law, the wrong of insurrection, the duty of political obedience, and the rightful conditions of free individualism and of just coercion; nor has any advocate of the Rights of Man ever upheld a loftier ideal of liberty before the people, or limned more clearly the ultimate conditions of all true progress, or cherished a deeper faith in the universal perfectibility of human nature.' [Hastie, xlii] Alas, despite this stirring encomium, which many, perhaps most, readers would find both surprising and implausible, Kant's political writings were to languish in obscurity until given a new lease of life by the translation of Mary Gregor almost a century after Hastie wrote. Kant published some other, smaller pieces on political themes[4] that are not without interest but, with the exception of 'On the Relation of Theory to Practice in the Right of a State,' in this chapter, I shall focus primarily on the 'Doctrine of Right'.

By incorporating his *Rechtslehre* in a work entitled *The Metaphysics of Morals*, Kant clearly envisaged the interpenetration of his moral and political philosophies.[5] After Machiavelli, it may have appeared that there was no necessary connection between politics and morals, perhaps even a necessary division. Kant, however, will have none of this. 'Kant revoked Machiavelli's separation between morals and politics,' writes Wolfgang Kersting, 'and by integrating political philosophy under the authority of pure practical reason re-created the old unity of morals and politics in a revolutionary new conceptual framework and on the basis of a revolutionary new theory of justification.' [Kersting, 343]

The 'Doctrine of Right' is divided into two parts: the first of which deals with what Kant call 'Private Right'. This is largely a treatment of property—what it is to have things external to oneself and how to acquire them.[6] The second part, 'Public Right', is Kant's account of civil society or the state.[7] After the initial publication of *The Metaphysics of Morals*, Kant added an 'Appendix' in which he responded to some critical comments by a reviewer, taking the opportunity to repeat and to clarify the text.[8] The subtitle of the first part of the 'Doctrine of Right' is 'The Sum of Laws That Do Not Need to be Promulgated,' whereas the subtitle of the second part is 'The Sum of Laws that Need to be Promulgated'. The significance of this contrast between non-promulgation and promulgation should become clearer as we proceed.

Both parts of the 'Doctrine of Right' are of interest to libertarians (and to liberals generally): the first, because of the close connection that libertarians discern between property and liberty; the second for obvious reasons. It must be said, however, that although there's much that a lover of political liberty can take from Kant's work, it would be going much too far to portray him as advocating an embryonic form of libertarianism.[9] 'The libertarian tendency to appeal to both Locke and Kant in support of their arguments betrays a tendency to conflate Locke's natural right to freedom with Kant's innate right to freedom,' writes Katrin Flikschuh. She continues, 'It is important to distinguish between them. While libertarians are often criticised for departing from question-begging premises, Kant's conception of innate right to freedom as a right that individuals possess "merely in virtue of their humanity" is grounded in his metaphysics of freedom as a (shared) idea of reason. Whether or not one finds Kant's account defensible is a separate question—the point is that, given his metaphysical presuppositions, Kant is an unlikely proponent of a libertarian conception of individual freedom as a natural right.' [Flikschuh, 123-124, n. 25]

FREEDOM, EQUALITY AND INDEPENDENCE

In the 'Introduction' to the 'Doctrine of Right' Kant makes a ringing claim that should warm the heart of every lover of liberty: 'Freedom,' he says, (and by 'freedom' here he has in mind not some transcendental or noumenal account of freedom but simply the condition of being unconstrained by another's choice) 'insofar as it can coexist with the freedom of every other in accordance with a universal law, is the only original right belonging to every man by virtue of his humanity.' [Kant 1797, 30] Kant draws a distinction between what we might call *negative* freedom, the freedom to act without external constraint, and *positive* freedom, which is the ability of the will[10] to be a law unto itself. Negative freedom is a necessary but not a sufficient condition of positive freedom.

In his 'On the Relation of Theory to Practice in the Right of a State,' Kant denies not only that the welfare of its citizens can provide the basis of state power but he also rejects the idea that the state can legitimately legislate for a specific concept of happiness for its citizens. 'No one,' he writes, 'can coerce me to be happy in his way (as he thinks of the welfare of other human beings); instead, each may seek his happiness in the way that seems good to him, provided he does not infringe upon the freedom of others to strive for a like end which can coexist with the freedom of everyone in accordance with a possible universal law (i.e. does not infringe upon this right of another.' [Kant

1793, 291] He adds, 'A government established on the principle of benevolence toward the people like that of a *father* toward his children — that is, a *paternalistic government* (*imperium paternale*), in which the subjects, like minor children who cannot distinguish between what is truly useful or harmful to them, are constrained to behave only passively, so as to wait only upon the judgment of the head of state as to how they *should be* happy and, as for his also willing their happiness, only upon his kindness — is the greatest *despotism* thinkable (a constitution that abrogates all the freedom of the subjects, who in that case have no rights at all).' [Kant 1793, 291] When he came to publish the 'Doctrine of Right' some four years later, Kant's views seem to have shifted significantly towards accepting, even endorsing, state interference in social matters. Now, he says the ruler can impose taxes not just for the defence of the state but 'to support organizations providing for the poor, foundling homes, and church organizations, usually called charitable or pious institutions.'[11] Why should those who have more be legally obliged to contribute to the support of those who have less? Because, Kant says, 'they owe their existence to an act of submitting to [the state's] protection and care, which they need in order to live.'[12] Despite this, Kersting claims that 'For Kant a community of right is not a community of solidarity among the needy, but a community for self-protection among those who have the power to act.' [Kersting, 345]

John Ladd writes, 'Kant's doctrine of justice and law turns on the concept of coercion. Law is conceived as a coercive order, and justice treats only what can be made a matter of coercion....The principles of justice themselves determine the legitimate and illegitimate uses of coercion. The legitimate use of coercion is coercion that accords with liberty, and the illegitimate use is one that transgresses liberty.'[13] Illegitimate coercion is violence (the libertarian would say 'aggression'), and violence and liberty are opposites. Freedom, as man's only original right, is the right to be free of violence. All of this is music to the ear of the libertarian. What Kant believes his conception of freedom implies is, however, not quite so musical. Whereas a libertarian would happily accept that our right to be free of violence imposes an obligation on others to refrain from being violent towards us, Kant goes further, believing that our original right gives us another right, this time the right to live under a political order and to require others to join us there. If what Kant means by political order is a *de facto* association of those who respect the principle of zero-aggression or non-violence, this isn't necessarily unacceptable to libertarians. But Kant goes much further than this. For him, the political order isn't the product of the free association of the non-violent but, as we shall see, the unitary authority which can legitimately command our obedience and to which we can offer no active resistance.

If freedom is man's only original right, isn't this right necessarily infringed upon by the existence and operation of the state? Kant rejects this conclusion. The state indeed employs coercion and that coercion can be taken to be a hindrance to freedom, but the state in using coercion isn't in fact hindering freedom but merely offering a hindrance to a hindrance to freedom, a hindrance to violence or aggression.[14]

In 'On the Relation of Theory to Practice in the Right of a State,' in addition to freedom, Kant also proposes independence and equality as principles that should ground any defensible conception of the state. [Kant 1793, 291-296] By *independence*, Kant has in mind the idea that although citizens are ultimately bound only by laws they give to themselves, not all who are bound by laws are equally capable of making them—'As for legislation itself, it is not the case that all who are free and equal under already existing public laws are to be held equal with regard to the right to give these laws.' [Kant 1793, 294] For Kant, women and children are intrinsically incapable of being independent in the appropriate sense, and among adult males, only those who are economically self-sufficient qualify. [see Kant 1793, 294-296] *Equality* is sometimes used by political philosophers to severely limit, if not effectively eradicate, any robust conception of freedom. But lovers of liberty need not be concerned here for, in this context, Kant intends equality to be understood purely formally, as equality before the law, and as such, equality is perfectly consistent with material inequalities of all sorts. 'Each member of a commonwealth has coercive rights against every other....But whoever is *subject* to laws is a subject within a state and is thus subjected to coercive right equally with all the other members of the commonwealth....But this thoroughgoing equality of individuals within a state, as its subject, is quite consistent with the greatest inequality in terms of the quantity and degree of their possessions, whether in physical or mental superiority over others or in external goods and in rights generally (of which there can be many) relatively to others....But *in terms of right*...they are nevertheless all equal to one another as subjects; for, no one of them can coerce any other except through public law...' [Kant 1793, 292]

KANT AND HOBBES

'On the Relation of Theory to Practice in the Right of a State' is subtitled, 'Against (*gegen*) Hobbes'. In what way, exactly, is this little treatise against Hobbes? Their disagreement seems to turn on their different conceptions of the social contract. For Kant, the social contract isn't an historical event ('as a fact it is indeed not possible' [Kant 1793, 296]) but is, rather, an idea of reason. This non-actual social contract functions to limit what the legislator can do; in this respect: the legislator must make laws 'in such a way that they could have arisen from the united will of a whole people...as if he [any citizen] has joined in voting for such a will.' [Kant 1793, 296-297] The will of the legislator, as legislator, can't be an arbitrary will. Citizens cannot be supposed to give their wills to laws that are intrinsically unjust. The criterion here isn't whether, as a matter of fact, the majority of citizens are in fact unhappy with a particular law but rather whether a given law is such that it would be 'self-contradictory that an entire people should agree' with it. [Kant 1793, 298] Not only is the contract non-actual, so too is our consent to it non-actual, our consent being deduced from its being an idea of Reason to which we cannot but give our consent.

For Hobbes, too, the social contract wasn't meant to be taken as an actual historical event nor was it a voluntary matter. On these two points, Hobbes and Kant agree. The difference between them is that Hobbes justifies his social contract in terms of the practical benefits that he believes accrue from it for each individual—freedom from fear and violence—whereas Kant justifies his social contract in terms of an idea of Reason that he believes we cannot coherently resist. Katrin Flikschuh writes, 'Kant follows Hobbes in regarding individuals' desires for external objects as inevitably conflictual and as requiring a political solution. However, Kant's solution differs from Hobbes' proposed *Leviathan State*. Hobbes conceives his political solution in terms of an all-powerful sovereign who constrains individuals' pursuit of their desires by means of his irresistible force. By contrast, Kant's solution is premised on individuals' capacity to conceive and to acknowledge the authority of a general law of external freedom...action in accordance with which makes possible the conflict-free coexistence of each with everyone else.' [Flikschuh, 100]

Kant was influenced in his thinking by Rousseau, whom he greatly admired, and never more so than in his distinguishing between the arbitrary will of an individual, which *is* coerced by a state that sets an authority over it, and the united will of all (practical reason itself)—what any man *would* will—which cannot conflict with his non-arbitrary will. Kant follows Rousseau in other respects too.

In his 'Conjectures on the Beginnings of the History of the Human Race,' a rational reconstruction of *Genesis*, Kant gives us an account of the emergence of reason from the matrix of instinct that could have come straight from the pen of Rousseau. In the beginning, Kant tells us, all was instinct. Instinct was man's only guide to action and he had no need of any other. While instinct ruled, all was well. But reason soon began to stir. By allowing man to institute comparisons, it moved him beyond the control of instinct. Reason, with the aid of the imagination, played the major role in the creation of artificial desires that aren't only unsupported by natural instinct but are in fact contrary to it. With this dubious advance, man's natural state has been irrevocably damaged; his eyes have been opened and he discovers in himself the power to choose. Hand in hand with the development of the power to choose goes a conscious awareness of the future, for choice is the selection of one among a set of possibilities and possibilities are essentially futural. By the power of choice, man is enabled to escape the bounds of temporal immediacy. He develops the capacity to plan and to prepare for far-off goals, and this is a decided practical advantage. But this advantage isn't acquired without some corresponding drawbacks. To become aware of the future is to realise that what it holds in store for us isn't always what we would desire; it is to find oneself afflicted with a burden of anxiety, a burden from which other animals are free. The transition man undergoes is from an animal condition to a human one, from domination by instinct to some measure of control over it, from a state of nature to a state of freedom. Kant notes, acutely, that the acquisition of reason wasn't an unmixed blessing for the individual man. As instrumental, reason can be a tool for good or for ill; by its use, evils were created of a kind and quantity unknown to man in his state of ignorant innocence. But though the individual man may not have been unduly appreciative of his change of state, the human species as a whole has benefitted from it.[15]

POSSESSION AND OWNERSHIP

It is possible (perhaps even probable) that the few who have read the 'Doctrine of Right' have wondered why Kant begins this treatise with an extensive account of property. Unless the purpose of this section is clearly grasped, the discussion may well appear to be interesting but its significance obscure. In brief, the argument is this: if we are to be able to have property in any full-blooded sense, then we are required to enter into a social contract. Outside the civic condition, our possessions wouldn't be secure and we wouldn't be able to use them as we wished. Our freedom would, therefore, be compromised. The internal logical dynamic of private right moves us inexorably towards both property and public right. [see Kersting, 348]

Kant begins his substantive discussion of 'Private Right' in *The Metaphysics of Morals* by distinguishing between what he calls sensible and intelligible possession, 'intelligible possession' being his term for ownership. Sensible possession is a factual matter: if I have a pen in my hand, I possess it; if a dog has a bone in its mouth, it possesses the bone. Intelligible possession, on the other hand, is a normative matter, a matter of right. 'That is *rightfully* mine,' writes Kant, 'with which I am so connected that another's use of it without my consent would wrong me.'[16] Kant, not particularly helpfully, characterises intelligible possession as 'the possession of an object *without holding it* (*detentio*)' but even if the mode of expression is obscure, the basic idea is reasonably clear. A little later, he says that the real definition of what can be externally mine is that 'I would be wronged by being disturbed in my use of it *even though I am not in possession of it.*'[17]

What does Kant think can be yours or mine? Three kinds of thing: external objects (things), another's choice (contracts), and, in a very politically incorrect move, wives, children and servants (persons as quasi-things).[18] Kant believes that it has to be possible to have any given thing—what he calls 'an object of choice'—as mine (or yours). If this weren't so, then some object of choice or other would have to be objectively and permanently a *res nullius*, that is, would have to such that no one could ever come to own it. An object of choice is something that a person can make use of by his physical power. If an object of choice wasn't within the rightful power of anyone, then 'freedom would be depriving itself of the use of its choice with regard to an object of choice, by putting *usable* objects beyond any possibility of being *used*; in other words, it would annihilate them in a practical respect and make them into *res nullius*, even though in the use of things choice was formally consistent with everyone's outer freedom in accordance with universal laws.'[19] If any given thing can be mine or yours, it follows that we can, in some sense, put 'all others under an obligation, which they wouldn't otherwise have, to refrain from using certain objects of our choice because we have been the first to take them into our possession.'[20]

In the absence of an explicit agreement between Tom and Jane, why should Tom accept the imposition of an obligation on him to refrain from interfering with what Jane unilaterally claims to be hers? The answer, according to Kant, is because Jane, in imposing this obligation on others, must accept the right of others to impose similar obligations upon her. Jane's assertion that this field belongs to her and that no one may interfere with her use of it implies that she is 'under an obligation to every other to refrain from using what is externally his.' Putting the same point negatively, Kant writes that 'I am therefore not under an obligation to leave external objects belonging to others untouched unless everyone else provides me assurance that he will behave in accordance with the same principle with regard to what is mine.'[21]

From a libertarian perspective, so far, so good. Now, however, Kant takes us in a direction where, it seems, no libertarian could follow. What he has told us so far about the non-contractual imposition of obligation upon others turns out not to have been the full story. If Tom could impose obligations on Dick merely by a unilateral act of will, this would, according to Kant, infringe upon Dick's freedom. That being so, it is 'only a will putting everyone under an obligation, hence only a collective general (*common*) and powerful will, that can provide everyone this assurance,' and this will can be found only in a civil, that is, a political, condition.[22]

Prior to the emergence of a civil condition or a state, are we then to take it that one can't in fact own anything? Kant denies this. In a non-civil state of nature, we can indeed take intelligible possession of things, we can own them, *but only in a provisional way.* 'Prior to a civil constitution (or in *abstraction* from it), external objects that are mine or yours must therefore be assumed to be possible, and with them a right to constrain everyone with whom we could have any dealings to enter with us into a constitution in which external objects can be secured as mine or yours.'[23] Prior to a civil condition (or considered apart from it), intelligible possession, ownership, is real but merely provisional. It becomes conclusive only in an actual civil condition. So, 'the way to have something external as one's own *in a state of nature* is physical possession which has in its favor the rightful *presumption* that it will be made into rightful possession through being united with the will of all in a public lawgiving, and in anticipation of this holds *comparatively* as rightful possession.'[24] I think it can fairly be said that most philosophical justifications of property before Kant's turn to a greater or lesser extent on the idea that property is essential to man's attainment of his ends. 'From Aristotle to Locke,' writes Kersting, 'theories of property were always embedded in pragmatic contexts and connected with consideration of human ends...' [Kersting, 349] Kant's account, in contrast, is resolutely detached from any such pragmatic considerations.

Over the years, various theories have been produced as to how it is possible for someone to originally acquire things external to him. Locke, notoriously, speaks of the mixing of labour and of improvement, Hume of factual possession and prescription; Kant, on the other hand, believes that I make something that isn't mine to be mine by bringing the object of my choice, something that I have the capacity to use, under my control. In so doing, I will it to be mine and have in prospect the idea of a possible united will.[25] In other words, I take factual possession of an object of choice that belongs to no one; I make evident that I have done so and that I intend to exclude all others from my object of choice; and by so doing, I bind others to agree with my choice. This last step is what takes me from mere sensible factual possession to normative intelligible possession, that is, to ownership and property. Since this last move is by far the most controversial aspect of Kant's (and not only Kant's) theory of original acquisition, I am going to give you his own words. The third aspect of original acquisition is, he says, '*Appropriation (appropratio*) as the act of a general will (in idea) giving an external law through which everyone is bound to agree with my choice.—The validity of this last aspect of acquisition, on which rests the conclusion "this external object is *mine*," that is, the conclusion that my possession holds as possession *merely by right (possessio noumenon*), is based on this: since all these acts *have to do with a right* and so proceed from practical reason, in the question of what is laid down as right, abstraction can be made from the empirical conditions of possession, so that the conclusion, "the external object is mine," is correctly drawn from sensible to intelligible possessions.'[26] Admittedly, this isn't the most perspicuous passage of prose ever penned but it is what it is.

The Lockean position on original acquisition, especially in light of the 'mixing of labour' metaphor, is often taken to imply that ownership is a two-place direct relationship, a right between a person and a thing.[27] Kant attacks this position, a position that he himself had once held.[28] Rights and obligations are correlative so that if such a direct right existed, the originally acquired object of choice would have to bear the corresponding obligation. Such an originally acquired object bearing this obligation would, as it were, be obliged to reject anyone else who tried to acquire it. But, as Kant points out in a scathing passage, in thinking this, a person would be thinking of my right 'as it were a guardian spirit accompanying the thing, always pointing me out to whoever else wanted to take possession of it and protecting it against incursion by them' which is, of course, absurd.[29] Some pages later, he returns to the attack, arguing that 'The first working, enclosing, or, in general, *transforming* of a piece of land can furnish no title of acquisition.' This is a common but, Kant believes, fundamentally mistaken, idea. How could such a misconception arise if not by the 'tacit deception of personifying things and of thinking of a right to things as being a right *directly* against them, as if someone could, by the work he expends upon them, put things under an obligation to serve him and no one else.'[30] If you were the only girl in the world, you couldn't acquire anything as property, since there would be no one to exclude from it. You would have sensible, but not intelligible, possession. 'What is called a right to a thing is only that right someone has against a person who is in possession of it in common with all others (in the civil condition).'[31]

In the choice between the two initial positions on the relationship of human beings to land, one of which is that everyone owns everything in common, and the other of which is that no one owns anything, Kant seems to choose the former position. 'All men are originally in common possession of the land of the entire earth.'[32] Doesn't this undermine what Kant has been saying? He thinks not, for he believes that I can't unilaterally lay an obligation on another to refrain from using what I have merely sensibly possessed; I can do so only through the unified choice of all who own all land in common. Moreover, what he means by possession in common is *not* what is usually meant by that expression and amounts to little more than saying that all human beings have a right to be wherever nature or chance has placed them.[33] This kind of accidental (yet in another sense necessary)[34] property of having to be in a particular place is distinguished from residence, which is acquired and lasting. Kant firmly rejects the idea of an original or primitive possession in common which, he says, 'can never be proved.'[35] What he means by original possession in common is 'a practical rational concept which contains a priori the principle in accordance with which alone people can use a place on the earth in accordance with principles of right.'[36]

In original acquisition, I occupy or take control (*occupatio*) of my object of choice (previously unowned) and I do so before anyone else.[37] Nevertheless, as we have seen, such acquisition, deriving from a unilateral will, can be only provisional. Conclusive acquisition derives from the will of all. He writes, 'the *rational title* of acquisition can lie only in the idea of a will of all united a priori (necessarily so united), which is here tacitly assumed as a necessary condition (*conditio sine qua non*); for a unilateral will cannot put others under an obligation they wouldn't otherwise have.—But the condition in which the will of all is actually united for giving law is the civil condition....Hence *original* acquisition can be only *provisional.—Conclusive* acquisition takes place only in the civil condition.'[38]

A standard objection to all forms of original acquisition is that they place no intrinsic limit on the amount of property that can be originally acquired so that some extrinsic principle of limitation must be accepted if some one person is not to acquire everything. Thus Locke, for example, produces two provisos, the first allowing the acquisition of perishables only to the extent that they do not spoil, and the second, more significant proviso, requiring that enough and as good of whatever it is that is acquired be left for others. Does Kant have an answer to this objection? Yes. His answer is, you can acquire whatever you can control, and the mark of control is simply your ability to defend what you acquire. 'My possession,'he writes, 'extends as far as I have the mechanical ability, from where I reside, to secure my land against encroachment by others...'[39] For Kant, it is in no way necessary that you do anything else to the land—you do not have to develop it, build on it, drain it, fence it off or do anything else, simply be able to defend it. Development is, at best, a sign of control—it isn't constitutive of it. Acquisition deriving from control has the advantage of allowing someone to acquire, let us say, a stand of forest, which he simply wants to admire aesthetically but not otherwise use.[40]

What moves man from the state of nature to a civil or political condition?[41] The answer is that, as illustrated by the account of property, in a state of nature, there can be no distributive justice. Kant accepts that in the state of nature there can be societies (conjugal or domestic) compatible with rights but he denies that these societies can have law. The state of nature permits only private right; for public right, we must enter into a civil union.[42] When men can't avoid living in close proximity, Kant thinks they are obliged to leave the state of nature and enter into 'a rightful condition, that is, a condition of distributive justice.'[43] This he calls the postulate of public right, a postulate that Katrin Flikschuh describes as 'famously obscure'. [Flikschuh, 111] In the state of nature, no one can be assured of what is his because 'No one is bound to refrain from encroaching on what another possesses if the other gives him no equal assurance that he will observe the same restraint towards him.'[44] Bernd Ludwig identifies this postulate as what is radically new in the 'Doctrine of Right', for it is by means of this postulate that, as Flikschuh notes, 'Kant succeeds in deriving individuals' (global) obligations of justice towards one another directly from their claims to external objects of their choice, rendering redundant any contractual political agreement to that effect.' [Flikschuh, 116]

THE STATE

Philosophers before Kant have connected the idea of property with the idea of the state. There is a tendency to prioritise one conception over the other, so that property may be taken to be the creation of the state (Hobbes) or it is held that the state exists to protect and defend property (Locke). For Kant, the two notions are co-implicative so that 'a justificatory interconnection of both property and the state, which sets both conceptions into a relations of mutual systematic dependence, replaces the independence of the state from property in Hobbes as well as the independence of property from the state in Locke.' [Kersting, 353]

Public Right, Kant defines, as 'a system of laws for a people' who, because they interact with one another 'need a rightful condition under a will uniting them.'[45] People thus related to each other are in what Kant calls a 'civil condition' and 'the whole of individuals in a rightful condition, in relation to its own members is called a state (*civitas*).'[46] A little later, he defines the state, somewhat more crisply, as 'a union of a multitude of human beings under laws of right.'[47]

There have been those, such as Hobbes, who seem to think that it is our actual experience of violence and disorder that impels us to move from a state of nature to a civil state. Kant believes that even were our actual experience to be of an entirely pacific nature, without public right 'individual human beings, peoples, and states can never be secure against violence from one another, since each has its own right to do *what seems right and good to it* and not to be dependent upon another's opinion about this.'[48] It is this radical insecurity and its concomitant practical limitation on freedom that Kant believes impels us rationally (not empirically) to leave the state of nature and enter into civil society. An individual must 'leave the state of nature, in which each follows its own judgment, unite itself with all others (with which it cannot avoid interacting), subject itself to a public lawful external coercion, and so enter into a condition in which what is to be recognized as belonging to it is determined *by law* and is allotted to it by adequate *power* (not its own but an external power); that is, it ought above all else to enter a civil condition.'[49]

Libertarians and other lovers of liberty can agree with much of this. Certainly, any society, if it isn't to dissolve into chaos, must have laws, and such laws can't simply be the arbitrary product of a legislator but must be of a kind that all could agree to abide by. For libertarians, the principle of zero-aggression applies to all, whether or not they have explicitly subscribed to it. It is no defence to a charge of murder to say that no one had informed you that it was prohibited and that, even if they had, you hadn't in fact agreed to be bound by such a law! Thus far, Kant and libertarians would agree. But Kant goes much further than any libertarian would, in the end, be prepared to go.

Every state, Kant believes, has three authorities: a sovereign or legislative authority (*potestas legislatoria*), an executive (*executoria*), and a judiciary (*iudiciaria*). The legislative authority, the sovereign, is simply the united will of the people. Whatever it legislates for the people is necessarily right since no one can wrong himself! The discerning reader should, at this point, hear echoes of Rousseau's General Will, hardly surprising given Kant's admiration for the Swiss/French thinker.[50] The relationship of the sovereign, executive and judiciary (which are, in effect, the people united as a whole) to the people taken as a collection of individuals is one of superior to inferior, of commander to those required to obey commands. The original contract is the means by which a people forms itself into a state. This, of course, as we have seen, isn't an actual historical event, but an idea. In making this contract, a people gives up the external freedom it possesses in a state of nature to resume it as members of a commonwealth. In so doing, a man hasn't 'sacrificed a *part* of his innate outer freedom for the sake of an end, but rather, he has relinquished entirely his wild, lawless freedom in order to find his freedom as such undiminished, in a dependence upon laws, that is, in a rightful condition, since this dependence arises from his own lawgiving will.'[51]

The ruler of the state is that moral person to whom executive authority belongs. The sovereign, the legislative person, can't also be the ruler, since the ruler is subordinate to the sovereign, which can depose the ruler or reform his administration but, significantly, can't punish him, for punishment is an executive act. Finally, neither the ruler nor the sovereign can judge but can only appoint judges.

Kant warns strongly against any attempt on the part of a people to inquire into the origin of their political authorities. For Kant, it matters not a whit whether 'a state began with an actual contract of submission (*pacta subiectionis civilis*) as a fact, or whether power came first and law arrived only afterwards.'[52] The only reason for such an enquiry would be a hope of discovering a disreputable origin of the authority and the use of this knowledge to resist it. 'If a subject, having pondered over the ultimate origin of the authority now ruling, wanted to resist this authority, he would be punished, got rid of, or expelled (as an outlaw, *exlex*) in accordance with the laws of this authority, that is, with every right.'[53] That this opinion is no matter of momentary philosophic spleen but a considered view becomes evident when Kant returns to make this point again a little later, saying that such an inquiry is futile, even conceding that we can deduce from the nature of uncivilised men that 'they were subjected to it [law] by force' but according this fact no political significance.[54]

It will come as no surprise to the reader to discover that Kant permits no active resistance by the people against its ruler, the agent of the sovereign, even if that ruler has proceeded contrary to law. The people may complain; they may not resist. 'The reason a people has a duty to put up with even what is held to be an unbearable abuse of supreme authority is that its resistance to the highest legislation can never be regarded as other than contrary to law, and indeed as abolishing the entire legal constitution. For a people to be authorized to resist, there would have to be a public law permitting it to resist, that is, the highest legislation would have to contain a provision that it is not the highest and that makes the people, as subject, by one and the same judgment sovereign over him to whom it is subject. This is self-contradictory.'[55]

Given Kant's premises, it is hard to deny the force of his logic; all the more reason, then, to call his premises into question. At the heart of his premises lies the presupposition that the legislative authority incorporates the united will of the people such that whatever it decides can't be wrong. We encountered this mysterious property of indefectible self-rule when we considered Rousseau's General Will and now it re-appears in Kant's conception of the people's united will. Rousseau's General Will could have been the object of Churchill's description of Russia—a riddle wrapped in a mystery inside an enigma—and Kant's united will is scarcely less mysterious or enigmatic. It must be noted that Kant *does* permit a kind of passive resistance which, however, can only take place through the people's representatives, which is more or less the standard position in the thinking of the Reformers and Kant was, of course, a Lutheran pietist. Kant takes this possibility of passive resistance as a sign of non-corruption, since, if the demands of government were always granted 'this would be a sure sign that the people are corrupt, that its representatives can be bought, that the head of the government is ruling despotically through his minister, and that the minister himself is betraying the people.'[56]

Wolfgang Kersting claims that Kant's denial of a right to resistance can be (and has been) misunderstood. He believes that it does not mandate that one should obey 'a regime that practices state-terror and murders entire groups of the population' or provide a justification for asserting the legitimacy of totalitarianism. [Kersting, 361] It is difficult, however, to reconcile Kersting's claim with what Kant has in fact written. As we have seen, passive resistance is possible but active resistance, even to an unbearable abuse of authority—and what could be more unbearable than state-terror and murder—Kant believes to be contrary to law. In any event, Kant's theory recognises no right of the people to sedition, rebellion or tyrannicide. If despite all this, a rebellion takes place, which is successful, then, in a very Hobbesian moment, the people are obliged to obey their new rulers! '[O]nce a revolution has succeeded and a new constitution has been established, the lack of legitimacy with which it began and has been implemented cannot release the subjects from the obligation to comply with the new order of things as good citizens, and they cannot refuse honest obedience to the authority that now has the power.'[57] Such a position may well be consistent with Kant's overall account but it is uncomfortably close to an unprincipled *realpolitik* of 'might makes right'.

This is not the only respect in which we find striking similarities between Kant and Hobbes. In his 'Idea of a Universal History based on the Principle of

World-Citizenship,' Kant plays some variations on a Hobbesian theme. Human society, he tells us, isn't the result of any superior display of rationality on the part of man; it is, rather the outcome of those very elements in him, such as pride, ambition and greed, that normally are held to be reprehensible. For Kant, antagonism is the motive force that pushes man, despite himself, into society. Man is torn between a propensity and an inclination. He wants to be completely free from all restraint, to have everything go according to his wish and will and to be bound by no obligations to others; at the same time he craves power, and the recognition of his superiority by others. His vanity demands that he achieve a rank among his fellows, whom he cannot tolerate, but from whom he cannot withdraw. Were it not for his unsocial sociability man would be one of a kind with the animals he has domesticated. Without his heartless competitive vanity and an apparently insatiable desire to possess and rule, man wouldn't possess the excellences he does. His natural capacities would lie rusty and unused. Man wishes concord; but Nature knows better what is good for the race; she wills discord. He wishes to live comfortably and pleasantly; Nature wills that he should be plunged from sloth and passive contentment into labour and trouble, in order that he may find means of extricating himself from them. Man's natural urges, the source of unsociableness and mutual opposition, from which so many evils arise, drive men to new exertions of their forces and thus to the manifold development of their capacities. (This idea of the emergence of social order from individual self-seeking behaviour was anticipated by Adam Smith and echoed, a little later, by Hegel.)

I wrote earlier that whether or not there can be a legitimate rebellion, a venerable topic that was considered in turn by Locke writing some years after Hobbes, Hobbes's thinking bears a striking resemblance to certain traditional Chinese ideas. In Chinese political thinking, the Emperor's authority depends upon his acquiring and retaining the mandate of heaven. If this is withdrawn, then his rule ceases to be legitimate. The evidence of its withdrawal, however, is considerably less mystical and consists largely in the occurrence of widespread natural, social or political disorder. So too, given that Hobbes believes that the function of the state and of government is to provide the security which is the very reason for its being, should it be unable to provide that security then, *de facto*, it has already ceased to govern. So, resistance to the authority of Leviathan can't be *prospectively* legitimate but, if such resistance is in fact successful, then it thereby becomes *retroactively* legitimate. McClelland makes the point that it is somewhat ironic that Hobbes's *Leviathan*, a masterpiece of social contract theory, is used by Hobbes to undermine the very thing that social contract was invented to establish, namely, the justification for disobeying our lawfully constituted authority! [McClelland, 193] It seems that much the same can be said of Kant in this regard, even given his overall rejection of the empirical in favour of the rational

There is no need to follow Kant's account of the details of the operation of the state—it follows more or less the usual pattern. There is, however, one notorious section of the 'Doctrine of Right' that causes even the most devoted Kantians to choke on their cornflakes and that is Kant's attitude to punishment.

The only justification for punishment, according to Kant, is the criminal's commission of a crime. Punishment 'can never be inflicted merely as a means to promote some other good for the criminal himself or for civil society. It must always be inflicted upon him only *because he has committed a crime,*' although if such justified punishment incidentally serves the ends of deterrence, so much the better.[58] Those who are jailed for their crimes can't expect the state to provide their bed and board free of charge[59] and so must cede their labour to the state. This reduces them effectively to the status of slaves, either for a specific time, or permanently, depending on the length of their sentences. Should a criminal be convicted of murder, Kant thinks the only fitting punishment for him is death. No other punishment will satisfy the dictates of justice. In a notorious passage, Kant even goes so far as to say, 'Even if a civil society were to be dissolved by the consent of all its members (e.g. if a people inhabiting an island decided to separate and disperse throughout the world), the last murderer remaining in prison would first have to be executed, so that each has done to him what his deeds deserve and blood guilt does not cling to the people for not having insisted upon this punishment; for otherwise the people can be regarded as collaborators in this public violation of justice.'[60]

INTERNATIONAL RELATIONS

Whereas the *citizens* of a state are all equal because of their common subjection to the state of which they are citizens, *states*, in their relations to each other 'are (like lawless savages) by nature in a non-rightful condition.'[61] Just as individuals are under a duty to enter into a civil condition, so too, states are obliged to leave their specific form of a state of nature. This time, however, their leaving it will lead not to the formation of a superstate—Kant explicitly rejects this idea as entailing the dissolution of the once separate states—but only to a federation, 'an alliance that can be renounced at any time and so must be renewed from time to time.'[62] States in a state of nature may war with each other and use their own citizens as soldiers to do so. They can do this, not because the state owns it citizens or their property, nor because the citizens owe their ruler a duty, but rather because the sovereign owes a duty to the people! The citizens, 'as co-legislating members of a state…must therefore give their free assent, through their representatives, not only to waging war in general but also to each particular declaration of war. Only under this limiting condition can a state direct them to serve in a way full of danger to them.'[63] Wars can't rightfully be punitive according to Kant, since punishment is a prerogative of a superior, and states, in their relationships to each other, have no superiors. In the conduct of a war, a state may use any form of defence, except those that would unfit its subjects to be citizens. Since such unfit means include spying, assassination, spreading disinformation and plundering the defeated enemy, it can be seen that Kant places some severe restrictions on the state's conduct of a war.

CONCLUSION

Kant's political philosophy is an attempt to show that man is inexorably compelled to move into civil society—the state—by the very logic of private right. If one wishes to have property rather than mere possession, then one must leave the state of nature, give up one's lawless freedom, and enter into a civil union with others in which one's freedom, although altered, is rather magnified than diminished. Kant, unlike Hegel, draws no distinction between a civil but apolitical condition and a political condition proper; for him, the civil condition just *is* political. Kant and the libertarian anarchist both accept the need for law and for order if men are to live together peacefully; anarchy, after all, isn't a state of disorder and lawlessness but rather a condition in which both law and order emerge from the spontaneous and contractual engagement of one person or group with another. But, unlike Kant, the libertarian can accept no quasi-Rousseauean 'united will of the people' embodied in unquestionable and irresistible political institutions to ground his conception of law and order.

Notes

1 1ˢᵗ edition 1781, 2ⁿᵈ edition 1787.

2 The German word *Recht* has a variety of meanings so that its translation 'is a perennial problem for translators.' [Kersting, 364, n. 1] English has just one word for law, whereas German has *Recht* and *Gesetz* and French has *droit* and *loi*. *Recht* and *droit* correspond, more or less, to the Latin, *ius*, and signify the entire body of laws and the principles underlying it, whereas *Gesetz* and *loi* correspond to the Latin, *lex*, and signify a particular law or statute. *Recht* also has the meaning of justice, and also right, as when one has a right against another person. On top of this broad, general linguistic usage, philosophers tend to add their own linguistic idiosyncrasies which adds to the hermeneutic fun.

3 Schopenhauer describes the *Rechtslehre* as 'deplorable' and claims that the 'influence of senility is preponderant' in the second part of *The Metaphysics of Morals*. [Schopenhauer 2010, 136]

4 Such works would include 'Idea of a Universal History based on the Principle of World Citizenship' (1784); 'Conjectures on the Beginnings of the History of the Human Race' (1786); and 'Toward Perpetual Peace' (1795). 'On the Relation of Theory to Practice in the Right of a State' is part II of 'On the Common Saying: That may be Correct in Theory, but it is of no Use in Practice' (1793). See Kant 1996 for a standard and convenient collection of Kant's writings on moral and political philosophy.

5 References will be to the Mary Gregor translation of *The Metaphysics of Morals* (Kant, 1797) by page number and also, in case the reader is using another translation, by section number; so, for example, Kant 1797, 51, §14. Italics in citations from the 'Doctrine of Right' are in the original, unless specifically stated to be otherwise.

6 Kant 1797, 37-86, §§1-42.

7 Kant 1797, 89-138, §§43-62.

8 Kant 1797, 'Appendix,' 125-138.

9 See Verhaegh 2004a, 2004b.

10 Just as German has two words, *Recht* and *Gesetz*, for law, so too, it has two words for will: *Der Wille* and *Die Willkür*. *Der Wille*, for Kant, resembles Rousseau's general will; it is the source of the principles of right and wrong and it is inerrant. *Die Willkür*, on the other hand, is that capacity that makes it possible for us as individuals to decide between alternatives. '*Der Wille*,' John Ladd writes, 'is the legislative Will that issues decrees, as it were, for the *Willkür*, which acts or fails to act conformably with them.' [Ladd, xxvi-xxvii]

11 Kant 1797, 100, §49.

12 Kant 1797, 101, §49.

13 Ladd, xviii-xix; see also Kersting, 346.

14 See Kant 1797, §§D & E, 25-26.

15 For a brief account of Kant on 'unsocial sociability' see Duchesne, 38-42 and Smith 2016, passim.

16 Kant 1797, 37, §1.

17 Kant 1797, 39, §5.
18 Kant 1797, 37-38, §4; see also 48, §10.
19 Kant 1797, 41, §6.
20 Kant 1797, 41, §6; see also 43, §7.
21 Kant 1797, 44, §8.
22 see Kant 1797, 45, §8.
23 Kant 1797, 45, §9. In my *Libertarian Anarchy*, I presented, without realising it, a quasi-Kantian quasi-Humean account of property. See Casey 2012b, 69-71.
24 Kant 1797, 46, §9.
25 See Kant 1797, 47, §10.
26 Kant 1797, 47, §10.
27 This position may be more characteristic of Locke's intellectual disciples than of Locke himself. For Locke, property was the resultant of a tripartite relationship between subject, object and God. [see Flikschuh, 118, n. 12]
28 'The body is mine for it is a part of my I and is moved by my faculty of choice. The entire animated or unanimated world that does not have its own faculty of choice is mine, in so far as I can compel it and move it according to my faculty of choice. The sun is not mine. The same holds for another human being, therefore nobody's property is a *Proprietat* or an exclusive property. But in so far as I want to appropriate something exclusively to myself, I will, at least, not presuppose the other's will or his action as being opposed to mine. I will therefore perform those actions that designate what is mine, cut down the tree, mill it, etc. The other human being tells me that this is his, for through the actions of his faculty of choice, it belongs to his own self, as it were.' [Kant 1764-65, 110]
29 See Kant 1797, 49, §11.
30 Kant 1797, 55, §17.
31 Kant 1797, 50, §11.
32 Kant 1797, 54, §16.
33 Kant 1797, 50, §13.
34 While on the earth, I have to be in some place or other—I must have a specific location—and so location is in this sense necessary; however, I do not have to be in *this* particular place rather than *that*, and so any given location is accidental.
35 Kant 1797, 51, §13.
36 Kant 1797, 51, §13.
37 See Kant 1797, 51, §14.
38 Kant 1797, 52, §15; see also §16.
39 Kant 1797, 56, §17.
40 Kant believes that his account of property and its acquisition, which makes one of property's constitutive elements the ability of its owner to dispose of it as he pleases, necessarily implies that only objects external to man can properly be said to be owned since a man, according to Kant, cannot dispose of himself as he pleases. A man, therefore cannot be said to own himself, though he can be his own master. As we have seen, Kant did not always hold this position. 'The body is mine,' he wrote, 'for it is a part of my I and is moved by my faculty of choice.' [Kant 1764-65, 110]
41 I am leaving to one side Kant's treatment of contract rights and of the rights to persons akin to rights to things [Kant 1797, 57-84, §§18-40] which, though interesting and certainly not uncontroversial, isn't directly relevant to my concerns in this volume.
42 See Kant 1797, 85, §41.
43 Kant 1797, 86, §42.
44 Kant 1797, 86, §42] 'A state of nature,' writes John Ladd, 'being one of war and violence, is considered by Kant to be incompatible with man's innate right to liberty. In such a state, man does, of course, possess a kind of lawless liberty, but he has no right thereto. His innate right extends only to lawful liberty, because it comes from nature as a moral lawmaker. That is why it is a demand of justice, incumbent on everyone, to quit the state of nature and why everyone has a right to employ force to make others join him in doing so.' [Ladd, xx]
45 Kant 1797, 89, §43.
46 Kant 1797, 89, §43.
47 Kant 1797, 90, §45.
48 Kant 1797, 90, §44.

49 Kant 1797, 90, §44.

50 At this point, Kant briefly rehearses the points he had made in 'On the Relation of Theory to Practice in the Right of a State' about freedom, equality and independence.

51 Kant 1797, 93, §47.

52 Kant 1797, 95, §49.

53 Kant 1797, 95, §49.

54 Kant 1797, 112, §52.

55 Kant 1797, 96-97, §49.

56 Kant 1797, 98, §49.

57 Kant 1797, 98, §49.

58 Kant 1797, 105, §49.

59 Commenting on the liberal trope of incarceration as 'paying your debt to society', Margaret Atwood remarks, 'the material benefit to society is not only zero, it's considerably less than zero, because it's not the jailed criminal who's actually paying for anything, it's the taxpayers.' [Atwood, 124]

60 Kant 1797, 106, §49.

61 Kant 1797, 114, §54.

62 Kant 1797, 115, §54.

63 Kant 1797, 116, §55.

Chapter 24

EDMUND BURKE

I believe in only one thing: liberty; but I do not believe
in liberty enough to want to force it upon anyone
—H. L. Mencken

Politics is the conduct of public affairs for private advantage
—Ambrose Bierce

Edmund Burke was born in Dublin in 1729 or 1730. He studied at Trinity College Dublin from which he graduated in 1748. Burke settled in London in 1750 where, some few years later, he produced his earliest works, *The Vindication of Natural Society* and *A Philosophical Enquiry into the Origin of the Sublime and Beautiful*. He had a varied but overall successful political career that lasted until his death in 1797 in which, although he never attained political office, he was none the less extremely influential.

When it comes to Burke's writing, the critics divide. William Pitt judged it to be a mass of rhapsodic effusion that commanded little admiration and no agreement. Thomas Paine spends the first ten or so pages of his *Rights of Man* attacking what he sees as Burke's unjustified and intemperate attack on the French. 'Everything which rancour, prejudice, ignorance or knowledge could suggest is poured in the copious fury of near four hundred pages. In the strain and on the plan Mr. Burke was writing, he might have written on to as many thousands. When the tongue or the pen is let loose in a frenzy of passion, it is the man, and not the subject, that becomes exhausted.' [Paine, 100] Marx, notoriously, wrote of Burke, in a footnote in *Capital*, that 'This sycophant, who, in the pay of the English oligarchy, played the part of romantic opponent of the French Revolution, just as, in the pay of the North American colonies at the beginning of the troubles in America, he had played the liberal against the English oligarchy, was a vulgar bourgeois through and through....true to the laws of God and Nature, he always sold himself in the best market!'[1] However accurate this expression of ire is as an indication of Marx's dislike for Burke, it is quite inaccurate as a description of Burke's attitude towards money and commerce. Burke, in fact, did not like the commercial forces that were emerging in his time to vie with the landed interests upon which, in Burke's view, the stability of the British constitution rested. 'Burke reveals himself... as hostile to the new moneyed, non-aristocratic interest across the Channel, that is to say the men who were lending to the government and thus acquiring vast powers....Burke neither supported [the bourgeoisie] nor had any way of knowing that half a century on they would have risen to irresistible political prominence.' [O'Keeffe, 104]

So, was Burke a mere gun for hire, as Marx none too subtly suggests? Did he choose sides to suit his purse? Jesse Norman evaluates this criticism with commendable clarity. If Paine and Marx are correct in their estimation of Burke's character, this 'cuts at the root not merely of Burke's achievement but of his moral authority….if Burke is simply a paid propagandist, a lackey wearing the livery of others…then for all his literary and intellectual brilliance he cannot be worth of our respect.' [Norman, 181] Norman, unsurprisingly, takes a positive view of Burke's life and achievements. Indeed, he not only defends Burke against his critics but goes so far as to portray him as 'the earliest post-modern thinker' and a 'more radical thinker even than Karl Marx himself.' [Norman, 183] One's views on this matter are likely to be coloured by one's political predispositions and about this, as about taste, there's no disputing. For the purposes of this chapter, I will take Burke's *bona fides* as a given and try to assess the value of his thought on its merits, independently of his personal history and circumstances.

A VINDICATION OF NATURAL SOCIETY

In 1756, at the tender age of 27, Edmund Burke published his first work, *A Vindication of Natural Society: or, A View of the Miseries and Evils arising to Mankind from every Species of Artificial Society.* [Burke 1997a, 129-184] It is written in the form of a letter from an unnamed noble writer coming to the end of his public life to another nobleman just entering upon his public career. As its title suggests, the *Vindication* purports to demonstrate the evils that accrue to mankind from what Burke terms 'artificial society,' which is to say, from society organised on the basis of political structures. Despite its being Burke's first publication and his only sustained theoretical treatment of politics, the *Vindication* attracts relatively little attention from scholars today, still less from the general reader. 'The *Vindication of Natural Society* and the *Philosophical Inquiry into the Origin of Our Ideas on the Sublime and Beautiful* have always seemed the wayward children in Burke's family of writings. They seem unrelated to the central concerns of his later work, and are usually mentioned in passing as youthful ventures designed merely to secure Burke's entrance into the public world of London culture.' So writes Isaac Kramnick in *The Rage of Edmund Burke: Portrait of an Ambivalent Conservative.* [Kramnick, 88] This common appraisal of the *Vindication* isn't one that Kramnick shares. Those scholars who do direct their attention towards the first of these wayward children by and large take it to be an early and not wholly successful attempt at satirising the Deistic writings of Bolingbroke.[2] Nevertheless, at the time of its publication, some of Burke's contemporaries took him to be in earnest in his denunciation of 'artificial society'. Some fifty years ago, Murray Rothbard published an article arguing that the arguments and conclusions of the *Vindication* should be taken literally. [Rothbard, 1958] Rothbard's effort at literal interpretation was immediately rejected by John C. Weston— '[T]he ironic intent [of the *Vindication*] is immediately clear to all serious students of Burke's thought'—and Rothbard's view cannot, on the whole, be said to have gained critical favour in the intervening years. [see Weston, 441]

So, just what does Burke have to say in the *Vindication*, taking it at face value?[3] He begins by reflecting on the changeableness of human nature, its constant restlessness. 'The Mind of man itself,' he writes, 'is too active and restless a Principle ever to settle on the true Point of Quiet. It discovers every Day some craving Want in a Body, which really wants but little. It every Day invents some new artificial Rule to guide that Nature which if left to itself were the best and surest guide.' [Burke 1997a, 137-138] Burke echoes the Lockean commonplace that the State of Nature is inherently inconvenient. These inconveniences include: 'Want of Union, Want of mutual Assistance, Want of a common Arbitrator to resort to in their Difference.' [Burke 1997a, 138] From the product of the union of the sexes comes man's first society with its resultant conveniences; this, Burke calls *Natural Society*. Had we but stopped at this point in our social development, all would be well but, impelled by our restless nature, unable to leave well enough alone, and impressed by the convenience of natural society, we supposed that a *Political Society* formed of the union of many families would be, by analogy, even better than natural society. [Burke 1997a, 138-139] Alas, it wasn't to be so.

Political societies, or states, have a double relation; *externally* to other states, and *internally* to their own citizens. The external relations of states are characterised by war: 'War is the Matter which fills all History, and consequently the only, or almost the only View in which we can see the External of political Society, is in a hostile Shape; and the only Actions, to which we have always seen and still see all of them intent, are such, as tend to the Destruction of one another.' [Burke 1997a, 141] Burke now proceeds to give an historical or quasi-historical account of the ravages of war that runs to several pages. [Burke 1997a, 142-151] The figures he mentions of those killed and the extent of the armies employed may, by modern standards of historical scholarship, be exaggerated but they were drawn from the data available to him at the time he wrote. This catalogue of death and destruction is, according to Burke, chargeable almost exclusively to Political Society: 'Political Society is chargeable with much the greatest Part of this Destruction of the Species.' [Burke 1997a, 152] Man in a state of nature has much less capacity for spectacular human destruction. 'In a State of Nature, it had been impossible to find a Number of Men, sufficient for such Slaughters, agreed in the same bloody Purpose; or allowing that they might have come to such an Agreement, (an impossible Supposition) yet the Means that simple Nature has supplied them with, are by no means adequate to such an end; many Scratches, many Bruises undoubtedly would have been received upon all hands; but only a few, a very few Deaths.' [Burke 1997a, 152] The staggering amount of destruction by human beings of one another evidenced in our sanguinary history isn't the result of some natural uncontrollable aggression inhabiting the breast of the individual: 'Whoever will take the pains to consider the Nature of Society, will find they result directly from its Constitution. For as *Subordination*, or in other Words, the Reciprocation of Tyranny, and Slavery, is requisite to support these Societies, the Interest, the Ambition, the Malice, or the Revenge, nay even the Whim and Caprice of one ruling Man among them, is enough to arm all the rest, without any private Views of their own, to the worst and blackest Purposes...' [Burke 1997a, 153]

From the aspect of the state's internal relations to its own subjects, Burke offers an argument against artificial (which is to say, political) Society that, even if all that he has offered so far should be rejected, would suffice to destroy its pretensions. No government, he believes, can exist without infringing the basic requirements of justice that are incumbent on every individual. All writers on politics agree—and they are supported in their agreement by experience—that all governments frequently violate the requirements of justice, substituting deception for truth, convenience for honesty, and subordinating all to the political interest. 'The Whole of this Mystery of Iniquity is called the Reason of State. It is a Reason, which I own I cannot penetrate. What Sort of a Protection is this of the general Right, what is maintained by infringing the Rights of Particulars? What sort of Justice is this, which is inforced by Breaches of its own Laws?' [Burke 1997a, 154] He finds it difficult to accept that political institutions that are deemed to be suitable for the furthering of the ends of human society should find it necessary to go against what every individual instinctively knows to avoid. 'But no wonder, that what is set up in Opposition to the State of Nature, should preserve itself by trampling upon the Law of Nature.' [Burke 1997a, 154]

Burke now proceeds to examine the various forms of government: despotism, aristocracy, and democracy, demonstrating the intrinsic shortcomings of them all.[4] In case it should be thought that the problems he notices are merely problems of application, he tells us plainly: 'In vain you tell me that Artificial Government is good, but that I fall out only with the Abuse. The Thing! The thing itself is the Abuse!' [Burke 1997a, 167] and he continues over another ten pages to exhibit the shortcomings of all forms of government. [Burke 1997a, 166-76]

He concludes by pointing out the appalling disparities of wealth that result from the creation of artificial society, with the consequence that only a few are really free while the many occupy a position of virtual slavery. Once again, he contrasts the artificial with the natural: 'The Poor by their excessive Labour, and the Rich by their enormous Luxury, are set upon a Level, and rendered equally ignorant of any Knowledge which might conduce to their Happiness. A Dismal View of the Interior of all Civil Society. The lower Part broken and ground down by the most cruel Oppression; and the Rich by their artificial Method of Life bring worse Evils on themselves, than their Tyranny could possibly inflict on those below them. Very different is the Prospect of the Natural State. Here there are no Wants which Nature gives, and in this State Men can be sensible of no other Wants, which are not to be supplied by a very moderate Degree of Labour.' [Burke 1997a, 180-81] So much for a summary of the contents of the *Vindication*.

Was Burke serious in saying all this or was he indulging in an elaborate exercise in satire, irony or parody? The majority of Burke interpreters take Burke's intent in the *Vindication* to be satirical or ironic. Ian Ousby, for example, remarks that the *Vindication* was 'an ironical treatise examining the divisions in society...' [Ousby, 136] Iain Hampsher-Monk notes that in the *Vindication*, Burke 'satirized the confident rationalism which the First Viscount Bolingbroke, in his posthumously published Philosophical Works (1754), had applied critically to religion.' [Hampsher-Monk 1998] He believes the *Vindication* to be 'an ironic 'defence' of the state of nature, exercised through a hyperbolically rationalist critique of existing society, in a kind of *reductio ad absurdum* of Deist arguments...' [Hampsher-Monk, §1] Some interpreters, without doubting the overall satirical or ironic purpose of the work, are none the less aware that its satire or irony wasn't immediately evident to some of its readers and, to the extent that this was so, the *Vindication* must be judged to have failed of its purpose. Others see an element of the double-edged in the *Vindication*.

So, then, firmly on the side of the satirical/ironic interpretation of the *Vindication* we have Ian Ousby, Iain Hampsher-Monk and also David Berman [2009], Peter Stanlis, F. P. Lock, George H. Smith [2014], John C. Weston, Liam Barry, Woodrow Wilson—yes, that Woodrow Wilson! Apart from some of Burke's contemporaries, one of the few people unequivocally on the non–satirical side of the fence is Murray N. Rothbard. Only one other person besides Rothbard that I know of has offered an argument against taking the *Vindication* as a satire, and he does so on the grounds that its claims conflict with the greater body of Burke's work. Patrick Ford argues, however, that the anarchism of the *Vindication* can be found in Burke's anti-revolutionary writings. 'An analysis of Burke's writings and speeches show that he had an affinity for liberty his entire life and almost always saw the State as the enemy of freedom *and* of traditional order.' [Ford, passim] To support his claim, he cites a passage from Burke's *Speech on Conciliation with America*: 'Pursuing the same plan (of punishing by the denial of Government) to still greater lengths, we wholly abrogated the antient government of Massachuset. We were confident, that the first feeling, if not the very prospect of anarchy, would instantly enforce a compleat submission. The experiment was tried. A new, strange, unexpected face of things appeared. Anarchy is found tolerable. A vast province has now subsisted, and subsisted in a considerable degree of health and vigour, for near a twelve-month, without Governor, without public Council, without Judges, without Executive Magistrates.'[5]

Together with Patrick Ford, Murray Rothbard takes a very different view of the *Vindication* from the majority of commentators, seeing it as 'perhaps the first modern expression of rationalistic and individualistic anarchism.' [Rothbard 1958, 114] Was he right to take this view? Although Rothbard acknowledges that scholars on the whole accept Burke's apparent revelation in the 'Preface' to the second edition of the *Vindication* that the work was intended to be a satire, he nevertheless believes that a sober analysis of its contents reveals little that is either satirical or ironic. Why did Burke reveal his real design in the 'Preface' to the second edition? In Rothbard's view, he did so because, upon the commencement of his political career, he found his widely known authorship of the *Vindication* to be an embarrassment and so attempted to pass it off as a kind of *jeu d'esprit*. 'If the work were really a satire,' asks

Rothbard, 'why only proclaim it as such when a rising political career was at stake?' [Rothbard 1958, 118]

At the time when he made his claim, Rothbard did so with some justification, for it seems to have been commonly accepted that the 'Preface' to the second edition of the *Vindication*, in which Burke is taken to have revealed its satirical purpose, appeared in 1765, nine years after the *Vindication*'s first publication. It was also accepted by some that the point of the revelation of the *Vindication*'s apparently real purpose in the Preface wasn't unrelated to Burke's parliamentary ambitions which became manifest about this time. T. W. Copeland quotes Robert Murray to the effect that 'when his [Burke's] election to parliament was likely in 1765, he published a new edition of his *Vindication of Natural Society*, and in the preface he assured his readers that the design of it was entirely ironical.' [cited in Copeland, 141] The point of Burke's clarification of purpose, according to Murray, was to limit any possible damage that an imprudent juvenile publication might do to his parliamentary career. Copeland points out that in holding this opinion, Murray appears to be relying on John Morley who wrote that 'It is significant that in 1765, when Burke saw his chance of a seat in parliament, he thought it worth while to print a second edition of his *Vindication* with a preface to assure his readers that the design of it was ironical.' [cited in Copeland, 141] But Copeland notes that the second edition of the *Vindication*, containing the 'Preface' with the admission of ironical intent was, in fact, produced in 1757, just one year after the original first edition and not nine years, as had been thought. Unfortunately, then, for the *ad hominem* aspect of Rothbard's argument, given that it now seems certain that the Preface appeared just one year after the *Vindication*'s original appearance (at which time Burke has no political prospects), it is unlikely that Burke used the revelation in the 'Preface' to explain its purpose away so as to smooth his path to a political career. [see Smith, 2014]

Rothbard may have been wrong (although justifiably so) in attributing Burke's apparent *volte face* to a desire to explain away something that might damage his embryonic parliamentary career but he can be forgiven for his failure to detect the satirical intent of the work itself when such an intent was equally undetectable to such an acute contemporary of Burke as William Godwin. So convincing was the case made for the shortcomings of 'artificial society' by Burke that even today, few readers of this pamphlet would, without exterior prompting, spontaneously take it to be either satirical or ironic. It has few of the usual hallmarks of satire: hyperbolic exaggeration, the presentation of patent absurdities as if they were commonplaces; the communication of local truths as if they were universal, as in Jane Austen's opening to *Pride and Prejudice*: 'It is a truth universally acknowledged that a single man in possession of a good fortune must be in want of a wife' which is a universal truth only if the universe is limited to early nineteenth-century matchmaking mothers with daughters to dispose of in marriage. Readers might care to recall the words of Burke's contemporary, Richard Hurd, who remarked that an erstwhile ironist 'should take care by a constant exaggeration to make the *ridicule* shine through the Imitation. Whereas this Vindication is everywhere enforc'd, not only in the language, and on the principles of L. Bol., but with so apparent, or rather so real an earnestness, that half his purpose is sacrificed to the other' [see Lock, 85] and the similar sentiments of William Godwin, the first chapter of whose *Enquiry Concerning Political Justice*, an anarchist critique of the State, is unashamedly modelled on the *Vindication*.

It isn't difficult to see why some readers of the *Vindication* took it at face value. The writing has a passionate intensity and its indignation has a ring of truth that belies any satirical or ironic reading. Isaac Kramnick points to the *Vindication*'s 'moving description of the grinding poverty of the poor and its radical assault on the oppression by the great and powerful who are responsible for the wretchedness of nine-tenths of humanity who "drudge through life".' [Kramnick, 90] Where is the irony in this? This indignation is, for Kramnick, no mere ironic moment for he believes that we can find in Burke's *Reformer* of 1748 a very similar exhibition of indignation, this time in a context that no one takes to be ironic or satirical. There Burke writes, of 'the natural equality of mankind,' and its degeneration into the rich in their gilded coaches and their velvet couches, 'followed by the miserable wretches, whose labour supports them." [Kramnick, 90] Similarly, the seriousness of the radical views expressed in the *Tracts Relative to the Laws Against Popery in Ireland* is never called into question but 'This is a radicalism quite akin to that of the *Vindication*, which may well explain why Burke never published *The Tracts* in his lifetime.' [Kramnick, 93] Here Burke is, according to Kramnick, saying that 'men set up artificial institutions of government and law to protect the cherished rights of natural society' but 'the tendency of these artificial institutions is to demolish natural equality and obliterate natural rights. This is a far cry from the Burke we are used to.'[6] In the end, however, Kramnick appears to come down on the side of the majority of Burke commentators in the irony-satire/non-irony-satire debate, writing that in the Preface to the *Vindication*, 'Burke...revealed to all the ironic intent of the book....The essay was no radical threat, he insisted, merely an ironic ploy with which to ridicule Bolingbroke's irreligion.' [Kramnick, 89] Nevertheless, he goes on to ask 'But was it pure irony? Is it, indeed, possible to write ironically without giving some weight to what is ridiculed?' [Kramnick, 89] His thesis is that Burke was an ambivalent conservative and that in the 1750s, he 'was wrestling with his own ambivalent social views' [Kramnick, 89] so that the *Vindication* was at one and the same time a radical manifesto *and* a conservative apologia. As such, Kramnick is persuaded that the *Vindication* is more than mere irony.

Perhaps the most nuanced approach to the *Vindication* is that taken by Frank Pagano who believes that it 'reveals the deepest grounds of his [Burke's] politics. It is his only purely theoretical writing on politics. It also is a poetic attack upon the pretensions of political theory and a defense of practice.' [Pagano, 446] Pagano believes that the *Vindication* has either been read too seriously or not seriously enough. He is in agreement with Liam Barry in holding that 'The reader should seek the meaning of the *Vindication* in a concealed, below the surface, plot.' [Pagano, 448] While he does not deny that there are elements of satire in the text, he also does not believe that they are structurally significant.

'It is not sufficient to read the work as a satire of one or more writers. This seems hardly hidden, and it is not, strictly speaking, part of the plot.' [Pagano, 448] In this, Pagano departs from the main current of commentators. On the other hand, he is also opposed to reading the *Vindication* as a straightforward account of Burke's political theory, taking the fictional form in which the work is written as being of more than stylistic significance. Why, one might wonder, does Burke choose this fictional form for his earliest work? Was it simply to conceal his identity as author? Hardly; that could have been done by removing his name from the title page of a straightforward dissertation. According to Pagano, 'Burke chooses the fictional form not so much because he wishes to conceal his thought, or merely to ridicule that of another, but because he finds fiction to be the best form by which to convey his ideas about politics.' [Pagano, 448] He believes that Burke deliberately juxtaposes a series of human inconsistencies in the *Vindication*, all the better to make evident the point that man is a creature constituted of clashing elements. This juxtaposition has, according to Pagano, 'led some readers to regard the work as a failure. Others adopt the one-sided interpretations mentioned above.' [Pagano, 448]

In holding this view, Pagano comes close to Kramnick's thesis that Burke was deeply ambivalent in his political views. The literary structure of the *Vindication*, then, according to Pagano, consists of a plot and an underplot. The plot is essentially a critique of liberal theory; the underplot is a conservative defence of liberal practice. The division of the text into plot and underplot finds justification, Kramnick believes, in Burke's preface in which he speaks of an under-plot that is more significant than the apparent design.

Although Pagano and Kramnick approach one another's positions, one difference between them might be that Kramnick, while arguing for an unresolved tension in the *Vindication*, does not explicitly locate the elements of this tension in a two-level structure, as does Pagano. On the surface, the level of the plot, the *Vindication* seems to support the judgement that 'viewed from the foundations, no society and no government are legitimate.' [Pagano, 449] The *Vindication* appears to condemn 'all civil society and neglects to vindicate... natural society.' [Pagano, 451] A return to man's natural condition not being possible, the recipient of the letter 'must either engage in politics or lead a meaningless life.' [Pagano, 452] According to Pagano, what looks to be the letter's advocacy of anarchy is a mere appearance which, when eliminated, leads the letter-writer to recommend a conservative position—the underplot. The apparently strong condemnation of the immorality of government—its 'Reasons of State'—what Burke calls 'this Mystery of Iniquity' is, in Pagano's judgement, simply part of a dialectical strategy. He writes: 'The Vindication *seems* to be a display of how liberal theories of right are continually violated by liberal schemes of government. It is this repeated history of failure that leads to the conclusion that civil society should be abandoned. Indeed, it is hard to see how this final conclusion is wrong if all the intermediate conclusions are correct. If no society secures right, and if, in the state of nature, right exists, a return to the state of nature and the abandonment of civil society would seem to be right.' [Pagano, 454. Emphasis added] But this is not Burke's real position. That position is, rather, to 'attack the premise that no society secures right.' [He, 455]

For Pagano, the *Vindication*, in the end, isn't an either-or but a both-and. Pagano concludes that 'the *Vindication* is a defense of both British artificial or civil religion and the Hobbesian-Lockean natural right because natural rights philosophy is part of the British civil religion....Thus Burke vindicates, at one and the same time, natural society and artificial society.' [Pagano, 461] Are those who take the *Vindication* at face value, either as being completely serious or completely satirical, wholly mistaken? No. This is because 'The letter's surface...is correct and much of its teaching unconcealed. Each individual criticism is nearly accurate. Although the work is not wholly a satire, its cumulative effect is satiric, because the assumption that reason can uncover the whole truth about society is wrong.' [Pagano, 462]

BURKE AND SOCIETY

In the BBC TV series, *Blackadder*, Edmund Blackadder, Prince George's devious factotum, puts his idiotic sidekick, Baldrick, forward as a candidate for election in a rotten borough. He is interviewed by an ever-so-slightly anachronistic BBC political correspondent who is told by Blackadder that 'we in the Adder Party are going to fight this campaign on issues, not personalities.' The interviewer asks why this is so, only to be blandly informed that it is 'because our candidate doesn't have a personality.'[7] In a similar way, much of the problem with trying to come to terms with Burke's political philosophy arises from that fact that he doesn't seem to have a political philosophy or, at least, not one that can simply be located in a treatise or text since Burke, apart from the *Vindication*, wrote no treatise specifically on political philosophy: 'Burke's political philosophy is nowhere systematically expounded, writes John Plamenatz, 'it is revealed, sometimes deliberately and sometimes only by implication, in his writings about particular affairs, English, American and French.' [Plamenatz, 333] What political philosophy he has, if he has one at all, must be gleaned from various passages in his voluminous writings. Truth to tell, Burke's theory is more of an anti-theory, his ideology, more of an anti-ideology. He is commonly taken to reject abstruse metaphysical reasoning about politics, in particular, certain accounts of the centrality of reason, in favour of instinct and history, and even if this claim is something of an exaggeration, it is hard to deny its fundamental accuracy. I think it might be fairer to characterise Burke as not so much denying reason a place in politics but as denying a certain abstract, detached and ahistorical view of reason that place. In his *Reflections on the Revolution in France*, he famously remarks that 'We are afraid to put men to live and trade each on his own private stock of reason; because we suspect that this stock in each man is small, and that the individuals would do better to avail themselves of the general bank and capital of nations and of ages.' [Burke 1790/2003, 74]

As was the case with Hume, Burke has no interest in speculating about the origins of society or the state, still less in drawing conclusions from any such conjectural history. He starts with the here and the now. Man is an inherently social being, living in and through society. Society isn't simply an assemblage of individuals but is permeated by institutions of various kinds, which institutions constrain, compete and cooperate with each other, contextualise and shape people's lives, and act as repositories of artistic, technical, social and political knowledge. [see Norman, 199] In a way that anticipates themes that will become familiar to us from the writings of Friedrich Hayek, Burke believes that society isn't the outcome of some grand design or some overall plan. It is, rather, the evolutionary resultant of how people have lived their lives in community over many years, the decisions they have made, individually and in community, the laws that have emerged to regulate their lives together, and the means they have devised to further their ends. A people isn't just a mass of individuals; it is a corporation, an artificial body, in which there are distinct and different yet cooperating parts. Society, at its root, depends upon attachments that precede reason and calculation such as love of one's family and locality and other attachments that radiate outwards from there into one's country and one's nation. Such attachments are constitutive of one's being; they aren't chosen arbitrarily. 'At bottom,' writes Sabine, 'these feelings are instinctive. They make up the massive substructure of human personality in comparison with which reason and self-interest are superficial. At the foundation of society and morals is the need that every man feels to be a part of something larger and more enduring than his own ephemeral existence.' [Sabine, 613]

For Burke, society isn't a product of reason alone. It depends, rather, on instinct and obscure propensities, even on what Burke, defiantly, calls prejudices, by which term he means judgements in *advance* of reason, not necessarily judgements *opposed* to reason. 'Prejudice,' writes Mansfield, 'is not opposed to reason but allied with it. Prejudice supplies the untaught, natural feelings that give permanence to reason....Burke's frank recognition that politics is inseparable from prejudice, that society can never be rational and enlightened, reminds one of Aristotle; but his confidence that prejudice contains sufficient latent wisdom does not. For Aristotle, latent wisdom indeed exists in political opinion, but not in the uncontradicted seclusion that Burke seems to suppose.' [Mansfield, 705] Prejudices are a form of pre-judgement in conformity with long-established customs or traditions, the repository of latent wisdom. The moral virtues trump the intellectual virtues; in particular, prudence, practical wisdom, trumps theoretical science, should the two conflict. If one removes reason and natural law as the foundation of society, one is left with a vacuum that must be filled. Burke filled it with tradition and the elevation of the community in place of the individual. As John Plamenatz remarks, 'Prejudice is not irrational. It is not belief that cannot be justified; it is only belief that most people never trouble to justify and are perhaps incapable of justifying for not knowing how to set about doing so.' [Plamenatz, 343] Prejudices function in the social order more or less as habits (understood in the Aristotelian sense of that term) function in the life of the individual. They are acquired through the exercise of judgement and embodied in our lived experiences, and they enable society as a whole to organise its affairs efficiently, without the need for constant heartfelt examination of circumstances. A prejudice 'enables the individual to live much better than he could live without it; it enables him to rely on much more than his own wisdom and therefore to satisfy many more wants than he could otherwise do.' [Plamenatz, 344]

In addition to the idea of prejudice, Burke also gives a central role in his social and political thinking to the notion of prescription. The claims that are made in a particular society about land ownership, about acceptable modes of government and so on, if they are a product of long usage and custom, must be deemed to have demonstrated their value, independently of any abstract theorising. [see Plamenatz, 341-342] Prescription is, as it were, a kind of socio-political 'survival of the fittest'. Use, long continued, gives title to property even should there be no knowledge of the circumstances of its original acquisition. The notion of prescription that is central to Burke's thought is taken from Roman law. Prescription means that what matters in respect of property is that it be handed on by a train of succession; what the situation was with respect to its original acquisition isn't important. A scheme of government must be presumed to be in order if the people governed by it have been so for long and have flourished under it. A government in place need show no justification for its continuation so long as no other government with a greater title should appear. Boucher's thesis is that 'Burke consciously tried to steer a path between utilitarian pragmatism and the absolutism of natural law by developing a view of the civil social person who was neither motivated wholly by self-interest, nor dependent upon an other-worldly criterion of conduct neglectful of his or her interests. Burke's emphasis upon prejudice, presumption, and prescription provides the basis for anchoring morality and political obligation to the collective wisdom of a community, and not to empirical rational calculation or abstract principles.' [Boucher, 284]There can be no doubt that Burke's conception of society is quasi-organic. Society grows and changes as if it were a living thing. Any attempt at sudden and complete reconstruction is likely to leave the patient dead, though the operation may be deemed successful! The moral dimension of human existence, then, isn't primarily a product of abstract reason but rather of custom, tradition and membership in a particular society. Man is truly human only in and through his social embeddedness.

There is much in what Burke says that resonates with our lived experience. We are constituted in large part by things outside our range of choice. Our language, our family, and our locality—all these are simply given to us whether we will or not. Does a libertarian have to deny any of this? I don't think so. Indeed, a libertarian can accept, to a large extent, the presumptive legitimacy of existing structures but without conceding any inviolable status to them, and a libertarian can be a gradualist in respect of change, although a rapid gradualist. Such is the complexity of existing institutions that any immediate radical change is likely to be wildly destructive and, in fact, inimical to a coherent and improved restructuring.

THE BRITISH CONSTITUTION

Burke held that the functional balance in the British Constitution of King, Lords and Commons is justified not by appeal to any grand theory but simply by prescription. In this, perhaps surprisingly, he finds himself on much the same ground as Hume who also argued that social and political arrangements are largely conventional and are justified, if justification is needed, by custom and use. Just as the ultimate justification of property is prescription, not some abstract conception of title, so too the ground of the constitution is also prescription. 'Our constitution is a prescriptive constitution; it is a constitution whose sole authority is that it has existed time out of mind...Prescription is the most solid of all titles, not only to property, but, which is to secure that property, to government....It is a presumption in favour of any settled scheme of government against any untried project....The individual is foolish; the multitude, for the moment, is foolish, when they act without deliberation; but the species is wise, and, when time it given to it, as a species it always acts right.' This is the wisdom of crowds with a vengeance![8]

Politics, for Burke, is an art, not a science, and it requires prudence, experience and knowledge of human nature. He agreed with Hume on the essentially conventional nature of society although he was inclined to regard some social conventions as more or less inviolable, among these being property, religion, and the framework of the British Constitution.[9] The constitution to which Burke was so attached was, in large part, a Whig invention, designed to limit the prerogatives of the king. Burke's view of the British Constitution isn't unlike the customary understanding of the common law. The common law isn't a creature of statute, made by a particular group of people on a wet Wednesday afternoon when they had nothing more exciting to do, but the product of particular real and significant decisions, honed and refined in the furnace of actual practice and detailed decision–making. It isn't made up in advance but elicited from the exigencies of disputes and the necessities of dispute resolution. Similarly, the British Constitution isn't made up from scratch but is a living and vital record of the political decisions and political arrangements that have been tried in the furnace of experience.

BURKE ON MANNERS AND PREJUDICE

Burke thought that manners mattered more than law and even more than morals inasmuch as both law and morals in large measure depend upon manners. In the first of his *Letters on a Regicide Peace*[10] he writes 'Manners are of more importance than laws. Upon them, in a great measure, the laws depend. The law touches us but here and there, and now and then. Manners are what vex or sooth, corrupt or purify, exalt or debase, barbarize or refine us, by a constant, steady, uniform, insensible operation, like that of the air we breathe in. They give their whole form and colour to our lives. According to their quality, they aid morals, they supply them, or they totally destroy them.' [Burke 1796, 126] Among the harshest things he has to say of those who make up the new French regime is that they have systematically set about destroying manners and natural piety.

I find myself in substantial agreement with Burke on this point. If we take manners to encompass all that is customary in society, then law and morals are phenomena emergent from such customs. We do not produce and maintain our manners primarily by some process of detached ratiocination. They arise naturally in the context of social relations. Such judgement as they embody is a kind of pre-reflective judgement, what Burke calls prejudice. Manners as prejudices allow us to act swiftly and surely and rightly in most circumstances without the need for agonised reflection and reasoning. At the root of manners is the notion of restraint, of limitation, of delayed gratification, and its product is a kind of social capital, just as the product of fiscal delayed gratification and restraint is economic capital. Burke contrasts this form of ordered liberty with mere licence, which is the freedom to do whatever one wants to do without regard to circumstances, one's own or others. Libertarianism is compatible with both Burkean liberty or with Burkean licence. A libertarian can arrive at substantially the same conclusions as Burke with this difference, that the restraints and limitations that channel our exercise of liberty must, with the exception of the restraint of actions aggressing against others, be self-imposed, self-accepted, and not imposed by the coercive power of the law. Just how close the Burkean position is to that of a culturally conservative libertarian should be evident from that seminal passage on manners from the *Letters on a Regicide Peace* just quoted.

Jesse Norman characterises the differences between liberalism (in both its classical variety and its libertarian mode) and Burke's approach in the following way. Liberalism 'emphasizes the primacy of the individual; Burke emphasizes the importance of the social order. Liberalism sees freedom as the absence of impediments to the will; Burke sees freedom as ordered liberty. Liberalism believes above all in the power of reason; Burke believes in tradition, habit and 'prejudice.' Liberalism emphasises universal principles; Burke emphasises fact and circumstance. Liberalism is unimpressed by the past; Burke quarries it. Liberalism admires radical change; Burke detests it. The liberal will cannot be made the subject of duties; Burke insists upon them.' [Norman, 282; see fig. 1]

BURKE AND ROUSSEAU

We saw that behind Burke's idea of tradition and custom is a notion of collective wisdom transcending that of the individual and that this idea isn't a million miles away from Rousseau's General Will. But that isn't the only respect in which the two supposedly diametrically opposed thinkers converge. Both also found a central place in their thinking for the emotions. David Boucher remarks that 'Burke certainly subscribes to some notion of a general will when he suggests that the collective rationality of a people must count for much more than individual reason, which is often flawed and subject to the pressures of the moment.' [Boucher, 292] Despite the similarities in their thinking, Burke held Rousseau in contempt and no doubt was genuine in holding this opinion. He saw Rousseau as the apostle of extreme individualism, as a man in the grip of an idea which, by jettisoning morals and law and manners, couldn't help but destroy society. He attacks Rousseau, describing him as a man who is 'a lover of his kind but a hater of his kindred,' a Mrs Jellyby *avant la lettre*, as it were.[11]

Yet, Rousseau and Burke had more in common that might at first appear to be the case. For both men, society, the group, was of more importance than the individual. Similarly, whereas Burke and Hume appear to, and do, agree in their overall conservative tendencies, there are significant differences between them also. Hume's cast of mind is essentially utilitarian and pragmatic; Burke, on the other hand, commended an attitude of reverence to the past and to tradition that Hume would have had no truck with. In the end, the philosopher who most resembles Burke is Hegel. Hegel attempts to give a systematic account of what in Burke is, at its best, inchoate and scattered.

Fig .1

Liberalism (and Libertarianism)	Burke
Individual	Social Order
Freedom as absence of impediment to the will	Freedom as ordered liberty
Reason	Tradition, habit, prejudice
Universal Principles	Facts, circumstances
The past is of no great significance	The past as the root of the present
Radical change	No radical change
The individual will is not subject to duties	The individual will is subject to duties

It is important always to bear in mind just how limited government was in Burke's time. This may be something that we know but there is perhaps a tendency to forget it and, anachronistically, to dress the government of the eighteenth century in twenty-first century clothes. The principal tasks of government in Burke's time were the maintenance of public order, defence against threats from abroad, the management of foreign affairs generally and to some extent trade. Apart from the administration of the Poor Law, an Elizabethan invention made necessary by the suppression of the monasteries, government had no interest in the provision of welfare. Governments thus limited in their aims and ambitions fit well Michael Oakeshott's description of the proper function of government. 'And the office of government is not to impose other beliefs and activities upon its subjects, not to tutor or to educate them, not to make them better or happier in another way, not to direct them, to galvanize them into action, to lead them or to co-ordinate their activities so that no occasion of conflict shall occur: the function of government is merely to rule....The image of the ruler is the umpire whose business is to administer the rules of the game, or the chairman who governs the debate according to known rules but does not himself participate in it.' [Oakeshott 1991, 427]

BURKE—DEFENDER OF LIBERTY?

In respect of his attitude towards liberty, Burke appears to be both Jekyll and Hyde. There is Burke the defender of the oppressed in Ireland, American and India; and then there is the Burke who castigates the French Revolution. 'How,' asks McClelland, 'could such a consistent defender of American liberties turn almost overnight into the scourge of the liberties of the French?' [McClelland, 422] The clash between the British Government and the American colonists resulted from a mutual assertion of abstract rights. On the British side, the parliamentary sovereign right to tax; on the American side, the assertion of the right to have taxation only if they had representation. Both sides were at fault, the British perhaps more so. But the case of the revolution in France was different. 'The only difference between the French and American cases is that the French Revolution began in the name of an ideology, while the Americans were eventually forced into ideology which made them revolutionaries.' [McClelland, 423]

It is often argued that Burke was inconsistent, inasmuch as he supported Ireland against oppression, the American colonists likewise, and the Indians against the depredations of the East India Company but objected strongly to the revolution in France. Was he inconsistent? Many of his contemporaries thought so but George Sabine thinks not. At the root of Burke's thinking was an unshakeable belief that political institutions were complicated systems founded on prescription and custom, growing from the past into the future, in which the accumulated wisdom of a people could be found. Against the common charge that Burke was inconsistent in supporting the American colonists while rejecting the French Revolution and all its works and pomps, Norman replies that in fact Burke accepted and gave his support to not one but five revolutions: the Glorious Revolution of 1688, the American War of Independence, the struggle for Corsican Independence, Polish resistance to Russian intervention in 1768, and resistance to the East India Company. [see Norman, 251-252] If this is so, what was so different about the French Revolution that it merited a very different response from Burke? The revolutions or resistances that Burke supported all involved a struggle against specific wrongs, in particular, against the arbitrary exercise of power. But the French Revolution wasn't of this kind. It wasn't an attempt to defend a particular way of life against aggression but rather the wholesale destruction of particular ways of life in the pursuit of abstract and rootless rights. Sabine thinks that whereas the revolution in France did not, in essentials, change any of Burke's ideas, it did deeply unsettle him, so much so that it 'unbalanced his judgment, revealed hatreds that had been decently masked, and produced a flood of irresponsible rhetoric in which his impartiality, his judgement of history, and his customary mastery of facts were largely lost.' [Sabine, 608]

In his *Speech on Conciliation with the Colonies*, Burke had claimed that the colonists had a great attachment to liberty, not to liberty as some ahistorical abstract principle but liberty as that had grown and developed in the context of English history and society. In a similar way, Burke is willing to endorse a notion of human rights provided that they aren't merely abstract, divorced from tradition, law, history and custom. Burke has no interest in abstract rights. What *are* these abstract rights? Where do they come from? Why these and only these rights? Such rights as engage his interest are the actual concrete rights embodied in political tradition and custom. He does not deny natural rights but sees them as applying only to men in a pre-political condition. But men today do not live in such a condition and it is absurd to base our conduct on rights that attach to it. Inasmuch as Burke is willing to recognise such things as natural rights, he recognises them only when clothed with the forms of actual embodiment in concrete political circumstances. His image is that natural rights are like light rays that pierce a dense medium and are thereby refracted. Burke isn't necessarily opposed to change but only to radical or revolutionary change that would have the effect of destroying the carefully cultivated garden of society and substituting in its place a ploughed field bereft of any living thing except weeds. Political change, for Burke, is conceived of as a kind of continuous organic growth, a change from seed to plant, from youth to age. 'In this Character of the Americans,' he writes, 'a love of Freedom is the predominating feature, which marks and distinguishes the whole....This fierce spirit of Liberty is stronger in the English colonies probably than in any other people of the earth....They are devoted not only to Liberty, but to Liberty according to English ideas, and on English principles. Abstract Liberty, like other mere abstractions, is not to be found'[12]

BURKE'S PRIMEVAL CONTRACT

Edmund Burke offers us an account of the foundations of political order that is, in essence, non-contractual. His account begins, perhaps oddly, with the claim that 'Society is indeed a contract' which might seem to undermine my statement that his account is non-contractual, but Burke's idea of the social contract is a very special one. Ordinary contracts, what Burke calls 'subordinate contracts for objects of mere occasional interest' concern themselves with such low matters as a 'partnership agreement in a trade of pepper and coffee, calico, or tobacco,' but the contract that concerns the very foundation of the state is not of this order. This contract, which has now, inexplicably, become a partnership, 'is to be looked on with other reverence, because it isn't a partnership in things subservient only to the gross animal existence of a temporary and perishable nature. It is a partnership in all science; a partnership in all art; a partnership in every virtue and in all perfection.'[13] And because the objects of this contract/partnership cannot, it seems be achieved immediately, nor even in a few generations, it turns out to subsist not only between one living being and another but also between the living, the dead and the unborn. It seems that this political partnership (which has once again been re-termed a contract) is a species of transcendent entity, of which particular political partnerships are mere local habitations: 'Each contract of each particular state is but a clause in the great primeval contract of eternal society, linking the lower with the higher natures, connecting the visible and invisible world, according to a fixed compact sanctioned by the inviolable oath which holds all physical and all moral natures, each in their appointed place.' [*Reflections*, 82-83]

The primeval and eternal partnership/contract (now become a compact) is, it appears, sanctioned by an inviolable oath, though what the wording of this oath is, who takes it and when it has been or is to be taken, is mysteriously left unspecified. This partnership/contract/compact has the further interesting characteristic that it is 'not subject to the will of those who by an obligation above them, and infinitely superior, are bound to submit their will to that law.' The eternal and primeval contract/partnership/ compact/law (it has now become a law) demands the submission of our wills. One may not, except under some kind of (unspecified) necessity that is not chosen but rather thrust upon one, refuse to submit to this contract/partnership/compact/law: 'The municipal corporations of that universal kingdom are not morally at liberty at their pleasure, and on their speculations of a contingent improvement, wholly to separate and tear asunder the bands of their subordinate community and to dissolve it into an unsocial, uncivil, unconnected chaos of elementary principles. It is the first and supreme necessity only, a necessity that is not chosen but chooses, a necessity paramount to deliberation, that admits no discussion and demands no evidence, which alone can justify a resort to anarchy.' [Burke 1790/2003, 82-83]

A voluntary and rational rejection of the transcendent, eternal and primeval contract/partnership/compact/law would, according to Burke, have devastating consequences. That way, it seems, madness lies: 'But if that which is only submission to necessity should be made the object of choice, the law is broken, nature is disobeyed, and the rebellious are outlawed, cast forth, and exiled from this world of reason, and order, and peace, and virtue, and fruitful penitence, into the antagonist world of madness, discord, vice, confusion, and unavailing sorrow.' [Burke 1790/2003, 82-83] It is interesting, however, to note that, some fifteen years before he wrote these words, Burke was somewhat less pessimistic about the consequences of a rejection of the transcendent political order on which he was to wax so eloquent: 'A new, strange, unexpected face of things appeared. Anarchy is found tolerable. A vast province has now subsisted, and subsisted in a considerable degree of health and vigour, for near a twelvemonth, without governor, without public council, without judges, without executive magistrates.'[14]

It is hard not to be carried away on the floodtide of Burke's eloquence, an eloquence he honed, no doubt, in Trinity College's debating society, in a tradition not yet atrophied. To appreciate the passage properly requires it to be read as a unit and not piecemeal as I have presented it. To subject it to such rude analysis as I have done might seem to be taking a spade to a soufflé (as someone once remarked about a critic of the writings of P. G. Wodehouse). Frank Turner remarks 'An unrestrained passion infuses his pages and drives his argument, while an ornate, distant, unfamiliar rhetoric interferes with the persuasiveness of his presentation—in fact, it almost blocks our access to it. Burke's pulsating emotion and the rhetorical vehemence of his assault on the political violence in France press the reader to take refuge in the very rationality he denounces.' [in Burke 1790/2003, xiv-xv] On the other hand, Conor Cruise O'Brien plays down the criticism of rhetorical excess: 'There is, in reality, very little rhetoric, quantitatively speaking...Most of the book...is made up of plain, cogent argument.' [in Burke 1790/2003, 219]

Whatever the merits of the claim and counter-claim in the context of Burke's *Essay* as a whole, the passage on the primeval contract just considered isn't a page from a novel nor yet a stanza of a poem nor a leader in a newspaper of record but is, presumably, a serious and rational attempt to reject mundane contractarianism as the root of the legitimacy of the political order. Shorn of its rhetoric, however, it appears to be entirely devoid of argument, amounting to a bare assertion that there's a great primeval eternal contract (in Burke's very special sense of that term) that demands our obedience. Where this contract came from, what its terms are, precisely why we are bound by it—none of these issues is explicitly articulated. Nor is it easy to see how Burke reconciles such sentiments with his commitment to Whiggery with its apotheosis of the so-called Glorious Revolution of 1688 which, ironically, justified itself by charging James II with breaking the original contract between king and people! [Turner ed., 24] The best that can be said for this passage is that it contains a tacit pragmatic appeal to much the same fear that one finds at the root of Hobbes's *Leviathan*, namely, that without the state chaos ensues. There is a deep irony in this, given that it would be harder to find two thinkers more diametrically opposed to one other than Burke and Hobbes and that 'What Burke deplored in his particular characterization of the policies of the new French Government was their embodiment of the absolutist state about which Hobbes had theorized.' [in Burke 1790/2003, xxv]

Commenting on this notorious passage, Sabine notes the conflation of the terms 'state' and 'society' and he writes that this is 'a serious confusion of words, since society, the state, and government have certainly very different meanings. Moreover, the interchange served a rhetorical need in Burke's argument. By it he implied that the revolutionary government in France, in overthrowing the monarchy, had become an enemy to French society and was destroying French civilization. Doubtless Burke meant to assert that this was true, but he had no right to cast the argument in a form that begged the question. Overthrowing a government and destroying a society are quite different things, and there are many sides of a civilization that depend very little on the state.' [Sabine, 615-616]

Not everyone is as sceptical about the Burkean super-contract as I am. Jesse Norman remarks, correctly, that Burke's contract is very different from that of Hobbes, Locke and Rousseau, and regards it as an 'extraordinarily interesting and powerful idea.' [Norman, 202] One might be tempted to say that Burke's contract is different from those of Hobbes, Locke and Rousseau simply because whatever their other merits or demerits, the contracts of Hobbes, Locke and Rousseau *are* contracts whereas Burke's contract is not! But perhaps there's more to it than that. Burke, despite his talk of contracts, is in fact much closer to Hume in holding that a contract—a real contract, not his metaphysical one—is unnecessary to ground political obligation, such obligation arising in some other way. I am in agreement with Burke in rejecting the contractual theories of Hobbes, Locke and Rousseau; I am in agreement with him in seeing *de facto* political orders as arising from a confluence of historical accidents, tradition, custom, caprice and acquiescence. Nevertheless, I see all this as merely an historical matter-of-fact description of the *status quo*, not a justification—and a justification is just what is needed.

What *is*, perhaps, defensible in Burke's thought is his reminder to us that human beings aren't disembodied rational beings but are fleshly creatures of experience, custom, habit, historical precedent and religion, and that there's a perpetual danger that a concern with abstract rights runs the risk of dissolving those prior and necessary human roots that perform the constitutive role for man in his social identity that memory does for his psychological identity. Moreover, to his eternal credit, Burke was forthright in his condemnation of the contempt for property evidenced in the land confiscations and fiscal depredations of the revolutionary French government, believing that such contempt for property couldn't but eventually extend to persons as well, a belief vindicated by history. 'Burke…understood one's own personhood and body to be a mode of property and thus considered that what had begun as confiscation of church lands could end in the deprivation of citizens' lives by the revolutionary state.' [Turner ed., xxxiii]

Indeed.

Notes

1 Marx 1867 [1978], 925-926, n. 13. For more on this, see O'Brien in Burke 1790 [1968], 18-19.

2 Henry St John, 1ˢᵗ Viscount Bolingbroke (1678-1751). Ian Harris, the author of the *Stanford Encyclopedia* entry on Burke, presents the more or less standard scholarly interpretation of the *Vindication*. 'This short work, he writes, 'was written in the persona of the recently deceased Henry St. John, Viscount Bolingbroke (1678–1751). Bolingbroke had been a Tory pillar of the state, and therefore of the church too; but the posthumous publication of his philosophical works revealed that far from being an Anglican, he had not been a Christian—but rather a deist. *A Vindication* suggested the ills that Bolingbroke had attributed to the artifice of revealed religion could be paralleled by those generated by civil society. One logic, indeed, was attributable on these terms to both Christianity and civil society: that just as the latter distributed the means of power unequally, so too did Christianity distribute those of salvation unequally (for not everyone had heard, and fewer believed, the Gospel). The deism of Bolingbroke implied the principle that God treated everyone impartially, and that the means to salvation were therefore to be found in a medium available to all, and thus available from the earliest point of human history, namely reason. It was easy to add, as Burke did, that if the principle that such an original nature was the mature expression of God's ordinances were to be applied to civil society, the normative result would be a regression from complex and therefore civilised forms to a simple society, even to animal-like primitiveness—some of the matter of *A Vindication* paraphrases Rousseau's *Discourse on Inequality* (Sewell 1938, 97–114). So Bolingbroke the deist and Bolingbroke the politician could be made to look very much at odds with each other. This gap offered Burke an opening. *A Vindication* satirized Bolingbroke's schizophrenic position, employing a good deal of transparent exaggeration to make 'his' criticisms of civil ('artificial') society seem very absurd: and Burke added a preface to the second edition which made the disjunctive alternatives clear so that even he who ran might read.' [Harris, 11-12]

3 I am aware that Burke is writing a fictional letter and that it is a critical solecism to assume that the views and opinions of characters in a work of fiction are those of the author. Nevertheless, although the *Vindication* is a work of fiction, it is a work of didactic fiction, so I am going to refer to its authorial voice simply as 'Burke'.

4 Burke 1997a, 155-158, 158-161, and 161-167.

5 'Conciliation with the Colonies,' in Burke 1756-1790, 228-229.

6 Kramnick, 93. Ian Harris, who, as we have seen, supports the standard interpretation that the *Vindication* is a satire of work of Bolingbroke comments, 'Yet it is hard not to recognize that Burke himself was telling the reader, in a way that entered the consciousness all the more forcibly because it accompanied entertainment, that civil society really did imply *some* evils, just as he identified losses as well as gains from progress in other connexions. Burke's *Vindication*, speaking in the voice of pseudo-Bolingbroke, lamented the situation of miners: and 'the innumerable servile, degrading, unseemly, unmanly, and often most unwholesome and pestiferous occupations' of 'so many wretches' was lamented by Burke

without any persona, thirty-four years later in *Reflections on the Revolution in France*. Such criticism, taken in itself, is undoubtedly telling. Burke never dissembled the existence of the real misery that he observed in civil society. Instead, he pointed out that wretched practices could not be detached from the larger pattern of habits and institution in which they were implicated, and that this pattern had a beneficial effect. Burke recognized misery, did not deny it, and therefore had a lively sense of the imperfection of arrangements, however civilized they might be. His sense of duality in nature and society resembles Adam Smith's.' [Harris, 12]

7 *Blackadder*, Series III, Episode 1, 'Dish and Dishonesty'.

8 'Reform of Representation in the House of Commons,' 1782, in Burke 1854-1856, Vol. VI, 146f.

9 According to McClelland, inheritance is the key idea to Burke's politics. 'Everyone in England, from the king downwards, has something valuable to hand on to his children. The king inherits his crown, the nobility its privileges, and the common people their rights and liberties. Each of these three instances of inheritance is consistent with, and indeed bolsters up, the others.' [McClelland, 417]

10 Its editor E. J. Payne believes *Letters on a Regicide Peace* to be Burke's masterpiece, rating it even higher than the *Reflections*.

11 See 'A Letter to a Member of the National Assembly,' in Burke 1854-1856, Vol. II, 535-541.

12 'Conciliation with the Colonies' in Burke 1756-1790/1993, 221-222.

13 *Reflections*, 82-83. This and subsequent references to the *Reflections on the Revolution in France* are to the Turner edition.

14 'Conciliation with the Colonies,' in Burke 1756-1790/2003, 228-229.

Chapter 25

HEGEL: TRANSCENDENT GENIUS OR MINDLESS CHARLATAN?

Although the state may originate in violence, it does not rest on it;
violence, in producing the state, has brought into existence
only what is justified in and for itself, namely, laws and a constitution
—Hegel

'The atmosphere of Hegel's State is the enclosed atmosphere
of the small, stuffy waiting rooms of Prussian officials, in which Professor Hegel
probably often waited, when intent upon minor academic intrigues.
It has absolutely no affinity or connection
with the colossal wickedness of Dachau or Auschwitz
—J. N. Findlay

It is unlikely that I shall be taken to say something wildly controversial if I remark that Georg Wilhelm Friedrich Hegel's works are neither easy to read nor easy to understand. During his lifetime, Hegel, controversial then as now, produced a body of work that some take to be the product of a transcendent genius; for example, Iris Murdoch, a philosopher whose judgement I respect, believes Hegel's writings to contain 'possibly more truth than any other' philosopher, and Roger Scruton, another philosopher whose judgement I respect, believes that the fundamental philosophy of conservatism has 'never been better captured than by Hegel in the *Phenomenology of Spirit...*'[1] On the other hand, Arthur Schopenhauer, who can't be found among the ranks of Hegel's admirers, describes Hegel's philosophy as the product of a 'gross, mindless charlatan.' [Schopenhauer 2010, 160] In case there should be any doubt as to what he means by describing Hegel as a charlatan, Schopenhauer characterises Hegel's philosophy as a 'colossal mystification that will certainly supply posterity with an inexhaustible theme of scorn for our time, a mystification crippling all intellectual powers, stifling all actual thought, and, by means of the most wicked misuse of language, putting in place the most hollow, most senseless, most thoughtless and...most stupefying verbiage of a pseudo-philosophy...' [Schopenhauer 2010, 16]

Among Hegel's most famous works are *The Phenomenology of Spirit* (1807), *The Science of Logic* (1812-1816) and *The Encyclopedia of the Philosophical Sciences* (1817), any one of which is guaranteed to test the intellect and the patience of would-be readers. Fortunately, for my particular purposes, the core of Hegel's thought on matters political can be found in one work, *The Philosophy of Right* (1821).

As with all Hegel's work,[2] this isn't light bedtime reading but when it is placed side by side with the intellectual marathons that are *The Phenomenology of Spirit* and the *Logic* it is, to switch metaphors in midstream, a comparative stroll in the park.[3] In the account that follows, I shall try to present what Hegel has to say on social and political matters as clearly and as charitably as possible. I can't guarantee to illuminate every dark place in Hegel's text (or indeed *any* dark place) and it is always possible that I may contribute some less than luminous interpretations of my own, but I console myself with the thought that even seasoned Hegel veterans can and do disagree among themselves about almost every sentence of the master's *oeuvre*.

Some early reviews of *The Philosophy of Right* were less than flattering.[4] Many reviewers saw it simply as an apology for the Prussian political status quo and, in subsequent years, it has been interpreted as a path-clearer for German Imperialism and even for National Socialism so that 'together with the thought that the roots of Marxism lie in Hegel's philosophy, this secured for Hegel a prominent if unenviable place in the popular demonology of totalitarianism.'[5] On the other hand, support for a more positive evaluation of Hegel's political thought hasn't been lacking, and many contemporary interpretations take it to be an attempt to provide a foundation for the emergent liberal state, an attempt not necessarily ineluctably linked either to its immediate political environment in Prussia or to subsequent German political developments.[6]

HEGEL THE LIBERAL?

It isn't obvious that Hegel's political philosophy provides support for the liberal state. At the heart of contemporary liberal politics is a certain view of man and society which makes society to be the resultant of the actions and interactions of isolated individuals, each seeking his own ends. This is certainly the classical liberal position and, suitably refined, the libertarian position too. On the other hand, the socialist position, and also the communitarian and the conservative position, tends to see society as having a measure of reality over, above and against the individuals who make it up.

Some take Hegel to be not so much a liberal as a critic of liberalism. Kenneth Westphal argues, to the contrary, that 'Hegel is a reform-minded liberal who based his political philosophy on the analysis and fulfillment of individual human freedom. Hegel gave this theme a profound twist through his social conception of human individuals. He argued that individual autonomy can be achieved only within a communal context.' [Westphal, 234] Thom Brooks states roundly that, 'The debate on whether Hegel's political philosophy is either conservative or liberal is now over. Today, the overwhelming majority of commentators accept that Hegel's views are best viewed as politically moderate, in between the extremes of conservatism and liberalism.'[7] Some may wonder if philosophical judgements are best determined by counting heads; others will perhaps be puzzled by the implication that conservatism and liberalism should be considered as extremes. Whether or which, Hegel does not simply reject liberalism outright; rather, he sees it as a partially correct but one-sided approach to man and society that is, as Allen Wood writes, 'salvageable only when placed in the context of a larger vision, which measures the subjective goals of individuals by a larger objective and collective good, and assigns to moral values a determinate, limited place in the total scheme of things.' [Wood 1991, xi]

A little later, Wood give gives us a succinct account of just what it is that Hegel finds objectionable about liberalism. Hegel's vision of society, he says, 'provides the basis for an indictment of any society which tries to call itself "free" even though it fails to offer its members any rationally credible sense of collective purpose, leaves them cynically discontented with and alienated from its political institutions, deprives them of a socially structured sense of self-identity, and condemns many of them to lives of poverty, frustration and alienation. It leads us to question the value of the formalisms — representative democracy, the market economy, the protection of individual liberties — with which liberals wish to identify "freedom", and to emphasize instead the social contents and consequences which liberals would usually prefer to leave "open" by excluding them from the domain of collective concern and control.' [Wood 1991, xxviii]

The core of the classical liberal position is the claim that society, however complex and developed it might be is, in the end, merely the resultant of the nexus of individual actions and interactions. By contrast, conservatives (and communitarians) tend to think of society in quasi-organic terms, as an entity that has a mode of being of its own over and above that of the individuals who are its elements, a mode of being that isn't merely an incidental outcome of the interaction of individuals seeking their own ends. In drawing this distinction, I am, of course, thinking of liberalism as that has been classically expressed in the thought of writers from Locke to Spencer, not liberalism as that concept is now commonly understood in the contemporary anglophone world. While the term *liberal* retains much of its original force in continental Europe, its contemporary anglophone use is 'virtually the opposite of its use during the nineteenth century, when liberal parties set out to propagate the message that political order exists to guarantee individual freedom, and that authority and coercion can be justified only if liberty requires them.'[8] Contemporary (anglophone) liberalism effectively hinges on the idea that the function of the state is to use its coercive power to distribute the good things of life to its substantially equalised citizens or, perhaps more accurately, to re-distribute them from one set of citizens to another. When it comes to liberty, contemporary liberalism prioritises personal (especially sexual) liberty while enthusiastically endorsing state control of the economy; contemporary conservatism, in contrast, prioritises economic liberty for the most part while, in the end, endorsing state control of morality and social order.

Hegel has been charged with prioritising the group or collective over the individual. Kenneth Westphal believes, however, that this accusation embodies a false dilemma that insists that either 'individuals are more fundamental than or are in principle independent of society, or vice versa: society is more basic than or "prior to" human individuals.' Hegel, according to Westphal, accepts neither side of this dichotomy, and points out that 'there are no individuals, no social practitioners, without social practices, and vice versa, there are no social practices, without social practitioners—without individuals who learn, participate in, perpetuate, *and who modify* those social practices as needed to meet their changing needs, aims and circumstances. The issue of the ontological priority of individual or society is bogus'[9] Well…not quite. It is true that at any given time, society and the individuals of which it is composed co-exist, and it may also be granted that our individual being is social through and through, much of what is important to us consisting of our relationships to others; nevertheless, one can conceive of individuals without society (even if only residually, like Robinson Crusoe on his island before the arrival of Friday) but a society without individuals is, strictly speaking, nothing. Was Hegel a social organicist, one who believes, as Burke appears to believe, that society is best imagined as a kind of living being, growing and developing in accordance with its own internal form? Westphal this time thinks that the answer to this question has to be yes, but he rejects the idea that Hegel's organicism was therefore conservative because Hegel, he writes, 'stressed that a society's practices are subject to rational criticism and revision.' [Westphal, 237]

FREEDOM AND *THE PHILOSOPHY OF RIGHT*

Hegel begins *The Philosophy of Right* by focusing on the individual, the bearer of what he calls an 'abstract right'. This is more or less where many other political thinkers (Locke, for example) start too but for Hegel, the right-bearing individual is merely the point of departure, not the point of arrival. For the liberal tradition, we start with the individual; what needs to be explained is how we get from the individual to society and to the state. Hegel seems to tell us a similar story but in fact his story is radically different. His individual isn't a completely developed entity that remains unchanged during its incorporation into society and state, with society and state merely playing the instrumental role of removing or limiting certain inconveniences that attach to individual life. On the contrary, for Hegel, the individual is, as it were, an abstraction, an abstraction that acquires flesh and bones only when incarnated in historical time and social space.

There is nothing about this contention that a libertarian need *necessarily* disagree with, even if he has some reservations about the mode of expression and the direction in which Hegel eventually takes it. As Murray Rothbard once remarked, libertarians often mistakenly assume 'that individuals are bound to each other only by the nexus of market exchange,' forgetting that 'everyone is necessarily born into a family' and 'one or several overlapping communities, usually including an ethnic group, with specific values, cultures, religious beliefs, and traditions' [Rothbard 1994, 1-2]

The Philosophy of Right can perhaps best be understood as a sustained reflection on the implications of freedom. As such, it might appear that it would be something that a history such as this, focused on the development of freedom, should welcome and celebrate. Hegel's conception of freedom, however, isn't simply the absence of constraint by others or the ability to act more or less as one wishes but, rather, the ability to set one's goals in a way that is genuinely in accord with one's status as a rational being. Our ability to make arbitrary and subjective choices is part of what it means to be free, but it is only a part. For Hegel, arbitrary freedom is not the whole story; we can't really be free if our freedom is confined simply to the pursuit of our own petty satisfactions but only if 'we successfully pursue ends larger than our own private good, indeed larger than anyone's private good.' [Wood 1991, xxiv]

Arbitrary freedom—freedom as the mere absence of constraint or as the ability to do as one pleases—is firmly rejected by Hegel as a complete or, in the end, even a coherent account of what freedom really is. He writes, 'The commonest idea we have of freedom is that of *arbitrariness*—the mean position of reflection between the will as determined solely by natural drives and the will which is free in and for itself. When we hear that freedom in general consists in *being able to do as one pleases*, such an idea can only be taken to indicate a complete lack of intellectual culture.'[10] In contrast to freedom as arbitrariness, true freedom has no necessary connection with the mundane world. Hegel believes that the free will 'has reference to nothing but itself, so that every relationship of *dependence* on something *other* than itself is thereby eliminated.' [Hegel, 54, §23] He adds, somewhat less perspicuously, 'It is *true*, or rather it is *truth* itself, because its determination consists in being in its *existence*—i.e. as something opposed to itself—what it is in its concept; that is, the pure concept has the intuition of itself as its end and reality'[11]

What is clear from the foregoing is that Hegel's concept of freedom isn't the bread and butter concept of the ability to act unconstrained by others that we normally and unreflectively entertain but is, rather, the power or ability to overcome the limitations of subjective particularity and to act in some kind of universal or objective way. So long as we are determined in any way by what is outside us, we aren't free. We can be free only if we can somehow take whatever might stand opposed to us and integrate it into our own projects. Allen Wood comments, 'freedom is possible only to the extent that we act rationally, and in circumstances where the objects of our action are in harmony with our reason.' [Wood 1991, xii] Moreover, if we shift our perspective from the individual in himself to the individual in society, Hegel believes that we shall come to see that freedom consists in the individual's identification of the institutions of his society as, in some sense *his* institutions. Zbigniew Pelczynski finds four different (but related) kinds of freedom in the *Philosophy of Right*: natural freedom; ethical freedom; civil freedom; and political freedom. Since these different forms of freedom correspond roughly to the major divisions of the *Philosophy of Right*, I shall use this classification to structure the following discussion.[12]

NATURAL FREEDOM

For Hegel, freedom and the will are intrinsically connected, freedom being 'just as much a basic determination of the will as weight is a basic determination of bodies....Will without freedom is an empty word, just as freedom is actual only as will or as subject.' [PR 35, §4] But will and thought are just two dimensions of reason so that freedom is, in the end, a matter of thought, of self-consciousness. A will that is determined merely by impulses and appetites is a purely natural will. Without a rational criterion, such a will is arbitrary. As already mentioned, many regard just such an arbitrary will as the prime example of a free will but Hegel rejects this view. The content of such a will, that which determines its object, is given to the will from outside itself and so the will in acting upon it isn't free. 'The common man thinks that he is free when he is allowed to act arbitrarily,' says Hegel, 'but this very arbitrariness implies that he is not free.' [PR 49, §15] If men were to act solely by virtue of their natural wills, the result would be a Hobbesian state of nature. Should we then aim to leave such arbitrariness completely behind us? Not quite. As Pelczynski notes, 'arbitrary choice has a place in a rational normative order, as Hegel admits in his account of civil society; in fact it is one of its fundamental constituents.' [Pelczynski 1984b, 66]

'A person,' says Hegel, 'has the right to place his will in any thing [*Sache*]' and in so doing, a person makes the thing to be his.' [PR 75, §44] Hegel sees ownership, at least in one of its aspects, as a direct relationship between an entity with a will and freedom—man—and entities without either will or freedom—things. He writes, 'to appropriate something means basically only to manifest the supremacy of my will in relation to the thing [*Sache*] and to demonstrate that the latter does not have being in and for itself and is not an end in itself.' [PR 76, §44] It can't be too much emphasised that property for Hegel is *not* primarily a matter of utilitarian material acquisition; on the contrary, property is central to the realisation of an individual's freedom and his assertion of identity and the embodiment of his personality. 'The starting point of the derivation of property rights,' writes Alan Ryan, 'is the claim that the object of right is freedom; rights are derived from the free will, not from their serving needs. The first and fundamental rights are those of persons, and persons exist in the first place as property-owners.' [Ryan, 184]

If Locke's notion of mixing one's labour with material things is less than completely perspicuous, Hegel's idea of placing one's will in something is perhaps even less so—how exactly does one perform this action? Placing one's will in an object isn't like putting one's socks in a drawer. It seems that one puts one's will into something if one possesses it, an action that can be performed either by grasping that thing, forming it, or marking it in some way. Even if, for the sake of argument, we accept that the idea of placing one's will in something is otherwise conceptually unproblematic and that it explains why and how a person could in principle own something (whereas a thing, not having a will, cannot own a person), it wouldn't yet explain how a person can own a specific something as against another person. Hegel's interest in property isn't the common one we tend to find in philosophers such as Locke or Hume for whom property is taken to satisfy some human need or to be advantageous to society as a whole. Although he doesn't deny that property *does* in fact satisfy human needs, Hegel none the less sees it as primarily a way in which human freedom is asserted: 'In relation to needs — if these are taken as primary — the possession of property appears as a means; but the true position is that, from the point of view of freedom, property, as the first *existence* [*Dasein*] of freedom, is an essential end for itself.'[13]

Hegel rejects many accounts of property that have been held by his predecessors. He rejects the Lockean notion of a right to property based on labour and the right that Locke believes we have to our own persons; he rejects the

Rousseauean conception of private property as the root of all evil; he rejects what he takes to be the hyper-individualism of Kant's account of property which leads inexorably to a social contract; and he also rejects the Humean conventionalist account of property and, through Hume, the utilitarian grounding of property and property rights. [see Ryan, 180 ff.] According to Westphal, whereas Hegel was in agreement with Hume that property rights weren't natural but conventional, unlike Hume, he argued that property conventions weren't primarily to be valued for their contribution to utility but for their contribution to freedom. [see Westphal, 247-248]

Although any given thing belongs to whoever is the first to take it into his possession, a person can't come to own something simply by willing that it be his; he must take possession of it in some way, and must do so in such a way that his act of possession can be recognised by others. [see PR 81, §§50, 51] Because natural objects differ from one another in so many ways, there are also many ways in which we can take control of any object. There is no single criterion that an act of possession has to meet in order to qualify as an act of possession. [see PR 82, §52] Despite the multiplicity of ways of taking possession of a thing, they all follow one of three patterns: either the immediate physical seizure of the object; or the giving of a form to it; or designating ownership of it by means of a sign.[14] Physical seizure is manifestly the most evident form of taking ownership but it is also the one that is most subjective, temporary and limited in scope. Giving form to an object can occur in many ways. Hegel counts tilling the soil, cultivating plants, domesticating animals, even conserving game, as instances of imparting form. And the third mode of taking possession, possession by designation is, Hegel thinks, the most complete mode of all. It consists of giving a sign to others that I have, in Hegel's terms, placed my will in an object. This giving of a sign is in fact implicit in the two other modes of taking possession, for in seizing a thing or giving form to it, I likewise give a sign to others in order to exclude them.[15] My use of a thing is not a *criterion* of ownership, merely a *sign* that I have taken possession of it. If I have the whole use of something, I am its owner.

Hegel's account of property grants that the uncoerced act of exchange between two human beings demonstrates that each recognises the other as the proprietor/owner, not merely the possessor, of whatever goods or services that are being exchanged. Hegel sees in this activity the manifestation of a common will (both parties desire the same exchange) which comes about precisely because even though each party to the exchange anticipates a gain, each evaluates the contemplated benefits from the exchange differently. If I propose to my newsagent to exchange €1.80 for a copy of *The Irish Times* and he is willing to accept my offer, our wills are at one in producing the exchange and in doing so because we each anticipate a relative improvement in our positions. I value a copy of *The Irish Times* more than the €1.80 I part with, and my newsagent values the €1.80 more than this particular copy of *The Irish Times* and so the exchange takes place.

My will is personal, the will of an individual, but it becomes objective when embodied in property. Private property is therefore an important dimension of subjectivity. Although Hegel is willing to subordinate the claims of private property to the state in certain circumstances, he rejects the idea that the state is entitled to prohibit private property altogether. He criticises Plato on this count, saying 'The Idea of Plato's republic contains as a universal principle a wrong against the person, inasmuch as the person is forbidden to own private property.' [PR 77, §46]

Libertarians generally subscribe to a thesis of self-ownership, basing their accounts of the ownership of external goods on the projection of our ownership of ourselves into the world outside us. Given Hegel's account of ownership as the placing of one's will in an object, we might wonder if he also subscribes to a thesis of self-ownership? Hegel does, in fact, accept a distinction of some sort between a person and his body, even going so far as to say that I 'possess my life and body, like other things [*Sachen*], only in so far as I so will it,' nevertheless, he rejects any form of radical dualism from an external point of view, a dualism that would allow another person to say that whereas he may have abused your body, he hasn't abused you. [PR 78, §47] 'Violence done to *my body* by others is violence done to me.'[16] I can alienate whatever of my property is external in nature and only what is external. Hegel recognises no right of an individual to commit suicide; no person has a right over his life because no person can have a right over himself. None the less, if I am required to give up my life by the state, I must surrender it! The reason for this is because the 'individual person [*einzelne*] is a subordinate entity who must dedicate himself to the ethical whole.' [PR 102, §70 Addition (H)]

Man is, on one level, a natural entity among other natural entities. As a natural entity, he does not possess himself originally but he comes to do so when he comprehends his freedom by means of his self-consciousness. In so doing, 'he takes possession of himself and becomes his own property as distinct from that of others.' [PR 86, §57] All alleged justifications of slavery depend upon taking man to be a natural entity and nothing else. All rejections of slavery as contrary to right depend upon regarding man as a spirit, as something free in itself. Both positions are partial and limited. Of the two sides of the antinomy, that 'which asserts the concept of freedom…has the advantage that it contains the absolute starting point — though only the starting point — on the way to truth.' [PR 87, §57]

When it comes to slavery, Hegel is prepared to apportion blame between slaves and the enslavers in a way that is likely to raise the hackles of the tender-hearted. He remarks, 'if someone is a slave, his own will is responsible, just as the responsibility lies with the will of a people if that people is subjugated. Thus the wrong of slavery is the fault not only of those who enslave or subjugate people, but of the slave and the subjugated themselves.' He concludes by remarking that slavery occurs 'in a world where a wrong is still right. Here, the wrong *is valid*, so that the position it occupies is a necessary one.' [PR 88, § 57] It might be objected that most workers alienate their physical or mental labour to their employers and in so doing, are engaged in a partial form of self-imposed slavery. Hegel accepts that I can alienate my labour to another and that if what was alienated was the whole of my time and the whole of my product, I would, in effect, be a slave. Even though an Athenian slave, let us say a pedagogue, might have had easier work to perform than a modern worker, unlike the modern worker 'he was nevertheless a slave, because the entire scope of his activity had been alienated to his master.'[17] None the less, Hegel concedes that slaves have an absolute right to free themselves [see PR 97, §66]

ETHICAL FREEDOM

If we are to survive, let alone flourish, then our natural freedom must be contained within a larger context in which everyone recognises and abides by certain rules as applying to all. Rules, considered from one angle, serve merely to constrain and limit our freedom [see PR 192, §149] but, from another angle, they make possible the tangible expression of our freedom in ways that wouldn't otherwise be possible. These common rules promote human flourishing, but their *raison d'être*, for Hegel, is their enlargement of practical freedom. Whether in the family, in civil society or even in the state, natural freedom will be constrained or, perhaps, channelled, but not eliminated: 'the ethical order must be shot through with personal rights and spheres of autonomy, and be acceptable to individual conscience.' [Pelczynski 1984b, 69]

Hegel is clear that the co-operative activity instanced in acts of uncoerced exchange in the market is different in kind from the exchanges that take place within the family. To put it crudely, family exchanges are based on love; commercial transactions are based on money. Paul Redding remarks, 'In the family the particularity of each individual tends to be absorbed into the social unit, giving this manifestation of *Sittlichkeit* [ethical life] a one-sidedness that is the inverse of that found in market relations in which participants grasp themselves in the first instance as separate individuals who then enter into relationships that are external to them.' [Redding, 35] Family members are, as it were, already in a relationship with each other before ever there's a question of the exercise of choice, whereas strangers are free to choose to enter into relationship with others or not to do so, as they see fit. Hegel judges—and in this he is surely correct—that the form of social life exemplified in the family and the form of life exemplified in the market are each one-sided. [see Rose 2007, 113-118] A major theme of this history has been the claim that the progress of freedom has been in large part the gradual, if fitful, detachment of the individual from the pre-choice nexus of family, clan and tribe, whatever form such families, clans and tribes may take. Despite this, I wouldn't wish to be taken to suggest that the ideal life for the free individual is an atomic existence in which every aspect of his life is regulated by market considerations and by market considerations only.

'One reason Hegel viewed human freedom as a social phenomenon,' writes Kenneth Westphal, 'is that through collective efforts to meet individual need, natural needs are elaborated into more-specific needs for the kinds of goods communities make available to their members. The social elaboration of needs transforms those needs from a natural level of mere givenness to a social level, indicating that humans come to give themselves their own needs.' He continues, 'One of Hegel's most brilliant insights is how the development of commerce contributes to the development of human enculturation, a collective process whereby we liberate ourselves from our naturally given needs and desires. Political economy is thus crucial for overcoming natural heteronomy and to achieving autonomy. Achieving autonomy from nature is central to Hegel's account of the family and civil society.' [Westphal, 245-246] It is hard to disagree with Westphal's assessment of what he calls 'Hegel's brilliant insight' but it is also hard to see how this insight is either original with or peculiar to Hegel. The contribution of commerce to the development of culture, in particular, its contribution to the functional prioritisation of liberty, is a commonplace of historical thought. Still, it is true that exchange and contract can't take place in the absence of some form of shared morality since those who engage in contracts and in exchanges necessarily experience a moral obligation to keep their bargains and to be honest in their dealings with others.

CIVIL FREEDOM

Civil society, for Hegel, is a kind of 'external' state. In this society, 'individuals seek to satisfy each others' needs through work, production and exchange'; there is a 'thorough-going division of labour and a system of social classes' and 'law courts, corporate bodies and public regulatory and welfare authorities' that 'promote security of property, livelihood and other rights.'[18] Civil society *is* the modern state, but only when it is perceived under a particular aspect, as a system of public authorities and autonomous bodies whose function it is to serve the economic and legal interests of individuals or groups. Hegel describes civil society as a stage intermediate between the family and the state proper, a stage, which has only effectively come into being in the modern world. Hegel credits Christianity with bringing individuality, the principle of subjective freedom, into the world: 'It was primarily in the Christian religion that the right of subjectivity arose, along with the infinity of being-for-itself; and in this situation, the totality must also be endowed with sufficient strength to bring particularity into harmony with the ethical unity.'[19]

All human beings have a need for food, drink, clothing and shelter. Animals can satisfy their limited needs in a limited number of ways. Man, however, multiplies his needs, and divides and differentiates them. This realm of needs and their satisfaction is a means of bringing men into contact with each other. 'I acquire my means of satisfaction from others and must accordingly accept their opinions. But at the same time, I am compelled to produce means whereby others can be satisfied. Thus, the one plays into the hands of the others and is connected with it. To this extent, everything particular [*alles Partikulare*] takes on a social character...'[20]

The multiplication of human needs, and their diversity, promotes the division of labour, which in turn makes the '*dependence* and *reciprocity* of human beings in the satisfaction of their other needs complete and entirely necessary.' [PR 233, §198] This mutual dependence and reciprocity resulting from the effort to provide for the satisfaction of our own individual needs, contributes to the satisfaction of the needs of all. 'By a dialectical movement, the particular is mediated by the universal so that each individual, in earning, producing, and enjoying on his own account [*für sich*], thereby earns and produces for the enjoyment of others.'[21] 'Civil society,' writes Westphal, 'comprises the institutions and practices involved in the production, distribution and consumption of products that meet a variety of needs and wants. Hegel called this the "system of needs".'[22]

The particular share any individual acquires of resources is conditional upon his original assets, his skill, and his mental and physical aptitudes. The resulting inequalities aren't in any way improper and the demand for material equality is, Hegel says, 'characteristic of an empty understanding, which mistakes this abstraction and *obligation* of its own for the real and the rational.' [PR 234, §200] Considered abstractly, all persons are equal simply as persons but this abstract form of equality has nothing in particular to do with equality of possessions, and those who think that it does are vacuous and superficial. Even if, *per impossibile*, an equality of goods were once introduced, Hegel points out that it 'would in any case be destroyed again within a short time, because all resources are dependent on diligence.' Following Fichte (to a degree), Hegel thinks that 'everyone ought to have property' but he robustly denies that 'justice requires everyone's property to be equal.'[23] [PR 80, 81, §49]

Hegel distinguishes several estates that subsist within civil society: the first (substantial) estate is agriculture; the second estate is trade and industry; and the third estate is the universal estate that concerns itself with governance. As others have done before him, Hegel takes the emergence of such states to be intrinsically connected with the invention of agriculture (and, he adds, marriage). Agriculture brings with it 'the cultivation of the soil, and in consequence exclusively private property...and it reduces the nomadic life of savages, who seek their livelihood in constant movement, to the tranquillity of civil law [*Privatrecht*] and the secure satisfaction of needs.' [PR 235, §203] Hegel links the introduction of agriculture, the abandonment of nomadism, and the emergence of the state to the institution of marriage which he sees as implying a care for the family as a permanent social entity which, in turn, implies some sort of semi-communal family property. With the emergence of trade and industry, the individual is wrenched from the bosom of the family. 'But civil society tears the individual [*Individuum*] away from family ties, alienates the members of family from one another, and recognizes them as self-sufficient persons.' [PR 263, §238] By means of this separation, the individual is at once liberated and challenged. 'In the estate of trade and industry, the individual [*Individuum*] has to rely on himself, and this feeling of selfhood is intimately connected with the demand for a condition in which right is upheld. The sense of freedom and order has therefore arisen mainly in towns. The first estate, on the other hand, has little need to think for itself; what it gains is an alien gift, a gift of nature. This feeling of dependence is fundamental to it, and may easily be coupled with a willingness to accept whatever may befall it at the hands of other people. The first estate is therefore more inclined to subservience, the second estate to freedom.' [PR 237, §204] The universal estate (by which Hegel seems to have in mind the class directly concerned with the administration of government) produces no wealth of its own and so its members must either have private means or receive an indemnity from the state. Readers may be forgiven if they suspect members of Hegel's third estate of bearing a striking and non-accidental resemblance to Plato's guardians.

Most political philosophers would see the administration of justice as an aspect, indeed a key aspect, of the state proper but Hegel characterises it rather as a significant dimension of civil society. Animals have instinct for their law; human beings have custom. Custom contains, as it were, the seeds of law, but custom is subjective and contingent. The codification of custom is a rudimentary legal code, a legal code that is characterised by formlessness, indeterminacy and incompleteness. [see PR 242, §211]

If laws are to be binding, they must be promulgated, but they cannot be promulgated if, as Hegel notes, they are displayed in such a way (as was done by Dionysius the Tyrant) that no citizen could read them or if, as in the case of Arthur Dent, the protagonist of Douglas Adams's *The Hitchhiker's Guide to the Galaxy*, who discovered that his house was to be demolished to make way for a local bypass, the notice of intent had been displayed in an unlit cellar of the local planning office in a locked filing cabinet with a sign on the door saying, *Beware of the Leopard.* Similarly, laws can be made effectively invisible if they are buried in great tomes that only the learned can access and read, a situation that more and more obtains.

Law aspires to be complete and self-contained but it requires constant revision in the light of circumstances. 'It is therefore mistaken.' Hegel writes, 'to demand that a legal code should be comprehensive in the sense of absolutely complete and incapable of any further determinations (this demand is a predominantly German affliction) and to refuse to accept…something allegedly imperfect on the grounds that it is incapable of such completion.' [PR 248, §216]

In a civil society, crime is no longer just a personal and individual violation but an affront to society. 'The fact that an injury to one member of society is an injury to all the others does not alter the nature of crime in terms of its concept, but in terms of its outward existence [*Existenz*]; for the injury now affects the attitudes [*Vorstellung*] and consciousness of civil society, and not just the existence [*Dasein*] of the immediately injured party. In heroic ages—see the tragedies of the ancients—the citizens do not regard the crimes which members of royal houses commit against each other as injuries to themselves.' [PR 250, §218]

Hegel draws a firm distinction between morality and law. 'Since morality and moral precepts concern the will in its most personal [*eigensten*] subjectivity and particularity, they cannot be the object [*Gegenstand*] of positive legislation.' [PR 244, §213] Pelczynski writes, 'The peculiarity of modern European culture…is that men conceive themselves not just as member of communities but also…as bearers of private rights against the state and possessors of legitimate particular and group interests. In Hegel's view Christianity had an equally profound effect on European culture….Under its influence men came to regard themselves as moral agents, acknowledging no higher authority than their own conscience or reason. Hegel calls the first tendency "particularity" and the second "subjectivity…" [Pelczynski 1971a, 7]

Trade and commerce must be free but ultimately subject to regulation for the good of civil society. Regulation is required to bring trade and commerce 'back to the universal, and to moderate and shorten the duration of those dangerous convulsions[24] to which its collisions give rise, and which should return to equilibrium by a process of conscious necessity.' [PR 262, §236] Civil society has an obligation to provide a livelihood for individuals and a duty to protect them against themselves. Here, civil society is acting as if it were a substitute family.[25] Since the emergence of civil society is responsible, in part, for the destruction of the family, it must, as it were, assume some of its functions. Since 'society has…taken from them the natural means of acquisition and also dissolved [*aufhebt*] the bond of the family in its wider sense as a kinship group — they are more or less deprived of all the advantages of society, such as the ability to acquire skills, and education in general, as well as of the administration of justice, health care, and often even of the consolation of religion. For the *poor*, the universal authority [*Macht*] takes over the role of the family with regard not only to their immediate deficiencies, but also to the disposition of laziness, viciousness, and the other vices to which their predicament and sense of wrong gives rise.' [PR 265, §241] Hegel has interesting things to say about the development of what he calls 'a rabble'. A rabble comes into existence when a large mass of people drops below a certain standard of living. When this happens, the feelings of self-respect that come from supporting oneself by one's own work are lost. It should be noted, however, that Hegel does not say that poverty is a sufficient condition for the development of a rabble. On the contrary, the creation of a rabble also requires a disposition to rebel against the rich, against society, against government. The members of a rabble 'become frivolous and lazy' and 'yet claim that they have a right to receive their livelihood.'[26]

The particular form of civil association that Hegel calls the corporation functions as if it were a second family.[27] A corporation 'has the right…to look after its own interests within its enclosed sphere, to admit members in accordance with their objective qualifications of skill and rectitude and in numbers determined by the universal context, to protect its members against particular contingencies, and to educate others so as to make them eligible for membership. In short, it has the right to assume the role of a *second* family for its members…' [PR 270-271, §252]

It can be seen then, that civil society, which results in part from the dissolution of the family, is a sphere in which our self-interest and our individual choices have the greatest scope. It is characterised by economic transactions, various forms of non-status based associations and 'the right to public assistance and protection against misfortune or the vagaries of the market.' [Pelczynski 1984a, 70] In contrast, the political state, properly speaking, performs functions of governance that civil society isn't capable of carrying out. [see PR 288, §267]

Hegel's distinction between civil society and the state proper seems to be an arbitrary, certainly an unusual, way of dividing what is normally conceived of as a single set of institutions.[28] Most thinkers conceive of the law and police as aspects or dimensions of the state proper. Hegel, one supposes, wasn't unaware of this possible criticism but it seemed important to him to distinguish between two forms of state, civil society, the external state, and the state proper, in virtue of their serving different ends: the civil state serving individual ends, and the political state proper serving the people as a whole. Michael Foster finds the distinction between civil society and the state proper unnecessary and confusing, remarking, 'The sphere in the realm of 'Sittlichkeit' which Hegel distinguishes from the State as "bürgerliche Gesellschaft" combines in itself (and we must add, confuses) *both* the determinations by which we have found it possible to differentiate 'society' from State. It is both economic society and civil society; it is the sphere in which both economic laws are fulfilled and civil law is enforced.' [Foster 1965, 150]

STATE FREEDOM

A question that has puzzled many readers of *The Philosophy of Right* is— what exactly is the distinction between civil society and the state? [see Avineri, 176-193] Zbigniew Pelczynski devoted an entire edited collection of papers to attempting to answer this question. He remarks, 'The distinction has been disputed, though on completely different grounds, by marxism and liberalism. Marxism is heavily indebted to the concept of civil society but it denies the Hegelian conception of the state as a political *community*...and regards the state as an apparatus of coercion and class exploitation superimposed on society.

Liberalism, on the other hand, treats the state and civil society as synonymous — a legal and institutional framework for the pursuit of individual interests.' [Pelczynski 1984, vii] I am in agreement with both the Marxists and the liberals on this topic! As a libertarian, I too regard the state as an apparatus of coercion; and insofar as the idea of the state could have any justification at all for me, then it could only have it if it were effectively reduced to a form of a voluntarily based civil society!

As we have seen, civil society is a kind of external state; the state proper, however, is more than this. 'It implies an institutional public forum in which matters concerning the community as a whole are debated and decided upon, and the decision carried out by the government. In this public or political arena the needs of civil society and of the national community are appraised and evaluated, and the unity of private interest and community values is realized in a conscious and organized manner.' [Pelczynski 1984b, 61] The reason for Hegel's positing the political state, the state proper, seems to be that certain aspects of civil society, such as commerce and trade, if left unregulated, would lead to economic and social instability. That being so, it is necessary to have institutions that can regulate the market and the other manifestations of civil society to prevent such instability. Hegel had read Adam Smith and agrees with him that in a market economy based upon an individual's search for the satisfaction of his needs, this individual search does, in fact, contribute to the satisfaction of the needs of all. Nevertheless, and this is the fateful move, Hegel also believes that the market economy, if unregulated by some element outside itself, will ineluctably produce a class of poor people. To think otherwise is, he believes, to see things only from the one-sided perspective of an a-familial economy based upon market exchange. That being so, 'the economy was to be contained within an over-arching institutional framework of the state, and its social effects offset by welfarist state intervention.'[29]

Hegel rejects the idea that the state is a result of a contract between everyone and the sovereign. 'This view,' he says, ''is the result of superficial thinking, which envisages only a single unity of different wills' which makes the state to be some kind of external association.'[30] The state isn't simply the result of an agreement between previously isolated individuals 'motivated by fear or enlightened self-interest. It is the result of an evolution of generations of individuals to form a historical community.' [Pelczynski 1971a, 4] If one starts from the asocial individual then the laws of society are inevitably taken to be a limitation of our natural freedom, a limitation we may be willing to accept in exchange for security. For Hegel, however, our belonging to society isn't a contingent matter.[31] A contract is made up of two identical wills, two arbitrary wills. 'But the state is constituted differently. No individual is entitled to break away from the state 'because the individual by nature is already by nature a citizen of it.' [PR 106, §74 Addition (H)] Whether an individual enters or leaves a state isn't a matter for the arbitrary will of the individual but a matter that the state itself must permit. The state, then, does not rest upon a contract. 'It is false to say that the arbitrary will of everyone is capable of founding a state: on the contrary, it is absolutely necessary for each individual to live within the state. The great advance made by the state in modern times is that it remains an end in and for itself, and that each individual may no longer base his relationship [*Beziehung*] to it on his own private stipulation, as was the case in the Middle Ages.'[32] Kenneth Westphal, notes, however that 'Hegel's objections to the social contract tradition do not…preclude him from sharing many issues and points of doctrine with that tradition.' [Westphal, 243] And Paul Redding notes, 'while Hegel is critical of standard "social contract" theories, his own conception of the state is still clearly a complicated transformation of those of Rousseau and Kant.'[33]

In a curious way, Hegel's description of the non-contingent connection of the individual to the state is strangely reminiscent of Burke's primeval and eternal contract that, we may remind ourselves, 'holds all physical and all moral natures, each in their appointed place.' Burke's special kind of social contract, we may remember, was 'not subject to the will of those who by an obligation above them, and infinitely superior, are bound to submit their will to that law.' The eternal and primeval contract demands the submission of our wills. One may not refuse to submit to it except under some kind of (unspecified) necessity that isn't chosen but rather thrust upon one. 'The municipal corporations of that universal kingdom are not morally at liberty at their pleasure, and on their speculations of a contingent improvement, wholly to separate and tear asunder the bands of their subordinate community and to dissolve it into an unsocial, uncivil, unconnected chaos of elementary principles. It is the first and supreme necessity only, a necessity that is not chosen but chooses, a necessity paramount to deliberation, that admits no discussion and demands no evidence, which alone can justify a resort to anarchy.' [Burke 1790/2003,

82-83] A voluntary and rational rejection of the transcendent, eternal and primeval contract would, according to Burke, have devastating consequences. He writes, 'But if that which is only submission to necessity should be made the object of choice, the law is broken, nature is disobeyed, and the rebellious are outlawed, cast forth, and exiled from this world of reason, and order, and peace, and virtue, and fruitful penitence, into the antagonist world of madness, discord, vice, confusion, and unavailing sorrow.' [Burke 1790/2003, 82-83]

If the reader also hears echoes of Plato in Hegel's claims, that's not surprising. For Plato, the end of the *polis* supersedes the ends of its component individuals. Only the *polis* is completely self-sufficient, as distinct from the individual or the family or, in Hegel's case, civil society. Part of what Hegel believes, a large part, comes from a yearning to return to the collectivism of the ancient world. 'Hegel's primary source of inspiration and model of political community,' writes Pelczynski, 'is to be found in Plato…the *Republic* seemed to him a work of true genius and a most profound theory expressing the essence of Greek society and culture. The fundamental presupposition of the *Republic* and ancient Greek political life generally (Hegel argues) was the absolute priority of the community over the individual.' [Pelczynski 1984b, 57] To be fair to Hegel, we must note that despite his admiration for the classical world in general (and Plato in particular), he has reservations about its suppression of individuality. He makes the point that the universal aspect of the state was indeed present to its thinking but that it neglected particularity, whereas 'the essence of the modern state is that the universal should be linked with the complete freedom of particularity [*Besonderheit*] and the well-being of individuals, and hence that the interest of the family and of civil society must become focused on the state….Thus, the universal must be activated, but subjectivity on the other hand must be developed as a living whole. Only when both moments are present [*bestehen*] in full measure can the state be regard as articulated and truly organized.' [PR 283, §260] He adds a little later, that 'In the states of antiquity, the subjective end was entirely identical with the will of the state; in modern times, however, we expect to have our own views, our own volition, and our own conscience. The ancients had none of these in the present sense; for them, the ultimate factor was the will of the state.'[34]

It is clear from all this that Hegel is anxious to preserve the moment of individual choice and individual freedom in his conception of the modern state. The problem is whether on his conception of the state such preservation is in fact possible. He writes: 'If the state is confused with civil society and its determination is equated with security and protection of property and personal freedom, the interest of individuals [*der Einzelnen*] *as such* becomes the ultimate end for which they are united; it also follows from this that membership of the state is an optional matter. — But the relationship of the state to the individual [*Individuum*] is of quite a different kind. Since the state is objective spirit, it is only through being a member of the state that the individual [*Individuum*] himself has objectivity, truth, and ethical life.' [PR, 276, §258] Beyond the need for regulation, then, the state proper also has to exist in order to allow the individual to realise his place in the most fully developed form of the ethical life of society. The state proper is necessary to reconcile and to hold in tension the elements of freedom and autonomy and the demands of morality. So, the state proper mustn't be confused with civil society, nor must its purpose or function be reduced merely to providing for the security and protection of property or promoting the personal freedom and interests of individuals.[35]

We have seen that despite his almost boundless admiration for Plato, Hegel deprecates the lack of respect for the individual revealed in Plato's thought. And even though he commends Rousseau for putting forward the idea that will is the principle of the state, he criticises him for thinking of the will in this context only as the individual will, with the result that the state is formed from a contract between individual wills each giving its express consent. This ends up 'by systematically rejecting all established order.' [Pelczynski 1984a, 59] Nevertheless, according to Hegel, 'the subjectivity of freedom (which is the *sole* content of the principle of the individual will) embodies only *one* (consequently one-sided) moment of the *Idea of the rational* will.' [PR 277, §258; see Westphal, 244] Hegel is critical of Rousseau's account of the general will for not achieving its stated purpose and of its remaining, in essence, merely the will of a collection of individuals or simply a majority will. Whether this criticism is justified or not, is another matter. To the casual eye, Rousseau's account and Hegel's seem, in the end, to come to much the same thing. [see Avineri, 183-184]

The latent collectivism of Hegel's judgement becomes glaringly obvious in a notorious purple passage that appears as an addition to §258 of *The Philosophy of Right*. Here, Hegel writes, 'The state in and for itself is the ethical whole, the actualization of freedom, and it is the absolute end of reason that freedom should be actual. The state is the spirit which is present in the world and which consciously realizes itself therein, whereas in nature, it actualizes itself only as the other of itself, as dormant spirit....The state consists in the march of God in the world, and its basis is the power of reason actualizing itself as will. In considering the Idea of the state, we must not have any particular states or particular institutions in mind; instead, we should consider the Idea, this actual God,[36] in its own right [*für sich*].'[37] Anticipating the objection that it is a little difficult to find any state that manifests its divinity in an obvious way, Hegel adds, 'The state is a work of art; it exists in the world, and hence in the sphere of arbitrariness, contingency, and error, and bad behaviour may disfigure it in many respects. But the ugliest man, the criminal, the invalid, or the cripple is still a living human being; the affirmative aspect — life — survives [*besteht*] in spite of such deficiencies, and it is with this affirmative aspect that we are here concerned.'[38]

Shlomo Avineri argues that what Hegel is trying to say in passages such as these isn't really so much that the state is the march of God through history but rather that 'the very existence of the state is part of a divine strategy, not a merely human arbitrary artefact.' [Avineri, 177]

Hegel's account of the operative structure of the state proper is of no particular interest, presenting, as it does, a detailed yet distressingly mundane account of the sovereign and his power (which many people consider a weak point of Hegel's account), the executive power and legislative power, and the state's role in international law and in world history. [PR 308, §273] 'Perhaps the greatest internal weakness in Hegel's organizational scheme is his account of the monarch,' writes Kenneth Westphal. J. N. Findlay remarks on Hegel's 'strange belief in hereditary monarchy as the crowning truth of the State Idea…', and Zbigniew Pelczynski comments that 'After the breath-taking conceptualization of the modern state in §260, Hegel's description of its political organization [including an hereditary monarchy] comes rather as an anti-climax.'[39] On the other hand, Thom Brooks remarks, 'Hegel is right to give the monarch the significance he does' and this significance 'is far greater than has been recognised. The constitutional monarch is a necessary part of Hegel's rational state that is simply too powerful for interpreters to continue to overlook or discount.'[40]

Now that we have had an overview of Hegel's entire scheme, let us ask the question again: why does Hegel feel the need to differentiate between civil society and the state proper? Do we not have law and policing in the civil condition? In the civil condition, law is indeed realised, but it is realised unconsciously; in the state proper, it becomes the object of conscious will. But *whose* will? The will of the ruler or the will of the subject? If the subject, civil society seems adequate for its purposes; it is only if ethical will is identified with the will of the ruler that the State would appear to become necessary. Legislation, for Hegel, is the expression of the general will of a political society but this general will is *not* a quasi-mechanical emergent property of social interchanges between individuals or social groups. In the state, all citizens must be able to recognise the general will as the expression of *their* will, and of their *wills*— that is, as *willed*.[41] For this willing to take place, there must be an express act on the part of whoever is playing the role of monarch in that society.

It is interesting that Hegel takes this approach, given that he has, in his account of market exchange in civil society, already indicated how a common will can emerge *without* its being that case that there has to be a source of that will other than the wills of the individual participants in the exchange. Given civil society, with its corporations, law and police, what need is there for what Hegel calls the 'political state'? As Michael Foster notes, '"Bürgerliche Gesellschaft" itself contains all the conditions essential for the realization of "Sittlichkeit", upon Hegel's own definition of that idea, and when Hegel first introduces the State as the actualization of "Sittlichkeit" he endows it with no characteristic not already possessed by "society" properly understood. Civil law is the system of law developed by logical necessity from the original principles of reason; "bürgerliche Gesellschaft" is the sphere in which this system is both "posited" and enforced. It embodies, that is to say, a system of reasonable determinations and presents them as objective to the reason of the subject; and in doing this it fulfils all the conditions necessary to the perfect realization of ethical freedom.' [Foster 1965, 154-155]

On reflection, one might say that Hegel has *three*, not two, conceptions of the state; civil society (the external state) and the state proper, which itself subdivides into the state as ethical community and the political state, the system of central government bodies. In §276 of *The Philosophy of Right*, Hegel presents us with the metaphor of the political state as the life or soul of an organic body, which is 'present at every point' of the body and which is such that any part of the body not animated by it must die. The political state, as the supreme ethical community, serves to bring everything together into a unified yet universal whole—individual, family, and civil society—all subject, in the end, to a supreme and independent public authority. Much of the heightened rhetoric in Hegel regarding the state—in particular, the notion that freedom is obedience to the state—is about the state as an ethical community rather than the administrative machinery of government. Michael Foster raises a problem, noting: 'if the ethical will is identified with the will of the ruler, then it will be true that the State is the necessary condition of its exercise, but it will be true also that its exercise is confined to a limited body of men. In their will alone "absolute Sittlichkeit" will be realized, and they alone will possess full ethical freedom; and the possession of this freedom and the realization of this Sittlichkeit will presuppose the existence of another body of men excluded from participation in either. But if this identification is not made, then...Hegel has no ground for making the transition from society to State at all.' [Foster 1965, 162]

It can, I think, fairly be said that the notions of natural, ethical and civil freedom aren't completely obscure. When we come to consider political freedom, however, clarity is a quality more in demand than in evidence. Pelczynski remarks that '"political freedom" is an elusive concept in the Philosophy of Right.' [Pelczynski 1984a, 71] Why should this be so? Pelczynski's explanation—that Hegel found it prudent to temper his theoretical zeal in the context of Prussian reaction—is maliciously tempting but not ultimately persuasive.[42] What exactly political freedom is and why it is important—indeed, why it is the culmination of the various forms of freedom—are matters that are never fully clarified by Hegel. Even Pelczynski, generally an admirer of Hegel's work, concedes that the place where public freedom is most clearly valorised is in Hegel's treatment of the corporation, which is a feature of the civil condition, not the political state proper.

To find an answer to our question, we must return to our starting point and remember that for Hegel freedom, to be truly freedom, must be self-conscious. And the case could be made that even though civil freedom is real and substantial, it isn't yet fully self-conscious. Shlomo Avineri writes, 'The rationality which permeates the world of man becomes apparent for the first time in the state, Hegel argues. In the family, it is still hidden behind feeling and sentiment; in civil society, it appears as an instrumentality of individual self-interest. Only in the sphere of the state does reason become conscious of itself; in other words, only in the state are the actions of man one with his intentions — man knows what he wants and acts according to it.' [Avineri, 178] The argument seems to run along these lines: first, in the civil condition there are laws and police-functions but not, it seems, of a high enough or of a universal enough nature to soar above the trailing clouds of particularity; second, even though Hegel recognises the emergent social function of elements of civil society, in particular, the market economy, the forces operating at this level are less than fully conscious and quasi-natural so that the 'unity and universality in civil society is achieved without the knowledge and will of its members.' [Pelczynski 1984b, 74] Political freedom is the place where Hegel believes his version of the Rousseauean general will finds a home. Transcending the individual wills of the citizens, Hegel's objective general will is at once more than the sum of its parts yet also capable of giving conscious expression to the individual subjective wills. 'It is through the *political* institution of the ethical community that the reconciliation of the subjective and objective aspects of the will is effected.' [Pelczynski 1984b, 75]

Well, perhaps.....but I'm not persuaded. Leaving aside for one moment, the rhapsody on unity and universality, in the end, the argument here seems to be that, without explicit direction and unitary control, an appropriate level of civil order cannot be maintained. There is nothing uncommon in this assertion, an assertion that lies at the root of much resistance to the idea of anarchy. What is surprising in Hegel's case is that in his conception of civil society, he very clearly recognised the emergence of order from the ground up. In doing so, he grants a key component of the anarchist's case. Shlomo Avineri argues that 'The state...is based on rational freedom, organized in such a way as to enable each to realize his freedom in conjunction with others, while in civil society one can realize one's ends only by disregarding everyone else's aims.' [Avineri, 179] Avineri isn't quite correct in this assertion; in civil society, one must in fact take others' ends into account, though one need not necessarily makes them one's own. One must necessarily mind one's own business; one need (and perhaps *should*) mind another's business only insofar as that business comes within the remit of one's own concerns. In the end, Hegel's motivation for introducing the state proper is both quasi-Hobbesian—without it, there will be social disorder—and quasi-Burkean (in a romantic mode)—only in the political state can the individual will find complete ethical fulfilment. A sceptic may be forgiven for thinking that if complete ethical fulfilment is possible only in the state proper, only those who are members of the universal estate will be the beneficiaries of it.

In the end, Zbigniew Pelczynski makes the best case possible for Hegel when he sympathetically characterises the distinction between civil freedom and political freedom in these words: 'The *raison d'être* of civil society and the justification of civil freedom is the private interest and subjective choice of the individual *bourgeois* which, mediated through a system of economic and social relations as well as laws, institutions and authorities, promotes the interest of the ethical community only indirectly and in the last resort. The *raison d'être* of political community and the justification of political liberty is the good of the ethical community itself, the common good or the public interest, which the fully self-conscious and self-determined *citizen* promotes for its own sake.' [Pelczynski 1984a, 76] On the other hand, Michael Foster unsympathetically remarks, 'I do not believe that it is possible to find in Hegel or to construe out of his words a single consistent doctrine of the relation of "bürgerliche Gesellschaft" to "Staat", or a single consistent account of the "transition" from the one to the other.' [Foster 1965, 151]

Hegel's account of the state is, J. N Findlay says 'an unedifying piece of writing, largely lacking in thought and argument, and without any deep coherence with his own principles. It describes with faithful accuracy the political arrangements of the monarchy in which Hegel spent his later years.[43] And it presents these arrangements as the final fruits of the historic development of Spirit. Hegel, it would seem from this work, was not really gifted with deep political and social understanding. He was profound in his appreciation of speculative puzzles, of aesthetic and religious experiences—of what constitutes the higher solitude of man—but he was not profound in his grasp of the political and the social.' [Findlay, 327] Some readers may find Findlay's trenchant judgement on Hegel's political thinking particularly apt—others not! Although Findlay's judgement may be a little harsh—after all, Hegel *has* his admirers—I find it difficult in the end not to agree with its substance. After all the huffing and puffing a conscientious reader has had to endure through many pages of dense prose, he finally arrives at the state proper, the apogee of Hegel's system, only to find that, in a Heath Robinsoneque revelation, the mountain has laboured to bring forth a mouse or, to change metaphors in midstream, he arrives at the Emerald City only to find that the great and terrible Wizard of Oz is a little old man with a bald head and a wrinkled face and a megaphone.

Burke and Hegel might both be characterised as philosophers of conservatism—Burke defending a praxis-based, tradition-embodied empirical form of conservatism whereas Hegel defended conservatism in a highly sophisticated rationalistic variety. In contrast to the conservatism of both Burke and Hegel, are the ideas of two towering figures of the nineteenth century—John Stuart Mill, the English utilitarian and putative defender of liberty, and Karl Marx, the apostle of a political creed that was to dominate a large part of the world for most of the twentieth-century.

Notes

1 Murdoch 1998, 146, Scruton 2014, 119.

2 *The Philosophy of Right*'s title in German is *Grundlinien der Philosophie des Rechts*, hereafter referred to in citations as PR. As already mentioned in the chapter on Kant—but the point is worth repeating—the German word '*Recht*' is notoriously difficult to translate idiomatically into English. In German there are two words for law, *Recht* and *Gesetz,* whereas English has just one, namely 'law'. *Recht* corresponds, more or less, to the Latin, *ius*, and signifies the entire body of laws and the principles underlying it, whereas *Gesetz* corresponds to the Latin, *lex*, and signifies a particular law or statute. Additionally, *Recht* means 'justice'. It also signifies a right, as when one has a right against another person. On top of this broad linguistic usage, philosophers (as we have seen, Kant, and here Hegel) tend to add their own idiosyncrasies. *The Philosophy of Right* is published in the form of text and notes by Hegel and additions contributed by his students based upon Hegel's lectures and comments. As Samuel Dyde remarks, 'It is but bare justice to the editors to say that these additions usually cast a welcome light upon the text.' [Dyde 1896 [2001], 10] In my citations from *The Philosophy of Right* I will note material that comes from these additions but I will treat it (not uncontroversially) as being as authentically Hegelian as Hegel's own text and notes.

3 Is it possible to read and properly understand *The Philosophy of Right* in isolation from Hegel's other works? Some say yes, others say no. [see Brooks 2007, 4ff.] In confining my attention in this chapter more or less exclusively to *The Philosophy of Right*, I am evidently coming down on the 'yes' side of this argument.

4 In 1843, Karl Marx produced a detailed (but unpublished in his lifetime) *Critique of Hegel's Philoso-*

phy of Right (*Zur Kritik der Hegelschen Rechtsphilosophie*). Among other things, Marx takes exception to the daunting level of abstraction of many of the arguments in Hegel's work and, substantively, he rejected both civil society and the state as being essentially alien to a truly human life. Since the time of Marx, criticisms of Hegel's work haven't been in short supply. If the measure of a thinker is the eminence of his critics, then Hegel must surely rank highly. Among his critics we find not only Marx but also Arthur Schopenhauer, Friedrich Nietzsche, Ludwiz Bolzmann, Bertrand Russell and, notoriously, Karl Popper in the second volume of his *The Open Society and its Enemies* in which, perhaps unfairly, he portrays Hegel as the *éminence grise* behind the rise of twentieth century totalitarianism. [see Kolakowski, 122-125]

5 Wood 1991, viii-ix; see, notoriously, Popper, 27-80, but see also Avineri, 176ff.

6 See Paul Franco, who presents an account of Hegel as steering a path between liberalism, traditionally construed, and communitarianism. [Franco, passim] What liberalism is, is contested. Westphal takes it to encompass two basic principles; (1) the principle of personal autonomy ('each person is competent to and ought to participate in making law'; and (2) the principle of justice ('there are standards any law must meet to be good or just.')

7 Brooks 2007, 1. On the other hand, David Rose believes that Hegel is 'a rational conservative who advocates reform when required, but views any attempt to rationally reconstruct the state according to the determinations and demands of pure reason or universal moral realism as a nonsensical and dangerous undertaking.' [Rose 2007, 7]

8 Scruton 2014, 65; see Gatti, 2.

9 Westphal, 236-237; italics in original.

10 Hegel, 48, §15. Unless otherwise indicated, words and phrases emphasised in quotations from Hegel are in the original.

11 Hegel, 54, §23. The difference in immediate intelligibility between these various passages illustrates a common experience in reading Hegel, where passages of relative lucidity compete with passages of almost complete obscurity, acquiring a *chiaroscuro*-like brilliance by contrast. David Berman contrasts the obscure style of writing, characteristic of the classic German philosophers—Kant, Fichte, Schelling and Hegel—with the clear style of writing of Hegel's most vituperative critic, Schopenhauer. [Berman 1995, xviii] For a succinct and accessible account of the metaphysical dimension of Hegel's account of the will, see Hampsher-Monk 1992, 429-431.

12 See Pelczynski 1984b, 64-76.

13 PR 77, §45; see also 78, §46, Addition (H), Findlay, 310 and Ilting, 93. Thom Brooks comments, 'we first grasp our freedom in the world as our freedom when we take possession of a thing. When we take possession of some thing, we create an external space where our freedom can become manifest.' [Brooks 2007, 32]

14 Hampsher-Monk notes that grasping, forming and marking are but 'imperfect representations of will.' One expresses the relationship between one's will and a thing most directly by making use of it. [Hampsher-Monk 1992, 435]

15 See PR 84-88, §§55,56 & 58; see Ryan 188 ff.

16 PR 79, §48; see Findlay, 311; see also Ryan 186 ff.

17 PR 98, §67; see also 96, §66.

18 Pelczynski 1984b, 61; see Pelczynski 1971a, 10ff.

19 PR 223, §185 Addition (H); see Pelczynski 1971a, 7. 'The truth is that the common-sense convictions which form part of the intellectual heritage of the modern world were acquired and formed under the long discipline of Christian faith, and that the Greeks did not possess them because they had not been educated in Christian doctrine....the logical connexion between Christian doctrine and the particular common-sense conviction that will is a part of human nature becomes clearer if we recognize that metaphysics forms a middle term between religious dogma and common sense. The doctrine that a positive element is essential to law implies a faculty of will in man, and is implied in its turn by the doctrine that the supreme law for man is the command of God that is to say that it belongs to its essence to issue from God's *will*. If we ask now for the source of that doctrine which attributes will to God, there can be no doubt about the answer; it is the revelation embodied in the Old Testament.' [Foster 1965, 135-136]

20 PR 230, §192 Addition (H).

21 PR 233, §199; see Rose 2007, 121ff.

22 Westphal, 257; see PR, 189 §188.

23 'Hegel is, like many writers of early modernity, an apologist for the emerging capitalist system and the institution of private property, but his defence does not rest on more common utilitarian arguments

or claims of systematic efficiency. Capitalism may well deliver what individuals want better than other systems, but—more significantly, and like Hegel's argument for private property in abstract right—it allows individuals to decide for themselves what they want. It is this implicit embodiment of freedom at the heart of capitalism that serves to justify it.' [Rose 2007, 120-121]

24 'Hegel,' writes David Rose, 'demonstrates an astute and unexpected sensitivity for the contingent evils of capitalism: poverty and the atomism of civil society. Capitalism ensures recognition as a free particular individual, but it needs to be regulated otherwise it undermines the "homeliness" of the state and leads to social atomism.' [Rose 2007, 127] Hegel will not be the last to make some such observation.

25 The existence and mode of operation of mutual aid societies or friendly societies is one of the best-kept secrets in social history. It's not clear that Hegel knew anything about them although it would seem from his comments on corporations that he would have approved of them if he had. These societies originated as early as the sixteenth century and continued well into the twentieth. By 1801, in Britain, there were 7,200 societies with around 700,000 adult male members, in a country of 9 million. In 1920, some 18 million Americans belonged to fraternal societies, some 30% of all adults over 20. These societies provided death benefits (often as much as was equivalent to a year's salary at the time), payable to survivors, unemployment assistance, accident insurance, financial aid to those seeking work, and health cover by means of contracts entered into between the societies and physicians. In the late nineteenth century, some of the larger societies built orphanages and old-age homes. [See Beito 1990 & 2000; see also Green 2000]

26 PR 266, §244 Addition (G).

27 J. N. Findlay is not impressed by the section in *The Philosophy of Right* on the Police and the Corporation (§§23-256) remarking, 'The Police (Public Authorities) and Corporations (Trade Guilds) now make a somewhat comic entrance on the dialectical stage' although Findlay is somewhat reticent about saying just *why* what Hegel has to say on these matters is comic.

28 Ilting credits Hegel with being 'the first to introduce a distinction between civil society and the state as two different spheres of public life and to attempt to give a theoretical foundation to this distinction.' [Ilting, 107].

29 Redding, 37-38; see also Pelczynski 1971a, 12.

30 PR 106, §75; see Ilting, 94.

31 Hegel, as Kant, regards the question of the historical circumstances of the origin of any particular state as being of no philosophical value or interest. It makes no difference, he says, 'what is or what the historical origin of the state in general (or rather of any particular state with its rights and determinations)…whether it first arose out of patriarchal conditions, out of fear or trust, out of corporations, etc., or how the basis of its rights has been understood and fixed in the consciousness as divine and positive right or contract, habit, etc.' [PR 276, §258]

32 PR 106, §74 Addition (H).

33 Redding, 37; see PR §75.

34 PR 285, §261 Addition (H).

35 See PR 276, 278, §258.

36 Remember Hobbes's 'mortal God'? But see Avineri, 177.

37 PR 279, §258, Addition (G).

38 PR 279, §258, Addition (G).

39 Westphal, 262; Findlay, 325; Pelczynski 1984b, 62.

40 Brooks 2007, 113; see also Pelczynski 1971a, 231ff, and Avineri, 185-189.

41 Is the general will merely the sum of individual wills or is it something totally other than individual wills, taken either one by one or, indeed, all together? [See Westphal, 241]

42 In 1819, in the various German states, as part of a wave of reaction to the liberal movements that had flourished during the Napoleonic 'German spring,' academic publications were censored and guidelines were produced for the removal from the universities of those whom the authorities regarded as demagogues. [see Wood 1991, vii-ix] Wood remarks that 'there is now a virtual consensus among knowledgeable scholars that the earlier images of Hegel, as the philosopher of the reactionary Prussian restoration and forerunner of modern totalitarianism, are simply wrong, whether they are viewed as accounts of Hegel's attitude toward Prussian politics or as broader philosophical interpretations of his theory of the state.' [Wood 1991, ix]

43 But see Westphal, 235, 237.

Chapter 26

JOHN STUART MILL

I would not give half a guinea to live under one form of government
rather than another. It is of no moment to the happiness of an individual
—Samuel Johnson

If all mankind minus one, were of one opinion, and only one person were
of the contrary opinion, mankind would be no more justified in silencing that
one person, than he, if he had the power, would be justified in silencing mankind
—John Stuart Mill

John Stuart Mill (1806-1873), the son of the economist James Mill, received one of the most truly extraordinary educations in human history. He started Greek at the age of three and was soon reading the Greek classics in literature and philosophy. He added Latin to his accomplishments at the age of eight, and all the time, in addition to his classical studies, he was learning mathematics, history and economics. Because of his father's standing, Mill was incredibly well connected with the most prominent people of his time— Bentham, Ricardo, Say, Saint Simon and Comte. It isn't every young boy who is taken for walks by Ricardo to chat about economics. Under the influence of his father and Jeremy Bentham, Mill became a utilitarian and claimed to have remained one (in some form or other) throughout his life, despite, in the opinion of some critics, holding views whose compatibility with utilitarianism is difficult to reconcile. It is easy to forget that Mill contributed to political economy as well as to ethics, politics and logic. He started in life as a free marketeer but not without accepting the necessity for state intervention in the economy if it were considered necessary for utilitarian purposes. In his later life, he moved inexorably in the direction of socialism, amending his *Principles of Political Economy* accordingly. This work, first published in 1848, was the Samuelson of its age, being the dominant textbook in economics for well over half a century until finally displaced by Marshall's *Principles of Economics* in 1919.

Mill's *On Liberty* was published in 1859 and was followed two years later by his *Considerations on Representative Government*. These are the two works that will primarily concern us here.[1] Mill's writings, in particular, his essay *On Liberty*, have had an enormous effect on modern social and political thought. For all that, however, Mill is *not* one of the world's great thinkers, least of all one of the most consistent. He has an annoying and persistent habit of giving with one hand and taking with the other. George Sabine, as usual, puts the matter clearly: 'On nearly every subject he was likely to begin with a general statement of principles which, taken literally and by itself, appeared to be as rigid and as abstract as anything that his father might have written. But having thus declared his allegiance to the ancestral dogmas, Mill proceeded to make concessions and restatements so far-reaching that a critical reader was left in doubt whether the original statement had not been explained away.' [Sabine, 706-707] Seemingly committed to a form of utilitarianism in the Benthamite tradition, Mill nevertheless rejected any unitary conception of happiness that could make utilitarianism workable. 'Mill was not willing to accept Bentham's greatest happiness principle for what in effect it was, namely, a rough and ready criterion for judging the utility of legislation.' [Sabine, 708] Mill was also not, to his credit, willing to sacrifice his native conviction that freedom and integrity were, in some sense, intrinsic goods, apart from any contribution their possession might make to some utilitarian notion of happiness or pleasure. There is a persistent tension between Mill's residual utilitarianism and his latent anti-utilitarian conception of the human good.

On Liberty

If a classic is a book that everybody thinks he has read but few in fact have, then John Stuart Mill's essay *On Liberty* is most definitely a classic.[2] Short though it is, I suspect that very few people have read it through from beginning to end and most people are therefore of the opinion that Mill is a doughty defender of the freedom of the individual against the combined forces of society and state. That opinion isn't entirely wrong although it isn't entirely right either. Those who would object to a portrayal of John Stuart Mill as the White Knight of liberty include Ayn Rand who trenchantly describes *On Liberty* as 'the most pernicious piece of collectivism ever adopted by suicidal defenders of liberty,'[3] and Quentin P. Taylor who argues that Mill was rather a socialist than any kind of free-market liberal. [see Taylor, passim]

Mill believes that the core thesis of *On Liberty* can be expressed in 'one very simple principle' that should govern the dealings of society with the individual, whether those dealings are exercised through legal means or by means of the moral coercion of public opinion. It is worth quoting the famous passage that contains this simple principle:

> [T]he sole end for which mankind are warranted, individually or collectively, in interfering with the liberty of action of any of their number is self-protection….the only purpose for which power can be rightfully exercised over any member of a civilized community, against his will, is to prevent harm to others. His own good, either rightfully physical or moral, is not a sufficient warrant. He cannot rightfully be compelled to do or forbear because it will be better for him to do so, because it will make him happier, because, in the opinions of others, to do so would be wise, or even right. These are good reasons for remonstrating with him, or reasoning with him, or persuading him, or entreating him, but not for compelling him, or visiting him with any evil in case he do otherwise. To justify that, the conduct from which it is desired to deter him, must be calculated to

produce evil to some one else. The only part of the conduct of any one, for which he is amenable to society, is that which concerns others. In the part that merely concerns himself, his independence is, of right, absolute. Over himself, over his own body and mind, the individual is sovereign. [*On Liberty* §I, 9, 14]

Even at the remove of over a hundred and fifty years, it is hard not to be moved by the obvious sincerity and forcefulness of this well-known passage. A clearer, more unambiguous, more succinctly stated defence of the liberty of the individual has surely never been produced by any other writer. And yet, and yet….there is a problem with this one very simple principle and it is this—what we have in this passage isn't obviously one, certainly isn't simple, and may not, in the end, even *be* Mill's guiding principle. Before taking a closer look at this supposedly one very simple principle, let us examine the broader context of Mill's thought.

Mill thinks it expedient to begin his treatment of liberty by considering one particular form of it which, he believes, is generally recognised by all shades of current opinion—liberty of thought. [*On Liberty* §1, 16, 19] The justification of this form of liberty isn't peculiar to it alone but has much wider application so that, if we can come to grips with it, we will find much that's applicable to other aspects of liberty as well. Mill lists four grounds on which both freedom of opinion and freedom of expression of opinion (not quite the same thing) can be shown to be necessary to the well being of mankind.[4] First, the silenced opinion may be true. Second, it may contain a portion of truth, even if is not completely true. Third, a received opinion which is wholly true, if it cannot be challenged, will be held 'in the manner of a prejudice, with little comprehension or feeling of its rational grounds' [*On Liberty* II, §43, 59] and fourth, such an opinion, if not subject to challenge, will be in danger of collapsing into a formal and inefficacious dogma. Of these four grounds, the latter two which relate to the prevention of dogmatism, and connected as they are to Mill's deeper concerns about human development, are much more important to Mill than the first two which focus on the discernment of truth. David Brink notes that 'Mill's claim that the value of freedom of expression lies in keeping true beliefs from becoming dogmatic reflects his view that freedoms of thought and discussion are necessary for fulfilling our natures as progressive beings.' [Brink, 62]

The basic principle of liberty is non-interference by individuals, groups of individuals, or governments with the actions of others, or with the thoughts or the expression of those thoughts by others. Mill believes that whereas thought as such is absolutely free, the expression of thought in action is subject to the condition of its not harming others. Nevertheless, the *expression* of thought is so close to thought itself that any social limitations on it should be minimal. Where, however, talk turns into action, then restraint may not only be permitted but may even be required. 'The implicit principle here,' writes Magid, 'is that as long as discussion remains discussion, it ought to be permitted absolute freedom; but once it passes beyond discussion to action, it ought to be treated as action.' [Magid, 799] Where opinions move closer to action, as in incitement, opinions can be controlled by social or political means. [*On Liberty* §III, 1, 62]

How does all this apply more widely, to matters beyond freedom of opinion or freedom of expression of opinion? Here, Mill expresses himself in a mode that Aristotle himself wouldn't have found alien. He believes that the human good lies in a kind of deliberative choosing which gives direction to one's life. If choice is to be genuine and informed, then not only must we have liberty of opinion and expression of opinion, we must also (within certain limitations) have liberty of action.[5]

One could make a case for the legal restriction of individual liberty on a number of grounds. One could restrict Jones' exercise of liberty for Jones's own good (paternalism); or to prevent him from acting immorally (moralism); or to prevent him offending another (offence-prevention); or, finally, to prevent his causing harm to others (harm-prevention). This gives Mill four possible grounds for restricting liberty: 1. paternalism; 2. moralism; 3. offence-prevention; and 4. harm-prevention. Mill isn't willing to concede that the immorality of a person's action just by itself is a legitimate ground for the legal restriction of his actions (number 2). Restriction of liberty on the grounds of mere offence (number 3) is ruled out by Mill when he writes 'The acts of an individual may be hurtful to others, or wanting in due consideration for their welfare, without going the length of violating any of their constituted rights. The offender may then be justly punished by opinion, though not by law.' [*On Liberty* §V, 3, 83] Mill subscribes whole-heartedly to the legal principle *volenti non fit injuria* (to one who is willing, there can be no injury) so that society has no justifiable interest in 'protecting' those who consent to actions that cause them harm.

Restricting a person's liberty for the good of that person (number 1) is a form of paternalism that Mill is prepared to tolerate only where the person in question, such as a child, is incapable of the proper exercise of liberty. This acceptable form of paternalism may then be employed in respect of individuals or, indeed, in respect of whole societies. It is important to realise that the prescriptions of *On Liberty* apply fully only to societies at a high stage of development, adult societies, as it were. Mill doesn't think that his reflections on liberty apply always and everywhere. The full benefits of liberty are confined to people (and societies) that are mature—liberty isn't something that is valuable unconditionally. If liberty is instrumentally valuable then, if the other constituent elements for human perfection are lacking, liberty, unable to bring about this condition all by itself, loses much of its value. Given that liberty is essentially instrumental for Mill and to be valued insofar as it contributes to a developed human life, some particular forms of liberty are going to be more important than others. Mill then rejects grounds 2 and 3 completely as possible grounds for the restriction of liberty, and accepts 1 only in a qualified way. So that leaves only the harm-prevention ground (number 4) in the running for a condition that might unconditionally restrict liberty. [see Brink, 55] I will continue the discussion of Mill's 'very simple principle' shortly but first, I should like to consider Mill's allegiance to utilitarianism.

WAS MILL A UTILITARIAN?

Despite his professed allegiance to utilitarianism, Mill's most significant contribution to social and political thought was his *On Liberty*, the arguments of which aren't always obviously in accord with that doctrine. 'For Mill freedom of thought and investigation, freedom of discussion, and the freedom of self-controlled moral judgment and action were goods in their own right.' [Sabine 708] Mill did in fact believe that freedom would be beneficial to society and in that sense, his support for it was utilitarian, but his commitment to freedom went well beyond utilitarian considerations. His real reason for supporting freedom was that 'it produces and gives scope to a high type of moral character. To hear public questions freely discussed, to have a share in political decisions, to have moral convictions and to take the responsibility for making them effective are among the ways in which reasonable human beings are produced.' [Sabine, 709]

Mill distinguishes, in a distinctly non-utilitarian way, between superior and inferior pleasures. Not all pleasures are commensurable. The pursuit of higher pleasures is productive of progress so that any society in which higher pleasures are to be produced needs social freedom. This distinction between higher and lower pleasures, however plausible in itself, fatally compromises the utilitarian side of Mill's thought. If pleasures aren't commensurable, then it is simply not possible to have a felicific calculus. How many lower pleasures does one higher pleasure equal? How many hamburgers balance Beethoven's *Eroica*? There can be no answer to these questions. McClelland plays down the significance of this problem, noting that 'Mill knew perfectly well that his additions to the utilitarian agenda were not amenable to the arithmetical rigours of the Benthamite felicific calculus...' but whether Mill knew this or not isn't strictly relevant to the conceptual knot at the heart of Mill's thought. [McClelland, 472]

How is Mill supposed to reconcile his utilitarianism and his liberalism? One can be a utilitarian and one can be a liberal but it isn't immediately obvious that one can simultaneously be both. Paul Kelly notes, 'We cannot simply explain away this inconsistency in terms of the peculiar point of each work, because even in *On Liberty* Mill claims that he builds his account of liberty on the foundations of utility.' [Kelly 2009b, 387-388] Henry Magid remarks that although Mill is still, in some residual sense, a utilitarian, 'the core has been so modified and expanded that the resultant theory has a cast different from that of original utilitarianism. Government does not exist merely to produce the maximum of that kind of pleasure that the citizens happen to prefer. Rather some types of pleasure are better than others, and the government has the responsibility for having its citizens educated to pursue the higher pleasures in place of the lower pleasures.' [Magid, 789-790] In the end, what Mill stood for was the valorisation of human dignity and moral responsibility; freedom, not just as a means to human fulfilment but as a constitutive part of that fulfilment; freedom as both an individual good and a social good; and a positive role for the state in offsetting the dangers of a dominant society. A libertarian can concur wholeheartedly with the first three of these positions (however much

Mill, as a utilitarian, might not have been philosophically entitled to hold them) but there is no way he could accept the fourth.

What is particularly striking about Mill's *On Liberty* is that his strategy isn't primarily to carve out a space for liberty against government intrusion; rather, it is intended to address the dangers to liberty presented by society. 'The threat to liberty which Mill chiefly feared was not government but a majority that is intolerant of the unconventional, that looks with suspicion on divergent minorities and is willing to use the weight of numbers to repress and regiment them.' [Sabine, 710] The state constrains the liberty of the individual formally through law but society constrains it informally by means of public opinion. The only way for individuals to defend themselves against both state and society was 'through eternal vigilance over the state and through self-assertion over prevailing opinion.' [McClelland, 474] Of the two threats to liberty, Mill believed that the threat from society is by far the more potent. The individual, then, needs to be protected, not only from the state, but also from society. 'Protection, therefore, against the tyranny of the magistrate is not enough: there needs protection also against the tyranny of the prevailing opinion and feeling; against the tendency of society to impose, by other means than civil penalties, its own ideas and practices as rules of conduct on those who dissent from them; to fetter the development, and, if possible, prevent the formation, of any individuality not in harmony with its ways, and compel all characters to fashion themselves upon the model of its own. There is a limit to the legit-imate interference of collective opinion with individual independence and to find that limit, and maintain it against encroachment, is as indispensable to a good condition of human affairs, as protection against political despotism.' [*On Liberty*, §I, 5, 9]

On this point, a libertarian is likely to find himself disagreeing with Mill. Provided no physical aggression is used to influence behaviour, there appears to be nothing obviously improper with social means of producing conformity—persuasion, exhortation, non-association (shunning)—all these are legitimate activities *if* unaccompanied by the initiation or the threat of the initiation of physical violence. Mill was right, of course, to grasp the practical significance of social pressure in inducing a measure of conformity to social norms but, whatever the force of such social pressure, and however unpleasant or obnoxious it might be, unless that pressure be physical, it cannot be of direct concern to a libertarian. If Mill had been a consistent utilitarian, then liberty would have had only an instrumental value as a means to man's overall happiness. But this wasn't Mill's view. For him, liberty of thought and speech and action was a good whether or not it made a contribution to happiness, although he did, in fact, think that liberty was and would be happiness-producing.

Mill appears to have three courses of action open to him: either he remains inconsistent in maintaining a non-instrumental conception of freedom and a distinction between higher and lower pleasures at the same time as he purports to be a utilitarian; or he keeps his utilitarianism and gives up non-instrumental freedom and the distinction between higher and lower pleasures; or he keeps non-instrumental freedom and the distinction between higher and lower pleasures but gives up utilitarianism. [see Brink, 56-58] In the end, then, Mill is an inconsistent utilitarian, a thinker whose ethical views were more Kantian than Benthamite. He desired freedom for thought and action, protected not only from the interference of the state but from the oppression of social majorities, but it is difficult to discern the principled basis on which he could make his case. Mill was concerned to delineate a sphere of activity for individuals in respect of which neither state nor society had a legitimate interest that would permit either to intervene, to supervise or to restrict. Sketching out such a sphere isn't especially difficult if one has at one's disposal a theory of natural rights but, of course, as a utilitarian, Mill had no such tools to hand. The result of the conceptual confusion at the base of Mill's thought is that his practical application of his principles was arbitrary so that for him, the prohibition on the sale of alcohol was an illegitimate restriction of liberty but the enforcement of mandatory public education was not. In the end, he was prepared to accept a plethora of regulations on business and enterprise, so much so that nothing is left of any commitment he may ever have had to *laissez faire*. Now, let us return to a more detailed account of Mill's notorious 'one very simple principle.'

ONE VERY SIMPLE PRINCIPLE?

The 'one very simple' passage contains at least three propositions that may or may not amount to the same thing but if they do—and that's a moot point—they do so in very different verbal ways. These three propositions are: (1) interference with the liberty of action of another is justified only by the end of self-protection; (2) the will of an agent can forcibly be overborne only to prevent harm to others; and (3) only conduct concerning others can be amenable to society. This last proposition makes no mention of harm but, instead, tells us that only conduct concerning (but not necessarily harmful to) others is amenable to society. Many commentators are either unaware of or, if aware of, ignore the complexities of this passage, reducing it, in effect, to proposition (2), and they focus their attention and their discussions only on this proposition which has come to be known as *the* 'harm principle'.

But matters become yet more complex. In chapter V of the essay, a remote region of this short work that only the most intrepid intellectual travellers ever reach, Mill presents two maxims which, he says, form the entire doctrine of his essay. These are: (a) 'the individual is not accountable to society for his actions in so far as these concern the interests of no person but himself'; and (b) 'for such actions as are prejudicial to the interests of others, the individual is accountable, and may be subjected either to social or to legal punishment, if society is of the opinion that the one or the other is requisite for its protection.' [*On Liberty*, §V, 2, 104] How do these two maxims, forming the entire doctrine of the essay, relate to the one simple principle that Mill had earlier described as the object of his essay? [*On Liberty*, §I, 9, 13] Proposition (a) is recognisably similar (though not identical) to (3) and whereas proposition (b) might be taken to be equivalent to (2), it makes no mention of 'harm', speaking instead of 'actions prejudicial to the interests of others.' Furthermore, it appears to run elements of (2) and (3) together and to extend them by hinting at a notion of society as something that can have opinions and, it seems, can also be the agent of the administration of punishment.

If Mill's 'one very simple principle' is dubiously one, it is clearly not simple.[6] Even assuming that we can reduce the three propositions in the passage to proposition (2), the so-called 'harm principle', we encounter further problems. The notion of harm in Mill's essay is systematically ambiguous as is evidenced by his use of a range of near-synonyms ('evil', 'injury', 'damage', 'hurt', 'concern', 'affect', 'regard' and 'molest') in his discussion and application of the principle. These near-synonyms fall into two broad classes: the morally neutral—'concern', 'affect', 'regard'; and the morally negative—'hurt', 'damage', 'injury', 'evil'. Since, however, it can be argued that everything everybody does concerns, affects or regards another in some way or other, however trivial, the seemingly morally neutral terms employed by Mill must be understood in a negative way if his principle isn't to become vacuous, that is, those actions that concern, affect or regard others, must affect or regard them in a harmful fashion.

Shoehorning 'harm' or its equivalent into the meaning of the neutral concepts employed by Mill, although necessary, is still not sufficient to avoid every difficulty. If Algernon takes the last cucumber sandwich before Jack can get to it, or if Tom buys the last seat for the opera as Harry stands fretting behind him in the ticket queue, Jack and Harry have been harmed. Even so, it's difficult to see how anyone could object to the actions of Algernon or Tom unless there's some other element of their conduct that is independently reprehensible, such as Algernon's rugby-tackling Jack to keep him from the sandwich or Tom's queue-jumping Harry. Towards the end of his essay, and somewhat belatedly, Mill recognises the point that an action that negatively affects the interests of another does not necessarily justify intervention by society. 'Whoever succeeds in an overcrowded profession, or in a competitive examination; whoever is preferred to another in any context for an object which both desire, reaps benefit from the loss of others, from their wasted exertion and their disappointment' but 'society admits no right, either legal or moral, in the disappointed competitors to immunity from this kind of suffering.' [*On Liberty*, §V, 3, 105] How, then, is Mill, or anyone else, to make a judgement that an action is harmful in the requisite sense? That brings us to a consideration of what appears to be Mill's fundamental operating principle in matters of human conduct.

Within a page of the occurrence of the passage containing the one very simple principle, Mill makes it clear that all ethical questions are to be referred to the principle of utility. 'I regard utility as the ultimate appeal of all ethical questions,' he writes, 'but it must be utility in the largest sense, grounded on the permanent interests of man as a progressive being.' [*On Liberty*, §1, 11, 15] Utility is a notoriously slippery notion but, unless it's to become irredeemably vague, it must at the very least amount to the claim that the moral status of human actions is to be determined by an evaluation of their consequences. If Mill means what he says here about the centrality of the principle of utility, he has a problem, for it is neither impossible nor even particularly difficult to conceive of circumstances in which considerations of utility might either demand the performance of acts that contravene the harm principle or the prohibition of acts that do not.

Consider the following cautionary tale. In the remote and isolated town of Desperation live a sheriff and ninety-nine other inhabitants. Some years earlier, the sheriff had been responsible for sending the Wild Bunch to jail and they have sworn vengeance on him. On escaping from jail, they ride into Desperation, corral everyone in the stockyard, and present them with the following choice: 'If you, the townspeople, shoot the sheriff, we'll ride out of town; if you don't shoot the sheriff, then we'll kill him and all of you too. You have fifteen minutes to decide.' What should the townspeople do? Ruling out miraculous rescues and escapes and assuming the sheriff is unwilling to shoot himself, there seem to be only two possibilities. If the townspeople shoot the sheriff, we end up with one dead body. If the townspeople don't shoot the sheriff, we end up with one hundred dead bodies. In each case, the sheriff dies. Now, a utilitarian approach to this problem seems to dictate that we should shoot the sheriff (better one dead body than one hundred dead bodies) but if killing someone isn't interfering with his liberty or overbearing his will, it's hard to know what is. It might be claimed that shooting the sheriff is consistent with propositions (1) and (2) of Mill's very simple principle. Proposition (1) allows for interference with the liberty of another for the purposes of self-protection and it could be argued that in shooting the sheriff the townspeople are simply protecting themselves. The problem with this claim is, I suggest, that the natural and plausible way to read (1) is that it permits one to interfere with the liberty of an aggressor against oneself when such interference is necessary to protect oneself from that aggressor. One may, of course, read (1) as permitting the kind of third party interference with liberty as sketched in the 'shoot the sheriff' scenario, but then (1) becomes intuitively much less plausible. Wouldn't (2), the 'harm principle', justify the townspeople's shooting the sheriff? Once again, a plausible reading of (2) requires the harm to emanate from the one whose will is overborne and not from some innocent third party such as the sheriff. Where liberty and utility clash, which is to take precedence?

There is a deeper problem underlying the whole of Mill's essay. Whom is it directed against? Who or what is Mill's target? Who or what does he think is the most significant threat to human liberty? 'Governments,' is Mill's occasional answer to this question, although he is relatively dismissive of the possibility of tyrannical governments in contemporary nineteenth century society. He accepts as a matter of historical fact that rulers were generally conceived as antagonistic to those whom they ruled and is refreshingly aware, on occasion, of the evils that governments may do, writing in his *Considerations on Representative Government* [hereafter CRG], 'Every kind and degree of evil of which mankind are susceptible, may be inflicted on them by their government; and none of the good which social existence is capable of, can be any further realized than as the constitution of the government is compatible with, and allows scope for, its attainment. Not to speak of indirect effects, the direct meddling of the public authorities has no necessary limits but those of human existence....' [§II, 2, 217] Nevertheless, he believes that the growth of representational democracies has increased the possibility that those who are ruled will identify their rulers as themselves and thus the antagonism between ruler and ruled will lessen or disappear. A welcome breath of realism makes itself apparent when Mill notes that 'The "people" who exercise the power are not always the same people with those over whom it is exercised; and the "self-government" spoken of is not the government of each by himself, but of each by all the rest.' [*On Liberty* II, 4, 8] In the end, however, damaging as government may be to the liberty of individuals, society is of much more concern to Mill as a source of threats to liberty than the state. Libertarians generally direct their hostility primarily against the state which they see as the great and unjustified limiter of man's freedom. The enemy of liberty, as Mill saw it, wasn't so much government or state but society. The dominant theme of *On Liberty* is the oppression that can be exercised by the majority in society against the minority. Of course, one way in which the majority can exercise such oppression is by means of government but it is not the only way nor, perhaps, the most significant way. The argument in *On Liberty*, then, isn't so much an appeal for relief from governmental interference but an argument for social tolerance. Kelly notes that 'Mill's real concern is not with the levers of public power or the direction in which they should be exercised. Rather, it is with the social threat to liberty, and in answer to this he offers a defence of an ideal of liberty and individuality as a philosophy of life.' [Kelly 2009b, 393] It is, I think, interesting to note that whereas one of the chapters in *On Liberty* is entitled 'Of the Limits to the Authority of Society over the Individual,' there is no corresponding chapter entitled 'Of the Limits to the Authority of the State over the Individual'.

Throughout the whole of his essay Mill is, I believe, guilty of the fallacy of misplaced concreteness. As Mill conceives it, society is an agent that can do things. 'Society can and does execute its own mandates'; there are certain conditions that 'society is justified at enforcing at all costs.'[7] Society isn't only an agent inasmuch as it apparently possesses the ability to do things, it is also a patient in that things can be done to it. Society protects us, and we, as a result, owe it a return for this protection. But society is neither an agent nor a patient. Society is not a real entity. The term 'society' is merely a convenient shorthand device used to refer to the aggregate of individual human actions and interactions, just as 'the market' is a shorthand way of referring to the aggregate of economic exchanges that take place between individuals. Society has no way of acting that isn't reducible to the actions of individual agents and society has no mode of being such that a person can claim to act as its agent. We owe society nothing because there is nothing to owe anything to. We may, and often do, owe this or that individual a debt but to whom, except by way of metaphor, do we pay a debt to society? Society can't do anything nor can anything be done to it. Carl Jung notes that 'Words like "Society" and "State" are so concretized that they are almost personified. In the opinion of the man in the street, the "State," far more than any king in history is the inexhaustible giver of all good; the "State" is invoked, made responsible, grumbled at, and so on and so forth. Society is elevated to the rank of a supreme ethical principle; indeed, it is even credited with positively creative capacities.' [Jung 1957, 385]

In case one might think that Mill is simply using the term 'society' as a shorthand device to refer to the aggregate of individual actions and interactions, several passages in the essay make it very clear that this is not so. Mill thinks there are positive acts that one may be compelled by society to perform. These include: giving evidence in court; sharing in common defence; and sharing in other works necessary to the interest of society of which one enjoys the protection. [*On Liberty*, §I, 11, 15] Mill also thinks one can be compelled by society to perform certain acts of individual beneficence such as saving another's life or protecting the defenceless against abuse. It is apparently one's duty to do such things: 'things which whenever it is obviously a man's duty to do he may rightfully be made responsible *to society* for not doing.'[8]

Given that utility is meant to be the ultimate arbiter in ethical matters for Mill, one may well wonder where this deontological notion of duty has suddenly sprung from but, leaving that intriguing avenue of enquiry to one side, we can see that Mill's principle, which is generally interpreted purely negatively, not only is consistent in his eyes with positive duties and obligations, it sometimes in fact requires them. These positive obligations aren't the consequences of contractual agreements freely entered into but result simply from our membership of society. Mill explicitly rejects any contractual foundation for society; 'society is not founded on a contract,' he says, 'and...no good purpose is answered by inventing a contract in order to deduce social obligations from it... [*On Liberty*, §IV, 3, 83] Those who look upon *On Liberty* as a charter document of libertarianism would do well to be concerned by the extensive list of liberty-restricting positive obligations that one acquires not as the result of any explicit agreement or the free assumption of responsibility but simply by virtue of living with others.

In addition to inappropriately concretising the notion of society, Mill also confounds the literal and the metaphorical senses of 'tyranny'. Governments exercise their tyranny by politico-legal means through instrumental agencies— armies, police forces or the like; society, in strong contrast, exercises its so-called tyranny only by means of social pressure. To call what governments do and what society does 'tyranny' is to call two very different things by one name; politico-legal coercion that is based on the use of force through specific agencies or ordinary criminal violence against a person or property isn't at all the same thing as social pressure unaccompanied by force or the threat of force. In the film *Ronin*, would-be tough guy Sean Bean challenges Robert de Niro with: 'You ever kill anybody?' to which de Niro responds with a superb put-down: 'I hurt somebody's feelings once.' Hurting someone's feelings isn't a nice thing to do but do not list it on your CV if you want a job with the Mafia. Mill is, no doubt, correct to be deeply suspicious of the potent force of public opinion but there's a difference in principle, not just in power or extent or efficiency, between commands and prohibitions accompanied by the threat of force or the actual exercise of force, on the one hand, and exhortations, expressions of disapproval and the like unaccompanied by force or the threat of force, on the other. The disapproval of one's peers, for example, however forcibly expressed and however much resented or unwelcome, isn't coercive and so can't be an expression of tyranny; taxation, by contrast, however personally affable your local inspector of taxes may be, *is* coercive and, I would argue, tyrannical.

But the distinction between acts of violence and acts of rudeness, though significant, isn't the central issue. One might kill another human being and be justified in so doing, and one might be rude to one's friend and not be justified. If the 'harm' principle is to be defensible, harm must be understood not just as factual damage to another's interests but, normatively, as *unjustified* damage. Taken normatively, the harm prohibited by the principle would cover those actions that infringe another's *rights* to person and property. The reason Algernon's taking of the last cucumber sandwich isn't prohibited by the harm principle (though it clearly injures Jack's interests, even if only slightly) is that Jack had no right (or no more right) to that sandwich than did Algernon. Unfortunately, Mill is unable to give such an account as his commitment to the principle of utility is coupled with a refusal to employ any abstract notion of right. 'I forego any advantage which could be derived to my argument from the idea of abstract right, as a thing independent of utility.' [*On Liberty*, §I, 11, 15]

So, Mill's one very simple principle isn't obviously one, clearly isn't simple, and may not in fact be his guiding principle. Mill conflates genuinely tyrannical actions (usually though not exclusively the product of government or government agencies) that *are* liberty-limiting with the merely metaphorically tyrannical non-liberty-limiting actions of individuals. This conflation results, at least in part, from Mill's tendency to think of society as something which can both do things and have things done to it, as an agent and a patient. Whatever metaphorical value such a conception of society may have and whatever linguistic convenience it provides, it makes no literal sense. Finally, Mill's commitment to utility as 'the ultimate appeal of all ethical questions' [*On Liberty*, §I, 11, 15] makes it difficult, if not impossible, for him to give a normative account of harm that alone could render the 'harm principle' coherent. Mills' 'one very simple principle' is definitely at the heart of *On Liberty*. It is thought provoking and, even today, still provocative and controversial. Nevertheless, the remainder of *On Liberty* needs to be considered if Mill's principle is to be properly evaluated.

Mill has been accused of being an illiberal liberal in attempting, as some critics see it, to substitute a kind of religion of humanity that everyone is going to be forced to accept as an alternative to the dominant if fading moral authority of Christianity. Some, such as Hamburger and Cowling, have taken Mill to be proposing the imposition of a tyranny exercised by a superior elite. Whatever the deficiencies in Mill's account of liberty, it is hard to see how such a charge could be justified. Extrapolating from one of Mill's own examples, it would seem that whereas Mill 'would have no trouble with restricting incitement to racial violence, he would also have no time for the idea of "hate speech", in which the mere expression of certain views is itself considered to be a harm. Holocaust deniers, racists, homophobes, heterophobes, and any other category of bigot are all entitled to hold, and be protected in expressing, their beliefs, on Mill's theory.' [Kelly 2009b, 395] And whereas it is true that Mill is unwilling to allow Christian beliefs to be forced coercively upon those who would otherwise not accept them, he does not deny that men are free to find consolation and significance in religious belief if that's what they freely choose to do.

CONSIDERATIONS ON REPRESENTATIVE GOVERNMENT

For Mill, although government is something we must have, not just any form of government will do. Mill robustly rules out the romantic idea that a despotic monarchy would be the best form of government if only we could be sure to find a good despot. 'I look upon this as a radical and most pernicious misconception of what good government is; which, until it can be got rid of, will fatally vitiate all our speculations on government.' [CRG §III, 1, 238] From his utilitarian perspective, Mill adopts the position that the function of government is twofold—the preservation of order, and the attainment of some measure of social progress and human development. Of the two functions, Mill is inclined to rate the second higher than the first. In *Considerations on Representative Government*, written some two years after *On Liberty*, Mill charges government not only with the standard tasks of creating happiness, or at least the conditions for happiness; he also wants it to become responsible for encouraging the greatest degree of mental cultivation in its citizens. This is a very old idea and one long thought dead whose corpse is none the better for being dragged unceremoniously out of its grave. Libertarians might be able to live with a government that provided peace and justice and confined itself strictly to that task but they can have no truck with a government that takes it upon itself to 'help' its citizens to achieve mental cultivation. When Mill takes the function of government to be not just the provision of the conditions conducive to happiness but also positively to encourage what one can only call the spiritual potential of its citizens, we see him shifting from a purely utilitarian conception of government to one that is closely related to one common to the classical conceptions of Greece and Rome. Although he acknowledges the bread-and-butter functions of government, he writes, 'the most important point of excellence which any form of government can possess is to promote the virtue and intelligence of the people themselves' and he continues, 'We may consider, then, as one criterion of the goodness of a government, the degree in which it tends to increase the sum of good qualities in the governed, collectively and individually; since, besides that their well-being is the sole object of government, their good qualities supply the moving force which works the machinery.' [CRG, §II, 21, 227]

In the old days, the struggle for liberty was between a people and its political rulers. Rulers then 'consisted of a governing One, or a governing tribe or caste, who derived their authority from inheritance or conquest, who, at all events, did not hold it at the pleasure of the governed....' [*On Liberty*, §I, 2, 5] Nowadays (nineteenth century nowadays) things are (or may be) different. If our rulers can be in some way identified with us, then there's no possible tension between a 'them' and an 'us'. There is no principled obstacle to a government's having popular support. But only some forms of popular government are conducive to the active participation of citizens, something that is desirable in any society that has learned the virtue of obedience. Popular government also is broadly protective of the rights of individuals and conducive to their moral advancement. Echoing ideas that comes to us from the Greeks, Mill says, 'the ideally best form of government is that in which the sovereignty, or supreme controlling power in the last resort, is vested in the entire aggregate of the community; every citizen not only having a voice in the exercise of that ultimate sovereignty, but being, at least occasionally, called on to take an actual part in the government, by the personal discharge of some public function, local or general.' [CRG, §III, 7, 244] Genuine popular government, he believes, is possible only in very small states, a point with which Rousseau would be in firm agreement. On the other hand, the benefits of advanced civilisation are only available in very large states. Is there some way to combine the benefits of popular government with the advanced civilisation that comes with large size? Yes. The answer lies, Mill thinks, in representative democracy. Much of the *Considerations on Representative Government* is, unsurprisingly, devoted to developing the details of a scheme for representative government. It isn't necessary to give or to grasp a blow-by-blow account of the details of Mill's scheme; it will be sufficient to appreciate the broad moves he makes.

Mill does not believe that just any form of government can be matched with just any form of society. The form of government that is best for a given society is related to that society's stage of development. He writes, 'the proper functions of a government are not a fixed thing, but different in different states of society; much more extensive in a backward than in an advanced state.' [CRG, §II, 2, 217] Civilisation, he thinks, requires the sacrifice of certain elemental freedoms. Whereas 'uncivilized races, and the bravest and most energetic still more than the rest, are averse to continuous labour of an unexciting kind,' what Mill calls 'real' civilisation requires the acceptance of the necessity of just such unexciting work and the mind must be 'disciplined into the habits required by civilized society.' [CRG, §II, 28, 232] One is reminded of the old bumper-sticker joke: 'Before the white man came to America, there were no taxes and men hunted and fished all day—and this is an improvement?'

Is democracy the best form of popular government? Democracy in a full-blooded sense has never been quite respectable as a political doctrine. After all, once the mob rules, who can tell what will happen? Mill is prey to conflicting tendencies. On the one hand, he is inclined to widen suffrage but then, the problem of mob rule rears its head. Should the people be given what they say they want or what their betters know to be really good for them? His utilitarian upbringing inclined him to the former; his perfectionist tendencies inclined him to the latter. Democracy has dangers, one of which is 'the danger of class legislation; of government intended for (whether really effecting it or not) the immediate benefit of the dominant class, to the lasting detriment of the whole.' [CRG, §VI, 19, 299] If representative government is to work, the people as a whole must be prepared to receive it, to preserve it, and to shoulder the burdens that it imposes upon them although Mill admits, in a revealing comment, that 'The natural tendency of representative government... is towards collective mediocrity...'[9]

In a Platonic moment, Mill believes that the core areas of government—legislative, judicial and executive—require a level of competence beyond the capacity of the man in the street and also beyond the capacity even of his representatives. Such governmental competences belong only to the expert. It isn't the function of the citizens' representatives to govern; rather, it is their task to control the experts who carry out the actual government. Mill writes, 'while it is essential to representative government that the practical supremacy in the state should reside in the representatives of the people, it is an open question what actual functions, what precise part in the machinery of government, shall be directly and personally discharged by the representative body....There is a radical distinction between controlling the business of government, and actually doing it. The same person or body may be able to control everything, but cannot possibly do everything; and in many cases its control over everything will be more perfect, the less it personally attempts to do.' [CRG, §V, 4-5, 271]

In Mill's representative democracy, not only is it the case that the people do not rule themselves directly, they aren't even ruled by their representatives. Rather, they are ruled by experts who are controlled (or meant to be controlled—not always the same thing) by their representatives. The function of the representative assembly is to monitor and control the government, 'to throw the light of publicity on its acts: to compel a full exposition and justification of any which anyone considers questionable; to censure them if found condemnable, and, if the men who compose the government abuse their trust, or fulfil it in a manner which conflicts with the deliberate sense of the nation, to expel them from office, and either expressly or virtually to appoint their successors.' [CRG, §V, 13, 282] If this sounds familiar that's hardly surprising, since this is more or less the orthodox current understanding of how our representatives should function. Of course, because of what is known as the agent/principal problem, it is very far from how they in fact *do* function, but this is just another example of the divergence of reality and ideality.

The agent/principal problem is the problem of aligning the interests of those whom you commission to look after your interests with *your* interests. Who does not know of boards of directors, nominally the employees or delegates of the shareholder owners of corporations, who act in every respect as if the property they administer is in effect theirs? There is a depressing similarity across all our 'liberal' democracies. Looking out at the country from which I write, Ireland, we have local governments with elected representatives who are relatively powerless to control or direct the actions of the county managers who are nominally their employees. We have university presidents who are in law the employees of Boards of Regents or Governing Authorities but who effectively dominate such bodies. In Mill's system of representative democracy, the agent/principal problem is exacerbated: their representatives are the agents of the people; and the experts are agents of the representatives. What chance would you give for either the wishes of the people or even the wishes of their representatives being attended to? Bad as things may be in the lack of accountability of our public representatives to the public they are meant to represent, they would hardly be better if our Prime Ministers, Cabinets Ministers, University Presidents and others were obliged to defer to unaccountable experts.

The key to the justification and popular acceptance of modern democracy is the idea of representation. Those who are governed are thought to be governed by those who represent them and thus, it is claimed, in being governed by those who represent them they are, in effect, governing themselves. This gets over the fundamental problem of why, in any political structure, some people rule and others are ruled. If rulers and ruled are, in effect, one and the same, then the problem of justifying the rule by one person or group of people of other people disappears. The justification of political governance, then, rests upon democracy, and the justification of democracy in turn rests upon representation. If the bough of representation were to break, then down would come the cradle of democracy, baby and all.

How are we to conceive of political representation? Is a political representative an agent of those whom he represents, limited to the carrying out of their instructions? Mill rejects this idea as Burke had previously rejected it. Or is the political representative a trustee, free to act in the interests of those whom he represents according to his own best judgment of what those interests are? Or is he neither an agent nor a delegate nor a trustee, being simply able to do more or less whatever he likes once elected? Or are there other possibilities in addition to these?

In what way are our political representatives *representative*? What does it mean for one man to represent another? Under normal circumstances, as our examples show, those who represent us do so at our bidding and cease to do so at our bidding. They act on our instructions within the boundaries of a certain remit and we are responsible for what they do as our agents. Furthermore, the central characteristic of representation by agency is that the agent is responsible to his principal and is bound to act in the principal's interest. Is this the situation with my so-called political representatives? Political representatives aren't (usually) legally answerable to those whom they allegedly represent. In fact, in modern democratic states, the majority of a representative's putative principals are in fact unknown to him. Can a political representative be the agent of a multitude? This also seems unlikely. What if the principals have interests that diverge from each other? A political representative must then of necessity cease to represent one or more of his principals. The best that can be done in these circumstances is for the politician to serve the many and betray the few.

If it is to be tenable, representative or indirect democracy requires a clear, robust, and defensible conception of representation. No such conception has been forthcoming to date, and it's doubtful if any ever will. Voltaire famously sneered that only three things were definitely true of the Holy Roman Empire: it wasn't holy, it wasn't Roman, and it wasn't an empire. Whatever truth there may be in Voltaire's epigram (and it's less obviously true than it might first appear— see Wilson 2016), two things are definitely true of representative democracy: it isn't democracy and it isn't representative. In the end, representation is a fig leaf that's insufficient to cover the naked and brutal fact that even in our sophis- ticated modern states, however elegant the rhetoric and however persuasive the propaganda, some rule and others are ruled. The only question is, as Humpty-Dumpty noted in *Through the Looking-Glass*, 'which is to be master — that's all.'[10]

Is there not always a danger that a supposedly popular government will descend into factionalism? Yes. Mill is suspicious of government by faction, however large that faction might be. He believes that if democracy amounts to government by a majority, which majority alone has representation, then the unrepresented minority cannot be certain its interests will be protected and so the purposes for which democracy exists will be frustrated. Mill fears, for example, that a representative body representing the interests of the working class will jeopardize the property rights of the wealthy, and thus 'undermine the economy of the nation.' [Magid, 795] To ensure that everybody was in fact represented, Mill proposed a complex system of proportional representation. History has shown that Mill was right to fear government by faction. Practical politics in most democracies is a contest between various gangs struggling to determine which of them can get its hands on the tiller of the ship of state. History has also shown that Mill was wrong to think that his proportional representation system would solve his problems. This wasn't because there was some particular flaw with his system of proportional representation but because there's a basic flaw with the whole notion of representation to begin with.

MILL—LIBERTARIAN?

Is Mill a libertarian? No—not quite. 'Mill's ideal of liberty,' writes Paul Kelly, 'is far less libertarian than is often supposed.' [Kelly 2009b, 394] Liberty isn't an overriding right but merely an instrument of perfection. David Brink comments succinctly, 'Mill's liberalism should not be confused with traditional libertarianism, which does recognize a right to liberty per se.' [Brink, 65] For Mill, liberty may be restricted not only if there is definite damage but even a definite risk of damage. That being so, Mill writes, 'the case is taken out of the province of liberty, and placed in that of morality or law.' [*On Liberty* §IV, 10, 91]

From a libertarian point of view, one of the most disturbing aspects of Mill's thought is the positive role he allocates to the government in educating the tastes and morals of its citizens. Even assuming that there's any role for government in the production of any kind of pleasure for anyone, there is a high quotient of 'we know what's good for you' in the suggestion that a task of government is steering (coercing?) citizens away from lower and towards higher pleasure. There is more than an echo in this suggestion of the German Idealist conception of autonomy, *true* freedom, as distinct from the merely vulgar freedom which concerns itself with non-interference, and there's also an anticipation of the contempt for the pleasures of the plebeians and the bourgeoisie one finds in some of the adherents of the twentieth century Frankfurt School. Mill accords a priority to the individual over society, a priority libertarians would happily endorse, but this priority isn't so much a priority of the individual as he in fact is in the raw but of the educated and cultured individual he may become.

Mill is prepared to argue that citizens of a representative government may be subject to positive obligations that restrict their freedoms, such as giving evidence in law cases, contributing to the common defence or other joint works 'necessary to the interests of the society of which he enjoys the protection,' and a certain level of Good Samaritanism, such as saving the lives of others or protecting them against abuse. [see *On Liberty* §I, 11, 15] Even intra-family relations should be subject to regulation; especially, Mill thinks, there should be compulsory education of children. 'Is it not almost a self-evident axiom, that the State should require and compel the education, up to a certain standard, of every human being who is born its citizen?' [*On Liberty* §V, 12, 116] Sometimes, it isn't immediately obvious whether these obligations are to be construed as moral or legal and whether the compulsion to be applied to the recalcitrant is moral suasion or physical force but I think the tendency of Mill's thought here inclines towards legal compulsion. Later in the essay, another passage gives weight to this interpretation. He writes, 'Though society is not founded on a contract...every one who receives the protection of society owes a return for the benefit.' This return includes not injuring the interests of others which can be conceived of as rights, and 'secondly, in each person's bearing his share... of the labours and sacrifices incurred for defending the society or its members from injury and molestation. These conditions society is justified in enforcing *at all costs* to those who endeavor to withhold fulfilment.' [*On Liberty* §IV, 3, 83; emphasis added] The thinking of earlier utilitarians, Bentham included, was that laws were, at best, necessary evils and should be as limited and as restricted as possible. This wasn't Mill's considered view. He was willing to have extensive systems of laws, provided they were productive of what he saw as the human good.

In economics, Mill was no supporter of *laissez faire*. He endorsed widespread regulation of business and industry. 'The significant feature of Mill's economics was that he substantially abandoned the conception of natural economic laws and in consequence the dogma of a self-regulating competitive economic system' [Sabine, 713] This abandonment of *laissez-faire* was just one dimension of a commitment to what would later come to be called a doctrine of positive freedom. In his *Principles of Political Economy*, he devotes an entire section to what he regards as the necessary (and multifarious) functions of government. Mill considers what is, in effect, the classical liberal (and libertarian) position and rejects it: 'We sometimes...hear it said,' he says, 'that governments ought to confine themselves to affording protection against force and fraud; that, these two things apart, people should be free agents, able to take care of themselves, and that so long as a person practices no violence or deception, to the injury of others in person or property, legislators and governments are in no way called on to concern themselves about him.'[11] Against this position, Mill raises the objection that nothing, except expediency, allocates government to one set of functions and not others, so that if a government is considered necessary for law, justice and security functions, there can be no principled objection to its taking responsibility for other functions as well. Libertarian anarchists would accept the principle underlying Mill's objection; that, indeed, is the substance of their objections to minarchism. Of course, libertarian anarchists run the argument precisely in the opposite direction, arguing that if government isn't necessary for health or welfare or education or the economy, there is no principled reason why it should be regarded as necessary for justice and security either.

The whole of Book V, chapter xi of the *Principle of Political Economy* is devoted to the topic of 'Of the Grounds and Limits of the Laissez-faire or Non-Interference Principle'. Mill is well aware of the objections to government intervention—its compulsory character; the necessity for taxation to fund its interventions; the increase in power and influence accruing to governments resulting from their interventions; the relative incompetence of government agents; and the depressing effect of government intervention on individual and collective action—but he nevertheless sees a role for government in the establishment of minimum wages,[12] the regulation of working hours,[13] the provision of public assistance,[14] and the prohibition of selling oneself into slavery, and certain forms of censorship.

It used to be believed that the government had a role in fixing prices and regulating manufacturing but Mill thinks that the benefits of free trade in relation to price and quality are now wisely recognised. On the other hand, Mill believes that 'individual liberty is not involved in the doctrine of Free Trade' so that regulations pertaining to adulteration or sanitary arrangements or dangerous working conditions do not constitute a violation of the principle of liberty. [*On Liberty* §V, 4, 105-106] I can see no obvious reason why Mill wants to or, indeed, can make a distinction in kind between individual freedoand free trade; free trade is, in the end, simply the exercise of individual freedom with respect tobuying and selling. Clearly, there are moral considerations that bear upon this form of social interaction but such moral considerations bear on all forms of social interaction. Trade will also have to operate under legal constraints that prohibit adulteration, deception, theft and so on, but libertarians would view such practices as violations of the zero-aggression principle and so their prohibition wouldn't be a restriction of liberty.

Cyril Northcote Parkinson believes Mill's position on government to be contradictory. 'His arguments about political equality can lead only to socialism. There can be no equality between millionaires and paupers. Votes for all are a mockery where there are vast differences in wealth. If citizens are to be politically equal it is absurd to allow one man to control six newspapers while another controls nothing—not even himself. But how can these inequalities be prevented? By just such governmental interference and confiscation as Mill has already rejected in the name of liberty. His two doctrines are incompatible. He wants to equalise citizens as voters while simultaneously freeing them as traders.' [Parkinson 1958, 222]

From all this, it can plainly be seen that Mill is recommending policies that are based not only on the harm principle of *On Liberty* but on a more positive principle which we might call the 'help principle'. Consider, again, Mill's endorsement of Good Samaritan laws. If I decline to rescue someone who is drowning, it is clear that he will suffer harm but it isn't at all clear that I should be in any way responsible for that harm unless we stipulate a pre-existent obligation (moral or legal?) to help others which my inaction violates—and where would such a pre-existent obligation come from? But if such an obligation to help others exists, how could it be confined within manageable limits such that every person's liberty isn't severely constrained? Mill's *On Liberty*, then, should, in the interests of truth in advertising, perhaps be re-titled *On Certain Kinds of Very Limited and Restricted Forms of Liberty*.

Notes

1 References are to the 1991 Oxford World's Classic version, edited by John Gray. Chapter and paragraph numbers are given first for those using other editions, then the page number in the Gray edition; so § I, 9, 14 = chapter 1, paragraph 9, page 14 in the Gray edition. For an accessible account of Chapter III of *On Liberty*, see Smith and Moore, 37-60.

2 A version of this section and the section entitled 'One Very Simple Principle?' was first published in *Philosophy Now* (Casey, 2009).

3 'An Untitled Letter' in Rand 1984, 153.

4 *On Liberty* II, §§41-43, 59.

5 See *On Liberty* §III, 1-10, 62-72.

6 See Kelly 2009b, 393 and Brink, 83.

7 *On Liberty*, §1, 5, 8, §IV, 3, 83.

8 *On Liberty* §I, 11, 15; emphasis added.

9 CRG, §IV, 2-3, 257, §VII, 13, 313.

10 David van Reybrouck's *Against Elections* provides a refreshingly iconoclastic approach to the supposedly intrinsic connection between democracy and elections. Against populists who claim to be able to discern the will of the people he writes, 'there's no such thing as one monolithic "people"…, nor is there anything that could be described as a "national gut feeling", and common sense is the most ideological thing imaginable. After all, "common sense" is an ideology that refuses to recognise its own ideological character…' On attempts to make representative democracy more responsive he comments, 'Nowadays it is often forgotten, but fascism and communism were originally attempts to make democracy more vital, based on the idea that if parliament was abolished, the people and their leader would be better able to converge (fascism) or the people could govern directly (communism).' [van Reybrouck, 18, 31]

11 Mill 1965, V, i. §2—800.

12 Mill 1965, II, xii, §1—355.

13 Mill 1965 V, xi, §12.

14 Mill 1965 V, xi, §13.

Chapter 27

BACK TO THE FUTURE: KARL MARX

Socialism in general has a record of failure so blatant
that only an intellectual could ignore or evade it
—Thomas Sowell

While the State exists, there can be no freedom.
When there is freedom, there will be no State
—Lenin

Irony: Taking a 170-year-old envy-based 'philosophy,'
which has led to the murder of several hundred million human beings
and the oppression of billions more, and calling it 'progressive'
—Larken Rose

Karl Marx was born in Trier, Germany's oldest city, in 1818. He began his academic life as a student of law at Bonn in 1835 before transferring to Berlin in 1836 where he, along with many others, came under the influence of Hegel's thought. He eventually obtained his doctorate from Jena in 1841 and a year later had a fateful first meeting with a fellow Rhinelander, Friedrich Engels, the man who was to be his close associate and co-worker for the rest of his life. Much debate has taken place as to the respective contributions of Marx and Engels to their collaborative work; some are anxious to take Engels out of the picture except as a kind of super-amanuensis; other see him as playing a significantly greater role in the partnership than is usually accorded to him. John Bowle writes, 'The Marx-Engels canon is thus framed and permeated by Engel's contribution.'[1] It can't be denied that during Marx's lifetime, Engels was content to remain in the background and modestly but incorrectly underestimated his own contribution to their common project. It is significant, however, that, as Leszek Kolakowski notes, 'subsequent generations of Marxists made more use, in expounding and advocating their doctrine, of Engels's writing than of Marx's, always excepting the first volume of *Capital*.' [Kolakowski, 259]

It is not a little ironic that Marx, the champion of the proletariat, was himself conspicuously shy of proletarian work. He lived much of his mature life as Engels's pensioner, Engels himself deriving his wealth from the cotton firm he inherited from his father! 'Making little effort to earn his living,' writes Cyril Parkinson, Marx 'sponged continually on others. Engels largely supported him out of what he could earn on the Manchester Stock Exchange and Marx accepted this help as no more than his due and too little for his needs.' [Parkinson, 50] Marx, writes Geoffrey Sampson, 'advocated socialism while leading a bourgeois and, in his later years, comfortable life (financed largely out of the profits of the cotton trade) in a society dominated by liberal ideology, thus demonstrating…that an individual's beliefs are not necessarily determined by his economic situation...' [Sampson, 92]

Together, Marx and Engels published the *Communist Manifesto* in 1848; Marx was just thirty years old. A year later, Marx moved to London where he would make his home for the rest of his life. Despite living in England for almost thirty years, Marx never learned to speak English well, interacted not at all with economists and, despite being a pensioner of the factory-owning Engels, never managed to visit a single English factory. [see Nasar 41, 11-47] His magnum opus, *Capital* (volume I), was published in 1867 and he continued organising this work until his death in 1883, although he appears to have written little new after 1869. The material that Engels would later publish as *Capital* volumes II and III was written between 1864-1865 and between 1867-1879.[2]

Despite that fact that his own background was Jewish, there are typical nineteenth century anti-semitic elements in Marx's thought. At times he expresses himself in ways which, even allowing for the endemic and casual anti-semitism of the age, is still shocking. He was particularly critical of what he saw as the Jewish concern with huckstering and money-making, a criticism that it might not be too far-fetched to see as not unconnected with his own need to rely on moneylenders that resulted from his own fiscal incompetence. Writing in an early essay, 'On the Jewish Question' he says 'Money is the jealous god of Israel, before which no other god can exist. Money humbles all of man's gods – and turns them into a commodity. Money is the universal *value* of all things, constituted for itself. It has therefore robbed the entire world, the world of men as well as nature, of their own value. Money is the estranged essence of man's labour and existence, and this estranged essence dominates him, and he worships it. The god of the Jews has become secularised; he has become a worldly god.' [Marx 1994, 54] Marx was a frustrated academic and he had the academic's typical contempt and scorn for those who work with their hands. He also appears to have absorbed the Aristotelian idea that the making of money from money was somehow unnatural.

If Marx loved workers, it was workers in the round and at a distance; individual workers earned nothing but his scorn, especially when they had the temerity to question his theorising. Proudhon, as a mere compositor, was the target of a vitriolic attack, but the man who was the object of Marx's most extraordinary vilification was his most significant ideological rival in the 1860s, Ferdinand Lasalle.[3] In a letter to Engels of 1862, Marx wrote about Lasalle, 'It is now quite plain to me — as the shape of his head and the way his hair grows also testify — that he is descended from the negroes who accompanied Moses' flight from Egypt (unless his mother or paternal grandmother interbred with a negro). Now, this blend of Jewishness and Germanness, on the one hand, and basic negroid stock, on the other, must inevitably give rise to a peculiar product. The fellow's importunity is also negro-like.'[4] In his *Statism and Anarchy*, Bakunin defended Lasalle against Marx, remarking that 'Marx complains bitterly that Lassalle (*sic*) robbed him, that he appropriated his ideas.

It is a particularly odd protest coming from a communist, who advocates collective property but does not understand that once an idea has been expressed it ceases to be the property of an individual....In contrast to his teacher Marx, who is strong on theory, on behind-the-scenes or underground intrigue, but loses all significance and force in the public arena, Lassalle seem to have been expressly created for open struggle in the practical realm....His like-minded comrades, the socialists, Marxists, and his teacher, Marx himself, concentrated against him the full force of their malicious envy. Indeed, they hated him as deeply as the bourgeoisie did; as long as he was alive, however, they could not give voice to their hatred because he was too strong for them.' [Bakunin 1873, 176, 177] 'Marx,' writes Max Eastman, 'had a bad character....He was a totally undisciplined, vain, slovenly, and egotistical spoiled child. He was ready at the drop of a hat with spiteful hate. He could be devious, disloyal, snobbish, anti-democratic, anti-Semitic, anti-Negro. He was by habit a sponge, an intriguer, a tyrannical bigot who would rather wreck his party than see it succeed under another leader.' [Eastman, 81-82] Cyril Parkinson describes Marx as, 'a Jew without a country, a professor without a university position and an author without a public,' and remarked that his 'worldly failure was complete, his inexperience quite exceptional, and his practical ignorance of the masses no less remarkable than the hatred he felt for people he had never even met.' [Parkinson 1970, 48]

The reader might well object at this point that whatever Marx's personal failings may (or may not) have been, they are not relevant to his writings; what matters are Marx's ideas, not his psychological processes or even his moral character. There is a measure of soundness in this objection but it cannot but be a matter of interest to uncover the source of Marx's passion, whatever it was that drove him to spend endless days virtually self-imprisoned in the British Museum. Reading Marx's major works, one might easily get the impression that he was an economist with an interest in political theory or, alternatively, a political theorist with an interest in economics. On the contrary, as John Bowle writes, 'A broad survey of their writings shows that Marx and Engels were at heart revolutionary romantics, in the tradition of 1789. Being Germans and authoritarians, they also believed that their goal could be won only through state power.' [Bowle, 299] What Marx really was, however, was a latter-day prophet fuelled by a passionate concern (like Rousseau, a concern demonstrated more in the abstract than the concrete) for those whom he took to be the downtrodden of this earth, a prophet[5] who looked forward to a secularised eschatological fulfilment in which all would be well, and all would be well, and all manner of things would be well. 'Like the Old Testament from which its style derives,' writes Parkinson, '*Das Kapital* is based upon revelation, not argument. Marx (like Isaiah) tells us what is going to happen. He does not explain how he comes to be so certain about it, nor why the change has to be regarded as progress.'[6]

All things considered, one very important fact to keep in mind when considering Marx's influence on others is the obvious but sometimes neglected fact that Marx was a communist! 'Marx's devotion to communism,' Rothbard writes, 'was his crucial focus, far more central than the class struggle, the dialectic, the theory of surplus value, and all the rest. Communism was the great goal, the vision, the desideratum, the ultimate end that would make the sufferings of mankind throughout history worthwhile....In the same way as the return of the Messiah, in Christian theology, will put an end to history and establish a new heaven and a new earth, so the establishment of communism would put an end to human history.' [Rothbard 1990, 123] Commenting on the Rothbardian (but not only Rothbardian) insight that Marx was essentially a millennial communist, an insight in many ways so obvious that, like the eponymous purloined letter in Edgar Allan Poe's short story, it can escape attention, Peter Boettke notes that crucial to the millennial argument that communism would end all human suffering is the claim that 'the future communist world would be a post-scarcity world. All economic problems would fade away and there would be no need to address the question of the allocation of scarce means among competing needs.'[7] But questions of scarcity can't simply be wished away. Boettke judges that Ludwig von Mises's insight that a socialist economy's inability to engage in economic calculation is what makes a socialist economy impossible 'is the most significant contribution to political economy made in the twentieth century.' [Boettke, 79 n. 2] Several attempts have been made to escape the force of the economic calculation argument, among them, the Trial and Error Method of Price Determination (or Shadow Market) and the so-called Competitive Solution but significantly, as Wilczynski notes, neither of these expedients has 'been applied in practice in any Socialist centrally planned economy, except in modified forms in Yugoslavia and Hungary.'[8] In essence, these expedients are akin to trying to play competitive poker with Monopoly™ money.[9]

   Much of the power of Marxism comes from its being an *ersatz* religion. Marx's writings have the character of a sacred text and the adherence of his followers the character of religious devotion.[10] Eric Voegelin says of Marx's writings that they have 'become the Koran of the faithful, supplemented by the patristic literature of Leninism-Stalinism.' [Voegelin 1952, 140] It may be a little unkind but, in connection with Marxism as an religion, I can't resist quoting from the twentieth century Russian author Alexander Zinoviev, who remarks, 'Don't believe anyone who tells you that he went through a great spiritual crisis when he discovered that Marxism was not the pinnacle of wisdom and nobility of thought but the nadir of dull-wittedness, superficiality and dishonesty. If anyone does experience a crisis, he's lying if he says it's because he's lost his faith in Marxism....it is impossible to lose one's faith in Marxism in the first place for the simple reason that it's impossible to believe in it in the first place. It is a phenomenon which does not belong in the realm of faith, but in that of quasi-faith or pseudo-faith.' [Zinoviev, 8]

   In this twenty-first century, which succeeds a twentieth century that was dominated in many ways by Marxism in various forms, some strong, some weak, it is salutary to remember that, in his lifetime, Marx was virtually unknown and his writings likewise. Parkinson remarks that, 'Later historians, recording the quarrels among these nineteenth-century revolutionaries, are apt to forget that these protagonists (whatever their later fame) were all then quite unknown. Marx was no more than a shabby refugee living in Soho or Hampstead and working daily at the British Museum....certainly as obscure as any, not so much criticized as ignored.' [Parkinson 1970, 50-51] It is doubtful that Marxism would have achieved any importance at all had it not been for its adoption as the official ideology of the Soviet Union. John Bowle goes so far as to say 'The cult of Marxism began only after the Russian Revolution gave it prestige,' a sentiment with which it is difficult to disagree. [Bowle, 300]

MARX'S WRITINGS

The two most prominent pieces in the Marxist canon are *The Communist Manifesto* and *Capital*. *The Communist Manifesto* owes no little of its prominence to its brevity, its clarity and its forceful writing. Not everyone, however, is equally enamoured of it. Although he regards it as a masterpiece of political propaganda and judges that it contains the essential doctrines of Marxism, John Bowle believes that 'The *Manifesto*, like the later nineteenth-century slogans of nationalism, breathes hatred and revenge: it is disfigured by vulgar abuse, and it ends with incitement to violence on a world scale.' [Bowle, 314] Whatever one's ultimate judgement on the intellectual value of *The Communist Manifesto*, it isn't boring. The same, however, can't be said for the second prominent member of the Marxist canon.

I am generally all in favour of the reading of original texts rather than just summaries or second-hand accounts. Nevertheless, some books should *not* be read cover to cover. When I was an adolescent and had more energy than sense, I managed to read John Locke's *Essay on Human Understanding* in its entirety, all two volumes and 996 pages of it. Despite my respect for Locke, this isn't something I could recommend to anyone—there are better things to do with one's time. Marx's *Capital*[11] is another book that should *not* be read from cover to cover, although I suspect that many people have come to the same conclusion as I have without the benefit of my advice. It is a huge, sprawling, badly organised tome. Here I am speaking of the first volume, the only one Marx himself completed. It has many of the vices of the caricature of German scholarship—ridiculous length and an extravagant display of needless scholarship[12]—with few of the virtues—clear analysis and logical rigour, although David McClelland bizarrely claims to find it 'witty in a heavy-handed Germanic sort of way!' [McClelland, 560] Bowle describes *Capital* as a 'massive, rancorous and obscure book' but 'less unreadable than its structure and opening chapters would suggest.' [Bowle, 332] Bowle's judgement of the combined work of Marx and Engels is also distinctly unfavourable; he describes their corpus of work as 'these obscure and voluminous writings.' [Bowle, 305]

There are passages in *Capital* that make sense even if one may not agree with them but there are also many passages that make no sense at all so that agreement or disagreement is simply not possible. For example, try to make sense of this brief sentence from Chapter 2, on the 'Process of Exchange'. 'What chiefly distinguishes a commodity from its owner,' writes Marx, 'is the fact that every other commodity counts for it only as the form of appearance of its own value.' [*Capital*, 179] One might say, in the words of Colonel Pickering in *My Fair Lady*, 'Come sir, you've picked a poor example.' Well, yes, it is a poor example but there are many more. Reading parts of *Capital* is not unlike reading the works of Hegel[13] (not a coincidence): the overall effect is rather like contemplating a masterpiece of *chiaroscuro*, when the merest banality can appear to be a stunning revelation because it is an area of light surrounded by a massive and ponderous darkness. All that being said, *Capital* gets better as it goes along and there are some parts that are capable of gripping the reader and arousing his righteous indignation, for example Part Eight, on the 'So-Called Primitive Accumulation'.[14]

Marx was sensitive to criticisms of his style. In a footnote to the Preface to the Second Edition of *Capital*, he writes, 'the mealy-mouthed babblers of German vulgar economics grumbled about the style of my book. No one can feel the literary shortcoming of *Capital* more strongly than I myself' but he then goes on to quote from a favourable Russian review which claimed that 'the author in no way resembles...the majority of German scholars, who...write their books in a language so dry and obscure that the heads of ordinary mortals are cracked by it.' [*Capital*, 99] Some, not many, have discovered literary merit in *Capital* that less percipient readers have been unable to discern. In his 'Introduction' to his book *Moneybags Must Be So Lucky: On the Literary Structure of 'Capital,'* Robert Paul Wolff writes 'As I worked through the extraordinary first chapter on value, with its bizarre mixture of classical economics and Hegelian metaphysics, couched in a bitterly satirical language quite unlike anything I have encountered elsewhere in political philosophy or the social sciences, I became more and more powerfully convinced that Marx's abstract theories of price and exchange, his angry critique of the injustices of capital, his complex conception of the objectively mystified character of bourgeois social reality, and his richly metaphorical invocation of the religious, political and literary images of the Western cultural tradition, were so integrally connected that each could be understood only in relation to all the others.' In the face of such fundamental disagreements, we can only conclude that it is futile to dispute about matters of literary taste—try reading *Capital* (not all of it!) for yourself and make up your own mind. *Capital* was originally meant to be a multi-volume enterprise but Marx was apparently incapable of fleshing out the architectonic of such a project. All we have from his own hand in finished form is the first volume, a volume which some believe has no obvious logical structure. Paul Johnson remarks, '*Capital* is a series of essays glued together without any real form.' He continues, 'The second and third volumes were produced by Engels after Marx's death from material that Marx, if he had wanted to, could very well have organized himself in the fifteen years that elapsed between the publication of *Capital* volume 1 and his death.' [Johnson, 55]

What, if anything, is new in *Capital*? What will we find there that isn't already contained in the earlier writings of Marx? Very little, unless it's the development along economic lines of a pre-reflective moral indignation at the widespread poverty of the nineteenth century, inserted into a theoretical economic frame which, based on a misguided concept of value, simply can't do the work it's supposed to do. But this is to get ahead of myself. Before moving on, it is worth noting, before anyone should become outraged at the extent of human poverty, that for almost all of history, the mass of human beings has lived at or just above (and often below) the level of grinding poverty.[15] This is the default position. It doesn't need a reason or an explanation. Poverty doesn't need to be explained; wealth does. Poverty comes about all by itself; wealth must be created. Of the 7 billion people alive on the planet, 1.1 billion subsist below the internationally accepted extreme-poverty line of $1.25 a day. What is striking about this statistic isn't the regrettably economically submerged 1.1 billion but the 5.9 billion who live above the poverty line, and that historically unique uplift of the majority of mankind out of poverty is due almost entirely to the operation of capitalism, a fact which receives some anticipatory recognition in the paean of praise to capitalism one finds in the opening section of *The Communist Manifesto*.[16]

Other than *Capital*, Marx's works vary in readability. Some are quite witty—for instance, 'The Eighteenth Brumaire of Louis Bonaparte' (1852)—others, such as the already-mentioned *The Communist Manifesto* (1848), are quickened by bombast, invective and anger. There are even two that are masterpieces of conspicuous brevity: the first of these being '[Theses] On Feuerbach' (1845), the second, which is perhaps the shortest and most accessible way into the core of Marx's thought, being his 'Preface' to *A Contribution to the Critique of Political Economy* (1859).[17] Later, following the pioneering work of Hans-Hermann Hoppe, I shall attempt to show that the overall thrust of some of Marx's analysis is, in fact, correct but seriously misapplied, much like a marksman (pun intended) who is dead on target—the wrong target.

Whatever the literary merits or demerits of Marx's work, there can be no doubt as to its theoretical shortcomings. In the section of *Capital* entitled 'Historical Tendency of Capitalist Accumulation' [*Capital*, chapter 32, 927-930] Marx prophesies an ever-decreasing number of capitalists ('One capitalist always strikes down many others...constant decrease in the number of capitalist magnates'), an ever-increasing level of poverty, oppression, degeneration and exploitation on the part of the proletariat ('the mass of misery, oppression, slavery, degradation and exploitation grows'), and an ever-rising level of anger in the proletariat as the result of their poverty and oppression ('there also grows the revolt of the working class, a class...united and organized by the very mechanism of the capitalist process of production'). I am not alone in pointing out the spectacular failure of these particular prophecies—the number of capitalists hasn't decreased, workers haven't become poorer, more oppressed, degraded and exploited, and we still await the running of blood in the gutters, but with ever decreasing trepidation.[18]

THE ALIEN WORLD OF MARXIST ALIENATION

The motive force of Marx's writing was a deep revulsion at certain aspects of modern life. His passion did not arise from any concern with abstract economics but from a visceral rejection of the exploitation he believed to be the inevitable accompaniment to capitalism. His study of economics was meant to explain this exploitation theoretically and practically to undermine it. It is vitally important to understand that Marx's objection to capitalism was *not* that it did not work; on the contrary, it worked all too well![19] If exploitation was the core topic of Marx's mature and late work, alienation was the topic of his earliest writings. The works of Marx, then, can be divided into two groups: the early ones dealing with the notion of alienation[20] and the later ones concerning themselves with exploitation. [see Mésáros] The notion of alienation comes to Marx from Hegel and is relayed by Marx to the twentieth century in the form of the disdain of the Frankfurt School thinkers for the ordinary man and his desires. The idea of exploitation lies at the heart of Marx's mature work and the explanation of this phenomenon is what Marx's economic thinking is all about.

Around the mid-1840s, Marx wrote what have now come to be called the *Economic and Philosophic Manuscripts* (1844, first published 1932).[21] These writings are best known for developing the concept of alienation, a notion that is, in essence, a form of romanticism, one that tends to excite the sympathies of the more tender-minded of philosophers. Marx adopts the standard conservative romantic technique of criticising contemporary capitalist society for its destruction of organic ties and loss of community. Unlike most romantics, however, it's important to note that Marx does not wish to restore some lost idyllic past and he isn't in any way a sentimental environmentalist. The cure for the present lies not in the past but in the future which comes about by 'strengthening man's power over nature' so that we can 'salvage what was of value in primitive society....The destructive effects of the machine cannot be cured by abolishing machines, but only by perfecting them.'[22] The notion of alienation, coming originally from Hegel, was used by Feuerbach to account for our investing a valuable part of our human nature in a God of our own creation, thereby alienating us from ourselves. Marx adopted Feuerbach's idea and applied it to the plight of the worker in a capitalist society.

Marx's alienation comes in four varieties: the worker is alienated from *the product of his work*; from his *act of working*; from *himself*; and from *other workers*. The worker is alienated from *the product of his work* because, Marx writes, 'the object which labor produces – labor's product – confronts it as *something alien*, as a *power independent* of the producer. The product of labor is labor which has been embodied in an object, which has become material: it is the *objectification* of labor....Under these economic conditions this realization of labor appears as *loss of realization* for the workers; objectification as *loss of the object and bondage to it;* appropriation as *estrangement*, as *alienation*. [Marx 1844, XXII] The product of the worker's labour is snatched away from him as soon as it is created, like a newborn baby ripped from the arms of its mother. [see Otteson 2003, 201]

What, precisely, is the significance of this criticism? Of course the product of labour is alien to the producer—that's the whole point of production! The ability to separate one's product from oneself is the fundamental difference between *techne* and *praxis*, between art and action; I can alienate the table that I make; I can't, strictly speaking, alienate my act of dancing or singing (except as recorded). The alienation of the worker from the products of his labour comes about whether the worker is working for himself or for another. The product of one's labour is alienated if, having it for one's own, one keeps it, one sells it or gives it away or, if working for another, one's labour has been purchased and the resultant object is alienated from its very first appearance.

Whatever value this concept has for Marx in these writings comes from a systematic ambiguity between the idea of alienation as simply a detachment of what is originally one's own and its transference to another (nothing particularly sinister here—my newsagent alienates a copy of the *Irish Times* to me every now and then without too much existential angst), and the idea of alienation as detaching a part of one's very self and placing it outside and against one. 'The *alienation* of the worker in his product means not only that his labor becomes an object, assumes an *external* existence, but that it exists independently, *outside him*, and alien to him, and that it stands opposed to him as an autonomous power. The life which he has given to the object sets itself against him as an alien and hostile force.'[23] The vocabulary of 'alien', 'hostile' and 'confronting' is tendentious in the extreme. For Marx, alienation is closer to the distressing appearance of the intestinal monster in the film *Alien* than to something simply produced by oneself which is physically detachable from oneself. Cases of self-surgery or science fiction to one side, this fraught Marxist notion of alienation is merely metaphorical.

But the worker isn't only alienated from the product of his labour; he is alienated from that very labour itself, from his *act of working*. 'What constitutes the alienation of labour? First, that the work is *external* to the worker, that it is not part of his nature; and that, consequently, he does not fulfil himself in his work but denies himself, has a feeling of misery rather than well-being, does not develop freely his mental and physical energies but is physically exhausted and mentally debased. The worker, therefore, feels himself at home only during his leisure time, whereas at work he feels homeless. His work is not voluntary but imposed, *forced labour*. It is not the satisfaction of a need, but only a *means* for satisfying other needs. Its alien character is clearly shown by the fact that as soon as there is no physical or other compulsion it is avoided like the plague. External labour, labour in which man alienates himself, is a labour of self-sacrifice, of mortification.'[24] What this passage amounts to is little more than the complaint that some of us find our work less than completely fulfilling. True, but so what? To complain about unfulfilling work is to complain about being human. I am pretty sure that our ancestors who were obliged to chase around all day after rapidly vanishing game on empty stomachs were alienated from their labour. But even so, not everybody is disenchanted with his work. Some people like performing boring and repetitive tasks; some people like to earn their money without having to think too hard or to assume too much responsibility. And, when it comes right down to it, one's work isn't the be all and end all of one's life. Most people have something in their lives that attracts their creative abilities but it need not necessarily be the occupation by which they earn their living.

Josef Wilczynski believes that alienation and socialism are not incompatible. In socialist societies, alienation 'has manifested itself in the persisting reappearance of poor work discipline, a high labour turnover, the neglect of and damage to socialized property, pilfering in factories and on farms, the embezzlement of public funds, elaborate ways of circumventing laws and regulations, the black market, dissent and conflicts between workers and management, enterprises and bureaucracy and between the individual person and the monolithic and ubiquitous state.' [Wilczynski, 11]

The other two categories of alienation follow along the same track and nothing essentially new is to be gathered from them. Man is alienated from *himself* in that he is producing in accordance with forces outside himself and not in accordance with his own intrinsic powers; and man is alienated from *other workers* because the relationship of exchange (which Marx seems to understand in a zero-sum sense) takes the place of the satisfaction of mutual need. Why Marx thinks that exchange could be anything other than the satisfaction of mutual need is a mystery but, apparently, he does.

THE EVIL OF EXPLOITATION

The account of the phenomenon of exploitation on which Marx's moral indignation is founded derives from the work of Engels (*Condition of the Working Class in England*) which itself was based on secondary (and dubious) sources rather than on direct and first-hand empirical evidence. Much of Engels's data were gleaned from the conditions that obtained *before* the Industrial Revolution, data which were then used as evidence to condemn the very conditions which replaced them! Paul Johnson comments, 'all the first part of Marx's scientific examination of working conditions under capitalism in the mid-1860s is based upon a single work, Engels's *Conditions of the Working Class in England*.....A great deal of the book, including all the examination of the pre-capitalist era and the early stages of industrialization, was based not on primary sources but on a few secondary sources of dubious value, especially Peter Gaskell's *The Manufacturing Population of England* (1833), a work of Romantic mythology which attempted to show that the eighteenth century had been a golden age for English yeomen and craftsmen. In fact, as the Royal Commission on Children's Employment of 1842 conclusively demonstrated, working conditions in the small, pre-capitalist workshops and cottages were far worse than in the big new Lancashire cotton mills. Printed primary sources used by Engels were five, ten, twenty, twenty-five or even forty years out of date....Marx cannot have been unaware of the weaknesses, indeed dishonesties, of Engels's book since many of them were exposed in detail as early as 1848 by the German Economist Bruno Hildebrand, in a publication with which Marx was familiar. Moreover Marx himself compounds Engel's misrepresentations knowingly by omitting to tell the reader of the enormous improvements brought about by enforcement of the Factory Acts and other remedial legislation since the book was published and which affected precisely the type of conditions he had highlighted.' [Johnson, 64, 65, 66]

There can be no denying that, by the standards of the twenty-first century, the working conditions of Lancashire mill workers were poor. But what isn't so often realised is just how much poorer were the working conditions in the countryside from which these mill workers fled. 'The reason that the poverty of early industrial England strikes us so forcibly is that this was the first time writers and politicians took notice of it and took exception to it, not because it had not existed before.' [Ridley, 220] Murray Rothbard writes:

Capitalism did *not*, therefore, tragically disrupt, as [Karl] Polanyi would have it, the warm, loving, "social" relations of pre-capitalist era. Capitalism took the outcasts of society: the beggars, the highwaymen, the rural over-populated, the Irish immigrants, and gave them the jobs and wages which moved them from destitution to a far higher standard of living and of work. It is easy enough to wring one's hands at the child labor in the new British factories; it is, apparently, even easier to forget what the child population of rural England was doing before the Industrial Revolution— and during the Revolution, in those numerous areas of England where the I.R. [Industrial Revolution] and the new capitalism had not yet penetrated: these children were dying like flies, and living in infinitely more miserable conditions. *This* is why we read nowadays, when it seems inexplicable to us, British and American writings of the period which praise the new factories for giving work to women and children! This praise was not due to their being inhuman monsters; it was due to the fact that, before such labor was available, and in those regions where such labor was not available, the women and children were living and suffering in infinitely worse conditions. Women, children, immigrants, after all, were not driven to the factories with whips; they went voluntarily and gladly, and that is the reason. [Rothbard 2004]

Marx was not only *not* a scientist, he was also an indifferent scholar, if by scholar one understands someone who dispassionately investigates his area of study and informs his position by considering positions opposed to his own and critically evaluating them.[25] As Karl Jaspers writes in an oft-quoted passage, Marx's approach was 'one of vindication of something proclaimed as the perfect truth with the conviction not of the scientist but of the believer.' [Jaspers, 1950] Joseph Tanner and F. S. Carey wrote that in parts of *Capital*, Marx used British Government Reports recklessly to prove the opposite of what they in fact established. So reckless, indeed, was his use of these sources that it cast a pall of suspicion over his other works. [Tanner & Carey, passim]

It is perhaps worth retelling a glaring (and oft-cited) example of Marx's unscientific economy with the truth. William Gladstone, in his Budget speech to the House of Commons in 1863, commented on what he called an 'intoxicating augmentation of wealth', remarking that it was *not* confined to persons in 'easy circumstances' but noting, with satisfaction, the extraordinary and unprecedented improvement in the average condition of the British labourer over a period of twenty years. To Marx, finishing *Capital*, this was a singularly inconvenient truth, a piece of evidence at odds with the entire tenor of his work, and he quoted Gladstone as saying that the augmentation of wealth was 'entirely confined to classes of property,' precisely the opposite of what Gladstone in fact said. [*Capital*, 806] It is difficult to see how this misrepresentation could be anything other than an intentional perversion of Gladstone's original statement. [see Kealey, 83-84] On this matter, Paul Johnson notes that 'Marx gave as his sources (sic) the *Morning Star* newspaper; but the *Star*, along with the other newspapers and *Hansard*, gives Gladstone's words correctly. Marx's misquotation was pointed out. Nonetheless, he reproduced it in Capital, along with other discrepancies, and when the falsification was again noticed and denounced, he let out a huge discharge of obfuscating ink; he, Engels and later his daughter Eleanor were involved in the row, attempting to defend the indefensible, for twenty years. None of them would ever admit the original, clear falsification and the result of the debate is that some readers are left with the impression, as Marx intended, that there are two sides to the controversy. There aren't. Marx knew Gladstone never said any such thing and the cheat was deliberate.' [Johnson, 67]

The moral force of all forms of socialism is derived from indignation at the perceived plight of the poor and needy and their apparent neglect by the impersonal[26] and harsh forces of capitalism. We all know, so we think, just how awful things were for the teeming masses of people in the late eighteenth, nineteenth, and early twentieth centuries. In the end, so the story goes, the state stepped in to clean up the social mess created by greedy and unscrupulous capitalists. That's the usual story, the story we all know. Except, of course, that we do *not* all know it and we don't all know it for the simple reason that it isn't true. Leaving aside the uncomfortable fact that a glaring problem with all forms of socialism is that other people's money[27] eventually runs out, what is often not realised is how much the lot of the really poor was *improved*, not worsened, by the industrial revolution. People did not leave idyllic conditions in the country voluntarily to subject themselves to appalling conditions in the city. They left the countryside for the city because they believed, correctly, that by so doing, they were bettering themselves. Life in the industrial cities may have been bad by our standards but it was judged by those who moved there at that time to be better than life in the country. As might be expected, estimates vary on the level of absolute destitution (the absolutely destitute are those without a minimally adequate supply of food, clothing and shelter) during the industrial revolution. Whatever the actual level, these people weren't condemned to die in the streets. Private contributions to the welfare of the poor were widespread. In fact, writes Walter Trattner, 'so rapidly did private agencies multiply that before long Americas's larger cities had what to many people was an embarrassing number of them. Charity directories took as many as 100 pages to list and describe the numerous voluntary agencies that sought to alleviate misery, and combat every imaginable emergency.' [Trattner, 92-93]

But, of course, charity and government relief were not (and are not) the only options. Throughout history, people have taken care of themselves and their dependents and their communities. Often ignored in accounts of the social situation during the time of the industrial revolution and its aftermath, is the existence and proliferation of mutual aid societies. These societies weren't charities, but voluntary organisations financially sustained by contributions from their members and controlled as mutual societies by those same members, and they provided unemployment assistance, made provision for health care expenses, disability, old-age payments and even insurance for funerals. 'Between 20 and 35 million Americans belonged to a mutual aid society in 1930, more than any other kind of organization besides churches.' [Brook & Watkins, 181] Very few people are aware of these societies. I have to confess, to my embarrassment, that I myself knew little or nothing about them until relatively recently. I can only exculpate myself, and others, by remarking that knowledge of these societies mysteriously disappeared down an Orwellian memory hole.[28]

HUNTER, FISHERMAN, SHEPHERD, CRITIC

Notoriously, Marx and Engels wrote in *The German Ideology* (1845-46) that 'as soon as the division of labour comes into being, each man has a particular, exclusive sphere of activity, which is forced upon him and from which he can't escape. He is a hunter, a fisherman, a shepherd, or a critical critic, and must remain so if he does not want to lose his means of livelihood; whereas in communist society, where nobody has one exclusive sphere of activity but each can become accomplished in any branch he wishes, society regulates the general production and thus makes it possible for me to do one thing today and another tomorrow, to hunt in the morning, fish in the afternoon, rear cattle in the evening, criticise after dinner, just as I have a mind, without ever becoming hunter, fisherman, shepherd or critic.'[29] Some unconvincing attempts have been made to suggest that this passage is a parody or a joke and shouldn't be taken seriously[30] but I can see no reason to justify this suggestion except a desire on the part of those who make it to cover up an obvious embarrassment.[31] Roger Scruton remarks that this notorious passage 'is the only attempt he [Marx] makes to describe what life will be like without private property—and if you ask who gives you the gun or the fishing rod, who organizes the pack of hounds, who maintains the coverts and the waterways, who disposes of the milk and the calves and who publishes the lit. crit., such questions will be dismissed as "beside the point", and as matters to be settled by a future that is none of your business.' And, Scruton continues, 'as to whether the immense amount of organization required for these leisure activities of the universal upper class will be possible, in a condition in which there is no law, no property, and therefore no chain of command, such questions are too trivial to be noticed.' Scruton concludes, 'it requires but the slightest critical address, to recognize that Marx's "full communism" embodies a contradiction: it is a state in which all the benefits of legal order are still present, even though there is no law; in which all the products of social cooperation are still in existence, even though nobody enjoys the property rights which hitherto have provided the sole motive for producing them.'[32]

In his highly coloured and entertaining defence of Marxism, Terry Eagleton bravely, if quixotically, adheres to the pre-revisionist understanding of this passage, holding that 'communism means an end to scarcity, along with an end to most oppressive labour.' [Eagleton, 91] This is romantic utopianism with a vengeance! Max Eastman writes, 'Although few seem to realize it, Marxism rests on the romantic notion of Rousseau that nature endows men with the qualities necessary to a free, equal, fraternal, family-like living together, and our sole problem is to fix up the external conditions. All Marx did about this with his dialectic philosophy was to change the tenses in the romance: Nature *will* endow men with these qualities *as soon as* the conditions are fixed up.' [Eastman, 29] This romanticism is a zombie horse that, however flogged to death it may appear to be, insists on rising from the dead again and again. André Gorz, for example, talks about our world as one which is 'out of joint', our societies as 'disintegrating' and our hopes and values as 'crumbling'. In case you may have forgotten or, more likely, never noticed this passage from Gorz in the first place, this apocalyptic crisis was supposed to have occurred—in 1983! We can be rescued from this dire state of affairs only by a 'total transformation' in which the way out of capitalism is by the abolition of wage labour and the institution of an income for life for all. [Gorz, 1, 77, 40-63]

Let us clarify a few points. First, even if, as a result of a division of labour,[33] I take advantage of the principle of comparative advantage to specialise in what I am good at, unless someone is pointing a gun at my head, I remain free to change professions. It may be unwise or inexpedient to do so but it isn't impossible. Second, if one is going to hunt, fish, rear cattle and be a critic, it is highly unlikely that one will be very good at all these activities. Put musician or physician on the list in place of hunter or fisherman and the Marx/Engels fantasy begins to look a lot less plausible, not that it was very plausible to begin with.[34] Thirdly, in what way can I act as I have a mind to if society regulates the general production?—please explain! If regulating society means allocating tasks to people then it's hard to see this as consistent with my being able to switch at will from one activity to another. 'If all the necessities of life are provided by individuals doing as they like,' writes Alan Carter, 'why is social planning needed? If all the necessities are not provided by individuals doing as they like, and if, therefore, developed technology is required to produce the remainder, who is to design, construct and service the machinery? And can it be assumed that those individuals will be able to do as they like—especially when individuals doing as they like are not, on this view, thought to provide all that is necessary?' [Carter, 12] The state, the regulator of society, expelled through the front door, sneaks back through the window.

Over time, however, it became apparent even to Marx that this idyllic picture was implausible. Intimations of a revision of his original romantic idyll appear as early as *Grundrisse der Kritik der Politischen Ökonomie* (*Outlines of a Critique of Political Economy*)[35] and in the third volume of *Capital* (which, it must be remembered, Marx did not publish himself) where he remarks, 'In fact, the realm of freedom actually begins only where labour which is determined by necessity and mundane considerations ceases; thus in the very nature of things it lies beyond the sphere of actual material production. Just as the savage must wrestle with Nature to satisfy his wants, to maintain and reproduce life, so must civilised man, and he must do so in all social formations and under all possible modes of production....Beyond it begins that development of human energy which is an end in itself, the true realm of freedom, which, however, can blossom forth only with this realm of necessity as its basis. The shortening of the working-day is its basic prerequisite.'[36] This is a very long way from the happy hunters, fishermen, pastoralists and critics of *The German Ideology*.

It isn't that Marx is unaware of the classical liberal position on the economic and social mutual benefits of exchange. In 'From the Paris Notebooks' (1844) he writes, 'The *communal being [Gemeinwesen] of man*, or men's self-activating and self-manifesting *human* being, their mutual complementing aimed at species-life, at authentic human being—all of this political economy comprehends only in the form of *exchange and trade*. *Society*, says Destutt de Tracy, is a *series of mutual exchanges*. It is exactly this movement of mutual integration. *Society*, says Adam Smith, is a *commercial society*. Each of its members is a *merchant*. Thus does political economy *fix* on the estranged form of sociable interaction and take it to be the form that is *essential, original* and adequate to the nature and destiny of man'[37] For Marx, no description of a human activity could be more damning than to describe it as commercial; no human occupation less worthy than that of the merchant. In his estimation, the classical liberal position makes human life in common to be little more than a matter of glorified huckstering. Marx cannot conceive of exchange as being anything other than sub-human—'men who are exchanging are not relating to one another as men.' [Marx 1994, 95] If it were urged against him that the division of labour, wage-labour, free market exchange and the apparently democratic political organisation consonant with all this were all of them spontaneous and natural, he wouldn't deny that this is so in some sense of the term 'natural' but would urge that this deforming and spontaneous self-seeking by individuals and groups be replaced by the exercise of *real* democracy in which people exercise a conscious and collective control over their economic and social conditions of existence.

Trying to make as much sense as possible of this idea we may take from it the following: man can create things that eventually come to stand over against him as somehow limiting his freedom; capitalism itself is the product of human actions, which then returns to channel other human actions and limit human potentiality; the division of labour, which removes us from an amateurish dabbling with many things to a professional concentration on what our abilities best suit us for is, in the end, according to Marx, a bad idea.

One thing, if 'thing' is the appropriate term, that can stand over against people by virtue of their social class is their very system of thought about the nature of the social relationships that enmesh them. To the extent that there's a lack of correspondence between the social relationships that really obtain and those that members of a particular class *believe* to obtain as a result of their membership of a class, to that extent their thinking reflects an ideology or, as it is sometimes phrased, it demonstrates a false consciousness. It doesn't appear as if Marx ever in fact used the specific term 'false consciousness' though he did discuss the substantive core of that concept in his treatment of ideology, in particular in *The German Ideology*.[38] However that may be, Marxists, in particular cultural Marxists, have used 'false consciousness' as a term of art to indicate the gap between the true nature of the social reality that people inhabit and the ideas of persons in a particular class about the nature of the social reality they inhabit, ideas that are subject to class-based systematic distortions and intellectual scotoses.[39]

As already mentioned, the father of the doctrine of false consciousness was Rousseau. Among Rousseau's intellectual offspring are radical gender feminists (such as Alison Jaggar) who believe that women who appear freely to choose what radical gender feminists disapprove of are systematically self-deceived. Jaggar writes, 'If individual desires and interests are socially constituted, however, the ultimate authority of individual judgment comes into question. Perhaps people may be mistaken about truth, morality or even their own interests; perhaps they may be systematically self-deceived about these matters or misled by their society.' [Jaggar, 44] Miraculously, however, even granting the social constitution of individual desires and interests, Jaggar believes that some women may manage to escape the maelstrom of male machinations. According to her, an adequate political psychology would recognise the ways in which 'certain historical circumstances allow specific groups of women to transcend at least partially the perception and theoretical constructs of male dominance.' [Jaggar, 150] What these mysterious liberating historical circumstances might be and precisely how they are supposed to bring about their selective release of some prisoners from the gaol of false consciousness is a little unclear. There is more than a touch of the *deus ex machina* ('…and then a miracle happens') about them.[40]

Unfortunately for its adherents, the notion of 'false consciousness' is incoherent. If false consciousness is thought of as the *universal* and *necessary* consequence of some kind of structural feature of our social/cultural/political reality, as something having universal extension, then it would seem that it should necessarily poison the well of thought from which we all drink— *everybody* should be infected by it and no one should be able to escape its reach. But the notion of 'false consciousness' only makes conceptual sense if it is possible to have a consciousness that is *not* false, otherwise, *everyone* is simply a victim of its conditioning, including those who accuse others of being held hostage by it.

Nevertheless, if the reach of false consciousness is less than universally (and necessarily) extensive, as, for instance, the radical feminist Alison Jaggar believes, if it applies only to some people or some groups but not to others, only to some beliefs but not to others, then independent criteria are required to show *which* person, group or belief is which, and *why*. It isn't enough simply to say '*your* beliefs are a manifestation of false consciousness but *mine* are not.' What special virtues—or, to take Jaggar's phrase, what historical circumstances— grant immunity from false consciousness to you or to your group? What is to prevent the victims of the putatively false consciousness from asserting in their turn that *you* and *your group* are the ones trapped in the web of false consciousness! It is hard to avoid the conclusion that the notion of 'false consciousness' isn't much more than a sophisticated form of the *argumentum ad hominem* used by a putatively enlightened class to pre-emptively dismiss the beliefs of its putatively unenlightened opponents.[41]

In essence, the doctrine of false consciousness, which is found not only in Marx but also in later thinkers such as Adorno, Althusser, Lacan, Deleuze, Badiou and Žižek, is a socio-political adaptation of the appearance-reality distinction popularised by Plato and subsequently by other revisionist metaphysicians. *This* is how things *seem to be*, Plato tells us, but *this* is how things *really* are. This is how things *seem to be* in our social and political worlds, our latter-day savants tell us, but what is *really* there, underlying the placid surface, is oppression, power structures, self-deception and domination. What you choose is what you *think* you want but what you *really* want is something entirely different. You may protest that you are free and self-determining but that's an illusion, the very protestation serving to conceal from you the extent to which you are unfree and conditioned. Even some economists, who really should know better, have been infected by the false consciousness bug. For a popular (if ephemeral) manifestation of this infection produced by two Nobel Laureates, see Akerlof & Shiller's *Phishing for Phools*. Consumers, they seem to think, don't know what they *really* want and so fall prey to, among other things, false advertising, disguised transaction costs and downright shysterism. But whether buyers know what they really want or not, it needs no ghost come from the grave to tell us that some people make foolish decisions and that some participants in the marketplace are rogues and vagabonds so that much heartache and many regrets could be prevented by the simple application of *caveat emptor* without ever needing to lose our shoes in the intellectual swamp of false consciousness. [see Galles, passim]

CLASS STRUGGLE, CAPITALISM, LABOUR AND EXPLOITATION

'The history of all hitherto existing society is the history of class struggles.' So begins *The Communist Manifesto*.[42] The same sentiment in almost the same words had appeared in the writings of Louis-Auguste Blanqui some years before Marx and Engels wrote the *Communist Manifesto*.[43] 'In all the revolutions, there have always been but two parties opposing each other; that of the people who wish to live by their own labor, and that of those who would live by the labor of others…. *Patricians and plebeians, slaves and freemen, guelphs and ghibellines, red roses and white roses, cavaliers and roundheads, liberals and serviles, are only varieties of the same species.*' [Blanqui, x] In fact, the notion of the class struggle goes back even further than Blanqui, and Marx himself was to describe Augustin Thierry as the 'father of the "class struggle".'[44] In any event, it doesn't really matter who invented the concept of class struggle or when it was invented; what concerns us is the use Marx makes of it.[45] It should be noted that apart from naming the classes currently in conflict, Marx gives no clear definition of what a class is and was still working on the idea when the manuscript included in *Capital* III was written, in which he once again took up the topic only to break off suddenly and never resume the discussion. If there is a core of truth to the idea of class it has to be something along the lines of a distinction between a group of human beings that labours and produces—wealth producers—and another group of human beings that lives off the work and product of the other—wealth consumers. As it happens, libertarian anarchists have no fundamental disagreement with class analysis along these lines and so do not find themselves in opposition to Marx on this point. The contentious issue is *which* human beings make up *which* class.

What has struck every reader with surprise or even astonishment is the praise Marx and Engels lavish on the achievements of the bourgeoisie in the first section of *The Communist Manifesto*. A full-blooded apologist could scarcely have written more fulsomely. According to Marx and Engels, the positive achievements of the bourgeoisie have been stunning, surpassing the building of the pyramids, Roman aqueducts and Gothic cathedrals, providing cheap and plentiful commodities, creating a large number of huge towns dwarfing the cities of the classical and medieval eras and, not least (and very politically incorrectly), rescuing 'a considerable part of the population from the idiocy of rural life.' [Marx & Engels 1848 [2002], 224] The short reign of the bourgeoisie has produced 'more massive and more colossal productive forces than have all preceding generations together. Subjection of Nature's forces to man, machinery, application of chemistry to industry and agriculture, steam-navigation, railways, electric telegraphs, clearing of whole continents for cultivation, canalization of rivers, whole populations conjured out of the grounds...'[46] In another surprising twist, Marx and Engels had nothing but scorn for socialist fellow travellers who wished to dispense with the price coordination supplied by the market. Marx and Engels were, writes Thomas Sowell, 'unsparing in their criticisms of their fellow socialists who wanted to replace price-co-ordination with central planning.' [Sowell 1996, 218] In *The Poverty of Philosophy*, as part of his general assault on the thinking of Proudhon, Marx specifically attacks Proudhon's notion that prices should be fixed by a central agency in proportion to the labour time needed to produce any given item, expressing scepticism that there is any necessary relation between labour time, utility and demand.

The achievements of the bourgeoisie, considerable as they are, have to be set against a long list of negatives. The rise to dominance of the bourgeoisie has, according to our authors, ended all 'feudal, patriarchal, idyllic relations,' 'torn asunder the motley feudal ties that bound man to his "natural superiors",' so that nothing remains to connect one person to another, even in the family, save the cash nexus. Religious fervour has been subordinated to egotistical calculation and intellectuals and professionals have become wage-labourers. Some of these supposed demerits of bourgeois life are somewhat tongue in cheek; there are other demerits, however that are not insignificant, not least of which is the concentration of property in the hands of the few, together with the political coalescence of independent provinces into nations.

Why did Marx and Engels give such lavish praise to the bourgeoisie's achievements? The answer would appear to be that the spectacular material abundance that the activities of the bourgeoisie had produced had brought matters to a head such that the next stage of social development, a return to the delights of primitive times *without* its material limitations, was now possible. The account in *The Communist Manifesto* recalls themes first developed in *The German Ideology* (1845/6) where communism was to become possible not

piecemeal but only all at once. In the communist world, labour would be transformed into a kind of self-activity and the state, the illusory community, would
be replaced by a real community. [Marx & Engels 1975-2001, 5, 78]

The spectacular results of bourgeois activity had brought about the conditions which undermined that very activity and, at the same time, created
the conditions in which communism could come to be. The spectacular and
energetic achievements of the bourgeoisie contain the seeds of the bourgeoisie's own destruction. The forces it has conjured up are like an out-of-control
genie—boom and bust and over-production leading to the condition of famine
amid plenty. Marx and Engels write, 'there is too much civilization, too much
means of subsistence, too much industry, too much commerce. The productive
forces at the disposal of society no longer tend to further the development of
the conditions of bourgeois property; on the contrary, they have become too
powerful for these conditions, by which they are fettered, and so soon as they
overcome these fetters, they bring disorder into the whole of bourgeois society,
endanger the existence of bourgeois property.'[47] As the bourgeoisie career
inexorably towards destruction, its correlative class, the proletariat, moves to
take power so that, in effect, the bourgeoisie have managed to become their
own gravediggers.

At this point, the topic shifts to the dehumanising effect that work in
the new bourgeois dispensation has upon the worker. This is, of course,
alienation making a reappearance. The division of labour and the extensive
use of machinery, between them bring it about that work loses its individual
character and its charm for the workman. It is hard not to see this theme as a
return to romanticism. Yes, there may have been some people whose work
was a pleasure but these were the privileged few. One of the reasons why the
cities grew to the extent that they did during the industrial revolution was that
country people voted with their feet and deserted the supposed idylls of the
countryside.

So, what is to be done? The Communist party, the organisers of the proletariat, must abolish private ownership of the means of production. Will such
destruction not destroy liberty also? No, it will destroy only bourgeois liberty
that the proletariat do not in any case enjoy. Bourgeois notions of freedom
are historically conditioned and have no absolute validity. All that bourgeois
freedom implies is the freedom to buy, sell and trade. 'Your very ideas,' say our
authors, 'are but the outgrowth of the conditions of your bourgeois production
and bourgeois property, just as your jurisprudence is but the will of your class
made into law for all, a will whose essential character and direction are determined by the economical conditions of existence of your class.'[48]

Having seized power, the Communists will abolish all property in land,
introduce a heavy progressive or graduated income tax, abolish the rights of
inheritance, confiscate the property of all emigrants and rebels, centralise credit
in the hands of the State, with a national bank funded by state capital enjoying
an exclusive monopoly, centralise the means of communication and transport
in the hands of the state, extend state ownership of factories and other instruments of production, require everyone to work to the same extent, abolish the

distinction between town and country and provide free education for all in public schools.[49] It is with a sinking heart that one realises that, even in those countries where Communists haven't seized power, much of this programme has in fact been implemented. Property in land may not have been formally abolished but heavy taxation and death (estate) duties mean that landowners in effect rent their land from the state. Inheritance hasn't been formally abolished but taxes and duties on death diminish significantly the capacity to bequeath.[50] Progressive (so-called) income tax is a standard feature of almost all Western democracies. The power of words is evident in this use of the term 'progressive' to conceal the fact that the compulsory payment (tax) for uninvited services is charged to the wealthier alleged beneficiaries of these services at a *proportionately* higher rate than to the poorer. Imagine what Mrs Johnson would think if, when she arrived at the supermarket checkout with exactly the same purchases as Mr Jones, she were to be asked to pay more for them because, as the cashier would point out reasonably, 'After all, you have more money!' Central banks (in effect state-owned even if legally independent) have, of course, become the organs of universal credit, producing intrinsically inflationary paper currency. Communications and transport are only now, fitfully, returning to semi-private ownership after a long period of ownership by the state thought the state still exercises significant control over both. State ownership of business enterprises is no longer fashionable and is mercifully declining but free and compulsory indoctrination for all in public schools is well established and unlikely to disappear in the near future.[51]

Eventually, according to Marx, all class distinctions will disappear and, with their disappearance and with the concentration of the means of production in the hands of the whole nation, public power will lose its political character. Goodbye state, hello stateless utopia. The seizure of the state by the proletariat, or its vanguard, the Communist Party, is easily to believe in; given our flawed human nature and the stubborn facts of history, the inevitable dissolution of the state after such a seizure is less easy to believe.

POLITICS AND ECONOMICS

One of the ideas central to Marxism is that economics grounds politics and not the other way around.[52] This idea can be found in Marx and Engel's writing as early as the *Holy Family* (1845), a manifesto of their joint apostasy from the liberal-socialist Hegelian Left.[53] It is reiterated in Engels's 1888 Preface to *The Communist Manifesto* where he writes of what he calls *The Communist Manifesto*'s fundamental proposition (which he attributes to Marx) which is that, 'in every historical epoch, the prevailing mode of economic production and exchange, and the social organization necessarily following from it, form the basis upon which is built up, and from which alone[54] can be explained, the political and intellectual history of that epoch; that consequently the whole history of mankind (since the dissolution of primitive tribal society, holding land in common ownership) has been a history of class struggles, contests between exploiting and exploited, ruling and oppressed classes; that the history of these class struggles forms a series of evolutions in which, nowadays, a

stage has been reached where the exploited and oppressed class—the proletariat—cannot attain its emancipation from the sway of the exploiting and
ruling class—the bourgeoisie—without, at the same time, and once and for all,
emancipating society at large from all exploitation, oppression, class distinctions and class struggles.' [Engels 1888, 202-203] The main points of this
fundamental principle are: 1. In every age, the dominant mode of economic
production and exchange, together with its associated form of social organisation, form a base upon which is constructed the political and intellectual life of
that age; 2. Human history is constituted by a series of class struggles forming
a series up to the present, and 3. The class struggle has now reached a stage
in which the emancipation of the exploited class, the proletariat, will end all
exploitation, oppression, class distinction and class struggle.

Although *Capital* has achieved universal fame, even if only the fame of the
purchased but largely unread,[55] Marx's economic theory is contained more
succinctly and comprehensibly in his earlier work, *A Contribution to the
Critique of Political Economy* (1859), a revised and rewritten version of the
first volume of the unpublished *Grundrisse*. In this short and clearly written
piece, we find many of the most important themes of Marxism presented with
a commendable clarity and vigour. Marx tells us that although he began his
academic life as a student of jurisprudence, by the mid 1840s, his investigation
had led him to grasp that a fundamental understanding of legal relationships
and political structures was not to be had by a direct study of these phenomena
but, rather, by realising that they are 'rooted in the material conditions of life'
and that the 'mode of production of material life conditions the social, political
and intellectual life-process generally. It is not the consciousness of men that
specifies their being, but on the contrary their social being that specifies their
consciousness.' [Marx 1996, 159; 160] The social being of men, in turn, is
conditioned by the currently operative material productive forces. Change,
when it comes, comes from the bottom up, not down from the top. 'With the
alteration of the economic foundation the whole colossal superstructure is more
or less rapidly transformed.'[56]

EXPLOITATION AGAIN AND THE LABOUR THEORY OF VALUE

Why does Marx think the buyer-seller nexus in respect of labour is necessarily exploitative? In brief, and crudely, it appears to be a matter of theft.
[but see Kolakowski, 325-332] The employer pays for x but obtains x+delta.
The price of labour is less than the price of the finished good produced by that
labour. By the same token, the price of all factors entering into the finished
good—material, rent, licensing fees, insurance, etc. are less than the price of
the finished good, assuming, as always, that the business is a going concern and
turning a profit. If not, the price of the finished good may in fact be less than its
factor prices. In an 1865 work, 'Value, Price and Profit, Marx gives us a short
account of his theory. He writes:

> For the present, I want to turn your attention to one decisive point.
> The *value* of the labouring power is determined by the quantity of labour

necessary to maintain or reproduce it, but the *use* of that labouring power is only limited by the active energies and physical strength of the labourer....We have seen that, to daily reproduce his labouring power, he must daily reproduce a value of three shillings, which he will do by working six hours daily. But this does not disable him from working ten or twelve or more hours a day. But by paying the daily or weekly *value* of the spinner›s labouring power the capitalist has acquired the right of using that labouring power during *the whole day or week*. He will, therefore, make him work say, daily*, twelve hours*. *Over and above* the six hours required to replace his wages, or the value of his labouring power, he will, therefore, have to work *six other hours*, which I shall call hours of *surplus labour*, which surplus labour will realize itself in a *surplus value* and a *surplus produce*....By advancing three shillings, the capitalist will, therefore, realize a value of six shillings, because, advancing a value in which six hours of labour are crystallized, he will receive in return a value in which twelve hours of labour are crystallized. By repeating this same process daily, the capitalist will daily advance three shillings and daily pocket six shillings, one half of which will go to pay wages anew, and the other half of which will form *surplus value*, for which the capitalist pays no equivalent. It is this *sort of exchange between capital and labour* upon which capitalistic production, or the wages system, is founded, and which must constantly result in reproducing the working man as a working man, and the capitalist as a capitalist. *The rate of surplus value*, all other circumstances remaining the same, will depend on the proportion between that part of the working day necessary to reproduce the value of the labouring power and the *surplus time* or *surplus labour* performed for the capitalist. It will, therefore, depend on the *ratio in which the working day is prolonged over and above that extent*, by working which the working man would only reproduce the value of his labouring power, or replace his wages.[57]

In short, the worker works for x hours to pay the cost of his maintenance, but the employer makes him work for x+delta and keeps the delta for himself; the employer pays for labour but gets labour power.[58] Exploitation, then, is a form of theft.[59] One might wonder why, in the absence of coercion, any worker would agree to such a bad bargain. If a gun is put to one's head, then yes, one will agree to do things that otherwise one would decline to do. But where is the gun in the circumstances of ordinary employment?

Capital (1867) makes extensive use of a network of inter-related concepts— use value, exchange value, surplus value, labour, labour power[60] and, of course, capital.[61] The cornerstone of this conceptual complex is the notion of the labour theory of value.[62] Crudely put, this amounts to the claim that the value of a commodity is a function of the amount of labour that went into its creation. Marx's account eventually involves a slightly more sophisticated version of this thesis, with brute labour being replaced by the idea of socially useful labour but the basic idea remains—the value of a commodity is determined by the amount of (qualified) labour that went into its production. As an empirical doctrine, the labour theory of value is manifestly false. 'If labor is the sole—or even main—source of value, writes Thomas Sowell, 'then in those economies where there is more labor input and less nonlabor input, output per capita and therefore real income would be higher. The opposite is blatant. In the most desperately poor countries, people work longer and harder for subsistence than in more elaborate and prosperous economies where most people never touch physical goods during the production process. Indeed, it is only in the latter countries that subsistence is sufficiently easy to achieve that it is taken for granted and that there is time and money to spend on books on the "exploitation" or "alienation" of labor.' [Sowell 1996, 226-227]

The labour theory of value was a commonplace of the standard economics of the period in which Marx was writing. Marx did not invent the concept; he merely took it over from existing economic theory, in particular, from the writings of David Ricardo. The whole of *Capital* can be seen as an exhibition of the problems that follow if this notion is taken seriously; to that extent, *Capital* is largely consistent. Paul Thomas writes: 'Most modern economists' accounts of what they call "Marxian economics" centre on the view that Marx vitiated his economic analysis by virtue of having inherited, uncritically, a labour theory of value from the classical political economists. The logical consistency and strength of Marx's subsequent analysis is then generally admitted.' [Thomas, 480] 'Modern economic thought has long abandoned the view that commodities exchange according to the working time stored up in them. Price is in fact determined by supply and demand; by the amount of capital invested, the scarcity of the raw material involved and many other factors.' (Bowle, 331) Nevertheless, the labour theory of value is economically obsolete and it was replaced *even during Marx's lifetime* by the concept of marginal utility.

The concept of marginal utility had three fathers: William Stanley Jevons, who first articulated the idea in a paper published in 1863 and included it in his *The Theory of Political Economy* in 1871 which made his name as the leading economist of the period; Carl Menger came up with the idea in his *Principles of Economics* in 1871, and Leon Walras in his *Éléments d'économie politiques pure* in 1874. The first volume of *Capital* was published in 1867 some years after the first appearance of Jevons paper but before its widespread dissemination. Still, Marx did not die until 1883 and it is hardly conceivable that he could have been unaware of the new marginal utility economics. As David Gordon notes, 'Although the marginalist or subjective revolution in economics began in the 1870s, a decade of great intellectual activity for Marx, he failed to note its occurrence.' [Gordon 1990, 13] Carl Menger writes:

There is no necessary and direct connection between the value of a good and whether, or in what quantities, labor and other goods of higher order were applied to its production. A non-economic good (a quantity of timber in a virgin forest, for example) does not attain value for men if large quantities of labor or other economic goods were applied to its production. Whether a diamond was found accidentally or was obtained from a diamond pit with the employment of a thousand days of labor is completely irrelevant for its value. In general, no one in practical life asks for the history of the origin of a good in estimating its value, but considers solely the services that the good will render him and which he would have to forgo if he did not have it at his command. Goods on which much labor has been expended often have no value, while others, on which little or no labor was expended, have a very high value. Goods on which much labor was expended and others on which little or no labor was expended are often of equal value to economizing men. The quantities of labor or of other means of production applied to its production cannot, therefore, be the determining factor in the value of a good. Comparison of the value of a good with the value of the means of production employed in its production does, of course, show whether and to what extent its production, an act of past human activity, was appropriate or economic. But the quantities of goods employed in the production of a good have neither a necessary nor a directly determining influence on its value. [Menger, 146-147]

Summing up, David Gordon writes, 'Instead of asking, as the classical economists did, what objective property of goods makes them valuable, these writers [Jevons et al.] placed value in the minds of consumers. Value arises from the subjective preferences, not from the cost of production; included in the cost theories spurned by this group is the labor theory.' [Gordon 1990, 13]

There are, then, fundamental problems with the conceptual structure of Marx's attack on capitalism. The labour theory of value isn't defensible and, to the extent that the remainder of Marx's ideas, for example, the key notion of exploitation, rests on that indefensible theory, Marx can't sustain it. Of course, if Marx's explanation of exploitation in *Capital* is rendered nugatory by his failure to come to terms with the marginal theory of utility it does *not* mean that there isn't exploitation and that if there were such exploitation it wouldn't be reprehensible. It *does* mean, however, that Marx hasn't established it by the means he has chosen.[63]

Some have attempted to salvage what they regard as the ship of Marxism while jettisoning its redundant supercargo. Over the years, efforts have been made to make and mend Marxism without much success but in the mid-twentieth century, a loose school of revisionist Marxism developed, sometimes called Analytical Marxism, that attempted to purge Marx's theories of their unacceptable elements and reconstruct what they regard as its central insights on firmer foundations. I can't devote much space to this neo-Marxism here save to say that the more it is defensible, the less it looks anything like Marxism, all such efforts resembling productions of *Hamlet* without the Prince of Denmark.[64]

By and large, the adherents of this school accept that the labour theory of value is dead in the water.[65] Jon Elster comments trenchantly, 'the [labour] theory is useless at best, harmful and misleading at its not infrequent worst.' [Elster, 120] If exploitation can't be explained by the labour theory of value, how then is it to be conceived? Where there is no manifest coercion or violence, how can it be that workers are exploited by capitalists? Our analytical Marxists propose different answers to this question: G. A. Cohen accepts that individual workers may be free to enter or leave capitalist employment but argues that they are collectively unfree to do so; John Roemer locates the root of exploitation in the differential ownership of capital assets. Assessing the efforts of these Marxist revisionists, David Gordon concludes that 'very little remains of Marxism when Elster and his colleagues are finished analysing and "defending" it....When all the criticisms are put together, analytical Marxism becomes a formidable weapon in the hands of anti-Marxists. As an instrument for a Marxist renascence, it fails.' [Gordon 1990, 28-29]

Whatever about its internal consistency, the whole enterprise that Marx is attempting in *Capital* is fundamentally wrong-headed. The value of a commodity is nothing objective and isn't to be found 'in' the commodity. Value isn't a property that a cat or a tree or a pen can possess in and of itself; it is a relational property. Value is what a desk is worth to John Grisham as John Grisham considers it suitable for writing legal thrillers upon. Moreover, labour isn't a thing; it can't be congealed, packaged, put into something, or reside somewhere. Labour is an activity of a human being and it exists only when that human being is labouring. For a source of the substantialist concept of labour, we can point the finger to a certain extent at the Lockean metaphor of 'mixing one's labour' from his *Second Treatise*. The more important concept in Locke, however, isn't mixing one's labour with some external object but that of 'improvement'; the labour-mixing image—and that's all it is, an image—is a way of capturing the intuition that when I form something by, say, carving it from a piece of wood or moulding a piece of clay, I thereby establish a pre-emptive claim to own it. There are, of course, other ways of establishing pre-emptive claims. So desks or books or donkeys or desktop computers are worth nothing in and of themselves; whatever value they have they have only in relation to those who are willing to exchange their money, goods or services for them.

This point is so fertile a source of misunderstanding that it's worth rehearsing. The fundamental problem with Marx's account, whether crude or sophisticated, is simply this: *Things have no value*, if value is thought of as something that inheres in them in an objective way. Things do not have value in themselves as they exist in nature, and they do not acquire value in themselves either as the result of a process of production. To try to discern the objective value of anything is to look for the wrong thing in the wrong place, much like the Sufi wise-fool, the Mulla Nasrudin, in the following story. 'Someone saw Nasrudin searching for something on the ground. "What have you lost, Mulla?" he asked. "My key," said the Mulla. So they both went down on their knees and looked for it. After a time the other man asked: "Where exactly did you drop it?" "In my own house." "The why are you looking here?" "There is more light here than inside my own house," replied the Mulla.' [Shah, 26] If you set out for your destination in the wrong direction, no amount of feverish stepping on the gas pedal is going to get you there; you need to turn around and go in the right direction. The concept of value permeating Marx's account is fundamentally misguided and no amount of elaborate logic chopping or subtle scholastic distinctions can make it right. The difference between Marx and the Mulla is that the Mulla is looking for the right thing in the wrong place, whereas Marx is looking for the wrong thing in the wrong place.

As was a commonplace among those who considered such matters, Marx believed that an uncoerced exchange involved an equality. If A is to be exchanged for B (and A and B aren't the same) there must be something that is identical to both which makes them equal to each other—and for Marx, that's labour. Of course, exchange isn't an equality—if it were, it wouldn't, under normal circumstances, take place. It is, rather, a mutual inequality. [see Gordon, 1990, 14] It is relatively easy to establish this point. Suppose your hobby is constructing replicas of famous buildings from lollipop sticks. You spend 20 years working on a lollipop replica of the Taj Mahal. At 40 hours per week by 50 weeks per year (you take two weeks' holiday) by twenty years, this comes to 40,000 hours. Let us take $5 as the going rate for labour. By my reckoning, your model is worth $200,000. Perhaps it is. Try selling it and see if anyone is willing to fork over anything near that amount. My guess is that you'll be sadly disappointed. The likelihood of finding someone who will pay that amount or anything even remotely near it for your replica is close to vanishing point. The element of truth in the labour theory of value is that if the cost of manufacturing a product (the cost to be determined by the price of material, labour, transport, overheads, etc.) is consistently greater than the price I can obtain for it in the market, I won't stay in business for very long.

Now, in case it should be forgotten, the point of the conceptual apparatus of the labour theory is to explain the notion of exploitation and it is this latter notion that really concerns Marx. David Gordon summarises the Marxist 'exploitation' account succinctly and sympathetically as follows: 'capitalism inevitably creates two classes: capitalists (owners of the means of production) and workers. The former, having brought it about that the latter have no choice but to work for them, extract profits through the worker's exploitation. It is no use talking of free economic activity in the context of a system in which the wealth held by the members of each of the two main classes varies so greatly. "Freedom" in such an arrangement is a sham: to talk of the justice of capitalism is to stand on empty verbiage.' [Gordon 1990, 47] If, as seems to be the case, Marx's theory of exploitation rests on the labour theory of value and if that theory turns out to be false, then Marx hasn't explained where the exploitation of workers come from. Nevertheless, even if the labour theory of value has to be abandoned, it does not follow that there isn't exploitation of the workers by capitalists. There might be an account of capital and labour that doesn't suffer from the problems of the labour theory of value so that 'it might still be true that workers sell their labor power and receive in return enough to sustain their labor, and that the difference in value between what they produce and what they receive as wages is the source of rent, interest, and profit, even if it is not the case that the values of goods, including labor, are determined by the socially necessary labor time required to produce them.' [Gordon 1990, 49]

Is the term 'exploitation' a purely economic descriptive notion or does it contain a normative element, a negative normative element? If the latter, what is the basis for the normative judgement? Even if is true that the value that a worker receives is less than the value he creates for his employer, why is that necessarily exploitation? Some passages in Marx clearly suggest a moralised conception of this notion. Take the following: 'Labour-power is not purchased under this system for the purpose of satisfying the personal needs of the buyer, either by its service or through its product. The aim of the buyer is the valorization of his capital, *the production of commodities which contain more labour than he paid for, and therefore contain a portion of value which costs him nothing* and is nevertheless realized through the sale of those commodities.' [*Capital*, 769; emphasis added] Taking something that one did not pay for which belongs to someone else sounds suspiciously like theft!

The exchange value of a widget is determined by the amount of socially necessary labour required to produce it.[66] The capitalist exploits the worker by purchasing his labour power and forcing him to work extra time beyond the time necessary to produce the widget. Surplus value, then, derives from unpaid working time. Where the few control all the capital, it's inevitable that the workers will be exploited. Given the labour theory of value, class conflict is unavoidable and the only solution is the removal of capital from the hands of the few by means of the collectivisation of the means of production. It might be urged that if the employer pays the worker less than the full value of his contribution the worker is disadvantaged. Again, if this amounts to the claim that such a procedure is unjust we have simply begged the question. What then could a non-question-begging account of disadvantage mean? Perhaps it is that workers are forced to work for their employers. If this were so, then workers would be at a disadvantage so the question now becomes, *are* workers forced to work for employers? On the face of it, this does not seem to be the case. They are free to work for themselves, or to form cooperatives and work for one another. Where is the coercion? Is the claim rather not so much that workers are coerced as that a worker is entitled to all that value that he creates? This might possibly be true but it isn't obviously true. Perhaps, after all, on a more adequate economic analysis, when all the factors of production are taken into account the worker *does* receive the full value of his labour so there's no exploitative gap to be explained.

An account of exploitation that does *not* depend essentially upon conceiving it in terms of the misappropriation of unpaid labour or surplus value is provided by Leszek Kolakowski. He points out that 'Marx himself ridiculed the utopians and Lasalle for holding that the worker should receive in the form of wages the whole equivalent of the values produced by him' but rather that 'surplus value...should accrue to society' in various ways that, in fact, it actually does under capitalism! Exploitation, then, concerns the lack of control by society over the use of surplus product and it is a matter of more or less, not something that can be totally eliminated. Kolakowski goes on to argue that, paradoxically, 'If, instead of private ownership, the power to control the means of production and distribution is confined to a small ruling group uncontrolled by any measure of representative democracy, there will be not less exploitation but a great deal more....From this point of view socialist communities at the present day are examples not of the abolition of exploitation but of exploitation in an extreme degree, since by cancelling the legal right of ownership they have destroyed the machinery which gave society control over the produce of its own labour.' In what must be a supreme example of meiosis, Kolakowski remarks that 'Although this account of exploitation appears to be in accordance with Marx's own views it is hard to reconcile with orthodox Marxism...'! [Kolakowski, 332, 333, 334]

CRITIQUE OF THE GOTHA PROGRAMME

In his *Critique of the Gotha Programme* (1875)[67] Marx commented on the proposed programme for the Socialist Worker's Party of Germany. A number of points of interest emerge from Marx's comments. In response to the Programme's call for equality, Marx notes that in the transitional stage between the existing economic, social and political order and the establishment of communist society, equality is unrealisable. But when communist society has been established 'after the subjection of individuals to the divisions of labour, and thereby, the antithesis between mental and physical labour, has disappeared; after labour has become not merely a means to live but the foremost need in life; after the multifarious development of individuals has grown along with their productive powers, and all the springs of co-operative wealth flow more abundantly—only then can the limited horizon of bourgeois right be wholly transcended, and society can inscribe on its banner: from each according to his abilities, to each according to his needs!' [Marx 1996, 214-215]

The Programme had committed the German Worker's Party to strive for a free state. Marx wants to know what such a beast would look like. He writes, 'Freedom consists in transforming the state from an agency superior to society into one thoroughly subordinated to it...'[68] In a communist society, what will be the status and function of the state? To this question, Marx replies, significantly, 'Between capitalist and communist society there is a period of revolutionary transformation of one into the other. There is also corresponding a period of political transition, in which the state can be nothing else but *the revolutionary dictatorship of the proletariat.*'[69]

Two particular targets of Marx's attack within the Programme are noteworthy. The Programme called for universal and compulsory school attendance. This seems not unlike Marx's own call in the *Communist Manifesto* for free education for all children in public schools. Nevertheless, Marx treats this aspect of the Gotha programme with utter scorn, holding that elementary state education is completely objectionable and calling for the separation of education from the influence of both Church and State. The Programme also called for the prohibition of child labour, and here Marx notes that such a prohibition would be 'incompatible with the existence of large-scale industry and hence an empty, pious wish.'[70] Moreover, if such a policy were to be implemented he thinks its effect would be reactionary because, provided there are appropriate safety measures for children 'an early combination of productive labour with instruction is one of the most powerful means for transforming present-day society.' [Marx 1996, 225]

THE REAL CLASS STRUGGLE

Marx's occasional piece, 'Civil War in France' (1871) contains some significant remarks on his estimation of the state. He writes, 'The centralised state power, with its ubiquitous organs of standing army, police, bureaucracy, clergy, and judicature—organs wrought after the plan of a systematic and hierarchic division of labour—originates from the days of absolute monarchy, serving nascent middle-class society as a mighty weapon in its struggles against feudalism....During the subsequent regimes the government...became not only a hotbed of huge national debts and crushing taxes; with its irresistible allurements of place, pelf and patronage, it became...the bone of contention between the rival factions and adventurers of the ruling classes...'[71] There is much here with which the anarchist can agree. The state is predicated upon a division of labour—it assumes a monopoly of legitimate violence since it assumes that a free market in the provision of such services is bound to be destructive. Moreover, states have consistently allied themselves with sectional interests—bankers, rent-seeking industrialists and the like. Libertarian anarchists need have no fundamental disagreement with the idea of class analysis just as such and so do not necessarily find themselves in opposition to Marx on this point. [see Hook, 323-346] The contentious issue is *which* human beings make up *which* class.[72]

According to Hans-Hermann Hoppe, Marxists believe that the history of mankind is in essence the history of struggles between pairs of classes; that the dominant class exploits the dominated class; that the dominant class employs the coercive force of the state to protect the 'relations of production' or property arrangements favourable to the dominant class which it does by means of laws that privilege the dominant class, together with the promulgation and maintenance of an ideology that legitimates these arrangements; that within the dominant class there exists an internal tendency towards centralisation and concentration and an external tendency towards conflict between the increasingly integrated groups; and that this centralisation and concentration and competition will lead to the emergence of a revolutionary class consciousness and the withering away of the state and the replacement of coercive government of man by man with an administration of things, all of this resulting in unprecedented economic prosperity. Hoppe believes that Marxism is essentially correct in all five points!—except for the small matter of misidentifying the classes! Because of this misidentification, based on an unsustainable (Hoppe calls it 'absurd') theory of exploitation, Hoppe believes that Marxism has brought the five claims into disrepute.

In his historical excursus, Marx correctly identifies slavery as a form of exploitation and, similarly, the feudal relationship between lord and peasant, and he is suitably indignant about the plunder and violence and conquest employed in establishing and maintaining these relationships.[73] He is similarly indignant about the violence involved in the appropriation of colonies.[74] So far so good. Unfortunately, Marx goes on to portray the employer/worker relationship as similarly exploitative. Hoppe believes, and I agree with him, that the situations are entirely different. He writes, 'Marx is engaged in a trick. In engaging in historical investigations and arousing the reader's indignation regarding the brutalities underlying the formation of many capitalist fortunes, he actually sidesteps the issue at hand. He distracts from the fact that his thesis is really an entirely different one: namely, that even if one were to have a "clean" capitalism so to speak, i.e., one in which the original appropriation of capital were the result of nothing else but homesteading, work, and saving, the capitalist who hired labour to be employed with this capital would none the less be engaged in exploitation.' [Hoppe 1993, 54] Now, as has already been shown, the labour theory of value is economically obsolete so that to the extent that a theory of exploitation depends upon it, its case is not proven. If exploitation can't be explained by the labour theory of value, it must be explained by factor Z, whatever that may be, but an analysis of the phenomenon of uncoerced exchange shows us that no such factor Z can be found.

Apart from any other deficiencies it may have, the Marxist analysis of exchange attaches no importance to the notion of time. But time is an essential feature of human life as a whole and is no less a significant feature of exchange. Just as a shopper who pays more for butter in one store than he would be obliged to pay in another isn't necessarily irrational, provided we take into account that it isn't just the butter itself which is purchased but the service, the splendour (or otherwise) of the store, the convenience, and so on, so too, time enters into exchanges. Other things being equal, we prefer something now to that same something later. The worker is paid now for goods whose value to the employer is only realised later. We can now see why the worker enters into an agreement that, on the Marxist analysis, is baffling. 'The laborer enters the agreement because, given his time preference, he prefers a smaller amount of present goods over a larger future one; and the capitalist enters it because, given his time preference, he has a reverse preference order and ranks a larger future amount of goods more highly than a smaller present one.' [Hoppe 1993, 56-57] As is the case with all non-coerced exchanges, both parties benefit.

So, then, is exploitation possible at all if the Marxist account is rejected? Yes, but for different reasons. A exploits B if A uses B's resources without B's permission, whether these are B's external resources or, in the extreme case, B himself. Slavery is the exploitation of the slave because the slave's property in himself is appropriated coercively by the slave owner. Serfdom is exploitation because the serf's property in the land he has homesteaded is appropriated by the feudal lord. Exploitation isn't merely some psychological dissatisfaction one may experience from an exchange. We often obtain less than we would like from an exchange—perhaps I am not paid as much as I think I am worth or my house sells for less than I would like—but as long as we are free to exchange or not exchange and our property isn't simply appropriated, we can't complain that we were exploited. Once, at the concession stand at a rugby game, I overheard someone complain of being 'ripped off' because he was asked to pay €5 for a hotdog, the term 'rip off' being a synonym for exploitation. But, of course, he wasn't obliged to buy the hotdog. He wouldn't have died if he had waited an hour or two to buy it somewhere else for less. Whether he knew it or not, since actions speak louder than words, his purchase of the hotdog testified to the fact that he was judging his immediate acquisition of the hotdog to be worth *more* than €5! Exploitation, then, properly understood, takes place whenever one person appropriates resources that he himself has neither homesteaded nor saved nor produced nor acquired from another by legitimate exchange. Thieves exploit those upon whom they predate; so too robbers and fraudsters. Unlike free and uncoerced exchange, exploitation is zero-sum; the exploiter's gain is the exploited's loss.

We can then divide mankind into two classes: those who live by homesteading, producing, exchanging; and those who live by exploiting them. It is here that the fundamental truth of class conflict lies and that's why the Marxist account of class conflict has a ring of truth. The whole of human history is a record of the conflict between producers and predators.[75] Marxism is correct to hold that class conflict is the key to the analysis of human society; Marxism is wrong to identify that conflict as obtaining between employer and worker and wrong not to see where it is really located; between the state and the state-supported entities, and the rest of society. It is true that Marxism portrays the state as the executive committee of the bourgeoisie and sees the close connection between big business and big government[76] but it misunderstands fundamentally the nature of that relationship. The cosy relationship that exists between the state and the beneficiaries of corporate welfare does not exist because the state is the resolute defender of private property but because the state is the dispenser of privileges and monopolies and rebates and bailouts, all of which protect its cronies from the full impact of free market competition. The relationship is particularly friendly between the state and the banks in their cooperative efforts to establish and maintain legalised counterfeiting. 'By offering to cut the banking elite in on its own counterfeiting machinations and allowing them to counterfeit on top of its own counterfeited notes under a regime of fractional reserve banking, the state can easily reach this goal and establish a system of state monopolized money and cartelized banking controlled by the central bank. And through this direct counterfeiting connection with the banking system and by extension the banks' major clients, the ruling class in fact extends far beyond the state apparatus to the very nervous [*sic*- nerve?] centers of civil society—not that much different, at least in appearance, from the picture that Marxists like to paint of the cooperation between banking, business elites and the state.' [Hoppe 1993, 66]

When the exploiting class is large and the exploited class relatively small, the exploitative relationship can be initiated and sustained by violence. When the exploiting class is small compared to the exploited class, then the maintenance of exploitation can't be sustained just by violence or by the threat of violence. In this case, it is essential that the exploited class must come to accept that the *status quo* is in order, and to that end, an appropriate ideology must be promulgated and widely accepted. That ideology typically contains a theory of democracy, constitutions, elections, a notion of representation, the necessity for state coercive institutions to preserve law and order and the necessity for the forcible redistribution of property to protect the poor, and the general dispensing of goodies to all and sundry (cleverly disguising the fact that these goodies are paid for by someone else), often accompanied by an historical account that conceals more than it reveals, and by the steady (and remunerative) work of the exploiters' willing little helpers—civil servants, the print and electronic media, schools and churches. It isn't necessary that those who are exploited enthusiastically accept the *status quo* (all the better for the exploiters if they do); it is enough if they passively acquiesce in it, accepting its inevitability as expressed in the common but false saying that only two things are inevitable in life, death and taxes. The emergence of the modern state is testimony to the successful deployment of an effective ideology, not least because of the uncritical acceptance by many people of a Marxist–inspired account of exploitation. People look for exploitation in the wrong place and fail to see the exploitation that's taking place right before their eyes.

In order for the state to function, the mass of the people has to believe in its legitimacy. The state therefore employs a class of professional apologists and controls the means of propaganda, often through dominance of the education system. The task of the State apologist is 'to convince the public that what the State does is not…crime on a gigantic scale, but something necessary and vital that must be supported and obeyed.' [Rothbard 2002, 169] In return for their services, the apologists are rewarded with power and status and allowed to share in the booty obtained from the masses. We are brought up to believe in the legitimacy of the state, our state-sponsored education confirms us in this belief, everything around us in society supports this belief and nothing appears to count against it.[77] The belief in the legitimacy of the state is all the more effectively planted in the minds of its citizens if it is never in fact argued for or justified (that might raise doubts) but simply conveyed inchoately as a foundational principle. Thus communicated, just as death is an inescapable fact of natural life, so too does the state and its legitimacy appear to be a fact of social life. Such is the power of being first in the field—'positioning' in advertising terms—that the state can literally get away with murder if it can foster the notion that what it does is legitimate. Rothbard claims that the man on the Clapham omnibus, after centuries of propaganda, 'has been imbued with the idea…that the government is his legitimate sovereign, and that it would be wicked or mad to refuse to obey its dictates.' The legitimacy of the state has been effectively and insidiously communicated to all by the state's apologists in the churches, the schools, the universities, the press, 'aided and abetted by all the trappings of legitimacy: flags, rituals, ceremonies, awards, constitutions, etc.'[78]

WHERE ARE WE NOW? TERRY EAGLETON'S APOLOGY FOR MARX

The post-2008 financial crisis had the incidental effect of throwing a lifeline to Keynesian economic theories and (changing metaphors) made it possible for Marxism to be taken off the life-support machine it had been on for a considerable time. The financial crisis is widely touted as a crisis of capitalism and thus is taken to show that Marx was right after all. This belief has found expression in many places—newspaper articles, posters, the Internet, television and radio programmes—but perhaps the most egregious and entertaining semi-scholarly expression of this view is Terry Eagleton's 2011 book, aptly entitled, *Why Marx was Right*. I choose Eagleton's book not because it's the most serious work of scholarship (on the contrary, it's a 200 page+ piece of invective, sometimes amusing, sometimes silly, but written throughout with style and panache) but because it says what oft was thought but ne'er so well expressed.[79] It is a remarkable demonstration of the capacity of dead horses to regain life once they cease to be flogged and so should encourage us to flog dead horses vigorously and ceaselessly. In this book, Eagleton takes ten common criticisms of Marx and attempts to rebut them one by one. The criticisms he considers (rephrased for brevity) are: 1. Marxism is irrelevant. It might have been relevant in the nineteenth century but not in our post-industrial Western societies; 2. The practical result of Marxism has been mass murder, terror and tyranny. Less dramatically, socialism means lack of freedom and a lack of material goods; 3. Marxism is a form of determinism, a secular version of Providence. As such, it is inimical to human freedom and dignity; 4. Marxism is utopian and out of touch with social and political reality; 5. Marxism is just a form of economic reductionism; 6. Marx was a materialist and an anti-humanist. His materialism and anti-humanism leads directly to the likes of Stalin; 7. Marx's class analysis is out-of-date. The revolutionary worker is a figment of the Marxist imagination; 8. Marxists advocate violent political action, revolution instead of evolution. The end justifies the means, regardless of whatever mayhem may ensue; 9. Marxism believes in an all-powerful state. Wherever Marxism has been put into practice, the socialists in power have ruled despotically; Party over people, the state over party, and a monstrous dictator over all;[80] and 10. Marxism has been superseded by feminism, environmentalism, anti-globalisation and the like. The contribution of Marxism to such movements has been at best marginal. Not all these criticisms are equally germane to my project in this chapter (for example, I am not really worried about Marxism's alleged supersession by feminism) but some of these common criticisms clearly are. Let us see what Eagleton has to say about them.

   In responding to the first criticism, that supposed irrelevancy of Marxism, the target of Eagleton's ire is, very often, the target of anarchists' ire as well! What Eagleton attacks as capitalism is what I and other libertarians would portray as 'crony capitalism'—big business, big labour, big finance, big whatever—all cronies of the state. (see his chapter 9) In fact (and in brief) Eagleton makes the common Marxist mistake of objecting to things that are in fact objectionable but mistaking the cause of their objectionability. In this case, Eagleton makes the seemingly ineradicable mistake of identifying crony capitalism with the operation of the free market.[81] He writes that Ronald Reagan and Margaret Thatcher helped 'to dismantle traditional manufacture, shackle the labour movement, let the market rip, strengthen the repressive arm of the state and champion a new social philosophy known as barefaced greed.' (Eagleton, 4) It is hard to know where to begin to comment soberly on this explosion of ire but I really only want to make one obvious point: whatever Reagan and Thatcher may have done during their tenures of office, whether they dismantled traditional manufacture, shackled the labour movement, strengthened the repressive arm of the state and championed a new social philosophy known as barefaced greed or not, the one thing they did *not* do was to let the market rip.

In another passage, Eagleton deprecates 'Spectacular inequalities of wealth and power, imperial warfare, intensified exploitation, and an increasingly repressive state...' (Eagleton, 8; see also 185) From a libertarian perspective, inequalities of wealth aren't by themselves morally or legally problematic. In fact, it's hard to see how it could be so for anyone who thinks about the matter seriously. Consider the following scenario. In the country of Plutopolis, half the people have an income of $1,000,000 a year and the other an income of $500,000. One half of the people are twice as rich as the other half; the income disparity is stark. In the country of Miserarium, on the other hand, every one has exactly the same income of $463.19 per year. Ask yourself where would you rather live? If you answer Miserarium, I would suspect your honesty or your sanity or both. So, unless one is motivated simply by envy and would prefer to have very little provided only that others were no better off, the moral and legal issue isn't inequality just as such, it's whether such inequality is the product of aggression or expropriation or theft or robbery or fraud; or whether it's the result of the free exchange of good and services.[82] Anarchists are also opposed to intensified exploitation but, unlike Marxists, they do not locate such exploitation in the operation of a free-market but in the nexus of state-banking-finance and all other beneficiaries of corporate welfare. And, of course, anarchists also deprecate the increasingly repressive state. Allister Heath remarks, 'Real business people, who make their money in open, competitive markets, are entitled to their vast wealth but crony capitalists, who rely on state privileges, do not deserve our support. The Left and the Right have both got it wrong here: the former wrongly attack all inequality; the latter wrongly defend all of it. The blunt reality is that all societies are highly unequal, even supposedly communist ones. What really matters is the source of the inequality: are the wealthy rich because they looted everybody else, as was inevitably the case in feudal, pre-commercial societies, or are they prosperous because they profited from serving the needs of others in a competitive market? Is a society open to new talent and ideas, and encouraging of social mobility, or is it controlled by a small economic and political aristocracy that doesn't let anybody else climb to the top? Whether inequality is good or bad depends on the answer to those questions...' [Heath 2014]

Eagleton concedes (how could he not) that what he calls capitalism has produced untold wealth in some parts of the world. This claim is evident, not to mention having Marx's own *imprimatur*.[83] But, Eagleton thinks, such wealth come at a cost, a cost of genocide, famine, imperialism and the slave trade. Once again, a libertarian can agree, in part, with Eagleton's point. Aggression against other peoples has historically been part of the changes that have taken place since 1750. But aggression isn't an intrinsic part of a free market—it *is* part of crony capitalism that, with the state as its friend, is only too happy to use aggression to attain its ends. Hans-Hermann Hoppe grants the essential correctness of the Marxist thesis, that 'much or even most of the initial capitalist property is the result of plunder, enclosure, and conquest,' finding himself in surprising agreement with Terry Eagleton who writes that 'Marx writes with scarcely suppressed outrage in Capital of the bloody, protracted process by which the English peasantry were driven from the land. It is this history of violent expropriation which lies beneath the tranquillity of the English rural landscape'[84] and Hoppe goes on to note that the export of capitalism to the Third World has been accompanied by force and violence. Once again, however, it must be clearly stated that the free market isn't at all the same thing as crony capitalism. [Hoppe 1993, 54] Allister Heath again, 'There are two ways businesses and investors can make money legally. The first is by providing goods and services that people want, by working out correctly what assets will be in most demand or by investing capital in successful projects, all activities that boost economic growth, increase employment, help develop poor economies and lift living standards….The second way that businesses and investors can make money is by getting the government to rig markets in their favour – by erecting barriers to entry to restrict competition, by providing them with cheap credit or by allowing them to use their political connections to grab contracts and other privileges. These gains are not the fruit of value-adding economic activity. Rather than helping to grow the economy, they often merely redistribute wealth.'

Eagleton manifests the academic's customary disdain of profit, regarding it, in orthodox Marxist fashion, as an expression of acquisitive self-interest (a morally suspect motive) and also, again as usual, seeing it in zero-sum terms. 'If you need to accumulate capital more or less from scratch, then the most effective way of doing so, however brutal, is through the profit motive. Avid self-interest is likely to pile up wealth with remarkable speed, though it is likely to amass spectacular poverty at the same time.' [Eagleton, 16; see also 59] Well, theft will amass capital very effectively, much more effectively and rapidly than making a profit in business, but no libertarian will endorse theft as a legitimate method of capital accumulation. Profits can be made only if a seller of goods and services is supplying what people in fact want to buy and where, pray tell, is the brutality in that! The making of profit does not, in a world in which uncoerced exchange is doubly positive sum, results in anyone's poverty. Eagleton's writing here is more impassioned than reasoned.

In another passage, Eagleton again concedes that capitalism is astonishingly productive and generates enormous wealth but argues that it does so 'in a way that cannot help putting it beyond the reach of most of its citizens.' If we are talking about the free market, that term being simply a placeholder for the nexus of uncoerced interactions between willing participants and not some reified process, it isn't clear why the generation of enormous wealth for X, Y, and Z 'cannot help' impoverishing A, B, and C—unless, that is, we make the mistake of thinking that there's a fixed quantity of wealth so that the more X, Y and Z have, the less is available for A, B and C. But Eagleton surely can't think of wealth in a 'steady-state' way as he has admitted the generative and productive power of capitalism; so why then does capitalism necessarily result in wealth for some and poverty for others? That can't happen on the free market, free exchange being mutually beneficial but, of course, in can and does happen in a system of crony capitalism.

Together with a frank (and welcome) admission by Eagleton that Maoism and Stalinism were 'botched, bloody experiments,' there's also a significant amount of special pleading and excusing and blaming of others for the botching and the blood. I hate to point this out but this is a justification not much above the level of 'two wrongs make a right'. Later in his book Eagleton writes, 'In its brief but bloody career, Marxism has involved a hideous amount of violence. Both Stalin and Mao Zedong were mass murderers on an almost unimaginable scale.' It would be hard to deny the truth of Eagleton's observation though some have tried, but he immediately goes on to say that whereas few Marxists today do in fact attempt to deny the enormities of Stalinism and Maoism, 'many non-Marxists would defend, say, the destruction of Dresden or Hiroshima.' [Eagleton, 184] Whether or not anyone (non-Marxist or otherwise) would defend the atrocities of Dresden or Hiroshima is entirely irrelevant to the infamy of Stalinism and Maoism. In fact, libertarian anarchists (and free-marketeers generally) are fully as opposed to imperial warfare as is Eagleton, not least because they know such warfare is paid for, in money and in the destruction of property and lives, by those who work and produce in every society and not by those who live parasitically off the proceeds of their labour.

Objectionable as this line of argument is, it's scarcely more objectionable than the economic naïvety demonstrated in Eagleton's charming but foolish idea of an economy that is neither centrally planned nor market-governed. [see Eagleton, 25ff.] In this unfocused vision, resources are allocated by negotiation (between whom?) and policy is determined by representative assemblies through a process of devolved and detailed planning. What is produced and how it is produced will be determined by 'social need rather than the private profit.' [Eagleton, 25] Under capitalism, Eagleton remarks, 'we are deprived of the power to decide whether we want to produce more hospitals or more breakfast cereals. Under socialism, this freedom would be regularly exercised.' [Eagleton, 25] One doesn't know whether to laugh or to weep. Without markets and a real (not just notional) price system, there's no rational way to determine production or allocation priorities, whether to produce more breakfast cereal or more hospitals. Central planning of a complex economy hasn't, doesn't, and can't work.

In terms of their continuing influence, Mill and Marx were two giants of the nineteenth century and their influence continues to be felt today, albeit in a muted form. But there is another tradition of political thought, largely but not exclusively confined to the nineteenth century, that has had nothing like the same effect on practical politics, yet it is one that presented, and continues to present, the most radical challenge of all to every form of liberal, conservative and socialist thought. I am speaking of anarchism. The next three chapters will explore this tradition in some detail, beginning with what I call the anarchist prophets (William Godwin and Max Stirner), continuing with the classical anarchists (Pierre-Joseph Proudhon, Mikhail Bakunin and Pyotr Kropotkin) and concluding with those anarchists who wrote in English (Josiah Warren, Lysander Spooner, Benjamin Tucker and Auberon Herbert).

Notes

1 Bowle, 307. Of the significant works in the Marx-Engels canon to which reference is made in this history, it is generally accepted that *The Holy Family* (1845), *The German Ideology* (1845-1846) and The *Communist Manifesto* (1848) were co-authored by Marx and Engels whereas the *Anti-Dühring* (1877-1878), *The Condition of the Working Class in England* (1845) and *The Origin of the Family, Private Property and the State, in the Light of the Researches of Lewis H. Morgan* (1884) were written by Engels alone with, in the case of the *Anti-Dühring*, some contributions from Marx. Marx appears to have been solely responsible for the first volume of *Capital* (1867) but its second and third volumes (1895 and 1894 respectively) were redacted by Engels.

2 Marx's writings are easily available. The series Cambridge Texts in the History of Political Thought has brought out two volumes—*Marx: Early Political Writings* (1994) and *Marx: Later Political Writings* (1996), which contain a wide selection of material. *Capital*, Vol. I (1867 [1976]) and *The Communist Manifesto* (1848a [2002]) are both available in Penguin editions. The standard published edition of Marx's works in English is the Lawrence & Wishart 50 volume set, usually available only in university libraries; however, a comprehensive set of the works of Marx and Engels is available online at https://www.marxists.org/archive/marx/works/date/. References to Marx's works in this chapter, unless otherwise noted, will be to the Penguin *Capital* and the Penguin *Communist Manifesto*, and to the Cambridge Texts editions.

3 Ferdinand Lasalle (1825-1864) was, as Leszek Kolakowski notes, 'Marx's chief rival as theoretician in the 1860s' and one who 'outclassed him as far as ideological influence in Germany was concerned.' [Kolakowski, 238]

4 *Marx & Engels Collected Works*, vol. XXX, 259; see Chaloner & Henderson 1975, 19-20.

5 Marx, remarks Cyril Parkinson, 'had all the single-minded purpose of a Hebrew prophet (which is what he was) and ruthlessly sacrificed his wife and family, friends and disciples. He had an abstract pity for the poor but his capacity for hatred was more obvious than his capacity for affection.' [Parkinson 1958, 152]

6 Parkinson 1970, 56-57.

7 Boettke, 80-81; but see Eagleton, 91.

8 Wilczynski 605-606 and 110-111; see also Wilczynski 516 and 302.

9 See Wilczynski, 158. For a succinct presentation of the history the socialist calculation debate, see Doherty, 76-81.

10 Parkinson remarks that 'If the political characteristics of Theocracy are to include a Founder, a mythology, a Sacred Book, a priesthood, a place of pilgrimage and an inquisition, Communism must be ranked among the great religions of the world.' [Parkinson 1958, 151]

11 As the concept central to his *magnum opus*, 'capital' receives several definitions from Marx. The most prosaic is the depiction of capital as a kind of protean entity which is now money, now commodities, 'constantly changing from one form into the other, without becoming lost in this movement.' [*Capital*, 255] Rather more colourfully, but obscurely, Marx characterises capital as an 'animated monster,' 'dripping from head to toe, from every pore, with blood and dirt.' [*Capital*, 1007, 926]

12 I am acutely aware that this very history is about the same, ridiculous length as *Capital* and, in the opinion of some, may also be judged to contain an extravagant display of needless scholarship! *Mea maxima culpa*.

13 Bowle writes that *Capital* is based on 'the original adaptation of Hegel and Feuerbach, on the concept of surplus value and on Ricardian and Malthusian economics, on the idea of scientific "law".' [Bowle, 340] Marx generates a dizzying network of scholastic concepts around the idea of surplus value—absolute surplus value, relative surplus value, surplus labour, indispensable labour time, indispensable labour, indispensable product, socially indispensable labour, surplus labour time, surplus product and surplus value. Readers who are interested in observing the bloodless ballet of these interrelated concepts and can withstand intellectual vertigo are referred to the relevant relatively crisp entries in Wilczynski.

14 *Capital*, chapters 26-33, 873-940.

15 'Modern humans first appeared about one hundred thousand years ago,' writes Steven Landsburg

and 'for the next 99,800 years or so, pretty much everyone lived just above the subsistence level—on the modern U.S. equivalent of $400 to $600 a year. In a few fortunate times and places, it was a bit more than that, but almost never more than about twice as much. There were usually tiny nobilities who lived far better indeed, but numerically those nobilities were quite insignificant. If you'd been born any time before the late eighteenth century, it is astronomically probable that you'd have lived on the equivalent of under $1000 a year—just like your parents and your grandparents, and just like your children and your grandchildren.' [Landsburg, 27]

16 At the time of the birth of Christ, economists estimate that the world's GDP was around 102 billion international dollars. 'Toward the end of the nineteenth century,' writes Peter Novak, 'during the golden age of shipping, that figure had climbed nearly a thousand percent to Int$1.1 trillion. By the close of the twentieth century, global GDP rose a further 3,000 percent to Int$33 trillion. That's 33,000 percent growth since the reign of the Roman emperor Augustus.' [Novak 2015, 23] He goes on to point out that in 'one of the great unreported stories of our time, the proportion of people living in extreme poverty in the world fell by half between 1990 and 2010, beating the United Nations' Millennium Development Goal by five years.' [Novak 2015, 25]

17 *Zur Kritik der politischen Ökonomie.* See Marx 1996. The *Contribution* was Marx's first major work in economics and treated themes that would become staples in Marxism: value, alienation, capital and labour.

18 John Maynard Keynes trenchantly described *Capital* as 'an obsolete economic textbook which I know to be not only scientifically erroneous but without interest or application to the modern world.' [Keynes, 300]

19 Marx & Engels 1848 [2002], 226.

20 See Kolakowski, 138-141; 172-173; 281-291.

21 The document known as the *Economic and Philosophic Manuscripts* is largely the product of editorial redaction by twentieth century editors, a redaction that not everyone has found acceptable. None of the material contained in it was published in Marx's lifetime. [see editor's comment in Marx 1994, ix-x.]

22 Kolakowski, 411; see 408-416.

23 Marx 1844, XXII; 1963a, 122-123, §XXII.

24 Marx 1844, XXIII; 1963a, 124-125, §XXIII.

25 'Marx had a brain like a high-powered locomotive engine,' notes Max Eastman, wryly, 'and when he set out to prove a thing, there was nothing for ordinary facts or practical considerations to do but get out of the way.' [Eastman, 95]

26 It is important to note that Marx's ire was directed towards capitalism as a system and not the moral imperfections of capitalists. In the 'Preface' to the first edition of *Capital*, he writes, 'To prevent possible misunderstanding let me say this. I do not by any means depict the capitalist and the landowner in rosy colours. But individuals are dealt with here only in so far as they are the personification of economic categories, the bearers [*Träger*] of particular class-relations and interests. My standpoint, from which the development of the economic formation of society is viewed as a process of natural history, can less than any other make the individual responsible for relations whose creature he remains, socially speaking, however much he may subjectively raise himself above them' [Marx 1986, 92; see Sowell 1996, 99, 153-154]

27 See William Baker's *Endless Money* for a post-2007/2008-financial-crisis economically and financially informed critique of the moral hazards of socialism.

28 See Beito 1990, Beito 2000, Gosden 1973, Meadowcroft & Pennington 2007, and Green 2000.

29 Marx & Engels 1975-2001, 5, 47; Marx 1994, 132.

30 Joseph O'Malley, editor of the Cambridge edition of *Marx: Early Political Writings*, remarks that this passage is oddly 'out of keeping with the critical thrust of chapter I as a whole, and clearly evoking Fourier's model of an agricultural utopia, this passage has been for Marx's severer critics evidence of his naivete or incoherence, and for many more sympathetic critics and commentators a source of embarrassment or perplexity. Some of the latter have pointedly ignored it. Some have suspected it to be a parody or a joke. Now, thanks to W. Hiromatsu's 1974 edition of the chapter on Feuerbach, which has been largely ignored in the West, we can see more clearly than before the places where Marx inserted words, comments, etc. into Engels' smooth copy. Hiromatsu's edition...has lead (*sic*) one commentator to conclude that the passage is Engels' (perhaps unconscious) parody of Fourier's utopia, into which Marx sarcastically or humorously inserted the "critical critics", against whom "The German Ideology" is largely directed. In this case, the passage should not be taken as a serious expression of Marx's ideas about either "communism" or the "abolition" of the division of labour.' [O'Malley 1994, xx, n.]

31 It is more than a shade ironic that in *The German Ideology*, Marx and Engels criticise Stirner's idea of the Ego as an idle fantasy while producing some idle fantasies of their own.

32 Scruton 2015, 5-6. For a succinct account of Stirner's thought in relation to that of Marx, see Kolakowski 163-171.

33 'As the division of labour is the primary source of social inequality and private property,' writes Kolakowski, 'the chief purpose of communism must be to abolish the division of labour.' [Kolakowski, 159]

34 It is true that Albert Schweitzer was simultaneously a superb musician, a physician and a theologian but the rarity of such as he only serves to underscore my point.

35 The *Grundrisse*, written between 1857 and 1858, was unpublished in Marx's lifetime (it appeared in English, edited and abbreviated, in 1971) but he revised, rewrote and published its first volume as *A Contribution to the Critique of Political Economy* in 1859.

36 *Capital*, Vol. III, Part VII, chapter 48, § 3.

37 Marx 1994, 95. Emphasis in original.

38 But see Kolakowski, 174-176. The Marxist notion of Class Consciousness (Engels and Lenin), and the related Hegelian-derived Marxists notions of Class-in-itself and Class-for-itself (Marx and Engels), the latter implying a *conscious* apprehension by members of a class of their class identity, imply the possibility of False Consciousness.

39 Marx's reductionism was to be just one of the three influential forms of 'nothing but-ness' that were to dominate and distort the intellectual, political and social life of the twentieth century. 'Between Marx and Freud, with Darwin behind them,' writes Richard Tarnas, 'the modern intelligentsia increasingly perceived man's cultural values, psychological motivations, and conscious awareness as historically relative phenomena derived from unconscious political, economic, and instinctual impulses of an entirely naturalistic quality.' [Tarnas, 329]

40 For a vivid critique of the use of the false consciousness weapon by gender feminists, see Sommers, 255-275.

41 False consciousness is just one local variation of a whole set of theories and theorists whose essential aim, if that's not a self-contradiction, is the reduction of human nature, human knowledge, human lived experience to some set of ahuman elements. Marx reduces human life to the play of economic forces, Darwin to the blind biological struggle for existence, Freud to repressed and distorted sexual mechanisms. Despite their scholastic differences, the two major schools of modern philosophy (the Anglo-American and the Continental) are reductionist, each denying, although for different reasons, human freedom, each asserting that human beings are 'nothing but' X (fill in the X according to taste). Of the two schools, the Anglo-American is scholastically sterile, saying less and less with an ever increasing technical sophistication; the Continental school is the more engaging. The 'nothing but' to which Continental philosophers reduce man and his experience include (power relations) for Michel Foucault and (texts) for the more ambitious Jacques Derrida who is not content to reduce just man to 'nothing but' but appears to encompass the whole of reality in his reductionism. [see O'Hear, 4-15, 108-112]

42 Marx & Engels 1848 [2002], 291. Bowle judges that in *The Communist Manifesto* Marx and Engels have created 'one of the great political myths of world history. That the *Manifesto* is based on assumptions divorced from reality, and upon a distorted view of the past; that its economics are unsound; and its prophecies erroneous, is irrelevant to its power.' [Bowle, 322-323] J. A. S. Grenville remarks that "Marx's theories about the conflict of classes and his call for fraternal working class solidarity bears little resemblance to the actual events of 1848. The influence of his teaching became profound only later in the century. The strongest force in Europe during the decades that followed was not the resultant movement of European society through class conflict but nationalism.' [Grenville, 97-98]

43 Louis-Auguste Blanqui (1804-1881), proto-socialist, part-time prisoner and full-time revolutionary 'inculcated the importance of revolutionary organization and helped to improve the technique of conspiracy.' [Kolokowski, 215] Marx also borrowed from Blanqui the idea of the Proletarian Revolution and the Dictatorship of the Proletariat. For an illuminating discussion of pre-Marxist treatments of class struggles, see Raico 2006. This part of my discussion relies heavily on Raico's article.

44 It is generally conceded, even by Marxists, that the ideas of class and class struggle aren't original with Marx. Terry Eagleton asks, 'Is what is peculiar to Marxism, then, the concept not of class but of class *struggle*? This is certainly closer to the core of Marx's thought but it is no more original to him than the idea of class itself.' [Eagleton, 31; see Bottomore and Rubel, 19] Brian Doherty comments, 'Early-nineteenth-century French liberal economists created a libertarian class analysis that was later warped by Marx. In the view of this school of French *economistes*, the relevant class distinction...lay

Freedom's Progress?

between the productive and the predatory—with the productive being anyone working in the market in any capacity, and the predatory being the state and its agents and dependents who steal from the productive. Here we see the vital libertarian distinction between *society* and *state*...' [Doherty, 32]

45 See Eastman, 8; see also Otteson 2014, 202ff.

46 Marx & Engels 1848 [2002], 224-225.

47 Marx & Engels 1848 [2002], 226.

48 Marx & Engels, 1848 [2002], 238-239.

49 Marx & Engels 1848 [2002], 243.

50 'Wasting the labour of the people "under the pretense of caring for them" is exactly what our governments do,' writes Cyril Parkinson. 'Freedom is founded upon ownership of property. It involves self-expression in terms of architecture and arts. It cannot exist where the rulers own everything, nor even when they concede some limited right of tenure. But the modern belief is that spendable income is a concession by the State. The taxation which is intended to promote equality, the taxation which exceeds the real public need, and above all the tax which is so graduated as to prevent the accumulation of private capital, is inconsistent with freedom. Against a State which owns everything, the individual has neither the means of defence nor anything to defend.' [Parkinson 1965, 76]

51 See Marx & Engels, 1848 [2002], 243-244.

52 The first writer I know of who postulated the priority of the economic to the political was James Harrington. Harrington's idea was that the structure of a government was ineluctably determined by the 'balance of dominion in the foundation', that is, by whom and by how many the material resources in a given state were controlled. Harrington saw government as being essentially determined by a society's underlying social and economic forces. Some inkling of this is present in the thought of the Levellers and especially in the thought of the Digger, Gerrard Winstanley; Harrington, however, is the first the make this thesis explicit, a good two hundred years before Marx wrote.

53 '*The Holy Family*,' writes Leszek Kolakowski, 'is a virulent, sarcastic, and unscrupulous attack on Marx's former allies, especially Bruno and Edgar Bauer. The work is diffuse and full of trivial mockery, puns on his adversaries' names, etc....Nevertheless it is an important document, bearing witness to Marx's final break with Young Hegelian radicalism: for its proclamation of communism as the working-class movement *par excellence* is presented not as a supplement to the critique of Young Hegelianism, but as something opposed to it.' [Kolakowski, 147]

54 'That ideological and political ideas are influenced by material or economic circumstances we should mostly admit,' writes Parkinson. 'That they are influenced by nothing else is a ridiculous over-simplification.' [Parkinson 1970, 54]

55 As also would appear to be the case with the *Bible* and Stephen Hawking's *A Brief History of Time.* The historian R. F. Foster speaks of 'books that fulfil a felt or perceived need among people, which may have everything to do with buying a book, but very little to do with reading it to the end.' [Foster 2002, 165]

56 Marx 1996, 160; see Wilczynski, 34.

57 §8 of 'Value, Price and Profit (1865), entitled 'Production of Surplus Value.'

58 "Exploitation,' writes Kolakowski, 'in his [Marx's] view, did not consist in a worker selling his labour below its value....For—and this is the corner-stone of Marx's analysis of capitalism in its mature form—wage-labour is based on the sale of labour-power, not the sale of labour.' [Kolakowski, 277, 278]

59 See Gordon 1993, 35. According to Peter Sloterdijk, the phenomenon of exploitation has re-appeared in a new and surprising way. 'Free-market authors have also shown how the current situation turns the traditional meaning of exploitation upside down. In an earlier day, the rich lived at the expense of the poor, directly and unequivocally; in a modern economy, unproductive citizens increasingly live at the expense of productive one—though in an equivocal way, since they are told, and believe, that they are disadvantaged and deserve more still. Today, in fact, a good half of the population of every modern nation is made up of people with little or no income, who are exempt from taxes and live, to a large extent, off the other half of the population, which pays taxes. If such a situation were to be radicalized, it could give rise to massive social conflict. The eminently plausible free-market thesis of exploitation by the unproductive would then have prevailed over the much less promising socialist thesis of the exploitation of labor by capital. This reversal would imply the coming of a post-democratic age.' [Sloterdijk, 5-7]

60 Kolakowski writes, 'the value of labour-power is the value of the products necessary to keep the labourer and his children alive and able-bodied.' [Kolakowski, 279]

61 Marx has a remarkably crude understanding of what production consists in—the immediate activity

of the labourers. Despite the title of his major work, *Capital*, he seems to have had no real conception of the function of capital in the production process, still less any conception of the role of the entrepreneur or even the manager. It is as if he thought that a film director contributed nothing to a film because he did not appear on screen or that a conductor made no contribution to the performance of the orchestra because he played no instrument. Together with the massive under-appreciation of the role of the capitalist in production goes a massive over-appreciation of the role of the manual labourer.

62 In the Marxist tradition, labour is used as something of a universal explanatory paradigm, a kind of conceptual Atlas, bearing a world of concepts on its shoulders. There is a labour theory of abstract thought, a labour theory of humanization, even a labour theory of language development! [see Engels 1884, 251-264; see Wilczynski, 298-299]

63 See Reisman 2012, ch. 1. Wilczynski notes that the labour theory of value has been subjected to severe criticism. 'It disregards the the role of non-labour factors of production and underestimates the part played by the demand side in price formation. There is a lack of consistency in Marx's analysis. In *Capital* vol. III, in contrast to vol. I, he implied that constant capital (like variable capital) was capable of creating value (as distinct from transferring value); in effect, Marx abandoned the theory. Marx himself probably realized that to demonstrate exploitation under capitalism, it was not necessary to have the labour theory of value, as exploitation could in fact be demonstrated by the inferior bargaining power of labour compared with the capitalists.' But if the labour theory of value is removed as the cornerstone of exploitation then exploitation, if it exists, is a merely factual feature of capitalism as it exists at a given time, not a necessary constitutive feature of it and, as Wilczynski notes, 'the strengthening of labour's bargaining power (through trade unions) would imply that exploitation could be removed within the framework of capitalism…' [Wilczynski, 300; see also 622]

64 The account that follows relies heavily on David Gordon's 1990 book, *Resurrecting Marx: The Analytical Marxists on Freedom, Exploitation, and Justice*. Readers requiring a fuller account of this latter-day attempt to raise Marx from the dead are referred to Gordon's calm, reasoned and devastating analysis. See also the essays published in Yuri Maltsev's *Requiem for Marx*, in particular, Hans-Hermann Hoppe's 'Marxist and Austrian Class Analysis'.

65 For a representative selection of analytical Marxism in action see Ian Steedman's *Marx after Sraffa*, Jon Elster's *Making Sense of Marx*, G. A. Cohen's *Karl Marx's Theory of History—A Defence*; and John Roemer's *Analytical Foundations of Marxist Economics*. Brian Doherty notes that 'if the labor theory of value was wrong, as Böhm-Bawerk proved, then pretty much everything else in Marx was wrong, since his intellectual edifice was built on that labor theory of value.' [Doherty, 73]

66 'What is socially necessary labour time?' asks Alexander Shand. He answers with an example. 'If, for example, the quantity produced of a good is too large for the market to clear at a particular price, then less of the good should have been made; not all the labour embodied in it was socially necessary. Whether or not some labour is socially necessary is ultimately determined by what happens in the market in the process of exchange, including what customers think something is worth.' [Shand, 58] Shand's answer may or may not be correct but if it is, it comes at a cost of burying the ostensibly objective factor of labour time under the mound of a distinctly subjective notion of customer valuation.

67 The *Critique* was written in 1875 but not published (by Engels) until 1891.

68 Marx 1996, 221; see van Dun 2009, 52.

69 Marx 1996, 222; emphasis in original.

70 Marx 1996, 225; but see Eagleton, 89.

71 Marx 1996, 181; see Hook, 339.

72 *Herr Eugen Dühring's Revolution in Science* (1878), more often known simply as *Anti-Dühring*, was written by Engels, with some contributions by Marx. Leaving aside the crude personal attack on Dühring, the essay recapitulates the Marxist materialist theory of history, a history governed by laws and the theory of surplus value and presents them as the two great discoveries of Marx by which socialism became a science. [see Bottomore and Rubel, 30] In the economic section of the work, which seems to come from the hand of Marx, we find again the idea that modern industry has called two opposed classes into being, the bourgeoisie and the proletariat. The forces of production created by the bourgeoisie can't be controlled by them and if catastrophe is to be avoided, there must be a revolution of the modes of production and distribution. When the time is right, the revolution will come and with it, the end of opposing classes.

73 See *Capital*, chapter 26, 873.

74 See *Capital*, chapter 33, 931.

75 For a feminist approach to this topic, see McElroy 2002b, 16-18.

76 See Hunter Lewis's *Crony Capitalism in America* for a detailed account of the incestuous back-slapping relationship between government, corporations, the medical establishment, the legal establishment and the labour unions.

77 See Wittgenstein 1969, §§ 117-119.

78 Rothbard 1973; in Stringham 2007, 35.

79 David Harvey's *The Enigma of Capital* is another latter-day re-presentation of Marxism given life by the economic downturn that started in 2008 but, though sober and scholarly, or perhaps because it *is* sober and scholarly, it can't compete in the popularity stakes with Eagleton's *jeu d'esprit*. At many points in his analysis, Harvey links what he is pleased to call capitalism to the machinations of the state in its various manifestations but despite this linkage he seems simply incapable of grasping the elementary fact that a market operating under state control, state restrictions, state regulations, state financial inducements, state legal privileges, all in the context of the state's control of the money supply, may be many things but the one thing that it is *not* is free. For a much more sophisticated, yet popular, defence of Marxism, a fascinating mixture of discernment and delusion, see Slavoj Žižek's *Trouble in Paradise*. There, Žižek writes, 'Communism remains the horizon, the *only* horizon, from which one can not only judge but even adequately analyse what goes on today....One should remain shamelessly orthodox Marxist...' [Žižek, 26, 27] For a more sober, if somewhat less engaging, treatment of similar matters, see G.A. Cohen's *Why Not Socialism?* For a spirited refutation of the attempts by Cohen (and others) to revivify Socialism (broadly understood), see James Otteson's superb, *The End of Socialism*. (Otteson's book is reviewed in Casey 2015.)

80 Some apologists for Marxism would like to divorce it from Leninism and hence, from Leninist atrocities. Augusto Del Noce comments, 'In all these interpretations Marxism becomes either a sort of ghost which, for all we know, may never have the opportunity to prove itself in history, or even a mere nineteenth-century utopia which the most mature Western thought has surpassed once and for all' He goes on to evaluate this claim thus: 'I totally disagree with these interpretations. In my opinion Marxism could become reality only in the exact way it did; therefore, it was verified in terms of its power, and at the same time refuted in terms of its outcome.' [Del Noce, 80] Max Eastman concludes, 'It is not enough to pick flaws in the tactics of Lenin; his basic understanding must be questioned. An honest, bold, loyal, and within its limits extremely highbrow attempt to produce though common ownership a society of the Free and Equal, produced a tyrant and a totalitarian state; there sprang up in its wake, borrowing its name and imitating its political procedures, other tyrants and totalitarian states...' [Eastman, 110]

81 See Harvey, passim, for an extended disquisition based on the same erroneous conflation of crony capitalism and the free market.

82 Something like a zero-sum dynamic obtains between equality and liberty. As Thomas Szasz notes, 'in proportion as we increase the importance of equality in human affairs, we inexorably diminish the importance of other values, such as liberty, responsibility, and justice. This...is the basis for the "anti-capitalist mentality" (von Mises) and the liberal infatuation with socialism (Communism).' [Szasz, 153]

83 'Marx and Engels were unsparing in their criticism of other revolutionaries who categorically opposed capitalism without regard to time, conditions, or the inherent constrains of technology,' writes Thomas Sowell. 'From a Marxian perspective, socialism became preferable to capitalism only *after* capitalism had created the economic prerequisites for socialism and after capitalism had exhausted its own potentialities as a system.' [Sowell 1996, 155]

84 Eagleton, 185. Eagleton can't resist using one wrong, the enclosure of the commons, to diminish another, in this case, the Cuban revolution.

Chapter 28

THE ANARCHIST PROPHETS—
GODWIN AND STIRNER

We anarchists do not want to emancipate the people;
we want the people to emancipate themselves
—Errico Malatesta

Liberty means responsibility. That is why most men dread it
—George Bernard Shaw

The most improper job of any man, even saints…
is bossing other men. Not one in a million is fit for it,
and least of all those who seek the opportunity
—J. R. R. Tolkien

I: WHAT IS ANARCHISM?

For many people, anarchy is just another word for chaos or disorder.[1] Without the State and its laws, they believe we would live in a world where everyone is free to grab anything he desires without the need to regard the persons or property of others. It may be that there are people who desire nothing more than to live in chaos and disorder[2] but anarchy, as that is conceived by those who have thought and written about it seriously, isn't the absence of order just as such but the absence of a certain kind of order, order produced by a top-down command and control structure, typically, but not exclusively, state government. Anarchists vigorously reject the implication that the absence of such top-down government is synonymous with disorder.[3] At the heart of the idea of anarchy as anarchists conceive it lies a deep-rooted resistance to having one's life and actions ordered by others.[4] Writing to his son Christopher in 1943, J. R. R. Tolkien remarked that 'My political opinions lean more and more to Anarchy (philosophically understood, meaning abolition of control, not whiskered men with bombs)…the most improper job of any man, even saints…is bossing other men. Not one in a million is fit for it, and least of all those who seek the opportunity.' [Tolkien, 74]

Even though anarchism may have been practically instantiated in the earliest human societies, anarchism as a self-conscious political creed is a relatively recent development. George Woodcock believes that anarchism's 'peculiar combination of moral visions with a radical criticism of society only begins to emerge in a perceptible form after the collapse of the medieval order.' [Woodcock, 37] Earlier movements, whether that of the Peasants' Revolt or Anabaptism, focused on a kind of egalitarianism but not necessarily on individualism. Historians of anarchism tend to 'fall into the error of assuming that the primitive or medieval folk community, based on mutual aid and roughly egalitarian by nature, is also individualistic; more frequently, of course, it is the reverse, inclined toward a traditional pattern in which conformity is expected and the exceptional resented.' [Woodcock, 40] John Bowle is more inclined to see anarchism as having a longer pedigree. For him, some manifestations of anarchism appear in classical and medieval times. The first stirring of the individualism characteristic of anarchism begins to appear in late-medieval Italy. Anarchist tendencies manifest themselves in a religious mode during the Reformation and then in an increasingly secular mode in Godwin, Fourier, Owen and Proudhon, Sorel and Kropotkin. Albert Meltzer takes an even longer focus than Bowle, noting that 'what might be called the Anarchist approach goes back into antiquity' and that we can see 'an Anarchism of sorts in the peasant movements that struggled against State oppression over the centuries.' [Meltzer, 12] Whatever the precise truth of the length of the anarchist pedigree, I think it can be accepted that anarchistic tendencies were present in various degrees in various societies before the self-conscious elaboration of anarchism as a political doctrine in the late eighteenth and early nineteenth centuries.

There is a reactionary and romantic strain in some forms of anarchism that gives rise to a longing for a simpler past, a rejection, sometimes explicit, sometimes implicit, of modern industrial society. 'The anarchist's cult of the natural, the spontaneous, the individual, sets him against the whole highly organized structure of modern industrial and statist society, which the Marxist sees as the prelude to his own Utopia. Even efforts to encompass the industrial world by such doctrines as anarcho-syndicalism have been mingled with a revulsion against that world, leading to a mystic vision of the workers as more regenerators; even the syndicalists could not foresee with equanimity the perpetuation of anything resembling industrial society as it exists at present.' [Woodcock, 23] The comic-book caricature of the anarchist as a bomb-throwing bearded Russian leftist isn't without some (remote) foundation in fact, given that the common understanding of anarchism is that it is predominantly if not exclusively a left-wing doctrine and one associated with those inclined to engage in what is sometimes euphemistically referred to as direct action. The activity of the British rioters of August 2011 was repeatedly referred to by the electronic and print media as an expression of anarchy.

To provide a better understanding of what libertarian anarchism is, I would like to show it in relation to the broader anarchist family. We'll see that all forms of anarchism have in common their rejection of the state but differ from one another primarily in respect of the position they adopt towards the implications of liberty and, in particular, in their attitude towards the nature, role and legitimacy of property in human society. In contradistinction to the relaxed approach I adopt here to the appropriate use of the term 'anarchism', others give an account that's more severely circumscribed. Meltzer, for example, is unwilling to characterize Godwin and Proudhon as anything other than mere precursors of anarchism and he denies the commonly held opinion that Bakunin was the founding father of anarchism, pointing out that Bakunin's conversion to anarchism was a late development. [Meltzer, 12, 15] Meltzer's harshest words, however, are reserved for those who believe there can be such a thing as anarcho-capitalism or libertarian anarchy. He writes: 'Commonsense shows that any capitalist society might dispense with a "State" (in the American sense of the word) but it couldn't dispense with organised government, or a privatised form of it, if there were people amassing money and others working to amass it for them. The philosophy of "anarcho-capitalism" dreamed up by the "libertarian" New Right has nothing to do with Anarchism as known by the Anarchist movement proper....What they [the anarcho-capitalists] believe in is in fact a limited State—that is, one in which the State has one function, to protect the ruling class, does not interfere with exploitation, and comes as cheap as possible for the ruling class.' [Meltzer, 50] On this way of looking at things, anarcho-capitalism simply can't be anarchism because capitalism and the state are inextricably linked (the first giving rise to the second or vice versa) or because capitalism[5] necessarily exhibits domineering hierarchical structures such as that between employer and employee. [see Meltzer, 50]

As with most interesting philosophical concepts, very little is uncontroversial about anarchism.[6] For historical reasons, anarchism has perhaps been most associated with socialist or quasi-socialist movements so that, as Novak puts it, 'anarchism is opposed to private ownership of land and capital.' [Novak 1958, 325] If this is so, then the term cannot be used by those who aren't opposed to private ownership of natural resources or capital. The object of Meltzer's scorn, Murray Rothbard, along with some others, attempted to make conceptual space for the term 'anarcho-capitalism' by distinguishing two different kinds of capitalism, remarking that 'the term 'capitalism was coined by its greatest and most famous enemy, Karl Marx' but that 'what Marx and later writers have done is to lump together two extremely different and even contradictory concepts and actions under the same portmanteau term.' These contradictory concepts Rothbard styles 'free-market capitalism' and 'state capitalism' and the difference between them is 'precisely the difference between, on the one hand, peaceful, voluntary exchange, and on the other, violent expropriation.' [Rothbard 1973, 419] David Osterfeld makes essentially the same point when he distinguishes between what he calls *economic capitalism* and *sociological capitalism*. Economic capitalism signifies 'production according to the dictates of the market' whereas sociological capitalism 'is defined in terms of... the ownership of the means of production by the 'bourgeois,' or ruling class.' [Osterfeld 1983, 505-506] Sociological capitalism finds expression in reality as what is often called 'mercantilism', which is, in part, an incestuous relationship between big business, banking and government, a position which has been vehemently excoriated in both its historic and in its current manifestations. Free market defenders of capitalism have economic capitalism in mind when engaged in their defence of it and are not only *not* committed to a defence of sociological capitalism but are, in fact, resolutely opposed to it. Needless to say, failure to keep these two very different accounts of capitalism apart has led to much confusion and 'critics and opponents of capitalism talked past each other when many were in basic agreement.'[7] Walter Block, too, distinguishes between *corporate state monopoly capitalism* and *anarcho- or laissez-faire capitalism* and remarks that 'these two systems are as different as night and day. They have nothing in common except for this highly unfortunate terminology that labels both 'capitalism''.'[8] The distinction is clear, even if the terminology varies: on the one hand, free-market capitalism or economic capitalism or anarcho/laissez-faire capitalism; on the other, state capitalism, sociological capitalism or corporate state monopoly capitalism.

Given the permanent possibility of confusion involved in using the term 'capitalism' which entails the necessity for constant clarification, it might be advisable to adopt another name to describe the position that Meltzer finds so objectionable. Of course, a mere change of names won't avert all criticism. Free-market capitalism by any other name, even when distinguished from state capitalism, would smell as rank to the Meltzers of this world. Noam Chomsky was once asked what he thought of anarcho-capitalism and despite conceding that he agreed with anarcho-capitalists on a range of issues, appreciating their willingness to publish his material when no one else would, and being complimentary about their commitment to rationality, he said that a society foolish enough to allow its implementation would be destroyed. 'Anarcho-capitalism... is a doctrinal system which, if ever implemented, would lead to forms of tyranny and oppression that have few counterparts in human history....The idea of 'free contract' between the potentate and his starving subject is a sick joke.'[9]

There are many futile activities and pursuits in this world of ours—state central planning and herding mice at crossroads are two that immediately spring to mind—but riding high in the futility charts must be verbal disputes about whether or not a hotly contested concept 'really' applies to this or that phenomenon. 'Is this *really* art?' we ask, with a heavy emphasis on the 'really,' attempting to smuggle in a judgement ('It's not very good, is it?') under the guise of a neutral classification. The concept of anarchy is one such highly contested concept and many who identify themselves as anarchists are unwilling to allow others to describe themselves as such. '*We* are really anarchists,' they say, '*you* are not!' [see Caplan, No Date] It's true that unless you want to end up talking to yourself like Humpty-Dumpty in *Through the Looking Glass*, a term can't be used to mean something completely at odds with its normal range of uses: 'I don't know what you mean by "glory",' Alice said. Humpty Dumpty smiled contemptuously. 'Of course you don't — till I tell you. I meant "there's a nice knock-down argument for you!"' 'But "glory" doesn't mean "a nice knock-down argument",' Alice objected. 'When *I* use a word,' Humpty Dumpty said, in rather a scornful tone, 'it means just what I choose it to mean — neither more nor less.' 'The question is,' said Alice, 'whether you **can** make words mean so many different things.' 'The question is,' said Humpty Dumpty, 'which is to be master — that's all.' [Lewis Carroll 1871, 80-81] But if words can't simply be used just any old way, neither is it the case the words are a kind of trade-mark which some groups have an exclusive right to use and others not. In a 1996 interview, Noam Chomsky conceded that 'No one owns the term 'anarchism.' It is used for a wide range of different currents of thought and action, varying widely.' [Lane, 1996] Eight years later, he was still of the same view: 'Anarchism is a very broad category; it means a lot of different things to different people.' [Pateman, 234]

Despite Meltzer's prescriptive urges, the range of appropriate uses of the term 'anarchy' is given by any good dictionary. The *Oxford English Dictionary* tells us that 'anarchy' derives from the Greek privative prefix αν, together with αρχός, meaning a leader or chief. It thus comes to have a root meaning of absence of leadership or absence of government, also having, as already mentioned, in its popular signification, the additional idea of lawlessness or disorder resulting from that absence. Less commonly, it can also mean a state of society without government but without any implication that the absence of government and presence of liberty spells disorder. Somewhat more rarely still, it can signify the absence or non-recognition of authority and order in any sphere whatsoever, for example, in morals or religion, and not only in society at large. As used by most anarchist thinkers, the terms 'anarchy' and 'anarchism' have no necessary connotation of lawlessness or disorder.

As I mentioned already, although anarchism is typically taken to be a doctrine that characteristically rejects the domination of people by the state—Woodcock gives his working definition of anarchy: 'a system of social thought, aiming at fundamental changes in the structure of society and particularly—for this is the common element uniting all its forms—at the replacement of the authoritarian state by some form of non-governmental cooperation between free individuals.' [Woodcock, 11]—it should rather be *formally* defined as the rejection of *any* form of non-voluntary domination of one person or group of people by another. Sometimes and by some people, it implies the rejection even of voluntary submission to the authority of another. [see Wolff 1970, passim]

If anarchism is *formally* defined as the rejection of *any* form of non-voluntary domination of one person or group of people by another, then it is an open question which modes of human interaction *materially* instantiate this non-voluntary domination. The commonest example of non-voluntary domination is, of course, the state but it may not the only one. Anarchists on the communist and collectivist end of the political spectrum appear to believe that the institution of private property necessarily gives rise to non-voluntary domination; so too the relationship of employer to employee. On the other hand, those who believe that we should be free to bind ourselves by entering into informal or contractual relations with others, even relations in which we voluntarily subordinate ourselves to others, do not accept the common claim of anarchists from the left end of the political spectrum that such relations are necessarily anti-anarchic. Our freedom to bind ourselves is, in the end, the limiting case of liberty. If we aren't free to bind ourselves then our liberty is compromised and we are not really free.

That form of anarchism that accepts this radical notion of freedom I call, for obvious reasons, libertarian anarchism. The libertarian anarchist has to be prepared to tolerate whatever arrangements may be arrived at by a particular social group provided only that no coercion is used and that the arrangements apply only to those who have freely signed up to them. John Sneed remarks that the function of an anarchist as anarchist isn't to endorse any particular economic system but 'to destroy the State in order to allow all economic systems to compete on a voluntary basis.' [Sneed 1977, 118]

George Woodcock takes the denial of authority to be characteristic of anarchism though not all who deny authority are necessarily anarchists. I am not so sure that this rejection of authority constitutes the most important or even the distinguishing feature of anarchism. Certainly, anarchists reject the forcible imposition of authority from above, the assumption on the part of some that they are entitled to rule—to employ allegedly legitimate force—against others. But there are at least two kinds of authority. The first is the authority of expertise (authority-E). You believe what your car mechanic tells you because he knows about cars and you do not or, perhaps more accurately, you *believe* (and hope) that he has this knowledge. So too with your doctor and your dentist. They have authority of expertise and you usually believe what they tell you because you believe they know more than you do about a particular subject matter. Others, however, have an authority that isn't necessarily connected to any real or supposed knowledge or expertise. It is merely a matter of the role that that person plays in a given social or political arrangement. This is the authority of office (authority-O). A policeman has this kind of authority. He may be an idiot or a genius, he may know a lot or a little, he may be helpful or arrogant—it doesn't really matter which—whatever the level of his expertise, by virtue of his office, he has authority.

There can be no sensible anarchist objection to authority of expertise. We are free to accept or reject such authority as we see fit. But even authority of office may be legitimate—provided we subscribe to it voluntarily. If I join a chess club, for example, I become part of an organisation with rules and regulations that I am obliged to observe as long as I wish to remain a member of that club. Should I come to find the authority of office exercised in that club oppressive, I am at liberty to try to change it for the better by constitutional means, and if I should fail to do so, I am free to leave. No one compels me to be a member of that club. It is hard to see how anything other than the most solitary primitive life could be lived without some structures of authority. What should matter to the anarchist, it seems to me, is not whether someone exercises authority over him but whether the authority that is exercised over him is one to which he freely subscribes.

The topic that fundamentally separates anarchists into different types is their approach to property. Individuals anarchists, and also, as we shall see, Proudhonian Mutualists, tend to regard property, properly conceived, as a guarantor of freedom and non-dominance. Collectivist and communist anarchists, on the other hand, tend to reject the notion of property out of hand. Peter Ryley notes the areas of agreement between these various forms of anarchism but remarks that their approach to property was the ground of their divide. 'Individualism drew on an older tradition that viewed forms of property as a guarantor of individual independence and economic security and as a device that ensured that the full value of labour was gained by the labourer. The distinction individualists drew was between valid and invalid forms of property. For communists, property was in itself a system of expropriation and an institution founded in injustice, which perpetuated exploitation.' [Ryley, 192] A standard criticism of libertarian anarchism is that it is a mere propaganda front for capitalism, the capitalism of big corporations, privileges, monopolies, and so on. This criticism is bold and dramatic but, alas, it is also inaccurate. Nothing could be further from the truth. Libertarian anarchism favours free markets—free markets in commodities, in labour, in capital, in ideas—free markets in everything. 'It has become commonplace,' notes Ryley, 'to associate markets with capitalism, as if the two were intrinsically linked. Nevertheless, the individualists challenged that notion and opposed the emerging corporate capitalism of their day. They argued that cooperative markets could only exist in the absence of the distorting medium of the state and through free currencies as the medium of exchange. Above all, the equality of each party in the process was to be ensured by extensive property rights.' [Ryley, xi]

Classical liberalism and anarchism are similarly sceptical in their evaluation of the state but differ in their degree of scepticism. Whereas liberalism, writes Peter Sloterdijk, 'wanted a minimal state that would guide citizens almost imperceptibly, leaving them to go about their business in peace,' anarchism, he says, 'called for the total death of the state.' Furthermore, both liberalism and anarchism hoped for the end of exploitation of the productive classes by the 'unproductive classes, that is, the nobility and the clergy.' Both movements were destined to be disappointed. Instead of its disappearing or even being reduced in size and scope, 'The modern democratic state gradually transformed into the debtor state, within the space of a century metastasizing into a colossal monster—one that breathes and spits out money.' And in the new social democratic order, a new class of exploiters replaced the nobility and clergy, a class comprising almost half the population of most modern states who are 'exempt from taxes and live, to a large extent, off the other half of the population, which pays taxes.' [Sloterdijk, 5-7]

Blithely ignoring debates as to who is and who isn't *really* an anarchist, in what follows I am going to deal in the chapters that follow with the following thinkers; William Godwin (who explicitly denies that he is an anarchist); Max Stirner, the apostle of egoistic individualism; Pierre-Joseph Proudhon and his Mutualism; after Proudhon, the Russian duo—Bakunin with his anarcho-collectivism and Kropotkin with his anarcho-communism.[10] Bakunin, the collectivist, substitutes for Proudhon's individual possession, possession by voluntary institutions, whereas Kropotkin goes yet further, arguing for communism and attacking the wage system. After the Russians, we come to the American Individualists: Josiah Warren, Lysander Spooner and Benjamin Tucker, and my account will finish with a cursory look at the English thinkers, Wordsworth Donisthorpe and Auberon Herbert.[11]

II: WILLIAM GODWIN

Many of us have had the annoying experience of being known relationally as 'Tom's brother' or 'Angela's sister' or 'Benjamin Britten's teacher'[12] instead of by our own names. If William Godwin (1756-1836) is looking down on this

world from another and a better place he must be permanently annoyed, for
he is known to history in the main for having been the lover and subsequently
the husband of Mary Wollstonecraft, the father of Mary Shelley (the author of
Frankenstein) and the father-in-law of the poet Percy Bysshe Shelley. Godwin
did, in fact, have a profound effect on Shelley, who came across his writings
in 1811 and was hugely influenced by him, becoming, in his turn, probably
the first major anarchist literary figure.[13] Godwin also influenced Robert Owen
and, through him, the American Individualist tradition and the trade union
movement generally.[14] William Thompson was another who was influenced
by Godwin and who in his turn had an influence on Marx. But Godwin has a
claim to fame in his own right, and not just as a father, father-in-law, husband,
lover or influencer. Even so, 'the irony remains,' George Woodcock remarks,
'that the influence of *Political Justice*, the most complete early exposition of
anarchist ideas, should have been diffused in English Literature and in the
English socialist movement, but should have been absent from the anarchist
movement itself until very late in its history. For Stirner and Proudhon do not
take up where Godwin left off; each of them begins anew on his own road
to freedom.' [Woodcock, 86] Despite his fame among his contemporaries,
Godwin's work is now generally either unknown or, if known, neglected.
Immensely famous in his own time, Godwin was one whose reputation shone
as brilliantly as a supernova and was as quickly extinguished.[15] Thomas Sowell
remarks of *Political Justice*, 'An immediate success upon its publication in
England in 1793, within a decade it encountered the chilling effect of British
hostile reaction to ideas popularly associated with the French Revolution....
By the time two decades of warfare between the two countries were ended at
Waterloo, Godwin and his work had been relegated to the periphery of intellectual life and he was subsequently best known for his influence on Shelley.
Yet no work of the eighteenth-century "age of reason" so clearly, so consis-
tently, and so systematically elaborated the unconstrained vision of man as did
Godwin's treatise.' [Sowell 1987, 23]

THE FIRST PHILOSOPHICAL ANARCHIST?

If Mark Philp is to be believed, Godwin was the first philosophical anarchist.
The vindication of this claim lies in Godwin's authorship of *An Enquiry
Concerning Political Justice*.[16] The French Revolution was the occasion for the
production of the *Enquiry* but Godwin's ideas long predated the stirring events
in Paris. He had a lifelong belief in the natural equality of all men such that if
one man were in the power of another, it could only be the result of conquest
or convention. He did not, in fact, describe himself as an anarchist because,
for him, this term had a purely negative connotation. He believed that human
society was natural and, moreover, that it was capable of functioning without
government. He argued for decentralisation and a voluntary sharing of goods,
and the means by which this desirable state of affairs was to be achieved was
education or propaganda, not political action. In this, he was at one with such
as Proudhon. In the end, whether he was the first philosophical anarchist or not,

Godwin's work certainly displays themes, and not a few arguments, that were to become staples in libertarian and anarchist writings.

GODWIN'S ETHICS

Godwin believes that the character of human beings is completely determined by their social environments. It isn't easy to see logically how this can be so but that's the position he holds. Man may not be perfect but he is perfectible, capable of indefinite improvement. Change the social environment, Godwin thinks, and you change men. A simple life would be conducive to the proper moral formation of all and would lead, eventually, to the elimination of crime and antisocial behaviour generally and even war. Godwin has a deep, if to twenty first-century eyes, naïve faith in the power of education. As later would Proudhon and Tolstoy, he places his faith in the power of reason to persuade men to adopt a proper perspective on social and political matters. Persuasion, however, is an individual matter and not a matter of collective policy formation. If people's opinions could be changed, he thought, then all would be remediated. Given the power of education to form or deform man, Godwin is anxious that such power shouldn't be in the hands of the state and he writes, 'the project of a national education ought uniformly to be discouraged on account of its obvious alliance with national government.' [Godwin, 353] Government is the most significant element in our social environment and it is not, Godwin believes, one for the good. He manifests an Enlightenment faith—one can only describe it as faith—in the power of reason to govern human life and foresees the eventual disappearance of any need for force and hence any need for government. Some two hundred years and several devastating wars and social catastrophes later, it's difficult to sustain such an optimistic and irrational faith. All of us—anarchists included—are obliged to make provision for the prevention and control of injustice, but anarchists would agree with Godwin that the state is neither the appropriate nor the best means by which this is to be done.

In Thomas Sowell's *A Conflict of Visions*, William Godwin is given as an example of one whose thinking approaches as near as is possible, to what Sowell calls an 'unconstrained vision'. Visions, for Sowell, are pre-rational (not necessarily *ir*rational) apprehensions of reality that provide the foundation on which theories are subsequently built. A constrained vision is one that accepts that there are more or less irremovable limitations or restrictions within which individuals and societies must operate; an unconstrained vision, on the contrary, accepts that such limitations or restrictions may exist but denies that they are irremovable. [see Sowell 1987, 18-39] Of such as Godwin, Sowell writes, '...human nature itself is a variable, and in fact the central variable to be changed.' [Sowell 1987, 86, 87] In contemporary western society, we can see the operation of an unconstrained vision in, for example, the increasing acceptance of transgender identity politics in which the connection between one's gender and one's biological sex is, at most, a tangential matter, if indeed one's biology offers any constraint or limitation at all. Taken to its extreme, the unconstrained vision leads towards the idea that man and the world are radically plastic and can be unmade and remade at will. But what is or can be anything is, in fact, nothing. In the words of W. S. Gilbert, 'When every one is somebod*ee*, Then no one's anybody!' [*The Gondoliers*] Even the most resolute unconstrained visionary is, in some matters at least, a fundamentalist realist and would baulk at crossing a busy highway at rush hour on his hands and knees while wearing a blindfold and ear plugs.

An issue on which moralists have differed over the ages is whether one owes the same moral consideration to all other human beings irrespective of their relationship to oneself (ethical universalism) or whether one owes greater consideration to one's family, kin, neighbours and community (ethical particularism). Among ancient Chinese thinkers, Mo Tze was an ethical universalist; Confucius, an ethical particularist. Godwin is an ethical Universalist. 'Does any person in distress apply to me for relief?' he writes. 'It is my duty to grant it, and I commit a breach of duty in refusing.' [Godwin, 56] How far do my obligations extend? As far, he thinks, as they may reach without injury to myself. 'But how much am I bound to do for the general weal, that is, for the benefit of the individuals of whom the whole is composed?' he asks, and he answers, 'Everything in my power.' [Godwin, 56] He even goes so far as to say that if my death should promote the general good more than my life, I should be content to die!

Can he really be serious? My *death*? *Everything* in my power? If I were to take everything that I have and give it to the poor—*all* the poor and not just those who happen to live in my vicinity—everybody would benefit by around €0.00000001 or perhaps not even that much. The result would be my complete impoverishment and the practical enrichment of no one else.[17] We might call this the Mrs Jellyby effect, after the character in Charles Dickens's *Bleak House*, who devotes all her time and energy (and the unpaid labour of her daughter) to relieving the plight of the natives of Boorie-goola-Gha on the left bank of the Niger. What's wrong with that, one might wonder? The problem is that Mrs Jellaby's ineffectual telescopic philanthropy is achieved at the cost of a filthy home, ragged and underfed children and a suicidal husband.[18]

Godwin doesn't believe that men have rights. He is a proto-utilitarian and thinks that what we tend to regard as rights—freedom of speech or conscience— are simply devices we need to help us find our way to moral truth. Rather than rights, we have reciprocal claims on one another. If there were such things as rights then it would have to be possible for them to cohere so that it wouldn't be possible for one man's right to clash with another's. But what we believe to be our rights cannot, he thinks, but clash and so it follows, he believes, that men cannot have rights. In an anticipation of Max Stirner (and Benjamin Tucker in his Stirnerite mode) Godwin puts it thus: 'My neighbour has as much right to put an end to my existence with dagger or poison, as to deny me that pecuniary assistance without which I must starve, or as to deny me that assistance without which my intellectual attainments or my moral exertions will be materially injured. He has just as much right to amuse himself with burning my house or torturing my children upon the rack, as to shut himself up in a cell careless about his fellow men, and to hide "his talent in a napkin".' [Godwin,

68] Individuals, then, have no rights and neither does society which, after all, is only a name for individuals in the aggregate. But although men have no rights, they do have duties. In fact, duties and rights are 'absolutely exclusive of each other.' [Godwin, 69] This is an interesting twist to the usual tale. Ordinarily, we are understood to have rights so that we may fulfil our duties—duties imply rights. In our contemporary world, we have witnessed the proliferation of rights and the diminution, some would say, the elimination of duties so that now all we have are rights and no duties. On the contrary, Godwin would have us believe that all we have are duties and no rights.

GODWIN ON LIBERTY OF THE PRESS

Godwin takes a proto-Millean line on the liberty of the press, arguing that 'Conscience and the press ought to be unrestrained, not because men have a right to deviate from the exact line that duty prescribes, but because society, the aggregate of individuals, has no right to assume the prerogative of an infallible judge, and to undertake authoritatively to prescribe to its members in matters of pure speculation.' [Godwin, 71] 'Persecution,' Godwin remarks, 'may make us hypocrites; but cannot make us converts.' [Godwin, 71] Pressure to behave will come not from above but from all around. He envisages a kind of permanent panopticon-like observance by all of all, the kind of situation that caused Mill concern in *On Liberty*. Woodcock remarks that even were the pressure of public opinion by all on all to be spontaneous and free, this 'does not entirely erase the distasteful picture of a future where mutual inspection and censorship will be the order of the day and public opinion will reign triumphant.' [Woodcock, 78] Woodcock thinks that public opinion may well be more intolerant than any state law. He writes: 'The anarchists accept much too uncritically the idea of an active public opinion as an easy way out of the problem of dealing with antisocial tendencies. Few of them have given sufficient thought to the danger of a moral tyranny replacing a physical one, and the frown of the man next door becoming as much a thing to fear as the sentence of the judge.' [Woodcock, 79] I can accept that there are dangers here, as Woodcock points out, but there still remains the fundamental difference that, frown as they will, if my neighbours can't employ force against me, I may still continue with the behaviour of which they disapprove. But the law doesn't just frown at me or refuse to associate with me or give me dirty looks; it will act against me and it is willing to use force to attain its ends.

GODWIN AND GOVERNMENT

What is the basis of human society? For Godwin, the answer is simple—it is our need for mutual assistance. Society is possible only on the basis of justice, which is the rule (or rules) emerging from and permitting the connection of one person with another. Since human beings are one and all morally equal to each other, if they come together with one another it can only be because they believe that this will be productive of their mutual advantage. 'Men would never have associated,' declares Godwin, 'if they had not imagined that in consequence of that association they would mutually conduce to the advantage and happiness

of each other. This is the real purpose, the genuine basis of their intercourse…'
[Godwin, 67] He distinguishes between the spheres of society and government
and declares that government mustn't interfere with the spontaneous development of society.

Practically, what are the possible areas of political concern? For Godwin,
these are government or general administration, the administration of justice
and law in respect of crime and the regulation of property, and education. If
human social relationships were free of transgression, government wouldn't
be necessary. 'Men associated at first for the sake of mutual assistance. They
did not foresee that any restraint would be necessary, to regulate the conduct of
individual members of the society, towards each other, or towards the whole.
The necessity of restraint grew out of the errors and perverseness of a few.'
[Godwin, 52] Like Tom Paine, Godwin believes government to be an evil,
although a necessary evil in present circumstances. In time, it will cease to be
necessary. In the meantime, a kind of radically decentralised democracy would
be an acceptable second best.

Since we are, as it were, stuck with government in the short term, our
immediate task is to minimise its capacity for evil. But is government necessarily evil? Isn't democracy the rule of the people by themselves? What could
possibly be objectionable about this? Democracy may be a form of self-rule
but, curiously, just like monarchy and oligarchy, it results in the same division
of men into two classes—those who rule and those who are ruled. Why should
this be, Godwin wonders? 'Why divide men into two classes, one of which is
to think and reason for the whole, and the other to take the conclusion of their
superiors on trust? This distinction is not founded in the nature of things; there
is no such inherent difference between man and man as it thinks proper to
suppose.' [Godwin, 271]

Even in politics, size matters; the bigger the state the worse it's likely to be.
'Great, complex, centralized states are harmful and unnecessary for the good
of mankind,' writes Woodcock. 'As they dissolve, localized forms of administration should take their place, in which the disadvantages of government may
immediately be mitigated by a diminished scope for ambition.'[19] In the small
communes, or parishes as Godwin calls them, little legislation would be needed
and there would be maximal participation in local administration. Offences
against justice could be dealt with by a system of juries, which juries could
also provide arbitration when necessary. In emergencies, parishes might need
to co-operate but such cooperation isn't without its own dangers, not least that
of the temptation for delegates to form parties that would tend to further their
own ambitions at the expense of their parishes.

Governments are responsible for many of the evils that afflict society. 'May it
not happen,' Godwin writes, 'that the grand moral evils that exist in the world,
the calamities by which we are so grievously oppressed, are to be traced to
political institution as their source, and that their removal is only to be expected
from its correction? May it not be found that the attempt to alter the morals of
mankind singly and in detail is an injudicious and futile undertaking; and that
the change of their political institutions must keep pace with their advancement

in knowledge, if we expect to secure to them a real and permanent improvement? To prove the affirmative of these questions shall be the business of this first book.'[20] John Bowle comments, 'William Godwin was plainly a doctrinaire. Yet his criticism of government has justice. Whatever the psychological miscalculations on which his remedies are based, and however fatuous his belief in the rationality of mankind, who can deny the vast iniquities which he so briskly pointed out?' [Bowle, 140]

Government, however necessary in the short term, is ultimately unjustifiable and no man of morals should associate with it. Godwin sketched a kind of communal association of leaderless units as the basic pattern for a libertarian society, another idea that was to resonate through libertarian and anarchist circles. Woodcock says of the *Enquiry* that it 'anticipates the various facets of the libertarian point of view' with 'astonishing completeness,' so much so that 'it still remains one of the most thorough expositions of anarchistic beliefs.' [Woodcock, 65] The tendency of authority, all authority, is to destroy life, so that the sooner political government is dissolved the better. 'With what delight must every well-informed friend of mankind look forward to the dissolution of political government, of that brute engine which has been the only perennial cause of the vices of mankind, and which has mischiefs of various sorts incorporated with its substance, and not otherwise to be removed than by its utter annihilation!' [Godwin, 306]

Godwin considers three possible justifications of political authority: force, divine right and contract. Force, Godwin dismisses immediately. If force were a sufficient justification for government, it would make every extant government to be right merely because it exists. Divine right as a justification for government Godwin also dismisses, pointing out, as Hume did, that it justifies *all* governments of whatever character unless and until we can discover an independent criterion that will enable us to distinguish between those governments of which God approves and those of which he does not. Of the three contenders, that leaves only contract to be considered. He asks, 'Who are the parties to this contract? For whom did they consent, for themselves only or for others? For how long a time is this contract to be considered as binding? If the consent of every individual be necessary, in what manner is that consent to be given? Is it to be tacit, or declared in express terms?' [Godwin, 83]

Godwin's objections to the contract theory are that a man can't be bound by a contract entered into by his progenitors. Contracts bind only those who are privy to them. Is acquiescence sufficient? No. Making a point later echoed by, among others, Lysander Spooner, Godwin remarks, if acquiescence justified government, then 'every government that is quietly submitted to is a lawful government, whether it be the usurpation of Cromwcl [*sic*] or the tyranny of Caligula. Acquiescence is frequently nothing more than a choice on the part of the individual of what he deems the least evil.' [Godwin, 84] Even if I were to enter explicitly into a contract, for how long is this contract supposed to subsist? For life? And if not for life, for how long? And just what indeed am I contracting to? Should I not know the terms and conditions—all of them? If I am to be bound by law should I not be presented with all the laws of the state?

'What then can be more absurd than to present to me the laws of England in fifty volumes folio and call upon me to give an honest and uninfluenced vote upon their whole contents at once?' [Godwin, 85] And am I deemed to have subscribed to laws yet to be made? Finally, if I refuse to contract, how can I be bound? 'If the people, or the individuals of whom the people is constituted, cannot delegate their authority to a representative; neither can any individual delegate his authority to a majority, in an assembly of which he is himself a member.' [Godwin, 86] Godwin concludes, 'No consent of ours can divest us of our moral capacity. This is a species of property which we can neither barter nor resign; and of consequence it is impossible for any government to derive its authority from an original contract.' [Godwin, 86] Well, if force, divine will and contract are the only possible grounds of government and all are to be dismissed, that seems to leave us only with the option of anarchy.

Not quite! Government, it turns out for Godwin, can after all be justified! Godwin manages to combine what is, in effect, a utilitarian conception of the function of government with a *soupçon* of Rousseau. Government exists for our mutual benefit. It is proper then that each man have some share in directing the common affairs of all. That being so, 'it seems necessary that he should concur, in electing a house of representatives, if he be the member of a large state; or, even in a small one, that he should assist in the appointment of officers and administrators; which implies, first, a delegation of authority to these officers, and, secondly, a tacit consent, or rather an admission of the necessity, that the questions to be debated should abide the decision of a majority.' [Godwin, 91]

Wait a minute! Didn't Godwin reject delegation and consent in his criticism of contract? It might have seemed so at the time but apparently not—and here comes the Rousseau twist. When it comes to matters common to all, matters concerning the common good, there must be a will that supersedes that of individuals. Delegation, properly understood, is not a matter of principal and agent but 'an act which has for its object the general good.' [Godwin, 92] Godwin is aware that some will see him as contradicting himself in this matter. 'It may perhaps by some persons be imagined, that the doctrine here delivered of the justice of proceeding in common concerns by a common deliberation, is nearly coincident with that other doctrine which teaches that all lawful government derives its authority from a social contract.' [Godwin, 92-93] I respectfully suggest the reason that someone might *think* Godwin is contradicting himself is because he *is* contradicting himself. Nevertheless, let us give him a chance to explain what looks like a blatant contradiction. He offers two points in an effort to distinguish his position from that of the contractualists. *First*, he says, the subject of common deliberation, which is the prerogative of government, is prospective rather than retrospective and that, it seems, is a significant difference. The *second* point of difference appears to be based on an analogy between the necessity for the exercise of private judgement in an individual and the corresponding necessity for common deliberation in a state. 'No individual,' Godwin says, 'can arrive at any degree of moral or intellectual improvement, unless in the use of an independent judgment.' So too 'No state can be well or happily administered, unless in the perpetual use of common deliberation respecting the measures it may be requisite to adopt.' [Godwin, 94] Godwin's first response seems to be quite beside the point, and his second response appears to be either question-begging or else to amount simply to the utilitarian claim the effective administration of a state requires common deliberation, not a particularly convincing argument when the justification of the state is the very point at issue. I hope I won't be thought to be unfair if I say that Godwin's reasoning here is less than completely persuasive and that the suspicion that he has contradicted himself hasn't been effectively countered.

Godwin has another argument for government that hinges upon its resemblance to law when law is properly understood. He argues that legislation is not, in fact, a matter that lies within society's competence. Reason is the only legislator 'and her decrees are irrevocable and uniform.' [Godwin, 95] Society may only interpret the law, not make it, 'like a British judge, who makes no new law, but faithfully declares that law which he finds already written.' [Godwin, 95] In much the same way, political authority is on a par with law. Just as law isn't made but declared, so too political authority—the use of coercion to enforce justice—has its proper area of operation and can't be justified outside it. And as human legislators aren't entitled to make what laws they please, so too, if political authority were to 'wander in the smallest degree from the great line of justice' then 'its authority is at an end, it stands upon a level with the obscurest individual, and every man is bound to resist its decisions' [Godwin, 95] Godwin distinguishes between obedience and mere compliance. 'I conform to the principles of justice, because I perceive them to be intrinsically and unalterably right. I yield to injustice, though I perceive that to which I yield to be abstractedly wrong, and only choose the least among inevitable evils.' [Godwin, 97]

This justification for government is somewhat less obscure than Godwin's earlier quasi-Rousseauean effort but to the extent that it has force, it offers little comfort to a statist unless one is prepared to be generous in one's estimate of the range of the legitimate concerns of justice. (As we shall see shortly, this is precisely Godwin's position.) Even libertarians are prepared to accept that someone (not necessarily any given particular person or agency to the exclusion of others) has the right to enforce the requirements of justice. But, then, libertarians, natural rights libertarians at least, circumscribe the bounds of justice tightly around the core of the zero-aggression principle, which is that no one may initiate or threaten to initiate physical violence against the person or property of another.

Godwin is, in fact, prepared to accept the use of force to repel force: 'The first and most innocent of all the classes of coercion is that which is employed in repelling actual force.' [Godwin, 371] He is unwilling, however, to sanction the use of force for punishment or for prior restraint, pointing out that the doctrine of prior restraint has been used 'to justify the most execrable of all tyrannies.' [Godwin, 372] In its place, Godwin proposes a vigilant use of public pressure. He writes, 'Why not arm myself with vigilance and energy, instead of locking up every man whom my imagination may bid me fear, that I may spend my days in undisturbed inactivity. If communities, instead of aspiring, as they have hitherto done, to embrace a vast territory, and to glut their vanity with ideas of empire, were contented with a small district with a proviso of confederation in cases of necessity, every individual would then live under the public eye, and the disapprobation of his neighbours, a species of coercion, not derived from the caprice of men, but from the system of the universe, would inevitably oblige him to reform or to emigrate.' [Godwin, 372]

There are a number of interesting points in this passage. First, one can agree with Godwin that smaller communities where people are known to one another and where one's actions, one's public actions at least, are observable by those whose respect and cooperation one desires, are more likely to be able to exercise informal sanctions. There are, of course, downsides to this, as Mill was to discuss at length in his *On Liberty*. Smaller communities are more likely to ride roughshod over the concerns and sensibilities of their members. Historically, in small communities, the options of reformation or emigration were, in fact, the operative conditions and were substantially effective. Nevertheless, until such time as our present day gigantic states are resolved into local self-governing communities, and even when they are, it may be necessary to exercise physical restraint on those with an insufficient appreciation of the difference between *meum* and *tuum*.

In the end, despite his reservations, Godwin is sufficiently a realist to recognise that coercion, as he calls it, may sometimes be necessary. 'I ought to take up arms against the domestic spoiler, because I am unable either to persuade him to desist, or the community to adopt a just political institution, by means of which security might be maintained consistently with the abolition of coercion.' [Godwin, 386] The critic might object that recourse to self-help must lead to anarchy-as-disorder. Godwin accepts that if in our present circumstances a country's government were suddenly to be dissolved, we would be relieved of some evils only to be visited by other, more severe, evils. 'We should have all the evils attached to a regular government,' he says, 'at the same time that we were deprived of that tranquillity and leisure which are its only advantages.' [Godwin, 387] However that may be, anarchy isn't necessarily worse than despotism, not least because despotism is perennial whereas anarchy is temporary. Moreover, anarchy would tend to induce a certain energy and wakefulness in people and foster a spirit of independence. In fact, mankind has lived in a state of anarchy not only in pre-civil societies but also, periodically, in times of revolution, even in historic times. 'Anarchy is,' he says, 'neither so good nor so ill a thing in relation to its consequences, as it has sometimes been represented.' [Godwin, 389]

PROPERTY

Godwin's attitude towards property is, in some ways, even more extreme than what one will find in the classical Continental anarchists, Kropotkin perhaps excepted. In matters of material goods, Godwin was a proto-socialist and a radical one at that. Those who have more than they really need have a positive duty in justice—in justice, note, not just in charity—to support those who do not. Godwin's conception of justice is rather positive than negative. Justice isn't merely a matter of zero-aggression or non-interference as it is for a libertarian but is rather a positive matter of rendering assistance to others who need it. Anticipating themes that will later find expression in such as John Rawls, Godwin believes that what we have and, indeed, what we are, we hold in a kind of trust for the use and benefit of all. Godwin believes that all men are entitled to a share of the common stock of human possessions, not only so much as will keep them in being but such as will provide for their well being. There is, however, a corresponding duty on all to perform their share of the common tasks. The dominant image here is agrarian, of happy peasants working together in the field. Godwin shares the bucolic romanticism that is common to many other anarchists and, like all romantics, he has reservations about the ultimate value of industrialism. He isn't alone in being attached to this romantic image. We find the same thing in Thomas More and Winstanley and in Kropotkin. Such a communal life requires a wholesale simplification of our needs and the elimination of luxury. The accumulation of property is inimical to such a simple life.

Of life in such a simple non-industrial community, Godwin tells us a story that will become standard for all utopian thinkers. Such an idyllic life would require a minimum of labour, leaving the maximum of our time and energy for other pursuits. The same story would be told again by Marx and the germ of it is, perhaps, worth repeating. In *The German Ideology* Marx writes that 'as soon as the division of labour comes into being, each man has a particular, exclusive sphere of activity, which is forced upon him and from which he cannot escape. He is a hunter, a fisherman, a shepherd, or a critic, and must remain so if he does not want to lose his means of livelihood'—and, of course, the division of labour is most highly developed in industrial societies. Nevertheless, in a communist society, on the other hand, 'where nobody has one exclusive sphere of activity but each can become accomplished in any branch he wishes, society regulates the general production and thus makes it possible for me to do one thing today and another tomorrow, to hunt in the morning, fish in the afternoon, rear cattle in the evening, criticise after dinner, just as I have a mind, without ever becoming hunter, fisherman, shepherd or critic.'[21] Others, including Kropotkin, repeat this fantasy.[22] If we abandon luxury the need for most of the work in which we currently engage will disappear. Such work as is needed won't be a great strain on anyone. 'If superfluity were banished, the necessity for the greater part of the manual industry of mankind would be superseded; and the rest, being amicably shared among all the active and vigorous members of the community, would be burthensome to none. Every man would have a frugal, yet wholesome diet.....all would have leisure to cultivate the kindly and philanthropical affections of the soul and to let loose his faculties in the search of intellectual improvement.' [Godwin, 423-424]

But what if I wish to acquire and retain property? Is it not mine, provided I haven't acquired it by force or by fraud? Godwin is willing to concede that your property is indeed yours but only in the sense that it is a trust that you are obliged to use for the 'increase of liberty, knowledge and virtue.' [Godwin, 56] In giving to another from what is mine, I do him no favours, but merely discharge an obligation. What if a man will say that he came honestly by his wealth, that he owes no debts and may dispose of his wealth as he pleases? Godwin rejects this argument completely. 'If justice have any meaning, nothing can be more iniquitous, than for one man to possess superfluities, while there is a human being in existence that is not adequately supplied with these.' [Godwin, 415]

Godwin considers the objection, often repeated since his time, that a system of equal property would lead to sloth. A critic might urge, 'Once establish it as a principle in society that no man is to apply to his personal use more than his necessities require, and you will find every man become indifferent to those exertions which now call forth the energy of his faculties….If each man found that, without being compelled to exert his own industry, he might lay claim to the superfluity of his neighbour, indolence would perpetually usurp his faculties, and such a society must either starve, or be obliged in its own defence to return to that system of injustice and sordid interest…' [Godwin, 430] Just how much work would be required to produce what we need? Godwin has already suggested that most manual labour would become unnecessary in his brave new world. [Godwin, 423-424] He now goes on to specify that the amount of work required of any man would be of 'so light a burthen as to assume the appearance of agreeable relaxation and gentle exercise, than of labour.' [Godwin, 431]How long would we have to work to produce our necessities? Godwin answers, 'half an hour a day, seriously employed in manual labour by every member of the community, would sufficiently supply the whole necessaries. Who is there that would shrink from this degree of industry?' This recurrent romantic fantasy isn't any more persuasive on its second appearance than it was on its first. In any event, our disposition of society must concern itself with men as they are, not with men as they might become and that renders Godwin's proposals moot in the extreme. Godwin's reply to such practical objections is that his proposal is to take hold only *after* we have experienced great intellectual improvement and in such circumstances, men won't relapse into indolence merely because of the equality of property. Perhaps he is right in making such a claim. Perhaps not. Who can tell? All in all, I hope I may be forgiven if I say that I find Godwin's reply to the 'indolence' objection to be less than persuasive, requiring, as it does, a reformation of human nature and a blithe misunderstanding of the relationship between human needs and human productivity. Despite his affinities with anarcho-collectivists and anarcho-communists in the matter of property, Godwin, like Stirner and Proudhon, is a staunch individualist and detests all forms of collectivism. He is deeply suspicious of any form of cooperation that might become institutionalised. In the end, then, despite his rejection of the anarchist label, William Godwin has a strong claim to be considered the first explicitly reflective anarchist thinker. He characterises government as a source of evil and is prepared to accept it as, at best, a necessary evil in mankind's current state of development.

III: MAX STIRNER

In the history of anarchism, Max Stirner (1806-1856), born Johann Kaspar Schmidt, stands alone—and that's just as it should be, for a more radical individualist thinker can scarcely be found. If Godwin's *Political Justice* was a supernova that blazed for a brief moment before dying as spectacularly as it had lived, Stirner's *The Ego and His Own [Der Einzige und sein Eigenthum]* had an even more brilliant, if briefer, moment of astronomical glory. What is striking about *The Ego and His Own* isn't that it had its Warholian fifteen minutes of fame but that it had any minute of fame at all! Engels wrote that 'Although Stirner's book *Der Einzige und sein Eigenthum* is forgotten, his notions and especially his critique of the State appear among the friends of anarchy.[23]

As anyone who has ever tried to read *The Ego and His Own* will know, it's a disorganised, rhapsodic effusion that induces a kind of intellectual vertigo, much ore surrounding some few nuggets of gold.[24] It is not a little ironic that Stirner himself notes 'What has here been set down roughly, summarily, and doubtless as yet incomprehensibly, will, it is to be hoped, become clear as we go on.' [Stirner, 26] The reader will have to be the judge as to whether Stirner's hopes have been realised. Stirner anticipates many themes that would become familiar years later in Nietzsche's writings and, in another mode, in the works of Ayn Rand but, unlike either Nietzsche or Rand, Stirner wouldn't go on to achieve any measure of permanent fame. Nietzsche, in fact, was one of the few to recognise the power and potential of Stirner's thought. According to Leszek Kolakowski, Nietzsche 'had read Stirner's work though he nowhere expressly refers to it.' [Kolakowski, 163] Apart from Nietzsche's knowledge of and possible use of Stirner's work, a much disputed topic, there was a temporary revival of interest in Stirner's ideas in the late nineteenth century and Benjamin Tucker, the American anarchist, published the first English edition *The Ego and His Own*.

STIRNER THE ANTI-RATIONALIST

Godwin, like the eighteenth century man he was, put his trust in reason; Stirner violently and passionately rejects reason and all its works and pomps. In so doing, he became one of the earliest of the modern irrationalists. 'In contrast to Godwin's stress on reason, Stirner speaks for the will and the instincts, and he seeks to cut through all the structures of myth and philosophy, all the artificial constructions of human thought, to the elemental self.' [Woodcock, 92] The individual, or rather the Ego, is what we know and it is the only thing we know and, recalling medieval metaphysical nominalism, each Ego is absolutely unique.

For Stirner, the Ego is considered 'not as a distinct individual, body or soul, but as pure self-consciousness, an ego in which existence and the awareness of existence are identical. "*Der Einzige*"—"the unique one"—is deliberately opposed to "*der Einzelne*", the "individual" of liberal philosophy.' [Kolakowski, 163]

Many anarchist thinkers have an operative principle—justice or reason or mutual aid—which supervenes on the tendency towards the atomistic fragmentation that anarchism is believed to encourage. Stirner has and wants nothing like this. He denies the existence of natural law; he denies the very idea of a common humanity. His ideal is the egoist, a bare individual set over against all collectivities and, indeed, other individuals. Each ego is a law unto itself. There are no rights, no duties, no immutable moral laws. The ego or self does not demand any right, nor does it recognise any. In a surprising twist, even freedom, which is normally *the* desideratum of libertarians everywhere, is subordinated to the uniqueness of the ego.[25] Stirner rejects any and every restriction on the individual—religion, state, society, principles and parties, even the abstract noun Man comes in for criticism. Each ego retreats into itself, somewhat like a political version of Leibniz's monads, and in this moment of retreat, the possibility or likelihood of conflict recedes. Egos can associate in Stirner's world but they do so spontaneously and only for as long as and to the extent that they wish to do so; a bizarre form of association, indeed!

Stirner approaches a kind of nihilism in his rejection of all absolutes. The state can't exist without the ascendency of one man over another and that's fundamentally incompatible with Stirner's idea of the ego. The state, the apotheosis of collective man, necessarily imperils freedom and so must be destroyed. 'The State,' he writes, 'always has the sole purpose to limit, tame, subordinate the individual—to make him subject to some *generality* or other; it lasts only so long as the individual is not all in all, and it is only the clearly marked *restriction of me*, my limitation, my slavery.' [Stirner, 227] But apart from the state, other people can also set themselves up as an obstacle to my freedom. Existence may then be, as for Hobbes, a 'war of each against all'. Anarchists commonly distinguish between the state and society, opposing the former while valorising the latter. Stirner's egoism leads him to reject both state *and* society. 'Therefore, we two, the State and I, are enemies. I, the egoist, have not at heart the welfare of this "human society," I sacrifice nothing to it, I only utilize it; but to be able to utilize it completely I transform it rather into my property and my creature; that is, I annihilate it, and form in its place the *Union of Egoists*.' [Stirner, 179]

Not only the state and society but *any* absolute at all constitutes an obstacle to my ego. The ego cannot recognise anything as superior to itself. *'What is sacred to me is not* my own…' [Stirner, 37] In saying this, Stirner opposes all sacred or quasi-sacred entities—Church, State, Society, Man, Morality—that can be set over against the individual. The individual cannot be subsumed in any of these quasi-sacred collectivities. *'Everything sacred is a tie, a fetter.'* [Stirner, 216] Stirner has no time for those who reject Christianity but hold on to a morality that's every bit as dominating. 'The same people who oppose Christianity as the basis of the State, who oppose the so-called Christian State, do not tire of repeating that morality is "the fundamental pillar of social life and of the State." As if the dominion of morality were not a complete dominion of the sacred, a "hierarchy."' [Stirner, 48-49]

STIRNER ON 'OWNNESS', ALTRUISM AND DUTIES

Freedom, the foundational principle of libertarianism, is contrasted unfavourably with what Stirner calls 'ownness'. 'What a difference between freedom and ownness! One can get *rid* of a great many things, one yet does not get rid of all; one becomes free from much, not from everything. Inwardly one may be free in spite of the condition of slavery, although, too, it is again only from all sorts of things, not from everything; but from the whip, the domineering temper, of the master, one does not as slave become *free*. "Freedom lives only in the realm of dreams!" Ownness, on the contrary, is my whole being and existence; it is I myself. I am free from what I am *rid* of, owner of what I have in my *power* or what I *control*. *My own* I am at all times and under all circumstances, if I know how to have myself and do not throw myself away on others. To be free is something that I cannot truly *will*, because I cannot make it, cannot create it: I can only wish it and—aspire toward it, for it remains an ideal, a spook. The fetters of reality cut the sharpest welts in my flesh every moment. But *my own* I remain.' [Stirner, 157]

It goes without saying that Stirner rejects any form of idealism or altruism. These are idols of our own construction that serve to obscure ourselves from ourselves. Even the search for freedom can be itself another idol. 'Thousands of years of civilization have obscured to you what you are, have made you believe you are not egoists but are called to be idealists ("good men"). Shake that off! Do not seek for freedom, which does precisely deprive you of yourselves, in "self-denial"; but seek for *yourselves*, become egoists, become each of you an *almighty ego*.' [Stirner, 164]

Stirner will have no truck with the idea of our having duties or, like Godwin, having natural rights: 'I do not demand any right, therefore I need not recognize any either. What I can get by force I get by force, and what I do not get by force I have no right to, nor do I give myself airs, or consolation, with my imprescriptible right.' [Stirner, 210] Moreover, like Godwin, he accepts that the consequence of this rejection of rights implies that a man may do as he pleases not only with himself and his own but also with the self of others. 'I secure my freedom with regard to the world in the degree that I make the world my own, "gain it and take possession of it" for myself, by whatever might, by that of persuasion, of petition, of categorical demand, yes, even by hypocrisy, cheating, etc.' [Stirner, 165]

STIRNER ON PROPERTY

Stirner's amoralism has consequences for his account of property. He writes, 'The Communists affirm that "the earth belongs rightfully to him who tills it and its products to those who bring them out." I think it belongs to him who knows how to take it, or who does not let it be taken from him, does not let himself be deprived of it. If he appropriates it, then not only the earth, but the right to it too, belongs to him. This is egoistic right: it is right for me, therefore it is right.' [Stirner, 191] Property and power go hand in hand. 'What then is *my* property? Nothing but what is in my *power*! To what property am I entitled?

To every property to which I—empower myself. I give myself the right of property in taking property to myself, or giving myself the proprietor's *power*, full power, empowerment.' [Stirner, 256] Stirner notes, neatly, that Proudhon's claim that property is theft is, in fact, a left-handed affirmation of property.[26] 'Is the concept "theft" at all possible, he asks, 'unless one allows validity to the concept "property"? How can one steal if property is not already extant? What belongs to no one cannot be *stolen*; the water that one draws out of the sea he does *not steal*. Accordingly property is not theft, but a theft becomes possible only through property.' [Stirner, 251]

Max Stirner is the most radical of radical thinkers. His egoistic individualism is the most extreme form of individualism to be found in any of the thinkers that we have considered or will consider. He was the first to outline themes that would subsequently find a more prominent home in thinkers such as Nietzsche and Ayn Rand. He rejected reason, natural law, rights, duties, and all absolutes, even a common humanity. Even freedom was less important to him than the radical uniqueness of the ego. Given all this, it hardly needs to be said that he rejects the state.[27]

Is it possible to be a Stirnerite egoist? Theoretically, yes; but the practical consequences are unliveable. While a Stirnerite could (and probably would) physically resist the initiation of violence against himself or his property, he would have no moral basis on which to resist such attacks. It has been said that Hobbes's anthropology implies that *homo homini lupus*—man is a wolf to man—but whether this is true of Hobbes's view of man in the state of nature or not, in neatly encapsulates Stirner's account of the ego.

Notes

1 The *Oxford English Dictionary* defines anarchy as: 'Absence of government; a state of lawlessness due to the absence or inefficiency of the supreme power; political disorder. In the sense of the term which makes it to be a lawless or disorderly state, *anarchy* is used as a term of reproach by Marxists who speak of the anarchy of capitalist production. But, as Ludwig von Mises points out, 'Even if the capitalistic method of production were "anarchistic," i.e., lacking systematic regulation from a central office…it is completely wrong to suppose they [capitalists] have no guide for arranging production to satisfy need.' The free market production of goods and services is orderly precisely *because* it is anarchistic, for capitalists, notes Mises, 'are bound, *by forces they are unable to escape*, to satisfy the needs of consumers as fully as possible, given the state of economic wealth and technology….consumer demand…determines the pattern and direction of production…' [Mises 1978, 156. Emphasis added]

2 For a graphic (if fictional) example of would-be lovers of disorder, see Montesquieu's fable in his *Persian Letters* of the wicked Troglodytes who reject kings, magistrates, contracts, and cooperation in favour of an aggressive hostility towards one another which eventually leads them all to destruction. [Montesquieu, letter 11, 15-18] In contrast, the good Troglodytes learn that 'the interest of the individual is always identical with the common interest, and that to attempt to separate oneself from it is fatal; that we should not find virtue arduous, or regard it as a painful exercise, and that justice to another is a charity to oneself.' [Montesquieu, letter 12, 18] Despite their newfound happiness, however, the good Troglodytes find that 'spontaneous political virtue becomes too much for them, and they choose a king to govern them.' [Shklar, 38]

3 Holding that law is governmental social control, Donald Black nevertheless accepts that there can be, and has been, social life without law. As he points out, 'law is an historical phenomenon, not universal, whereas anarchy is found in all societies to some degree. In a modern society, for

example, much anarchy appears in the social life of children, among friends and colleagues, within families and subcultures, among transients, isolates, disreputables, and others on the edges of social life, and also between people separated by great distances in social space, foreigners of all kinds. Much appears among nations as well.' [Black, 124]

4 For an account of the intellectual adventures of the term 'anarchy' in English political thought in the seventeenth and eighteenth centuries, see Watner 1986, passim.

5 I have a certain sympathy with Meltzer here—not much, but some. The term 'capitalism' carries so much emotional and conceptually confusing baggage, either positive or negative depending on one's point of view, that it can scarcely be used in a neutral or descriptive way.

6 I refer the reader to the following: for a convenient compendium of original writings, see Graham 2005 and Graham 2009; for a somewhat broader perspective but still from within the individual anarchistic tradition, see Caplan (No Date); for a sophisticated critique of philosophical anarchism, see Gans, passim.

7 Osterfeld 1983, in Stringham 2007, 506.

8 Block 2006, 40; see Long in Long & Machan 2008, 139 n. 17.

9 Lane 1996; see also Pateman, passim, especially 133-135, 234-235.

10 There is also anarcho-syndicalism which makes the revolutionary trade union the organ of the struggle for freedom and the basis of the new order. The reality of the various protean anarchist movements is characterised by a kind of Byzantine complexity.

11 For a summary account and introduction to a wide range of contemporary anarchist thinkers see *Anarchist Academics* at Anon (2010). Some of the thinkers treated in this admirably eclectic and catholic collection include Bruce Benson, Bryan Caplan, David Friedman, David Prychitko, Gary Chartier, Hans-Hermann Hoppe, Ivan Illich, Jan Narveson, Murray Bookchin, Murray Rothbard, Noam Chomsky, Robert Paul Wolff, Roderick Long, Simon Critchley and Walter Block.

12 Frank Bridge, in case you are wondering. Bridge was a fine composer in his own right who deserves better of history and of the musical public than to be known simply as Britten's teacher.

13 Oscar Wilde's *The Soul of Man under Socialism* was a late, literary manifestation of Godwinism.

14 Less obviously, perhaps, Godwin also influenced the Irish Liberator, Daniel O'Connell. 'William Godwin's emphasis on moral force democracy as an instrument of change permanently influenced his [O'Connell's] politics.' Besides Godwin, other contemporary thinkers contrived to move O'Connell in a (for the time and context) surprising liberal direction. 'Adam Smith persuaded him of the merits of a free economy, Thomas Paine strengthened O'Connell's democratic conviction and challenged his Catholic faith. He would return to Catholicism from Deism, but he never reneged on democracy, freedom of conscience, religious toleration, separation of church and state, the equality of all people, and laissez-faire.' [McCaffrey, 5]

15 I exaggerate—I should say 'almost as quickly'. A supernova's starring role lasts just under two minutes. Godwin's lasted somewhat longer than that.

16 The Oxford World Classics publication of this work is based on the first edition of 1793. The second (1796) and third (1798) editions made extensive changes but, as Mark Philp, the editor of the Oxford edition says, 'while the first edition may not represent Godwin's final thoughts, it more perfectly captures the spirit of the time in which he was writing than later editions.' [in Godwin 1793, xxxvi] All subsequent references to Godwin's work, unless otherwise indicated, are to the Oxford edition of the *Enquiry*.

17 As we shall see below, John Rawls's Difference Principle in his seminal book, *A Theory of Justice*, permits inequality in a society provided that it benefits the least well-off. If there is only one society—all human beings, everywhere—then this would require massive and radical redistribution of wealth. Not surprisingly, then, in his later work, *The Law of Peoples*, Rawls restricts the reach of the Difference Principle and permits it to operate only within particular societies. [See Rawls 1971; see also Rawls 1999]

18 In his day, Godwin achieved notoriety for his unorthodox views on marriage. He wished to abolish marriage, not to promote free love or sexual promiscuity but to show people that sex wasn't important! Intellectual affinity was what really mattered and since love marriages often yoked people of different intellectual capacities together (like Mr and Mrs Bennet in *Pride and Prejudice*), he wanted them to be able to separate once their sexual passion was spent.

19 Woodcock, 76. See Kohr, passim.

20 *Enquiry*, 3rd edition 1798, chapter 1.

21 Marx & Engels 1975-2001, 5, 47; Marx 1994, 132.

22 This particular horse isn't quite dead yet. In his 2015 book, *PostCapitalism*, Paul Mason argues that we have reached the end of the capitalist road; the problem of production has largely been solved and there remains only the problem of distribution. Utopia, it seems, is just around the corner.

23 Engels, in Anon. 1972, 30.

24 For an account of Marx's reaction to Stirner, see Kolakowski, 163-171. Kolakowski writes: 'In *The German Ideology* Marx and Engels criticize Stirner unmercifully….Marx denounces as unreal the notion of a human being whose whole life is only a kaleidoscope of self-consciousness and who can be indifferent or insensitive to the physical and social changes which in fact condition mental ones….It is a pious illusion to expect individuals to live together without the aid of the community and its institutions….the idea of individual liberation based on Stirner's category of the unique Ego is an idle fantasy.' [Kolakowski, 168, 169, 170]

25 It is one of the supreme existential ironies of history that Stirner, the arch-apostle of radical egoism, should have died from the most trivial of causes—an infection resulting from an insect bite.

26 As we shall shortly see, Proudhon's dictum is less obviously a rejection of property as a whole than these three words would suggest.

27 Stirnerite tendencies towards the elevation of the individual and the unique can be found in thinkers less dramatic but more coherent than Stirner. For example, F. C. S. Schiller, the Pragmatist/Humanist, had at the core of his thought 'the conviction that all acts and all thoughts are irreducibly the products of individual human beings, and are therefore inescapably associated with the needs, desires and purposes of men. Thus such terms as "truth" and "reality" denote nothing absolute; rather, they are intertwined with human intentions and deeds. Man makes his "truth" just as he makes his other values, "beauty" and "goodness."….There is therefore genuine novelty in our growing universe, and no theoretical limit to man's freedom.' [Abel, 8]

Chapter 29

THE CLASSICAL ANARCHISTS: PROUDHON, BAKUNIN AND KROPOTKIN

No man who knows aught, can be so stupid to deny that
all men naturally were born free
—Milton

When plunder has become a way of life for a group of people
living together in society, they create for themselves
in the course of time a legal system that authorises it,
and a moral code that glorifies it
—Bastiat

I: PIERRE-JOSEPH PROUDHON

Born in Franche-Comté, Pierre-Joseph Proudhon's background was that of a solidly provincial French peasant, although his father had been an artisan rather than a farmer. [see Droz, 73-74] Proudhon had the peasant's deep-rooted suspicion of industrial society; moreover, his rural and provincial upbringing infused him with a vision of the ideal society that was never to leave him, despite his long sojourn in Paris. He had some formal education early in life but because of family circumstances he had to choose a practical trade. In his case, he chose printing. Some early works written as entries to an essay contest won him a scholarship and he took himself off to Paris where, in 1840, he produced the first work that attracted attention, his *What is Property?*[1]

There can be little doubt that Proudhon was one of the most important social and political thinkers of the nineteenth century. His ideas on anarchy, property, land and labour influenced many subsequent thinkers, whether they adopted, adapted, or even rejected them. 'Proudhon,' writes Kolakowski, 'also exerted a strong influence over Bakunin, particularly from the anarcho-syndical point of view….he was also looked up to by later anarchists such as Kropotkin.' [Kolakowski, 210] Despite his personal importance and his contemporary and subsequent influence on others, it is hard to deny that Proudhon's writings aren't completely coherent—they may even be contradictory—not least because he never seems to have reread his own work! [see Kolakowski, 203-204]

PROUDHON—*WHAT IS PROPERTY?*

What is Property? opens with the ringing and notorious claim that property is theft. Startling and unambiguous as this phrase may appear to be, it doesn't in fact mean what it is often taken to mean—it is *not* a universal condemnation of all and every form of property. In fact, it could hardly be that and remain coherent, for, as Stirner astutely remarked, theft is the unjust and unlawful appropriation of another's property—without property, there can be no theft! What Proudhon's notorious claim condemns is property inasmuch as it is employed by someone to exploit the labour of others without effort on the property owner's part. Proudhon was in fact quite happy to endorse a notion of property as the possession and use of one's own house and land and tools, inasmuch as these were employed by and for oneself without, as he saw it, the exploitation of others. Proudhon, then, wasn't a communist and his endorsement of a certain kind of property was to separate him from other anarchists.

Proudhon believes that one has an absolute right to what one produces (*jus in re*) but one does *not* have an absolute right over the means of production (*jus ad rem*). What is produced is proper to the producer; what it is produced from is common. The material of which anything is made is ultimately given to us by nature and so belongs to all. Furthermore, our technological knowledge is also common. One might wonder why a producer has a right to his product, given that the material of which it is made has ultimately to be taken from the common stock which belongs to all. In the making of his product, the producer has *de facto* arrogated to himself exclusively what, on Proudhon's premises, belongs to all. The objection then might be made that a producer cannot own what he produces unless he antecedently owns the material that's used in the production. Those with communist inclinations, then, raise an objection somewhat along these lines: why, they ask, should we arrogate the product to the producer? Why not have means *and* ends both be common? This proposal Proudhon rejects. If the commonality of the means of production tends towards equality, the commonality of everything would, he thinks, be destructive of independence, and the importance of independence was a theme that runs throughout his work. 'Property, in fact, springs from man's desire to free himself from the slavery of communism, which is the primitive form of association,' writes Woodcock. 'But property, in its turn, goes to the extreme, and isolated equality by the right of exclusion and increase, and supports the acquisition of power by the privileged minority. In other words, it leads to unjust authority.' [Woodcock 1962, 106]

Proudhon's position, then, is an intermediate one between two extremes. At one extreme, with its commonality of means and commonality of product, communism preseves equality but denies independence. At the other extreme, the individuality of means and the individuality of product preserves independence but denies equality. Proudon's position, with its commonality of means and individuality of product preserves both independence and equality. In summary, then, Proudhon, in *What is Property?* rejects government and unworked property and advocates the organisation of society on the basis of free contractual relationships between workers.

Like Stirner, Proudhon valued individual freedom and was chary of associations and movements. Unlike Stirner, however, Proudhon wasn't opposed to society; if Stirner is the egoistic individualist, Proudhon, if it isn't a contradiction in terms, could be said to be the social individualist. 'To Stirner,' says Woodcock, 'the individual is all, and society his enemy. To Proudhon the individual is both the starting-point and the ultimate goal of our endeavours, but society provides the matrix...within which each man's personality must find its function and fulfilment.' [Woodcock 1962, 99] Proudhon believes, as most anarchists do, that man is inherently social but that, while this is so, his individuality must not be submerged in any form of social entity, not even in the family. Society isn't merely an aggregate of individuals but has its own character that is distinct from its constituent elements.

PROUDHON AND THE REVOLUTION

Proudhon took part in the February Revolution of 1848 but afterwards remarked that it was a revolution without ideas. Over the succeeding years, he directed his attention towards theory-in-practice, publishing a number of periodicals, standing for election to the Constituent Assembly and trying to get a People's Bank up and running. Of these enterprises, the periodicals were successful but participation in the constituent Assembly and the attempted constitution of the People's Bank were not. Eventually, the Assembly tired of Proudhon's provocative activities and he was tried and convicted on charges of sedition and sentenced to a fine and three year's imprisonment. The three years in what was, in effect, a kind of house arrest gave Proudhon the time and the solitude necessary to study, think and write. During his confinement, he wrote three books, continued to edit his periodicals and even found time to get married.

Proudhon's 1851 work, *The General Idea of the Revolution*, portrays the revolution (presumably a revolution *with* ideas) as a kind of natural and irresistible force resembling the Nemesis of the ancients. This idea of a fateful force as an agent of change was to become another standard element in anarchist thought, one echoed later by Kropotkin in a Darwinian mode. The French Revolution had been, at best, only a political revolution. The underlying economic structures had remained essentially unchanged. Association, flexible and dynamic association—and remember how chary Proudhon was of any form of association—if used as a means and not as an end in itself, could help to bring about the social republic. The root of association is contract, and contract, a horizontal form of relationship between equals, opposes government, which is a vertical relationship between unequals. 'The idea of contract excludes that of government,' writes Proudhon. 'Between contracting parties there is necessarily a real personal interest for each; a man bargains with the aim of securing his liberty and his revenue at the same time. Between governing and governed, on the other hand, no matter how the system of representation or delegation of the governmental function is arranged, there is *necessarily* an alienation of part of the liberty and means of the citizen.' [Proudhon 1851, 113] Contract horizontalises the vertical and makes the involuntary and unfree into the voluntary and free. The new order, then, is modelled on economic rather than political patterns. Practically, the realisation of this ideal will involve decentralisation and some kind of federalism, as well as worker control of the means of production.

PROUDHON AND ORDER

What of law and order? How shall this be supplied in the absence of coercive government? Proudhon tells us:

> In place of laws, we will put contracts. — No more laws voted by a majority, nor even unanimously; each citizen, each town, each industrial union, makes its own laws. In place of political powers, we will put economic forces. In place of the ancient classes of nobles, burghers, and peasants, or of business men and working men, we will put the general titles and special departments of industry: Agriculture, Manufacture, Commerce, &c. In place of public force, we will put collective force. In place of standing armies, we will put industrial associations. In place of police, we will put identity of interests. In place of political centralization, we will put economic centralization. Do you see now how there can be order without functionaries, a profound and wholly intellectual unity? You, who cannot conceive of unity without a whole apparatus of legislators, prosecutors, attorneys-general, custom house officers, policemen, you have never known what real unity is! What you call unity and centralization is nothing but perpetual chaos, serving as a basis for endless tyranny; it is the advancing of the chaotic condition of social forces as an argument for despotism — a despotism which is really the cause of the chaos. Well, in our turn, let us ask, what need have we of government when we have made an agreement? Does not the National Bank, with its various branches, achieve centralization and unity? Does not the agreement among farm laborers for compensation, marketing, and reimbursement for farm properties create unity? From another point of view, do not the industrial associations for carrying on the large-scale industries bring about unity? And the constitution of value, that contract of contracts, as we have called it, is not that the most perfect and indissoluble unity? [Proudhon 1851, 245-246]

There is so much here that echoes down the corridors of anarchism, and almost everything Proudhon proposes, with the possible exception of economic centralisation, would be acceptable to libertarian anarchists. Law will be replaced by arbitration, education will be a matter for parents and teachers, and everywhere, almost everywhere, we shall have decentralisation, including the decentralisation of nation states.

PROUDHON AND MUTUALISM

In 1849, Proudhon was arrested for insulting Louis-Napoléon Bonaparte and was confined to prison until 1852. On his release from his not very onerous confinement, Proudhon soon found himself in trouble with the authorities again. The official reaction to his publication *Of Justice in the Revolution and in the Church* encouraged his flight over the border to Belgium. Proudhon developed some more concrete political ideas in his 1863 work, *The Principle of Federation*, in which federal forms of association replace nationalism. His anarchism wasn't violent but tended towards the idea of a society's organising itself on the basis of spontaneous self-governing producers. From here to the notion of federation was a short step. Bowle remarks that Proudhon's self-governing federal society was 'incompatible with industrial capitalism' but, given Proudhon's suspicions of industrial society in the first place, this would not have been problematic for him. [Bowle, 156]

Although anarchy—society without government—has been the predominant mode of social organisation for most of human history, its very predominance meant that it was theoretically invisible so that it had rarely if ever been reflectively appropriated and rationally expressed.[2] Just as one can reason without learning logic, and speak without formally learning grammar, so one can live in anarchy without being able to speak or write about anarchism. [see Graham 2005, xi] Proudhon was the first person to coin the term 'anarchist' and to so describe himself, saying, 'Although a firm friend of order, I am (in the full sense of the term) an anarchist.'[3] The position he espoused must, in all justice, be described as a form of anarchism although its attitude to property diverges sharply from that of anarcho-communism, anarcho-collectivism and anarcho-syndicalism.

As we have seen, Proudhon is notorious for his epigram that 'property is theft', which would seem to place him in the company of anarcho-communists. Proudhon also said, however, that 'Property is liberty'! How may these statements be reconciled? In fact, Proudhon used the term 'property' in one sense to denote (and to deprecate) the idea of ownership by those who had no continuing contact with whatever it was they allegedly owned, whereas he had no difficulty with the idea that land belonged to those who in fact used or possessed it. The idea that property is legitimate only to the extent that it is possessed and used was to loom large in the thought of Josiah Warren and Benjamin Tucker. This is hardly surprising in the case of Tucker, given the enormous influence Proudhon's writings had on him. Nevertheless, Warren's thoughts on this matter were completely independent of, and indeed prior to, Proudhon's.

'Property,' writes Proudhon, 'is the suicide of society. Possession is a right; property is against that right. Suppress property while maintaining possession, and by this simple modification of the principle, you will revolutionize law, government, economy, and institutions; you will drive evil from the face of the earth.' [Proudhon 1840, 215; in Graham 2005, 37] Proudhon distinguished sharply between one form of property (let us call it Property-C) inasmuch as it was the outcome of conquest or exploitation and maintained only by the exercise of state power, and another form of property (Property-L), inasmuch as it was the outcome of labour and intrinsically independent of state power for its maintenance. The former kind of property is theft; the latter is freedom. Proudhon's Mutualism, unlike the communist and collectivist forms of anarchism, defends private property, property-L, provided that fundamental human equality isn't thereby endangered. In common with other forms of anarchism, Mutualism rejects the state.[4] In place of the state, mutualism allows, at best, a federation of free communes. The economic system is to be based upon the free association of individual workers or, when the nature of their work required it, some kind of syndicalist arrangement. The products of individual workers and cooperatives would be traded in the market. Mutualism also proposes the disruption of the system of state-sponsored banking monopoly and the provision of a system of free credit. Property (property-L) is to counteract the power of the State, and in so doing to insure the liberty of the individual.

Proudhon's concessions to private property, limited as they were, and his exaltation of it as a bulwark against the state, were not well received by some other anarchists. Other aspects of his Mutualism also fell under suspicion. Kropotkin, for example, was as opposed to a Mutualist form of money and credit as he was to any other form of money and credit and Bakunin ridiculed the Mutualist idea of contract or convention as implying the idea that individuals were, before such conventions, pre-social. If the anarcho-communists and anarcho-collectivists think Proudhon makes too many concessions to property and individual rights, others might think that he hasn't gone far enough. Mutualism is opposed to what Proudhon regards as the theft of labour but, by allowing currently unused land to be re-appropriated, it could be claimed that the labour invested in the land by the owner not currently in possession has been misappropriated. Mutualists, in turn, find the libertarian anarchist theory of property acquisition or property justification to be less than convincing and, along with Georgists[5] (ancient and modern) and latter-day left-libertarians, reject the idea that land can ever be property in a full-blooded sense since it isn't the product of labour.

Marx was initially very favourably impressed by Proudhon's thought and he wrote to him in 1846 to propose collaboration. Proudhon, however, was wary of any form of association with such as Marx and, indeed, wary of the idea of revolution as a means of social reform. In his reply to Marx, he warned of the dangers of their becoming leaders in a new form of intolerance. Proudhon's response disappointed Marx and ended direct contact between them which perhaps explains, in part, Marx's abusive attack on Proudhon in *The Poverty of Philosophy*. 'Marx, who greeted [Proudhon's] first publication as a political event comparable with Sieyès's *Qu'est-ce que le Tiers Etat?*, was mercilessly sarcastic at the expense of *La Philosophie de la misère*, reproaching Proudhon with ignorance of economics, the fanciful use of misunderstood Hegelian schemas, a moralistic conception of socialism, and a reactionary petty-bourgeois Utopia.' [Kolakowski, 209] *Ad hominem* abuse to one side, Marx's criticism of Proudhon would seem to come down to three basic points: Proudhon substitutes moral indignation for economic analysis; Proudhon's individualism is, in essence, a romantic advocacy of a return to medieval methods of production; and Proudhon's application of Hegel's schemata is arbitrary. [see Kolakowski, 225-226] Anarchism as a whole, and Proudhonism in particular, is to be criticised for being a form of petit-bourgeois socialism, failing to appreciate or, even worse, rejecting the fundamental importance of class conflict. [see Anon. 1972, 9] It isn't clear to what extent Marx's criticism of Proudhon is to the point. Leszek Kolakowski notes that 'Despite Marx's scornful criticism, it is not the case that Proudhon regarded actual social conditions and economic forces as the embodiment of abstract philosophical categories antecedent to social reality. On the contrary, he is at pains to state that the intellectual organization of social reality in abstract categories is secondary to that reality. The first determinant of human existence is productive work, while intellectual activity is the outcome of such work.' [Kolakowski, 205]

Friedrich Engels wrote to Marx, 'I am half through Proudhon's book [*Idée générale de la révolution au XIXe siècle*] and think that your opinion is completely justified. His appeal to the bourgeoisie, his return to Saint-Simon and a hundred other things in the critical part alone confirm that he regards the industrial class, the bourgeoisie and proletariat, as intrinsically identical and brought into contradiction only by the non-completion of the revolution.... Our propositions that the historically decisive impetus comes from material production, the class struggle, etc., have been largely accepted, mostly in a distorted form, and on this—by means of pseudo-Hegelian jugglery—the experiment is based of seemingly merging the proletariat once more in the bourgeoisie.'[6] In a letter, some years later, Marx wrote, 'Under the *pretext of freedom*, and of anti-governmentalism or anti-authoritarian individualism, these gentlemen...actually preach ordinary bourgeois economy, only Proudhonistically idealised! Proudhon did enormous mischief.'[7] There is a measure of irony in Marx's attack on Proudhon inasmuch as Proudhon's position was an attempt to maintain a kind of dialectical tension between opposed and competing tendencies, an attempt one would have thought that would have been music to Marx's ears. Woodcock remarks, 'And here it is worth emphasizing the persistence of the idea of conflict in Proudhon's thoughts; he lived for the struggle more than for the victory....At most he sees a possible truce between the contradictory forces in the universe and in society; but stress and tension are inevitable and desirable.' [Woodcock 1962, 114] Marx is right about one thing, however, and that is that Proudhon, despite the notoriety of his slogan that 'Property is theft' is no communist, regarding communism as a system of social organisation that's incompatible with human dignity, not to mention leading inexorably to universal poverty, on the one hand, and, on the other, to an omnipotent state.

II: Mikhail Bakunin

Mikhail Bakunin (1814-1876) is, perhaps, the least original but certainly not the least inspiring of our classical anarchists. His life and times seems like a script for a Hollywood movie (picture Bakunin as Liam Neeson with a full-length beard!) A man of action, if largely ineffective action, a conspirator, a revolutionary enthusiast, he was incapable of sustained literary reflection. 'Bakunin,' writes Kolakowski, 'had not the gifts of a theoretician or a founder of systems. He was full of inexhaustible revolutionary energy, bent on destructive aims and inspired by anarchistic Messianism.' [Kolakowski, 248] Even his greatest admirer could scarcely describe Bakunin as a systematic thinker. His writings are fragmentary and incomplete. *God and the State*, his most famous (though not necessarily his most important) work is a case in point. 'It is,' writes Paul Avrich, 'disjoined, repetitious, poorly organized, and full of digressions.' [Avrich, vii] Despite these admitted defects, however, it is also 'forceful and energetic, and packed with arresting aphorisms that testify to Bakunin's remarkable intuitive gifts.' [Avrich, vii]

The textual history of *God and the State* illustrates the confused and confusing state of most of Bakunin's output. It first appeared in print in 1882 after Bakunin's death, published by some colleagues of his who did not realise that it was simply part of a larger project with the wildly improbable if entrancing title of *The Knouto-Germanic Empire and the Secret Revolution*, which Bakunin worked on between 1870 and 1872. After its publication, it achieved wide circulation and was translated into many languages, the English translation being published by Benjamin Tucker.

The national origin of our anarchists is reflected in their writings. Godwin couldn't be anything other than English, Proudhon is ineffably French, and it is impossible to imagine Bakunin as anything other than Russian. His family were landowners, his father a disciple of Rousseau. After an early, if brief, obligatory stint in the army, he moved to Moscow where he met Nicholas Stankevich. One of his first intellectual attractions was Hegelianism and a possible career as a professor of philosophy seemed to be opening out for him. In pursuit of his plans, he went to live in Berlin for a couple of years but it was during a trip to Dresden that his conversion to anarchism was initiated when he became a Young Hegelian.

In his earliest writings, produced around this time, there appear traces of the eschatological tone that was to be a dominant feature of his thought. 'Let us put our trust,' he writes, 'in the eternal spirit which destroys and annihilates….The urge to destroy is also a creative urge.' [Bakunin, *The Reaction in Germany*, 1842] In Switzerland, Bakunin would meet his first militant revolutionary in Wilhelm Weitling who implanted in Bakunin's mind the core anarchist idea that the perfect society stands in no need of government requiring, at most, an administration, no laws but only mutual obligations. His involvement with Weitling was brought to the attention of the Russian authorities, who commanded Bakunin to return to Russia. He refused to return and was condemned in his absence to penal servitude in Siberia. From Switzerland he went to Paris, there to meet, among others, Proudhon and Marx. He became intimate with Proudhon and regarded him reverentially as the master even though he was later to reject Proudhon's attenuated conception of property as possession and his scheme of mutual banking.

Anarchism wasn't Bakunin's only interest. He was an early adherent of pan-Slavism and his activities in this cause took him on insurrectionary journeys to Poland and Bohemia before he arrived in the Duchy of Anhalt where he wrote his *Appeal to the Slavs*. At this stage in his intellectual career, Bakunin wasn't yet completely committed to anarchism; he 'had not developed his later conceptions of libertarian organization' and 'his rejection of the bourgeois state at this time was not incompatible with the vision of a revolutionary dictatorship.' [Woodcock, 144]

ADVENTURES OF A WOULD-BE REVOLUTIONARY

Bakunin in many ways reminds one of the archetypal Irishman who, landing on the wharves of New York to find a fight in progress, inquired if this was a private fight or whether anyone could join in. A revolt broke out in Dresden in 1849 and even though it wasn't his fight, Bakunin joined in. When the revolt was defeated, Bakunin was captured, sentenced to death and imprisoned. After a year, he was handed over to the tender mercies of the Austrians who once again imprisoned him, sentenced him to death and passed him on to the Russians. Since he was already under condemnation in Russia, the Russians simply put him in the Peter-Paul Fortress in St Petersburg without benefit of trial, in which less than comfortable surroundings he was to remain for the next six years. A combination of pressure from his relatives and an apology to the Tsar for his offences against autocracy (either cringing or cunning, depending on one's reading of it) sufficed to secure his transfer from prison to exile in Siberia in 1857. In Siberia, he lived for the next four years, during which time he married and tried to persuade the Governor (who was his cousin) to become a revolutionary dictator! Under the less-than-vigilant eye of the next Governor (another family connection!) he was able to travel down the river Amur and eventually to board an American ship by which, in a truth-imitating-fiction Phileas Fogg manner, he travelled to San Francisco via Japan, then on to New York and finally to London.

Most men would have been content with a quiet life after the experiences Bakunin had had over a period of ten years. Not Bakunin. In 1863, an insurrection broke out in Poland. Nothing daunted by his previous perfect history of failure, Bakunin, with equal measures of enthusiasm and incompetence, joined an expedition of 200 Poles that was supposed to arrive in Lithuania, there to arouse the populace to attack the Russian flank. The captain of the ship on which they were travelling refused to land them in Lithuania and returned them to Sweden. This experience, finally, was sufficient to reduce to vanishing point Bakunin's enthusiasm for pan-Slavism and to allow him to turn his boundless energy to other matters. In 1864, he left London for Italy where he settled for the remainder of his life.

He founded a shadowy organisation called the International Brotherhood in 1866, whose *Revolutionary Catechism* demonstrated a definite move towards anarchism in its opposition to authority, to the state and to religion, while its internal organisation moved in quite an opposite un-libertarian direction. With all its defects, the International Brotherhood did finally force Bakunin to clarify his thinking on political matters and moved him inexorably in the direction of anarchism where he was, and continued to be, heavily influenced by Proudhon. Although Bakunin would never become a fully-fledged communist in the manner of a Kropotkin, he went beyond Proudhon, ever the individualist, in accepting the necessity for association as a central principle for economic organisation. For Bakunin, it was going to be groups of workers, not individuals, that would become the unit of social organisation. 'With Bakunin,' writes Woodcock, 'the main stream of anarchism parts from individualism, even in its mitigated Proudhonian form; later, during the sessions of the International, the collectivist followers of Bakunin were to oppose the Mutualist followers of Proudhon—the other heirs of anarchy—over the question of property and possession.' [Woodcock, 152] The International Brotherhood was succeeded by the International Alliance of Social Democracy whose programme emphasised the principle of federalism. Nation states were to disappear and to be replaced by a worldwide union of free associations. The Alliance sought admission as a body to the International (International Working Men's Association) but Marx, suspicious of an organisation dominated by the formerly pan-Slavic Proudhonist Bakunin, brought about the rejection of its application, ostensibly on the grounds that there was only room for one such international organisation. The Alliance was formally dissolved and its branches became sections of the International. 'The struggle against anarchism attained the highest pitch in the First International,' writes N. Y. Kolpinsky. 'In the International, Marx and Engels led the struggle against 'every brand of anarchist ideology, a struggle which they carried to an organisational demarcation between the truly revolutionary majority of the Association and the anarchist organisations.' [Kolpinsky 14, 15] As Kolpinsky sees it, 'Bakunin and his followers set themselves the task of fighting the influence of Marxism, and taking over leadership of the International, setting up for that purpose their own organisations—the International Alliance of Socialist Democracy....From 1868 on, with the establishment of the Alliance, an acute ideological struggle developed in the International.... Marx and Engels demonstrated that the anarchist dogmas about "abolishing the state" as the first step in the revolution, destroying authority of every kind, and introducing total decentralization as a necessary condition of the revolution, were quite untenable.....In their critique of anarchism, Marx and Engels stressed the fact that the Bakuninists were trying to split the working-class movement and to demolish the unity that had already been gained...'[8]

Of the events of this period, Friedrich Engels later wrote: 'Marx and I, ever since 1845, have held the view that *one* of the final results of the future proletarian revolution will be the gradual dissolution and ultimate disappearance of that political organisation called *the State*....At the same time we have always held, that in order to arrive at this and the other, far more important ends of the social revolution of the future, the proletarian class will first have to possess itself of the organised political force of the state and with this aid stamp out the resistance of the Capitalist class and re-organise society....The Anarchists reverse the matter. They say, that the Proletarian revolution has to *begin* by abolishing the political organisation of the State....Does it require my express assertion that Marx opposed these anarchist absurdities from the very first day that they were started in their present form by Bakunin?....The Anarchists tried to obtain the lead of the International, by the foulest means, ever since 1867 and the chief obstacle in their way was Marx. The result of the five year's struggle was the expulsion from the International, at the Hague Congress, Sept. 1872, of the Anarchists from the International, and the man who did most to procure that expulsion was Marx.'[9]

Earlier, Engels had written, 'Bakunin maintains that it is the *state* which has created capital, that the capitalist has his capital *only by the grace of the state*.

As, therefore, the state is the chief evil, it is above all the state which must be done away with and then capitalism will go to blazes of itself. We, on the contrary, say: Do away with capital, the concentration of all means of production in the hands of the few, and the state will fall of itself. The difference is an essential one: Without a previous social revolution the abolition of the state is nonsense; the abolition of capital is precisely the social revolution and involves a change in the whole mode of production. Now then, inasmuch as to Bakunin the state is the main evil, nothing must be done which can keep the state—that is, any state, whether it be a republic, a monarchy or anything else—alive.'[10] Despite Engels's assessment of the point of difference between the communists and the anarchists, Kolakowski, however believes otherwise. 'On this point, the disagreement was not essential, for Marx, like Bakunin, considered that existing political institutions would have to be destroyed, while Bakunin agreed that the state had arisen historically as an instrument of private property....the dispute therefore came down to whether the socialist revolution could do away with all forms of statehood at the outset.' [Kolakowski, 254] Here, for once however, I believe that Kolakowski errs and that Engels is correct in his evaluation of the significance of the point at issue between Marx and Bakunin.

Bakunin had joined the International in 1864 and, having struggled against its Marxist wing, he was eventually expelled from it in 1872.[11] This was the occasion for his *Statism and Anarchy*, subtitled 'The Struggle of the Two Parties in the International Working Men's Association', in which he predicted that the Marxist dictatorship of (meaning 'by') the proletariat would turn into the dictatorship of (meaning 'over') the proletariat. It also gave him to opportunity to state in, for him, a reasonably comprehensive way his vision of an anarchist society. Bakunin rejected completely the communist strategy of taking over the state for its own purposes, believing that there was no way in which a state could operate without domination and slavery. In *Statism and Anarchy*, his major work, he wrote a sublimely scathing but also coherent and strangely prescient and prophetic passage which, to allow its full flavour to be experienced, I quote at some length:

We have already expressed several times our profound aversion to the theory of Lassalle and Marx, which recommends to the workers, if not as their ultimate ideal, then at least as their immediate and principal objective, the creation of a people's state. As they explain it, this will be nothing other than 'the proletariat raised to the level of a ruling class.'
If the proletariat is to be the ruling class, it may be asked, then whom will it rule? There must be yet another proletariat which will be subject to this new rule, this new state. It might be the peasant rabble, for example, which, as we know, does not enjoy the favor of the Marxists, and which, finding itself on a lower cultural level, will probably be governed by the urban and factory proletariat. Or, if we look at this question from the national point of view, then, presumably, as far as the Germans are concerned it is the Slavs who, for the same reason, will occupy in regard to the victorious

German proletariat the same position of servile domination that the latter now occupies in relation to its own bourgeoisie.

If there is a state, then necessarily there is domination and consequently slavery. A state without slavery, open or camouflaged, is inconceivable— that is why we are enemies of the state….It always comes down to the same dismal result: government of the vast majority of the people by a privileged minority. But this minority, the Marxists say, will consist of workers. Yes, perhaps of former workers, who, as soon as they become rulers or representatives of the people will cease to be workers and will begin to look upon the whole workers' world from the heights of the state. They will no longer represent the people but themselves and their own pretensions to govern the people. Anyone who doubts this is not at all familiar with human nature. [Bakunin 1873, 177-178]

In the light of subsequent histories of Germany and Russia, I leave it to readers to judge for themselves whether Marx or Bakunin had the better of their disagreement.

In the late 1860s, Bakunin came under the influence of a young student from Moscow, Sergei Nechayev, an association that was to cause him and his followers some embarrassment. From this period of Bakunin's life, we have the *Revolutionary Catechism* and the *Principles of Revolution* and other publications which preach indiscriminate destruction in the name of revolution and the doctrine that the end justifies the means, any means. There can be no doubt that Bakunin, like many anarchists, was emotionally attracted to the idea of destruction as a process of eschatological purification by which the old world could be made ready for its new creation but there's little to suggest that, in practice, despite his penchant for manning barricades at the drop of a hat, that Bakunin was an advocate of total and mindless destruction. Much scholarly debate has been occasioned by whether these inflammatory documents were written by Bakunin or even endorsed by him. Given that he made no protest over their publication, it would seem that they must have had at least his tacit approval. Nechayev engaged in other unsavoury activities that did nothing to enhance Bakunin's reputation and which have provided Marxist opponents of Bakuninism ever since with ammunition to use against it.[12]

In 1874 an insurrection threatened to break out in Bologna. Sure enough, Bakunin was immediately on the scene, only to witness the would-be uprising end in farce before it had even begun. His exit from Bologna, disguised as a priest with a basket of eggs on his arm, is the stuff of comic opera. He was to die some two years later in 1876 and Woodcock writes that those who attended his funeral 'were already turning the anarchist movement—his last and only successful creation—into a network that within a decade would have spread over the world and would bring a terror into the minds of rulers that might have delighted the generous and Gothic mind of Michael Bakunin…' [Woodcock, 170]

There are echoes of a Stirner-like egoism in some of Bakunin's writings.[13] The socialist, according to Bakunin, 'is distinguished from the strict republican by his *frank and human egotism*; he lives for himself, openly and without fine-sounding phrases.'[14] Bakunin continues, 'The strictly political republican is a stoic; he recognizes no rights for himself but only duties…that of eternal devotion to his country, of living only to serve it, and of joyfully sacrificing himself and even dying for it.' [Graham 2005, 81] On the other hand, the socialist 'insists upon his positive rights to life and to all of its intellectual, moral, and physical joys. He loves life, and he wants to enjoy it in all its abundance.' [Graham 2005, 81] The Robespierrean republican deals with the citizen, the socialist republican deals with the man. The former is a nationalist, the latter an internationalist. Liberty for the Republican is the liberty of the willing slave, willing to sacrifice himself and others. Bakunin is an individualist. 'History is made,' he says, 'not by abstract individuals, but by acting, living and passing individuals. Abstractions advance only when borne forward by real men.' [Bakunin 1871, 58]

BAKUNIN ON THE STATE AND AUTHORITY

Whereas some anarchists are suspicious of any and all forms of authority, Bakunin's attitude is much more nuanced. It goes without saying that he rejects authority where that authority amounts to coercion, whether from the side of the Church or the side of the State. He notes that the Church has been a willing ally of the State for most of its existence. But Bakunin is perfectly happy to accept the authority of expertise from those who are genuinely expert in their areas of expertise, whether in boot-making or architecture. He isn't willing to have it imposed on him but he is willing, sometimes having taken a second opinion, to accept it.

The state is the primary instrument of authority as coercion or domination. The state, according to Bakunin, '*is the most flagrant, the most cynical, and the most complete negation of humanity.*'[15] This is so because sovereign states presuppose the existence of other sovereign states, all hostile to and threatening each other. Between these states, war is 'the supreme law, an unavoidable condition of human survival.' [Graham 2005, 83] Internally, the morality of the state is dominated by its own interest in its preservation and in the extension of its power. Bakunin points out that the state makes it possible for us to valorise actions that in other situations would clearly be deprecated. 'Thus, to offend, to oppress, to despoil, to plunder, to assassinate or enslave one's fellowman is ordinarily regarded as a crime. In public life, on the other hand, from the standpoint of patriotism, when these things are done for the greater glory of the State, for the preservation or the extension of its power, it is all transformed into duty and virtue.' [Graham 2005, 83-84]

In a wonderfully purple passage, Bakunin fulminates against the state, saying, 'since the birth of the State, the world of politics has always been and continues to be the stage for unlimited rascality and brigandage, brigandage and rascality which, by the way, are held in high esteem, since they are sanctified by patriotism, by the transcendent morality and the supreme interest of the State. This explains why the entire history of ancient and modern states is merely a series of revolting crimes; why kings and ministers, past and present, of all times and all countries—statesmen, diplomats, bureaucrats, and warriors—if judged from the standpoint of simple morality and human justice, have a hundred, a thousand times over earned their sentence to hard labour or to the gallows. There is no horror, no cruelty, sacrilege, or perjury, no imposture, no infamous transaction, no cynical robbery, no bold plunder or shabby betrayal that has not been or is not daily being perpetrated by the representatives of the states, under no other pretext than those elastic words, so convenient and yet so terrible: *"for reasons of state."'* [Graham 2005, 84]

It is a common strategy to attempt to provide a justification for the state by claiming that it represents us so that it does not, appearances to the contrary notwithstanding, really coerce us. In *Statism and Anarchy*, Bakunin attacks the idea of political representation. He has in his sights here not just the bourgeois extant governments but also the anticipated revolutionary governments that are expected to succeed them. 'Both the theory of the state and the theory of so-called revolutionary dictatorship are based on this fiction of pseudo-representation—which in actual fact means the government of the masses by an insignificant handful of privileged individuals, elected (or not even elected) by mobs of people rounded up for voting and never knowing what or whom they are voting for—on this imaginary and abstract expression of the imaginary thought and will of all the people, of which the real, living people do not have the faintest idea.' [Bakunin 1873, 136-137] All governments, revolutionary or bourgeois, share exactly the same basic characteristics. 'The only difference between revolutionary dictatorship and the state is in external appearances. Essentially, they both represent the same government of the majority by a minority in the name of the presumed stupidity of the one and the presumed intelligence of the other.' [Bakunin 1873, 137]

Bakunin is scathing about the alleged representative nature of the representative system in politics writing, 'the whole deception of the representative system lies in the fiction that government and a legislature emerging out of a popular election must or even can represent the real will of the people.' [Graham 2005, 87] The interests of rulers and ruled are not only *not* coincident, they are in fact opposed. 'However democratic may be their feelings and their intentions, once [rulers] achieve the elevation of office they can only view society in the same way as a schoolmaster views his pupils, and between pupils and masters equality cannot exist. On one side there is the feeling of a superiority that is inevitably provoked by a position of superiority; on the other side, there is a sense of inferiority which follows from the superiority of the teacher....' [Graham 2005, 88]

Defenders of representative democracy will say, of course, that the voters have their say in elections and can always vote for someone else if not satisfied with their prior choice. But they miss the point that once elected, our alleged representatives can do pretty much what they want, untrammelled by the prospect of immediate recall. If my lawyer fails to act according to my instructions, I can fire him immediately; not so with my political representative. 'It is true that all our legislators...are elected...by the people. It is true that on election day even the proudest of the bourgeoisie...are obliged to pay court to Her Majesty, The Sovereign People…But once the elections are over, the people return to their work and the bourgeoisie to their profitable businesses and political intrigues….In reality, the control exercised by voters on their elected representatives is a pure fiction. But since, in the representative system, popular control is the only guarantee of the people's freedom, it is quite evident that such freedom in its turn is not more than a fiction.' [Graham 2005, 88-89] Representative democracy advertises itself as promoting the election of anyone sufficiently energetic and dedicated who can persuade enough people to vote for him. Maybe so, but as Bakunin points out, 'this does not prevent the formation in a few years' time of a body of politicians, privileged in fact though not in law, who, devoting themselves exclusively to the direction of the public affairs of a country, finally form a sort of political aristocracy or oligarchy.' [Bakunin 1871, 32]

If Proudhon is the person most associated with the development of Mutualism, and Kropotkin is the person most closely associated with Anarcho-Communism, Mikhail Aleksandrovich Bakunin holds the dominant position (if that's not a contradiction in terms) in Anarcho-Collectivism.[16] Needless to say, whatever differences he and other collectivists may have with anarcho-communists on other matters, in their rejection of the state they are entirely in accord with them. The state, says Bakunin, 'is an abstraction which consumes the life of the people. But for an abstraction to be born, develop, and continue to exist in the real world, there must be a real collective inter-ested in its existence.' This collective is 'the governing and property-owning class, which is to the State what the sacerdotal class of religion, the priests, is to the Church.'[17] Whereas both anarcho-communism and anarcho-collectivism both propose the common ownership of the means of production, they differ significantly on the allocation of the results of that production. Where anarcho-communism believes in a non-market, moneyless distribution according to need, anarcho-collectivism holds to a distribution according to deed. This requires a wage system of some kind and therefore some sort of money. 'The important difference between anarcho-communism and anarcho-collectivism,' writes Osterfeld, 'is that while for the former the wage-system and all other market phenomena will be abolished, the collectivists retain not only a modified wage system but other exchange relationships as well.'[18] Some anarcho-collectivists saw their position merely as a stage on the way to anarcho-communism but others saw it as terminal.[19]

BAKUNIN AND MARX

Perhaps what Bakunin is best known for in the history of political thought is his being the locus of the only serious opposition to Marxism in the interne-cine struggles that took place in socialist circles in the mid-nineteenth century. Despite all his shortcomings, personal and authorial, he saw clearly the author-itarian implications of Marxist socialism. 'It was in the conflict between Bakunin and Marx within the International,' writes Woodcock, 'that the irrec-oncilable differences between the libertarian and the authoritarian conceptions of socialism were first developed, and in this struggle the faction that Bakunin

led gradually shaped itself into the nucleus of the historic anarchist movement.'
[Woodcock, 136]

Within the International, the contest between Bakunin and Marx grew ever
more intense. Both men had some characteristics in common. Both were
Hegelians or post-Hegelians in philosophy, both were autocratic in temperament and both were lovers of intrigue. There were differences too. 'Bakunin,'
writes Woodcock, 'had an expansive generosity of spirit and an openness of
mind which were both lacking in Marx, who was vain, vindictive, and insufferably pedantic.' [Woodcock, 158] These personality differences were reflected
in their political philosophies. Bakunin was a libertarian, Marx an authoritarian; Bakunin was a federalist, Marx a centralist; Bakunin sought to destroy
the state, Marx to take it over; Bakunin espoused worker control of the means
of production, Marx espoused their nationalisation.

State and Anarchism is perhaps most well known for its direct attack on
Marx. Although granting that Marx is intelligent and well read, and conceding
the soundness of much of his criticism of Proudhon, Bakunin also remarks that
Marx is 'ambitious and vain, quarrelsome, intolerant, and absolute....There
is no lie or calumny that he would not invent and disseminate against anyone
who had the misfortune to arouse his jealousy—or his hatred, which amounts
to the same thing. And there is no intrigue so sordid that he would hesitate to
engage in it if in his opinion...it might serve to strengthen his position and his
influence or extend his power.' [Bakunin 1873, 141] Bakunin goes on to say that
'we energetically reject any attempt at a social organization devoid of the most
complete liberty for individuals as well as associations, and one that would call
for the establishment of a ruling authority of any nature whatsoever, and that,
in the name of this liberty—which we recognize as the only basis for, and the
only legitimate creator of, any organization, economic or political—we shall
always protest against anything that may in any way resemble communism or
state socialism....' [Graham 2005, 82]

Bakunin expresses his opposition to those who wish to overthrow existing
states only to set up states of their own. 'We are the natural enemies of such
revolutionaries—the would-be dictators, regulators, and trustees of the revolution—who even before the existing monarchical, aristocratic, and bourgeois
states have been destroyed, already dream of creating new revolutionary states,
as fully centralized and even more despotic than the state we now have. These
men are so accustomed to the order created by an authority, and feel so great a
horror of what seems to them to be disorder but is simply the frank and natural
expression of the life of the people, that even before a good, salutary disorder
has been produced by the revolution they dream of muzzling it by the act of
some authority that will be revolutionary in name only, and will only be a new
reaction in that it will again condemn the masses to being governed by decrees,
to obedience, to immobility, to death; in other words, to slavery and exploitation by a new pseudo-revolutionary aristocracy....' [Graham 2005, 85-86]

To repeat a point I made earlier but which bears repetition, Bakunin makes
the excellent, indeed I believe unanswerable, point in respect of the communist
theory of the people's state in which the proletariat will be raised to the level

of the ruling class. He asks, 'If the proletariat is to be the ruling class...whom will it rule? There must be yet another proletariat which will be subject to this new rule, this new state." [Bakunin 1873, 177] If it is the case that the entire nation will rule but no one will be ruled then 'there will be no government, there will be no state...' [Bakunin 1873, 178] Of course, what the dictatorship of the proletariat really means is the proletariat's being dictated *to* by a small minority, the 'government of the vast majority of the people by a privileged minority...' [Bakunin 1873, 178]. If such a state were really a people's state what need would there be to abolish it. On the other hand, if its abolition is necessary 'for the real liberation of the people, then how do they dare call it a people's state?' [Bakunin 1873, 179]

Indeed.

III: PYOTR KROPOTKIN

If Bakunin was Superman, the man of fire and brimstone, Pyotr Alexeyevitch Kropotkin (1842-1921) was Clark Kent, the man of tea and crumpets. If Bakunin was the man of action, Kropotkin was the man of reflection. Despite their temperamental and intellectual differences, however, Bakunin and Kropotkin were at bottom not totally dissimilar. Real as their real intellectual and temperamental differences were, they were perhaps exaggerated by circumstances. As a creature of the early nineteenth century, Bakunin was, at heart, a romantic revolutionary, translating the Hegelian Dialectic into a doctrine of salvation through destruction; Kropotkin, on the other hand, born in the mid-nineteenth century was a non-apocalyptic evolutionary. Bakunin has the street fighter's appreciation for the concrete and the practical; Kropotkin inspired more visionary and optimistic, if less practical, schemes.

Like Bakunin, Kropotkin too was a member of the Russian nobility. As a member of the Corps of Pages, he was one of a very select few whose prospects for personal advancement were gold-plated. As a Sergeant in the Corps, he was for a year the personal page of the new Tsar Alexander II. A number of things drew him away from a military career, among them, his nascent liberal tendencies, which weren't lessened by the idiocies of military life, but, perhaps most significantly, a growing passion for the sciences. Kropotkin's liberal and scientific ambitions prompted him to apply for a commission in a regiment stationed in Russia's Wild East, Siberia. Unlike Bakunin, Kropotkin arrived in Siberia by his own choice and as a free man. One of his responsibilities was to inspect the penal system in operation there. His experience of the brutalities of this system was to shake his faith in the wisdom of the state and put him on the road that would eventually take him to anarchism. Kropotkin's scientific energies found expression in his geographic work, an exploration of the Siberian highlands, and the subsequent account of the glacial age and the desiccation of East Asia.

While in Siberia, Kropotkin made the acquaintance of the poet M. L. Mikhailov, who introduced him to the writings of Proudhon. Having read Proudhon's *Economic Contradictions*, Kropotkin came to regard himself as a socialist. In 1866, he resigned his commission and returned to St Petersburg to begin the life of an academic. After some years, his expertise as a geographer attracted the attention of the Russian Geographical Society which offered him a secretaryship. At this point, Kropotkin's liberal and scientific impulses came into conflict. He declined the offer of the secretaryship, believing that he had no right to indulge his academic interests while so many people were without the basic necessaries of life.

As many Russians before and after him have done, Kropotkin decided to travel to the West. He settled for a time in Zurich and became part of the large Russian colony there, reading widely and deeply in socialist and revolutionary literature. From Zurich he went to Geneva where he made the acquaintance of Nicolai Zhukovsky, an associate of Bakunin and an advocate of populist agitation. Exciting as all this theoretical exploration was to him, Kropotkin felt the need for some practical experience of the working class so, on Zhukovsky's recommendation, he went to live among the people of the Jura. Here, he found the practical exemplification of all the theoretical material he had been reading about, which brought about in him what can only be described as a conversion experience. He wrote: 'The theoretical aspects of anarchism as they were then beginning to be expressed in the Jura Federation, especially Bakúnin; the criticism of state socialism—the fear of an economic despotism, far more dangerous than the merely political despotism—which I hear formulated there; and the revolutionary character of the agitation, appealed strongly to my mind. But the equalitarian relations which I found in the Jura Mountains; the independence of thought and expression which I saw developing in the workers, and their unlimited devotion to the cause appealed even more strongly to my feelings; and when I came away from the mountains, after a week's stay with the watchmakers, my views upon socialism were settled; I was an anarchist.' [Kropotkin 1899b, 267]

KROPOTKIN, THE EARLY ANARCHIST YEARS

Kropotkin returned to St Petersburg as an apostle of anarchism, there to join the not-particularly anarchist Chaikovsky Circle but, more importantly, to begin what would be a long and prolific literary career. His thought at this time seems to have been a mixture of elements from Proudhon and Bakunin with a slight bias in favour of the latter. As a member of the Chaikovsky Circle, he engaged in propaganda work for which he arrested and imprisoned in the Peter-and-Paul fortress in 1874. Two years later he escaped from the St Petersburg military hospital, travelling first to England and then back to Switzerland. 'In Kropotkin's incomparable account in his memoirs,' writes Marshall Shatz, 'the meticulously organized plot had all the ingredients of a spy-thriller: safe houses, a coded message hidden in a watch, a heart-stopping getaway through the streets of the capital.'[20]

Around this time, his understanding of what anarchism was began to develop. He wrote, 'I gradually came to realize that anarchism represents more than a mere mode of action and a mere conception of a free society; that it is a part of a philosophy, natural and social, which must be developed in a quite different way from the metaphysical or dialectic methods which have been employed in sciences dealing with man. I saw that it must be treated by the same methods as natural science…' [Kropotkin 1899b, 403]

Though never a card-carrying agitator in the manner of Bakunin, Kropotkin was at this time still attracted to practical organisation so that his writings were only a part of his overall enterprise. Among the most significant of his publications was the production of the anarchist newspaper, *Le Révolté*, for which at the start he did most of the writing. 'Kropotkin's early articles in *Le Révolté* were concerned mostly with current issues, treated with an optimism that saw in every strike or bread riot a hopeful omen of the disintegration of the great national states which he saw as the particular enemies of peace and social justice.' [Woodcock, 185] Some of Kropotkin's books, including *The Conquest of Bread*, were made up in large part of articles written for *Le Révolté* and Kropotkin's later Parisian publication, *La Révolte*. His extensive writings in French and English in the 1880s were to be seminal, for all his thought and his later writings are, in effect, expansions and buttressing of his ideas of this period.

Kropotkin was rounded up in a general prosecution of anarchists in France in 1883 and he spent some time in the prison of Clairvault. In typical Kropotkin fashion, he spent this time in an extremely productive manner, writing articles, conducting classes for other inmates, and even working in the prison garden. After intense public pressure from some of the most important and distinguished men of the period, the French government eventually released him and in 1886 he returned to England, which was to be his home for the next thirty years. From this time on, influenced in no small way by his contact with the English socialist movement, he turned more and more to theoretical work and began to emphasise the evolutionary rather than the revolutionary elements in social change.

KROPOTKIN—*THE STATE* AND *MUTUAL AID*

The major works of this later period of Kropotkin's life were *The State* (1897) and *Mutual Aid* (1902). The latter work was perhaps influenced by his discovery of the writings of William Godwin. Kropotkin certainly elaborates on the Godwinian theme of universal benevolence but these ideas had been present in any event, even if embryonically, in *The Conquest of Bread*. In the writing of *Mutual Aid*, Kropotkin availed himself of the information about animal and human cooperation he had gained during his time in Siberia. Mutual aid, Kropotkin believes, is the norm rather than the exception among animal species, including man. A Darwinian struggle for existence isn't primarily an intra-human contest but a contest between human societies and nature. Man is and has always been ineluctably social, so much so that even when the coercive instrument of the state arose, human voluntary cooperation did not cease. Woodcock remarks that '*Mutual Aid* creates, of course, no departure in libertarian thought. It represent rather the classic statement of the idea common to most anarchists, that society is a natural phenomenon, existing anterior to the appearance of man, and that man is naturally adapted to observe its laws without the need for artificial regulations.' [Woodcock, 201]

Woodcock believes that Kropotkin, and indeed many other anarchists, are insufficiently sensitive to the liberty-restricting activities of social groups other than the state. 'A taboo-ridden native of the primitive Congo,' writes Woodcock, 'had in reality far less freedom of action than a citizen of the England in which Kropotkin himself lived with such slight interference. A stateless society, in other words, may be very far from a free society so far as the personal lives of its members are concerned.' [Woodcock, 202] It is true that the state isn't the only enemy of liberty, and it is also true that social pressures to conform can be immense. But to repeat a point made earlier, there is a difference in kind between conformity induced by violence or the threat of violence and conformity induced by other means. It could be put to Woodcock that he, as a Millean, is over-sensitive to the liberty-restricting aspects of social pressure. Mill is acutely aware of the lateral social pressures to conform—this is a very large theme in his *On Liberty*—but is overly sanguine when it comes to the deleterious effects of government on liberty.

Kropotkin and Anarcho-Communism

It could be asked, what, if anything, is significantly different about Kropotkin's form of anarchism as compared to that of Proudhon or Bakunin? Kropotkin diverges from both when it comes to the issue of access to goods and services. For both Bakunin and Proudhon, though in slightly different ways, the distribution of goods and services is to be directly related to a worker's contribution. For Kropotkin, however, all this is a remnant of a wage system, and a wage system he takes to be just another form of compulsion that has no place in a free society. Kropotkin asks, 'How, then, shall we estimate the share of each in the riches which all contribute to amass? Looking at production from this general, synthetic point of view, we cannot hold with the collectivists that payment proportionate to the hours of labour rendered by each would be an ideal arrangement, or even a step in the right direction.' [Kropotkin 1892, 32] Access to goods and services is to be based on need, not on the specific contributions of any one person or group. 'Anarchist communism called for the socialization not only of production but of the distribution of goods,' writes Marshall Shatz, 'the community would supply the subsistence requirements of each individual free of charge, and the criterion "to each according to his labour" would be superseded by the criterion "to each according to his needs".'[21]

This, of course, is a form of communism.[22] Kropotkin didn't invent communism but he certainly popularised it. Even in Kropotkin's time, the idea wasn't new, and had found expression in many earlier thinkers. 'The feature that distinguishes anarchist communism from other libertarian doctrines is the idea of free distribution, which is older than anarchism itself,' writes Woodcock. 'Sir Thomas More advocated it in the sixteenth and Winstanley in the seventeenth century; it was a feature of Campanella's City of the Sun, and even in the phalansteries[23] imagined by Fourier the rare individuals who couldn't be charmed into finding work attractive would still have their right as human beings to receive the means of living from the community.' [Woodcock, 188]

As with all forms of anarchism, anarcho-communism rejects the state, arguing that it is in no way coincident with society. Kropotkin remarks, 'Men lived thousands of years before the first States were constituted...for us modern Europeans the centralized States date but from the sixteenth century.'[24] He goes on to say, 'But ours is neither the communism of Fourier and the phalansterians, nor of the German state socialists. It is anarchist communism, communism without government—the communism of the free. It is the synthesis of the two ideals pursued by humanity throughout the ages—economic and political liberty.' [Kropotkin 1892, 35-36] He remarks, 'It is above all over the question of the State that socialists are divided....There are those, on the one hand, who hope to achieve the social revolution through the State by preserving and even extending most of its powers to be used for the revolution. And there are those like ourselves who see the State, both in its present form, in its very essence, and in whatever guise it might appear, as an obstacle to the social revolution, the greatest hindrance to the birth of a society based on equality and liberty....' [Kropotkin 1897, 9]

State and government mustn't be confused. 'State and government are two concepts of a different order. The State idea means something quite different from the idea of government. It not only includes the existence of a power situated above society, but also of a territorial concentration as well as the concentration in the hands of a few of many functions in the life of societies. It implies some new relationship between members of society that did not exist before the formation of the State. A whole mechanism of legislation and of policing has to be developed in order to subject some classes to the domination of others.' [Kropotkin 1897, 10] Nor must the state be confused with society. 'Man lived in Societies for thousands of years before the State had been heard of...so far as Europe is concerned the State is of recent origin—it barely goes back to the sixteenth century...' [Kropotkin 1897, 10] 'Man,' Kropotkin says, 'did not create society; society existed before Man. We now also know...that the point of departure for mankind was not the family but the clan, the tribe.' [Kropotkin 1897, 12] Society is based on a certain elemental human solidarity. *Mutual Aid* is an extended illustration of Kropotkin's belief that 'it is not love and not even sympathy upon which Society is based in mankind. It is the conscience [consciousness]—be it only at the stage of an instinct—of human solidarity.' [Kropotkin 1902a, xvi] This is what Kropotkin calls 'mutual aid'. Love and sympathy, and morality generally, are developments based upon this more primary instinct. In *Mutual Aid*, Kropotkin shows this principle working in animal societies, in what he calls savage and barbarian human societies, in the medieval city and, finally, among ourselves.

Anarcho-communism not only rejects the state, it also rejects private property and capitalism. Even more strikingly, it also rejects money and markets. As a form of communism, it favours the common ownership of the means of production but, again, as distinct from other forms of anarchism, it also favours common ownership of the products of labour as well. The reason for its rejection of the private ownership of the products of labour is logical if not particularly practical. Anarcho-communists argue that without such common ownership of the products of labour, it is likely that individuals will eventually accumulate capital, with the consequent reappearance of different and antagonistic social classes. Money and trade and markets are to be abolished: money, because it quantitatively and arbitrarily distinguishes between the value of one worker's output and another and, apart from the ever-present danger of capital accumulation, inhibits the qualitative distribution and consumption of goods; markets and trade, because (perhaps) of an implicit recognition that markets and trading invariably give rise to money but also because markets underpin the notion that consumption should be proportioned to deeds rather than needs.

Kropotkin is refreshingly direct in his comments on taxation. Taxation, he says, is 'an institution originating purely with the State—the formidable weapon used by the State, in Europe as in the young societies of the two Americas, to keep the masses under its heel, to favour its minions, to ruin the majority for the benefit of the rulers and to maintain the old divisions and castes.' [Kropotkin 1897, 54]

How is anarchism to be given practical effect? In some minds, anarchism is inextricably associated with violence, whether rightly or wrongly. Kropotkin's attitude towards violence was somewhat ambivalent. In his earlier years he was sympathetic to the need for violence but as he got older he disapproved of individual acts of terrorism and regarded assassinations as effectively useless and even demoralising. If not violence, then what? Cooperation, voluntary cooperation. At this point, the idea of the commune comes to the fore. Communes, associations of people with common interests will arise voluntarily, and the association of such associations will produce a form of overall cooperation that will replace the state. Communes will be responsible for the expropriation and collectivisation of the means of production. Kropotkin believed that the economy could be coordinated by a horizontal network of associations, membership of which would be voluntary. 'Railways were constructed piece by piece,' he remarks, 'the pieces were joined together, and the hundred different companies, to whom these pieces belonged, gradually came to an understanding concerning the arrival and departure of their trains.... All this was done by free agreement, by exchange of letters and proposals, and by congresses at which delegates met to discuss well-specified points, and to come to an agreement about them, but not to make laws....there is no European central government of railways!' [Kropotkin 1892, 117, 118]

Lying behind Kropotkin's thought is a key assumption—all things are for all. Everything of value in human life is the result of the collective contribution of all in which the specific contributions of individuals cannot be distinguished. What is made by all should be enjoyed by all. The means of production, he says, 'being the collective work of humanity, the product should be the collective property of the race. Individual appropriation is neither just nor serviceable. All belongs to all. All things are for all men, since all men have need of them, since all men have worked in the measure of their strength to produce them, and since it is not possible to evaluate everyone's part in the production of the world's wealth.' [Kropotkin 1892, 19] So, then, individual appropriation isn't permissible but neither is its polar opposite, state ownership. Voluntary cooperation is capable of supplying the necessary degree of organisation required for communal enterprises. As we have seen, Kropotkin points to the international postal union, among other forms of voluntary non-state arrangements, to illustrate the way in which such cooperation could function.

In the anarcho-communist society, there would be a form of property but it would be one based on and limited to immediate and necessary use. The farmer cultivating just enough land or the family living in a house with just enough space for them or the worker working with just enough tools—all these would be entitled to retain possession of those things they were using and nothing else for as long as and only for as long as they were using them; 'everyone, whatever his grade, in the old society, whether strong or weak, capable or incapable, has, before everything, *the right to live*, and…society is bound to share amongst all, without exception, the means of existence it has at its disposal.' [Kropotkin 1892, 28]

Organisation we must have if men are to flourish but the good of organisation isn't only or even best supplied by government. The kind of organisation conducive to human flourishing will arise when 'men at last attempt to free themselves from every form of government and to satisfy their need for organization by free contracts between individuals and groups pursuing the same aim. The independence of each small territorial unit becomes a pressing need; mutual agreement replaces law in order to regulate individual interests in view of a common object—very often disregarding the frontiers of the present states.' [Kropotkin 1892, 36] Distribution of the products of the economy would be based on need, not on the individual contributions of particular workers. The contributions of individuals would, in any case he thinks, be difficult if not impossible to discern, for anarcho-communists believe, a belief echoed by egalitarian thinkers before and since, that wealth is in the main a product of the collective contributions of our ancestors and our contemporaries. Everyone produces everything; everyone should share in everything. (Against this claim, a defender of private property might respond that whereas extant property is indeed the resultant of the efforts of many, they do not therefore have a claim on it if they have already been remunerated for their efforts.)

Kropotkin makes the point that the fundamental material needs of humanity could be provided for by a small amount of labour on the part of everyone. He has a delightfully romantic and unreal conception of what life would be like under anarcho-communism, not unlike the earlier ideas of William Godwin and Richard Owen. According to Kropotkin, five hours' work a day by those between the ages of twenty to fifty or thereabouts would be sufficient to provide enough for all. The accusation of being unrealistically utopian is often levelled against anarchists as a whole but, in the case of anarcho-communism, the accusation would seem not to be without merit, although Kropotkin was swift to reject it: 'Far from living in a world of visions and imagining men better than they are, we see them as they are; and that is why we affirm that the best of men is made essentially bad by the exercise of authority.' [Kropotkin 1896, in Graham 2005, 144] After the necessary work has been done, all time and effort could be dedicated to the development of the spirit.

What of the objection that in an anarchist society based on need, some will inevitably free ride on the efforts of others? Kropotkin concedes that some people may behave in this way but he is confident that the majority of people will naturally behave socially since man is by nature social. But what of the idlers and malingerers? Are they to be allowed to sponge off others? How can they be prevented from so doing if there is no coercive authority to prevent them?

Here, Kropotkin has recourse to the idea of lateral social pressure and, if necessary, ostracism. He writes, 'if you are absolutely incapable of producing anything useful, or if you refuse to do it then live like an isolate man or like an invalid....You are a man and you have the right to live. But as you wish to live under special conditions, and leave the ranks, it is more than probable that you will suffer for it in your daily relations with other citizens. You will be looked upon as a ghost of bourgeois society, unless some friends of yours, discovering you to be a talent, kindly free you from all moral obligation towards society by doing all the necessary work for you. And finally, if it does not please you, go and look for other conditions elsewhere in the wide world, or else seek adherents and organize with them on novel principles.' [Kropotkin 19892, 139]

George Woodcock is disturbed by this idea of lateral social pressure and seems to think it irreconcilable with the principles of anarchism. He remarks, 'A free society where the outsiders, those who are not 'in the ranks', are subjected to the moral condemnation of their neighbours may seem self-contradictory.' 'Yet Godwin propounded the same idea a hundred years before Kropotkin, and it is not out of keeping with the strain of puritanism which disturbingly recurs throughout the libertarian tradition; like all theoretical extremists, the anarchist suffers acutely from the temptations of self-righteousness.' [Woodcock, 193] Woodcock's Millean disquiet isn't completely wrongheaded. Certainly, as Mill recognised, there can be a form of non-violent social pressure, characteristic of, though not confined to, small communities. But the non-violent nature of such pressure is vitally important. If you are willing to maintain your idiosyncratic and asocial proclivities, then do so. No one will physically harm you. But no one is required to associate with you or deal with you, and if they choose not to do so then that's their prerogative. Moreover, Woodcock's characterisation of such lateral pressure as a form of puritanism isn't necessarily justified. In a liberal anarchist society, it might well be the puritan who is the one who is pressured into conformity or flight.

Late in life, Kropotkin wrote the entry on 'Anarchism' for *The Encyclopaedia Britannica* (1910) In this piece, he presents anarchism as a form of left-wing socialism, writing, 'As to their economical conceptions, the anarchists, in common with all socialists, of whom they constitute the left wing, maintain that the now prevailing system of private ownership in land, and our capitalist production for the sake of profits, represent a monopoly which runs against both

the principles of justice and the dictates of utility.' [Kropotkin 1910, 234-235]
He denies any possibility of self-reform by the state. 'The state organization,
having always been....the instrument for establishing monopolies in favour
of the ruling minorities, cannot be made to work for the destruction of those
monopolies.' [Kropotkin 1910, 235]

He is aware of the wider anarchist family. He was one of the first to give
Godwin his due as a precursor of anarchism. 'It was Godwin,' he writes,
'who was the first to formulate the political and economical conceptions of
anarchism, even though he did not give that name to the ideas developed in
his remarkable work.' [Kropotkin 1910, 238] Stirner, too, is recognised for
his contributions: 'individualist anarchy found...its fullest expression in Max
Stirner....Stirner...advocated not only a complete revolt against the state and
against the servitude which authoritarian communism would impose upon
men, but also the full liberation of the individual from all social and moral
bonds—the rehabilitation of the 'I', the supremacy of the individual, complete
"amoralism" and the "association of the egotists".' [Kropotkin 1910, 240-241]
Kropotkin's comments on Proudhon extend beyond a consideration of the
Frenchman himself to a consideration, brief but notable, of some anglophone
contributors to anarchism. 'The ideas of Proudhon,' he says, 'found quite a
considerable following in the United States, creating a school of thought, of
which the main writers are Stephen Pearl Andrews, William Grene, Lysander
Spooner....A prominent position among the individualist anarchists in America
has been occupied by Benjamin R. Tucker, whose journal *Liberty* was started
in 1881 and whose conceptions are a combination of those of Proudhon with
those of Herbert Spencer.' [Kropotkin 1910, 243-244]

IV: ANARCHO-SYNDICALISM

Anarcho-syndicalism is opposed both to capitalism and to what it regards as
the capitalist state. Whereas the anarcho-communists put their faith in unspecified voluntary associations, the anarcho-syndicalists find their operative
organisations ready to hand in the form of trade unions. The Kropotkinian idyll
re-emerges in the claim by some anarcho-syndicalists that the needs of all can
be met without requiring from the workers more than a few hours' work per
day. The 'Pittsburgh Proclamation', in which this claim is made, goes on to
call for the 'destruction of the existing class rule...by...energetic, relentless,
revolutionary and international action,' the cooperative organisation of production, exchange between cooperative units without commerce or profit and 'the
regulation of all public affairs by free contracts between the autonomous...
communes and associations.'[25]

According to Emma Goldman, syndicalism 'has grown out of the disappointment of the workers with politics and parliamentary methods,' as a
result of which it has 'turned its back upon parliamentarianism and political
machines, and has set its face toward the economic arena wherein a lone
gladiator Labour can meet his foe successfully.'[26] Whereas for anarcho-
communists and anarcho-collectivists, the means of production belong to all, for

the anarcho-syndicalists the means of production in a particular industry, once appropriated from the capitalists, would belong to those who work in that industry; the workers' control of the means of production is thereby particularised and limited by industry. Ironically, the workers as the now-owners of the industry must make what are essentially entrepreneurial decisions, the decisions formerly made by the capitalists; what to manufacture and what to cease manufacturing, what plant and machinery to employ, whether to expand or contract and so on.

A further dilemma arises in relation to the disposability of a given worker's share in the industry. If workers aren't allowed to dispose of their quotal shares, then those who prevent them from so doing are in reality the real owners of the industry; if they *are* allowed to dispose of their shares, then it seems impossible in principle to prevent a re-emergence of the distinction between owner and worker the obliteration of which was the very point of syndicalism.[27]

I think it's reasonably clear from the foregoing that all these forms of left-anarchism are unanimous in their rejection of the coercive state but also, to different degrees, either suspicious or completely dismissive of the idea of the private ownership of external goods, deeming such ownership to be restrictive of human liberty. It also appears that, at the root of the left-libertarian position (which we find today in the work of Peter Vallentyne, Michael Otsuka and others) is the belief that natural resources belong to everyone in some *a priori* egalitarian manner so that robust ownership of them by individuals (such as, for example, ownership without positive obligations to others) is unjustified.[28] For the left-libertarians, this rejection of the robust ownership of natural resources requires their *de jure* owners to pay a rent or tax as a matter of justice to those who are excluded from their possession. This rent or tax would have to be paid to and distributed by some agency which, for these purposes at least, would constitute a *de facto* state inasmuch as it would have to have the power to compel the payment of the rent or tax. Insofar as there appears to be an argument for the left-anarchist and left-libertarian approach to the ownership of external resources, it seems to depend on the claim that since natural resources aren't created by any human being, we have no reason to believe that the original appropriators of any portion of land are entitled to all its benefits. In contrast, libertarian anarchism regards the robust ownership of external resources as an intrinsic element in human liberty.

Notes

1   For an accessible and evenhanded treatment of Proudhon's merits and failings, see Kolakowski, 203-211.

2   See Scott 1985, 1998, and 2009, passim.

3   Proudhon 1840 [1994], 205.

4   Before he died, Proudhon seems to have modified his opposition to the state somewhat, conceding the legitimacy of a form of decentralized form of federal government. See Proudhon 1863/5 in Graham 2005, 72-74.

5   Georgists are followers of the American economist and philosopher Henry George (1839-1887) who, in a series of seminal (and in their time, immensely influential) works, explored the thesis that the economic value which derived from land should belong equally to all members of a community but,

that being granted, people own the value that they create themselves. See George 1879, 1884 and 1898.

6 A letter from Engels to Marx, 21 August 1851, in Anon. 1972, 41.

7 A letter from Marx to L. Kugelmann, 9 October 1866, in Anon. 1972, 45.

8 Kolpinsky, 16, 17, 19. For Engels account of the ideological struggle in the International, see his letter to C. Cariero, 1-3 July 1871, in Anon. 1972, 49-52; for Marx's account, see his letter to F. Bolte, 23 November 1871, in Anon. 1972, 57-59.

9 From 'On the Occasion of Karl Marx's Death,' published in *Der Sozialdemokrat*, no. 21, 17 May 1883, in Anon. 1972, 173.

10 In a letter from Engels to T. Cuno, 24 January 1872, in Anon. 1972, 71-72.

11 'Marx and Bakunin were engaged in a conflict in which it is hard to distinguish political from personal animosities,' writes Kolakowski, concluding, 'Politics apart, the history of Marx's relations with Bakunin does not show the former in a favourable light. His charge that Bakunin was using the International for personal advantage was groundless, and his efforts to have Bakunin expelled were finally successful (in 1872) thanks in the main to the Nechayev letter, for which Marx must have known that Bakunin bore no responsibility.' [Kolakowski, 247, 248]

12 Max Eastman remarks, 'Nechayev was denounced even by his sufficiently violent colleague, the anarchist Bakunin, as a dangerous fanatic, who "when it is necessary to render some service to what he calls 'the cause'...stops at nothing—deceit, robbery, even murder." But Lenin startled his early friends by defending this madman and honoring his memory.' [Eastman, 86]

13 Engels write, '...Finally, came Stirner, the prophet of contemporary anarchism—Bakunin has taken a great deal from him....Stirner remained a curiosity, even after Bakunin blended him with Proudhon and labelled the blend "anarchism"...' [Engels, in *Die Neue Zeit* Nos. 4 & 5, 1886, in Anon. 1972, 175]

14 Graham 2005, 81; italics in original.

15 Graham 2005, 83. Italics in original.

16 For a brief historical treatment of the Tsarist Russia common to both Bakunin and Kropotkin, see Droz, 181-189.

17 Bakunin 1869, in Graham 2005, 87.

18 Osterfeld, in Stringham 2007, 509.

19 For an accessible and evenhanded treatment of Bakunin's merits and failings, see Kolakowski, 246-256.

20 Shatz, in Kropotkin 1892, xiii.

21 Shatz in Kropotkin 1892, xvi.

22 Anarchism and socialism are solidly linked in the public mind but, as James Buchanan notes, 'Socialist organization...must be and can only be antithetic to anarchy, despite the surprising linkage of these two contradictory organizational norms in much of romantic literature.' [Buchanan 2000, 24] For a pithy demolition of the intellectual pretensions of anarcho-communism, see Rothbard 2000b.

23 A phalanstery can be imagined as a kind of proto-kibbutz. For Fourier, it was the basic unit of social organisation, about a square mile in size, with common buildings such as schools, dining halls, and some private dwellings, with a population of around 2,000 people. A phalanstery would, according to Fourier, strike a balance between the demands of society and the needs of the individual. For a brief account of Fourier's life and work, see Kolakowski, 198-203.

24 Kropotkin 1896, in Graham 2005, 142.

25 From 'The Pittsburgh Proclamation,' in Graham 2005, 192-93.

26 Goldman 1913, in Graham 2005, 203.

27 See Osterfeld 1983, in Stringham 2007, 510-11.

28 See Vallentyne 2010 and Otsuka 2003.

Chapter 30

THE ANGLOPHONE ANARCHISTS: WARREN, SPOONER, TUCKER AND HERBERT

Representative government is artifice, a political myth,
designed to conceal from the masses the dominance of a self-selected,
self-perpetuating, and self-serving traditional ruling class
—Giuseppe Prezzolini

Political language…is designed to make lies sound truthful
and murder respectable
—George Orwell

Proudhon, Bakunin and Kropotkin have one thing in common apart from their anarchism. For none of them is English his first language. It might appear that the anarchist tradition is strictly non-anglophone but this isn't so. England and the USA produced their own variety of anarchists, the American thinkers being better known than the English. Benjamin Tucker is by far the most prominent of the anglophone anarchists though he was by no means the only one nor was he the first. In fact, the elements of his anarchism were bequeathed to him by the much older, and possibly first, American anarchist, Josiah Warren and Tucker's work was, to a great extent, a systematic development of Warren's ideas. [see Riggenbach 2011a] Tucker expressly dedicates his *Instead of a Book* 'To the Memory of My Old Friend and Master Josiah Warren Whose Teachings were My First Source of Light.'[1] Lysander Spooner is yet another native American product with his own perspective on political matters. Auberon Herbert is an English (not just English-speaking) anarchist who, while one of the most significant anarchistic writers of all is, at the same time, perhaps one of the most neglected. [see Doherty, 37-52]

I: JOSIAH WARREN

Josiah Warren (1798-1874) was a jack-of-all-trades—inventor, musician, author—and largely an autodidact, with all the advantages and disadvantages that autodidacticism usually brings in its train. Crispin Sartwell says of him that he was 'both a genius and a crank of nearly the first order' and it is hard to disagree with this assessment.[2] Marrying at an early age, he and his family were members of the New Harmony socialist community established by Robert Owen.[3] Inspired rather than discouraged by the failure[4] of the New Harmony project, Warren went on to establish several communities of his own: the aptly (or otherwise) named *Utopia* in 1847, and the prophetically named *Modern*

Times in 1851. Sartwell notes that his experience in New Harmony 'was central to Warren's life and thought, and many of his ideas can be seen as attempts to understand and correct the failures of that community while retaining the energy and idealism that first drew him there.' [Sartwell 2011, 21] Although Benjamin Tucker's *Liberty* rightly takes pride of place as the most significant and influential individualist anarchist publishing venture, it was preceded by some 50 years by Warren's The *Peaceful Revolutionist*, admittedly far less successful or influential but still not without significance.

WARREN THE EXTREME INDIVIDUALIST

Philosophically, Josiah Warren is an extreme individualist, almost a nominalist. He holds that ultimately only individuals are real. His thinking is centred on a few basic principles, the most important of them, from the point of view of liberty, being individualism and self-sovereignty. Warren's individualism is radical and extends not only to politics but also to metaphysics and episte-mology.[5] For Warren, what exists are individuals and only individuals. Anything else is a collection, composite or mixture of individuals. No two individuals are alike or interchangeable and no individual remains the same over time. 'Not only are no two minds alike now, but no one remains the same from one hour to another.' [Warren 2011, 65] Warren is a radical individualist in the mould of Stirner but, like Godwin, he is also an environmental determinist. In a manner that anticipates certain aspects of Marx's thought, Warren believes that what we are is a dynamic intersection of environmental influences. If taken to its logical conclusion, this account of the individual would lead to its dissolution into its constituent parts and those parts, in turn, into—well, who knows? The position is hardly coherent.

Warren's individualism affects not only his understanding of the nature of reality but also his understanding of language. Language—and our knowledge is inextricably connected with language—makes use of concepts and concepts are ineluctably general. That being so, language inevitably distorts the reality it is supposed to describe and represent.[6] Applying all this to politics, Warren sees its basic problem as the perpetual attempt to subordinate the individual to the group. Politics 'necessarily de-individualizes its subjects, treating them en masse or in classes.' [Sartwell 2011, 7] Every piece of writing, constitutions included, however it may be produced, can be understood only by individuals and by each individual only in his own way. 'Words are the principal means of our intellectual intercourse, and they form the basis of all our institutions; but here again this subtle individuality sets at nought the profoundest thoughts and the most careful phraseology. There is no certainty of any written laws, or rules, or institutions, or verbal precepts being understood in the same manner by any number of persons.' [Warren 2011, 58] It follows from this that the idea that a constitution can regulate and order a society is chimerical. 'A creed, a constitution, laws, articles of association, are all liable to as many different interpretations as there are parties to it; each reads it through his own mental spectacles, and that which is blue to one is yellow to another, and green to a third although all give their assent to the words, each one gives assent to his peculiar interpretation of them, which is only known to himself, so that the difference between them can be made to appear only in action; which, as soon as it commences, explodes the discordant elements in every direction, always disappointing the expectation of all who had calculated on uniformity or conformity.' [Warren 2011, 75-76] Sartwell comments, 'To freeze a dynamic social order into a document is mere folly: you simply launch into the interminable, and in principle insoluble, process of interpretation.' [Sartwell 2011, 7] The apparent social stability provided by law is an illusion. Laws are expressed in words and words are infinitely interpretable. That being so, it is 'individuals rather than laws that govern....there is no security in laws. We must seek it elsewhere.'[7]

Taken to an extreme, Warren's individualism is self-stultifying. The very notion of individuality is itself conceptual and universal: it is simply not possible to talk about anything except at the simplest level (and possibly not even here) without making use of universal concepts. Sartwell makes this point well: 'As soon as Warren starts founding disciplines and capturing in a term ("individuality") the essence of the universe, or the basis of all justice and social arrangements ("self-sovereignty"), he is doing what the discipline he invented demands he not do.' [Sartwell 2011, 9] The consistent anti-universalist must either simply assert the anti-universalist thesis or demonstrate it by means of some argument. The simple assertion of the anti-universalist thesis carries no weight for what is simply asserted can simply be denied. It follows, then, that the anti-universalist must demonstrate the anti-universalist thesis by means of argument. But if an argument for the anti-universalist thesis is to be other than accidentally persuasive, it must be valid, and an argument is valid if and only if it exhibits the property of valid implication, that is, if and only if it is a token of the universal type 'valid implication'. Thus, in order to prove the anti-universalist thesis, the anti-universalist would be forced to make covert use of universalism. Hence, the anti-universalist is caught in an existential contradiction, a contradiction between the content of what is being asserted by the anti-universalist in asserting the anti-universalist thesis and what the anti-universalist is implicitly committed to in making that assertion. Warren, then, has a point but he takes it too far. If we were to take him literally, we should have to stop reading what he himself has written for it is a presupposition of reading a document that some form of commonality of judgement is possible, minimally, between the author and at least one (ideal) reader. Nevertheless, Warren is correct in his scepticism of the value of constitutions as instruments of legal or political stability. In the end, a written document means only what its authorised interpreters say it means, whatever the intentions of its authors might have been, supposing those to exist and to be ascertainable.

The idea of a Rousseauean General Will is anathema to Warren. 'Good thinkers never committed a more fatal mistake than in expecting harmony from an attempt to overcome individuality, and in trying to make a state or nation an individual. The individuality of each person is perfectly indestructible. A state or nation is a multitude of indestructible individualities and cannot, by any possibility, be converted into anything else.' [Warren 2011, 62] For Warren, the sovereignty of the individual must always be respected. No one may be compelled to do or to refrain from doing something even where the compulsion is well intended. Warren takes the typical political philosopher—Hegel, Marx or Rousseau—to be engaged in a Procrustean attempt to eradicate a messy and indigestible subjectivity from the world so that his neat and orderly scheme can find application without being disturbed by the exigencies of individuality, much like the bus driver who, when told that several of his would-be passengers had complained that he wasn't stopping to pick them up, replied, 'I can't stop—it ruins the schedule!'

So, we have individuals. Now what? A consequence of being an individual, for Warren, is that each person, each individual, is entitled to full control of himself, his body, and his actions. If it is going to be difficult to reconcile self-sovereignty with any notion of coercive government, so much the worse for coercive government. Warren is of the opinion that the leading idea in all forms of political association has been to submerge the individual in the group whereas what is in fact required for the harmonious adjustment of society is precisely the contrary—the raising of the individual above the group. He writes, 'in all forms of organized society, the first and great leading idea was and is to sink the individual in the state or body politic, when nothing short of the very opposite, which is, raising every individual above the state, above institutions, above systems, above man-made laws, will enable society to take the first successful step toward its harmonious adjustment.' [Warren 2011, 63; see 104]

Warren on the State

It hardly needs to be said that Warren has a less than elevated opinion of the nature and function of the state. The state, we are told, exists to secure our persons and our property but its record in providing this security is less than stellar. Rather than improving the human condition, states worsen it. Claiming to secure person and property, Warren writes, states 'have spread wholesale destruction, famine, and wretchedness in every frightful form over all parts of the earth, where peace and security might otherwise have prevailed. They have shed more blood, committed more murders, tortures, and other frightful crimes in the struggles against each other for the privilege of governing, than society would or could have suffered in the total absence of all government whatever.'[8] It should be remembered that this passage was written in the early nineteenth century—what would Warren have written had he had our experience of the supremely sanguinary twentieth century? Even when not engaged in slaughter, governments interfere in our everyday lives in a multitude of ways. They 'invade the private household' and 'impertinently meddle with, and in their blind and besotted wantonness, presume to regulate the most sacred individual feelings.' [Warren 2011, 73]

Unlike Stirner, Warren isn't opposed to an individual's associating with others—and we may remember that even Stirner contemplated the bizarre possibility of a union of egotists. What is important to Warren isn't whether individuals do or do not associate with one another but whether such associating is voluntary. We not only do not compromise our liberty but, on the contrary, we exercise it when we associate with others in pursuance of a common goal. 'No subordination can be more perfect than that of an orchestra, but it is all voluntary.'[9] In cooperative ventures, our liberty isn't compromised if 'each one is the supreme judge at all times of the individual case in hand, and is free to act from his own estimate of the advantages to be derived to himself or others.' But if 'the decision or will or others is made the rule of action, contrary to his views or inclination' then a person's legitimate liberty is violated.[10]

At one point, Warren comes very close to enunciating the principle of zero-aggression. He is considering whether there can be any proper function for government and he writes, 'The whole proper business of government is restraining offensive encroachments, or unnecessary violence to persons and property, or enforcing compensation therefore; but if, in the exercise of this power, we commit any unnecessary violence to any person whatever or to any property, we, ourselves, have become the aggressors, and should be resisted.' [Warren 2011, 144] A latter-day libertarian anarchist would find little to disagree with in this except to recognise the right to resist or restrain aggression as a right that belongs to all and not simply to some designated body.

If an act is aggressive then it may rightfully be resisted. But when is an act aggressive? Sometimes we have no difficulty in telling whether it is or it isn't; on other occasions, however, we simply aren't sure. The same problem can arise in respect of trespass against property. What constitutes a trespass is sometimes clear, sometimes not. Clear and distinct property titles are perhaps the best way to avoid unnecessary disputes but sometimes even with well-drawn boundaries disputes can neither be avoided nor easily resolved.[11]

On economic matters, Warren accepted the orthodoxies of his day, among them, although in a convoluted way, what in effect amounted to the labour theory of value. This led him, as it did Marx, into an intellectual morass when it came to dealing with money, interest, credit and exchange, a morass from which he was unable to extricate himself. Given that all his significant writing was done long before the theory of marginal utility was clearly formulated, Warren's economic perplexities are both understandable and excusable. (The same, however, can't be said for the economic theories of Benjamin Tucker.) Warren's contribution to the case of individualistic anarchism was important not only because of its intrinsic merits but also because it founded a native American strain of anarchistic thought that permitted the European imports to be both more easily assimilated but also to be modified to suit the American genius.

II: LYSANDER SPOONER

Lysander Spooner (1808-1887) was a thinker who rivalled Josiah Warren in originality and excelled him in logical acumen and clarity of expression. A lawyer by training and by instinct, he was a master not only of logic but also of rhetoric. This combination of logical rigour with rhetorical invective is truly stimulating, even today, some hundred and fifty years after he wrote.

SPOONER ON JUSTICE AND RIGHTS

Spooner has a simple theory of justice. It is essentially a version of the classic conception of justice as rendering to others what is their due. What, then, are the elements of justice for Spooner? Negatively, as one might expect, justice enjoins us not to steal from another or to rob another or otherwise to interfere with another's property. Likewise, one may not, in justice, initiate the assault or the homicide of another. Are these the sum total of our just obligations? No. There may be some positive ones, but these, as will be seen, all depend on prior voluntary commitments. We can't acquire them without doing something. So, for example, we have an obligation to pay our debts, and to return borrowed property and to make reparations for injury. Of course, if we haven't contracted any debts or borrowed any property or caused any injury to another, then we have no positive obligations to discharge in justice. Spooner remarks, 'So long as these conditions are fulfilled, men are at peace and ought to remain at peace, with each other.' [Spooner 1992, 11] Of course, human life isn't only a matter of justice. We may believe that we have obligations that go beyond justice, obligations to relieve the distress of others, to feed the hungry and to clothe the naked. But, Spooner contends, such obligations are *moral* obligations, not obligations of justice and so aren't amenable to any form of physical compulsion. We may be compelled by force, if necessary, to do our legal duties, that is, duties in justice, but although others may attempt to persuade us to fulfil our moral obligations, they may not justifiably use force to achieve their ends.

A man may choose to pursue his just deserts by himself or, if he so chooses, to associate with or to employ others for that purpose. He may not, however, be forced to accept another's assistance if he does not desire to do so. Spooner writes, 'such associations can be rightful and desirable only in so far as they are purely voluntary. No man can rightfully be coerced into joining one, or supporting one, against his will....If he chooses to depend, for the protection of his own rights, solely upon himself, and upon such voluntary assistance as other persons may freely offer to him when the necessity for it arise, he has a perfect right to do so.' [Spooner 1992, 13] Expressing what will become a standard theme in libertarian literature, Spooner makes the point that there is no principled difference between various forms of association for mutual assistance. 'An association for mutual protection against injustice is like an association for mutual protection against fire or shipwreck. And there is no more right or reason in compelling any man to join or support one of these associations, against his will, his judgment, or his conscience, than there is in compelling him to join or support any other, whose benefits (if it offer any) he does not want, or whose purposes or methods he does not approve.' [Spooner 1992, 13]

The basic principles of natural law and natural justice, are, Spooner thinks, easily known, so easily known that children acquire them without difficulty. Human beings come to know this natural law 'long before they have learned the meanings of the words by which we describe it.' [Spooner 1992, 15] Natural law and natural justice are implicit in human practice before ever they are reflectively appropriated in thought. Unless there be such a thing as natural justice and unless it exists by nature and not merely by convention, there can be no crime. Absent natural justice and what appear to be crimes are merely a particular set of natural events in the world like the falling of the rain or the sighing of the breeze. Conversely, if we recognise some actions as criminal, then this way of understanding them is either purely conventional and subject to arbitrary, sometimes radical, alteration, or these actions are always and every-where a violation of some natural principle of justice. The rights corresponding to justice—the right not to be assaulted or to be robbed or to be murdered—belong to man simply as man. They can't be given to a man or taken from him, nor can he give them away; they are imprescriptible and inalienable. Laws that are the product of a legislature either give effect to natural justice (in either its positive or negative form) or they do not. If they do, that's well and good; if not, it is 'an assumption of authority and dominion, where no right of authority or dominion exists. It is, therefore, simply and always an intrusion, an absurdity, an usurpation, and a crime.' [Spooner 1992, 18]

If natural justice is easily known, universal, and the rights associated with it inalienable and imprescriptible, what need have we of legislation? The short answer is, none. Nevertheless, legislation we have, and in abundance. Why? Spooner's answer is simple and stark. Whenever society has advanced so that it produces more than the mere means of subsistence, some group of people 'have associated and organized themselves as robbers, to plunder and enslave all others, who had either accumulated any property that could be seized, or had shown by their labor, that they could be made to contribute to the support or pleasure of those who should enslave them.' [Spooner 1992, 20-21] This theft and enslavement was institutionalised in the form of governments and enforced by the making of laws. The laws thus made by these bands of robbers have 'no more real obligation than have the agreements which brigands, bandits, and pirates find it necessary to enter into with each other, for the more successful accomplishment of their crimes, and the more peaceable division of their spoils.' [Spooner 1992, 22] Legislation, then, is the means by which the few hold the many in a state of subjection and have done so ever since states came into being.

SPOONER ON LAW AND MORALITY

Spooner's distinction between the realm of *law*, which deals with crime, and the realm of *morality*, which concerns itself with virtues and vices, is the subject of a treatise, entitled, not surprisingly, 'Vices are not Crimes'. [see Spooner 1992, 25-52] 'Vices,' Spooner says, 'are those acts by which a man harms himself or his property. *Crimes* are those acts by which one man harms the person or property of another.' [Spooner 1992, 25] For Spooner, and for libertarians generally, it is vitally important to make and maintain this distinc-tion. To treat vices as crimes and to punish them accordingly is to infringe the vicious person's rights, property or liberty. If all vices were punished as crimes then everyone would be in prison with no one outside to lock the prison door. If, on the other hand, only some vices are treated as crimes, what will serve as the basis for such an arbitrary distinction? Will the members of a legislature pass laws against the vices of others while ignoring their own? Suitably authorised agencies have the right to punish crimes because they are the delegates of individuals who also have that right. But as no individual has the right to punish the vices of another, so no group can have that right delegated to them.

SPOONER ON GOVERNMENT AND CONSENT

Against Spooner's position that governments are merely robbers who have acquired a veneer of respectability, it may be argued that they are legitimate inasmuch as their authority rests on the consent of the governed. In response, Spooner would argue that the authority of a government can't be simply a matter of numbers, otherwise any group of people x+delta could claim to govern any group of people of size x. I can't lawfully dispose of your property or person and I still couldn't do so lawfully even if all those who lived in my community agreed with my attempted disposition but you did not. To make the legitimacy of a government to be a matter of a majority is to rest it upon a contest between two groups of men. Even were it to be the case that governments have, if not the enthusiastic support, at least the acquiescence of the many, why should that matter? 'Men are dunces for uniting to sustain any government, or any laws, *except those in which they are all agreed.*'[12]

Perhaps it could be argued against Spooner that, 'we are a nation and the nation has a right to determine its own activities and it can do so only by legislation.' This, of course, raises the questions, 'what is a nation and how do nations come to be?' How is it, asks Spooner, that each of many millions of men 'comes to be stripped of all his natural, God-given rights, and to be incorporated, compressed, compacted, and consolidated into a mass with other men, whom he never saw; with whom he has no contract; and towards many of whom he has no sentiments but fear, hatred and contempt?' [Spooner 1992, 59] If a nation, and the government by which it is directed, is to exist by right at all, then it can only do so by consent.

Well, it might be said, at least in the case of the USA, there is such consent and it is manifested in and through the US Constitution.[13] Spooner has no doubt that the US Constitution purports to be a contract embodying consent. He believes, in fact, that the only way to conceive of that Constitution in such a way that it would have legal effect *is* for it to be a contract of some kind. 'It has no authority or obligation at all *unless as a contract between man and man.*'[14] Although he believes that the US Constitution is a much better document than it is generally taken to be, he argues vigorously against its being acceptable or its being in fact accepted.[15] Spooner's thesis is absolutely clear: 'The Constitution has no inherent authority or obligation.' [Spooner 1992, 77]

If the US Constitution is a contract, who are the parties to it? Spooner remarks, the Constitution 'does not so much as even purport to be a contract between persons now existing. It purports, at most, to be only a contract between persons living eighty years ago." [Spooner 1992, 77] According to

Spooner, only those people who were in fact around when it was approved could possibly be candidates for position of contractor. Does that mean that all the people living in the USA eighty years before Spooner wrote are to be taken to be parties to the Constitution? No—only those people legally entitled and competent to make contracts among those alive at the time are in the running[16] but not even all these were, in fact, parties to the Constitution for, as Spooner notes, 'we know, historically, that only a small portion even of the people then existing were consulted on the subject, or asked, or permitted to express either their consent or dissent in any formal manner.' [Spooner 1992, 77] He points out that the number of people who consented to the Constitution of the USA wasn't very numerous. Women and blacks were excluded. Property qualifications excluded anywhere from one half to three quarters of the white male adults and of the remaining small amount of potentially qualified voters, how many in fact exercised their franchise?

Spooner examines the opening lines of the US Constitution and asks who the 'We' in 'We, the people of the United States....' is meant to be. He replies that it can only mean individuals, acting freely and voluntarily. Such authority as the document has, it has only between those who, as a matter of fact, consented. He invites us to imagine another, rather less grandiose, agreement, in which, we might say, 'We, the people of Philadelphia, agree to maintain a school....for ourselves and our children.' Such an agreement would, of course, be binding only on those who in fact agreed, and any attempt to legally compel those who had not consented to contribute to the maintenance of the school would be a form of extortion. References to posterity can't be taken to imply that there was any intention or any acknowledgement of a right or power to bind posterity

According to Spooner, those who consented to the Constitution, whatever their number may have been, only bound themselves and no others. Still further, even those who explicitly consented did not bind themselves for ever, for no time element is mentioned in the passage—according to Spooner, this makes it merely an association during pleasure, even between the original consenting parties. Since the original parties to the purported contract that is the Constitution were no longer alive in 1870 when Spooner was writing,[17] he believes it follows that '*the Constitution, so far as it was their contract, died with them.* They had no power or right to make it obligatory upon their children. It is not only plainly impossible, in the nature of things, that they *could* bind their posterity, but they did not even attempt to bind them.' [Spooner 1992, 77] If those now alive aren't bound by those who established the Constitution, have they somehow bound themselves? Clearly, they could bind themselves by explicit ratification. Failing that, are there any other ways in which they might do so? What of the claim that voting in a political system implies *de facto* consent to that system? Spooner writes:

>...without his consent having ever been asked, a man finds himself environed by a government that he cannot resist; a government that forces him to pay money, render service, and forego the exercise of many of his natural rights, under peril of weighty punishments. He sees, too, that other

men practise this tyranny over him by the use of the ballot. He sees further that, if he will but use the ballot himself, he has some chance of relieving himself from this tyranny of others, by subjecting them to his own. In short, he finds himself, without his consent, so situated that, if he use the ballot he may become a master; if he does not use it, he must become a slave. And he has no other alternative than these two. In self-defence, he attempts the former. His case is analogous to that of a man who has been forced into battle, where he must either kill others, or be killed himself. Because, to save his own life in battle, a man attempts to take the life of his opponents, it is not to be inferred that the battle is one of his own choosing. Neither in contests with the ballot—which is a mere substitute for a bullet—because, as his only chance of self-preservation, a man uses a ballot, is it to be inferred that the contest is one into which he voluntarily entered…[18]

Only if the act of voting were truly voluntary, could a person be said to support the Constitution under which he votes. But for many people it is not so much voluntary as it is a necessity or a matter of self-defence. [see Spooner 1992, 80-81] Some vote to have some small say in the disposition of the money that is taken from them in taxes. Were such taxation not to occur, they wouldn't have any inclination to vote. Of course, in reality one's voting makes no difference whatsoever to the disposition of the revenue collected by such taxation. 'To take a man's property without his consent, and then to infer his consent because he attempts, by voting, to prevent that property being used to his injury, is a very insufficient proof of his consent to support the Constitution.' [Spooner 1992, 81-82] On the related matter of taxation as an indication of tacit consent, Spooner writes:

No attempt or pretence, that was ever carried into practical operation amongst civilized men—unless possibly the pretence of a "Divine Right," on the part of some to govern and enslave others—embodied so much shameless absurdity, falsehood, impudence, robbery, usurpation, tyranny, and villainy of every kind, as the attempt or pretence of establishing a government by consent, and getting the actual consent of only so many as may be necessary to keep the rest in subjection by force. Such a government is a mere conspiracy of the strong against the weak. It no more rests on consent than does the worst government on earth. What substitute for their consent is offered to the weaker party, whose rights are thus annihilated, struck out of existence, by the stronger? Only this: Their consent is presumed!...As well might the highwayman pretend to justify himself by presuming that the traveller consents to part with his money. As well might the assassin justify himself by simply presuming that his victim consents to part with his life. As well might the holder of chattel slaves attempt to justify himself by presuming that they consent to his authority, and to the whips and the robbery which he practises upon them. The presumption is simply a presumption that the weaker party consent to be slaves. [Spooner 1992, 75-76]

Taxes, being compulsory, provide no evidence that taxpayers support the constitution. Spooner compares the tax collector unfavourably to a highwayman!

> The highwayman takes solely upon himself the responsibility, danger, and crime of his own act. He does not pretend that he has any rightful claim to your money, or that he intends to use it for your own benefit. He does not pretend to be anything but a robber. He has not acquired impudence enough to profess to be merely a 'protector,' and that he takes men's money against their will, merely to enable him to 'protect' those infatuated travellers, who feel perfectly able to protect themselves, or do not appreciate his peculiar system of protection. He is too sensible a man to make such professions as these. Furthermore, having taken your money, he leaves you, as you wish him to. He does not persist in following you on the road, against your will; assuming to be your rightful 'sovereign,' on account of the 'protection' he affords you. He does not keep 'protecting' you, by commanding you to bow down and serve him; by requiring you to do this; and forbidding you to do that; by robbing you of more money as often as he finds it for his interest or pleasure to do so; and by branding you as a rebel, traitor, and an enemy to your country, and shooting you down without mercy, if you dispute his authority, or resist his demands. He is too much of a gentleman to be guilty of such imposture, and insults, and villainies as these. [Spooner 1992, 85]

Spooner makes the even more radical claim that not only does the Constitution not bind anyone now, but that it never did bind anyone. He makes much of the fact that no one signed the document and that the general principle of law and reason is that a written instrument does not bind until and unless it is signed. He instances the formalisation of wills and deeds and the requirement that they be signed, sealed, witnessed and acknowledged. He then says, 'And yet we have what purports, or professes, or is claimed, to be a contract—the Constitution—made eighty years ago, by men who are now all dead, and who never had any power to bind us, but which (it is claimed) has nevertheless bound three generations of men, consisting of many millions, and which (it is claimed) will be binding upon all the millions that are to come; but which nobody ever signed, sealed, delivered, witnessed, or acknowledged; and which few persons, compared with the whole number that are claimed to be bound by it, have ever read, or even seen, or ever will read, or see. And of those who ever have read it, or ever will read it, scarcely any two, perhaps no two, have ever agreed, or ever will agree, as to what it means.' [Spooner 1992, 91]

Spooner concludes that, despite its pretensions, the US Constitution is not a contract, that it binds nobody and never did bind anybody, and that those who claim to act by its authority are acting without authority. There is nothing to stop anyone who thinks the Constitution to be worthy of being signed signing it and agreeing with others who do likewise that they will make laws for each other within its remit, allowing non-signers to live in peace. Appearances to the contrary notwithstanding, then, the government of the USA does not in fact rest upon any consent of the people of the USA.

III: Benjamin Tucker

Whatever reservations other writers might have had about describing themselves as anarchists, Benjamin Tucker (1854-1939) had none. In a letter to the New York *Tribune* (4 December 1898), he asserts that he was the first Anglo-Saxon to originate an anarchist newspaper in English, a publication which he modestly describes as 'the pioneer and principal organ of modern individualist Anarchism.' He claims to have published what he describes as 'the chief Anarchistic works' in English, to be the author of a textbook on anarchism, and to have been friends with, and learned from, Josiah Warren, Stephen Pearl Andrews, and Lysander Spooner. All this would appear to be true.

Liberty

The anarchist newspaper to which Tucker refers was *Liberty*, for the late nineteenth and early twentieth centuries the most important publication of its kind in any language and even today an invaluable resource for libertarians.[19] Wendy McElroy notes that 'In the late nineteenth century, Tucker and *Liberty* formed the vital core around which a radical individualist movement reconstituted itself and grew.' [McElroy 1997, 423] The editorial line of *Liberty* was the rejection of authority, authority being conceived of as the imposition of the will of one man upon the will of another, whether by religion, by politics, or by public opinion. In fact, Tucker defines government in terms of authority, describing it as 'the subjection of the *non-invasive* individual to a will not his own.' [Tucker 1897, 39] The point of the inclusion of the term 'non-invasive' in this definition is precisely to prevent resistance to invasive individuals from falling under the rubric of government. 'The Anarchists,' writes Tucker, 'are opposed to all government, and especially to the State as the worst governor and chief invader. From *Liberty*'s standpoint, there are not three positions, but two: one, that of the authoritarian Socialists, favouring government and the State; the other, that of the Individualists *and* Anarchists, against government and the State.' [Tucker 1897, 39-40] Although the state isn't the only possible invader of this kind, it is by far the commonest and most potent of them. So Tucker, in *Liberty*, rejects the state and advocates its replacement by a series of voluntary arrangements.

Tucker the Stirnerite

Tucker began his anarchist life as a natural rights exponent in the manner of Lysander Spooner, holding that every individual has the natural freedom to do whatever he will with himself and his property 'as long as he does not trespass upon the equal freedom of any other person.' [*Liberty* 24, 2] By the late 1880s, however, he had become an advocate of a kind of Stirnerite egoism.[20] Not everyone was happy with this transition on his part.[21] Victor Yarros [1865-1956] who, ironically, began *his* intellectual life as an egoist and ended it as a social democrat, observed that 'Every reader [of *Liberty*] knows that in 1886

Mr. Tucker was not an egoist, either in his views or in his phraseology. Yet, when the revolution took place and he became an egoist, he made no formal retraction and took no vow of modesty.' [*Liberty* 201, 3] Tucker responded by saying, 'From the start I have known that self-interest is the mainspring of conduct and that the ego is supreme. I had not, however carefully thought out or even considered the bearing of this philosophy upon the question of obligation. I took society for granted and assumed the desire of man for society, and it was from this standpoint that I had loosely talked of natural rights. But Stirner's book caused me to ask myself, If the individual does not wish society, is he under any obligation to act socially? And I no sooner asked it than I answered it in the negative.' [*Liberty* 201, 4]

In considering the relationship that should exist between the state and the individual most people make use of some theory of ethics, some account of moral obligation, Not anarchists, according to Tucker! 'The idea of moral obligation, of inherent rights and duties,' says Tucker, 'they totally discard. They look upon all obligations, not as moral, but as social, and even then not really as obligations except as these have been consciously and voluntarily assumed. If a man makes an agreement with men, the latter may combine to hold him to his agreement; but, in the absence of such agreements, no man, so far as the Anarchists are aware, has made any agreement with God or with any other power of any order whatsoever. The Anarchists are not only utilitarians, but egoists in the farthest and fullest sense. So far as inherent right is concerned,' Tucker concludes, 'might is its only measure.' [Tucker 1897, 24] Laws prohibiting the invasion of one man's person or property by another are social, not moral. Rights-talk might still be acceptable as a *façon de parler*, such rights, however, being in no way natural but arising from agreements or contracts between people.

John Kelly, writing in *Liberty*, attacked this account as incoherent. It is impossible, he says, 'to base a society upon contract unless we consider a contract as having some binding effect, and that the binding effect of a particular contract can't be due to the contract itself. That is to say, no special obligations could be created for us by a contract unless we were under some general obligations towards each other already....I believe, therefore, that while the individual is, and must ever be, for himself the arbiter of right and wrong, these latter exist independently of him, and that moral progress consists in the approximation of the various individual conceptions...to conformity with the objective reality. As I look at it, men have not to create justice, but merely to discover what justice is and live in accordance therewith.' [*Liberty* 104, 7] Another of Tucker's interlocutors, William Hanson, had held that 'The existence of one person is equalled by the existence of another. So long as two persons stand thus related, neither invading the life or liberty of the other, then there is no right and no wrong. But the moment either invades the life, liberty, or property of the other, right and wrong and morality begin.' [*Liberty*, 261, 2] Tucker rejects Hanson's argument, remarking that one man's existence may be equalled by another's only if they are equally able to maintain their existence but, if not, they are unequal and so there is no moral obligation why one 'should not subordinate or destroy the other.' [*Liberty* 261, 3] 'Why,' responds Tucker, 'is one man bound to refrain from injuring another? ...I know plenty of reasons why it is expedient for one man to refrain from injuring another....But if my reasons do not commend themselves to his judgment; if my view of expediency does not coincide with his,—what obligation is there upon him to refrain? [*Liberty* 261, 3]

Tucker may have rejected Hanson's argument but he hasn't rebutted it. Although Hanson invited misunderstanding by his use of the ambiguous term 'existence', his argument hinges on the *moral* equality of any two human beings, not on their being in some sense *physically* equal. Tucker's attempt to reject Hanson's argument may be met in the following way. If I am unwilling to accept that other people have the right to dispose of themselves and their lawfully acquired property as they see fit without interference from me or from another then I must be prepared either to defend a form of special pleading ('I am unique so that I may infringe upon the liberty of others but they must respect mine') or to concede that others have the right to violate my own liberty when and if they can. Neither of these alternatives is logically self-stultifying but both are radically implausible. The special pleading alternative is an ever-popular option with those who wish to accord themselves a special and superior moral status but they usually find themselves in a minority of one on this matter. The 'I can do anything I like to you and you can do anything you like to me' position, apart from being practically unlikely, makes it impossible for morality to get any purchase in human life. Morality-as-expediency is an unstable compound that either turns into morality (and on what basis could Tucker justify this?) or returns to an amoral expediency. Morality having been expelled from the house of humanity through the front door finds the back door locked when it tries to sneak back in.

Tucker's Stirnerite positivism led him to ever more extreme (and in my judgement) indefensible views. 'I am asked by a correspondent,' he writes, 'if I would "passively see a woman throw her baby into the fire as a man throws his newspaper"....it is highly probable that I would personally interfere in such a case. But it is as probable, and perhaps more so, that I would personally interfere to prevent the owner of a masterpiece by Titian from applying the torch to the canvas. My interference in the former case no more invalidates the mother's property right in her child than my interference in the latter case would invalidate the property right of the owner of the painting. If I interfere in either case, I am an invader, acting in obedience to my injured feelings.'[22] If the ownership of a child were on all fours with the ownership of a painting then Tucker's argument goes through. But whether or not a baby can be owned in precisely the same way as a material object is precisely the point at issue. The status and appropriate treatment of children is a problematic issue for many libertarians (see, for example, Rothbard 2002, chapter 14) but Tucker's position comes perilously close to being a counsel of despair. Devoid of any rights-based defence for his positions, he becomes increasingly reliant on utilitarian considerations. He writes, 'I deny that the thing fundamentally desirable is the minimum of invasion. The ultimate end of human endeavour is the minimum of pain. We aim to decrease invasion only because, as a rule, invasion increases the total of pain....But it is precisely my contention that this rule, despite the immense importance which I place upon it, is not absolute...' [*Liberty* 324, 4]

TUCKER ON PROPERTY

If there are no natural rights, then property can't be a natural right either. Tucker's position on land ownership mirrored that of his mentor Josiah Warren and the land reformer George Henry Evans. Only land that was occupied and used could be owned, and only for so long as it was used and occupied. [*Liberty* 331, 4] He attacked Spooner who adhered to a Lockean-type labour-investment land-acquisition theory. Tucker wonders what would follow from Spooner's conception. 'Evidently that a man may go to a piece of vacant land and fence it off; that he may then go to a second piece and fence that off; then to a third, and fence that off; then to a fourth, a fifth, a hundredth, a thousandth, fencing them all off; that, unable to fence off himself as many as he wishes, he may hire other men to do the fencing for him; and that then he may stand back and bar all other men from using these lands, or admit them as tenant at such rental as he may choose to exact.' [*Liberty* 180, 4] In return, however, several pertinent objections to the conjoint condition of occupancy and use were raised by some of Tucker's correspondents, notably Steven Byington, for example: is a property to be considered abandoned if a man leave it for a vacation elsewhere; if an owner, desirous of selling his property continues to occupy it but not use it, does he then cease to own it? Tucker's response to these objections is a blithe non-answer. He regards objections such as these to be mere matters 'of human device or administrative detail, not to be discussed in these columns unless the attempt be to show that such device is impossible.' [*Liberty* 331, 4]

But the Tucker/Warren doctrine on property rights won't do. The occupy/ use criterion of land ownership rules out any just practice of land rental, even if I, the landowner, want to rent it to you and you, the would-be tenant, want to rent it from me. Rothbard writes, 'once a piece of land passes justly into Mr. A's ownership, he cannot be said to truly own that land unless he can convey or sell the title to Mr. B; and to prevent Mr. B from exercising his title simply because he doesn't choose to use it himself but rather rents it out voluntarily to Mr. C, is an invasion of B's freedom of contract and of his right to his justly-acquired private property.' [Rothbard 2000a, 210] The individual anarchists' problem with land ownership stems ultimately from the economic doctrine of the labour theory of value. This doctrine, which also undermines Marx's critique of capitalism, lies at the root of the individual anarchists' dismissal of the legitimacy of rent, interest and profit and from this follows their rejection of a full-blooded account of land ownership.

Consistent with his denial of natural rights, Tucker regarded property as a social convention and not a matter of right. From the point of view of his conception of anarchism, however, property is that which a man produces for himself or acquires from another without force or fraud or by contract. 'It will be seen from this definition,' he says, 'that Anarchistic property concerns only products. But anything is a product upon which human labor has been expended, whether it be a piece of iron or a piece of land.' He adds the following note:

'It should be stated, however, that in the case of land, or of any other material the supply of which is so limited that all cannot hold it in unlimited quantities, Anarchism undertakes to protect no titles except such as are based on actual occupancy and use.' [Tucker 1897, 61]

But if property is only a social convention and not a matter of right, does Tucker's anarchy recognise the propriety of compelling people to observe such conventions? Tucker answers that 'the only compulsion of individuals the propriety of which Anarchism recognizes is that which compels invasive individuals to refrain from overstepping the principle of equal liberty.' The role played in Tucker's earlier thought by natural rights was replaced by the concept of 'equal liberty' which, as Tucker frankly admits, is simply a social convention. His defence of this position is startlingly and unconvincingly circular. He writes, 'Anarchism protects equal liberty...not because it is a social convention, but because it is equal liberty,—that is, because it is Anarchism itself.'[23] This circular argument, like all circular arguments is formally valid (any proposition can be said, vacuously, to follow from itself) but there is no genuine advance in knowledge. For example, in triumphantly demonstrating to my own satisfaction that "Might is Right" follows inexorably from the proposition "Might is Right" I may persuade myself of the truth of that proposition but I am unlikely to persuade anyone else of that truth or, indeed, of the value of my inference.

The poser of the original question on property to Tucker, the indefatigable Mr Blodgett, returned to this topic of 'equal liberty'. What, he asks, is so special about one social convention as distinct from another. If it is proper to compel the observance of one social convention, why not compel the observance of others. 'If "there are no natural rights," there is no occasion for conscientious or other scruples, providing the power exists.' [Tucker/Blodgett 1897, 63] If one rules out any operative notion of natural rights, all that's left is expediency. 'There certainly can be no more reason why Anarchists, who deny every obligation on the ground of right, should be consistent in standing by the platform put forward when weak, than that ordinary political parties should stand by their promises made when out of power.' [Tucker/Blodgett 1897, 63] When all is said and done, 'equal liberty' is but a catch-phrase which 'sounds nice, but when we criticise it, it is hollow. For instance, "equal liberty" may give every one the same opportunity to take freely from the same cabbage patch, the same meat barrel, and the same grain-bin. So long as no one interferes with another, he is not overstepping the principle of "equal liberty," but when one undertakes to keep others away, he is, and you can only justify the proscription by saying that one ought to have liberty there, and the others had not,—that those who did nothing in the production ought not to have "equal liberty" to appropriate. But if nobody has any "natural rights," then the thief not only does not interfere with the "equal liberty" of others, but he does them no wrong.' [Tucker/Blodgett 1897, 63]

Tucker's response to Blodgett's question is far from satisfactory. He simply states that an anarchist takes no satisfaction in enforcing any social convention other than that of equal liberty. If he were to do so, he would cease to be an anarchist and 'the remaining Anarchists would still be entitled to stop him from invading [enforcing] them.' One might wonder what kind of entitlement this could be, natural rights having been removed from consideration. The remaining anarchists could, of course, do whatever they wished but so too, it seems, could anyone else who was unpersuaded by the obviousness of Tucker's notion of equal liberty. Tucker suspects that Blodgett may not be sufficiently acute to perceive the distinction he (Tucker) is drawing but if Blodgett fails to perceive this distinction this may well be because here we have a distinction without a difference. Blodgett's response bears out my interpretation. He comments, 'You (Tucker) accept my statement that it is as proper to enforce one social convention as another, provided there is any satisfaction in doing so. I find the difference between an Anarchist and a Governmentalist is nothing here. If there is any difference in the action of the two, it is not a difference in the principles which control it. There might be a difference in method, and a difference in the *kind* of social conventions which they wish to enforce. On both these points I suppose I should have some sympathy with the Anarchists like you. But when we prevent another from doing as he otherwise would, we govern him in that particular, and I see no advantage in denying it, or in trying to find another term to express the fact.' [Tucker/Blodgett 1897, 66]

TUCKER ON THE STATE

Some people claim that the state originates in contract and that those living today who did not consent to that contract are yet bound by it. Tucker, of course, echoing Spooner, rejects this claim completely. There never was such a contract and even had there been 'it could not impose a shadow of obligation on those who had no hand in making it.' [Tucker 1897, 32] What if we were to conceive of the state not as a quasi-mechanical outcome of a contract but as a kind of organism? Would that not change our approach to it? Tucker thinks not. Organisms have no greater degree of permanence than contractually-constituted institutions. 'But,' he asks, 'what is history but a record of the dissolution of organisms and the birth and growth of others to be dissolved in turn? Is the State exempt from this order? If so, why? What proves it? The State is an organism? Yes; so is a tiger. But unless I meet him where I haven't my gun, his organism will speedily disorganize. The State is a tiger seeking to devour the people, and they must either kill or cripple it. Their own safety depends upon it.' [Tucker 1897, 33] The 'state as organism' argument rests, in the end, on a conflation of state and society. Human society could not cease to exist without taking its constituent individual human beings with it; the disappearance of the state, on the other hand, would have no such disastrous consequences. 'The State, unlike society, is a discrete organism. If it should be destroyed to-morrow, individuals would still continue to exist. Production, exchange, and association would go on as before, but much more freely, and all those social functions upon which the individual is dependent would operate in his behalf more usefully than ever. The individual is not related to the State as the tiger's paw is related to the tiger. Kill the tiger, and the tiger's paw no longer performs its office; kill the State, and the individual still lives and satisfies his wants. As for society, the Anarchists would not kill it if they could, and could not if they would.' [Tucker 1897, 36]

But if there is no state, what is to prevent one man or one group of men from invading another? Tucker gives what is now the classic libertarian response to this question. The abolition of the State, he says, 'will leave in existence a defensive association, resting no longer on a compulsory but on a voluntary basis, which will restrain invaders by any means that may prove necessary.' But, it might be objected, this is to replace like with like, for the state just *is* such a defensive institution. Not quite, says Tucker. The state is not, or not just, a defensive institution. It is also an aggressor. 'Why, the very first act of the State, the compulsory assessment and collection of taxes, is itself an aggression, a violation of equal liberty, and, as such, vitiates every subsequent act, even those acts which would be purely defensive if paid for out of a treasury filled by voluntary contributions.' [Tucker 1897, 25] To tax a man to pay for protection he did not ask for and which he does not desire is to violate his liberty and, in making him pay for it, adds insult to injury. Taxation apart, most of the laws made by our erstwhile protector the state serve only to crib, cabin and confine our personal liberties and to grant monopolies and privileges to commercial, industrial and financial enterprises. In saying all this, Tucker echoes one of his inspirations, Proudhon, who wrote, memorably, that 'To be governed is to be watched, inspected, spied upon, directed, law-ridden, regulated, penned up, indoctrinated, preached at, checked, appraised, seized, censured, commanded, by beings who have neither title nor knowledge nor virtue. To be governed is to have every operation, every transaction, every movement noted, registered, counted, rated, stamped, measured, numbered, assessed, licensed, refused, authorized, indorsed, admonished, prevented, reformed, redressed, corrected. To be governed is, under pretext of public utility and in the name of the general interest, to be laid under contribution, drilled, fleeced, exploited, monopolized, extorted from, exhausted, hoaxed, robbed; then, upon the slightest resistance, at the first word of complaint, to be repressed, fined, vilified, annoyed, hunted down, pulled about, beaten, disarmed, bound, imprisoned, shot, machine-gunned, judged, condemned, banished, sacrificed, sold, betrayed, and, to crown all, ridiculed, derided, outraged, dishonored.' [Proudhon 1851, Epilogue]

Tucker was presented by one of his correspondents, Frederic Perrine, with the common objection that as long as we live within the borders of a state and benefit from so doing, we owe it our taxes. If we do not wish to stay and be bound, then we should leave. Tucker points out that this argument simply assumes that the state is some kind of voluntary organisation. If it were so then the argument would have traction for 'such voluntary association would be entitled to enforce whatever regulations the contracting parties might agree upon within the limits of whatever territory, or divisions of territory, had been brought into the association by these parties as individual occupiers thereof, and no non-contracting party would have a right to enter or remain in this domain except upon such terms as the association might impose.' [Tucker 1897, 44] But if a person takes his pre-existent property into a voluntary association with others then, upon secession from or the dissolution of such voluntary association, he retains his pre-existent property and returns to the *status quo ante*. 'But,' Tucker notes, 'no individual to-day finds himself under any such circumstances. The States in the midst of which he lives cover all the ground there is, affording him no escape, and are not voluntary associations, but gigantic usurpations. There is not one of them which did not result from the agreement of a larger or smaller number of individuals, inspired sometimes no doubt by kindly, but oftener by malevolent, designs, to declare all the territory and persons within certain boundaries a nation which every one of these persons must support, and to whose will, expressed through its sovereign legislators and administrators no matter how chosen, every one of them must submit. Such an institution is sheer tyranny, and has no rights which any individual is bound to respect; on the contrary, every individual who understands his rights and values his liberties will do his best to overthrow it.' [Tucker 1897, 45]

Could it be argued that it is possible for men to agree to form an association from which it wouldn't be possible to secede? Tucker thinks one could go through a form of such a contract but it would only be a form. 'Contract,' he remarks, 'is a very serviceable and most important tool, but its usefulness has its limits; no man can employ it for the abdication of his manhood. To indefinitely waive one's right of secession is to make one's self a slave. No, no man can make himself so much a slave as to forfeit the right to issue his own emancipation proclamation. Individuality and its right of assertion are indestructible except by death. Hence any signer of such a constitution as that supposed who should afterwards become an Anarchist would be fully justified in the use of any means that would protect him from attempts to coerce him in the name of that constitution.' [Tucker 1897, 48] On this conception of the matter, a man isn't free to alienate his freedom.

In his chapter entitled 'State Socialism and Anarchism: How Far they Agree, and Wherein They Differ' Tucker describes State Socialism as *the doctrine that all the affairs of men should be managed by the government, regardless of individual choice*. Anarchism, by contrast, is described as *the doctrine that all the affairs of men should be managed by individuals or voluntary associations, and that the State should be abolished*. [Tucker 1897, 7, 9] Tucker's description and analysis of Marxist State Socialism is right on the money. The State Socialist solution to the existence of class monopolies was to create and maintain one gigantic state monopoly! The cure for monopolies is, apparently, a monopoly of monopolies. 'The government must become banker, manufacturer, farmer, carrier, and merchant, and in these capacities must suffer no competition. Land, tools, and all instruments of production must be wrested from individual hands, and made the property of the collectivity. To the individual can belong only the products to be consumed, not the means of producing them.' [Tucker 1897, 7] But, of course, the effects of this monopoly of monopolies—the state— wouldn't be only economic. Such liberty as any one might exercise, he would exercise only by permission of the state. Moreover, the influence of the state would extend more and more into ever more areas of human life; 'the community, through its majority expression, will insist more and more in prescribing the conditions of health, wealth, and wisdom, thus impairing and finally destroying individual independence and with it all sense of individual responsibility.' [Tucker 1897, 8]

In a chilling and prescient passage that deserves to be quoted in full, Tucker sketches the brave new world of State Socialism:

> Whatever, then, the State Socialists may claim or disclaim, their system, if adopted, is doomed to end in a State religion, to the expense of which all must contribute and at the altar of which all must kneel; a State school of medicine, by whose practitioners the sick must invariably be treated; a State system of hygiene, prescribing what all must and must not eat, drink, wear, and do; a State code of morals, which will not content itself with punishing crime, but will prohibit what the majority decide to be vice; a State system of instruction, which will do away with all private schools, academies, and colleges; a State nursery, in which all children must be brought up in common at the public expense; and, finally, a State family, with an attempt at stirpiculture, or scientific breeding, in which no man and woman will be allowed to have children if the State prohibits them and no man and woman can refuse to have children if the State orders them. Thus will Authority achieve its acme and Monopoly be carried to its highest power. [Tucker 1897, 8-9]

How far-fetched and hyperbolical this prognostication must have seemed in 1890, but how much of it has been realised not only in political regimes that are overtly socialist but even in those that purport *not* to be socialist.

As Tucker sees it, the approach of the founders of individual anarchism, Warren and Proudhon, to the problem of class monopolies wasn't to monopolise the monopolies but to attack the notion of authority that lies at the bottom of all monopolies and to substitute in its place, liberty, specifically, freedom of competition. Their attachment to the labour theory of value distorted, in part, their application of this principle of competition in the economic arena but the principle has wider application to all forms of social organisation, including the state. Tucker wasn't the originator of individualist anarchism. He had predecessors in Warren, Andrews and Spooner. But although 'the basis of a systematic philosophy existed in the writings of theorists such as Warren and Spooner, it lacked cohesion. Not until Tucker's publication of *Liberty* did radical individualism become a distinct, independent movement functioning in its own name and seeking its own unique goal.' [McElroy 12997, 432]

IV: THE ENGLISH INDIVIDUALISTS

Around the time Benjamin Tucker was publishing *Liberty* in the USA, some English writers who were described as Individualists were producing work on related themes: Wordsworth Donisthorpe, Auberon Herbert,[24] Josephine Butler and, to some extent, Herbert Spencer.[25] Tucker corresponded with and gave a platform to these English Individualists.[26] Whereas Tucker explicitly characterised himself as an anarchist, Donisthorpe and Herbert did not. Those who adopt a proprietary attitude to the terms 'anarchism' and 'anarchist' and who are inclined to link anarchism definitionally with some form of socialism are happy to take the anti-socialist Donisthorpe and Herbert at their words and so deny their anarchist credentials. Nevertheless, matters aren't quite that simple. Their rejection of socialism, as Tucker's rejection of socialism, was of *state* socialism and it is possible, remarks Peter Ryley, 'to establish an association between individualism and a libertarian approach to early socialist thought.'[27]

Tucker took Donisthorpe's (and Joseph Hiam Levy's) Individualism to be what he (Tucker) meant by anarchy and held that the Individualists' rejection of the term 'anarchist' was based on mistakenly understanding anarchism to be a rejection of all forms of order and the dissolution of all law. To repeat a point I made earlier in my discussion of Tucker, he wrote 'From *Liberty's* standpoint, there are not three positions, but two: one, that of the authoritarian Socialists, favoring government and the State; the other, that of the Individualists *and* Anarchists, against government and the State.'[28] Donisthorpe identified anarchy with Hobbes's war of all against all and so, not unnaturally, was disinclined to find it desirable. Although he believed that some form of governance was necessary to protect the weak against the strong, he did not believe that this could be provided only by a unique and omnipotent state.

AUBERON HERBERT

However unlikely a proto-anarchist Donisthorpe may have been, he was nowhere near as unlikely as the other major English Individualist thinker of this period, Auberon Herbert. Herbert was by birth part of the English Establishment—the third son of the third Earl of Carnarvon, married to the daughter of another Earl, and a Liberal MP for Nottingham for five years. Who knows where his political career might have taken him had he not had the good (or bad) luck to encounter Herbert Spencer in 1873? This was his Road to Damascus experience and Herbert's wonderful and beautifully written description of it is worth recounting.[29] 'I went into the House of Commons, as a young man,' he writes,

> believing that we might do much for the people by a bolder and more unsparing use of the powers that belonged to the great lawmaking machine….It was at that moment that I had the privilege of meeting Mr. Spencer, and the talk which we had…set me busily to work to study his writings….I lost my faith in the great machine; I saw that thinking and acting for others had always hindered, not helped, the real progress; that all forms of compulsion deadened the living forces in a nation; that every evil violently stamped out still persists, almost always in a worse form, when driven out of sight….I no longer believed that the handful of us—however well-intentioned we might be—spending our nights in the House, could manufacture the life of a nation, could endow it out of hand with happiness, wisdom and prosperity, and clothe it in all the virtues. I began to see that we were only playing with an imaginary magician's wand; that the ambitious

work we were trying to do lay far out of the reach of our hands….It was a work that could be done in one way—not by gifts and doles of public money, not by making that most corrupting and demoralizing of all things, a common purse; not by restraints and compulsions of each other; not by seeking to move in a mass, obedient to the strongest forces of the moment, but by acting through the living energies of the free individuals left free to combine in their own way, in their own groups, finding their own experience, setting before themselves their own hopes and desires, and ever as the foundation of it all, respecting deeply and religiously alike their own freedom, and the freedom of others. [Herbert 1978, 260-261]

Herbert chose to describe the position he developed as 'Voluntaryism', thereby emphasizing, obviously, the central role that voluntary action was to play in his conception of the good society. The core of Herbert's Voluntaryism is an anti-state libertarianism. Like Donisthorpe, Herbert explicitly rejected the application of the label 'anarchist' to himself though it's reasonably clear that what he meant by the anarchism he rejected involved the use of force and was linked in his mind to the caricature anarchism of the bomb-throwing bearded Russian variety.

HERBERT, ADHERENT OF NATURAL RIGHTS AND DEFENDER OF PROPERTY

Tucker, at least the latter-day Tucker, was an anti-natural rights Stirnerite; Donisthorpe inclined towards a kind of libertarian Burkeanism; but Herbert held to a full-blooded natural rights account of man and society. He asks us to consider this question: 'if men have no rightful claim to possess any sovereignty over the bodies and minds of each other; if that sovereignty only belongs to the man's own self; if the attempt to have and to exercise power over each other has been the most fruitful cause both of the past and the present misery of the world; if force has never permanently bettered and never can permanently better any of us, but only unfits us for our struggle in a world, where we must depend for our success, sooner or later, at some point or other, notwithstanding all ingenious systems of external protection, upon the selves that are within us, upon our own choice of what is right, and our own power to abide by that choice; then what is the practical aim we must put before ourselves in politics, what measures and what form of Government will give the truest expression to these convictions?' [Herbert 1885, 31-32] Underlying Herbert's question is a commitment to two principles; self-sovereignty, and the illegitimacy of any attempt on the part of one man to coerce another.

In answer to his own question, then, Herbert thinks we must have a system of complete liberty in which there can be no coercion in matters of social conduct, religion, education, trade, occupations or work. Liberty and liberty alone makes us to be moral beings and 'allows the better and higher part of our nature to rule in us…' [Herbert 1908, 70] If liberty isn't allowed to operate, if some men set out to rule over others, then our moral world implodes. [see Herbert 1908, 68] In such a system of liberty, 'men will be entirely content to further their own interests by means of their own efforts and their own voluntary and self-directed associations; and content in social matters to obtain acceptance for their views by such moral influence as each is able to gain in the universal moral conflict. There must be the complete renouncement of force,—that force which all the present Governments of the world employ without hesitation— as the instrument by which the condition of men is to be improved; and in its place the following out and perfecting by voluntary means of that good, whatever it may be, which seems to each man or each group of men the truest and highest.' [Herbert 1885, 32-33]

What role is there for government in this system of voluntary interaction? A government has only one purpose—the defense of every person and property from attack. This, for Herbert, is the only justification for government. The inclusion of property as an item to be defended by government sets Herbert off from the American anarchists and also, if not quite as sharply, from Donisthorpe. Herbert is quite clear and equally emphatic about the central role of private property in a Voluntaryist political order. 'Private and personal property must be fully and completely recognized, whether it be the property of the rich or of the poor man. We must close our ears to the careless and unthoughtful denunciations of property, and see that without the fullest recognition of property there can be no real liberty of action. It is idle to say in one breath that each man has the right to the free use of his own faculties, and in the next breath to propose to deal by the power of the State with what he acquires by means of those faculties, as if both the faculties and what they produced belonged to the State and not to himself. Private property and free trade stand on exactly the same footing, both being essential and indivisible parts of liberty, both depending upon rights, which no body of men, whether called Governments or anything else, can justly take from the individual.'[30]

Contemporary libertarian anarchists are often accused of being mere propertarians because of their strong defence of property rights, both rights in the property of one's self and in external goods. It is interesting, then, to see this theme appearing and being so strongly defended by an earlier thinker. Herbert writes, 'We Voluntaryists believes (*sic*) that no true progress can be made until we frankly recognise the great truth that every individual who lives within the sphere of his own rights, as a self-owner, and has not first aggressed upon others by force or fraud, and thus deprived himself of his own rights of self-ownership by aggressing upon those same rights of all others, is the one and the only true owner of his own faculties, and his own property.' [Herbert 1897, 5] Thus, self-ownership. But there is more. 'We claim that the individual is not only the one true owner of his faculties, but also of his property, because property is directly or indirectly the product of faculties, is inseparable from faculties, and they must rest on the same moral basis, and fall under the same moral law, as faculties. Personal ownership of our own selves, of our own faculties, necessarily includes personal ownership of property.' [Herbert 1897, 5]

With property protected, men are free to associate in any way they choose, just so long as that association is voluntary. The flourishing mutual associations of the period, known as friendly societies, provided a concrete example of people providing for themselves, their dependents, co-workers and, in some cases even non-subscribers, without any need for coercive governmental redistribution that would undermine their liberty. For Herbert, 'State socialism is not only coercive; it is morally corrupting. This is because people will give up their natural rights to self-ownership and receive, instead, what the state deigns to give them in exchange. It is a system based on compulsion and forced obedience.' [Ryley, 73] Some socialist critics of Individualism generally, and of Herbert's Voluntaryism specifically, portray it as libertarianism for the wealthy and the privileged. Peter Ryley remarks, however, that this 'would be to do [Herbert] a disservice. He saw liberty as the only way to emancipate the working class…' [Ryley, 72] 'It is idle to talk of freedom,' Herbert writes, 'and, while the word is on one's lips, to attack property. He who attacks property, joins the camp of those who wish to keep some men in subjection to the will of others.' [Herbert 1978, 347-348] He concedes that, as things stand, the greater part of property belongs to the richer classes but he urges, in a way that conjures up memories of Proudhon's Mutualism, that 'it will not be so, as soon as ever you, the workers, take out of the hands of the politicians, and into your own hands, the task of carving out your own fortunes….In every city and town and village they [the workers] must form their associations for the gaining of property; they must put their irresistible pence and shillings together, so that, step by step, effort upon effort, they may become the owners of land, of farms, of houses, of shops, of mills, and trading ships…'[31]

The question might be asked how Herbert could be thought of as an anarchist if he allows for even the minimal government that he in fact does allow for. 'We ought not to direct our attacks—as the anarchists do—*against all government*,' he writes, 'against government in itself, as the national force machine, against government strictly limited to its legitimate duties in defense of self-ownership and individuals rights, but only against the overgrown, the exaggerated, the insolent, unreasonable, and indefensible forms of government which are found everywhere today, and under which, those who govern, usurp powers of all kinds, that do not and cannot belong to them…'[32] Despite these pro-government sentiments, Herbert was implacably opposed to taxation. In words that call to mind the similar sentiments expressed by Lysander Spooner he writes, 'The citizens of a country who are called upon to pay taxes have done nothing to forfeit their inalienable right over their own possessions…and there is no true power lodged in any body of men, whether known under the title of governments or of gentlemen of the highway, to take the property of men against their consent. The governments which persist in levying taxes by force, simply because they have the power to do so, will one day be considered as only the more respectable portion of that fraternity who are to be found in all parts of the world, living by the strong hand on the possessions of those who are too weak to resist them.' [Herbert 1978, 163] Herbert's approved government, then, was to be a voluntary organisation limited to the enforcement and defence of rights and supported by voluntary contributions.

Herbert's idea that a limited government could be supported by what he termed 'voluntary taxation' was vigorously attacked by Joseph Levy. A lively debate between Herbert and Levy ensued in which Herbert gave as good as he got by attacking in turn Levy's idea of 'compulsory co-operation.' 'Levy realized that taxation was the very essence of government as it had always existed,' writes Watner, 'Nor could he accept Herbert's analysis of the essential distinction between individualism and anarchism as being based on whether or not a central agency of defense was retained in their respective ideal societies....[he] was correct in asserting that Herbert had not thought through the problems of voluntary taxation.' On the other hand, 'Herbert realized that Levy's theory of individualism was marred by the existence of compulsory taxation in a society trying to maximize freedom....However Herbert erred in not realizing that "freely competing judicial agencies would have to be guided by a body of absolute law to enable them to *distinguish* objectively between defense and invasion."'[33]

Herbert did not describe himself as an anarchist; indeed, he explicitly rejected that label. As he saw it, anarchism tended towards a kind of unsystematic coercive form of violence and coercion of any form was anathema to him.[34] Moreover, he thought that non-coercive forms of anarchism aren't really anarchist. What such erstwhile anarchists sought, Herbert thought, wasn't the abolition of government as such but the abolition of a central, domineering government and its replacement by a kind of decentralized voluntary government. In Herbert's view, such a government, with its sole function of defence, is simply a convenient way of laying off what is essentially our individual right of self-defence. 'Let us never yield to the superstition of magnifying the Governments of our own creation. Whilst we concede the power to Governments to protect every man in his person and in his property from the attacks of other men, rather than leave this power in the hands of men individually, let me repeat that it is a mere survival of old forms of thought to suppose that there is any odour of divinity about whatever form of Government it may be,— Imperial or Republican,—that we set up.' [Herbert 1885, 33-34]

Contemporary libertarian thinkers suggest that law, justice and security could be provided by privately organised and privately managed defence associations. These could be run for profit or they could be mutual. Much as individuals in a Voluntaryist society could do, anarchist groups can also associate freely and there might well be ascending orders of organisation as necessary—all voluntary and contractual. In the end, Herbert's support for government is distinctly less damaging to his anarchist credentials than might appear at first glance. Ryley comments, I believe correctly, 'surely what he was advocating is not a government as commonly understood, but the very self-regulating community that stands at the heart of all anarchist thought.' If this be so, then Herbert's 'disavowal of anarchism is unconvincing to say the least.' [Ryley, 74] And Benjamin Tucker remarked, on the occasion of Herbert's death, that he was 'a true anarchist in everything but name. How much better...to be an anarchist in everything but name than to be an anarchist in name only.' [*Liberty*, Vol. 15, No. 6, 16]

This all-too-brief account of Herbert's writings may convey the impression that I believe Auberon Herbert to be pretty much the staunchest and least compromised anglophone defender of liberty produced by the nineteenth century. If so, that would be because that is what I do think. He is a forceful, elegant, passionate yet translucently clear writer who avoids almost (but not quite) all the traps that have, to some extent, managed to snare his predecessors and contemporaries. He is not utopian; he is not a covert lover of violence; he is not an egoist; and he robustly defends the legitimacy of and necessity for private property if freedom is to be defended.

Notes

1 Given this dedication, it is surprising to find the normally reliable commentator Crispin Sartwell warning us sternly that 'It is one of the greatest errors in superficial readings of Warren to connect him to the later thought of Benjamin Tucker, Ayn Rand, and Murray Rothbard, even though the term "individualist" is used to describe them all.' [Sartwell 2011, 47] It is certainly true that the thought of these four individuals isn't identical in all respects but why that should be an obstacle to *connecting* them in some way or other isn't immediately clear to me.

2 *The Practical Anarchist: Writings of Josiah Warren*, ed. and intro. Crispin Sartwell. New York: Fordham University Press, 2. Hereafter, references to this work will be as Warren 2011, when Warren's writings are in question, and as Sartwell 2011, when Sartwell's 'Introduction' is referred to.

3 For a brief account of Richard Owen's life and work, see Kolakowski, 193-198.

4 With delightful understatement, Sartwell describes the New Harmony undertaking as 'something of a disaster.' [Sartwell 2011, 21] In truth, it was a total fiasco, held together for as long as it survived only by the overwhelming charismatic force of Owen's personality. 'Owen's experiments,' writes Max Eastman, 'did not fail, nor Lenin's either, because of the "habits of the individual system" prevailing in its members. It failed, rather, because of the impulses of the social animal prevailing in them....It is no accident that Owen's community—and the others like it—throve only so long as the founder stayed on hand to boss it.' [Eastman, 107; see also 93-99]

5 As we shall see, Benjamin Tucker became an avowed Stirnerite egoist but Josiah Warren's radical individualism runs him a close second.

6 The distorting effect of language on thought was a central theme of Alfred Korzybski and the discipline of General Semantics that he founded.

7 Warren 2011, 108-109. See also 180-181.

8 Warren 2011, 73; see 108.

9 Warren 2011, 143; see Butler 1980, 440-442.

10 Warren 2011, 79; see 134ff.

11 See Warren 2011, 171; see also Casey 2012a & Butler 1980, 446-447. Josiah Warren was followed, for a time, by the protean thinker, Stephen Pearl Andrews (1812-1886). [see Riggenbach 2011b] In his 1854 work, *The Constitution of Government in the Sovereignty of the Individual*, Andrews adopts, without radically extending, Warren's notions of individuality and sovereignty. 'Individuality is a universal law which must be obeyed if we would have order and harmony in any sphere, and, consequently, if we would have a true constitution of human government, then the absolute Sovereignty of the Individual necessarily results.' [Andrews, 28] Accepting that government may be a temporary necessity, Andrews looks forward to its eventual dissolution when the purposes which it serves—the restraint of encroachments and the management of combined interests—are provided for the practical adoption of a principle of mutual recognition of the pre-eminence of the rights of individuality. He writes, 'it is not only possible and rationally probable, but that it is rigidly consequential upon the right understanding of the constitution of man, that all government, in the sense of involuntary restraint upon the Individual, or substantially all, must finally cease, and along with it the whole complicated paraphernalia and trumpery of Kings, Emperors, President, Legislatures, and Judiciary.' [Andrews, 42]

12 Spooner 1992, 57. Emphasis in original.

13 The presentation of Spooner's ideas in the remainder of this section is a version of material that first appeared in Casey 2012b, 128-145.

14 Spooner 1992, 77. Emphasis added.

15 It is possible to argue, as Sheldon Richman has persuasively done, that the U.S. Constitution

was never intended to be, as it is commonly believed to have been, 'a landmark in the long and continuing struggle for liberty' but rather the charter document of a counter-revolutionary movement
of conservatives seeking to institutionalise a national government with 'the unlimited power to tax,
to maintain a permanent debt through a central bank, to regulate and promote trade, and to keep a
standing army...' [Richman 2016, 1]
16 'And it can be supposed to have been a contract then only between persons who had already
come to years of discretion, so as to be competent to make reasonable and obligatory contracts.'
[Spooner 1992, 77]
17 "Those persons, if any, who did give their consent formally, are all dead now. Most of them
have been dead forty, fifty, sixty, or seventy years." [Spooner 1992, 77]
18 Spooner 1992, 67. I make no apology for citing some long passages from Spooner. Given that
his writings are so little known, it is difficult otherwise to get the flavour of his style which, to me
at any rate, is a truly delightful blend of icy logic and flaming invective.
19 References to Tucker will, in the main, be either to an issue of *Liberty* (by issue number and
page number*)*, or to *Instead of a Book* (which is largely made up of excerpts from *Liberty*).
20 The English Individualist John Badcock Jr. was another Stirnerite. [see Watner 1982a, 60]
21 For a concise account of the natural rights/egoism debate within the pages of *Liberty*, see
McElroy 1998, 426-428.
22 *Liberty* 321, 1; see also 235, 2 and 320, 4 & 5.
23 Tucker 1897, 63; see Watner 1977, 317.
24 Murray Rothbard took 'Aubrey Herbert' as a pen name for some of his early writings!
25 A proper consideration of the contribution to political philosophy of Herbert Spencer, one of the
now-neglected giants of nineteenth thought, would simply take us too far afield. Another thinker
of an individualist, quasi-anarchist feminist persuasion worthy of an extensive treatment is Josephine Butler whose 'own advocacy of radical decentralization was not fully anarchist, yet her class
and gender critique would clearly make such an association intellectually comfortable, whilst her
combination of feminism and libertarianism with a class analysis was the basis of individualism.'
[Ryley, 59]
26 Apart from Donisthorpe and Herbert, Tucker also extended publication hospitality to Joseph
Hiam Levy, Joseph Greevz Fisher, John Badcock Jr., Albert Tarn, Henry Seymour, M. D. O'Brien,
J. M. Armsden, W. C. Crofts and A. E. Porter. Of these, Carl Watner writes, 'This disparate group of
activists and thinkers were truly individualists; no two were wholly alike in their philosophy. What
united them was their general adherence to a doctrine of individual freedom in economic enterprise
and social relations, which they believed should not be restricted by governmental regulations.
Every one of the group mentioned had at least minor differences with Tucker and the editorial
doctrines of *Liberty*.' [Watner 1982a, 60]
27 Ryley, 52; see also Ryley 51-85.
28 Tucker 1897, 39-40; see McElroy 2012.
29 'Auberon Herbert,' writes Brian Doherty, 'a disciple of Spencer's, stayed truer to Spencer's
original anarchist vision and was a direct inspiration to a squad of 1950's American libertarian
anarchists who adopted his term "voluntaryism." Herbert was that rare anarchist philosopher who
was a practicing politician before his ideological maturation.' [Doherty, 35-36]
30 Herbert 1885, 33; see also Herbert 1978, 384-386. Some lively debates between Herbert and
Tucker on the topic of property (and others) grace the pages of *Liberty*.
31 Herbert 1978, 348; see 304-305.
32 Herbert 1978, 375-376; emphasis in original; see also 383-384.
33 Watner 1982a, 63, 64. For a succinct yet illuminating account of the Herbert-Levy dispute,
see Watner 1982a, 61-67. Many of the issues and controversies to be found in the pages of *Liberty*
are still with us today, with current arguments on the nature and limitations (if any) of liberty, the
meaning and justification of self-ownership, government vs governance, protective associations,
and the rights and limits of property all bearing an uncanny resemblance to those discussed in
Liberty over a hundred years ago.
34 See Herbert 1978, 191-226—'The Ethics of Dynamite'.

Chapter 31

TWENTIETH-CENTURY TRIBALISMS—FASCISM, NATIONAL SOCIALISM AND BOLSHEVISM

How fortunate for leaders that men do not think
—Adolf Hitler

The world is bursting with sin and sorrow.
Am I to be champion of the Decalogue, and to be
eternally raising fleets and armies to make all men good and happy?
—Sydney Smith

A man is likely to mind his own business when it is worth minding.
When it is not, he takes his mind off his own meaningless affairs
by minding other people's business....
Those who see their lives as spoiled and wasted crave
equality and fraternity more than they do freedom.
If they clamor for freedom, it is but freedom
to establish equality and uniformity
—Eric Hoffer

The political events that took place in 1920s and 1930s Italy and Germany with their associated ideologies of Fascism and National Socialism were unique, unprecedented and largely inexplicable phenomena, the political equivalent of geological erratics. These political singularities were brought into being by a specific combination of post-World War I angst, the worldwide economic recession of the late 1920s[1] and the inability of liberal democracies to cope with those problems. [see Wiskemann, 13-51] World War II was fought to exterminate the aggression of Fascism and National Socialism and it did this so successfully that apart from some few insignificant pockets here and there, these movements have been virtually eliminated from contemporary societies. To twenty-first century eyes, it seems as if 'Fascism, ignominiously struck down in the course of the Second World War, quickly lost whatever cachet it briefly enjoyed among some intellectuals in the West, to be reduced to little more than a public expression of private pathologies.' [Gregor 2009, 1]

This is the story that's commonly told and it isn't without its charm; unfortunately, it has the slight disadvantage of not being entirely true. Despite the standard historically pious account of the eradication of fascism, much of what fascism (and national socialism and bolshevism[2]) stood for and stands for is still with us—it hasn't gone away, you know. Wesley Riddle writes, 'The spirit of fascism is alive and well in the United States, and it is not only—not even primarily—the parley of the right. There are, to use Friedrich Hayek's words, "totalitarians in our midst." Indeed, the Welfare State bears the fundamental characteristics of fascism, that is, government control of the use and disposal of private property and government confiscation of the wealth of productive members of society to support welfare schemes and to buy political patronage.'[3] [Riddle, 156-157]

Fascism and National Socialism and, as I shall argue, Leninism/Stalinism (Bolshevism, for short) were *not* political singularities but were rather particular forms of a broader set of phenomena whose roots reach back into the nineteenth century, to Bergson, to Sorel, to Nietzsche, to the Romantic movement and still further back to the French Revolution and Rousseau. As Karl Popper remarks, 'Modern totalitarianism is only an episode within the perennial revolt against freedom and reason.' [Popper, 60] We might substitute 'fascism' for 'totalitarianism' in Popper's remark and it would be equally true. Fascism did not come from nowhere. It did not suddenly spring into being out of thin air. 'Italian fascism,' writes Richard Griffiths, 'was not so much the creator of a tradition, as one manifestation, albeit a particularly successful one, of a series of concerns that were in the air.' [Griffiths, 11]

'THE COLONEL'S LADY AN' JUDY O'GRADY ARE SISTERS UNDER THEIR SKINS'[4]

In the course of this book I have often mentioned that philosophical concepts are, by their very nature, contested, and the same is true for certain key political concepts. The subjects of this chapter—fascism, national socialism, and marxism in its twentieth century political instantiation of bolshevism— are concepts concerning the use of which there are no neutral positions. Take fascism. Some would confine the use of this term strictly to the early twentieth century Italian experience while others would endorse a broader usage that would permit its application to political movements in Spain and Portugal and elsewhere.[5] Is there a generic fascism of which there are particular types, the two most prominent instantiations being Mussolini's Italy and Hitler's Germany, with others bringing up the rear? Or is fascism, as already suggested, a political movement peculiar to Italy, differing not only from Hitler's National Socialism (as Gregor suggests) but from all other putative fascisms in other countries as well? Was National Socialism a form of fascism or something completely different? 'Fascist movements,' writes Robert Paxton, 'varied so conspicuously from one national setting to another, moreover, that some even doubt that the term fascism has any meaning other than as a smear word. The epithet has been so loosely used that practically everyone who either holds or shakes authority has been someone's fascist.'[6]

A. James Gregor appears to deny the identity of national socialism and fascism, writing, 'National Socialism was an anomalous fascist power. Its charismatic object of loyalty...proved to be not the nation, the characteristic object of loyalty for true fascism, but an ill-defined and ill-assessed racial confraternity.' [Gregor 1969, xiv] John Lukacs too denies that there's a general form of fascism. For him, fascism is ineluctably Italian whereas national socialism is a type or kind, of which German National Socialism was just one particular historical manifestation. 'National Socialism was more universal and more powerful and more enduring than was fascism,' writes Lukacs. [Lukacs, 117] The application of the term 'fascist' to Hitler's national socialism was, he believes, an attempt on the part of the Soviet Union to put some distance between what was going on in Germany and its own increasingly national form of socialism. 'Stalin had good reasons to insist on this kind of terminology. National, instead of "international" socialism was more and more applicable to Stalin's Russia in the 1930s, whence it was best to avoid the usage of such a term. At the same time the overall application of "fascism" to all right-wing, and strongly anti-communist, parties and practices and phenomena was very useful for international communist and left-wing rhetoric and practice.' [Lukacs, 108]

What of marxism in its Bolshevist incarnations?[7] Is *that* completely different from fascism and national socialism and something *sui generis* or does it instantiate elements of fascism or national socialism in some significant respect? As we have just seen, John Lukacs believes that Bolshevism was just one particular instantiation of a generic national socialism whereas National Socialism was another, the type or kind 'national socialism' as a whole being distinct from the type or kind 'fascism'. There may be some who will maintain that the Russian experiment wasn't in any real sense an implementation of Marxism, perhaps even that Marxism has never really been concretely implemented at all. But, as Augusto Del Noce notes, no Marxist can consistently hold this position since Marx placed 'the criterion of truth of his philosophy in empirical verification, in the historical result it has produced....Marxism could become reality only in the exact way that it did; therefore, it was verified in terms of its power, and at the same time refuted in terms of its outcome.'[8] Since 1989, marxism has all but ceased to be an effective political force, but its cultural influence continues unabated. 'Today Marxism no longer fuels a revolutionary faith in the Communists themselves, but its philosophical negations have penetrated mainstream opinion.' [Del Noce, 83]

Roger Griffin argues that 'there can be no objective definition of fascism, since, like all generic conceptions in the human sciences, "fascism" is at bottom an ideal type. In other words, it ultimately results from an act of idealizing abstraction which produces an artificially tidy model of the kinship that exists with a group of phenomena which, despite their differences, are sensed to have certain features in common.' [Griffin, 2]

It is hard to disagree with this claim, nonetheless, I shall argue that Fascism and National Socialism (and Bolshevism) are all forms of fascism, broadly understood, which developed in more or less relative isolation from each other. They were products of similar but nationally modified sets of circumstances. Stanley Payne, the historian of fascism, argues that, despite the controversies over the term's meaning and application, 'it is useful to treat fascism as a general type or generic phenomenon for heuristic and analytic purposes...' [Payne 1995, 4] Mussolini was to acknowledge that 'Fascism and Nazism are two manifestations of the parallel historical situations which link the life of our nations, resurrected to unity in the same century and through the same action.'[9] Hitler was somewhat less concerned about doctrinal convergence between Fascism and his National Socialism. What he admired in Mussolini wasn't any particular doctrine or policy but Mussolini's skilful employment of the Sorelian myth and his rhetorical ability.

Fascism did not materialise magically from nowhere at the wave of Mussolini's wand. It is true that Italian Fascism took time to develop a reasonably clear ideological content but it did eventually arrive at one. A. James Gregor believes that 'Fascism, as a social and political philosophy, was essentially the product of the genius of Giovanni Gentile.' [Gregor 1969, 5] The works of Gentile, he believes, compare 'more than favourably with Lenin's rationale and perhaps favourably with the philosophical efforts of Marx as well. ...Gentile's arguments appear and reappear in all the official Fascist attempts at rational vindications of policy. Gentile's argument proved essential to standard Fascist apologetics.'[10]

Just as Mussolini did not conjure up fascism all on his own, so too, Hitler did not single-handedly invent national socialism. The idea of a form of socialism that would be confined to or directed towards the nation was already current in France in the Cercle Proudhon in the early years of the twentieth century. Friedrich Hayek notes, 'the support which brought [National-Socialist] ideas to power came precisely from the socialist camp.' [Hayek 1944, 125] If anything constituted the distinctive heart of National Socialism it was the *Führerprinzip* (with Hitler as *Führer*), the racial superiority of the Germans versus the racial inferiority of the Jews and Slavs and others, and war as an instrument of policy and substance. As early as 1939, Stephen King-Hall saw the content of National Socialist doctrine as consisting of nationalism taken to the extreme, the subordination of the individual to the community and the *Führerprinzip*, together with the addition of positive racism (Nordicism) and negative racism (anti-Semitism) and anti-communism. [see King-Hall, 23]

As should be obvious by now, there's no universal agreement on what the essential constituents, if any, of fascism, national socialism and bolshevism might be, but here, in no particular order, are some of the usual suggestions: these movements appear to approve of collectivism, nationalism, authoritarianism, totalitarianism, corporatism, militarism and violence, and to disapprove of Jews, capitalism, democracy, materialism, parliamentarianism and liberal decadence. In addition to delineating these general characteristics which the three movements all share to some extent or other, it doesn't seem to me to be possible to make sense of this seemingly heterogeneous collection of characteristics without taking an interpretative stand that can't be other than controversial.

I believe that the outstanding and dominant characteristic that fascism, national socialism and bolshevism together exhibit is *tribalism*, the exaltation of the group over the individual, whether that group is a nation or a race or a class or a tribe. 'Tribalism has immense power, as anyone who has ever been caught up in the emotions of a crowd can testify. To surrender the lonely self to something larger, more powerful and elementary, is one of the deepest instincts of mankind.'[11] Tribalism is a venerable characteristic of all human societies. We can find this expressed in popular culture in Mr Spock's portentous enunciation in *The Wrath of Khan* (1982) that 'The needs of the many outweigh the needs of the few...or the one.' In this chapter, I shall characterise fascism, national socialism and bolshevism as modern forms of tribalism in which the state attempts, with various degrees of success, to exercise total or near-total control over all political and social matters. I am not the first or indeed the only person to defend this kind of interpretation. Writing of the distinguished historian Pitirim Sorokin, Frank Cowell remarks that, for Sorokin, 'it is possible to understand the similarity which makes recent Communist, Fascist and Nazi systems species or classes of the same genus or large class of totalitarian state among which are to be found the state systems of ancient Egypt, Peru, Mexico and of China...' [Cowell 1952, 167] Before addressing the topic of tribalism directly, however, I first want to take a brief look at the philosophy underlying these apparently diverse movements, in particular fascism, before trying to show that a significant part of their appeal lies in their ability to provide for their adherents a form of transcendence.

Irrationalism—the Philosophy of Fascism

What philosophy, then, lies behind fascism?[12] Does any? The temptation is to say that fascism has no philosophy, for it is quite widely believed that fascism has no intellectual foundation of its own and that, at best, it wears intellectual clothing borrowed from other movements of thought and is quite content with this second-hand intellectual sartorialism. The same view is commonly expressed regarding national socialism. But, remarks Friedrich Hayek, 'It is a common mistake to regard National-Socialism as a mere revolt against reason, an irrational movement without intellectual background.' [Hayek 1944, 124] Most commentators agree in characterising fascism as anti-rational, as a movement that valorises belief and will and action over reasoning and reflection. An anonymous pro-fascist article of 1925 argued that 'Reasoning does not communicate, emotion does. Reasoning convinces, it does not attract. Blood is stronger than syllogisms.' [in Griffin, 55] Fascism, then, is a political fact but it's generally thought, and not only by its opponents, that there really is no such thing as fascist theory. 'We aren't effete thinkers,' the fascists seem to say, 'we are men of action.' That may indeed be what fascists think but anti-intellectualism is itself a kind of intellectual position in just the way that the plain bluff man of common sense who wants no truck with high-fa-lutin' philosophy is, of necessity, in the grip of a philosophy himself. As J. S. McClelland points out, it should be obvious that '"anti-intellectualism" is an intellectual position which has to be argued just as hard as the "intellectual" position it attacks.' [McClelland, 714] Anti-intellectualism, then, is itself an intellectual position (even if only latently so) and 'fascism's anti-rationalism hasn't prevented it from producing a vast amount of highly particular ideological writings, some of them displaying great erudition and theoretical verve...' [Griffin, 6]

The nineteenth century had seen a depreciation of reason by various thinkers and a corresponding elevation of instinct and will. For these thinkers, reason was sterile and life denying, whereas will was creative and life affirming. The opposition of reason and will is a common motif of fascism. Fascist thinkers oppose the living body of action and will to the frozen corpse of reason and calculation. Ethically, the desire for happiness or well-being is unfavourably contrasted with heroism and duty, and self-sacrifice and discipline and duty are favourably contrasted with the liberal attachment to freedom and equality.

Who were these nineteenth century progenitors of irrationalism? Among others, Henri Bergson, Georges Sorel, Friedrich Nietzsche and Jules Soury. All these thinkers in one way or another were critics of rationalism, mistrusting reason or allowing reason to possess, at best, an instrumental value. They tended to elevate something other than reason—*élan vital*, violence, will, action—to the primary position. 'The anti-rationalists were, in general, men who had become convinced that "unconscious," "instinctive," or "paralogical" elements were of primary importance in determining individual and collective response to the environment.' [Gregor 1969, 63] A cross-connection between nineteenth century anarchism and irrationalism can be found in the writings of Stirner. 'What strikes one at once about *The Ego and His Own* is its passionate anti-intellectualism,' writes George Woodcock. Stirner 'cuts through all the structures of myth and philosophy, all the artificial constructions of human thought, to the elemental self....The human individual is the only thing of which we have certain knowledge, and each individual is unique....Rights do not exist; there is only the might of the embattled ego.' [Woodcock, 92, 93] Schopenhauer is *the* pre-eminent philosopher of the will, where will is presented as a supra-human and a-rational force that expresses itself blindly and treats with contempt and disdain the individual desires of the little human animals whose destiny it determines. For Schopenhauer, the commonplace man is to be superseded by a kind of latter-day quasi-Buddhist saint. For Nietzsche, who despised the common man every bit as much as Schopenhauer, it is the hero,[13] not the saint, who is to supersede the common man.[14] If Schopenhauer was an Eastern philosopher in Western guise, Henri Bergson wasn't so very different. As Buddhists are happy to use reason to demonstrate its own limitations, so too, Bergson used reason to demonstrate the limits of the intellect. Reason and intellect have their uses but only as instruments for the movement of the *élan vital*, the creative life force. 'Bergson supposed the mind to be natively endowed with such an intuition, akin to instinct and more deeply rooted in life than is reason, but largely atrophied in human development by man's overdependence on intelligence.'[15]

Neither Schopenhauer nor Bergson had any particular interest in the application of their ideas to politics. The first person to attempt the more or less systematic application of the philosophy of irrationalism to politics was Georges Sorel. This he did in his 1908 work, *Reflections on Violence*, in which capitalism played the role that Schopenhauer had attributed to the will, that of blindly bringing higher forms of social life into being without intending to do so. Sorel provided a unique blend of ideas from sources as diverse as Nietzsche, Vico and Bergson. John Bowle goes so far as to say that if one is to understand the twentieth century 'one must take account of Sorel....his criticisms can be answered: they cannot be ignored.' [Bowle, 402] Sorel isn't the easiest author to read and, by general consent, his writings are confused and sometimes even contradictory. Why, given his admitted contradictions and confusions, is Sorel important? He is important because as well as being part of the movement of anti-intellectualism made popular by Bergson and others, Sorel also managed to combine 'Marx's belief in the class war with a Nietzschean understanding of myth, and a new understanding of the subconscious mind.'[16] It is arguable that he contributed three ideas that were to become centrally important to fascism—*syndicalism*, the importance of *violence* or direct action, and the notion of the *myth*.

Sorel began his political life as a *syndicalist*. Syndicalism is a form of socialism that puts a priority on trade unions as the means of overall social organisation. 'Syndicalism informed corporatist theory,' writes Jonah Goldberg, 'by arguing that society could be divided by professional sectors of the economy, an idea that deeply influenced the New Deals of both FDR and Hitler.' [Goldberg 2008, 36] We shall see a little later just how important corporatist ideas would be for fascism.[17]

Sorel's thought is particularly stark inasmuch as, despite his roots in anarcho-syndicalism, which isn't normally noted for extraordinary militancy, he proposed that a healthy society was one in which conflict and *violence* played a constitutive part. For Sorel, 'Violence was important in itself, whether it pursued a practical end or not. The violent act was useful as providing the "extreme moments" which sustained the class struggle and, through that, the health and vigour of society as a whole.' [Griffiths, 14] To those who had been through the conflagration that was World War I, a little street violence was nothing to get too upset about. On a slightly higher level, violence could be seen to have a number of functions, among them the ability to create an heroic group consciousness and also to be an instrument for the achievement of policy. The Sorelian view of violence was that it was a means of defence against the tyranny of the democratic state, a view that was ripe for an alliance with the Bismarckian view that violence was a tool for the achievement of the state's purposes. Hitler was to combine the two views so that 'the Sorelian violence of a mass movement could be used to capture state power, whose legitimate violence could then be used in the pursuit of Nazi foreign policy ends: first the Party and the SA, and then the Wehrmacht.' [McClelland, 722]

Sorel proposed the idea of *myth* as an organising principle whose function was to guide and motivate action regardless of its truth. For Sorel, myth isn't the product of reasoned investigation but the result of intuition. Henri Bergson, one of Sorel's sources, spoke of intuition as a capacity that 'transcends the intellect' and whose 'immediate truths…are independent of, and antecedent to, the truth conditions governing physical science.' [Gregor 2009, 97] As Sorel puts it, perhaps less than perspicuously, a myth is 'a body of images which, by intuition alone, and before any considered analyses are made, is capable of evoking as an undivided whole the mass of sentiments which corresponds to the different manifestations of the war undertaken by socialism against modern society.' [Sorel, 57] This Sorelian idea of myth was taken up by Mussolini whose operational myth was that the Italian nation was the spiritual descendant of Ancient Rome. In 1922, Mussolini wrote, 'We have created our myth. The myth is a faith, a passion. It is not necessary for it to be a reality. It is a reality in the sense that it is a stimulus, is hope, is faith, is courage. Our myth is the nation, our myth is the greatness of the nation! And to this myth, this greatness, which we want to translate into a total reality, we subordinate everything else. For us the nation is not just territory, but something spiritual....A nation is great when it translates into reality the force of its spirit.'[18] Griffin adds, 'Hitler, who owed no direct debt to Sorel, had his notion of a *Weltanschauung* [world view] that played the same role in his thought as myth did for Sorel and Mussolini. If Ancient Rome played the part of myth for Mussolini, race, blood and soil was Hitler's version.

The Sorelian myth, then, is a vital part of any fascist ideology. Griffin's definition of fascism is that it is 'a genus of political ideology whose mythic core in its various permutations is a palingenetic [rebirth] form of populist ultra-nationalism.' [Griffin, 4] For Fascism proper, it is the nation which is to be reborn; for National Socialism, the *Volk*, for Bolshevism, the proletariat. Fascism proper is a type of political organisation based on a set of fundamental principles the essence of which is a kind of ultra-nationalism built on the idea of a rebirth of the nation. This myth of rebirth in Fascism was the means by which a humdrum political ideology was transmuted into an immanently transcendent *ersatz* religion. That Fascism was intended to be a new religion was well understood by the Vatican. In his 1931 encyclical, *Non abbiamo bisogno*, Pope Pius XI accused Fascism of attempting to inculcate in the young a 'statolatry', a pagan worship of the state. [Pius XI, §44]

The function of the Sorelian myth was to generate the psychic energy that would lead to action, action untrammelled by the limitations of rational thought. Reason had its place, of course, but only as an instrument or a tool. What mattered most was the will, a will to believe (William James), a will to power (Friedrich Nietzsche), a will to act. If such action involved violence or even terror, so be it; yet another idea that has its roots in the French Revolution. All human life was characterised by struggle, intellectual or physical and it isn't an accident that Hitler called his *magnum opus*, *Mein Kampf—My Struggle*. Sorel understood that 'what counted in politics were myths for which men would die.' [Bowle, 399] Mussolini and Hitler had both been impressed by the fact that in the First World War, soldiers had been willing to fight and die not for socialism or for any other idea but for the nation, for Italy or for Germany, a fact all the more impressive when one remembers that Italy and Germany as nations were relatively recent creations, going back in time not much further than fifty or sixty years.

Nationalism, in one form or another, writes Gregor, 'was the 'organizing or functional myth of 'fascism.' [Gregor 1969, 153] Roger Griffin agrees, arguing that what he calls the mythic core of Fascism is the idea of a nation [*Volk*, proletariat] as an organism or group that can degenerate or be regenerated, the nation [*Volk*, proletariat] as a kind of hyper-person. Its core is the idea of a re-birth, a new beginning. 'The mythic core that forms the basis of my ideal type of generic fascism,' writes Griffin, 'is the vision of the (perceived) crisis of the nation as betokening the birth pangs of a new order. It crystallizes in the image of the national community, once purged and rejuvenated, rising phoenix-like from the ashes of a morally bankrupt state system and the decadent culture associated with it.' [Griffin, 3] Nationalism, for the Fascist, is the belief that the nation has an intrinsically higher level of being than the individuals of which it is constituted. Those individuals, in turn, give meaning to their lives only inasmuch as they contribute to the flourishing of the nation. What has been said of fascism applies *mutatis mutandis* to national socialism and bolshevism.

Transcendence

So, then, there is after all a philosophy of sorts behind fascism—the depression of the pretensions of reason and thought and the exaltation of instinct and feeling. But there is more to the appeal of fascism than a warmed-over version of nineteenth-century irrationalism. The mass of men isn't moved by rational subtleties, even the rational subtleties of irrationalism! The appeal of fascism can be comprehended only if it is seen to be an attempt—in its time, a very successful attempt—to overcome what are taken to be the limitations of individualism, selfishness and materialism, in the interests of a higher end, an attempt to achieve a kind of transcendence through political means.[19] I use the term 'transcendence' here to signify simply the desire each man has to belong to or be part of something more than the humdrum little world inhabited by his own little self, whatever that something more might be. [see Tallis 2010, passim] The aim of many men isn't to exalt the self but rather to lose it. 'Their chief desire,' writes Eric Hoffer, 'is to escape that self—and it is this desire which manifests itself in a propensity for united action and self-sacrifice. The revulsion from an unwanted self, and the impulse to forget it, mask it, slough it off and lose it, produce both a readiness to sacrifice the self and a willingness to dissolve it by losing one's individual distinctness in a compact collective whole.' [Hoffer, 58, §43]

It is hard to disagree with Christopher Booker when he writes, 'All human beings belong to families, communities, tribes or nations which provide them with a central part of their sense of identity.' [Booker, 551] Liberal democracy had dramatically revealed its limitations in the mass slaughter of World War I and its aftermath. 'It is hard, nowadays,' writes Griffiths, 'to realise the feeling of disarray in the western democracies at this time. There was a real sense of doubt, even among democracy's strongest supporters, as to its capacity to survive the crisis.' [Griffiths, 59] Eric Hoffer notes, 'There was no likelihood of a genuine revolutionary movement arising in Wilhelmian Germany. The Germans were satisfied with the centralized, authoritarian Kaiser regime, and even defeat in the First World War did not impair their love for it. The revolution of 1918 was an artificial thing with little popular backing. The years of the Weimar Constitution that followed were for most Germans a time of irritation and frustration. Used as they were to commands from above and respect for authority, they found the loose, irreverent democratic order all confusion and chaos. They were shocked to realize that they had to participate in government, choose a party, and pass judgment upon political matters. They longed for a new corporate whole, more monolithic, all-embracing and glorious to behold than even the Kaiser regime had been—and the third Reich more than answered their prayer.' [Hoffer, 47-48, §35]

Gerald M. Platt writes of the individual's need to make sense of his place in the world and the devastation that occurs when such a place can't be found. He remarks, 'The loss of familiar social orders and one's place in them is potentially chaotic. People who can't sustain a biographically achieved sense of personal identity, continuity, feelings of worthiness, self-esteem, membership in a community and so on, are easily overwhelmed by affective experiences. When these conditions are widespread the society is undergoing a sense-making crisis.'[20] J. S. McClelland remarks that 'Fascism makes perfectly good sense as an anti-Marxist but still revolutionary[21] response to the apparent failures of liberal democracies in their troubled period after the First World War. Fascism can be seen as an attempt to reintegrate societies that were going through the painful process of becoming mass societies, or were seen to be going through such a process. No doubt fascists exaggerated the extent to which their societies were disintegrating into heaps of atomised, anomic individuals....but the fact remains that fascism was a way of getting out of what appeared to be enervated liberal democracies with some form of social integration left intact.' [McClelland, 736-737] From the fascist perspective, both liberalism and socialism were failed political experiments. 'Fascism transcends democracy and liberalism,' wrote Asvero Gravelli, the director of Antieuropa, in 1930. 'Its regenerating action is based on granite foundations: the concept of hierarchy, the participation of the whole people in the life of the State, social justice through the equitable distribution of rights and duties; the injection of morality into public life; the prestige of the family; the moral interpretation of the ideas of order, authority, and freedom.' [in Griffin, 66-67]

In his brilliant essay, 'The Masses in Representative Democracy,' Michael Oakeshott characterises what the calls the 'mass man' as the obverse of the individual who emerged decisively in Europe in the fourteenth and fifteenth centuries. According to Oakeshott, the aim of the mass man is to 'assimilate the world to his own character by deposing the individual and destroying his moral prestige.' [Oakeshott 1991a, 372] The mass man has no friends, for friendship is a relation between individuals; in its place, he substitutes comradeship. He has feelings rather than thoughts, impulses rather than opinions, and above all else, he requires to be led. For such men, leaders are never lacking. Private property is a material dimension of individuality and so must be abolished, and an equality which permits no one to differ essentially from another is the basis of his morality: 'All must be equal and anonymous units in a "community".' [Oakeshott 1991a, 375] In words that have a familiar and ominous ring, Oakeshott explains that for the mass man, government was understood to be 'the exercise of power in order to impose and maintain the substantive condition of human circumstance identified as "the public good"; to be governed was, for the "anti-individual", to have made for him the choices he was unable to make for himself. Thus, "government" was cast for the role of architect and custodian, not of "public order" in an "association" of individuals pursuing their own activities, but of "the public good" of a "community". The ruler was recognized to be, not the referee of the collisions of individuals, but the moral leader and managing director of "the community". And this understanding of government has been tirelessly explored over a period of four and a half centuries from Thomas More's *Utopia* to the Fabian Society, from Campanella to Lenin. [Oakeshott 1991a, 377]

The widespread social, political, religious and personal dislocation and disorientation produced by the First World War, and the economic devastation following on from the Great Depression, provided the perfect conditions for those proposing to the bewildered masses a way of understanding the chaos in which they found themselves and also, more importantly, a way out of that chaos towards a new and better order. The social disruption that followed the war was not so much a function of any deep trauma as it was simply the result of 'the prolonged break in the civilian routine of the millions enrolled in the national armies.' [Hoffer, 49, §36]

Man is a strange animal. Once his primary biological requirements are met, his need for satisfaction isn't sated but rather displaced. His day-to-day self is seldom so prepossessing that when his gaze turns inward he can bear to contemplate its magnificence for long, and when his safety and security is guaranteed, and the memory of need and danger distant, his defining affective state isn't one of gratitude but boredom. Despair, disgust and boredom are an ever-present nuisance in time of contentment to man, but you could travel through the entire universe, like Bowerick Wowbagger, the Infinitely Prolonged,[22] and still be unable to find an anxious pig or a parrot suffering from existential angst. Dogs don't get bored when there's nothing to do, and cats just go to sleep but, as the novelist and philosopher Walker Percy notes, 'a man in the world has the unique capacity for being delighted with the world and himself and his place in the world, or being bored with it, anxious about it, or depressed about it.' [Percy 2000a, 127]

Who could possibly feel as alive as the man who has just escaped death! Martin Bell, one-time war correspondent of the BBC comments: 'I'm the happiest that I've ever been. The turning point was nearly getting killed in a war zone. After that, every day has been like the first day of the rest of my life. I am living not on borrowed time, but on donated time. Every day I wake up happy to be alive.' [Bell 2005]

Imagine you get up on a Monday morning, have the same skimpy and rushed breakfast you always have, go to work to the same place where you have worked for the last 15 years to face the same tasks you have faced since what seems like the dawn of creation. At work, you collapse and are rushed to hospital. They run some tests on you and inform you that you are in the advanced stages of pancreatic cancer with just two months to live. Later that afternoon, an embarrassed house doctor comes back to tell you that the hospital confused your records with those of another man with the same name and that there's nothing really wrong with you that eating a regular breakfast and a good holiday won't cure. How do you feel? As if reprieved at the last minute from the firing squad. How does the world look to you now? Suddenly, everything is vibrant, coloured and alive.

Émile Durkheim gave us the technical term *anomie* to describe the condition that results from the deterioration or dissolution of social bonds between individuals and their social groups, a condition that has become increasingly characteristic of Western societies in the last two hundred years. 'When people are bored,' writes Hoffer, 'it is primarily with their own selves that they are bored. The consciousness of a barren, meaningless existence is the main fountainhead of boredom. People who are not conscious of their individual separateness, as is the case with those who are members of a compact tribe, church, party, etcetera, are not accessible to boredom. The differentiated individual is free of boredom only when he is engaged either in creative work or some absorbing occupation or when he is wholly engrossed in the struggle for existence. Pleasure-chasing and dissipation are ineffective palliatives. Where people live autonomous lives and are not badly off, yet are without abilities or opportunities for creative work or useful action, there is no telling to what desperate and fantastic shifts they might resort in order to give meaning and purpose to their lives.' [Hoffer, 54, §41]

Of course, there's nothing like a real threat to shake us out of our lassitude, and that's why war is (or at least can be) exciting. War is unpredictable and dangerous—peacetime is, in contrast, safe but boring. Even if it is conceded that much of a soldier's life is a succession of humdrum days, still, the presence of even a remote possibility of death lends a certain zest to life. Of course, this in no way provides a justification for war, for, as Benjamin Constant remarks, 'I have sometimes wondered what one of these men who wish to repeat the deeds of Cambyses, Alexander or Attila would reply if his people spoke to him and told him: nature has given you a quick eye, boundless energy, a consuming need for strong emotion, an inexhaustible thirst for confronting and surmounting danger, for meeting and overcoming obstacles. But why should we pay for thee? Do we exist only so that they may be exercised at our expense? Are we here only to build, with our dying bodies, your road to fame? You are bored by the inactivity of peace. Why should your boredom concern us?' [Constant 1988, 82]

Fascism offered a form of transcendence, then, one that took its inspiration from a common experience of the First World War. The war had shown that people from different regions of Italy, speaking different dialects, could sink their differences in pursuit of a common goal. What if the unified and concerted action demanded and produced by the war could be reproduced in peacetime and directed positively towards the good of the nation? What could not be achieved if the petty squabbling and the friction produced by each man's pursuit of his own narrow interests, so evident in liberal democracies, could be superseded by the coordinated cooperation of all for the good of all?

Even the home of the brave and the land of the free seems to have been afflicted with doubts about the ability of liberal democracy to cope with the post-war problems. It is an old political maxim that one should never let a good crisis go to waste and, if such crises do not occur naturally, why then, they can always be contrived.[23] 'In times of crisis, during floods, earthquakes, epidemics, depressions and wars, separate individual effort is of no avail, and people of every condition are ready to obey and follow a leader. To obey is then the only firm point in a chaotic day-by-day existence.' [Hoffer, 109, §93] President Roosevelt announced in his Inaugural Address of 4 March in the fateful year of 1933 that he was unhesitatingly assuming 'the leadership of the great army of our people dedicated to a disciplined attack upon our common problems.' The militaristic imagery is obvious and worrying but even more worryingly, Roosevelt went on to say that although he hoped that the normal balance of executive and legislative authority would be adequate to meet the crisis, he wasn't ruling out a temporary departure from that balance should that, in his judgement, become necessary. To the ears of the historically sensitive auditor, this statement cannot but fail to be resonant of the *Führerprinzip* of another leader who also took power in 1933. Roosevelt announced: 'In the event that Congress should fail to take one of these two courses, and in the event that the national emergency is still critical, I shall not then evade the clear course of my duty that will then confront me.' This duty, it seems, would be to ask Congress to give him broad executive power to 'wage a war' (again note the militaristic language) 'against the emergency, as great as the power that would be given to me if we were in fact invaded by a foreign foe.' Some might think that it would be going too far to describe this as incipient fascism but if it isn't exactly fascism as we have come to know and love it, it isn't a million miles away from it either. Riddle comments that 'The fact that the people looked to a single man, i.e. to the Chief Executive to lead them like a herd, testifies to the recent modern stature assumed by the Presidency. Progressive nationalism and total war had resulted in the growth of executive bureaucracy and increasing popular identification of the President as the Leader, America's counterpart to *Il Duce* and *der Führer*.' [Riddle, 144-145] Remarking on the imperialisation and autocratisation of the American Presidency, Robert Nisbet notes that 'Present-day royalism in the federal government began with FDR. Few then present are likely to forget the excitement generated by his seeming assumption during the Hundred Days of just about all the powers of government. Congress was for the time relegated to the shades; the air was filled with alphabetical symbols of the agencies, bureaus, strategies he was pursuing on his own.... Royalism the essence of Roosevelt's wartime stance....his consultation of the Congress, once the war was entered, was infrequent and minimal. So was his consultation of the Cabinet.'[Nisbet 1988, 80]

In the early decades of the twentieth century, the view of many was that something new and better was needed in place of the tired and ineffective nostrums of liberal democracy. A veteran of the war, Edgar Jung, wrote in 1927, 'A German resurgence demands ideas which are deeper and more in harmony with the German people, calls for a bold act of spiritual renewal so as to overcome the poverty of German thinking and German impotence.' [in Griffin, 107] Not just a new political order was needed, thought Ernest Jünger, but a new type of person who would exhibit a 'contempt for pleasure', a 'warrior-like mentality', a feeling for 'virile and unconditional judgements.' [in Griffin, 111] As is well known, Hitler believed that what had happened in the conduct of the final year of the war and in its political aftermath in Germany with the establishment of the Weimar Republic was a gross betrayal of the German people and a demonstration of national decadence.[24] In his speech to the court in Munich after his failed putsch of 1923, Hitler said, 'if the two million who lie buried in Flanders and Belgium were to rise from the dead and be asked whether they would be prepared to recognize the state of affairs brought about by that act of high treason [the establishment of the Weimar Republic]…they would all shout: Never! We did not fall in battle so that in five years more could be ripped away from Germany thanks to this new and so-called legalized constitutional state than had been gained in the previous 150 years with the blood of hundreds of thousands, indeed of millions.' What happened at the end of the war was, he said, 'a crime against the German people, a stab in the back against the heroically fighting army, against the German people, German freedom, and the German nation.' [in Griffin, 117]

There is to be found in fascism and its sister movements, then, a kind of immanent transcendence in which individuals are encouraged to go beyond the limitations of their petty existence to find fulfilment in advancing the destiny of the nation, the race or the working class. Fascism and national socialism and bolshevism make use of the religious language of sacrifice and redemption, a usage that has led some thinkers to classify them as forms of religion. To justify the claim that these movements are *ersatz* religions would take a book in itself. Fortunately, although the point tends to escape the attention of current scholars—Roger Griffin, for one, argues that fascism 'lacks a genuine metaphysical dimension and is the utter antithesis and destroyer of all genuine religious faith' [Griffin, 5] though he seems to have softened his attitude more recently—it was readily apparent to contemporaries of those movements and to many scholars since. Giovanni Amendola, the editor of *Il Mondo*, noted that Fascism had pretentions to being a religion that desired the conversion of Italians to the true political faith. [see Burleigh, 2] 'The fascist moment that gave birth to the "Russian-Italian method", writes Goldberg, 'was in reality a religious awakening in which Christianity was to be either sloughed off and replaced or "updated' by the new progressive faith in man's ability to perfect the world.' [Goldberg 2008, 139]

Jonah Goldberg's definition of fascism focuses explicitly on its religious dimension. He describes fascism as a 'religion of the state' which 'assumes the organic unity of the body politic and longs for a national leader attuned to the will of the people. It is totalitarian in that it views everything as political and holds that any action by the state is justified to achieve the common good. It takes responsibility for all aspects of life, including our health and well being, and seeks to impose uniformity of thought and action whether by force or through regulation and social pressure. Everything, including the economy and religion, must be aligned with its objectives.' [Goldberg 2008, 23] But it wasn't only opponents and critics of fascism and national socialism and bolshevism that characterised them as secular religions. In 1925, Mussolini spoke of himself as a Messiah who had begun by talking to fifty disciples and who then went on to evangelise many more with faith, devotion and sacrifice while, in the same year, Hitler compared himself to Christ who, according to

Hitler, 'rose in a rotten world, preached the faith, was at first scorned, and yet out of this faith a great world movement had been made.'[25]

Fascism and national socialism and bolshevism all rejected a consumerist materialism, a selfish and unpatriotic classical liberalism and an ineffective and decadent democracy. They castigated the desire for liberty and equality and happiness as petty-minded and bourgeois when compared to the challenge of service, devotion and discipline required of the patriotic citizen. In his 'Berlin Speech', in addition to the virtues of discipline, courage, tenacity and patriotism, Mussolini demanded from youth 'scorn for the comfortable life...' [in Griffin, 79] Oswald Mosley, the leader of the British Union of Fascists, wrote in 1935 that 'you find in Fascism, taken from Christianity....the immense vision of service, of self-abnegation, of self-sacrifice in the cause of others, in the cause of the world, in the cause of your country; not the elimination of the individual, so much as the fusion of the individual in something far greater than himself....' [in Griffin, 173-174]

The appeal of Fascism and National Socialism was, in the end, grounded in a kind of transcendence, a call to go beyond the narrow and petty limits of one's individual needs and desires to further the cause of something greater than oneself, whether that cause was the Volk or the State or the Nation or the Race or the Proletariat. The attraction of this challenge to rise above oneself is perfectly understandable. Many people live lives of outstanding ordinariness from which they try to escape in different ways. Standard operating practice here is, of course, the consumption of large amounts of alcohol, with drug-taking as an increasingly popular option as well. Some people live for Saturday afternoon football when they can lose their petty identities and become part of their team, experiencing joy or despair in a way not otherwise possible for them. Some people seek escape from the tedium of daily life in the vain search for the perfect sexual experience or the even vainer search for the perfect sexual partner, others in the never-ending pursuit of wealth and fame or yet more wealth or yet more fame.

History and literature reveal that many people experience their own selves as fleeting and insubstantial and their lives as basically meaningless. As Prospero says in Shakespeare's *The Tempest*, 'Our revels now are ended. These our actors, as I foretold you, were all spirits, and are melted into air, into thin air: And like the baseless fabric of this vision, The cloud-capp'd tow'rs, the gorgeous palaces, the solemn temples, the great globe itself, yea, all which it inherit, shall dissolve, and, like this insubstantial pageant faded, leave not a rack behind. We are such stuff as dreams are made on; and our little life is rounded with a sleep.'[26] Given the fragility and seeming insubstantiality of their lives, people seek to attach their evanescent selves to something greater and more significant than their tiny egos, something more important, more permanent and lasting. As Arthur Koestler notes, the worst evils in human relationships come not from selfishness or self-assertion but from a kind of misplaced effort at transcendence. He notes, 'the trouble with our species is not an excess of *aggression*, but an excess capacity for fanatical *devotion*.' [Koestler, 14] When we rid ourselves of our narrow, feeble, limited, hateful self, we give up not only whatever advantages may accrue to us but we also rid ourselves of responsibility. As Eric Hoffer notes, 'there is no telling to what extremes of cruelty and ruthlessness a man will go when he is freed from the fears, hesitations, doubts and the vague stirrings of decency that go with individual judgment. When we lose our individual independence in the corporateness of a mass movement, we find a new freedom—freedom to hate, bully, lie, torture, murder and betray without shame and remorse.' [Hoffer, 93, §77]

Emilio Gentile defines political religion[27] as 'a form of sacralisation of politics of an exclusive and integralist character…[that]…rejects coexistence with other political ideologies and movements, denies the autonomy of the individual with respect to the collective, prescribes the obligatory observance of its commandments and participation in its political cult, and sanctifies violence as a legitimate arm of the struggle against enemies, and as an instrument of regeneration.' Note these points well: political religions, including fascism and national socialism, are committed to the intolerance of political alternatives, an insistence on obedience and the use of violence to achieve their objectives and *the rejection of individual autonomy and the prioritisation of the collective*. Furthermore, Fascism, as a political religion, is a jealous god who will suffer no other god before it so that its intolerance extends beyond the boundaries of the merely political to include any rival centre of authority. 'It adopts,' says Emilio Gentile, 'a hostile attitude toward traditional institutionalised religions, seeks to eliminate them, or seeks to establish with them a relationship of symbiotic coexistence, in the sense that the political religion seeks to incorporate traditional religion within its own system of beliefs and myths, assigning it a subordinate and auxiliary role.' [Gentile, 30]

If Giovanni Gentile was the philosopher of Fascism, Martin Heidegger would have liked to be the philosopher of National Socialism. Heidegger believed that 'he could endow Hitler and the Nazi movement in general with the philosophy it needed to fully realise itself as the most valid "counter-movement against Nihilism", and so become the saving force of the West that it promised to be. He thought he knew better how the Nazi ideology ought to be articulated than the official ideologists and the other Nazi interpreters of Nietzsche, such as Kriek and Bäumler.' In the late 1920s, Heidegger 'so fused and confused his terms that,' as Karl Löwith remarked, 'it was not clear to his hearers whether they ought to begin reading the pre-Socratics or to join the SA.' [Redner, 60, 61]

Eric Voegelin characterises political ideologies as efforts to create quasi-religious communities that are, however, divorced from any real connection with the transcendent and turned inwards immanently instead of transcendently outwards. Class, state, race or nation—all are tried as God-substitutes.[28] Many of the ideas that informed fascism were 'in the air' in the nineteenth century but the attempted 'religionisation' of politics goes all the way back to the French Revolution and to Rousseau. Vilfredo Pareto commented that the vast majority of fascists 'followed a line of conduct to the pursuit of an almost mystical ideal: the celebration of national sentiment and the power of the State, the reaction against pseudo-liberal, pacifist, and humanitarian forms of democratic ideology.' In Italy, he wrote, 'Fascism has succeeded in...giving to the nationalist religion the goal of defending the State and brings about social renewal: this is where the essence of the Fascist Revolution basically lies.'[29]

In the light of all this, it might be granted that fascism and national socialism were (or are) forms of *ersatz* religion but surely, it will be objected, bolshevism couldn't have been one? Alas, yes. Marcin Kula writes, 'Although communism always fought against religion, paradoxically, it came to resemble it in a number of ways.' It is an indisputable fact, he says, 'that communism was never and nowhere free of quasi-religious elements.' [Kula, 371] Augusto Del Noce notes that the 'Marxist revolution keeps the appearance of a religion because it requires a conversion, since it marks a transition to a higher reality and to a reality that is totally "other," even if absolutely not transcendent or supernatural.' [Del Noce, 76] Peter Grieder writes, 'it is perhaps helpful to conceptualise National Socialism and Communism (particularly during the Stalinist period) as political religions....the titanic totalitarian movements of the twentieth century can usefully be interpreted as attempts to re-deify a godless universe through the worship of new, and as it turned out, false gods. With regard to Communist ideology, both former proponents and opponents subscribe to this view....The party was to Communists what the medieval Church was to Catholics: the source of all truth and redemption....As for the Nazis, it is virtually certain that they would have tried to supplant Christianity with their own quasi-religious *völkisch* ideology if they had won the war.' [Grieder, 573] Bolshevism is, in many ways, an immanent Manichaean Christian heresy—a struggle between good and evil forces but with those forces firmly located in the here and now, with the inexorable dynamic of history playing the role of Providence. As is often the case with the sceptic in the community of the faithful, hypocrisy is a necessary tool of survival.[30] After this detour through the themes of irrationalism and transcendence, we can now return to our consideration of fascism, national socialism and bolshevism as modern forms of tribalism.

TRIBALISM

If there is a transcendent and religious side to Fascism and National Socialism and Bolshevism—and I hope I have shown that there is—there's also a much more obvious, mundane and less contentious side to these movements. The second of Emilio Gentile's four-point characterisation of fascism was its rejection of the autonomy of the individual with respect to the collective. This point is, I believe, the most politically significant of all and the one most relevant to the effect such movements have on our freedom. Fascism, national socialism and bolshevism, in their different ways, are all forms of collectivism for which the individual is nothing and the collectivity everything, a claim encapsulated in the Fascist saying 'everything for the state; nothing against the state; nothing outside the state.' 'Fascism,' writes Gregor, 'aspired to a complete identification of the individual and the collective will.' [Gregor 1969, 322]

Much the same point is made by Llewellyn Rockwell in his study contrasting fascism and capitalism when he notes that 'The state, for the fascist, is the instrument by which the people's common destiny is realized, and in which the potential for greatness is to be found. Individual rights, and the individual himself, are strictly subordinate to the state's great and glorious goals for the nation. [Rockwell, ix] Bolshevism, fascism and national socialism all reject the priority of the individual. Without society the individual isn't *really* an individual, isn't *truly* human and cannot be so unless the interests of the "totality" and the individual ultimately coincide. On this point, bolshevism, fascism, national socialism, and even the more extreme variants of communitarianism, all meet.[31]

Alfredo Rocco, the Fascist Minister of Justice, in 1925, rejected the claim that Fascism undermines the status of the individual. According to him, Fascism does *not* submerge the individual in the group, it merely 'subordinates him but does not eliminate him...For Fascism, society is the end, individuals the means, and its whole life consists in using individuals as instruments for its social ends...Fascism...faces squarely the problem of the right of the state and the duty of individuals. Individual rights are only recognized in so far as they are implied in the rights of the state.'[32] One might well wonder just how much of substance is left in the individual once he has been subordinated, treated as a means to an end, instrumentalised and granted only those rights that the state is prepared to give him. With friends like that, Fascism scarcely needs enemies; with a denial like that, what need have we of an affirmation?

Fascism and national socialism and bolshevism are ultimately not something new but a return to one of the oldest form of social organisation, the tribe, but this time, the tribe on a very grand scale. In 'The Roots of War,' Ayn Rand wrote that 'the ideological root of statism (or collectivism) is the *tribal premise* of primordial savages who, unable to conceive of individual rights, believed that the tribe is a supreme, omnipotent ruler, that it owns the lives of its members and may sacrifice them whenever it pleases to whatever it deems to be its own "good".' [Rand 1967b, 31] The battle, as always, is between the collective and the individual and 'it does not matter if the individual is subsumed by the State, the Race, or the Collective....whether individual liberty is crushed by *welfare* socialism or *national* socialism.' [Riddle, 157] The individual had to be persuaded that what he really was wasn't just an isolated social atom but his people, his nation, his party and his state. 'Society and the state, for Gentile and for Fascist ethicists in general,' writes Gregor, had a 'logical, factual, and moral priority over the individuals of whom it was composed.' [Gregor 1969, 218] The collective is prior to the individual. The state is absolutely sovereign. There are no limitations to which it is subject.

The liberal distinction between society and state is a distinction without a difference. Without the state there is and can be no society. 'Social life without the state would be impossible....The Marxist distinction between the state which governs men and the non-state of the communist future which will govern things was, for Mussolini, devoid of meaning.'[33] Gregor emphasises the importance of myth, a Sorelian myth of course, that facilitates the collectivisation of the individual. 'The sentiments of collectivities are influenced by emotive suasion. As a consequence, an organizing or functional myth is generated which captures the collective imagination. Such a myth is a collection of propositions, neither necessarily consistent nor true, that effectively mobilize sentiment. ...Their chief function is to reduce the collective will to obedience.' [Gregor 1969, 87]

The priority of the collective over its constituent members was, as we have seen, characteristic of Greece and Rome. Not even Aristotle was able to escape the gravitational pull of the tribalism of the *polis* and Plato, of course, had no desire whatsoever to attempt an escape from tribalism but enthusiastically returned its embrace. Not only are national socialism and fascism and bolshevism new forms of tribalism, they are also, to use Christian categories, forms of idolatry, conflating the created with the Creator, a small piece of the spatio-temporal world with the divine. This tendency has many fathers, going back well into prehistory and finding modern expression in the thought of Machiavelli, among others.

For Mussolini, the nation had its own moral being as a kind of metaphysical parent whose children we are and on whom we depend for our very existence. For the tribalist, 'Individuals are products and not creators of society and the state.'[34] For the fascist, freedom is activity in conformity with law, a law determined by the guardians of the nation. This elevated conception of liberty is contrasted favourably with the vulgar liberal conception of freedom as mere instinct or caprice or choice. Just as an individual person has a coherent set of ends which exclude other ends, so too, the hyper-personal nation cannot tolerate whatever is inconsistent with its ends. The individual is subordinate to the nation and its ends and there's no room for individual rights that can be opposed to the achievement of the ends of the nation.

Using this new, improved account of liberty, the usual dangerous distinction between an agent's merely apparent will and what is deemed to be his *real* will is maintained. 'The right to restrain individual action is sanctioned by the restraining agencies acting to effect what is understood to be the *real* will of the individuals involved....This real will, essential to the real or ultimate interests of the individual, is understood to be occasionally at variance with the individual's immediate impulse. The state has the moral right to act in the name of that will in restraining the individuals.' [Gregor 1969, 222] So, if you are restrained in your actions and your choices by your political betters, do not be ungrateful, do not resent it, and do not resist. Like a loving parent, your state is restraining you only for your own good and because, unlike you, it knows what is really good for you.

There are two types of human being; those who know, the elite, and those who do not, the peasants, and it is only right and proper that those who know should govern those who do not. If this sounds familiar, that's because we have heard this siren song before, from Plato, from Hegel and from Mill. A. James Gregor puts it crisply when he says that 'the very essentials of syndicalism and nationalism were fundamentally collectivist both in the philosophic and sociological sense. Fascism was the product of a collectivist tradition. It found its origins in Marxism and in the sociological tradition of Gumplowicz, Pareto, and Michels.' [Gregor 1969, 168]

THE US FASCIST EXPERIENCE

It seemed to many that fascism could provide a more coherent kind of political representation than was possible in a liberal state and could also organise the working class better than socialism. The fascist criticisms of the representational ambitions of liberal democracy are hard to resist. What matters to each person are the unique circumstances of his life, his ambitions, his dreams, not some abstract entity called justice or the like, whereas the ideal liberal voter is supposed to vote only for the common good when he enters the polling booth. In a liberal democracy, then, according to fascist thought, 'the matter of voting is something of a charade in which an unreal man does something which to him must seem rather trivial if he thinks about the matter clearly or at all,' a sentiment that eerily echoes Mark Twain's reputed aphorism that if voting made any difference they wouldn't let us do it! [McClelland, 730] It is important to realise that in their origin, elections and voting had little to do with democracy and by the 1920s their disconnect had become apparent. 'Contemporary democratic governments,' writes Bernard Manin, 'have evolved from a political system that was conceived by its founders as opposed to democracy.... what today we call representative democracy has its origins in a system of institutions...that was in no way initially perceived as a form of democracy or of government by the people.'[35] It might not be all that fantastic to wonder if, in the twenty-teens, we are once again approaching a situation in which the democratic limitations of representative democracy are becoming daily more evident. [see van Reybrouck, passim] However that may be, the fascist critique of the putative representational nature of liberal democracy is one thing: its valorisation of the collective and its demonisation of the individual, however, is quite another.

Although the philosophical and ideological antecedents of fascism go back to the nineteenth century, the rise of fascism as a political force is very much an effect of the moral, spiritual, economic and social implications of the First World War. It shouldn't come as a surprise, but it almost invariably does, to realise that the first concrete expression of fascism in its totalitarianism mode wasn't Mussolini's Italy or Hitler's Germany but Woodrow Wilson's USA! Jonah Goldberg argues that 'during World War I, America became a fascist country, albeit temporarily. The first appearance of modern totalitarianism in the Western world wasn't in Italy or Germany but in the United States of America. How else,' he continues, except as totalitarian, 'would you describe a country where the world's first modern propaganda ministry was established; political prisoners by the thousands were harassed, beaten, spied upon, and thrown in jail simply for expressing private opinions; the national leader accused foreigners and immigrants of injecting treasonous "poison" into the American bloodstream; newspapers and magazines were shut down for criticizing the government; nearly a hundred thousand government propaganda agents were sent out among the people to whip up support for the regime and its war; college professors imposed loyalty oaths on their colleagues; nearly a quarter-million goons were given legal authority to intimidate and beat "slackers" and dissenters; and leading artists and writers dedicated their crafts to proselytizing for the government.'[36]

Woodrow Wilson and his associates were adherents of the socio-religious movement called Progressivism.[37] Progressivism was a development of certain residual puritanical elements in American society and, more directly, an offshoot of the 'postmillennial pietist Protestantism that had conquered Yankee areas of northern Protestantism by the 1830s.' [Rothbard 1999e, 249] Christopher Lasch notes the close connection between Progressivism and the latent paternalism of the nascent welfare state, remarking that the new paternalism that emerged in the second half of the nineteenth century 'found political expression in the progressive movement and later in the New Deal, and gradually worked its way into every corner of American society. [Lasch, 222]

Rothbard remarks that Pietists, as postmillenialists,[38] attempted 'to use local, state, and finally federal governments to stamp out sin, to make America and eventually the world holy, and thereby to bring about the Kingdom of God on Earth.' [Rothbard 1999e, 249; see also 252] With evident sincerity, Wilson's son-in-law could write to him, describing him as God's chosen instrument! [see Rothbard 1999e, 251] Progressivism was driven by a quasi-religious certainty that its adherents knew what was good, not only for themselves, but for everyone else as well. Progressivists brought us Prohibition[39] and eugenics[40] in the 1920s and latter-day progressivists bring us the war on smoking and the crusades against fat, salt, sugar, obesity and drugs.[41] But that's all right. They know what's good for you and, let's be honest; you're really not capable of looking after yourself, are you?

Progressivism had all the religious impulses and fervour of Puritanism but its goal wasn't the greater glory of God (*ad maiorem gloriam Dei*) but the greater glory of the race and of the nation. This movement, a grandchild of the French Revolution (and a great-grandchild of the ideas of Rousseau), was characterised by imperialism, nationalism, militarism, racism, eugenicism, welfarism and statism. If any elements of Christianity remained for progressivists, it was a Christianity shorn of its transcendent beliefs. The Social Gospel was Christianity firmly harnessed to the needs of the state, a domesticated, tame and docile Christianity. Progressivists 'had an abiding faith in the basic goodness of man given the right environment, and they felt sure they could figure out scientific solutions to all problems through government studies, then shape the appropriate environments using government power.' [Riddle, 138]

Wilson was a state worshipper, a believer in the state as an organic expression of the people. What of individual rights? The *Declaration of Independence*, Wilson thought, talked a great deal of nonsense about such things. 'We are not bound to adhere to the doctrines held by the signers of the Declaration of Independence,' he wrote; 'we are as free as they were to make and unmake governments. We are not here to worship men or a document. [...] Every Fourth of July should be a time for examining our standards, our purposes, for determining afresh what principles, what forms of power we think most likely to effect our safety and happiness. That and that alone is the obligation the Declaration lays upon us.' [Pestritto, 99] Society is a living organism and the Constitution, if it is to be fit for purpose, must be a living Constitution. 'All that progressives ask or desire, writes Wilson, 'is permission—in an era when 'development,' 'evolution,' is the scientific word—to interpret the Constitution according to the Darwinian principle; all they ask is recognition of the fact that a nation is a living thing and not a machine.' [Pestritto, 121] On the value of the Constitution as a protector of individual rights, the judgement of Wilson's fellow professor and eminent Constitutional theorist, John W. Burgess, could scarcely be more different. At the end of the nineteenth century, he writes, it was 'a principle of our constitutional law...that the individual citizen and person in these United States was exempt from any power or control by the United States Government, except when such power or control was expressly vested by the Constitution of the United States in said government, or reasonably and neces-sarily implied in such expressly vested power or control.' [Burgess, 18] The turning point, he believes, came in 1898. Up to that point, individual liberty had been consistently protected by the courts against government interference; after that point, the direction was completely reversed. [see Burgess, 1] It is worth nothing that Burgess's arguments were made more than ten years before Franklin D. Roosevelt's spectacular assault on the political independence of the Supreme Court.

Herbert Croly, editor of the *New Republic*, author of the bible of Progres-sivism, *The Promise of American Life*, and one of the gurus of Wilsonian Progressivism, endorsed war as a policy instrument. War was good for unifying the country and for imperial expansion. 'War,' he wrote, 'may be and has been a useful and justifiable engine of national policy' and he supported both colonialism and imperialism. [Croly, 314] He wrote, 'colonial expansion by modern national states is to be regarded, not as a cause of war, but as a safety valve against war. It affords an arena in which the restless and adventurous members of a national body can have their fling without dangerous conse-quences, while at the same time it satisfies the desire of a people for some evidence of and opportunity for national expansion.' [Croly, 320-321] And speaking of what he calls the Asiatic and African peoples, Croly remarks that 'A European nation can undertake the responsibility of governing these polit-ically disorganized societies without any necessary danger to its own national life. Such a task need not be beyond its physical power, because disorganized peoples have a comparatively small power of resistance, and a few thousand resolute Europeans can hold in submission many million Asiatics.' Not only is there little danger to Europeans in engaging in such imperialistic adven-tures but we may be assured that it is actually good for those who come under European control inasmuch as 'at least for a while the Asiatic population may well be benefited by more orderly and progressive government. Submission to such a government is necessary as a condition of subsequent political develop-ment.' [Croly, 319] Some of the baleful effects of Wilson's Progressivism are to be seen not only in respect of the governance of the United States but also globally in his post-World War I dismemberment of the crumbling Ottoman Empire, the geopolitical results of which are still with us a hundred years later in the Balkan tensions and the intractable Middle East disputes.[42]

War has also been used by latter-day Progressivists as an instrument for the righting of wrongs and the promotion of the good around the world. The USA, the UK and the European Union are particularly prone to intervene militarily in conflicts that cannot conceivably be construed as a threat to their national security—Haiti, Panama, El Salvador, Grenada, Nicaragua, Bosnia & Herzegovina, Syria, Iraq, Libya, Kosovo, Macedonia and the Democratic Republic of Congo, to name just a few. The use of war for secular missionary purposes was deprecated long ago by Sydney Smith when he wrote to Lady Grey, 'For God's sake, do not drag me into another war! I am worn down, and worn out, with crusading and defending Europe, and protecting mankind; I must think a little of myself. I am sorry for the Spaniards—I am sorry for the Greeks—I deplore the fate of the Jews; the people of the Sandwich Islands are groaning under the most detestable tyranny; Bagdad is oppressed—I do not like the present state of the Delta—Thibet is not comfortable. Am I to fight for all these people? The world is bursting with sin and sorrow. Am I to be champion of the Decalogue, and to be eternally raising fleets and armies to make all men good and happy? We have just done saving Europe, and I am afraid the consequence will be, that we shall cut each other's throats. No war, dear Lady Grey!—no eloquence; but apathy, selfishness, common sense, arithmetic! I beseech you, secure Lord Grey's sword and pistols, as the housekeeper did Don Quixote's armour. If there is another war, life will not be worth having. I will go to war with the King of Denmark if he is impertinent to you, or does any injury to Howick; but for no other cause.'[43]

The chaos of individualism could only be overcome by an heroic leader who can transcend the petty limitations of liberal democracy, Jeffersonian individualism being 'abandoned for the benefit of a genuinely individual and social consummation.' [Croly, 188] Speaking about the traditional American conception of freedom, Croly wrote, 'Up to a certain point that freedom has been and still is beneficial. Beyond that point it is not merely harmful; it is by way of being fatal. Efficient regulation there must be; and it must be regulation that will strike, not at the symptoms of the evil, but at its roots. The existing concentration of wealth and financial power in the hands of a few irresponsible men is the inevitable outcome of the chaotic individualism of our political and economic organization....In becoming responsible for the subordination of the individual to the demand of a dominant and constructive national purpose, the American state will in effect be making itself responsible for a morally and socially desirable distribution of wealth.' [Croly, 28-29] If that passage is reminiscent of National Socialist *Gleichshaltung* and Italian Corporatism[44] it's because it is the native American version of the same thing.

The writer of the *Foreword* to the recent Princeton publication of Croly's Progressivist classic is anxious to dispel any such idea that there might be a substantive connection between Croly's work and fascism. He concedes that Croly believed in the virtues of 'nationalism and even imperialism' but believed that the expansion of the state was justifiable on the basis that 'a robust federal government would create a national community and something Croly called "the national spirit." This last idea sounds vaguely menacing—a phrase that certain European dictators would later exploit for horrific purposes. Yet Croly, apparently, meant nothing of the sort.' [Foer 2014, xxvii] I see. Croly uses more or less the same language as Mussolini to express more or less the same ideas as Mussolini but somehow manages to mean something radically different from Mussolini. Foer does concede that 'Croly's emphasis on nationalism—and the special role that he assigned to enlightened elites—contained faint resonances with European fascism' but he goes on to assure us that Croly's admiration for Mussolini was only for the early Mussolini, which he withdrew when Mussolini's authoritarianism became evident.

Modern liberalism is, in many ways, the successor to Wilsonian Progressivism. The aim of the liberal enterprise is to 'transform a democratic republic into an enormous tribal community, to inspire in every member of society from Key West, Florida, to Fairbanks, Alaska, that same sense of belonging—"we're all in it together!"—that we allegedly feel in a close-knit community.' Goldberg notes that 'ever since the New Deal, liberals have been unable to shake this fundamental dogma that the state can be the instrument for a politics of meaning that transforms the entire nation into a village.' [Goldberg 2008, 159-160] Robert Nisbet notes the curious evisceration of the primary meaning of the term 'liberal' as pertaining to individual freedom and its replacement by a crass materialistic form of equality: 'Liberalism had its notable reversal of values in the United States during the New Deal. The New Deal is second only to World War I under Wilson as a cause of the steady politicization of a doctrine founded originally on the freedom of the individual. The central value of contemporary American liberalism is not freedom but equality; equality defined as redistribution of property.' [Nisbet 1988, 63] There are, of course, many kinds of equality—equality of goods, of services, of opportunities, of legal standing— and it is not immediately obvious what makes equality of distribution of goods and services so special that all other forms of equality are crowded out. An assumption lying behind 'equality-as-distribution-of-goods-and-services' is that goods and services, in some quasi-magical way, are to be found just lying around, waiting to be distributed. But, as James Otteson remarks, 'goods do not appear out of nowhere: every particle of them is produced by human labor and thus costs scarce resources that might otherwise have been expended elsewhere.' [Otteson 2014, 81] Leaving this (quite large) problem of production to one side, there's yet another nagging problem for socialists. Suppose that by some superhuman effort we arrive at that happy day when equality in the possession of goods or access to services has been achieved—what happens the day after? Some people will consume their shares, some will save, and yet others will trade. Within a very short space of time, the balance of equality will once again be disturbed. Do we interfere yet again? How often and how constant must our interference be? Otteson calls this the 'Day Two' problem. And the problem is worse that it may first seem. 'With each iteration of the process there would be successively less to redistribute, owing to a number of factors: first, there are the losses constituted by the wealth going to the redistributors, who are not themselves engaged in wealth-producing activity; second, there is the disincentive such policy provides for others to continue producing wealth;

and third, there is a tragedy-of-the-commons dynamic initiated by converting wealth production from a positive-sum enterprise into a zero-sum bounty or prize.' [Otteson 2014, 87]

The effects of the 1929 Wall Street Crisis weren't only economic but also social and political. Many saw it as signifying the inability of a free market system to prevent recurrent crises and looked for some other way to regulate human affairs. As a consequence, we got Roosevelt's New Deal in the USA and the beginning of the rise of Keynesian interventionism worldwide. Franklin Delano Roosevelt is often portrayed as if his policies were the antithesis of the laissez-faire-defending Herbert Hoover but, as Robert Nisbet points out, Hoover was anything but an apostle of laissez-faire. 'An engineer by profession, he tasted of social engineering under Wilson in World War I. He was food administrator for the United States and important in a variety of other government connections. He was the strongest member of the Harding and Coolidge administrations, always known for his keen interest in the use of the national government to build up the country. When depression came, Hoover launched a considerable number of governmental schemes and programs for relief of the people—many of them to survive and be used by Roosevelt in his first term of office. Hoover really began modern peacetime political and social engineering; Roosevelt simply enlarged upon it.' [Nisbet 1988, 66-67]

Hitler and Roosevelt shared more important things than the same accession year. Both were elected because they presented themselves as having and were believed to have the capacity to put life into exhausted political systems. Both came up with New Deals for those who had lost or were in fear of losing their social and economic status at a time of change. 'The Nazi regime, born of the post-Great War crisis in Germany, was a kind of Germanic New Deal.' [King-Hall, 34] If we were to compare one New Deal to another in terms of their impacts, Hitler's New Deal would come out on top except in respect of militarism and re-armament where the US New Deal easily outpaced it![45] The official National Socialist newspaper, the *Völkischer Beobachter*, congratulated Roosevelt on ending market speculation by, as they put it, his adoption of National Socialist means,[46] and Mussolini took FDR to be 'one of us', someone who knew that the market couldn't be left to its own devices—a mantra whose chant is still to be heard today in Rome and Berlin and Washington. Writing in 1933, Mussolini acknowledged that Italian Fascism and the newly arrived National Socialists have both 'annihilated demo-social-liberal forces' and claimed to detect 'fascist seeds' in England, France and even in the USA. 'Roosevelt,' he wrote, 'is moving, acting, giving orders independently of the decision or wishes of the Senate or Congress. There are no longer intermediaries between him and the nation. There is no longer a parliament but an "état majeur". There are no longer parties, but a single party. A sole will silences dissenting voices. This has nothing to do with any demo-liberal conception of things.' [in Griffin, 73]

Before Fascism became inextricably linked with anti-Semitism and the horror of the Holocaust, there was nothing particularly controversial in characterising FDR's policies as fascist. The application of this term to his policies was often intended as a compliment. This, of course, is no longer so and one often finds writers employing locutions such as 'X [fill in the name] was no fascist but....' Indeed, with something less than his usual clarity, Jonah Goldberg writes, 'Franklin Roosevelt was no fascist...But many of his ideas and policies were indistinguishable from fascism.'[47] One is left wondering how, if Roosevelt's ideas were indistinguishable from fascism, he managed to preserve himself free from the stain of that original political sin. Jim Powell, too, though scathing in his attack on what he calls FDR's folly, is surprisingly reticent about characterising the New Deal as fascist in orientation, writing, 'The New Deal was the American version of the collectivist trend that became fashionable around the world, so it perhaps shouldn't be surprising that New Deal utterances by FDR and his advisers sounded similar to fascist doctrines associated with Italian dictator Benito Mussolini.' [Powell, 76] One does not have to jump over some insuperable evidential gap to conclude that the reason they sounded similar to fascist doctrines was because they *were* fascist doctrines! Once fascism is understood for what it is, FDR's New Deal can be seen to be, in essence, fascistic.[48] It was seen to be so by many in its own time, as well as being a re-incarnation of Wilsonian Progressivism for a new era.[49] Gian Migone notes that 'on at least one occasion he [Roosevelt] called Mussolini "that admirable Italian gentleman"...' but he denies that Roosevelt had any Fascist sympathies, describing him instead as a 'closet Wilsonian'. [Migone, xxvi, xxxii] If, however, one regards Wilsonianism as a form of proto-fascism, then there's at best a nominal difference between being a closet Wilsonian and a Fascist sympathiser.

The supposed threat of Fifth Column activities was used by Roosevelt to discredit any opposition to his plans for war. 'Roosevelt effectively used the Fifth Column issue to discredit and disgrace his isolationist opponents.' He did not merely attack their views, 'he also challenged their loyalty. FDR lumped those who were, in fact, spies in the employ of Hitler together with his isolationist critics.' [MacDonnell, 139] Roosevelt's treatment of Charles Lindberg was particularly disgraceful. Lindbergh had accused the US Administration of recklessly leading America towards war only to be vilified by Roosevelt as a covert National Socialist. Howard Ickes, the Secretary of the Interior, described Lindbergh as America's No 1 Nazi fellow traveller.[50] Using the criteria employed by Roosevelt to make this judgement, it is hard to see how the George Washington of the Farewell Speech would have escaped the isolationist and, anachronistically, the covert National Socialist label! Among the largely cowed and compliant press, the *Chicago Tribune* was the only nationally significant newspaper to take issue with Roosevelt's employment of Fifth Column scaremongering that the paper took to be a way of promoting his interventionist programmes. Robert Higgs writes:

> In the depths of the Great Depression, the federal government employed the wartime measures as models for dealing with what Franklin Roosevelt called "a crisis in our national life comparable to war." Hence the War Finance Corporation came back to life as the Reconstruction Finance Corpo-

ration, the War Industries Board as the National Recovery Administration, the Food Administration as the Agricultural Adjustment Administration, the Capital Issues Committee as the Securities and Exchange Commission, the Fuel Administration as the Connolly Act apparatus for cartelizing the oil industry and the Guffey Act apparatus for cartelizing the bituminous coal industry. The military mobilization of young men came back as the quasi-military Civilian Conservation Corps. The Muscle Shoals hydroelectric munitions facility became the germ of the Tennessee Valley Authority. The wartime U.S. Housing Corporation reappeared first as part of the Public Works Administration in 1933 and then as the U.S. Housing Authority in 1937. The New Deal's federal social security program harked back to the wartime servicemen's life insurance and the payments made to the soldiers' dependents. The temporary wartime abandonment of the gold standard became permanent in 1933-1934, when the government nationalized the monetary gold stock and abrogated all contractual obligations, both public and private, to pay gold. Along with the revived agencies came many of the wartime planners, including [Bernard] Baruch, Felix Frankfurter, George Peek, Hugh Johnson, John Hancock, Leon Henderson, and John Dickinson, not to mention FDR himself, as advisers or administrators. Obviously the wartime precedents were crucial in guiding the New Dealers and helping them to justify and gain acceptance of their policies. [Higgs, 380]

Wilson's World War I alphabet agencies pale into insignificance beside the creations of Franklin Delano Roosevelt's inventive genius. He produced the SEC (Securities and Exchange Commission), CCC (Civilian Conservation Corps), FERA (Federal Emergency Relief Administration), CWA (Civil Works Administration), NRA (National Recovery Administration), AAA (Agricultural Adjustment Administration), and so on. In 1941, after the attack on Pearl Harbour, internment camps for Japanese or Japanese-Americans were set up by the WCCA (Wartime Civil Control Administration), a decision supported by the shameful Supreme Court decision in *Korematsu v. United States* (1944). [see Levy & Mellor, 127-142] The independence from political interference of the US Supreme Court, such as it had been, had earlier been seriously undermined by Roosevelt's threat to pack the court if it continued to resist his New Deal projects. [see Hall, 233-234] The court-packing scheme was disguised, very thinly disguised, as a plan for court reform but this transparent euphemism fooled no one, not even members of Roosevelt's own party. As it happened, Justices Hughes and Roberts were effectively intimidated by the threat and ceased to resist FDR's plans and, within a short space of time, retirements and deaths enabled FDR to appoint to the Court justices more sympathetic to his projects—Frankfurter, Douglas and Murphy. In *United States vs Carolene Products Co.* [304 U.S. 144, 1938], the Roosevelt court distinguished, albeit in a tentative way, between what it deemed to be *fundamental* liberties—such as freedom of speech, the right to vote—and *nonfundamental* liberties—property rights and freedom of contract.[51] The process of driving a coach and four through the provisions of the US Constitution, a process whose roots reach back at least to the 1861-1865 domestic armed conflict and probably even earlier, now attained an unstoppable momentum. As Roger Pilon of the Cato Institute noted in remarks he made to a House of Representatives Subcommittee in 1997, 'a document of delegated, enumerated, and thus limited powers became in short order a document of effectively unenumerated powers, limited only by rights that would thereafter be interpreted narrowly by conservatives on the Court and episodically by liberals on the Court. Both sides, in short, would come to ignore our roots in limited government, buying instead into the idea of vast majoritarian power—the only disagreement being over what rights might limit that power and in which circumstances.'[52]

Roosevelt's Civilian Conservation Corps (CCC), which recruited some 2.5 million men, was a para-military force designed to take young men off the streets and out of the civilian work force. Hitler said of *his* programmes that they would do exactly the same thing! The CCC wasn't the only para-military organisation set up under Roosevelt. Even more ominous was the National Recovery Administration. This was led by Hugh Johnson who, not coincidentally, had been a military liaison to the War Industries Board in WWI and director of the WWI draft. Who can fail to see in the Blue Eagle, symbol of National Recovery, with its lightning bolts and industrial cogwheel, a startling and graphic resemblance to the National Socialist swastika? *(See Fig. 1)*

The public display of the Blue Eagle was a sign of compliance with the NRA's demands. In order to keep prices high, price controls were implemented and no one was allowed to undersell. Farm animals were destroyed and agricultural crops left to rot in the field. Higgs again:

> "It is not possible," said William Graham Sumner, "to experiment with a society and just drop the experiment whenever we choose. The experiment enters into the life of the society and never can be got out again." World War I, the New Deal, and World War II gave rise to the greatest experiments in collectivization America had ever experienced. These experiments radically transformed the political economy institutionally and ideologically. The political economy of 1948 bore scarcely any resemblance to that of 1912, and the changes gave every indication of being irreversible. In the process by which this radical transformation occurred, the military draft played a central part. Conscription made possible the creation of a huge armed force in 1917-1918, which in turn required massive amounts of complementary resources. To get these resources the government had to raise taxes enormously, go deeply into debt, and impose a great variety of controls on the market economy; that is, it had to override traditional limitations on government action and to disallow long-standing economic liberties.

> In light of the apparent success of the policies employed during World War I, the temptation to impose similar policies during the Great Depression proved irresistible. In large part the New Deal consisted of quasi-war

policies to deal with a pseudo-war emergency. Participation in World War II, with its global reach and voracious demand for resources, increased every aspect of the process by an order of magnitude: the draft permitted the creation of a huge army, which gave rise to vast military resource requirements that could be met expeditiously only by imposition of a command-and-control system throughout the economy. By the late 1940s the three great experiments had entered, institutionally and ideologically, into the life of the society. With all the fundamental barriers to the growth of government having been battered down during war and pseudo-war emergencies, nothing substantial remained to impede the relentless growth of government. [Higgs, 387-388]

Fig. 1

TOTALITARIANISM

The absolute sovereignty of the state led inexorably to totalitarianism, legitimising 'the extension of state control into every aspect of human concern.' [Gregor 1969, 158] The term 'totalitarian' was coined in the 1920s by Giovanni Amendola.[53] Totalitarianism is thought of as having the following features: an official ideology to which all must conform, an ideology directed towards a state of human perfection controlled by a single mass party under the direction of a leader and his associates, a system of terror exercised by the party and its police, a monopoly of control of mass communication, a monopoly control of combat weapons, and central control and direction of the economy.[54] According to Peter Grieder, totalitarianism is 'the concerted but disguised attempt by a state to exercise total control over, coerce, integrate, manipulate, mobilise and seduce its population in the name of an ideology' whether or not such ambitions were in fact realised or not.[55] A. James Gregor's account is broadly in line with Grieder's. For him, totalitarian regimes are characterised by an ideology which is critical of the past while making chiliastic claims for the future, by a mass movement organised in a single party under the control of a supposedly charismatic leader with his accompanying tutelary elite, by a monopoly or near monopoly of the means of coercion (and communication), and by the centralised and bureaucratic control of the entire economy. [see Gregor 1969, 7]

'Totalitarian' is now a bad word, a word that describes something intrinsically sinister. But it wasn't always so. When fascism was fashionable, totalitarianism was also in vogue. The disappearance of the word does not mean that the reality it names has also disappeared. In fact, it is still with us but it is now much more likely to be called 'holism' or 'inclusivity'. Totalitarianism can be a father who smacks you around the head to make you do what you are told *for your own good*, or a mother who talks at you incessantly to make you do what whatever it is she wants you to do *for your own good*. Today, the paternal variety of totalitarianism is out of fashion and the maternal variety is in the ascendant. Goldberg writes, 'liberalism today sees no realm of human life that is beyond political significance, from what you eat to what you smoke to what you say. Sex is political. Food is political. Sports, entertainment, your inner motives and outer appearance, all have political salience for liberal fascists. Liberals place their faith in priestly experts who know better, who plan, exhort, badger, and scold.' [Goldberg 2008, 14] Gregor agrees, writing, 'in the twentieth century [political life] has become increasingly integrative and totalitarian, in the sense that no aspect of life is conceived to be, in principle, private and unpolitical. With the decline of religion, politics has become its secular surrogate...' [Gregor 1969, 1]

All forms of latter-day tribalism love collectivities, nations, groups, all of which take precedence over the individual and his petty needs and concerns. Fascism, for example, is impatient with political disagreements and urges that we go beyond politics in the interests of the nation. Fascists believe fervently that a better world can be made here and now, even if some people have to be discommoded, sometimes radically discommoded,[56] in the process. Common to both Fascism and National Socialism was the idea that internal conflict within a state or society was a waste of energy and resources and that 'a country ought to be able to develop all its resources cooperatively, without the waste and friction of the class struggle, and with a fair distribution of the product between capital and labor.' [Sabine, 885] If all internal divisions are to cease and all internal competitive differentiation is to disappear, then the state becomes all in all. There can be nothing apart from the state—no unions or trade organisations, no independent businesses, no rival centres of authority or control. If the group is to come together as one, all divisions must be submerged and all the sources of division must be suppressed as much as possible. One tried and tested method of getting squabbling combatants to unite is to give them a common enemy and the best way to do this is to have them fight a war. 'There's a war on, you know' is the *Dad's Army* catchphrase used to put an end to all 'selfish' objections. 'The only condition that submerges the divergent social and economic interests of a modern nation is preparation for war,' writes Sabine. 'Accordingly fascism and national socialism were in essence war governments and war economies set up not as expedients to meet a national emergency but as permanent political systems.' [Sabine, 887] If one wants to suppress civil liberties then one really needs a war, if not a war on other flesh and blood people then a war on inanimate object or abstract entities such as a war on drugs or a war on poverty or a war on terror.

In totalitarian systems, religion becomes subordinate to the state; likewise education. 'No area of privacy remained that an individual could call his own and no association of individuals which was not subject to political control.' [Sabine, 916] In Italy, for example, education was completely subordinated to the ends of the state, including education in the universities. Giuseppe Bottai, Mussolini's Minister of Education from 1936-1943 wrote in 1928 that 'The role of the university under Fascism lies in laying the basis for living culture, one which creates a class of men able to provide leadership in politics, science, and art. The university must adapt so as to be able to fulfil a task of this sort.... if the need for a cultural revolution is above all palpable in legal, political, economic, and social studies, it is no less urgent in other types of study, which often pursue lines of enquiry which still conflict with the fascist train of the character and mind of Italians.' [in Griffin, 62]

Under totalitarianism, intermediate organisations and bodies of all sorts were either eliminated or else dominated, including all forms of mutual aid organisations, as well as labour unions and business organisations. The effect of all this was to create a social wasteland between the state and the individual. On one side, the state; on the other, a mass of socially naked individuals.[57] 'Though the individual was "organized" at every turn, he stood more alone than ever before....totalitarian society was truly atomic. The people were literally the "masses," without information except what propaganda agencies chose to give them and without power to combine for any purposes of their own.' [Sabine, 919; see Malan, passim]

The net result of all this centralisation was, as one might expect, chaos and confusion. Overlapping and multiple forms of control were set up and, needless to say, individuals attempted to carve out their own particular spheres of influence without regard to the overall impact such carving up would have on the whole. Sabine notes that 'National socialist totalitarianism never achieved a rational division of functions in any branch of government, or an organization into governing agencies with legally defined powers that acted predictably according to known rules.' [Sabine, 917] The law became merely a mode of occasional decision-making to be administered in accordance with a subjective estimation of what constituted wrongdoing.

According to corporatist doctrine, employers and employees were supposed to be represented in the running of firms. In effect, however, the result was just the same as occurred in Germany. Firms lost their freedom of action and both management and labour became mere tools of the state. Ultimate control was put into the hands of state functionaries. This passage from one of Sir Oswald Mosley's lieutenants, Alexander Raven Thomson, illustrates several themes in Fascism; its idealism (anti-materialism), its organicism, its transcendent ambitions, and its corporatism. 'The corporate state,' Thomson writes, 'is the organic form through which the nation can find expression. Fascism is no materialist creed like Communism, which sets up, as its only purpose, the material benefit of the masses. Fascism is essentially idealistic....Fascism recognises the nation as an organism with a purpose, a life and means of action transcending those of the individuals of which it is composed....the Corporate State must not be considered solely as a means of good government. It is also the means of self-expression of the nation as a corporate whole in the attainment of its national destiny.'[58] Italian corporatism found its Teutonic twin in the National Socialist doctrine of *Gleichshaltung*. This doctrine, which sounds distinctly harmless in its English translation of 'co-ordination', demands the orientation of all activities, all organisations and institutions—churches, schools, universities, clubs, trades unions, industry, agriculture, trade, radio, newspapers, cinema and literature—so that all think in line with the *Führer*.

Central control, central planning is not only characteristic of Fascism and National Socialism but also, notoriously, of Bolshevism. For all of these regimes, the achievement of the nation's ends implies a central direction of all its activities and the elimination of distracting tendencies that might deflect it from its goals. Griffin writes, 'the convinced fascist is a utopian, conceiving the homogeneous, perfectly co-ordinated national community as a total solution the problems of modern society.' [Griffin, 6] Given the complexity of any society of even a moderate size, such massive attempts at central control and direction are never likely to succeed but it does not prevent the attempts from seriously disrupting the lives of individuals and communities.

Despite their international ambitions, all these regimes in the end converged on a form of nationalism. This narrowing of focus might cause doctrinal difficulties for Bolshevism but not for Fascism or National Socialism. The philosopher, Ugo Spirito, writing in 1932, argues that, in contrast to socialism, Fascism looks to a system of international collaboration in which, without succumbing to what he calls the 'anarchy of individualistic *laissez-faire*', every country will organise its own economy in a planned way which 'takes account of the organization prevailing in other countries and comes to an arrangement with them on how best to co-ordinate different programmes.' [in Griffin 69] Some Fascist thinkers thought of Fascism's flirtation with private property as a mere transitional stage. Ugo Spirito, for example, thought that Fascism would ultimately 'divest itself of residual capitalist elements to become an "integral corporativism" in which private property would no longer constitute loci of particular interests independent of, and conceivably opposed to, the interests of the state.' [Gregor 1969, 293] The terms used to describe this post-transitional stage are revealing: 'Fascist Communism,' 'Fascist Bolshevism,' and 'Fascist Socialism'.

A NOTE ON ANTI-SEMITISM AND EUGENICISM

Fascism, in its Italian incarnation, had no intrinsic connection to anti-Semitism and wasn't to acquire any until it came under the influence of National Socialism in the late 1930s. In fact, as Griffiths notes, Fascism 'benefited from Jewish funders in its early days, and ...was joined by a higher percentage of the small Italian Jewish population than of the Gentile population.' [Griffiths, 38] There is no intrinsic connection between anti-Semitism and Fascism. Gregor notes, 'anti-Semitism, political and economic conservatism, and contempt for the working classes have never been necessary or sufficient conditions for admission into the class of individuals that could be historically identified as "fascists." Many prominent Fascists in Italy (Gentile among them) were never anti-Semitic, anti-radical, or anti-labor even for tactical reasons. Many movements generally identified as "fascist" were neither conservative or anti-Semitic, nor did they manifest "racial antagonism" in any meaningful sense of the term.' [Gregor 1969, 25] Not only is anti-Semitism not peculiar to Fascism, it is also not even an exclusive possession of the political Right. 'The French Left had, in the last decades of the nineteenth century, found anti-Semitism to be a particular effective weapon...' [Griffiths, 19]

The idea of race and the supposed significance of racial differences was a commonplace of late nineteenth and early twentieth century thought despite its being an imprecise and, to the extent that it had any content, a biological rather than a sociological category. The Aryan or Nordic race, as the culture-creating race, was supposed to play a particularly important role in civilisation in contrast to the merely culture-bearing races and, of course, in strong contrast to the culture-destroying race. Anti-Semitism was a social given of almost all late nineteenth century European society, particularly in the countries of Central and Eastern Europe but also in France. Existing alongside anti-Semitism and often interrelated with it was a conception of history as a struggle between different races. The major theorists of race theory were the Englishman Houston Chamberlain and the Frenchman Arthur de Gobineau. Not only did anti-Semitism link up with race theory but it also managed, quite frequently, to become associated with anti-capitalism as well when Jews were taken to be the primary movers and shakers of capitalism!

As a form of ultra-nationalism, fascism is necessarily racist but such racism does not *necessarily* lead to eugenics or genocide or anti-Semitism or hatred of other nations or of groups perceived to be different. In practice, of course, fascism can give life to such tendencies if they are already present in a community. Fascism does not require the active persecution of other races or cultures but can, in fact, content itself with a kind of racial or cultural apartheid.

In National Socialism, of course, anti-Semitism plays an important role if only as an adjunct of its central focus on race theory. Because National Socialism is so inextricably associated with anti-Semitism, anti-Semitism is often taken to be a defining feature of fascism. It has therefore become difficult to characterise political movements as fascist if anti-Semitism does not feature prominently in them. Among other things, the effect of National Socialist race theory was to support eugenic legislation so as to purify the race by exterminating physical and mental defectives and to keep *the* culture-destroying race, the Jews, in check. Eugenics wasn't, however, a National Socialist invention but an eminently respectable social engineering project[59] benefitting from the support of all supposedly right-thinking people everywhere, including William Beveridge,[60] Bertrand Russell, H. G. Wells, Winston Churchill,[61] Neville Chamberlain[62] and John Maynard Keynes in Great Britain, [see Sewell, 54, 76] and Charles Davenport, Oliver Wendell Holmes, Margaret Sanger[63] and Presidents Theodore Roosevelt[64] and Wilson[65] in the USA.[66] The eugenics movement in the United States, which had widespread support from the cultural elite, received institutional validation from the Supreme Court ruling in *Buck v. Bell* (1927) that permitted the Commonwealth of Virginia to sterilise the unfit.[67] In the first half of the twentieth century, over 50,000 people were forcibly sterilised in the USA. The US experiment was an inspiration to Hitler who, it is believed, wrote appreciative letters to Leon Whitney, President of the Eugenics Society, and to Madison Grant, author of *The Passing of the Great Race*.[68]

The anti-egalitarian and anti-humanist tendency in National Socialism is starkly and chillingly displayed in a memorandum of 1925 written by Franz Pfeffer von Salomon in which he argued that 'No pity is to be shown to those who occupy the lower categories of the inferior groups: cripples, epileptics, the blind, the insane, deaf and dumb, children born in sanatoria for alcoholics or in care, orphans, criminals, whores, the sexually disturbed, etc....Nor should we mourn the dumb, the weak, the spineless, the apathetic, those with hereditary diseases, the pathological, because they go under innocently....' [in Griffin, 119] David Klinghoffer remarks, 'The key elements in the ideology that produced Auschwitz are moral relativism aligned with a rejection of the sacredness of human life, a belief that violent competition in nature creates greater and lesser races, that the greater will inevitably exterminate the lesser, and finally that the lesser race most in need of extermination is the Jews.' He adds, 'All but the last of these ideas may be found in Darwin's writing.'[69] But, however eye-catching and spine-chilling the doctrines of eugenicism and racism may be, and however important a role they may have played in National Socialism, they do not, I believe, constitute the core of tribalism as such.

FASCISM, NATIONAL SOCIALISM AND BOLSHEVISM—CHILDREN OF THE LEFT

To use the term 'fascism' as a general term of abuse for those on the right of the political spectrum is, as Griffiths points out, a 'gross over-simplification,' (I would even say 'misrepresentation') 'given the left-wing characteristics to be found in most varieties of fascism.' [Griffiths, 1] Griffith goes on to claim that, in fact, 'most of the major figures [in fascism] appear to have come originally from the Left.' [Griffiths, 126] Llewellyn Rockwell agrees with this assessment, pointing out that 'All the biggest and most important players within the fascist movement came from the socialists' and that 'It was a threat to the socialists because it was the most appealing political vehicle for the real-world application of the socialist impulse. Socialists crossed over to join the fascists en masse.' [Rockwell, 14] Jonah Goldberg notes, 'fascism, properly understood, is not a phenomenon of the right at all. Instead, it is, and always has been, a phenomenon of the left. This fact—an inconvenient truth if there ever was one—is obscured in our time by the equally mistaken belief that fascism and communism are opposites. In reality, they are closely related, historical competitors for the same constituents, seeking to dominate and control the same social space.' [Goldberg 2008, 7]

Marxism in its various manifestations and fascism in all its forms are often taken to be polar opposites but this is not, in fact, so. 'The typology employed to classify the various contending political systems before the War was fundamentally mistaken,' argues Gregor. 'Marxism-Leninism and the subsequent variants that proliferated after the termination of hostilities shared more features with paradigmatic Fascism than they did or do with liberalism...' [Gregor 1969, 331] It might be objected that Communism and National Socialism were cordial enemies. Yes, they quarrelled but this was just a quarrel between totalitarian kissin' cousins. 'Both movements deified the state, abhorred individualism, were intensely collectivist in outlook, and character-ized themselves as "Socialist".' [Grieder, 575] The transition from Communist to National Socialist and vice versa was a common phenomenon. Communists turned into National Socialists (before the war) and National Socialists into Communists (after the war) with relative ease.

All the evidence suggests that fascism in all its forms and communism in its bolshevist incarnation do *not* in fact occupy different ends of a one-dimensional left-right political spectrum but, to switch metaphors in mid-stream, are more like rival suitors for the same fair maiden. 'The notion that communism and Nazism are polar opposites stems from the deeper truth that they are in fact kindred spirits....Both ideologies are reactionary in the sense that they try to re-create tribal impulses. Communists champion class, Nazis race, fascists the nation. All such ideologies...attract the same *types* of people.' [Goldberg 2008, 74] Both fascism and communism are forms of socialism—one national, the other putatively international—and socialism is really just a new name for the old reality of tribalism. The quarrel between bolshevism and fascism is a family quarrel and, like all family quarrels, is bitter and vicious especially since, as Gregor remarks, 'both paradigmatic Fascism and contemporary Marxism are rooted in the same ideological traditions and share some critical normative convictions.' [Gregor 1969, 333] The essential family connections of fascism and bolshevism aren't recognised only by those with an anti-socialist axe to grind. Leon Trotsky remarked that 'Stalinism and Fascism, in spite of a deep difference in social foundations, are symmetrical phenomena. In many of their features—their authoritarianism, totalitarianism, corporatism, their monopoly on coercion and communication and their cult of 'the leader'—they show a deadly similarity.'[70]

The standard interpretation of National Socialism from those on the political left is to see it as the last gasp of capitalism and as the epitome of conservatism. But 'Hitler despised the bourgeoisie, traditionalists, aristocrats, monarchists, and all believers in the established order.' [Goldberg 2008, 59] Just as Fascism was through and through socialist, so too was National Socialism, at least in origin. Well aware of Hitler's intentions, conservatives and capitalists tended to loathe the National Socialists, while the bulk of National Socialist support came from the working classes. It is true that fascism tends to be authoritarian[71] and also true that some forms of conservatism tend towards the authoritarian, but, unless one is prepared to commit the fallacy of the undistributed middle, fascism isn't therefore intrinsically conservative. Nevertheless, not all author-itarian regimes are necessarily fascist. Griffin writes of the twentieth century quasi-fascist regimes 'whose fundamental aim is the reactionary one of using mechanisms of intensive social engineering and repression to maintain the social status quo.' [Griffin, 9] Examples of such quasi-fascist (and conserva-tive) states would be Franco's Spain, Dollfuss's Austria and Salazar's Portugal. These all lack the mythic core of fascism, which is the notion of the funda-mental regeneration or rebirth of the nation.

Just as anti-Semitism is taken to be characteristic of the political right, so anti-capitalism is often taken to be a characteristic of the political left. But it is often not realised that anti-capitalism has been just as characteristic of many thinkers who would be placed, as fascists generally are, on the political right even if, as we have seen, such positioning is suspect. Capitalism was taken by these fascist thinkers to be destructive of the traditional values of agrarian society, much as Marx and Engels had portrayed it in the opening pages of the *Communist Manifesto*. 'Fascists, particularly during the decade between 1930 and 1940, never tired of affirming their radicalism, their rejection of capitalism as an economic system and their preoccupation with the well-being and syndical organization of the working classes.' [Gregor 1969, 24] Fascist anti-capitalist criticism portrayed capitalism as creating and supporting individual selfishness as opposed to generating the good of society as a whole. This criticism led to the development of corporatist theories of society, originally modelled on the medieval guilds, but going well beyond the medieval version in postulating a vision of society as a complex of interlocking, mutually cooperative (instead of conflicting) bodies which would practically organise and also give political expression to everyone in society.

The anti-capitalist strain in National Socialism which, as a practical factor, ended with the murder of Gregor Strasser in 1934, was an important element in its early years. Capitalism, the early National Socialists alleged, was yet another factor in the debasement and depersonalisation of German society and an important contributor to what many people, not just members of the National Socialist party, considered to be the endemic social and political chaos of post-war Germany. Gottfried Feder writes that 'Today chaos reigns on earth, confusion, struggle, hate, envy, conflict, oppression, exploitation, brutality, egotism....the will to put a stop to chaos, to put in order a world out of joint, and to keep order as guardians...that is the enormous task which National Socialism has set itself...Our aim is: Germany's rebirth carried out in a German spirit to create German freedom...' [in Griffin, 121-122] Both Fascism and National Socialism made some practically necessary concessions to elements of capitalism later in their development but they never lost their socialist ambitions to control it if they couldn't eliminate it altogether. Even granting the relative soft-pedalling of the original stark National Socialist anti-capitalist rhetoric in the mid 1930s, the effect of National Socialist policy when in power was to leave the legal order of private property intact but effec-tively to exercise micro-control of every aspect of the economy through a totalitarian policy of *Gleichshaltung*. 'Though inter-war Marxists saw fascism as a permutation of capitalism's onslaught against socialism,' writes Griffin, 'fascists conceived themselves as superseding its basic principles of laissez-faire individualism and the profit motive through the introduction of a nationally and socially healthy system: indeed a form of socialism purged of materialism and internationalism.' [Griffin, 141] What was needed in the economy was the same martial virtue exhibited by soldiers in war. Business leaders couldn't be allowed to operate their businesses with an eye merely to profits—such a vulgar mercenary concern is rank capitalism, and capitalism and Marxism, as Werner Daitz asserts, 'grow from the same root'. [in Griffin, 141] It is worth quoting more extensively from Daitz's article to demonstrate the rooted anti-capitalist animus of National Socialism, an animus that persisted even as late as 1936.

> We therefore demand in the economy a soldierly conduct within and without. For, if the leader of a business runs it without regard to the economic independence of the nation, but only with a view to the highest possible profits, it will inevitably destroy the social peace within his company. His employees will be bound to adopt the same attitude... and for their part strive for the highest possible wage without regard for social peace and the state of the company. For Marxism always follows capitalism like its shadow. Both grow from the same root—Jewish merce-nariness [*Gelddenken*, lit. "money thinking"] which always finds a way of infiltrating Nordic economic thought once intellect has corrupted it. In the interests of a supposedly higher financial return, both destroy Blood and Soil, the biological foundations of their national culture [*Volkstum*] and hence of their own existence...' [Daitz, in Griffin, 141]

Despite the overwhelming evidence to the contrary, some commentators firmly associate fascism with capitalism as its promoter and defender. 'Fascism' write G. D. H & M. I. Cole,' is State-controlled Capitalism operated in the interests of the broad mass of property-owners....It must be nationalist because the national State is the only available instrument for guarding the rights of property against Socialist attack.'[72] Some fourteen years later, however, G. D. H. Cole seems to have changed his opinion, arguing against what he calls the 'erroneous belief' that Fascism was a form of Capitalism. Instead, he points out, correctly, that the 'great capitalists' were 'controlled by it...compelled to subordinate their money-making impulses to the requirements of the Fascist State...'[73]

In his splendid analysis of fascism and its relation to capitalism, Llewellyn Rockwell points out that fascist economies, although nominally free-market, are dictated to and heavily constrained by bureaucrats. Producers (whether conceived of as workers or business owners) are syndically organised into cartels that are the recipient of government largesse (banks, insurance companies, car firms, etc). Fascist governments borrow and spend recklessly to sustain national economic and ideological goals. If all this sounds familiar that isn't surprising: most western states still operate on these principles, even if, these days, economic goals take precedence over ideological goals.

Appearances to the contrary notwithstanding, then, fascism isn't pro-capitalist nor is it intrinsically conservative. If its fundamental myth of social and political rebirth is taken seriously, then nothing from the past is sacred unless it contributes to the new vision of things. As the phoenix rises from its ashes, so the new order comes into being on the ruins of the old. Particular fascist movements may make tactical alliances with conservatives if that promotes their ends but such alliances won't outlast their usefulness

In the end, the evidence for the left-wing heritage of both Fascism and National Socialism is incontestable.[74] The programme of the newly-formed (1919) *Fasci di Combattimento*, as published in Mussolini's newspaper *Il Popolo d'Italia*, was resolutely left-wing and solidly nationalist. It included demands for lowering the voting age to eighteen, abolishing the Senate and creating instead a Technical Council on labour, industry, commerce and agriculture [anticipations of corporatism] and for an expansive Italian foreign policy. Its social demands included an eight-hour working day, a minimum wage, worker participation in industry, the management of industry to be given over to proletarian organisations, the requirement that owners of property cultivate their lands on penalty of confiscation, the provision of state secular education, a progressive tax on capital amounting to a partial expropriation of all riches and the confiscation of ecclesiastical property and revenues. [see Schnapp, 3-6]

When it came time to formulate the policies of the newly emerged National Socialist party in 1920, this is what, among other things, these policies expressed in the NSDAP[75] (National Socialist) party programme demanded: a greater Germany, living room for the population of the German nation (which did not include Jews), the subordination of individual activity to the general interest and the general good, the ruthless prosecution of all those whose activities are deemed injurious to the common interest, the abolition of unearned income, the confiscation of all war profits, the nationalisation of corporations, profit-sharing in large industrial enterprises, the reconstruction of the national system of education whose curricula must be brought into line with practical life, the creation of a German national press and the prohibition and prosecution of newspapers whose output was not conducive to the national welfare, and the establishment of a strong central state power for the Reich. The original 1920 programme demanded the expropriation of land for communal purposes without compensation but this expropriation was 'clarified' in 1928 so that the expropriation was to be limited to land that had been illegally acquired or land that wasn't administered in accordance with the national welfare. [see NSDAP 1920] Frank McDonough, the author of *Hitler and Nazi Germany*, describes these seemingly obvious anti-capitalist demands as being limited and 'socialist' (the inverted commas are his) which is as much as to say not *really* socialist at all. [see McDonough, 11] As is the case with the Programme of the *Fasci di Combattimento*, it requires unparalleled, not to say perverse, hermeneutical abilities to deny the obviously anti-capitalist and socialist thrust of these measures and to interpret such demands as being characteristic of right-wing or conservative thinking.

Early in this chapter, I mentioned that there is no universal agreement on what the essential constituents, if any, of fascism, national socialism and bolshevism might be but that among the likely candidates were the approval of collectivism, nationalism, authoritarianism, totalitarianism, corporatism, militarism and violence and the disapproval of Jews, capitalism, democracy, materialism, parliamentarianism and liberal decadence. Whatever the prevalence of one or more of these elements in either Fascism, National Socialism or Bolshevism, we are now in a position to summarise our discussion and to conclude that these movements flourished on the basis of the social and economic disorientation resulting from the First World war, that they were all forms of one-party dictatorship, whether totalitarian or authoritarian, that they all shared a contempt for reason and for evidence and for argument, substituting dogmatism and fanaticism in their place, and that each of them was, in its own way, an expression of tribalism in a twentieth century mode. [see Sabine 922-923] In *Genesis*, God says, 'Let us make man in our image, after our likeness.' [*Genesis*, I:26] The proponents of the new tribalisms all had in common the ambition to remake man in *their* image, after *their* likenesses. I do not think it unfair to say that the results of these spectacular twentieth century experiments in social and political reconstruction were somewhat less than edifying. That, unfortunately, won't prevent those who never learn anything from history from re-running the experiments, and with that thought in mind, I return to where I began.

The political changes that took place in 1920s and 1930s Italy, Germany and Russia, with their associated ideologies of Fascism, National Socialism and Bolshevism, were, as historical events, unique, but they were *not* unprecedented and they were *not* inexplicable. Still more to the point, *they are not unrepeatable*, in essence if not in every point of detail. The startling events of the year 2016—the British referendum vote to leave the European Union, the election of Donald Trump to the US Presidency, the rise and rise of the Front National in France, the re-emergence of nationalist movements in Austria, Hungary, Poland and even in Germany, all of them with more or less explicit commitments to forms of what I can only call, with full knowledge of the term's historical resonance, national socialism—all these phenomena manifest to a greater or lesser degree and in various ways a rejection of liberal attitudes to free speech, free thought, free action, free trade and the free movements of people. To me they suggest that what Francis Fukuyama described as the end of history might just have been the end of just one very specific and contingent historical phase and the beginning of another in which what seemed like eternal political verities are perhaps now undergoing a radical realignment. Who can tell what the future holds? I certainly cannot and it would be foolish, especially in a book whose focus is on what has been, to make predictions about what is to come. But it is interesting to speculate about the extent to which the political trends of the early to middle twenty-first century will resemble the political movements of the early to middle twentieth century. Time will tell.

The twentieth century, the century of the new tribalisms, witnessed two spectacular world conflicts (or one world conflict in two parts, if you prefer) with massive destruction of life and property, and many more minor yet bloody conflicts. The twenty-first century has so far avoided wars on the scale of the 1914-1918 and 1939-1945 engagements but it has tried to make up for it with some remarkably limited but destructive conflicts, including those in Afghanistan, Algeria, Central African Republic, Chad, Colombia, Ivory Coast, Darfur, Ethiopia-Somalia, Iraq, Libya, and Syria. All these conflicts have to do, in one way or another, with who is to exercise political control over their respective regions. War and politics seem to go hand in hand. Why is war an endemic feature (if it *is* an endemic feature) of human societies?

Notes

1 'After the First World War,' writes David van Reybrouck, 'love of electoral democracy cooled markedly. The economic crisis of the 1920s and 1930s fragmented support and anti-parliamentary totalitarian models gained in popularity all over Europe. [van Reybrouck, 48]

2 From now on, I shall adopt the now standard convention of using capital-letters to refer to the specific historical instantiations of these ideal types and lower case letters to refer to the ideal types themselves. So, 'F'—Fascism refers to the Italian political movement; 'f'—fascism refers to the ideal type. In citations, capitalisation/non-capitalisation will as in the original.

3 See below, the section: 'Fascism, National Socialism and Bolshevism—Children of the Left.'

4 'When you get to a man in the case/ They're like as a row of pins/ For the Colonel's Lady an' Judy O'Grady/ Are sisters under their skins!' [Rudyard Kipling, *The Ladies*]

5 See Gregor 2009, 1-20. It could be argued that some movements often portrayed as being fascist, such as those in Spain and Portugal, were really either conservative movements at heart or embryonic fascistic movements that stalled at a certain stage of development. Paul Gottfried's *Fascism: The Career of a Concept* arrived on my desk too late to have its arguments substantially included in this chapter but it would seem, from a cursory examination of its contents, that Gottfried supports my contention that the term *fascism* has become a generic (and thus conceptually diffuse) term of abuse used for people who do not share its user's political prejudices, and that Fascism was, in essence, a movement not of the political Right but of the political Left.

6 Paxton, 8; see 206-220.

7 According to William Randolph Hearst (writing in 1918), the Bolsheviks were 'representatives of the most democratic government in Europe' and Bolshevism was '*the truest democracy in Europe, the truest democracy in the world today.*' [Hearst 1918, emphasis in original] Hearst might be forgiven for his naïve enthusiasm in 1918; it is a little more difficult to forgive or even to understand his support for Bolshevism for the next sixteen years. On the credit side, Hearst strongly opposed American involvement in World War I, or at least he did so until the U.S. entered the war on the Allied side on 6 April 1917, at which time his sentiments shifted seamlessly from pro- to anti-German.

8 Del Noce, 80; see also 64.

9 From the 'Berlin Speech', in Griffin, 79.

10 Gregor 1969, 27. Augusto Del Noce argues that 'Fascism is actually a heresy of Communism based on the thesis that Marxist revolutionary thought must be sublated, a sublation that supposedly can be achieved by accepting the Idealistic critique of Marxist philosophy.' [Del Noce, 54] Writing of Gentile, Harry Redner comments, 'In 1923 Gentile began his political career as an Idealist philosopher who happened to become a Fascist; by the early 1930s he had ended up as a Fascist who happened to be an Idealist philosopher.' [Redner, 55]

11 Sacks, 47. It is worth noting that although Sacks recognises the dangerous attraction of tribalism and the evils to which it leads, he also argues strongly that 'universalism is an inadequate response to tribalism, and no less dangerous' because 'it leads to the belief…that there is only one truth about the essentials of the human condition, and it holds true for all people at all times.' [Sacks, 50] This belief in the efficacy of universalism, Sacks terms 'Plato's Ghost'. If tribalism tends to elevate the accidental differences of race or language or culture to the level of absolutes, a bland universalism can tolerate only those differences that make no difference.

12 Whatever I say about fascism in the remainder of this chapter is to be taken to apply *mutatis mutandis* to national socialism and bolshevism, and vice versa, unless the context clearly indicates otherwise.

13 'The conception of man as being not so much a rational as an heroic animal was not invented by the revolt against reason; it is a typical tribalist idea.' [Popper, 74]

14 Although fascism was happy to adopt the Nietzschean idea of the hero, the superman, and adapt it to its own purposes, it was blind to the primacy Nietzsche gives to the individual and to his abhorrence of the state.

15 Sabine, 893. Not everyone is fully persuaded of the genuineness of the claims of national socialism and fascism to be heirs to the tradition of philosophic irrationalism. George Sabine writes, 'Philosophic

irrationalism had formed a persistent strand in European thought throughout the nineteenth century, and while fascism and national socialism were less than philosophically reputable, they constantly sought to enhance their standing by claiming affinity with this.' [Sabine, 888] Sabine is correct to say that fascism and national socialism claim affinity with nineteenth century proponents of irrationalism but he is, I believe, on the basis of the evidence, incorrect to suggest that this claim is meretricious.

16 Bowle, 413. Bowle believes that Sorel's thought can be summed up under four topics: the decadence of bourgeois culture; the necessity of and importance of myth; the General Strike (a widespread revolutionary state of mind) as the instrument for the destruction of the state; and moral redemption via the proletariat. [see Bowle, 402]

17 H. L. Mencken wrote an brilliant critique of New Deal presuppositions in his 'New Deal No. 1', first published in the Baltimore *Evening Sun* in December 1934. See Mencken, 209-213.

18 In Griffin, 44. Sorel's own myth was the idea of the general strike, an idea somewhat less potent, perhaps, than that of the nation.

19 No one in any way interested in this topic should fail to read Michael Oakeshott's brilliant essay, 'The Masses in Representative Democracy.' [see Oakeshott 1991a]

20 In Griffin 291. Viktor Frankl also wrote incisively and movingly in *Man's Search for Meaning* of the fundamental importance of meaning for human life. See also Christopher Booker's discussion of what he calls the 'Rebellion against "The One"' in George Orwell's *Nineteen Eighty-Four* in Booker, 499-503.

21 A. James Gregor writes, 'Fascism is identified as the first revolutionary mass movement regime which aspired to commit the totality of human and natural resources of an historic community to national development' [Gregor 1969, xii]

22 Wowbagger is a character in Douglas Adams's *The Hitchhiker's Guide to the Galaxy* five-volume (yes, five!) trilogy who, having become immortal as the result of an accident involving a particle accelerator, a pair of rubber bands and a liquid lunch, eventually gives himself the task of insulting everybody in the universe as a way of relieving the tedium of having to live forever. The apathy of athanasia is a staple of high and low art—see Wagner's *The Flying Dutchman*, Flann O'Brien's *The Third Policeman* and, one of my favourite films, *Groundhog Day*.

23 It has often been remarked that the founders of religions—Gautama and Jesus, for example—possess charisma, the dynamic energy of which is eventually translated into the static building blocks of an institution. Whether this is so or not, a crisis, or what is termed a crisis even if it is not, is, for many politicians, too good an opportunity to be frittered away in the evanescence of the moment. If the crisis can be used to bring about institutional change, then its effect, otherwise transitory, will become permanent. 'In a constitutional democracy,' writes Thomas Sowell, 'a crisis cannot be made to last indefinitely because alternative versions of events cannot [as in totalitarian states] be suppressed. Real crises must be utilized to establish enduring institutions. The Great Depression of the 1930s was a landmark in this respect. The monetary system—the gold standard—was permanently changed. Labor-management relations were permanently changed by the Wagner Act, adding legal sanctions against employers to other union powers. The permissible limits of price competition were permanently reduced by the Robinson-Patman Act, "fair trade" laws, and a host of special restrictions and subsidies applying to sugar, the maritime industry, and others.' [Sowell 1996, 327]

24 Indeed, historians have struggled to explain the German Army's dramatic reversal of fortune between the end of 1917 when the British and French armies were in total disarray and, with the withdrawal of Russia from the war, forty extra divisions became available for use by the Germans on the Western front. [see Stevenson, passim]

25 Franz von Papen commented caustically on the National Socialist mystical faith in the mighty *Führer*. [see Burleigh, 3] Max Eastman remarks on the 'bigotry and Byzantine scholasticism which has grown up around the sacred scriptures of Marxism. Hegel, Marx, Engels, Plekhanov, Lenin—these men's books contained for the Bolsheviks the last word of human knowledge. They were not science, they were revelation.' [Eastman, 11-12]

26 *The Tempest*, Act 4, Scene 1.

27 Gentile distinguishes between *political religion* and *civil religion*. Civil religion is a 'form of sacralisation of a collective political entity that is not identified with the ideology of a particular political movement, affirms separation of Church and state, and, though postulating the existence of a deistically conceived supernatural being, coexists with traditional religious institutions without identifying itself with any one particular religious confession, presenting itself as a common civic creed above parties and confessions. It recognises broad autonomy for the individual with regard to the sanctified collectivity,

and generally appeals to spontaneous consensus for observing the commandments of public ethics and the collective liturgy.' [Gentile, 30]

28 See Voegelin 1938, passim. It is often thought that the term 'political religion' had its origin in the early work of Eric Voegelin but the term antedates Voegelin by many years, having been used as early as the French Revolution and in 1838 by Abraham Lincoln to express the attitude of Americans to the US Constitution. [see Gentile, 25; see also Gray, passim]

29 In an interview of 1923, in Griffin, 249; 250.

30 For a brilliantly scathing indictment by Czesław Miłosz of the necessity to practise various forms of hypocrisy in the people's democracies in order not to attract the attention of the Grand Inquisitors, see his chapter 'Ketman', in Miłosz, 54-81.

31 Karl Popper, in the second volume of his *The Open Society and its Enemies (Hegel & Marx)* describes Hegelianism as 'the essence of tribalism' [Popper, 30] and says of Hegel that 'he represents the "missing link", as it were, between Plato and the modern form of totalitarianism.' [Popper, 31]

32 Quoted in Gregor 1969, 185.

33 Gregor 1969, 153-154. See also 189.

34 Gregor 1969, 171-172; see also 145.

35 Manin, 1. 'Elected representatives, it was firmly believed, should rank higher than most of their constituents in wealth, talent, and virtue. The fraction of the population constituting the electorate varied from country to country at the time representative government was established....But whatever the threshold was, measures were taken to ensure that representatives were well above it. What counted was not only the social status of representatives defined in absolute terms, but also (and possibly more importantly) their status relative to that of their electors. Representative government was instituted in full awareness that elected representatives would and should be distinguished citizens, socially different from those who elected them.' [Manin, 94]

36 Goldberg 2008, 11-12. See also, Gordon 1990, passim. See Peterson for an account of the propaganda campaign waged against American neutrality, and see Mead 36-41 on the enduring Anglo-American alliance against the various historical incarnations of 'the evil one'.

37 For a quick but reasonably comprehensive overview of Progressivism and Liberalism, see http://www.heritage.org/initiatives/first-principles/progressivism-and-liberalism, accessed 20 July 2016. See Leonard, passim.

38 Postmillenialism is the doctrine that Christ's second coming will happen *after* the Kingdom of God had been established on earth for a thousand years.

39 The eminent Constitutional theorist John W. Burgess, reflecting on Prohibition, wonders 'whether, in having recourse to political and legal means, we have taken a road which leads to the loss of liberty and of the sense of personal responsibility and to despotic government' [Burgess, 88] Prophetically, he wrote in 1923, 'It remains to be seen whether National prohibition will, in the long run, prove any more effective than State prohibition, and also whether, in relying upon law, we shall neglect the moral influences, which are so much more valuable to the formation of character.' [Burgess, 88]

40 See Sewell, 65-66, 67-68 and 87. Patrick Newman, reviewing Thomas Leonard's *Illiberal Reformers*, writes, 'Of prime concern to the progressives was their theory of race suicide—that newly arriving ethnic immigrants were outbreeding the Anglo-Saxons and diluting the overall racial pool of America....' He continues, 'A prominent progressive professor....worried in 1902 about the race suicide implications of allowing Chinese immigrants to enter the country again when the Chinese Exclusion Act of 1882 was up for renewal, and wrote that white workers could not compete with the Chinese since they were unable to "live upon a handful of rice for a pittance," and the Chinese, "who with their yellow skin and strange debasing habits of life seemed to them hardly fellow men at all but evil spirits, rather.... This progressive was none other than Woodrow Wilson, who would become president a decade later.'

41 Although its ultimate origins were Christian, Progressivism was itself evangelised by the emergent anti-liberalism of the later nineteenth century, until it 'rejected the liberal conception of man' and 'installed in its place a therapeutic conception which acknowledges irrational drives and seeks to divert them into socially constructive channels....Instead of regulating the conditions of work alone, it now [regulated] private life as well, organizing leisure time on scientific principles of social and personal hygiene.' [Lasch, 224]

42 See Fromkin, 253-262 and passim. A nostalgic longing for empire can still sometimes be found among some latter-day Progressivists. See Daniel McCarthy's (2014), 'Why Liberalism Means Empire' but see also Sheldon Richman's (2014) rebuttal.

43 Excerpt from a letter of Sydney Smith to Mary, Countess Grey, wife of Earl Grey (Prime Minister

from 1830-1834), 19th February 1823, in Holland, 235-236. Smith (1771-1845) was a renowned Anglican clergyman, humourist and wit.

44 The Fascist theory of the Corporate State was formulated by Gentile.

45 For a comprehensive, critical account of the New Deal, see Powell 2003.

46 Schivelbusch, 190; see also 19-20.

47 Goldberg 2008, 123, 156-157.

48 'To classic American republicans,' writes Brian Doherty, 'Roosevelt seemed to be setting up the equivalent of the most ancient forms of tyranny, the god-king....The combination of alphabet agencies, Social Security, and relentless barrages of war whooping and propaganda, plus a reign that seemed to be growing as long as any pharonic family with term after unprecedented term—what did this all add up to? All hail God-King Roosevelt!' [Doherty, 65]

49 Roosevelt's visceral dislike for British Imperialism led him to be extraordinarily sympathetic to the Soviet Union. Roosevelt, writes Robert Nisbet, 'made no bones, during World War II, about his preference for Stalin's Communism over Churchill's British imperialism....Despite the totalitarian structure of the Soviet Union and its appalling record, it was not this nation that FDR foresaw as the enemy of democracy but rather British imperialism.' [Nisbet 1988, 72]

50 The 1942 film, *Keeper of the Flame*, was a not-so-thinly-veiled attack on Charles Lindbergh. See Cole 1974 and 1983, passim. See also Cull, passim and Denson 2006, 101-172; 173-180.

51 'Once the Supreme Court accepted the New Deal,' writes Kermit Hall, 'the justices abruptly withdrew from the field of economic regulation. This reflected a monumental change in the Court's attitude toward property rights and entrepreneurial liberty.' [Hall, 799] The tentative 'preferred-position' theory first expressed in *Carolene* would later blossom in the Warren Court. [see Schwartz, 281-284]

52 In Powell, 220; see Burgess, passim. Ambrose Bierce quipped that a conservative was 'a statesman who is enamored of existing evils, as distinguished from the liberal, who wishes to replace them with others.

53 A literary anti-totalitarian classic, a critique of the power of tyrannical political regimes to control people not just by violence but by the power of ideas, is Miłosz's *The Captive Mind*.

54 For Thomas Sowell, totalitarian ideology is characterised by the localisation of evil in some group or other, the localisation of wisdom in some person or other, a single scale of values against which all decisions are to be made, a presupposition that there exists sufficient knowledge to achieve its goals, a problem to be solved which is so urgent that all manner of ruthlessness is justified. [see Sowell 1996, 308, also 306-314]

55 Grieder, 565; see also 564.

56 Radically discommoded = df. 'killed'.

57 The elimination of groups intermediate between the individual and the state is not a characteristic necessarily confined to fascism. Robert Nisbet notes that the contemporary American giant state consists of 'a horde of loose individuals, of homunculi serving as atoms of the Giant's body, as in the famous illustration of Leviathan in Hobbes's classic.' [Nisbet 1988, 137]

58 In Griffin, 176; see also D'Annunzio's outline of Corporatism in Griffin, 36-37.

59 It shouldn't come as a shock to readers to learn that some eugenicists were collectivists at heart, displaying scant respect for individual human beings. Thomas Sowell remarks that Francis Galton denied that individuals were 'special or significant', insisting that 'each of us is merely a bud or outgrowth of a larger, organic system.' [Sowell, 53; see also 60] See the Social Sciences and Humanities Research Council of Canada's website, http://eugenicsarchive.ca/ for original material on the eugenics movement.

60 Before his apotheosis as a demiurge of the British Welfare State, William Beveridge argued that those who were unemployable and so dependent upon the State ought to be maintained in public institutions. The price they were obliged to pay for their public support, however, was the loss of their civil rights to vote *and to become fathers*. [see Sewell, 73 and Greenleaf, 270]

61 'The multiplication of the feeble-minded is a very terrible danger to the race.' [memo to the Prime Minister, Herbert Asquith, 1910; see Brignell 2010a]

62 Prime Minister of the United Kingdom in 1937 and sometime chairman of the Birmingham branch of the Eugenic Society.

63 Sanger wrote, '...the campaign for Birth Control is not merely of eugenic value, but is practically identical in ideal with the final aims of Eugenics.' [Sanger 1921, 5] See her delightfully entitled chapter 'The Fertility of the Feeble-Minded' in Sanger 1922, 80-104 in which she writes, 'The feeble minded woman is twice as prolific as the normal one.' [Sanger 1922, 86] Sanger's *Birth Control Review*, which ran from 1917-1940, contains pieces on various aspects of eugenics written by a variety of the

twentieth-century's great and the good.

64 'I wish very much that the wrong people could be prevented entirely from breeding,' wrote Roosevelt, 'and when the evil nature of these people is sufficiently flagrant, this should be done. Criminals should be sterilized and feeble-minded persons forbidden to leave offspring behind them.' [Hagedorn ed., Vol. XII, 201; see Brignell 2010b]

65 As governor of New Jersey, Wilson in 1911 signed a eugenic sterilisation bill according to which the feeble-minded could be forced to undergo sterilisation.

66 See Wade, 26-38; and see Sewell, 49-106.

67 An account of the gory details of this case, a case designed to give the US Supreme Court the opportunity to constitutionally legitimate eugenics, can be found in Sewell, 97-100.

68 See Kühl, passim; and see Sewell, 112-113, 126-127 and 133-134.

69 Klinghoffer, online; see Sewell, 129-142.

70 Trotsky, 278; see Gregor 1969, 346.

71 Some thinkers distinguish between totalitarianism and authoritarianism, authoritarianism supposedly being less ambitious in its goals, contenting itself merely with the suppression of liberty and all opposition but without necessarily requiring the destruction of the institutions of civil society. [see Grieder 564-565] For John Lukacs, fascism was authoritarian whereas national socialism and communism were totalitarian. I find Lukacs's claim paradoxically revisionary since the term 'totalitarian' was produced from the womb of Italian Fascism and was adopted by Mussolini himself. Whatever the ultimate truth of the matter, if there is any such thing, I see no vital difference in kind between totalitarianism and authoritarianism, at most, a difference of degree.

72 Cole, 1934, 55-56; quoted in Griffin, 267.

73 Cole 1948 [2011], 149f.; 147.

74 See Gottfried, chapter 5. Despite the evidence overwhelmingly linking fascism to socialism, this doesn't prevent a kind of ideological game of 'Pin the tail on the donkey' taking place between liberals (in the modern sense of that term) and conservatives, each side attempting to characterise the other as the fellow-traveller of fascism. Thomas Sowell remarks that 'Adherents of both the constrained and the unconstrained visions each see fascism as the logical extension of the adversary's vision. To those on the political left, fascism is "the far right." Conversely, to Hayek, Hitler's "national socialism" (Nazism) was indeed socialist in concept and execution.' [Sowell 1987, 114-115]

75 NSDAP stands for the *Nationalsozialistische Deutsche ArbeiterPartei*—the National Socialist German Workers' Party—the official name for the party known to us slangily as the Nazi party. It is an interesting matter of linguistic usage that the Communist Party is never referred to in formal contexts as the 'Commie Party' whereas the National Socialist German Workers Party is routinely referred to as the 'Nazi' party, this nickname having the effect of pushing the 'Socialist' element of the Party's name well into the background. 'Hitler wouldn't have called himself a Nazi,' remarks Mark Forsyth. 'Indeed, he became quite offended when anyone did suggest he was a Nazi. He would have considered himself a National Socialist. *Nazi* is, and always has been an insult.' [Forsyth, 111; see 111-114] David Mamet remarks, 'the sibilant in the acronym NAZI stands for Socialist. They, like the Italian Fascists and the pre-Bolshevik Communists, believed, in their beginnings, in Social Justice, and the Fair Distribution of goods. But these sweet ideas are encumbered in execution by the realization that *someone*, finally, has to do the work; their adamant practice will quite soon reveal this: "Oh. We will need slaves." These slaves may be called, variously, the Rich, the Jews, the Kulaks, the Gypsies, Armenians, countercultural elements, and so on, but they are chosen not for their odious qualities but for their supine or defenseless nature.' [Mamet, 32]

Chapter 32

WAR

It is sweet and fitting to die for your country
—Horace

A churl [of a tax-collector] was affronting me and I killed that clown
O God! Is this a cause for enmity?
—Muireadhach Albanach Ó Dálaigh

No nation could preserve its freedom in the midst of continual warfare
—James Madison

In the last days of World War I,[1] just before going over the top of the trenches in yet another futile attack, the idiot-savant Private Baldrick says to Captain Blackadder (who has been trying desperately not to get himself killed) 'I have a plan, sir.' 'Really, Baldrick?' replies Blackadder, 'A cunning and subtle one?' 'Yes, sir.' 'As cunning as a fox who's just been appointed Professor of Cunning at Oxford University?' 'Yes, sir.' [A voice is heard shouting: *On the signal, company will advance!*] Blackadder remarks resignedly, 'Well, I'm afraid it'll have to wait. Whatever it was, I'm sure it was better than my plan to get out of this by pretending to be mad. I mean, who would have noticed another madman round here?'[2]

In the early 1970s, having lived and worked in the Netherlands for a year, I decided to cycle home to Ireland. After a detour through the ironically named Dutch Alps, I eventually found myself cycling across the plateau of Picardy in northern France. I rode past a graveyard with neat gravestones all in a row. And then I rode past another. And then another. Lots of graveyards, with lots of gravestones and, lying beneath them, lots of soldiers killed in the war to end all wars. And I wondered, as so many have wondered before me, just what it was that all these men gave their lives for.[3] Did they really find it sweet and fitting to die for their countries? As Eric Bogle wrote in his song, 'Green Fields of France"

> And I can't help but wonder, now Willie McBride,
> Do all those who lie here know why did they die?
> Did you really believe them when they told you 'The Cause?'
> Did you really believe that this war would end wars?
> Well the suffering, the sorrow, the glory, the shame
> The killing, the dying, it was all done in vain,
> For Willie McBride, it all happened again,
> And again, and again, and again, and again.[4]

Freedom's Progress?

But the millions of men who died or were maimed and the women who were widowed and the children who were left fatherless weren't the only casualties of the war. Something else died on the green fields of France. 'European liberalism,' writes Bruce Porter, 'finally perished on the battlefields of Verdun and the Somme.'[5] The effects of the death of liberalism were to resonate throughout the entire twentieth century and are still being felt today.[6]

The discrepancy between the avowed aims of war and other less than reputable reasons for it are sometimes evident even to the military mind. A famous (or notorious) attack on war as a 'racket' was made in 1935 by the decorated Marine General, Smedley Darlington Butler, a racket being defined by him as 'something conducted for the benefit of the very few, at the expense of the very many.' [Butler 2003, 23] The principal beneficiaries of war, according to Butler, were the 'Munitions makers. Ship builders. Manufacturers. Meat packers. Speculators.' [Butler 2003, 25] In making this claim, Butler anticipated by some twenty-six years, the substance of Dwight Eisenhower's warnings in his 'Farewell Address' of the dangers presented by what he termed 'the military-industrial complex'. Both military men, however, while clearly perceiving the close connection between the armed forces and industrial and commercial interests, were conspicuously blind to the connecting link between them which is, of course, the state.

Not everyone is persuaded of the futility of war. In his 2014 book, *War! What is it Good For?: Conflict and the Progress of Civilization from Primates to Robots*, Ian Morris, in a neo-Hobbesian vein, robustly defends the thesis that war has been central to human development![7] Perhaps I'm myopic, but I find it a little difficult to see what significant contribution to human development was made by, for example, the atomic devastation of Hiroshima and Nagasaki in 1945,[8] the slaughter of as many as half of the 600,000 population of Nanking by the Japanese in 1937 (Japan disputes the numbers killed), the German blitz of Rotterdam, of London and Coventry and other British cities, and the Allied bombing of Hamburg, Berlin and Dresden.[9] About the razing of Dresden, Kurt Vonnegut writes: 'Dresden was surely among the World's most lovely cities. Her streets were broad, lined with shade-trees. She was sprinkled with countless little parks and statuary. She had marvellous old churches, libraries, museums, theaters, art galleries, beer gardens, a zoo, and a renowned university....In the Swastika's shadow those symbols of the dignity and hope of mankind stood waiting, monuments to truth. The accumulated treasure of hundreds of years, Dresden spoke eloquently of those things excellent in European civilization wherein our debt lies deep....In February 1945, American bombers reduced this treasure to crushed stone and embers; disembowelled her with high-explosives and cremated her with incendiaries. The atom bomb may represent a fabulous advance, but it is interesting to note that primitive TNT and thermite managed to exterminate in one bloody night more people than died in the whole London blitz.' [Vonnegut 2009a, 36-37] Perhaps the military achievements of the Dresden holocaust more than compensated for the collateral damage? Perhaps, if one believes that a two-day disruption of the local railroads were worth the death of a hundred thousand non-combatants and the destruction of an entire historic city.[10]

WAR AND HUMAN NATURE

Is there something fundamentally wrong with human beings? No visitor to earth from another planet could fail to observe and to be puzzled by our propensity to kill one another with alacrity. Is it the case that our ordinary lives are so boring that war and violence provide some relief from its deadening grip?[11] There is some evidence to support this view, not least, the esteem in which warriors have been held in many societies. Tacitus's comments on the Germans of his time are illustrative of the *mores* of a warrior culture. 'For the Germans,' he writes, 'have no taste for peace; renown is more easily won among perils, and a large body of retainers cannot be kept together except by means of violence and war. They are always making demands on the generosity of their chief, asking for a coveted war-horse or a spear stained with the blood of a defeated enemy....The wherewithal for this openhandedness comes from war and plunder. A German is not so easily prevailed upon to plough the land and wait patiently for harvest as to challenge a foe and earn wounds for his reward. He thinks it tame and spiritless to accumulate slowly by the sweat of his brow what can be got quickly by the loss of a little blood.' And what do such men do when not fighting? 'When not engaged in warfare they spend a certain amount of time in hunting, but much more in idleness, thinking of nothing else but sleeping and eating. For the boldest and most warlike men have no regular employment, the care of house, home, and fields being left to the women, old men, and the weaklings of the family.'[12]

There can be no doubt, then, that war offers many men an escape from the dull hand of daily drudgery. It must also be said that it offers the opportunity to some men to demonstrate one cardinal virtue above all the others—courage. As an example of this, consider the military career of one of the most extraordinary (yet relatively little known) soldiers of all time, General Sir Adrian Carton de Wiart. His life was like something out of an extravagant action-hero film—no, strike that, like something out of several extravagant action-hero films, each more unlikely than the other.

Born in 1880 to an aristocratic Belgian father and an Irish mother, he was socially very well connected; one of his cousins was Count Henri Carton de Wiart, Prime Minister of Belgium and another, Baron Edmond Carton de Wiart was political secretary to the Belgian King. de Wiart was educated in England. While at Oxford, he abandoned his academic studies to enlist and serve in the Boer War, under a false name. Wounded in the stomach and groin, he was invalided home. Commissioned shortly afterwards, he saw action in South Africa again and spent some time in India. In 1908 he married. Nothing unusual there you might think but de Wiart didn't marry just anyone. Oh no. His wife was Countess Friederike Maria Karoline Henriette Rosa Sabina Franziska Fugger von Babenhausen. When the First World War broke out, de Wiart was serving in Africa where he was shot in the face, his injuries costing him the loss of an eye and part of his ear. Need I say that thereafter he wore an eye patch! Back in Europe where the real action was and where he wanted to be, he fought on the Western Front, commanding, in succession, three infantry battalions and a brigade. He was wounded seven times in, among other places, the skull, ankle, hip, and ear, while also losing his left arm. Now one-eyed and one-armed, he was beginning to resemble an army version of Admiral Nelson.

He was awarded the Victoria Cross, the British Army's highest award for gallantry, for his actions during the war but, typically, made no mention of it in his autobiography. The VC citation reads: 'For most conspicuous bravery, coolness and determination during severe operations of a prolonged nature. It was owing in a great measure to his dauntless courage and inspiring example that a serious reverse was averted. He displayed the utmost energy and courage in forcing our attack home. After three other battalion Commanders had become casualties, he controlled their commands, and ensured that the ground won was maintained at all costs. He frequently exposed himself in the organisation of positions and of supplies, passing unflinchingly through fire barrage of the most intense nature. His gallantry was inspiring to all.'

Active in the British Military Mission in Poland in the inter-war period (his French opposite number was Charles de Gaulle), he became acquainted with Ignacy Paderewski, the Polish Prime Minister. His advice was sought by the Nuncio, Cardinal Achille Ratti (afterwards Pius XI) on whether or not to evacuate the diplomatic corps from Warsaw. He saw action again in 1920, when the Red Army were at the gates of Warsaw, fighting off an attack by Red Cavalry on a train on which he was travelling. When things quieted down, between 1924 and 1939, he lived in Poland on an estate, the use of which he was given, by Prince Karol Mikołaj Radziwiłł.

On the outbreak of World War II, de Wiart was reinstated in the army by special appointment. Most men would have been happy to have been given a desk job but not de Wiart. Just before he reached the age of 60, he took active command of a military expedition to Norway. Eventually deemed to be too old to serve in active command, he was given the task in 1941 of being head of the Military Mission to Yugoslavia. On the way there, his plane crashed[13] and, after swimming to shore, he was captured by the Italians (of course). A high-profile prisoner, de Wiart had for his fellow prisoners General Sir Richard O'Connor and Thomas Daniel Knox, the Earl of Ranfulrly. He attempted escape on five occasions, succeeding once in tunnelling out and avoiding captivity for eight days, despite not speaking Italian and despite his distinctive appearance (one arm, one eye, multiple wounds). He was eventually released as part of the Italian plan to get out of the war.

There's a ForrestGumpish-like photograph of de Wiart at the Cairo Conference of 1943, standing behind and alongside Chiang Kai-shek, Franklin Delano Roosevelt, General Somervell, General Stilwell, Admiral Mountbatten and Winston Churchill: de Wiart slumming it once again. After Cairo, he was sent on a mission to China where he liaised for the remainder of the war with the Nationalist Chinese government. The war over, de Wiart retired to County of Cork (my native county), there to fish contentedly for salmon and shoot at snipe and there, eventually, to die at the age of 83. Among his decorations were VC (the Victoria Cross). KBE (Knight Commander of the Order of the British Empire), CB (Companion of the Order of the Bath), CMG (Companion of the Order of St Michael and St George), DSO (Companion of the Distinguished Service Order), Officer of the Order of the Crown (Belgium), Croix de guerre (Belgium), Silver Cross (Knight) of the Order of Military Virtue (Poland), Cross of Valour (Poland—twice!), Commander of the Legion of Honour (France) and Croix de guerre (France).

The occasional flippancy in my account of General de Wiart's life and career is evinced simply by its quasi-fantastic character. In fact, I have nothing but admiration for his single-minded courage and dedication to what he saw as his duty shown by this extraordinary man; what a pity that it took state-organised human conflict and destruction to produce this courage and dedication.

If war isn't just a product of boredom or the ever-present desire to live off the proceeds of armed robbery, is it the case, as Arthur Koestler has speculated, that man is 'an aberrant biological species, an evolutionary misfit, afflicted by an endemic disorder which sets it apart from all other animal species...' [Koestler 1979, 5] Are human beings naturally bellicose? [see Beyer 40-50] Freud seems to have thought so, holding that man naturally exhibits a lust for hatred and destruction that inevitably issues in war. It is true that men may kill when moved by anger or when consumed by lust, but war isn't just the spontaneous killing of one man by another. War is, perhaps paradoxically, a social event, requiring a high level of human cooperation in the slaughter of conspecifics; it is, curiously, the organised production of radical disorganisation. In fact, *pace* Freud, it takes a great deal of propaganda and desensitisation to persuade normal human beings that killing one another is a good thing. The point of much military training is to persuade soldiers to obey without thinking and to treat their enemies as if they were less than human.[14] It really helps if you can't see the face of the person you are attempting to kill; this might explain in part why, with the advance of sophisticated weapons that enable us to kill at ever-increasing distances, the death toll of modern wars has risen spectacularly.[15] [see Spiller, 239 ff.]

How is it possible for people to behave as callously to one another as they do in time of war? How can people who would feel revulsion and shame at kicking a dog, torture and kill other human beings? The Polish Reserve Police Battalion 101 was instructed to shoot 1,800 Jews from the village of Jozefow. They did— men, women, children, old people, all shot at close range. The members of the Battalion were all ordinary workingmen, not specially trained and hardened killers. Few of them declined to act, though they were given the opportunity to do so. Their primary reaction to their deeds was initially one of depression and anger. Nevertheless, the second time around, their negative emotional reactions were less severe. The killing escalated. In just a few days, 35,000 Jews from various work camps were killed. [see Hedges, 87-88]

War involves killing people, and killing people is usually prohibited both morally and legally. To those who aren't conditioned to it, to bring about or even to witness the violent death of another human being is repulsive. Whatever one might do when angry or fearful, killing another human being isn't something most of us can do in cold-blood. To make it acceptable to a normal human being, it has to be dressed up in a form of drama in which we become actors. 'The indispensability of play-acting in the grim business of dying and killing is particularly evident in the case of armies. Their uniforms, flags, emblems, parades, music, and elaborate etiquette and ritual are designed to separate the soldier from his flesh-and-blood self and mask the overwhelming reality of life and death.' [Hoffer, 65, §47]

If war is to be distinguished from mere violence, the killing it involves must be justified. Kaldor remarks, 'Men go to war for a variety of individual reasons— adventure, honour, fear, comradeship, protection of "home and hearth"—but socially organized legitimate violence needs a common goal in which the individual soldier can believe and which he shares with others. If soldiers are to be treated as heroes and not as criminals, then heroic justification is needed to mobilize their energies, to persuade them to kill and risk being killed.' [Kaldor, 28] One way to justify organized violence against other human beings is to distinguish between an in-group and an out-group, between us and them, where *we* (the in-group) are fully human and *they* (the out-group) are not. So, all human beings observe prohibitions on killing and stealing but these prohibitions apply only between members of the in-group; the killing of or stealing from members of out-groups is not only *not* prohibited, it is actively condoned and encouraged. The relation of one group to another is one of 'isolation, suspicion, hostility. But within a tribe the situation is quite otherwise….the members of a group have a united and common interest against every other group.' [Davie, 16] If a group is to be able to preserve itself in the face of the enmity of other groups, it must adopt effective means of settling or avoiding in-group disputes that would weaken it as a whole.[16] Maurice Davie notes that 'There are two codes of morals, two sets of mores, one for comrades inside and another for strangers outside, and both arise from the same interests. Against outsiders it is meritorious to kill, plunder, practice blood revenge and steal women and slaves, but inside the group none of these things can be allowed because they would produce discord and weakness.'[17] As Caesar remarked of the Germans, 'Robberies beyond the bounds of each community have no infamy, but are commended as a means of exercising youth and diminishing sloth.'[18] And just in case one is inclined to think that the distinction between in-group and out-group with their associated *mores* is a thing of the dim and distant past, one might reflect that cross-border cattle-raiding between England and Scotland is an enterprise that ceased only relatively recently. Slavoj Žižek writes, 'One thing that never ceases to surprise the naïve ethical consciousness is how the very same people who commit terrible acts of violence towards their enemies can display warm humanity and gentle care for the members of their own group…This limitation of our ethical concern to a narrow circle seems to run counter to our spontaneous insight that we are all humans, with the same basic hopes, fears and pains, and therefore the same justified claim to respect and dignity.' [Žižek 2009, 40-41] But the possessors of a naïve ethical consciousness get things precisely backwards. There is nothing at all spontaneous about the insight that we are all humans and share our humanity in common—what *is* spontaneous is the deep-rooted perception that 'we' are not 'they' and 'they' are not 'us'. And there's nothing at all surprising in our ability to care for kin and kindred while simultaneously hating those who are not 'us'—what *is* surprising is the slow and intermittent progress that has been made throughout history in the extension of our ethical concern to the stranger and the enemy, even if that extension is partial and fitful and subject to calamitous regression.

Arthur Koestler believes that there is a problem with the serendipitous evolutionary development of the human brain, with the later neo-cortex sitting on top of the older brain but not being sufficiently integrated with it. He thinks that evolution blundered in what he describes as 'the rapid, quasi-brutal *superimposition* (instead of *transformation*) of the neocortex on the ancestral structures and the resulting *insufficient coordination* between the new brain and the old, and *inadequate control* of the former over the latter.' [Koestler, 11] We have, as it were, a penthouse brain, with rickety staircases and a lift that works only intermittently, thus ensuring less than perfect coordination between the penthouse and the other floors of the building. Human violence is often attributed to some inbuilt tendency on the part of the individual human being to be aggressive. Nevertheless, Koestler believes, and in this I think he is correct, that our problem isn't primarily individual aggression, which accounts for only a tiny amount of the damage we do to one another, but rather our very sociability which, wrongly placed, leads to fanaticism. The trouble with our species, he writes, 'is not an excess of *aggression*, but an excess capacity for fanatical *devotion*. Even a cursory glance at history should convince one that individual crimes committed for selfish motives play a quite insignificant part in the human tragedy, compared to the numbers massacred in unselfish loyalty to one's tribe, nation, dynasty, church, or political ideology, *ad majorem gloriam dei*....Homicide committed for personal reasons is a statistical rarity in all cultures, including our own. Homicide for *un*selfish reasons, at the risk of one's own life, is the dominant phenomenon in history.' [Koestler, 14] Whereas large-scale human conflict normally occurs between one group and another, conflict sometimes occurs *within* groups, and even though inhibitions against intra-group homicide are necessarily strong, they aren't insuperable. [see Gat, 46-47] Nevertheless, appearances to the contrary notwithstanding, and *pace* Hobbes, human beings have been quite successful in keeping intra-group individual deviant behaviour under control.[19] For a social group to exist at all implies that the modes of social control, formal and informal, are effective. If not, the group would cease to exist. Lawrence Keeley, too, emphasises the *social* nature of warfare: 'Warfare is ultimately not a denial of the human capacity for social cooperation, but merely the most destructive expression of it.' [Keeley, 158] A 2014 study in the *New Scientist* would seem to provide some recent evidence for Koestler's and Keeley's claim: 'Contrary to popular perception, people are rarely violent simply because they lose control and fail to think about right and wrong....Across cultures and history, there is generally one motive for hurting or killing: people are violent because it feels like the right thing to do. They feel morally obliged to do it....Violence is not the breakdown of morality—it is motivated by moral emotions and judgements.' [Fiske & Rai, 30]

Thinkers of a romantic disposition are inclined to believe that life before what we are pleased to consider civilisation was neither nasty, brutish, nor short, but when it comes to the incidence and character of inter-group violence, the evidence does not support this pious belief.[20] The two basic positions in respect of the naturalness of war are exemplified in the writings of Hobbes and Rousseau. For Hobbes, the human state of nature was one of constant war of all with all whereas, according to Rousseau, aboriginal man lived harmoniously with his fellow men and with nature until the serpent of agriculture brought in its train property, class division and war. [but see Gat, 5; 134] This long-running debate has been effectively settled by anthropological research. It is now established beyond rational dispute that hunter-gatherer groups and tribes did *not* inhabit some aboriginal Garden of Eden. Violence was endemic among them, 'resulting in very high homicide rates among hunter-gatherer peoples, much higher than in any modern industrial society. And yes, intergroup fighting and killing were widespread among them.' [Gat, 13] The truth would seem to be not that hunter-gatherer groups and tribes fought all the time with one another; but they did fight with one another on and off and, when they did, casualties were relatively high. [see Gat, 15-16] Jared Diamond comments, 'It may astonish you readers, as it initially astonished me, to learn that trench warfare, machine guns, napalm, atomic bombs, artillery, and submarine torpedoes produce time-averaged war-related death tolls so much lower than those from spears, arrows, and clubs.' [Diamond 2012, 140] What Diamond means by 'lower' here is the level of deaths as a percentage of the relevant social groups over an alternating period of war and peace, not absolute numbers. The reason for this remarkable fact is that warfare between hunter-gather groups and tribes involved the entire population of men, women and children, with the losers in serious conflicts being killed in large part or sometimes even massacred, though the absolute numbers were low.[21] Contrary to what is popularly believed, then, the level of individual participation in pre-civilised inter-group conflict and the casualty rate of participants tended, if anything, to be *higher* than those of many modern, civilised wars. 'Although modern conscript armies during active warfare generally represent a high percentage of the male population,' writes Lawrence Keeley, 'on many occasions nonstate societies mobilize a higher proportion of their manpower. In World War II, neither the Soviet Union nor the United States...managed during the whole war to mobilize any greater proportion of its manpower than have some tribes and chiefdoms.' [Keeley, 34] In respect of the prevalence and importance of war to non-state societies (bands, tribes, and chiefdoms) as opposed to states, Keeley concludes that 'There is simply no proof that warfare in small-scale societies was a rarer or less serious undertaking than among civilized societies. In general, warfare in prestate societies was both frequent and important. If anything, peace was a scarcer commodity for members of bands, tribes, and chiefdoms than for the average citizen of a civilized state.' [Keeley, 39; see Beyer, 41]

Throughout human history, most killing has been done by one social group or another—band, tribe, chiefdom or state. Political organisation at some level or other, then, appears to be a necessary condition of war, and in being disposed towards war, the modern state is no more morally reprehensible than any other level of political organisation, somewhat less so, in fact, if we consider injuries and deaths in proportional terms. But although it's true that the *percentage* of participants and casualties in state wars may be lower than in pre-state wars, the *absolute numbers* killed and injured simply do not compare. This is so because, although the proportion killed is smaller than in pre-state wars, it's a smaller proportion of a much larger number of people; 30% of 10,000 is 3,000, 1% of 50,000,000 is 500,000. To kill other human beings in really large numbers it takes a great degree of social organisation, usually a nation state. This being so, it is more than a little unexpected to find Lawrence Keeley, who very clearly establishes in his *War before Civilization*, the ubiquitously social (and political) roots of war, recommending as an antidote to war, 'an effective political organization with legislative, judicial, and police powers, whether its scale comprises a family band, a village, a tribe, a chiefdom, a city-state, a nation, or the whole earth.' [Keeley, 181] Effective political organisations are likely to be just as effective at waging wars as they are at doing anything else and the economies of scale available to the larger political unit means that it can attain its war-related purposes using a smaller percentage of its population. In any event, the pertinent issue isn't whether proportionally more people were killed in inter-band, inter-village, inter-tribe or inter-state conflict, but the radical imbalance between the numbers killed in socially organised inter-group conflict and those killed by individual violence.

The number of people killed in the twentieth century in state-sponsored conflicts or state-related victimization is, at a conservative estimate, between 175,000,000 and 180,000,000.[22] By contrast, although it is impossible to say for sure, the number of people killed in the twentieth century by what we might call normal criminal homicide or in inter-tribe violence is nowhere near that number. The figure derived from the same source as that for state-originated deaths gives us roughly eight million non-state homicides worldwide in the twentieth century, which is less than five per cent of the state-related figure. Matthew White, the author of the source from which these figures derive, appears eager to absolve the state of responsibility for these deaths, remarking 'Governments don't kill people; people kill people.' This, of course, is true but completely misses the essential difference between deadly force employed for personal gain or revenge or hatred and the deadly force employed by agents of states or would-be states in inter- and intra state conflicts.

It is a commonplace that persons are prepared to do things as part of a group that they would never contemplate doing when acting alone and this degree of cooperation is possible only because of man's possession of language. Language and ritual is what constitutes a group as a group. To be identified as Big-endian or a Little-endian[23] requires the telling and the believing of a story and the promotion of actions consistent with those beliefs. Koestler notes, 'man's deadliest weapon is *language*.'[24] Without language, man wouldn't be man. There would be no literature, no social life as we know it—but also, no war. So, it isn't personal self-assertion or some defect in individual psychology or even a psycho-developmental defect endemic in the human race that is responsible for man's inhumanity to man. Paradoxically, it is precisely the same positive attribute—what Koestler calls the integrative tendency or what I would call self-transcendence through the social—that is responsible both for social cohesion *and* also responsible for large-scale human destruction. The paradox, a la Koestler, is that 'the act of identification with the group is a *self-transcending* act, yet it reinforces the *self-assertive* tendencies of the group.'[25]

WAR AND THE STATE

On however limited a scale it may occur, war is a socio-political activity, not the expression of individual aggression or hostility. Diamond defines war as 'recurrent violence between groups belonging to rival political units, and sanctioned by those units.' [Diamond 2012, 131] Although it should come as no surprise to anyone to find that there is a close association between war and the development and operation of that most typical of contemporary political orders, the state, it must be conceded that war has been characteristic of *all* human groups at *all* times.[26]

War has the effect of uniting a group in the way that almost nothing else can. The effect of external pressure on the group is to force it to bond ever more tightly together to resist attack. Maurice Davie notes, 'war exerts a supreme integrating force. Rude societies undergo remarkable changes when war converts the unordered populace into a disciplined army under a leader with powers of life and death….the warriors submit their unruly wills to a leader, and private quarrels are sunk in a larger patriotism.' [Davie, 162-163] The unity of the group makes possible coercive regimes that, at other times, would be unacceptable to those subject to those regimes.[27] War is also extremely useful to political leaders, allowing them to divert the attention and deflect the attacks of their would-be political opponents. In Shakespeare's *Henry IV (Part II)*, the English King remarks to his son that he has distracted his mighty nobles by diverting their attention from himself to the troubles in the Holy Land (why does this sound so familiar?), 'Lest,' he said, 'rest and lying still might make them look/ Too near unto my state.' He recommends to his son, as standard operating procedure, to 'busy giddy minds/ With foreign quarrels'—good advice to rulers then and still good advice today.[28]

The Romans provided for the institution of a dictator in times of national emergency and, as we have already noted, closer to our own time, Franklin Delano Roosevelt's inauguration speech of 1933 contains intimations of a willingness to assume dictatorial powers if he deemed such to be necessary. If one wants coercive powers and one wants them to be unchecked, then, as Hermann Goering noted, the tried and tested winning strategy is to persuade one's fellow countrymen that they are under attack or are about to be attacked.

We got around to the subject of war again and I [Gustave Gilbert] said that, contrary to his attitude, I did not think that the common people are very thankful for leaders who bring them war and destruction.

'Why, of course, the people don't want war,' Goering shrugged. 'Why would some poor slob on a farm want to risk his life in a war when the best that he can get out of it is to come back to his farm in one piece. Naturally, the common people don't want war: neither in Russia nor in England nor in America, nor for that matter in Germany. That is understood. But, after all, it is the leaders of the country who determine the policy and it is always a simple matter to drag the people along, whether it is a democracy or a fascist dictatorship or a Parliament or a Communist dictatorship.'

'There is one difference,' I pointed out. 'In a democracy the people have some say in the matter through their elected representatives, and in the United States only Congress can declare wars.'

'Oh, that is all well and good, but, voice or no voice, the people can always be brought to the bidding of the leaders. That is easy. All you have to do is tell them they are being attacked and denounce the pacifists for lack of patriotism and exposing the country to danger. It works the same way in any country.'[29]

Those who opposed America's entry into the World Wars, such as Charles Lindbergh, were reviled as 'isolationists', sometimes even as enemy fellow-travellers and traitors. It has been said that the first casualty of war is truth but, if so, its second casualty must be the vilification of any form of opposition or resistance to that war. Davie concludes, 'War exerts perhaps the greatest integrative force known; its effect has always been to tighten the reins of government….In time of war personal rights must yield to the superior right of life of the unified community.' [Davie, 164]

Military command is strictly necessary only in time of war but those who exercise it are understandably often loath to give it up when the war ends. A permanent state of war or a permanent readiness for war is a way of maintaining the necessity for military command and the concomitant requirements of all in society to yield to its exigencies. 'The state was established,' says Davie, 'when a chieftain and his war band got permanent possession of a definite territory of considerable area occupied by a large number of people engaged in the arts of agriculture and industry. The chief characteristics of the state thus formed are the predominance of military power, and loyalty to a sovereign exercising authority over the geographical area rather than to a tribe or organization based on blood relationship.' [Davie, 166] Franz Oppenheimer takes more or less the same view as Davie. 'The State, complete in its genesis, essentially and almost completely during the first stages of its existence, is a social institution, forced by a victorious group of men on a defeated group, with the sole purpose of regulating the dominion of the victorious group over the vanquished, and securing itself against revolt from within and attacks from abroad. No primitive state known to history originated in any other manner.' [Oppenheimer, 43-44] He continues, '[The State's] purpose, in every case, is found to be the political means for the satisfaction of needs. At first, its method is by exacting a ground rent, so long as there exists no trade activity the products of which can be appropriated. Its form, in every case, is that of dominion, whereby exploitation regarded as "justice," maintained as a "constitution," insisted on strictly, and in case of need enforced with cruelty.' [Oppenheimer, 112-113] With the emergence of war and state the original *de facto* horizontal equality of members of the social group tends to be disrupted and eventually destroyed by the emergence of the vertical political means of command and control. '"Where war is carried on and booty acquired, greater differences arise, which find their expression in the ownership of slaves, women, arms and spirited mounts." The ownership of *slaves!* The nomad is the inventor of slavery, and thereby has created the seedling of the state, the first economic exploitation of man by man.' [Oppenheimer, 64]

All the great empires of the ancient world—Babylonia and Assyria, Persia and Macedonia, Egypt, Rome and China—have their origin in war. War leaders eventually become kings or emperors. Davie argues that 'The state, therefore, owes its origin to war....The state normally arises from the conquest of a comparatively peaceful agricultural group by an invading nomadic war band....The success of the invading host is rooted in its military superiority. But conquest does not lead to the formation of a state unless the conquered people is agricultural.' [Davie, 174] In essential agreement with Davie is Albert Keller who writes in his *Homeric Society*, 'the state is in origin a product of war and exists primarily as an enforced peace between conquerors and conquered.' [Keller, 248] 'History lessons,' says John Keegan, 'remind us that the states in which we live, their institutions, even their laws, have come to us through conflict, often of the most bloodthirsty sort.' [Keegan, 4]

WAR AND THE RISE OF THE MODERN STATE

War, then, isn't in essence a matter of individual violence writ large. It takes a social group of some kind—in modern times, a state—to make a war; but wars also make states. The causation is reciprocal. 'The machinery of the modern state,' writes Bruce Porter, 'is derived historically from the organizational demands of warfare, and states as we know them today trace their origins and development in large measure to the crucible of past wars.' [Porter, xix] It may be objected that war, or, at least, inter-group violence, has been a constant factor of human society since time immemorial so that to tie it to the emergence of the state is, to put it mildly, counter-intuitive. On the other hand, Mary Kaldor claims, 'The notion of war as state activity was firmly established only towards the end of the eighteenth century.' [Kaldor, 17] The Romans did indeed fight as a state, or a proto-state, but their opponents weren't other states but whole societies. So too, the struggles between the Greek city-states were between the citizens of those city-states and their armies were composed of citizen militias. After the fall of the Western Roman Empire, there was, of course, much fighting but again, not between states as such. Standing armies as we now know them, with their regiments, their ranks, their barracks, and so on, are of relatively recent origin.[30]

Bruce Porter believes that if the state is to be conceived of as a sovereign power exercising a monopoly of force over a specific geographical area and its population, then the state 'simply did not exist in the medieval world. The state as we know it is a relatively new invention, originating in Europe between 1450 and 1650.' [Porter, 6] Since its emergence during this period, the state has taken on a variety of forms. First, there was the *quasi-dynastic state* with roots in its medieval past but, more significantly, with limited sovereignty, even if this was coupled with unlimited ambition. 'The European state was no more than a private dynasty, more than a cluster of feudal realms, but it was not yet widely perceived as the political incarnation of a sovereign people.' [Porter, 106] Second, we see the emergence of the *nation state*, erupting in the French Revolution and dominating the nineteenth century. Here, for the first time, we see the attempted identification of the nation, a cultural entity, with the state, a political entity. 'Originating in war and propagated by invading armies, this nationalism transformed dynastic states into true nation states….multinational empires split into a host of new states…[and]…wars of national unification welded disparate principalities into unitary states….This period essentially ended after the First World War, which precipitated the final disintegration of the Austro-Hungarian and Ottoman empires, creating a boomlet of new nation-states on the periphery of Europe.' [Porter, 106] Third, we see the emergence of the *collectivist state* in the twentieth century. This state is characterised by the mass participation of its citizens in its politics, at least in principle, but, even more significantly, the extension of the state's remit to the control of the economy and to the provision of welfare for all its citizens. All these various forms of state were the products of war: the Dynastic State (1648-1789) was a product of the Thirty Years War; the Nation-State was a product of the French Revolutionary Wars and their aftermath (1789-1914); and the Collectivist State resulted from World War I and World War II (1914-present).

The nature of war and the manner of its conduct is intimately connected to the emergence of the various types of state. Kaldor writes, 'What we tend to perceive as war, what policy makers and military leaders define as war, is, in fact, a specific phenomenon which took shape in Europe somewhere between the fifteenth and eighteenth centuries….It was a phenomenon that was intimately bound up with the evolution of the modern state.' [Kaldor, 15] In the seventeenth and eighteenth centuries, war was a conflict between absolutist states, concerned with settling dynastic disputes and border conflicts. The combatants were professional armies, sometimes mercenary, and the wars were financed by taxation and borrowing. In the nineteenth century, war was a conflict between the newly emerging nation states. This time, the disputes did not concern dynastic succession or border arrangements but national goals. The combatants were professional but also included some conscripts, and in addition to the normal increase in taxation required to fund these wars, there was also a rapid expansion of bureaucracy and administration. The early twentieth century gave us the phenomenon of the world war or war between coalition of states, or states made up of multiple nations, or empires. The issue at stake here was the triumph of various ideologies. The armies were again professional, conscript and massive. The whole economy was mobilised to support the war—tax, bureaucracy, and property confiscation. The mid to late twentieth century saw conflict between blocs. Once again, the conflict was ideological. The armies were no longer mass conscript but increasingly technologically sophisticated and professional. The whole was again support by the usual fiscal measures but also saw the emergence of a symbiotic alliance between the military establishment and the industries supplying the technology. During the entire modern period, war demanded a 'centralized, "rationalized", hierarchically ordered, territorialized modern state.' [Kaldor 17]

The general condition for modern war, then, especially the two great wars of the twentieth century, is to be found in the modern sovereign state. This state regards itself as 'the supreme and ultimate form of human society, subject to no law of man and only subject to the laws of God in so much as in time of danger, or war, each Sovereign State claimed, or sought, a monopoly of Divine favour.' [King-Hall, 20] Given the nature of sovereignty as that is understood to be characteristic of the modern state, should unresolvable disputes arise between them, no recourse could be had to anything other than brute force.

War tends to promote territorial enlargement and integration, the cult of the great leader, and the internal repression of a state's citizens. Europe went from having roughly one thousand political units of various kinds in the 1300s to around twenty-five in 1900.[31] War between states tends to encourage warring factions within the state to submerge their differences. War tends to centralise power and promote the emergence and enlargement of bureaucracies. War invariably increases the government's fiscal depredations upon its own population in the form of taxes, confiscations, conscriptions, or massive borrowings to be set against future tax income. As Porter notes, 'few states are able to sustain wars out of current revenue alone, wars almost invariably add to the public debt; historically, a vast portion of the public debt of European countries has accumulated during wartime.' [Porter, 16] The levels of centralisation, taxation, and bureaucracy attained in war never return to pre-war levels but ratchet up to new heights.

'Given the close linkage between war and state formation,' writes Porter, 'it can hardly be regarded as coincidental that both the Puritan revolution in England and the secular Revolution in France culminated in military rule.' [Porter, 133] One made a general Lord Protector; the other made a general an Emperor. Napoleon was responsible for the complete rationalisation and centralisation of power in France by means of the dismemberment of the *pays d'états* and the creation of *départements*, the establishment of the Ministries of the Interior and the Ministry of Police, the first to regulate pretty much all activities in France—commerce, transport, education, scientific establishments; the second to censor, carry out surveillance, and control movement by means of identity cards and passports, the latter device still with us. The multiple local legal codes, some four hundred of them, were swept away in the Code Napoléon, a uniform body of law applicable to all. Napoleon, the general, restructured France in the image of a well-organised army. 'Napoleon's enduring bequest to France was his forging of a centralised nation-state infused with a secular spirit, substantially divested of traditional impediment to state power, and possessed of a uniform system of administration and laws.' [Porter, 140-141]

Strife between states involves each state in aggression against its own citizens—by confiscation (tax, inflation, property destruction, etc.), enslavement (draft), injury and death. Among these varied forms of internal aggression, taxation could only be efficiently gathered if the internal structure of each state is stable and the means of exercising violence limited to the state and its officials. The establishment of law, order and justice within the state provided a stable platform for 'taxation and borrowing and for legitimacy.' [Kaldor, 20] In one of his more lucid moments, Rousseau saw that the waging of inter-state wars required the establishment of increasing methods of internal state control.[32] He wrote, 'The whole life of kings, or of those on whom they shuffle off their duties, is devoted solely to two objects: to extend their rule beyond their frontiers and to make it more absolute within them. Any other purpose they may have is either subservient to one of these aims, or merely a pretext for attaining them. Such pretexts are "the good of the community," "the happiness of their subjects," or "the glory of the nation": phrases for ever banished from the council chamber, and employed so clumsily in proclamations that they are always taken as warnings of coming misery and that the people groans with apprehension when its masters speak to it of their "fatherly solicitude"....war and conquest without and the encroachments of despotism within give each other mutual support.' Rousseau noted that 'money and men are habitually taken at pleasure from a people of slaves to bring others beneath the same yoke; and that, conversely, war furnishes a pretext for exaction of money and another, no less plausible, for keeping large armies constantly on foot, to hold people in awe. In a word, anyone can see that aggressive princes wage war at least as much on their subjects as on their enemies, and that the conquering nation is left no better off than the conquered.'[33]

WAR—TAX AND BUREAUCRACY

The human suffering and physical devastation are obvious enough consequences of war, though not so obvious as to prevent its constant recurrence. What isn't so often noted is the staggering financial cost of war resulting not only from the damage and destruction of property which has to be replaced, but from the finance needed to pay, transport and supply the soldiers who are to partake in this unique form of social interaction.[34] C. Northcote Parkinson remarks that from war 'we inherit the grisly legacy of taxation. Horses, chariots and arms have to be paid for. Taxes bring with them all the attendant horrors of arithmetic, estimates, assessment and accounts. War is thus accompanied by and largely responsible for a vastly more complicated administration.' [Parkinson 1958, 51] 'One factor in the collapse of laissez-faire during World War I,' notes Bruce Porter, 'was the enormous cost of the war, which dwarfed all previous European conflicts in the magnitude of resources required for its waging. The result was an extremely robust fiscal-military cycle of bureaucratic expansion, centralization, and increased taxation. The percentage of national income devoted to military spending in all the major powers rose on the average from slightly over 4 percent to between 25 and 33 percent over the course of the war.'[35]

In earlier and more innocent times, the extraordinary revenues granted to the king in time of war (purportedly for the provision of defence against external aggression) were intended to be once-off subsidies subject to parliamentary approval. So used are we to thinking of the English Parliament as the supreme legislative body that it can be difficult to grasp that even as late as the seventeenth century it was little more than a 'glorified tax-collection agency' that was 'summoned by the king when he needed revenue and dissolved at his discretion.' [Fawcett, 87] When approval wasn't forthcoming from parliaments (by whatever name known), 'government used financial expedients: forced loans, borrowing from foreign bankers, currency debasement, and the sale of assets.' [Ames and Rapp, 170] War taxes were temporary and conditional; kings, of course, wanted them to be permanent and unconditional. The solution? Let war be perpetual! In France, by the middle of the fifteenth century, given the state of almost perpetual war in which the country found itself, extraordinary taxes had become ordinary; in England, by contrast, the exaction of extraordinary royal taxes did not escape the watchful eye of Parliament. Francis Fukuyama believes that it is to the credit of the Glorious Revolution that it legitimated taxation inasmuch as taxes were levied now by Parliament and Parliament was based upon consent. Well, not quite. What the Glorious Revolution did was to create a Pooh Bah-esque situation in which any real distinction between the executive power that demanded taxes and the body that was supposed to represent the interests of the taxpayers was eliminated, thus making effective opposition to taxes practically impossible.[36] In the end, however, the ever-increasing costs of war steadily eroded the distinction between the extraordinary and the ordinary not just in England but more or less everywhere in Europe. Ames and Rapp note that the transition from feudal levies to professional armies connected with the displacement of cavalry and its replacement by massed infantry required substantial financial support: 'the birth of tax systems in Western Europe is tied to this military transition....modern taxation supplanted feudal dues in part because of the need for liquid funds to pay modern standing armies. [Ames and Rapp, 170; 174]

Fukuyama notes that the bulk of the budgets of early modern states went on military expenses. The making of the modern state and the making of war go hand in hand, and money, other people's money, lots of it, is required for both. 'Towns everywhere housed bureaucrats, great and small, who existed above all to tax, to police and to regulate society.' [Hufton 1994, 40] Ninety percent of the budget of the Dutch Republic was spent on war in the period of their long struggle with the Spanish King; ninety eight percent of the Habsburg Empire's budget went to finance its wars with Turkey and the Protestant powers in the seventeenth century. From the beginning of the seventeenth century to its end, the budget of France rose five- to eightfold, while the British budget increased sixteen-fold from 1590 to 1670. The size of the French army increased proportionately, from 12,000 men in the thirteenth century to 50,000 in the sixteenth, to 150,000 in the 1630s, to 400,000 in Louis XIV's reign. [Fukuyama 2011, 330] The absolutism of the absolutist monarchs of the late seventeenth and eighteenth centuries was an absolutism in spirit which, given the limitations of communication and transport, was incapable of being fully materially realised. Subject to the same practical limitations, war also was limited. During this period, the size of armies increased enormously. The French army in the early eighteenth century stood at 150,000, reaching a peak of almost 400,000 during the War of the Spanish Succession. By 1708 the Russian army had reached an establishment of 113,000 men under Peter the Great and exceeded 200,000 by the time his reign ended. The cost of maintaining these military establishments was enormous. 'The army enforced collection of the tax by brute force, its inevitable abuses spurring the flight of the populace beyond the ever-more-distant frontier.' [Porter, 117] The bulk of tax went to support those very tax-collecting troops: in Prussia 80% of tax revenue; in Russia, between 80% and 95%. In lock step with the development of the expanded armies went a correspondingly expanded bureaucracy to administer the troops and the money.

Modern states generally excel medieval polities in their creative capacities for the exaction of revenue. Generally, but not always. The case of Philip IV of France is exemplary in this regard. Philip sought to bring the quasi-independent fiefs of Gascony (in the far south-west) and Flanders (in the far north-east) under his control. To fund this expensive undertaking, he had recourse to a number of inventive financial expedients. 'The clergy were compelled to vote supplies....From 1294 the laity were gathered together to vote aides. In 1292 an indirect sales-tax was introduced....In addition, the king persecuted the Templars and the Jews, whose assets he confiscated; and he sought immediate relief by debasing the coinage and by borrowing freely from Italian bankers, later repudiating his debts.' [Hay, 131] Nothing, it would appear, changes. Modern governments seemed to have taken King Philip's correspondence course. It might seem from all this that taxes were raised primarily so that wars could be fought. It is difficult, however, not to entertain the cynical suspicion that wars were fought so that taxes might be imposed and collected. Indeed, Tom Paine wrote, 'In reviewing the history of the English government, its wars and taxes, an observer, not blinded by prejudice, nor warped by interest, would declare that taxes were not raised to carry on wars, but that wars were raised to carry on taxes.' [Paine 2000, 94]

At the nascent stage of state formation, kings had to recruit their forces from the contributions of semi-independent feudal barons but, as the modern state took shape, monarchs were able to 'consolidate territorial borders and to centralize power by using their growing economic assets, derived from customs duties, various forms of taxation and borrowing from the emergent bourgeoisie, to raise mercenary armies which gave them a certain degree of independence from the barons.' [Kaldor, 18] Perhaps the significant, or at least, one of the most significant moves, was the move from baronial levies and mercenary troops to the creation of a standing army permanently at the disposal of the monarch, garrisoned in barracks, and drilled into obedience. 'The establishment of standing armies under the control of the state was an integral part of the monopolization of legitimate violence which was intrinsic to the modern state.' [Kaldor, 19] Standing armies, however, are expensive. To keep a large number of men hanging around in barracks engaged in non-productive activities, to house, feed and pay them, takes a great deal of money. In the eighteenth century, almost all the state's revenues went towards paying for this army. The average would seem to have been around 75% or so. New bureaucracies emerged to make tax gathering more efficient. If money was to be borrowed, banking has to be regularised, this to include the creation of central banks, and a distinction drawn between the personal finances of the monarch and the state's finances.

In the eighteenth century, wars were fought with one eye on cost, so that battles were avoided if at all possible, manoeuvring, retreats and advances were substituted, and armies wintered while fighting was suspended. That all changed with the Napoleonic mass levies. Human life was cheap in a conscript army. If one lost 50,000 men, there were always another 50,000 men to replace them. The Napoleonic model went into abeyance for most of the nineteenth century only to reappear with a vengeance in the twentieth. The wars of the first half of the twentieth century were total wars involving not just a professional military force financed by heavy taxation and massive borrowing (although they did all that) but also involved the entire civilian population to provide men and material. All the resources of the nation were directed towards the war. Economic enterprises became targets. Indiscriminate bombing of civilians was justified to destroy enemy morale.

By the end of the seventeenth century, the king was no longer first among equals but preeminent over all. The ability of the nobility to be a counter-force to the monarch had more or less vanished for good as they were transformed from quasi-independent mini-monarchs to courtiers dancing attendance on the king. The Reformation had effectively eliminated the Church's power to be an alternative source of authority. In Protestant states, the church became in effect a government department, and even in Catholic countries, it came under increasing *de facto* state control. 'In no Protestant country did the Church provide a truly effective obstacle to state control. In the main its authority and privileges were not such as to incur the opposition of secular powers nor did it feel the uncomfortable blast of the impious Enlightenment except perhaps in Scotland.' [Hufton, 58] The king no longer lived from his own private resources but, increasingly, from his ability to extract resources from a defined territory. It was no longer possible for a kingdom to be administered person-ally by a king and his closest advisers. Expansive administrative apparatuses, modelled on those pioneered by the Church as early as the eleventh century, were established and the tentacles of the state began to spread, with an attempt to homogenise language, laws, and customs through the various kingdoms. [see Fukuyama 2011, passim] To set up such complex structures required the cooperation of those groups in society which possessed the resources necessary for infrastructural expansion, namely administrative, financial, and military expertise, ready cash, and the personal authority associated with social standing. These groups in turn sought to negotiate or extract terms of service that would protect or extend their privileges, status, and income in the face of the potentially unlimited and arbitrary authority of the patrimonial monarch or prince. [Ertman, 8]

Remarking on the expansion in the size of bureaucracies, Antony de Jasay writes, 'it has been estimated that over the period from 1850 to 1890 the number of British government employees grew by about 100 per cent and from 1890 to 1950 by another 1000 per cent...' Commensurate with the expansion in size was the expansion in budget: 'public expenditure in the nineteenth century averaged about 13 percent of GNP, after 1920 it never fell below 24 per cent, after 1946 it was never less than 36 per cent and in our day it is, of course, just below or just above the half-way mark depending on how we count public expenditure.' [de Jasay 1998, 86.] It is said that as a rule what goes up must come down but taxes are a depressing exception to this rule. Even when war taxes are lowered, eventually, they rarely if ever return to their pre-war level. In the USA, the introduction of income tax on a regular basis required the passage of the sixteenth Amendment to the Constitution in 1913. In a forty-year period, the French had rejected some two hundred bills that attempted to introduce income tax. Income tax was introduced for the first time in July 1914. The dates for the American and French acceptance of income tax are significant. Even with the stupendous rise in taxes in the countries at war, the income wasn't sufficient to pay for the war. The rest of the money was borrowed—spend today, pay tomorrow—which meant that tax rates would stay high for years after the conclusion of the war. 'In the British case...just servicing the war debt required an annual postwar expenditure equivalent to 175 percent of the entire national budget in 1913.' [Porter, 163] Olwen Hufton remarks that armies need 'massive bureaucracies to sustain them and that the work of government was directed above all to ensuring the revenues needful to keep them up and indeed extend them.' [Hufton 1994, 95] She notes, as we have seen Tilly, Ertman and others do, that the costs of servicing the debts incurred to pay for the armies and navies were the really significant elements in a state's expenditure, compared to which, in the early days at least, the state's expenditure on all other items paled into insignificance.

WAR AND THE STATE IN THE USA

The absolute state of the late seventeenth and early eighteenth century was not the nation state. There was no belief at this time that nation and state should necessarily coincide. This was to become the dominant ideology of the nineteenth century. 'Nationalism,' writes Porter, 'is also a powerful collective emotion fixated on the mystical and mythical image of the nation. It is a kind of modern tribalism or political religion capable of eliciting strenuous exertions, supreme sacrifices, and deeply felt hostility—above all in war and in connection with war.' [Porter, 122] It is possible to see the nation-state as the more or less inevitable end result of the consistent development of the dynamics of absolutism. The idea of the nation as it merges with politics to produce the nation-state is more than the innocent, vague and ill-defined feeling of social solidarity we may have with those who speak the same language and follow the same customs that we do. It achieves a mythic reality that goes well beyond the mild emotion of social identification. 'The potency of myth is that it allows us to make sense of mayhem and violent death....By turning history into myth we transform random events into a chain of events directed by a will greater than our own....Most national myths, at their core, are racist. They are fed by ignorance....And many intellectuals are willing to champion and defend absurd theories for nationalist ends.' [Hedges, 23-24]

Nationalism has been instrumental in the growth of the American state, and war has been instrumental to nationalism. 'Throughout the history of the United States,' writes Porter, 'war has been the primary impetus behind the growth and development of the central state. It has been the lever by which presidents and other national officials have bolstered the power of the state in the face of tenacious popular resistance. It has been a wellspring of American nationalism and a spur to political and social change.' [Porter, 291]

The American domestic conflict of 1861-1865, usually referred to as the American Civil War, had a major impact on taxation, bringing into existence the first tax on income in US history and, ominously, being the occasion of the creation of the Bureau of Internal Revenue. Although the income tax was repealed in the 1870s, many of the other wartime taxes remained in place. Along with the war and the tax increases, we saw an expansion in bureaucracy. Woodrow Wilson believed that the principal achievement of the Civil War had been the creation of a national consciousness, from a libertarian point of view, not an unmixed blessing. It could be argued that the Civil War turned the states that were loosely united into the nation state that is the United States. I think it is significant that from this time onwards the term 'United States', although grammatically plural, now usually takes a singular verb. Robert Nisbet, however, argues that 'It was hard to find a truly national culture, a national consciousness, in 1914. The Civil War had, of course, removed forever philo-sophical, as well as actively political, doubts of the reality of the Union as a sovereign state. But in terms of habits of mind, customs, traditions, folk litera-ture, indeed written literature, speech accent, dress, and so forth, America could still be looked at as a miscellany of cultures held together, but not otherwise much influenced, by the federal government in Washington.' [Nisbet 1988, 2]

War is usually the occasion for the restriction or elimination of civil liberties and this was so no less in the USA than elsewhere. Robert Nisbet believes that that the involvement of the United States in the First World War had a radically transformative effect on its nature: 'The present age in American history begins with the Great War,' he writes. 'When the guns of August opened fire in 1914, no one in America could have reasonably foreseen that within three years that foreign war not only would have drawn America into it but also would have, by the sheer magnitude of the changes it brought about on the American scene, set the nation on another course from which it has not deviated significantly since.' [Nisbet 1988, 2]

In his 1915 State of the Union Address, two years before the USA entered World War I, Woodrow Wilson declared, 'There are citizens of the United States, I blush to admit, born under other flags but welcomed under our generous naturalization laws…who have poured the poison of disloyalty into the very arteries of our national life; who have sought to bring the authority and good name of our Government into contempt…such creatures of passion, disloyalty and anarchy must be crushed out.' Wilson assured the American people that disloyalty would be strongly repressed since any disloyal person had forfeited his right to civil liberties. In making these declaration, Wilson, as was the case with Lincoln some fifty years earlier, seemed to suffer from a form of selective amnesia. While President of Princeton University, he had published a book entitled *Constitutional Government in the United States* in which he had maintained that unrestrained criticism and outspoken argument for change were the essence of a constitutional system! In a comment that could have been (and perhaps was) designed to fit Wilson, H. L. Mencken is scathing of what he calls the 'professional world-saver' whose 'whole life has been devoted to the art and science of spending other people's money. He has saved millions of the down-trodden from starvation, pestilence, cannibalism, and worse—always at someone else's expense, and usually at the taxpayer's.' [Mencken, 427]

Wilson's activities weren't without precedent and it must be conceded that the tendency to ride roughshod over freedom in times of war isn't just a twentieth century phenomenon, During the 1861-1865 American domestic conflict, Lincoln suspended *habeas corpus* on eight occasions, once nation-wide, and even went to the extent of defying a writ of *habeas corpus* issued by Chief Justice Taney of the Supreme Court. During this conflict, between thirteen thousand and thirty eight thousand men were imprisoned by military authorities, most for draft evasion, but some merely for exercising their right to free speech. The most spectacular instance of repression was the case of former Congressman Clement Vallandigham in 1863, who was tried by a military commission and imprisoned for characterising the war as cruel and unneces-sary, for asserting his first Amendment rights and for urging the voters to kick Lincoln out. In fact, Vallandigham was imprisoned for doing little more than that which Lincoln himself had done in criticising President Polk during the war of 1848! Another case of selective amnesia.[37] 'Many libertarians tend to be sensitive to the quasi-tyrannical means Lincoln used; while not necessarily sympathetic to Confederate values, they sense that the issues involved are more complicated than Lincoln's triumphalism and regret some of the powers of the centralized federal state that arose in the aftermath of, and to a large degree as a result of, the Civil War.'[38]

Abraham Lincoln has become, remarks H. L. Mencken, 'the American solar myth, the chief butt of American credulity and sentimentality.…the varnishers and veneerers have been busily converting Abe into a plaster saint, thus making him fit for adoration in the Y. M C. A.'s.' [Mencken, 221] He adds that Lincoln's Gettysburg speech 'is poetry, not logic; beauty, not sense. Think of the argument in it. Put it into the cold words of everyday. The doctrine is simply this: that the Union soldiers who died at Gettysburg sacrificed their lives to the cause of self-determination.…It is difficult to imagine anything more untrue. The Union soldiers in that battle actually fought *against* self-determination; it was the

Confederates who fought for the right of their people to govern themselves.'[39] It is more than a little ironic that Lincoln, in a speech in Congress (12 January 1848) of which he was inordinately proud, declared that 'Any people anywhere, being inclined and having the power, have the right to rise up, and shake off the existing government and form a new one that suits them better. This is a most valuable—a most sacred right—a right which we hope and believe is to liberate the world.' Lincoln adds: 'Nor is this right confined to cases in which the whole people of an existing government may choose to exercise it. Any portion of such people that can *may* revolutionize, and make their *own* of so much of the territory as they inhabit. More than this, a *majority* of any portion of such people may revolutionize, putting down a *minority*, intermingled with, or near about them, who may oppose their movement. Such minority was precisely the case of the Tories of our own Revolution.' [Lincoln, passim] Nothing in the actual record of Lincoln's speech corresponds precisely to the generally received impression of his speech. The passage nearest to it is one in which, speaking of revolution, Lincoln described it as 'one of the most sacred of rights—the right which he [Lincoln] believed was yet to emancipate the world; the right of a people, if they have a government they do not like, to rise and shake it off.' This right of revolution could not be a perfect right 'if it could not be exercised until every individual inhabitant was in favor of it....Minorities must submit to majorities.'[40]

It may come as a surprise to some to learn that Abraham Lincoln did not, in fact, deliver *the* Gettysburg Address! The Gettysburg Address was actually delivered by one Edward Everett, then esteemed as a great orator, now almost completely forgotten. Lincoln's remarks, the exact words of which are disputed, were not at the top of the bill, coming a long way down on the afternoon's proceedings. The immediate newspaper reaction to Lincoln's remarks was divided. Whereas the *Chicago Tribune* thought that Lincoln's remarks would 'live among the annals of the war', the *Chicago Times* was of the opinion that 'The cheeks of every American must tingle with shame as he reads the silly, flat, and dishwattery [*sic*] remarks of the man who has to be pointed out as the President of the United States.' Taking issue with the content as well as with the manner of Lincoln's speech, the *Chicago Times* described them as 'a perversion of history so flagrant that the most extended charity cannot view it as otherwise than willful.' *The Harrisburg Patriot and Union* was willing to 'pass over the silly remarks of the President' whereas the *Providence Daily Journal* thought the President's words were beautiful, touching, inspiring and thrilling. The *Times* of London was singularly unimpressed, remarking that 'The ceremony was rendered ludicrous by some of the sallies of that poor President Lincoln. Anything more dull and commonplace it would not be easy to produce.' Lincoln himself is said to have remarked, on perceiving the audience's reaction, 'It's a flat failure and the people are disappointed.'[41] Whatever the truth of the matter, however, Lincoln's Gettysburg remarks have moved from the profane world of fact to the sacred realm of legend and back again, and as the reporter in *The Man Who Shot Liberty Valence* noted 'When the legend becomes fact, print the legend.'

Even before America's entry into World War I, the National Defense Act gave the President the authority to place orders with private firms that took priority over all other orders and contracts. Resistance to such orders permitted effective confiscation. [see Raico 1999, 231] Wilson arrested and jailed dissidents at a rate of knots that would have left Mussolini dizzy, and the very first ministry of propaganda was established in the USA to aid the war effort.[42] 'With U.S. entry into World War I, the federal government expanded enormously in size, scope, and power. The government virtually nationalized the ocean shipping industry. It did nationalize the railroad, telephone, domestic telegraph, and international telegraphic cable industries. It became deeply engaged in manipulating labor-management relations, securities sales, agricultural production and marketing, the distribution of coal and oil, international commerce, and the markets for raw materials and manufactured products. Its Liberty Bond drives dominated the financial capital markets. It turned the newly created Federal Reserve System into a powerful engine of monetary inflation to help satisfy the government's voracious appetite for money and credit. In view of the more than 5,000 mobilization agencies of various sorts— boards, committees, corporations, and administrations—contemporaries who described the government's creation as "war socialism" were well justified.' [Higgs, 376-377]

Not everyone was enthusiastic for war,[43] and the myth that the outbreak of the war was greeted with universal acclaim is just another one of those facts that everybody knows that just ain't so.[44] There were those, of course, for whom the U.S.'s entry into the war was a matter of the utmost significance. At the outbreak of the war in 1914, the House of Morgan was named as 'sole purchasing agent in the United States, for the duration of the war, for war material for Britain and France. Furthermore, the Morgans also became the sole underwriter for all the British and French bonds to be floated in the U.S. to pay for the immense import of arms and other goods from the United States. *J. P. Morgan and Company now had an enormous stake in the victory of Britain and France, and the Morgans played a major and perhaps decisive role in maneuvering the supposedly "neutral" United States into the war on the British side.*'[45]

The Espionage Act of 15 June 1917,[46] passed by Congress with some amendments, made it an offence to interfere with the draft or to spread rumours intended to undermine the war effort. It penalised those convicted of wilfully obstructing the enlistment services with fines as much as $10,000 and imprisonment as long as 20 years. Among the publications closed down under the terms of this act was Max Eastman's *THE MASSES*. The most spectacular and bizarre conviction obtained under this Act had to be that of Robert Goldstein who had produced a motion picture about the American Revolution in which British soldiers were depicted bayonetting women and children in the Wyoming Valley massacre of 1778. For this antique negative depiction of the USA's current ally in the war against Germany, Goldstein received a 10-year jail sentence! Robert Higgs records that 'In California the police arrested Upton Sinclair for reading the Bill of Rights at a rally. In New Jersey the police arrested Roger Baldwin for publicly reading the Constitution,' and Geoffrey Stone notes that 'Against this background, and especially in light of the severity of the sentences meted out, no sensible person dared criticize the Wilson administration's policies.'[47]

The Espionage Act wasn't enough. On 16 May 1918, the so-called Sedition Act (shades of John Adams!) was passed by Congress.[48] It amended section 3 of the 1917 Espionage Act and forbade anyone to 'wilfully utter, print, write, or publish any disloyal, profane, scurrilous, or abusive language about the form of government of the United States, or the Constitution of the United States, or the military or naval forces of the United States, or the flag...or the uniform of the Army or Navy of the United States, or any language intended to bring the form of government...or the Constitution...or the military or naval forces of the United States into contempt, scorn, contumely, or disrepute...' or discouraging the sale of war bonds. [see Burgess, 77f.] It led to the banning of 75 periodicals and the denial of postal privileges to over four hundred publications, the arrest of thousands without just cause, and the support by the Justice Department of the quarter of a million volunteers of the American Protective League (APL) whose function it was to spy upon their fellow citizens.[49] Under the auspices of the APL, Americans of German extraction or origin 'were stoned, beaten, flogged, harassed, jailed, ostracized, and jeered. The teaching of German in public schools was banned in several states, and the burning of books in the German language was widespread.'[50] [Mead, 39]

Perhaps the most egregious infringement of individual rights was conscription. Some wondered why, in the grand crusade against militarism, the USA were adopting conscription, the very emblem of militarism. The Speaker of the House, Champ Clark (D-Mo.), remarked that 'in the estimation of Missourians there is precious little difference between a conscript and a convict.' [Raico 1999, 236] Despite the 'involuntary servitude' section of the Constitution, the Supreme Court looked into its collective heart and mysteriously found conscription to be constitutional.[51] John W. Burgess, a distinguished Professor of Constitutional Law at Columbia University, robustly denied that the authorisation by statute of the levying of a conscript army for service in a foreign war was justified by the Constitution. This power, he said, 'is the most despotic power which government can exercise.' [Burgess, 63; see 55ff.] Ayn Rand noted that 'the draft is clearly unconstitutional. No amount of rationalization, neither by the Supreme Court nor by private individuals, can alter the fact that it represents "involuntary servitude".' [Rand 1967a, 257] In the event, 24 million men were registered and 3 million were drafted. [see Compton] 'To insure that the conscription-based mobilization could proceed without obstruction, critics had to be silenced....These suppressions of free speech [made legal by the Espionage and Seditions Acts] subsequently upheld by the Supreme Court, established dangerous precedents that derogated from the rights previously enjoyed by citizens under the First Amendment.' [Higgs 1999, 378] The supposed great dissenter on the Supreme Court, Mr Justice Holmes, was singularly and strikingly non-dissenting when it came to judicially evaluating cases brought under the wartime acts. H. L. Mencken writes, 'In three Espionage Act cases, including the Debs case, one finds a clear statement of the doctrine that, in war time, the rights guaranteed by the First Amendment cease to have any substance, and may be set aside summarily by any jury that has been sufficiently inflamed by a district attorney itching for higher office.' [Mencken, 258] 'The government,' writes Robert Higgs, 'further subverted the Bill of Rights by censoring all printed materials, peremptorily deporting hundreds of aliens without due process of law, and conducting—and encouraging state and local governments and vigilante groups to conduct—warrantless searches and seizures, blanket arrests of suspected draft evaders, and other outrages too numerous to catalog here.' [Higgs 1999, 378. See Bourne 1919]

War is *the* great stimulus to the restriction of civil liberties,[52] a form of aggression by the state against its own citizens. 'War,' writes Tom Palmer, 'challenges lawfulness at every turn. It undermines the rule of law. It concentrates power in the executive branch of government. It provides a ready-to-hand justification for every abuse of power.' [Palmer 2014a, 12] The cry 'There's a war on' is all the justification that is needed to stifle dissent. The Committee on Public Information with George Creel as its head, set up by Wilson just seven days after the United States of America's entry into the war, 'played a key role in raising anti-German hysteria.' [MacDonnell, 23] This Committee was responsible for the release of government news at home and foreign propaganda. Whereas the Committee wasn't technically able to censor, its close links to the Justice Department and to the Post Office effectively shaped censorship policy. 'What we had to have,' wrote George Creel, 'was no mere surface unity, but a passionate belief in the justice of America's case that should weld the people of the United States into one white-hot mass instinct with fraternity, devotion, courage, and deathless determination. The *war-will*, the will to win, of a democracy depends upon the degree to which each one of all the people of that democracy can concentrate and consecrate body and soul and spirit in the supreme effort of service and sacrifice. What had to be driven home was that all business was the nation's business, and every task a common task for a single purpose.' [Creel, 5] In his account of the matter, written soon after the war, Creel made this point emphatically if disingenuously when he wrote, '*In no degree was the Committee an agency of censorship, a machinery of concealment or repression. Its emphasis throughout was on the open and the positive. At no point did it seek or exercise authorities under those war laws that limited the freedom of speech and press.*' [Creel, 4; emphasis in original] He went on to say that the Committee on Public Information did not call what they did propaganda, 'for that word, in German hands, had come to be associated with deceit and corruption.' [Creel, 4] Indeed.

After the War, of course, remorse set in. 'Americans came to cast a jaundiced eye upon the work of the Creel committee, blaming the Committee on Public Information for fostering a national climate of intolerance and hysteria,' writes MacDonnell. 'Additionally, President Wilson's establishment of a centralized propaganda agency seemed to be a dangerous concentration of power in the hands of government.' [MacDonnell, 144] The Supreme Court had another mysterious change of heart and, now that it made little or no practical difference, overruled the majority of its World War I decisions, implicitly acknowledging that the convictions obtained under them were unconstitutional and had violated the First Amendment. 'In period of war fever,' writes Geoffrey Stone, 'we are likely to lose our sense of perspective and needlessly sacrifice fundamental liberties—particularly the fundamental liberties of those we already fear and despise. In both of these episodes, the President, the Congress, and the Supreme Court all failed in their responsibility to preserve and protect the Constitution, and the public sat by silently or, worse, cheered them on.' [Stone 2007, 84]

War is the opportunity for central planning with a vengeance. Just as the body, in conditions of extreme cold, focuses on the preservation of the essential internal organs and abandons, if necessary, its extremities, so too, a planned economy abandons all the messiness associated with freedom and individual choice in the interests of perceived planned efficiencies. The Government took to itself the power to intervene directly in the economy under the National Defense Act and the Army Appropriations Act. By and large, transport, industry and agriculture came under direct Federal control. In 1918, at the height of its powers, the War Industries Board controlled all available resources and could fix prices, at least, wholesale prices. It also set production schedules, 'allocated resources, standardized procedures, coordinated purchase, covered costs, and guaranteed profits.' [Riddle, 140-141] Retail prices soared. More than anything else, the government's organisation of the economy for war determined how the central government would grow in the United States in the twentieth century, and conscription, more than anything else, determined how the government would organize the economy for war. So, in a multitude of ways, the original and limited military draft shaped not only the contours of the nation at war but also the course of its politico-economic development throughout the succeeding years. [Higgs, 376] Mencken remarked, sardonically, that 'Most of England's appalling troubles today are due to a bad guess: she went into the war on the wrong side in 1914….The United States made a similar mistake in 1917. Our real interests at the time were on the side of the Germans….But we succumbed to a college professor who read Matthew Arnold…' [Mencken, 218, 219]

Like the prospect of death, war tends to concentrate the mind wonderfully. In time of war, local differences and quarrels are sunk in the fight against the common enemy. 'The chief appeal of war to social planners isn't conquest or death but mobilisation. Free societies are disorganized. People do their own thing, more or less, and that can be downright inconvenient if you are trying to plan the entire economy from a boardroom somewhere. War brings conformity and unity of purpose. The ordinary rules of behavior are mothballed. You can get things done: build roads, hospitals, houses.' [Goldberg, 149] If only, dream our political leaders, society could be politically organized on a war footing all the time! Increased bureaucratic control came courtesy of the doubling of the Federal bureaucracy and increased central control of the economy via the National War Labor Board which involved itself in industrial relations, working conditions, overtime and unionisation. [see Riddle, 140-141]

The cost of the US's involvement in World War I was enormous, around $33.5 billion, plus another $13 billion in veterans' benefits and interest on the war debt. And then there's the small matter of '130,000 combat deaths,

35,000 men permanently disabled, and perhaps also the 500,000 influenza deaths among American civilians from the virus the men brought home from France.' [Raico 1999, 239] The nature of the horrors of World War I is reasonably well known. What is hard to conceive is the sheer *scale* of the human casualties. In its first two years, more people died in World War I than died in the French Revolution and the Napoleonic conflicts, the minor wars of the nineteenth and early twentieth centuries, including the Crimean, Franco-Prussian and Boer Wars, the Civil War in the USA and the war between Russia and Japan *combined.* World War II was even more devastating, not least in respect of civilian deaths. Before World War I, Napoleon's conscript army had been the largest force ever assembled in modern times, amounting to just under two million men. The combined armies of Britain, France and Germany in World War I came to almost 28 million men. In addition to all this, 'The indirect costs, in the battering of American freedoms and the erosion of attachment to libertarian values, were probably much greater. But as Colonel House had assured Wilson, no matter what sacrifices the war exacted, "the end will justify them"—the end of creating a world order of freedom, justice, and everlasting peace.' [Raico 1999, 239] Denson remarks that, 'In the war-torn 20th century, we rarely hear that one of the main costs of war is a long-term loss of liberty to winners and losers alike. There are the obvious and direct costs of the number of dead and wounded soldiers, but rarely do we hear about the lifetime struggles of combat veterans to live with their nightmares and injuries. Nor do we hear much about the long-term hidden costs of inflation, debts, and taxes. Other inevitable long-term costs of war that aren't immediately obvious are damages caused to our culture, to our morality, and to civilisation in general. Two of the primary methods by which most modern governments conduct wars are conscription and propaganda. The winners have always written the history, and after the war, propaganda is often adopted as "history" and eventually becomes a myth or legend. We need to pierce through the veils of myth and propaganda to see what the true costs of war have been, especially to American liberty.' [Denson 1999, xxv]

As is the case with all our pleasures, wars have to be paid for. There are three ways to do this—by borrowing, by taxation, or by inflating the currency. There is also just plain stealing, otherwise known as requisitioning or confiscation, but that, in essence, is just a form of taxation in kind. 'Governments have at their disposal three methods for financing a war: taxation, borrowing from the public, and monetary inflation or the creation of new money,' writes Joseph Salerno. 'Governments may also resort to coercive requisitioning, that is, confiscating the material resources and conscripting the labor services they deem necessary for the war effort without compensation or in exchange for below-market prices and wage rates. Historically, a combination of these methods has generally been used to effect the transfer of resources from civilian to military uses during a large-scale war. From the viewpoint of technical economic theory, however, the government could always realize the funds necessary to carry out its war aims exclusively from increased taxation and non-inflationary borrowing on capital markets. As Schumpeter pointed out with regard to Austria, immediately after

World War I, "It is clear that strictly speaking we could have squeezed the necessary money out of the private economy just as the goods were squeezed out of it. This could have been done by taxes which would have looked stifling, but which would in fact have been no more oppressive than the devaluation of money which was their alternative.'" [Salerno, 437-438]

On the tax side of things, the ratification of the Income Tax Amendment 'paved the way for a massive increase in taxation once America entered the war. Taxes for the lowest bracket tripled, from 2 to 6 percent, while for the highest bracket they went from a maximum of 13 percent to 77 percent. In 1916, fewer than half a million tax returns had been filed; in 1917, the number was nearly three and half million, a figure which doubled by 1920. This was in addition to increases in other federal taxes. Federal tax receipts "would never again be less than a sum five times greater than prewar levels."' [Raico 1999, 233] The Constitutional scholar John W. Burgess interprets the Sixteenth Amendment as investing the Government 'with entirely unlimited power in the levying and collection of the most comprehensive of all taxes, the income tax, the tax which can take, thus unlimited, the entire product of all property and all labor. There is now nothing in our Constitution, as I understand it,' he writes, 'to prevent the government from exercising completely arbitrary, despotic and discriminating powers over the property of the individual through the levy and collection of this unlimited tax upon incomes...' [Burgess, 50; see 42-54] These prophetic words were written in 1923.

And then there is inflation, the unholy spirit of the unholy trinity of inflation, taxation and borrowing. 'Through the recently-established Federal Reserve System,[53] the government created new money to finance its stunning deficits, which by 1918 reached a billion dollars each month—more than the total annual federal budget before the war. The debt, which had been less than \$1 billion in 1915, rose to \$25 billion in 1919. The number of civilian federal employees more than doubled, from 1916 to 1918, to 450,000. After the war, two-thirds of the new jobs were eliminated, leaving a "permanent net gain of 141,000 employees—a 30 percent 'ratchet' effect."' [Raico 1999, 233] Joe Salerno notes, 'war is enormously costly, and inflation is a means by which governments attempt, more or less successfully, to hide these costs from their citizens. For war not only destroys the lives and limbs of the soldiery, but, by progressively consuming the accumulated capital stock of the belligerent nations, eventually shortens and coarsens the lives and shrivels the limbs of the civilian population. Whereas the enormous destruction of productive wealth that war entails would become immediately evident if governments had no recourse but to raise taxes immediately upon the advent of hostilities, their ability to inflate the money supply at will permits them to conceal such destruction behind a veil of rising prices, profits, and wages, stable interest rates, and a booming stock market.' [Salerno, 434] The efficiencies, such as they are, are achieved by massive appropriation of individual resources, by rationing, deprivation, and disorder, high costs and waste. The perceived efficiency of the planned wartime economy over the perceived inefficiency of the peacetime economy is an illusion. The wartime planned economy satisfies the desires of a few, very few people (even if it does that) whereas the peacetime economy satisfies the desires of all, at least to some extent. It isn't coincidental that when governments want the people to rally around, they declare a war. In these days, the wars are not so much on other people as they are on abstract objects and modes of behavior—wars on cancer, on drugs, on obesity, on smoking, on climate change; the experts have spoken, the debate is finished, now let the war begin.

During the course of the war, all the states involved in it took ever more direct control of the economic assets of their citizens—railroads, shipping, armaments. Controls were imposed on currency and finance, on wages and prices and labour relations, on foodstuffs. Rationing was introduced which aimed to limit consumption. All these control required controllers and the bureaucrats blossomed like mushrooms. Of all these controls, perhaps the most significant was that exercised over the currency and over finance. The gold standard, with its built-in limitations on the money supply, was inimical to the reckless expenditure required by war and became one of its casualties. The gold standard 'never recovered from the impact of the war; it was briefly revived in 1925, but Britain abandoned it forever in 1931. Without gold as a peg, currency stability became more dependent than ever on the macroeconomic skills of state officials and central treasuries.' [Porter, 167] I hope I won't be taken to be overly cynical if I wonder what these macroeconomic skills are and how they are manifested? The last lingering elements of a gold standard was finally taken off its life-support machine in the 1970s and since then the entire world has been engaged in a gigantic sociological-political-financial experiment with fiat currencies underpinned by nothing at all, like the grin of the fabled Cheshire Cat.

'In its formative years,' writes Bruce Porter, 'the New Deal derived considerable inspiration from Woodrow Wilson's wartime administration. The National Industrial Recovery Act of 1933, one of the legislative milestones of the "Hundred Days," established the National Recovery Administration consciously modelled after the War Industries Board of 1918-1920.' [Porter, 277] Bad as the bureaucratic expansion of government had been in WWI, it paled into insignificance beside the WWII expansion. If progression was the innovation of WWI in respect to tax, 'withholding' was the innovation of WWII. Introduced as a temporary measure, needless to say it became permanent. 'By making income taxation largely invisible and hence less painful, withholding not only helped finance the war effort but greatly facilitated postwar revenue extraction and the permanent maintenance of a large federal bureaucracy.' [Porter, 283] The growth of the regulatory state was further enhanced by World War II so that our mid-twentieth century world found itself with states regulating, sometimes even owning, coal mines, railroads, airlines, steelworks, electricity and gas utilities. Porter writes, 'The contrast between the liberal Britain and France of 1914 and the highly regulated, economically engaged states that emerged after 1945 was striking.' [Porter, 169]

World War I had been enormously expensive: 'World War I destroyed globalization, disrupted economic growth, severed physical, financial, and trade links, bankrupted governments and businesses, and led weak or populist regimes to rely on desperate measures that were supposed to head off revolutions but just as often hastened them. When the war was over, the victors as well as the vanquished were crippled by colossal debts and subjected to vicious attacks of inflation and deflation.' [Nasar, 205] But bad as World War I had been, World War II was even worse. 'World War II was 10 times more expensive than World War I,' writes Robert Higgs. 'Many new taxes were levied. Income taxes were raised repeatedly, until the individual income tax rates extended from a low of 23 percent to a high of 94 percent. The income tax, previously a "class tax" became a "mass tax" as the number of returns grew from 15 million in 1940 to 50 million in 1945. Even though annual federal revenues soared from $7 billion to $50 billion between 1940 and 1945, most war expenses still had to be financed by borrowing. The national debt held by the public went up by $200 billion, or more than five-fold. The Federal Reserve System itself bought some $20 billion of government debt, thereby acting as a de facto printing press for the Treasury. Between 1940 and 1948 the money stock (Ml) increased by 183 percent, and the dollar lost nearly half its purchasing power.'[54]

War tends to give the lie to the state's proud claim to be the protector of life and property. Bruce Porter notes that 'over 100 million persons died violently in the twentieth century either as victims of war or of state genocide, a toll that eclipses the total losses of all previous wars or massacres in all ages of human history combined.' [Porter, 21] Porter's figure of 100 million is on the conservative end of the scale. Others put the figure closer to 200 million. But what's a million or two here or there? And, of course casualties weren't confined to military personnel: 'In the wars of the twentieth century not less than 62 million civilians have perished, nearly 20 million more than the 43 million military personnel killed.' [Hedges, 13] The financial cost of the various conflicts in Iraq, Afghanistan and Pakistan between 2001 and 2014 comes to $4,374 billion; the human cost, in direct war deaths, amounts to between 300,000 and 350,000, made up of 6,800 US Military, 6,787 US Contractors, 31,900 Allied Military and Police, 174,000-220,000 civilians, 78,000-88,000 Opposition Forces and just under 800 journalists and humanitarian workers.[55]

WAR AND THE TOTALITARIAN STATE

By its very nature, totalitarianism has been half in love with easeful death. 'The antecedents of totalitarianism all shared a common thread: a belief in the achievement of human progress through violence and conflict.' [Porter, 205] Conflict, strife, struggle are thought to be the very stuff of life—and death. Totalitarian societies are civil societies organised as if they were armies. 'The defining attribute of the totalitarian state was perpetual mobilization for war— war against foreign adversaries, both real and imagined, and war against its own population.' [Porter, 195]

It can be no surprise to find that those who have been militarised by their service in the war were receptive to the siren song of the totalitarian state. Life in a genuine civil society is hard, not least because one has to take responsibility for oneself. To those used to the comradeship of the trenches, the challenge of self-sufficiency came as an unwelcome shock. Little wonder, then, that the offer of the incipient totalitarian states to replicate the solidarity and comradeship of war in civilian society was well nigh irresistible to many. Half of all National Socialist recruits 'were veterans of World War I, a figure far higher than the population as a whole.' [Porter, 219] Another factor that made the social environment propitious for the new tribalism was the devastating effect of the war on the institutions of civil society. Little remained between the naked individual and the state. The choice seemed to be—on your own or with everyone together. Of course, there were gaps between the totalitarian ambitions of the new tribal states and their ability to implement totalitarianism in fact. Of the various states that took this route, Stalinist Russia was perhaps the most successful in deleting intermediate social institutions, certainly more successful than National Socialist Germany and conspicuously more successful than Fascist Italy.

In war, all power and control moves inexorably towards the centre. A war, any war, is essential to keep it there. If an external enemy can't be found, then an internal enemy must be discovered or manufactured. Many candidates have played the role of internal enemy—Jews, saboteurs, Trotskyites, kulaks. Whereas a war against internal enemies, real or imagined, was a feature of all totalitarian states, it took a particularly virulent form in the Soviet Union. The Russian Civil War, so-called, which lasted from 1918-1921, rivalled the extent of World War I. Less striking but equally as deadly were the wars of Stalinist forced collectivisation, which resulted not only in fighting between the peasants and Soviet troops but in engineered famines in the Ukraine and Kazakhstan. In this piece of social engineering, a mere 11 million people died. The Purge of 1936-1938 reduced the Russian population by another 3 million. 'Stalin's purges were a unique form of "statistical terror," purely prophylactic in nature, intended to atomize society and destroy or deter any conceivable opposition even before said opposition existed. The guilt or innocence of his victims was beside the point; millions died for the sole purpose of keeping hundreds of millions in a state of constant fear.' [Porter, 204] When one adds up all the figures, the number of victims of the Soviet Union's aggression against its *internal* enemies comes to around 51 million over the thirty-six years between 1917 and 1953.[56]

It isn't common to link warfare and welfare. One seems to be organised mass social destruction; the other, organised mass social construction. Yet they are linked. Porter writes, 'the historical linkages between war and the welfare state are too close and too extensive to dismiss as mere coincidences of chronology.' [Porter, 180] The beginnings of the welfare state is to be found in Bismarck's Prussia in the wake of the Franco-Prussian war but it becomes more widely instantiated only during and after World War I, until finally it achieves the status of an unquestioned, perhaps even fundamental, part of the role of the state after World War II.

If the seventeenth-eighteenth century absolutist state gave us centralisation and the explosion of the military, and the nineteenth century nation-state gave us the fusion of nationalism and statism, the twentieth century gave us the state in which almost all the citizens were supposed to have a say in its direction while the state intervened in the economy and provided, or attempted to provide, for the welfare of all its citizens. It comes as a surprise to many people to learn that the first extensive state provision of social security measures took place not in Britain or the United States or even in France but in Prussia. In the 1880s, Bismarck provided sickness insurance, accident insurance and old age insurance. 'By the turn of the century the militarized, Prussianized German state had the most comprehensive system of labor protection and social welfare provision of any country in Europe.'[57] Where Prussia led, France followed, albeit at a temporal distance of fifteen to twenty years so that by the early 1900s it had in place provision for health care assistance, social insurance and old age pensions. In Britain, welfare spending went from 4% before the First World War to about 8% after it to around 18% in 1950. 'The mass state, the regulatory state, the welfare state—in short, the collectivist state that reigns in Europe today—is an offspring of the total warfare of the industrial age.' [Porter, 192] For most of its history, the modern state, whether quasi-dynastic, national or collectivist, had spent most of its revenue on war and war related activities. By the middle of the twentieth century, welfare spending overtook warfare spending, even in the United States, which also maintained the largest single military establishment in the world. Between 1950 and 1980, welfare spending went from being just over 26% of the federal spending to just over 54%.

Conservatives tend to be accepting of warfare and distrustful of welfare; modern liberals welcome welfare and deprecate warfare. Both would resist any claim that the two are closely connected, and yet it is so. Moreover, systems of social welfare, even if productive in the short term of improvements in living standards for a segment of the population, aren't necessarily expressive of any real charitable sentiment. Augusto Del Noce notes 'the common sentiment is that poverty is disgusting and therefore must be pushed out of sight. Welfare systems also serve the purpose of shielding people from depressing feelings of charity and compassion. The atomized individual is more and more imprisoned in radical egocentrism.' [Del Noce, 128]

All good things, even this history, must come to an end but the question is, where? Our ruminations so far have brought us into the twentieth century in its consideration of war and the emergence of the new tribalisms. It is tempting, and not only for reasons of exhaustion (yours and mine!) to leave matters there but there are some individual twentieth century political philosophers who simply can't be ignored. In the next chapter, I give a brief account of five twentieth century thinkers who are important, positively or negatively, in the history of political thought from the perspective of liberty—Ayn Rand, Friedrich Hayek, Robert Nozick, Murray Rothbard and John Rawls. There are many more thinkers who might well merit inclusion in a history such as this. In his monumental history of the libertarian movement in America, *Radicals for Capitalism*, Brian Doherty writes, 'Five thinkers form the spine of the story this book tells, five people without whom there would have been no uniquely libertarian ideas or libertarian institution of any popularity or impact in America in the second half of the twentieth century. Those five are…Ludwig von Mises,

Friedrich A. Hayek, Ayn Rand, Murray Rothbard, and Milton Friedman. Four men and one woman; four Jews and one Catholic; four economists and one novelist; four minarchists…and one anarchist…; two native-born Americans and three immigrants; two Nobel Prize winners and three who remained not only aloof from most professional and intellectual accolades but generated a heated hostility from cultural gatekeepers…' [Doherty, 8-9] Doherty's list includes three of the thinkers I discuss (Hayek, Rand and Rothbard) and two I do not, not because they are not worthy of inclusion but simply because if this book is ever to finish, a line, however arbitrary, must be drawn somewhere.

Notes

1 An accessible and very useful source for online primary material relating to the First World War can be found at http://www.firstworldwar.com/index.htm.
2 *Blackadder Goes Forth*, Series 4, Episode 6.
3 My grandfather served in this war and two of my great-uncles died in it; one at the Somme, the other at the fiasco that was Gallipoli.
4 You can hear the whole of Bogle's song sung by The Fureys at https://www.youtube.com/watch?v=ntt3wy-L8Ok.
5 Porter, 161. I recommend Bruce Porter's book, *War and the Rise of the State* where, in a relatively brief compass, one can find the answer to everything one wanted to know about war and the state but was afraid to ask. Not that I agree with everything Porter has to say—in fact, I disagree strongly with his optimistic evaluation of the virtues and strength of democracy—but the overall thrust of his book, especially its demonstration of the intimate connection between war and the state, is undeniably correct. See also Strachan 2003, passim.
6 For a brief historical survey of classical liberalism, see Droz, 45-61.
7 Morris, 2014. See Davies, 2015 for a considered critical review of Morris's book.
8 Perhaps the most common justification for the use of nuclear weapons against Japan was that it shortened the war and saved lives. On this point, the most senior US military officer during World War II, Fleet Admiral William Leahy wrote, 'It's my opinion that the use of this barbarous weapon at Hiroshima and Nagasaki was of no material assistance in our war against Japan. The Japanese were already defeated and ready to surrender because of the effective sea blockade and the successful bombing with conventional weapons…My own feeling was that in being the first to use it, we had adopted an ethical standard common to the barbarians of the Dark Ages. I was not taught to make wars in that fashion, and that wars cannot be won by destroying women and children.' [Leahy, 441]
9 Michael Walzer writes, 'The greater number by far of the German civilians killed by terror bombing were killed without moral (and probably also without military) reason,' and he quotes Churchill as remarking that '"The destruction of Dresden remains a serious query against the conduct of Allied bombing."' [Walzer, 261; but see Raico 199a, passim]
10 Compare Walzer, 260-268. See https://www.youtube.com/watch?v=yGcO6zZ4MRM for some footage and stills of the Dresden bombing.
11 In his delightfully quixotic, brilliant and very funny book, *Lost in the Cosmos: The Last Self-Help Book*, Walker Percy sketches a conversation between a dysfunctional bunch of refugees aboard an inter-stellar spaceship fleeing from a destroyed planet Earth, and their potential hosts. These hosts, recognising the unstable and murderous propensities of human beings and the danger they would present to their own civilisation, decline to accept them and redirect them to planet PC7, remarking 'You can take your chances with each other. They, too, are a curious, inquisitive, murderous civilization. NH3 breathers, nuclear, but not as advanced as you. They are sentimental, easily moved to tears, and kill each other with equal ease….They like wars too, pretend not to, but get in trouble during an overly long peace. Right now they are bored to death and spoiling for a fight.' [Percy 1984, 212-213.]
12 Tacitus, *Germania*, §§14, 15; 1970,113-114; 2009, 670-671.

13 In fact, he survived not one but *two* plane crashes.

14 Jeremy Black remarks that 'among the Native population of North America, there appears to have been no sharp distinction between raiding other human groups and hunting animals. The two activities merged. In part, this may be because non-tribal members were not viewed as human beings, or at least as full persons. Although the context was very different, the treatment of enemies as beasts or as subhuman can also be seen in the case of some conflicts by modern and earlier states.' [Black 2003, 1]

15 Slavoj Žižek writes, 'although our power of abstract reasoning has developed immensely, our emotional-ethical responses remain conditioned by age-old instinctual reactions of sympathy to suffering and pain that is witnessed directly. That is why shooting someone point-blank is for most of us much more repulsive than pressing a button that will kill a thousand people we cannot see...' [Žižek 2009, 36-37]

16 As Eric Hoffer notes, 'Hatred is the most accessible and comprehensive of all unifying agents.' But however effective hatred may be as a unifying agent, it comes at a cost, and that cost is the diminution or loss of many values we should otherwise cherish, leading, in the end, to a kind of internal corrosion of opposing groups. [Hoffer, 85, §65]

17 Davie, 18; see Stevens, 42.

18 *Commentarii de Bello Gallico*, Book VI.

19 Hard as it may be to believe, some thinkers are even *more* pessimistic than Hobbes. Blaise Pascal remarks that 'All men naturally hate one another. They employ lust as far as possible in the service of the public weal. But this is only a pretence and a false image of love; for at bottom it is only hate.' [Pascal, *Pensées*, Section VII, §451]

20 See Keeley, 22ff; see Diamond 2012, 129-170.

21 The proximate reasons for inter-tribal warfare seem to come down to the following: revenge; women; pigs, cattle or other basic economic units; slaves, sorcery or land. [see Diamond 2012, 157-159]

22 Although the era of the world war with staggering casualties may have passed us by (or maybe not), wars are still being fought for political reasons all over the world. In the Democratic Republic of Congo alone, approximately 6,000,000 people have died since the late 1990s. [Marshall, 123] As I write (2016), between sixty and seventy countries are involved in wars of varying degrees of scope and seriousness.

23 I have in mind here the rival parties (thinly disguised versions of Whigs and Tories) in Jonathan Swift's satire, *Gulliver's Travels*, not the rival versions of computer architecture.

24 Koestler 1979, 15. Slavoj Žižek makes a similar point in a slightly different mode when he asks, 'What if, however, humans exceed animals in their capacity for violence precisely because they *speak*?' [Žižek 2009, 52; see also 56-62]

25 Koestler 1979, 82. See also Spiller, passim. See (above) the chapter on 'Twentieth-Century Tribalisms' for more on this topic. For a perspective on war from a politically realist perspective, see Hanson.

26 The subsequent discussion focuses more or less exclusively on war in connection with the modern state. See Rothbard 2000c.

27 Judith Shklar remarks that 'The willingness, indeed eagerness, of the Roman people to go to war was used by its various rulers to control the citizens. While a warring people was bound to be turbulent, the prospect of foreign war always pulled them together.' [Shklar, 57]

28 Shakespeare, *Henry IV*, Part II, Act 4, Scene 5.

29 These comments were made by Hermann Goering on 18 April 1946 to Gustave Gilbert, a German-speaking intelligence officer who had access to the prisoners kept in Nuremberg jail and who recorded the conversation in his notebooks which were later published in *The Psychology of Dictatorship*.

30 'The regiment,' notes Keegan, 'was a device for securing the control of armed force to the state.' [Keegan, 12] In earlier times, armies were raised by individual lords when needed and their loyalty, such as it was, was to those lords. Keegan again, 'Attempts to make armed forces more effective, by conceding greater independence to landholders in the worst-troubled areas or paying knights to serve under arms, only heightened the problem; the landholders declined to muster when called, built stronger castles, raised private armies, waged war in their own right—sometimes against the sovereigns.' [Keegan, 13]

31 See Anon (no date A) for a timelapse video of boundary changes in Europe over 1,000 years.

32 In a speech to the Constitutional Convention of 29 June 1787, James Madison too noted that 'The means of defense against foreign danger historically have become the instruments of tyranny at home.'

33 Rousseau, 1756 (1917), 95; 96-97; quoted in Kaldor, 21.

34 The financial cost of the Iraq and Afghan military adventures has been estimated to be in the region of $4 trillion, and rising. [see Palmer 2014a, 8]

35 Porter, 162. Margaret Atwood remarks, dryly, 'you can float many a heft tax scheme on the back of a righteous-sounding and energizing war. Wars focus the attention; people don't want to feel or even appear disloyal at such times. Scare them with the thought that they themselves may be looted and pillaged by bands of slavering, subhuman barbarians who will roast and eat their children and ravish and eviscerate their women—don't laugh, it's happened—and they'll fork over with remarkable docility, if not eagerness. Just to remind you: the income tax was begun in Great Britain in 1799, to finance the Napoleonic Wars. In the United State, it began in 1862, to support the Civil War. In Canada, in 1917, incomes were first taxed as a temporary measure to finance the First World War. And taxes are like zebra mussels: once they've been introduced, they're very hard to get rid of. The wars the incomes taxes were meant to pay for have come and gone, but the income taxes themselves persist.' [Atwood, 136] In the United Kingdom for the tax year 2013-2014, income tax still accounted for over 27% of receipts. National insurance contributions and value added tax (VAT) each accounted for another 18%. The remainder of tax revenue was contributed by a bewildering but ingeniously devised variety of taxes, including (but not confined to)—corporation tax, fuel duties, capital gains tax, inheritance tax (death duties, to you and me), duties on tobacco, wines and spirits, bank levies, business rates, council tax, climate change levies and a landfill tax. [data taken from Murphy 2016a, 32]

36 It is one of history's ironies that when the English Parliament succeeded in the seventeenth century struggle between itself and the king, it would give rise to a situation in which the new executive power would be drawn from the ranks of Parliament so that there was no longer any real distinction between the tax-seekers and the tax-approvers and therefore no genuine possibility of resistance to extraordinary ordinary taxation. As Walter Bagehot note, 'The House of Commons—now that it is the true sovereign, and appoints the real executive—has long ceased to be the checking, sparing, economical body it once was. It is now more apt to spend money than the minister of the day.' [Bagehot, 103]

37 See Stone, 1-40, Neely, passim, DiLorenzo, 154-156 and Denson 2006, 33-96; 173-180. Some years after the war, Vallandigham, a lawyer, accidentally shot himself while demonstrating that it was possible to shoot oneself accidentally when drawing a pistol from one's pocket. His client was acquitted; Vallandigham died.

38 Doherty, 27. Louis Menand, while accepting the orthodox dogma that 'The war was fought to preserve the system of government that had been established at the nation's founding', nevertheless also concedes that after the war 'The United States became a different country.' [Menand, ix] He points out that one effect of the secession of the Confederate States was that it allowed the North to act without restraint [his word is 'interference'!] from the South so that the federal government became, in his words, the 'legislative engine of social and economic progress.' [Menand, x] Two conspicuous and ominous acts of the unrestrained-by-the-South Congress were the creation of the first 'significant' national currency and 'the first system of national taxation.' [Menand, x]

39 Mencken, 223. Such non-poetic elements that the Address possesses are not beyond reproach, its very opening statement— 'Four score and seven years ago our fathers brought forth on this Continent a new Nation'—being in fact false. Joseph Ellis comments, 'In 1776 thirteen American colonies declared themselves independent states that came together temporarily to win the war, then would go their separate ways. The government they created in 1781, called the Articles of Confederation, was not really much of a government at all and was never intended to be. It was, instead, what one historian has called a "Peace Pact" among sovereign states that regarded themselves as mini-nations of their own, that came together voluntarily for mutual security in a domestic version of a League of nations....the transition from the Declaration of Independence to the Constitution cannot be described as natural. Quite the contrary, it represented a dramatic change in direction and in scale, in effect from a confederation of sovereign states to a nation-size republic, indeed the largest republic ever established.' [Ellis 2016, xi, xiii; see Stewart 2013]

40 The record of Lincoln's speech can be found in *The Congressional Globe* (First Series), *Sketches of the Debates and Proceedings; The First Session of the Thirtieth Congress,* published by

Blair and River, Washington 1848. Available online at http://digital.library.unt.edu/ark:/67531/metadc30771/m1/206/sizes/m/?q=lincoln, accessed 31 July 2016, 154-156.

41 It should be noted that the exact wording of some of the newspaper reports varies from source to source.

42 See Higgs 1999, passim and Gordon 1999, passim.

43 Not everyone in Britain was enthusiastic for war either. Britain's entering the war was no foregone conclusion. Opinion in Britain was deeply divided. Even the Cabinet was divided. Douglas Newton's *The Darkest Days* is a fascinating, if not uncontroversial, account of the weeks leading up to the declaration of war. For a more standard account, see Strachan, passim.

44 See Ferguson 1999, 174-211, and Hochschild, passim.

45 Rothbard 1997, 128; emphasis added. For a comprehensive discussion of the factors leading to the U.S.'s entry into World War I, see Tansill 1938, passim. For a discussion of the role of British Naval Intelligence in relation to the sinking of the *Lusitania*, see Raico 1999a, 332 ff.

46 *The Statutes at Large of the United States of America*, April 1917 to March 1919, Chapter 30 (217-219), available at http://www.constitution.org/uslaw/sal/040_statutes_at_large.pdf, accessed 15 April 2016.

47 Higgs 1999, 378; Stone 2007, 56.

48 The Act is officially listed as 'Espionage Offenses' and can be found in *The Statutes at Large of the United States of America*, April 1917 to March 1919, Chapter 75 (553-554), available at http://www.constitution.org/uslaw/sal/040_statutes_at_large.pdf, accessed 15 April 2016.

49 See MacDonnell 25-26 and Higgs, 1999, passim.

50 'During wartime,' writes Tom Palmer, 'criticism is characterized as treasonous, defeatist, and unpatriotic. Civil liberties are abandoned, censorship imposed, newspapers shut down, and spying on citizens authorized. Fellow citizens are designated enemies, demonized, harassed, arrested, interned, expelled, or killed.' [Palmer 2014a, 13]

51 The ways of Supreme Courts are mysterious indeed, some cynics might say even arbitrary and fickle. The Irish Prime Minister (Taoiseach) Jack Lynch once remarked of the Irish Supreme Court that 'It would be a brave man who would predict these days, what was or was not contrary to the Constitution.' Following the High Court case of *Ryan v. The Attorney General* [1965 Ir 294 in which it was claimed that the Irish Constitution [*Bunreacht na hÉireann*] contained unenumerated rights, the Supreme Court 'enthusiastically embraced the idea and went on to use it as the basis for some of the most important decisions the court ever took.' [MacCormaic, 334; see Casey 2004, and Casey 2005]

52 War is not, however, the only instrument employed for the restriction of civil liberties nor is the state the only agent of repression. Over the last thirty years or so, driven by the social censorship of a so-called liberal elite, free speech has been under attack ('you can't say *that*!) in both society at large and, bizarrely, in our universities. [see Lukianoff, passim]

53 Murray Rothbard notes that 'the Federal Reserve System coincided with the outbreak of World War I in Europe, and it is generally agreed that it was only the new system that permitted the U.S. to enter the war and to finance both its own war effort, and massive loans to the allies; roughly, the Fed doubled the money supply of the U.S. during the war and prices doubled in consequence.' [Rothbard 1997, 120]

54 Higgs, 381-382. For a discussion of factors leading to the U.S. entry into World War II, see Tansill 1952, passim. Here is a sample of what you will find there: 'It was entirely fitting,' writes Charles Tansill, 'that [Henry L.] Stimson became Secretary of War in 1940; no one deserved that title quite as well as he. The entry in his *Diary* for November 25, 1941, is illuminating. With regard to Japan "the question is how we should maneuver them into the position of firing the first shot without allowing too much danger to ourselves." On the following day Secretary Hull answered this question by submitting an ultimatum that he knew Japan could not accept. The Japanese attack upon Pearl Harbor fulfilled the fondest hopes of the Roosevelt Cabinet.' [Tansill 1952, viii]

55 See http://costsofwar.org/ for details and references; also Palmer 2014a, 8.

56 This period covers events from the Civil War and the Volga Famine through various collectivisations, dekulakisations, deportations and purges up to post-World War II repatriations. [See Marsh 144]

57 Porter, 159. 'Following a visit to Germany,' writes Ralph Raico, 'Lloyd George and Churchill were both converted to the Bismarckian model of social insurance schemes.' [Raico 1999a, 328]

Chapter 33

Rand, Hayek, Nozick, Rothbard and Rawls

There are only two rules of governance in a free society:
Mind your own business. Keep your hands to yourself
—P. J. O'Rourke

⌐It is terrible to contemplate how few politicians are hanged
—G. K. Chesterton

A libertarian is someone who has graduated from thinking that
there are problems with the state to realizing that the state is the problem.
— Jakub Bożydar Wiśniewski

I: Ayn Rand

W ho is Ayn Rand? If one were to ask this question of any
reasonably educated politically literate person, one would stand a pretty
good chance of getting an answer, a dusty answer[1] perhaps, but an answer
nonetheless. In a contest of public recognition, readership, and following, Ayn
Rand (1905-1982) would win hands down over Hayek, Rawls, Nozick and
even Murray Rothbard. 'The Russian-born novelist and philosopher Ayn Rand
was the most popular libertarian of all and simultaneously the most hated,'
writes Brian Doherty. She must be regarded, Doherty continues, as 'the most
influential libertarian of the twentieth century to the public at large' despite
her explicit and vehement rejection of that label. [Doherty, 11] In 2007, fifty
years after its first publication, her novel, *Atlas Shrugged* sold almost 200,000
copies. I suspect that this yearly total probably exceeds the combined lifetime
sales of Hayek, Rawls, Nozick and Rothbard. The great disparity in sales
tells us nothing, of course, of the relative intellectual worth of these authors'
productions but it is evidence of their reach and influence. Whatever one thinks
of Rand's work, and however much she may be despised and ignored by the
great and the good, the great unwashed have taken her to their hearts. For a
woman who has been dead for over thirty years and who, during her lifetime
and after, was in receipt of more than her fair share of obloquy, she is perhaps
more influential today than she has ever been.[2]

Why? Douglas Rasmussen thinks she is newsworthy for a variety of substantive reasons, including 'her ability to note with dramatic force the immorality
and hypocrisy of our current political age; her commitment to individual rights;
her holding liberty and capitalism inviolate; her rejection of "moral cannibalism" in any form; her advocacy of moral individualism; her recognition

of a moral order grounded in human nature; and her realization that reality was not only intelligible but open to the possibilities for human achievement far more wondrous than ever realized.' [Rasmussen, in Various 2010] Perhaps so. These are all good reasons for her to attract attention. But this wouldn't explain why thinkers who have proposed much the same ideals aren't sought out by the general public with the same fervour as she is. Neera Badhwar agrees with Rasmussen's account of why Rand is in the news; but she adds that 'she would not be any more in the news than Mises, Hayek, or Bastiat if she had not expressed these ideas in fiction, especially *Atlas Shrugged*. Her fiction....appeals not only to our reasoning capacities, but also to our imaginative and emotional capacities.' [Badhwar, in Various 2010] Michael Huemer is of the same mind as Badhwar, remarking that the reason Rand is making the headlines while other liberty-promoting thinkers are not is that Rand 'is the most compelling *writer* of the group. More importantly, Rand was not only a philosopher, but a compelling *novelist*.' [Huemer, in Various 2010] Of course, Rand isn't the first philosopher to have achieved renown largely through the medium of novels. Rousseau, too, owed most of his fame not to his treatises but to his novels, *La Nouvelle Héloïse* and *Émile* and, in more recent times, we have had the novels of Iris Murdoch and Jean-Paul Sartre to entertain and edify us.

Badhwar and Huemer are right, I believe, in thinking that Rand's fiction is the key to her widespread popularity. For every person who is wildly excited by the play of abstract philosophical ideas, there are thousands whose imaginations are fired and whose intellects are captivated by the stirring depiction of the human drama. Rand herself speaks of 'the sterile, uninspiring futility of a great many theoretical discussion of ethics, and the resentment which may people feel toward such discussions: moral principles remain in their minds as floating abstractions, offering them a goal they can't grasp and demanding that they reshape their souls in its image, thus leaving them with a burden of undefinable moral guilt.' [Rand 1975a, 9-10]   Many people have come to a vividly experienced love of liberty through the reading of Rand's novels. Even though her non-fiction writing is strong and characterful—I find her essays exciting and entrancing[3]—her fiction outsells her nonfiction by several orders of magnitude. Huemer notes: 'The lesson for defenders of freedom seems clear. We need more novelists, screenwriters, and other artists.' [Huemer, in Various 2010] Man may not be able to live without reason but reason alone rarely spurs him to action.

Not everyone is as enthusiastic about Rand's writing as Badhwar and Huemer. Antony Flew remarks that it is unfortunate that 'Rand's novels are so full of long philosophical speeches and that her contributions to philosophy are so largely a matter of quoting the speeches from her novels. Her moral ideas could have been much better illustrated with the help of detailed accounts of paradigm lives, both good and bad, and developed in contrast or relation with certain classical philosophers.'[4]

So, what is it then that keeps Rand in the public eye? Is it her ideas? Is it her novels? I believe it is both. Rand's ideas aren't that terribly different (in many respects) from that which can be found in other writers but her organisation and presentation of these is concrete, dynamic and novel. What is unique in Rand is the combination of her ideas about freedom and individuality embodied in a fictional setting that many people find imaginatively gripping and intellectually satisfying. [see Sciabarra, 1995]

Rand and her Inspirations

Rand's ideas are a combination of classical and modern themes. Her basic philosophical orientation is Aristotelian, though just how much of Aristotle's work she read is a moot point. In fact, it's quite hard to determine just how much of *any* philosopher Rand read.[5] She portrays Kant as the great intellectual Satan but this depiction of Kant is hard to reconcile with the writings of the mild-mannered man from the cultural backwater of Königsburg. Rand manages to update Aristotle without losing what is essential to him. She is a metaphysical and epistemological realist, as is Aristotle, but she abandons Aristotle's *polis*-based account of politics for a liberal conception of politics centred on freedom. She 'attempts to combine an essentially classical or premodern view of man with a modern political doctrine....the argument...is that freedom of action in society is a function of what is proper to living a good human life...' [Den Uyl and Rasmussen, 179] When she depicts virtue as constitutive of what it is to lead a good life, she is channelling Aristotle. From her classical heritage also comes the idea that self-interest, properly understood, and morality, properly understood, cannot genuinely conflict. Nor could the self-interest of one person genuinely conflict with the self-interest of another, provided that self-interest is properly understood. These ideas may seem strange to us today but, as Roderick Long notes, they were commonplaces of the Classical tradition. Long also notes the diverse sources of Rand's philosophical inspiration, remarking that she 'sets out to found a classical liberal conception of politics (including strong individual rights to negative liberty) upon a classical Greek conception of human nature and the human good.' He goes on to note, however, that she 'adds to her ethics a spirit of heroic exaltation drawn from Nietzsche and the French Romantics.' [Long, in Various 2010]

Rand's Aristotelianism and liberalism enter into an uneasy alliance with a strain of ethical egoism coming from Nietzsche and Stirner though, once again, it isn't easy to tell just how much of either man's works she read. Whether or which, there appears to be an unresolved strain in Rand's work: is her ideal human being the Aristotelian great-souled man (*megalopsuchos*) or the Nietzschean Übermensch or the Stirnerite Egoist? 'In her choices as a novelist, if not explicitly in her nonfiction, Rand retained a streak of Nietzsche.' Her work 'vibrates with unresolved tension between glorifying man qua man, the greatness possible in man, and glorifying only the Great Man. This was left over from the earlier Nietzscheism that she officially disavowed...' [Doherty, 228, 542]

If freedom and the individual are characteristic themes in Rand's thought, another central notion is the associated idea of rights. For Rand, a right isn't an entitlement to things but rather the freedom to act. 'Even property rights are not conceived by her to be rights to things, but only the freedom to pursue courses of action with respect to material goods.' [Den Uyl and Rasmussen, 169] Rand's society is composed of individuals who each have rights to life liberty and property that each must respect. Rights, for Rand, are essentially negative, putting others under an obligation not to interfere with one another, not claim rights that oblige others positively to do things for others.[6] Rights for Rand are natural and covalent with man's rational nature and not something conferred either by society or by government.

Michael Huemer is one of those who sees a fundamental tension between Rand's egoistic ethics and the remainder of her work. If Huemer is right about this, this tension would appear to be an instance of the unresolved strain I already mentioned between Rand's Aristotelian and classical liberal heritage, on the one hand, and, on the other hand, her 'spirit of heroic exaltation' which, I believe derives in a diluted form from Nietzsche and Stirner. Rand claims that every person is an end in himself. This idea, although arguable, isn't novel. Even Rand's intellectual nemesis, Kant, held this position. There is, however, a possible ambiguity in this claim. I can regard myself as an end in myself (indeed, it is hard to see how I could *not* do so) and then, either regard others merely as means to my ends or regard them as ends in themselves. The former alternative is compatible with ethical egoism; the latter alternative is not. Huemer remarks that regarding others merely as means to my ends would make a defence of individual rights obscure, while regarding others as ends in themselves 'could not be advanced by a true egoist, who must hold that it is obligatory to treat other persons (and everything else) as mere means to one's own welfare.' [Huemer, in Various 2010]

RAND'S POLITICAL PHILOSOPHY

What is Rand's political philosophy? Putting it as succinctly as possible, I would have to say that, as a political theorist, Rand is essentially a minarchist (minimal government) libertarian—*libertarian* because of the obvious emphasis she places on the importance of human liberty for an adequate human life, and *minarchist* because she believes that the basic condition that will permit men to associate together needs to be framed by a unitary code of law administered by a unitary enforcement body—this for her is the state. It is important to note that Rand rejected the description of herself as a libertarian, largely because she identified libertarianism with anarchism. But not all libertarians are anarchists; some, such as Murray Rothbard are; others, such as Tibor Machan, are not.

Individuals have the right to defend themselves against aggression [Rand 1963b, 126] but the use of physical force cannot, she believes, be left at the discretion of individual citizens. [see Rand 1963b, 127] Why not? Because it would threaten the peaceful coexistence of all. Imagine what would happen, Rand muses, if someone had his wallet stolen 'and broke into every house in the neighbourhood to search for it, and shot the first man who gave him a dirty look, taking the look to be proof of guilt.' [Rand 1963b, 127] Indeed. Rand's example, lurid and tendentious as it may be, illustrates the dangers of self-help remedies against aggression—a tendency to shoot first and ask questions later, allied to yet another tendency to raise the violence stakes, seeking two eyes for an eye and two teeth for a tooth. Traditional societies that had no official organisations dedicated to preventing and investigating crime tended to repress the use of self-help remedies against criminal acts (except in cases of emergency) and to recommend instead having recourse to the appropriate socially sanctioned methods of adjudication and punishment. [see Berman 1983, passim]

Order, for Rand, requires law and that law must be objective and it must be objectively enforced by an institution—*one* institution—charged with protecting rights. The function of government is limited to protecting individuals against the criminal invasion of their persons or property by other individuals or organisations. There is, then, and there can only be one system of law and one system of law adjudication and one system of law enforcement. In her essay on 'The Nature of Government,' Rand defines government as 'an institution that holds the exclusive power to *enforce* certain rules of social conduct in a given geographical area' and as '*the means of placing the retaliatory use of physical force under objective control…*'[7] This is a more or less standard Weberian conception of the state and relatively uncontroversial. But there are people—anarchists—who wonder 'whether government as such is evil by nature and whether anarchy is the ideal social system.' [Rand 1963b, 131] These people, she thinks, confuse the inadequacies and evils of particular governments with the nature of government as such. Without government, society would be at the mercy of criminals. But, it might be asked, could we not have multiple governments, competing with each other for business? After all, competition is generally good for keeping businesses honest, including businesses that provide services, so why shouldn't the services of policing, security and courts be provided by multiple suppliers as well? Wouldn't the provision of these services in this way be less expensive and more efficient than its provision by monopoly and, more importantly, wouldn't it be voluntary?

Rand's response to this suggestion is swift and scathing. Suppose, she asks, 'Mr. Smith, a customer of Government A, suspects that his next-door neighbor, Mr. Jones, a customer of government B, has robbed him; a squad of Police A proceeds to Mr. Jones house and is met at the door by a squad of Police B, who declare that they do not accept the validity of Mr. Smith's complaint and do not recognize the authority of Government A. What happens then? You take it from there.' [Rand 1963b, 132] I suspect we are supposed to imagine scenes of carnage as competing defence agencies fight it out, like rival bootlegging gangs in 1920s Chicago. But why should this be so? Right now, we have competing defence agencies—that is, governments—all around the world and they manage to get along with each other, at least most of the time. It is even possible for people living in different jurisdictions to sue and be sued. Even within the USA there are multiple legal jurisdictions, and multiple police services operating at different levels, yet somehow managing to cooperate rather than engage in deadly physical attrition. In the commercial sphere, we have multiple insurance agencies supplying insurance services for people who are geographically intermingled with each other and yet they too manage to deal with one another without employing violence.[8] Rand rejects anarchism because she sees it as undermining the stable structure of law and law-enforcement that men living together require if they aren't to become involved in endlessly escalating inter-personal violence. In this, her reasoning is strikingly similar to Locke's portrayal of the inconveniencies of the state of nature. If anarchy necessarily involved either no legal system or a chaos of competing and irreconcilable legal systems, then it would be hard to disagree with Rand on the necessity for a minimal government.[9] But anarchism, at least libertarian anarchism, is opposed neither to law, nor to a convergence of laws, nor to the enforcement of laws. Still less is it a supporter of chaos.

Rand believes that libertarians are essentially subjectivists in ethical matters. Ronald Merrill expresses her reservations thus: "the key problem with libertarianism is its aversion to grounding political principles in moral philosophy.' [Merrill, 180] This negative judgement of libertarians would appear to derive from Rand's inability or unwillingness to distinguish between some and all, between what is incidental to libertarianism and what is necessary.[10] But to reject government as anarchists do isn't to reject law and order; to reject a monopoly supplier of justice isn't to reject justice, any more than to reject a monopoly supplier of apples requires one to give up munching Granny Smiths. Once again, Rand seems to think that libertarians are substantively committed to various let-it-all-hang-loose doctrines. She fails to appreciate the difference between, on the one hand, denying that laws can properly be used to enforce certain policies that infringe human freedom and, on the other, commending certain uses of freedom. It is perfectly consistent, for example, to deny that it's a function of government to make and enforce laws concerning drug use without being committed to the view that drug use is a good thing. It is perfectly possible, even if not very common, to be a libertarian and to hold socially conservative views on the necessity for a flourishing society to have and to embody restrictions that are the product of socially informal sanctions.

Rand's general criticism of the various forms of tribalism is sharp and unanswerable but, bizarrely, she characterises libertarianism as a form of rightist tribalism! There are, she says, 'tribalists...who claim to be rightists. They are champions of individualism, they claim, which they define as the right to form one's own gang and use physical force against others—and they intend to preserve capitalism, they claim, by replacing it with anarchism (establishing "private" or "competing" governments, i.e. tribal rule). The common denominator of such individualists is the desire to escape from *objectivity*...'[11] Since Rand doesn't name names, it's difficult to know who exactly she has in mind here. Certainly, there are people who reject any notion of objectivity, and some of them would claim to be anarchists. It does not follow from this, however, that all anarchists reject the notion of objectivity. Nor does the anarchist notion of competing defence agencies amount to the reintroduction of tribalism. Rand distinguishes between a tribe and an association, the latter being ruled by ideas and not men. 'All proper associations are formed or joined by individual choice and on conscious, intellectual grounds (philosophical, political, professional, etc.)—not by the physiological or geographical accident of birth, and not on the ground of tradition.'[12] Ironically, this is precisely the basis upon which libertarian anarchism works so on Rand's definition there's no way that anarchist groups can be said to be tribes.

Let us line up the points of agreement and disagreement between Rand and libertarian anarchists. Libertarian anarchists accept, as does Rand, the legitimacy of the use of retaliatory force. Libertarian anarchists, at least natural law libertarian anarchists, accept the necessity for objective laws; so too does Rand. In agreement with Rand, libertarian anarchists believe that laws (but not necessarily legislation) should be enforced. The only significant point on which libertarian anarchists and Rand differ is that libertarian anarchists believe that retaliatory force, objective laws and their enforcement can best be provided by multiple competing providers, relating to one another more or less as insurance companies do at present, rather than by a single agency with a monopoly on the legitimate use of force.

Apart from her misdirected critique of libertarianism generally and libertarian anarchism in particular, how does Rand positively justify government? She doesn't seem to have an answer to this question except to repeat that she believes that the provision of law and its enforcement can be provided only by a monopoly provider. Without such a monopoly provider, she seems to believe that there can be no objective law, no objective rules of evidence and no objective control over the use of retaliatory force. 'What is missing,' admits Roland Merrill, and it is a crucial admission, 'in the Objectivist politics is a positive theory of the origin of government. What is government? What justifies it? Why should rational men submit to it? How does it, or should it, originate?' [Merrill, 182] Where does a Randian government get its authority? Does it derive it from the consent of the governed; or is it simply the case that a government mysteriously manifests itself and once in place simply repels all other contenders? If the source of a government's authority is the consent of the governed, how is this consent to be elicited? It seems that Rand has no answer to these simple and obvious questions. Ronald Merrill bluntly says, 'Rand simply dodges the issue.' [Merrill, 183]

Where will Rand's minimal government get its money from? Rand accepts that taxation involves the initiation of force and so it is, on her own principles, impermissible. If that is so, government financing (and the government must be financed somehow) must be voluntary.[13] Her concrete suggestion is a stamp tax on contracts. But since the government is a monopoly provider and customers aren't free to go elsewhere, how would the imposition of such a tax not amount to the initiation of force, since the government monopoly can only be maintained by force? Rand appears to dodge several questions concerning the financing of other government services—police, military, and so on. Answers to these problems, it seems, are for the future. She writes, 'The question of how to implement the principle of voluntary government financing—how to determine the best means of applying it in practice—is a very complex one and belongs to the field of the philosophy of law. The task of political philosophy is only to demonstrate the nature of the principle and to demonstrate that it is practicable.'[14]

In fact, the problem government funding, voluntary or otherwise, is *not* that complex a question and it does *not* belong to the field of the philosophy of law, and even if it did, it would still need some kind of answer. Ronald Merrill is extremely charitable to Rand when he says that 'she was not primarily a political philosopher interested in working out all the details...' [Merrill, 184] This judgement just will not do as a defence of Rand's lack of detail. Rand isn't being asked to work out all the details; she is just being asked to answer some obvious basic questions in this area, and she appears to have no answers to them, except to kick the questions into the long grass. In the end, Merrill admits what by now should be obvious, namely, that 'Objectivist political theory is vulnerable to the anarcho-libertarian critique because Rand's work in this area failed to delve to the roots of the subject and deal with the inherent weakness of Locke's concept of government.' [Merrill, 185]

II: Friedrich Hayek

Born in Vienna to a notable and well-connected family (he was second cousin to Ludwig Wittgenstein), Friedrich Hayek (1899-1992) served in the First World War, after which he took degrees in law (1921) and political science (1923) from the University of Vienna, while also studying philosophy, economics and psychology. His initial attraction to socialism was eradicated by his reading of Ludwig von Mises's *Socialism*. In 1973, Hayek wrote of the effect of Mises's *Socialism* on him as follows: 'To none of us young men who read the book when it appeared the world was ever the same again. ...Not that we at once swallowed it all. For that it was much too strong a medicine and too bitter a pill...[but]...though we might try to resist, even strive hard to get the disquieting considerations out of our systems, we did not succeed. The logic of the argument was inexorable.' [Hayek 1992, 133] He attended Mises's *Privatseminar*, along with many other subsequently distinguished students. With Mises's assistance, Hayek became the director of the Austrian Institute for Business Cycle Research before he joined the staff of the London School of Economics in 1931. His time in London brought him into contact with many important and influential people, including John Maynard Keynes, whose *General Theory* he notoriously declined to subject to the critique it so eminently deserved. Hayek left London for Chicago in 1950 and later, in the late 60s, moved to Freiburg. After Freiburg, Salzburg, then back, for the last time, to Freiburg.

Although Hayek was initially best known for his work as an economist—his Nobel Prize was awarded for work done on the Business Cycle—his attention turned in the mid-to-late 1940s to social and epistemological matters. These were to be his principal concerns for the remainder of his life. In these fields, he produced a series of works whose sheer size and concentrated reasoning inhibits effective condensation. Apart from his wartime *The Road to Serfdom*, Hayek produced *The Constitution of Liberty*, the three-volumed *Law, Legislation and Liberty*, and his final attack on Socialism, *The Fatal Conceit*. The remarks that follow are largely confined to the first two of these works. In addition to his work in economics,[15] certain aspects of Hayek's social and political thought are welcome and constructive contributions to libertarian theory. This would include his thorough investigation and elaboration of the notion of spontaneous order and his extensive work on law. Other aspects of his work are, however, not quite so welcome and constructive as contributions to the advancement of liberty.

ORDER AND DESIGN, LAW AND LEGISLATION

Man's basic social life is ordered but isn't designed or planned by anyone. It emerges from the interactions among individual human beings. Even if some modes of social interaction could have been designed (but weren't) other basic modes of social order can't have been designed, for example, language. In a similar way, attempting to centrally plan a society is a bad idea even if it were realisable, which it is not. No one person, no one institution, has all the requisite information to make the 'best' decision. Computers won't help. It isn't the speed of the calculation that's the problem; it is, rather, not being able to have access to all the constantly shifting and changing data.[16]

Similar considerations apply to law. Hayek distinguished insightfully between law and legislation. Law is a systematically ambiguous term and much confusion in discussion results from failure to disambiguate it: it can mean either those regulations that are made by those who consider themselves or are considered by others to be legislators (law as legislation); or it can mean those rules that have emerged spontaneously in a community as a means of permitting the members of that community to live together in harmony, to resolve disputes and, where possible, to prevent them arising (law proper). Both forms of law are meant to apply to all within the scope of a given jurisdiction, but whereas this is unproblematic for law proper, since such law emerges dynamically within the society to which it applies, it isn't always unproblematic for law as legislation which can be, and often is, selectively applied to some but not others in a society. Law proper is therefore coeval with society and must be antecedent to language, ethics and the more idiosyncratic elements of culture. Without common rules, human beings couldn't live together in peace and so society would be impossible. That being so, as Hayek notes, it would have to be the case that 'Long before man had developed language to the point where it enabled him to issue general commands, an individual would be accepted as a member of a group only so long as he conformed to its rules.' [Hayek 1982, I 72]

LIBERTY AND COERCION

So far, so good. Hayek's approach to law is not only consistent with libertarianism, but is a generally useful analytic tool. Hayek's views on politics, however, in particular his views on liberty and coercion, will be less acceptable to libertarians. [see Barry 1979, 54-75] Problems here emerge as early as the 1944 work, *The Road to Serfdom*. For example, what exactly does Hayek mean in *The Road to Serfdom* when he says that 'there is nothing in the basic principles of liberalism to make it a stationary creed'? If there are, as he says, 'no hard and fast rules fixed once and for all' just what is the essence of liberalism? According to him, we are to make use of the spontaneous forces of society— but only *as much as possible*. We are not to rule out coercion completely but only use *as little as possible*. And the principle of *laissez-faire* is merely a rule of thumb, and a rough one at that. [see Hayek 1944, 13] We get a better idea of what all this means a little later in the book when he tells us that opposition to socialist central planning is not to be taken as an endorsement of 'a dogmatic laissez-faire attitude.' [Hayek 1944, 27] The forces of competition are the best way of co-ordinating human affairs because they make no use of coercion but, 'where it is impossible to create the conditions necessary to make competition effective, we must resort to other methods of co-ordinating individual efforts.' [Hayek 1944, 27] But competition cannot be allowed free rein in all areas so that not all uses of coercion are disallowable. 'To prohibit the use of certain poisonous substances, or to require certain sanitary arrangements, is fully compatible with the preservation of competition....Nor is the preservation of competition incompatible with an extensive system of social services—so long as the organisation of these services is not designed in such a way as to make competition ineffective over wide fields.' [Hayek 1944, 28]

In all this, Hayek is taking an essentially Smithian line that there are some public goods that will be undersupplied by a free market among individuals and which therefore can only be supplied by a state. 'Thus neither the provision of signposts on the roads, nor, in most circumstances, that of the road themselves, can be paid for by every individual user. Nor can certain harmful effects of deforestation, or of some methods of farming, or of the smoke and noise of factories, be confined to the owner of the property in question or to those who are willing to submit to the damage for an agreed compensation. In such instances we must find some substitute for the regulation by the price mechanism.' [Hayek 1944, 29]

Not only are public goods to be supplied by the state, so also is a measure of social security. Hayek distinguishes between two kinds of security—limited and absolute. The former, such as a minimum of food, shelter and clothing, he thinks, can be guaranteed in a wealthy society 'without endangering general freedom.' [Hayek 1944, 90] Furthermore, he sees no reason why a state 'should not assist the individuals in providing for those common hazards of life against which, because of their uncertainty, few individuals can make adequate provision,' so that the case for the state's providing comprehensive social insurance is very strong. Even though Hayek concedes that democratic government might conceivably 'be as oppressive as the worst dictatorship,' none of this is particularly encouraging for a libertarian. [Hayek 1944, 52]

Some fifteen or so years after *The Road to Serfdom*, in *The Constitution of Liberty*, Hayek defines freedom as the absence of coercion. 'We are concerned in this book with that condition of men in which coercion of some by others is reduced *as much as is possible* in society. This state we shall describe throughout as a state of liberty or freedom.'[17] What then is coercion? Hayek's initial account links freedom to the idea of a person's not being subject to the arbitrary will of another or others. Later, his account is that coercion occurs when 'one man's actions are made to serve another man's will, not for his own but for the other's purpose.'[18] Apart from 'coercion', the most significant words in Hayek's account are 'as much as is possible.' Why is this? Because, it seems, 'Coercion, however, cannot be altogether avoided because the only way to prevent it is by the threat of coercion.' Really? 'Free society has met this problem by conferring the monopoly of coercion on the state and by attempting to limit this power of the state[19] to instances where it is required to prevent coercion by private persons.' [Hayek 2006, 19-20] As the mapmakers say, 'Here be dragons.' So, it appears then that for Hayek, coercion is a seemingly ineliminable fact of social and political life. We have a choice. We can have it everywhere in society, abounding and uncontrolled, or we can confine it to one particular institution and attempt to control its use there.

But coercion is *not* equivalent to every form of influence by which one man may attempt to move another; moreover, even in cases of genuine coercion, the will of the one coerced is free. If a mugger puts a gun to your head and says, 'Give me your wallet, punk, or I'll blow your *&%$£+@ head off,' you can choose either to refuse and take your chances or to give him your wallet. If you do give him your wallet, you are being coerced but you can choose not to be if you're willing to take the consequences. 'Coercion occurs when one man's actions are made to serve another man's will, not for his own but for the other's purpose. It is not that the coerced does not choose at all; if that were the case, we shouldn't speak of his "acting." If my hand is guided by physical force to trace my signature or my finger pressed against the trigger of a gun, I haven't acted. Such violence, which makes my body someone else's physical tool, is, of course, as bad as coercion proper and must be prevented for the same reason. Coercion implies, however, that I still choose but that my mind is made someone else's tool, because the alternatives before me have been so manipulated that the conduct that the coercer wants me to choose becomes for me the least painful one. Although coerced, it is still I who decide which is the least evil under the circumstances.'[20] Aristotle made a similar point when he distinguished between voluntary actions and non-voluntary actions. A non-voluntary action is one that you perform which, under normal circumstances you would not, as, for example, a ship's captain, who jettisons his supercargo to save the ship and crew. Non-voluntary actions are, strictly speaking, voluntary but the insertion of the 'non-' indicates that one's choice in this instance is based on one's estimate of the lesser of two (or more) evils.

Why, Hayek asks, is coercion bad? The answer, one might think, is because it is a violation of a person's freedom. That is *not* the answer that Hayek gives. His answer is oddly utilitarian: 'Coercion is bad because it prevents a person from using his mental powers to the full and consequently from making the greatest contribution that he is capable of to the community.' [Hayek 2006, 118] This latent Mill-like consequentialism has, well, consequences, not the least of which is that it prevents Hayek from distinguishing successfully between the factual physical reality of force or violence and the normative moral/legal/political reality of coercion.

The clearest instances of coercion occur when there is a threat of force or violence, but Hayek won't allow coercion to be confined to such manifest examples, remarking that 'the threat of physical force is not the only way in which coercion can be exercised.' [Hayek 2006, 119] This refusal to confine coercion to physical force or the threat of it has immediate consequences, for when Hayek goes on to give a short list of examples of coercion, three of the four are physical whereas the fourth is not. He says, 'True coercion occurs when armed bands of conquerors make the subject people toil for them, when organized gangsters extort a levy for "protection," when the knower of an evil secret blackmails his victim, and, of course, when the state threatens to inflict punishment and to employ physical force to make us obey his commands.' [Hayek 2006, 121] The conquerors, the gangsters and the state all threaten physical violence; the blackmailer, in his capacity of blackmailer does not, as morally repulsive as his actions may be.

Hayek seems to see coercion as stretching out along a continuum, ranging, at one end, from the most obvious and crude physical threats to, at the other end, unpleasant social behaviour. What kind of actions could we locate at the lower end of the coercion scale? Well, Hayek has in mind 'a morose husband, a nagging wife, or a hysterical mother may make life intolerable unless their every mood is obeyed.' [Hayek 2006, 122] But this is nonsense. If these things are to count as coercion, then the concept has been inflated well past the point of usefulness. The relevant continuum is where we have physical violence or the threat to initiate physical violence at one end and absolutely nothing like this at the other. As usual, in any continuum, around the midpoint we will have cases where it can be difficult to judge whether what we have is coercion or not, but such difficulties do not prevent us from seeing clearly that the extremities are, on the one hand, clearly coercive and, on the other, non-coercive. Hayek seems to recognise this point himself when he says, 'coercion can be so defined as to make it an all-pervasive and unavoidable phenomenon.' [Hayek 2006, 122]

ROTHBARD'S CRITIQUE OF HAYEK ON COERCION

Although Rothbard appreciates Hayek's definition of freedom in *The Constitution of Liberty* as 'the absence of coercion,' he has significant problems with Hayek's extremely wide definition of coercion. For Hayek, coercion includes the aggressive use of physical violence but it also includes what Rothbard regards as peaceful and non-coercive actions. Hayek appears to regard all violence as being necessarily aggressive. In failing to distinguish between aggressive and defensive violence, Hayek's' account is defective in yet another respect. "Hayek's justification of the existence of the State, as well as its employment of taxation and other measures of aggressive violence, rests upon his untenable obliteration of the distinction between aggressive and defensive violence, and his lumping of all violent action into the single rubric of varying degrees of "coercion."" [Rothbard 2002a, 226]

However problematic it may be to include such actions as, for instance, nagging under the rubric of coercion, even more problematic for critics such as

Rothbard is Hayek's inclusion under the heading of coercion of certain refusals to exchange. The kind of thing Hayek has in mind is a situation where, given conditions of widespread unemployment, an employer might use the threat of dismissal to obtain concessions not originally contracted for. [see Barry 1979, 73] But whatever the ultimate *moral* status of such a threat, Rothbard is clear that dismissal is simply a 'refusal by the capital-owning employer to make any further exchanges with one or more people' and, as such, is an exercise of freedom. Another example of coercion given by Hayek that Rothbard finds unacceptable is that of the monopolist who refuses to sell a vital commodity to others *in extremis* except on terms that they find harsh and unwelcome. Once again, Rothbard says that assuming there's no antecedent wrongdoing by the monopolist, whatever the *moral* implications of his action may be, it can't be considered coercion. Rothbard concludes, "[Hayek's] middle-of-the-road failure to confine coercion strictly to violence pervasively flaws his entire system of political philosophy." [Rothbard 2002, 225]

Coercion is either legitimate or it isn't. If it isn't, then it's not obvious why it becomes legitimate when monopolised by the state. Coercion isn't just physical force or the threat of such force; it is the *wrongful* (initiatory) use of or threat of force. Physical force or violence is wrong when it's *initiated* by one man or one group of men against another; it isn't wrong, when it's employed to defend an innocent person against the initiation of force by another. Hayek concedes that the state employs coercion. It does so in respect of taxation and various compulsory services, such as serving in the armed forces via conscription or doing jury duty. Is such coercion not a restriction of my freedom? Apparently not.[21] The reason for this surprising answer is that the very predictability of such demands by the state somehow evacuates them of their harmful character. Lest I be accused of misrepresenting Hayek on this matter, I am going to quote him here. He writes, 'Though…[tax and conscription] are not supposed to be avoidable, they are at least predictable and are enforced irrespective of how the individual would otherwise employ his energies; this deprives them largely of the evil nature of coercion. If the known necessity of paying a certain amount of taxes becomes the basis of all my plans, if a period of military service is a foreseeable part of my career, then I can follow a general plan of life of my own making and am as independent of the will of another person as men have learned to be in society. Though compulsory military service, while it lasts, involves severe coercion, and though a lifelong conscript couldn't be said ever to be free, a predictable limited period of military service certainly restricts the possibility of shaping one's life less than would, for instance, a constant threat of arrest resorted to by an arbitrary power to ensure what it regards as good behavior.' [Hayek 2006, 125-126]

This is nonsensical doublespeak. Yes, a broken leg is a less serious medical condition than pancreatic cancer but it's still not a condition one would wish to have. Compulsory military service for a limited time is better than compulsory military service for life but it's still a restriction and limitation of my freedom. Hayek's argument seems to amount to the fatuous claim that coercion by the state, because it is predictable and relatively impersonal isn't 'really' coercion because, after all, it might be worse. Rothbard has no difficulty exposing the absurdity of such a principle, pointing out that, on Hayek's principles, 'if everyone knew in advance that he would be tortured and enslaved one year out of every three, neither would this be coercion.' [Rothbard 1958b] If earlier Hayek had indefensibly widened the notion of coercion to include non-aggressive actions, in other respects, he narrows the notion of coercion to exclude clearly aggressive actions. 'In order to "limit"' State coercion… Hayek asserts that coercion is either minimized or even does not exist if the violence-supported edicts are not personal and arbitrary, but are in the form of general universal rules, knowable to all in advance…' [Rothbard 2002a, 226] But such an account is scarcely plausible, given that it's easy to conjure up examples of patently unjustifiable actions and policies that could none the less be generally known in advance, say, for example, a policy of culling 30% of female infants under the age of two every four years.

In a 'Memorandum to the Volker Fund' which he wrote in 1958, Rothbard anticipates some of the points he will make years later in *The Ethics of Liberty* but he is much more forthright and scathing in the Memorandum than he is in the relevant section of *The Ethics of Liberty*. Expressing surprise and distress, he describes *The Constitution of Liberty* as being 'an extremely bad, and I would even say evil, book.' [see Gordon 2007, 68] Rothbard notes that although Hayek begins well by defining freedom as the absence of interpersonal coercion, when he comes to define coercion 'the descent into the abyss begins.' For instead of defining coercion as physical violence or the threat thereof…he defines it to mean: specific acts of one person with the intent of harming another. If one were to open a grocery store next to Monopoly, Inc., the only grocery store in the village, it's very likely that this would have a damaging economic effect on Monopoly's revenues but it wouldn't be a coercive act. Nevertheless, suppose one bore a grudge against Monopoly Inc. for the high prices they had charged one for graphic novels when a boy, and had opened one's store with the specific intention of causing harm to Monopoly, then it appears that the act *would* be coercive. Rothbard is rightly puzzled at this strange outcome of the inflated conception of coercion.

The problem then, is this. Hayek's political inclinations are those of a classical liberal; his moral inclinations, however, are utilitarian. Being unable to make use of a notion of natural law that would allow him to distinguish between the physical reality of violence and the moral reality of coercion, Hayek has no principled position from which to take a consistent stand for freedom. Part of the antipathy experienced by some to the idea of natural law arises from the mistaken notion that it necessarily has theological implications and is essentially a form of 'Divine Command' ethical theory. Frank van Dun expresses the view that the term 'natural' in 'natural law' is to be taken literally, holding that natural law 'refers to the natural, physical world of living human beings.' [van Dun 2001, 3] Likewise, the 'law' in 'natural law' isn't to be understood as a kind of super-statute, a kind of command or directive of some celestial or transcendental lawgiver. It is, instead, to be taken as referring to 'the order or bond of conviviality that has its natural foundation in the plurality and diversity of distinct and separate persons.' [van Dun 2001, 3] Similarly, the renowned legal theorist, Lon Fuller states clearly that 'These natural laws have nothing to do with any "brooding omnipresence in the skies"....They remain entirely terrestrial in origin and application.' These natural laws aren't residents of some Empyrean region that descend on us from on high. 'They are not "higher" laws; if any metaphor of elevation is appropriate they should be called "lower" laws. They are like the…laws respected by a carpenter who wants the house he builds to remain standing and serve the purpose of those who live in it.' [Lon Fuller 1964, 96] If this naturalistic conception of natural law is taken seriously then whatever other objections may be made to it, as least some of the more egregious ones will have been eliminated.[22]

In the end, for Hayek, the freedom of an individual may be limited for all sorts of purposes that others, beside the particular agent, consider good. This is what permits Hayek to endorse a whole range of options that would be unacceptable to libertarians, including redistributive taxation policies, state support for, and control of, education, and so on.[23] Because of his reputation and renown, Hayek tends to 'crowd-out' other more plumb-line defenders of liberty, just as we shall see Nozick do with libertarians. Hayek is a kind of classical liberal, someone who prioritises freedom but not in any absolute way. But one can't be a little bit unfree without compromising liberty any more than one can be a little bit pregnant. Practically, the restrictions Hayek endorses may be slight by the standards of current Welfarism but there's nothing intrinsically to prevent their extension, and that, historically, is just what happened. Interestingly, Rothbard doesn't see Hayek as a liberal but as a neo-conservative inasmuch as '[Hayek] believes that we must blindly follow traditions even if we can't defend them.' [Rothbard, 1958b] Rothbard sums up Hayek's overall position in the following way: traditional social institutions are to be accepted on blind faith and without adequate reason; reason can't discover moral principles or justice; the argument for freedom rests on ignorance; and freedom means equality under the law, whatever the content of legal rules.

According to Brian Doherty, *The Constitution of Liberty* 'clarifies Hayek's many differences with other strains of twentieth-century libertarianism. Hayek makes this distinction between him and other libertarians quite clear toward *Constitution*'s end. He pledges no fealty to liberty for its own sake or for the sake of rights or justice. If anything is an unquestioned and unquestionable good to Hayek, it is diversity, growth, change, and progress in both knowledge and material goods. The free market and the unhampered price system are good, then, because they allow dispersed knowledge to be transmitted and brought to bear on the real world.'[24] In the end, it's hard to disagree with Doherty's judgement that Hayek was 'the least *libertarian* of the major libertarian influences of the twentieth century, by many other libertarians' lights.' [Doherty, 98]

III: ROBERT NOZICK

If one mentions the topic of libertarianism to anyone with pretensions to a liberal education, one is like to elicit, 'Ah, you mean that book by Nozick,

whatitsname again?, mm…—*Anarchy somethingorother.....*' And therein lies
the problem. On the one hand, Robert Nozick (1938-2002) made the topic of
libertarianism academically visible and gave it a temporary veneer of academic
respectability in Cambridge, Massachusetts and Other Important Places, but
the very fact that he occupies the libertarian foreground for most people means
that he has made it well nigh impossible for them to see anything libertarian
standing behind him. This is a problem, for concealed behind him stands almost
everything of libertarian interest. Apart from Murray Rothbard, other libertarians obscured by the prominence of Nozick include Jan Narveson, Anthony
de Jasay, David Friedman and Randy Barnett. [see Doherty, 495-498] That's
not to say that *Anarchy, State and Utopia* isn't interesting. It is—and clever,
and controversial and engagingly written in a masterly self-deprecating style.
Nozick was one of those annoyingly intelligent and articulate people we have
all known who have more good ideas before mid-morning coffee than most
of us have in a year, but *Anarchy, State and Utopia* is *not* the only significant
work in libertarian literature; it wasn't the first, and it certainly won't be the
last. Its publication in 1974, however, created something of a sensation in the
normally sedate world of academic philosophy. Here we had a Harvard philosopher defending a form of libertarianism, when libertarianism of any kind is
a position that your average liberal academic reflexively considers as attractive as an Ebola sandwich. I believe that Eric Mack understates the position
when he remarks that *Anarchy, State, and Utopia* 'shocked the philosophical
world with its robust and sophisticated defense of the minimal state…' [Mack
2015, 2] To the majority of the largely liberal-leaning academic community,
Nozick's book must have seemed an egregious case of wilfully defending the
indefensible. In addition to *Anarchy, State, and Utopia*, for which he is best
known, Nozick published other significant books—*Philosophical Explanations* (1981), *The Examined Life* (1989), *The Nature of Rationality* (1993),
Socratic Puzzles (1997), and *Invariances* (2001). Nevertheless, I think it fair
to say that whatever the merits of these later works, they are overshadowed
by the notoriety of *Anarchy, State, and Utopia*. Nozick must have felt like
some composers, such as Ravel with his *Bolero* and Barber with his *Adagio for
Strings*, in being simultaneously gratified and frustrated by the fame of just one
particular work to the virtual obliteration of all their others.

Despite Murray Rothbard's direct and immediate personal influence on
many central figures in contemporary libertarianism, and his direct if mediated
influence on very many others by means of his scholarly and popular publications, his most significant influence on contemporary academic discussions
of political thought has been uncharacteristically indirect. Nozick credits
his interest in libertarianism to a long conversation he had with Rothbard
sometime in the late 1960s. 'It was a long conversation about six years ago
with Murray Rothbard,' he says, 'that stimulated my interest in individualist
anarchist theory.' [Nozick 1974, xv] Eric Mack writes, 'The major force in
his conversion to libertarian views was his conversations at Princeton with his
fellow philosophy graduate student, Bruce Goldberg. It was through Goldberg
that Nozick met the economist Murray Rothbard….Nozick's encounter with

Rothbard and Rothbard's rights-based critique of the state...lead [*sic*] Nozick to the project of formulating a rights-based libertarianism that would vindicate the minimal state.' [Mack 2015, 3] Despite his explicit acknowledgement of Rothbard's influence, Rothbard's writings on libertarianism aren't directly discussed in the text of *Anarchy, State and Utopia*, his ghostly intellectual presence being confined to just a few minor footnotes.

ANARCHY, STATE AND UTOPIA

Nozick starts *Anarchy, State and Utopia* with a bang. 'Individuals have rights, and there are things no person or group may do to them (without violating their rights). So strong and far reaching are these rights that they raise the question of what, if anything, the state and its officials may do. How much room do individual rights leave for the state?' [Nozick 1974, ix] That is his starting point. His conclusion will be that 'a minimal state, limited to the narrow functions of protection against force, theft, fraud, enforcement of contracts, and so on, is justified; that any more extensive state will violate persons' rights not to be forced to do certain things, and is unjustified;[25] and that the minimal state is inspiring as well as right.' [Nozick 1974, ix] Nozick's project, then, is to justify a neo-Lockean minimalist night-watchman state, a state with very narrowly circumscribed responsibilities. He specifically denies that the state can be used for paternalistic purposes or for coerced charity.

If Nozick was reticent about explicitly discussing Rothbard, Rothbard did not return the compliment. One of the most scintillating sections of *The Ethics of Liberty* is a chapter entitled 'Robert Nozick and the Immaculate Conception of the State.' Building on the work of Roy Childs and Randy Barnett, Rothbard subjects the central thesis of *Anarchy, State and Utopia* to a withering criticism. His summary of its central thesis is succinct. It is, he says, 'an "invisible hand" variant of a Lockean contractarian attempt to justify the State, or at least a minimal State confined to the function of protection.' [Rothbard 2002, 231] He outlines the steps in Nozick's thesis as follows: 'Beginning with a free-market anarchist state of nature, Nozick portrays the State as emerging, by an invisible hand process that violates no one's rights, first as a dominant protective agency, then to an "ultraminimal state," and then finally to a minimal state.' [Rothbard 2002, 231] If Nozick's account of the necessary and inevitable emergence of the state from a condition of anarchy by means of libertarian principles is defensible, Rothbard's anti-state anarchic position is seriously undermined.

The Rothbard-Nozick tension is merely one aspect of a larger dispute with the libertarian camp. Although all parties to the dispute are keen to defend the claim that the free market is either the proper or the best way to provide for the range of services that human beings need, they differ on the critical question of the provision of those services that are often held to be the core services of government—the creation and maintenance of order and the preservation of the peace via a resolution of disputes. The term 'minarchism' was coined by Samuel Konkin in 1971 to apply to those libertarians who believe that compulsory government in some form is necessary. Minarchists believe that the free market can provide all the services human beings require *except* the core functions of government, law, justice and security; anarchists believe that *all* services, including the allegedly core functions of government, are sustainable without the use of a coercive agency exercising a monopoly of legitimate force over a specified geographical area. [see Long & Machan] Nozick's theory, then, is a paradigm example of minarchism.

Although it might seem to be a mere matter of historical detail, Rothbard believes it to be theoretically important to ask whether any state has in fact come into being by means of the Nozickean process. With all the available evidence apparently pointing in the other direction, Rothbard judges that the answer to this question has to be in the negative: '[E]very State where the facts are available originated by a process of violence, conquest, and exploitation...' [Rothbard 2002, 231] One may wonder whether Rothbard's opinion in this matter is, in fact, historically accurate. One thinks, for example, of Switzerland and Vatican City. Nevertheless, despite these possible exceptions—and one would have to admit that Switzerland and Vatican City are neither of them your standard state—the history of the majority of states, if not of all states, supports Rothbard's opinion. The practical effect of this for Nozick's position, according to Rothbard, is that no state is in fact justified (since none of them has arisen via the prescribed Nozickean process). He believes that Nozick, to be consistent, should join with him in calling for the abolition of all existing states; only then could we see whether or not a minimal state would inevitably come into being without violating anyone's rights.

Whatever misgivings one might have about Nozick's project as a whole, from a libertarian perspective, it can't be denied that it starts with the right question. 'Why not,' asks Nozick, 'have anarchy? Since anarchist theory, if tenable, undercuts the whole subject of *political* philosophy, it is appropriate to begin political philosophy with an examination of its major theoretical alternative.' [Nozick 1974, 4] He adds, wryly, that 'Those who consider anarchism not an unattractive doctrine will think it possible that political philosophy ends here as well'! [Nozick 1974, 4]

As I have already mentioned, *Anarchy, State, and Utopia* is notorious for its no-holds-barred statement of rights.[26] I repeat the ringing announcement from the start of the book: 'Individuals have rights, and there are things no person or group may do to them (without violating their rights). So strong and far reaching are these rights that they raise the question of what, if anything, the state and its officials may do. How much room do individual rights leave for the state?' [Nozick 1974, ix] Having such a stark conception of rights, Nozick has to be able to justify the coming-into-being of a minimal state. Can he do this? Let's take Nozick's argument in the order in which he presents it.

In a state of libertarian nature, everyone has the right to resist and punish aggression. Of course, not everyone is in a position physically so to do nor, even if such were physically possible, would it necessarily fit with the principle of comparative advantage and the division of labour for each man to be his own defender and avenger. So, just as with many services that we require, it is more than likely that some people will offer their services to others to provide protection and vindication, and thus protective agencies will emerge, much as in the last several hundred years, the desire to protect oneself against the costs of catastrophic disasters has led to a system of pooling of risks that has resulted in the emergence of insurance firms. Any individual may exercise the right to defend and vindicate himself if he so chooses but, practically speaking, it makes economic sense for the non-specialist to pay others to provide such services for him. In the normal course of events, then, a plurality of protective agencies will arise, each offering a range of services at a range of prices and which protective agency (if any) one selects to protect one will depend upon normal commercial and personal considerations.

Where an aggressor and the one aggressed against both belong or subscribe to the same protective agency, then any dispute is resolvable internally; but what will happen if the aggressor and the one aggressed against belong or subscribe to different agencies? It is possible that the matter might be resolved by violence but, given the high transaction costs of violence, both to the agencies involved and eventually to their clients, it's highly unlikely that agencies would voluntarily choose to take this path. It is much more likely that an inter-agency dispute will be referred to a third party for resolution. Nozick contends that such appeals to a third party will lead inevitably to the emergence of a unified federal judicial system of which all the protective agencies are mere components.

At this point, Nozick's argument runs into trouble. 'The fact,' writes Rothbard, 'that every protective agency will have agreements with every other to submit disputes to particular appeals courts or arbitrators does *not* imply "one unified federal judicial system".' [Rothbard 2002, 234] Nozick's argument commits a basic logical fallacy. Just as from every wife's having a husband it does not follow that there is some one particular man who is husband to every woman; so too, if every intra-agency dispute is referred to a third part arbitrator, it does not follow that there has to be some one specific third party arbitrator to which every dispute is referred. Even in our present non-libertarian society, there are thousands of non-state arbitrators making a living by resolving disputes. Indeed, so clogged is the state courts' system that many corporations include a private arbitration clause in their contracts in an effort to avoid inevitable delays and to achieve decisions that are competent and minimally predictable.

Nozick believes that there's something special about the provision of protection services that militates against the emergence and continuing existence of different agencies: '[U]nlike other goods that are comparatively evaluated, maximal competing protective services cannot coexist; the nature of the service brings different agencies not only into competition for customer's patronage, but also into violent conflict with each other.'[27] Nevertheless, the evidence of history and contemporary experience shows Nozick's thesis of the inevitability of the emergence of a dominant protective agency to be indefensible. In Europe for many hundreds of years, multiple overlapping and competing legal jurisdictions competed and cooperated, most having no connection with the state's coercive apparatus,[28] and even today, the existence of thousands of arbitrators, lawyers, private protection agencies and insurance companies testifies to the viability of having multiple agents and agencies competing to provide insurance, arbitration and protection services. If a natural monopoly were to emerge anywhere, it should surely emerge in the area of insurance, but in fact, there's a significant amount of competition between rival insurance companies and no indication that a super-insurance agency either has or must inevitably emerge. In fact, if anything, there is every market incentive for different agencies *not* to compete aggressively with one another and to work out in advance of any disputes how those would be resolved. There's no more a necessary momentum towards one super-agency than there is towards any natural monopoly. The same rules apply here. If the super-agency that arose through natural monopoly supplies its services well and at a reasonable rate, competitors are kept out by market forces. If the super-agency starts to provide a poor service or to increase its charges significantly then competitors will enter the field and, unless driven from it by force by, let us say, a proto-state, they will provide the necessary competition to keep the quality of services up and prices down. There is, then, no antecedent reason to think that in some special way, the provision of defence and justice is, unlike everything else, a natural monopoly. So, Nozick's argument falls at the first fence. Although it's always *possible* that a dominant protective agency could *in fact* emerge, there is no inevitability about such an event's occurring and, as we have seen, given normal competitive pressure, every likelihood that it won't in fact occur. For the sake of argument, however, let us grant Nozick his first step and move on to a consideration of the second. How does one get from a dominant protective agency to an ultraminimal state? The story here is that the dominant protective agency, observing that remaining small-time operators engage in risky procedures against its clients, would have the right to prohibit such procedures and, in so doing, it would take on the mantle of a state, even if only an ultraminimal state, whose remit extended solely to security issues.[29] Although it's easy to see why an agency might have at least an interest and possibly some rights in respect of the activities of other agencies that bear upon its clients, we might well wonder why the dominant protective agency should have any particular rights where the alleged risky behaviour of the small-time operators does not involve *its* clients. Still more to the point, we might ask why, in cases of inter-agency conflict, the dominant agency should have the right (as distinct from the power) to prohibit the risky procedures of the small-timers *and not vice versa*? After all, if there are risks involved in having multiple agencies (and there would appear to be such risks), what of the risks involved in having a single agency with no competitors?

It is at this point that the notorious chapter 'Prohibition, Compensation, and Risk' of *Anarchy, State, and Utopia* comes into play. In this chapter, Nozick, for no immediately obvious reason, significantly weakens his conception of rights. Rights were to be originally thought of as *absolute* barriers against the actions of others—'there are things no person or group may do to them (without violating their rights)'; now, however, it turns out, that even if Tom has a right against Dick that Dick not interfere with his pizza eating, none the less Dick *may* so interfere provided he is willing to compensate Tom for this interference in some way. Tom's right is no longer absolute. This surprising turn of events pivots on yet another distinction, one between *property* rules (which are absolute) and *liability* rules (which are not). Property rules are non-compensable; liability rules are. Eric Mack remarks that 'the view that rights in themselves are claims protected by liability rules does not comport well with the overall tone of *Anarchy, State, and Utopia*. Nozick does not begin this work by declaring that there are things that may not be done to individuals *unless, of course, they are duly compensated*.'[30] It's hard to disagree with Mack's assessment here except, perhaps, to suggest that it is somewhat understated.

The reason for what Mack calls the 'surprising' attenuation of Nozick's conception of rights becomes obvious in the remainder of Part I. On the basis of original strong conception of rights enunciated boldly at the start of *Anarchy, State, and Utopia*, Nozick wasn't going to be able to get to his minimal state so the conception of rights simply had to be modified. Now, if this surprising or, as I would prefer to call it, this do-it-yourself modification of rights is rejected, Nozick's project of justifying the minimal state is stopped dead in its tracks, regardless of any other deficiencies in his argument.[31] But perhaps Nozick can overcome this objection and push on to his conclusion.

The suggestion that those agencies whose activities are prohibited should be satisfied to be compensated by the dominant protective agency is untenable. What form will the compensation take? What amount of compensation will be offered? Who will be the judge of its adequacy? What if no amount of compensation is acceptable? Why should the ultraminimal state not simply do whatever it likes, to whomever it likes, in whatever way it likes, paying whatever kind and amount of compensation it likes, if any? The only defensible answer to this question has to rest on the assertion of the basic libertarian principle of zero-aggression. 'No one has the *right* to coerce anyone not himself directly engaged in an *overt* act of aggression against rights.' [Rothbard 2002, 239] Once it is conceded that an agency has to right to use violence to prohibit risky behaviour by other agencies, there's no principled stopping place that can prevent the extension of this concession, and the ultraminimal state rather quickly becomes the minimal state.

Nozick's second step, going from the dominant protective agency to the ultraminimal state, is similarly unjustified but, for the sake of argument, let us leave our objections to this step to one side and consider Nozick's third step, that which takes us from the ultraminimal state to the minimal state. Nozick's argument here is that the ultraminimal state is obliged to compensate the potential customers of the small-time agencies whose risky activities it has had to restrict, by providing them with protective services and, in so doing, *de facto*, the minimal state emerges. Once again, the principled point concerning the insufficiency of compensation as a legitimation of criminal action is irrefutable. A willingness to make compensation is not, and never can be, a justification of criminal action; it can be, at best, an attempt to remediate the criminal action by restoring the situation that existed before the crime was committed. My burglary of your house can't be justified by my subsequent willingness to compensate you for your loss, particularly if I am to be the one who determines the method and quantity of compensation. '[C]ompensation, in the theory of punishment, is simply a method of trying to recompense the victim of crime; it must in no sense be considered a moral sanction for the crime itself.' [Rothbard 2002, 241]

Nozick himself would appear to have had some misgivings, remarking that 'a system permitting boundary crossing, provided compensation is paid, embodies the use of persons as means: knowing that they are being so used, and that their plans and expectations are liable to being thwarted arbitrarily, is a cost to people; some injuries may not be compensable; and for those that are compensable, how can an agent know that the actual compensation payment won't be beyond his means.' [Nozick 1974, 71] But the key problem isn't only whether or not a given rights-transgressor may not be able to afford compensation; it is, rather, whether or not compensation is *antecedently* acceptable to the one whose rights are transgressed. All this talk of compensation rests on the illegitimate assumption of commensurable utility scales but, if Austrian economics has shown anything to be beyond question, it's the ultimately subjective nature of people's value scales. "[T]he existence of only *one* fervent anarchist who *could not* be compensated for the psychic trauma inflicted on him by the emergence of the State is enough by itself to scuttle Nozick's allegedly non-invasive model for the original of the minimal state. For that absolutist anarchist, no amount of compensation would suffice to assuage his grief." [Rothbard 2002, 242-243]

Rothbard adopts Roy Childs' brilliant 'Nozick-in-reverse argument' in which Childs demonstrates that if we were to start with the minimal state, the invisible hand would lead us inexorably to the ultra-minimal state; the same process would take us from the ultra-minimal state to the dominant protective agency and thence to a plurality of agencies, no one of which is necessarily dominant.[32] Let us start with the assumption that we have a minimal state. Now let another agency which mirrors the procedures of the minimal state come into being. By hypothesis, the activities of this new agency can't be any riskier than those of the minimal state. The new agency can charge less for its services since the minimal state, as distinct from the ultraminimal state, has to pay compensation to those who would have used agencies with risky procedures. Since these compensation payments aren't legally mandatory, the minimal state, now under pressure from its competitor, is more likely than not to cease making them. In doing so, it ceases to be a minimal state and becomes an ultra-minimal state. Those who were in receipt of compensation can now choose to patronise the new agency. If the price differential disappears, as is likely to happen if the formerly minimal state ceases having to provide the payment of compensation, the new agency will have to differentiate itself from the (now) ultraminimal state by other means, such as the provision of better or different services. But there's nothing magical about the number two. If there can be two such agencies, there can be a third, and if a third, then a fourth. The ultraminimal state is now simply the dominant agency among a plurality of agencies. Since, however, there is no economic imperative unsupported by coercion that guarantees any business its dominant position, there's every likelihood that the owners and operators of the once minimal state, then ultraminimal state, and now (for the moment) dominant agency will be unable to maintain its market dominance vis-à-vis the new, aggressive agencies and instead of being first among equals will simply become one among equals.[33] 'The sinister minimal state is reduced, by a series of morally permissible steps which violate the rights of no one, to merely one agency among many. In short, the invisible hand strikes back.' [Childs 1977, 32-33] Rothbard then summarises his argument against Nozick's argument:

(1) no existing State has been immaculately conceived, and therefore Nozick, on his own grounds, should advocate anarchism and then wait for his State to develop; (2) even if any State *had* been so conceived, individual rights are inalienable and therefore no existing State could be justified; (3) every step of Nozick's invisible hand process is invalid: the process is all too conscious and visible, and the risk and compensation principles are both fallacious and passports to unlimited despotism; (4) there is no warrant, even on Nozick's own grounds, for the dominant protective agency to outlaw procedures by independents that do not injure its own clients, and therefore it cannot arrive at an ultra-minimal state; (5) Nozick's theory of 'non-productive' exchanges is invalid, so that the prohibition of risky activities and hence the ultra-minimal state falls on that account alone; (6) contrary to Nozick, there are no 'procedural' rights,' and therefore no way to get from his theory of risk and non-productive exchange to the compulsory monopoly of the ultra-minimal state; (7) there is no warrant, even on Nozick's own grounds, for the minimal state to impose taxation; (8) there is no way, in Nozick's theory, to justify the voting or democratic procedures of any State; (9) Nozick's minimal state would, on his own grounds, justify a maximal State as well; and (10) the only 'invisible hand' process, on Nozick's own terms, would move society from his minimal State back to anarchism.' [Rothbard 2002, 252-53]

Nozick's admittedly ingenious attempt to justify the minimal state on libertarian principles fails. He can have a robust conception of rights, rights that guarantee that there are things that no one may do to another without violation, or he can have a minimalist state—he can't have both.

If part I of Nozick's *Anarchy, State and Utopia* has been the subject of legitimate criticism by libertarians, part III has perhaps suffered undue neglect. One point in that section is worthy of remark. Nozick firmly denies that a libertarian world will be a product of uniformity. 'The conclusion to draw is that there will not be one *kind* of community existing and one kind of life led in utopia. Utopia will consist of utopias, of many different and divergent communities in which people lead different kinds of lives under different institutions. Some kinds of communities will be more attractive to most that others; communities will wax and wane. People will leave some for others or spend their whole lives in one. Utopia is a framework for utopias, a place where people are at liberty to join together voluntarily to pursue and attempt to realize their own vision of the good life in the ideal community but where no one can impose his own utopian vision upon others.' [Nozick 1974, 311-312]

IV: MURRAY ROTHBARD

Wendy McElroy claims that Murray Rothbard (1926-1995) created the modern libertarian movement inasmuch as 'modern libertarianism is an identifiable structure of interconnected beliefs, and Rothbard was the first theorist to make those connections complete.'[34] In her view, Rothbard was a system builder who put together in a unique fashion elements that did not necessarily originate with him. The elements which she believes Rothbard integrated into a coherent whole include a 'basic Aristotelian or Randian approach; the radical civil libertarianism of nineteenth century individualist-anarchists, especially Lysander Spooner and Benjamin Tucker; the free market philosophy of Austrian economists, in particular Ludwig von Mises, into which he incorporated sweeping economic histories; and, the foreign policy of the American Old Right – that is, isolationism' [McElroy 2000]. Joseph Stromberg concurs with McElroy's claim, making the point that whereas others had contributed various bits and pieces to the libertarian project, Rothbard attempted a grand synthesis of all that was worth preserving and carrying forward: 'Before Rothbard there had been classical liberals teetering on the edge of anarchism. There had been free-market anarchists. There had been Austrian School economists. There had been upholders of natural law and natural rights. There had been 'isolationists,' revisionist historians, and proponents of a critical sociology of the state. Murray Rothbard's goal was a grand synthesis of all these forms of knowledge. The result was a powerful vehicle of political understanding and the intellectual weaponry with which to begin the process of fundamental change.' [Rockwell 1995, 45] If Ayn Rand 'is the libertarian figure with the highest profile outside the movement, Rothbard is the major libertarian whom a typical American, layperson or academic, is least likely to know about.' [Doherty, 13]

From a European perspective, there's something quintessentially American about Rothbard—in the way he spoke, the way he wrote, in the issues he chose to focus on. David DeLeon, writing on the theme of anarchism in America notes that although the nineteenth-century American anarchist Lysander Spooner and others explicitly influenced Rothbard, the social development of the United States was such that most anarchists were the 'automatic product of the American environment.' [DeLeon 1978, 127] Of his American anarchist predecessors, Rothbard himself wrote: 'Lysander Spooner and Benjamin R. Tucker were unsurpassed as political philosophers and…nothing is more needed today than a revival and development of the largely forgotten legacy they left to political philosophy.' [Rothbard 2000c, 205] Spooner and Tucker outlined 'the way in which all individuals could abandon the State and cooperate to their own vast mutual benefit in a society of free and voluntary exchanges and interrelations.'[35]

ROTHBARD ON ZERO-AGGRESSION

For Rothbard, 'The libertarian creed rests upon one central axiom: that no man or group of men may aggress against the person or property of anyone else,' aggression being defined as 'the initiation of the use or threat of physical violence against the person or property of anyone else.' [Rothbard 2006, 27] It is important to note that this isn't a pacifist's charter. What is ruled out by the nonaggression axiom is the *initiation* of violence or the threat of violence against another's person or property; it does *not* rule out the use of violence in the defence of one's person or property. One may, of course, decline to defend one's person or property by force but if so, that is one's own choice.

Although particular individuals have aggressed and still do aggress against other persons and property, Rothbard believes that, throughout history, 'there has been one central, dominant, and overriding aggressor upon all of these rights: the State.' [Rothbard 2006, 28] What is special and significant about Rothbard's treatment of the state and its agents is that he insists that the consistent libertarian should hold it accountable to the same moral norms as every other actor or agent: 'the libertarian refuses to give the State the moral sanction to commit actions that almost everyone agrees would be immoral, illegal, and criminal if committed by any person or group in society.' [Rothbard 2006, 28] Once it is conceded that the state and its agents must be subject to the same moral law as everyone else, many political problems simply disappear. Murder is murder, whether committed by an individual or by the state through its agents; theft is theft, whether committed by an individual or by the state through its agents. The transparently obscurantist device of calling these ethical violations by other names succeeds only so long as people are willing to believe that taxation isn't really theft and wars of aggression do not really involve murder. It is testimony to the power of long usage and propaganda that so many people do so believe. [see Doherty, 266-270]

ROTHBARD ON HUMAN NATURE

Rothbard writes that man's nature is such that 'each individual person must, in order to act, choose his own ends and employ his own means to attain them. Possessing no automatic instincts, each man must learn about himself and the world, use his mind to select values, learn about cause and effect, and act purposively to maintain himself and advance his life. Since men can think, feel, evaluate, and act only as individuals, it becomes vitally necessary for each man's survival and prosperity that he be free to learn, choose, develop his faculties, and act upon his knowledge and values. This is the necessary path of human nature; to interfere with and cripple this process by using violence goes profoundly against what is necessary by man's nature for his life and prosperity. Violent interference with a man's learning and choices is therefore profoundly 'antihuman'; it violates the natural law of man's needs.' [Rothbard 2006, 33]

In *The Ethics of Liberty*, Rothbard provides a fuller account of the concept of natural law than the one he presents in *For a New Liberty*. In contradistinction to his mentor Mises, Rothbard held that not only means but also ends were amenable to rational evaluation. 'In natural-law philosophy, then, reason is not bound...to be a mere slave to the passions, confined to cranking out the discovery of the means to arbitrarily chosen ends. For the ends themselves are selected by the use of reason...'[36] Natural law allows Rothbard to go beyond the limitations of praxeology (praxeology being the study of those aspects of human action that can be grasped *a priori*, the study concerned with the conceptual analysis and logical implications of preference, choice, means-end schemes, and so forth.) For Rothbard, 'natural law provides man with a "science of happiness," with the paths which will lead to his real happiness.' [Rothbard 2002, 12]

The sceptic might raise the question about why any particular end, such as life or the quality of life, has to be the object of human choice. Rothbard addresses this objection in *The Ethics of Liberty* using an argument not unlike that which would be later used by Hans-Hermann Hoppe: '[A] proposition rises to the status of an *axiom* when he who denies it may be shown to be using it in the very course of the supposed refutation. Now, *any* person participating in any sort of discussion, including one on values, is, by virtue of so participating, alive and affirming life. For if he were *really* opposed to life, he would have no business in such a discussion, indeed he would have no business continuing to be alive. Hence, the supposed opponent of life is really affirming it in the very process of his discussion, and hence the preservation and furtherance of one's life takes on the stature of an incontestable axiom.' [Rothbard 2002, 32-33]

One further very important task which natural law allows Rothbard to perform is to distinguish very clearly between that law which is discoverable by the use of reason, on the one hand, and either custom or the arbitrary will of legislators, on the other. One might be tempted to think that a natural law approach is necessarily one that is conservative in its orientation but nothing could be further from the truth. Customs, habits, traditions, statutes—all these are brought to the bar of reason to be judged and, if found wanting, to be rejected. '[T]he fact that natural-law theorists derive from the very nature of man a fixed structure of law independent of time and place, or of habit or authority or group norms, makes that law a mighty force for radical change.' [Rothbard 2002, 20]

It is important to be clear that it isn't Rothbard's intention in either *For a New Liberty* or *The Ethics of Liberty* to provide a complete or comprehensive ethical system. He intends only to set out the essence of a political philosophy of liberty based on a very sharply focussed concept of justice. That a man should be *free* to perform act X and that no one may justly prevent him by force from so doing does *not* settle the question of whether, within the scope of a larger and more comprehensive ethics, it is *right* for him so to do. Followers of classical eudaimonistic ethics who accept the traditional idea that the virtues are co-implicative might worry that Rothbard's notion of justice, being so sharply separated from the other virtues, can't be fully rounded. To this, the response must be that although the concept of justice deployed by Rothbard isn't fully rounded, it is not intended to be fully rounded, merely basic. Nevertheless, it is in no way antagonistic to or subversive of a complete ethical system; rather it is fully compatible with any complete ethical system whose principles or applications do not violate the essence of liberty.[37]

LIBERTY AND POWER

The tension between liberty and power is the dynamic upon which almost all of Rothbard's work turns. The market, the network of free uncoerced exchanges, is the locus of liberty; the primary locus of power is the state. *Power and Market*, which was published in 1970, was originally intended by Rothbard to form part of *Man, Economy and State*–indeed, chapter 12 of *Man, Economy, and State* is a truncated form of *Power and Market*). The two works are now published together as was originally intended. [Rothbard 2004] Here, I want to focus on those parts of *Power and Market* that could be seen as providing a bridge between the purely economic aspects of Rothbard's thought and the more specifically political. David Gordon is right to emphasise that '*Power and Market* does not contain Rothbard's ethical system; it is a work of praxeology and is thus value free.' [Gordon 2007, 23] None the less, the topics that Rothbard broaches here are germane to the system of political ethics he developed in his later works.

In *Power and Market*, Rothbard applies the results of his economic work primarily though not exclusively to the realm of power, namely the state, examining particularly its modes of intervention in the market. Rothbard provides a typology of intervention that, as far as I can tell, is both original and novel. Intervention is the violent intrusion by an agent into free social or market relations. Intervention can be autistic, binary or triangular. (For Rothbard, 'autism' was a technical economic term, not to be confused with its use in medicine and psychiatry.) In autistic intervention, the intervener (I) either interferes with the person of (S), an individual subject, or commands (S) to perform or to refrain from performing action (A), where that action or interference bears on (S)'s person or property alone. In binary intervention, the intervener (I) forces (S) to exchange with (I) or elicits a 'gift' from (S). In triangular intervention, the intervener (I) compels or prohibits exchanges between pairs of subjects (S1) and (S2). [Rothbard 1962, 1058] All three forms of intervention are hegemonic, that is to say, they belong in the arena of command and obedience, in contrast to the voluntary contractual relationships characteristic of the market. Human relations can be (i) one-one, (ii) one-many, (iii) many-one or (iv) many-many. Following the principle of methodological individualism, cases (ii), (iii) and (iv) ultimately reduce to (i). The market, however complex it may be, is analytically reducible to a complex of two-party exchanges. Human relations are either hegemonic (vertical), based upon command and obedience, or free (horizontal) and based upon agreement or contract. Where the relationship is hegemonic, as we have seen, there are only three basic possibilities

Rothbard instances murder and assault as examples of autistic intervention. These would be examples of S's having to suffer radical interference with his person. Other instances of interference with S's actions would include forcing him to speak or not to speak, to observe a particular religious practice or to refrain from so doing. Instances of binary intervention aren't hard to come by—taxes, conscription, compulsory jury service and, Rothbard adds provocatively, highway robbery. Price controls, minimum wage laws, conservation laws, patents, anti-trust laws, licences and tariffs are all examples of triangular intervention. Those on the left side of the political spectrum tend to object to autistic intervention and are libertarian in this area, while usually being in favour of triangular intervention. Those on the right side of the political spectrum, in contrast, tend to object to triangular intervention and so are libertarian in this dimension, while being neutral or actively supporting autistic intervention, particularly in regard to the enforcement of public morals. Both sides take binary intervention to be unproblematic. The consistent libertarian, however, objects to all three kinds of intervention.

The final chapter of *Power and Market* provides a tabular representation of the implications of holding either to a market principle or to a hegemonic principle in one's political society, which I present here in a slightly adapted form [Rothbard 1962, 1365]:

	Market Principle	Hegemonic Principle
Freedom	Individual Freedom	Coercion
Utility	General mutual benefit—maximized social harmony	Exploitation—benefit of one group at the expense of another
Conflict/Harmony	Mutual Harmony	Caste conflict
Violence	Peace	War
Power	Power of man over nature—most efficient satisfaction of consumer wants	Power of man over man—disruption of want satisfaction

THE STATE AND SOCIETY

Given one's ownership of one's self and one's ownership of those things that one has properly appropriated, there may well be times when another person will attempt to interfere with one's use of one's property. The world isn't now, never has been, and never will be, a utopia and there will always be those who prefer to live parasitically and criminally upon the efforts of others. To the extent that such people succeed in their efforts, to that extent is one's liberty abridged. For really impressive interference with liberty, however, we must go not to your average criminal, but to an institution that takes aggression to a completely new level. '[L]ibertarians regard the State as the supreme, the eternal, the best organized aggressor against the persons and property of the mass of the public. *All* States, everywhere...' [Rothbard 2006, 56]

Rothbard's definition of the state is two-fold. The state is that organisation that (i) 'acquires its revenue by physical coercion' and (ii) 'achieves compulsory monopoly of force and ultimate decision-making power over a given territorial area.' [Rothbard 2002, 172] In both these aspects, the state interferes with the property and liberty of the individual. Through taxation, the state aggresses against the property of the individual, and through the variety of compulsory monopolies it enjoys, the state aggresses against the free exchange of goods and services in the area of which it claims control. 'If, then, taxation is compulsory, and is therefore indistinguishable from theft, it follows that the State, which subsists on taxation, is a vast criminal organization, far more formidable and successful than any 'private' Mafia in history. Furthermore, it should be considered criminal not only according to the theory of crime and property rights as set forth in this book, but *even* according to the common apprehension of mankind, which always considers theft to be a crime.' [Rothbard 2002, 166]

Human beings organise themselves in multifarious ways either for their mutual betterment or for the criminal exploitation by one group of another. The state, on one level, is just another organisation. The state differs from all other non-criminal organisations, however, inasmuch as it receives its income by coercion and violence or the threat of coercion or violence. [Rothbard 2002, 162] Not content to extract money with menaces from those it holds captive, the state also takes it upon itself to interfere, often radically, in the lives of those whom it is pleased to regard, with proprietorial pride, as *its* citizens. The state is also the quintessential monopoly and the services it provides, such as they are, are provided inefficiently and expensively. The monopoly power of the modern state extends widely and with various degrees of incompetence 'over police and military services, the provision of law, judicial decision-making, the mint and the power to create money, unused land...streets and highways, rivers and coastal waters, and the means of delivering mail.' [Rothbard 2002, 162]

Some thinkers attempt to justify the state by claiming that the state *is* us or, less radically, that the state *represents* us, and so what may appear to be an interference with liberty is simply an appearance. Manifestly, the state is *not* us (the common experience of oppression testifies to this) nor, somewhat less obviously, can it be said to represent us in any significant sense. [See Rothbard 2002, 164-166]

The conflation of state and society is a fruitful source of confusion. Of course, human beings aren't isolated individuals; of course we live in and can flourish only in society where 'society' denotes the sum of the complex, overlapping system of voluntary and status relationships between individuals. But it's a gross mistake to conclude from this that because we need society that therefore we need the state. 'The great *non sequitur* committed by defenders of the State, including classical Aristotelian and Thomist philosophers, is to leap from the necessity of *society* to the necessity of the *State*.' [Rothbard 2002, 187] Not only is the state not equivalent to society, it isn't, properly, even part of society, unless we are prepared to recognise criminal gangs as part of society as well. '[T]he State is an inherently illegitimate institution of organized aggression, of organized and regularized crime against the persons and property of its subjects. Rather than necessary to society, it is a profoundly antisocial institution which lives parasitically off the productive activities of its subjects.' [Rothbard 2002, 187]

There may be those who think that Wendy McElroy overstated her case in claiming that Rothbard created the modern libertarian movement. Looking at the evidence objectively, however, one has to admit that even though many of the ingredients of contemporary libertarianism were originated and developed by his predecessors—the anarchism of Benjamin Tucker and Lysander Spooner, the economics of Ludwig von Mises and other Austrians, the anti-war sentiments of the Old Right—Rothbard brought all these elements together in a new and potent theoretical and practical synthesis which, powered by his rhetorical and dialectical skills, created a new platform on which subsequent defenders of liberty could stand.

V: John Rawls

It is generally agreed among philosophers that Alasdair MacIntyre more or less single-handedly revived the study of substantive ethics in the anglophone world with the publication of his *After Virtue* (1981), followed by *Whose Justice, Which Rationality* and *Three Rival Version of Moral Inquiry*. Much the same could be said of the contribution of John Rawls (1921-2002) to the study of political philosophy in the anglophone world. His 1971 work, *A Theory of Justice*, is generally agreed to have been *the* seminal work in political philosophy in the second part of the twentieth century and to have reignited the fading embers of political philosophy as an academic discipline. It may also have the dubious distinction of being the only work in political philosophy to have given birth to a musical, called (what else?), '*A Theory of Justice: The Musical!*,' which features John Rawls as the good guy (of course!) and Robert Nozick and Ayn Rand as the bad guys (no surprise there either) with Hobbes, Locke, Rousseau, Mill, Bentham, Sidgwick, Wollstonecraft and Marx playing supporting roles.

A Theory of Justice ignited a veritable firestorm of responses, criticisms, arguments and counter-arguments so that its secondary literature is voluminous. Rawls's work has since been criticised and commented on by almost every political philosopher of distinction. Nozick wrote *Anarchy, State and Utopia* at least partly in response to *A Theory of Justice*. Michael Walzer and Michael Sandel wrote critiques of *A Theory of Justice* from a communitarian perspective. Marxists, feminists and a whole bunch of other 'ists' have all criticised Rawls's book for a variety of reasons. For a book to produce commentary and criticism on an industrial scale must surely constitute evidence of its greatness. Well, perhaps—or perhaps not. Ayn Rand wrote, presciently, in 1973, just two years after the book's publication that, 'within a few years of the book's publication, commentators will begin to fill libraries with works analysing, "clarifying" and interpreting its mysteries. Their notions will spread all over the academic map, ranging from the appeasers, who will try to soften the book's meaning—to the glamorizers, who will ascribe to it nothing worse than their own pet inanities—to the compromisers, who will try to reconcile its theory with its exact opposite—to the *avant garde*, who will spell out and demand the acceptance of its logical consequences. The contradictory, antithetical nature of such interpretations will be ascribed to the book's profundity—particularly by those who function on the motto: "If I don't understand it, it's deep."…. Within a generation, the number of commentaries will have grown to such proportions that the original book will be accepted as a subject of philosophical specialization, requiring a lifetime of study—and any refutation of the book's theory will be ignored or rejected, if unaccompanied by a full discussion of the theories of all the commentators, a task which no one will be able to undertake.'[38] Yes. Quite.

Rawls produced a slightly different version of the book in 1975 and then a more substantially revised version in 1999. Rawls's significantly slimmer book, *The Law of Peoples*, which concerns itself with issues of global justice, was also published in 1999. Before that, *Political Liberalism* had been published in 1993. This work addresses the problem of how people who have significantly different substantive philosophical and religious commitments could converge on a liberal democratic regime. In 2001, *Justice as Fairness: A Restatement* appeared which was intended to re-present the central arguments of *A Theory of Justice*. An edition of Rawls's lectures on the history of political philosophy was brought out posthumously in 2007 under the revealing title, *Lectures on the History of Political Philosophy*.

A THEORY OF JUSTICE

A Theory of Justice could perhaps be described as an attempt to reconcile the first two legs of the French Revolution's motto: Liberty, Equality and Fraternity—whether the exclusion of Fraternity from the discussion is illiberal or inegalitarian is a matter Fraternity will have to take up with Rawls. The first characteristic of *A Theory of Justice* that will be noticeable to any reader of this classic work (and, like many classics one wonders how many people have in fact read it) is that it is long—almost 600 pages. Its second characteristic is its restrained New Englandish prose style that, even by normal academic standards, makes it both worthy and excruciatingly dull. It isn't, at least not on the surface, an exciting book, but do not be misled by appearances—it isn't exciting under the surface either. No one has ever been or will ever be induced to rush to man the barricades for the cause of justice on reading this book. An early reviewer wrote, '*A Theory of Justice* is a book which risks the fate of being much discussed but little read. Its high level of abstraction and its self-conscious circularity of argument will frustrate and at times infuriate even those who are deeply concerned with its themes.' [Grey 1973, 327] Ayn Rand asked, somewhat more trenchantly, 'Is *A Theory of Justice* likely to be widely read? No. Is it likely to be influential? Yes—precisely for that reason.'[39]

Rawls's theory of justice is, essentially, a new-look social contractarianism. The standard model of all contract theories involves people getting together to agree on how they will conduct their affairs in common. Rawls's contract theory has just such a get-together but his one, which is called the original position, has some unusual features.[40] The most prominent aspect of the original position is that in it, decisions are to be made behind what Rawls calls the veil of ignorance. The simple yet ingenious idea of the veil of ignorance is that if, prior to agreement, we were to know our strengths and weaknesses, our characters and our particular views of what is good for man, we would necessarily be influenced by such considerations in arriving at an agreement with others who might well have quite different natural endowments and significantly different views of the good. Behind the veil of ignorance, however, 'no one knows his place in society, his class position or social status: nor does he know his fortune in the distribution of natural assets and abilities, his intelligence and strength, and the like. Nor, again, does anyone know his conception of the good, the particulars of his rational plan of life, or even the special features of his psychology such as his aversion to risk or liability to optimism or pessimism.' Rawls assumes that 'the parties do not know the particular circumstances of their own society. That is, they do not know its economic or political situation, or the level of civilization and culture it has been able to achieve. The persons in the original position have no information as to which generation they belong.' [Rawls 1999, 118] Does anything survive this particularly severe case of collective amnesia? Yes, some bits and pieces. The veiled amnesiacs know the general facts about society; they understand politics and economics and psychology. Conveniently, they know just whatever it is that they need to know that would affect their choice of the principles of justice. [see Rawls 1999, 119]

There is a delightful air of arbitrariness, not to say unreality, about all this, which should tickle the funny bones of aficionados of science fiction. Behind the veil of ignorance we don't know anything about ourselves—our sex, our ages, our abilities, whether we are risk-averse or willing to live dangerously—but we *do* know all about politics, economics, and psychology; quite how this is possible is something of a mystery. Of all categories of people, academics probably come closest in reality to matching Rawls's ideal candidate for a place behind the veil. It is no criticism of Rawls's ideas, say their defenders, to point out their unreality. They aren't meant to be real—they are meant to sketch a kind of thought experiment. Thought experiments generally divide people into two groups—those who think their very extremity makes them a complete waste of time and those who think they can be useful in allowing us to test our intuitions in a hypothetical setting. I have no objection to thought experiments in principle but I think it might be granted that the further they move away from reality, the less is their ability to provide some traction to our intuitions. In any event, one might wonder just why we have the general capacities that Rawls allows and not others? Also, if the denizens of the original position do not know what their other attributes and abilities are and what their conception of the good is we might wonder how they are supposed to make their choices and evaluate their outcomes. Some such misgiving seems to have occurred even to Rawls. He writes, 'The notion of the veil of ignorance raises several difficulties. Some may object that the exclusion of nearly all particular information makes it difficult to grasp what is meant by the original position.' [Rawls 1999, 119] Exactly so. Were we to be denuded of the knowledge Rawls would denude us of in the Original Position, there's hardly a sense in which we would be persons at all; above all, there would seem to be no position from which an inhabitant of this shadowy region could make a reasonable choice.[41]

The images of the original position and the veil of ignorance are striking but they aren't Rawls's only interesting conceptual devices; there is also his notion of reflective equilibrium. The central idea here is that we have first order judgements about what justice consists in and second-order principles that may or may not justify them. Reflective equilibrium is meant to be the process (and the outcome of the process) by which we balance our first and second order judgements, giving absolute priority to neither. In trying to understand what a writer is up to, it's often useful to know what position he is arguing against. Reflective Equilibrium is directed against those who would give absolute priority to some moral principle or set of moral principles, as, for example, Nozick does in *Anarchy, State, and Utopia*.

So, behind the veil of ignorance, what principles of justice governing rights and duties and the distribution of goods would our socially and psychologically emaciated human beings choose? Since no one knows what position he is going to occupy after the agreement, Rawls believes that the rational choice for all inhabitants of the original position to make is to adopt a kind of maximin strategy, that is, to choose principles of justice that would in some way maximise the position of the least well off in the resultant society. Of course, this prioritises those who are risk-averse. What if people aren't risk-averse? There is nothing intrinsically irrational in gambling that one might be one of the better off and making one's choice accordingly. Rawls's seemingly neutral position in fact makes a substantive choice of character in prioritising the riskophobe over the riskophile.

Two Principles of Justice

Rawls produces two basic principles of justice, the first one dealing with liberty, and the second with equality. The principles are ordered so that the first takes priority over the second. The first principle of justice is that 'each person is to have an equal right to the most extensive scheme of equal basic liberties compatible with a similar scheme of liberties for others.'[42] What kinds of liberties does Rawls have in mind? Well, the liberty to vote and to stand for public office, freedom of speech, freedom of assembly, freedom of conscience, freedom from arbitrary arrest and the freedom to own personal property. Is anything excluded from Rawls's list? Yes. The freedom to own property that constitutes the means of production is *not* included in this list, nor is the freedom to contract in a *laissez-faire* manner. Rawls's list is patently non-neutral in a significant number of ways, in what is included and what is excluded, and in the conflation of freedom 'tos' with freedom 'froms' which already compromises the notion of liberty on offer here.

The second principle of justice, the one relating to equality, comes in two parts. Here are Rawls's *ipsissima verba*: 'Social and economic inequalities are to be arranged[43] so that they are both (a) to the greatest expected[44] benefit of the least advantaged and (b) attached to offices and positions open to all under conditions of fair equality of opportunity.' [Rawls 1999, 72] Part (a) is generally referred to as the Difference Principle and this, it is generally agreed, is the really significant principle of equality.[45] Rawls, then, is advocating a kind of egalitarianism but not a mechanically mathematical one. Inequalities may result from his principles of justice but not in such a way as to discriminate unfairly against the worst off in society.

Underlying Rawls's principles is a certain conception of desert that it's important to be clear about. Rawls believes that much of what comes to us is a matter of good fortune. Our families, our education, our circumstances generally—these are all matters of luck. We did nothing to deserve them. One might argue that whatever luck one might have had, still one has to do something with it, to develop one's skills and talents, or to work at one's education. This is where Rawls becomes more radical. Our capacities to work hard are themselves matters of luck. One's very character, one's dispositions, these too are matters of luck and the notion of desert has no application here. We shouldn't benefit from our talents because we have done nothing to deserve them.

At this point, we are approaching sheer nonsensicality. If everything is a matter of luck then luck ceases to have any intellectual traction. Luck, as a concept, has significance only if it can be contrasted with what isn't luck. I work for a day and receive $20—not luck; I walk down the street and pick up a $20 bill—luck. But if everything is luck, then the notion of desert goes out the window and *nobody* deserves anything any more or any less than any other person. David Gordon writes, 'if you don't deserve your talents or personality traits, what is left? Rawls has evacuated persons of their attributes, leaving virtually nothing behind. Further, suppose Rawls is right that people do not deserve their superior abilities—that is, they do not acquire these talents by superior moral merit. It does not follow that they aren't entitled to benefit from them. Why does the fact that you do not "deserve," in Rawls's sense, your superior talents imply that they ought to be transferred to society to be managed for the benefit of the least well off? Rawls, though ostensibly devoted to liberty, winds up with a system in which society controls virtually all the important human attributes.' [Gordon 2008]

Nozick was critical of this aspect of Rawls's thought also. He wrote, 'If nothing of moral significance could flow from what was arbitrary, then no particular person's existence could be of moral significance, since which of the many sperm cells succeeds in fertilizing the egg cell is (so far as we know) arbitrary from a moral point of view. This suggests another, more vague, remark directed to the spirit of Rawls' position rather than to its letter. Each existing person is a produce of a process wherein the one sperm cell which succeeds is no more deserving than the millions that fail. Should we wish that process had been "fairer" as judged by Rawls' standards, that all "inequities" in it had been rectified? We should be apprehensive about any principle that would condemn morally the very sort of process that brought us to be, a principle that therefore would undercut the legitimacy of our very existing.' [Nozick 1974, 226*] Of course, a sperm cell isn't something that can be the subject of moral evaluation. In the case in point, it isn't something that can be deserving or undeserving. What is absurd about Rawls's position is that it would require us to think of a person as a sort of bare particular, shorn of all that makes it human, which could then be judged to be deserving or not of the attachment of talents and dispositions. Just as it would be meaningless to make a sperm cell an object of moral evaluation, so too it's absurd to attempt to apply moral judgements to a human being denuded of all significant human attributes.

In enunciating his Difference Principle, Rawls is trying to steer a path between allowing for any distributional outcome consistent with the freedom to own, produce and contract, on the one hand [Liberty], and, on the other hand, requiring a strictly equal division of all production among the members of a society [Equality]. He wants to have his cake and eat it too; but the Difference Principle is unstable and collapses either on the side of liberty or on the side of equality.[46] Given that all human capacities and talents are matters of moral luck, there is to be a bottom-line equality in the distribution of wealth created by a community. Once a bottom-line equality is achieved, however, inequalities are permitted. This is how Thomas Grey puts the argument: 'How can I justly bargain for more than an equal share by threatening to withhold my scarce talents? It must be because I have some special claim on these talents and their fruits. But if they are considered a social asset—as Rawls apparently regards them—I can have no such special claim. On the other hand, if my talents and the fruits of the use I choose to make of them belong to me, then there can be no justified coercion of me if I do not choose to share them with others. The inequalities that Rawls would permit suggest some acquiescence in this view. But those who press this view to its limits will reject the notion that greater equality of income is a legitimate aim of public policy. The persistence of such views, especially among the strong and productive, would introduce a fatal instability into a society nominally committed to Rawls' difference principle.' [Grey 1973, 325]

RAND'S CRITIQUE OF RAWLS

Ayn Rand doesn't often direct detailed critical attention to the work of other contemporary thinkers. When she does, however, the combination of her intellectual penetration and literary dexterity can be devastating. Her critique of some of the core contentions of Rawls's *A Theory of Justice* is priceless. Rawls accepts that it is a natural fact that some people are born in one way and some in other ways. This is just a brute fact of nature; it's neither just nor unjust, the notion of justice having no application at this point. Nevertheless, Rawls thinks that whatever the initial distribution of gifts and talents and abilities may be, they are to be put to use for the benefit of all, especially the least advantaged. How does this follow from the naturally unequal distribution of capacities and talents? Rand remarks, 'If a natural fact is neither just nor unjust, by what mental leap does it become a *moral* problem and an issue of *justice*?'[47] Rand's attack on the whole idea of a lottery of individual gifts and talents is masterly. She describes it as a kind of fairy tale, 'the notion that man, before birth, is some sort of indeterminate thing, an entity without identity, something like a shapeless chunk of human clay, and that fairy godmothers proceed to grant or deny him various attributes ("favors"): intelligence, talent, beauty, rich parents, etc. These attributes are handed out "arbitrarily" (this word is preposterously inapplicable to the processes of nature), it is a "lottery" among pre-embryonic non-entities, and—supposedly adult mentalities conclude—since a winner could not possibly have 'deserved" his "good fortune,' a man does not deserve or earn anything after birth, as a human being, because he acts by means of "undeserved," "unmerited," "unearned" attributes. Implication: to earn something means to choose and earn your personal attributes *before* you exist.'[48] In connection with Rawls's thought experiment of the veil of ignorance and the choice of principles to be made from behind it (see the discussion below), Rand says, 'I submit that it is impossible for men to make any choice on the basis of ignorance, i.e. using ignorance as a criterion: if men do not know their own identities, they will not be able to grasp such things as "principle to live by," "alternative" or what is a good, bad or worst "possible outcome."'[49]

With Rawls clearly in mind, Rand has this to say about obscurity in writing: 'if you want to propagate an outrageously evil idea…your conclusion must be brazenly clear, but your proof unintelligible. Your proof must be so tangled a mess that it will paralyze a reader's critical faculty—a mess of evasions, equivocations, obfuscations, circumlocutions, non sequiturs, endless sentences leading nowhere, irrelevant side issues, clauses, sub-clauses and sub-sub-clauses, a meticulously lengthy proving of the obvious, and big chunks of the arbitrary thrown in as self-evident, erudite references to sciences, to pseudo-sciences, to the never-to-be-sciences, to the untraceable and the improvable—all of it resting on a zero: the *absence* of definitions.'[50] F. C. S. Schiller is of a similarly cynical if somewhat more charitable opinion, writing, 'The obscurity of many philosophers is notorious and indisputable; but it may be explained as a defence-reaction. They write obscurely in order to be respected by academic colleagues who dare not criticize what they are not sure they have understood, and in order not to be found out.'[51] [Schiller, 14]

ACCOMMODATING DIFFERENT CONCEPTIONS OF THE GOOD

It is hardly a secret that different people can have quite different religious moral and political commitments. In the past, this situation has led to much violence and suffering as one group has attempted to force its views upon others which, not surprisingly, resisted. In much of the world, such conflicts no longer lead to our killing each another (though there are parts of the world where this still happens), but the fundamental differences haven't gone away. The problem remains of how to construct a political order that can accommodate people with substantially different conceptions of the good—political, moral or religious.

In *Political Liberalism* (1993), Rawls's introduces the idea of what he calls, 'public reason'. Political reasoning can proceed only on the basis of reasons that are shared among all people and not on the basis of reasons that are peculiar to particular people or traditions. All well and good, but what if there are no such public reasons? What then? Public reasons seem to hinge upon such values as equality and fairness and freedom but, it might be argued, not everyone accepts these values as ultimate. Rawls attempts to evade this objection by arguing that although the justification of such values may differ from group to group, none the less, all groups can, despite their different justifications of them, adhere to these values. Public reasons, then, emerge as a kind of neutral area, which permits those with very different views to co-exist and co-habit.

Unfortunately, this 'public reasons' approach would appear to be question-begging. What Rawls is offering us is a no-perspective theory of perspectives or the idea that neutral values are nobody's values. At the bottom of this is a fundamental circularity. To those who have really strong conceptions of the good, Rawls's public reasons won't count for much. Public reasons are, in fact, just one substantive (if emaciated) position among others and not some neutral zone where all can meet.[52] The notion of public reasons (and also the notion of overlapping consensus) simply assumes that there is a common core on which adherents of diverse moral, social and political doctrines can agree. This depends on one very large presupposition—that each of these different positions has, as it were, a reasonable core (as distinct, presumably from the unreasonable outer belt) and that this reasonable core is the same for all. But why should a position have any reasonable core? And even if it did, why should it be the same for all? And who judges what is or what isn't reasonable? Once again, this is simply a way to gloss over the fact that all positions require justification and no position is specially privileged—there are no neutral positions. Public reason is a quasi-substantive moral notion masquerading behind a mask of neutrality. David Gordon comments, 'Rawls's idea of public reason has little to recommend it. Rawls has simply defined a notion of social stability to suit his theory. He never shows that something bad will happen if a society isn't "stable" in his sense. Why can't a society like our own, with considerable religious and philosophical disagreements, continue to flourish without the crutch of public reason? Unless one defines a society so that it must include common adherence to a political doctrine, it isn't clear why social order demands agreement. Would not coercive efforts to enforce such a political orthodoxy on people with strong religious beliefs be likely to reduce social stability rather than promote it?' [Gordon 2008]

THE LAW OF PEOPLES

In *The Law of Peoples*, a late work, Rawls turns his attention to international politics. He distinguishes between what he calls 'well-ordered people,' some of whom are liberal and others merely decent. International order requires us to tolerate decent people even though they may have state religions and deny people equality of opportunity on religious grounds. If a people is neither liberal nor decent—if it violates human rights or is aggressive— it is an outlaw and military intervention may be justified! Such peoples deserve neither respect nor toleration. None of this is revolutionary. In reality, it's just an attempt to rationalise a particular Western perspective on international politics. What is most interesting about *The Law of Peoples* is that Rawls rejects the claim that his Difference Principle should be applied globally. David Gordon makes the excellent point that Rawls's attempt to restrict the application of the Difference Principle within 'peoples' (that is, within nations, states) rather than between or among them, forces him to undermine his own position. Take the example of Butterflyland and Beehive, two countries that start out with more or less the same level of resources. The inhabitants of Beehive work hard while the feckless inhabitants of Butterflyland laze the summer away. In time, of course, Beehive is doing quite well but Butterflyland is running into trouble. Should some of Beehive's resources be taken to help out the inhabitants of Butterflyland? Rawls thinks not. (see *The Law of Peoples*, 117) Well, why not? Gordon quotes Rawls at this point, who says, 'Surely there is a point at which a people's basic needs (estimated in primary goods) are fulfilled and a people can stand on its own' and Gordon asks, acutely, 'Why does not an analogous point drastically limit the scope of the difference principle within a society?' [Gordon 2000]

It can't be denied that Rawls's work has dominated political philosophy for the last forty years, nor can it be denied that it is a gallant attempt to promote the marriage of freedom and equality. Still, for the reasons I have noted, this shotgun Rawlsian marriage is headed for divorce.

Notes

1 'Ah, what a dusty answer gets the soul/ When hot for certainties in this our life!' wrote the Victorian poet George Meredith, in his sonnet sequence *Modern Love*, sonnet 50.
2 Rand is conspicuous in being one of few female writers to espouse the cause of liberty. Two others made significant contributions, even if they didn't quite achieve her fame; Isabel Paterson (*The God of the Machine*) and Rose Wilder Lane (*The Discovery of Freedom*). [see Doherty, 113-147, 225-243, 542-546]
3 Rand's reflections on the nature and function of art, deepened by her experience as a scriptwriter and novelist, are particularly insightful. 'Art,' she writes, 'is not the "handmaiden" of morality, its *basic* purpose is not to educate, to reform or to advocate anything….The basic purpose of art is *not* to teach, but to *show*—to hold up to man a concretized image of his nature and his place in the universe.' [Rand, 1975a, 10-11] For Rand, 'Art is the concretization of metaphysics.' It particularises man's concepts and 'allows him to grasp them as if they were percepts.' [Rand 1975a, 8]
4 Flew, in Den Uyl and Rasmussen 1984, 187-188]
5 'Rand was not erudite; most of her education in contemporary philosophy came from things she was told by philosopher friends…' [Doherty, 540] Now that I come to think of it, Ludwig Wittgenstein wasn't particularly well-read in philosophy either.
6 See 'Man's Rights' in Rand 1964a, 108-117.
7 Rand 1963b, 125, 128; emphasis in original.
8 For some short but insightful critiques of Rand on government, see Coulam 1960, Dykes 1998, Dykes 2007 and Sloman 1993.
9 In *Atlas Shrugged*, Galt's Gulch appears to operate without any government. [see Rand 1957, 701-815 (Part III, chapters 1 & 2)]
10 On Rand's fraught relationship with libertarianism and libertarians, in particular with Murray Rothbard, see Doherty, 261-265.
11 'The Missing Link', in Rand 1984, 59.
12 'The Missing Link' in Rand 1984, 61.
13 Rand 1964c, 135. Auberon Herbert too thought of government as something that could be financed by means of voluntary contributions.
14 Rand 1964c, 135; see also Boaz, 163.
15 The importance of Hayek's work in economics was (eventually) recognised by the award of a Nobel Prize in 1974. In the late 1930s, Hayek struggled unavailingly against the spread of Keynesian ideas. He is said to have regretted that he didn't develop a systematic and exhaustive refutation of the economics contained in Keynes's *General Theory*. His reason for not doing so was that he expected Keynes to change his mind, something for which Keynes was noted. 'Much of Keynes's fascination for his contemporaries,' remarks Robert Lekachman, 'was his capacity

to advocate radically opposed ideas at different periods in his life....Keynes himself was the sort of restless, responsive intellectual who adjusts his theories to the changing shape of the outside world....If Keynes had survived into the 1960s, he would surely be busy inventing a new and better post-Keynesian doctrine...' [Lekachman, 4, 5; see Wapshott, passim] For an entertaining and instructive video on Keynes versus Hayek, see Papola and Roberts.

16 Thomas Sowell acknowledges his intellectual debt to Hayek in his superb and must-read *Knowledge and Decisions* [see Sowell 1996, xxii]. It is easy to see why. The first part of Sowell's book analyses 'some more or less enduring features of various social processes, and their implications for the coordination of fragmented individual knowledge.' [Sowell 1996, 163] The theme of the second part of Sowell's book is, in his own words, contained in the following two sentences: 'Even within democratic nations, the locus of decision making has drifted away from the individual, the family, and voluntary associations of various sorts, and toward government. And within government, it has moved away from elected officials subject to voter feedback, and toward more insulated governmental institutions, such as bureaucracies and the appointed judiciary.' [Sowell 1996, 164] Given his admiration for experts, the putative apostle of liberty, J. S. Mill, might have been happy with this drift of decision-making, but no genuine lover of liberty could possibly be content with it.

17 Hayek 2006, 11, emphasis added.

18 Hayek 2006, 11; 117.

19 Hayek adopts the usual Weberian definition of the state as 'the human community that (successfully) claims the monopoly of the legitimate use of physical force.' [Hayek 2006, 370; Weber, 78]

20 Hayek 1960, 117. See Barry 1979, 71.

21 Justice for Hayek is not so much a matter of giving to each his due but rather 'the application of equal abstract rules to everyone, irrespective of the particular content of those rules.' [Doherty, 221] This is a peculiar concept of justice, a concept more applicable perhaps to the notion of fairness, but it will explain to some extent why Hayek is able to countenance what to your average libertarian is coercion (taxation and conscription) as long as such were rule-based and applied equally to everyone. [see Doherty, 220]

22 For a contemporary, sophisticated account of natural law, see Barden & Murphy's *Law and Justice in Community*. They take natural law to be not an extrinsic imposition, something handed down from above as it were, but as something intrinsic to our moral experience, writing 'humans have always lived together: civil society is a social order and not a contract-based organization.... The intrinsic demand to act reasonably and responsibly gives rise to what we term the 'natural law', and that which is intrinsic to the social order is what we term the 'naturally just'.' [Barden & Murphy, 2010, 191]

23 It is difficult, for example, to see how Hayek would respond effectively from a libertarian perspective to the claim put forward by Liam Murphy and Thomas Nagel that 'Private property is a legal convention, defined in part by the tax system; therefore, the tax system cannot be evaluated by looking at its impact on private property, conceived as something that has independent existence and validity.' [Murphy & Nagel, 8; see Fried, 85-94; see also LeFevre, passim] Murphy & Nagel's argument is rehearsed by Richard Murphy in his *The Joy of Tax*.

24 Doherty, 224; see also 100-111, 217-224, 546-555.

25 Nozick's expanded treatment of this point involves him in direct conflict with John Rawls. Despite this, Nozick is typically gracious in his evaluation of Rawls's work. He describes *A Theory of Justice* as 'a powerful, deep, subtle, wide-ranging, systematic work in political and moral philosophy....a fountain of illuminating ideas.' [Nozick 1974, 183]

26 A distinction can be made between claim rights and liberty rights. A liberty right is simply the absence of an obligation—I have a liberty right to X if I have no obligation not to do X. So, for example, I have a liberty right to eat cold pizza on a Sunday morning if I have no obligation not to eat cold pizza on a Sunday morning. A claim right is an entitlement to have others act or refrain from acting in certain ways. In the case of my pizza eating propensities, my liberty right is matched by my claim right against others that they not interfere with its exercise. The *locus classicus* for a sophisticated typology of rights is Wesley Hohfeld's 1919 paper.

27 Nozick 1974, 17. Nozick's claim here is very similar to that made by Ayn Rand some ten years earlier. As I mentioned earlier, she surmises, suppose 'Mr. Smith, a customer of Government A, suspects that his next-door neighbor, Mr. Jones, a customer of government B, has robbed him; a squad of Police A proceeds to Mr. Jones house and is met at the door by a squad of Police B, who

declare that they do not accept the validity of Mr. Smith's complaint and do not recognize the authority of Government A. What happens then? You take it from there.' [Rand 1963b, 132]

28 See Berman 1983.

29 In the context of discussing Nozick's story about competing defence agencies and the rise of a dominant one, Doherty remarks that 'Nozick then summoned a new principle, one not usually included in the anarcho-libertarian vision of rights: the notion that even in a perfectly libertarian world it is appropriate to prohibit actions if they pose an undue risk to cause harm to others—even before the harm is actually done. However, if you enforce a prohibition on someone before any harm is committed, you owe him compensation.' [Doherty, 487]

30 Mack 2014; emphasis in original.

31 One such deficiency would be Nozick's tendency to think of a dominant protective *association* made up of different agencies (and so susceptible to internal competitive pressures) as if it were itself a single agency. 'Nozick faces a problem even if he succeeds in showing that the *confederation* of agencies that emerges from such networking may permissibly eliminate its non-outlaw competitors. For, there may still be too much competition *among the confederates* that make up the dominant association for it to qualify as a state.' [Mack 2015, 24; see also Childs 1977]

32 Rothbard 2002, 250-251; see Childs 1977, 32-33.

33 A process very like this took place in Ireland a few years ago when private companies were allowed to compete with local councils for the provision of refuse collection and disposal services. First one, then another private company entered the market. The local council had to lower its prices to stay in competition. No longer the monopolist provider of such services, it's now simply one among others.

34 McElroy 2000. Some of the material in this section first appeared in Casey, 2010 where a fuller account of Rothbard's life and work can be found. See also Doherty, 243-247, 265-270, and 558-568.

35 Rothbard 2000, 205-206; see Gordon 2007, 13.

36 Rothbard 2002, 7; see also, 206-214.

37 Despite the clarity of Rothbard's writing, it hasn't prevented him from being misunderstood. One commentator goes so far as to link Rothbard with Stirner, identifying both thinkers as aiming for a society of egoists as their social ideal. [see Rapp, 29]

38 Rand 'An Untitled Letter' in Rand 1984, 158-159.

39 Rand 'An Untitled Letter' (1973) in Rand 1984, 156.

40 It is tempting, but the temptation must be resisted, to think of Rawls's original position as a latter-day equivalent of the State of Nature beloved of earlier contractarian thinkers: Rawls writes, 'the original position is not to be thought of as a general assembly which includes at one moment everyone who will live at some time; or, much less, as an assembly of everyone who could live at some time. It is not a gathering of all actual or possible persons.' [Rawls 1999, 120]

41 Anthony O'Hear sees *A Theory of Justice* as a 're-fashioned Hobbesianism.' He remarks, 'the detail of Rawls' own theory is not what is relevant here. What is relevant is his conception of society as a contract between anonymous and mutually unknown individuals.' [O'Hear, 64, 65]

42 Rawls 1999, 53. The original formulation was slightly different. It read, 'each person is to have an equal liberty to the most extensive basic liberty compatible with a similar liberty for others.' [Rawls 1971, 60] What the significance of this change in wording is supposed to be is not entirely clear to me.

43 One wonders *who* is to do what is blandly described as 'arranging' and *how* this 'arranging' is to be done. It would be difficult to better Thomas Sowell's acerbic comments on this point. He remarks that 'the bland and innocuous word "arrange"' covers 'a pervasive exercise of power necessary to supersede innumerable individual decisions throughout the society by sufficient force or threat of force to make people stop doing what they want to do and do instead what some given principle imposes.' [Sowell 1996, 331]

44 The word 'expected' does not appear in the 1971 formulation. Once again, the precise difference the addition of this word is supposed to make is unclear to me.

45 See Rawls 1971, 302; rev. ed. 47.

46 An early reviewer, Thomas Grey, pointed out this serious problem with the Difference Principle. [Grey 1973] Grey's objection, along with much other relevant material, is discussed in Palmer 2007.

47 'An Untitled Letter' in Rand 1984, 148.

48 'An Untitled Letter' in Rand 1984, 149.

49 'An Untitled Letter' in Rand 1984, 151.

50 'An Untitled Letter' in Rand 1984, 157.

51 Schiller adds, later, that 'The academic pedant always thinks in his heart, and occasionally all but says, "What *I* can understand, I despise."' [Schiller, 102]

52 In *Political Liberalism*, Rawls modifies his account of the principles of justice. The principle of liberty now is expressed as a person's having a claim rather than a right to what is now described as 'a fully adequate scheme of equal basic rights and liberties' (before this, the phrase used was just 'a system of basic liberties').

Chapter 34

A VALEDICTION

If people have to choose between freedom and sandwiches
they will take sandwiches
—Lord Boyd-Orr

Liberty, as it is conceived by current opinion, has nothing inherent about it;
it is a sort of gift or trust bestowed on the individual by the state
pending good behaviour
—Mary McCarthy

Every normal man must be tempted, at times, to spit on his hands,
hoist the black flag, and begin slitting throats
—H. L. Mencken

We have almost come to the end of our long journey together, and although we have touched on much (you might think much too much!), we have had to neglect still more. Many other writers and topics could, and perhaps should, have been included but that would have been to make what is an already extremely long book start to approach the size of *The Hitchhiker's Guide to the Galaxy*[1]—that way madness lies. So, let the journey we have undertaken together be a framework into which other themes, other topics, other thinkers can be inserted as the spirit moves. In this final chapter, I shall recall some topics that have emerged in the course of our journey.[2]

WHY NOT LET THE DEAD BURY THE DEAD?

You might have wondered on occasion why we should have bothered with so much old stuff? Who cares what Plato or Aristotle or John of Salisbury thought? Why should we read Bodin or Machiavelli or for that matter anyone else who lived and wrote before our glorious twenty-first century? The short answer to that question is—because history isn't as the Whig historians would have us believe. It is *not* the case that each day in every way things get better and better.[3] Good ideas aren't always taken up—sometimes, as with the Althusian ideas of federation and sovereignty they are simply ignored or largely forgotten—and bad ideas, such as the labour theory of value and its friends, aren't always consigned to the dustbin. If, for example, Althusius's ideas on federation, a Russian doll-like set of vertically arranged interlocking but detachable entities with sovereignty located firmly in the base units had been adopted instead of Bodin's idea of sovereignty located in the ruler, we could well have had a very different political history in the West over the last 400 years. In a similar way, the example of the polycentric legal orders of the Middle Ages shows us that many different modes of political and legal organisation can co-exist and interact and even compete, and so should encourage us to believe that as the present is different from the past, so too the future will be different from the present.

On the other hand, many are the bad ideas that, despite their demonstrable and demonstrated idiocy, refuse to go away, vampire notions that just won't stay in their graves. Prominent among these vampire notions are the interconnected ideas of exploitation, alienation and the labour theory of value, notions whose zombie-like indestructibility derives from the radical inability of Marxists and their socialist fellow travellers to appreciate the nature and function of capital. This may seem surprising given that Marx wrote a large volume on that very subject but such is indeed the case. Marx and his latter-day disciples are prey to the ever-popular illusion that consumption is the key to economic prosperity and that capitalists, by exploiting their workers and by hoarding their ill-gotten gains, are guilty not only of theft but of bringing the whole economy to ruin. The argument given here is simply a form of the *post hoc, ergo propter hoc* fallacy—if B follows or is associated with A, then A must be the cause of B. Decreased spending is associated with the bust phase of the boom/bust cycle so our Marxists come to think that the bust is *caused* by the decreased spending. This is not so, and the very last thing that's required in a bust phase of a boom/bust cycle is exogenous stimulation of the economy. The economic 'hair of the dog' solution is just as ineffective in economics as it is in drinking excessive amounts of alcohol and it simply postpones or prolongs the inevitable retrenchment/hangover. One can spend now and save later or save now and spend later; what one cannot do is spend now and spend later. Of course, the inconvenient truth is that capital is the very first requirement of genuine economic development, but capital can be acquired only by a restriction on consumption and by a deferral of immediate gratification. Saving is the key to prosperity, not just for the bloated capitalists and the bourgeoisie but for everybody; not just for the eccentric individualist but for society as a whole.

The Marxist misunderstanding of capital did not collapse with the demolition of the Berlin wall. A most unlikely publishing sensation of 2014 was a massive volume by the French economist Thomas Piketty entitled *Capital in the Twenty-First Century* which, as the title suggests, seems to present itself as a kind of *Das Kapital* brought up to date. Friends and foes alike have taken Piketty to be a Marxist of some variety but the man himself has explicitly repudiated that description![4] Whether or not Piketty is a Marxist, his account of capital and capitalism is just as unsuccessful as that given by Marx, with abstract economic aggregates such as 'national income' and 'return to capital' twirling around each other in a bloodless ballet of abstractions. Conflating real wealth with monetary instruments, Piketty is animated throughout by an egalitarian envy of those who have more money than others and, not surprisingly perhaps, he earns the praise of those, such as governments, who have a vested interest in relieving the rich of what such governments regard as their ill-gotten gains. 'Piketty,' writes Deirdre McCloskey, 'focuses…on the great evil of very rich people having seven Rolex watches by mere inheritance. Liliane Bettencourt, heiress to the L'Oréal fortune…the third richest woman in the world, who "has never worked a day in her life, saw her fortune grow exactly as fast as that of...Bill Gates". That is bad, Piketty says, which is his ethical philosophy in full.' [McCloskey 2014, 86]

Perhaps the book's most egregious error is the idea that capital is a kind of economic cornucopia whose gifts never fail but which automatically, even mechanically, produces ever-growing wealth for its owners as if it were the economic equivalent of a perpetual motion machine.[5] Profit, profit, profit is all that capital can ever bring, never, it seems, a loss. This, of course, *is* true of the kind of government-sponsored crony capitalism that we witness in enterprises that are euphemistically considered 'too big to fail' but it is *not* true of free-market capitalism. [see McCloskey, 84] Socialists everywhere are prey to the nightmare, a nightmare that Piketty shares, that in a free market economy, one person or one group could end up owning everything and so controlling everyone. But von Mises's revolutionary insight into the dynamics of economic calculation, applied by Murray Rothbard to the theory of the firm, demonstrates that the free market, absent government regulation or legal control, imposes inherent limits on the size of a firm. In order for any entity—government *or* firm—to engage in rational calculation, it must be possible for it to relate its operation to an external market. To the extent that such a market shrinks, to that extent the possibility of rational calculability declines. If there were ever to be only one firm, one owner of everything, then rational calculability would disappear altogether. 'One big cartel would not be able rationally to allocate producers' goods at all and hence could not avoid severe losses. Consequently, it could never really be established, and, if tried, would quickly break apart.' [Rothbard 2009, 659]

AIDS TO FREEDOM

Early man tended to see himself as a member of the tribe first and as an individual second, if at all. Certainly, when we come to look at our early history we can see that the early Greeks tended to take the *polis* to be the primary reality and to regard the individuals of which it was composed as secondary. The Sophists were perhaps the first thinkers to offer a serious challenge to this conception, even if that challenge wasn't immediately successful. Sir Henry Maine is famous for maintaining that the development of society consists primarily in the move from status to contract, from societies ordered on the basis of *who you are* to societies ordered on the basis of *what you can do*. I echo this idea in my contention that the progress of liberty has largely consisted in a slow and imperfect transition from collectivism to individualism, from the primacy of the tribe or the group or the collective to the primacy of the individual person. Such a transition is neither automatic nor complete, nor are relapses impossible. The lure of the collective exercises a perennial magnetic attraction for the human spirit. Fascism, Bolshevism and National Socialism— each was a return to tribalism in one form or another and many aspects of our current welfare states continue to embody tribalist impulses.

The formation of Europe is often seen to be the blending of Greek philosophy, Roman Law and Christianity into a new and potent socio-political-religious brew, and so in many ways it was. But what is often neglected is the contribution made by the political practices of the barbarian tribes. The ninth century inherited the Roman and Patristic teaching on the divine source of secular authority and the corresponding obligation on Christians to offer no resistance to their rulers and to obey them in all things save a direct command to violate God's laws. But this inherited tradition came into sharp conflict with the indigenous beliefs and practices of the Germanic tribes, one significant aspect of which was that the authority of rulers was limited and the obligation of those who were ruled to offer obedience to that authority was conditional. The clash between these two theoretical tectonic plates is the source of much of the apparently confused political discussions and political practices not only of this period but also of the following centuries. The traditions of the Germanic tribes were innocent of any subscription to the theory of unlimited and absolute obedience to one's rulers. As Carlyle remarks, the Teutonic tradition 'knew nothing of an unlimited authority in the ruler, but a great deal of the relation of the king to his great or wise men, and even to the nation as a whole.' [Carlyle I, 220] For people in the ninth century, the law was the law of the community, not a mere matter of the king's will; the king, as part of the community, was as bound by that law as anyone else. The laws, says Carlyle, have been made 'with the general consent of the faithful subjects of the king....the king does not make laws by his own authority, but requires the consent and advice of his wise men and, in some more or less vague sense, of the whole nation.' [Carlyle I, 234; 238] At this time, kings came to be kings by a process that to us appears confused, not to say irrational. The process combined elements of divine sanction, election and hereditary succession, elements that might well seem to us to be incompatible and even contradictory but which seemed perfectly in order to the people of that time. The element of election in this process is of great interest to those of us keeping an eye on liberty. Perhaps of even greater interest is that in this process of election, there was a mutual exchange of promises between king and people or, at least, between king and the great men in the land. This made the kingly appointment both contractual and conditional.

Christianity was another important contributor to the eventual emancipation of the individual from the group, fitful and slow as that emancipation may have been. Although Christianity made no immediate impact on its social and political surroundings, it eventually contributed to the emancipation of the individual in two ways. First, in its idea of man as *imago dei*, as a being made in the image and likeness of God, *an absolutely free and unconstrained God*, it gave a dignity to the human individual that he rarely if ever had had before, even if, in reality, that dignity was honoured more in the breach than in the observance. Second, the Church eventually came to constitute a rival institution to any and all political regimes. As the Western world began to settle down after the fall of Rome, there would be not one but two *loci* of authority, neither of which would have a complete claim to the total allegiance of the individual. In the tension between the *regnum* and the *sacerdotium*, a space was created that permitted freedom to flourish.[6] This freedom took concrete form in the

High Middle Ages in the emergence of commerce, technology, the cities and the universities, all these institutions and practices forming the social spine of a world that is recognisably modern and is still with us today.

The fracturing of Christendom resulting from the Reformation coincided with the beginnings of the modern state. It could be argued that the rise of the modern state contributed to this fracturing or that the fracturing of Christendom contributed to the rise of the state—in fact, it is likely that the direction of causation was reciprocal. In the new states, Protestant and Catholic alike, the churches were in almost every case subordinated to the states' political purposes, no longer able to provide significant opposition to the emerging centralisation of political power and its extension into ever increasing areas of human life. So dominant is this new dispensation of the centrality and necessity of the state that it is practically impossible for us to imagine that things could ever have been or could ever be different. The history of political philosophy from the sixteenth century onwards is a history severely constrained, for the most part, by its unspoken and unchallenged presuppositions. In political philosophy, the question is nearly always, what is the best kind of state?— rarely the more basic question, is the state either necessary or desirable? The anarchist movement of thought, beginning with Godwin, is to the modern state what the Sophists were to the *polis*.

A Few Last Words on Liberty

It should be obvious at this point that I believe liberty to be an important matter—but I do *not* believe that it is the *only* important matter. There is more to life than liberty, just as there are more interesting things to eat and drink than bread and water, however essential bread and water might be. Murray Rothbard remarked that 'Only an imbecile could ever hold that freedom is the highest or indeed the only principle or end of life.' For him, such a claim is scarcely coherent or meaningful. He agreed with Lord Acton that 'freedom is the highest *political* end, not the highest end of man per se.' [Rothbard 1984, 95] Liberty is the foundation stone of any and all acceptable social orders, but liberty by itself doesn't determine whether any of these orders is otherwise desirable.

Misunderstandings can and do arise from a failure to recognize the severely limited scope of libertarianism. It isn't intended to be, nor is it, a complete ethical or political system; it is rather an overarching constraint on any such system. Libertarianism does *not* imply that all modes of conduct are equally valuable or have equal merit. There may well be those who believe this and who think of themselves as libertarians but such a view, despite Russell Kirk's assertion that liberty unconstrained descends into a maelstrom of licence, isn't a necessary consequence of libertarianism as such.[7] A libertarian may choose to be a libertine but there's nothing in libertarianism to constrain him to be one. Tibor Machan asks, 'Is libertinism implicit in the advocacy of liberty as the highest political principle?' and he answers, 'No—libertarianism only prohibits the forcible squelching of indecent conduct, not its vigorous criticism, opposition, boycott or denunciation in peaceful ways.' [Machan, 49] Libertarianism is compatible with a whole variety of ethical positions. Any system of morality or politics that does not infringe upon individual liberty is acceptable to libertarianism; any system that infringes upon individual liberty is not. Thomas Sowell notes that, 'Logically, one can be a thorough libertarian, in the sense of rejecting government control, and yet believe that private decision-making should, as a matter of morality, be directed toward altruistic purposes. It is equally consistent to see this atomistic freedom as the means to pursue purely personal well-being. In these senses, both William Godwin and Ayn Rand could be included among the contributors to libertarianism.' [Sowell 1987, 116]

The basic principles of conservatism were laid out in various of his writings by Russell Kirk; most famously, perhaps, in *The Conservative Mind* in the form of 6 canons. While the number of canons or principles vary from presentation to presentation, the substantive content remains more or less constant. In *The Politics of Prudence*, we are presented with 10 Principles: 1.the moral order is enduring—human nature is a constant and moral truths are permanent; 2. conservatives adhere to custom, convention and continuity; 3. conservatives believe in prescription, that which has been established by immemorial usage; 4. conservatives are guided by the principle of prudence; 5. conservatives pay attention to the principle of variety—equality before the law levels all ranks—in all other respects inequality is the norm; 6. conservatives are chastened by their principle of imperfectibility—no perfect social order is attainable, utopias are not in sight and are not to be sought; 7. freedom and property are closely linked; 8. conservatives uphold voluntary community and oppose involuntary collectivism; 9. conservatives see the need for prudent restraints on power and on human passions; and 10. conservatives understand that permanence and change must be recognised and reconciled.[8]

Libertarians may adhere to none, some, or all of these principles. *This* libertarian: recognises an enduring moral order and the constancy of human nature; grants the heuristic and presumptive value of custom, convention, continuity and prescription; whole-heartedly recognises and values the differences that make a difference; ruefully recognises (in others) and confesses (in himself) human imperfectibility, and neither expects nor seeks the fantasy of a utopia, for here we have no abiding city; willingly grants—indeed, insists upon—the close connection between freedom and property; rejects involuntary collectivism and welcomes the creation and sustaining of voluntary communities; recognises prudence as the first of the cardinal virtues, seeing restraint as a form of social capital and, as such, the foundation of the moral individual, civil society and political order; and is happy to seek a balance between permanence and change.

More generally, libertarianism, just as such, does not deny the importance of love, community, discipline, order, learning, or any of the many other values that are essential to human flourishing. Libertarians as much as anyone else can cherish these values but, however much they might cherish them, they reject any and all attempts to produce and maintain them by force, coercion or intimidation. They regard such attempts as both wrong in themselves and as ineffective. As Tibor Machan puts it, 'force is permissible and useful only in repelling force, not in building character, love, faith, scientific knowledge, etc.' [Machan, 39] In the end, as Rothbard notes, the question for the libertarian is this: 'Should virtuous action (however we define it) be compelled, or should it be left up to the free and voluntary choice of the individual?' [Rothbard 1984, 92] No third road is possible here; one must choose compulsion or liberty.

Robert Nisbet isn't alone in claiming that for libertarians 'individual freedom, in almost every conceivable domain, is the *highest of all social values*' and is so 'irrespective of what forms and levels of moral, aesthetic, and spiritual debasement may prove to be the unintended consequences of such freedom.'[9] On the contrary, I should say that for libertarians, liberty is the *lowest* of social values, lowest in the sense of most fundamental, a necessary condition of a human action's being susceptible of moral evaluation in any way at all. Libertarians are sometimes portrayed as if they necessarily considered social disorder to be something desirable. Nothing could be further from the truth. Although there may be individual libertarians who, bizarrely, judge that a disordered, Hobbesian-state-of-nature is a consummation devoutly to be wished, most libertarians desire to live in an ordered society. The question isn't really *whether* order is desirable; it is *what kind of order* is desirable, *where* that order is to come from and *how* it is to be maintained.

For the libertarian, as for Johannes Althusius and many others, genuine order arises intrinsically from the free interaction among individuals and among groups of individuals; it does not descend extrinsically from on high. As is clearly shown in the world of commerce, high-level order can emerge without an orderer. Each individual consumer, each firm, orders its own affairs and the relations it has with others. Out of this nexus of relationships emerges a higher-level order that isn't the design of any one person. No one person or agency, for example, is required to organise the production, transport, distribution and sale of food in a given country. Food producers, transport firms, wholesalers and retailers, each working to their own ends, produce an ordered and flexible outcome that isn't planned by any one person or agency.

Libertarians are free to take a variety of positions towards the significance of custom, habit and tradition. Nothing in libertarianism mandates a particular stance. Although some libertarians adopt a hostile attitude towards custom, habit and tradition and, in particular, towards religious traditions, this wasn't the position of Murray Rothbard, the pre-eminent libertarian of the latter half of the twentieth century. As I already mentioned, in an essay he wrote on Frank Meyer who sought to 'fuse' the conservative's reverence for tradition with the libertarian's love of liberty, Rothbard remarked that custom 'must be voluntarily upheld and not enforced by coercion' and that 'people would be well advised (although not forced) to begin with a presumption in favor of custom…'[10] If it be granted that one shouldn't be coerced into observing customs or traditions Rothbard, for one, was more than happy to go along with much of conservative thought. He called his fellow libertarians to order, remarking that libertarians often mistakenly assume 'that individuals are bound to each other only by the nexus of market exchange' forgetting that 'everyone is necessarily born into a family' and 'one or several overlapping communities, usually including an

ethnic group, with specific values, cultures, religious beliefs, and traditions.'
[Rothbard 1994, 1-2]

The libertarian relies on a sharp distinction between what is required
only by morality and what is required only by legality, although, of course,
there are areas where morality and legality overlap. In the 'Preface', I made
mention of what I called the 'Boundary Problem.' Thomas Sowell uses the
term 'precisional fallacy' to describe the use of fuzzy boundary issues to
collapse distinctions that are, in fact, quite clear. 'The precisional fallacy is
often used polemically,' he says. 'For example, an apologist for slavery raised
the question as to where precisely one draws the line between freedom and
involuntary servitude, citing such examples as divorced husbands who must
work to pay alimony. However fascinating these where-do-you-draw-the-
line questions may be, they frequently have no bearing at all on the issue at
hand. Wherever you draw the line in regard to freedom, to any rational person
slavery is going to be on the other side of the line. On a spectrum where
one color gradually blends into another, you cannot draw a line at all—but
that in no way prevents us from telling red from blue (in the center of their
respective regions). To argue that decisive distinctions necessarily require
precision is to commit the precisional fallacy.' [Sowell 1996, 292] Legality is
determined by considerations of justice and justice, in turn, is a function of non- or
zero-aggression. Whatever is done, provided it involves no aggression or
threat of aggression, is *ipso facto* just; it is not, however, *ipso facto* moral.
Rothbard distinguishes emphatically between 'a man's *right* and the morality
or immorality of his exercise of that right.' The possession of a right is one
thing; its exercise is quite another. The moral or immoral ways of exercising
that right 'is a question of personal ethics rather than of political philosophy,'
whereas political philosophy is concerned 'solely with matter of right, and of
the proper or improper exercise of physical violence in human relations.' It
can hardly be said too often or too bluntly that, despite the suspicions of Kirk
and others, libertarianism is *not* the same thing as libertinism. Libertarianism
will not admit the physical restraint or physical punishment of acts that do not
aggress against others but it nowhere implies moral approval of such acts or
rules out their restraint by other methods.

Libertarian thought is premised on the appropriate contractual or consensual
relationships that should obtain between adult human beings, in respect of their
property in themselves and their property in external resources. For the most
part, what is *not* explicitly considered in libertarian thought is the intergenera-
tional aspect of relationships between those who are complete self-owners and
those who are not yet so—between parents and children. This relationship is
diachronic rather than synchronic and is based not on contract but on status, on
custom and on culture.

Edmund Burke is correct in thinking that man is an inherently social being,
living in and through society. Society, in turn, isn't simply a random assemblage
of individuals but is a network of individual relationships existing under various
conceptual descriptions and it is permeated and interpenetrated by institutions
of various kinds, which institutions constrain, compete and cooperate with each

other, contextualise and shape people's lives, and act as repositories of artistic, technical, social and political knowledge. Society *is* real—not in the way in which a garden gnome is real but real in much the same way that the market is real. Society isn't the outcome of some grand design or some overall plan. It is, rather, the evolutionary resultant of how people have lived their lives over many years, the decisions they have made, individually and together, the laws that have emerged to regulate their lives in community, and the means they have devised to further their ends. We are constituted in large part by things outside our range of choices. Our language, our family, and our place of origin—all these are simply given to us whether we will or not.[11]

'The effective organ for the transmission of cultural information is the family,' writes David Mamet. 'Not only attitudes but mechanisms for social interaction are learned from earliest infancy....If the family as a cohesive covenantal unit does not exist, attitudes toward these universal situations must be learned by the individual late in life, when he is both conscious of and burdened by his pressing personal needs....He is, then, prey to his intellect....But the intellect is an inadequate organ for working out the myriad interactions of a society.' [Mamet, 164] He continues, 'the interactions of the family were not based upon reason, and so, not liable to casuistry. They were based upon the generationally bequeathed experience of previous families; experience so deep and ingrained that it could neither be absorbed nor parsed by reason....The child imbibes the lessons of civic virtue, religious devotion, marital behavior, restraint, self-esteem and self-sufficiency in the home. If the home is destroyed, or its influence negated or derided (as it was both by Welfare, and as it is in today's Liberal Arts "education"), he is hard-pressed to come, through the force of his own reason, to a practicable ethical view of the world.' [Mamet, 165-166]

In their focus on that which is simply given to us, on tradition, conservatives have identified something of great importance. It is undeniable that much of what we are is simply given to us and isn't a matter of choice. The family we belong to, the nation we conceive of as ours, the language we speak, the way we speak it, indeed, many of our ideas—all these are important, perhaps constitutive, parts of what we are, parts of our very identity, if you will, and yet *not* a matter of choice. [see Sacks, passim] Much, if not most, of our social life is made possible by the production in us of largely unconsciously acquired cultural norms. If we have to think about them consciously all the time and entertain them subject to constant revision then, like the caterpillar who, when he began to wonder how he walked, got his legs all tangled up, we too are rendered socially incompetent. It is as if all our social relationships were occurring for the first time and we had no past experience to fall back on in guiding us towards the appropriate forms of behaviour. The result is deeply unsettling, when not actively destructive. David Mamet writes, 'under the Statist revision of the Obama administration, racial tensions have devolved to acrimony unknown in this country for decades. Sexual relations are universally subject to constant revision, and limits on language and behaviour, once imposed unconsciously, and learned in family, community, and school, are returned to the conscious mind, erasing spontaneity and ease, and replacing them with consternation and fear.' [Mamet, 107-108]

A libertarian can happily accept the presumptive legitimacy of existing cultural, social and moral norms; moreover, a libertarian can (and I believe, should) be a gradualist (although a rapid gradualist) in respect of necessary or desirable changes. Such is the complexity of existing social institutions that any sudden or radical change is likely to be wildly destructive and perhaps even inimical to their coherent and improved restructuring. In his 'Ivan Karamazov's Mistake,' Ralph C. Wood rejects what he regards as the common misinterpretation of significance of the 'Grand Inquisitor' chapter in Dostoevsky's *The Karamazov Brothers*. 'It has become commonplace,' he says, 'to regard Ivan Karamazov's "Legend of the Grand Inquisitor" as a prescient parable glorifying human freedom and defending it against the kind of totalitarian threats it would face in the twentieth century.' But, Wood believes, Dostoevsky is using this chapter to attack a secular notion of freedom. 'It is astonishing, he writes, 'that so many readers have taken the Grand Inquisitor's conception of freedom as if it were Dostoevsky's own—and also as if it were true.' Dostoevsky defends, not a Western liberal notion of freedom, but a more adequate (for him) Orthodox, communal conception of freedom. This communal freedom is premised on the idea that our responsibilities 'come to us less by our own choosing than through a thickly webbed network of shared friendships and familial ties, through political practices and religious promises. In a very real sense, such "encumbrances" choose us before we choose them. There is no mythical free and autonomous self that exists apart from these ties. There are only gladly or else miserably bound persons—namely, persons who find their duties and encumbrances to be either gracious or onerous.'

This Dostoevskian/Woodian conception of freedom appears, on the face of it, to be restrictive and to be more than a libertarian would be prepared to accept; but Wood goes on to note that 'Our freedom resides rather in becoming communal selves *who freely embrace our moral, religious, and political obligations*' and this freedom to embrace or not to embrace is all that a libertarian requires. [emphasis added] Our moral, cultural and social norms, though given to us pre-reflectively, are capable of being reflectively appropriated, and a large part of our maturation as human beings consists in just such an appropriation.

Still, the libertarian may (and I believe should) agree with Augusto Del Noce when he notes that the subjugation of man's sensuous and appetitive faculties is a primary function of reason which, as subjugator, acts repressively. The subjugation of the lower by the higher is necessary to produce properly functioning individuals and properly functioning societies. [see Del Noce, 141] A libertarian of this persuasion will want the subjugation to emerge from within the individual and the society, especially from the family, and not merely to be imposed on either from outside. The law that the libertarian follows is the law given by the reflective self and not by another; it is autonomous, not heteronomous.

Libertarianism differentiates itself from liberalism (in both its classic and its modern incarnations) and also from conservatism in rejecting the use of force in all cases except those of resisting or punishing aggression. The modern liberal is (or was, until recently) content to use the power of the state to enforce

his economic views on all to produce what he considers to be the correct distribution of goods and services, while claiming as large a space as possible for
personal, especially sexual, morality; the conservative, on the other hand,
generally wishes to leave as much space as possible for economic activities,
while recruiting the state to enforce his moral views on others. Unlike the libertarian for whom liberty operates as a principle across the whole range of human
endeavour, both the liberal and the conservative are selective in those spheres
in which they will allow liberty to operate. Where a libertarian differs from
the conservative in respect of customs, habits, and traditions isn't necessarily
in his lack of appreciation of their social, moral and cultural value but simply
in refusing to allow their maintenance or propagation by means of force or
coercion. If coercion is ruled out, then many libertarians are only too willing to
entertain a presumption in their favour.

SOCIAL CAPITALISM

Men act to improve their situations. In order for us to act, something about our
current situation must be apprehended as being capable of improvement and
we act to bring that improvement about. A man came across his friend banging
his head against a wall and asked him why he was doing this. 'Because,'
replied his friend, 'it feels so good when I stop.' A being perfectly satisfied
in every way wouldn't act—it's a moot point whether he *could* act![12] Just as
in economics, equilibrium is ever tended towards but never reached, because
of the constantly changing, kaleidoscopic nature of the world, so too, in our
human lives, complete satisfaction is never attained but is, at best, intended.
Our ever-changing physiological conditions, force us to act to preserve homeo-
stasis. But we are also psychologically unstable and, if St Augustine is to be
believed, spiritually unstable. 'You have made us for yourself, O Lord,' he
wrote, 'and our hearts know no rest until they rest in Thee.' We can live hand
to mouth, as our remote ancestors did, or we can try in a more ordered and
long-term way to improve our situations—the way we do this economically is
by the creation of capital.

What should be a libertarian's approach to social order? As long as one
respects the primacy of liberty in matters of zero-aggression, one is a libertarian. Whatever else one may wish to commit to is a matter of indifference to
the libertarian *qua* libertarian. Nevertheless, I believe that a civilised existence
requires both freedom *and* order; that just as a sound economy requires capital
which is produced by saving and by delayed gratification,[13] so too, cultural
capital is similarly produced by delayed gratification: 'the essential mechanism
of societal preservation is not inspiration, but restraint.' [Mamet, 171] Freedom
without order is like a sudden explosive release of energy, pointless and destructive; order without freedom is like the body in the library, a lifeless corpse.
Freedom and order together are necessary to produce a living, vital society.

Progressives, so-called, whether Marxists, Freudians, Rousseaueans, Deconstructionists—all of them latter-day Platonists[14] in one form or another—have
consistently disparaged, attacked and attempted to undermine the social world
and the bourgeois virtues created and sustained by the experiences of ordinary

people, with a view to reconstructing reality in line with their preferred dogma. 'Every form of progressivism bases itself on the claim of a special, "scientific," knowledge of what is wrong with humanity and how to fix it.' [Codevilla, 37] It is true that our perceptions are, in part, constituted by us. Aquinas, no epistemological or social radical, wrote, *quidquid recipitur, recipitur secundum modum recipientis*—whatever is received, is received according to the mode of the receiver—but that, while true and important, does not make reality to be *merely* conventional. As Thomas Sowell sardonically remarks, 'Would anyone walk into a lion's cage because both the lion and the cage, as we see them, are ultimately things constructed in our brains? More importantly, why not? Only because the verification processes so deftly made to disappear in theory could become very quickly, very brutally, and very agonizingly apparent. That is also the very reason why dogs do not run into a roaring flame and why bats swerve to avoid colliding with a stone wall. All these differently constructed worlds are subjected to verification processes. All these creatures' worlds, like our own, are indeed "perceptions" but they are not *just* perceptions.'[Sowell 1996, xv] There are, then, limits to our ability to reconstruct reality, whether that reality is physical or social. Everything is what it is and not another thing, even if we have difficulty from time to time grasping just *what* it is that something is. Reality is not a shapeless mass of play dough that can be shaped however we wish. There is, writes Sowell, 'an independent reality which each individual perceives only imperfectly, but which can be understood more fully with feedback that can validate or invalidate what was initially believed.' [Sowell 1996, xv]

Edmund Burke thought that manners mattered more than law and even more than morals, inasmuch as both law and morals in large measure depend upon manners. In his 'First Letter on a Regicide Peace' he writes, 'Manners are of more importance than laws. Upon them, in a great measure, the laws depend. The law touches us but here and there, and now and then. Manners are what vex or sooth, corrupt or purify, exalt or debase, barbarize or refine us, by a constant, steady, uniform, insensible operation, like that of the air we breathe in. They give their whole form and colour to our lives. According to their quality, they aid morals, they supply them, or they totally destroy them.'[15] We do not produce and maintain our manners primarily by some process of detached reason. They arise naturally from social relations. Such judgement as they embody is a kind of pre-reflective judgement, what Burke calls 'prejudice'. Manners, as prejudices, allow us to act swiftly and surely and rightly without the need for agonised reflection and reasoning. At the root of manners is the notion of restraint, of limitation, of delayed gratification, and its product is a kind of social capital, just as the product of fiscal delayed gratification and restraint is economic capital. Burke contrasts this form of ordered liberty with mere licence, which is the freedom to do whatever one wants to do without regard to circumstances. Will you have ordered liberty, or will you have licence? Which shall it be?

Libertarianism is compatible with both Burkean liberty and with Burkean licence. A libertarian can arrive at substantially the same conservative conclusions as Burke, with this important difference, *that the restraints and*

limitations that channel our exercise of liberty must, with the exception of the
restraint of actions aggressing against others, be self-imposed, self-accepted,
and not imposed by the coercive power of the law. When manners decline as
the result of cultural decay, then the law (or rather legislation) rushes in to fill
the vacuum. Matters that in a culturally rich society are dealt with by informal
sanctions, such as speech that is intended to be crude, insulting and hurtful,
now have to be overtly regulated by laws, with consequent intrusions upon our
liberty. But the law is a blunt and crude instrument and such micro-regulation
is both ineffective and also stifling. Man does not live by legislation alone.[16]
A society replete with minute and detailed legislation is a society whose stock
of social capital has declined and is declining. This, I suggest, is an accurate
account of many contemporary Western societies. Whether these societies can
replenish their social capital is a matter for conjecture. Some societies have
done so in the past—but others have not, and have perished.

Are conservatism and libertarianism intrinsically opposed to each other or is
it possible to be both conservative and libertarian? The answer to this question,
like the answer to many others, is—it depends.[17] It depends primarily on the
position one starts from. As we have seen, conservatism is rooted in a disposition to resist rapid and fundamental change and to accept only those changes
that are, as it were, reformative and organic. The conservative values order and
virtue above all else whereas liberty for him is only one value among others
and is in no way preeminent. The libertarian, in contrast, takes liberty to be
the fundamental and necessary precondition of a life that's truly human. It is
not the only value that libertarians can hold—most libertarians recognise the
values of love, friendship, altruism, courage, charity—but none of the other
values can come to be unless we are able to act free from coercion. It is true that
behavioural simulacra of these virtues can be produced by coercion, by regulation and by force but they are ghoulish animated corpses from which the real
life has departed. If one starts from a conservative position, holding to conservative values, one will always be prepared, in principle, to sacrifice freedom to
other more important values. One can be, at best, a libertarian for the sunny day
but not for the days of snow and ice. If one starts from a libertarian position,
one can adopt and adapt conservative values in a way that supplements and
embodies one's commitment to freedom provided that, in so doing, one does
not compromise one's primary commitment to freedom. If one starts from a
conservative position, one is unlikely ever to become libertarian or to endorse
libertarianism, unless one undergoes a political philosophical conversion. On
the other hand, if one starts from a libertarian position one can, without necessarily being obliged to, accept the heuristic value of tradition and the antecedent
(yet rebuttable) normativity of custom and habit. I have tried to show that libertarianism isn't necessarily reducible to libertinism. One more or less certain
way to prevent its collapse into libertinism is for it to adopt the cultural core
values of conservatism and this libertarians are free to do. Conservatism, on the
other hand, is always at the mercy of the questions—whose tradition? which
customs? what habits? If it develops a principled and rational response to these
questions then it has ceased to be radically conservative and has begun to move

in a direction that, I believe, will lead it to espouse the fundamental position of liberty as the necessary condition of all the virtues and thus to transmute into a form of libertarianism.

That freedom and individuality aren't incompatible with conservatism can be seen in this passage from *the* philosopher of conservatism, Roger Scruton, who writes of the moment when the significance of the laws formulated by the British Labour Party became clear to him:

> I was suddenly struck by the impertinence of a political party that sets out to confiscate whole industries from those who had created them, to abolish the grammar schools to which I owed my education, to force schools to amalgamate, to control relations in the workplace, to regulate hours of work, to compel workers to join a union, to ban hunting, to take property from a landlord and bestow it on his tenant, to compel businesses to sell themselves to the government at a dictated price, to police all our activities through quangos designed to check us for political correctness. And I saw that this desire to control society *in the name of equality* expressed exactly the contempt for human freedom that I encountered in Eastern Europe. *There is indeed such a thing as society; but it is composed of individuals. And individuals must be free, which means being free from the insolent claims of those who wish to redesign them.* [Scruton 2014, 12; emphasis added]

I should point out, however, that despite appreciating the value of the free individual, Scruton is not, in the end, a classical liberal, still less, a libertarian. In *How to be a Conservative*, he concludes, 'the role of the state is, or ought to be, both less than the socialists require, and more than the classical liberals permit.' Why, one might wonder, should the state have a greater role than would be consistent with classical liberalism? Because, answers Scruton, civil society 'depends upon attachments that must be renewed and, in modern circumstances, these attachments cannot be renewed without the collective provision of welfare.' [Scruton 2014, 135] A conservative libertarian could accept Scruton's point about attachments that must be renewed, without also accepting his claim that they can only be renewed today on the back of the collective provision of welfare by the state. This is, perhaps, an instance where the old jibe that 'liberals make foolish changes and conservatives conserve them' has some relevance. In any event, just how Scruton's acceptance of the necessity for the collective provision of welfare through the instrumentality of the state, with its staggering economic costs, now and hereafter, not to mention its corrosive effect on the voluntary forms of human association that conservatives such as Scruton value—'schools, churches, libraries, choirs, orchestras, bands theatre groups, cricket clubs, football teams' and the core of the free individual, [Scruton 2014, 120; see also 42ff.]— is consistent with his rejection of the insolent claims of state-sponsored social engineers isn't immediately clear to me.

It is, then, I believe, perfectly possible to be a political libertarian and cultural liberal. It is also possible to be, as I am, a political libertarian and a cultural conservative. These cursory remarks are merely a suggestive sketch of the overall defensibility of that position but its comprehensive articulation and defence is a matter for another (much shorter) book.

My concern in this book has been largely with ideas and their social and political implementation. I haven't completely ignored practical, economic and technological issues but they have formed a background to my overall purpose. Without going all Marxist, however, it cannot be denied that the structures of production condition, even if they don't determine, our social and political forms of organisation. An issue that will have (and to some extent is already having) a dramatic impact on our social and political thinking is the radically changing nature of work. To a large extent, our economies have been, and largely still are, based on rewarding people for their contributions to productivity, in other words, for the work they do. But more and more categories of work can now be done by mechanical and electronic robots more rapidly, more efficiently and more cheaply than by human hands and brains. These robots are capable of performing not just brute physical labour but, increasingly, what has traditionally regarded as white-collar work, including medical diagnoses and legal research. Previous technological changes have had the effect of drastically reducing or even destroying whole categories of employment while, simultaneously, permitting the creation of new types of work which were capable of absorbing many of the newly unemployed. In the current context, however, it is difficult to see where the blue *and* white collared about-to-be- unemployed will go for work or what they will do when they get there; the future, the not so distant future, will bring about an unprecedented and critical situation in which masses of people are not only unemployed but unemployable. *What* effects these new robot technologies will have on our social and political structures is unforeseeable; *that* it will have a seismic effect on them, however, is readily foreseeable. Every crisis, it has been said, is an opportunity but whether this crisis is a disaster in waiting or an opportunity for lovers of liberty to begin the process of bringing about a world consistent with the principles of liberty remains to be seen.

> Historically, freedom is a rare and fragile thing.
> It has emerged out of the stalemates of would-be oppressors....
> everywhere there are those prepared to scrap it for other things
> that shine more brightly for the moment....
> Freedom is not simply the right of intellectuals to circulate
> their merchandise. It is, above all, the right of ordinary people
> to find elbow room for themselves and a refuge
> from the rampaging presumptions of their 'betters."
> —Thomas Sowell

Notes

1 Not Douglas Adams's five volume trilogy but the mythical encyclopedia of that name at the centre of that trilogy which is, in Adams's modest description of it, 'More popular than *The Celestial Home Care Omnibus*, better selling than *Fifty-three More Things to do in Zero Gravity*, and more controversial than Oolan Colluphid's trilogy of philosophical blockbusters *Where God Went Wrong, Some More of God's Greatest Mistakes* and *Who is this God Person Anyway?* It's already supplanted the *Encyclopedia Galactica* as the standard repository of all knowledge and wisdom for two important reason. First, it's slightly cheaper; and secondly it has the word DON'T PANIC printed in large friendly letters on its cover.'

2 Some of the material in this chapter found earlier expression in Casey 2010, Casey 2012b and Casey 2014.

3 To paraphrase Émile Coué de la Châtaigneraie's mantra—'*Tous les jours à tous points de vue ils ne vont pas de mieux en mieux.*

4 See Daniel Ben-Ami, Isaac Chotiner and Doug Saunders.

5 As Deirdre McCloskey notes, 'The classical and Marxist idea that capital begets capital, "endlessly," is hard to shake.' [McCloskey 2011, 142]

6 'The western Church was always to assert that whatever duty might be owed by men to their earthly rulers, only the Church could tell them what their final duty was, for it was owed to God. Church and State in the west would, therefore, have to live together side by side, sometimes amicably, sometimes quarrelling, sometimes one being dominant in practical or political terms, sometimes the other. From this tension would grow liberty.' [Roberts 1997, 94]

7 See Kirk 1984, passim. In his appreciative account of Kirk's life and works, John Pafford remarks that Kirk's 'vitriolic denunciation of libertarianism represented his genuine convictions and, perhaps, an annoyance with himself for having been attracted to it earlier'—the zeal of the unconverted, as it were. [Pafford, 28]

8 Kirk, 2007-2016. An example of what a lack of prudence can lead to in the political realm can be seen in the disorder produced in the Roman constitution by the tribunes Tiberius and Gaius Gracchus and the consequent civil strife of Marius and Sulla, Pompey and Caesar, and Octavian and Antony. [see Plutarch 1999, 83-115]

9 Nisbet 1984, 21. Those, like Nisbet, who are sceptical of the overarching value of freedom in human life will sometimes ask questions like, '"What freedom does a starving man have?" The answer is that starvation is a tragic human condition—perhaps more tragic than loss of freedom. That does not prevent these from being *two different things*. No matter what ranking may be given to such disagreeable things as indebtedness and constipation, a laxative will not get you out of debt and a pay raise will not insure "regularity." Conversely on a list of desirable things, gold may rank much higher than peanut butter, but you cannot spread gold on a sandwich and eat it for nourishment. The false issue of *ranking* things cannot be allowed to confuse questions of *distinguishing* things.' [Sowell 1996, 117; emphasis in original]

10 Rothbard 1984, 102, 103.

11 'I owe to others my life, my language, my family, my locality, my nation, my culture, my education, my horizons and aspirations,' writes Anthony O'Hear, before going on to concede, with Burke, that 'if men dissolve their ancient corporation, in order to regenerate their community, in that state of things each man has a right, if he pleases, to remain an individual. In such circumstances, if anyone is then forced into the fellowship of another, this is conquest and not compact.' [O'Hear, 61, 63]

12 God, as always, is a special case.

13 For another, not unrelated, extraordinarily rich account of the virtues of the world of the bourgeoisie, see the astonishing series of encyclopedic books by Deirdre McCloskey: *The Bourgeois Virtues* (2007), *Bourgeois Dignity* (2011), and *Bourgeois Equality* (2016). McCloskey writes, 'modern capitalism does not need to be offset to be good. Capitalism can on the contrary be virtuous. In a fallen world the bourgeois life is not perfect. But it's better than any available alternative.' [McCloskey 2007, 1] Capitalism, McCloskey claims, 'nourishes lives of virtue in the non-self-interested sense, too. The more common claim is that virtues support the market...I say that the market supports the virtues.' [McCloskey 2007, 4] Matt Ridley notes the widespread but profoundly mistaken sentiment that capitalism and markets are 'necessary evils, rather than inherent goods' and the corresponding belief that 'free exchange encourages and demands selfishness,

whereas people were kinder and gentler before their lives were commercialised, that putting a price on everything has fragmented society and cheapened souls.' [Ridley, 102] The truth is otherwise. 'In market societies, if you get a reputation for unfairness, people will not deal with you. In places where traditional honour-based feudal societies gave way to commercial, prudence-based economies—say Italy in 1400 Scotland in 1700, Japan in 1945—the effect is civilising, not coarsening.' [Ridley, 103]

14 It is perhaps worth repeating here what I wrote above in the Preface: 'A problem bequeathed to philosophy by Socrates (through Plato) is the belief, still held by some philosophers to this day, that in order to know what a given concept means and to be justified in using it, one has to be able to produce on demand the necessary and sufficient conditions for its instantiation. This may well be in order for certain disciplines, such as mathematics, where one can often state such conditions—for example, a triangle is a plane figure bounded by three straight lines—but it is most certainly *not* the case in more humdrum and empirically messy areas of life. Who, offhand, can give the definition of a tree? But one's inability to define a tree satisfactorily does not significantly prevent one from identifying an entity as a tree or speaking meaningfully about trees, and having one's identification be accurate for practical purposes most of the time. Of course, there may occasionally be boundary problems so that while there are trees that are unambiguously trees and bushes that are unashamedly bushes, there may be bushes that are suspiciously arboreal, not to mention trees that appear to have a hankering to transgenerate into bushes. But this confused and confusing boundary area between trees and bushes does not prevent us from being clear about most trees and most bushes most of the time. The classical argument form known as the *sorites*—a first cousin of the Socratic obsession with necessary and sufficient conditions—uses the phenomenon of borderline cases between bushes and trees (or any other two pertinent entities) to conclude that, in the end, there's really no difference between bushes and trees at all.' In a related discussion, Thomas Sowell provides a penetrating account of the intellectualist bias, writing 'Explicit articulation—in words or symbols—is central to the intellectual process. By contrast the enormously complex information required to make life itself possible, which has systemically evolved and exists in unarticulated form in the genetic code, is not intellectual....Conversely, the forms of articulation may be elaborate and impressive and yet the substance of what is elaborated simple or even trivial.' [Sowell 1996, 334; see 334-338]

15 Burke 1796, 126. A similar point has been made more recently by Thomas Sowell. 'Informal relationships are not mere minor interstitial supplements to the major institutions of society,' writes Sowell. 'These informal relationships not only include important decision-making processes, such as the family, but also produce much of the background social capital without which the other major institutions of society could not function nearly as effectively as they do. Language has already been mentioned as an informally produced system. Morality is another major item of background social capital, without which the cost of operating everything from credit cards to courts of law would be far more expensive—perhaps prohibitively so. The same could be said for hygiene, civility, and other informally transmitted characteristics without which many (or all) formal organizations would incur huge costs of operation, if they could operate at all.' [Sowell 1996, 30]

16 Donald Black notes that '*Law varies inversely with other social control....Law* itself is social control, but many other kinds of social control also appear in social life, in families, friendship, neighborhoods, villages, tribes, occupations, organizations, and groups of all kinds.' [Black 1976, 6, emphasis in original]

17 See Casey, 2011. On a personal note, if it hasn't otherwise become blatantly obvious by now, I should confess that politically I am a libertarian, culturally I am a conservative, and religiously I am a Catholic. Unless one has the intellectual flexibility of a White Queen, to be libertarian, conservative and Catholic all at the same time obviously requires (minimally) that libertarianism, conservatism and Catholicism be coherent. Claims have been made from time to time asserting the incoherence of libertarianism and conservatism or the incoherence of libertarianism and Catholicism but I reject all such claims. Libertarianism requires only adherence to the non-aggression principle or, as I now prefer to call it, the zero-aggression principle; after that, one can be as egalitarian and liberal (in the contemporary sense of the term) or as conservative as one pleases. Similarly, while some libertarians, perhaps most, are committed to beliefs, policies or activities that are incompatible with Catholicism, libertarianism just as such is not at all incompatible with Catholicism. [see McNerney, passim]

BIBLIOGRAPHY

The bibliography lists the primary sources that I have consulted in the writing of this book, together with the works of other historians of political thought as well as some significant social and economic historians, a selection of secondary scholarly books and articles, together with some more popular and accessible books and articles that I consider meritorious, illuminating or controversial. Where possible, I have given an internet address for the works cited so that readers without access to a comprehensive library may readily consult the material. When an author has a single entry in the Bibliography, in-text references will be by author's last name and page number (or other identifier) within square brackets; for example **[Cahill, 148]** refers to page 148 of Thomas Cahill's *How the Irish Saved Civilization*. Where an author has more than one entry in the Bibliography, or where there is more than one author with the same last name, in-text references will be by author's last name, *date*, and page number (or other identifier) within square brackets; for example, references to different books by Jared Diamond might be to **[Diamond 2012, 131]** or **[Diamond 2006, 27]**, whereas references to **[Nelson 1988, 212]** and **[Nelson 2009, 625]** would be to the entries for Janet Nelson and Mark T. Nelson respectively. Where two dates are given for a publication in the bibliography, the first is typically the date of the current publication, the second the date of original publication or as near to it as can be ascertained. To situate the sources historically in the body of the text, in-text references will normally be to the original date of publication, sometimes accompanied by the date of current publication: thus the work referred to in the text as **[Marx & Engels 1848 [2002], 226]** will be found in the Bibliography as **Marx, Karl and Friedrich Engels. (2002 [1848])** while a textual reference to **[Bakunin 1873, 177-178]** will be found below as **Bakunin, Mikhail. (1900 [1873])**.

Abdel Haleem, M. A. S. 'Introduction,' in *The Qur'an*, trans. M. A. S. Abdel Haleem. Oxford: Oxford University Press, ix-xxxvi. [Oxford World's Classics]

Abel, Reubel. (1966) 'Introduction' to Schiller 1966, 7-11.

Adam, Sibyl, Luis Abolafia Anguita et al. (2015) 'Open Letter to Dr. David Duncan and Dr. Adrian Lee regarding the University Press Release on "International Men's Day",' available at https://docs.google.com/a/ucd.ie/document/d/19i_5G_jQ6Ob-GF2gdexi-MUI6cQ7_FV4Fo7KRhypLv3A/mobilebasic#ftnt1, accessed 8 June 2016.

Adams, Charles. (1999 [1998]) *Those Dirty Rotten Taxes: The Tax Revolts that Built America*. New York: Simon & Schuster.

Adams, Charles. (2001 [1993]) *For Good and Evil: The Impact of Taxes on the Course of Civilization*, 2nd ed. New York: Madison Book.

Adams, Matthew S. (2013) 'Max Stirner/The Practical Anarchist: Writings of Josiah Warren/A British Anarchist Tradition: Herbert Read, Alex Comfort and Colin Ward/ The Politics of Postanarchism,' in *European Review of History*, Vol. 20, No. 2, 309-314.

Adcock, Frank Ezra. (1957) *The Greek and Macedonian Art of War*. Berkeley, California: The University of California Press.

Aitchison, Jean. (2001 [1981]) *Language Change: Progress or Decay?*, 3rd ed. Cambridge: Cambridge University Press.

Akerlof, George A. & Robert J. Shiller. (2015) *Phishing for Phools: The Economics of Manipulation & Deception*. Princeton, New Jersey: Princeton University Press.

Akhavi, Shahrough. (2011) 'The Muslim Tradition of Political Philosophy,' in Klosko, 789-802.

Alexis-Manners, Nekeisha. (2005) 'Deconstructing Romans 13: Verse 1-2,' available at http://www.docstoc.com/docs/20066808/Deconstructing-Romans-13, accessed 13 August 2013.

Allawi, Ali A. (2009) *The Crisis of Islamic Civilization*. New Haven, Connecticut: Yale University Press.

Allen, John William. (1928) *A History of Political Thought in the Sixteenth Century*. London: Menthuen & Co. Ltd.

Allen, William. (1975 [1584]) 'A True, Sincere, and Modest Defence of English Catholics,' in Zuck, 188-190.

Allison, Lincoln. (1984) *Right Principles: A Conservative Philosophy of Politics*. Oxford: Blackwell.

Althusius, Johannes. (1964/1995 [1614]) *Politica. An Abridged Translation of Politics Methodologically set forth and Illustrated with Sacred and Profane Examples*, ed. and trans. Frederick S, Carney. Indianapolis: Liberty Fund. Available at http://files.libertyfund.org/files/692/0002_Bk.pdf, accessed 1 December 2013.

Althusius, Johannes. (2006 [1617]) 'Selections from the *Dicaeologicae*' trans. Jeffrey J. Veenstra, introduction by Stephen J. Grabill, in *Journal of Markets and Morality*, Vol. 9, No. 2, 399-483.

Ambrose. (c. AD 390) 'Letter to Theodosius,' no. 40, in Migne, *Patrologia Latina*, vols 14-17. English translation available at http://www.newadvent.org/fathers/340940.htm, accessed 22 September 2013.

Ames, Edward & Rapp, Richard T. (1977) 'The Birth and Death of Taxes: A Hypothesis,' in the *Journal of Economic History*, Vol. 37, No. 1, 161-78.

Anderson, Scott. (2011) 'Coercion,' in *Stanford Encyclopedia of Philosophy*, available at http://plato.stanford.edu/archives/win2011/entries/coercion/, accessed 7 September 2013.

Andrews, Stephen Pearl. (1854) *The True Constitution of Government in the Sovereignty of the Individual*, 3rd ed. New York: T. L. Nichols. Available at https://archive.org/details/scienceofsociety00andrrich, accessed 22 June 2014.

Angold, Michael. (2002 [2001]) *Byzantium: The Bridge from Antiquity to the Middle Ages*. London: Phoenix Press.

Anon. (1515) 'The Document of Articles of the Black Forest Peasants,' in Baylor, 243-245.

Anon. (1525a) 'The Forty-six Frankfurt Articles,' in Baylor, 246-253.

Anon. (1525b) 'The Memmingen Federal Constitution (Bundesordnung),' in Baylor, 239-242.

Anon. (1525c) 'To the Assembly of the Common Peasantry,' in Baylor, 101-129.

Anon. (1570) 'An Homily against Disobedience and Wylful Rebellion,' in Wootton, 2003, 94-98.

Anon. (1645) 'England's Miserie and Remedie,' in Wootton, 2003, 276-282.

Anon. (1647) 'An Agreement of the People for a Firm and Present Peace, upon Grounds of Common-Right and Freedom; as It was Proposed by the Agents of the Five Regiments of Horse; and Since by the General Approbation of the Army, Offered to the Joint Concurrence of All Free COMMONS of ENGLAND,' (excerpt) in Wootton, 283-285 and in Sharp 1998, 92-101.

Anon. (1653/4) Commonwealth Instrument of Government. Available at http://www. fordham.edu/halsall/mod/1653intrumentgovt.asp, accessed 3 January 2014.

Anon. (1937) *Bunreacht na hÉireann (Constitution of Ireland)*. Dublin: Government Publication Office.

Anon. (1972) *Anarchism and Anarcho-Syndicalism*, with preface by N. Y. Kolpinsky. Moscow: Progress Publishers.

Anon. (2007 [1625]) *Altera secretissima instructio* (trans. Thomas Hobbes) in Noel Malcolm, *Reason of State, Propaganda, and the Thirty Years War: An Unknown Translation* by Thomas Hobbes. Oxford: Clarendon Press.

Anon. (2010) *Anarchist Academics*. Books LLC. Available at http://en.wikipedia. org/wiki/Category:Anarchist_academics?CFID=2279783&CFTOKEN=26993018, accessed 6 June 2014.

Anon. (2011) 'Women and Men in Ireland,' Central Statistics Office Report, available at http://www.cso.ie/en/media/csoie/releasespublications/documents/otherreleases/ 2011/Women,and,Men,in,Ireland,2011.pdf., accessed 6 May 2015.

Anon. (c. 1100) 'Select Passages from the *Norman Anonymous*,' in Douglas & Greenaway, 725-28.

Anon. (no date A) 'Stunning 1000 Years of European Borders Change – Timelapse Video' available at http://www.v8j.com/stunning-1000-years-of-european-borders-change-timelapse-video-695/#, accessed 10 June 2014.

Anon. (no date B) 'AntiFemComics,' available at https://www.google.ie/search?q=An-tiFemComics&biw=1660&bih=1239&tbm=isch&tbo=u&source=univ&sa=X-&ved=0ahUKEwjA_ofvx5jNAhVJJsAKHa49D2UQsAQIGg#imgrc=XdHT-QK1o-JgtBM%3A, accessed 8 June 2016.

Appell, George N. (1984) 'Freeman's Refutation of Mead's Coming of Age in Samoa: The Implication for Anthropological Inquiry,' in *The Eastern Anthropologist*, Vol. 37, 183-214. A revised version of this article is available online at http://www.gnappell. org/articles/freeman.htm, accessed 1 October 2016.

Aquinas, St Thomas. (1252-1256) *Commentary on the Sentences of Peter Lombard (In Sent.)*, D. 44, a. 2, available at http://dhspriory.org/thomas/Sent2d44q2a2.htm, accessed 5 September 2016.

Aristotle. (1885 [?]) *The Politics of Aristotle*, trans. Benjamin Jowett. Oxford: Clarendon Press. Available at https://archive.org/details/politicsaristot05arisgoog, accessed 4 November 2016.

Aristotle. (1928) *Metaphysics*, trans. W. D. Ross, 2nd ed. Oxford: Clarendon Press. [The Works of Aristotle, Vol. VIII, *Metaphysica*]

Aristotle. (1991) *The Art of Rhetoric*, trans. Hugh Lawson-Tancred. London: Penguin.

Arrian. (1971 [c. AD 117]) *The Campaigns of Alexander*, trans. Aubrey de Sélincourt. London: Penguin. [A translation of *Anabasis Alexandrou*]

Ascheim, Steve. (1996 [1995]) *Culture and Catastrophe: German and Jewish Confrontations with National Socialism and Other Crises*. London: Palgrave Macmillan.

Ashton, Robert. (1989 [1978]) *The English Civil War: Conservatism and Revolution, 1603-1649*. London: Phoenix Giant.

Atwood, Margaret. (2008) *Payback: Debt and the Shadow Side of Wealth*. London: Bloomsbury.

Augustine, Aurelius. (1962) *The Political Writings of St. Augustine*, ed. Henry Paolucci. Chicago: Henry Regnery Company.

Augustine, Aurelius. (1972 [413-426]) *City of God*, trans. Henry Bettenson. London: Penguin Books.

Augustine, Aurelius. (1982 [410]) *On the Literal Interpretation of Scripture* [*De Genesi ad Litteram*], trans. annotated by John Hammond Taylor. New York: Newman Press.

Augustine, Aurelius. (1988-2000 [434]) *Tractates on the Gospel of John*, (multi-volume) trans. John W. Rettig. Washington D.C.: The Catholic University of America Press. Available at http://www.newadvent.org/fathers/1701.htm, accessed 22 December 2013. See also http://www.documentacatholicaomnia.eu/02m/0354-0430,_Augustinus,_In_Evangeliumnnis_Tractatus_CXXIV,_MLT.pdf, accessed 8 September 2013.

Augustine, Aurelius. (2001) *Political Writings*, (eds) E. M. Atkins and R. J. Dodaro. Cambridge: Cambridge University Press.

Austin, Victor Lee. (2009) *Up with Authority: Why We Need Authority to Flourish as Human Beings*. London: T&T Clark International.

Avineri, Shlomo. (1972) *Hegel's Theory of the Modern State*. Cambridge: Cambridge University Press.

Avrich, Paul. (1970) 'Introduction,' in Bakunin 1871.

Aylmer, G. E. (ed.) (1975) *The Levellers in the English Revolution*. London: Thames & Hudson.

Azumah, John Alembillah. (2001) *The Legacy of Arab-Islam in Africa*. London: One World Publications.

Badhwar, Neera K. & Roderick T. Long. (2013) 'Ayn Rand,' in *Stanford Encyclopedia of Philosophy*, available at http://plato.stanford.edu/archives/sum2013/entries/ayn-rand/, accessed 7 September 2013.

Badinter, Elisabeth. (2006) *Dead End Feminism*, trans. Julia Borossa. Cambridge: Polity Press. First published in 2003 as *Fausse route* by Le Livre de Poche.

Bagehot, Walter. (2001 [1867]) *The English Constitution*, ed. Miles Taylor. Oxford: Oxford University press. [Oxford World Classics]

Baggini, Julian. (2015) *Freedom Regained: The Possibility of Free Will*. London: Granta.

Bailie, William. (1906) *Josiah Warren: The First American Anarchist*. Boston: Small, Maynard & Co.

Baker, Mark C. (2002 [2001]) *The Atoms of Language*. Oxford: Oxford University Press.

Baker, William W. (2010) *Endless Money: The Moral Hazards of Socialism*. Hoboken, New Jersey: John Wiley & Sons, Inc.

Bakunin, Mikhail. (1842) 'The Reaction in Germany,' in Graham 2005, 43-44. Available at http://www.marxists.org/reference/archive/bakunin/works/1842/reaction-germany.htm, accessed 6 June 2014. See also Graham 2005 79-96, 101-105.

Bakunin, Mikhail. (1900 [1873]) *Statism and Anarchy*, trans. and ed. Marshall S. Shatz. Cambridge: Cambridge University Press. [Cambridge Texts in the History of Political Thought]

Bakunin, Mikhail. (1970 [1871]) *God and the State*, intro. Paul Avrich. New York: Dover.

Bakunin, Mikhail. (2009 [1870]) *Letters to a Frenchman on the Present Crisis*. The Anarchist Library. Available at https://ia600804.us.archive.org/13/items/al_Michail_Bakunin_Letters_to_a_Frenchman_on_the_Present_Crisis_a4/Michail_Bakunin__Letters_to_a_Frenchman_on_the_Present_Crisis_a4.pdf, accessed 8 June 2014.

Ball, Terence & Richard Bellamy. (eds) (2003) *The Cambridge History of Twentieth Century Political Thought*. Cambridge: Cambridge University Press.

Baltzly, Dirk. (2012) 'Stoicism,' in *Stanford Encyclopedia of Philosophy*, available at http://plato.stanford.edu/archives/win2012/entries/stoicism/, accessed at 7 September 2013.

Barber, Michael. (2012) 'Alfred Schutz,' in *Stanford Encyclopedia of Philosophy*, available at http://plato.stanford.edu/archives/win2012/entries/schutz/, accessed 7 September 2013.

Barden, Garrett & Tim Murphy. (2010) *Law and Justice in Community*. Oxford: Oxford University Press.

Barfield, Owen. (1977) *The Rediscovery of Meaning and Other Essays*. San Rafael, California: The Barfield Press.

Barfield, Owen. (1988 [1957]) *Saving the Appearances: A Study in Idolatry*, 2nd ed. Middletown, Connecticut: Wesleyan University Press.

Barfield, Owen. (2007 [1953]) *History in English Words*. Great Barrington, Massachusetts: Lindisfarne Books. [First published by Faber & Faber (London) in 1953; rev. ed. Eerdmans (Grand Rapids, Michigan) in 1967]

Barker, Ernest. (1918) *Greek Political Theory*. London: Methuen.

Barnes, Jonathan. (1987) 'New Light on Antiphon,' in *Polis*, vol. 7, 2-5.

Barnett, Randy E. (1977) 'Whither Anarchy? Has Robert Nozick Justified the State?,' in *Journal of Libertarian Studies*, Vol. 1, No. 1, 15-21.

Barrow, John D. (1992 [1990]) *Theories of Everything: The Quest for Ultimate Explanation*. London: Vintage. [Originally published by Oxford University Press, 1990]

Barry, John M. (2012 [2011]) *The Creation of the American Soul: Roger Williams, Church and State, and The Birth of Liberty*. London: Duckworth Overlook.

Barry, Norman P. (1979) *Hayek's Social and Economic Philosophy*. London: The Macmillan Press Ltd.

Barry, Liam. (1952) *Our Legacy from Burke*. Cork: Paramount Print.

Bastiat, Claude Frédéric. (1998 [1850]) *The Law*, trans. Dean Russell. Irvington-on-Hudson, New York: Foundation for Economic Education.

Bastiat, Claude Frédéric. (2007 [2011]) *The Bastiat Collection*. 2nd edition. Auburn, Alabama: The Ludwig von Mises Institute.

Batnitzky, Leora. (2010) 'Leo Strauss,' in *Stanford Encyclopedia of Philosophy*, available at http://plato.stanford.edu/archives/win2010/entries/strauss-leo/, accessed 7 September 2013.

Battenhouse, Roy W. (ed.) (1955) *A Companion to the Study of St. Augustine*. New York: Oxford University Press.

Bauer, Péter Tamás. (1976 [1971]) *Dissent on Development*, rev. ed. Cambridge, Massachusetts: Harvard University Press.

Bautier, Robert-Henri. (1971) *The Economic Development of Mediaeval Europe*, trans. Heather Karolyi. London: Thames & Hudson. [Series: Library of European Civilization]

Baylor, Michael. (2011) 'Political Thought in the Age of the Reformation,' in Klosko, 227-246.

Baylor, Michael. (ed.) (1991) *The Radical Reformation*. Cambridge: Cambridge University Press. [Cambridge Texts in the History of Political Thought] [A very useful sourcebook containing material from various figures of the so-called Radical Reformation. Shorter excerpts can be found in Zuck]

Beard, Henry & Christopher Cerf. (1992)*The Official Politically Correct Dictionary and Handbook*. London: Grafton.

Beard, Henry & Christopher Cerf. (1994) *Sex & Dating: The Official Politically Correct Guide*. London: HarperCollins.

Beardslee, John Walter, Jr. (1918) *The Use of* Phusis *in Fifth-Century Greek Literature*. Chicago: Chicago University Press.

Becker, Anna. (2014) 'Jean Bodin on Oeconomics and Politics,' in *History of European Ideas*, Vol. 40, No. 2, 135-154.

Becker, Carl Lotus. (1932) *The Heavenly City of the Eighteenth-Century Philosophers*, 2nd ed. New Haven, Connecticut: Yale University Press. [2nd edition published in 2003]

Beecher, Jonathan. (2011) 'Early European Socialism,' in Klosko, 369-392.

Beiser, Frederick C. (ed.) (1993) *The Cambridge Companion to Hegel*. Cambridge: Cambridge University Press.

Beito, David. (1990) 'Mutual Aid for Social Welfare: The Case of American Fraternal Societies,' in *Critical Review*, 709-736.

Beito, David. (2000) *From Mutual Aid to the Welfare State: Fraternal Societies and Social Services, 1890-1967*. Chapel Hill, North Carolina: University of North Carolina Press.

Bell, Martin. (2005) 'Agony can be Ecstasy,' *The Times*, 20 September.

Ben-Ami, Daniel. (2014) 'Poor Marx for Thomas Piketty,' available at http://daniel-benami.com/2014/05/09/poor-marx-for-thomas-piketty/, accessed 22 December 2015.

Benewick, Robert & Philip Green. (eds) (1998) *The Routledge Dictionary of Twentieth-Century Political Thinkers* 2nd ed. London: Routledge.

Berens, Lewis H. (1961 [1906]) *The Digger Movement in the Days of the Commonwealth as Revealed in the writings of Gerrard Winstanley, the Digger, Mystic and Rationalist, Community and Social Reformer*. London: Holland Press & Merlin Press. Excerpts from Winstanley's major works with interspersed commentary.

Berlin, Isaiah. (1969) *Four Essays on Liberty*. Oxford: Oxford University Press. [Contains the well-known essay 'Two Concepts of Liberty,' as well as 'Political Ideas in the Twentieth Century,' 'Historical Inevitability,' and 'John Stuart Mill and the Ends of Life.'

Berman, Constance Hoffman. (2010 [2000]) *The Cistercian Evolution: The Invention of a Religious Order in Twelfth-Century Europe*. Philadelphia: University of Pennsylvania Press.

Berman, David. (1995) 'Introduction' to Schopenhauer 1995, xvii-xxxix.

Berman, David. (2009 [2005]) *Berkeley and Irish Philosophy*. London: Bloomsbury.

Berman, Harold J. (1983) *Law and Revolution: The Formation of the Western Legal Tradition*. Cambridge, Massachusetts: Harvard University Press.

Berman, Harold J. (2003) *Law and Revolution II: The Impact of the Protestant Reformations on the Western Legal Tradition*. Cambridge, Massachusetts: The Belknap Press (Harvard University Press).

Bernal, Martin. (1992) 'Review of Patterson's Freedom,' in *American Journal of Sociology*, Vol. 97, No 5, 1471-1473.

Berns, Laurence. (1987) 'Thomas Hobbes,' in Strauss & Cropsey, 396-420.

Berns, Walter. (1984) 'The Need for Public Authority,' in Carey, 25-33.

Bertram, Christopher. (2012) 'Jean Jacques Rousseau,' in *Stanford Encyclopedia of Philosophy*, available at http://plato.stanford.edu/archives/win2012/entries/rousseau/, accessed 7 September 2013.

Beyer, Anna Cornelia. (2014) *Inequality and Violence: A Re-appraisal of Man, the State and War*. Farnham, Surrey: Ashgate.

Beza, Theodore. (1554) 'On the Authority of the Magistrates to Punish Heretics,' in Zuck, 143-144.

Beza, Theodore. (1574) 'The Rights of Rulers and Duty of Subjects,' in Zuck, 169-172.

Bingham, John. (2016) 'The Scilly Isles? Is that in Scotland,' *The Telegraph*, 21 September, available at http://www.telegraph.co.uk/news/2016/09/21/the-scilly-isles-is-that-in-scotland/, accessed 21 September 2016.

Bishop, Morris. (1971) *The Penguin Book of the Middle Ages*. London: Penguin.

Black, Antony. (1970) *Monarchy and Community: Political Ideas in the Later Conciliar Controversy: 1430-1450*. Cambridge: Cambridge University Press.

Black, Antony. (1979) *Council and Commune: The Conciliar Movement and the Council of Basle*. London: Burns & Oates.

Black, Antony. (1988a) 'The Conciliar Movement,' in Burns 1988, 573-587.

Black, Antony. (1988b) 'The Individual and Society,' in Burns 1988, 588-606.

Black, Donald. (1976) *The Behavior of Law*. New York: Academic Press.

Black, Jeremy. (2003) *War: An Illustrated History*. Gloucestershire: Sutton Publishing Limited.

Black, Jeremy. (2011) *Slavery: A New Global History*. London: Robinson.

Blanqui, Jérôme-Adolphe. (1837) *Histoire de l'Economie Politique en Europe depuis les anciens jusqu'à nos jours*. Paris: Guillaumin.

Blaug, Mark. (1997) *Economic Theory in Retrospect*, 5th ed. Cambridge, Cambridge University Press.

Block, Walter. (1980) 'On Robert Nozick's "On Austrian Methodology",' in *Inquiry*. 23 (4), 397-444.

Block, Walter. (2006) 'Kevin Carson as Dr. Jekyll and Mr. Hyde,' in *The Journal of Libertarian Studies*, Vol. 20 No. 1, 35-46.

Blum, Jerome. (1961) *Lord and Peasant in Russia from the Ninth to the Nineteenth Century*. Princeton, New Jersey: Princeton University Press.

Boaz, David. (ed.) (1997) *The Libertarian Reader: Classic & Contemporary Writings from Lao-Tzu to Milton Friedman*. New York: The Free Press.

Bobonich, Chris. (2013) 'Plato on Utopia,' in *Stanford Encyclopedia of Philosophy*. Available at http://plato.stanford.edu/entries/plato-utopia/, accessed 22 December 2013.

Bodin, Jean. (1945 [1566]) *Method for the Easy Comprehension of History*. trans. Beatrice Reynolds. New York: Columbia University Press.

Bodin, Jean. (1955 [1576]) *Six Books of the Commonwealth*, abridged and trans. Marian J Tooley. Oxford: Blackwell. Available online at http://www.constitution.org/bodin/bodin.txt, accessed 28 November 2013. Tooley's 'Introduction' separately available online at http://www.constitution.org/bodin/bodin_0.htm.

Bodin, Jean. (1962 [1576]) *The Six Bookes of a Commonweal*, trans. Richard Knolles, ed. Kenneth Douglas McRae. Cambridge: Harvard University Press.

Bodin, Jean. (1975 [1593?]) *Colloquium of the Seven about Secrets of the Sublime*. trans. Marion Leathers Kuntz. Princeton, N. J.: Princeton University Press.

Bodin, Jean. (1992 [1576]) *On Sovereignty: Four Chapters from The Six Books of the Commonwealth*, trans. and ed. Julian H. Franklin. Cambridge: Cambridge University Press.

Boettke, Peter J. (2012) *Living Economics: Yesterday, Today, and Tomorrow*. Oakland, California: The Independent Institute.

Böhm-Bawerk, Eugen von. (1890 [1884]) *Capital and Interest: A Critical History of Economic Theory*. London: Macmillan and Co. Available at http://lf-oll.s3.amazonaws.com/titles/284/0188_Bk.pdf, accessed 25 April 2014.

Böhm-Bawerk, Eugen von. (1975) *The Exploitation Theory of Socialism-Communism*. South Holland, Illinois: Libertarian Press.

Bolton, Whitney F. (ed.) (1975) *The English Language*. London: Sphere Books. [Sphere History of Literature in the English Language Volume 10]

Booker, Christopher. (2004) *The Seven Basic Plots: Why We Tell Stories*. London: Bloomsbury.

Bottomore, Thomas Burton & Maximilien Rubel. (1963) 'Introduction' to Marx 1963.

Boucher, David & Paul Kelly. (eds) (1998) *Social Justice: From Hume to Walzer*. London: Routledge.

Boucher, David & Paul Kelly. (eds) (2009) *Political Thinkers: From Socrates to the Present*, 2nd ed. Oxford: Oxford University Press. A set of essays by individual authors on various political thinkers.

Boucher, David. (2009) 'Burke,' in Boucher & Kelly 2009, 282-302.

Bouillon, Hardy & Harmut Kliemt. (eds) (2007) *Ordered Anarchy: Jasay and his Surroundings*. London: Ashgate.

Bourne, Randolph Silliman. (1918) 'War is the Health of the State,' an excerpt from *Untimely Papers*, New York: B. W. Huebsch 1919 (ed. James Oppenheim), available at http://www.antiwar.com/bourne.php, accessed 9 June 2014. *Untimely Papers* is available at https://archive.org/details/untimelypapers00bourgoog, accessed 9 June 2014. See also Bourne 1992, 355-395.

Bourne, Randolph Silliman. (1992) *The Radical Will: Selected Writings 1911-1918*. Berkeley, California: The University of California Press.

Bowen, Elizabeth. (1945) 'Notes on Writing a Novel,' in *Orion—A Miscellany* (Vol. II). London: Nicholson and Watson. Available at http://www.narrativemagazine.com/issues/fall-2006/classics/notes-writing-novel-elizabeth-bowen, accessed 19 March 2016.

Bowle, John. (1954) *Politics and Opinion in the 19th Century*. London: Jonathan Cape.

Boyd, J. P. (ed.) (1950) *The Papers of Thomas Jefferson*. Princeton, New Jersey: Princeton University Press.

Bracton, Henry de. (1235-1260 [1977]) *Bracton on the Laws and Customs of England* [*De Legibus et Consuetudinibus Angliae*], trans. Samuel E. Thorne. Cambridge, Massachusetts: The Belknap Press of Harvard University Press, 1977. Published in Association with the Selden Society. The [searchable] text is available online at http://bracton.law.harvard.edu/, accessed 8 September 2013.

Bradbury, Ray. (2008 [1954]) *Fahrenheit 451*. London: HarperVoyager.

Bradshaw, Leah. (2015) 'Review of Larry Siedentop's *Inventing the Individual*,' *The Review of Politics*, Vol. 77, No 03, 487-490.

Brafman, Ori & Rod A. Beckstrom. (2006) *The Starfish and the Spider: The Unstoppable Power of Leaderless Organizations*. London: Portfolio. A delightful and entertaining account of the strength and value of leaderlessness in a variety of contexts.

Brailsford, Henry Noel. (1961) *The Levellers and the English Revolution*, ed. Christopher Hill. London: The Cresset Press.

Braitmichel, Caspar. (1565) 'The Beginnings of the Anabaptist Movement,' in Zuck, 68-70.

Brand, Hanno. (ed.) (2005) *Trade, Diplomacy and Cultural Exchange: Continuity and Change in the North Sea Area and the Baltic, c. 1350-1750*. Hilversum, The Netherlands: Uitgeverij Verloren.

Brecht, Arnold. (1968) 'Approaches' in 'Political Theory' in *International Encyclopedia of the Social Sciences*. Available at *Encyclopedia.com* at http://www.encyclopedia.com/topic/Political_philosophy.aspx, accessed 20 April 2015.

Brett, David. (2009) *A Book around the Irish Sea: History without Nations*. Dublin: Wordwell.

Brignell, Victoria. (2010a) 'The Eugenics Movement Britain Wants to Forget,' *New Statesman*, 9 December 2010. Available at http://www.newstatesman.com/society/2010/12/british-eugenics-disabled, accessed 5 October 2016. Available at http://www.newstatesman.com/society/2010/12/disabled-america-immigration, accessed 5 October 2016.

Brignell, Victoria. (2010b) When America Believed in Eugenics,' New Statesman, 10 December 2010

Brink, David. (2009) 'Mill's Moral and Political Philosophy,' in *Stanford Encyclopedia of Philosophy*. Available at http://plato.stanford.edu/entries/mill-moral-political/, accessed 4 March 2014.

Brook, Yaron & Don Watkins. (2012) *Free Market Revolution: How Ayn Rand's Ideas Can End Big Government*. New York: Palgrave Macmillan.

Brooks, David. (2011 [2000/2004]) *The Paradise Suite: Bobos in Paradise* and *On Paradise Drive*. New York: Simon & Schuster.

Brooks, Thom. (2007) *Hegel's Political Philosophy: A Systematic Reading of the Philosophy of Right*. Edinburgh: Edinburgh University Press.

Brown, Michael. (2016) *The Irish Enlightenment*. Cambridge, Massachusetts: Harvard University Press.

Brown, Peter. (1967) *Augustine of Hippo: a Biography*. London: Faber. New revised edition, Berkeley, California: University of California Press, 2000.

Brown, Peter. (2012) *Through the Eye of a Needle: Wealth, the Fall of Rome, and the Making of Christianity in the West, 350-550 AD*. Princeton, New Jersey: Princeton University Press.

Brown, Peter. (2015) *The Ransom of the Soul: Afterlife and Wealth in Early Western Christianity*. Cambridge, Massachusetts: Harvard University Press.

Browne, Sarah & Jesse Jones. (2016) 'Burn in Flames: Post-Patriarchal Archive in Circulation,' in *feminists@law*, Vol. 6, No 1, available at http://journals.kent.ac.uk/index.php/feministsatlaw/article/view/265/840, accessed 17 January 2017.

Brutus, Stephanus Junius. [Hubert Languet? Philip de Mornay?] (1994 [1579]) *Vindiciae, contra Tyrannos: or, concerning the Legitimate Power of a Prince over the People, and of the People over a Prince*, ed. and trans. George Garnett. Cambridge: Cambridge University Press. Available in an earlier translation at http://www.constitution.org/vct/vindiciae.htm, accessed 30 August 2013. Also available at http://lonang.com/library/reference/vindiciae-contra-tyrannos-1579/, accessed 5 July 2016.

Buchanan, George. (2004 [1579]) *A Dialogue on the Law of Kingship among the Scots*. ed. and trans. Roger A. Mason and Martin S. Smith. Aldershot: Ashgate. Available online in an earlier version at http://www.portagepub.com/dl/caa/buchanan.pdf?, accessed 14 September 2013 (trans. Robert MacFarlane, Colorado Springs, Colorado: Portage Publications, 2009 [London: S. Hamilton (for T. Cadell, Jun. and W Davies in the Strand), Fleet Street, 1799]).

Buchanan, James M. (2000 [1975]) *The Limits of Liberty: Between Anarchy and Leviathan*. Indianapolis, Indiana: The Liberty Fund. [Volume 7 in the Collected Works of James M. Buchanan]

Bullinger, Heinrich. (1975) 'A History of the Reformation (recalling 1525),' in Zuck, 64-66.

Bunge, Mario. (1979) 'A Systems Concept of Society: Beyond Individualism and Holism' in *Theory and Decision*, Vol. 10, 13-30.

Burg, David F. (2004) *A World History of Tax Rebellions: An Encyclopedia of Tax Rebels, Revolts and Riots from Antiquity to the Present*. New York: Routledge.

Burgess, John William. (1923) *Recent Changes in American Constitutional Theory*. New York: Columbia University Press.

Burke, Edmund. (1854-56), *The Works of the Right Honourable Edmund Burke. 6 vols. [Speech on Conciliation with the Colonies (1745)—vol. I, 464-471.]* London: Henry G. Bohn.

Burke, Edmund. (1968 [1790]) *Reflections on the Revolution in France*, ed. Conor Cruise O'Brien. London: Penguin Books.

Burke, Edmund. (1993 [1756-1790]) *Pre-Revolutionary Writings*, ed. Ian Harris. Cambridge: Cambridge University Press. [Cambridge Texts in the History of Political Thought. This collection contains, *inter alia*, 'Extempore Commonplace on The Sermon of our Saviour on the Mount'; *A Vindication of Natural Society*; *A Philosophical Enquiry into the Origin of our Ideas of the Sublime and Beautiful*; *Tracts on the Popery Laws*; *Thoughts on the Cause of the Present Discontents*; and *Conciliation with America*]

Burke, Edmund. (1996) *The Writing and Speeches of Edmund Burke, vol. III—Party, Parliament, and the American War 1774-1780*), eds W. M. Elofson, Paul Langford et al. Oxford: Clarendon Press.

Burke, Edmund. (1997a) *The Writings and Speeches of Edmund Burke, vol. I—The Early Writings*, eds T. O. McLoughlin, James T Boulton et al. Oxford: Clarendon Press.

Burke, Edmund. (1997b [1756]) *A Vindication of Natural Society*, in Burke 1997a, 129-184.

Burke, Edmund. (1999 [1796]) *Letters on a Regicide Peace*, ed. E. J. Payne. Indianapolis, Indiana: Liberty Fund. Available at http://lf-oll.s3.amazonaws.com/titles/658/0005-03_Bk.pdf, accessed 17 April 2014.

Burke, Edmund. (1999) *Select Works of Edmund Burke*, ed. E. J. Payne. Indianapolis, Indiana: Liberty Fund, available at http://www.econlib.org/library/LFBooks/Burke/brkSWv4.html, accessed August 2013.

Burke, Edmund. (2003 [1790]) *Reflections on the Revolution in France*, ed. Frank M. Turner. New Haven, Connecticut: Yale University Press. With essays by Darrin M. McMahon, Conor Cruise O'Brien, Jack N. Rakove, Alan Wolfe.

Burleigh, Michael. (2000) 'National Socialism as a Political Religion,' in *Totalitarian Movements and Political Religions*, Vol. 1, No. 2, 1-26.

Burns, James Henderson. (ed.) (1988) *The Cambridge History of Medieval Political Thought, c. 350-c. 1450.* Cambridge: Cambridge University Press. [The two volumes in this superb history contain individual articles, many of which will be separately cited]

Burns, James Henderson. (ed.) (1991) *The Cambridge History of Medieval Political Thought, 1450-1700.* Cambridge: Cambridge University Press.

Burns, Tony. (2009) 'Aristotle,' in Boucher & Kelly 2009, 81-99.

Burrow, John. (2007) *A History of Histories: Epics, Chronicles, Romances and Inquiries from Herodotus and Thucydides to the Twentieth Century*. London: Allen Land.

Bury, John Bagnall. (1920) *The Idea of Progress*. London: Macmillan and Co.

Butler, Ann Caldwell. (1980) 'Josiah Warren and the Sovereignty of the Individual,' in *The Journal of Libertarian Studies*, Vol. 4, No. 4, 433-448.

Butler, Smedley D. (2003 [1935]) *War is a Racket*, intro. Adam Parfrey. Port Townsend, Washington: Feral House. [This edition also contains *Common Sense Neutrality* and *An Amendment for Peace. War is a Racket* was originally published by Round Table Press, Inc. (New York, 1935)]

Butterworth, Charles E. (2011) 'Arabic Contributions to Medieval Political Theory,' in Klosko ed., 164-179.

Bydeley, Steve. (2009) 'Submit to Governing Authorities? (Romans 13),' available at http://www.beinaberean.org/writings/romans13.html, accessed 5 September 2014.

Cahill, Thomas. (1995) *How the Irish Saved Civilization: The Untold Story of Ireland's Heroic Role from the Fall of Rome to the Rise of Medieval Europe*. New York: Doubleday. [Despite its extravagantly hyperbolical title, this is an engaging account of the early medieval period with a focus on the literary, cultural and religious contributions of Irish culture to European civilisation]

Calvin, John. (1559) 'On Civil Government [*Institutio Christianae Religionis*, Book IV, chapter 20],' in Höpfl, 47-86.

Cambiano, Giuseppe. (1987) 'Aristotle and the Anonymous Opponents of Slavery,' in Finley, 22-41.

Campos, Paul F. (1998) *Jurismania: The Madness of American Law*. New York: Oxford University Press.

Canning, Joseph. (1996) *A History of Medieval Political Thought (300-1450)*. London: Routledge.

Caplan, Bryan. (2011) 'Anarchist Theory FAQ or Instead of a FAQ, by a Man Too Busy to Write One, version 5.2,' available at http://econfaculty.gmu.edu/bcaplan/anarfaq. htm accessed 4 June 2014.

Caplan, Bryan. (no date) 'Appendix: Defining Anarchism,' available at http://econfaculty.gmu.edu/bcaplan/def.htm, accessed 4 June 2014.

Carcopino, Jérôme. (1941) *Daily Life in Ancient Rome*, trans. E. O. Lorimer, ed. Henry T. Rowell. Harmondsworth, Middlesex: Penguin.

Carey, G. W. (ed.) (1984) *Freedom and Virtue: the Conservative/Libertarian debate*. Lanham, Maryland: University Press of America.

Carey, Nessa. (2012 [2011]) *The Epigenetics Revolution: How Modern Biology is Rewriting Our Understanding of Genetics, Disease and Inheritance*. London: Icon Books.

Carlyle, A. J. (1928) *A History of Mediaeval Political Theory in the West. Vol. 3.— Political Theory from the Tenth Century to the Thirteenth*. London: William Blackwood & Sons.

Carlyle, R. W. & A. J. Carlyle. (1903) *A History of Mediaeval Political Theory in the West. Vol. 1—The Second Century to the Ninth*. London: William Blackwood & Sons.

Carlyle, R. W. & A. J. Carlyle. (1909) *A History of Mediaeval Political Theory in the West. Vol. 2.—The Political Theory of the Roman lawyers and the Canonists, from the Tenth Century to the Thirteenth Century*. London: William Blackwood & Sons.

Carlyle, Thomas. (2005 [1850]) *Latter-Day Pamphlets*. New York: Elibron Classics.

Carneiro, Robert L. (1970) 'A Theory of the Origin of the State,' in *Science* (new series), vol. 169, no. 3947, 733-38.

Carney, Frederick S. (1964) 'Translator's Introduction,' in Althusius 1964, ix-xxxiii.

Carroll, Lewis. (1972 [1871]) *Through the Looking Glass*. London: Hart-Davis, MacGibbon.

Carter, Alan B. (1988) *Marx: A Radical Critique*. Brighton, Sussex: Wheatsheaf Books.

Carver, Terrell. (1982) *Marx's Social Theory*. Oxford: Oxford University Press.

Carver, Terrell. (2011) 'The Marxian Tradition,' in Klosko, 393-413.

Casey, Gerard. (1992) 'Minds and Machines,' in *American Catholic Philosophical Quarterly*, Vol. 66 No. 1, 57-80. Available at http://www.ucd.ie/philosophy/staff/gerardcasey/casey/MndMchnes.pdf, accessed 6 July 2014.

Casey, G. (2004) 'The 'Logically Faultless' Argument for Unenumerated Rights in the Constitution,' *Irish Law Times,* 22 (16): 246-248.

Casey, G. (2005) 'Are there Unenumerated Rights in the Irish Constitution?' *Irish Law Times,* 23 (8): 123-127.

Casey, Gerard. (2008) 'An Argument for Essentialism,' in *Linguistic and Philosophical Investigations*, Vol. 7, 15-18.

Casey, Gerard. (2009) 'One Very Simple Principle,' *Philosophy Now*, Vol. 76, 26-27.

Casey, Gerard. (2009a) 'Teaching Philosophy to the Gifted Young,' in *Gifted Education International*, Vol. 25, 246-258.

Casey, Gerard. (2010) *Murray Rothbard*. London: Continuum. Volume 17 in the series MAJOR CONSERVATIVE AND LIBERTARIAN THINKERS, series ed. John Meadowcroft.

Casey, Gerard. (2010a) 'Reflections on Legal Polycentrism,' in *Journal of Libertarian Studies*, Vol. 22, 22-34.

Casey, Gerard. (2010b) 'Constitutions of No Authority: Spoonerian Reflections,' in *The Independent Review*, Vol. 14, No. 3, 325-340.

Casey, Gerard. (2011) 'Conservatism and Libertarianism: Friends or Foes?' in Özsel, 33-53.

Casey, Gerard. (2012) 'Seeing Ourselves as Others See Us: The Place of Reason in Adam Smith's *Theory of Moral Sentiments*,' in Edmondson & Huelser, 79-93.

Casey, Gerard. (2012a) 'Ownership and Possession—Where Do You Draw the Line? Sound recording, available at http://mises.org/media/7487/Ownership-and-Possession-Where-Do-You-Draw-the-Line?ajaxsrc=audio, accessed 11 July 2014.

Casey, Gerard. (2012b) *Libertarian Anarchy: Against the State*. London: Continuum.

Casey, Gerard. (2012c) 'Thinking Critically about Critical Thinking,' in *Critical Thinking and Higher Order Thinking*, (ed.) Mike Shaughnessy. New York, Hauppauge: Nova Science Publishers, 23-39.

Casey, Gerard. (2014) 'The Limits of Liberty, or Hurrah for Repression!' A talk given at the 2014 Annual Meeting of the Property and Freedom Society in Bodrum, Turkey. Available at https://www.youtube.com/watch?v=5iZMw0z2IMg, accessed 23 July 2015.

Casey, Gerard. (2015) 'Review of James R. Otteson's *The End of Socialism*,' in *The Review of Austrian Economics*, published online, 29 January 2015.

Casey, Gerard. (2016) 'Review of Edward Peter Stringham's *Private Governance: Creating Order in Economic and Social Life*,' in *The Independent Review*, Vol. 21, No. 01, 150-153. Available at http://www.independent.org/publications/tir/article.asp?a=1149, accessed 19 June 2016.

Catlin, George. (1996 [1875]) *Life among the Indians*. London: Bracken Books. [Originally published in London & Edinburgh in 1875 by Gall & Inglis]

Chadwick, Nora. (1970) *The Celts*. London: Penguin.

Chaffey, Tim. (2011) 'An Examination of Augustine's Commentaries on Genesis One and Their Implications on a Modern Theological Controversy,' in *Answers Research Journal*, Vol. 4. 89-101, available at https://assets.answersingenesis.org/doc/articles/pdf-versions/Augustine_Genesis_1_theology.pdf

Chaloner, W. H. & W. O. Henderson. (1975) 'Marx/Engels and Racism,' in *Encounter* (July 1975), available at http://www.paulbogdanor.com/antisemitism/marxracism.pdf, accessed 11 January 2015.

Chanda, Nayan. (2008) *Bound Together: How Traders, Preachers, Adventurers and Warriors Shaped Globalization*. New Haven, Connecticut: Yale University Press.

Chaplin, Jonathan. (2008) 'Representing a People: Oliver O'Donovan on Democracy and Tradition,' in *Political Theology*, Vol. 9 No. 3, 295-307.

Charles I. (1642) 'His Majesties Answer to the Nineteen Propositions of Both Houses of Parliament' (excerpts), in Wootton, 2003, 171-174.

Chartier, Gary. (2014) *Radicalizing Rawls: Global Justice and the Foundations of International Law*. London: Palgrave Macmillan.

Chesterton, Gilbert Keith. (1933) *St. Thomas Aquinas*. New York: Sheed & Ward.

Chesterton, Gilbert Keith. (1987) *The Essential Chesterton*, ed. P. J. Kavanagh. Oxford: Oxford University Press.

Childs Jr, Roy A. (1977) 'The Invisible Hand Strikes Back,' in *Journal of Libertarian Studies*, Vol. 1 No. 1, 23-33.

Chotiner, Isaac. (2014) 'Thomas Piketty: I Don't Care for Marx,' available at http://danielbenami.com/2014/05/09/poor-marx-for-thomas-piketty/, accessed 22 December 2015.

Christoyannopoulos, Alexandre. (2011) *Christian Anarchism: A Political Commentary on the Gospel* (abridged). Exeter: Imprint Academic.

Cicero, Marcus Tullius. (1927 [45 BC]) *Tusculan Disputations*, trans. J. E. King. Cambridge, Massachusetts: Harvard University Press. [Loeb Classical Library]

Cicero, Marcus Tullius. (1998 [54-51BC]) *The Republic & The Laws*, trans. Niall Rudd. Oxford: Oxford University Press. [Oxford World's Classics]

Cicero, Marcus Tullius. (2000 [44BC]) *On Obligations*, trans. P. G. Walsh. Oxford: Oxford University Press. [Oxford World's Classics]

Cicero, Marcus Tullius. (2016) *How to Win an Argument: An Ancient Guide to the Art of Persuasion*, ed. and trans. James M. May. Princeton, New Jersey: Princeton University Press.

Cipolla, Carlo M. (1993) *Before the Industrial Revolution: European Society and Economy, 1000-1700*, 3rd ed. New York: W. W. Norton.

Claessen, Henri M. & Skalnik, Peter. (eds) (1978) *The Early State*. The Hague: Mouton Publishers.

Clark, Gregory. (2009) *A Farewell to Alms: A Brief Economic History of the World*. Princeton, New Jersey: Princeton University Press.

Clark, Peter. (2000) *British Clubs and Societies 1580-1800: The Origins of an Associated World*. Oxford: Oxford University Press.

Clastres, Pierre. (1989) *Society against the State: Essays in Political Anthropology*, trans. Robert Hurley in collaboration with Abe Stein. New York: Zone Books. Originally published as *La Société contre l'état* in 1974 by Editions de Minuit.

Clay, Diskin. (2006) 'Introduction,' in Marcus Aurelius's *Meditations*, Penguin, xi-xlv.

Coady, C. A. J. (2012) 'The Problem of Dirty Hands,' in *Stanford Encyclopedia of Philosophy*, available at http://plato.stanford.edu/archives/sum2011/entries/dirty-hands/, accessed 7 September 2013.

Cobban, Alan B. (1988 [1975]) *The Medieval Universities: Their Development and Organization*. Berkeley: University of California Press. [First published in London by Menthuen Press]

Cochran, Gregory & Henry Harpending. (2009) *The 10,000 Year Explosion: How Civilization Accelerated Human Evolution*. New York: Basic Books.

Codevilla, Angelo M. (2016) 'The Rise of Political Correctness,' in *Claremont Review of Books* (Fall 2016), 37-43.

Coggan, Philip. (2011) *Paper Promises: Money, Debt and the New World Order*. London: Allen Lane.

Cohen, Gerald Allen. (1978) *Karl Marx's Theory of History: A Defence*. Princeton, New Jersey: Princeton University Press.

Cohen, Gerald Allen. (1995) *Self-ownership, Freedom, and Equality*. Cambridge: Cambridge University Press.

Cohen, Gerald Allen. (2009) *Why Not Socialism?* Princeton, New Jersey: Princeton University Press.

Cole, George Douglas Howard & Margaret I. Cole. (1934) *A Guide to Modern Politics*. London: Victor Gollancz.

Cole, George Douglas Howard. (2011 [1948]) *The Meaning of Marxism*. London: Victor Gollancz Ltd. Reprinted by Routledge (2011).

Cole, Wayne S. (1974) *Charles A. Lindbergh and the Battle Against American Intervention in World War II.* New York: Harcourt Brace Jovanovich.

Cole, Wayne S. (1983) *Roosevelt and the Isolationists.* Omaha: University of Nebraska Press.

Coleman, Janet. (1988) 'Property and Poverty,' in Burns 1988, 607-648.

Coleman, Janet. (2011) 'Medieval Political Theory c. 1000-1500,' in Klosko, 180-205.

Collins, Jeffrey. (2011) 'The Early Modern Foundations of Classic Liberalism,' in Klosko, 258-281.

Compton, John W. (2014) *The Evangelical Origins of the Living Constitution.* Cambridge, Massachusetts: Harvard University Press.

Comyn, David & Patrick S. Dineen. (eds. and transs.) (1902-1914) *Foras Feasa ar Éirinn: The History of Ireland by Geoffrey Keating D. D.* London: Irish Texts Society. Available online at http://www.ucc.ie/celt/online/T100054/, accessed 12 January 2017; see also http://vanhamel.nl/codecs/Comyn_and_Dinneen_1902-1914, accessed 12 January 2017.

Constant, Benjamin. (1988 [1819]) 'The Liberty of the Ancients compared with that of the Moderns,' in Constant 1988, 309-328.

Constant, Benjamin. (1988) *Constant: Political Writings*, ed. and trans. Biancamaria Fontana. Cambridge: Cambridge University Press.

Constant, Benjamin. (2003 [1815]) *Principles of Politics Applicable to All Governments*, ed. Etienne Hofmann, trans. Dennis O'Keeffe. Indianapolis, Indiana: Liberty Fund. Available at http://lf-oll.s3.amazonaws.com/titles/861/0452_LFeBk.pdf, accessed 25 April 2014.

Conti, Alessandro. (2011) 'Wyclif,' in *Stanford Encyclopedia of Philosophy*, available at http://plato.stanford.edu/entries/wyclif/, accessed 11 October 2016.

Conway, Robert Seymour. (1928 [1923]) *The Making of Latin: An Introduction to Latin, Greek and English Etymology*, 2nd ed. London: John Murray.

Copeland, T. W. (1938) 'Burke's *Vindication of Natural Society*,' in *The Library*, 4th Series XVIII.

Copley, James. (1961) *Shift of Meaning.* Oxford: Oxford University Press.

Corpus juris cononici. *Decreti Gratiani*, available at http://digital.library.ucla.edu/canonlaw/, accessed June 2013.

Cottrell, Leonard. (1955) *Life under the Pharaohs.* London: Pan.

Coulam, Paul. (1996) 'For a New Libertarianism: Problems and Perspectives in the Thought of Ayn Rand, Murray Rothbard and David Friedman,' *Philosophical Notes No. 39.* London: Libertarian Alliance.

Cowell, Frank Richard. (1952) *History, Civilization and Culture: An Introduction to the Historical and Social Philosophy of Pitirim A. Sorokin.* London: Adam and Charles Black.

Cowell, Frank Richard. (1956 [1948]) *Cicero and the Roman Republic.* London: Penguin. [More about the Roman Republic than about Cicero, but a treasure chest of information about the governance of Rome and the daily life of the Romans.]

Cowling, Maurice. (1963) *Mill and Liberalism.* Cambridge: Cambridge University Press.

Crane, Tim. (ed.) (1998) *Routledge Encyclopedia of Philosophy*, available at https://www-rep-routledge-com.ucd.idm.oclc.org/, accessed 1 September 2015. [Originally edited by Edward Crane, the *Encyclopedia* is now available on line via subscription]

Crawford, Michael. (ed.) (2007) *Anthropological Genetics: Theory, Methods and Applications.* Cambridge: Cambridge University Press.

Creel, George. (1920) *How We Advertised America: The First Telling of the Amazing Story of the Committee on Public Information that Carried the Gospel of Americanism to Every Corner of the Globe*. New York: Harper & Brothers Publishers.

Croly, Herbert. (2014 [1909]) *The Promise of American Life*. Princeton, New Jersey: Princeton University Press.

Crossley, David. (2011) 'Francis Herbert Bradley's Moral and Political Philosophy,' in *Stanford Encyclopedia of Philosophy*, available at http://plato.stanford.edu/archives/spr2011/entries/bradley-moral-political/, accessed 7 September 2013.

Crowder, George. (1991) *Classical Anarchism: The Political Thought of Godwin, Proudhon, Bakunin, and Kropotkin*. Oxford: Clarendon Press.

Crystal, David. (2010 [1987]) *The Cambridge Encyclopedia of Language*, 3rd ed. Cambridge: Cambridge University Press.

Cudd, Ann. (2012) 'Contractarianism,' in *Stanford Encyclopedia of Philosophy*, available at http://plato.stanford.edu/archives/fall2012/entries/contractarianism/, accessed 7 September 2013.

Cull, Nicholas John. (1995) *Selling War: The British Propaganda Campaign Against American Neutrality in World War II*. New York: Oxford University Press.

D'Agostino, Fred, Gerald Gaus and John Thrasher. (2012) 'Contemporary Approaches to the Social Contract,' in *Stanford Encyclopedia of Philosophy*, available at http://plato.stanford.edu/archives/win2012/entries/contractarianism-contemporary/, accessed 7 September 2013.

d'Entrèves, Alexander Passerin. (1939) *The Medieval Contribution to Political Thought: Thomas Aquinas, Marsilius of Padua, Richard Hooker*. Oxford: Oxford University Press.

d'Entrèves, Alexander Passerin. (1967) *The Notion of the State: An Introduction to Political Theory*. Oxford: Clarendon Press.

d'Entrèves, Alexander Passerin. (ed.) (1959) *Aquinas: Selected Political Writings*. Oxford: Blackwell.

Daitz, Werner. (1936) '*Weltanschauung und Wirtschaft*' ('World-view and economy), in *Nationalsozialistiche Monatschriften* 7/70, 54-60; excerpt in Griffin, 141-142.

Dalberg-Acton, John Emerich Edward. (1907) *The History of Freedom and Other Essays*. London: Macmillan and Co. Limited. Available at http://lf-oll.s3.amazonaws.com/titles/75/0030_Bk.pdf, accessed 25 April 2014.

Dalton, Dennis. (2011) 'Hindu Political Philosophy,' in Klosko, 803-820.

Damrosch, Leo. (2007 [2005]) *Jean-Jacques Rousseau: Restless Genius*. New York: Houghton Mifflin Company.

Daniels, Norman. (ed.) (1983 [1975]) *Reading Rawls: Critical Studies of* A Theory of Justice. Oxford: Blackwell. Contains articles by, among others, Thomas Nagel, Ronald Dworkin, H. L. A. Hart and A. K. Sen.

Davidson, James Dale & William Rees-Mogg. (1999) *The Sovereign Individual*. London: Touchstone.

Davie, Maurice R. (1929 [2003]) *The Evolution of War: A Study of its Role in Early Societies*. Mineola, New York: Dover Publications Inc.

Davies, Norman. (1999) *The Isles: A History*. London: Papermac.

Davies, Norman. (2011) *Vanished Kingdoms: The History of Half-Forgotten Europe*. London: Allen Lane.

Davies, Stephen. (2015) 'Blood and Leviathan,' a review of Ian Morris's *War! What is it Good For?: Conflict and the Progress of Civilization from Primates to Robots*,' available at http://reason.com/archives/2015/06/27/blood-and-leviathan, accessed 28 June 2015.

Davis, David Brion. (1998) 'Introduction: The Problem of Slavery,' in Drescher and Engerman, ix-xviii.

Davis, Robert C. (2003) *Christian Slaves, Muslim Masters: White Slavery in the Mediterranean, The Barbary Coast, and Italy, 1500-1800*. London: Palgrave Macmillan.

Dawson, Christopher. (1959 [1954]) *Medieval Essays*. New York: Image Books.

Dawson, Christopher. (2009 [1933]) 'St. Augustine and His Age,' in Christopher Dawson, *Enquiries into Religion and Culture* Washington D. C.: Catholic University of America Press, 164-213.

Day, Vox. (2008) *The Irrational Atheist: Dissecting the Unholy Trinity of Dawkins, Harris, and Hitchens*. Dallas, Texas: Benbella Books, Inc.

de Benoist, Alain. (1999) 'The First Federalist: Johannes Althusius,' in *Krisis*, Vol. 22, 2-34. Trans. Julia Kostova. Available at http://www.alaindebenoist.com/pdf/the_first_ federalist_althusius.pdf, accessed 1 December 2013. Page references are to the online English version.

de Coulanges, Numa Denis Fustel. (2006 [1874]) *The Ancient City: A Study of the Religion, Laws, and Institutions of Greece and Rome*, trans. Willard Small. Mineola, New York: Dover Publications, Inc. First published as *La cité antique* by L. Hachette et cie, Paris in 1864. Available online in a 2001 edition from Batoche Books (Kitchener, Ontario) at http://socserv.socsci.mcmaster.ca/econ/ugcm/3ll3/fustel/AncientCity.pdf, accessed 10 September 2015. Also available from Johns Hopkins Press (Baltimore, Maryland) in a 1980 reprint of the Doubleday Anchor Book of 1956. This is a classic work that although to some extent necessarily dated is still a mine of information.

de Jasay, Anthony. (1991) *Choice, Contract, Consent: A Restatement of Liberalism*. London: Institute of Economic Affairs.

de Jasay, Anthony. (1997) *Against Politics: On Government, Anarchy and Order*. London: Routledge.

de Jasay, Anthony. (2010) *Political Philosophy, Clearly: Essays on Freedom and Fairness, Property and Equalities*, ed. Hartmut Kliemt. Indianapolis: The Liberty Fund.

de la Boétie. Étienne. (1975 [1552-1553]) *The Politics of Obedience: The Discourse of Voluntary Servitude*, trans. Harry Kurz, intro. Murray N. Rothbard. Auburn, Alabama: The Mises Institute. Available at https://mises.org/library/politics-obedi-ence-discourse-voluntary-servitude, accessed 20 June 2016. [Originally published in Montreal by Black Rose Books]

de la Mettrie, Julien Offray. (1912 [1748]) *Man a Machine*, trans. Gertrude C. Bussey. Chicago: Open Court.

de Las Casas, Bartolomé. (1992 [1552]) *In Defense of the Indians*, ed. and trans. Stafford Poole. De Kalb, Illinois: Northern Illinois University Press.

de Mariana, Juan. (1599) 'Whether it is Right to Destroy a Tyrant?,' in Zuck, 192-195.

de Mesquita et al. (2005) *The Logic of Political Survival*. Cambridge, Massachusetts: MIT Press.

de Mesquita, Bruce Bueno & Alastair Smith. (2012 [2011]) *The Dictator's Handbook*. New York: Public Affairs. [In some ways, a popular version of de Mesquita 2005; cf. CGP Grey 2016 & 2016a]

de Molinari, Gustave. (1904) *The Society of Tomorrow: A Forecast of its Political and Economic Organisation*, trans. P. H. Lee Warner. London: T. Fisher Unwin.

de Roover, Raymond. (1967) *San Bernardino of Siena and Sant'Antonino of Florence: The Two Great Economic Thinkers of the Middle Ages*. Boston: Baker Library, Harvard Graduate School of Business Administration.

de Tocqueville, Alexis. (1985 [1945]) *Democracy in America*. [Second Part] New York: Alfred Knopf.

de Waal, Frans. (2006a) 'Morally Evolved: Primate Social Instincts, Human Morality, and the Rise and Fall of "Veneer Theory",' in Macedo & Ober, 1-58.

de Waal, Frans. (2006b) 'Response to Commentators: The Tower of Morality,' in Macedo & Ober, 161-81.

Dealey, James Quayle. (1921) *State and Government*. New York: D. Appleton and Company.

Deane, Herbert A. (1963) *The Political and Social Ideas of St. Augustine*. New York: Columbia University Press.

Deane, Phyllis. (1978) *The Evolution of Economic Ideas*. Cambridge: Cambridge University Press.

Del Noce, Augusto. (2014) *The Crisis of Modernity*, ed. and trans. Carlo Lancellotti. Montreal & Kingston: McGill Queens University Press.

DeLeon, David. (1978) *The American as Anarchist: Reflections on Indigenous Radicalism*. Baltimore, Maryland: The Johns Hopkins University Press.

Dempsey S. J., Bernard W. (1935) 'Just Price in a Functional Economy,' in *The American Economic Review*, Vol. 25, No. 3, 471-486.

Dempsey S. J., Bernard W. (1943) *Interest and Usury*. Washington, D.C., Catholic University Press.

Den Uyl, Douglas J. & Douglas B. Rasmussen. (eds) (1984) *The Philosophic Thought of Ayn Rand*. Chicago: University of Illinois Press.

Denck, Hans. (1525/6) 'On the Law of God,' in Baylor, 130-151.

Deneen, Patrick. J. (2016) 'Res Idiotica,' available on the Website *Front Porch Republic*, at http://www.frontporchrepublic.com/2016/02/res-idiotica/, accessed 17 April 2016.

Denson, John V. (1999b) 'War and American Freedom,' in Denson 1999a, 1-51.

Denson, John V. (2006) *A Century of War: Lincoln, Wilson and Roosevelt*. Auburn, Alabama: Ludwig von Mises Institute.

Denson, John V. (ed.) (1999a) *The Costs of War: America's Pyrrhic Victories,* 2nd expanded edition. London: Transaction Publishers. Available at https://mises.org/library/costs-war-americas-pyrrhic-victories, accessed 15 April 2016.

Derenghem, Émile. (1958) *Muhammad and the Islamic Tradition*, trans. Jean M. Watt. New York: Harper & Brothers. [Originally published in 1956 as *Mahomet et la Tradition islamique*, Paris; Seuil.]

Deutsch, David. (2011) *The Beginning of Infinity: Explanation that Transform the World*. London: Penguin.

Deveraux, Daniel. (2011) 'Classical Political Philosophy: Plato and Aristotle,' in Klosko, 96-119.

Diamond, Jared. (1987) 'The Worst Mistake in the History of the Human Race,' in *Discover* (May), 64-66. Available on the *Discover* site (but not in the original paginated version) at http://discovermagazine.com/1987/may/02-the-worst-mistake-in-the-history-of-the-human-race, accessed 11 October 2016. Also available at http://www.sigervanbrabant.be/docs/Diamond.PDF, accessed 11 October 2016.

Diamond, Jared. (2006) *Collapse: How Societies Choose to Fail or Succeed*. London: Penguin.

Diamond, Jared. (2012) *The World until Yesterday: What Can We Learn from Traditional Societies?* London: Allen Lane.

DiLorenzo, Thomas J. (2003 [2002]) *The Real Lincoln: A New Look at Abraham Lincoln, His Agenda, and an Unnecessary War*. New York: Three Rivers Press.

Dobbin, Robert. (2012) *The Cynic Philosophers from Diogenes to Julian*. London: Penguin Books.

Doherty, Brian. (2007) *Radicals for Capitalism: A Freewheeling History of the Modern American Libertarian Movement*. New York: Public Affairs. [This is a must-read, riveting account of the history of Libertarianism in America, clear, comprehensive and constructive.]

Donisthorpe, Wordsworth. (1889) *Individualism: A System of Politics*. London: Macmillan and Co. Available at http://lf-oll.s3.amazonaws.com/titles/291/1233_Bk.pdf, accessed 25 April 2014.

Donisthorpe, Wordsworth. (1895) *Law in a Free State*. London: Macmillan and Co. Available at http://lf-oll.s3.amazonaws.com/titles/290/0803_Bk.pdf, accessed 14 April 2014.

Donnelly, James S. (1989) 'The Land Question in Nationalist Politics,' in Hachey & McCaffrey, 79-98.

Dostoevsky, Fyodor. (2007 [1879-1880]) *The Karamazov Brothers*, trans. Constance Garnett. Ware, Hertfordshire: Wordsworth Classics.

Douglas, David C. & George W. Greenaway. (eds) (1953 [1981]) *English Historical Documents*, 2nd ed. London: Eyre Methuen

Drescher, Seymour & Stanley L. Engerman. (eds) (1998) *A Historical Guide to World Slavery*. Oxford: Oxford University Press.

Droz, Jacques. (1967) *Europe between Revolutions (1815-1848)*. London: Fontana/Collins. [Fontana History of Europe]

Duchesne, Ricardo. (2012) *The Uniqueness of Western Civilization*. Leiden: Brill.

Dudley, Leonard. (2012) *Mothers of Innovations: How Expanding Social Networks Gave Birth to the Industrial Revolution*. Newcastle: Cambridge Scholars Publishing.

Duffy, Eamon. (2005 [1992]) *The Stripping of the Altars: Traditional Religion in England c.1400-c.1580*, 2nd ed. New Haven, Connecticut: Yale University Press.

Duncan, David Ewing. (1998) *The Calendar: The 5000-Year Struggle to align the Clock and the Heavens—and What Happened to the Missing Ten Days*. London: Fourth Estate.

Duncan, Graeme. (1973) *Marx and Mill: Two Views of Social Conflict and Social Harmony*. Cambridge: Cambridge University Press.

Dunning, William Archibald. (1896) 'Jean Bodin on Sovereignty,' in *Political Science Quarterly*, Vol. 11, No. 1, 82-104.

Dunning, William Archibald. (1905) *A History of Political Theories from Luther to Montesquieu*. New York: The Macmillan Company. Available for reading online at https://archive.org/details/ahistorypolitic07dunngoog, accessed 7 February 2014.

Duplessis-Mornay, Philip. (1579) 'A Defense of Liberty against Tyrants' in Zuck, 174-176.

Dyde, Samuel Waters. (1896 [2001]) 'Translator's Preface' to Hegel 1820/21 [2001].

Dykes, Nicholas. (1998) 'Mrs Logic and the Law: A Critique of Ayn Rand's View of Government,' in *Philosophical Notes No. 50*. London: Libertarian Alliance. Available at http://www.libertarian.co.uk/lapubs/philn/philn050.pdf, accessed 18 August 2014.

Dykes, Nicholas. (2007) 'The Facts of Reality: Logic and History in Objectivist Debates about Government,' in *Philosophical Notes No. 79*. London: Libertarian Alliance. Available at http://www.libertarian.co.uk/?q=node/620, accessed 18 August 2014.

Eagleton, Terry. (2011) *Why Marx Was Right*. New Haven, Connecticut: Yale University Press.

Earle, Timothy K. (1993) *Chiefdoms: Power, Economy, and Ideology*. Cambridge: Cambridge University Press.

Earle, Timothy K. (1997) *How Chiefs Come to Power*. Stanford, California: Stanford University Press.

Eastman, Max. (1955) *Reflections on the Failure of Socialism*. San Diego, California: Viewpoint Books. [Originally published in New York by the Devin-Adair Company]

Eatwell, Roger. (2003) 'Reflection on Fascism and Religion' in *Totalitarian Movements and Political Religions*, Vol. 4, No. 3, 145-166.

Edmonds, David & John Eidinow. (2006) *Rousseau's Dog: A Tale of Two Great Thinkers in the Age of Enlightenment*. London: Faber & Faber.

Edmondson, Ricca & Karlheinz Huelser. (eds) (2012) *The Politics of Practical Reasoning: Integrating Action, Discourse and Argument*. Lanham, MD: Rowman and Littlefield (Lexington Books).

Edwards, Robin. (2013) 'Our Island Coastline,' in Jebb & Crowley, 47-53.

Eire, Carlos M. N. (2016) *Reformations: The Early Modern World, 1450-1650*. New Haven, Connecticut: Yale University Press.

Eisenstein, Elizabeth L. (2005 [1983]) *The Printing Revolution in Modern Europe*. Cambridge: Cambridge University Press. [An abridgement of Eisenstein's 1979 two-volume *The Printing Press as an Agent of Change*]

Elazar, Daniel J. (1964) 'Althusius' Grand Design for a Federal Commonwealth,' in Althusius 1964, xxxv-xlvi.

Eller, Vernard. (1987) *Christian Anarchy: Jesus' Primacy over the Powers*. Grand Rapids, Michigan: William B. Eerdmans Publishing Company.

Elliott, J. H. (1968) *Europe Divided (1559-1598)*. London: Fontana/Collins. [Fontana History of Europe]

Ellis, George F. R. (2005) 'Physics and the Real World,' in *Physics Today*, Vol. 57 No. 7, 49-54.

Ellis, Joseph. (2016) *The Quartet: Orchestrating the Second American Revolution, 1783-1789*. New York: Vintage. [A division of Penguin Random House LLC]

Ellul, Jacques. (1991 [1988]) *Anarchy and Christianity*, trans. Geoffrey W. Bromiley. Grand Rapids, Michigan: William B. Eerdmans Publishing Company.

Elshtain, Jean Bethke. (2009) 'St Augustine,' in Boucher & Kelly 2009, 118-131.

Elster, Jon. (1985) *Making Sense of Marx*. Cambridge: Cambridge University Press.

Elton, G. R. (1963) *Reformation Europe (1517-1559)*. London: Fontana/Collins. [Fontana History of Europe]

Engels, Friedrich. (1888) 'Preface to the English Edition of the [*Communist Manifesto*] of 1888,' in Marx & Engels (1848 [2002]), 199-204.

Engels, Friedrich. (1958/71 [1848]) *The Condition of the Working Class in England*, trans. and eds W. O. Henderson & W. H. Chaloner. Oxford: Blackwell.

Engels, Friedrich. (1972 [1884]) *The Origin of the Family, Private Property and the State, in the Light of the Researches of Lewis H. Morgan*. London; Lawrence & Wishart.

Ertmann, Thomas. (1997) *Birth of the Leviathan: Building States and Regimes in Medieval and Early Modern Europe*. Cambridge: Cambridge University Press.

Evans, Peter B., Dietrich Rueschemeyer & Theda Skocpol. (eds) (1985) *Bringing the State Back In*. Cambridge: Cambridge University Press.

Evans, Richard J. (1997 [2000]) *In Defence of History*. London: Granta.

Fabre, Cecile. (2002) 'Justice, Fairness, and World Ownership,' in *Law and Philosophy*, Vol. 21, No. 3, 249-273.

Fabre, Cecile. (2003) 'Justice and the Compulsory Taking of Live Body Parts,' in *Utilitas*, Vol. 15, No. 2, 127-150.

Fabre, Cecile. (2006) *Whose Body is it Anyway? Justice and the Integrity of the Person*. Oxford: Clarendon Press.

Fagan, Brian. (2004) *The Long Summer: How Climate Changed Civilization*. New York: Basic Books.

Farb, Peter. (1977 [1974]) *Word Play: What Happens When People Talk.* London: Hodder and Stoughton.

Farrell, Warren. (1994 [1993]) *The Myth of Male Power: Why Men are the Disposable Sex.* New York: Berkley Books.

Fawcett, Bill. (2012) *Trust Me, I Know What I'm Doing: 100 More Mistakes That Lost Elections, Ended Empires, and Made the World What It Is Today.* New York: Berkley Books.

Federici, Michael P. (2002) *Eric Voegelin: The Restoration of Order.* Wilmington, Delaware: ISI Books.

Feinman, G. M. & Joyce Marcus. (eds) (1998) *Archaic States.* Sante Fe: School of American Research Press.

Femia, Joseph V. (2003) 'Machiavelli,' in Boucher & Kelly 2009, 139-162.

Ferguson, Kitty. (2011 [2008]) *Pythagoras: His Lives and the Legacy of a Rational Universe.* London: Icon.

Ferguson, Niall. (1999 [1998]) *The Pity of War.* London: Penguin.

Ferguson, Niall. (2008) *The Ascent of Money: A Financial History of the World.* London: Penguin.

Ferguson, Yale H. (1963) 'Chiefdoms to City-States: the Greek Experience,' in Earle 1993, 169-192.

Fernández-Armesto, Felipe. (ed.) (1997 [1994]) *The Times Guide to the Peoples of Europe,* rev. ed. London: Times Books.

Feser, Edward. (2006) *The Cambridge Companion to Hayek.* Cambridge: Cambridge University Press.

Feser, Edward. (2007) *Locke.* Oxford: Oneworld.

Fetscher, Iring. (2006) 'Republicanism and Popular Sovereignty,' in Goldie & Wokler, 573-597.

Figgis, John Neville. (1907) *Studies of Political Thought: From Gerson to Grotius,* 1414-1625. Cambridge: Cambridge University Press.

Filmer, Robert. (1680 [1635/40]) *Patriarcha or the Naturall Power of Kinges Defended against the Unnatural Liberty of the People.* London: Matthew Gillyflower and William Henchman. 1680 edition available at http://oll.libertyfund.org/titles/filmer-patriarcha-or-the-natural-power-of-kings, accessed 21 March 2014. Readable version available at http://oll.libertyfund.org/titles/filmer-patriarcha-or-the-natural-power-of-kings, accessed 7 April 2014.

Filmer, Robert. (1949 [1635/40-1680]) *Patriarcha and Other Political Works of Sir Robert Filmer,* ed. Peter Laslett. Oxford: Blackwell. (As well as the *Patriarcha,* the Laslett volume contains *The Freeholder's Grand Inquest touching the King and His Parliament* [1647/48], *Observations upon Aristotle's Politiques touching Forms of Government* [1652], *Directions for Obedience to Government in Dangerous or Doubtful Times, Observations concerning the Originall of Government* [1651/52], *The Anarchy of a Limited or Mixed Monarchy* [1648], and *The Necessity of the Absolute Power of all Kings.* [1648]) Reprinted by Transaction in 2009.

Filmer, Robert. (1991 [1680]) *Patriarcha and other Writings,* ed. Johann P. Sommerville. Cambridge: Cambridge University Press. [Cambridge Texts in the History of Political Thought]

Filmer, Robert. (2003 [1652]) *Observations upon Aristotle's Politiques,* (excerpts), in Wootton ed. 2003, 110-120.

Findlay, John Niemeyer. (1958) *Hegel: A Re-Examination.* London: George Allen & Unwin.

Finkel, Michael. (2009) 'The Hadza,' in *National Geographic*, December, available at http://ngm.nationalgeographic.com/2009/12/hadza/finkel-text/1, accessed 3, September 2015. [Page numbers refer to the online edition]

Finley, Moses I. (1998 [1980]) *Ancient Slavery and Modern Ideology*, expanded edition, ed. Brent D. Shaw. Princeton, N. J.: Markus Wiener Publishers.

Finley, Moses I. (ed.) (1987) *Classical Slavery*. London: Frank Cass.

Finnis, John. (1998) *Aquinas: Moral, Political and Legal Theory*. Oxford: Oxford University Press.

Finnis, John. (2011) 'Aquinas' Moral, Political, and Legal Philosophy,' in *Stanford Encyclopedia of Philosophy*, available at http://plato.stanford.edu/archives/fall2011/entries/aquinas-moral-political/, accessed 7 September 2013.

Fischer, Tibor. (2009 [1994]) *The Thought Gang*. London: Vintage Books.

Fisher, Nicolas Ralph Edmund. (2001 [1993]) *Slavery in Classical Greece*. 2nd ed. London: Bristol Classical Press.

Fiske, Alan Page & Tage Shakti Rai. (2014) 'Violence for Goodness' Sake,' in *New Scientist*, Vol. 222, No. 2997, 30-31.

Fleischacker, Samuel. (2013) 'Adam Smith's Moral and Political Philosophy,' in *Stanford Encyclopedia of Philosophy*, available at http://plato.stanford.edu/archives/spr2013/entries/smith-moral-political/, accessed 7 September 2013.

Flikschuh, Katrin. (2000) *Kant and Modern Political Philosophy*. Cambridge: Cambridge University Press.

Flynn, John T. (1955) *The Decline of the American Republic*. New York: The Devin-Adair Company.

Foer, Frank. (2014) 'Foreword' to Croly 1909.

Foer, Joshua. (2012 [2011]) *Moonwalking with Einstein: The Art and Science of Remembering Everything*. London: Penguin.

Forster, E. M. (2011 [1928]) *The Machine Stops*. London: Penguin. [Modern Classics]

Forsyth, Mark. (2013) *The Etymologicon: A Circular Stroll through the Hidden Connections of the* English Language. London: Icon.

Forsyth, Mark. (2014) *The Elements of Eloquence: How to Turn the Perfect English Phrase*. London: Icon.

Fortescue, John. (1997 [1468-71]) *The Laws and Governance of England [Of the Difference between an Absolute and a Limited Monarchy]*, ed. with introduction by Shelley Longwood as *On the Laws and Governance of England*. Cambridge: Cambridge University Press.

Forth, Christopher E. (2009) 'Imagining Our Ancient Future,' in *Science* (New Series), Vol. 325 No. 5941, 677-678.

Fortin, Ernest L. (1987) 'St. Augustine,' in Strauss & Cropsey, 176-205.

Fortin, Ernest L. (1987a) 'Thomas Aquinas,' in Strauss & Cropsey, 248-75.

Foster, Michael Beresford. (1965) *The Political Philosophies of Plato and Hegel*. New York: Russell & Russell. Available at https://ia800207.us.archive.org/4/items/politicalphiloso00fost/politicalphiloso00fost.pdf, accessed 7 December 2016.

Foster, R. F. (2002 [2001]) *The Irish Story: Telling Tales and Making it Up in Ireland*. Oxford: Oxford University Press.

Foucault, Michel. (1981) 'Sexuality and Solitude,' in *London Review of Books*, Vol. 3, No 9, 21 May 1981. Available at http://www.lrb.co.uk/v03/n09/michel-foucault/sexuality-and-solitude, accessed 19 October 2016.

Fox, Claire. (2016) *'I Find That Offensive!'* London: Biteback Publishing. [Series: Provocations]

Fox, John. (1570) 'To the True and Faithful Congregation of Christ's Universal Church,' in Zuck, 200-204.

Francis, Mark. (2007) *Herbert Spencer and the Invention of Modern Life*. Ithaca, New York: Cornell University Press.

Francis, Richard C. (2011) *Epigenetics: How Environment Shapes our Genes*. New York: W. W. Norton & Company.

Franco, Paul. (2002) *Hegel's Philosophy of Freedom*. New Haven, Connecticut: Yale University Press.

Frank, Joseph. (1955) *The Levellers: A History of the Writings of Three Seventeenth Century Social Democrats: John Lilburne, Richard Overton, William Walwyn*. Cambridge, Massachusetts: Harvard University Press.

Frankfort, Henri. (1948) *Kingship and the Gods: A Study in Near Eastern Religion as the Integration of Society and Nature*. Chicago: University of Chicago Press. [An Oriental Institute Essay]

Frankfort, Henri et al. (1949) *Before Philosophy: The Intellectual Adventure of Ancient Man*. London: Pelican. [Originally published as *The Intellectual Adventure of Ancient Man* by the University of Chicago Press, 1946.]

Frankl, Viktor. (2006 [1946]) *Man's Search for Meaning: An Introduction to Logotherapy*. Boston: Beacon Press.

Franklin, Julian H. (1992) 'Introduction' to Bodin *On Sovereignty* (1992), ix-xxvi.

Franklin, Julian H. (2009) *Jean Bodin and the Rise of Absolutist Theory*. Cambridge: Cambridge University Press.

Franklin, Julian H. (ed.) (1969) *Constitutionalism and Resistance in the Sixteenth Century: Three Treatises by Hotman, Beza & Mornay*, trans. Julian H. Franklin. New York: Pegasus.

Frayn, Michael. (2006) *The Human Touch: Our Part in the Creation of a Universe*. London: Faber & Faber.

Freedman, Lawrence. (ed.) (1994) *War*. Oxford: Oxford University Press. [Oxford Readers]

Freeman, Derek. (1983) *Margaret Mead and Samoa: The Making and Unmaking of an Anthropological Myth*. Cambridge, Massachusetts: Harvard University Press.

Freeman, Derek. (1999) *The Fateful Hoaxing of Margaret Mead: A Historical Analysis of Her Samoan Research*. Boulder, Colorado: Westview Press.

Freeman, Kathleen. (1971 [1947]) *Ancilla to the Pre-Socratic Philosophers: A Complete Translation of the Fragments in Diels, Fragmente der Vorsokratiker*. Oxford: Blackwell. Available at http://www.sacred-texts.com/cla/app/, accessed 13 June 2014.

Freeman, Samuel. (2012) 'Original Position; in *The Stanford Encyclopedia of Philosophy*, available at http://plato.stanford.edu/archives/spr2012/entries/original-position/, accessed 14 July 2014.

Fried, Charles. (2007) *Modern Liberty and the Limits of Government*. New York: W. W. Norton & Company. [Very much worth reading]

Frisby, Dominic. (2013) *Life after the State: Why We Don't Need Government*. London: Unbound.

Fromkin, David. (1989) *A Peace to End All Peace: The Fall of the Ottoman Empire and the Creation of the Modern Middle East*. New York: Henry Holt and Company.

Fukuyama, Francis. (2011) *The Origins of Political Order*. London: Profile Books.

Fukuyama, Francis. (2015 [2014]) *Political Order and Political Decay: From the Industrial Revolution to the Globalization of Democracy*. London. Profile Books.

Fuller, Lon L. (1964) *The Morality of Law*. New Haven, Connecticut: Yale University Press.

Furedi, Frank. (2013) *Authority: A Sociological History*. Cambridge: Cambridge University Press.

Gabb, Sean. (2016) 'The Greatness of Margaret Thatcher: An Alternative View,' available at https://thelibertarianalliance.com/2016/09/02/the-greatness-of-margaret-thatcher-an-alternative-view/#more-33430, accessed 3 September 2016.

Gaismayr, Michael. (1526) 'A Plan of Reform,' in Zuck, 21-24. [1526]; 'Territorial Constitution for Tyrol' in Baylor, 254-260.

Galles, Gary M. (2016) 'Review of George A. Akerlof & Robert J. Shiller's *Phishing for Phools: The Economics of Manipulation & Deception,*' available at http://www.independent.org/publications/tir/article.asp?a=1149, accessed 19 June 2016.

Gallus, Nicholas et al. (1550) 'A Confession of the Magdeburg Pastors Concerning Resistance to the Superior Magistrate,' in Zuck, 137-138.

Gammie, John G. (1986) 'Herodotus on Kings and Tyrants: Objective Historiography or Conventional Portraiture?' in *Journal of Near Eastern Studies*, Vol. 45, No. 3, 171-195.

Gans, Chaim. (1992) *Philosophical Anarchism and Political Disobedience*. Cambridge: Cambridge University press.

Garlan, Yvon. (1987) 'War, Piracy and Slavery in the Greek World,' in Finley 1987, 7-21.

Garnsey, Peter. (1996) *Ideas of Slavery from Aristotle to Augustine*. Cambridge: Cambridge University Press.

Gat, Azar. (2006) *War in Human Civilization*. Oxford: Oxford University Press.

Gatti, Hilary. (2015) *Ideas of Liberty in Early Modern Europe: From Machiavelli to Milton*. Princeton, New Jersey: Princeton University Press.

Gauthier, David. (1998) 'David Hume, Contractarian,' in Boucher & Kelly 1998, 17-44.

Gentile, Emilio. (2005) 'Political Religion: A Concept and its Critics—A Critical Survey, trans. Natalia Belozertseva,' in *Totalitarian Movements and Political Religions*, Vol. 6, No. 1, 19-32.

George, Henry. (1931 [1879]) *Progress and Poverty: An Inquiry into the Cause of Industrial Depressions and of Increase of Want with Increase of Wealth*. London: The Henry George Foundation. Available at http://www.econlib.org/library/YPDBooks/George/grgPP26.html, accessed 9 January 2014. Available at http://lf-oll.s3.amazonaws.com/titles/328/0777_Bk.pdf, accessed 25 April 2014.

George, Henry. (1931b [1884]) *Social Problems*. London: The Henry George Foundation.

George, Henry. (2006 [1898]) *The Science of Political Economy*. New York: Cosimo Classics.

Gere, Cathy. (2009) *Knossos and the Prophets of Modernism*. Chicago: University of Chicago Press.

Gierke, Otto. (1900) *Political Theories of the Middle Ages*, trans. Frederic William Maitland. Cambridge: Cambridge University Press. Available at http://lf-oll.s3.amazonaws.com/titles/2562/Gierke_PoliticalTheories1634_Bk.pdf, accessed 25 April 2014. Also available at http://socserv2.mcmaster.ca/~econ/ugcm/3ll3/gierke/MedPol-Theo.pdf, accessed 19 May 2014.

Gierke, Otto. (1950 [1913]) *Natural Law and the Theory of Society: 1500 to 1800*, trans. with introduction by Ernest Barker in two volumes. Cambridge: Cambridge University Press. [A translation of five subsections of the fourth volume of von Gierke's *Das deutsche Genossenschaftsrecht*. A facsimile of the Cambridge edition was produced by The Lawbook Exchange, Ltd. (Clark, New Jersey) 2001]

Gigot, Francis E. S.S. (1901) *Special Introduction to the Study of the Old Testament—Part I, The Historical Books*. New York: Benziger Brothers.

Gilbert, Gustave. (1950) *The Psychology of Dictatorship: Based on an Examination of the Leaders of Nazi Germany*. New York: The Ronald Press Company.

Giles of Rome (Aegidius Romanus). (1986) *On Ecclesiastical Power*, trans. R. W Dyson. Woodbridge, Suffolk: The Boydell Press. [A translation of the *De Ecclesiastica Potestate* of Aegidius Romanus]

Giles of Rome. (2001) 'On the Rule of Princes (selection),' in McGrade et al., 200-215.

Giles of Rome. (2004) *On Ecclesiastical Power*, ed. and trans. R. W. Dyson. New York: Columbia University Press. [A critical edition and translation of Giles's *De Ecclesiastica Potestate* by R. W Dyson]

Gimpel, Jean. (1976) *The Medieval Machine: The Industrial Revolution of the Middle Ages*. London: Penguin. First published as *La Révolution industrielle du moyen âge* (1974).

Ginther, James R. (2012) 'Between *Plena Caritas* and *Plenitudo Legis*: The Ecclesiology of the *Norman Anonymous*,' in North, 141-62.

Gisin, Nicolas. (2016a) 'Time Really Passes, Science Can't Deny That,' Available at http://arxiv.org/pdf/1602.01497v1.pdf, accessed 20 May 2016. [Talk presented at the Conference 'Time in Physics' at the ETH-Zurich, September 2015]

Gisin, Nicolas. (2016b) 'Physics Killed Free Will and Time's Flow. We Need Them Back,' in *New Scientist*, issue 3074. [18 May 2016]

Glaeser, Edward. (2011 [2012]) *Triumph of the City: How Urban Spaces Makes Us Human*. London: Pan Books.

Gnuse, Robert. (2011) *No Tolerance for Tyrants: The Biblical Assault on Kings and Kingship*. Collegeville, Minnesota: Liturgical Press.

Godfrey of Fontaines. (2001 [1295/96]) 'Are Subjects Bound to Pay a Tax when the Need for it is not Evident?' in McGrade et al., 315-320.

Godwin, William. (1946 [1793]) *An Enquiry Concerning Political Justice, and its Influence on General Virtue and Happiness*, ed. F. E. L. Priestly. Toronto: University of Toronto Press.

Godwin, William. (2013 [1793]) *An Enquiry Concerning Political Justice*, ed. Mark Philp. Oxford: Oxford University Press. Available at http://oll.libertyfund.org/titles/godwin-an-enquiry-concerning-political-justice-in-2-vols, accessed 4 June 2014. Excerpts from this book can be seen in Graham 2005 between 12-22, 171-173.

Goertz, Hans-Jürgen. (1996 [1980]) *The Anabaptists*, trans. Trevor Johnson. Routledge: London.

Goldberg, Jessica L. (2015 [2012]) *Trade and Institutions in the Medieval Mediterranean: The Geniza Merchants and their Business World*. Cambridge: Cambridge University Press.

Goldberg, Jonah. (2008) *Liberal Fascism: The Secret History of the American Left from Mussolini to the Politics of Meaning*. New York: Doubleday.

Goldberg, Steven. (1973) *The Inevitability of Patriarchy*. New York: William Morrow and Company. [see also 'Steven Goldberg on Patriarchy,' available at http://www.goldberg-patriarchy.com/logic.html, accessed 16 November 2016]

Goldie, Mark & Robert Wokler. (eds) (2006) *The Cambridge History of Eighteenth-Century Political Thought*. Cambridge: Cambridge University Press. [A superb collection of individually authored pieces on a wide-range of eighteenth-century thinkers and ideas]

Goldie, Mark. (2006) 'The English System of Liberty,' in Goldie & Wokler, 40-78.

Goldie, Mark. (2011) ''Absolutism,' in Klosko, 282-295.

Goldwin, Robert A. (1987) 'John Locke' in Strauss & Cropsey, 476-512.

Gontier, Thierry. (2013) 'From "Political Theology" to "Political Religion": Eric Voegelin and Carl Schmitt,' in *The Review of Politics*, Vol. 75 No. 1, 25-43.

Goodman, Christopher. (1558) 'How Superior Powers Ought to be Obeyed,' in Zuck, 150-152.

Gordon, Barry J. (1964) 'Aristotle and the Development of Value Theory' *The Quarterly Journal of Economics*, Vol. 78 No. 1, 115-128.

Gordon, David. (1990) *Resurrecting Marx: The Analytical Marxists on Freedom, Exploitation, and Justice*. London: Transaction Books.

Gordon, David. (1993) 'The Marxist Case for Socialism,' in Maltsev, 33-50.

Gordon, David. (1999) 'A Common Design: Propaganda and World War,' in Denson 1999a, 301-319.

Gordon, David. (2000) 'Review of John Rawl's *The Law of Peoples*,' in *The Mises Review*, Vol. 6, Number 4. Available at http://mises.org/misesreview_detail.aspx?-control=172, accessed 13 July 2014.

Gordon, David. (2007) *The Essential Rothbard*. Auburn, Alabama: Ludwig von Mises Institute.

Gordon, David. (2008) 'Going Off the Rawls,' in *The American Conservative*, Vol. 7, No. 15, 24-27, available at http://www.theamericanconservative.com/articles/going-off-the-rawls/, accessed 14 July 2014.

Gornitz, Vivien. (2007) 'Sea Level Rise, After the Ice Melted and Today,' NASA GISS Science Briefs, available at http://www.giss.nasa.gov/research/briefs/gornitz_09/, accessed 21 August 2016.

Gornitz, Vivien. (2009a) 'Ancient Cultures and Climate Change,' in Gornitz 2009, 6-10.

Gornitz, Vivien. (ed.) (2009) *Encyclopedia of Paleoclimatology and Ancient Environments*. Dordrecht: Springer.

Gorz, André. (1985 [1883]) *Paths to Paradise: On the Liberation from Work*, trans. Malcolm Imrie. London: Pluto Press.

Gosden, P. H. J. H. (1973) *Self-Help: Voluntary Associations in Nineteenth Century Britain*. London: B. T. Batsford.

Gottfried, Paul. (2016) *Fascism: The Career of a Concept*. DeKalb, Illinois: Northern Illinois University Press.

Gourevitch, Victor. (1997a) 'Introduction,' in Rousseau 1997a, ix-xxxi.

Gourevitch, Victor. (1997b) 'Introduction,' in Rousseau 1997b, ix-xxxi.

Grabill, Stephen J. (2006) 'Introduction' to Althusius 2006, 403-416.

Grafton, A., Glenn W. Most & Salvatore Settis. *The Classical Tradition*. (2010) Cambridge, Massachusetts: The Belnap Press of Harvard University Press.

Graham, Gordon. (2002) *The Case against the Democratic State*. Thorverton, Essex: Imprint Academic.

Graham, Robert. (ed.) (2005) *Anarchism: A Documentary History of Libertarian Ideas: Volume One: From Anarchy to Anarchism (300CE to 1939)*. Montreal: Black Rose Books.

Graham, Robert. (ed.) (2009) *Anarchism: A Documentary History of Libertarian Ideas: Volume Two: The Anarchist Current (1939-2006)*. Montreal: Black Rose Books.

Gratian. (1993 [c. 1140]) *Gratian: The Treatise on Laws* (*Decretum DD. 1-20*) *with the Ordinary Gloss*, eds A. Thompson and J. Gordley. Washington D. C.: The Catholic University of America Press.

Graver, Margaret. (2013) 'Epictetus,' in *Stanford Encyclopedia of Philosophy* 2013, available at http://plato.stanford.edu/archives/spr2013/entries/epictetus/, accessed 7 September 2013.

Gray, John. (2003 [2002]) *Straw Dogs: Thoughts on Human and Other Animals*. London: Granta.

Gray, Phillip. W. (2007) 'Political Theology and the Theology of Politics: Carl Schmitt and Medieval Christian Political Thought,' *Humanitas*, Vol. 20, nos 1-2, 175-200.

Grebel, Conrad et al. (1524) 'A Letter to Thomas Muentzer' in Zuck, 55-61; 'Letter to Thomas Müntzer' in Baylor, 36-48.

Green, David. (2000) *Reinventing Civil Society: The Rediscovery of Welfare Without Politics*. London: Civitas (Institute for the Study of Civil Society).

Green, Thomas Hill. (1906) 'Lecture on Liberal Legislation and Freedom of Contract' in *Works of Thomas Hill Green*, ed. R. L. Nettleship. London: Longmans, Green and Co., 365-386.

Greenaway, James. (2012) *The Differentiation of Authority: The Medieval Turn toward Existence*. Washington, D.C.: The Catholic University of America Press.

Greene, Joshua. (2014 [2013]) *Moral Tribes: Emotion, Reason, and the Gap between Us and Them*. London: Atlantic Books.

Greenfield, Kent. (2012) *The Myth of Choice: Personal Responsibility in a World of Limits. London: Biteback Publishing*. [First published by Yale University Press in 2011]

Greenleaf, W. H. (2003 [1983]) *The Rise of Collectivism* [The British Political Tradition, Vol. One]. London: Routledge.

Gregor, A. James. (1969) *The Ideology of Fascism: The Rationale of Totalitarianism*. New York: The Free Press.

Gregor, A. James. (2009) *Marxism, Fascism, and Totalitarianism*. Stanford, California: Stanford University Press.

Gregory VII. (1081) 'Letter to Bishop Hermann of Metz,' 15 March 1081. Available at http://avalon.law.yale.edu/medieval/inv14.asp, accessed 10 October 2013.

Greif, Avner. (2006) *Institutions and the Path to the Modern Economy: Lessons from Medieval Trade*. Cambridge: Cambridge University Press.

Grenville, J. A. S. (1976) *Europe Reshaped (1848-1878)*. London: Fontana/Collins. [Fontana History of Europe]

Grey, C. G. P. (2016) 'The Rules for Rulers,' available at https://www.youtube.com/watch?v=rStL7niR7gs, accessed 5 November 2016. Cf. de Mesquita 2005 & 2012.

Grey, C. G. P. (2016a) 'Death and Dynasties,' available at https://mail.google.com/mail/u/0/#inbox/158403f12ed49d8e?projector=1, accessed 8 November 2016. Cf. de Mesquita 2005 & 2012.

Grey, Thomas C. (1973) 'The First Virtue,' in *Stanford Law Review*, Vol. 25, 286-327.

Grice-Hutchinson, Marjorie. (1952) *The School of Salamanca: Readings in Spanish Monetary Theory, 1544-1605*. Oxford: Clarendon Press.

Grieder, Peter. (2007) 'In Defence of Totalitarianism Theory as a Tool of Historical Scholarship' in *Totalitarian Movements and Political Religions*, Vol. 8, Nos 3-4, 563-589. [The journal is now titled, *Politics, Religion & Ideology*.]

Griffel, Frank. (2014 [2007]) 'Al-Ghazali,' in *Stanford Encyclopedia of Philosophy*, available at http://plato.stanford.edu/entries/al-ghazali/, accessed 30 June 2016.

Griffin, Roger. (ed.) (1995) *Fascism*. Oxford: Oxford University Press. [Oxford Readers] An exceptionally useful collection of excerpts from the writings of, among others, Mussolini, D'Annunzio, George, Spengler, Hitler, Goebbels, Goering, Heidegger, Mosley, Primo de Rivera, Doriot, Quisling, Codreanu et al.

Griffiths, Richard. (2005 [2000]) *Fascism*. London: Bloomsbury. [First published by Duckworth as *An Intelligent Person's Guide to Fascism* in 2000]

Groarke, Louis. (2008) 'Callicles,' in O'Grady, 101-110.

Grotius, Hugo. (2004 [1609]) *The Free Sea*, ed. with introduction by David Armitage, trans. Richard Hakluyt. Indianapolis, Indiana: Liberty Fund. Reprinted and translated many times. The translation and edition by Ralph van Deman Magoffin (Oxford: Oxford University Press, 1916) contains a facsimile of the 1633 edition.

Grotius, Hugo. (2005 [1625a]) *The Rights of War and Peace*, ed. with Introduction by Richard Tuck. Indianapolis, Indiana: Liberty Fund. Reprinted and translated many times since. Jean Barbeyrac's 1735 edition, with extensive notes and commentary, was the most important; it was translated into English and published in London by Innys et al. in 1738.

Grotius, Hugo. (2005 [1625b]) 'Prolegomena to the First Edition of *De Jure Belli ac Pacis*,' in Grotius 1625a, Book III, 1745-1762.

Guizot, François. (1828 [1997]) *The History of Civilization in Europe*, trans. William Hazlitt, ed. Larry Siedentop. Indianapolis, Indiana: Liberty Fund.

Gurevich, Aaron. (1995) *The Origins of European Individualism*, trans. Katherine Judelson. Oxford: Blackwell.

Gurney, John. (2013) *Gerrard Winstanley: The Digger's Life and Legacy*. London: Pluto Press.

Gutgesell, Manfred. (2007) 'Economy and Trade,' in Schulz & Seidel, 371-375.

Guthrie, William Keith Chambers. (1969 [1971]) *The Sophists*. Cambridge: Cambridge University Press. [First published as part 1 of *A History of Greek Philosophy, Volume III*, 1969]

Guyer, Paul. (ed.) (1992) *The Cambridge Companion to Kant*. Cambridge: Cambridge University Press.

Hachey, Thomas E. & Lawrence J. McCaffrey. (1989) *Perspectives on Irish Nationalism*. Lexington, Kentucky: the University Press of Kentucky.

Hagedorn, Hermann. (ed.) (1926) *The Works of Theodore Roosevelt* (National Edition). New York: Charles Scribner's Sons.

Haidt, Jonathan. (2016) 'Two Incompatible Sacred Values in American Universities,' available at https://youtu.be/Gatn5ameRr8, accessed 19 December 2016.

Hakim, Catherine. (2015) *Supply and Desire: Sexuality and the Sex Industry in the 21st Century*. London: IEA. [IEA Discussion Paper No. 61]

Hale, J. R. (1971) *Renaissance Europe (1480-1520)*. London: Fontana/Collins. [Fontana History of Europe]

Hall, Kermit L. (ed.) 2005) *The Oxford Guide to the Supreme Court*, 2nd ed. Oxford: Oxford University Press.

Halter, Helene M. (1995) *Bodin and Althusius on the Nature of Sovereignty*. A Thesis in the Department of Political Science, Concordia University. Available at http://spectrum.library.concordia.ca/2630/1/MM01313.pdf, accessed 1 December 2013.

Hamburger, Joseph. (1999) *John Stuart Mill on Liberty and Control*. Princeton, New Jersey: Princeton University Press.

Hampsher-Monk, Iain. (1992) *A History of Modern Political Thought: Major Political Thinkers from Hobbes to Marx*. Oxford: Blackwell.

Hampsher-Monk, Iain. (1998) 'Edmund Burke,' in Edward Craig (ed.), *Routledge Encyclopedia of Philosophy*, available at https://www-rep-routledge-com.ucd.idm.oclc.org/, accessed 1 September 2015.

Hampsher-Monk, Iain. (2006) 'British Radicalism and the anti-Jacobins,' in Goldie & Wokler, 660-687.

Hanke, Lewis. (1959) *Aristotle and the American Indians: A Study of Race Prejudice in the Modern World*. London: Hollis & Carter.

Hannam, James. (2009) *God's Philosophers: How the Medieval World laid the Foundations of Modern Science*. London: Icon Books.

Hansen, Mogens Herman & Thomas Heine Nielsen. (eds) (2004) *An Inventory of Archaic and Classical Poleis*. Oxford: Oxford University Press.

Hanson, Victor Davis. (2010) *The Father of Us All: War and History, Ancient and Modern*. New York: Bloomsbury Press.

Harari, Yuval Noah. (2015 [2011]) *Sapiens: A Brief History of Humankind*, trans. Yuval Harari, aided by John Purcell & Haim Watzman. New York: Harper. [First published in Hebrew by Kinneret, Zmora-Bitan, Divr. Published also in a slightly different form in Great Britain in 2014 by Harvill Secker]

Hardy, Edward R. Jr. 'The City of God,' in Battenhouse, 257-283.

Harrington, James. (1977 [1656-1660a]) *The Political Writings of James Harrington*, ed. J. G. A. Pocock. Cambridge: Cambridge University Press.

Harrington, James. (1992 [1656-1660b]) *The Commonwealth of Oceana & A System of Politics*. ed. J. G. A. Pocock. Cambridge: Cambridge University Press. [Cambridge Texts in the History of Political Thought] Available at http://files.libertyfund.org/files/916/0050_Bk.pdf and http://www.constitution.org/jh/oceana.htm, accessed 9 January 2014.

Harrington, James. (2003 [1659]) *The Art of Lawgiving in Three Books*, (excerpts), in Wootton, 2003, 395-417.

Harris, Ian. (2012) 'Edmund Burke,' in *Stanford Encyclopedia of Philosophy*, available at http://plato.stanford.edu/archives/spr2012/entries/burke/, accessed 7 September 2013.

Hartmann, Klaus. (1984) 'Towards a New Systematic Reading of Hegel's *Philosophy of Right*,' in Pelczynski 1984, 114-136.

Harvey, David. (2011 [2010]) *The Enigma of Capital and the Crises of Capitalism*. London: Profile Books.

Haskins, Charles Homer. (1927) *The Renaissance of the Twelfth Century*. Cambridge, Massachusetts: Harvard University Press.

Hasnas, John. (2006) *Trapped: When Acting Ethically is Against the Law*. Washington, D. C.: Cato Institute.

Hastie, William. (1891) 'Translator's Introduction' to Kant (1891 [1797]), vii-xliv.

Haworth, Alan. (1994) *Anti-Libertarianism: Markets, Philosophy and Myth*. London: Routledge. [see Haworth 1998 and Lester 1997 & 2002]

Haworth, Alan. (1998) 'Letter,' in *Journal of Applied Philosophy*, Vol. 15 No. 3, 311-312.

Hay, Denys. (1964 [1953]) *The Medieval Centuries*. London: Menthuen & Co. Ltd.

Hayek, Friedrich A. (1944) *The Road to Serfdom*. London: Routledge & Kegan Paul.

Hayek, Friedrich A. (1982) *Law, Legislation and Liberty: A New Statement of the Liberal Principles of Justice and Political Economy*. London: Routledge. This single volume edition contains Vol. 1, *Rules and Order* (1973), Vol. 2, *The Mirage of Social Justice* (1976), and Vol. 3, *The Political Order of a Free People* (1979); each of the three volumes is independently paginated.

Hayek, Friedrich A. (1988) *The Fatal Conceit: The Errors of Socialism*, ed. W. W. Bartley III. Chicago: University of Chicago Press.

Hayek, Friedrich A. (1992) *The Fortunes of Liberalism: Essays on Austrian Economics and the Ideal of Freedom*. Indianapolis, Indiana: The Liberty Fund.

Hayek, Friedrich A. (2006 [1960]) *The Constitution of Liberty*. London: Routledge & Kegan Paul.

Haywood, John. (2008 [2000]) *Historical Atlas of the Medieval World: AD600-1492*. New York: Metro Books.

Hearnshaw, F. J. C. (1967 [1933]) *Conservatism in England*. New York: Howard Fertig.

Hearst, William Randolph. (1918) 'In Self-Defense We Should Hasten to Aid and Hearten Russia's Revolutionary Government,' *New York American* (1 March).

Heath, Allister. (2014) 'It's Time to Reject Crony Capitalism and Embrace the Real Thing,' in *The Telegraph*, 21 January, available at http://www.telegraph.co.uk/finance/economics/10587534/Its-time-to-reject-crony-capitalism-and-embrace-the-real-thing.html, accessed 27 March 2014.

Heath, Malcolm. (2008) 'Aristotle on Natural Slavery,' in *Phronesis* Vol. 53, No. 3, 243-270.

Hedges, Chris. (2002) *War Is A Force That Gives Us Meaning*. New York: Public Affairs [Perseus Books Group].

Hegel, G. W. F. (1956 [1837]) *The Philosophy of History*, trans. J. Sibree. Mineola, New York Dover Publications, Inc.

Hegel, G. W. F. (1991 [1820/21]) *Elements of the Philosophy of Right*, ed. Allen W. Wood, trans. H. B. Nisbet. Cambridge: Cambridge University Press.

Hegel, G. W. F. (2001 [1820/21]) *Philosophy of Right*, trans. S. W. Dyde. Kitchener, Ontario: Batoche Books, 2001.

Henderson, Ernest F. (1910) *Select Historical Documents of the Middle Ages*. London: George Bell and Sons. A listing of the Dictates and a brief discussion of their authoritativeness can be found at http://www.unamsanctamcatholicam.com/history/79-history/215-revisiting-dictatus-papae.html, accessed 4 May 2014.

Henry of Ghent. (2001 [c. 1290] 'Is a Subject Bound to Obey a Statute when it is not Evident that it Promotes the Common Utility?' in McGrade et al., 307-314.

Herbert, Auberon. (1885) *The Right and Wrong of Compulsion by the State: A Statement of the Moral Principles of the Party of Individual Liberty, and the Political Measures Founded upon Them*. London: Williams and Norgate. Available at http://lf-oll.s3.amazonaws.com/titles/906/0486_Bk.pdf, accessed 25 April 2014.

Herbert, Auberon. (1897) *The Principles of Voluntaryism and Free Life*. Burlington, Vermont: Free Press Association. Available via Nabu Public Domain Reprints. Also in Herbert 1978, 369-16.

Herbert, Auberon. (1899) 'Lost in the Region of Phrases,' in Herbert 1978, 241-258.

Herbert, Auberon. (1908 [1906]) *The Voluntaryist Creed & A Plea for Voluntaryism*. London: Henry Frowde (W. J. Simpson, at the Oxford University Press). Available at http://lf-oll.s3.amazonaws.com/titles/1026/0545_Bk.pdf, accessed 25 April 2014. 'A Plea for Voluntaryism' is also to be found in Herbert 1978, 315-368.

Herbert, Auberon. (1978 [1885]) *The Right and Wrong of Compulsion by the State, and Other Essays*, ed. Eric Mack. Indianapolis, Indiana: The Liberty Fund. This volume contains, among others, the title essay, 'The Choices between Personal Freedom and State Protection' and 'A Plea for Voluntaryism'. I would place Herbert's work in the 'must-read' category for all libertarians. Available at http://oll.libertyfund.org/titles/herbert-the-right-and-wrong-of-compulsion-by-the-state-and-other-essays-1978-ed, accessed 6 July 2014.

Hergot, Hans. (1527) 'On the New Transformation of the Christian Life,' in Baylor, 210-225.

Herodotus. (2003 [c. 415 BC]) *The Histories*, trans. Aubrey de Sélincourt, rev. John Marincola. London: Penguin.

Hexter, Jack H. *The Vision of Politics on the Eve of the Reformation*. London: Allen Lane, 1973.

Heyes, Cressida. (2016) 'Identity Politics,' in *Stanford Encyclopedia of Philosophy*, available at https://leibniz.stanford.edu/friends/members/view/identity-politics/a4/, accessed 20 August 2016.

Higgs, Robert. (1987) *Crisis and Leviathan: Critical Episodes in the Growth of American Government*. New York: Oxford University Press.

Higgs, Robert. (1999) 'War and Leviathan in Twentieth-Century America: Conscription as the Keystone,' in Denson 1999a, 375-388 and in Higgs 2004, 163-175.

Higgs, Robert. (2004) *Against Leviathan: Government Power and a Free Society.* Oakland, California: The Independent Institute.

Highsmith, Patricia. (1983) *Plotting and Writing Suspense Fiction.* New York: St. Martin's Griffin.

Hill, Christopher. (1972) *The World Turned Upside Down: Radical Ideas during the English Revolution.* London: Temple Smith.

Hill, Christopher. (1973) 'Introduction,' in Winstanley 1973, 9-68.

Hill, Robert S. (1987) 'David Hume,' in Strauss & Cropsey, 535-558.

Hirsi Ali, Ayaan. (2016 [2015]) *Heretic: Why Islam Needs a Reformation Now.* New York: Harper.

Hirst, Derek. (1986) *Authority and Conflict: England 1603-1658.* London: Edward Arnold.

Hobbes, Thomas. (1996 [1651]) *Leviathan*, ed. Richard Tuck. Cambridge: Cambridge University Press.

Hochschild, Adam. (2012 [2011]) *To End All Wars: A Story of Protest and Patriotism in the First World War.* London: Pan Books.

Hoffer, Eric. (1951) *The True Believer: Thoughts on the Nature of Mass Movements.* New York: Harper & Row. [Republished in 1966 by Perennial Classics. Since the pagination of the two versions differ, references to Hoffer shall be by page number (to the original 1951 edition) and by section number (common to both editions.)]

Hofmann, Melchior. (1530) 'The Ordinance of God,' in Zuck, 84-87.

Hohfeld, Wesley. (1919) *Fundamental Legal Conceptions*, W. Cook (ed.), New Haven: Yale University Press.

Holland, Saba. (1855) *A Memoir of the Reverend Sydney Smith. By his Daughter, Lady Holland. With a Selection from his Letters*, ed. Mrs. Austin, 2 vols. London: Longman, Brown, Green, and Longmans.

Holmes, George. (1975) *Europe: Hierarchy and Revolt (1320-1450).* London: Fontana/Collins. [Fontana History of Europe]

Holmes, Hannah. (2011 [2008]) *A Natural History of Ourselves.* London: Atlantic Books.

Holton, James E. (1987) 'Marcus Tullius Cicero,' in Strauss & Cropsey, 155-175.

Honderich, Ted. (1990) *Conservatism.* London: Penguin.

Hook, Sidney. (2002 [1933]) *Towards the Understanding of Karl Marx.* Amherst, New York: Prometheus Books. [Expanded edition, ed. Ernest B. Hook; first published by John Day Company, New York]

Höpfl, Harro. (ed.) (1991) *Luther and Calvin on Secular Authority.* Cambridge: Cambridge University Press. [Cambridge Texts in the History of Political Thought]

Hopkins, Katie. (2016) 'Whatever the Feminist Online Lynch Mob Say, Ched Evans is Innocent. But Britain's Saturday Night Binge-Culture is as Guilty as Sin,' *MailOnline*, 17 October 2016, available at http://www.dailymail.co.uk/sport/ched_evans/index.html, accessed 27 October 2016.

Hoppe, Hans-Hermann. (1989) *A Theory of Socialism and Capitalism.* Norwell, Mass.: Kluwer Academic Publishers.

Hoppe, Hans-Hermann. (1993) 'Marxist and Austrian Class Analysis' in Maltsev, 51-74.

Hoppe, Hans-Hermann. (2001) *Democracy: The God that Failed.* Piscataway, New Jersey: Transaction publishers.

Hoppe, Hans-Hermann. (2006) *The Economics and Ethics of Private Property.* Auburn: Alabama: Ludwig von Mises Institute.

Hoppe, Hans-Hermann. (2012) *The Great Fiction: Property, Economy, Society, and the Politics of Decline*. Baltimore, Maryland: Laissez Faire Books.

Hoppe, Hans-Hermann. (2015) *A Short History of Man: Progress and Decline (An Austro-Libertarian Reconstruction)*. Auburn, Alabama: The Mises Institute. Available at https://mises.org/search/site/a%20short%20history%20of%20man, accessed 10 May 2016.

Hornberger, J. G. (2010) 'Conservatism vs. Libertarianism,' available at http://www. fff.org/ comment/ com0604c.asp on 14 December 2010; uploaded 12 April 2006, accessed 17 April 2014.

Hörnqvist, Mikael. (2011) 'Renaissance Political Philosophy,' in Klosko, 206-226.

Hornung, Erik. (1982) *Conceptions of God in Ancient Egypt: The One and the Many*, trans. John Baines. Ithaca, New York: Cornell University Press.

Hotman, François. (1573) 'Francogallia' in Zuck, 164-167.

Houlden, J. L. (1973) *Ethics and the New Testament*. Harmondsworth, Middlesex: Penguin.

http://www.ts.mu.edu/readers/content/pdf/1/1.4/1.4.1.pdf, accessed 5 December 2013.

Howe, Stephen. (1998) *Afrocentrism: Mythical Pasts and Imagined Homes*. London: Verso.

Hubmaier, Balthasar. (1525) 'The Article-Letter of the Black Forest Peasants,' in Zuck, 18-19. [Hubmaier's authorship of this piece is in question]

Hubmaier, Balthasar. (1527) 'On the Sword,' in Zuck ed., 77-79; in Baylor, 181-209.

Hueglin, Thomas. O. (1999) *Early Modern Concepts for a Late Modern World: Althusius on Community and Federalism*. Waterloo, Ontario: Wilfred Laurier University Press. Accessible via Project Muse at http://muse.jhu.edu/books/9780889207677 , accessed 13 June 2014.

Hufton, Olwen (1994) *Europe: Privilege and Protest 1730-1789*. London: Fontana Press. [Fontana History of Europe]

Hume David. (1983 [1754/1761]) *The History of England*, ed. William B. Todd. Indianapolis: Liberty Classics.

Hume, David. (1820) *Private Correspondence of David Hume with Several Distinguished Persons between the Years 1761 and 1776*. London: Henry Colburn and Co.

Hume, David. (1888 [1740]) *A Treatise of Human Nature*, ed. L. A. Selby-Bigge. Oxford: Clarendon Press.

Hume, David. (1987 [1741-1777]) *Essays: Moral, Political, and Literary*, ed. Eugene F. Miller, rev. ed. Indianapolis, Indiana: Liberty Fund.

Hume, David. (1987 [1741a]) 'That Politics may be Reduced to a Science,' in Hume 1987, 37-41.

Hume, David. (1987 [1741b]) 'Of the First Principles of Government,' in Hume 1987, 32-36.

Hume, David. (1987 [1748a]) 'Of the Original Contract,' in Hume 1987, 465-487.

Hume, David. (1987 [1748b]) 'Of Passive Obedience,' in Hume 1987, 488-492.

Hume, David. (1987 [1777]) 'Of the Origin of Government,' in Hume 1987, 37-41.

Hummel, Jeffrey Rogers. (2014 [1996]) *Emancipating Slaves, Enslaving Free Men: A History of the American Civil War*, 2nd ed. Chicago: Open Court.

Hunton, Philip. (1643) 'A Treatise of Monarchy' (excerpts), in Wootton, 175-211.

Hurd, Richard. (1756) 'Letter from Hurd to William Mason, 16 June 1756,' in Whibley.

Hurmence, Belinda (ed.) (1984) *My Folks Don't Want Me to Talk about Slavery*. Winston-Salem, North Carolina: John F. Blair Publisher.

Hut, Hans. (c. 1527) 'On the Mystery of Baptism,' in Baylor, 152-171.

Hutchinson, W. T., & al. (eds) (1962-1977). *The Papers of James Madison*. Chicago: University of Chicago Press.

Ibn Khaldûn. (1967 [1377]) *The Muqaddimah: An Introduction to History*, 2ⁿᵈ ed., trans. Franz Rosenthal, abridged and ed. N. J. Dawood. Princeton, New Jersey and London: Princeton University Press, 1967. [Bollingen Series] The abridged edition was first published jointly by Routledge & Kegan Paul Ltd., and Martin Secker and Warburg Ltd., London.

Ilting, K.-H. (1971) 'The Structure of Hegel's Philosophy of Right,' in Pelczynski 1971, 90-110.

Imbrie, John and Katherine Palmer Imbrie. (1986) *Ice Ages: Solving the My*stery. Cambridge, Massachusetts: Harvard University Press.

Irenaeus. (AD 175-185]) *Against Heresies*. [*Adversus haereses*], available at http://www.newadvent.org/fathers/0103.htm, accessed 7 September 2013.

Irwin, William. (ed.) (2002) *The Matrix and Philosophy: Welcome to the Desert of the Real*. Peru, Illinois: Open Court Publishing Company.

Isaac, Ephraim. (1998) 'Biblical Literature: Hebrew Scriptures,' in Drescher and Engerman, 91-98.

Isocrates. (1929 [393/2 BC]) 'Against the Sophists,' 160-177 in *Isocrates II*, trans. George Norlin. London: William Heinemann Ltd. [The Loeb Classical Library]

Jacobs, Jane. (1970) *The Economy of Cities*. London: Vintage Publishers.

Jacobsen, Thorkild. (1949) 'Mesopotamia,' in Frankfort 1949, 137-234.

Jaeger, Werner. (1934) *Aristotle: Fundamentals of the History of his Development*. Oxford: Clarendon Press.

Jaggar, Alison. (1983) *Feminist Politics and Human Nature*. Brighton, Sussex: The Harvester Press. [US edition published by Rowman & Allanheld]

James VI & I. (1598) 'The Trew Law of Free Monarchies,' in Wootton ed., 2003, 99-106.

James VI & I. (1610) 'A Speech to the Lords and Commons of the Parliament at White-Hall,' in Wootton ed., 2003, 107-109.

Jamroziak, Emilia. (2013) *The Cistercian Order in Medieval Europe, 1090-1500*. London: Routledge.

Jaspers, Karl. (1950) 'Marx und Freud,' in *Der Monat*, Vol. xxvii, No. 3, 141-150.

Jaspers, Karl. (1953 [1949]) *The Origin and Goal of History*, trans. Michael Bullock. London: Routledge and Kegan Paul. First published as *Vom Ursprung und Ziel der Geschichte*. München: Piper Verlag.

Jászi, Oscar & John D. Lewis. (1957) *Against the Tyrant: The Tradition and Theory of Tyrannicide*. New York: The Free Press.

Jebb, Matthew and Colm Crowley. (eds) (2013) *Secrets of the Irish Landscape: The Story of the Irish Landscape is the Story of Ireland*. Cork: Atrium Press.

Jenkins, Scott. (2011) 'What does Nietzsche Owe Thucydides?' in *Journal of Nietzsche Studies*, Vol. 42, 32-50.

Jennings, Jeremy. (2011) 'Early Nineteenth-Century Liberalism,' in Klosko, 331-347.

Jespersen, Otto. (1982 [1905]) *Growth and Structure of the English Language*, 10ᵗʰ ed. Oxford: Basil Blackwell.

Jespersen, Otto. (1992 [1924]) *The Philosophy of Grammar*. Chicago: The University of Chicago Press.

John of Salisbury. (1927/1963 [1159]) *The Statesman's Book of John of Salisbury, being the Fourth, Fifth, and Sixth Books, and Selections from the Seventh and Eighth Books, of the Policraticus*. trans. John Dickinson. New York: Alfred A. Knoff, Inc. [Reissued by Russell Y Russell, Inc.]. Available at http://www.constitution.org/salisbury/policrat456.htm, accessed 3 September 2013.

John of Salisbury. (1938 [1159]) *Policraticus—of the Frivolities of Courtiers and the Footprints of Philosophers*. trans. J. B. Pike. Minneapolis: The University of Minnesota Press.

John of Salisbury. (1991 [1159]) *Policraticus: of the Frivolities of Courtiers and the Footprints of Philosophers*. trans. and ed. by Cary J. Nederman. An abridged version in the series, Cambridge Texts in the History of Political Thought. Cambridge: Cambridge University Press.

Johnson, Paul. (2007 [1988]) *Intellectuals: From Marx and Tolstoy to Sartre and Chomsky*. New York: Harper Perennial.

Jones, Peter. (2008) *Vote for Caesar: How the Ancient Greeks and Romans Solved the Problems of Today*. London: Orion Books. An enchanting introduction to Greek and Roman culture.

Jun, Nathan. (2012) 'Review of Crispin Sartwell (ed.), *The Practical Anarchist: Writings of Josiah Warren*,' in *Anarchist Studies*, Vol. 20 No 1, 115-116.

Jung, Carl G. (1957) 'Man and his Future,' in Jung 1998, 357.

Jung, Carl G. (1998 [1983]) *The Essential Jung: Selected Writings*, ed. Anthony Storr. London: Fontana Press

Justinian. (1853 [AD 533]) *Institutes*, trans. Thomas Collett Sandars. London: John W. Parker and Son.

Justinian. (1985 [AD 530-33]) *The Digest of Justinian*, in four vols., trans. Alan Watson. Philadelphia: University of Pennsylvania Press.

Kahn, Andrew. (2008) 'Introduction' to Montesquieu 1721, vii-xxx.

Kahneman, Daniel. (2011) *Thinking, Fast and Slow*. London: Penguin Books.

Kaku, Michio. (2015) *The Future of the Mind: The Scientific Quest to Understand, Enhance, and Empower the Mind*. New York: Anchor Books.

Kaldor, Mary. (2012 [1998]) *New and Old Wars: Organized Violence in a Global Era*, 3rd ed. Stanford, California: Stanford University Press.

Kanfer, Stefan. (1997) 'Isaac Singer's Promised City,' in *City Journal*, available at http://www.city-journal.org/html/7_3_urbanities-isaac.html, accessed 12 January 2016.

Kant, Immanuel. (1764) 'Observations on the Feeling of the Beautiful and Sublime,' in Kant 2011, 11-62.

Kant, Immanuel. (1764-65) 'Remarks in the *Observations on the Feeling of the Beautiful and Sublime*,' in Kant 2011, 65-202.

Kant, Immanuel. (1891 [1797]) *The Philosophy of Law: An Exposition of the Fundamental Principles of Jurisprudence as The Science of Right*, trans. W. Hastie. Edinburgh: T. & T. Clark. Available at http://lf-oll.s3.amazonaws.com/titles/359/0139_Bk.pdf, accessed 23 February 2015. [A translation of the first part of *The Metaphysics of Morals*.]

Kant, Immanuel. (1953 [1783]) *Prolegomena to any Future Metaphysics that will be able to present itself as a Science*, trans. Peter G. Lucas. Manchester: Manchester University Press.

Kant, Immanuel. (1963 [1786]) 'The Conjectural Beginnings of Human History,' in Lewis White Beck ed., *Kant: On History*. New York: Bobbs-Merrill.

Kant, Immanuel. (1965 [1797] *The Metaphysical Elements of Justice* (Part I of *The Metaphysics of Morals*), trans. John Ladd. Indianapolis, Indiana: Bobbs-Merrill Educational Publishing. [A translation of *Metaphysische Anfangsgründe der Rechtslehre*, Part I of *Metaphysik der Sitten*]

Kant, Immanuel. (1970) *Kant's Political Writings*, ed. Hans Reiss, trans. H. B. Nisbet. Cambridge: Cambridge University Press. Available (in part) at http://www.bard.edu/library/arendt/pdfs/Kant-Political.pdf, accessed 8 March 2015. This convenient volume contains, among other pieces, Kant's 'Idea for a Universal History with a Cosmopolitan Purpose'; 'An Answer to the Questions: "What is Enlightenment?"'; 'On the Common Saying: "This may be True in Theory, but it does not Apply in Practice'; 'Perpetual Peace: A Philosophical Sketch'; *The Metaphysics of Morals*;

Kant, Immanuel. (1996 [1793]) 'On the Common Saying: That May Be Correct in Theory, but It Is of No Use in Practice,' in Kant 1996, 273-309.

Kant, Immanuel. (1996 [1797]) *The Metaphysics of Morals*, trans. and ed. Mary Gregor. Cambridge: Cambridge University Press. [Cambridge Texts in the History of Philosophy]

Kant, Immanuel. (1996) *Practical Philosophy*, trans. Mary Gregor. Cambridge: Cambridge University Press. [The Cambridge Edition of the Works of Immanuel Kant, general editors, Paul Guyer and Allen W. Wood]

Kant, Immanuel. (2011) *Observations on the Feeling of the Beautiful and Sublime and Other Writings*, eds Patrick Frierson and Paul Guyer. Cambridge: Cambridge University Press. [Cambridge Texts in the History of Philosophy] Available at http://users.clas.ufl.edu/burt/touchyfeelingsmaliciousobjects/KantObservationsontheFeelingoftheBeautifulandSublimeandOtherWritingsCambridge.pdf, accessed 4 January 2017.

Karlstadt, Andreas. (1524) 'Letter from the Community of Orlamünde to the People of Allstedt,' in Baylor, 33-35.

Karlstadt, Andreas. (1524a) 'Whether One Should Proceed Slowly,' in Baylor, 49-73.

Karsten, Frank and Karel Beckman. (2012) *Beyond Democracy*. CreateSpace Independent Publishing Platform.

Kaye, Joel. (2000) *Economy and Nature in the Fourteenth Century: Money, Market Exchange, and the Emergence of Scientific Thought*. Cambridge: Cambridge University Press.

Kealey, Terence. (1996) *The Economic Laws of Scientific Research*. London: Macmillan Press Ltd. [Covers a much wider range of topics—history, economics, politics—and in a much more engaging way than its title would suggest.]

Kealey, Terence. (2008) *Sex, Science & Profits*. London: Heinemann. [Reprinted by BCA]

Keegan, John. (1994) *A History of Warfare*. New York: Vintage.

Keeley, Lawrence H. (1999) *War Before Civilization: The Myth of the Peaceful Savage*. Oxford: Oxford University Press.

Keller, Albert Galloway. (1906) *Homeric Society: A Sociological Study of the Iliad and the Odyssey*. New York: 1902.

Kelley, Donald. (2011) 'The Influence of Roman Law,' in Klosko, 156-163.

Kelly, Fergus. (1988) *A Guide to Early Irish Law*. Dublin: Dublin Institute for Advanced Studies.

Kelly, Paul. (2009a) 'Hume,' in Boucher & Kelly 2009, 225-244.

Kelly, Paul. (2009b) 'J. S. Mill on Liberty,' in Boucher & Kelly 2009, 381-399.

Kennedy, John T. (2011), 'The Fundamental Fallacy of Government,' available at http://www.anti-state.com/kennedy/kennedy1.html >, accessed 22 May 2014.

Kennedy, Paul. (1989) *The Rise and Fall of the Great Powers: Economic Change and Military Conflict from 1500 to 2000*. London: Fontana Press.

Kerford, George B. (1981) *The Sophistic Movement*. Cambridge: Cambridge University Press.

Kershaw, Stephen. (2010) *A Brief Guide to Classical Civilization*. London: Robinson.

Kersting, Wolfgang. 'Politics, Freedom, and Order: Kant's Political Philosophy,' in Guyer, 342-366.

Keynes, John Maynard. (1963) *Essays in Persuasion*. New York: W. W. Norton & Co.

King-Hall, Stephen. (1939) *History of the War, Volume I: The Cause of the War*. London: Hodder & Stoughton.

King, P. D. (1988) 'The Barbarian Kingdoms,' in Burns 1988, 123-153.

King, Richard. (2013) *On Offence: The Politics of Indignation*. London: Scribe.

Kingdon, Robert M. (1991) 'Calvinism and Resistance Theory, 1550-1580,' in Burns 1988, 193-218.

Kirk, Russell. (1984) 'Libertarians: The Chirping Sectaries,' in Carey, 113-124.

Kirk, Russell. (2007-2016) 'Ten Conservative Principle,' available at http://www.kirkcenter.org/index.php/detail/ten-conservative-principles/, accessed 23 January 2017.

Kirzner, Israel M. (2001) *Ludwig von Mises: The Man and his Economics*. Wilmington, Delaware: ISI Books.

Klinghoffer, David. (2008) 'An Important Historic Sidebar,' available at http://www.nationalreview.com/article/224233/dont-doubt-it-david-klinghoffer, accessed 16 May 2015. [*National Review* online]

Klosko, George. (ed.) (2011) *The Oxford Handbook of the History of Political Philosophy*. Oxford: Oxford University Press. A superb collection of brief, scholarly yet very accessible essays by different authors on a wide range of political themes and periods.

Klosko, George. (2011a) 'Contemporary Anglo-American Political Philosophy,' in Klosko 2011, 456-479.

Kluger, Jeffrey. (2009) *Simplexity: Why Simple Things Become Complex (And How Complex Things Can Be Made Simple)*. New York: Hyperion.

Knowles, David. (1962) *The Evolution of Medieval Thought*. London: Longman.

Knox, John. (1558) 'The Appellation,' in Zuck, 154-155.

Knox, John. (1561) 'The Interview with Mary Queens of Scots,' in Zuck, 155-156.

Knox, John. (1564) 'Debate with Lethington,' in Zuck, 156-158.

Koestler, Arthur. (1979) *Janus: A Summing Up*. London: Picador.

Kohr, Leopold. (1991 [1957]) *The Breakdown of Nations*. Totnes, Devon: Green Books. First published by Routledge & Kegan Paul in 1957.

Kolakowski, Leszek. (1978) *Main Currents of Marxism: Its Rise, Growth and Dissolution*, trans. P. S. Falla. Oxford: Oxford University Press. [In 3 volumes—Vol. I: The Founders; Vol. II: The Golden Age; Vol. 3: The Breakdown]

Kolpinsky, N. Y. (1972) 'Preface' to Anon. (1972).

Konstan, David. (2012) 'Epicurus,' in *Stanford Encyclopedia of Philosophy*, available at http://plato.stanford.edu/archives/win2012/entries/epicurus/, accessed 7 September 2013.

Kramer, Samuel Noah. (1981) *History Begins at Sumer*. Philadelphia: University of Pennsylvania Press.

Kramnick, Isaac. (1977) *The Rage of Edmund Burke: Portrait of an Ambivalent Conservative*. New York: Basic Books.

Kraut, Richard. (ed.) (1992) *The Cambridge Companion to Plato*. Cambridge: Cambridge University Press.

Kretzmann, Norman, Anthony Kenny & Jan Pinborg (eds) (1982) *The Cambridge History of Later Medieval Philosophy: From the Rediscovery of Aristotle to the Disintegration of Scholasticism 1100-1600*. Cambridge: Cambridge University Press.

Kretzmann, Norman and Eleonore Stump. (eds) (1993) *The Cambridge Companion to Aquinas*. Cambridge: Cambridge University Press.

Kropotkin, Peter. (1903) *Modern Science and Anarchism*. Philadelphia: The Social Science Club of Philadelphia. Available at http://theanarchistlibrary.org/library/petr-kropotkin-modern-science-and-anarchism, accessed 4 June 2014.

Kropotkin, Peter. (1910) 'Anarchism,' in *The Encyclopaedia Britannica*, 11th ed., reprinted in Kropotkin 1892, 233-247]

Kropotkin, Peter. (1939 [1902b]) *Mutual Aid: A Factor of Evolution*. London: Penguin Books.

Kropotkin, Peter. (1987 [1897]) *The State: Its Historic Role*. London: Freedom Press.

Kropotkin, Peter. (1989 [1899b]) *Memoirs of a Revolutionist*, intro. George Woodcock. Montréal: Black Rose Books. Available at http://theanarchistlibrary.org/library/petr-kropotkin-memoirs-of-a-revolutionist, accessed 17 June 2014.

Kropotkin, Peter. (1995 [1892]) *The Conquest of Bread and Other Writings*. ed. Marshall Shatz. Cambridge: Cambridge University Press,] [Cambridge Texts in the History of Political Thought]

Kropotkin, Peter. (1998 [1886-1907]) *Act for Yourselves: Articles from Freedom 1886-1907*. London: Freedom Press.

Kropotkin, Peter. (1998 [1899a]) *Fields, Factories and Workshops Tomorrow*. London: Freedom Press.

Kropotkin, Peter. (2006 [1902a]) *Mutual Aid: A Factor of Evolution*. Mineola, New York: Dover.

Kühl, Stefan. (1994) *The Nazi Connection: Eugenics, American Racism and German National Socialism*. New York: Oxford University Press.

Kula, Marcin. (2005) 'Communism as Religion' in *Totalitarian Movements and Political Religions*, Vol. 6, No. 3, 371-381.

Ladd, John. (1965) 'Introduction' to Kant 1797 [1965], ix-xxxi.

Lahey, Stephen E. (2003) *Philosophy and Politics in the Thought of John Wyclif*. Cambridge: Cambridge University Press.

Lahey, Stephen E. (2013) 'John Wyclif's Political Philosophy' *Stanford Encyclopedia of Philosophy*, available at http://plato.stanford.edu/archives/sum2013/entries/wyclif-political/, accessed 7 September 2013.

Lahr, M. Mirazón et al. (2016) 'Inter-group Violence among early Holocene Hunter-Gatherers of West Turkana, Kenya,' in *Nature*, Vol. 529, 394-398.

Laks, André & Glenn W. Most. (eds) (2016) *Sophists, Part 1*, trans. André Laks & Glenn W. Most. Cambridge, Massachusetts: Harvard University Press. [Loeb Classical Library, Vol. VIII of the nine volume edition of Early Greek Philosophy, LCL 531]

Lambertini, Roberto. (2014 [2001]) 'Giles of Rome,' in *Stanford Encyclopedia of Philosophy*, available at https://leibniz.stanford.edu/friends/members/view/giles/a4/, accessed 1 September 2015.

Landau, Iddo. (2006) *Is Philosophy Androcentric?* University Park, Pennsylvania: The Pennsylvania University Press.

Landes, David. (1999 [1998]) *The Wealth and Poverty of Nations*. London: Abacus. [First published in the USA by W. W. Norton & Company (1998), and in Great Britain by Little, Brown and Company (1998)]

Landsburg, Steven E. (2009 [2007]) *More Sex is Safer Sex: The Unconventional Wisdom of Economics*. London: Pocket Books.

Lane, Melissa. (2011) 'Ancient Political Philosophy,' in *Stanford Encyclopedia of Philosophy*, available at http://plato.stanford.edu/archives/fall2011/entries/ancient-political/, accessed 7 September 2013.

Lane, Melissa. (2014) *Greek and Roman Political Ideas*. London: Penguin.

Lane, Tom. (1996) 'On Anarchism: Noam Chomsky interviewed by Tom Lane,' available at http://www.chomsky.info/interviews/19961223.htm, accessed 4 June 2014.

Lasch, Christopher. (1996 [1995]) *The Revolt of the Elites and the Betrayal of Democracy*. New York: W. W. Norton & Company.

Laslett, Peter. (1949) 'Introduction' to Filmer 1949, 1-43.

Laszlo, Ervin. (1972a) *The Systems View of the World: The Natural Philosophy of the New Developments in the Sciences*. New York: George Braziller.

Laszlo, Ervin. (1972b) *Introduction to Systems Philosophy: Towards a New Paradigm of Contemporary Thought*. New York: Harper & Row.

Laszlo, Ervin. (2010 [2006]) *The Chaos Point: The World at the Crossroads*, rev. ed. London: Piatkus.

Lavery, Jonathan. (2008) 'Protagoras,' in O'Grady ed., 30-44.

Lawson-Tancred, Hugh C. 'Introduction' to Aristotle 1991, 1-61.

Lazaridis, Iosif et al. (2014) 'Ancient Human Genomes Suggests Three Ancestral Populations for Present-Day Europeans,' in *Nature* Vol. 513. 409-413.

Le Fanu, James. (2009) *Why Us? How Science Rediscovered the Mystery of Ourselves*. New York: Pantheon Books.

Leahy, William D. (1950) *I Was There: The Personal Story of the Chief of Staff to Presidents Roosevelt and Truman Based on His Notes and Diaries Made at the Time*. New York: Whittlesey House.

Lecky, William. (1981 [1896]) *Democracy and Liberty*, 2 vols. Indianapolis: Liberty Fund.

Lee, Alexander. (2009) 'Roman Law and Human Liberty,' in *Journal of the History of Ideas*, Vol. 70, No. 1, 23-44.

Lee, Daniel. (2016) *Popular Sovereignty in Early Modern Constitutional Thought*. Oxford: Oxford University Press.

Leeson, Peter T. (2007) 'An-*arrgh*-chy: The Law and Economics of Pirate Organization,' in *Journal of Political Economy*, Vol. 115, No. 6, 1049-1094.

LeFevre, Robert. (2007 [1966]) *The Philosophy of Ownership*. Auburn, Alabama: The Ludwig von Mises Institute.

Lehner, Ulrich L. (2016) *The Catholic Enlightenment: The Forgotten History of a Global Movement*. Oxford: Oxford University Press.

Leith, Sam. (2012 [2011]) *You Talkin' to Me?: Rhetoric from Aristotle to Obama*. London: Profile Books.

Lekachman, Robert. (1967 [1966]) *The Age of Keynes: A Biographical Study*. London: Penguin.

Leonard, Thomas C. (2016) *Illiberal Reformers: Race, Eugenics and American Economics in the Progressive Era*. New Haven, Connecticut: Princeton University Press.

Lester, J. C. (1997) 'Review of Alan Haworth's Anti-Libertarianism,' *Journal of Applied Philosophy*, vol. 14 No 1, 92-93. Available at http://www.la-articles.org.uk/antilib. htm, accessed 25 March 2016.

Lester, J. C. (2002) 'Behind the Caricature,' available at http://www.la-articles.org.uk/ antilib.htm, accessed 25 March 2016.

Levy, Robert A. & William Mellor. (2008) *The Dirty Dozen: How Twelve Supreme Court Cases Radically Expanded Government and Eroded Freedom*. New York: Sentinel.

Lewis, Bernard. (2012) *Notes on a Century: Reflections of a Middle East Historian*. London: Penguin.

Lewis, Clive Staples. (1987) 'The Humanitarian Conception of Punishment,' in *Amcap Journal*, Vol. 13, No. 1, 147-48.

Lewis, Davis. (2002 [1969]) *Convention: A Philosophical Study*. Oxford: Blackwell.

Lewis, Hunter. (2013) *Crony Capitalism in America: 2008-2102*. AC2 Books.

Lilburne, John et al. (1648) "The Petition of 11 September 1648,' in Sharp 1998, 131-139.

Lilburne, John, William Walwyn, Thomas Prince and Richard Overton. (1649) 'An Agreement of the Free People of England,' in Sharp 1998, 168-178.

Lilburne, John. (1645) 'On the 150th Page,' in Sharp 1998, 3-8.

Lilburne, John. (1646) 'The Freeman's Freedom Vindicated,' in Sharp 1998, 31-32.

Lilburne, John. (1649a) 'England's New Chains Discovered,' in Sharp 1998, 140-157

Lilburne, John. (1649b) 'The Young Men's and the Apprentices' Outcry,' in Sharp 1998, 179-201.

Lincoln, Abraham. (1848) 'Speech in the United States House of Representatives, 12 January,' available at http://teachingamericanhistory.org/library/document/the-war-with-mexico-speech-in-the-united-states-house-of-representatives/, accessed 31 July 2016.

Lloyd, Peter. (2016) *Stand By Your Manhood: An Essential Guide for Modern Man.* London: Biteback Publishing.

Lock, F. P. (1998) *Edmund Burke, Volume I (1730-1784).* Oxford: Oxford University Press.

Locke, John. (1960 [1689]) *Two Treatises on Government*, ed. Peter Laslett. rev. ed. Cambridge: Cambridge University Press.

Locke, John. (1988 [1689]) *Two Treatises on Government.* Cambridge: Cambridge University Press.

Long, A. A. (2006) *From Epicurus to Epictetus: Studies in Hellenistic and Roman Philosophy.* Oxford: Clarendon Press.

Long, Roderick T. & Tibor R. Machan. (eds) (2008) *Anarchism/Minarchism: Is Government Part of a Free Country?* Aldershot, Hampshire: Ashgate Publishing.

Lopez, Robert S. (1967]) *The Birth of Europe.* New York: M. Evans & Co. Inc. [Rowman & Littlefield]

Lopez, Robert S. (1976) *The Commercial Revolution of the Middle Ages, 950-1350.* Cambridge: Cambridge University Press.

Lord, Carnes. (1987) 'Aristotle,' in Strauss & Cropsey, 118-154.

Lotzer, Sebastian. (1525) 'The Twelve Articles of the Peasants,' in Zuck, 14-16; in Baylor, 231-238.

Lovett, Frank. (2013) 'Republicanism,' in *Stanford Encyclopedia of Philosophy*, available at http://plato.stanford.edu/archives/spr2013/entries/republicanism/, accessed 7 September 2013.

Ludwig, Emil. (1936) *The Nile: The Life-Story of a River.* London: George Allen & Unwin Ltd.

Lukacs, John. (2002) 'The Universality of National Socialism (The Mistaken Category of "Fascism"),' in *Totalitarian Movements and Political Religions*, Vol. 3, No. 1, 107-121.

Lukianoff, Greg. (2014) *Unlearning Liberty: Campus Censorship and The End of American Debate.* New York: Encounter Books.

Lunn-Rockliffe, Sophie. (2011) 'Early Christian Political Philosophy,' in Klosko ed., 142-155.

Luscombe, David E. (1982) 'The State of Nature and the Origin of the State,' in Kretzmann, Kenny and Pinborg, 757-770.

Luscombe, David E. (1988) 'Introduction: The Formation of Political Thought in the West,' in Burns 1988, 157-173.

Luscombe, David E. and G. R. Evans. (1988) 'The Twelfth-Century Renaissance,' in Burns 1988, 306-338.

Luther, Martin. (1523) 'On Secular Authority,' in Höpfl, 1-43.

MacCormaic, Ruadhán. (2016) *The Supreme Court.* Dublin: Penguin Ireland.

MacDonnell, Francis. (2004 [1995]) *Insidious Foes: The Axis Fifth Column and the American Home Front.* Guilford, Connecticut: The Lyons Press. Previously published by Oxford University Press.

Macedo, Stephen and Josiah Ober. (eds) (2006) *Primates and Philosophers: How Morality Evolved.* Princeton, New Jersey: Princeton University Press.

Macfarlane, Alan. (1978) *The Origins of English Individualism: The Family, Property, and Social Transition*. Oxford: Basil Blackwell.

Machan, Tibor. (1984) 'Libertarianism: The Principle of Liberty,' in Carey, 35-58.

Machiavelli, Niccolò. (1988 [1513 (1532)]) *The Prince*, eds Quentin Skinner & Russell Price. Cambridge: Cambridge University Press. [Cambridge Texts in the History of Political Thought]

Machiavelli. Niccolò. (1970 [1518/19 (1531)]) *The Discourses*, ed. Bernard Crick, trans. Leslie J. Walker. London: Penguin.

Mack, Eric. (2009) *John Locke*. London: Continuum.

Mack, Eric. (2011) 'Libertarianism,' in Klosko, 673-688.

Mack, Eric. (2015) 'Robert Nozick's Political Philosophy,' in *The Stanford Encyclopedia of Philosophy*, available at http://plato.stanford.edu/archives/sum2015/entries/nozick-political/, accessed 8 July 2015.

Mackay, Thomas. (ed.) (1981 [1891] *A Plea for Liberty: An Argument against Socialism and Socialistic Legislation*. Indianapolis, Indiana: Liberty Classics. Available at http://lf-oll.s3.amazonaws.com/titles/313/0071_Bk.pdf, accessed 6 July 2014.

MacMullen, Ramsay. (1986) 'What Difference Did Christianity Make?,' in *Historia: Zeitschrift für Alte Geschichte*, Bd. 35, H. 3, 322-343.

Magid, Henry M. (1987) 'John Stuart Mill,' in Strauss & Cropsey, 784-801.

Mahoney, Daniel J. (2005) *Bertrand de Jouvenel: The Conservative Liberal and the Illusions of Modernity*. Wilmington, Delaware: ISI Books.

Maier, Hans. (2007) 'Political Religions: a Concept and its Limitations,' in *Totalitarian Movements and Political Religions*, Vol. 8, No. 1, 5-16. Translated by Jodi Bruhn.

Maine, Henry Sumner. (1883) *Dissertations on Early Law and Custom*. London: John Murray. Available at http://oll.libertyfund.org/titles/maine-dissertations-on-early-law-and-custom, accessed 25 April 2014.

Maine, Henry Sumner. (1890) *On Early Law and Custom*. London: John Murray.

Maine, Henry Sumner. (1906 [1861]) *Ancient Law: Its Connection with the Early History of Society and its Relations to Modern Ideas*, 4th American from the 10th London edition. New York: Henry Holt and Company. Available at http://lf- oll.s3.amazonaws.com/titles/2001/1376_Bk_Sm.pdf, accessed 25 April 2014.

Maine, Henry Sumner. (1976 [1885]) *Popular Government*. Indianapolis, Indiana: Liberty Fund.

Maitland, Frederic William. (2003) *State, Trust and Corporation*, eds David Runciman and Magnus Ryan. Cambridge: Cambridge University Press.

Mäkinen, Viripi. (2001) *Property Rights in the Late Medieval Discussion on Franciscan Poverty*. Leuven, Belgium: Peeters.

Malan, Koos. (2012) *Politocracy*. Pretoria: Pretoria University Law Press.

Malcolm, Noel. (2007) '"Reason of State" and Hobbes,' in Anon. 2007, 92-123.

Malik, Kenan. (2014) *The Quest for a Moral Compass: A Global History of Ethics*. London: Atlantic Books.

Malinowski, Bronislaw. (1926) *Crime & Custom in Savage Society*. London: Routledge & Kegan Paul, Ltd. [The International Library of Psychology Philosophy and Scientific Method]

Mallock, William Hurrell. (1918) *The Limits of Pure Democracy*. London: Chapman and Hall, Ltd.

Maltsev, Yuri N. (ed.) (1993) *Requiem for Marx*. Auburn, Alabama: Ludwig von Mises Institute.

Mandeville, Bernard. (1970 [1714]) *The Fable of the Bees*. London: Penguin. An online version is available at http://lf-oll.s3.amazonaws.com/titles/846/0014-01_Bk.pdf, accessed 6 April 2014.

Manin, Bernard. (1997) *The Principles of Representative Government*. Cambridge: Cambridge University Press. Available at http://www.thetimes.co.uk/article/against-elections-the-case-for-democracy-by-david-van-reybrouck-5z8hzn0m2, accessed 4 November 2016.

Mamet, David. (2012) *The Secret Knowledge: On the Dismantling of American Culture*. New York: Sentinel. [A division of Penguin Books]

Mann, Joel E. and Getty L. Lustila. (2011) 'A Model Sophist: Nietzsche on Protagoras and Thucydides,' in *Journal of Nietzsche Studies*, Vol. 42, 51-72.

Mansfield, Harvey, J. (1987) 'Edmund Burke,' in Straus & Cropsey, 687-709.

Mantz, Felix. (1525)'A Protest and Defense,' in Zuck, 62-63. [1525]; 'Protest and Defense' in Baylor, 95-100.

Marcellinus, Ammianus. (1950 [post AD 378]) *Res gestae*, ed. and trans. J. C. Rolfe. Cambridge, Massachusetts: Harvard University Press. [Loeb Classical Library] Available online at http://penelope.uchicago.edu/Thayer/E/Roman/Texts/Ammian/28*.html, accessed 9 September 2015.

Marcus Aurelius. (2006 [AD 161-180]) *Meditations*, trans. Martin Hammond, intro. Diskin Clay. London: Penguin.

Marks, Jonathan M. (2003) *What it Means to be 98% Chimpanzee: Apes, People, and their Genes*. Berkeley and Los Angeles: University of California Press.

Markus, Robert Austin. (1970) *Saeculum: History and Society in the Theology of St Augustine*. Cambridge: Cambridge University Press.

Markus, Robert Austin. (1988) 'The Latin Fathers,' in Burns ed. 1988, 92-122.

Marshall, Tim. (2016 [2015]) *Prisoners of Geography: Ten Maps that Tell You Everything You Need to Know about Global Politics*. London: Elliott and Thompson Limited.

Marsilius of Padua. (1956 [1324]) *Defensor pacis*, trans. with introduction by Alan Gewirth. New York: Columbia University Press.

Marsilius of Padua. (1993 [c. 1342]) *Defensor minor*, ed. and intro. Cary J. Nederman, *Marsiliglio of Padua: Writings on the Empire*. Cambridge: Cambridge University Press, 1993.

Martin, James J. (1970) *Men Against the State: The Expositors of Individualist Anarchism in America, 1827–1908*. Colorado Springs, CO.: Ralph Myles Publishers.

Marx, Karl & Friedrich Engels. (1839-1895) 'Online Versions of the Works of Marx and Engels in Chronological Order,' available at Marxist Internet Archive, https://www.marxists.org/archive/marx/works/date/, accessed 25 March 2014.

Marx, Karl and Friedrich Engels. (1965 [1852] *Selected Correspondence*. Moscow: Progress Publishers.

Marx, Karl & Friedrich Engels. (1968) *Selected Works*. London: Lawrence and Wishart.

Marx, Karl & Friedrich Engels. (1975-2001) *Karl Marx Friedrich Engels Collected Works*, in 50 vols. London: Lawrence and Wishart. A listing of the contents of these volumes is available at https://www.marxists.org/archive/marx/works/cw/, accessed 28 March 2014.

Marx, Karl & Friedrich Engels. (1996 [1848b]) *Manifesto of the Communist Party*, in Marx 1996, 1-30.

Marx, Karl & Friedrich Engels. (2002 [1848]) *The Communist Manifesto*, trans. Samuel Jones, introduction and notes Gareth Stedman Jones. London: Penguin. An inexpensive edition with extensive commentary and notes.

Marx, Karl. (1844) 'Economic and Philosophical Manuscripts,' available at https://www.marxists.org/archive/marx/works/1844/manuscripts/labour.htm, accessed 29 July 2015. For an accessible print version, see Marx 1963a.

Marx, Karl. (1865) 'Value, Price and Profit' Speech to the International Working Men's Association,' available at https://www.marxists.org/archive/marx/works/1865/value-price-profit/index.htm, accessed 28 March 2014. In Marx & Engels (1975-2001), 101-147.

Marx, Karl. (1963 [1961]) *Karl Marx: Selected Writings in Sociology and Social Philosophy*, trans. Thomas Burton Bottomore, eds T. B. Bottomore and Maximilien Rubel. 2nd ed. London: Penguin. [Originally published in 1956 by C. A. Watts]

Marx, Karl. (1963a) *Karl Marx: Early Writings*, trans. and ed. Thomas Burton Bottomore. London: C. A. Watts & Co. Ltd. [This collection contains 'On the Jewish Question,' 'Contribution to the Critique of Hegel's Philosophy of Right: Introduction,' and 'Economic and Philosophical Manuscripts']

Marx, Karl. (1967 [1835-1847]) *Writings of the Young Marx on Philosophy and Society* trans. and ed. Lloyd D. Easton and Kurt H. Guddat. Garden City, New York: Anchor Books.

Marx, Karl. (1973 [1857-1858]) *Grundrisse: Foundations of the Critique of Political Economy (Rough Draft)*, trans. Martin Nicolaus. London: Allen Lane.

Marx, Karl. (1976 [1867]) *Capital: A Critique of Political Economy*, Volume One, trans. Ben Fowkes. London: Penguin Books.

Marx, Karl. (1978 [1885]) *Capital: A Critique of Political Economy*, vol. two, trans. David Fernbach. London: Penguin Books.

Marx, Karl. (1994 [1844a]) 'On the Jewish Question,' in Marx 1996, 28-56.

Marx, Karl. (1994 [1845]) 'On Feuerbach,' in Marx 1996, 116-118.

Marx, Karl. (1994) *Marx: Early Political Writings*, ed. and trans. Joseph O'Malley. Cambridge: Cambridge University Press. [Cambridge Texts in the History of Political Thought. This collection contains 'From the Critique of Hegel's Philosophy of Right (§§261-313)'; 'On the Jewish Question'; 'A Contribution to the Critique of Hegel's Philosophy of Right: Introduction'; 'From the Paris Notebooks'; 'Critical Marginal Notes on "The King of Prussia and Social Reform. By a Prussian"'; 'Points on the State and Bourgeois Society'; 'On Feuerbach'; 'From "The German Ideology"; Chapter One, "Feuerbach"'; 'From *Poverty of Philosophy*'; and 'Address on Poland']

Marx, Karl. (1996 [1851-1852]) 'The Eighteenth Brumaire of Louis Bonaparte,' in Marx 1996, 31-127.

Marx, Karl. (1996 [1875]) *Critique of the Gotha Programme*, in Marx 1996, 208-226.

Marx, Karl. (1996) *Marx: Later Political Writings*, ed. and trans. Terrell Carver. Cambridge: Cambridge University Press. [Cambridge Texts in the History of Political Thought. This collection contains *Manifesto of the Communist Party*; *The Eighteenth Brumaire of Louis Bonaparte*; 'Introduction' to the *Grundrisse*, 'Preface' to *A Contribution to the Critique of Political Economy*; *The Civil War in France*; *Critique of the Gotha Programme*; and '"Notes" on Adolph Wagner']

Marz, Zander. (2013) *Beyond the Government-Haunted World: A Comic Guide to Voluntaryism, Free Markets, and the Non-Aggression Principle*. Inspired Arts Press. [This is *the* book to give to your children and to read yourself when they're not around]

Mason, Paul. (2015) *PostCapitalism: A Guide to our Future*. London: Allen Lane.

Maxwell, John Francis. (1975) *Slavery and the Catholic Church*. London: Barry Rose Publishers.

May, Larry. (ed.) (2008) *War: Essays in Political Philosophy*. Cambridge: Cambridge University Press.

McArthur, Neil. (2011) 'The Scottish Enlightenment,' in Klosko, 319-330.

McCaffrey, Lawrence J. (1989) 'Components of Irish Nationalism,' in Hachey & McCaffrey, 1-19.

McCarthy, Daniel. (2014) 'Why Liberalism Means Empire,' in *The American Conservative* (16 July), available at http://www.theamericanconservative.com/articles/why-liberalism-means-empire/, accessed 30 September 2014.

McClelland, J. S. *A History of Western Political Thought*. New York: Routledge, 1996.

McCloskey, Deirdre Nansen. (2007 [2006]) *The Bourgeois Virtues: Ethics for an Age of Commerce*. Chicago: University of Chicago Press.

McCloskey, Deirdre Nansen. (2011 [2010]) *Bourgeois Dignity: Why Economics Can't Explain the Modern World*. Chicago: University of Chicago Press.

McCloskey, Deirdre Nansen. (2014) 'Measured, Unmeasured, Mismeasured, and Unjustified Pessimism: A Review Essay of Thomas Piketty's *Capital in the Twenty-First Century*,' in *Erasmus Journal for Philosophy and Economics*, Vol. 7, No. 2, 73-115, available at http://cjpc.org/pdf/7-2-art-4.pdf, accessed 9 June 2015.

McCloskey, Deirdre Nansen. (2016) *Bourgeois Equality: How Ideas, not Capital or Institutions, Enriched the World*. Chicago: University of Chicago Press.

McCord, William. (1992) 'Review of Orlando Patterson's *Freedom*,' in *Contemporary Sociology*, Vol. 21, No. 2, 176-178.

McCullock, Matt. (2006) 'Johannes Althusius' *Politica*: The Culmination of Calvin's Right of Resistance.' *The European Legacy: Toward New Paradigms*, Vol. 11 No. 5, 485-499.

McDonough, Frank. (1999) *Hitler and Nazi Germany*. Cambridge: Cambridge University Press.

McElroy, Wendy. (ed.) (2002a) *Liberty for Women: Freedom and Feminism in the Twenty-first Century*. Chicago: Ivan R. Dee.

McElroy, Wendy. (1997) 'Benjamin Tucker, *Liberty*, and Individualist Anarchism,' in *The Independent Review* Vol. 2, No. 3, 421-434. Available at http://www.independent.org/pdf/tir/tir_02_3_mcelroy.pdf, accessed 2 June 2014. Also available as Chapter 1 in McElroy 2003.

McElroy, Wendy. (2000) 'Murray N. Rothbard: Mr. Libertarian,' available at http://www.wendymcelroy.com/rockwell/mcelroy000706.html, accessed 29 June 2014.

McElroy, Wendy. (2002b) 'Introduction' to McElroy 2002a.

McElroy, Wendy. (2003) *The Debates of Liberty: An Overview of Individualist Anarchism, 1881-1908*. Lanham, Maryland: Lexington Books.

McElroy, Wendy. (2012) '*LIBERTY'S* Connection to Other Publications,' available at http://www.wendymcelroy.com/libdebates/apx1pubs.html, accessed 6 July 2014.

McEvedy, Colin. (1982) *The New Penguin Atlas of Recent History*. London: Penguin.

McEvedy, Colin. (1992) *The New Penguin Atlas of Medieval History*. London: Penguin.

McEvedy, Colin. (2002 [1967]) *The New Penguin Atlas of Ancient History*, 2nd ed. London: Penguin.

McEvedy, Colin. (2002 [1982]) *The New Penguin Atlas of Recent History*, 2nd ed. London: Penguin.

McGrade, Arthur S., John Kilcullen & Matthew Kempshall. (eds) (2001)*The Cambridge Translations of Medieval Philosophical Texts. Volume Two: Ethics and Political Philosophy*. Cambridge: Cambridge University Press. [Contains translations of works not readily available in English, by such as Albert the Great, Bonaventure, Giles of Rome, Henry of Ghent, William of Ockham, John Wyclif and others.]

McInerny, Ralph. (1992) *Aquinas on Human Action: A Theory of Practice*. Washington, D.C.: The Catholic University of American Press.

McIntosh, Jane & Clint Twist. (2001) *Civilizations*. London: BBC Worldwide Limited

McIntyre, Alison. (2011) 'Doctrine of Double Effect,' in *Stanford Encyclopedia of Philosophy*, available at http://plato.stanford.edu/archives/fall2011/entries/double-effect/, accessed 7 September 2013.

McNeill, William H. (1965 [1963]) *The Rise of the West: A History of the Human Community*. New York: Mentor. [cf. Duchesne]

McNerney, John. (2016) *Wealth of Persons: Economics with a Human Face*. Eugene, Oregon: Cascade Books.

Mead, Margaret. (1928) *Coming of Age in Samoa: A Psychological Study of Primitive Youth for Western Civilization*. New York: William Morrow & Company. Available at https://archive.org/details/comingofageinsam00mead, accessed 1 October 2016.

Mead, Walter Russell. (2008 [2007]) *God and Gold: Britain, America, and the Making of the Modern World*. London: Atlantic Books.

Meadowcroft, John and Mark Pennington. (2007) *Rescuing Social Capital from Social Democracy*. London: Institute of Economic Affairs.

Melquior, J. G. (1991) *Foucault*, 2nd ed. London: Fontana Press.

Meltzer, Albert. (1996) *Anarchism: Arguments For and Against*. Edinburgh: AK Press.

Menand, Louis. (2001) *The Metaphysical Club: A Story of Ideas in America*. New York: Farrar, Straus and Giroux. [A fascinating account, historical and conceptual, of the development of a peculiarly American cast of mind in the lives and works of Oliver Wendell Holmes, Jr., William James, Charles Sanders Peirce and John Dewey.]

Mencken, H. L. (1982 [1916]) *A Mencken Chrestomathy: His Own Selection of his Choicest Writings*, ed. and annotated by H. L Mencken. New York: Vintage Books.

Menger, Carl. (1976/2007 [1871]) *Principles of Economics*, trans. James Dingwall and Bert F. Hoselitz, intro. F. A. Hayek. Auburn, Alabama: Ludwig von Mises Institute.

Merrill, Ronald E. (1998) *The Ideas of Ayn Rand*. Chicago: Open Court.

Mésáros, István. (1975) *Marx's Theory of Alienation*, 4th ed. London: Merlin Press.

Metzger, Bruce M. & Michael D. Coogan. (eds) (1993) *The Oxford Companion to the Bible*. Oxford: Oxford University Press.

Migone, Gian Giacomo. (2015 [1980]) *The United States and Fascist Italy: The Rise of American Finance in Europe*, trans. Molly Tambor. Cambridge: Cambridge University Press. [First published as *Gli Stati Uniti e il fascismo. Alle origini dell'egemonia Americana in Italia* by Feltrinelli Editore, 1980]

Miles, Rosalind. (2001 [1988]) *Who Cooked the Last Supper? The Women's History of the World*. New York: Three Rivers Press. [Originally published as *The Women's History of the World* in 1988 by Penguin (London)]

Mill, John Stuart. (1859) *On Liberty*. 4th ed. London: Longman, Roberts, & Green Co. Available at http://www.econlib.org/library/Mill/mlLbty.html, accessed 3 March 2014.

Mill, John Stuart. (1861) *Considerations on Representative Government*, in Mill 1991, 205-470.

Mill, John Stuart. (1965 [1848]) *Principles of Political Economy, with some of the Applications to Social Philosophy*. Vols. II & III of Mill 1965-1991. [Now available from Liberty Fund]

Mill, John Stuart. (1965-1991) *Collected Works of John Stuart Mill*, 33 vols. ed. J. Robson. Toronto: University of Toronto Press.

Mill, John Stuart. (1991) *On Liberty and Other Essays*, ed. John Gray. Oxford: Oxford University Press. [Oxford World's Classics]

Mill, John Stuart. (1991a [1859]) *On Liberty*, in Mill 1991, 5-128.

Mill, John Stuart. (1994 [1848]) *Principles of Political Economy and Chapters on Socialism*, ed. Jonathan Riley. Oxford: Oxford University Press. A selection of material from *Principles of Political Economy*, including segments from Books II and III and all of Books IV and V.

Mill, John Stuart. (2006 [1848]) *Principles of Political Economy with some of their Applications to Social Philosophy*, 2 vols. Indianapolis, Indiana: Liberty Fund.

Miller, Clyde Lee. (2013) 'Cusanus, Nicolaus [Nicolas of Cusa],' in *Stanford Encyclopedia of Philosophy*, available at http://plato.stanford.edu/archives/sum2013/entries/cusanus/, accessed 7 September 2013.

Miller, Dale E. (2010) *J. S. Mill: Moral, Social and Political Thought*. Cambridge: Polity Press.

Miller, Fred. (2102) 'Aristotle's Political Theory,' in *Stanford Encyclopedia of Philosophy*, available at http://plato.stanford.edu/archives/fall2012/entries/aristotle-politics/, accessed on 7 September 2013.

Millman, Brock. (2002) 'The Lloyd George War Government, 1917-1918,' in *Totalitarian Movements and Political Religions*, Vol. 3, No. 3, 99-127.

Miłosz, Czesław. (1980 [1953]) *The Captive Mind*, trans. Jane Zielonko. London: Penguin Books.

Milton, Giles. (2004) *White Gold: The Extraordinary Story of Thomas Pellow and North Africa's One Million European Slaves*. London: Hodder & Stoughton.

Milton, John. (1644) 'Areopagitica,' in Milton 2003, 236-273.

Milton, John. (1649) 'The Tenure of Kings and Magistrates,' in Milton 2003, 273-307.

Milton, John. (1654) 'Second Defence [of the English People],' in Milton 2003, 308-330.

Milton, John. (1660) 'The Ready and Easy Way to Establish a Free Commonwealth, in Milton 2003, 330-353.

Milton, John. (2003 [1991]) *The Major Works, including Paradise Lost*, eds Stephen Orgel & Jonathan Goldberg. Oxford: Oxford University Press.

Mises, Ludwig von. (1969 [1944]) *Omnipotent Government: The Rise of the Total State and Total War*. Grove City, Pennsylvania: Libertarian Press, Inc.

Mises, Ludwig von. (1978 [1931]) *On the Manipulation of Money and Credit: Three Treatises on Trade-Cycle Theory*, trans. Bettina Bien Greaves, ed. Percy L. Greaves Jr. Indianapolis, Indiana: Liberty Fund.

Mises, Ludwig von. (1996 [1949]) *Human Action: A Treatise on Economics*. 4th ed. San Francisco: Fox & Wilkes.

Mises, Ludwig von. (1998 [1949]) *Human Action: A Treatise on Economics*. Auburn, Alabama: Ludwig von Mises Institute.

Mitsis, Phillip. (2011) 'Hellenistic Political Theory,' in Klosko, 120-141.

Modugno, Roberta A. (2009) *Murray N. Rothbard vs. the Philosophers: Unpublished Writings on Hayek, Mises, Strauss, and Polanyi*. Auburn, Alabama: Ludwig von Mises Institute.

Mommsen, Theodore E. (1942) 'Petrarch's Conception of the "Dark Ages",' in *Speculum*, Vol. 17, No 2, 226-242.

Montesquieu (Charles-Louis de Secondat, Baron de La Brède et de Montesquieu). (1721 [2008]) *Persian Letters*, trans. Margaret Mauldon. Oxford: Oxford University Press. [Oxford World's Classics]

Moore, James. (2006) 'Natural Rights in the Scottish Enlightenment,' in Goldie & Wokler, 291-316.

Moran, Caitlin. (2011) *How to be a Woman*. London: Ebury Press.

Morgan, Lewis H. (1877) *Ancient Society or Researches in the Lines of Human Progress from Savagery, through Barbarism to Civilization*. New York: Henry Holt and Company.

Morrall, John B. (1970 [1967]) *The Medieval Imprint: The Founding of the Western European Tradition*. London: Pelican.

Morrall, John B. (1971) *Political Thought in Medieval Times* 3rd ed. London: Hutchinson University Library.

Morris, Christopher W. (2011) 'The State,' in Klosko ed., 544-560.

Morris, Colin. (1972) *The Discovery of the Individual, 1050-1200*. London: SPCK. [Series: Church History Outlines, ed. V. H. H. Green]

Morris, Ian. (2014) *War! What is it Good For?: Conflict and the Progress of Civilization from Primates to Robots*. New York: Farrar, Straus and Giroux.

Moss, Laurence S. and Christopher K. Ryan. (eds) (1993) *Economic Thought in Spain: Selected Essays of Marjorie Grice-Hutchinson*. Cheltenham: Edward Elgar.

Mumford, Lewis. (1961) *The City in History: Its Transformations, and its Prospects*. New York: Houghton Mifflin Harcourt.

Müntzer, Thomas & Heinrich Pfeiffer. (1524) 'The Eleven Mühlhausen Articles,' in Baylor, 227-230.

Müntzer, Thomas. (1521) 'The Prague Manifesto [Protest],' in Zuck, 32-34; 'The Prague Protest' in Baylor, 1-10.

Müntzer, Thomas. (1524) 'A Highly Provoked Defense,' in Zuck, 39-44; 'A Highly Provoked Defence' in Baylor, 74-94.

Müntzer, Thomas. (1524a) 'A Sermon before the Princes on Daniel Chapter Two,' in Zuck, 36-37; 'Sermon to the Princes,' in Baylor, 11-32.

Müntzer, Thomas. (1525) 'Confession,' in Zuck, 46.

Müntzer, Thomas. (1525a) 'Recantation,' in Zuck, 47.

Murdoch, Iris. (1994) *Metaphysics as a Guide to Morals*. London: Penguin.

Murdoch, Iris. (1998 [1997]) *Existentialists and Mystics: Writings on Philosophy and Literature*, ed. Peter Conradi. London: Penguin. [A collection of Murdoch's articles, books chapters and books reviews, first published in 1997 by Chatto & Windus]

Murphy, Liam & Thomas Nagel. (2005) *The Myth of Ownership: Taxes and Justice*. Oxford: Oxford University Press.

Murphy, Jessica. (2016) 'Canadian Professor Jordan Peterson Takes on Gender Neutral Pronouns.' Available at http://www.bbc.com/news/world-us-canada-37875695, accessed 5 November 2016.

Murphy, Richard. (2016a [2015]) *The Joy of Tax: How a Fair Tax System can Create a Better Society*. London: Corgi.

Musset, Lucien. (1993 [1965]) *The Germanic Invasions: The Making of Europe, 400-600 A.D.,* trans. Edward and Columba James. New York: Barnes and Noble. [Originally published in 1965 as *Les Invasions: Les Vagues Germaniques* by Presses Universitaires de France]

Nanos, Mark D. (1996) *The Mystery of Romans: The Jewish Context of Paul's Letter*. Minneapolis: Fortress.

Nasar, Sylvia. (2011) *Grand Pursuit: The Story of the People who made Modern Economics*. London: Fourth Estate.

Nathanson, Paul & Katherine K. Young. (2001) *Spreading Misandry: The Teaching of Contempt for Men in Popular Culture*. Montreal & Kingston: McGill-Queen's University Press.

Nathanson, Paul & Katherine K. Young. (2006) *Legalizing Misandry: From Public Shame to Systemic Discrimination against Men*. Montreal & Kingston: McGill-Queen's University Press.

Nathanson, Paul & Katherine K. Young. (2015) *Replacing Misandry: A Revolutionary History of Men*. Montreal & Kingston: McGill-Queen's University Press.

Nederman, Cary J. (1993) 'Introduction' to Marsilius of Padua's *Defensor minor* in Marsilius of Padua, ix-xxiii.

Nederman, Cary J. (2004) 'Political Philosophy,' in *Europe, 1450 to 1789: Encyclopedia of the Early Modern World*. Available at *Encyclopedia.com* at http://www.encyclopedia.com/topic/Political_philosophy.aspx#2, accessed 20 April 2015.

Nederman, Cary J. (2009) 'Marsiglio of Padua,' in Boucher & Kelly 2009, 148-62.

Nedham, Marchamont. (1777 [1656]) *The Excellencie of a Free State*. London: Millar, Cadell, Kearsly and Parker. Available at http://www.constitution.org/cmt/nedham/free-state.htm, accessed 13 January 2014.

Nedham, Marchamont. (2011 [1656]) *The Excellencie of a Free-State*, ed. Blair Worden. Indianapolis, Indiana: Liberty Fund. Available at http://files.libertyfund.org/files/2449/Nedham_Excelencie1594_LFeBk.pdf, accessed 13 January 2014.

Neely, Mark E., Jr. (1991) *The Fate of Liberty: Abraham Lincoln and Civil Liberties*. New York: Oxford University Press.

Neiman, Susan. (2014) *Why Grow Up?: Subversive Thoughts for an Infantile Age*. London: Penguin.

Nelson, Janet. (1988) 'Kingship and Empire,' in Burns 1988, 211-251.

Nelson, Mark T. (2009) 'A Problem for Conservatism,' in *Analysis* Vol. 69, No 5, 620-630.

Neufeld, Matthew G. (1994) 'Submission to Governing Authorities: A Study of Romans 13: 1-7,' in *Direction*, Vol. 23, No. 2, 90-97, available at http://www.directionjournal.org/issues/gen/art_849_.html, accessed 12 August 2013.

Neuhouser, Frederick. (2000) *Foundations of Hegel's Social Theory: Actualizing Freedom*. Cambridge, Massachusetts: Harvard University Press.

Neuwirth, Robert. (2001) *Stealth of Nations: The Global Rise of the Informal Economy*. New York: Anchor Books.

Newman, Patrick. (2017) 'Review of Thomas Leonard's *Illiberal Reformers: Race, Eugenics and American Economics in the Progressive Era*,' in *The Independent Review*, Vol. 21, No. 3 (Winter 2017), available at http://www.independent.org/publications/tir/article.asp?a=1189, accessed 22 December 2016.

Newton, Douglas. (2014) *The Darkest Days: The Truth behind Britain's Rush to War, 1914*. London: Verso.

Nicholas, Barry. (1962) *An Introduction to Roman Law*. Oxford: Clarendon Press, 1962.

Nicholson, Peter. (2009) 'The Sophists,' in Boucher & Kelly 2009, 29-46.

Nisbet, Robert. (1984) 'Uneasy Cousins,' in Carey, 13-24.

Nisbet, Robert. (1988) *The Present Age: Progress and Anarchy in Modern America*. Indianapolis, Indiana: Liberty Press.

Nock, Albert Jay. (1928) *On Doing the Right Thing*. New York: Harper & Brothers Publishers, 1928.

Nock, Albert Jay. (2011 [1922]) *The Myth of a Guilty Nation*. Auburn, Alabama: Ludwig von Mises Institute.

Nordau, Max. (1883) *The Conventional Lies of our Civilization*. Chicago: Laird & Lee.

Norman, Edward. (2007) *The Roman Catholic Church: An Illustrated History*. London: Thames & Hudson.

Norman, Jesse. (2013) *Edmund Burke: Philosopher, Politician, Prophet*. London: William Collins.

North, Douglass C. (1977) Markets and Other Allocations systems in History: The Challenge of Karl Polanyi,' in *The Journal of European Economic History*, Vol. 6, No. 3, 703-716. Available at http://www.jeeh.it/articolo?urn=urn:abi:abi:RIV.JOU:1977;3.703&ev=1, accessed 21 May 2016.

North, William (ed.) (2012) *Haskins Society Journal 22: Studies in Medieval History*. Woodbridge: The Boydell Press.

Norton, David Fate. (1982) *David Hume: Common-Sense Moralist, Sceptical Metaphysician*. Princeton, New Jersey: Princeton University Press.

Novak, D. (1958) 'The Place of Anarchism in the History of Political Thought,' in *The Review of Politics,* Vol. 20 No. 3, 307-29.

Novak, Peter. (2015) *Humans 3.0: The Upgrading of the Species*. London: The Friday Project [Harper Collins]

Nowrasteh, Alex. (2013) 'Karl Polanyi's Battle with Economic History,' available at http://www.libertarianism.org/blog/karl-polanyis-battle-economic-history, accessed 21 May 2016.

Nozick, Robert. (1974) *Anarchy, State and Utopia*. New York: Basic Books.

Nozick, Robert. (1977) 'On Austrian Methodology,' in *Synthese*, Vol. 36, No. 3, 353-392.

NSDAP. (1920) 'Programme of the NSDAP,' 24 February 1920. Available at http://www.hitler.org/writings/programme/, accessed 10 May 2014.

Nyquist, Mary. (2013) *Arbitrary Rule: Slavery, Tyranny, and the Power of Life and Death*. Chicago: University of Chicago Press.

O'Brien, J. C. 'The Instauration of the New Man of Marxism,' in Wood 1993, 181-194.

O'Connor, Frank. (1950) *Leinster, Munster & Connaught*. London: Robert Hale Limited, 1950.

O'Donovan, Oliver. (1996) *The Desire of the National: Rediscovering the Roots of Political Theology*. Cambridge: Cambridge University Press.

O'Donovan, Oliver. (2008) *The Way of Judgment*. Grand Rapids, Michigan: Wm. B. Eerdmans Publishing Co.

O'Grady, Patricia. (ed.) (2008) *The Sophists: An Introduction*. London: Duckworth.

O'Hear, Anthony. (2003 [2001]) *Philosophy in the New Century*. London: Continuum.

O'Keeffe, Dennis. (2010) *Edmund Burke*. New York: Continuum. Volume 6 in the series MAJOR CONSERVATIVE AND LIBERTARIAN THINKERS, series ed. John Meadowcroft.

O'Keeffe, Matthew. (1992) 'World Ownership is not Compatible with Self-Ownership: A Defence of Robert Nozick against G. A. Cohen,' London: Libertarian Alliance. Available at http://www.libertarian.co.uk/lapubs/philn/philn020.pdf, accessed 25 July 2014.

O'Malley, Joseph. (1994) 'Introduction,' to Marx 1994, vii-xxiv.

O'Neill, William F. (1971) *With Charity Toward None: An Analysis of Ayn Rand's Philosophy*. Totowa, New Jersey: Littlefield, Adams and Co.

O'Rourke, P. J. (1995) *Age and Guile Beat Youth, Innocence, and a Bad Haircut*. London: Picador.

Oakeshott, Michael. (1991 [1962]) *Rationalism in Politics and other Essays*, new and expanded edition. Indianapolis, Indiana: Liberty Press.

Oakeshott, Michael. (1991a) 'The Masses in Representative Democracy,' in Oakeshott 1991, 363-383. First published in 1961 in *Freedom and Serfdom: An Anthology of Western Thought*, ed. Albert Hunold, Dordrecht: D. Reidel.

Oakley, Francis. (2003) *The Conciliarist Tradition: Constitutionalism in the Catholic Church 1300-1870*. Oxford: Oxford University Press.

Oakley, Francis. (2010) *Empty Bottles of Gentilism: Kingship and the Divine in Late Antiquity and the Early Middle Ages (to 1050)*. New Haven, Connecticut: Yale University Press. [The Emergence of Western Political Thought in the Latin Middle Ages] This volume, and the other two volumes in this series by Oakley, are essential reading for those wishing to obtain an in-depth account of the emergence, the development, the continuities and discontinuities, of western political thought in the so-called middle ages. A magnificent work of rehabilitation and revelation.

Oakley, Francis. (2012) *The Mortgage of the Past: Reshaping the Ancient Political Inheritance. (1050-1300)*. New Haven, Connecticut: Yale University Press. [The Emergence of Western Political Thought in the Latin Middle Ages]

Oakley, Francis. (2015) *The Watershed of Modern Politics: Law, Virtue, Kingship, and Consent (1300-1650)*. New Haven, Connecticut: Yale University Press. [The Emergence of Western Political Thought in the Latin Middle Ages]

Ober, Josiah & Stephen Macedo. (2006) 'Introduction' to Macedo and Ober ix-xix.

Ober, Josiah. (2015) *The Rise and Fall of Classical Greece*. Princeton, New Jersey: Princeton University Press. [A brilliant account of Greek exceptionalism, tracing the connection between the political and the economic.]

Ogg, David. (1965) *Europe of the Ancien Régime (1715-1783)*. London: Fontana/ Collins. [Fontana History of Europe]

Ogle, Arthur Bud. (1978-1979) 'What is Left for Caesar? A Look at Mark 12:13-17 and Romans 13:1-7,' in *Theology Today*, Volume 34, No. 3, 254-264.

Oliver, J. Michael. (2013 [1973]) *The New Libertarianism: Anarcho-Capitalism*. CreateSpace.

Olson, Mancur. (1993) 'Dictatorship, Democracy, and Development,' in *American Political Science Review*, Vol. 87 No. 3, 567-76.

Onuf, Nicholas Greenwood. (2013 [1989]) *World of Our Making: Rules and Rule in Social Theory and International Relations*. London: Routledge. [Originally published by the University of South Carolina Press in 1989]

Opitz, Edmund A. (1995) *Leviathan at War*. Irvington-on-Hudson, New York: The Foundation for Economic Education.

Oppenheimer, Franz. (1926 [1914]) *The State: Its History and Development Viewed Sociologically*, trans. John M. Gitterman. New York: Vanguard Press. Available at http://library.mises.org/books/Franz%20Oppenheimer/The%20State%20Its%20 History%20and%20Development%20Viewed%20Sociologically.pdf, accessed 6 May 2014.

Ormerod, Henry A. (1997 [1924]) *Piracy in the Ancient World: An Essay in Mediterranean History*. Baltimore, Maryland: The Johns Hopkins University Press.

Ossewaarde, M. R. R. (2007) 'Three Rivals Version of Political Enquiry: Althusius and the Concept of Sphere Sovereignty,' in *The Monist*, Vol. 90 No 1, 106-125. Available at http://doc.utwente.nl/57991/1/Sphere_Sovereignty_-_the_Monist.pdf, accessed 1 December 2013.

Osterfeld, David. (2007) 'Freedom, Society, and the State; An Investigation into the Possibility of Society without Government (excerpt),' in Stringham, 504-537

Otsuka, Michael. (2003) *Libertarianism without Inequality*. Oxford: Clarendon Press.

Otteson, James R. (2014) *The End of Socialism*. Cambridge: Cambridge University Press.

Otteson, James R. (ed.) (2003) *The Levellers: Overton, Walwyn, and Lilburne*, 5 vols. Bristol: Thoemmes Press.

Ousby, Ian. (1996) *The Cambridge Paperback Guide to Literature in English*. Cambridge: Cambridge University Press.

Overton, Richard & William Walwyn. (1646) 'A Remonstrance of Many Thousand Citizens,' in Sharp 1998, 33-53.

Overton, Richard. (1646) 'An Arrow against All Tyrants,' in Sharp 1998, 54-72.

Oyer, John S. (1994) *Lutheran Reformers against Anabaptists: Luther, Melanchthon and Menius and the Anabaptists of Central Germany*. The Hague: Martinus Nijhoff.

Özsel, Doğancan. (2011) *Reflections on Conservatism*. Newcastle upon Tyne: Cambridge Scholars.

Pafford, John M. (2011) *Russell Kirk*. London: Bloomsbury. [Major Conservative and Libertarian Thinkers]

Pagano, F. N. (1983) 'Burke's View of the Evils of Political Theory: or, A Vindication of Natural Society,' in *Polity* Vol. 16, 446-462.

Pagden, Anthony. (2011) 'The School of Salamanca,' in Klosko, 246-257.

Page, Leslie R. (1987) *Karl Marx and the Critical Examination of his Works*. London: The Freedom Association.

Paglia, Camille. (1991) *Sexual Personae: Art and Decadence from Nefertiti to Emily Dickenson*. New York: Vintage Books.

Paglia, Camille. (1992) *Sex, Art, and American Culture*. New York: Vintage Books.

Paine, Thomas. (1948 [1775-1791]) *The Selected Works of Tom Paine*, ed. Howard Fast. London: The Bodley Head.

Paine, Thomas. (1995 [1775-76/1791]) *Rights of Man, Common Sense and other Political Writings*, ed. Mark Philp. Oxford: Oxford University Press.

Paine, Thomas. (2000) *Paine: Political Writings*, ed. Bruce Kuklick. Cambridge: Cambridge University Press.

Palmer, Frank. (1971) *Grammar*. London: Penguin.

Palmer, Frank. (1975) 'Language and Languages,' in Bolton, 12-37.

Palmer, Tom G. (1997) 'The Literature of Liberty,' in Boaz 1997, 415-453.

Palmer, Tom G. (2007) 'No Exit: Framing the Problem of Justice,' in Bouillon and Kliemt, 21-56.

Palmer, Tom G. (2009) *Realizing Freedom: Libertarian Theory, History and Practice*. Washington, D. C.: Cato Institute.

Palmer, Tom G. (2014a) 'Peace is a Choice,' in Palmer, 2014, 5-17.

Palmer, Tom G. (2014b) The Philosophy of Peace or the Philosophy of Conflict,' in Palmer, 2014, 103-125.

Palmer, Tom G. (ed.) (2014) *Peace, Love, & Liberty*. Ottawa, Illinois: Jameson Books.

Paolucci, Henry. (ed.) (1962) *The Political Writings of St. Augustine*. Chicago: Gateway.

Papola, John & Russ Roberts. (2010) 'Fear the Boom and Bust,' video, available at https://www.youtube.com/watch?v=d0nERTFo-Sk, accessed 1 June 2016.

Pardey, Eva. (2007) 'The Royal Administration and its Organization,' in Schulz & Seidel, 357-363.

Parens, Joshua and Joseph C. Macfarland. (2011 [1963]) *Medieval Political Philosophy: A Sourcebook*, 2nd ed. Ithaca, New York: Cornell University Press.

Parker, Geoffrey. (1979) *Europe in Crisis (1598-1648)*. London: Fontana/Collins. [Fontana History of Europe]

Parkinson, Cyril Northcote. (1958) *The Evolution of Political Thought*. Boston: Houghton Mifflin Company. [An unusual (and witty) approach to this topic]

Parkinson, Cyril Northcote. (1965 [1960]) *The Law and the Profits*. London: Penguin.

Parkinson, Cyril Northcote. (1970 [1967]) *Left Luggage: From Marx to Wilson*. London: Penguin.

Parliament of England. (1628) 'Petition of Right,' in Wootton, 2003, 168-171.

Parliament of England. (1689) 'The Bill of Rights,' available at http://www.fordham. edu/halsall/mod/1689billofrights.asp, accessed 3 January 2014.

Parrish, John M. (2007) *Paradoxes of Political Ethics: From Dirty Hands to the Invisible Hand*. Cambridge: Cambridge University Press.

Parsons, Wilfrid, S. J. (1940) 'The Influence of Romans XIII on Pre-Augustinian Christian Political Thought,' in *Theological Studies*, Vol. 1, No. 4 337-364. Available at

Parsons, Wilfrid, S.J. (1941) 'The Influence of Romans XIII on Christian Political Thought II: Augustine to Hincmar,' in *Theological Studies*, Vol. 2, No. 3 325-346. Available at http://www.ts.mu.edu/readers/content/pdf/2/2.3/2.3.2.pdf, accessed 5 December 2013.

Partridge, Eric. (1963 [1947]) *Usage and Abusage*. London: Penguin.

Pateman, Barry. (ed.) (2005) *Chomsky on Anarchism*. Edinburgh: AK Press.

Patrologia Graeca (Migne). Available at http://irishpilgrim.blogspot.ie/2009/06/mignes-patrologiae-cursus-completus.html, accessed 13 June 2014.

Patterson, Orlando. (1982) *Slavery and Social Death: A Comparative Study*. Cambridge, Massachusetts: Harvard University Press.

Patterson, Orlando. (1991) *Freedom—Volume I: Freedom in the Making of Western Culture*. New York: Basic Books.

Patterson, Thomas C. (1997) *Inventing Western Civilization*. New York: Monthly Review Press.

Payne, Stanley G. (1995) *A History of Fascism, 1914-1945*. Madison, Wisconsin: University of Wisconsin Press.

Payne, Stanley G. (2000) 'Fascism and Communism,' in *Totalitarian Movements and Political Religions*, Vol. 1, No. 3, 1-15.

Payne, Stanley G. (2002) 'Emilio Gentile's Historical Analysis and Taxonomy of Political Religions' in *Totalitarian Movements and Political Religions*, Vol. 3, No. 1, 122-130.

Paxton, Robert O. (2005 [2004]) *The Anatomy of Fascism*. London: Penguin. [First published in the USA by Alfred A; Knopf (2004) and in Great Britain by Allen Lane (2004)]

Peake, Mervyn. (1999) *The Gormenghast Trilogy: Titus Groan, Gormenghast, Titus Alone*. London: Vintage Books.

Pelczynski, Zbigniew. (1984b) 'Political Community and Individual Freedom in Hegel's Philosophy of State,' in Pelcznski 1984, 55-76.

Pelczynski, Zbigniew. (1971a) 'The Hegelian Conception of the State,' in Pelczynski 1971, 230-241.

Pelczynski, Zbigniew. (1971b) 'Hegel's Political Philosophy: Some Thoughts on its Contemporary Relevance,' in Pelczynski 1971, 1-29.

Pelczynski, Zbigniew. (1984) *The State and Civil Society: Studies in Hegel's Political Philosophy*. Cambridge: Cambridge University Press.

Pelczynski, Zbigniew. (1984a) 'Introduction: The Significance of Hegel's Separation of the State and Civil Society,' in Pelcznski 1984, 1-13.

Pelczynski, Zbigniew. (ed.) (1971) *Hegel's Political Philosophy: Problems and Perspectives*. Cambridge: Cambridge University Press.

Penman, Jim. (2015) *Biohistory*. Newcastle upon Tyne: Cambridge Scholars Publishing.

Pennington, Kenneth. (2011) 'Rights,' in Klosko, 530-543.

Percy, Walker. (1984 [1983]) *Lost in the Cosmos: The Last Self-Help Book*. New York: Washington Square Press.

Percy, Walker. (2000) *Signposts in a Strange Land*. New York: Picador.

Percy, Walker. (2000a) 'Is a Theory of Man Possible?,' in Percy 2000, 111-129.

Pestritto, Ronald J. (ed.) (2005) *Woodrow Wilson: The Essential Political Writings*. Lanham, Maryland: Lexington Books [Rowman & Littlefield Publishers, Inc.]

Peterson, H. C. (1939) *Propaganda for War: The Campaign against American Neutrality, 1914-1917*. Norman, Oklahoma: University of Oklahoma Press.

Pettit, Philip and Christian List. (2011) *Group Agency: The Possibility, Design, and Status of Corporate Agents*. Oxford: Oxford University Press.

Philips, Obbe. (1560, recalling 1533-36) 'A Confession,' in Zuck, 108-115.

Philo. (1941 [c. AD 30]) *Every Good Man is Free, On the Contemplative Life. On the Eternity of the World. Against Flaccus. Apology for the Jews. On Providence*. Harvard: Harvard University Press. [Loeb Classical Library No. 363]

Philp, Mark. (2009) 'William Godwin,' in *Stanford Encyclopedia of Philosophy*, available at http://plato.stanford.edu/entries/godwin/, accessed 3 April 2014.

Philp, Mark. (2013) 'Introduction' to Godwin 1793, ix-xxxiv.

Philpott, Daniel. (2011) 'Sovereignty,' in Klosko, 561-572.

Pieper, Josef. (1964 [1962]) *Guide to Thomas Aquinas*, trans. Richard and Clara Winston. New York: Mentor-Omega

Piketty, Thomas. (2014) *Capital in the Twenty-First Century*. Cambridge, Massachusetts: Belknap Press.

Pinker, Steven. (2014) *The Sense of Style*. London: Penguin.

Pirenne, Henri. (1956 [1925]) *Medieval Cities: Their Origins and the Revival of Trade* trans. Frank D. Halsey. Garden City, New York: Doubleday Anchor Books.

Pius XI. (1931) 'Non abbiamo bisogno,' available at http://www.vatican.va/holy_father/pius_xi/encyclicals/documents/hf_p-xi_enc_29061931_non-abbiamo-bisogno_en.html accessed 10 May 2014.

Plamenatz, John. (1963) *Man and Society: A Critical Examination of Some Important Social and Political Theories from Machiavelli to Marx, Vol. 1*. London: Longman. An old but excellent treatment of political thinkers, from Machiavelli to Rousseau.

Plant, Raymond. (2011) 'Freedom,' in Klosko ed., 624-636.

Plato. (1957 [c. 355-347 BC]) *Statesman*, 2ⁿᵈ ed., ed. and trans. J. B. Skemp. Bristol Classical Press. [Republished by Hackett Publishing Company, 1992]

Plato. (1968 [380 BC] *The Republic of Plato*, 2ⁿᵈ ed., trans. Alan Bloom. New York: Basic Books. Available at http://www.inp.uw.edu.pl/mdsie/Political_Thought/Plato-Republic.pdf, accessed 7 November 2016.

Plato. (1970 [348 BC]) *The Laws*, trans. T. J. Saunders. London: Penguin 1970.

Plato. (1992 [380 BC]) *Republic*, trans. H. D. P. Lee and Desmond Lee. London: Penguin.

Plato. (1995 [c. 355-347 BC]) *Statesman*, ed. Julia Annas and Robin Waterfield, trans. Robin Waterfield. Cambridge: Cambridge University Press. [Cambridge Texts in the History of Political Thought]

Plutarch. (1960 [c. AD 100]) *The Rise and Fall of Athens*, trans. Ian Scott-Kilvert. London: Penguin. [Also known as *Lives of the Noble Greeks and Romans* or *Parallel Lives* or *Plutarch's Lives*. Contains the lives of Theseus, Solon, Themistocles, Aristides, Cimon, Pericles, Nicias, Alcibiades and Lysander]

Plutarch. (1973 [c. AD 100]) *The Age of Alexander*, trans. Ian Scott-Kilvert. London: Penguin. [Also known as *Lives of the Noble Greeks and Romans* or *Parallel Lives* or *Plutarch's Lives*. Contains the lives of Agesilaus, Pelopidas, Dion, Timoleon, Demosthenes, Phocion, Alexander, Demetrius and Pyrrhus]

Plutarch. (1999 [c. AD 100]) *Roman Lives*, trans. Robin Waterfield. Oxford: Oxford University Press. [Also known as *Lives of the Noble Greeks and Romans* or *Parallel Lives* or *Plutarch's Lives*. Contains the lives of Cato the Elder, Aemilius Paullus, Tiberius and Gaius Gracchus, Marius, Sulla, Pompey, Caesar and Antony]

Pocock, J. G. A. (1992) 'Introduction' to Harrington 1992, vii-xxv.

Polansky, David. (2015) 'Nietzsche on Thucydidean Realism,' in *The Review of Politics*, Vol. 77, 425-448.

Polanyi, Karl. (1944) *The Great Transformation*. New York: Farrar & Reinhart. Published in England in 1945 as *Origins of our Time: The Great Transformation*. A second edition was published in 2001 by the Beacon Press (Boston) with a foreword by Joseph Stiglitz.

Polybius. (2010 [c. 160 BC]) *The Histories*, trans. Robin Waterfield. Oxford: Oxford University Press. [Oxford World Classics]

Ponet, John. (1556) 'A Short Treatise on Politike Power,' in Zuck, 146-149.

Popper, Karl. (1966 [1945]) *The Open Society and its Enemies: Hegel and Marx*, 6ᵗʰ ed. London: Routledge & Kegan Paul

Porter, Bruce D. (1994) *War and the Rise of the State: The Military Foundations of Modern Politics*. New York: The Free Press.

Postan, M. M. (1975 [1972]) *The Medieval Economy & Society*. London: Penguin.

Powell, Jim. (2003) *FDR's Folly: How Roosevelt and His New Deal Prolonged the Great Depression*. New York: Three Rivers Press.

Proudhon, Pierre-Joseph (1923/1969 [1851]) *The General Idea of the Revolution in the Nineteenth Century*, trans. John Beverley Robinson. New York: Haskell House Publishers Ltd. Available at http://libcom.org/files/Proudhon%20-%20General%20 Idea%20of%20the%20Revolution.pdf, accessed 4 June 2014. Also available at http:// fair-use.org/p-j-proudhon/general-idea-of-the-revolution/, accessed 2 June 2014.

Proudhon, Pierre-Joseph. (1863) *The Principle of Federation and the Need to Reconstitute the Party of Revolution*, trans. Richard Vernon. Available at http://www.ditext. com/proudhon/federation/federation.html, accessed 2 June 2014. All of Part I and the first chapter of Part II are translated.

Proudhon, Pierre-Joseph. (1994 [1840]) *What is Property?* ed. and trans. Donald R. Kelley and Bonnie G. Smith. Cambridge: Cambridge University Press.

Proudhon, Pierre-Joseph. (2009 [1853]) *The Philosophy of Progress*, trans. Shawn P. Wilbur. Left Liberty. Available at http://invisiblemolotov.files.wordpress. com/2009/04/npl-201-progress.pdf, accessed 2 June 2014.

Purdy, Herbert. (2016) *Their Angry Creed*. LPS Publishing.

Pye, Michael. (2014) *The Edge of the World: How the North Sea Made Us Who We Are*. London: Viking.

Qiaomei, Fu et al. (2016) 'The Genetic History of Ice Age Europe,' in *Nature,* published online 2 May 2016.

Quinton, A. (1978) *The Politics of Imperfection: The Religious and Secular Traditions of Conservative Thought in England from Hooker to Oakeshott*. London: Faber.

Raab, Dominic. (2009) *The Assault on Liberty: What Went Wrong with Rights*. London: Fourth Estate.

Raekstad, Paul Alexander. (2011) *Class and State in the Political Theory of Adam Smith: A Chapter in the History of a Neglected Strand of Political Thought*. Masters Thesis, University of Oslo. Available at https://www.duo.uio.no/bitstream/ handle/10852/24836/Raekstad.pdf?sequence=3, accessed 16 March 2014.

Raico, Ralph. (1996) 'Classical Liberal Roots of the Marxist Doctrine of Classes,' in Maltsev, 189-220. Also available from Mises Daily at http://mises.org/daily/2217, accessed 20 March 2014.

Raico, Ralph. (1999) 'World War I: The Turning Point,' in Denson 1999a, 203-247.

Raico, Ralph. (1999a) 'Rethinking Churchill,' in Denson 1999a, 321-360.

Ramsay, Maureen. (1997) *What's Wrong with Liberalism?: A Radical Critique of Liberal Political Philosophy*. London: Leicester University Press.

Rand, Ayn. (1963) *For the New Intellectual*. New York: Signet. Apart from the eponymous essay, this book also contains excerpts from *We the Living, Anthem, The Fountainhead* and *Atlas Shrugged*.

Rand, Ayn. (1963a) 'Collectivized Ethics,' in Rand 1964a, 93-99.

Rand, Ayn. (1963b) 'The Nature of Government,' in Rand 1964a, 125-134; also in Rand 1967a, 378-387.

Rand, Ayn. (1964a) *The Virtue of Selfishness*. New York: Signet.

Rand, Ayn. (1964b [1963]) 'Racism,' in Rand 1964a, 147-157.

Rand, Ayn. (1964c) 'Government Financing in a Free Society,' in 1964a, 135-140.

Rand, Ayn. (1965) 'The New Fascism: Rule by Consensus,' in Rand 1967a, 226-248

Rand, Ayn. (1967a) *Capitalism: The Unknown Ideal*. New York: Signet.

Rand, Ayn. (1967b [1966]) 'The Roots of War,' in Rand 1967a, 30-39; in Opitz, 18-25.

Rand, Ayn. (1967c) *Introduction to Objectivist Epistemology*. New York: Mentor.

Rand, Ayn. (1975) *The Romantic Manifesto*, 2nd rev. ed. New York: Signet.

Rand, Ayn. (1975a) 'The Psycho-Epistemology of Art,' in Rand 1975, 3-13.

Rand, Ayn. (1984) *Philosophy: Who Needs It.* New York: Signet.

Rand, Ayn. (1999 [1957]) *Atlas Shrugged.* London: Penguin.

Rand, Ayn. (1999) *Return of the Primitive: The Anti-Industrial Revolution,* ed. Peter Schwartz. New York: Meridian. [A new expanded edition of *The New Left: The Anti-Industrial Revolution* originally published in 1971]

Rand, Ayn. (2008 [1939]) *Anthem.* BN Publishing.

Rapp, John A. (2012) *Daoism and Anarchism: Critiques of State Autonomy in Ancient and Modern China.* London: Continuum. [Contemporary Anarchist Studies]

Rashdall, Hastings. (1936a) *The Universities of Europe in the Middle Ages,* Vol. I Salerno—Bologna—Paris, eds F. M. Powicke and A. B. Emden. Oxford: Clarendon Press.

Rashdall, Hastings. (1936b) *The Universities of Europe in the Middle Ages,* Vol. II Italy—Spain—France—Germany—Scotland, etc., eds F. M. Powicke and A. B. Emden. Oxford: Clarendon Press.

Rashdall, Hastings. (1936c) *The Universities of Europe in the Middle Ages,* Vol. III English Universities—Student Life, eds F. M. Powicke and A. B. Emden. Oxford: Clarendon Press.

Rauscher, Frederick. (2102) 'Kant's Social and Political Philosophy,' in *Stanford Encyclopedia of Philosophy,* available at https://leibniz.stanford.edu/friends/members/view/kant-social-political/a4/, accessed 23 February 2015.

Rawls, John. (1999 [1971]) *A Theory of Justice,* rev. ed. Oxford: Oxford University Press.

Rawls, John. (1999) *The Law of Peoples.* Cambridge, Massachusetts: Harvard University Press.

Rawls, John. (2001) *Justice as Fairness: A Restatement,* ed. Erin Kelly. Cambridge, Massachusetts: Belknap Press. [This is essentially a revision and development of *A Theory of Justice* in the light of criticisms and commentary.]

Rawls, John. (2008) *Lectures on the History of Political Philosophy.* Cambridge, Massachusetts: Belknap Press.

Read, Leonard E. (1996) 'Conscience on the Battlefield,' in Opitz, 63-78.

Redding, Paul. (2011) 'German Idealism,' in Klosko ed., 348-368.

Redding, Paul. (2014) 'Georg Wilhelm Friedrich Hegel,' in *Stanford Encyclopedia of Philosophy,* available at https://leibniz.stanford.edu/friends/members/view/hegel/a4/, accessed 23 February 2015.

Redford, James. (2001) 'Jesus is an Anarchist,' 19 December 2001 [4 December 2011], available at http://ia700307.us.archive.org/25/items/JesusIsAnAnarchist/Redford-Jesus-Is-an-Anarchist.pdf, accessed 12 August 2013.

Redner, Harry. (1997) *Malign Masters: Gentile, Heidegger, Lukács, Wittgenstein: Philosophy and Politics and in the Twentieth Century.* London: Macmillan Press Ltd.

Reeve, C. D. C. (2009) 'Plato,' in Boucher & Kelly 2009, 62-80.

Reilly, Robert R. (2011 [2010]) *The Closing of the Muslim Mind: How Intellectual Suicide Created the Modern Islamist Crisis.* Wilmington, Delaware: Intercollegiate Studies Institute.

Reisman, George. (1998) *Capitalism.* Ottawa, Illinois: Jameson Books.

Reisman, George. (2012) *Warren Buffet, Class Warfare, and the Exploitation Theory.* Laguna Hill, California: TJS Books.

Renfrew, Colin. (2007) *Prehistory.* London, Phoenix.

Rescorla, Michael. (2011) 'Convention,' in *Stanford Encyclopedia of Philosophy,* available at http://plato.stanford.edu/entries/convention/, accessed 22 May 2014.

Richman, Sheldon. (2014) Does Freedom Require Empire?' in *Counterpunch* (5-7 September), available at http://www.counterpunch.org/2014/09/05/does-freedom-require-empire/#.VBS_m7DMQyo.gmail, accessed 30 September 2014.

Richman, Sheldon. (2016) *America's Counter-Revolution: The Constitution Revisited.* Ann Arbor, Michigan: Griffin & Lash.

Riddle, Wesley Allen. (1994) 'War and Individual Liberty in American History,' in Opitz, 135-158.

Ridley, Matt. (2011 [2010]) *The Rational Optimist: How Prosperity Evolves.* London: Fourth Estate.

Riedemann, Peter. (c. 1545) 'Concerning Community of Goods,' in Zuck, 128-130.

Riggenbach, Jeff. (2011a) 'Josiah Warren: The First American Anarchist,' available at http://mises.org/daily/5067/Josiah-Warren-The-First-Amercan-Anarchist, accessed 21 June 2014.

Riggenbach, Jeff. (2011b) 'Stephen Pearl Andrews's Fleeting Contribution to Anarchist Thought,' available at http://mises.org/library/stephen-pearl-andrewss-fleeting-contribution-anarchist-thought, accessed 3 January 2015.

Riley, Peter. (2006) 'Social Contract Theory and its Critics,' in Goldie & Wokler, 347-375.

Risse, Thomas. (ed.) (2011) *Governance without a* ~~State?~~*: Policies and Politics in Areas of Limited Statehood.* New York: Columbia University Press.

Roberts, John Morris. (1993) *History of the World.* London: BCA. [First published in 1976 as *The Hutchinson History of the World*; available in various editions, including one updated and revised by Odd Arne Westad and published by Penguin in 2007]

Roberts, John Morris. (1997 [1996]) *The Penguin History of Europe.* London: Penguin Books.

Robinson, Dave & Oscar Zarate. (2011) *Introducing Rousseau: A Graphic Guide.* London: Icon Books.

Robinson, Steven R. 'The Political Background of the Sophists at Athens,' in O'Grady ed., 21-29.

Rockwell, Llewellyn H. Jr. (2011) 'What is Fascism?,' in *The Free Market*, Vol. 29, No. 7, 1-6.

Rockwell, Llewellyn H. Jr. (2013) *Fascism vs. Capitalism.* Auburn, Alabama: Mises Institute. Available at http://library.mises.org//books/Llewellyn%20H%20Rockwell%20Jr/Fascism%20versus%20Capitalism.pdf, accessed 2 May 2014.

Rockwell, Llewellyn H. Jr. (ed.) (1995) *Murray N. Rothbard: In Memoriam.* Auburn, Alabama: Ludwig von Mises Institute.

Roemer, John. (1981) *Analytical Foundations of Marxist Economics.* Cambridge: Cambridge University Press.

Rommen, Heinrich A. (1998 [1936]) *The Natural Law: A Study in Legal and Social History and Philosophy.* Indianapolis: Liberty Fund. First published as *Die ewige Wiedekehr des Naturrechts* by Verlag Jakob Hegner, 1936.

Roosevelt, Franklin D. (1933) 'Inaugural Address,' available at http://www.pbs.org/newshour/spc/character/links/roosevelt_speech.html, accessed 1 May 2014.

Rose, Carol M. (1985), 'Possession as the Origin of Property,' in *The University of Chicago Law Review,* 52 (1), 73-88.

Rose, David. (2007) *Hegel's Philosophy of Right.* London: Continuum.

Rose, Larken. (2005) *How to Be a Successful Tyrant: The Megalomaniac Manifesto.* Port Orange, Florida: IMAGE Team Publishing.

Rose, Larken. (2011) *The Most Dangerous Superstition.* [No publisher or place listed]

Rosen, Stephen Peter. (2005) *War and Human Nature.* Princeton, New Jersey: Princeton University Press.

Rosenthal, Edward C. (2005) *The Era of Choice: The Ability to Choose and its Transformation of Contemporary Life*. Cambridge, Massachusetts: The MIT Press.

Rossiter, C. (1982) *Conservatism in America*, rev. ed. New York: Knopf.

Rothbard, Murray N. (1958) 'A Note on Burke's Vindication of Natural Society,' *Journal of the History of Ideas*, Vol. 19, 114-118.

Rothbard, Murray N. (1958b) 'Confidential Memo on F. A. Hayek's *Constitution of Liberty*,' (Rothbard Papers, held at the Ludwig von Mises Institute). Also in Modugno, 61-70.

Rothbard, Murray N. (1973) 'A Future of Peace and Capitalism,' in James H. Weaver (ed.), *Modern Political Economy*. Boston: Allyn and Bacon.

Rothbard, Murray N. (1975) 'Introduction' to de la Boétie, 1975.

Rothbard, Murray N. (1984) 'Frank S. Meyer: The Fusionist as Libertarian Manqué,' in Carey, 91-111.

Rothbard, Murray N. (1990) 'Marx as Millennial Communist,' in *The Review of Austrian Economics*, Vol. 4, 123-179.

Rothbard, Murray N. (1994) 'Nations by Consent: Decomposing the Nation State,' in *The Journal of Libertarian Studies*, Vol. 11, No. 1, 1-10.

Rothbard, Murray N. (1995a [2006]) *Economic Thought Before Adam Smith*. Auburn, Alabama: Ludwig von Mises Institute.

Rothbard, Murray N. (1995b [2006]) *Classical Economics*. Auburn, Alabama: Ludwig von Mises Institute.

Rothbard, Murray N. (1997) *The Case against the Fed*. Auburn, Alabama: Ludwig von Mises Institute.

Rothbard, Murray N. (1997a) *The Logic of Action One: Method, Money, and the Austrian School*. Cheltenham, UK: Edward Elgar.

Rothbard, Murray N. (1997b) *The Logic of Action Two: Applications and Criticism from the Austrian School*. Cheltenham, UK: Edward Elgar.

Rothbard, Murray N. (1997c [1976]) 'Ludwig von Mises and Economic Calculation under Socialism,' in Rothbard 1997a, 397-407. First published in *The Economics of Ludwig von Mises*, ed. Lawrence Moss, Kansas City: Sheed and Ward, 66-77.

Rothbard, Murray N. (1997d [1957a]) 'The Single Tax: Economic and Moral Implications,' in Rothbard 1997b, 294-305. First published as a paper by the Foundation for Economic Education in 1957.

Rothbard, Murray N. (1997e [1957b]) 'A Reply to Georgist Criticisms,' in Rothbard 1997b, 306-310. First published as a paper by the Foundation for Economic Education in 1957.

Rothbard, Murray N. (1999a) *Conceived in Liberty. Volume I: A New Land, A New People: The American Colonies in the Seventeenth Century*. Auburn, Alabama: Ludwig von Mises Institute.

Rothbard, Murray N. (1999b) *Conceived in Liberty. Volume II: 'Salutary Neglect'" The American Colonies in the First Half of the Eighteenth Century*. Auburn, Alabama: Ludwig von Mises Institute.

Rothbard, Murray N. (1999c) *Conceived in Liberty. Volume III: Advance to Revolution, 1760-1775*. Auburn, Alabama: Ludwig von Mises Institute.

Rothbard, Murray N. (1999d) *Conceived in Liberty. Volume IV: The Revolutionary War, 1775-1784*. Auburn, Alabama: Ludwig von Mises Institute.

Rothbard, Murray N. (1999e) 'World War I as Fulfillment: Power and the Intellectuals,' in Denson 1999a, 249-299.

Rothbard, Murray N. (2000 [1974]) *Egalitarianism As a Revolt Against Nature and Other Essays*. Auburn, Alabama: Ludwig von Mises Institute.

Rothbard, Murray N. (2000a) 'The Spooner-Tucker Doctrine: An Economist's View,' in Rothbard 2000, 205-18.

Rothbard, Murray N. (2000b) ''Anarcho-Communism,' in Rothbard 2000, 199-204.

Rothbard, Murray N. (2000c) 'War, Peace, and the State,' in Rothbard 2000, 115-132.

Rothbard, Murray N. (2002 [1982]) *The Ethics of Liberty*. New York: New York University Press.

Rothbard, Murray N. (2004 [1961]) 'Down with Primitivism: A Thorough Critique of Polanyi,' available at https://mises.org/library/down-primitivism-thorough-critique-polanyi, accessed 21 May 2016.

Rothbard, Murray N. (2006 [1973]) *For a New Liberty, the Libertarian Manifesto*. Auburn, Alabama: Ludwig von Mises Institute.

Rothbard, Murray N. (2009 [1962]) *Man, Economy, and State: A Treatise on Economic Principles (with Power and Market)* 2nd ed. Auburn, Alabama: Ludwig von Mises Institute.

Rothmann, Bernhard. (1534) 'A Confession of Faith and Life of the Church of Christ of Muenster,' in Zuck, 89-93.

Rothmann, Bernhard. (1534a) 'A Restitution…of Christian Teaching, Faith and Life… through the Church of Christ at Muenster,' in Zuck, 99-101.

Rothmann, Bernhard. (1534b) 'Concerning Revenge,' in Zuck, 102-104.

Rousseau, Jean-Jacques. (1917 [1756]) 'Criticism of Saint Pierre's Project,' in *A Lasting Peace through the Federation of Europe and 'the State of War*, trans. Charles Edwyn Vaughan. London: Constable. Avail at http://lf-oll.s3.amazonaws.com/titles/1010/0147_Bk.pdf, accessed 3 April 2014.

Rousseau, Jean-Jacques. (1969) *Œuvres Complètes, vol. iv*. eds Bernard Gagnebin & Marcel Raymond. Paris: Gallimard.

Rousseau, Jean-Jacques. (1997a) *The Discourses and Other Early Political Writings*, ed. and trans. Victor Gourevitch. Cambridge: Cambridge University Press.

Rousseau, Jean-Jacques. (1997a1 [1750]) *Discourse on the Sciences and Arts* (First Discourse), in Rousseau, 1997a, 1-28.

Rousseau, Jean-Jacques. (1997a2 [1754]) *Discourse on the Origin and Foundations of Inequality Among Men* (Second Discourse), in Rousseau, 1997a, 111-188.

Rousseau, Jean-Jacques. (1997a3 [1756]) 'Letter from J. J. Rousseau to M. de Voltaire,' in Rousseau 1997a, 232-246.

Rousseau, Jean-Jacques. (1997b) *The Social Contract and other Later Political Writings* in Victor Gourevitch (ed. and trans.). Cambridge: Cambridge University Press.

Rousseau, Jean-Jacques. (1997b1 [1754]) *Discourse on Political Economy*, in Rousseau 1997b, 3-38.

Rousseau, Jean-Jacques. (1997b2 [1762]) *Of the Social Contract*, in Rousseau 1997b, 39-152.

Rousseau, Jean-Jacques. (1997b3 [1781]) *Essay on the Origin of Languages*, in Rousseau 1997, 247-299.

Rowe, Christopher & Malcolm Schofield. (eds) (2000) *The Cambridge History of Greek and Roman Political Thought*. Cambridge: Cambridge University Press.

Rozeff, Michael S. (2005) 'The Power to Destroy,' in *The Free Market*, No. 8, available at https://mises.org/library/power-destroy-0, accessed 8 December 2016.

Rubenstein, Nicolai. (1991) 'Italian Political Thought,' in Burns 1991, 30-65.

Rudé, George. (1964) *Revolutionary Europe (1783-1815)*. London: Fontana/Collins. [Fontana History of Europe]

Ruthven, Malise. (1990) *A Satanic Affair: Salman Rushdie and the Rage of Islam*. London: Chatto & Windus.

Ruwart, Mary J. (1992) *Healing Our World: The Other Piece of the Puzzle*. Kalamazoo, Michigan: SunStar Press.

Ryan, Alan. (1984) 'Hegel on Work, Ownership and Citizenship,' in Pelczynski 1984, 178-196.

Ryley, Peter. (2013) *Making Another World Possible: Anarchism, Anti-Capitalism and Ecology in Late 19th and Early 20th Century Britain*. London: Bloomsbury.

Sabine, George H. (1963 [1937]) *A History of Political Theory* 3rd ed. London: George G. Harrap & Co. Ltd. [For many years, this was *the* standard work in the field and for some, it still is. Still very much worth reading]

Sacks, Jonathan. (2003 [2002]) *The Dignity of Difference: How to Avoid the Clash of Civilizations*, rev. ed. London: Continuum.

Sahlins, Marshall. (1974) *Stone Age Economics*. Aldine Transaction.

Salami, Minna. (2015) 'Philosophy has to be about More than White Men,' *The Guardian* (23 March), available at http://www.theguardian.com/education/comment-isfree/2015/mar/23/philosophy-white-men-university-courses, accessed 3 April 2015.

Salerno, Joseph T. (1999) 'War and the Money Machine: Concealing the Costs of War Beneath the Veil of Inflation,' in Denson 1999a, 433-453.

Salomon, Max. (1991) 'Der Begriff des Natturrechts bei den Sophisten,' in *Zeitschrift der Savigny-Stiftung für Rechtsgeschichte, Römische Abteilung*, 129-67.

Sampson, Geoffrey. (1979) *Liberty & Language*. Oxford: Oxford University Press. [This book is an attack on the anti-liberal political implications of Chomsky's linguistic rationalism]

Sandel, Michael J. (1998 [1982]) *Liberalism and the Limits of Justice* 2nd ed. Cambridge: Cambridge University Press.

Sandel, Michael J. (2012) *What Money Can't Buy: The Moral Limits of Markets*. New York: Penguin.

Sanger, Margaret. (1921) 'The Eugenic Value of Birth Control Propaganda,' in *The Birth Control Review*, October 1921, 5. Available at http://birthcontrolreview.net/Birth%20Control%20Review/1921-10%20October.pdf, accessed 5 October 2016.

Sanger, Margaret. (1922) *The Pivot of Civilization*. New York: Brentano's Publishers. Available at http://birthcontrolreview.net/Birth%20Control%20Review/1921-10%20October.pdf, accessed 5 October 2016.

Saravia, Luís. (1544) *Instrucción de mercaderes muy provechosa...cambios licitos y reprobados*. Medina del Campo, 1544; reprint Madrid: Coleccion de Joyas Bibliograficas, 1949. Trans. M. Grice-Hutchinson, *Early Economic Thought*.

Sartwell, Crispin. (2011) 'Introduction' to Warren 2011, 1-53. [*The Practical Anarchist: Writings of Josiah Warren*, ed. Crispin Sartwell]

Sartwell, Crispin. (2008) *Against the State*. Albany, New York: State University of New York Press.

Sass, Stephen L. (1998) *The Substance of Civilization: Materials and Human History from the Stone Age to the Age of Silicon*. New York: Arcade Publishing.

Sattler, Michael. (1527a) 'The Schleitheim Confession of Faith [Seven Articles],' in Zuck, 72-75.

Sattler, Michael. (1527b) 'The Schleitheim Articles,' in Baylor, 172-180.

Saunders, Doug. (2014) 'Thomas Piketty: "You do need some inequality to generate growth",' available at http://www.theglobeandmail.com/report-on-business/economy/fixing-capitalisms-growth-pains/article18586580/, accessed 22 December 2015.

Saunders, Jason. (1966) *Greek and Roman Philosophy after Aristotle*. New York: The Free Press.

Saunders, Trevor J. (1970) 'Introduction' to Plato, *The Laws* trans. T. J. Saunders. London: Penguin 1970, 17-41.

Saunders, Trevor J. (1992) 'Plato's Later Political Thought,' in Kraut, 464-492.

Schall, James V. (1994) 'On the Place of Augustine in Political Philosophy: A Second Look at Some Augustinian Literature,' in *The Political Science Reviewer*, Vol. 23 No 1, 128-165.

Schall, James V. (1996) 'The "Realism" of Augustine's "Political Realism",' in *Perspectives on Political Science*, Vol. 25 No. 3, 117-123.

Schildhauer, Johannes. (1985) *The Hansa: History and Culture*, trans. Katherine Vanovitch. Leipzig; Edition Leipzig.

Schiller, Ferdinand Canning Scott. (1934) *Must Philosophers Disagree?* London: Macmillan and Co. Ltd.

Schiller, Ferdinand Canning Scott. (1966) *Humanistic Pragmatism: The Philosophy of F. C. S. Schiller*, ed. Reuben Abel. New York: The Free Press.

Schivelbusch, Wolfgang. (2006) *Three New Deals: Reflections on Roosevelt's America, Mussolini's Italy, and Hitler's Germany, 1933-1939*. New York: Metropolitan Books.

Schmidtz, David and Jason Brennan. (2010) *A Brief History of Liberty*. Oxford: Wiley-Blackwell.

Schmidtz, David. (2011) 'Property,' in Klosko, 599-610.

Schmitt, Carl. (1996) *The Concept of the Political*, trans. George Schwab. Chicago: The University of Chicago Press.

Schnapp, Jeffrey Thomson. (2000) *A Primer of Italian Fascism*, trans. Jeffrey T. Schnapp, Olivia E. Sears and Maria G. Stampino. Lincoln, Nebraska: University of Nebraska Press.

Sciabarra, Chris Matthew. (1995) *Ayn Rand: The Russian Radical*. University Park, Pennsylvania: University of Pennsylvania Press.

Sciabarra, Chris Matthew. (2000) *Total Freedom: Toward a Dialectical Libertarianism*. University Park, Pennsylvania: University of Pennsylvania Press.

Schneider, Thomas. (2007) 'Sacred Kingship,' in Schulz & Seidel, 323-329

Schopenhauer, Arthur. (1896 [1851]) *On Human Nature: Essays in Ethics and Politics*. Mineola, New York: Dover Publications Inc. [A selection from the chapters 'Zur Ethik' and 'Zur Rechtslehre und Politik' of Schopenhauer's Parerga and other posthumous writings.]

Schopenhauer, Arthur. (1966 [1819]) *The World as Will and Representation*, trans. E. F. J. Payne. New York: Dover Publications.

Schopenhauer, Arthur. (1970 [1851]) *Essays and Aphorisms*, trans. R. J. Hollingdale. London: Penguin. [A selection from *Parerga and Paralipomena*]

Schopenhauer, Arthur. (1995 [1819]) *The World as Will and Idea*, trans. Jill Berman, ed. and abridged David Berman. London: Everyman.

Schopenhauer, Arthur. (2010 [1839/1840]) *The Two Fundamental Problems of Ethics: Treated in Two Academic Prize Essays*. Oxford: Oxford University Press. [Oxford World's Classics] This edition contains Schopenhauer's two prize essay submissions, 'On the Freedom of the Will' (1839) and 'On the Basis of Morals' (1840).

Schultz, Regine and Matthias Seidel. (2007) *Egypt: The World of the Pharaohs*. Potsdam: H. F. Ullmann. [Tandem Verlag]

Schumpeter, Joseph. (1964 [1953]) *History of Economic Analysis*. London: Allen & Unwin.

Schwartz, Bernard. (1993) *A History of the Supreme Court*. Oxford: Oxford University Press.

Scott, James C. (1985) *Weapons of the Weak: Everyday Forms of Peasant Resistance*. New Haven, Connecticut: Yale University Press.

Scott, James C. (1998) *Seeing Like a State: How Certain Schemes to Improve the Human Condition Have Failed*. New Haven, Connecticut: Yale University Press.

Scott, James C. (2009) *The Art of Not Being Governed*. New Haven, Connecticut: Yale University Press.

Scott, James C. (2012) *Two Cheers for Anarchism*. Princeton, New Jersey: Princeton University Press.

Scott, Jonathan. (2004) *Commonwealth Principles: Republican Writings of the English Revolution*. Cambridge: Cambridge University Press.

Scruton, Roger. (1980) *The Meaning of Conservatism*. London: Macmillan. [3rd edition, St Augustine's Press, London]

Scruton, Roger. (2007) *A Political Philosophy: Arguments for Conservatism*. London: Bloomsbury.

Scruton, Roger. (2014) *How to be a Conservative*. London: Bloomsbury.

Scruton, Roger. (2015) *Fools, Frauds and Firebrands: Thinkers of the New Left*. London: Bloomsbury.

Seaman, Lewis Charles Bernard. (1973) *Victorian England: Aspects of English and Imperial History, 1837-1901*. London: Methuen & Co. Ltd.

Sedley, David. (2013) 'Lucretius,' in *Stanford Encyclopedia of Philosophy*, available at http://plato.stanford.edu/archives/fall2013/entries/lucretius, accessed 10 January 2014.

Segal, Ronald. (2001) *Islam's Black Slaves: The Other Black Diaspora*. New York: Farrar, Straus and Giroux.

Sen, Amartya. (1999) *Development as Freedom*. New York: Basic Books.

Seneca, Lucius Annaeus. (1964 [AD 56-62]) *de Beneficiis* (volume III of *Seneca—Moral Essays*, trans. John W. Basore. London: William Heinemann Ltd. [The Loeb Classical Library]

Seneca, Lucius Annaeus. (1969 [c. AD 62]) *Letters from a Stoic*, selected and trans. Robin Campbell. London: Penguin.

Seneca, Lucius Annaeus. (2007) *Dialogues and Essays*, trans. John Davie. Oxford: Oxford University Press.

Service, Elman R. (1975) *Origins of the State and Civilization: The Process of Cultural Evolution*. New York: W. W. Norton & Company Inc.

Sewell, Dennis. (2009) *The Political Gene: How Darwin's Ideas Changed Politics*. London: Picador.

Sexby, Edward (alias William Allen). (1657) 'Killing Noe Murder,' in Wootton, 2003, 360-388.

Shah, Idries. (1973 [1966]) *The Exploits of the Incomparable Mulla Nasrudin*. London: Picador.

Shand, Alexander. H. (1984) *The Capitalist Alternative: An Introduction to Neo-Austrian Economics*. New York: New York University Press.

Sharp, Andrew. (ed.) (1998) *The English Levellers*. Cambridge: Cambridge University Press. [Cambridge Texts in the History of Political Thought]

Shatz, Marshall. (2011) 'Anarchism,' in Klosko, 725-736.

Shaw, Chris. (2016) 'Jeffersonian Governance, Burkean Conservatism, and Anarchism,' available at https://thelibertarianalliance.com/2016/07/22/jeffersonian-governance-burkean-conservatism-and-anarchism/, accessed 29 July 2016 from The Libertarian Alliance Blog.

Sheehan, Jonathan & Dror Wahrman. (2015) *Invisible Hands: Self-Organization and the Eighteenth Century*. Chicago: The University of Chicago Press.

Shklar, Judith N. (1987) *Montesquieu*. Oxford: Oxford University Press. [Series: Past Masters]

Shortridge, Andrew & Dirk Baltzly. (2008) 'Antiphon,' in O'Grady, 2008, 83-92.

Shortridge, Andrew. (2008) 'Law against Nature?,' in O'Grady, 2008, 194-203.

Sidney, Algernon. (2003 [1698]) *Discourses Concerning Government* (excerpts), in Wootton, 417-445.

Siedentop, Larry. (2015 [2014]) *Inventing the Individual: The Origins of Western Liberalism*. London: Penguin. An accessible, entertaining and illuminating treatment of social, political and cultural history that should be on everyone's reading list.

Silvermintz, Daniel. (2008) 'Thrasymachus,' in O'Grady, 2008, 93-100.

Simmons, A. John. (1993) *On the Edge of Anarchy: Locke, Consent, and the Limits of Society*. Princeton, New Jersey: Princeton University Press.

Simons, Menno. (1552) 'A Reply to False Accusations,' in Zuck, 123-126.

Simons, Menno. (1554) 'My Conversion, Call, and Testimony,' in Zuck, 117-121.]

Skemp, J. B. (1952) 'Introductory Essays,' in Plato 1957.

Skinner, Quentin. (1977) *The Foundations of Modern Political Thought, Vol. 1—The Renaissance*. Cambridge: Cambridge University Press.

Skinner, Quentin. (1978) *The Foundations of Modern Political Thought, Vol. 2—The Age of Reformation*. Cambridge: Cambridge University Press.

Skinner, Quentin. (1998) *Liberty before Liberalism*. Cambridge: Cambridge University Press.

Slaughter, Thomas P. (1986) *The Whiskey Rebellion: Frontier Epilogue to the American Revolution*. Oxford: Oxford University Press.

Sloman, Richard. (1993) 'Liberty Defined: An Objectivist Anarchist Manifesto,' in *Philosophical Notes No. 28*. London: Libertarian Alliance. Available at http://www.libertarian.co.uk/lapubs/philn/philn028.pdf, accessed 18 August 2014.

Sloterdijk, Peter. (2010) 'A Grasping Hand – The Modern Democratic State Pillages its Productive Citizens,' trans. Alexis Cornel, in *City Journal*, Vol. 20, No. 1, 5-7. Available at http://www.city-journal.org/html/grasping-hand-13264.html, accessed 31 August 2016. Also available at http://www.forbes.com/2010/01/27/free-market-democracy-modern-opinions-contributors-peter-sloterdijk.html, accessed 31 August 2016.

Smith, Adam. (1976 [1759]) *The Theory of Moral Sentiments*, eds D. D. Raphael and A. L. Macfie. Oxford: Oxford University Press,

Smith, Adam. (1976 [1776]) *An Inquiry into the Nature and Causes of the Wealth of Nations*, eds R. H. Campbell, A. S. Skinner, and W. B. Todd. Oxford: Oxford University Press.

Smith, Adam. (1978 [1762/66]) *Lectures on Jurisprudence*, eds R. L. Meek, D. D. Raphael, and P. G. Stein. Oxford: Oxford University Press.

Smith, Craig. (2006) *Adam Smith's Political Philosophy: The Invisible Hand and Spontaneous Order*. London: Routledge.

Smith, George H. (2013) *The System of Liberty: Themes in the History of Classical Liberalism*. Cambridge: Cambridge University Press.

Smith, George H. (2014) 'Edmund Burke, Intellectuals, and the French Revolution, Part 2,' available at http://www.libertarianism.org/columns/edmund-burke-intellectuals-french-revolution-part-2, accessed 19 April 2014.

Smith, George H. (2016) 'Immanuel Kant on Spontaneous Order,' available at http://www.libertarianism.org/columns/immanuel-kant-spontaneous-order, accessed 15 June 2016.

Smith, George H. & Marilyn Moore. (eds) (2015) *Individualism: A Reader*. Washington, D. C.: The Cato Institute.

Sneed, John D. (1977) 'Order without Law: Where will Anarchists keep the Madmen?,' in *Journal of Libertarian Studies,* Vol. 1 No. 2, 117-124.

Snell, Bruno. (1953 [1946]) *The Discovery of the Mind*, trans. T. G. Rosenmeyer. Oxford: Basil Blackwell. [Originally published in German as *Die Entdeckung des Geistes* in Hamburg in 1946]

Sommers, Christina Hoff. (1994) *Who Stole Feminism? How Women have Betrayed Women*. New York: Touchstone.

Sommerville, Johann. (2011) 'The Social Contract (Contract of Government),' in Klosko, 573-585.

Sorel, Georges. (1950 [1908]) *Reflections on Violence*. London: Collier-Macmillan. Originally published as *Réflexions sur la violence*.

Southern, R. W. (1967 [1953]) *The Making of the Middle Ages*. London: Hutchinson & Co. (Publishers) Ltd.

Sowell, Thomas. (1987) *A Conflict of Visions: Ideological Origins of Political Struggles*. New York: William Morrow. Essential reading! [For a short YouTube presentation of the central idea of the book, see https://www.youtube.com/watch?v=OGvYqaxSPp4 (4 November 2008), accessed 19 April 2016] A revised edition of the book was published in 2007 by Basic Books (New York).

Sowell, Thomas. (1996 [1980]) *Knowledge and Decisions*. New York: Basic Books. [Few books deserve to be read from cover to cover. This is an exception. Essential reading!]

Sowell, Thomas. (2011) *Economic Facts and Fallacies*, 2nd ed. New York: Basic Books.

Spencer, Herbert. (1851) *Social Statics or The Conditions Essential to Human Happiness Specified, and the First of Them Developed*. London: John Chapman.

Spencer, Herbert. (1937 [1862]) *First Principles*, 6th ed. London: Watts & Co.

Spencer, Herbert. (1978 [1897]) *The Principles of Ethics*, 2 Vols. Indianapolis, Indiana: The Liberty Press.

Spencer, Herbert. (1982 [1884]) *The Man versus the State*. Indianapolis, Indiana: The Liberty Fund.

Spencer, Herbert. (1994) *Political Writings*. Cambridge: Cambridge University Press. [Contains *The Proper Sphere of Government* and *The Man versus the State*]

Spiller, Roger. (2005) *An Instinct for War: Scenes from the Battlefields of History*. Cambridge, Massachusetts: The Belknap Press.

Spooner, Lysander. (1870) *No Treason. No. VI. The Constitution of No Authority*. Boston: Self-Published. Available at http://files.libertyfund.org/files/2194/Spooner_1485_Bk.pdf, accessed 9 January 2014.

Spooner, Lysander. (1992) *The Lysander Spooner Reader*, ed. George H. Smith. San Francisco: Fox & Wilkes.

Spufford, Francis. (2010) *Red Plenty*. London: Faber & Faber.

Stanlis, Peter. J. (1965 [1958]) *Edmund Burke and the Natural Law*. Ann Arbor, Michigan: University of Michigan Press.

Stark, Rodney. (2007 [2006]) *Cities of God: The Real Story of How Christianity Became an Urban Movements and Conquered Rome*. New York: HarperOne.

Starnes, Todd. (2016) '"His Majesty": Student Singled-Handedly Defeats and Army of Gender Neutral Activists,' available at http://www.foxnews.com/opinion/2016/09/30/his-majesty-student-single-handedly-defeats-army-gender-neutral-activists.html, accessed 2 November 2016.

Stayer, James M. (1972) *Anabaptists and the Sword*. Lawrence, Kansas: Coronado Press.

Stearns, Stephen C., Sean G. Byars et al. (2010) 'Measuring Selection in Contemporary Human Populations,' in *Nature Reviews Genetics*, Vol. 11, No, 9, 611-622.

Steedman, Ian. (1977) *Marx after Sraffa*. London: New Left Books.

Steigmann-Gall, Richard. (2004) 'Nazism and the Revival of Political Religion Theory,' in *Totalitarian Movements and Political Religions*, Vol. 5, No. 3, 376-396.

Steinberg, Justin. (2009) 'Spinoza's Political Philosophy,' in *Stanford Encyclopedia of Philosophy*, available at http://plato.stanford.edu/archives/spr2009/entries/spino-za-political/, accessed 7 September 2013.

Stevens, Anthony. (2004) *The Roots of War and Terror*. London: Continuum.

Stevenson, David. (2011) *With Our Backs to the Wall: Victory and Defeat in 1918*. London: Allen Lane.

Stewart, Doug. (2013) 'My Great-Great-Grandfather Hated the Gettysburg Address. 150 Years Later, He's Famous for It,' available at http://www.smithsonianmag.com/history/my-great-great-grandfather-hated-the-gettysburg-address-150-years-later-hes-famous-for-it-180947746/?no-ist, accessed 1 October 2016.

Stone, Geoffrey R. (2007) *War and Liberty: An American Dilemma: 1790 to the Present*. New York: W. W. Norton & Company.

Stone, Isodor Feinstein. (1989) *The Trial of Socrates*. New York: Anchor Books (Random House), 1989.

Stone, Christopher D. (1972) 'Should Trees have Standing?—Toward Legal Rights for Natural Objects,' in *Southern California Law Review* Vol. 45, 450-501.

Storr, Will. (2013) *The Heretics: Adventures with the Enemies of Science*. London: Picador.

Stoye, John. (1969) *Europe Unfolding (1648-1688)*. London: Fontana/Collins. [Fontana History of Europe]

Strachan, Hew. (2003) *The First World War*. London: Simon & Schuster.

Strauss, Leo and Joseph Cropsey. (eds) (1987) *History of Political Philosophy*. Chicago: University of Chicago Press.

Strayer, Joseph R. (1970) *On the Medieval Origins of the Modern State*. Princeton, New Jersey: Princeton University Press.

Stringham, Edward (ed.) (2007) *Anarchy and the Law: The Political Economy of Choice*. New Brunswick: Transaction Publishers.

Stringham, Edward. (2015) *Private Governance: Creating Order in Economic and Social Life*. New York: Oxford University Press.

Strogatz, Steven. (2003) *SYNC: The Emerging Science of Spontaneous Order*. London: Penguin.

Strong, Derek Ryan. (2014) 'Proudhon and the Labour Theory of Property,' in *Anarchist Studies*, Vol. 22 No 1, 52-65.

Struve, Tilman. (1984) 'The Importance of the Organism in the Political Theory of John of Salisbury,' in Wilks, 303-317.

Stuart, Doug. (2014, 26 April) 'Does Inerrancy Disprove Libertarianism?,' available at http://libertarianchristians.com/2014/04/26/does-inerrancy-disprove-libertarianism/comment-page-1/#comment-6186, accessed 28 April 2014. Links to, *inter alia*, 'Romans Chapter 13' (Chuck Baldwin), 'Against Empire: A Yoderian Reading of Romans,' 'Does "Romans 13" Opposes Liberty?,' 'Romans 13 and Anarcho-Capitalism,' 'Hitler's Favorite Bible Verse,' 'Romans 13 and National Defense,' 'The Bible, government and Christian Anarchy,' 'More Indictment of the Mistranslated Romans 13,' 'New Testament Theology of the Stat, part 1,' 'Theology doesn't begin and end with Romans 13,' 'Stanley Hauerwas on Romans 13,' 'The State and Christian Obedience: John Howard Yoder on Romans 13,' 'Reading Romans 13 with John Howard Yoder (Again!)' and many other interesting links.

Stump, Eleonore & Norman Kretzmann. (eds) (2001) *The Cambridge Companion to Augustine*. Cambridge: Cambridge University Press.

Su, Rong, James Rounds & Patrick Ian Armstrong. (2009) 'Men and Things, Women and People: A Meta-Analysis of Sex Differences in Interests,' *Psychological Bulletin*, Vol. 135 No. 6, 859-884.

Sullivan, Roger. (1996) 'Introduction' to Kant (1996 [1797]), vii-xxvi.

Sumner, William Graham. (1959 [1906]) *Folkways: A Study of the Sociological Importance of Usages, Manners, Customs, Mores, and Morals*. New York: Dover Publications, Inc.

Szasz, Thomas. (1990) *The Untamed Tongue: A Dissenting Dictionary*. La Salle, Illinois: Open Court.

Tacitus, Publius Cornelius. (1970 [AD 98]) *The Agricola and the Germania*, trans. H. Mattingly, rev. S. A. Handford. London: Penguin.

Tacitus, Publius Cornelius. (2009 [AD 98-116]) *Annals, Histories, Agricola, Germania*, trans. Alfred John Church and William Jackson Brodribb. New York: Everyman's Library.

Taleb, Nassim Nicholas. (2012) *Antifragile*. London: Allen Lane.

Tallis, Frank. (2005) *Love Sick*. London: Arrow Books.

Tallis, Raymond. (2010) *Michaelangelo's Finger: An Exploration of Everyday Transcendence*. London: Atlantic Books.

Talmon, Jacob Leib. (1951) *The Origins of Totalitarian Democracy*. London: Secker & Warburg.

Tannehill, Morris & Linda Tannehill. (2007 [1970]) *The Market for Liberty*. Auburn, Alabama: The Mises Institute. Available at http://library.mises.org/books/Morris%20and%20Linda%20Tannehill/The%20Market%20for%20Liberty.pdf, accessed 14 May 2014.

Tanner, Joseph Robson and Frank Stanton Carey. (1885) *Comments on the use of the Blue Books made by Karl Marx in Chapter XV of Le Capital*. Cambridge: Cambridge Economic Club.

Tansill, Charles Callan. (1938 [1942]) *America Goes to War*. Boston: Little, Brown and Company.

Tansill, Charles Callan. (1952) *Back Door to War: The Roosevelt Foreign Policy, 1933-1941*. Westport, Connecticut: Greenwood Press, Publishers.

Tarnas, Richard. (1991) *The Passion of the Western Mind: Understanding the Ideas that have Shaped our World View*. London: Pimlico.

Tate, J. P. (2014) *Feminism is Sexism*. Marston Gate: Amazon.co.uk Ltd.

Tavris, Carol and Elliot Aronson. (2013 [2007]) *Mistakes Were Made (but not by me): Why We Justify Foolish Beliefs, Bad Decisions and Hurtful Acts*. London: Pinter & Martin.

Taylor, C. C. W. & Mi-Kyoung Lee. (2012) 'The Sophists,' in *Stanford Encyclopedia of Philosophy*, available at http://plato.stanford.edu/archives/spr2012/entries/sophists/, accessed 7 September 2013.

Taylor, Quentin P. (2016) 'Was John Stuart Mill actually a Socialist?' in *The Independent Review*, Vol. 21, No. 01, 73-94.

Tennant, Michael. (2005a) 'Christianarchy?,' in *Strike the Root*, available at http://www.strike-the-root.com/51/tennant/tennant5.html, accessed 12 August 2013.

Tennant, Michael. (2005b) 'Government as Idolatry,' in *Strike the Root*,. available at http://www.strike-the-root.com/51/tennant/tennant5.html, accessed 12 August 2013.

Tesón, Fernando R. 'Hugo Grotius on War and the State' a forum discussion of the ONLINE LIBRARY OF LIBERTY available at http://oll.libertyfund.org/pages/lm-grotius, with contributions by Eric Mack, Paul Carrese and Hans W. Blom. Accessed 15 April 2014.

Teubner, Gunther. (ed.) (1997) *Global Law without a State*. Aldershot, Hampshire: Dartmouth Publishing Company.

Thatcher, Margaret. (1987) 'Interview,' in *Woman's Own*, 31 October.

The Estates General of the United Netherlands. (1581) 'An Act of Abjuration,' in Zuck, 183.

The Twelve Elders of Münster. (1534) 'Thirteen Statements of the Order of [Private] Life,' in Zuck, 95-97.

Theodoret. *On Divine Providence*. Migne, *Patrologia Graeca*.

Thiselton, Anthony C. (1993) 'Hermeneutics,' in Metzger & Coogan, 279-280.

Thomas, Paul. (2009) 'Marx and Engels,' in Boucher & Kelly 2009, 474-490.

Thucydides. (1954 [431 BC]) *History of the Peloponnesian War*, trans. Rex Warner. London: Penguin Books.

Thucydides. (2013 [431 BC]) *The War of the Peloponnesians and the Athenians*, ed. and trans. Jeremy Mynott. Cambridge: Cambridge University Press. [Series: Cambridge Texts in the History of Political Thought]

Tierney, Brian. (1955) *Foundations of the Conciliar Theory: The Contributions of the Medieval Canonists from Gratian to the Great Schism*. Cambridge: Cambridge University Press.

Tierney, Brian. (1982) *Religion, Law and the Growth of Constitutional Thought*. Cambridge; Cambridge University Press.

Tierney, Brian. (1988) *The Crisis of Church and State, 1050-1300*. Toronto: University of Toronto Press.

Tierney, Brian. (2001 [1997]) *The Idea of Natural Rights*. Grand Rapids, Michigan: William B. Eerdmans Publishing Co.

Tierney, Brian. (2014) *Liberty and Law: The Idea of Permissive Natural Law 1100-1800*. Washington, D. C.: The Catholic University of America Press.

Tilly, Charles. (ed.) (1975) *The Formation of National States in Western Europe*. Princeton, New Jersey: Princeton University Press.

Tilly, Charles. (1985) 'War Making and State Making as Organized Crime,' in Evans, Rueschemeyer and Skocpol, 169-191.

Tilly, Charles. (1992) *Coercion, Capital, and European States, AD 990-1992*. Oxford: Blackwell.

Tolkien, J. R. R. (1954) *The Fellowship of the Ring: Being the First Part of the Lord of the Rings*. New York: Houghton Mifflin Company.

Tolkien, J. R. R. (1981) *The Letters of J. R. R. Tolkien*, ed. Humphrey Carpenter. London: George Allen & Unwin.

Tomaselli, Sylvana. (2013) 'Mary Woolstonecraft,' in *Stanford Encyclopedia of Philosophy*, available at http://plato.stanford.edu/archives/sum2013/entries/wollstonecraft/, accessed 7 September 2013.

Tooley, Marian J. (1955) 'Introduction' to Jean Bodin's *Six Books of the Commonwealth* Oxford: Blackwell, vii-xxxix, available online at http://www.constitution.org/bodin/bodin_0.htm, accessed 28 November 2013.

Trask, Robert Lawrence & Bill Mayblin. (2005 [2000]) *Introducing Linguistics*. Royston, Cambridgeshire: Icon Books.

Trattner, Walter I. (1994) *From Poor Law to Welfare State: A History of Social Welfare in America*. New York: Free Press.

Trigger, Bruce G. (2005) 'Going Still Further?' in Yoffee et al., 256-258.

Trigger, Bruce G. (2007) *Understanding Early Civilizations*. Cambridge: Cambridge University Press.

Troeltsch, Ernst. (1931) *The Social Teaching of the Christian Churches*, 2 vols, trans. Olive Wyon. London & New York.

Trotsky, Leon. (1937) *The Revolution Betrayed*, trans. Max Eastman. New York: Doubleday, Doran & Co.

Tuchman, Barbara W. (1979 [1978]) *A Distant Mirror: The Calamitous 14ᵗʰ Century*. London: Penguin.

Tuck, Richard. 'Introduction' to Hobbes 1996, ix-xlv.

Tucker, Benjamin. (1881-1908) *Liberty*. Available at http://travellinginliberty.blogspot. ie/2007/08/index-of-liberty-site.html, accessed 2 June 2104. Also at http://www. scribd.com/doc/180757753/Liberty-Whole-Volume-One, accessed 3 June 2014.

Tucker, Benjamin. (1926) *Individual Liberty: Selections from the Writings of Benjamin R. Tucker*, ed. C. L. S. New York: Vanguard Press. Available at https://mises.org/ system/tdf/Individual%20Liberty_3.pdf?file=1&type=document, accessed 1 August 2016.

Tucker, Benjamin. (2005 [1897]) *Instead of a Book, by a Man Too Busy to Write One*, 2ⁿᵈ ed. New York: Benj. R. Tucker, Publisher. Available at https://ia600406.us.archive. org/4/items/cu31924030333052/cu31924030333052.pdf, accessed 2 July 2014. Also available at http://fair-use.org/benjamin-tucker/instead-of-a-book/index, accessed 20 June 2014.

Turchetti, Mario. (2012) 'Jean Bodin,' in *Stanford Encyclopedia of Philosophy*, available at http://plato.stanford.edu/archives/win2012/entries/bodin/, accessed 7 September 2013.

Tuttle, Lisa. (1986) *Encyclopedia of Feminism*. New York: Facts on File Publications.

Twain, Mark. (1880) 'The Awful German Language,' available at https://drive.google. com/a/ucd.ie/file/d/0B4xHZbr3vgOmYm5teGlsSzQ4a28/view, accessed 9 February 2015. [Originally published in *A Tramp Abroad*, available in various editions]

Ullmann, Walter. (1966 [1961]) *Principles of Government and Politics in the Middle Ages*, 2ⁿᵈ ed. London: Menthuen & Co Ltd.

Ullmann, Walter. (1967 [1966]) *The Individual and Society in the Middle Ages*. London: Menthuen & Co Ltd.

Ullmann, Walter. (1975) *Law and Politics in the Middle Ages: An Introduction to the Sources of Medieval Political Ideas*. London: The Sources of History Limited. [Series: The Sources of History: Studies in the Uses of Historical Evidence (general editor G. R. Elton)—this series is now published by Cambridge University Press]

University of Oxford. (1683) 'The Judgment and Decree of the University of Oxford, Passed in their Convocation, July 21, against Certain Pernicious Books and Damnable Doctrines, Destructive to the Sacred Persons of Princes, Their State and Government, and of All Humane Society' 1683, in Wootton ed., 2003, 120-126.

Ure, Percy Neville. (1951) *Justinian and his Age*. London: Pelican.

Vallentyne, Peter (2010 [2002]), 'Libertarianism,' in *The Stanford Encyclopedia of Philosophy*, available at http://plato.stanford.edu/entries/libertarianism/, accessed 4 June 2014.

van Dun, Frank. (2009) 'The Logic of Law,' in *Libertarian Papers*, Vol. 1, Art. No. 36, 1-55.

van Dun, Frank. (2011) 'Natural Law, Liberalism, and Christianity,' in *Journal of Libertarian Studies*, Vol. 15, No. 3, 1-36.

van Laarhoven, Jan. (1984) 'Thou Shalt Not Slay a Tyrant! The So-Called Theory of John of Salisbury,' in Wilks, 319-341.

van Reybrouck, David. (2016 [2013]) *Against Elections: The Case for Democracy*, trans. Liz Waters. London: The Bodley Head. [Originally published as *Tegen Verkiezingen* by De Bezige Bij]

Various. (1320) 'The Declaration of Arbroath.' National Archives of Scotland. Translation of the Declaration of Arbroath – revised version (2005), based on Sir James
Fergusson, The Declaration of Arbroath 1320 (1970), 5-11, with reference to A. A. M.
Duncan, 'The Nation of Scots and the Declaration of Arbroath' (Historical Association pamphlet, 1970), pp. 34-37 and D. E. R. Watt (ed.) *Scotichronicon* Vol. 7 (1996),
4-9, translation compiled by Alan Borthwick, June 2005. Available at http://www.nas.
gov.uk/downloads/declarationArbroath.pdf, accessed 30 November 2016.

Various. (1523) 'The Second Zurich Disputation,' in Zuck, 52-54.

Various. (1647) 'The Putney Debates' (excerpt), in Sharp 1998, 102-130.

Various. (1647) 'The Putney Debates' (excerpt), in Wootton, 2003, 285-317.

Various. (2010) 'What's Living & Dead in Ayn Rand's Moral & Political Thought,'
available at http://www.cato-unbound.org/issues/january-2010/whats-living-dead-
ayn-rands-moral-political-thought, accessed 7 July 2014. A set of essays on the
contemporary significance of Ayn Rand by Douglas Rasmussen, Roderick Long,
Michael Huemer and Neera Badhwar.

Vawter, Bruce, CM. (1964 [1957]) *A Path through Genesis*. London: Sheed & Ward.

Verhaegh, Marcus. (2004a) 'The A Priori of Ownership: Kant on Property,' available
at https://mises.org/library/priori-ownership-kant-property, accessed 4 January 2017.

Verhaegh, Marcus. (2004b) 'Kant and Property Rights,' in *Journal of Libertarian
Studies*, Vol. 18, No 3, 11-32. Available at https://mises.org/system/tdf/18_3_2.
pdf?file=1&type=document, accessed 4 January 2017.

Vincent, John. (1996 [1995]) *An Intelligent Person's Guide to History*. London:
Duckworth.

Vinx, Lars. (2010) 'Carl Schmitt,' in *Stanford Encyclopedia of Philosophy*, available
at http://plato.stanford.edu/archives/fall2010/entries/schmitt/, accessed 7 September
2013.

Viola, Frank & George Barna. (2008 [2002]) *Pagan Christianity*, rev. ed. Carol Stream,
Illinois: BarnaBooks (Tyndale House Publishers).

Voegelin, Eric. (1952) *The New Science of Politics: An Introduction*. Chicago: The
University of Chicago Press. [Charles R. Walgreen Foundation Lectures]

Voegelin, Eric. (1986 [1938]) *Political Religions*, trans. T. J. DiNapoli and E. S. Easterly
III. Lewiston, New York: The Edwin Mellen Press. [Volume 23 in Toronto Studies in
Theology]

Voegelin, Eric. (1998) *The Collected Works of Eric Voegelin*, Vol. 21, *History of Political
Ideas*, Vol. III, *The Later Middle Ages*, ed. David Walsh. Columbia, Missouri: University of Missouri Press. References to this book will be by local volume number and
page, e.g. III, 27—Volume III, page 27.

Voegelin, Eric. (1998) *The Collected Works of Eric Voegelin*, Vol. 23, *History of Political
Ideas*, Vol. V, *Religion and the Rise of Modernity*, ed. James L. Wiser. Columbia,
Missouri: University of Missouri Press. References to this book will be by local
volume number and page, e.g. V, 132—Volume V, page 132.

Vogt, Katja. (2011) 'Ancient Skepticism,' in *Stanford Encyclopedia of Philosophy*,
available at http://plato.stanford.edu/archives/win2011/entries/skepticism-ancient/,
accessed 7 September 2013.

Vogt, Katja. (2013) 'Seneca,' in *Stanford Encyclopedia of Philosophy* 2013, available
at http://plato.stanford.edu/archives/sum2013/entries/seneca/, accessed 7 September
2013.

Vondung, Klaus. (2005) 'National Socialism as a Political Religion: Potentials and
Limits of an Analytical Concept,' in *Totalitarian Movements and Political Religions*,
Vol. 6, No. 1, 87-95.

Vonnegut, Kurt. (2009) *Armageddon in Retrospect and other New and Unpublished Writings on War and Peace*. London: Vintage Books.

Vonnegut, Kurt. (2009a) "Wailing Shall be in All Streets, ' in Vonnegut 2009, 32-45.

Waddington, Conrad Hal. (1977) *Tools for Thought*. St Albans, Hertfordshire: Paladin.

Wade, Nicholas. (2014) *A Troublesome Inheritance: Genes, Race and Human History*. New York: The Penguin Press.

Walker, Rebecca. (1992) 'Becoming the Third Wave,' in *Ms. Magazine*, Vol. 11, No. 2 (2): 39–41.

Wallace, David Foster. (2006a) *Consider the Lobster, and Other Essays*. New York: Back Bay Books. [An Imprint of Little, Brown and Company]

Wallace, David Foster. (2006b) 'Authority and American Usage', in Wallace 2006a, 66-127.

Waltz, Kenneth N. (1954) *Man, the State and War: A Theoretical Analysis*. New York: Columbia University Press.

Walvin, James. (2007) *A Short History of Slavery*. London: Penguin Book.

Walwyn, William (and on behalf of John Lilburne, Thomas Prince and Richard Overton). (1649) 'A Manifestation,' in Sharp 1998, 158-167.

Walwyn, William. (1644) 'The Compassionate Samaritane: Liberty of Conscience Asserted and the Separatist Vindicated,' in Wootton, 247-271.

Walwyn, William. (1646) 'Toleration Justified and Persecution Condemned,' in Sharp 1998, 9-30.

Walwyn, William. (1647) 'Gold Tried in the Fire,' in Sharp 1998, 73-91.

Walzer, Michael. (2006 [1977]) *Just and Unjust Wars: A Moral Argument with Historical Illustrations*, 4th ed. New York: Basic Books.

Wannenwetsch, Bernd. (2008) 'Soul Citizens: How Christians Understand their Political Role,' in *Political Theology*, Vol. 9 No. 3, 373-394.

Wapshott, Nicholas. (2011) *Keynes Hayek: The Clash that Defined Modern Economics*. New York: W. W. Norton & Company.

Warren, Josiah (1840-1873) 'Notebook D,' in Sartwell 2011, 124-138.

Warren, Josiah. (1833) 'The Peaceful Revolutionist,' in Sartwell 2011, 99-123.

Warren, Josiah. (1842) 'Manifesto,' in Warren 2011, 237-241.

Warren, Josiah. (1863) 'True Civilization,' in Warren 2011, 139-183. Available at http://dwardmac.pitzer.edu/anarchist_archives/bright/warren/truecivtoc.html, accessed 20 June 2014. See also the Josiah Warren Project at http://www.crispinsartwell.com/josiahwarren.htm, accessed 20 June 2014.

Warren, Josiah. (2011) *The Practical Anarchist: Writings of Josiah Warren*, ed. and intro. Crispin Sartwell. New York: Fordham University Press. [See reviews by Jun and by Adams 2013]

Warren, Josiah. (c. 1850) 'A Few Words to the Writer in a Paper Called "the Circular" on the Sovereignty of the Individual,' in Warren 2011, 235-236.

Warren, Mark E. (2011) 'Democracy,' in Klosko, 517-529.

Watner Carl. (1982b) 'The Proprietary Theory of Justice in the Libertarian Tradition,' in *The Journal of Libertarian Studies*, Vol. 6, Nos 3-4, 289-316.

Watner, Carl. (1977) 'Benjamin Tucker and His Periodical, Liberty,' in *The Journal of Libertarian Studies*, Vol. 1, No. 4, 307-318.

Watner, Carl. (1982a) 'The English Individualists as They Appear in *Liberty*,' in *The Journal of Libertarian Studies*, Vol. 6, No. 01, 59-82.

Watner, Carl. (1986) '"Oh, Ye are for Anarchy!": Consent Theory in the Radical Libertarian Tradition,' in *The Journal of Libertarian Studies*, Vol. 8, No. 1, 111-137.

Watner, Carl. (2005) '*Quod Omnes Tangit*: Consent Theory in the Radical Libertarian Tradition in the Middle Ages' in *The Journal of Libertarian Studies*, Vol. 19, No. 2, 67-85.

Watson, Alan. (ed.) (1985 [AD 530-33]) *The Digest of Justinian*, trans. Alan Watson, in four vols. Philadelphia: University of Pennsylvania Press. [see Justinian]

Weber, Max. (1948) *Essays in Sociology*. London: Routledge & Kegan Paul, 78.

Weinstein, David. (2011) 'Nineteenth- and Twentieth-Century Liberalism' in Klosko, 414-435.

Weinstein, David. (2012) 'Herbert Spencer,' in *Stanford Encyclopedia of Philosophy*, available at http://plato.stanford.edu/archives/fall2012/entries/spencer/, accessed 7 September 2013.

Weithman, Paul. (2001) 'Augustine's Political Philosophy,' in Stump and Kretzmann, 234-252.

Wells, Spencer. (2004) *The Journey of Man: A Genetic Odyssey*. New York: Random House.

Wente, Margaret. (2016) 'The Professor vs. the Pronoun Warriors,' available at http://www.theglobeandmail.com/opinion/the-professor-vs-the-pronoun-warriors/article32474079/, accessed 24 October 2016.

West, Ed. (2016) 'Why Do We Indulge the Crimes of the Left?' in *The Spectator* (12 June 2016). Available at http://blogs.spectator.co.uk/2016/06/indulge-crimes-left/, accessed 12 June 2016.

Weston, J. C. Jr. (1958) 'The Ironic Purpose of Burke's *Vindication* Vindicated,' in *Journal of the History of Ideas* Vol. 19, 435-441.

Westphal, Kenneth. (1993) 'The Basic Context and Structure of Hegel's *Philosophy of Right*,' in Beiser, 234-269.

Whatmore, Richard. (2011) 'Enlightenment Political Philosophy,' in Klosko, 296-318.

Whelan, Robert. (1999) *Wild in Woods: The Myth of the Noble Eco-Savage*. London. IEA.

Whibley, Leonard. (ed.) (2014 [1932]) *Correspondence of Richard Hurd and William Mason*, ed. Cambridge: Cambridge University Press.

White Jr., Lynn. (1964 [1962]) *Medieval Technology & Social Change*. Oxford: Oxford University Press.

Whitehead, A. N. (1929) *Process and Reality: An Essay in Cosmology.* Cambridge: Cambridge University Press. [Corrected edition published in 1978 in New York by the Free Press, eds, David Ray Griffin & Donald W. Sherburne.

Wickham, Chris. (2005) *Framing the Early Middle Ages: Europe and the Mediterranean, 400-800*. Oxford: Oxford University Press.

Wickham, Chris. (2009) *The Inheritance of Rome: A History of Europe from 400 to 1000*. London: Allen Lane.

Wickham, Chris. (2015) *Sleepwalking into a New World: The Emergence of the Italian City Communes in the Twelfth Century*. Princeton, New Jersey: Princeton University Press.

Widerquist, Karl. (2010) 'What Does Prehistoric Anthropology have to do with Modern Political Philosophy? Evidence of Five False Claims [USBIG Discussion Paper],' available at http://works.bepress.com/widerquist/19, accessed 3 July 2013.

Wilczynski, Josef. (1981) *An Encyclopedic Dictionary of Marxism, Socialism and Communism*. London: The Macmillan Press.

Wilks, Michael. (ed.) (1984) *The World of John of Salisbury*. Oxford: Basil Blackwell. [Published for the Ecclesiastical History Society]

William of Orange. (1975 [1581] 'An Apology against the King of Spain,' in Zuck, 178-181.

Williams, George H. (2000 [1962]) *The Radical Reformation*. 3ʳᵈ ed. Truman State University Press.

Williams, Roger. (1644) *The Bloudy Tenent of Persecution, for Cause of Conscience, Discussed, in a Conference betweene Truth and Peace* (excerpts), in Wootton ed., 238-247.

Williams, Roger. (2001 [1644]) *The Bloudy Tenent of Persecution, for Cause of Conscience, Discussed, in a Conference betweene Truth and Peace*, ed. Richard Groves. Macon, Georgia: Mercer University Press.

Williams, Thomas. (2013) 'John Duns Scotus,' in *Stanford Encyclopedia of Philosophy*, available at http://plato.stanford.edu/archives/sum2013/entries/duns-scotus/, accessed 7 September 2013.

Wilson, Edward O. (1978) *On Human Nature*. Cambridge, Massachusetts: Harvard University Press.

Wilson, John A. (1949) 'Egypt,' in Frankfort 1949, 39-133.

Wilson, Peter H. (2016) *The Holy Roman Empire: A Thousand Years of Europe's History*. London: Allen Lane. [A superb, thematically arranged history of an unfairly maligned political institution]

Wilson, Woodrow. (1914 [1896]) *Mere Literature and Other Essays*. Boston and New York: Houghton Mifflin Co.

Wimsatt, William K. & Monroe C. Beardsley. (1954) *The Verbal Icon: Studies in the Meaning of Poetry*. Lexington, Kentucky: The University of Kentucky Press.

Winstanley, Gerrard. (1649) 'The New Law of Righteousnes,' available at http://www.diggers.org/diggers-ENGLISH-1649/NEW-LAW-OF-RIGHTEOUSNESS-1648-Winstanley.pdf, accessed 8 January 2014.

Winstanley, Gerrard. (1650a) 'A New-Yeers Gift for the Parliament and Armie' (excerpt), in Wootton, 2003, 317-333.

Winstanley, Gerrard. (1650b) 'A New-year's Gift for the Parliament and Armie,' in Winstanley 1973, 159-210.

Winstanley, Gerrard. (1973 [1651-1652]) *The Law of Freedom and other Writings*. ed. Christopher Hill. London: Penguin Books. The most convenient collection of Winstanley's basic works.

Winstanley, Gerrard. (2010) The Complete Works of Gerrard Winstanley, 2 vols. eds Thomas N. Corns, Ann Hughes, and David Loewenstein. Oxford: Oxford University Press.

Wiskemann, Elizabeth. (1966) Europe of the Dictators. London: Fontana/Collins. [Fontana History of Europe]

Witt, Emily. (2017) 'Assertive Sexuality—Yet Again, We Must Fight the Politicisation of Sex,' in The Guardian, available at https://www.theguardian.com/commentis-free/2017/jan/01/we-must-fight-politicisation-of-sex-again, accessed 1 January 2017.

Witte, John. (2009) 'A Demonstrative Theory of Natural Law: Johannes Althusius and the Rise of Calvinist Jurisprudence,' in *Ecclesiastical Law Journal*, Vol. 11 No. 3 (2009), 248-265.

Wittgenstein, Ludwig. (1969) *On Certainty*, ed. G. E. M. Anscombe and G. H. von Wright, trans. Denis Paul and G. E. M. Anscombe. Oxford: Blackwell.

Wokler, Robert. (2006) 'Ideology and the Origins of Social Science,' in Goldie & Wokler, 688-709.

Woldring, Henk E. S. (1998) 'The Constitutional State in the Political Philosophy of Johannes Althusius,' in *European Journal of Law and Economics*, vol. 5, no. 2, 123-132.

Wolff, Robert Paul. (1998 [1970]) *In Defense of Anarchism*. Berkeley, California: University of California Press. Excerpt in Graham 2009, 326-328.

Wolff, Robert Paul. (2013 [1988]) *Moneybags Must be so Lucky: On the Literary Structure of* Capital. Wellington, New Zealand: Society for Philosophy and Culture. [First Published by University of Massachusetts Press Amherst, 1988]

Wolin, Sheldon S. (1968) 'Trends and Goals' in 'Political Theory,' in *International Encyclopedia of the Social Sciences*. Available at *Encyclopedia.com* at http://www. encyclopedia.com/topic/Political_philosophy.aspx, accessed 20 April 2015.

Wong, David. (2011) 'Confucian Political Philosophy,' in Klosko, 771-788.

Wood, Alan W. (1981) *Karl Marx*. London: Routledge and Kegan Paul.

Wood, Alan W. (1991) 'Editor's Introduction' to Hegel 1820.

Wood, Ellen Meiksins. (2012) *Liberty and Property: A Social History of Western Political Thought from Renaissance to Enlightenment*. London: Verso.

Wood, John Cunningham (ed.) (1993) *Karl Marx's Economics: Critical Assessments,* (2nd Series). London: Routledge.

Wood, Ralph C. 'Ivan Karamazov's Mistake,' *First Things*, December 2002, available at https://www.firstthings.com/article/2002/12/ivan-karamazovs-mistake, accessed 5 September 2016.

Woodcock, George. (1962) *Anarchism*. London: Penguin. Available at http://libcom. org/files/Woodcock,%20George%20-%20Anarchism,%20A%20History%20Of%20 Libertarian%20Ideas%20And%20Movements.PDF, accessed 10 January 2014. A superb overview of anarchists and anarchism.

Woodcock, George. (1987) *Pierre-Joseph Proudhon: A Biography*. New York: Black Rose Books. Available at https://libcom.org/files/Proudhon%20-%20A%20 Biography.pdf, accessed 2 June 2014.

Woodhouse, A. S. P. (ed.) (1974 [1938]) *Puritanism and Liberty: Being the Army Debates (1647-9) from the* Clarke Manuscripts *with Supplementary Documents*. 2nd ed. Chicago: The University of Chicago Press. Available at http://files.libertyfund. org/files/2183/Clarke_1346_Bk.pdf, accessed 8 January 2014.

Wootton, David (ed.) (2003 [1986]) *Divine Right and Democracy: An Anthology of Political Writing in Stuart England*. Indianapolis, Indiana: Hackett Publishing Company, 2003. Originally published by Penguin Books, 1986. A convenient yet extensive collection of primary texts from this period, with an excellent introduction and brief but valuable suggestions for further reading.

Wootton, David. (1991) 'Leveller Democracy and the Puritan Revolution,' in Burns 1991, 412-442.

Worden, Blair. (1991) 'English Republicanism,' in Burns 1991, 443-475.

Wright, Robert. (2000) *Nonzero: The Logic of Human Destiny*. New York: Vintage Books.

Wyclif, John. (2001 [c. 1377]) 'On Civil Lordship,' in McGrade et al., 587-654.

Wylie, Ida Alexa Ross. (1948) "The Quest of Our Lives,' in *Reader's Digest*, May Issue.

Xenophon. (1923 [c. 371 BC]) *Memorabilia*, trans. E. C. Marchant, in *Xenophon in Seven Volumes* [Loeb Classical Library]: Cambridge: Harvard University Press. Available in a translation by H. G. Dakyns at http://www.gutenberg.org/files/1177/1177-h/1177-h. htm, accessed 22 December 2013.

Xenophon. (1949 [c. 370 BC]) *The Persian Expedition*, trans. Rex Warner. London: Penguin.

Yoder, John Howard. (1994 [1972]) *The Politics of Jesus: Vicit Agnus Noster*, 2nd ed. Grand Rapids, Michigan: Eerdmans

Yoder, John Howard. (2001 [1984]) *The Priestly Kingdom: Social Ethics as Gospel*, 2nd ed. Notre Dame, Indiana: University of Notre Dame Press.

Yoffee, Norman, et al. (2005) 'Review Feature: *Myths of the Archaic State: Evolution of the Earliest Cities, States, and Civilizations* by Norman Yoffee,' in *Cambridge Archaeological Journal*, Vol. 15 No. 2, 251-268.

Zagorin, Perez. (2003) *How the Idea of Religious Toleration Came to the West*. Princeton, New Jersey: Princeton University Press.

Zinoviev, Alexander. (1986 [1980]) *The Madhouse*. London: Paladin.

Žižek, Slavoj. (2009 [2008]) *Violence: Six Sideways Reflections*. London: Profile.

Žižek, Slavoj. (2015 [2014]) *Trouble in Paradise: From the End of History to the End of Capitalism*. London: Penguin.

Zmirak, John. (2001) *Wilhelm Röpke: Swiss Localist, Global Economist*. Wilmington, Delaware: ISI Books.

Zuck, Lowell H. (ed.) (1975) *Christianity and Revolution: Radical Christian Testimonies 1520-1650*. Philadelphia: Temple University Press. [A very useful sourcebook containing many short excerpts from various figures of the so-called Radical Reformation. Longer and more complete versions of some of this material can be found in Baylor]

Zumbrunnen, John. (2002) '"Courage in the Face of Reality": Nietzsche's Admiration for Thucydides,' in *Polity*, Vol. 35, No. 2, 237-263.

INDEX